REFORMING THE FRENCH LAW OF OBLIGATIONS

The 2005 *Avant-projet de réforme du droit des obligations et de la prescription*, also dubbed the *Avant-projet Catala*, proposes the most far-reaching reform of the French Civil code since it came into force in 1804. It reviews central aspects of contract law, the law of delict and the law of unjustified enrichment. There is currently a very lively debate in France as to the merits or demerits of both the particular draft provisions and the general idea of recodification as such.

This volume is the first publication to introduce the reform proposals to an English speaking audience. It contains the official English translation of the text, and distinguished private lawyers from both England and France analyse and assess particularly interesting aspects of the substantive draft provisions in a comparative perspective. Topics covered include negotiation and renegotiation of contracts, *la cause*, the enforcement of contractual obligations, termination of contract and its consequences, the effects of contracts on third parties, the definition of *la faute*, the quantification of damages, and the law of prescription. The volume also contains an overall assessment of the draft provisions by one of the most senior French judges who chaired the Working Party on the *Avant-projet*, established by the French Supreme Court, the Cour de cassation.

The book is indispensable for comparative private lawyers and lawyers with a particular interest in French law. It is also of use to all private lawyers (both academics and practitioners) looking for information on recent international and European trends in contract and tort.

Volume 9 in the Series: Studies of the Oxford Institute of European and Comparative Law

Studies of the Oxford Institute of European and Comparative Law

Editor

Professor Stefan Vogenauer

Board of Advisory Editors

Professor Mark Freedland, FBA
Professor Stephen Weatherill
Professor Derrick Wyatt, QC

Reforming the French Law of Obligations

Comparative Reflections on the Avant-projet de réforme du droit des obligations et de la prescription ('the Avant-projet Catala')

Edited by

JOHN CARTWRIGHT
STEFAN VOGENAUER
and
SIMON WHITTAKER

·H A R T·
PUBLISHING

OXFORD AND PORTLAND, OREGON
2009

Published in North America (US and Canada) by

Hart Publishing
c/o International Specialized Book Services
920 NE 58th Avenue, Suite 300
Portland, OR 97213-3786
USA
Tel: +1 503 287 3093 or toll-free: (1) 800 944 6190
Fax: +1 503 280 8832
Email: orders@isbs.com
Website: www.isbs.com

Hart Publishing Ltd, 16C Worcester Place, Oxford, OX1 2JW
Telephone: +44 (0)1865 517530 Fax: +44 (0)1865 510710
Email: mail@hartpub.co.uk
Website: http//:www.hartpub.co.uk

British Library Cataloguing in Publication Data
Data Available

ISBN: 978-1-84113-805-3

Typeset by Forewords, Oxford
Printed and bound in Great Britain by
TJ International Ltd, Padstow

Preface

This volume in the Studies of the Oxford Institute of European and Comparative Law is the product of a colloquium held at St John's College, Oxford, in March 2007, the purpose of which was to discuss the *Avant-projet de réforme du droit des obligations et de la prescription* both from an internal French perspective and from wider perspectives of comparative law.

The *Avant-projet*, drawn up by a group of distinguished French jurists and retired judges under the leadership of Pierre Catala, was presented to the French Minister of Justice in September 2005. If enacted, it would lead to the most far-reaching reform of the French Civil Code since it came into force in 1804, and would fundamentally alter many central aspects of contract law, the law of delict and the law of unjustified enrichment. There is currently a very lively debate in France as to the merits or demerits of both the particular draft provisions and the general idea of recodification as such. These discussions are not only of interest to French lawyers, since one of the main aims of the *Avant-projet* is to update the French Civil code in order to make it more attractive as a model for other jurisdictions and to give French legal thought more weight in the continuing debates on the future of harmonisation of the laws of contract and tort in Europe: to enhance the 'exportability' of French law. To this end, various official translations of the *Avant-projet* were commissioned, amongst them one into English by two of the co-editors of this volume, John Cartwright and Simon Whittaker.

The purpose of the volume is to make both this translation and the original text of the *Avant-projet* accessible to an English speaking audience, together with discussion of particularly interesting aspects of the substantive draft provisions in a comparative perspective. Eight topics are dealt with first from an internal French perspective by French lawyers, and then subjected to a comparative assessment by contributors from other jurisdictions. Other contributions within the volume include an overall assessment of the draft provisions by one of the most senior French judges who headed a Working Party on the *Avant-projet* established by the French Supreme Court, the Cour de cassation.

The colloquium was organised by the Institute of European and Comparative Law at Oxford and supported financially by the *Association Sorbonne-Oxford pour le droit comparé*, whose founding members are the Université de Paris I, the Institute of European and Comparative Law of the University of Oxford and Clifford Chance. The objects of the *Association* are to develop exchanges, teaching and research in the field of

Anglo-French comparative law between the two universities. The *Association* is funded principally by Clifford Chance, and we should like to thank the *Association*, and Clifford Chance in particular, for their support which enabled us to bring scholars to Oxford in order to participate in the colloquium. We were very pleased that Michael Elland-Goldsmith, partner of Clifford Chance and Secrétaire Général—and long-standing supporter—of the *Association*, was able to participate in the colloquium. It is with great sadness that we record his premature death in June 2007.

We should also like to thank Jenny Dix, Administrator of the Institute of European and Comparative Law, for her invaluable assistance throughout the preparation for, and the running of, the colloquium; Janice Feigher and James Dingley of Clifford Chance, who took notes of the discussions at the colloquium; the President and Governing Body of St John's College, Oxford, for their hospitality; Jonathan Bremner, Wendy Kennett, Marina Milmo and Peter Wilson, for their assistance in translating papers that had originally been written in French; Adam Sher, for his help in editing the contributions; Pierre Catala and *La documentation française* for allowing us to reproduce the text of the *Avant-projet*; and most particularly, of course, the participants at the colloquium, both those who presented papers (which are now, in their revised forms, contained in this volume) and those who attended and made a very significant contribution to the discussion.

Since the Oxford colloquium, in the wake of the *Avant-projet*, various steps have been taken towards the reform of the laws of contract and prescription. Some of these developments took place only after submission of the manuscripts to the publishers. They concern many of the topics covered in this volume, and particularly those dealt with in chapters 4, 5, 16 and 17. It was not possible to update all the contributions in the light of these most recent developments but we are grateful to Richard Hart for allowing us to change the end of the penultimate section of chapter 1 in order to give a very brief account of the current state of the debate.

John Cartwright
Stefan Vogenauer
Simon Whittaker
Oxford
December 2008

Contents

I. The Perspective of the Judiciary

18 The Work of the Cour de cassation on the *Avant-projet de réforme*
PIERRE SARGOS

J. Summaries of the Discussions and Emerging Themes

19 Summaries of the Discussions
SIMON WHITTAKER, STEFAN VOGENAUER AND JOHN CARTWRIGHT

20 Emerging Themes
HUGH BEALE, PHILIPPE THÉRY AND GERHARD DANNEMANN

Contributors

Hugh Beale is Professor of Law at the University of Warwick; from 2000 to 2007 he was a Law Commissioner for England and Wales.

Jean-Sébastien Borghetti is Professor of Private Law at the University of Nantes.

John Cartwright is Professor of the Law of Contract at the University of Oxford and Tutor in Law at Christ Church, Oxford; and Professor of Anglo-American Private Law at the University of Leiden.

Gerhard Dannemann is Professor for British Legal, Economic and Social Structures at the Humboldt-Universität zu Berlin.

Muriel Fabre-Magnan is Professor of Private Law at the University of Paris I (Panthéon-Sorbonne).

Bénédicte Fauvarque-Cosson is Professor of Law at the University of Paris II (Panthéon-Assas).

Paula Giliker is Professor of Comparative Law at the University of Bristol.

Yves-Marie Laithier is Professor of Law at the University of Reims.

Denis Mazeaud is Professor of Private Law at the University of Paris II (Panthéon-Assas).

Lucinda Miller is Lecturer of Laws at University College London.

Pauline Rémy-Corlay is Professor of Comparative Law and Private International Law at the University of Paris XI, Faculté Jean Monnet, and Director of the Institut Charles Dumoulin.

Judith Rochfeld is Professor of Private Law (French and European) at the University of Paris I (Panthéon-Sorbonne).

Solène Rowan is a Fellow in Law at Queens' College, Cambridge.

Pierre Sargos was a Président de chambre à la Cour de cassation (France).

Ruth Sefton-Green is Maître de conférences at the University of Paris I (Panthéon-Sorbonne).

Philippe Théry is Professor of Law at the University of Paris II (Panthéon-Assas), Director of the Institut d'études judiciaires and formerly French Deputy Director at the Oxford Institute of European and Comparative Law.

Stefan Vogenauer is Professor of Comparative Law at the University of Oxford. He is a Fellow of Brasenose College and Director of the Oxford Institute of European and Comparative Law.

Simon Whittaker is Fellow and Tutor in Law at St John's College, Oxford and Professor of European Comparative Law at the University of Oxford.

Robert Wintgen is Professor of Law at the University of Paris X (Nanterre).

List of Abbreviations

ABGB	Allgemeines Bürgerliches Gesetzbuch (Austria, 1811)
AC	Law Reports, Appeal Cases (Third Series) (1891–)
App Cas	Law Reports, Appeal Cases (Second Series) (1875–1890)
AEPL Code	Code européen des contrats: Avant-projet, Livre premier, edited by the Academy of European Private Lawyers (Revised edn, Milan, Giuffrè, 2004)
AJ fam	Actualité juridique famille
Art(s)/art(s)	Article(s)
Ass plén	Assemblée plénière de la Cour de cassation
B & Ad	Barnewall and Adolphus' Reports, King's Bench (ER 106)
BGB	Bürgerliches Gesetzbuch (Germany, 1900)
BGH	Bundesgerichtshof
BGHZ	Entscheidungen des Bundesgerichtshofs in Zivilsachen
B & S	Best and Smith's Reports, Queen's Bench (ER 121–122)
Bull civ	Bulletin des arrêts de la Cour de cassation, Chambres civiles
Bull crim	Bulletin des arrêts de la Cour de cassation, Chambre criminelle
CA	Cour d'appel; Court of Appeal
Cass civ	Chambre civile de la Cour de cassation
Cass civ (1), (2) and (3)	Première, deuxième and troisième chambre civile de la Cour de cassation
Cass com	Chambre commerciale de la Cour de cassation
Cass crim	Chambre criminelle de la Cour de cassation
Cass mixte	Chambre mixte de la Cour de cassation
Cass soc	Chambre sociale de la Cour de cassation
Ch réun	Chambres reuniés de la Cour de cassation
Cass	Corte di cassazione
CC	Conseil Constitutionnel
Cc	Code civil
Cf/cf	Compare
Ch/ch	Chapter
Ch	Law Reports, Chancery Division (1890–)
Chron	Chroniques
CISG	UN Convention on the International Sale of Goods (1980)

CLR	Commonwealth Law Reports (Australia)
Clunet	Journal du droit international ('Clunet')
Cmnd	command (identifier for published parliamentary papers)
COM	European Commission Documents
concl	conclusions
Contrats Concur Consom	Contrats-Concurrence-Consommation
D	Recueil Dalloz
D aff	Recueil Dalloz, Cahier droit des affaires
Defr	Répertoire du notariat Defrénois
DH	Dalloz, Recueil hebdomadaire de jurisprudence (1924–1940)
Dig	Digesta (Digest of Justinian)
DLR (4th)	Dominion Law Reports (Fourth Series) (Canada) (1984–)
DP	Dalloz, Recueil périodique et critique de jurisprudence, de législation et de doctrine (1825–1940)
EC	European Community
ed(s)	editor(s)
edn	edition
EEC	European Economic Community
Eg/eg	for example
EGLR	Estates Gazette Law Reports
El & Bl	Ellis & Blackburn's Reports, Queen's Bench (ER 118–120)
ER	English Reports
ERCL	European Review of Contract Law
ERPL	European Review of Private Law
et al	and others, *et alii*
EWCA Civ	Decision of the Court of Appeal (Civil Division)
EWHC	Decision of the High Court
Exch	Exchequer Reports (1847–1856)
F(F)	French franc(s)
Fasc	fascicule
Gaz Pal	Gazette du Palais
HL	House of Lords
HMSO	Her Majesty's Stationery Office
HR	Hoge Raad
ICLQ	International and Comparative Law Quarterly
Inst	Institutiones (Institutes of Justinian)
IR	informations rapides
IRLR	Industrial Relations Law Reports
J	Mr Justice

JBL	Journal of Business Law
JCP	Juris-classeur périodique, La semaine juridique
JCP E	Juris-classeur périodique, La semaine juridique, entreprises et affaires
JCP G	Juris-classeur périodique, La semaine juridique, édition générale
JO	Journal officiel de la République Française
Law Com	Law Commission
LBC	Law Book Company
LC	Lord Chancellor
LGDJ	Librairie générale de droit et jurisprudence
LJ	Lord Justice of Appeal
Lloyd's Rep	Lloyd's List Law Reports
LPA	Les petites affiches
LQR	Law Quarterly Review
LR Ex	Law Reports, Exchequer Cases (1865–1875)
LR HL	Law Reports, English & Irish Appeals (1866–1875)
LR QB	Law Reports, Queen's Bench (First Series) (1865–1875)
LS	Legal Studies
Ltd	Limited
MA	Massachusetts
MBC	Metropolitan Borough Council
McGill LJ	McGill Law Journal
MPC	Metropolitan Police Commissioner (London)
N/n	Note
NBW	Nieuw Burgerlijk Wetboek (The Netherlands, 1992)
NH	New Hampshire Reports
NJW	Neue Juristische Wochenschrift
NJW-RR	Neue Juristische Wochenschrift—Rechtsprechungsreport
No(s)/no(s)	Number(s)
obs	observation
OJ	Official Journal of the European Communities
OJLS	Oxford Journal of Legal Studies
OR	Obligationenrecht (Switzerland, 1912)
Pan	Panorama
para(s)	paragraph(s)
PECL	Principles of European Contract Law (1995/2000)
PETL	Priniciples of European Tort Law (2005)
PICC	UNIDROIT Principles of International Commercial Contracts (2004 edn)
pr	principium
PUF	Presses Universitaires de France

QB	Court of Queen's Bench; Law Reports, Queen's Bench Division (1891–1901, 1952–)
QBD	Queen's Bench Division of the High Court of Justice; Law Reports, Queen's Bench Division (1875–1890)
rapp	rapport
RDC	Revue des contrats
Req	Chambre des requêtes de la Cour de cassation
Resp civ et assur	Responsabilité civile et assurance
RG	Reichsgericht
RGAT	Revue générale des assurances terrestres
RGZ	Entscheidungen des Reichsgerichts in Zivilsachen
RIDC	Revue internationale de droit comparé
RID éco	Revue internationale de droit économique
RJ com	Revue de jurisprudence commerciale
RJDA	Revue de jurisprudence de droit des affaires
RJPF	Revue juridique personnes et famille
RJQ	Recueil de jurisprudence du Quebec
RRJ	Revue de la recherche juridique, Droit prospectif
RTD civ	Revue trimestrielle de droit civil
RTD com	Revue trimestrielle de droit commercial et de droit économique
RTD fam	Revue trimestrielle de droit familial
S	Recueil Sirey
S(s)/s(s)	Section(s)
SCR	Supreme Court Reports (Canada)
Somm	sommaires
Somm com	sommaires commentées
UCC	Uniform Commercial Code (USA)
UDC	Urban District Council
UKHL	Decision of the House of Lords
UKPC	Decision of the Privy Council
ULR	Uniform Law Review/Revue de droit uniforme
vol(s)	volume(s)
WLR	Weekly Law Reports
Yale LJ	Yale Law Journal
ZEuP	Zeitschrift für Europäisches Privatrecht

Part I

Introducing the
Avant-Projet de réforme

1

The Avant-projet de réforme: *An Overview*

STEFAN VOGENAUER

O
N 22 SEPTEMBER 2005, the French Minister of Justice received a group of distinguished law professors, led by Pierre Catala, professor emeritus of the University of Paris II. The group submitted a major proposal for the reform of the law of obligations and the law of prescription, the *Avant-projet de réforme du droit des obligations et de la prescription.* This proposal represents the most ambitious attempt at reforming the core areas of French private law since 1804. These areas are contained in Titles III, IV and XX of the third Book of the Code civil, and concern the entire law of obligations (contract, quasi-contract and civil liability) and, as far as the law relating to limitation periods is concerned, almost every action brought in private law. Some of the most interesting parts of the *Avant-projet* will be analysed and assessed in the other contributions to this volume. It is the purpose of this chapter to provide an overview of the background, the genesis, the structure, the content and the reception of the reform proposals, as well as a bibliography of French and international literature on the *Avant-projet.*

I. BACKGROUND

The *Avant-projet* was written against the background of the impending bicentenary of the Code civil. Anniversaries are opportunities for reflection and reorientation, and the run-up to the 2004 festivities was no exception. French lawyers displayed a mixture of nostalgia, discontent and fear. Whilst they were justifiably proud of the Code's republican and egalitarian values, its international success and its longevity, they had long been aware that this *véritable Constitution de la France,* this *ciment de la société*[1] and

---

[1] Y Lequette, 'Quelques remarques à propos d'un Code civil européen de Monsieur von Bar' D 2002 chron 2202.

monument du droit[2] had lost much of its lustre. The reasons were twofold: (a) the Code had become outdated, and (b) its influence abroad was in decline.

(a) Codification, Decodification and Recodification

The Code civil is the oldest surviving post-Enlightenment code. It embodies the very idea of codification: full, comprehensive, systematic and coherent legislation for a particular area of the law, combined with complete abrogation of the previous law relating to the same subject-matter. Whether all these aims were actually achieved in 1804 is open to debate, but as time progressed doubts with regard to the completeness of the Code increased. On the occasion of the Code's centenary there was already doubt as to whether the Code still represented a full and comprehensive representation of private law, and throughout the twentieth century it became more and more obvious that it did not. As in many other European systems, the era of codification had been followed by that of 'decodification'.[3]

To some extent, this development was simply a consequence of the general phenomenon of *la crise* or *le déclin de la loi*[4]—indeed, of *la désacralisation de la loi*.[5] The prestige of legislation as a source of law has dramatically declined since the Second World War. The Constitution of the Fifth Republic weakened the authority of parliament by allocating central legislative powers to the executive to such an extent that the equation of *la loi* and *la volonté générale* has become more of a fiction than ever before. The quality of modern legislation is generally perceived to be poor. At the same time, the number of enactments on the statute book has increased hugely. The fragmentation and disintegration of the written law particularly affects the codes. True, many modern 'codes' were enacted throughout the twentieth century, particularly after the *Commission supérieure de codification* had been established with a view to simplifying and clarifying the law in 1989.[6] However, these are not systematic and intellectually coherent

---

[2] G Cornu, 'Un Code civil n'est pas un instrument communautaire' D 2002 chron 351.

[3] N Irti, *L'età della decodificazione* (Milan, Giuffrè, 1st edn 1979, 3rd edn 1989); K Schmidt, *Die Zukunft der Kodifikationsidee: Rechtsprechung, Wissenschaft und Gesetzgebung vor den Gesetzeswerken des geltenden Rechts* (Karlsruhe, CF Müller, 1985); S Genner, *Dekodifikation: Zur Auflösung der kodifikatorischen Einheit im schweizerischen Zivilrecht* (Basel, Helbing & Lichtenhahn, 2006). For France, see B Oppetit, 'La décodification du droit commercial français' in *Etudes offertes à René Rodière* (Paris, Dalloz, 1981) 197.

[4] B Mathieu, *La loi* (2nd edn, Paris, Dalloz, 2004) 75 who gives a comprehensive account of this development at 71–114.

[5] M Jéol, 'La Cour de cassation juge du droit' in Cour de cassation (ed), *L'image doctrinale de la Cour de cassation* (Paris, La documentation française, 1994) 37, 41 n 1.

[6] Décret no 89-647 du 12 septembre 1989 relatif à la composition et au fonctionnement de la Commission supérieure de codification, JO 13 September 1989, 11560. For an overview, see E Steiner, *French Legal Method* (Oxford University Press, 2002) 49–52.

enactments all of a piece, meant to replace and abrogate the previous law. Unlike the traditional codes, they are mere consolidating measures, essentially collections of single statutes and statutory instruments which attempt to restate in one document the law in a particular area which was previously scattered in different places.[7] As far as the ancient codes are concerned, major law reform with regard to matters falling into their scope is not necessarily achieved by amending the codes, but rather by enacting specific statutes. Legislation on important areas of private law, such as labour law, insurance law, consumer law, unfair competition and special types of contracts, has been enacted over the decades, but it has not been incorporated into the Code civil.

As a result, the Code civil has been little amended since 1804. A number of unsuccessful attempts at wholesale revision have been made. A first reform commission was established on the occasion of the centenary in 1904, but it was bound to fail, as it had no clear agenda and hardly any institutional support. In the inter-war period, the Working Group for a Franco-Italian project for a Code of obligations produced a draft that was published in 1927 but never reached the statute book.[8] Finally, a new *Commission de réforme* was established under the chairmanship of Professor Julliot de la Morandière in June 1945.[9] However, its members were deeply divided over the ambit of the social reforms that might be introduced by way of revision of the Code, so the Commission ultimately fell apart and its drafts were never submitted to parliament. The only successful major reform of the Code was the complete modernisation of family law which was achieved under the direction of Professor Carbonnier between 1964 and 1978. By contrast, the law of obligations has remained virtually untouched: 254 of its 286 original articles are still in force today, and only very few additions have been made to bring up the number of articles to 296.

In the face of legislative inertia, the courts assumed the task of adjusting the Code civil to modern conditions. Their law-making function, widely interpreted as a mere complement to the efforts of parliament during the nineteenth century and the first half of the twentieth century, became more and more visible. Particularly in the fields of contract law and delictual

[7] For a comprehensive account, see M Suel, *Essai sur la codification à droit constant: précédents—débuts—réalisation* (2nd edn, Paris, Journal Officiel de la République Française, 1995).

[8] See the contributions and the bibliography in M Rotondi (ed), *Le projet franco-italien du code des obligations* (1980). For a contemporary perspective, see GS Vesey-FitzGerald, 'The Franco-Italian Draft Code of Obligations' (1932) 14 Journal of Comparative Legislation and International Law (3rd series) 1.

[9] L Julliot de la Morandière, 'La réforme du Code civil' D 1948 chron 117. The results of the work of the Commission were published in nine volumes: *Travaux de la Commission de réforme du Code civil* (Paris, Recueil Sirey, 1947–57).

liability, the Cour de cassation shaped entirely new doctrines. The extent to which the judiciary has become the motor of law reform can be gathered from the fact that recent legislative intervention in the law of obligations has been mostly reactive, rather than proactive. Legislation was enacted in a fashion commonly associated with English statute law, ie to supplement or overrule case-law that had developed in areas where the existing legislation did not provide sufficient guidance.[10] As a consequence of these developments, a simple reading of Titles III and IV of the third Book of the Code civil does not even permit a remote knowledge of the laws of contract and delict today.[11]

This state of affairs is not only undesirable. In the light of the *jurisprudence* of the Conseil constitutionnel it is also bordering on the unconstitutional. In a landmark decision of 1999, the Conseil held that 'the objective of intelligibility and accessibility of the law' is of 'constitutional force', deriving from the Declaration of the Rights of Man and of the Citizen of 1789.[12] This was recently reaffirmed, the Conseil adding that this objective imposes an 'obligation to adopt sufficiently precise and unambiguous provisions' on the legislator.[13] Whilst these dicta only apply to newly enacted legislation, they may be seen as an exhortation also to render comprehensible old legislation that has become outdated and opaque.[14] A similar line was taken by the Conseil d'Etat which in its Annual Report 2006 deplored the lack of legal certainty resulting from the 'complexity' of the law.[15]

A comprehensive recodification of the third Book of the Code civil would increase the accessibility and the intelligibility of the law of obligations. It would help to modernise the law, so as to keep pace with changing social and economic realities, and it would rationalise the law by integrating relevant legal instruments and by restructuring general private law into one code. All of these aims had been pursued in other legal systems that had recently recodified their private laws, or at least important parts of it: the Netherlands in 1992,[16] Québec in 1994 and Germany in

---

[10] A famous example is the Loi no 2002-303 du 4 mars 2002 relative aux droits des malades et à la qualité du système de santé, JO 5 March 2002, 4118; see P Jourdain, 'Loi "anti-Perruche": une loi démagogique' D 2002, 891.

[11] P Catala, 'L'avant-projet de réforme des obligations et le droit des affaires' RJ com 1 May 2007, no 3, 182, 183.

[12] CC decision 99-421 DC of 16 December 1999, JO 22 December 1999, 19041. See also the Loi no 2003-591 du 2 juillet 2003 habilitant le gouvernement à simplifier le droit, JO 3 July 2003, 11192.

[13] CC decision 2006-540 DC of 27 July 2006, JO 3 August 2006, 11541.

[14] The point is made by P Sargos, 'The Work of the Cour de cassation on the *Avant-projet de réforme*', ch 18 below, 383, 386.

[15] J de Claussade, 'Sécurité juridique et complexité du droit' in Etudes et documents du Conseil d'Etat 57 (2006) 225.

[16] For a recent assessment of the reforms, see E Hondius, 'Les bases doctrinales du nouveau Code néerlandais' in C Ophèle and P Remy (eds), *Traditions savantes et codifications* (2007) 257.

2002.[17] These were the examples that the drafters of the *Avant-projet* wished to follow.[18]

(b) European and Global Challenges

But there is more to a codification than just a rational way of presenting the entire law in a given area. Historically, the idea of codification was closely connected to that of state-building and nationhood.[19] The major European civil codes are therefore important symbols of national unity and identity. French lawyers are particularly aware of this. As a consequence, many of them regard the recent proposals for a Europeanisation of contract law emerging from the European Commission and culminating in a 'Draft Common Frame of Reference' with great scepticism, if not outright hostility.[20] But defending the virtues of French contract law in order to counter the proposals for European harmonisation or even to convince those elaborating such proposals to adopt the solutions of French law will be difficult as long as the Code civil does not reflect the actual state of the law in this area. A recodification of French contract law is therefore seen as a strategic means to influence or even stop the project of an *Eurocode*: 'we have not got the Franc anymore, but the Code remains!'.[21]

However, the widespread opposition of French lawyers to the Europeanisation of contract law is due to a fear of a loss of *influence*, as much as of identity. The spectacular success of the Code civil and its export throughout the world during the nineteenth century turned France into one of the few legal systems that exerted such a dominant influence on other jurisdictions that the country is generally regarded as the 'lead jurisdiction' of an entire legal family that stretches from Chile to Vietnam.[22] Such cultural hegemony easily translates into competitive advantages for French businesses that operate internationally and for the lawyers advising them. Choices like that of the sixteen sub-Saharan and mostly francophone countries of the *Organisation pour l'Harmonisation en Afrique du Droit des*

[17] R Zimmermann, *The New German Law of Obligations: Historical and Comparative Perspectives* (Oxford University Press, 2005).

[18] P Catala, 'Présentation générale de l'avant-projet' in *Avant-projet de réforme du droit des obligations et de la prescription: Rapport remis au garde des Sceaux* (Paris, La documentation française, 2006) 11 (see below pp 465–7).

[19] See, recently, PAJ van den Berg, *The politics of European codification: a history of the unification of law in France, Prussia, the Austrian Monarchy and the Netherlands* (Groningen, Europa Law Publishing, 2007).

[20] For a particularly vivid example, see Lequette, n 1 above.

[21] L Vogel, 'Recodification civile et renouvellement des sources internes' in *Le Code civil 1804–2004: Livre du bicentenaire* (Paris, Litec, Dalloz, 2004) 159, 163, 165. See also C Jamin, 'Vers un droit européen des contrats? (Réflexions sur une double stratégie)' RJ com 2006, 94, 101–4.

[22] For a recent overview of the international influence of the Code civil, see B Fauvarque-Cosson and S Patris-Godechot, *Le Code civil face à son destin* (2006) 161–4, 201–58.

Affaires (OHADA) which decided to turn to the UNIDROIT Principles of International Commercial Contracts,[23] rather than to the Code civil when they looked for a uniform contract law Act a few years ago, set French lawyers' alarm bells ringing.[24]

The fear of losing out in an increasingly globalised competition between legal systems was intensified with the *electrochoc*[25] of the 2004 World Bank Report on 'Doing Business'. This purported to provide compelling evidence that the economies of states with legal systems based on French legal heritage were lagging behind.[26] Both the assumptions on which the Report was based and its methodological approach were fundamentally flawed. Nevertheless, French lawyers immediately engaged in a spirited counter-offensive. The *Association Henri Capitant des Amis de la Culture Juridique Française*—a venerable academic society that has the object of establishing and facilitating international contacts between lawyers and, ultimately, promoting French law abroad—published a two-volume refutation of the Report[27] and various other initiatives were founded in order to defend and openly promote the 'economic attractiveness' of French law.[28] Their shared concern is to ensure the competitiveness and the 'exportability' of French law in the face of what is perceived as an open bid for legal hegemony by common law systems. The defects in French law are mostly seen as formal, rather than substantive shortcomings. One of these is, again, the outdated and inadequate codification of the law of contract. Intelligibility and accessibility of the law are also important in order to secure its exportability. Again, a reform of the Code civil seemed to be a means to achieve this end. The aim of creating 'an exportable model, likely to influence foreign legislators, particularly the European legislator' is therefore mentioned again and again by supporters of the *Avant-projet*.[29]

---

[23] M Fontaine, 'The Draft OHADA Uniform Act on Contracts and the UNIDROIT Principles of International Commercial Contracts' [2004] ULR 573. The draft Act is currently under consideration by the OHADA member states: R Michaels, 'Preamble I' in S Vogenauer and J Kleinheisterkamp (eds), *Commentary on the UNIDROIT Principles of International Commercial Contracts (PICC)* (Oxford University Press, 2009) paras 123–5.

[24] Catala, above n 11, 184.

[25] Fauvarque-Cosson and Patris-Godechot, above n 22, 153.

[26] World Bank, *Doing Business in 2004: Understanding Regulations* (Washington DC, World Bank and Oxford University Press, 2004).

[27] Association Henri Capitant, *Les droits de tradition civiliste en question: A propos des Rapports* Doing Business *de la Banque Mondiale* (2 vols, Paris, Société de législation comparée, 2006). Other major publications include Fauvarque-Cosson and Patris-Godechot, above n 22; F Rouvillois (ed), *Le modèle juridique français: un obstacle au développement économique?* (Paris, Dalloz, 2005).

[28] These include the *Programme internationale de recherche Attractivité Economique du Droit* http://www.gip-recherche-justice.fr/aed.htm and the *Fondation pour le droit continental* http://www.fondation-droitcontinental.org/1.aspx.

[29] D Mazeaud, 'Observations conclusives' RDC 2006, 177, 179. See also P Catala, 'La genèse et le dessein du projet' RDC 2006, 11, 17.

II. GENESIS

The Code civil is thus perceived as being outdated and as losing its international influence. These are the defects that the *Avant-projet* sets out to remedy, as can be seen in the penultimate paragraph of its Introduction: the purpose of the reform proposals is to 'give France a civil law adapted to its time and a voice at the table of Europe'.[30] Indeed, the idea to embark on the *Avant-projet* arose in late January 2003, in the wake of a colloquium which compared French contract law and the Principles of European Contract Law (PECL).[31] Initially, a group of six law professors devoted themselves to the task.[32] Other participants were invited, and in the end thirty-seven people were involved in the project. Three of these were retired judges of the Cour de cassation. All the others were active or retired law professors, most of them based at one of the two leading Law Faculties of France, Paris I (Panthéon-Sorbonne) and Paris II (Panthéon-Assas).[33] The legal professions were not formally involved, but some of their members were occasionally consulted.[34]

Therefore, in an interesting parallel to the international proposals for contract law reform referred to in the previous section of this paper, the *Avant-projet* is a purely private initiative by legal academics. The group received institutional support from the *Association Henri Capitant*. The political authorities, whilst not formally involved, were broadly supportive: the project received some encouragement from the President of the Republic who, in his speech on the occasion of the bicentenary of the Code civil, suggested that a reform of the law of obligations should be implemented within five years;[35] the Ministry of Justice seems to have provided some technical assistance; and the text was published by the official governmental publishing agency, *La documentation française*.

At a very early stage, the group split into two distinct teams. The first, led by Professor Catala, dealt with contract and quasi-contracts. The work on contract was subdivided into eighteen topics which were each then dealt with by up to three contributors. The second team tackled civil liability. It was directed by Professor Geneviève Viney, the leading authority in this area of the law, and Professor Georges Drury. Professor Philippe Malaurie took on the third major part of the *Avant-projet*, the law of prescription.

---

[30] Catala, above n 18, 16 (see below p 477).

[31] The proceedings of this colloquium can be found in P Rémy-Corlay and D Fenouillet (eds), *Les concepts contractuels français à l'heure des Principes du droit européen des contrats* (2003).

[32] The genesis of the project is discussed in more detail by Catala, above n 18, 12–3 (see below pp 465–7, 469–71). See also P Catala, 'Il est temps de rendre au Code civil son rôle de droit commun des contrats' JCP G 2005 I 170, 1739; Catala, above n 29, 11–4.

[33] A list of the participants can be found below pp 461–3.

[34] J Cartwright, 'Reforming the French Law of Prescription: An English Perspective', ch 17 below, 359, 378–80, highlights the contrast with the broad consultation mechanisms employed by the Law Commissions in the United Kingdom.

[35] Catala, above n 32, 1741.

After the initial elaboration of the outlines of the project,[36] these sub-teams prepared first drafts within less than eight months which were then subjected to criticism by the entire group. In a final stage, the original group of participants implemented the suggestions emerging from this process, harmonised the substance of various drafts and took care to achieve uniformity of style. Much of the redrafting was done by the late Gérard Cornu, another law professor, who was well known for his particularly succinct style of legal writing. Work on the *Avant-projet* was finished in early summer 2005, only thirty months after it had begun.

III. STRUCTURE, PRESENTATION AND STYLE

Le plan, as every French lawyer knows, is the most important aspect of any piece of legal writing. The structure of the *Avant-projet* is particularly clear. The present Titles III and IV ('Contracts and Conventional Obligations'; 'Obligations Without Agreement') of the third Book of the Code civil are merged into a single new Title III 'On Obligations'. This, in turn, is introduced by a short Preliminary Chapter on 'The Source of Obligations' and then divided into three Sub-titles, dealing with 'Contracts and Obligations Created by Agreement in General' (Sub-title I), 'Quasi-Contracts' (Sub-title II) and 'Civil Liability' (Sub-title III), respectively. The first Sub-title has seven Chapters, the length of which varies greatly; the second Sub-title is divided into three very short Chapters; and the third Sub-title comprises four Chapters. The reform proposals for Title XX of the third Book ('Prescription and Possession') are dealt with separately.

The presentation of the reform proposals is somewhat less straightforward. The draft black letter rules of the *Avant-projet* are interspersed with 'Notes', 'General observations' and 'Comments' without it being obvious how these different categories interrelate. Sometimes the annotations to the black letter rules are also relegated to footnotes. Furthermore, the black letter rules are preceded by introductory notes of the respective drafters. There is a single block of such *exposés des motifs* for the two Sub-titles on contracts and quasi-contracts which is preceded by a short introduction written by Professor Cornu.[37] Separate *exposés* precede the Sub-title on civil liability and the Title on prescription, written by Professors Viney and Malaurie, respectively.[38] No doubt this partitioning reflects the division of labour between the different teams working on the

---

[36] For reflections on the expediency and the feasibility of reform, see the contributions in issue 4/2004 of the Revue des contrats, summarised in English by G Alpa, 'Harmonisation and Codification in European Contract Law' in S Vogenauer and S Weatherill (eds), *The Harmonisation of European Contract Law: Implications for European Private Laws, Business and Legal Practice* (Oxford, Hart Publishing, 2006) 149, 165–9.

[37] See below pp 479–623.

[38] See below pp 809–33, 881–99.

Avant-projet, but the position of the introductory note on civil liability in particular is bound to confuse the reader. It would also have facilitated the accessibility and the comprehensibility of the text if the format of the *exposés des motifs* had been harmonised so that the reader would not be left guessing whether different heading systems and other formal features are of significance or not.

The drafting of the *Avant-projet* deliberately follows the classic style of the great French codes.[39] The widely admired style of French legislation is characterised by linguistic elegance, brevity, simplicity of composition and the broad generality of its provisions. It places stronger emphasis on principle than on concrete instances, avoids enumerations, does not attempt to foresee all conceivable future cases and therefore relies on the judge to fill in the detail. For an English observer, used to the prolix and casuistic nature of British Acts of Parliament, this is extremely laconic.[40] There is only one feature of the *Avant-projet* that breaks with the French, and indeed with the continental, style of legislative drafting. Ignoring the ancient maxim *omnis definitio in iure civili periculosa est*,[41] it introduces a host of legal definitions, all in all roughly thirty. This has been justified as promoting both pedagogical aims and legal certainty,[42] but it could just as easily be argued that it betrays the academic provenance of the project.

IV. CONTENT

With a project of this size and ambition, form is of course subordinate to substance. The *Avant-projet* is explicitly designed to be a modification of the Code, and not a decisive break with the past, *une réforme d'adaptation et non de rupture*.[43] The spirit is one of continuity, not of revolution. This can be seen from the fact that the drafters went to great lengths to retain the wording and the numbering of central provisions, such as articles 1134 and 1135, which they obviously regarded as part of the cultural heritage of the Code. The essentially conservative character of the project is emphasised in the very first paragraph of the general introduction by Professor Catala and its appeal to customs, traditions and the saying of Portalis that 'it is right to save everything that it is not necessary to destroy'.[44] The impression is reaffirmed by some figures provided by

[39] Catala, above n 11, 185.
[40] See the comments by J Cartwright and S Whittaker, 'La réforme du droit des obligations traduite en anglais' D 2007, 712; S Whittaker and J Cartwright, 'Translating the *Avant-projet de réforme*', below ch 21.
[41] Javolen, Ulpian Dig 50.17.202.
[42] P Catala, 'Bref aperçu sur l'avant projet de réforme du droit des obligations' D 2006, 535, 537.
[43] Catala, above n 11, 184, 185. See also Catala, above n 18, 13 (see below p 471). For a similar assessment, see Jamin, above n 21, 102.
[44] Catala, above n 18, 11 (see below p 465).

Professor Catala after the publication of the *Avant-projet*.[45] According to these, the draft Title on obligations contains 488 provisions, as compared to the 296 articles in the present Titles III and IV of the third book. There are 406 draft provisions on contracts. Of these, 113 remain unchanged and 69 only change their language, but not their substance; 140 draft articles (34 per cent of the contract law provisions) codify the exiting law, normally by restating the case-law of the Cour de cassation; and only 84 (21 per cent) are full-blown innovations.[46] The picture is different in the proposed Sub-title on civil liability where the number of articles increases from 6 to 64, partially because of the famously laconic style of the current provisions on delict, partially because it is suggested to deal with contractual and delictual liability together.

One of the innovations is the proposed Preliminary Chapter to draft Title III, another prologue with 'pedagogical character'.[47] It lists the various sources of obligations and defines them, notably by introducing the notion of *acte juridique*. The seven Chapters of Sub-title I on contracts mostly reproduce the subdivisions of the current Code civil. Chapter I, however, includes a new Section 2 on the 'Formation of Contracts', a topic that is famously absent from the present Code civil: draft articles 1104–1107 contain an elaborate set of rules on offer and acceptance, pre-contractual liability and pre-contracts.[48]

Chapter II deals with the requirements for the validity of contracts. Noteworthy provisions include article 1113-2 on fraud originating from a third party, article 1114-3 on the exploitation of the other party's weakness, article 1122-2 on abusive terms (which can only be revised or struck out if there is a special provision to this effect) and articles 1121-3 to 1121-6 which reduce the scope for unilateral determination of the contract price. Surprisingly, the Chapter retains the doctrine of *la cause*, one of the particuliarities of French private law that even some French lawyers are no longer willing to defend (articles 1124 to 1126-1).[49] As opposed to this, the law of representation, one of the areas where the present Code is still stuck in the eighteenth century *ius commune*, only offering the instruments of mandate and *gestion d'affaires*, is finally enshrined in the text of the Code (articles 1119 to 1120-1). The Chapter also suggests adding a new Section on formalities, particularly the form of electronic contracts, all whilst maintaining the principle of informality (article 1127). Finally, the present articles 1304–1314 and 1338–1340 Cc are regrouped in a new Section on sanctions for invalidity (articles 1129–1133).

[45] Catala, above n 42, 535–6.
[46] The most important of these are listed by Catala, above n 18, 14 (see below pp 471–3).
[47] Catala, above n 42, 536.
[48] B Fauvarque-Cosson, 'Negotiation and Renegotiation: A French Perspective', below ch 2; J Cartwright, 'Negotiation and Renegotiation: An English Perspective', below ch 3.
[49] J Rochfeld, 'A Future for *la cause*? Observations of a French Jurist', below ch 4; R Sefton-Green, '*La cause* or the Length of the French Judiciary's Foot', below ch 5.

Chapter III, on the 'Effects of Contracts', retains the pivotal articles 1134 and 1135 Cc, reuniting the latter with the present article 1160. Draft articles 1135-1 to 1135-3 provide an elaborate mechanism for renegotiations in cases where a serious imbalance arises as a result of supervening events in the performance of a contract, but they deliberately stop short of giving the judge the power to adapt the contract.[50] The second Section of the Chapter introduces the technique of classification of the contract (articles 1142–1143). It also concerns some interesting changes in the rules on contractual interpretation, most notably by codifying the judge-made doctrines of *acte clair* and *dénaturation* (articles 1138 and 1141), by elevating *raison* and *équité* to general criteria of interpretation (article 1139) and by providing for an interpretation against the party under whose 'dominant influence' the contract was made without limiting this to consumer or standard-form contracts (article 1140-1). Sections 3 and 4 of the Chapter retain the fundamental distinction between *obligations de donner* and *de faire*, and add, controversially, the category of *obligations de donner à usage* (article 1146).[51] The fifth Section suggests wide-ranging changes in the provisions on non-performance,[52] the sixth Section introduces a completely new set of articles on restitution after the retroactive destruction of a contract, and the seventh and final Section codifies much of the case-law on the effects of contracts on third parties.[53]

Chapters IV, V and VII on the modalities, the extinction and the proof of obligations suggest only relatively marginal changes. By contrast, Chapter VI on 'Transactions Relating to Rights Under Obligations' is entirely new. It dedicates four Sections to the assignment of rights under obligations, personal subrogation, novation and delegation. Some of the provisions are highly innovative.

Sub-title II retains the outdated historical reference to 'Quasi-contracts' in its heading; but at least 'quasi-delict' does not make a reappearance. The Sub-title essentially codifies the case-law on *gestion d'affaires*, undue payment and *enrichissement sans cause*. The latter doctrine would be introduced into the Code for the first time, but it would continue to lead a backyard existence (articles 1336–1339). Subtitle III on civil liability attempts to unify contractual and extra-contractual liability. It contains

---

[50] Fauvarque-Cosson and Cartwright, above n 48.

[51] For the Section on performance, see Y-M Laithier, 'The Enforcement of Contractual Obligations: A French Perspective', below ch 6; L Miller, 'The Enforcement of Contractual Obligations: Comparative Observations on the Notion of Performance', below ch 7.

[52] M Fabre-Magnan, 'Termination of Contract: A Missed Opportunity for Reform', below ch 8; S Whittaker, '"Termination" for Contractual Non-performance and its Consequences: French Law Reviewed in the Light of the *Avant-projet de réforme*', below ch 9.

[53] D Mazeaud, 'Contracts and Third Parties in the *Avant-projet de réforme*', below ch 10; S Vogenauer, 'The Effects of Contracts on Third Parties: The *Avant-projet de réforme* in a Comparative Perspective', below ch 11.

central definitions of the types of reparable losses (articles 1343–1346),[54] creates a regime of liability which is generally more favourable to victims of personal injury (articles 1341, 1351, 1373, 1382-1), formally recognises the rule of *non cumul* (article 1341), broadens strict liability (article 1362) and liability in general,[55] makes the controversial suggestion of introducing punitive damages (article 1371),[56] and proposes, against the case-law of the Cour de cassation, that the victim should be required to mitigate his losses (article 1373). The draft Title on prescription maintains the link of prescriptive and acquisitive prescription that goes back to Roman law and has long been abandoned by other legal systems. It is, however, extremely innovative in cutting down the number of special limitation periods and by significantly shortening the general period from thirty to three years (article 2274).[57]

As far as the provisions on contract are concerned, the *Avant-projet* firmly remains within the French tradition of distinguishing general 'civil contracts' from 'commercial contracts'. The latter concern the legal relationships between merchants. They are governed by the Code civil, unless the Code de commerce provides to the contrary or commercial usages lead to a different result. The *Avant-projet* does not suggest the integration of the contract law rules of the Code de commerce into the Code civil. Indeed, it explicitly rejects this idea in its article 1103(2). Draft article 1306 provides a good example of the continuing bifurcation. It mirrors article 1341 Cc which stipulates that contracts over a certain sum or value (currently exceeding €1,500) can only be proved in writing. Article 1341(3) expressly provides that the provision is subject to special provisions for commercial transactions, and article L 110-3 Code de commerce indeed supersedes the evidentiary requirement by stating that commercial contracts can be proved 'by any means'. Instead of transferring this rule into the Code civil, the *Avant-projet*, in its article 1306(3), simply suggests the retention of the reference to the Commercial code that is currently contained in article 1341(3).

A similar vision of the contract law of the Code civil as a 'general law of contract' (*droit commun*) that applies to all citizens equally is reflected in the decision not to integrate rules for the protection of consumers which are currently dealt with in another special code, the Code de la consommation. This is again made clear in article 1103(2). The reform proposals certainly show a general concern for protecting the weaker party against

[54] P Rémy-Corlay, 'Damages, Loss and the Quantification of Damages in the *Avant-projet de réforme*', below ch 14.

[55] J-S Borghetti, 'The Definition of *la faute* in the *Avant-projet de réforme*', below ch 12; P Giliker, 'The Role of *la faute* in the *Avant-projet de réforme*', below ch 13.

[56] S Rowan, 'Comparative Observations on the Introduction of Punitive Damages in French Law', below ch 15.

[57] R Wintgen, 'Reforming the French Law of Prescription: A French Perspective', below ch 16; Cartwright, above n 34.

unfair exploitation, and sometimes they adopt principles from consumer law for the general law of contract, such as the pre-contractual duty of information imposed on parties with superior knowledge in article 1110 of the *Avant-projet*. Draft article 1122-2 on abusive terms mentions consumers by way of example. But the *Avant-projet* contains only one explicit consumer protection rule—draft article 1382-2(2)—which imposes severe restrictions on the validity of exemption and limitation clauses employed by businesspeople. The *Avant-projet* therefore adopts a very different approach from the 2002 reform of the German law of obligations. This had the incorporation of special consumer protection legislation into the Civil code as one of its main aims.[58] As opposed to this, the Code civil, as is emphatically stated in the general introduction to the *Avant-projet*, 'addresses all citizens alike, looking after them with Republican equality from their first breath to their last'.[59]

The need for a general law of contract to strike a balance between the needs of commerce and the protection of consumers was emphasised at the outset of the *Avant-projet*.[60] However, whilst the reform proposals stress the importance of freedom of contract and party autonomy, it cannot be overlooked that they give greater attention to considerations of substantive fairness than the Code of 1804.[61] This can be seen by the increased role of good faith, although the doctrine is not elevated to an overarching general principle of law, as it can be found in the laws of Germany, the Netherlands and the United States.[62] But there is a stronger emphasis on duties of co-operation, information, loyalty, etc (articles 1104, 1110, 1150, etc), and there are a number of provisions designed to safeguard the contractual equilibrium (articles 1114-3, 1122-2, 1135-2, etc). As a consequence, the role of the judge *vis-à-vis* the parties has been strengthened: a term may be revised or suppressed in the case of a significant disequilibrium, renegotiation of the contract may be ordered in case of supervening circumstances and the debtor may be granted time to perform before the contract can be resolved for non-execution.[63]

V. RECEPTION

Once the *Avant-projet* had been submitted to the Ministry of Justice, the Minister initiated a round of consultation with the legal professions. In

---

[58] Zimmermann, above n 17, 159–228.
[59] Catala, above n 18, 12 (see below p 467).
[60] *Ibid*.
[61] *Ibid*, 15 (see below p 475): a 'spirit of solidarity'.
[62] See § 242 BGB, arts 6:2, 6:248 NBW, §§ 1-201(20), 1-302(b), 1-304, 2-103(j) UCC and § 205 Restatement 2d Contracts.
[63] J-P Ancel, 'Le référé-contrat' D 2006, 2409.

response, three major reports were published, one by the Cour de cassation,[64] one by the Chambre de commerce et d'industrie de Paris (CCIP),[65] and another one by the National Bar Council, the Conseil national des barreaux.[66] They were broadly favourable to the reform and its aims, but contained many, partly conflicting, proposals for amendments. The Bar Council deplored the complexity of the draft provisions and suggested, *inter alia*, changes to the draft articles on proof. The Cour de cassation, in a very thoughtful contribution, criticised individual features of the *Avant-projet*, notably the retention of the doctrine of *la cause* and the timid approach towards supervening circumstances. By contrast, the Paris Chamber of Commerce regarded the draft articles on supervening circumstances as too far-reaching. It also opposed the extension of principles derived from unfair contract terms legislation beyond the strict consumer context, the general tendency to extend liability and the introduction of punitive damages. All three bodies were generally supportive of the proposed changes to the law of prescription.

At the same time, the *Avant-projet* was subjected to extensive academic scrutiny. The Revue des contrats organised a major colloquium on the reform of the law of contract on 25 October 2005 and another one dealing with the reform proposals on civil liability on 12 May 2006. The proceedings of both colloquia were published,[67] as were many other academic comments, some of which even contained alternative drafts for parts of the project.[68] At least one of the leading French textbooks on the law of obligations has systematically incorporated references to the *Avant-projet*.[69] The academic analysis was, by its very nature, conducted in a critical spirit, focusing on the perceived weaknesses of the reform proposals. But criticism was constructive, measured, and, on the whole, much more sympathetic

---

[64] Cour de cassation, *Rapport du groupe de travail de la Cour de cassation sur l'avant-projet de réforme du droit des obligations et de la prescription* (2007), http://www.courdecassation.fr/jurisprudence_publications_documentation_2/autres_publications_discours_2039/discours_22 02/2007_2271/groupe_travail_10699.html. See Sargos, above n 14.

[65] Chambre de commerce et d'industrie de Paris, *Pour une réforme du droit des contrats et de la prescription conforme aux besoins de la vie des affaires* (2006), http://www.etudes.ccip.fr/archrap/pdf06/reforme-droit-des-contrats-kli0610.pdf. See also D Kling and A Outin-Adam, 'Réforme du droit des obligations: La CCIP réagit au rapport Catala' LPA 16 January 2007, no 12, 3; V Charbonnier, 'La CCIP souligne l'urgence d'une modernisation du droit des contrats' Droit et patrimoine 2007, no 155, 10.

[66] Conseil national des barreaux, *Projet de rapport du groupe de travail chargé d'étudier l'avant-projet de réforme du droit des obligations et du droit de la prescription* (2006), http://www.cnb.avocat.fr/PDF/2006-11-09_obligations.pdf. See also C Jamin, 'Les avocats et l'avant-projet de réforme du droit des obligations et du droit de la prescription' JCP G 2006 Actualités 479, 1927.

[67] The contributions were published in issues 1/2006 and 1/2007 of the Revue.

[68] L Aynès and A Hontebeyrie, 'Pour une réforme du Code civil en matière d'obligation conjointe et d'obligation solidaire' D 2006, 328. See also D Mazeaud, above n 53.

[69] P Malinvaud, *Droit des obligations* (10th edn, Paris, Litec, 2007).

towards the proposals than, for instance, the academic reactions to the first draft preceding the 2002 German reform of the law of obligations.[70]

The reform proposals have also been cited in the courts. Their solutions were sometimes approved,[71] sometimes rejected.[72] It has been argued, although this is hard to prove, that the courts generally take account of the project in developing the law when they feel that its propositions go into the right direction.[73]

Finally, the *Avant-projet* has received international attention. It has been translated into English, German, Italian and Spanish. Further translations into Arabic and Japanese are envisaged.[74] Comparative lawyers have analysed its provisions.[75] The leading English-language account on the French law of obligations frequently refers to it.[76] It has even served as a point of reference for the current Japanese Civil Code (Law of Obligations) Reform Commission and the Working Group preparing the third edition of the UNIDROIT Principles.[77]

Immediately after the publication of the *Avant-projet* it was hoped that, after conclusion of the consultation exercise mentioned above, the reform proposals would be scrutinised by the Conseil d'Etat and would then be introduced into the legislative process.[78] However, complaints about a lack of political enthusiasm for the implementation of the project were voiced as early as January 2007.[79] Soon thereafter, in June of the same year, the Senate took the initiative on a reform of the law of prescription.[80] This proposal developed into a wholesale revision of Title XX of Book III of the Code civil which came into force on 19 June 2008.[81] Although the introductory report referred to the draft bill as 'the legislative translation' of the draft provisions prepared by Professor Malaurie,[82] the final product bears

---

[70] W Ernst and R Zimmermann (eds), *Zivilrechtswissenschaft und Schuldrechtsreform* (2001).

[71] See the opinion of the *Conseiller rapporteur* in Ass plén 14 April 2006, published as B Petit, 'Les critères de la force majeure' RJDA 2006, 679, 687.

[72] See the opinion of the Premier avocat général M Garrizzo in Ass plén 6 October 2006, D 2006, 2825.

[73] L Leveneur, 'Réforme du droit des obligations: effervescence autour de l'avant-projet' Contrats Concur Consom September 2006, 1, referring to Cass mixte 26 May 2006, Contrats Concur Consom September 2006, no 153.

[74] Catala, above n 32, JCP 1740.

[75] See the bibliography below. The *Association Henri Capitant* held a conference on the international reception of the *Avant-projet* on 1 April 2008, the proceedings of which will be published under its auspices.

[76] J Bell, S Boyron and S Whittaker, *Principles of French Law* (2nd edn, Oxford University Press, 2008) 294-452.

[77] UNIDROIT 2008, Study L—Doc 105 (Draft Chapter on Unwinding of Failed Contracts) 6; UNIDROIT 2008, Study L—Doc 108 (Draft Chapter on Conditional Obligations) 6, 7.

[78] Catala, above n 32, 1741.

[79] D Mazeaud and T Revet, 'Editorial' RDC 2007, 3; D Mazeaud and T Revet, 'Editorial' RDC 2007, 219, 220.

[80] Rapport no 338 (2006–2007) de M Jean-Jacques Hyest, déposé au Sénat le 20 juin 2007.

[81] Loi no 2008-561 du 17 juin 2008 portant réforme de la prescription en matière civile, JO 18 June 2008, 9856.

[82] Rapport no 432 (2006–2007) de M Jean-Jacques Hyest, déposé au Sénat le 2 août 2007, p 5.

little resemblance to the corresponding parts of the *Avant-projet*. The material was completely restructured and spread over two new Titles XX (on extinctive prescription) and XXI (on acquisitive prescription). Most importantly, the general limitation period which starts to run as soon as the creditor has knowledge or ought to have knowledge of the relevant circumstances is five, rather than three years; the long-stop period is twenty, rather than ten years (new articles 2224, 2232 Cc).

In June 2008, when this chapter was submitted for publication, the fortunes of the *Avant-projet's* provisions on contracts, quasi-contracts and civil responsibility were far from clear. No legislative initiatives seemed to be on their way. However, the election of a new President, who appointed a high-flying Minister of Justice, had helped to revive the project. In September 2007, the Minister announced that she intended to engage in a modernisation of the entire law of obligations.[83] The three major reforms of the Code civil that were enacted after the publication of the *Avant-projet* showed that substantial changes of the Code can be made relatively swiftly if there is a political will to change the law. They led to the adoption of an entirely new fourth Book 'On Securities' (articles 2284–2488),[84] the introduction of the trust-like device of *fiducie* in a new Title XIV in the third Book of the Code (articles 2011–2031)[85] and a wholesale revision of the laws of succession and donations by way of recodifying the first two Titles of the third Book (articles 720-1100).[86] If this pace of change was anything to go by, some form of legislative implementation of the *Avant-projet* did not seem impossible.

Nevertheless, in July 2008 many French lawyers were taken by surprise when it transpired that the Ministry of Justice had finalised a first legislative proposal for the reform of the law of contract.[87] This document, usually referred to as the *Projet de la chancellerie*, had been drafted by a small Working Group comprising four judges who were seconded to the Ministry and Professor Bénédicte Fauvarque-Cosson of the University of Paris II. It was officially presented to the public at a conference organised by the Revue des contrats on 24 September 2008.[88] The 195 articles of the

---

[83] Discours de Madame Rachida Dati, garde des Sceaux, ministre de la Justice, au 103ème Congrès des Notaires de France, 24 September 2007, http://www.presse.justice.gouv.fr.

[84] Ordonnance no 2006-346 du 23 mars 2006 relative aux sûretés, JO 24 March 2006, 4475. For overview see Ph Simler, 'La réforme du droit des sûretés: un livre IV nouveau du Code civil' JCP G 2006 I 124; S Piedelièvre, 'Premier aperçu sur la réforme du droit des sûretés par l'ordonnance du 23 mars 2006' Defr 2006, 791.

[85] Loi no 2007-211 du 19 février 2007 instituant la fiducie, JO 21 February 2007, 3051. For a first assessment, see the contributions in D 2007, 1346–75.

[86] Loi no 2006-728 du 23 juin 2006 portant réforme des successions et des libéralités, JO 24 June 2006, 9513.

[87] Ministère de la Justice, *Projet de réforme du droit des contrats*, July 2008. The draft has not been published but is available at http://www.dimitri-houtcieff.fr/files/projet_droit_des_contrats_blog8_2_.pdf. For a short overview, see B Fauvarque-Cosson, D 2008, 2965.

[88] The contributions will be published in issue 1/2009 of the Revue.

Ministry draft take up and develop many of the ideas of the *Avant-projet de réforme*. For example, they contain a set of definitions, a number of provisions on the pre-contractual negotiations and the formation of contracts, a regime for representation and a rule on the consequences of supervening events. However, the last mentioned provision, article 136 of the draft, shows that some solutions of the *Projet de la chancellerie* go far beyond the *Avant-projet* and display a much greater willingness to bring the Code civil in line with the contract laws of other European jurisdictions and the current international proposals for contract law reform: article 136 authorises the courts to adapt or terminate contracts if the parties refuse to renegotiate or the renegotiation fails, provided the parties agree to judicial adaptation.[89] The Ministry draft also codifies three 'guiding' or 'governing principles' of contract law: freedom of contract, *pacta sunt servanda* and good faith (articles 15–18), whilst the *Avant-projet de réforme* stops short of establishing an overarching principle of *bonne foi*.[90] Finally, the Ministry draft, in its articles 49 and 85–87, suggests abolishing the doctrine of *cause* and replacing it with the notion of 'interest' (*intérêt*).[91] All of these innovations have been subject to vivid criticism by legal scholars,[92] but feelings have run particularly high with regard to the suppression of *la cause*.[93] By contrast, the legal professions and the Paris Chamber of Commerce were broadly supportive.[94]

The latest twist in the saga of French contract law reform was the submission of another set of reform proposals to the Ministry of Justice in December 2008. This draft is the result of a Working Group led by François Terré, professor emeritus of the University of Paris II and President of the *Académie des sciences morales et politiques*. The establishment of the Working Group had been encouraged by the then Minister of Justice in 2006. The Ministry also provided some intellectual and

---

[89] Cf above p 13.

[90] Cf above p 15.

[91] Cf above p 12. The reconceptualisation of *cause* as 'interest' has long been advocated by Judith Rochfeld, most recently in her contribution to this volume, above n 49.

[92] For fundamental attacks, see R Cabrillac, 'Le projet de réforme du droit des contrats: Premières impressions' JCP G 2008 I 190; A Ghozi and Y Lequette, 'La réforme du droit des contrats: brèves observations sur le projet de la chancellerie' D 2008, 2609. For a much more positive assessment, see M Fabre-Magnan, 'Réforme du droit des contrats: "Un très bon projet"' JCP G 2008 I 199; D Mazeaud, 'Réforme du droit des contrats: haro, en Hérault, sur le projet!' D 2008, 2675.

[93] C Larroumet, 'De la cause de l'obligation à l'intérêt au contrat (à propos du projet de réforme du droit des contrats)' D 2008, 2441; P Malinvaud, 'Le "contenu certain" du contrat dans l'avant-projet "chancellerie" de code des obligations ou le *stoemp* bruxellois aux légumes' D 2008, 2551; O Tournafond, 'Pourquoi il faut conserver la théorie de la cause en droit civil français' D 2008, 2607.

[94] 'Projet de réforme du droit des contrats', Lettre du Conseil national des barreaux no 59, November 2008; Chambre de commerce et d'industrie de Paris, *Vers un droit des contrats modernisé et mieux adapté à la vie des affaires: Réaction de la CCIP à la consultation de la Chancellerie de juillet 2008* (2008), http://www.etudes.ccip.fr/archrap/pdf08/reforme-droit-des-contrats-kli0810.pdf.

financial support. The Drafting Committee of the Group consisted of seven law professors and a representative of the Paris Chamber of Commerce. Approximately a dozen further academics and practitioners contributed to the effort. The black letter rules of the Academy draft, or *Projet Terré*, were published alongside a number of articles on the fundamental issues of the reform and some short reports on the proposed development of particular doctrines of contract law.[95] In some areas, the Academy draft closely follows the *Avant-projet de réforme*. These include the essential conditions for the validity of contracts, in particular the requirement of consent. However, with regard to the more controversial issues, the *Projet Terré* rather sides with the *Projet de la chancellerie* with which it shares its much more comparative and international outlook: some fundamental contract law standards, such as freedom of contract and good faith, are codified at the outset – albeit without explicitly ascribing to them the status of 'governing principles' (articles 3–6); the judicial power to adapt the contract in the light of supervening circumstances is not only acknowledged, but even subjected to less restrictive requirements (article 92); and the doctrine of *cause* is discarded without replacing it with a proxy, such as 'interest' (article 13).

It is to be expected that the *Projet Terré* will exert a strong influence in the further elaboration of the *Projet de la Chancellerie*. A revised draft of the latter is expected in early 2009 and could be submitted to the Conseil d'Etat and Parliament later in the year. The Ministry has already signalled that, once the revision of contract law has been concluded, it will embark on a reform of the law concerning civil liability, the one area of the *Avant-projet de réforme* that it has not yet tackled.

VI. CONCLUSIONS

It has not been the purpose of this contribution to assess the merits and demerits of the *Avant-projet*. This will be done by the authors of the following chapters. I would like to conclude with three short observations.

First, the *Avant-projet* is a powerful statement of the role of *la doctrine* in France.[96] It shows a corporate body of legal scholarship that proposes a major reform which is aimed not only at restructuring and reconceptualising the law, but makes decidedly political suggestions, such as the introduction of punitive damages or the expansion of civil liability in general. It would perhaps go too far to speak of this 'collective legislative

---

[95] F Terré (ed), *Pour une réforme du droit des contrats: Réflexions et propositions d'un groupe de travail sous la direction de François Terré* (Paris, Dalloz, 2009).

[96] For the role of legal scholarship in France, see P Jestaz and C Jamin, *La doctrine* (Paris, Dalloz, 2004). For an overview in English, see P Jestaz and C Jamin, 'The Entity of French Doctrine: Some Thoughts on the Community of French Legal Writers' (1998) 18 LS 415.

doctrine' as a 'source of law',[97] but it is difficult to imagine a similar collaborative and proactive effort in Britain.

Second, the *Avant-projet* displays a major defect for a project that is explicitly designed to influence the international contract law discourse: an almost total absence of comparative reasoning.[98] With very few exceptions, notably the *exposé des motifs* regarding the law of prescription, developments outside France are either ignored or dealt with by simple assertions that a particular solution is better than that of the various international reform proposals.[99] The report of the Cour de cassation shows how comparatively little effort is needed to put the *Avant-projet* in the context of European contract law.[100] But, as the *doyen* of French comparative legal studies, Professor Tallon, has said, the project 'is meant to be Franco-French. . . . It remains firmly attached to rules that are strongly criticised internally and largely abandoned in modern legislation' abroad.[101]

This leads to a third, and final, point. As a consequence of the essentially conservative character of the *Avant-projet*, the reform proposals suggest retaining a number of doctrines and institutions that have been left behind in other countries or have always been considered too quirky to be adopted, such as *la cause, non cumul* or *quasi-contrat*. All of these may make perfect sense in the context of French private law. But it is vain to hope that their codification or recodification will enhance their exportability, or indeed the exportability of French law in general. If an international audience is to be persuaded that it should adopt any of these features it will need much more convincing than the mere enactment of a few articles in the Code civil.

Overall, however, it cannot be denied that the *Avant-projet* is an impressive achievement. It has launched a debate on the modernisation of the French law of obligations that was long overdue. It brought together some of the most distinguished legal scholars of this generation. Regardless of whether the reform proposals will be implemented or not, they represent an invaluable snapshot of contemporary French private law and will be of interest for years to come.

---

[97] P Deumier, 'Sources du droit en droit interne: La doctrine collective législatrice—une nouvelle source du droit?' RTD civ 2006, 63.

[98] In a similar vein, Jamin, above n 21, 102; Jamin, above n 66, 1928; E Hondius, 'The Two Faces of the Catala Project—Towards a New General Part of the French Law of Obligations' (2007) 15 ERPL 835, 839.

[99] For a detailed comparison of the *Avant-projet* and the PECL, see B Fauvarque-Cosson and D Mazeaud, 'L'avant-projet français de réforme du droit des obligations et du droit de la prescription et les principes du droit européen du contrat: variations sur les champs magnétique dans l'univers contractuel' LPA 24 July 2006, no 146, 3.

[100] See above n 64.

[101] D Tallon, 'Teneur et valeur du projet appréhendé dans une perspective comparative' RDC 2006, 131, 131–2. See also B Fauvarque-Cosson, 'La réforme du droit français des contrats: perspective comparative' RDC 2006, 147, 166.

BIBLIOGRAPHY

Ancel, Pascal, 'Das Projekt Catala zur Reform des Schuldrechts in Frankreich – einige Aspekte' in O Remien (ed), *Schuldrechtsmodernisierung und Europäisches Vertragsrecht* (Tübingen, Mohr Siebeck, 2008) 45.

——, 'Le référé contrat' D 2006, 2409.

——, 'Présentation des solutions de l'avant-projet' RDC 2007, 19.

——, 'Quelques observations sur la structure des sections relatives à l'exécution et à l'inexécution des contrats' RDC 2007, 105.

Arteil, David, 'L'effet des conventions à l'égard des tiers dans l'avant-projet de réforme du droit des obligations' LPA 15 November 2006, no 228, 11.

Assié, Francis, 'L'inexécution d'un contrat invoquée par un tiers' RJDA 2007, 3.

Aubert, Jean-Luc, 'Quelques remarques sur l'obligation pour la victime de limiter les conséquences dommageables d'un fait générateur de responsabilité : À propos de l'article 1373 de l'avant-projet de réforme du droit des obligations' in M Fabre-Magnan et al (eds), *Etudes offertes à Geneviève Viney* (Paris, LGDJ, 2008) 55.

Aynès, Laurent, 'La trajectoire du droit des contrats' RJ com 19 November 2005, 182.

——, 'Les effets du contrat à l'égard des tiers' RDC 2006, 63.

Aynès, Laurent and Antoine Hontebeyrie, 'Pour une réforme du Code civil en matière d'obligation conjointe et d'obligation solidaire' D 2006, 328.

Beale, Hugh, 'La réforme du droit français des contrats et le "droit européen des contrats": perspective de la Law Commission anglaise' RDC 2006, 135.

Béhar-Touchais, Martine, 'De l'influence éventuelle de l'avant-projet de réforme de la responsabilité civile sur le droit des pratiques restrictives et des contrats de distribution' Revue Lamy de la concurrence 1 July 2006, 41.

Bénabent, Alain, 'Autour de la méthode générale, ainsi que des nullités et autres sanctions' RDC 2006, 33.

——, 'Les difficultés de la recodification: les contrats spéciaux' in *Le Code civil 1804-2004: Livre du bicentenaire* (Paris, Litec, Dalloz, 2004) 245.

Boillot, Christine, 'Les perspectives renouvelées des rapports entre action paulienne et nullités de la période suspecte à travers l'avant-projet Catala et la réforme du 26 juillet 2005' in M Fabre-Magnan et al (eds), *Etudes offertes à Geneviève Viney* (Paris, LGDJ, 2008) 113.

Bouteille, Magali, 'Regard critique sur la modalité conditionnelle dans l'avant-projet de réforme du droit des obligations et de la prescription' D 2008, 1848.

Brissy, Stéphane, 'L'avant-projet de réforme du droit des obligations: une source d'évolution pour le droit du travail?' Droit social 2007, no 1, 8.

Brun, Philippe, 'Avant-projet de réforme du droit des obligations: le fait d'autrui—Présentation sommaire' RDC 2007, 103.

Cartwright, John and Simon Whittaker, 'La réforme du droit des obligations traduite en anglais' D 2007, 712.

Catala, Pierre, 'Au-delà du bicentenaire' RDC 2004, 1145.

——, 'Bref aperçu sur l'avant projet de réforme du droit des obligations' D 2006, 535.

——, 'Cession de créance et subrogation personnelle dans l'avant-projet de réforme du droit des obligations' in *Libre droit: Mélanges en l'honneur de Philippe Le Tourneau* (Paris, Dalloz, 2008) 213.

——, 'Colloque sur l'avant-projet de réforme du droit de la responsabilité: Ouverture' RDC 2007, 7.

——, 'Il est temps de rendre au Code civil son rôle de droit commun des contrats' JCP G 2005 I 170, 1739.

——, 'Interprétation et qualification dans l'avant-projet de réforme des obligations' in M Fabre-Magnan et al (eds), *Etudes offertes à Geneviève Viney* (Paris, LGDJ, 2008) 243–57.

——, 'La délégation dans l'avant-projet de réforme du droit des obligations' in *Etudes offertes au Doyen Philippe Simler* (Paris, Litec, Dalloz, 2006) 555.

——, 'La genèse et le dessein du projet' RDC 2006, 11.

——, 'L'avant-projet de réforme des obligations et le droit des affaires' RJ com 1 May 2007, no 3, 182.

Cabrillac, Rémy, 'Réforme du droit des contrats: révision-modification ou révision-compilation?' RDC 2006, 25.

Chabas, François, 'Observations sur le fait personnel et le fait des choses' RDC 2007, 73.

Chagny, Muriel, 'La notion de dommages et intérêts punitifs et ses répercussions sur le droit de la concurrence' JCP G 2006 I 149, 1223.

Chambre de commerce et d'industrie de Paris, *Pour une réforme du droit des contrats et de la prescription conforme aux besoins de la vie des affaires* (2006).[102]

Charbonnier, Vanessa, 'La CCIP souligne l'urgence d'une modernisation du droit des contrats' Droit et patrimoine 2007, no 155, 10.

Conseil national des barreaux, *Projet de rapport du groupe de travail chargé d'étudier l'avant-projet de réforme du droit des obligations et du droit de la prescription* (2006).[103]

Cornu, Gérard, 'Étude législative' RDC 2006, 19.

Cour de cassation, *Rapport du groupe de travail de la Cour de cassation sur l'avant-projet de réforme du droit des obligations et de la prescription* (2007).[104]

---

[102] http://www.etudes.ccip.fr/archrap/pdf06/reforme-droit-des-contrats-kli0610.pdf.

[103] http://www.cnb.avocat.fr/PDF/2006-11-09_obligations.pdf.

[104] http://www.courdecassation.fr/jurisprudence_publications_documentation_2/autres_publications_discours_2039/discours_2202/2007_2271/groupe_travail_10699.html.

Deckert, Katrin, 'La réforme du droit français des obligations: une perspective allemande' (2007) 15 ERPL 765.

Delebecque, Philippe, 'L'exécution forcée' RDC 2006, 99.

Deumier, Pascale, 'Sources du droit en droit interne: La doctrine collective législatrice—une nouvelle source du droit?' RTD civ 2006, 63.

Dubuisson, Bertrand, 'Les responsabilités du fait d'autrui (articles 1355 à 1362): point de vue d'un juriste belge' RDC 2007, 125.

Dufour, Olivia, 'Rapport Catala: l'ambitieuse réforme du droit des obligations' LPA 5 October 2005, no 198, 3.

Durry, Georges, 'Colloque sur l'avant-projet de réforme du droit de la responsabilité: Conclusion' RDC 2007, 181.

Editorial, 'Réforme du droit des obligations' D 2005, 2961.

Emy, Philippe, 'A propos de l'opposabilité d'une cession de créance: Réflexions sur l'avant-projet de réforme du droit des obligations' D 2008, 2886.

Fages, Bertrand, 'Autour de l'objet et de la cause' RDC 2006, 37.

——, 'Réforme de la responsabilité du fait d'autrui et sort réservé aux sociétés mères' RDC 2007, 115.

Fasquelle, Daniel and Rodolphe Mésa, 'La sanction de la concurrence déloyale et du parasitisme économique et le Rapport Catala' D 2005, 2666.

Faure-Abbad, Marianne, 'La présentation de l'inexécution contractuelle dans l'avant-projet Catala' D 2007, 165.

Fauvarque-Cosson, Bénédicte, 'L'avant-projet français de réforme du droit des obligations et de la prescription: présentation générale' (2007) 15 ERPL 761.

——, 'La réforme du droit français des contrats: perspective comparative' RDC 2006, 147.

——, 'Towards a New French Law of Obligations and Prescription?' ZEuP 2007, 428.

—— and Denis Mazeaud, 'L'avant-projet français de réforme du droit des obligations et du droit de la prescription et les principes du droit européen du contrat: variations sur les champs magnétiques dans l'univers contractuel' LPA 24 July 2006, no 146, 3.

—— and Denis Mazeaud, 'Nouvelles de France: vers une réforme possible du droit des contrats . . . ' in A Brzozowski et al (eds), *Towards Europeanization of Private Law: Essays in Honour of Professor Jerzy Rajski* (Warsaw, Beck, 2007) 497.

Fenouillet, Dominique, 'Les effets du contrat entre les parties: ni révolution, ni conservation, mais un 'entre-deux' perfectible' RDC 2006, 67.

Ferrante, Alfredo, 'Una primera aproximación al *Avant-Projet Catala* y a la nueva responsabilidad civil en el Derecho Francés' InDret: Revista para el Análisis del Derecho 1/2008.

Forest, Grégoire, 'Avant-projet de réforme du droit des obligations et contrats préparatoires à la vente immobilière' LPA 11 July 2006, no 137, 6.

García Cantero, Gabriel, 'Notes comparatives sur le régime de la représent-ation contenu dans l'avant-projet de réforme du droit des obligations' (2007) 15 ERPL 781.

Ghestin, Jacques, 'Le futur: exemples étrangers. Le Code civil en France aujourd'hui' RDC 2004, 1169.

Giliker, Paula, 'Codifying Tort Law : Lessons from the Proposals for Reform of the French Civil Code' (2008) 57 ICLQ 561.

Guégan-Lécuyer, Anne, 'Vers un nouveau fait générateur de responsabilité civile: les activités dangereuses (Commentaire de l'article 1362 de l'Avant-projet Catala)' in M Fabre-Magnan et al (eds), *Etudes offertes à Geneviève Viney* (Paris, LGDJ, 2008) 499.

Hécart, Charles, 'L'article 1342 de l'avant-projet Catala: quelle cohérence?' D 2006, 2268.

Hondius, Ewoud, 'The Two Faces of the Catala Project—Towards a New General Part of the French Law of Obligations' (2007) 15 ERPL 835 = in *Liber Amicorum Guido Alpa: Private Law Beyond the National Systems* (London, British Institute of International and Comparative Law, 2007) 526.

Huet, Jérôme, 'Des distinctions entre les obligations' RDC 2006, 89.

——, 'Observations sur la distinction entre les responsabilités contractuelle et délictuelle dans l'avant-projet de réforme du droit des obligations' RDC 2007, 31.

Jacometti, Valentina and Barbara Pozzo, 'L'avant-projet Catala dans la per-spective de recodification du droit italien des obligations' (2007) 15 ERPL 821.

Jamin, Christophe, 'Vers un droit européen des contrats? (Réflexions sur une double stratégie)' RJ com 2006, 94.

——, 'Les avocats et l'avant-projet de réforme du droit des obligations et du droit de la prescription' JCP G 2006 Actualités 479, 1927.

Jourdain, Patrice, 'Présentation des dispositions de l'avant-projet sur les effets de la responsabilité' RDC 2007, 141.

Kling, Didier and Anne Outin-Adam, 'Réforme du droit des obligations: la CCIP réagit au rapport Catala' LPA 16 January 2007, no 12, 3.

Lambert-Faivre, Yvonne, 'Les effets de la responsabilité (les articles 1367 à 1383 nouveaux du Code civil)' RDC 2007, 163.

Lando, Ole, 'L'avant-projet de réforme du droit des obligations et les Prin-cipes du droit européen du contrat: analyse de certaines différences' RDC 2006, 167.

Leduc, Fabrice, 'La responsabilité du fait personnel – La responsabilité du fait des choses' RDC 2007, 67.

Lehmann, Matthias, 'Le projet Catala et le droit allemand' RDC 2007, 1427.

Leveneur, Laurent, 'Réforme du droit des obligations: effervescence autour de l'avant-projet' Contrats Concur Consom September 2006, 1.

Le Tourneau, Philippe, 'Brefs propos critiques sur la "responsabilité contractuelle" dans l'avant projet de réforme de la responsabilité' D 2007, 2180.

——, 'Les responsabilités du fait d'autrui dans l'avant-projet de réforme' RDC 2007, 109.

—— and Jérôme Julien, 'La responsabilité extracontractuelle du fait d'autrui dans l'avant-projet de réforme du Code civil' in M Fabre-Magnan et al (eds), *Etudes offertes à Geneviève Viney* (Paris, LGDJ, 2008) 579.

Lienhard, Claude, 'Réparation intégrale des préjudices en cas de dommage corporel: la nécessité d'un nouvel équilibre indemnitaire' D 2006, 2485.

Lorenz, Stephan, 'La responsabilité contractuelle dans l'avant-projet: un point de vue allemand' RDC 2007, 57.

Malaurie, Philippe, 'Présentation de l'avant-projet de réforme du droit des obligations et du droit de la prescription' RDC 2006, 7.

Mazeaud, Denis, 'Les conventions portant sur la réparation' RDC 2007, 149.

——, 'Colloque sur la réforme du droit des contrats: Observations conclusives' RDC 2006, 177.

Méadel, Juliette, 'Faut-il introduire la faute lucrative en droit français ?' LPA 17 April 2007, no 77, 6.

Messaï-Bahri, Soraya, 'La sanction de l'inexécution des avant-contrats au lendemain de l'avant-projet de réforme du droit des obligations' LPA 24 July 2006, no 146, 12.

Mignot, Marc, 'Aperçu critique de l'avant-projet de loi sur la prescription' RRJ 2007, 1639.

——, 'Regards critiques sur l'avant-projet de loi relatif à la délégation de personne' Revue Lamy Droit civil 1 February 2007, 27.

Nelter, Marie-Catherine, 'Les innovations majeures de l'avant-projet de réforme du droit des obligations' Contrats Concur Consom December 2005, 4.

Niemiec, Amélie, 'L'avant-projet de réforme du droit des obligations et du droit de la prescription: une véritable codification de la rencontre de volontés' LPA 2008, no 17, 11.

Paisant, Gilles, 'Le code de la consommation et l'avant-projet de réforme du droit des obligations, quelle influence et quelle harmonisation ?' JCP G 2006 Actualités 429, 1737.

Petit, Florent, 'Réflexions sur la sécurité dans la cession de créance dans l'avant-projet de réforme du droit des obligations' D 2006, 2819.

Pignarre, Geneviève, 'L'obligation de donner à usage dans l'avant-projet Catala: Analyse critique' D 2007, 384.

Poumarède, Matthieu, 'Les régimes particuliers de responsabilité civile, ces oubliés de l'avant-projet Catala' D 2006, 2420.

Radé, Christophe, 'Brefs propos sur une réforme en demi-teinte' RDC 2007, 77.

Rémy, Philippe, 'Réviser le titre III du livre troisième du Code civil' RDC 2004, 1169.

Rochfeld, Judith, 'La proposition de réforme des sanctions de l'inexécution du contrat dans l'avant-projet de réforme du Code civil français et l'influence européenne' in R Schulze (ed), *New Features in Contract Law* (Munich, Sellier, 2007) 197.

——, 'Remarques sur les propositions relatives à l'exécution et à l'inexécution du contrat: la subjectivation du droit de l'exécution' RDC 2006, 113.

Rouhette, Georges, 'Regard sur l'avant-projet de réforme du droit des obligations' RDC 2007, 1371.

Savaux, Éric, 'Brèves observations sur la responsabilité contractuelle dans l'avant-projet de réforme du droit de la responsabilité' RDC 2007, 45.

Sefton-Green, Ruth, 'The DCFR, the *Avant-projet Catala* and French Legal Scholars: A Story of Cat and Mouse?' (2008) 12 Edinburgh Law Review 351.

Sériaux, Alain, 'Vanitas vanitatum: De l'inanité d'une refonte du livre III du titre III du Code civil' RDC 2004, 1187.

Sonnenberger, Hans Jürgen, 'Der Vorentwurf der Reform des Code civil' ZEuP 2007, 421.

Stoffel-Munck, Philippe, 'Autour du consentement et de la violence économique' RDC 2006, 45.

Tallon, Denis, 'La rénovation du titre III, livre III du Code civil: une approche comparative' RDC 2004, 1190.

——, 'Teneur et valeur du projet appréhendé dans une perspective comparative' RDC 2006, 131.

Veille, 'La CCIP propose des amendements à l'avant-projet Catala', JCP G 2006 Actualités 542.

Viney, Geneviève, 'Colloque sur l'avant-projet de réforme du droit de la responsabilité: Présentation des textes' RDC 2007, 9.

——, 'Le droit de la responsabilité dans l'avant-projet Catala' in *La création du droit jurisprudentiel: Mélanges en l'honneur de Jacques Boré* (Paris, Dalloz, 2007) 473.

Wessner, Pierre, 'Les effets de la responsabilité civile dans la perspective d'une révision du Code civil français: quelques observations débridées d'un juriste suisse' RDC 2007, 171.

Whittaker, Simon, 'La responsabilité pour fait personnel dans l'avant-projet de réforme du droit de la responsabilité: donner voix aux silences du Code civil' RCD 2007, 89.

Zimmermann, Reinhard, '"Extinctive" Prescription under the *Avant-projet*' (2007) 15 ERPL 805.

——, '*Restitutio in integrum*: The Unwinding of Failed Contracts under the Principles of European Contract Law, the UNIDROIT Principles and the *Avant-projet d'un Code Européen des Contrats*' [2005] ULR 719.

Part II

Assessing the
Avant-Projet de réforme

A

Negotiation and Renegotiation

2

Negotiation and Renegotiation: A French Perspective

BÉNÉDICTE FAUVARQUE-COSSON

NEGOTIATION AND RENEGOTIATION; the topic is original and stimulating. It brings together two phases of the contract which we hardly ever study together. In the life of a contract these phases are sometimes separated by years. Looking at these two phases together leads one to wonder whether it is possible—or necessary—to align their respective regimes. There is indeed a certain logic in not adopting two entirely distinct regimes, for instance one which would require good faith and the other not, or one which would admit performance in kind, contrary to the other. However, how far should the rules of one influence those of the other, and, above all, which of the two regimes will guide the other? Should renegotiations be aligned with negotiations or vice versa?

Thus, comparisons become entangled: comparisons with other legal systems, but also, and perhaps first of all, comparisons of these two stages within one legal system. It is appropriate to deal with negotiations first, then with renegotiations. It is the logical order of the outcome of the contract. Besides, by explicit reference to this chapter, the authors of the *Avant-projet* clearly took the decision to align the regime of renegotiations in part with that of pre-contractual negotiations.

Negotiations, taken in a wide sense, include contracts to negotiate,[1] pre-contracts, offer and acceptance. Without going here into the details of the provisions of the *Avant-projet* relating to the formation of a contract, we shall merely point out, in different cases, either the signs of acceptance of existing law, or, on the contrary, a reaction against it.

In relation to the former tendency, it will be noted that the offeror is bound, under the sanction of having to pay damages, to keep his offer open for a reasonable period (article 1105-2 of the *Avant-projet*), and silence

---

[1] Contracts to negotiate give rise to a basic, general obligation and, in accordance with the expressed will of the negotiating parties, to specific obligations.

does not in principle count as acceptance (article 1105-6). We can also see the recognition of a number of different types of contracts which punctuate the negotiation of a contract, worked out by practice, and their regime defined by the case-law of the Cour de cassation. Thus, the following now have a place in the Code civil: agreements in principle (article 1104-2), unilateral promises to contract (article 1106) and pre-emption agreements (article 1106-1 of the *Avant-projet*).

In relation to the second tendency—going against the existing law—we can mention the following:

- The rule according to which death or incapacity of the offeror occurring within the period expressly stated for keeping the offer open, is no longer an obstacle to the formation of a contract (article 1105-4).
- The ineffectiveness of the revocation by the promisor, during the option period granted to the beneficiary of a unilateral promise to contract, so that acceptance by the beneficiary, during that option period, will result in the (forced) formation of the promised contract (article 1106-3).

The same principle inspires the provisions relating to the non-performance of a pre-emption agreement.

This chapter will concentrate on the pre-contractual period during which there is, as yet, neither a contract to negotiate, nor a pre-contract, nor a specific offer. It is therefore that period of non-law, full of mysteries and paradoxes,[2] when everything could lead one to believe that each party has the power to defend his interests without any limitations. Indeed, the Code civil, and nearly two centuries later the Vienna Convention on the International Sale of Goods (CISG), shine by their silence on this question. Happily, the *Avant-projet* has filled this silence by introducing good faith in the pre-contractual period, taking its inspiration for so doing from French case-law and the Principles of European Contract Law (PECL). This requirement of good faith is also to be found at the renegotiation stage.

I. NEGOTIATION

The draft Code civil of year VIII provided that 'agreements must be *entered into* and performed in good faith'.[3] In the end, the Code civil limited the influence of good faith to only the stage of performance of the contract. Even today, article 1134(3) Cc provides only that 'agreements must be performed in good faith'.

---

[2] D Mazeaud, 'Mystères et paradoxes de la période précontractuelle' in *Le contrat au début du XXI siècle: Etudes offertes à Jacques Ghestin* (Paris, LGDJ, 2001) 637.

[3] F Terré, P Simler and Y Lequette, *Les obligations* (Paris, Dalloz, 2005) no 43, n 2.

Once the place actually given to good faith during negotiations has been assessed (section I(a) below), its consequences as regards sanctions have still to be measured (section I(b) below).

(a) Good Faith During Negotiations

(i) Articles 1104 and 1104-1 of the Avant-projet

Article 1104 of the *Avant-projet* provides:

> The parties are free to begin, continue and break off negotiations, but these must satisfy the requirements of good faith.
>
> A break-down in negotiations can give rise to liability only if it is attributable to the bad faith or fault of one of the parties.

Article 1104-1 of the *Avant-projet* provides:

> The parties may, by agreement in principle, undertake to negotiate at a later date a contract whose elements are still to be settled, and to work in good faith towards settling them.

Are these provisions innovative? It rather looks like a codification of recognition, indeed a codification of 'established law', inspired mainly by French case-law which did not wait for the *Avant-projet* before recognising the requirement to negotiate in good faith,[4] showing in so doing its capacity to innovate and its true role as a law-maker.[5]

The way forward had been opened up by the Italian Civil Code of 1942, which was the first to recognise a general obligation to negotiate in good faith. Since then, article 2.1.15 of the UNIDROIT Principles of International Commercial Contracts and article 2:301 of the PECL sanction in a general way negotiations contrary to good faith.

Looking at just the PECL, it can be noted that:

- Article 2:301(1) lays down a principle of freedom in the conduct and the breaking-off of negotiations: 'A party is free to negotiate and is not liable for failure to reach an agreement'.
- Article 2:301(2) tempers it: 'However, a party which has negotiated or broken off negotiations contrary to good faith and fair dealing is liable for the losses caused to the other party'.

---

[4] *Ibid*, no 185.

[5] In the same way, in practice it was possible to use the gaps in the Code to invent a contractual framework for contractual negotiations, subject to mandatory legal rules, already fairly numerous, which surround the pre-contractual period, whether in the special area of consumer law or even sometimes in the general law of contracts—an offer in writing, mandatory references to be included in the offer, an obligation on the offeror to keep the offer open, a period of reflection for the recipient of the offer, the right to change one's mind.

A regret could then be expressed: if, as *le doyen* Gérard Cornu noted in the Introduction to the *Avant-projet*, advances in contractual fairness 'are accompanied—in direct correlation—by the greater significance given to good faith',[6] why not give it the rank of an actual fundamental principle, in a general preliminary provision, in a similar way to that of the PECL or the UNIDROIT Principles?[7]

French law tries, as indeed do the PECL or the UNIDROIT Principles, to reconcile the notions of freedom of negotiations and legal certainty, as well as reconciling them with good faith. For its part English law, which is very attached to freedom as well as legal certainty, has excluded good faith from pre-contractual negotiations, for the very purpose of safeguarding certainty. The decision in *Walford v Miles*,[8] delivered by the House of Lords in 1992, is to this day a leading and symbolic authority, and one which has to be linked to the rejection in English law of a general obligation to inform (*emptor debet esse curiosus*).[9]

However, are good faith and certainty truly irreconcilable? The Green Paper on the reform of the Community *acquis* in the matter of consumer protection, on the contrary, understands good faith as a means of ensuring certainty for both consumers and professionals![10]

The opening and breakdown of negotiations are placed under the theme of the freedom not to contract, so that the breakdown of contractual negotiations cannot give rise to liability. But the problem is that in business practice, negotiating a contract, which is often prolonged and expensive, involves large financial outlays. This regime, which is based on freedom, therefore appears ill adapted as it is a source of uncertainty. This is in fact the reason why parties often put their negotiations within the framework of contracts to negotiate. In the absence of such contracts can the law, confronted with abusive or disloyal conduct on the part of one of the parties, reply that 'no one is better served than by himself' and that the claimant should have arranged the pre-contractual period through a

---

[6] G Cornu, 'Introduction' in *Avant-projet de réforme du droit des obligations et de la prescription: Rapport remis au garde des Sceaux* (Paris, La documentation française, 2006) 19, 20 (see below p 483).

[7] D Mazeaud and B Fauvarque-Cosson, 'L'avant-projet français de réforme du droit des obligations et du droit de la prescription' [2006] ULR 103.

[8] *Walford v Miles* [1992] 2 AC 128 (HL).

[9] On these questions, see J Cartwright, 'Negotiation and Renegotiation: An English Perspective', below ch 3.

[10] Commission (EC), 'Green Paper on the Review of the Consumer *Acquis*' COM (2006) 744 final, 8 February 2007, para 4.3 of Annex I. According to the Commission 'The main advantage of an overarching general clause for consumer contracts in the horizontal instrument would be the creation of a tool which would provide guidance for the interpretation of more specific provisions and would allow the courts to fill gaps in the legislation by developing complementary rights and obligations. It could therefore provide a safety net for consumers and create certainty for producers by filling gaps in legislation. In addition, a general provision may also be a useful tool when interpreting clauses contained in offers or contracts and it may as well respond to the criticism that certain directives or provisions are not time-proof'.

contract? In short, can the law be content with giving the following reply: if the risks of a breakdown have not been shared out—since it is indeed the sharing out of risks that is the question—too bad for the improvident, good luck for the fickle and even the dishonest?

There is no legal system, not even English law,[11] in which contractual freedom reigns without limit. The requirement of good faith or loyalty is found, in various degrees, in most foreign laws. Thus, German, Dutch and Swiss law confirm that contractual negotiations must be conducted and concluded in good faith.

(ii) Duties imposed in the name of good faith

In concrete terms, the operation of good faith is represented by three types of duties the breach of which amounts to a contractual fault: transparency, confidentiality, consistency.

Under the *duty of transparency*,[12] each negotiating party is bound to inform his partner of all matters that would enlighten him when reaching his decision and to be decisive in his giving consent. Born from the requirement of good faith, the pre-contractual obligation to inform usually falls on the vendor.[13]

The pre-contractual obligation to inform, created by the courts and then recognised by the Code de la consommation, is governed by extremely detailed rules in the *Avant-projet*. The rules governing that obligation are included in the Chapter on the validity of contracts,[14] but would have been better placed in the Sub-division on formation of contracts.

The PECL are more reserved. Section 3 of Chapter 2, relating to liability during negotiations, makes no mention of any obligation to inform. A little later, article 4:107 on fraud indeed allows a remedy in favour of the party who

> has been led to conclude [the contract] by the other party's fraudulent representation . . . or fraudulent non-disclosure of any information which in accordance with good faith and fair dealing it should have disclosed.

However, a contract must have been concluded. One may doubt that British interpreters would deduce from that provision the existence of a

[11] On the possible development of English law, see Cartwright, above n 9.

[12] P Malaurie, L Aynès and P Stoffel-Munck, *Les Obligations* (2nd edn, Paris, Defrénois, 2005) no 776.

[13] It has happened that a purchaser, better informed than the vendor because of his profession, has been held bound to inform a vendor of the bad deal he was about to make, but the third Civil chamber of the Cour de cassation has recently put an unequivocal stop to this in ruling that 'a purchaser, even if a business or professional, is not bound by an obligation to inform the vendor of the value of the goods purchased': Cass civ (3) 17 January 2007, D 2007, 1051 obs D Mazeaud (criticising the decision) and 1054 obs P Stoffel-Munck (approving it).

[14] On the obligation to inform, see arts 1110 and 1110-1 of the *Avant-projet*. See also, on fraud through concealment, art 1113-1 of the *Avant-projet*.

pre-contractual obligation to inform, sanctioned *per se*—ie independently of a fraud having a decisive impact on the party's giving of consent.

French case-law imposes a *duty of confidentiality* on negotiating parties who must not reveal information and *a fortiori* should not use it. Following the same line of thought, article 2:302 of the PECL provides:

> If confidential information is given by one party in the course of negotiations, the other party is under a duty not to disclose that information or to use it for its own purposes whether or not a contract is subsequently concluded.

Finally, a *duty of consistency* in the conduct of negotiations is imposed by French law. In the past, the courts required an intention to cause damage or bad faith. Now they regard as sufficient the brutal or deliberate character of the breaking-off of negotiations, without legitimate reason. Thus, parties who start negotiating without any intention of negotiating seriously, and perhaps with the intention of dissuading their partner from entering into negotiations for the same purpose with a third party, could find themselves liable. In the name of good faith, case-law requires parties to 'abstain from reprehensible conduct, capable of causing damage'.[15] The limits of this duty to abstain must be defined. A negotiating party will not be liable if he carries on parallel negotiations with others or if he hides their existence from the other party.[16] The position would be different if there were contracts to negotiate under the terms of which the negotiating parties had undertaken obligations of exclusivity or sincerity.

Echoing the above, article 2:301(3) of the PECL provides that:

> It is contrary to good faith and fair dealing, in particular, for a party to enter into or continue negotiations with no real intention of reaching an agreement with the other party.

(b) Sanctions

(i) Damages or Performance in Kind?

Where unfairly broken-off negotiations were conducted without a contract to negotiate, the negotiating party who is the victim of the breaking-off is entitled only to damages. The case-law refuses to order an unfair negotiating party to resume negotiations with a view to concluding the contract. The PECL take the same approach. This solution stems from obvious practical considerations, but also from the principle of contractual freedom and the requirement of free consent as a precondition for making contracts.[17] Some legal systems sanction the breaking-off of negotiations by

---

[15] CA Versailles 5 March 1993, RTD civ 1993, 752.

[16] Cass com 15 December 1992, RTD civ 1993, 577.

[17] It may be thought that the application of the PECL would lead to an identical solution. Under the terms of art 2:103(1)(a) there 'is sufficient agreement if the terms have been

enforced performance in kind, but this is rather exceptional. The best known example is that of Dutch case-law, famous for having accepted that where negotiations have reached a very advanced stage, a negotiating party, victim of an unfair breaking-off, may require the continuation of negotiations and even the enforced conclusion of the contract under negotiation.[18]

On the other hand, a different fate may be reserved for the unfair breaking-off of a partial agreement or a pre-contract. In that regard, one must mention the innovative provisions of the *Avant-projet* on unilateral promises to contract (article 1106), and pre-emption agreements (article 1106-1). Under the terms of article 1106:

> Revocation by the promisor during the period allowed to the beneficiary to express his agreement cannot prevent the contract which was promised from being formed.

Therefore, in spite of such a revocation, acceptance by the beneficiary during the option period will lead to the enforced creation and execution of the contract. This provision goes against the current case-law which sanctions, based only on damages, the revocation by the promisor during the option period allowed to the beneficiary of a unilateral promise to contract.[19] In addition, article 1106-1, relating to pre-emption agreements, influences the controlling court, which will now accept that as long as he proves bad faith on the part of the third party, the beneficiary of a pre-emption agreement may have the contract entered into in breach of a pre-emption agreement declared void, and the rights and obligations of the third party substituted.[20]

(ii) Nature of the Liability

To sanction the unfair break-off of negotiations, French law uses the mechanism of pre-contractual liability, which is included in the category of delictual liability governed by articles 1382–1386 Cc. The position is only different where negotiations take place within the framework and under

---

sufficiently defined by the parties so that the contract can be enforced'. It follows that, in case of partial agreement on the essential elements, the contract under negotiation is entered into and its enforced performance is possible.

[18] An astonishing solution, especially for English lawyers!—although, through the means of proprietary estoppel, English law occasionally also sanctions unfairness and inconsistency, even going as far as granting title to property to the injured party. German law, before the 2002 reform, allowed performance in kind in certain exceptional cases, for instance where the victim had given up a more advantageous contract through the other party's fault (BGH 24 June 1998, NJW 1998, 2900).

[19] Cass civ (3) 15 December 1993, D 1994 Somm 507 obs O Tournafond, D 1995 Somm 230 obs L Aynès, Defr 1994, 795 obs PH Delebecque, JCP 1995 II 22366 obs D Mazeaud, RTD civ 1994, 588 obs J Mestre; Cass civ (3) 26 June 1996, D 1997 Somm 169 obs D Mazeaud.

[20] Cass mixte 26 May 2006, D 2006, 1861 note P-Y Gautier and D Mainguy, D 2006 Pan 2644 obs B Fauvarque-Cosson, Defr 2006, 1207 obs E Savaux, JCP 2006 II 10142 obs L Leveneur, RDC 2006, 1080 obs D Mazeaud, RTD civ 2006, 550 obs J Mestre and B Fages.

the provisions of a contract to negotiate. In that case, the liability of a negotiating party who is in breach either of his obligation to negotiate in good faith or of his undertaking of confidentiality or exclusivity, is of a contractual nature.

A double issue is at stake in the question of the delictual or contractual nature of the liability: on the one hand, under national law, the question is to know whether the rules of contractual liability—article 1147 Cc—or the general rules of delictual liability—article 1382 Cc—apply. If it is an international contract, this question also determines the operation of various rules for the conflict of jurisdictions and conflict of laws.

Germany, and some countries with legal systems based on the German model, consider that this liability is of a contractual nature. In this respect they are following Ihering's doctrine, developed in 1861, which is based on a tacit pre-contract pursuant to which negotiating parties would mutually guarantee to each other loyalty and co-operation during negotiations and would implicitly be liable towards each other for faults committed in the course of these negotiations. Although the BGB of 1900 only partly recognised the doctrine of *culpa in contrahendo*, the case-law later extended it.[21] The reform of the law of obligations in Germany in 2002 gave effect to this case-law.[22]

Despite the propensities of these laws to admit tacit agreements, the case-law in France, Belgium and Luxembourg maintains that it is a matter of delictual liability.[23]

In *Tacconi v Wagner* the European Court of Justice (ECJ) also ruled in favour of delictual liability.[24] In that case, the German seller claimed that the break-off of negotiations was neither delictual not contractual, but was an autonomous matter not covered by Community provisions, justifying

---

[21] There were no general rules applying to the whole of this matter in the BGB of 1900. The introduction of pre-contractual liability stemming from *culpa in contrahendo* is a creation of the courts and academic writing. It has a considerable practical importance and a wide scope.

[22] The new § 311(2) BGB specifies that a contractual relationship giving rise to accessory obligations within the meaning of § 241(2) may arise even before the contract is formed. It lists a number of situations, including the entering into negotiations, that is the period stretching from the start of negotiations to the final formation of the contract. By virtue of this relationship, the parties to a contract are bound by reciprocal obligations of care as regards the other party's rights, property and interests, § 241(2). Failure to comply with these obligations therefore amounts to a contractual breach, a key notion of the new liability system. This will be sanctioned by application of the general rules of § 280 and following. It follows that the victim may apply either for simple reparation for the damage which was caused to him (§ 280(1)), or reparation replacing the performance of the contract (§ 282), or the reimbursement of expenses which he has incurred (§ 284). The extent of the reparation is then no longer limited to a negative interest, which is criticised by an important trend amongst academic writers which preferred the more restrictive solutions of the BGB.

[23] In Italy, the Corte di cassazione decided in favour of delictual liability but under the influence of Mengoni, the lower courts occasionally opt for contractual liability.

[24] Case C–334/00 *Fonderie Officine Meccaniche Tacconi SpA v H Wagner Sinto Maschinen-fabrik GmbH (HWS)* [2002] ECR I–7357, JCP 2003 I 152 obs G Viney, Defr 2003 no 13 obs R Libchaber.

the application of article 2 of the Brussels Convention,[25] and therefore the jurisdiction of the German court of the place of its domicile instead of that of the Italian court of the place where the harmful event had occurred (article 5(3)). This argument could have succeeded since, in the past, the ECJ had already refused the alternative between articles 5(1) and 5(3) of the Convention—ie between contractual and delictual liability. Similarly, with respect to the *action paulienne* and quasi-contracts, it also referred to article 2. So why not adopt the same solution in the matter of break-off of negotiations? However, the ECJ preferred to follow the more classical route of the majority opinion, rather than to have a new look at the question by opening a third route 'which would loosen the running knot of the classical construction'.[26]

The Federal Court of the Swiss Confederation, on the other hand, adopted the principle that pre-contractual liability was based on 'disappointed trust' and that it had a specific nature, relating to neither one nor the other liability—and therefore to neither one nor the other traditional regime.[27]

Would there not be here a solution which would draw closer the legal systems which use liability, of whatever sort, and English law which refuses to compel parties to pursue negotiations in good faith,[28] but at the same time providing for exceptions, in particular where there is a special relationship between the parties and where because of his *reliance* on it, the innocent party, who believed that a contract would be entered into, suffered loss? One thus finds the notion of a liability based on *reliance* and on loss suffered as a result of this reasonable trust.[29]

In fact, the putting into operation of the principle of *promissory estoppel*, or indeed, as in Australia, of a unitarian doctrine of *estoppel*, occasionally leads common law judges 'to sanction initiatives undertaken too lightly more severely than French courts do for unfair breaking-off'.[30]

[25] Convention of 27 September 1968 on Jurisdiction and the Enforcement of Judgments in Civil and Commercial Matters ('Brussels Convention'); see now Council Regulation (EC) 44/2001 of 22 December 2000 on Jurisdiction and the Recognition and Enforcement of Judgments in Civil and Commercial Matters [2001] OJ L/12/1.

[26] Libchaber, above n 24. However, is Community law not the first to want to free itself from the dual liability, as shown by the regime of liability for defective products, arising from Council Directive (EEC) 85/374 of 25 July 1985 on the approximation of the laws, regulations and administrative provisions of the Member States concerning liability for defective products [1985] OJ L/210/29?

[27] H-P Walter, 'La responsabilité fondée sur la confiance dans la jurisprudence du Tribunal fédéral' in C Chappuis and B Winiger (eds), *La responsabilité fondée sur la confiance* (Zurich, Schulthess, 2001) 151; see also D Philippe, 'La bonne foi dans la relation entre les particuliers: A. Dans la formation du contrat (rapport belge)' in *La bonne foi* (Travaux de l'association Henri Capitant, vol XLIII) (Paris, Litec, 1992) 66, 72-73.

[28] *Walford v Miles*, above n 8.

[29] For more developments on the role of reliance and estoppel in contract and tort see B Fauvarque-Cosson (ed), *L'estoppel et la protection de la confiance légitime* (Paris, Société de législation comparée, 2007).

[30] On these questions, see H Muir-Watt, 'Les pourparlers: de la confiance trompée à la relation de confiance' in P Rémy-Corlay and D Fenouillet (eds), *Les concepts contractuels français à l'heure des Principes du droit européen des contrats* (Paris, Dalloz, 2003) 53, 56.

Although notions and concepts differ, solutions are in fact often rather close. Thus the Court of Appeal of Versailles held that,

> in abandoning a project for purely internal reasons and leaving the other party to hope, for nearly 4 years, that a final agreement would be reached, that party through its failure to behave fairly caused the latter loss for which it owes reparation.[31]

An important question remains: that of the amount of reparation.

(iii) The Amount of Reparation

In French law, a negotiating party who is the victim is entitled to claim reparation of the *loss* he suffered as a result of the wrongful breaking-off of the negotiations: thus, for instance, the financial outlay he might have made because of the negotiations, the cost of preliminary studies, expenses for advice, etc. He will then have to be put back in the situation in which he would have been if he had not entered into negotiations with the party responsible for the wrongful breaking-off.

What of the *loss of profit*? Could a creditor be indemnified for the loss of a chance to enter into the final contract?

The PECL are silent on this point. French case-law, on the other hand, has evolved. At first reticent, it subsequently accepted compensation for the loss of a chance, after having examined the factual circumstances allowing a determination of whether the success of negotiations was likely.

French academic writers, however, have been divided: some authors wanted to exclude the profit that a negotiating party could have gained from an effective formation and performance of the contract under negotiation, because, on the one hand, even when conducted in good faith, negotiations would not necessarily have led to the formation of the contract under negotiation, and on the other hand, a contrary solution would have led to effect being given, 'indirectly . . . to a contract which was not entered into'.[32] Others, on the contrary, recognised the principle of reparation of harm consisting in the loss of a chance to make a profit out of the conclusion and performance of the negotiated contract, resulting from the wrongful breaking-off of the contractual negotiations. To identify the loss to be the subject of reparation they suggested that the decision be based on the 'degree of progress of the negotiations'.[33]

Finally, in the *Manoukian* judgment, the Commercial chamber held that a negotiating party, victim of a wrongful breaking-off of negotiations, could not obtain reparation for the loss consisting in the loss of a chance to make

---

[31] RTD civ 1996, 145 obs J Mestre.
[32] Malaurie et al, above n 12, no 464.
[33] G Viney, *Traité de droit civil: Introduction à la responsabilité* (Paris, LGDJ, 1995) no 198. See also Cass civ (2) 12 June 1987, RTD civ 1988, 107 obs J Mestre.

a profit out of the formation and performance of the contract under negotiation.[34] In 2006, a judgment of the third Civil chamber of the Cour de cassation confirmed that solution:

> [A] fault committed in the exercise of the right to break off unilaterally pre-contractual negotiations is not the cause of the loss consisting in the loss of a chance to obtain the profits which the conclusion of the contract led one to expect.[35]

If one follows this case-law, not only is lost profit no longer subject to reparation, but the only reparation will be of loss arising from a fault committed by a negotiating party in the break up of negotiations, so that loss the reparation of which used to be easily accepted could now be considered as irreparable.[36]

In some legal systems, the extent of compensation is limited to the *reliance interest* in contrast to the *expectation interest*. Thus, in common law systems where compensation is based on protection of reliance (*reliance interest*), the objective is to erase the inconsistency by putting the victim back into the position in which he would have been if he had not acted on the faith of the act found by the court (compensation for financial outlay). The purpose of German law, before the reform of 2002, was to put the partner back in the position in which he would be if the fault had not been committed. Since the reform, reparation may in certain cases go beyond just the negative interest.

II. RENEGOTIATION

As regards renegotiations,[37] the solutions adopted by the *Avant-projet* include truly innovative provisions which must be examined by themselves before putting them back into a comparative perspective.

(a) Articles 1135 to 1135-1 of the *Avant-projet*[38]

(i) Freedom to Include Express Terms

Article 1135-1 of the *Avant-projet* provides:

---

[34] Cass com 26 November 2003, D 2004, 869 note A-S Dupré Dallemagne, JCP G 2004 I 163 obs G Viney; JCP E 2004, 738 obs Ph Stoffel-Munck; RDC 2004, 257 obs D Mazeaud; RTD civ 2004, 80 obs J Mestre and B Fages.

[35] Cass civ (3) 28 June 2006, JCP 2006 II 10130 obs O Deshayes; D 2006, 2963 note D Mazeaud.

[36] On this point see Mazeaud, above n 35.

[37] D Mazeaud, 'La révision du contract' LPA 30 June 2005, no 37, 4.

[38] Art 1135-2 of the *Avant-projet* would go beyond the current legal rules, in providing for renegotiations by order of the court.

> In contracts whose performance takes place successively or in instalments, the parties may undertake to negotiate a modification of their contract where as a result of supervening circumstances the original balance of what the parties must do for each other is so disturbed that the contract loses all its point for one of them.

This provision confirms the parties' freedom to include express renegotiation clauses. But what is the point of such a provision? Is not contractual freedom the general rule in French law? Therefore, did this freedom not exist already and why did it have to be reaffirmed? Is this method not a source of uncertainty? Such a provision indeed creates a non-prescriptive right, a contemporary tendency which the Conseil Constitutionnel tends to censure. Furthermore, does one not run the risk, interpreting that provision *a contrario*, of concluding that a clause could not take effect where loss of point was only partial? On reflection, is the fact that the authors of the proposals felt the need to carve this possibility into legal stone not revealing of a resistance towards renegotiations, particularly where they have not been provided for by an express term?[39]

(ii) In the Absence of an Express Term

Article 1135-2 of the *Avant-projet* provides:

> In the absence of such an express term, a party for whom a contract loses its point may apply to the President of the *tribunal de grande instance* to order a new negotiation.

What exactly does the expression 'the party for whom the contract loses its point' mean? The criterion is rather vague and unnecessarily distinct from the expression in article 1135-1, 'all its point'. Must the assessment be made by reference to this criterion of a party's point or would it not be better to introduce a reference to a contract which has 'become excessively onerous' or 'very seriously unbalanced', which would be more objective? Besides, should not a requirement of posteriority be added—a change that occurred after the formation of the contract—and another of exteriority— the parties have no control over that change?

---

[39] Compare with D Mazeaud, above n 37: 'One measures with this provision all the loathing towards the only thought of revision of a contract which drove its authors, since they felt obliged to engrave in the marble of the law a solution which even the most fervent worshippers of the principle of the inviolability of contracts never dared to put into question, even as lip service—that is, the parties' freedom to include a clause under the terms of which they would renegotiate their contract in the case of changes of circumstances which fundamentally undermine its economic balance. Therefore one measures through this provision, which in giving *carte blanche* to contractual freedom in this matter gives credence to the (to say the least) surprising idea that in the absence of this legal safeguard it had no vocation to spread its wings, all the road which remains to be travelled for the doctrine of unforeseeasbility to enter into our customs'.

(iii) Failure of Renegotiations

Article 1135-3 of the *Avant-projet* provides:

> Where applicable, these negotiations should be governed by the rules provided by Chapter I of the present Title.[40]
>
> In the absence of bad faith, the failure of the negotiations gives rise to a right in either party to terminate the contract for the future at no cost or loss.

The *Avant-projet* puts renegotiations in line with pre-contractual negotiations. They recognise the same principle of the parties' freedom, with the same limits. However, should not a stricter regime be provided—ie a stronger requirement of good faith—because the parties are already bound by a contract and their respective legitimate expectations may be more important? It is true that in practice, in so far as the lower courts have an unfettered discretion in assessing what is contrary to good faith, or more precisely, a 'failure in the absence of bad faith', they will be able to be more demanding at the renegotiations stage.

The failure of renegotiations, in the absence of bad faith, opens for each party the right to terminate the contract in the future 'at no cost or loss'. The provision is sparing. It says both too much and too little.

As for saying too much: why should termination systematically take place 'at no cost or loss'? Could this not lead to unfairness where the defendant incurred a costly financial outlay for which he cannot be compensated, even in part, by the party for whom the contract lost its point? The Chambre de Commerce et d'Industrie de Paris has suggested that this part of the provision be deleted.[41]

As for saying too little: could not at least an obligation be imposed to give reasons for a refusal to revise the renegotiated contract?

(b) Comparative Perspective

Just for once, the comparison will be made starting with the French law currently in force, followed by the recent academic codifications.

(i) Comparison with the French Law Currently in Force

In French law, an express renegotiation clause gives rise to a duty to renegotiate, which divides in the following way:

---

[40] That is art 1102-1107 of the *Avant-projet*, including arts 1104 to 1104-1 mentioned above, see p 35.

[41] Chambre de commerce et d'industrie de Paris, *Pour une réforme du droit des contrats et de la prescription conforme aux besoins de la vie des affaires* (2006) http://www.etudes.ccip.fr/archrap/pdf06/reforme-droit-des-contrats-kli0610.pdf, pp 73–4.

- an obligation to achieve a result: starting the renegotiations;
- an obligation to take necessary steps to achieve a result which, in practice, means that the parties must abstain from making unreasonable proposals.

The duty to renegotiate pursuant to an express term does not therefore force the parties to modify a renegotiated contract but only to renegotiate it loyally—hence the parallel with negotiations for a contract in good faith.

A judgment delivered on 3 October 2006 restates this principle. The Cour de cassation, relying on the unfettered discretion of the lower court, dismissed the claim on the ground that the terms in dispute

> in no way imposed an obligation on one party to accept the modifications proposed by the other party and to amend the contract

and that the failure of the renegotiations could not be blamed on the company 'in the absence of unfair conduct on its part'.[42] In fact, the mere fact that the company refused to accept the substantial change in the price of the contract

> could not be characterised as fault on its part, whatever the economic imbalance claimed by company M which had to bear the consequences of its lack of foresight in the choice of index as the basis of the indexation clause.

Assuming that a duty to renegotiate is established and broken, what will then be the sanction of the duty to renegotiate in good faith? Damages or performance in kind?

The *Avant-projet* is silent on this specific question, but forcefully confirms the principle of performance in kind. Accordingly, could the demands of good faith, combined with the parties' intention—as shown by the very existence of a revision clause—not be said to impose on the parties not only an obligation to make reasonable proposals in the course of renegotiations, but also and above all to accept these proposals?[43] The duty of good faith would then be doubled with a true duty of co-operation. For the time being, the courts have not accepted it.

In the case of renegotiations, numerous writers have spoken out against performance in kind, on the ground that it is simply inconceivable. Some, on the contrary, consider that

> there is nothing to stop the courts from condemning the debtor of such an obligation 'to do' to perform in kind, in accordance with the current interpretation of article 1142.[44]

---

[42] Cass com 3 October 2006, D 2007, 765 note D Mazeaud.
[43] See B Oppetit, 'L'adaptation des contrats internationaux aux changements de circonstances: la clause de "hardship"' Clunet 1974, 974, 805.
[44] L Aynès, 'L'imprévision en droit privé' RJ com 2005, 397 no 26. The author here specifically refers to case-law on mediation clauses. One can indeed make a parallel with the judgment of

This amounts to saying that, in some cases, a party could be held to be bound to accept reasonable modification proposals. Without going that far, should one not, at the very least, deal specifically with the case of a contracting party who holds a unilateral right to modify the contents of a contract? Where the exercise of this right of unilateral modification results in a serious contractual imbalance, to impose a renegotiation of that contract could be conceivable, whether an express term to that effect was provided or not—or even to allow an adjustment by the courts.[45]

Traditionally, the case-law considers that in case of failure of renegotiations the contract remains in force (unless there is a contrary provision). Applying the general rules in the matter, each party then retains a right of unilateral termination, at least in the case of a contract for an indefinite term.[46] In the *Avant-projet*, this right unilaterally to terminate the contract also exists where the contract is for a fixed term.

(ii) Comparison with the PECL and the UNIDROIT Principles

In the PECL as well as in the UNIDROIT Principles, the failure of contractual renegotiations can justify the intervention of the courts to resolve the crisis. Furthermore, the PECL and the UNIDROIT Principles recognise not only judicial modification but also, and even primarily, judicial termination.

In accordance with article 6:111(3) of the PECL:

If the parties fail to reach an agreement within a reasonable time, the court may:
(a) end the contract at a date and on terms to be determined by the court; or
(b) adapt the contract in order to distribute between the parties in a just and equitable manner the losses and gains resulting from the change of circumstances.

Similarly, in the UNIDROIT Principles, article 6.2.3 provides that:

(1) In case of hardship the disadvantaged party is entitled to request renegotiations . . .
(2) . . .
(3) Upon failure to reach agreement within a reasonable time either party may resort to the court.

the Cass mixte, 14 February 2003, Bull mixt no 1, on mediation clauses: the court sanctioned the breach of such a clause by ruling that the claim was inadmissible.

[45] The idea was raised in connection with judgments delivered by the Commercial chamber of the Cour de cassation on 3 November 1992 (Defr 1993, 1377 obs J-L Aubert, JCP 1993 II 22164 obs G Virassamy, RTD civ 1993, 124 obs J Mestre) and 24 November 1998 (Contrats Concur Consomm 1999 comm no 56 obs M Malaurie-Vignal, Defr 1999, 371 obs D Mazeaud, JCP 1999 I 143 obs C Jamin, RTD civ 1999, 98 obs J Mestre, RTD civ 1999, 646 obs P-Y Gautier).

[46] Compare with the standard hardship clause published by the International Chamber of Commerce in 2003. In case of failure of the renegotiations set up under that clause, 'the party invoking this Clause is entitled to termination of the contract'.

(4) If the court finds hardship it may, if reasonable,
  (a) terminate the contract at a date and on terms to be fixed, or
  (b) adapt the contract with a view to restoring its equilibrium.

These provisions, which assume a trust in the national courts, would have favoured the maintaining of the contract more if they had reversed or arranged the order of things in a hierarchical way: the court could first adapt the contract, and if it considers that in the event it is not possible, terminate it.

III. CONCLUSION

At first glance, the topic of contractual negotiations and renegotiations reveals the existence of deep differences between French and English contract law, one being attached to the principle of good faith, the other one to that of legal certainty.

Contractual freedom dominates French law as well as English law. Free to conceive their contract, to draw its contents, to determine its balance, the parties to the contract must carry the responsibility of the bad exercise of their freedom. On the other hand, it is normal that the bad faith of the other party be sanctioned. Should one see it as an attack on, or as an exception to, this freedom? Is it not, on the contrary, the necessary corollary to that freedom—and even of legal certainty—which can only blossom within loyalty?

Besides, should not the entry into force of good faith, at the stage of renegotiations of a contract,[47] soon lead English courts to soften their refusal to take it into account at the stage of pre-contractual negotiations— a refusal sometimes thought by British authors to be excessive?

At the same time it will be noted that, like the English courts, the Cour de cassation is not indifferent to the way parties intended to apportion the risks of their contract. Thus, as has been seen, it recently refused to impose the modification of a contract, in spite of the presence of an express term providing for modification, on the ground that a company had to bear the consequences of its lack for foresight in the choice of index as the basis for its indexation clause.[48]

When all is said and done, would the true breaking-point rather not lie elsewhere? Do the French and English legal systems not converge in their refusal to let the courts intervene (a 'judge-proof' contract), contrary to European and international models which allow the courts to modify or terminate a contract? It must be noted that English courts give themselves more often than one thinks a certain power over a contract, for instance in

---

[47] On this case-law, and the signs of a possible evolution, including in relation to the obligation to negotiate in good faith, see the paper by Cartwright, above n 9.

[48] See above n 42.

discovering implied terms. Furthermore, the doctrine of frustration allows a court to put a contract aside, admittedly in restrictive conditions, but more flexible that those which justify, in French law, a debtor's exemption of liability on the ground of *force majeure*.

How much longer will the dogma of an inviolable contract, timeless and closed to any intervention by the courts, stand in France? How many years will go by before this fearsome warning by the authors of the *Leçons de Droit Civil* ceases to resonate?

> It would be extremely dangerous to leave contracts to the judge's discretion; intervening in the performance of an agreement with his personal feeling for equity and the general interest, he would ruin the contract, and put at risk the whole economy, by removing certainty in contractual relationships.[49]

---

[49] H, L and J Mazeaud and F Chabas, *Leçons de droit civil*, vol II-1: *Obligations—théorie générale* (9th edn, ed by F Chabas, Paris, Montchrestien, 1998) no 730.

3

Negotiation and Renegotiation: An English Perspective

JOHN CARTWRIGHT

T
HE TREATMENT IN the *Avant-projet de réforme du droit des obligations et de la prescription* of the questions of negotiation and renegotiation of a contract is very interesting in itself. In broad terms, the provisions on *negotiation* are conservative but welcome—the opportunity has been taken to put into the text of the Code provisions which reflect the law as it has already been established by the courts, but which have hitherto not found expression in the legislative texts. If implemented, it will bring the Code up to date. The provisions on *renegotiation*, however, are more controversial—partly for the very reason that they are relatively conservative, giving only a limited role to the court in solving the problems which arise during the lifetime of the contract. This has been explored in the previous chapter by Bénédicte Fauvarque-Cosson. But the comparisons between English law and the proposals of the *Avant-projet* are also of real interest, and can give a greater sharpness to the debate within French writing about the merits of the proposals on, in particular, renegotiation, whilst at the same time raising some fundamental questions about the merits of the existing rules of English law. It is these latter issues that will form the basis of the discussion in this chapter.

I. NEGOTIATION

The starting-point is a comparison of the different legal approaches of the two systems to contractual negotiations—the different approaches to the legal status to be accorded to the relationship between parties by virtue of their negotiating for a future contract. In brief, English law is reluctant to characterise the negotiations as constituting a legally protected relationship at all. French law, however, gives a certain scope of protection to the parties during the negotiations. This difference is also reflected in the different

willingness of the two systems to allow the parties expressly to undertake obligations to negotiate their future contract.

(a) English Law: No General Duty between Negotiating Parties

Traditionally, the approach of English law to the duty between negotiating parties is very restrictive.[1] As a general rule there is no inherent (implied) duty of good faith, loyalty or co-operation between parties negotiating for a contract, and the parties cannot even create an express legal obligation to conduct their negotiations in good faith. Negotiating parties do not owe each other any general duty of disclosure, even where one party realises that the other is making a serious mistake about the subject-matter of the contract. Breaking-off negotiations does not constitute a wrong—does not as such constitute a tort. Even the malicious breaking-off of negotiations does not constitute a wrong: how can it, if there is no duty to negotiate, nor even any general duty to behave in a particular way during the negotiations?

This does not mean that liability cannot arise during the negotiations. Certain particular forms of (mis-)conduct can give rise to liability in tort. Certain types of pre-contractual contract can be entered into by the parties to regulate their negotiations. The law of unjust enrichment may sometimes provide a particular solution to the difficulties which have arisen during negotiations which have broken down. And the doctrine of estoppel may be invoked on occasion. But these are seen as piecemeal solutions to the piecemeal problems which arise between negotiating parties, rather than constituting a general theory of 'precontractual liability'. It is worth exploring the reasons for this approach in English law.

In the first place, the reluctance to admit generalised duties between negotiating parties may follow from the reluctance of English law to work from general principles. The common law develops from the cases, problems which have arisen and for which remedies have been found (or refused) within the existing law.[2] To impose liability for conduct during the negotiations presupposes that there is a relevant source of obligation; and so the search for a remedy is focused on the question whether there has been a breach of a contractual obligation, or a tort, or a claim has arisen for unjust enrichment. The negotiations are not a relationship which gives rise to obligations *sui generis*. By definition, they are not inherently contractual; and the difficulty in fitting them within the law of tort or unjust enrichment is the particular nature of those sources of obligation.

---

[1] For more detailed discussion see J Cartwright, *Contract Law: An Introduction to the English Law of Contract for the Civil Lawyer* (Oxford, Hart Publishing, 2007) ch 4 ('The Negotiations for a Contract'), from which material in the first section of this chapter is drawn.

[2] See Cartwright, *ibid*, ch 2.

The law of tort can be invoked to remedy misconduct during negotiations. But it is a law of *torts*, made up of a set of compartmentalised wrongs, designed to protect different interests and in different circumstances.[3] Precontractual negotiations are not in themselves a protected interest within the law of tort. The precontractual context in which tortious liability can most easily arise is where one party has made a fraudulent statement on which the other party has relied. One might say that there is a general duty in English law to be honest in communicating information. But the English way of looking at it is not to see a general duty of honesty, but to say that the *dishonest* misrepresentation (a statement or conduct which communicates false information) is a wrong, actionable in the tort of deceit, if intended to be acted upon and in fact acted upon by the other party in such a way that he suffers loss. But deliberate silence does not normally constitute an actionable wrong in English law.[4] Similarly, although English law has a tort of negligence which imposes liability on a party who fails to fulfil his duty to take reasonable care in favour of a party to whom the duty was owed, and who suffers loss in consequence of the breach of duty, the only context in which this tort can generally be applied between negotiating parties is where the wrongful conduct consists in giving inaccurate information: misrepresentations.[5] The courts have not taken the view that the relationship between negotiating parties itself gives rise to mutual duties of care within the law of tort.[6]

The law of contract can sometimes be used by the parties to regulate their negotiations. But the usefulness of contractual obligations during the precontractual phase is limited. Contracts can be used to provide for the payment of sums incurred in anticipation of the contract being concluded, in the event that the negotiations do not succeed—and, in the absence of an express contract to this effect, the law of unjust enrichment may sometimes be able to offer some similar protection to the party who incurs expenditure, or confers a benefit on the other, in anticipation of a contract and which goes beyond the normal preparatory work for such a contract.[7] And a contract can be used to keep an offer open (an *option* contract) or to

---

[3] AM Dugdale (ed), *Clerk & Lindsell on Torts* (19th edn, London, Sweet & Maxwell, 2006), para 1-19; *OBG Ltd v Allan* [2007] UKHL 21, [2008] 1 AC 1 [32] (Lord Hoffmann, approving P Cane, 'Mens Rea in Tort Law' (2000) 20 OJLS 533, 552).

[4] *Peek v Gurney* (1873) LR 6 HL 377, 391, 403 (HL); *Smith v Hughes* (1871) LR 6 QB 597 (QB). For the tort of deceit see *Clerk & Lindsell on Torts*, above n 3, ch 18; and (in the particular context of precontractual misrepresentations) J Cartwright, *Misrepresentation, Mistake and Non-Disclosure* (2nd edn, London, Sweet & Maxwell, 2007) ch 5.

[5] *Esso Petroleum Co Ltd v Mardon* [1976] QB 801 (CA). For the tort of negligence see *Clerk & Lindsell on Torts*, above n 3, ch 8; and (in the particular context of precontractual misrepresentations) Cartwright, above n 4, ch 6.

[6] Cf *Martel Building Ltd v Canada* (2000) 193 DLR (4th) 1.

[7] *William Lacey (Hounslow) Ltd v Davis* [1957] 1 WLR 932 (QB); *British Steel Corp v Cleveland Bridge and Engineering Co Ltd* [1984] 1 All ER 504 (QB). See generally G Jones, *Goff and Jones: The Law of Restitution* (7th edn, London, Sweet & Maxwell, 2007), ch 26.

prevent one party from negotiating with third parties for a fixed period (a *lock-out* contract). But a contract cannot—even expressly—simply impose on the parties the obligation to negotiate, nor to negotiate in good faith. One reason is that the content of such an obligation is uncertain; and that even if one were to recognise the obligation (and somehow define the circumstances of its breach) one could not define the loss which flows from the breach. Lord Ackner said in *Walford v Miles*[8] that:

> The reason why an agreement to negotiate, like an agreement to agree, is unenforceable is simply because it lacks the necessary certainty . . .

and that such an agreement could be given content only by implying into it a test for whether the negotiations have been terminated properly. But:

> How can a court be expected to decide whether, subjectively, a proper reason existed for the termination of negotiations? The answer suggested depends upon whether the negotiations have been determined 'in good faith' . . .

And such a test of 'good faith' would itself be uncertain. This reluctance to accept 'contracts to negotiate' is not new. In *Courtney & Fairbairn Ltd v Tolaini Brothers (Hotels) Ltd*[9] Lord Denning MR said:

> If the law does not recognise a contract to enter into a contract (when there is a fundamental term yet to be agreed) it seems to me it cannot recognise a contract to negotiate. The reason is because it is too uncertain to have any binding force. No court could estimate the damages because no one can tell whether the negotiations would be successful or would fall through: or if successful, what the result would be. It seems to me that a contract to negotiate, like a contract to enter into a contract, is not a contract known to the law.

The rejection of the duty between negotiating parties is not, however, simply based on a reluctance to define general principles, or a pragmatic concern with the difficulty of defining with certainty the content of the obligation or the remedy to which breach of it might give rise. There is a more fundamental reason of principle. This was put most forcefully by Lord Ackner in *Walford v Miles* in terms which are linked to the argument based on lack of certainty but in fact go much deeper:[10]

> [T]he concept of a duty to carry on negotiations in good faith is inherently repugnant to the adversarial position of the parties when involved in negotiations. Each party to the negotiations is entitled to pursue his (or her) own interest, so long as he avoids making misrepresentations. To advance that interest he must be entitled, if he thinks it appropriate, to threaten to withdraw from further negotiations or to withdraw in fact in the hope that the opposite party may seek to reopen the negotiations by offering him improved terms. [Counsel arguing that liability be imposed should in the case], of course, accepts that the

---

[8] [1992] 2 AC 128, 138 (HL).
[9] [1975] 1 WLR 297, 301 (CA).
[10] Above n 8.

agreement upon which he relies does not contain a duty to complete the negotiations. But that still leaves the vital question: how is a vendor ever to know that he is entitled to withdraw from further negotiations? How is the court to police such an 'agreement'? A duty to negotiate in good faith is as unworkable in practice as it is inherently inconsistent with the position of a negotiating party. It is here that the uncertainty lies.

The very relationship between the parties during negotiations is 'adversarial'; the parties are at arm's length, each entitled to act in his own interest until the moment at which the contract is concluded. Each party bears the risk of the success of the negotiations unless there is a specifically identifiable reason for shifting that risk; and therefore each party incurs expenditure or otherwise acts at his own risk in the hope of a future contract; but he is not as a matter of general principle entitled to rely on the (future) contract, or on the other party during the negotiations, unless there is a specific, definable justification for it. Lord Ackner spoke of one party incurring liability to the other for misrepresentation—which we have already mentioned. But the starting point is of *no duty* between negotiating parties.

This policy—and the reluctance of the courts to allow the law of tort or unjust enrichment to displace the balance of risk during the negotiations—can be seen in other cases. The English courts reject the idea of a generalised duty of disclosure:[11]

> [E]ven if the vendor was aware that the purchaser thought that the article possessed that quality, and would not have entered into the contract unless he had so thought, still the purchaser is bound, unless the vendor was guilty of some fraud or deceit upon him, and . . . a mere abstinence from disabusing the purchaser of that impression is not fraud or deceit; for, whatever may be the case in a court of morals, there is no legal obligation on the vendor to inform the purchaser that he is under a mistake, not induced by the act of the vendor.

And the Supreme Court of Canada has rejected a general extension of the tort of negligence to contractual negotiations on a similar basis:[12]

> It would defeat the essence of negotiation and hobble the marketplace to extend a duty of care to the conduct of negotiations, and to label a party's failure to disclose its bottom line, its motives or its final position as negligent. Such a conclusion would of necessity force the disclosure of privately acquired information and the dissipation of any competitive advantage derived from it, all of which is incompatible with the activity of negotiating and bargaining.
> . . . [T]o impose a duty in the circumstances of this appeal could interject tort law as after-the-fact insurance against failures to act with due diligence or to hedge the risk of failed negotiations through the pursuit of alternative strategies or opportunities.

---

[11] *Smith v Hughes*, above n 4, 607 (Blackburn J).
[12] *Martel Building*, above n 6, [67]–[68].

However, there are two separate issues which must be disentangled.

First, the rejection by English law of the general (mutual) protection of the parties during the negotiations through any generalised principle of good faith, loyalty or co-operation. Negotiations are not, in this sense, a 'relationship' to which the law gives significance and protection. The law may recognise that a party during the negotiations has committed a particular wrong (such as a fraudulent misrepresentation) or has undertaken a specific, clear and certain obligation by entering into a particular form of express contract (such as a contract to keep open an offer—an option contract); or has changed the normal balance of risk during the negotiations by asking the other party to begin performance in anticipation of the contract being concluded (and so has incurred liability to pay for the anticipatory performance rendered). But these are all exceptions to the general allocation of risk—'no general liability, because no general duty'— and the law requires express wrongdoing (such as a statement, not simply silence), an express contractual promise (there is no inherent, implied obligation to keep an offer open) or a request for anticipatory performance to be rendered.

Secondly, however, English law goes further: even where the negotiating parties *do* wish to impose a general duty in relation to their negotiations—a duty to co-operate, to act in good faith—then this cannot be allowed in law. The argument at this point falls back on the more pragmatic one of certainty. We have seen that in *Walford v Miles* Lord Ackner regarded the point of principle (negotiations are inherently adversarial) and the practical problem of certainty (in particular, the meaning of a duty to negotiate 'in good faith') as interdependent. However, it is not self-evident that they cannot be separated. It has the result that the parties are unable to contract *into* a duty of good faith in their negotiations. And so the express intentions of the parties can be defeated. A court should be slow to reach such a conclusion. Moreover, an agreement to negotiate can be saved if the parties include within their agreement criteria for the resolution of any differences between the parties which are sufficiently certain to be operated by the court—such as a recognised form of dispute resolution[13] or terms which expressly state (or which allow the court to imply) that the difference is to be resolved by the imposition of 'reasonable' terms.[14] And especially in commercial cases the courts are reluctant to hold that they cannot give

[13] *Cable & Wireless plc v IBM United Kingdom Ltd* [2002] EWHC 2059 (Comm), [2002] 2 All ER (Comm) 1041 (provision that parties shall 'attempt in good faith to resolve any dispute or claim' arising out of the contract was saved by a provision that if the negotiations failed the differences would be settled by alternative dispute resolution).

[14] *Foley v Classique Coaches Ltd* [1934] 2 KB 1, 10 (CA) (sale of petrol 'at a price to be agreed by the parties in writing and from time to time' with arbitration clause to resolve disputes over price: implied term that the petrol should be supplied at a reasonable price). See also *Sudbrook Trading Estate Ltd v Eggleton* [1983] 1 AC 444 (HL).

effect to the parties' clearly expressed agreement.[15] But if there is simply a bare agreement to negotiate, or to negotiate in good faith, at present the English courts cannot give effect to it. Admittedly, even if we were to accept that the parties could contract expressly to negotiate in good faith, there may be consequential practical difficulties—such as the remedy for breach of such an obligation.[16] But this occurs elsewhere. The Court of Appeal has accepted that there can be a duty to consider properly conforming tenders, even though it is not obvious that any loss flows from a breach of the obligation if the claimant cannot show that his tender would have been accepted.[17] And the House of Lords in *Walford v Miles* was content to accept the notion of a lock-out contract, as long as the terms of the lock-out were sufficiently certain, although the breach of a lock-out contract may not easily give rise to a remedy because the claimant may not be able to establish that he lost a real or substantial chance of the contract.[18]

(b) French Law: The Move Towards a Protected Relationship?

In French law the position is rather different. As the previous chapter by Bénédicte Fauvarque-Cosson makes clear, although the 1804 Code civil did not make any special provision for negotiations, by the later stages of the twentieth century the case-law had developed a view of the negotiating process within which the parties can undertake duties towards each other—impliedly, as well as expressly. And these duties are brought together under the general principle of good faith.

The starting-point is the right to break off negotiations. Merely starting negotiations does not carry with it a duty to continue, or to reach a concluded contract. But through a range of particular instances which the courts have accepted as giving rise to liability, we can say that a more generalised, unifying duty of good faith in the negotiations has been accepted than has ever been contemplated by the courts in England. This is partly a result of the different approaches to legal rules and general principles in the two jurisdictions: French law works from general legal rules,

---

[15] *Cable & Wireless*, above n 13, [25] (Colman J): 'This may seem a somewhat slender basis for distinguishing this type of reference from a mere promise to negotiate. However, the English courts should nowadays not be astute to accentuate uncertainty (and therefore unenforceability) in the field of dispute resolution references.'

[16] Lord Denning MR in *Courtney & Fairbairn*, above, text to n 9.

[17] *Blackpool and Fylde Aero Club Ltd v Blackpool Borough Council* [1990] 1 WLR 1195 (CA) (an *implied* contractual duty to consider tenders).

[18] *Dandara Holdings Ltd v Co-operative Retail Services Ltd* [2004] EWHC 1476 (Ch), [2004] 2 EGLR 163. In practice, it is advisable to include an express promise to reimburse the expenditure which will have been wasted in the event of the negotiations failing by virtue of the breach of the 'lock-out'.

and the French courts deduce a general principle from specific instances more easily than the English.[19] The French courts have developed general (although defined) duties of disclosure between negotiating parties.[20] They devised the rule that, once an offer has been made, the offeror must give the offeree a reasonable opportunity of considering it;[21] it would be wrong to withdraw it abruptly and without good reason.[22] And the breaking-off of negotiations at an advanced stage by a party who has watched the other incur expenses is wrongful if there is no adequate justification for it. This became generalised in the form of propositions used by the courts such as:[23]

> Iveco had brutally and unilaterally broken off these far-advanced negotiations, and had failed to comply with the rules of good faith in commercial relations.

The liability in such cases is generally in tort: there is 'precontractual fault' on the part of the party who breaks off or otherwise conducts himself contrary to the requirements of good faith during the negotiations.[24] The generality of the law of tort—under which a party who breaks off negotiations by his 'fault' is liable to compensate the 'loss' which he has thereby 'caused'—gives French law the facility to impose liability in this context. This contrasts not only with the reluctance of the English courts to characterise the breaking-off of negotiations as wrongful, but also with the lack in English law of a general basis of liability under which the courts would be able to place such a claim. The English courts could find a home for such a claim if they so desired: it could be the duty of care in the tort of negligence. But we have already seen the reluctance of the common law courts to impose such a general duty, or to develop the duty of care in this respect. That reluctance of the English courts rests on the underlying principle: the very relationship between the parties to a negotiation is inherently adversarial and the courts should not develop implied duties to reverse that balance of risk. French law has developed general duties which can arise and be found to have been broken—if the lower court hearing the case so decides on the facts.

---

[19] R David and HP de Vries, *The French Legal System* (New York, Oceana, 1958) 81–5.

[20] J Ghestin, 'The Pre-contractual Obligation to Disclose Information: French Report' in D Harris and D Tallon (eds), *Contract Law Today: Anglo-French Comparisons* (Oxford, Clarendon Press, 1989) 151; cf B Nicholas, 'English Report', *ibid*, 166; B Nicholas, *The French Law of Contract* (2nd edn, Oxford, Clarendon Press, 1992) 102–6.

[21] Cass civ (1) 17 December 1958, D 1959, 33. This is a matter of fact for the sovereign power of assessment of the lower courts: Cass civ (3) 10 May 1972, Bull civ III no 297. See generally P Malaurie, L Aynès, P Stoffel-Munck, *Les Obligations* (2nd edn, Paris, Defrénois, 2005) no 470.

[22] Cass com 20 March 1972, JCP 1973 II 17543; Malaurie et al, above n 21, no 464.

[23] Cass com 22 April 1997, D 1998 J 45 ('la société Iveco avait rompu brutalement et unilatéralement des négociations très engagées, et avait manqué aux règles de bonne foi dans les relations commerciales').

[24] Malaurie et al, above n 21, nos 464, 470. For more detail, see B Fauvarque-Cosson, 'Negotiation and Renegotiation: a French Perspective', ch 2 above.

In this respect, the *Avant-projet* takes the law which has already been developed by the case-law, and proposes to articulate the general requirement of good faith in the revised Code itself:

> Article 1104: The parties are free to begin, continue and break off negotiations, but these must satisfy the requirements of good faith.
> A break-down in negotiations can give rise to liability only if it is attributable to the bad faith or fault of one of the parties.

The freedom of negotiation is the principle. That must be the starting-point, as has been stated by the courts in many cases.[25] But the freedom is not unlimited. It may be abused. The sanction for such abuse is liability in damages—tort liability for 'bad faith or fault'.[26] French law therefore not only strikes a different balance of risk between the parties (although negotiations are free, the freedom is limited), it uses a general principle of good faith (which English law rejects) and has no difficulty in finding the remedy for the breach of the duty of good faith in this context (since it can be fitted quite comfortably within civil liability).

The *Avant-projet* also makes explicit provision for the parties to regulate their negotiations by contract:

> Article 1104-1: The parties may, by an agreement in principle, undertake to negotiate at a later date a contract whose elements are still to be settled, and to work in good faith towards settling them.

This seems unexceptional. If the law imposes a general obligation to conduct negotiations in good faith, then it cannot be objectionable to permit the parties expressly to agree to this. For the French lawyer, the significance is to move the precontractual obligations into the contractual regime, rather than the tort regime.[27] But the notion of an obligation to work in good faith towards settling the details of a contract under negotiation does not raise any eyebrows. The unity of this area, and the balance between freedom in negotiations and the limits to this freedom, are made explicit in the *Exposé des motifs* to the Section on *Formation of Contracts* in the *Avant-projet* written by Philippe Delebecque and Denis Mazeaud:

> [T]hese rules are based on a trio of principles: freedom, loyalty and certainty.
> First, *freedom* in the period of precontractual negotiations (articles 1104 to 1104-2). The negotiating parties are free to enter into discussions, to carry on their negotiations and to end them how and when they see fit. In principle, they

---

[25] Eg Cass civ (3) 16 October 1973, D 1974 IR 35: 'Le droit de rompre des pourparlers ne dégénère en abus que si celui qui en use commet un ou plusieurs faits constitutifs de faute dans l'exercice de ce droit' ('the right to break off negotiations is only abused if the party who does so commits one or more acts which constitute fault in the exercise of this right').

[26] This formulation is rather curious, since the liability in tort arises from *fault*; and it is hard to see how 'bad faith', *independently of fault* could give rise to liability.

[27] This has a greater significance for French law because of the rule of *non-cumul* which denies concurrence of liability in contract and tort: Malaurie et al, above n 21, no 1010.

will not incur liability in this negotiating phase . . .

Secondly, *loyalty*. Precontractual freedom is indeed tempered and limited by a requirement of loyalty which is intended to impose a certain code of ethics in the period leading towards the conclusion of a contract, in so far as contractual negotiations are often marked by their length and often involve significant financial outlay. Also, the requirement of good faith provides guidance for negotiating parties during the negotiations, and especially at the moment of breaking them off. Similarly, the freedom to enter into minor contracts which mark out and provide a framework for the negotiations is constrained by the requirement of good faith.

Thirdly, *certainty*. The proposed rules are driven by the imperative to ensure legal certainty during the precontractual period. And so, first, an offeror's unilateral power of revocation is negatived when his offer, addressed to a particular person, carries his undertaking to maintain it during a specified period. In such a situation, the revocation of the offer will not prevent the formation of the contract if it is accepted within the specified period, nor will the offeror's death or incapacity during the period for acceptance. Just as certainty is assured by this provision for the recipient of the offer, and in particular respect for his legitimate belief that the offer will be maintained, so certainty for the offeror is promoted by the rule which provides that the contract is concluded only at the moment of receipt of the acceptance. Thus, the offeror is contractually bound only once he has actually been able to have notice of the will manifested by his partner, and cannot be bound in law without such knowledge. This solution, moreover, automatically reinforces his power to revoke his offer unilaterally. Secondly, the new rules aim to protect the legitimate expectations of the beneficiary of a pre-emption agreement or a unilateral promise to contract. In harmony with the provisions to the effect that one party may not unilaterally revoke a contract, and with the provisions governing enforced performance, and motivated by a concern not to undermine the preliminary contracts which are most commonly used in practice, the withdrawal by the offeror is sanctioned in the strongest possible manner. Indeed, the offeror's refusal to conclude the promised contract, or his concluding with a third party a contract of which he had given a preferential or exclusive right to the offeree, are not an obstacle to the conclusion of the promised contract with the offeree.

(c) Essential Differences in the Approach to the Negotiations

In summary, therefore, English law and French law take a different view about:

- the relationship between negotiating parties;
- the point, in advance of the contract being formed, at which one party begins to have some responsibility for the other;
- the role that the law of tort (and other legal principles) can play to support these underlying policies of the law of contract;

- the possibility for the parties to enter into express contractual obligations to regulate their negotiations.

These are not simply questions of presentation, or form, or 'legal technique'. English law has the tools at its disposition to impose more general duties between negotiating parties if the courts so desire. But, as a matter of principle, they resist it. To this extent, the values underlying the different legal systems' views of the contractual negotiating phase differ. This is not to say that the two systems do not both take a significant position on the risk allocation of the negotiations, and the role of their legal rules in the protection of the negotiating parties. But the position taken—and the party to be protected—is different. English law focuses on the freedom of each party to withdraw until the contract is concluded; one party is not entitled to rely on the contract being concluded, and therefore acts at his own risk until that moment unless the other party has done something to justify his assumption of risk: such as by making a misrepresentation; or having broken a contractually binding promise to maintain his offer; or having induced the other to begin to render the anticipated contractual performance or otherwise to act so as to incur expenditure beyond that which is within the normal pre-contract risk. To go beyond this, to impose a greater duty, would be to undermine each party's security in the negotiations—the certainty that they are not yet bound. The security of negotiations rests on the freedom from liability *vis-à-vis* the other party before the key moment at which risk is fixed—the moment at which the contract is formed. In this respect, English law is inward-looking: each party is entitled to look to his own interests.

French law, by comparison is less inward-looking: it respects the freedom of each party as the starting-point of principle, but it also expects each party to look outwards during the negotiations—to take some account of the other party's position. Just as an English lawyer sees the English approach as based on certainty for the negotiating parties, so the French lawyer will see the French approach as based on certainty. However, the balance is struck differently—and in French law the imposition of the duty of good faith during negotiations is seen not only as tempering the freedom in negotiations, but even as giving certainty (for each party *vis-à-vis the other*) through the careful imposition of duties—and therefore liability—during the precontractual stage.[28]

But the reluctance in English law to admit duties of good faith in negotiations even extends to the rejection of an expressly agreed obligation to negotiate. This is the point at which we might start to raise substantial questions. The rejection of generalised duties between negotiating parties is based on a position of principle: the inherently adversarial nature of their

[28] See the discussion of 'certainty' by Philippe Delebecque and Denis Mazeaud, quoted above p 60.

relationship. That is based on a value judgment about the proper (implied) balance of risk between negotiating parties—and one which is different from that taken in French law. But if the parties themselves *choose* to go beyond this, to agree expressly that their negotiations are not to be based on this narrow view—that, in effect, their negotiations *are* a relationship in which they accept that the law should have a role to protect each of them against the other's bad faith or failure to proceed in a fair, loyal and timely manner with the negotiations—why should the law not respect this? The only answer which the courts have been able to advance is one based on a lack of certainty in the content of such an obligation. But it is surely not impossible for the courts to construct criteria to determine whether one party has failed to do that which he promised expressly to the other party.

So much for the general approach to *negotiations* for a future contract. How does this then relate to the two systems' approaches to the *renegotiation* of an existing contract?

II. RENEGOTIATION

(a) French Law: A Link between Negotiation and Renegotiation

The *Avant-projet* draws a link between negotiation and renegotiation. This is not, perhaps, surprising. Having taken the opportunity to introduce into the Code the general propositions that *negotiations* must be conducted in good faith,[29] and that the parties may 'by an agreement in principle, undertake to negotiate at a later date a contract whose elements are still to be settled, and to work in good faith towards settling them',[30] it is a small step to saying that the parties may enter into a binding agreement to *re*negotiate in the event of certain defined supervening events. This is done in articles 1135-1 to 1135-3:

> Article 1135-1: In contracts whose performance takes place successively or in instalments, the parties may undertake to negotiate a modification of their contract where as a result of supervening circumstances the original balance of what the parties must do for each other is so disturbed that the contract loses all its point for one of them.

> Article 1135-2: In the absence of such an express term, a party for whom a contract loses its point may apply to the President of the *tribunal de grande instance* to order a new negotiation.

> Article 1135-3: Where applicable, these negotiations should be governed by the rules provided by Chapter I of the present Title.

---

[29] Art 1104, set out above p 59.
[30] Art 1104-1, set out above p 59.

> In the absence of bad faith, the failure of the negotiations gives rise to a right in either party to terminate the contract for the future at no cost or loss.

These provisions have already been discussed and subjected to some criticism in the previous chapter by Bénédicte Fauvarque-Cosson. For present purposes, it is sufficient to note that article 1135-1 relates only to the inclusion of renegotiation clauses in contracts for successive or instalment performance, and where there is a supervening event of such seriousness that 'the contract loses all its point' for one of the parties. And it is curious that this provision might be interpreted *a contrario* as *limiting* the range of permissible express renegotiation clauses to such situations. But the principal interest of this new provision is in the power of the court under article 1135-2 to *order* a new negotiation—a novelty, but which at the same time limits the power of the court. Only the party 'for whom the contract loses its point' may invite the court to make such an order.[31] And if the negotiations fail, the court has no power to impose a new contract: either party can simply terminate it without—except in the case of bad faith—any other remedy such as damages or any other mechanism for adjustment of benefits already conferred, a rule which could present serious difficulties for one of the parties if the contract is terminated at a point when the parties' performances do not yet correspond, such as where one party is required by the contract to pay only for complete performance but the contact is terminated after a significant performance has already been rendered by the other.[32]

But renegotiations are expressly linked to the general rules for negotiations by the first paragraph of article 1135-3. So the symmetry is maintained: parties may negotiate freely, but their negotiations are subject

---

[31] The purpose of the limits set out in art 1135-1 make sense when read with art 1135-2—the court's power arises only in such cases. It would surely have been better to separate out the parties' own power to define the circumstances in which there is to be a renegotiation (which need not be so narrowly limited?) and the circumstances in which the court may itself intervene on the initiative of one of the parties in the circumstances as they have now arisen, rather than in the circumstances as defined in advance by the contract. But then in both cases the (re)negotiations can properly be subject to the same regime of good faith. However, the explanation of art 1135-1 by Alain Ghozi in the *Exposé des motifs* of the *Avant-projet* (quoted below) appears to assume that even an express renegotiation clause should be limited to the case of the contract having 'lost all its point'—in the interests of certainty of transactions.

[32] This problem—the absence of an adjustment mechanism on termination of a contract—was addressed to some extent in relation to frustration in English law by the Law Reform (Frustrated Contracts) Act 1943. Termination for frustration presents other difficulties, however: it is automatic, rather than by act of either party; and although it is limited to cases where in the light of the changed circumstances since the formation of the contract performance of the contract would be illegal, impossible or 'radically different from that which was undertaken by the contract', *Davis Contractors Ltd v Fareham UDC* [1956] AC 696, 728–9 (HL), it is certainly more widely available than where there is *force majeure* in French law, and perhaps more widely than cases covered by art 1135-1 of the *Avant-projet* (it is not limited to the case of successive or instalment contracts; and the requirement that 'the contract loses all its point' may be narrower—although this test itself is open to some interpretation). On frustration, see H Beale (ed), *Chitty on Contracts* (29th edn, London, Sweet & Maxwell, 2004) ch 23.

to the requirements of good faith. Moreover they may enter into an agreement of principle which binds them to negotiate in good faith. Similarly, they may in the principal contract bind themselves to *re*negotiate in certain defined circumstances. And, in those limited circumstances, the court may (on the initiative of one party) order the parties to renegotiate even in the absence of an express renegotiation clause—but the renegotiations are subject to the same regime as initial contractual negotiations.

A balance is here being struck between the power of the parties and the power of the court to readjust the contract—and the *Avant-projet* comes down quite firmly against the larger scope of judicial intervention which has been adopted in other European jurisdictions and in the Principles of European Contract Law and the UNIDROIT Principles.[33] This is the issue on which there might be some serious debate. On the more general issue, however—the principle that there can be an express renegotiation clause, and that if such a clause becomes operative (or if the parties for other reasons, such as a court order, find themselves having to renegotiate a contract) the parties will be subject to the overriding duty to conduct themselves in good faith during the (re)negotiations—there is surely no debate. Given that negotiating parties are in general subject to the duty of good faith, and that parties can in law bind themselves to negotiate (in good faith) a future contract, it is but a small step to say that they can similarly bind themselves to renegotiate; and that the renegotiations, if begun, are subject to the duty of good faith. The discussion by Alain Ghozi of articles 1135-1 to 1135-3 in the *Exposé des motifs* to the *Avant-projet* emphasises certainty but also the significance of the law's encouraging and supporting the parties themselves to negotiate solutions to serious problems as they arise, as well as to plan for such situations in advance in the contact itself:

> [T]here is no better solution than one which will have been negotiated by the parties in question themselves. Therefore, there is deliberately no provision made for supervening circumstances. The success of settlement as an alternative means of resolving disputes which has always been recognised and in our own day calls for the development of mediation as another negotiated means of resolution of disputes bears sufficient witness to this. Furthermore, practitioners know this well, and include renegotiation clauses to deal with the situation of supervening serious difficulties. Also, negotiation by the parties is once again to be encouraged by placing it at the centre of the law itself, though it was thought necessary to structure the circumstances in which negotiations should take place in these situations so as to deal both with cases where the parties themselves have been silent on the matter and where the parties' negotiations have broken down. This is the purpose of the provisions as proposed.
>
> Parties to contracts are encouraged to include renegotiation clauses in their contracts to govern cases where a change of circumstances has the effect of dis-

---

[33] Discussed by Fauvarque-Cosson, above n 24.

turbing the original balance of what is required of them under the contract to the extent that the contract loses all its point for one of them (article 1135-1). In order to guarantee the certainty of transactions, modification is tied to the loss of point to the contract, and this test acts both as a measure of the seriousness of the imbalance and as its proof. The solution to the problem of supervening circumstances is therefore found in negotiation, thereby solving a contractual difficulty through contract itself. In the absence of an express renegotiation clause (a possibility which ought not to be ignored), a party for whom a contract loses its point may apply to the court (specifically, to the President of the *tribunal de grande instance*), which may order a negotiation aimed at saving the contract (article 1135-2). If this fails, and putting aside cases of bad faith, either party would have the right to claim the prospective termination of the contract without payment of expenses or damages (1135-3): once the point of the contract has disappeared, so too should the contract itself. Implicit in this is that a person who wishes to see the contract maintained will have to make those concessions which are necessary to allow the other party a minimum of benefit to encourage him to carry on with their contractual relationship.

(b) English Law: Breaking Down the Resistance to a Duty to (Re)Negotiate?

Much of the approach contained in the discussion by Alain Ghozi, set out above, applies similarly to English law. The doctrine of frustration is not so narrowly confined as the doctrine of *force majeure* in French law, but still it is narrow and it is for the parties themselves either to provide for future uncertainties in the contract itself, or to negotiate a solution in the case of supervening circumstances which are not provided for in the contract and which terminate the contract on the grounds of frustration. Parties do commonly include clauses—often termed *force majeure* or 'hardship' clauses—in contracts which are to be performed in the future, and in particular where the contract is a long-term performance contract.[34] However, when it comes to the question of what provision can be made in the contract for the resolution of the consequences of supervening circumstances, English law takes a narrower position than French law. In English law there is no general duty to negotiate a future contract; and the parties cannot in law bind themselves to negotiate a contract. We have seen already that two principal reasons are generally given for this: the inherently adversarial position of the negotiating parties; and the fact that the only way of giving content to such an agreement would be to imply a duty of good faith in negotiations—which is too uncertain as a standard for the English courts. There is therefore an inherent difficulty in English law in making provision for future supervening circumstances by means of a

---

[34] E McKendrick (ed), *Force Majeure and Frustration of Contract* (2nd edn, London, Lloyd's of London Press, 1995).

clause requiring the parties to renegotiate in the light of the circumstances when they are eventually known.

There have, however, been some signs recently of a reluctance on the part of the English courts to press too far the argument which rejects the duty to negotiate in good faith. The context in which the question has arisen is the strongest case for rethinking the traditional approach: an express clause providing for renegotiation of the contract.

In *Petromec Inc v Petroleo Brasilieiro SA*[35] Longmore LJ discussed (obiter) whether an express obligation to negotiate is enforceable. The clause in question imposed on the parties to a contract relating to the upgrading of a vessel the duty to negotiate in good faith the 'reasonable extra costs' of the works which would be due in certain specified circumstances. So the contract already contained an objectively revisable price; the obligation to negotiate in good faith was only supplemental to this, to provide the mechanism for the parties to negotiate the revision. Longmore LJ said:[36]

> The traditional objections to enforcing an obligation to negotiate in good faith are (1) that the obligation is an agreement to agree and thus too uncertain to enforce, (2) that it is difficult, if not impossible, to say whether, if negotiations are brought to an end, the termination is brought about in good or in bad faith, and (3) that, since it can never be known whether good faith negotiations would have produced an agreement at all or what the terms of any agreement would have been if it would have been reached, it is impossible to assess any loss caused by breach of the obligation.

But he noted that, in the particular case, these were not serious objections because the court could ascertain the 'reasonable costs' involved if the negotiations broke down (there was no real uncertainty); it would in fact be sufficiently clear in this case whether the parties had acted in bad faith in not concluding an agreement on the revised sums payable (in practice, the bad faith would be likely to be linked to whether one party had made fraudulent misrepresentations about its intention to continue the negotiations); and the court could assess the losses which would flow from the breakdown of the negotiations (because the court could assess the 'reasonable' costs which should have been agreed). But Longmore LJ went further, and raised the more general question of whether it is appropriate for English law to maintain such a sharp, principled objection to clauses imposing the obligation to negotiate in good faith:[37]

> It is not irrelevant that [this clause] is an express obligation which is part of a complex agreement drafted by City of London solicitors and issued under the imprint of Linklater & Paines (as Linklaters were then known). It would be a

---

[35] [2005] EWCA Civ 891, [2006] 1 Lloyd's Rep 121.
[36] *Ibid* [116].
[37] *Ibid* [121].

strong thing to declare unenforceable a clause into which the parties have deliberately and expressly entered. I have already observed that it is of comparatively narrow scope. To decide that it has 'no legal content' to use Lord Ackner's phrase[38] would be for the law deliberately to defeat the reasonable expectations of honest men, to adapt slightly the title of Lord Steyn's Sultan Azlan Shah lecture delivered in Kuala Lumpur on 24 October 1996 (113 LQR 433 (1977)[39]). At page 439 Lord Steyn hoped that the House of Lords might reconsider *Walford v Miles* with the benefit of fuller argument. That is not an option open to this court.

Below the level of the House of Lords, then, it is not yet safe to assume that even in the strongest case—the express renegotiation clause—will the duty to negotiate in good faith be accepted in law.

The question ought to be simply one of certainty in the particular case. We have seen that, in the case of an alleged obligation to negotiate a contract, the courts tend to entangle two issues: the inherently adversarial relationship involved in negotiations; and the lack of certainty in the notion of a duty to negotiate (or to negotiate 'in good faith'). The first issue speaks against an implied obligation to negotiate, but not against an expressly agreed obligation. In that case, only the question of the certainty of the obligation arises. And one is left wondering whether the English courts could not construct criteria to determine what is to be expected of parties engaging in negotiations in good faith, on the facts of a particular case. Lessons might even be learnt here from those other legal systems— including French law—which apply such a principle and which take into account, for example, the way in which each party has behaved towards the other during the negotiations (including statements made); the abruptness of breaking off; and the legitimacy of the reasons for breaking off.[40] This would not have to involve the imposition of a general duty of good faith which upsets the normal risk allocation, but would give content to an expressly agreed obligation rather than defeating the intentions of the parties by rejecting out of hand the very notion of an obligation to renegotiate. By entering into a contract containing such a clause the parties have already created a relationship which undermines their right to rely on the inward-looking, self-interested right to walk away from the negotiations without giving any reason and even in the knowledge that the failure of the negotiations might leave the other party with losses.

[38] The phrase referred to, *Walford v Miles* [1992] 2 AC 128, 138 (HL), runs as follows: 'A duty to negotiate in good faith is as unworkable in practice as it is inherently inconsistent with the position of a negotiating party. It is here that the uncertainty lies. In my judgment, while negotiations are in existence either party is entitled to withdraw from those negotiations, at any time and for any reason. There can be thus no obligation to continue to negotiate until there is a "proper reason" to withdraw. Accordingly a bare agreement to negotiate has no legal content.'
[39] The lecture was published under the title 'Contract Law: Fulfilling the Reasonable Expectations of Honest Men' in (1997) 113 LQR 433.
[40] Malaurie et al, above n 21, no 464; F Terré, P Simler and Y Lequette, *Droit civil: Les obligations* (9th edn, Paris, Dalloz, 2005) no 185.

One has to consider how far to press this argument. The first stage is to say that the court should be willing to examine more closely the objections to express renegotiation clauses based on the argument of uncertainty, so as to avoid defeating the parties' intentions. But from that one could then try to construct a secondary argument which strikes much more fundamentally at the objections to duties to negotiate in good faith. Renegotiation is different from negotiation. The parties are already in a contractual relationship—and so are they necessarily, as regards serious supervening circumstances, in an 'inherently adversarial relationship'? If not, then (and unlike in the case of initial negotiations) can we consider even *implied* duties to renegotiate? This would surely be a step too far for the English courts. There is no general (implied) duty to perform the contract in good faith, nor to exercise one's contractual rights in good faith. The parties can (and, in commercial contracts, commonly do) provide for future difficulties by 'hardship' and 'termination' clauses. But criteria are necessary to determine when such clauses should become enforceable (ie when the hardship or change of circumstances is sufficiently serious to permit the clause to be invoked). If the parties make express provision, that should be given force. But beyond the express contractual provision (the express allocation of the risk of supervening circumstances) the doctrine of frustration applies. Unless that doctrine is itself to be rewritten, there is no role in English law for an implied duty to renegotiate. The problem at the moment is that a strict reading of the cases—and the legacy of, in particular, *Walford v Miles*—means that even express hardship clauses may fail because the duty to renegotiate has not been accepted as having sufficient content that the operation of such a clause can be controlled by the courts. So parties are often left simply to negotiate their way out of serious supervening circumstances, unaided by the legal process even where they had sought to provide for it.

(c) Parallels and Differences

In both of our legal systems there is a link between negotiations and renegotiations, although these have not always been juxtaposed in legal writing. Negotiations are about the formation of a contact; renegotiations are typically a response to a serious problem which has arisen during the performance of the contract. So they tend to be seen as different problems. But it can be instructive to look at them together.

In English law, there has until now been a reluctance to treat the negotiations for a (new) contract as inherently deserving of the law's protection; and this has been carried over to the case of renegotiations. There is no implied duty to negotiate in good faith (or any other equivalent or related general principle), but nor can an express duty to negotiate be accepted.

The implied duty is rejected both on principle (the inherent nature of negotiations) and on the grounds of a lack of certainty. The rejection of the express duty ought to stand or fall by reference only to the question of certainty. There appears to be some unease about the rigidity of the English approach—and Longmore LJ in the *Petromec* case has recently declared his dissatisfaction with the outright rejection of an express duty to negotiate in good faith. But this was in the context of a *renegotiation* clause. And here it is most likely that such an express clause will be found: commercial parties, particularly in long-term contracts, may need to write into their contract the possibility of a renegotiation in the event of some serious change of circumstances. But the law presents an obstacle—an undesirable obstacle, which forces the parties back into negotiations (with, of course, no legal protection greater than they had for the initial negotiations) if they are to avoid the operation of either the unmodified contract or its automatic termination under the doctrine of frustration, depending on whether the change falls within that doctrine. It may not be a surprise that the question of whether to maintain the strict *Walford v Miles* approach should have arisen in the contract of an express term within a contract imposing on parties a duty to renegotiate in good faith. The fact that there is already a contract, under which performance has become problematic or there are other factual problems of performance, and which the parties have deliberately sought to anticipate and provide for, gives a different feel to the question—and makes the pressure to give effect to the clause all the stronger.

French law starts from a quite different point: the general duty of good faith in negotiations. But now that this has been developed through the case-law, and will become expressly provided for in the Code if the *Avant-projet* is implemented, the link to the existing duty to perform in good faith becomes even clearer. The *Avant-projet* makes the link express by imposing on the new negotiations the general provisions relating to negotiations (including good faith).

The question is how far to press the link in each system. As Bénédicte Fauvarque-Cosson notes in her chapter, there could be an argument that the existence of the contract strengthens the relationship and therefore inherently strengthens the duty to (re)negotiate. Given that there is already a duty under article 1134(3) of the Code to *perform* in good faith, it would be a natural step to say that this can give rise to a duty to engage (in good faith) in renegotiations if the circumstances so require. The *Avant-projet* is in this sense articulating in article 1135-2 an approach which fits with the existing view of contractual obligations in French law, and also—because of the existing contractual relationship—could impose not simply a duty to conduct renegotiations in good faith, but even to *begin* negotiations. But the *Avant-projet* is reluctant to go quite so far. It limits the intervention of the judge to the case where he is invited by a party for whom the contract

has 'lost its point'. So, too, the *Avant-projet* has not gone as far as, for example, the Principles of European Contract Law in giving expression to the general principle of good faith. It is not a general, overarching principle of the law of contract, but is used in particular contexts, to temper other rules, and to deal with particular problems (such as the negotiating phase). No doubt a case can be made that this is too cautious, and that a more generalised application of the principle of good faith should have been employed, backed up by stronger sanctions (such as a stronger duty of renegotiation).

In English law, however, even if an express duty to conduct negotiations (in good faith) could be developed, it would not be so obviously acceptable for the court to impose such a duty. The absence of general duties to perform a contract in good faith or to exercise one's contractual rights in good faith would be likely to present an insuperable obstacle to the development of an implied duty to enter into renegotiations to resolve the difficulties arising out of supervening circumstances. The doctrine of frustration is the end-stop in English law for changes in circumstances where the parties have not made provision in their contract.

What is notable, however, is that the *Avant-project* allows the judge to order renegotiations, and to control the conduct of the negotiations through the general principle of good faith; but not to impose a new contract. This is contrary to the approach taken in many other European jurisdictions, but demonstrates an interesting similarity to the English approach. The two systems differ as regards the values underlying the negotiations when they have been engaged: English law gives a greater freedom to the parties to break off negotiations without sanction, and is reluctant to see the negotiations as a legally protected relationship; French law expects each party to take more account of the interests of the other and so is much more inclined to impose liability during the negotiations. French law goes much further than English law in implying duties between negotiating parties; and is even able now to contemplate giving the judge the power to order the parties to negotiate. But in the end, for both systems, the formation of the contract itself still belongs to the parties, not to the judge.

B

A Future for la cause?

4

A Future for la cause? *Observations of a French Jurist*

JUDITH ROCHFELD

A T A TIME when the majority of European countries have put to one side the idea of cause and when the various projects of European harmonisation do not refer to it, French law remains attached to this concept. The *Avant-projet de réforme du droit des obligations et de la prescription* drafted under the presidency of Professor Catala has therefore, after some prevarication, maintained the place and the importance of this concept. Witness article 1124, which provides:

> A contract is valid where the undertaking has a cause which is real and lawful which justifies it.[1]

This approach contrasts sharply with that chosen by the Principles of European Contract Law (PECL). The latter, in particular under the influence of German law, have eliminated the requirement that a contract must have a cause in order to be valid. Article 2:101(1) of the PECL refers only to the need for a 'sufficient agreement' in order for the contract to be validly formed.

The above statement could be said merely to represent an academic mindset which is particular to the defence of a national characteristic, were it not for the fact that the French courts have, over the course of the last twenty years, given back both strength and usefulness to the concept of cause. They have renewed the definition of cause, its use and its sanctions—at least in relation to the control of the existence of cause, a control which will alone be considered in the discussion which follows and which is to be distinguished from the control of the legality and the morality of the contract, which is also carried out in French law through the concept of cause.[2] In doing so, the French courts have forged an instrument that is

---

[1] See generally arts 1124 to 1126-1.

[2] French academic commentators traditionally contrast the control of the absence of cause on the one hand and the control of the morality or legality of cause on the other hand, pursuant to a

useful in the fight for the protection of the interests of each party in a contract, through the defence of the interest that each pursues in exchange for the sacrifice to which he consents. This instrument can be of assistance to anyone, irrespective of status—consumer, business and professional alike. Paradoxically, it would therefore appear that, more than ever before, surrounded by a universe which is unaware of it, French law has marked out a future for cause.

For all that, consideration of this future comes down, on the one hand, to examining the relevance of the control which is exercised and, on the other hand, to integrating the developments which this concept and its uses have undergone in the particular context in which French contract law will in the future need to evolve, namely that of European harmonisation.[3] Nevertheless, in order to respond to the first question, it would appear necessary to set out the controls which are effected through the requirement of the existence of cause, before examining the justifications for the protection which it gives and its growing scope. This will allow us to respond to the second question: the identification of the presence of the same control or equivalent controls in the European provisions, even though what one might call the 'explanatory nature' which guides all the applications of cause in French law is not present there.[4] One may think, for example, within the PECL, of article 4:109, which specifies the sanction of subjective *lésion*. It permits a party to a contract to avoid the contract or to adapt it where the excessive benefit or unfair advantage which unbalances the contract is the result of an abuse by the other contracting party which has been committed based a situation of economic or intellectual dependence.[5] Certainly, the control here would be exercised according to different premises and a different approach: that of unfair conduct or an abuse of weakness which is manifested by a particular result, namely the imbalance in the content of the contract. It is therefore not a direct control of the imbalance itself, but rather of the behaviour and the positions of the parties influencing the content of the contract. That does not, however, detract from the fact that this control can ensure, even in part, the control of the balance of the parties' obligations.[6] Equally, the nullity of particular

---

functional distinction. See, for example: J Flour, J-L Aubert and E Savaux, *Droit civil, Les obligations, L'acte juridique* (12th edn, Paris, Sirey, 2006) nos 253–70; F Terré, P Simler and Y Lequette, *Droit civil: Les obligations* (9th edn, Paris, Dalloz, 2005) nos 331–69; and equally the leading case employing this distinction: Cass civ (1) 12 July 1989, Bull civ I no 293, Defr 1990, 358 obs J-L Aubert, D 1991 Somm 320 obs J-L Aubert, JCP G 1990 II 21546 note Y Dagorne-Labbé, RTD civ 1990, 468 obs J Mestre, Gaz Pal 1991.1.374 note F Chabas.

[3] This will be the object of the discussion with our respondent: see R Sefton-Green, '*La cause* or the Length of the French Judiciary's Foot', below ch 5.

[4] Cf the criticisms of this fragmentary approach, which was followed in the drafting of the Civil code of Québec, made by G Cornu, *Regards sur le titre III du Livre III du Code civil* (Paris, Les cours de droit—DEA de droit privé à Paris II, 1975–6) no 253.

[5] See also art 30(3) AEPL Code.

[6] On this comparison, see D Mazeaud, 'La matière du contrat' in P Rémy-Corlay and

clauses which have not been the subject of individual negotiation, in cases where they instil in the contract 'a significant imbalance in the parties' rights and obligations', should be compared with the control exercised through cause in French law.[7]

The passages that follow therefore aim to set out the range of controls which are at work in French law, in order to provide the elements for comparison and to open up the discussions mentioned above. In a series of steps which are intended to be as clear and as informative as possible (rather than purely logical and rational) we will make our way from studying the renewal of the definition of cause (section I), to the renewal of the uses to which cause is put—that is to say the controls which are founded upon it (section II)—and end by considering the renewal of the sanctions for the absence of cause (section III).

I. THE RENEWAL OF THE DEFINITION: FROM COUNTERPARTY TO INTEREST

The definition of cause in French law has never been clear; far from it. The Code civil does not help much in this regard. It certainly imposes cause as one of the four conditions for the validity of a contract: article 1108.[8] But it contents itself with providing that 'an obligation without cause or with a false cause, or with an unlawful cause, can have no effect'—article 1131[9]—leaving it to the interpreter to give substance to this multifaceted concept.

For all that, and even if it has come about only after much prevarication,

D Fenouillet (eds), *Les concepts contractuels français à l'heure des Principes du droit européen des contrats* (Paris, Dalloz, 2003) 81; and 'La cause' in *1804–2004: Le Code civil, un passé, un présent, un avenir* (Paris, Dalloz, 2004) 469; G Wicker, 'Force obligatoire et contenu du contrat' in P Rémy-Corlay and D Fenouillet (eds), *Les concepts contractuels français à l'heure des Principes du droit européen des contrats* (Paris, Dalloz, 2003) 151; J Beauchard, 'L'absence de cause dans les principes européens des contrats' in *Apprendre à douter—questions de droit, questions sur le droit: Etudes offertes à Claude Lombois* (Presse universitaire de Limoges, 2004) 819. Note also the control of good faith and reasonableness established by these Principles (see Wicker, above).

[7] Art 4:110, PECL; see also art 30(4) AEPL Code. Elsewhere, in relation to the second role of cause, the requirements of French law will be subject to little disruption, as the various projects leave the sanction of public policy and public morality to each state (other than the respect due 'to imperative rules' set out by the PECL: cf arts 1:101 and 15:101, 15:102). See J Hauser 'L'ordre public et les bonnes moeurs' in P Rémy-Corlay and D Fenouillet (eds), *Les concepts contractuels français à l'heure des Principes du droit européen des contrats* (Paris, Dalloz, 2003) 105.

[8] Art 1108 Cc: 'Four conditions are essential for the validity of an agreement: the consent of the party who binds himself; his capacity to contract; a definite object which forms the subject-matter of the undertaking; a lawful cause in the obligation.'

[9] See also art 1132, which provides that a 'contract is no less valid, for the cause not being expressed', which is considered to be a rule of proof, and art 1133, which affirms that 'the cause is unlawful where it is prohibited by legislation, and where it is contrary to public morality or to public policy'.

the majority of academic commentators have reached agreement on some traditional elements of the definition.

First, in relation to the 'voluntarist' foundations of modern contracts—according to which the contract is regarded as a meeting of wills with the goal of producing legal effects—the consensus has been to adopt the concept of 'final' cause: it embodies the idea of an objective which leads each one of the parties to enter into a contract; that which they hope to achieve by agreeing to place themselves under obligations.

Secondly, in order to assess this final cause, a psychological notion, the question has been raised of the degree to which the court will intervene in researching the intentions of the parties, and then, once this question has been resolved, of the intensity of the control applied to the elements thereby identified. In relation to the first point, the question consisted in determining whether the control should be confined to what is apparent from the contractual structure—notably the visible counter-performances which make up the elements of the exchange—or whether it should also be applied to the motivations of each of the parties. The response was, in a period of individualism, mistrustful of judicial interference—that of the Code civil and the nineteenth century—that the judge should intervene as little as possible: the freedom of contract, recognised as the foundation of the undertaking, had to be exercised in its full force, without external assessment. As a result, the control was presented as being concentrated upon an appreciation of the existence of visible counter-performances, making the engagements undertaken immediately comprehensible. The latter were defined in quite an objective manner as those normally expected in the type of contract which had been concluded. The motives of the parties were left to one side, being considered only in relation to the control of the lawfulness of the cause (another part of the majority opinion therefore held to the separation referred to above of the control of cause according to a functional distinction between the control of the absence of cause—and its objective assessment—and the control of the lawfulness of the cause—and its subjective assessment, which extended to the deter-mining motives of the parties). As to the second point, following the same line of thought, control was constructed as a rather superficial control of the presence of the visible elements of exchange: it sufficed for the judge to verify that a contractual counter-performance existed, whatever its make-up or its importance, any objective outside assessment of what would have been a reasonable contractual counter-performance being kept to a minimum.[10] This situation corresponded with the majority of contracts: bilateral contracts which were *commutative*—embodying an exchange not dependent on the occurrence of an outside event.

---

[10] Save in the case of a contractual counter-performance which did exist, but which was derisory, which was considered to be equivalent to an absence of cause.

It is these two foundation stones of the definition of cause which must be subjected to re-evaluation in the light of the evolution which has taken place in this area over the last few years, notably in the case-law since the beginning of the 1990s. Beyond the contractual counter-performances which could be objectively determined, interest has also been integrated into the definition of cause: one may define it as the interest pursued by each of the contracting parties through the contract they have concluded. As a result, the definition of cause has, on the one hand, become more concrete, including the real interest presented by the contract (section I(a) below). This definition, on the other hand, as a result of this addition, has become more 'subjective', being capable of embracing the precise individual goals pursued by the parties (section I(b) below).

(a) The 'Concretisation' of Cause: The Consideration of the Real Interest

A first current development may be described as the 'concretisation' of cause. It relates, in the first instance, to the evolution in the definition of this concept. The concept of cause has become more concrete, in the sense that it no longer refers to a contractual counter-performance of any nature, whatever its substance or significance, but to a 'real' contractual counter-performance, which includes the consideration of the interest which it represents. Next, and in consequence, this definition goes beyond the idea of contractual counter-performance: through the concept of interest, the definition of cause can include situations where no contractual counter-performance appears from the contractual structure, but where an interest is nevertheless pursued, as a result of the existence of another contract, a third party or according to another timetable (before or after the contractual structure under consideration).[11]

As to the first point, that of taking into account the interest represented by the contract in the definition of cause, one may note a number of judgments in which the courts were not content with the abstract definition of a contractual counter-performance of whatever nature, but verified that the contract genuinely had an interest for the person undertaking the obligation. This search by the courts is revealed, notably, by phrases stating that the obligation undertaken by one of the parties did or did not constitute a 'real interest' for the other, 'a genuine counter-performance', a 'serious' counter-performance or a counter-performance which was not 'derisory'.

For example, in a decision of 13 October 2004, the third Civil chamber

[11] For a more detailed discussion of interest, see J Rochfeld, *Cause et type de contrat* (Paris, LGDJ, 1997) nos 76–114, and 'v Cause' in *Encyclopédie Juridique Dalloz* (Paris, 2006) nos 25–45; and more recently J Ghestin, *Cause de l'engagement et validité du contrat* (Paris, LGDJ, 2006) nos 113–22.

of the Cour de cassation was faced with the sale of a right to a lease by the lessee and the acquisition of the right by the lessor. In the abstract, this operation would not appear to involve any counter-performance for the benefit of the lessor: as he was already the owner of the premises, the transfer of property which constituted the abstract counter-performance resulting from the type of contract 'sale' could not operate for his benefit. The court, however, refined the analysis, searching for the real interest pursued by the lessor. It therefore held that

> the acquisition by the lessor of the right to the lease put up for sale by his lessee, which permitted the lessor to recover the material enjoyment of the demised premises, has a cause.

The cause was therefore assessed not from a formal point of view—from which it appeared to be non-existent[12]—but from the point of view of the concrete interest represented by the performance: recovering the material enjoyment of the premises.[13]

The same line of thought, though in the face of the converse situation, in which a counter-performance seemed to be present, can be found in a judgment of 24 March 1993. In this case an assignment was annulled on the grounds of absence of cause because, upon analysing the contractual counter-performance in question, it emerged that it presented no utility whatsoever: it concerned the assignment of his clientele by a taxi driver. The right to present his successor to the administration had been removed by *décret*. As a result, the assignment of the clientele, which was the only thing capable of constituting the contractual counter-performance, was of no interest to the assignee, who could be registered on the same timescale by the administration.[14]

These decisions show that it is not sufficient for there to be a contractual counter-performance of any nature, whatever its substance or significance. Rather, there must be a contractual counter-performance which is of genuine interest to the other contracting party.

Embarking upon the second aspect of the 'concretisation' of cause through the integration of interest into its definition, we should note that cause is no longer systematically associated with the idea of contractual counter-performance. Two situations must be distinguished.

Where this counter-performance exists within the contractual structure—which is the position in most cases if one considers bilateral contracts

---

[12] Compare the decision to this effect in an earlier case: Cass 19 December 2000, appeal no 99-16085, unpublished, where the absence of three distinct persons led to a finding of absence of cause in relation to the assignment of the lease.

[13] Cass civ (3) 13 October 2004, D 2004 AJ 3140 obs Y Rouquet, D 2005, 1617 note E Monteiro, D 2005 Pan 1090 obs L Rozès, RTD civ 2005, 130 obs J Mestre and B Fages, Defr 2005, 1245 obs J-L Aubert, RDC 2005, 1009 obs D Mazeaud.

[14] Cass civ (1) 24 March 1993, appeal no 91-13459, unpublished.

where the terms of the exchange are apparent (transfer of title to a thing in exchange for the payment of the price in a contract of sale; delivery and quiet enjoyment of premises in exchange for payment of rent in a contract of letting)—one tends today not to stop there, but also to consider the interest which the contractual counter-performance represents. That is the meaning of the statement made above. The counter-performance manifests the interest which is sought—though in truth it usually masks it, in that the counter-performance suffices in the majority of cases to justify the undertaking without the need for any deeper search.

Where this counter-performance does not exist or is not immediately apparent from the contractual structure in question—eg in the case of the sale of a company which is in significant debt for the symbolic price of €1 or in the case of a promise to pay a sum of money the cause of which is not apparent on the face of the contractual structure—it is necessary to search for the real interest pursued by the party who appears to impoverish himself. Today the courts tend, more so than before, to undertake this exercise.

From a reading of cases that have been decided, there are three situations corresponding to this tendency on the part of the courts.

The first is traditional, even if it has only rarely and only recently been presented in academic writing as a situation in which the courts search for interest. It concerns unilateral contracts. For example, in the case referred to above of a promise to pay a sum of money, the contractual structure does not reveal immediately the interest of one of the parties: the one who pays without apparently receiving anything in return. It is therefore necessary to go beyond the contractual structure and analyse the benefit previously received or some other thing which justifies such an obligation.

The second situation is where the contract appears to be devoid of any counter-performance for the benefit of one of the contracting parties, but where that contracting party nevertheless has an interest in it. This may be provided for him through another contract or by a third party, the particular agreement therefore forming part of a greater whole. One may think in particular of the sale of greatly indebted companies for the symbolic price of €1. In the past, these contracts were regarded as sales without a price that was real and serious and were therefore annulled. Renewed analysis of cause and the more realistic approach that goes with it have permitted these contracts to be upheld where it turned out that, beyond the formal scope of the contract, a real interest was being pursued by each of the parties. This could be the discharge of the debts of the company and the avoidance of proceedings being brought against the seller; or the restarting of business activity and the maintenance of his post as a director. It could equally be an interest resulting from the relationship of that contract with other contracts. For example, the third Civil chamber, in a famous judgment of 3 March 1993, upheld the sale of a plot of land

for 1 FF.[15] The court confirmed the approach of the lower court according to which this sale was 'a necessary condition for the achievement' of a wider 'operation' which could not

> be dissociated from that in relation to the buildings or from the discharge of the debts of the (transferor) company by the (transferee) company.

The transferor therefore had an interest in 'the totality of the operations concerning the sale of the company', 'which formed an indivisible whole' together with those relating to the land and which 'permitted the discharge of debts and the pursuit of the business activities of the company'. The lower court even stated that the transferor

> had a great interest in the performance [of the contract] both in his personal capacity to avoid proceedings from his creditors and in his capacity of shareholder in the [transferee] company in which he, together with his wife, held almost half the shares.

The court therefore deduced that 'in the general economic context of the contract, the sale of the land had a cause and had a real counter-performance'. One notes here the use—the importance of which will be seen again below—of the expression 'the economic context of the contract',[16] which marks this deeper search for understanding of atypical contractual structures.

The third situation concerns contracts where the counter-performance does not arise from the nature of the contractual structure, nor is it furnished by the other contracting party, but rather by a third party. One may refer, in this regard, to the 'exteriorisation' of cause. In the same way, it is because one is able to search for the interest pursued that it is now possible to make the link between an obligation undertaken within a particular structure and a counter-performance provided by a third party.

To conclude on this point, it is necessary to note that the developments in the direction of a 'concretisation' of the definition of cause, described above, lead to the calling into question of two traditional ideas which have been put forward in French law.

The first is the association of cause and *objet*—subject-matter: in the 'majority' view, the *objet* of the obligation of one of the contracting parties—the performance or abstention which he undertakes—constitutes the cause of the obligation of the other contracting party; that which

---

[15] Cass civ (3) 3 March 1993, Bull civ III no 28, JCP G 1994 I 3744 obs M Fabre-Magnan, RTD civ 1994, 124 obs P-Y Gautier. See also Cass civ (1) 3 July 1996, Bull civ I no 286 (below n 21) referring to 'the desired economic outcome'; Cass civ (3) 16 February 2000, appeal no 98-14153, unpublished.

[16] On this concept for a critical commentary see J Moury, 'Une embarrassante notion: l'économie du contrat' D 2000 Chron 382; less critical: A Zelcevic-Duhamel, 'La notion d'économie du contrat en droit privé' JCP G 2001 I 300 (warmer); S Pimont, *L'économie du contrat* (Presses universitaires Aix-Marseille, 2004); A Arsac-Ribeyrolles, *Essai sur la notion d'économie du contrat* (doctoral thesis, Clermont-Ferrand, 2005).

justifies why that party consents to a sacrifice. We have, however, noted above the situations in which no contractual counter-performance is present within the contractual structure in question, where the *objet* of the obligation of one of the contracting parties does not constitute the cause of the obligation of the other. There may, therefore, be a cause in the absence of an *objet*.[17]

The second way in which traditional positions have been called into question relates to the scope of control: it has generally been limited to the framework of the exchange, that is to say the particular contract which was subjected to the assessment of the court—though it may nevertheless be noted that unilateral contracts have always found their cause outside the framework of the particular contract in question. If one accepts the need to search for the real interest which is being pursued, one will sometimes move outside the contractual framework in order to find it.[18]

Moreover, this more extended consideration of the interest which is sought opens up a second new direction: the recognition of the aims individually defined by the parties—which are said to be 'subjective'.

(b) The 'Subjectivisation' of Cause: The Consideration of Individually Defined Aims

The second current movement may be described in terms of the 'subjectivisation' of cause. It comes down to the fact that the courts are willing to search for and to analyse the cause of the obligation of each of the parties, as they have each individually defined it, without confining themselves to a pre-established definition of a contractual counter-performance. On the one hand, in the majority of academic writing, not only is cause defined as a contractual counter-performance, but it is also described as that normally associated with the type of contract in question: one may describe this as the 'typical' cause. On the other hand, the courts have long been reluctant to recognise overtly that they could undertake an assessment of the specific aim pursued by the parties: the 'atypical' cause. For many years, the courts used indirect methods to reach the same result—the 'interpretation' of the factors which the parties regarded as essential; the consideration of one factor or one condition as being 'decisive' for or 'essential' to consent. It is only in the last few years (from the 1990s) that the courts have accepted that they should undertake this exercise directly and draw the resulting conclusions in relation to the control that they exercise. While the

---

[17] The truth of this statement depends, of course, on the meaning given to the concept of *objet*. See A-S Lucas-Puget, *Essai sur la notion d'objet du contrat* (Paris, LGDJ, 2005) for a broadening and rereading in the direction proposed by G Ripert and J Boulanger, *Traité de droit civil (d'après le traité de Planiol)*, vol II (Paris, LGDJ, 1957) no 241.

[18] For a similar approach see J Ghestin, referring to the 'contractual perimeter' in 'Existence de la cause et périmètre contractual', note on Cass civ (1) 13 June 2006, D 2007, 277.

dominant position may be correct where the parties content themselves with entering a well-known contractual structure (such as sale or lease) without making any changes—which is certainly the most common situation and which serves to mask the diversity of potential hypotheses—it is no longer correct where they move away from those typical structures in order to construct the content of their contract around a specific aim. Two types of atypical contract may be distinguished.

This tendency relates, in the first place, to innominate contracts; or, more precisely, to contracts which are completely atypical in the sense that they are not referable to a particular recognition or a particular regime imposed by legislation—the idea of a nominate contract in French law—but to the existence of a frame of reference, to the approach of a court to the counter-performance which is normally expected. Because they concern new contractual structures—whether individually negotiated or not—the aims pursued by each of the parties are unknown: the contract and the aims are atypical, elaborated individually by the contracting parties. The courts must therefore find the interest pursued—which may consist in a contractual counter-performance—by means of an analysis of what specifically the contracting parties were aiming to achieve. This phenomenon has always existed, because previously unknown types of contract have always been appearing. For example, in the 1970s, whereas the contract between a painter and the owner of an art gallery—today referred to as a 'contract of patronage'—was not yet known, the Cour de cassation approved the decision of the lower court which had discovered the cause of the obligations born of such an engagement: for the owner in the right of 'first viewing' accorded by the painter for five years in relation to all his work and, for the painter in the obligation to pay him 10,000 FF each month.[19] We should merely note that the recognition of this 'individual' or 'subjective' aim is now made more overtly in the case-law. It appears, notably, in the expressions referring to the analysis of a 'desired counter-performance' or resulting from the 'economic context' or even from 'the desired economic outcome'.

This tendency relates, secondly, to contracts whose normal aims and interests are known and which it is easy for the judge to analyse (sale, lease, etc). Sometimes, however, the contracting parties will redefine their aims in a new direction—and the relevant obligations to allow them to pursue this course. In the case-law, this phenomenon appears under the expressions 'desired counter-performance', counter-performance resulting from the 'economic context of the contract', even (rather inappropriately) elements comprising the 'essential condition' or 'decisive condition' of the will of one of the parties.[20] For example, in a decision generally regarded as lying

---

[19] Cass civ (1) 8 June 1971, Bull civ I no 187.

[20] The concept of a 'condition' usually denotes a modality of the obligation, that is to say a future and uncertain event which affects the existence or the enforceability of an obligation. It could not apply to an essential element.

at the heart of this movement, that of the first Civil chamber of the Cour de cassation of 3 July 1996, the court had to consider the existence of a counter-performance, for the benefit of a couple who had signed up to a 'contract for the creation of a "video point club"'. This contract could be seen either as being something completely new, or as being constructed on the foundation of a known contract: that of hire of video cassettes, the contract being concluded between the couple constituting the video point club and the business supplying them with the cassettes. If the latter approach is adopted, it is necessary to take the view that the contracting parties have added an objective of financial viability to the counter-performances which are normally to be expected under the contract of hire: the hire of cassettes must be integrated into the creation and functioning of a commercially viable contract. This was the approach taken by the court, which accepted that they should consider the 'desired economic outcome' of the agreement,[21] that is to say to consider the specific goal pursued by the contracting parties. As a result, they enlarged the control of cause and the domain of nullity (see below). This movement shows, therefore, that even where there does exist a counter-performance or an interest for each one of the contracting parties, a contract may be annulled if its advantages do not correspond to those which were sought.

In conclusion regarding this evolution of the definition of cause, one may note that the two movements described above, of 'concretisation' and of 'subjectivisation', have been separated for the sake of clarity, but are in reality related. It is because the consideration of the real interest which was sought has entered into the definition of cause that it is possible to understand and to look for the interest individually pursued by the parties and defined by them beyond the typical counter-performance or that specified by a particular contract.

The evolution in the definition of cause has, of course, consequences for the control of its existence.

II. THE RENEWAL OF THE USES OF CAUSE: FROM AN ABSTRACT CONTROL OF BALANCE TO A CONTROL OF THE REAL UTILITY OF THE CONTRACT

The control of the absence of cause was for a long time limited to that of the formal existence of a counter-performance. It therefore remained rather superficial: for the contract to be validated it was enough that there existed apparent elements of exchange, whatever their makeup or the

---

[21] Cass civ (1) 3 July 1996, Bull civ I no 286, D 1997, 500 note P Reigné, JCP G 1997 I 4015 obs F Labarthe, Defr 1996, 1015 note P Delebecque, RTD civ 1996, 903 obs J Mestre. The case is translated in Hugh Beale et al, *Ius Commune Casebooks for the Common Law of Europe: Cases Materials and Text on Contract Law* (Oxford Hart Publishing, 2002) 137.

interest they represented. The extension of the definition of cause to an interest has, as we have seen, two consequences: the reinforcement of the control in the sense of a strengthening of the rigour of the examination of the interest represented; and its refinement, in the sense of an assessment of the specific interest pursued when that interest has been specified by the parties. In all these cases, the control consists in the need for a real, reasonable interest in the contract.

In the current case-law, this control will manifest itself in two different ways, corresponding to two methods of assessing the reasonable interest pursued, following on from whether the parties have or have not set out the definition of this interest—these two ends of the spectrum are not separated by a hermetically sealed barrier but, rather, represent a gradation. In cases where the parties have simply entered into a typical contractual structure, pursing the goal which normally goes with such a structure, the courts tend to impose an inviolable minimum content ('typical' cause) (section II(a) below). Conversely, where the parties take the trouble to set out this interest, the refinement of the control tends towards verification by the courts that this interest does indeed correspond with the 'desired' interest, having regard to the economic context of the contract ('atypical' cause) (section II(b) below). These advances lead one to compare the control founded upon cause with certain current propositions put forward by academic writers which contain ideas of proportionality or of coherence (section II(c) below).

(a) The Imposition of a Minimum Inviolable Reasonable Interest, or Typical Cause

In contracts which relate to a specific type regulated by legislation or as a result of case-law, the counter-performances or interests expected are known (even if their definition, as well as the qualification of the various obligations or elements of which they are composed, may vary): transfer of title against price in sale; delivery and quiet enjoyment of premises against rent in letting; transmission of 'know-how' against payment of a fee in the contract of franchise,[22] etc. It is therefore easy to determine the reasonable interest which is pursued, by reference to this pre-definition. It should nevertheless be highlighted that—in contrast with the mere idea of a counter-performance—it is necessary, for the contract to be valid, that the specified counter-performance is not just any counter-performance, but one that genuinely conforms to that which relates to the type of contract which has been chosen. To confine oneself to a formal control therefore comes down to validating contractual structures which present any counter-

---

[22] See below n 23.

performance, even if the counter-performance in question does not conform to the typical counter-performance of the particular type of contract.
Reinforcing the control in this way comes down to controlling that the
elements of the exchange do indeed correspond to those attaching to the
type of contract which has been concluded. For example, this type of
assessment is particularly noticeable in relation to the contract of franchise:
the courts verify that, notwithstanding certain elements of exchange, the
franchisor does indeed furnish the interest which is usually expected,
namely the transmission of know-how. If not, even if certain counter-
performances are effected, the contract will be annulled for absence of
cause.[23]

Two consequences flow from this. The first consists in the annulment of
contracts which do not present the interest which is normally expected,
even if they do present some interest.

The second consequence, which is an extension of the first, lies in the
reinforcement of the inviolable minimum contractual content which makes
up the typical cause, that is to say the totality of obligations which permit
the typical goal to be reached. This trend can be seen in the case-law in the
expression through which the courts impose the 'essential elements' of the
contract, or its 'fundamental obligations'. In doing so, they make manifest
the idea that it is impossible to undermine these essential elements, particularly through a clause inserted in the contract which prevents them from
being accomplished. We should therefore note a reinforcement of the
control by the courts which seeks to impose the inviolable minimum
relating to each type of contract. This approach marks a return of the
'essence' of contract, in the sense of the *essentialia* of Roman law, that is to
say a return of the inviolability of the essential elements making up the
minimum of each type of contract. This new direction stands out, on the
one hand, against a period in which freedom of contract has been
presented as all-powerful. It is carried out, on the other hand, through the
concept of cause, which performs not only a modelling function—the goal
pursued determines the reasonable interest normally expected from this
type of contract—but equally a function of imposing order—it determines
the essential elements of the contract which may not be undermined.

By way of illustration of this trend, we should of course note the famous
Chronopost judgment of the Commercial chamber of 22 October 1996 and
its repercussions. We will come back to this in relation to sanctions, but it
should also be mentioned in so far as it puts into effect the following line of
reasoning: the obligation of punctuality which concretises the goal pursued
by the client of the express parcel delivery company—the interest of this
creditor resides not merely in a delivery, but in a delivery within the stipulated time—may not be undermined by a clause which purports to negate

---

[23] For example Cass com 30 January 1996, appeal no 94-13792, unpublished.

it. Accordingly, as the Court stated, a limitation clause which negates this objective is to be struck out.[24] One may equally cite the decisions through which the Cour de cassation denied to the lessor the possibility of exonerating himself through a term of the contract from the obligation of delivery set out in article 1719(1) Cc (even though this article described this obligation as relating to 'the nature of the contract' and not to its 'essence') or from the obligation of ensuring the quiet enjoyment of the premises.[25] Recently, on 1 June 2005 the Cour de cassation affirmed in the same way that

> the lessor cannot, by means of a clause relating to the execution of works, free himself from his obligation to deliver the demised premises.[26]

While this solution may seem novel, in reality it is not: the Chambre des requêtes of the Cour de cassation had already adopted such an approach as long ago as 1863.[27]

The importance of this control in relation to contracts which have not been individually negotiated must be highlighted. At first glance, it may look like the imposition, in the name of an objective norm of control, of a reasonable interest exterior to the contracting parties evaluated by the court. In reality, one may analyse it in the opposite way: as an indication of a genuine understanding by the courts of the way in which contracts which have not been individually negotiated work (*adhésion*: contracting on the basis of signing up to one party's standard terms). On the one hand, via this approach the courts impose the inviolable minimum on a contracting party who wishes it and who could avoid it in the definition of the content of the contract as a result of his bargaining power—and of the lack of bargaining power of his contractual partner. The courts therefore show the stronger contracting party that, once the type of contract has been chosen, it is not

---

[24] Cass com 22 October 1996, Bull civ IV no 261, D 1997 Somm 175 obs P Delebecque, RTD civ 1997, 418 obs J Mestre, D 1997, 121 note A Sériaux, JCP G 1997 I 4002 obs M Fabre-Magnan, Contrats Concur Consom 1997 comm no 24 obs L Leveneur, Defr 1997, 333 obs D Mazeaud, P Delebecque, D aff 1997 Chron 235; C Larroumet 'Obligation essentielle et clause limitive de responsabilité' D 1997 Chron 145.

[25] Cass civ (1) 11 October 1989, Bull civ I no 317; Cass civ (3) 5 June 2002, Bull civ III no 123, RDC 2003, 118 obs G Lardeux; see also in relation to performance Cass civ (1) 23 February 1994, Bull civ I no 76.

[26] Cass civ (3) 1 June 2005, Bull civ III no 119, RTD civ 2005, 780 obs J Mestre and B Fages, Defr 2006, 439 obs L Ruet. We should note here the mingling of the 'essence' and the 'nature' of the contract, the judgment stating that it resulted from the 'nature' of the contract (in relation to this point see also the above-mentioned observations of G Lardeux under Cass civ (3) 5 June 2002, above n 25).

[27] Cass Req 19 January 1863, DP 1863.1.248: 'a contract cannot legitimately exist if it does not contain the obligations which are of its essence and if it does not produce a legal bond which constrains the contracting parties to perform them; it is of the essence of the contract of letting that the lessor binds himself to provide the lessee with the enjoyment of the thing which has been let and to maintain it, for the duration of the letting, in a fit state for the purpose for which it is intended to be used'.

possible to undermine that which is normally expected by the other contracting party. On the other hand, and above all, this movement is founded on a genuine analysis of the scope of consent given by a party's signing up to standard terms:[28] in the full knowledge of the other contracting party, or even misdirected by the other contracting party and its advertising material—witness, for example, in relation to the *Chronopost* case, the importance of the advertising material relating to punctuality—the party signing up to the terms has merely signed up to a contractual formula proposed by the other contracting party because it allowed him to pursue his particular goal. He signs up, therefore, to a type of contract and to its inviolable minimum content. He expects from it the interest which is normally expected. In doing so, he has given his agreement to the contractual minimum, to the contractual goal and the obligations which allow it to be attained, with the full knowledge of his partner. It is upon this foundation that the contractual domain is determined. Any clause or element which contradicts this goal may be considered as not forming part of the agreement.

(b) The Control of the Reasonable Interest According to the 'Desired Economic Outcome' or Atypical Cause

The subjectivisation of cause through the increased consideration of interest, as set out above, has extended the scope of control and the reach of nullity: a contract may be annulled due to absence of cause as defined by the parties even though there is an element of exchange ('desired' counter-performance of cause resulting from the 'economic context of the contract).

This evolution began with the decisions relating to 'sales' entered into for tax purposes. In relation to such contracts, rather than contenting themselves with the assessment of an objective counter-performance, which attached to the type of contract in question ('sale') and, in consequence, stopped at the stage of the control of the presence of a transfer of title in favour of the buyer, the courts pushed the analysis further and considered the specific goals being pursued: if the contractual structure did not, from the start, benefit from the tax advantages promised by its inventor, the contract would be annulled.

This movement was given its official baptism by the decision of 3 July 1996 referred to above. In this case, the agreement establishing a business which hired out video cassettes which could not, from the outset, be viable in a town which did not have enough inhabitants was annulled on the ground that

---

[28] This analysis is particularly well presented in the *conclusions* of Advocate-General Charbonnier in the decision of Cass civ (1) 19 December 1990, RGAT 1991, 155.

relating as it did to the hiring of video cassettes for the running of a business, the performance of the contract according to the economics desired by the parties was impossible.[29]

Since then the judgments controlling the possibility of attaining, from the outset, specific objectives of viability which have been defined by the parties have multiplied. A recent case of 29 March 2006 will serve as an example. The third Civil chamber was faced with a contract for the purchase of a 'hotel room' by a husband and wife, which was coupled with their signing up to the terms of a joint venture 'having as its object to share in the fruits and the costs of the hotel restaurant' which would be managed by another company.[30] The Court pronounced the nullity of the sale for absence of cause, stating that the counter-performance pursued by the 'purchasers' by means of this 'sale' lay

> not only in the assurance that their investment would generate a profit, but equally in the assurance and guarantee . . . that they would never have to bear the losses of the hotel, these being borne by [the seller] by reason of a contract to stand surety.

Absence of cause was found here as a result of the 'impossibility of realising a profit', a specific goal of viability, expressly coupled with this 'sale'.[31]

We should note that, in parallel with the reinforcement of the imposition of an inviolable minimum in relation to typical contracts, this phenomenon reflects the admission of the control of individually defined counter-performances and accompanies this control with contractual 'engineering'.

In the extension of this trend and the reports made above relating to the definition of a subjective cause, one should equally note the admission of the control of goals which have been individually defined—which can be understood through the concept of interest—beyond the context of a particular contract: the interest may be pursued by means of other contracts (within a group operation) or furnished by a person other than the contractual counter-party. For example, in a recent decision of 13 June 2006, the Cour de cassation analysed a contract providing for the transfer of the master tapes and the related rights of a producer for the symbolic sum of 1 FF. This price, which had been regarded as 'derisory' by the Cour d'appel and as vitiating the contract by reason of an absence of cause, was analysed in a more refined way by the Cour de cassation. The Cour de cassation reproached the lower court for having failed to ask whether

---

[29] Cass civ (1) 3 July 1996, above n 21.

[30] Cass civ (3) 29 March 2006, Bull civ I no 88, JCP G 2006 I 153 obs A Constantin, RDC 2006, 1072 obs D Mazeaud.

[31] It should be noted that if this is the result of problems relating to the performance of the contract, an assessment of the existence of cause can be invoked only if the contractual structure itself contained a contradiction or a defect inhibiting the pursuit of the goal of profitability from the outset.

even without looking at the publishing contract, the contract of transfer was not to be placed within an economic operation constituting an indivisible contractual grouping in such a way that it could not be annulled for absence of cause.[32]

Nevertheless, in relation to this trend, we should note two points that have been the focus of criticism. Numerous critics have pointed to the calling into question of legal certainty: many contracts could be threatened if every party to a contract who is dissatisfied, eg as a result of the absence of profitability, could obtain nullity of the contract.[33] One may, however, moderate the position by insisting on the need to respect strict conditions for annulment to be obtained, which relate to the need for a clear definition of the scope of the contractual domain, a notion that is of great importance in this context.[34] The insertion of an element as forming part of the cause must be conditional upon the utility of this element for the pursuit of the particular goal, on the one hand; and on the express stipulation of its causal nature, on the other. The contract must therefore demonstrate, by its plain terms, that the two parties knew of this goal and had admitted it into their relations as such. There is therefore no obstacle to its absence resulting in nullity. It should also be noted that in the examples referred to above, the particular objective had entered into the contractual domain. For example the couple in the 'video point club' case had signed up to the contract proposed by the professional party who had drafted the agreement. The professional party had full knowledge of this goal and had expressly inserted it in the contract. He had even used it as part of his submissions.

Elsewhere, however, a second line of criticism has concerned the mingling that this control appeared to introduce of the assessment of the existence of cause in the formation of a contract and the evaluation of the defective performance of a contract. These criticisms rely legitimately on the reference made in some of the judgments forming part of this trend, to the consideration of the performance of the contract which has been rendered impossible due to the 'desired economic outcome' or the unviable commercial outcome. The criticisms are legitimate in so far as cause intervenes traditionally as an element in the assessment of the contractual structure and not in the assessment of the proper and satisfactory performance of the contract. The criticism may therefore be accepted. It does not, however, invalidate the control which is effected: the control relates only to cases where the contractual structure does not permit the defined

---

[32] Cass civ (1) 13 June 2006, Bull civ I no 306, D 2006 Pan 2642 obs S Amrani-Mekki, D 2007, 277 note J Ghestin.

[33] Cf Labarthe, above n 21; Mestre, above n 21.

[34] On the definition of the contractual domain, cf H Capitant, *De la cause des obligations* (3rd edn, Paris, Dalloz, 1927) no 4; and on its importance as a factor promoting legal certainty within a control which is being widened cf Rochfeld, *Cause et type de contrat*, above n 11, nos 266–83 and Rochfeld, 'v Cause', above n 11, nos 78-80.

goal to be achieved, from the beginning, whatever the performance. Merely because some of the decisions place themselves at the frontier between these two poles does not mean that the whole movement should be called into question.

Finally, in light of these evolutions, it is helpful to examine the role of this control in comparison with two emerging ideas to which some would like to tie it, namely proportionality and coherence.

(c) Cause, Proportionality and Coherence

(i) Cause and Proportionality

Some see, in these new directions, the emergence of a control of proportionality, that is to say a control of the quantitative balance of the contractual counter-performances.[35] Recent decisions which have sanctioned nullity contracts which presented only a 'derisory counter-performance' for the other contracting party are relied upon in this regard. For example, in a decision of 8 February 2005, the Commercial chamber of the Cour de cassation considered that the undertaking of one of the parties consisted

> in obtaining his supplies exclusively from [the supplier] and had by way of counter-performance the undertaking [by the supplier] to act as guarantor in relation to 20% of the loan made to the distributors.

However, '[the supplier] was [himself] guaranteed by [third parties] who had agreed to act as guarantors'. As a result, the supplier 'had failed to show that he had taken on any real risk'. The decision of the Cour d'appel that 'the obligation undertaken by the [supplier] was derisory' was therefore confirmed.[36] Following the same line of thought, in a decision of 10 May 2005, the first Civil chamber considered a contractual counter-performance to be derisory in light of the 'economic context of the contract'.[37] Elsewhere, competition law, in its rules which sanction abuses committed as a result of a situation of dependence, independently of their repercussions on the free workings of the markets, uses considerations of proportionality and of equivalence: it stigmatises abuses consisting in taking advantages

---

[35] Cf S Le Gac-Pech, *La proportionnalité en droit privé des contrats* (Paris, LGDJ, 2000); and in a more reserved manner D Mazeaud, 'Le principe de proportionnalité et la formation du contrat' LPA 30 September 1998, no 117, 12, who denounces, in relation to this idea, the risk of uncertainty for contracts; for an application limited to situations of particularly serious substantive inequality of bargain founded on the abuse of economic power see, J-P Chazal, 'Théorie de la cause et justice contractuelle' JCP G 1998 I 159.

[36] Cass com 8 February 2005, Bull civ no 21, D aff 2005, 639 and D 2005, 2841 obs S Amrani-Mekki, JCP G 2005 Pan 463, RDC 2005, 684 obs D Mazeaud, RDC 2005, 771 obs M Béhar-Touchais.

[37] Cass civ (1) 10 May 2005, Bull civ I no 203, D 2005 IR 1379, JCP G 2005 I 181 obs H Perinet-Marquet, RTD civ 2005, 778 obs J Mestre and B Fages.

without any counter-performance in return, or advantages that are disproportionate in the light of the performances provided in return.[38] We
should note, finally, that on one occasion, though in the name of the
sanction of the false cause of a promise to pay—a relatively unusual
situation—the Cour de cassation has effected a partial reduction in the
counter-performance to that which it would have been in the absence of a
mistake as to the sum due—a quantitative alteration.[39] The debate clearly
remains open. It should nevertheless be highlighted that, in the present
writer's view, the notion of cause should remain on the qualitative level of
the assessment of the interest presented by the contract, so that the
contract corresponds to the genuine understanding of the spirit of the
transaction. The control of the absence of cause should therefore intervene
only at the margins of this preoccupation with the equivalence of the
parties' obligations, namely where a manifestly disproportionate contractual counter-performance verges on a derisory counter-performance,
resulting in an absence of cause—which seems, to the present writer, to be
the tenor of the relevant decisions.

(ii) Cause and Coherence

The control of absence of cause and its new directions do, however, involve
more in the way of links with the notion of coherence, a notion that is
currently on the rise in French law.[40] A failure to respect this coherence has
therefore sometimes been sanctioned through a finding of absence of cause,
whether by means of an explicit or implicit reference to this notion. For
example, on its implicit foundation, any term of an insurance contract
which 'deprives [it] of effect',[41] or 'of all effectiveness' or which is 'entirely
contrary' to the guarantee formally accorded by the policy[42] or which
frustrates the 'goal'[43] will be held invalid.

On the express foundation of cause, two judgments which point to the
link between cause and the requirement of coherence should be referred to
in more detail. The first is the aforementioned famous *Chronopost*

---

[38] Art 442-6(2) of the Code commercial, which stigmatises in particular the fact of 'obtaining,
or seeking to obtain from a trading partner any advantage unrelated to a commercial service
effectively rendered or which is manifestly disproportionate to the value of the service
rendered'; for a comparison with absence of cause see J Rochfeld's commentary on the Loi
no 2001-420 du 15 mai 2001 relative aux nouvelles régulations économiques, JO 16 May 2001,
7776, 'Nouvelles regulations économiques et droit commun des contrats' RTD civ 2001, 671.

[39] Cass civ (1) 11 March 2003, Bull civ I no 67, RTD civ 2003, 287 obs J Mestre and B Fages,
RDC 2003, 39 obs D Mazeaud, JCP G 2003 I 142 obs J Rochfeld.

[40] D Houtcieff, *Le principe de cohérence en matière contractuelle* (Presses universitaires
Aix-Marseille, 2001) nos 401–503 on the coming together of, but equally on the distinction
between, these two notions; for a synthesis of the applications in the case-law cf D Mazeaud obs
on Cass com 8 March 2005, RDC 2005, 1015.

[41] Cass civ (1) 21 May 1990, Bull civ I no 114; Cass civ (1) 17 February 1993, Bull civ I no 73.

[42] Cass civ (1) 3 July 1990, RGAT 1990, 888 note R Bout.

[43] Cass civ (1) 25 May 1992, Bull civ I no 151.

decision, in which the Cour de cassation stated that a limitation clause should be struck out if it 'undermined the scope of the obligation undertaken'.[44] The second decision extends this principle to a contractual grouping: having regard to the link between a finance leasing contract (of 'very particular equipment') and an advertising contract, the Cour de cassation held an express clause of division (*clause de divisibilité*) to be unenforceable on the ground that it 'contradicted the general economic context of the contract'. By the findings that performance under the advertising contract had ceased, that this was 'the only cause' of the finance leasing contract and that 'the two contracts were interdependent', the court found that it was incoherent to provide that the one should continue on the coming to an end of the other. As a result, notwithstanding any contrary provision, the ending of performance of the advertising contract entailed the termination of the finance leasing contract.[45] It should be noted that one particular factor tends to reinforce the coming together of cause and of the requirement of coherence: the generalisation of the process of concluding contracts where one party has taken the initiative in the drafting of the agreement, without the other being able to question the stipulations, leads to more frequent insertion of clauses that seek to undermine a stated goal.

In conclusion, the evolution of the uses of cause in relation to the control of its existence is particularly interesting in so far as it reveals three broad movements which underlie French contract law and inspire important changes in it—changes to which the evolution of other concepts equally bears witness, eg the heightened control of the respect of good faith in performance, abuse of rights, etc.[46]

First, one may note—as has already been mentioned—a return to 'essence': while a contract was for many years presented as a place where all-powerful wills meet, there are now limits which they cannot overcome, an inviolable minimum which cannot be called into question once the goal and the particular type of contract or contractual structure has been set out.

Secondly, this movement marks the permeation into French law of preoccupations with contractual inequality which go beyond the area of consumer law—to which these considerations have, for many years, been relegated. Inequality of bargaining power now entails consequences, as a matter of general law, for the control of the balance of the content of the contract.

---

[44] Cass com 22 October 1996, above n 24.

[45] Cass com 15 February 2000, Bull civ IV no 29, RTD civ 2000, 325 obs J Mestre and B Fages, Defr 2000, 1118 obs D Mazeaud, D 2000 Somm 364 obs P Delebecque.

[46] On these movements see (amongst others) D Mazeaud, 'Loyauté, solidarité, fraternité, la nouvelle devise contractuelle' in *L'avenir du droit: Mélanges en hommage à François Terré* (Paris, Dalloz, 1999) 603; C Jamin, 'Plaidoyer pour le solidarisme contractuel' in *Le contrat au début du XXI siècle: Etudes offertes à Jacques Ghestin* (Paris, LGDJ, 2001) 441; C Thibierge-Guelfucci, 'Libres propos sur la transformation du droit des contrats' RTD civ 1997, 357.

Finally, this movement highlights the increasing interventionism of the courts in relation to contracts and the participation of the courts in the elaboration of what counts as reasonable contractual content.

We will find these ideas once again when we turn to consider the developments relating to the sanction of the absence of cause.

III. THE RENEWAL OF THE SANCTION: FROM THE NULLITY OF THE CONTRACT TO THE ERADICATION OF CLAUSES UNDERMINING GOALS

The traditional sanction of absence of cause was nullity. Its regime, however, was that of absolute nullity. The nature of the sanction was justified by the idea that a contract could not exist without a cause, one of its essential elements. The regime of the sanction resulted from the traditional conception of nullities, which rested upon the importance of the absent element (according to whether it represented a condition of the existence or a condition of the validity of the contract). The recent evolution touches upon both of these points.[47]

(a) The Recognition of the Protection of Individual Interests: Relative Nullity

The first evolution, which occurred in the 2000s (even though the debates and academic criticisms are longstanding), relates to the regime of nullity: the courts have placed it in conformity with the modern conception of this sanction, founded upon the criteria of the interest protected by the sanction. The control of absence of cause, protecting in the first place the individual interests of the person for whom the contract presents no advantage, now results in relative nullity. As a result, this sanction may be invoked only by the person benefiting from the protection, within a period of five years, and the unbalanced contract may be affirmed. This solution was first affirmed in a timid way in 1999 in relation to insurance contracts (for absence of risk).[48] It was made into a principle by two judgments of the Cour de cassation in 2001 and in 2004.[49] The *Avant-projet* has taken

---

[47] In relation to these issues cf P Simler, 'La sanction de l'absence de cause' in *Etudes sur le droit de la concurrence et quelques thèmes fondamentaux: Mélanges en l'honneur d'Yves Serra* (Paris, Dalloz, 2006) 409.

[48] Cass civ (1) 9 November 1999, Bull civ I no 293, Defr 2000, 250 obs J-L Aubert, D 2000, 507 note A Cristau.

[49] Cass civ (1) 20 February 2001, Bull civ I no 39: 'the action in nullity . . . aims only at the protection of the individual [of the person seeking nullity] whose proprietary interests are alone in question'; Cass civ (1) 29 September 2004, Bull civ I no 216; and even more recently Cass civ (3) 29 March 2006, above n 30, stating that 'the action seeking the nullity of a contract for absence of cause resulting from the impossibility of realising a profit aims only at the protection of the interests of the claimant' and confirming relative nullity.

note of this evolution: article 1124-1 states that 'absence of cause is sanctioned by relative nullity of the contract'.[50] The biggest change is, however, to be found elsewhere.

(b) The Defence of the Essence of Contract: The Invalidation of a Clause Undermining the Goal

The most spectacular change lies in the sanction of the absence of cause. Traditionally, the entirety of the contract was affected: the contract was either annulled or preserved in its entirety. Notably, the courts had always refused to control the counter-performance relating to each individual clause.[51] This remains the case, but an additional sanction has appeared from the 1990s onwards: the eradication, on the foundation of article 1131 Cc, of any clause fettering, from the outset—that is to say, on the face of the contractual structure—the achievement of the interest represented by the contract. This evolution has been noted by the *Avant-projet* in article 1125(2), which provides that

> Any term of the contract which is incompatible with the real character of its cause is struck out.

In relation to its development, this sanction was applied in the first place to the clause requiring a 'claim by the victim' in contracts for liability insurance: a term which required that this claim by the victim be made within the period of the contract, even though the victim could not know of the harm he had suffered, was regarded as being capable of

> depriving the insured of the benefit of the insurance by reason of a fact which could not be laid at his door and . . . creating an unlawful advantage without cause for the benefit of the insurer who would thereby receive premiums without any counter-performance.

The Cour de cassation therefore decided that 'this clause [was] to be struck out'.[52] The remedy of striking out was definitively established by the famous *Chronopost* judgment of the Commercial chamber of 22 October 1996. In this decision, a derisory limitation clause, which applied to the

---

[50] The same article states that 'unlawfulness of cause taints the contract with absolute nullity'.

[51] See, nevertheless, by way of exception Cass civ (1) 15 February 1972, Bull civ I no 50; Cass com 4 July 1972, Bull civ IV no 213; Cass com 3 February 1975, Bull civ IV no 32; Cass com 22 July 1978, Bull civ IV no 141.

[52] Cass civ (1) 19 December 1990, Bull civ I no 303, JCP 1991 II 21656 note J Bigot, RTD civ 1991, 325 obs J Mestre and above n 28, a solution followed in numerous cases in the same area, notably Cass civ (1) 28 April 1993, Bull civ I nos 148 and 149; Cass civ (1) 9 May 1994, Bull civ I no 168; Cass civ (1) 16 December 1997, D 1998, 287 note Y Lambert-Faivre, JCP G 1998 II 10018 rapp P Sargos. A much discussed issue then arose in banking law in relation to the striking out of clauses which regulated the determination of value dates, Cass com 6 April 1993, Bull civ IV no 138, D 1993, 310 note C Gavalda, JCP G 1993 II 22062 note J Soufflet, LPA 14 April 1993 no 45, 12, RTD com 1993, 549 obs M Cabrillac and B Teyssié.

non-performance of an express parcel delivery company, was struck out: whilst the contract contained a promise of fast and punctual delivery, this clause effectively removed any sanction of this essential obligation. Permitting the debtor to consider himself not bound to perform, it was regarded as undermining the objective of the contract:

> [A] limitation clause, which undermined the obligation undertaken [the essential obligation of transporting the parcel in question in the relevant time] was to be struck out.[53]

It should, however, be noted that innovative as this evolution may seem, it is in reality no more than a resurgence of an ancient sanction. In the decision of 1863 referred to above, the court had already held invalid a clause of a lease which provided that the lessor was to be exonerated from all responsibility for failures in the performance of his obligation to maintain or repair the demised premises.[54]

Since then, this sanction has been generalised, and if one undertakes a synthesis of its applications in the case-law, one will find that they are to be found principally in relation to three types of clause.

First, without cause being expressly relied upon, this sanction permits the eradication of exclusion clauses which undermine an essential obligation, that is to say suppressing one or more fundamental obligations which are implied into the type of contract in question. For example, a lessor cannot escape his essential obligation to provide a minimum of quiet enjoyment[55] or—as the Cour de cassation found in a decision on 1 June 2005—from his obligation to deliver the demised premises, by inserting a clause permitting him to undertake all necessary works and thereby depriving the lessee of any use of the premises while these works were undertaken.[56]

---

[53] Cass com 22 October 1996, Bull civ IV no 261, F Terré, Y Lequette and H Capitant, *Les grands arrêts de la jurisprudence civile*, vol II (11th edn, Dalloz, 2000) no 156 and references—the case is translated in Beale et al, above n 21, 136. Lastly in this direction (outside the situation of a standard form of contract containing such a clause) Cass com 30 May 2006, Bull civ IV no 134, D 2006, 2288 note D Mazeaud, D 2006 Pan 2646 obs B Fauvarque-Cosson, RDC 2006, 1075 obs Y-M Laithier, RDC 2006, 1224 obs S Carval, RTD civ 2006, 773 obs P Jourdain.

[54] Cass req 19 January 1863, DP 1863.1.248, above n 27, striking down an exclusion clause allowing the lessor to dispense with his obligation to permit the lessee to have quiet enjoyment of the premises and to keep them in good repair.

[55] Cass soc 25 October 1946, D 1947, 88, RTD civ 1947, 65 note J Carbonnier, Gaz Pal 1946.2.259, JCP 1947 II 3400 obs P Esmein. See also: in the case of leasing, the lessor cannot include a provision to escape his obligation to transfer the enjoyment of the subject-matter of the leasing: Civ (1) 11 October 1989, Bull civ I no 317, D 1991, 25 note P Ancel; in a contract to use a safe, the bank must of necessity undertake an obligation to keep watch on it: Civ (1) 15 November 1988, Bull civ I no 318, D 1989, 349 note P Delebecque, RTD civ 1990, 666 obs P Jourdan (the decision, however, appealed to gross fault in the performance, objectively understood—ie by reference to the essential obligation).

[56] Cass civ (3) 1 June 2005, Bull civ III no 119, RTD civ 2005, 780 obs J Mestre and B Fages, Defr 2006, 439 obs L Ruet: 'The lessor cannot, by means of a clause relating to the undertaking of works, escape from his obligation to deliver the demised premises'; the clause in question providing that 'the lessor must bear without any indemnity and whatever their scale or duration

Secondly, the eradication of a clause may concern stipulations relating to liability. In relation to clauses of these nature, only exclusion or limitation clauses which are derisory (condition 1) relating to liability which is the result of the non-performance of an essential obligation (condition 2) should be subject to attack. One may legitimately take the view that this type of stipulation causes the liability which attaches to the non-performance of this obligation to disappear or reduces it to such an extent that the liability appears to be miniscule. In consequence, it suppresses the constraining nature of the essential obligation, which becomes purely optional for the party who is notionally subject to it.[57] It is therefore the character of its being optional, attached to the essential obligation, which assimilates it to the case of absence of cause. For this type of reasoning to be admissible it is, moreover, necessary that this absence exist from the beginning: that is to say the opposition between the clause and the constraining nature of the essential obligation must be plain from the very structure of the contract. The conditions for the performance of the contract do not enter into the equation. The Cour de cassation laid itself open to criticism in the famous *Chronopost* decision by, on the one hand, not insisting on the derisory nature of the limitation clause, and, on the other, in relation to the evaluation of the effect of its insertion on the contractual structure.[58] These imperfections have been remedied in subsequent judgments.[59]

any works which may become useful or necessary on the demised premises or in the building of which they form part'.

[57] Cf for the premises underlying this reasoning B Starck, 'Observations sur le régime juridique des clauses de non-responsabilité ou limitatives de responsabilité' D 1974 Chron 25: 'An obligation devoid of any sanction is not an obligation'.

[58] Cf for example C Larroumet under Cass com 22 October 1996, D 1997 Chron 145; A Sériaux, 'L'affaire Chronopost: arrêt de principe ou accident de parcours ?' note under Cass com 22 October 1996, D 1997, 121.

[59] Cf CA Caen 5 January 1999, JCP G 2000 I 215 obs J Rochfeld; Cass com 17 July 2001, JCP G 2002 I 148 obs G Louiseau in relation to a limitation clause in a contract for the maintenance of computer equipment which required action within '48 hours' which was found to be derisory: it 'amounted to depriving of all effect the essential obligation undertaken by this company'. It should also be noted that this idea undergoes an extension where assessments are made in relation to contractual performance: in the assessment of gross fault which renders limitation and exclusion clauses ineffective (within the meaning of article 1150 Cc) the 'causal' nature of the unperformed obligations has intervened as an objective criterion (does the non-performance undermine the essential obligation?) in addition to the traditional subjective assessment; cf esp Cass civ (1) 18 January 1984, Bull civ I no 27, JCP G 1985 II 20372 note J Mouly, RTD civ 1984, 727 obs J Huet—gross fault of the manager of a lottery (*loto*) office for not having forwarded a bulletin to the processing centre; Cass civ (1) 15 November 1988, Bull civ I no 318, D 1989, 349 note P Delebecque, RTD civ 1990, 666 obs P Jourdain—gross fault of a banker for the non-performance of his obligation to keep watch on a safe; Cass com 9 May 1990, Bull civ IV no 142, RTD civ 1990, 666 obs P Jourdain—gross fault in the failure on the part of the publisher of a telephone directory to include the telephone number of an artisan; *contra*, for a calling into question of this objective assessment in cases where the clause is the result of the nature of a particular standard form contract, Cass mixte 22 April 2005, RDC 2005, 651 with opinion of the Advocate-General de Gouttes, RDC 2005, 673 obs D Mazeaud, 753 obs P Delebecque,

Thirdly, and finally, this sanction is applied in relation to clauses which, without suppressing one of the essential obligations of the contract or removing its constraining nature, opposes or limits the scope of the contract to such an extent that one of the parties loses his interest in the contract. One may refer to the aforementioned example of the 'clause of claim' by the victim of the contract for liability insurance and, more generally, to all exclusion clauses which reduce to nothing a guarantee which has been entered into.[60]

The emergence of this sanction may be explained in several different ways. In terms of its appropriateness, in the first place, this sanction deals with the general situation of the unilateral drafting of contractual provisions by one party who is in a stronger bargaining position and who imposes them on the other contracting party. The latter signs up to them *en bloc*, without playing any role in their negotiation. In these situations, the traditional solution of the nullity of the whole contract is unsuitable: the party whose obligation is without cause is deprived of the interest which he hoped to gain from the contract; he must conclude another contract which, as a result of the proliferation of standard terms, will very often contain a clause in exactly the same terms. The striking out of these stipulations therefore permits the advantage which is naturally expected to be reintegrated into the contract—rather than wiping out the contract and, with it, the pursuit of the relevant interests.[61] Striking out therefore restores that interest to the contract.

As a matter of law, then, one may consider that the striking out of the relevant clause intervenes as a sanction which takes proper account of the reality of the acceptance of one of the parties *en bloc* to the contractual content which has been predefined by the other party. In this type of situation, one of the parties has given his consent only to the relevant goal and to the minimum contractual content that this goal entails. He has done so with the full knowledge of his contractual counter-party. This minimum contractual content cannot, therefore, be called into question by a clause

D 2005, 1832 obs J-P Tosi, D 2005, 2844 obs B Fauvarque-Cosson, JCP G 2005 II 10066 note G Loiseau, RTD civ 2005, 604 obs P Jourdain, RTD civ 2005, 779 obs J Mestre and B Fages. Following the same line of thought, though without the detour through the finding of gross fault, an exclusion clause may be struck out if it purports to cover non-performance of the fundamental or essential obligation, cf Cass civ (1) 23 February 1994, Bull civ I no 76, JCP G 1994 I 3809 obs G Viney, D 1995, 214 note N Dion, Contrats Concur Consom 1994 com no 82 obs G Raymond and no 94 obs L Leveneur, RTD civ 1994, 616 obs P Jourdain (clause in a parking contract evading the obligation to look after the vehicle).

[60] Cf Cass civ (1) 19 December 1990, above n 28, in relation to the clause labelled 'claim by the victim'.

[61] Cf, however, the nuances in relation to exclusion clauses, for example Cass com 9 July 2002, Bull civ IV no 121, JCP G 2002 II 10176 note G Loiseau and M Billiau and JCP G 2002 I 184 obs J Rochfeld where the striking out of a limitation clause for absence of cause led to the application of the general law of carriage of goods, that is to say, of the standard form of 'parcel service' contract which provided for the same amount; moreover, only a 'gross fault of the carrier could lead to [its] disapplication'; cf Cass com 24 March 2004, appeal no 02-19865, unpublished.

which undermines that goal, because such a clause cannot be considered to form part of the agreement of wills.

If one accepts this explanation, one is also led to accept, over and above the change in the effect of the sanction, a change in the nature of the sanction. It differs profoundly from the nullity traditionally applied in relation to absence of cause. The analysis moves, in effect, towards non-existence—the distinction between the two approaches has implications in relation to the legal regime: non-existence does not have to be pronounced by the judge, who is content to implement its consequences when he is faced with non-performance; it is not subject to prescription.[62] The reasoning is as follows: striking out a clause amounts to recognising that that stipulation has never formed part of the agreement which has been given *en bloc* by one party to the goal of the contract with the full knowledge of the other contracting party. As a result, it does not form part of the minimum contractual content to which the consent of the party who signed up to the terms was directed. And, at an even earlier stage, as it goes against this consent, it equally cannot form part of the content of the contract. It is in this way that one may take the view that the clause does not form part of the agreement. This sanction therefore permits us to deal with the nature of the process of the conclusion of contracts by signing up to one party's standard terms.

In summary, the sanctions are remarkable in the way that they illustrate the movements which have been set out above. First, the development in the case-law of the consideration and the control of the real interest in the contract: the sanction brings that interest back into the contract, on the foundation of an analysis of the true meeting of minds of the parties. That is why if at first glance one may consider that there is a repairing of the contract by the courts, it is more a case of the reintegration of the interest upon which the parties were agreed in choosing the particular type of contract or in constructing a particular contractual structure.

Secondly, this evolution forms part of the return to 'essence' adverted to above. Any clause which undermines the inviolable minimum obligational content of the contract is struck out.

Thirdly, the sanction shows the renewed vocation of the general law and of the control of the absence of cause in particular in restoring a balance in the content of the contract, beyond that which is founded on the status of the parties—consumer or business or professional.[63] Through this, the

---

[62] For a similar approach see also V Cotterau, 'La clause réputée non écrite' JCP G 1993 I 3691 no 1; J Kullmann, 'Remarques sur les clauses reputées non écrites' D 1993 Chron 61; S Gaudemet, *La clause réputée non écrite* (Paris, Economica, 2006). See also, *contra*, those who defend the concept of nullity: B Teyssié, 'Réflexions sur les conséquences de la nullité d'une clause d'un contrat' D 1976 Chron 281; C Guelfucci-Thibierge, *Nullité, restitutions et responsabilité* (Paris, LGDJ, 1992) nos 490–500.

[63] On this point see, especially, J-M Gueguen, 'Le renouveau de la cause en tant qu'instrument de justice contractuelle' D 1999 Chron 355; compare the control effected on the foundation of

notion of absence of cause has therefore become a weapon in the fight against iniquitous clauses, introduced by reason of the inequality in the bargaining power of the parties.

Ultimately, the developments which this sanction have undergone are perhaps those which show most clearly the very modern nature of the uses of the notion of cause in the case-law.

IV. CONCLUSION

Looking at French law and its evolution in this area, one may therefore conclude that cause not only has a future, but that the way in which its control is now effected demonstrates a remarkable enrichment and vitality in the uses to which the notion is put.

'Vitality' because the notion focuses attention on modern issues in contract law in such a way that its definition and assessment are permeated by current ideas: proportionality, coherence, control of one-sided bargaining power in the definition of the content of a contract; the rebalancing of the content of a contract . . .

'Vitality' also because its control marks, on the one hand, the taking into account of the reality and the generality of the process of the formation of contracts by signing up to one party's standard terms, beyond the area of consumer law. It seeks to react against the imbalance in the strength of the parties in the negotiation and the exercise of unilateral powers by the imposition of an inviolable minimum contractual content. On the other hand, this control is accompanied by an exercise of sophisticated contractual engineering through the verification of the balance of the contractual obligations and their relevance to the pursuit of the particular goals in question.

That is not to say, however, that there can be no debate. Indeed, the points made above tend merely to open up discussion. Such debate could relate to the legitimacy of using an instrument which relates to the control of the content of a contract and the fight against inequalities relating to it, rather than the use of techniques which are targeted at the behaviour of the contracting parties, or their relative strength, in order to found such a control. All the more so given that the latter approach appears to be given priority in other neighbouring legal systems and at the level of principles of European law. Debate could equally be conducted in relation to the sanctions and the judicial interventionism which this control highlights. It

the weapons used in the fight against *clauses abusives*, CA Toulouse 8 November 1995, D aff 1996 Chron 386 which identifies as abusive 'a clause exonerating the vendor from liability in the case of late delivery' because 'it results in the suppression of any right to compensation in the case of the failure by the business or professional party to perform his obligation of delivery', an obligation which was regarded as essential.

remains the case, however, that whatever conceptual label is chosen (and there is no question, in the present writer's view, of continuing to insist on the maintenance of the notion of cause in a context in which it is not recognised) the assessments and controls which are currently founded upon the concept of cause in French law must be preserved: the control of the existence of a real interest in the contract; the reintegration of the expected benefit; the consideration of the way in which contracts were concluded in order to assess the balance of their content in addition to the sanction of clauses which undermine the goal which is being pursued.

5

La cause *or the Length of the French Judiciary's Foot*

T O AN OUTSIDER, the *Avant-projet de réforme du droit des obli-gations et de la prescription* has adopted an attitude of 'if it ain't broken, don't fix it' towards reforming the doctrine of cause—*la cause*. Merely incorporating the last twenty years' case-law into the text does not look like a real reform. What has changed? Nothing?

This approach is backed up by the explanation given in the notes of the *Avant-projet*, that cause, as a condition of contractual validity, is part of French legal tradition.[1] Is the proposition that French law must keep the doctrine of cause because of legal tradition sufficient and convincing? Even though French jurists may be attached to cause as a concept, it is very doubtful whether the person in the street is attached to cause in quite the same way. It is suggested that legal culturalist or even traditionalist arguments do not compel *per se*:[2] this is not a good reason to keep the doctrine of cause. It is hoped that if the *Avant-projet* decided to keep cause, thus remaining at odds with the more limited conditions of validity contained in the Principles of European Contract Law, for example[3]—though this is not a compelling reason either[4]—there must be a better reason than this. It is perhaps not surprising, for those who have some acquaintance with French law, that the French academics who voluntarily undertook to reform the

---

* My warmest thanks to Stephen Smith for his helpful comments on an earlier version of this chapter.

[1] J Ghestin, 'Exposé des motifs: Validité—Cause (art 1124 à 1126-1)' in *Avant-projet de réforme du droit des obligations et de la prescription: Rapport remis au garde des Sceaux* (Paris, La documentation française, 2006) 37–42 (see below pp 521–33).

[2] R Sefton-Green, 'The European Union, Law and Society: Making the Societal-Cultural Difference' in T Wilhelmsson, E Paunio and A Pohjolainen (eds), *Private Law and the Many Cultures of Europe* (The Hague, Kluwer, 2007) 37–55.

[3] See art 2:101(1) PECL, which requires a mere offer and acceptance to form a contract.

[4] The fact that the PECL do not provide for cause is not a compelling reason for getting rid of it since the PECL have no mandatory force and are themselves the product of an academic exercise.

Code civil have made no mention at all of the policy considerations[5] behind the doctrine of cause, or indeed, more simply of the reasons why it is considered to be a useful concept.[6] In the light of reform, legal concepts must surely be maintained on the double condition of serving a useful function and doing it in the best way possible. Evaluating whether a legal concept achieves its end-purpose in the best way possible entails an enquiry into its legitimacy.[7] This paper uses the criteria of utility and legitimacy to evaluate cause.

Cause as a legal concept is remarkably opaque, not to say incomprehensible, for anyone who is not a specialist on the subject. To a layperson, it appears that judges use the doctrine of cause in a way that allows them to act with unfettered discretion, opacity and unpredictability. When proposing to reform the law, why not refashion an appropriate legal tool that is transparent for everyone, and does not represent the French judiciary as having a varying length of foot?

My objections are therefore partly addressed at the role that cause is playing, but more specifically at the way in which this is being done. The thrust of the argument will be to investigate why the doctrine of cause is useful and whether cause is best suited to do the task for which it is presently being used. This role will be analysed and assessed in the light of comparative—and notably English—law. It is a perfect terrain for comparative law, because in many of the instances brought before the Cour de cassation, English law would produce the opposite result. This enquiry therefore aims at discovering why this is so.

What, then, is the doctrine of cause used for and why? In reply to the enquiry as to what purpose the doctrine serves, an examination of the *Avant-projet* helps us to identify the dual function attributed to cause. Firstly, the doctrine enables a judicial assessment of the parties' substantive bargain: see article 1125. Secondly, it allows judicial elimination of terms that are incompatible with the contract's fundamental obligations, or the core of the contract: see article 1125(2). In reply to the question as to why the doctrine of cause is used, we can notice that the doctrine is, by its nature, a corrective post hoc instrument, in that it allows either for the whole contract to be annulled (*nullité relative*) or for a clause to be severed (*réputée non écrite*). It is therefore necessary to identify both the end-purpose and justification of this judicial interference with the contract.

Furthermore, in order to assess the utility of cause, it is necessary, as a starting point, to examine its rationale, ie the underlying values. The first

---

[5] H Beale, 'La réforme du droit français des contrats et le "droit européen des contrats": perspective de la *Law Commission* anglaise' RDC 2006, 135.

[6] See, however, X Lagarde, 'Sur l'utilité de la théorie de la cause' D 2007, 740 for a recent critical enquiry.

[7] See SA Smith, *Contract Theory* (Oxford University Press, 2004) 7, who suggests four criteria to assess contract theories: fit, morality, coherence and transparency. This chapter raises several objections to cause in that it fails to meet the criteria of coherence and transparency.

part of this chapter tests the hypothesis that the values protected by French case-law on cause, set out in the *Avant-projet*, are fair exchange[8] (or substantive justice[9]) and making good choices.[10] If this hypothesis is substantiated, this may explain how and why French judges use cause as a paternalistic protective device to annul contracts. The second part of this chapter examines the legitimacy of this judicial intervention[11] into the contract.

I. FAIR EXCHANGE AND MAKING GOOD CHOICES

The *Avant-projet* provides two very different functions for cause; indeed at first sight this difference seems insurmountable, as if one concept is being used to treat entirely different legal issues.[12] The first allows a judicial assessment of the parties' substantive bargain (section I(a) below). The second allows for a judicial elimination of clauses incompatible with the contract's fundamental obligations (section I(b) below).

(a) Judicial Assessment of the Parties' Substantive Bargain

Article 1125 of the *Avant-projet* distinguishes between two different situations where cause might be considered absent: when the exchange (or bargain) is illusory or derisory. We will need to examine whether the distinction contained in article 1125 is one of nature or of degree. I suggest that the criterion of an illusory or derisory cause is linked to the idea that a contract is underpinned by a fair exchange. The idea of fair exchange is of course more obvious in the case of a derisory cause, than of an illusory cause. In any event, when drawing up a comparison with English law, it is apparent that this approach clashes with the classic explanation given by English judges that the law will not allow a party to escape from a bad bargain. Moreover, the rule that consideration does not need to be adequate[13] also springs to mind. This rule appears to be in opposition with

---

[8] J Gordley, 'Equality in Exchange' (1981) 69 California Law Review 1587.

[9] SA Smith, 'In Defence of Substantive Justice' (1996) 112 LQR 138–58.

[10] J Gordley, 'Contract Law in the Aristotelian Tradition' in P Benson (ed), *The Theory of Contract Law: New Essays* (Cambridge University Press, 2001) 262–334.

[11] The legitimacy of paternalism is, of course, highly controversial, particularly for libertarians. See JS Mill, *On Liberty* (1859), in J Grey and GW Smith, *John Mill: Liberty in Focus* (London, Routledge, 1991) 23, 30–31.

[12] The allegation that this leads to a conceptual incoherence is however rebutted by Gordley, above n 10, who argues that the idea of a fair exchange explains why controls can be made of the substance of the contract, from two aspects eg the regulation of a fair price and also of the contract's auxiliary clauses.

[13] *Bolton v Madden* (1873) LR 9 QB 55, 57 (QB) (Blackburn J): 'the adequacy of the consideration is for the parties to consider at the time of making the agreement, not for the Court when it is sought to be enforced'.

the *Avant-projet* stating that if a bargain contains a derisory cause the contract will be invalid for absence of cause, but this suggestion should be treated with caution as it is all too easy, and not particularly helpful, to fall into the trap of assimilating cause and consideration.

The suggestion that there is a link between fair exchange and cause needs to be explored further from several vantage points, before the provisions of article 1125 of the *Avant-projet* can be discussed in depth.

(i) The Relevance of Fair Exchange to Contract Law

It is suggested that French law's conception of cause can be linked to the idea that a contract is built upon a fair exchange. Is fair exchange relevant to contract law? Contract law generally respects the choices of parties provided the conditions of validity are respected. Cause, as a condition of validity, allows French law to interfere with parties' choices. James Gordley has outlined three major reasons for enforcing promises, the third of which may provide a key to open the door to the doctrine of cause.[14] First, from a utilitarian point of view, traceable to Jeremy Bentham, the choices of contracting parties are respected because they reveal certain preferences for satisfaction. An extension of this conception is to put rationality at the apex of contract law, which requires that parties act rationally, or think coherently, when they make contracts.[15] The second justification for enforcing contracts, traceable to Hegel and Kant, concentrates on choices that are explicable in terms of freedom[16] and personal autonomy.

The third justification is that making choices can be linked to the Aristotelian idea of the virtue of prudence, that when people makes choices their choices are right or wrong, measurable by standards of virtue, prudence and also justice. Contracts of exchange are justified if they fulfil the virtue of commutative justice. Conversely, if they do not respect the virtues of prudence, and particularly commutative justice, which requires a fair exchange, then a contract will not be considered valid. According to this latter viewpoint, individuals' decisions can be trumped, or a contract can be annulled, when contracting parties' choices are wrong, from an Aristotelian point of view.[17] This evaluation of people's choices is a justification for paternalistic intervention, although of course there are many others. In a similar vein, Antony Kronman has explained paternalistic legislation as a means of protecting people against their bad judgment.[18] The suggestion that French judges consider that parties' choices are invalid on the basis

---

[14] Gordley, above n 10, 268–71.
[15] *Ibid*, 279, n 52 citing EJ Weinrib.
[16] According to Gordley, above n 10, 278; C Fried, *Contract as Promise: A Theory of Contractual Obligation* (Cambridge, MA, Harvard University Press, 1981) follows this tradition, as the centrality of the promise is linked to this conception of freedom.
[17] Gordley, above n 10, 280–85.
[18] AT Kronman, 'Paternalism in the Law of Contract' (1983) 92 Yale LJ 763, 790.

that they have exercised bad judgment and that their choices do not correspond to commutative justice needs to be explored further.

(ii) Fair Exchange and Rationality

Patrick Atiyah has suggested that a link between fair exchange and rationality exists:

> We do not generally ask why a person consents to arrangements because most
> people do not consent without good and adequate reasons. Unfortunately, human
> experience demonstrates that this general assumption is not universally valid.
> People do occasionally consent to arrangements on inadequate or irrational
> grounds.[19]

In my view, French and English law do not give the same priority to the
three focus points outlined above. This might explain why French judges
will annul contracts for absence of cause, in situations where English law
considers the contract perfectly valid. To give an example of how civilians
and common lawyers perceive contracting parties' capacity for rationality
differently, Judith Rochfeld suggests that a contracting party, in the pursuit
of his or her interest, will agree to make a sacrifice in exchange.[20] This
metaphor clashes with the premise that I consider English law uses—that
contracting parties act as rational agents, even if it is accepted that their
rationality is limited. Indeed, it is because their rationality is limited that
parties can and do make bad bargains. An inference can be drawn from the
use of this metaphor: French law is wary of selfish individualistic
behaviour, whereas English law expects people to behave reasonably and
rationally. Contracting parties do not make sacrifices in the eyes of English
law; it is normal in the business world, to give something in return for
something. The French adage *donnant donnant* reflects the same idea. However, French law does intervene when people behave irrationally; cause is
instrumentalised by the judges to protect contracting parties' irrationality.
Is this legitimate,[21] and if so, in what circumstances? It is recalled that
article 1125 of the *Avant-projet* limits judicial intervention to two circumstances: when what is agreed in exchange is illusory or derisory.

(iii) Cause as a Justification and Rationality

Does the law need to be involved or concerned about why people make
contracts, whether they have a real justification? Does this mean a justifi-

---

[19] PS Atiyah, 'Contract and Fair Exchange' in PS Atiyah, *Essays on Contract* (Oxford, Clarendon Press, 1986) 329, 353.

[20] See J Rochfeld, 'A Future for *la cause*? Observations of a French Jurist', ch 4 above.

[21] See Atiyah, above n 19, on whether paternalistic intervention is defensible, legitimate, etc. This question will be treated below, pp 117–19.

cation that exists or simply one that is valid? If the cause is absent when the bargain is illusory, this suggests that there is no check on the quality of the justification, whether it is good or bad, but just whether it exists.[22] In other words, two people can contract to do something that appears daft and unjustified to others, but as long as their contract is not immoral, contrary to public policy, etc, the law has no say as to whether their reasons are good or bad. The bargain must exist; it cannot be a figment of parties' imagination. This leaves room for a certain amount of contractual freedom but also a large margin of manoeuvre for interpretation.[23] What does it mean to say the bargain must exist and not be illusory? If contracting parties are deemed to be rational agents, even if rationality is limited, is this not axiomatic? If I make a contract with a rail transport company to go to the moon, the bargain does not exist, it is illusory. A common lawyer might be tempted to suggest that it is a matter of plain common sense that such contracts will not be enforced. Is not an article in the Code repeating what amounts to common sense somewhat superfluous?

Moreover, it can be inferred from case-law that judges do not merely check the existence of the parties' reasons for making a contract; they also evaluate party choices. This is why the hypothesis that illusory cause is linked to the idea of rationality, of making good choices in the Aristotelian sense, will be examined in more detail. Does making choices, contained under the banner of freedom of contract, mean making good choices, ie behaving rationally, or does it include behaving irrationally and how and why does the law set limits? If judges have jurisdiction to determine whether a party's choice is good or bad, rational or irrational, this jurisdiction is based on a subjective and normative evaluation and involves intruding in the contract on paternalistic grounds. It should already be clear that French and English law do not have the same attitude towards this question.

(iv) A Classification Exercise

One way of assessing the necessity of cause is to evaluate the well-known case-law and match it against the articles of the *Avant-projet*. An attempt at classifying how such cases would be determined under the new provisions,

---

[22] This interpretation excludes considerations of Aristotelian virtues.

[23] See Ghestin, above n 1, 38 (see below p 525), which indicates that what is agreed in exchange (*la contrepartie*) is subject to varying parameters and is a question of interpretation. It is suggested that the Cour de cassation will have control over this interpretation though on one level it is difficult to see why. The interpretation of the bargain, what has been agreed, is a matter of fact whereas the Cour de cassation only has jurisdiction over questions of law (at least in theory). This shows that the dividing line does not make much sense (at least to a common lawyer) and that, more importantly, any control or judicial intervention in relation to cause, involves casuistic considerations, see below pp 118–19.

as well as to consider how these fact-hypotheticals would be decided under English law, follows.

Two categories can be identified, the first involves cases where the question of whether or not the cause is illusory are considered. It is argued that the judges' intervention in these cases is highly objectionable. The second category concerns cases where the cause is allegedly derisory. Judicial interference on this ground is less objectionable, for reasons that will be identified subsequently.

1. Cases where the cause is illusory   As an abundant legal literature on the case indicates,[24] the decision of the first Civil chamber of the Cour de cassation of 3 July 1996 approved the annulment of the contract to hire video cassettes in a rural community for lack of cause: is this simply a bad bargain and would it fall under the definition of the *Avant-projet* as an illusory exchange? The hirers could rent out the video cassettes in the rural community; they simply were going to run at a loss. It can be assumed, in the absence of evidence to the contrary, that the hirers accepted that risk when the contract was made: they knew what they were doing, they acted freely, rationally and perhaps improvidently. However, the reasons why the judges felt it was necessary to annul this contract are not explained at all.[25] Did the judges annul the contract because they felt the hirers had not made a good choice[26] or because they felt sympathetic to their plight? Ad hoc intuitive paternalism would be frowned upon by the common law.[27]

An English court would not even consider annulling this contract; it would have no basis to do so.[28] Once the hirers have started to perform, which appears to be the case here, there seems no good reason in English

---

[24] Cass civ (1) 3 July 1996, Bull civ I no 286, D 1997, 500 note P Reigné, JCP G 1997 I 4015 obs F Labarthe, Defr 1996, 36381 note P Delebecque, RTD civ 1996, 903 obs J Mestre—the case is translated in Hugh Beale et al, *Ius Commune Casebooks for the Common Law of Europe: Cases Materials and Text on Contract Law* (Oxford, Hart Publishing, 2002) 137. See also J Rochfeld, *Cause et type de contrat* (Paris, LGDJ, 1999) 241–3.

[25] See Lagarde, above n 6, 741–2, who suggests this might be a borderline case of mistake. In the event that the case cannot be categorised as mistake, cause is adapted to fit the case. The judges may well stretch the doctrine of cause to fit the necessary role, thus employing a legal fiction.

[26] One could argue that the hirers did not made a good choice or did not act rationally since they chose to enter into an unprofitable contract. This line of argument fails to convince of course since risk taking involves that very exercise.

[27] See MJ Trebilcock, *Limits of Freedom of Contract* (Cambridge, MA, Harvard University Press, 1993) 147, 158. See D Kennedy, 'Distributive and Paternalistic Motives in Contract and Tort Law with Special Reference to Compulsory Terms and Unequal Bargaining' (1982) 41 MLR 536. Ad hoc (intuitive) paternalism is highly political and therefore can only be exercised by those who have legitimacy to do so. It is controversial that judges should have such legitimacy, see below pp 118–19.

[28] If the contract was merely executory, ie performance had not yet commenced, there might be an argument for feeling sympathetic to the hirers, especially if they had made investments (reliance) and then realised that the operation was not going to be profitable. However, the law does not or should not operate according to our sympathetic feelings! I am grateful to Stephen Smith for having drawn my attention to this point.

law why the judges should save them from what turned out to be a bad bargain. As positive law stands at present, this case reflects a perfect divergence of approach between English and French law.

Other examples from case-law indicate that cause may fulfil a function that would come under a totally different legal classification or appellation in English law. There are a number of instances where reference is made to cause, but it is not the basis of the decision, and one may wonder whether cause is not superfluous, even though partisans of the doctrine of cause have a tendency to see it everywhere.[29]

In a decision of the third Civil chamber of the Cour de cassation of 7 February 1996,[30] concerning a contract for the sale of land, a deposit was paid upon the conclusion of the contract in which it was stipulated that the vendor could keep the deposit if the purchaser changed his mind, 'for whatever reason'. After a part of the building collapsed, the purchaser decided, quite rationally it could be argued, to pull out of the sale and reclaimed his deposit. The Cour de cassation refused to accept the vendor's interpretation that he could keep the deposit, indicating implicitly that such a contract was without a cause. It is suggested that this might fall under the category of an inexistent or illusory cause.

Under English law, there might be an argument for stating that there is unjust enrichment if the vendor keeps the deposit, and the legal basis would be explained as a total failure of consideration.[31] If this analysis is correct, French and English law would converge on this solution, though not for the same reasons. Here it would appear that recourse to the absence of cause means something very different in the two cases mentioned above.[32] This lends weight to the perception that common lawyers have of cause as being multifaceted, even if French jurists defend it as a unitary notion. It is difficult to understand how a notion that plays so many different roles is a unitary one.[33]

---

[29] See, for example, Cass com 15 February 2000, Bull civ IV no 29, where the court indicates that the cause of a hire-purchase contract was a prior contract to diffuse advertisements. In the event of the termination of the first contract, the lack of cause (the first contract) is used to justify termination of the second. On one view, reference to cause is redundant here.

[30] Cass civ (3) 7 February 1996, appeal no 93-17873, unpublished.

[31] Another case which might fit into this category is the decision of the first Civil chamber of the Cour de cassation concerning the assignment by a taxi driver of his clientèle. In fact, an authorisation was required so that this assignment was held to be without a cause. See Cass civ (1) 24 March 1993, appeal no 91-13459, unpublished. In English law this might be analysed as unjust enrichment for total failure of consideration since the assignor could not transfer the clientele without obtaining the authorisation. This could also be analysed as a failure of a condition precedent so that the contract is never formed.

[32] For further heterogenous examples see, for example, the decision of the first Civil chamber of the Cour de cassation of 15 June 1994, Bull civ I no 215, concerning a surgeon's assignment of incorporeal rights and sale of shares in company. If the assignment of incorporeal rights could not take place, because they did not exist, this could again be analysed as an unjust enrichment on the grounds of a total failure of consideration.

[33] Ghestin, above n 1, 37 (see below p 521).

The cases where the Cour de cassation has held that there is a valid cause are equally significant. An example can be found in the decision of the third Civil chamber of 13 October 2004 for the sale of the lease by the lessee to the assignee of the lessor.[34] From a common lawyer's perspective this is a valid contract, indeed it is difficult to understand why any court would even agree to hear claims contesting its validity. This observation gives rise to concern: firstly, that cause is sufficiently unclear as a legal concept so that the risk of vexatious litigation is high. Secondly, the enquiry into the parties' justification for making a contract is actually a question of factual consideration. It is not predictable whether or not a justification may be considered real or valid. In other words, the reasons for the judges determining what is or is not a valid cause are not clear. The judicial justification for cause being present or absent looks arbitrary from the outside.

So far, the hypothesis that a fair exchange may explain what might fall under the new heading of an illusory cause has not been demonstrated. However, it looks as if judges can annul contracts on the grounds that parties have failed to make good choices. English judges are not entitled to do this. It is therefore not axiomatic why a contract is annulled for absence of cause. From a common lawyer's viewpoint, the kind of situations that might correspond to the idea of illusory cause, and thus justify annulling the contract, fail to meet the criteria of both coherence and transparency.

2. Cases where the cause is derisory   The underlying idea of fair exchange is highlighted in the hypotheses of a derisory cause, since it is clear that the annulment of the contract is founded on a material evaluation of the equivalence of the exchange.[35] Once again, it is not that surprising that French law recognises this idea since *lésion* is explicitly recognised for certain kinds of contracts, unlike in English law.[36] Even if the Cour de cassation does not require a strict equivalence of undertakings,[37] it is apparent that an imbalance[38] suffices to merit annulling the contract. Once again, these cases clash with English law's view of bounded rationality. These cases could be equally stigmatised as bad bargains; in any event, English judges would not annul them. However, we will see that the French courts do not annul

---

[34] Cass civ (3) 13 October 2004, Bull civ III no 170. The idea that the lease has a value and can be assigned to a third party including the assignee of the lessor does not require any particular comment. It seems self-evident that the (new) lessor's property will become more valuable if the lessor recovers the leasehold.

[35] Gordley, above n 10.

[36] Art 1118 Cc.

[37] An argument used by the detractors of the use of cause as *lésion qualifiée*.

[38] The existence of an imbalance means a substantive and not a procedural imbalance and does not therefore correspond to the hypotheses covered by art 4:109 PECL. None of the cases under the heading of cause give any indication of procedural irregularities, excessive influence, etc on the facts. Or rather, if these elements are present, they are not transparent and they are therefore discounted.

contracts on the basis that the cause is derisory very often,[39] so that the cases where the contract is not annulled are equally revealing.[40] The crucial question here is then to examine why and when it is necessary to annul contracts for a derisory cause: these must be cases where the unfairness of the exchange is manifest.

One case where the contract is annulled on the basis that the undertakings are disproportionate and would arguably fit into the category of a derisory cause is the decision of the Commercial chamber of 14 October 1997.[41] The facts are as follows: SNC agreed to buy its beer exclusively from GBN (a beer manufacturer) in exchange for which GBN was to obtain a loan of 40,000 FF and guarantee it for SNC. The contract contained a penalty clause, which would be considered valid under French law (though note that the clause would not be valid under English law). SNC breached the contract and GBN applied the penalty clause accordingly. SNC succeeded in having the contract annulled for absence of cause, on the basis that the parties had disproportionate undertakings, or, more precisely, because GBN's undertakings were derisory.[42] A similar case confirmed this solution in 2005.[43] For a common lawyer, this case is difficult to understand and gives rise to conflicting interpretations, in the absence of sufficient facts. On the one hand, it is difficult to see why GBN's undertakings are derisory. Can it be inferred that GBN never actually gave the guarantee it promised, for example? On the other hand, the relationship between GBN and SNC can be analysed as a one-way or 'tied' contract; SNC is tied in to buying its beer exclusively from the beer manufacturer (GBN) who does nothing in return. In addition, information about the fairness of the price of beer is lacking.

Why, then, has French law decided to relieve SNC of its improvident, yet apparently rational choice? Here the court seems to be conveying the message that the contract is not a fair exchange. As already suggested, an explanation may lie in the externalities; this is a case of exclusive distribution which economists would analyse as a choice made in the absence of alternatives.[44] However, it also appears that the penalty clause was excessive. Since French judges have a moderating power to reduce the amount of penalty, why did the judges neglect to use this power? It would

---

[39] For a survey of the case-law, see J Ghestin, *Cause de l'engagement et validité du contrat* (Paris, LGDJ, 2006) 174–80.

[40] The cases where contracts are not annulled are quite revealing, often because the nominal or low price is explicable in terms of the overall transaction, so is not considered unfair. See, for example, Cass civ (1) 19 December 1995, Bull civ I no 481; Cass civ (3) 3 March 1993, Bull civ III no 28; Cass civ (1) 13 June 2006, Bull civ I no 306.

[41] Cass com 14 October 1997, appeal no 95-14285, unpublished.

[42] '. . . au regard de l'engagement de l'exploitant de la brasserie, "l'avantage procuré par la société GBN apparaît dérisoire," la cour d'appel en a justement déduit que le contrat litigieux était nul pour absence de cause'.

[43] See Cass com 8 February 2005, Bull civ IV no 21 for the same solution on analogous facts.

[44] See Trebilcock, above n 27, 158, n 31, citing Sunstein.

seem more reasonable, to a common lawyer, to reduce the amount of the clause to a liquidated damages clause in the event of breach and leave the contract on foot. Once again, annulling the contract, especially when other remedies were available, is tantamount to allowing a party to escape from a bad bargain.

Any speculation about the policy reasons behind this decision is just as uncertain or illusive as the real reasons themselves, since they are totally opaque. If French law wants to use the idea of a derisory cause to protect, or even ultimately prevent, parties from entering into contracts with unfair prices, it is arguable that the doctrine of cause may not be the best way of conveying the message that such contracts are considered unfair, since the judges' reasons for annulment are not transparent.

Other cases that fit into this category are admittedly much clearer and fit quite neatly the analysis that there is no fair exchange. For example, the Commercial chamber of the Cour de cassation's decision of 30 January 1996[45] that annulled a contract of franchise on the basis that since the franchisor provided no *savoir faire*, the contract has no cause on the basis that undertakings agreed in exchange were 'disproportionate'.[46] Could or would an English court annul such a contract? It is difficult to find a legal basis for replying in the affirmative. If parties make irrational or imprudent choices, they are not protected under English law, perhaps because one is deemed to look after one's own interests and this may be perceived as a way of ensuring that people assume their own responsibilities.

To conclude on this part we have seen that many cases show a divergence of result, and more particularly of outlook, about whether and when the law should intervene into the substance of the contract. The proposition that French law annuls contracts for absence of cause on the basis there is no fair exchange has been examined. This seems to be the case when the cause can be qualified as derisory or disproportionate. English law does not promote the idea of a fair exchange to the same extent, nor does it appear to be over-concerned about the rationality of contracting parties' behaviour, ie whether they have made good choices. In the eyes of English law, the rationality of choice is an individual matter, or more simply an aspect of freedom or personal autonomy and does not, therefore, require judicial intervention. Whether it is necessary or useful to protect contracting parties against their irrational choices is clearly a question of policy, about which there is bound to be disagreement. I hope to have shown that French case-law promotes this value by instrumentalising the cause, and the

---

[45] Cass com 30 January 1996, appeal no 94-13792, unpublished.

[46] See also Cass civ (1) 10 May 2005, Bull civ I no 203 for another example. This case concerns a licence/user of land for the life of the licensees upon payment of the sum of 300,000 FF, in return for which licensor had to pay all charges, repairs, etc. The licensor found himself liable for very onerous repairs and succeeded in annulling the contract for absence of cause. This might be qualified as a derisory cause under the new provisions.

Avant-projet would, for the most part, allow it to continue to do so. My reservations are focused on the legitimacy of this judicial control, a point that is reinforced by the next example.

(b) Judicial Elimination of Terms of the Contract that are Incompatible with the Contract's Core

Article 1125(2) of the *Avant-projet* gives judges a lot of manoeuvring room to eliminate terms that that are 'incompatible with the real character of its cause'. The meaning of this text is unfathomable; the criticism is directed at the text and not the translation. The text requires a paraphrase. It is suggested that article 1125(2) means that judges can strike out terms of the contract that clash with the real reason for the contract's existence, in other words, the core, the substance, the foundation of the contract. If we look at the applications in positive law of judicial elimination of contract terms, common lawyers may well have a strong sense of *déjà vu*. This possibility to set aside contractual terms when they are incompatible, or as used to be said 'repugnant',[47] to the core of the contract is highly reminiscent of the doctrine of fundamental breach.[48]

Once again, it is necessary to identify what is behind this provision. The lacuna in French law here is that there is no mechanism to regulate unfair contract terms contained in standard form contracts as between parties acting in the course of business (business to business, B2B). Whether there should be any legislative control is of course a question of policy. Briefly, controversy ranges over three identifiable foci. First, an argument based on pure freedom of contract refuses to recognise the need to regulate in the first place. A second angle focuses on the degree of regulation and the scope of its application. For example, it may be necessary to investigate whether all standard form contracts should be regulated or whether some standard form contracts in certain areas (eg financial services, insurance) should be excluded. Should regulation be directed only at standard form contracts or is this criterion unhelpful and should individually negotiated contracts (eg between a big and small business) also fall within the ambit of regulation? A third more interventionist position promotes regulating all standard-term B2B contracts and perhaps certain individually negotiated B2B contracts, depending on the relative bargaining power or status of the parties. Such regulation is subject to certain qualifications but would have the net effect of eliminating a distinction between B2B and B2C (business to consumer) contracts. Of course, the permutations of these respective

---

[47] See GL Williams, 'The Doctrine of Repugnancy' (1943) 59 LQR 343–58, (1944) 60 LQR 190–4.

[48] R Sefton-Green, *La notion d'obligation fondamentale: comparaison franco-anglaise* (Paris, LGDJ, 2000).

positions are numerous, but this particular discussion lies outside the scope of this chapter.[49]

To defend the need to regulate these kinds of contract, it is worth mentioning that contracting parties do not always have actual freedom in this sort of situation, even if they have theoretical freedom. When such contracts are made, a form of limited freedom exists in that one party does not have a choice; there is no pressure or duress, there is simply no alternative.[50] This is a sufficient argument for some form of state intervention that is paternalistic in nature. Furthermore, it should be noticed that English law has regulated such contracts since 1977, as section 3 of the Unfair Contract Terms Act 1977 allows the courts to assess the fairness, or rather the reasonableness, of a contractual term, as defined by the guidelines set out in schedule 2. French law is sorely lacking here, as no statutory provisions to regulate B2B contracts of any kind exist. This may be a side effect of the presence of a Code de la consommation, a point that will be dealt with later.

If we recognise the need to regulate potentially unfair contract terms in B2B contracts, we then need to examine how to do so. Yet again, the same criticisms of the *Avant-projet* reappear; these policy issues require an open discussion and a political decision is required about where and how to draw the line. This does not appear to have happened—yet! Secondly, in the absence of such transparency, the crucial question remains: what is the best legal instrument to achieve this aim? Article 1125(2) of the *Avant-projet* merely ratifies messy and spotty case-law and is unimaginative. In short, it simply preserves the status quo. However, this article should be read in conjunction with the specific provisions of the *Avant-projet* (article 1382 and following) dealing with exclusion and limitation clauses. It can be observed that these provisions take a middle stance and aim to regulate certain unfair terms contained in B2B contracts within stated limits.[51] It is contended that article 1382 and following give much clearer guidelines than article 1125(2), which runs the risk of being superfluous as well as distinctly controversial.

When examining the case-law where the doctrine of cause has been used as the legal basis for eliminating an unfair contract term, the *Chronopost*

---

[49] I am grateful to Hugh Beale for having raised the complexity of the debate in discussion at the colloquium. The Law Commission has made recommendations and drafted legislation on unfair terms, published in February 2005 and still awaiting parliamentary discussion time: Law Commission & Scottish Law Commission, 'Unfair Contract Terms' (Law Com No 292, Scot Law Com No 199, HMSO, 2005).

[50] Trebilcock, above n 27, 162; MJ Trebilcock, 'An External Critique of Laissez-Faire Contract Values' in FH Buckley (ed), *The Fall and Rise of Freedom of Contract* (Durham and London, Duke University Press, 1999) 79, 92.

[51] See in particular, art 1382-2: 'A party to a contract cannot exclude or limit the reparation for harm caused to his co-contractor by his deliberate or gross fault or by a failure to perform one of his essential obligations.'

saga comes to mind.[52] This serial and no doubt 'strategic litigation'[53] has given birth to a veritable cornucopia of legal literature.[54] In order to justify eliminating contract terms in B2B contracts, French judges first referred to a party's behaviour using a subjective approach through the application of *faute lourde*.[55] This criterion was rendered objective by concentrating on the nature of the obligation, rather than the party's behaviour and led to the emergence of a fundamental obligation (*l'obligation esentielle*).[56] After the first *Chronopost* explosion in 1996, the Cour de cassation retreated, in the decision of the Chambre mixte of 22 April 2005 when it reduced *faute lourde* to its subjective appreciation,[57] confirmed by the Commercial chamber on 13 June 2006,[58] but also contested by the same chamber on 30 May 2006[59] which reintroduced the objective test, focusing on the nature of the obligation, an approach that had already been used by the first Civil chamber in 2004.[60] Indeed the saga continues, as even more recently, the Commercial chamber resuscitated its duadic juxtaposition of cause and a fundamental obligation in a decision of 13 February 2007.[61] In short, two mechanisms coexist which enable judges to eliminate post hoc exclusion or limitation of liability clauses.

---

[52] Cass com 22 October 1996, Bull civ IV no 261—the case is translated in Beale et al, above n 24, 136; CA Caen 5 January 1999, JCP 2000 I 215 obs J Rochfeld. The epithet of 'saga' comes from a case note by D Mazeaud, 'Saga "*Chronopost*": les maîtres du temps perdent une manche' D 2006, 2288. See for the next instalment of the saga, below n 61.

[53] Strategic litigation predicates that 'powerful actors on the market use litigation about the relevant rules in order to try and persuade the courts to accept rules that protect the interests of those powerful actors'; see H Collins, 'Regulating Contract Law' in C Parker, C Scott, N Lacey and J Braithwaite (eds), *Regulating Law* (Oxford University Press, 2004) 20–22.

[54] Sefton-Green, above n 49, 155–65.

[55] By an extensive interpretation of art 1150 Cc, in which fraud is a ground for setting aside exclusion or limitation clauses by which *faute lourde* ('gross fault') is considered equivalent to fraud (*dol*).

[56] By a *condition substantielle*; see, for example, Cass civ (1) 2 December 1997, Bull civ I no 349.

[57] Cass mixte 22 April 2005, Bull civ mixte no 4: 'Constitue une faute lourde un comportement d'une extrême gravité, confinant au dol et dénotant l'inaptitude du débiteur de l'obligation à l'accomplissement de la mission contractuelle qu'il avait acceptée'.

[58] Cass com 13 June 2006, Bull civ IV no 143.

[59] Cass com 30 May 2006, Bull civ IV no 132: 'Attendu qu'en statuant ainsi, sans rechercher si la clause limitative d'indemnisation dont se prévalait la société Chronopost, qui n'était pas prévue par un contrat-type établi par décret, ne devait pas être réputée non écrite par l'effet d'un manquement du transporteur à une obligation essentielle du contrat, la cour d'appel n'a pas donné de base légale à sa décision.'

[60] Cass civ (1) 22 June 2004, appeal no 01-00444, unpublished: 'Mais attendu, d'abord, qu'ayant constaté, par motifs adoptés, que le départ du vol avait été différé de 24 heures et que l'importance de ce report ne permettait pas de l'assimiler à un "simple retard", la cour d'appel, caractérisant ainsi le retard excessif pour lequel le transporteur ne saurait s'exonérer à l'avance de toute responsabilité sans porter atteinte à l'essence du contrat de transport aérien de personnes, a pu écarter l'application de la clause relative à la non garantie des horaires invoquée par la société Corsair international.'

[61] Cass com 13 February 2007, Bull civ IV no 43. YM Sérinet, 'La descendance ambiguë des *Chronopost*: l'arrêt *Faurecia*' JCP G 2007 II 10063.

It has already been indicated that this is a messy, inconsistent and unpre-dictable way of proceeding. How can contracting parties know what sort of clauses will be valid or invalid when even the same chamber of the Cour de cassation contradicts itself about what is the relevant criterion to apply? Moreover, in my view, the doctrine of cause is not the best legal tool to deal with this problem.

The positive law definition that allows judges to eliminate such clauses is that the clause empties the contract of its substance; this then requires an enquiry into what is the substance, the core, the minimum requirements of the contract. I have argued that this consideration is purely descriptive and casuistic.[62] The main utility of such an exercise occurs when the Code civil cannot provide a comprehensive list of the core terms of the contract, since the contract is innominate, or concerns a string of contracts, about which predefined rules cannot be laid down. These cases can be contrasted with those in which a similar exercise is carried out, but in reality reference to cause is superfluous.[63]

In other cases, the definition of the core of the contract has descriptive value, but no more. This involves the judges interpreting each and every contract on its facts. It follows that there are no possible guidelines to follow if judges are merely carrying out a factual enquiry in order to determine which terms are core terms that cannot be rendered devoid of substance by other unfair terms, in a wide sense, ie not only exclusion and limitation clauses. In other words, this interpretation exercise allows judges to act with unfettered discretion, which might well be considered objec-tionable. The notes of the *Avant-projet* merely indicate that this provision lays down a 'necessary consistent logic', relegating to scholars (*la doctrine*) the job of connecting it to a 'principle of consistency' at a later date.[64] However, this does not enlighten us much further as to how and why judges may determine when contract terms are incompatible with the core content.

It is possible that the whole issue of whether judges should have juris-diction to interfere and eliminate contract terms in B2B contracts has deliberately been hidden under the carpet to avoid making an open policy decision. No doubt, members of the group drafting the *Avant-projet* would have disagreed about the need to regulate the terms of such contracts, or to what extent. Indeed, some would dismiss this question as one of consumer

---

[62] Sefton-Green, above n 49, 300–04.

[63] For instance, causalists will point to decisions about leases in which an unfair contract term has been removed on the ground that it contradicts an essential term of the contract, such as the lesssor's obligation to deliver. See for an example, Cass civ (3) 1 June 2005, Bull civ III no 119. In this instance it is suggested that no recourse need to be made to cause, nor is the analysis anything other than descriptive since the Code civil specifically enumerates the fundamental obligations of the lessor, from which there is no derogation.

[64] Ghestin, above n 1, 39 (see below p 527).

protection, belonging to the Code de la consommation. Several observations follow.

First, we can notice that the PECL contain article 4:110 that looks fairly similar to the main provisions of the Unfair Contract Terms Directive of 1993[65] in that it allows terms to be set aside which 'contrary to the requirements of good faith and fair dealing, cause a significant imbalance in the parties' rights and obligations'.[66] Defenders of greater intervention into unfair contract terms contained in B2B contracts may argue that this provision does not go far enough, since judges can only eliminate terms when they cause a 'significant imbalance'. Indeed, some would argue that it is crucial to leave the doctrine of cause to play this role as it can be cumulated, even in B2C contracts, with a claim that a clause is invalid under the Directive, as transposed into the Code de la consommation. It is contended that a *lex specialis* argument applies and that consumers will not have recourse to the doctrine of cause, or only as a subsidiary argument. Moreover, using cause is a last resort, in my view, since its application is entirely unpredictable.

Secondly, although the objection about the narrow scope of the criterion of a significant imbalance is well founded, objections to the use of cause to play this role still lie. In my view cause does not solve the problems that arise in relation to unfair contract terms; it is ineffective, or even inefficient, since it does not act as a deterrent to prevent such contract terms from being used. This kind of post hoc control is inevitably inadequate. The evidence stares us in the face: why are there so many *Chronopost* decisions, for example? A better means of regulation needs to be found, as demonstrated by the fact that Chronopost has carried on contracting with such unfair contract terms ever since 1996.[67] It is perhaps no coincidence that Chronopost has a monopoly in the public sector to provide a fast postal service. Parties contracting with Chronopost have no choice about accepting these unfair contract terms. Hence Chronopost has the power to carry out strategic litigation. This is clearly unsatisfactory, not to mention unfair.

Thirdly, the present case-law is a nightmare to follow, with different chambers of the Cour de cassation in disagreement even after a decision of the Chambre mixte. A number of rules coexist, depending on whether

---

[65] Council Directive (EC) 93/13 on unfair terms in consumer contracts [1993] OJ L/95/29.

[66] Art 4:110 PECL: 'A party may avoid a term which has not been individually negotiated if, contrary to the requirements of good faith and fair dealing, it causes a significant imbalance in the parties' rights and obligations arising under the contract to the detriment of that party, taking into account the nature of the performance to be rendered under the contract, all the other terms of the contract and the circumstances at the time the contract was concluded'. Comment A to art 4:110 explicitly says that the provision extends the scope of the general clause in the 1993 Directive to contracts between private persons and to commercial contracts.

[67] N Molfessis, 'Remarques sur l'efficacité des décisions de justice (à propos des effets de l'arrêt Chronopost)' RTD civ 1998, 213.

Chronopost is delivering for a domestic or transnational transaction. This is clearly untidy and could be improved. Nor is Chronopost the only business affected by this contradictory case-law.[68]

On the basis that the doctrine of cause has a minimal impact as a corrective device, it is suggested that the time has come for explicit recognition that standard form B2B contracts need effective regulation. Continuing to use cause, in addition to *faute lourde*, seems to offer a backdoor route of protection that does not go far enough. Would it not be more effective to use pre-emptive regulatory techniques by setting out explicit limits prohibiting the use of certain terms, or to set out guidelines about what is and is not considered unfair?[69] This would surely have the benefit of making the message clearer to contract-makers and perhaps have more effect. My objection here is not that French judges eliminate contract terms, but the way in which they do so: there are no visible guidelines for their intervention; hence they appear to be acting with discretion. To put it simply, the doctrine of cause will suffice as a corrective device, if there is no alternative, but *de lege ferenda*, a more effective means of regulation can surely be found. Is this not the purpose of law reform?

II. THE LEGITIMACY OF JUDICIAL INTERVENTION: PATERNALISM

Many objections to the court's jurisdiction to interfere on the grounds of fair exchange or substantive fairness have already been developed elsewhere in Anglophone legal literature.[70] It has been demonstrated that English courts refuse to interfere on similar grounds. It is incontrovertible that this is a controversial power. If judges exercise this power, it needs to be carefully delineated and controlled.

The French judiciary's use of the doctrine of cause to protect parties from imprudent and improvident bargains goes beyond the realm of fair exchange and impinges on an evaluation of the virtues of party choice. If English judges are reluctant to control unfair exchanges, ie the unfair price of contracts, *a fortiori* they will be even less inclined to enter into this sort of subjective, value-judgmental exercise. Objections can operate on two levels, first at the extent to which judges interfere in parties' contractual

---

[68] See, for example, Cass com 17 July 2001, appeal no 98-15678, unpublished, where a clause in a contract of computer maintenance limited liability of the service to interventions occurring within 48 hours, thus depriving the company of receiving the benefit of the fundamental obligation of the contract. See also the latest decision of the Commercial chamber of 13 February 2007, above n 61.

[69] See Unfair Contract Terms Act 1977 which has adopted this kind of approach to the regulation of unfair contract terms in B2B contracts.

[70] See Smith, above n 9, 138, n 3.

choices; secondly, the question of how this intervention is justified ('legitimacy') is of particular concern.

(a) Evaluating the Extent of Judicial Intervention

We have seen that the degree of French judges' intervention can be distinguished: a stronger form in respect of the illusory cause, a lesser in respect of the derisory cause. These two degrees of intervention might correlate to the distinction made between soft and hard paternalism.[71]

When judges eliminate unfair contract terms, is this soft or hard paternalism? Here the distinction is more blurred as a categorical answer cannot be given.[72] The answer will partly depend on our views about whether or when unfair terms need to be regulated, as already explained. The suggestion that French judges use the doctrine of cause in a paternalistic fashion, or to promote paternalistic goals (including that of perfectionism) is deliberately provocative. It would be presumptuous to attempt to give definitive replies. My purpose has been to elucidate a much-needed debate.

(b) Justification for Judicial Intervention: The Acid Test

The objections to the manner in which French judges intervene in the contract can be summarised in a short list, as follows:

1. The judicial use of the doctrine of cause leads to unpredictable solutions, which gives the impression that judges use the doctrine as corrective device in an arbitrary fashion.
2. The doctrine of cause can be contested on the grounds that it is not a legal concept but a casuistic instrument. It involves a factual interpretation of the contract. Interpreting the contract cannot, by definition, involve the use of notion, even less a unitary notion, since interpretation is by its nature, heteronomous. Furthermore, interpretation by recourse to the subjective intentions of the parties is required when examining whether cause is present or not in a given contract. This

[71] See FH Buckley, 'Perfectionism' (2005) 13 Supreme Court Economic Review 133, who suggests that soft paternalism fills in the gaps or second guesses a person's choices with the goal of giving effect to his true desires whereas hard paternalism, sometimes called perfectionism, trumps or overrules a person's choices even when these represent his true wishes, on the basis that the individual does not know what it good for him.

[72] One way of answering the question would be to identify whether or not the clause represents a party's true desires and or whether the party who accepts but does not proffer the clause was capable of knowing or understanding what was in his best interest. It may be impossible to adduce such evidence. Considerations will turn on casuistic factors, such as the degree of freedom, or choice, the contracting party had when accepting an unfavourable clause, etc.

can be criticised since it creates evidential difficulties, though this is a common law way of looking at the world.[73] The fact that judges use casuistic reasoning is not in itself shocking and would be an odd criticism to be formulated by a common lawyer. However, it gives rise to uncertainty, a qualified objection,[74] and lack of transparency, if effected under the name of a legal concept.

3. If the doctrine of cause is used as a palliative for unfairness in contract-making, clearer guidelines about when this palliative may be applied are required. The explanations given in decisions about what judges are actually doing when they use the doctrine, either to annul the contract or to eliminate a contract term, are opaque. If judges have and use guidelines, they are not visible. Thus the transparency criterion is not satisfied.

4. Paternalistic intervention requires legitimacy to avoid the criticism of an unjustified intrusion. To put it simply, one might ask why judges should decide what is good for us and be able to determine whether our choices are right or wrong, rational or not?[75] It has been suggested that paternalism may be legitimate if justified by reference to a common consensus, though it is usually admitted that this is the domain of the legislator.[76] Between libertarianism and paternalism there is a huge gap and we may not agree to what extent intrusion is warranted, or not. To exercise paternalistic intervention, judges need legitimacy and their use of the doctrine of cause suggests that their capacity for intrusion is quite large. The French judges' instrumentalisation of cause to substitute party choices for their own seems to reach quite close to the mark. As already suggested, this is a highly subjective exercise as it involves making value-judgments that run the risk of being arbitrary. This appears to be unjustified paternalism, on one level, not necessarily because no justification exists, but because none is given.

In conclusion we have seen that cause is required as a condition of validity in French contract law as evidence of the contract being made with a reason, as a guarantee of the rationality of the contracting parties, that good choices have been made. This in turn means that the doctrine of cause is used to protect parties from their irrationality and the *Avant-projet*

---

[73] Common lawyers consider, for example, that allowing the judges to investigate subjective intentions of the parties incites the parties to tell lies. French jurists consider that disregarding the parties' subjective intentions does not give enough weight to party autonomy. These viewpoints are diametrically opposed.

[74] It is admitted that legal uncertainty may be qualified as a relative consideration, since it has to be reconciled with other policy considerations.

[75] See MR Marella, 'The Old and New Limits to Freedom of Contract in Europe' (2006) 2 ERCL 257, 261–5.

[76] See Trebilcock, above n 27, 163 citing Milton Friedman and Dicey.

would enable judges to follow this path. This may appear to be justified in cases where freedom is de facto limited because of externalities; in other words, parties do not actually have a choice, they contract in the absence of an alternative. The difficulty of giving such a paternalistic device to the judges, either to annul contracts on the grounds of absence of cause, or to eliminate a contract term because it deprives a contract of its core, is that their decisions appear arbitrary, unjustified and equally irrational. Is this the best and most legitimate way of guaranteeing rational contracting behaviour in order to find an equilibrium between individual freedom, legal certainty and a certain degree of fair exchange or substantive fairness? In the light of the above, three propositions are offered to rebut these lack of legitimacy objections and to stimulate further debate:

1. Eliminate the doctrine of cause or give it a residual role, instead of distorting its function and creating a misleading concept.[77]
2. Insert express provisions that allow judges to interfere with contracts where fair exchange, or *lésion qualifiée*, is of concern. This would require a fuller discussion about the appropriate field of application.
3. Find a better, more effective, means of regulating unfair terms in B2B contracts. Since the judges' power to intervene is controversial, this would have the effect of limiting the potential controversy by spelling out and restricting this power.

---

[77] This seems to be the result obtained by the Civil Code of Québec which contains a provision on cause (arts 1410–1411) although it is rarely used in practice.

C

Enforcement of Contractual Obligations

6

The Enforcement of Contractual Obligations: A French Perspective

YVES-MARIE LAITHIER

U NDER THE HEADING of enforcement, English-speaking commentators generally deal with the judicial sanctions applicable where a contract is not performed.[1] But a more complete analysis of the provisions of the *Avant-projet de réforme du droit des obligations et de la prescription* leads us to accept a broader meaning to cover voluntary performance as well as the enforced performance of contractual obligations. According to the normal definition, performance is voluntary where the debtor fulfils the contract spontaneously; it is enforced where the court orders the debtor to perform his obligations to the creditor. These are two different modes of performance, but juxtaposing them seems all the more permissible in so far as what separates them is not so much a difference in nature as the degree of constraint applied to the debtor.[2]

In this area the policy aim of the *Avant-projet* is perfectly clear: the actual performance of contractual obligations is the 'focal point',[3] the objective to be attained. This choice can be linked to article 1134(1), whose numbering and wording—which is slightly mysterious—are unchanged, probably because of the high symbolic value of that provision.

One can only express satisfaction with this policy choice. First, because the preference for the performance of obligations is only an aim and not a dogma, as shown by, for example, the adoption of the right of withdrawal (article 1134-1 of the *Avant-projet*); or that of unilateral termination (article 1158). Secondly, because that aim is perfectly legitimate. It is

---

[1] For example, EA Farnsworth, *Contracts* (4th edn, New York, Aspen Publishers, 2004); SA Smith, *Atiyah's Introduction to the Law of Contract* (6th edn, Oxford, Clarendon Press, 2006).

[2] In particular, P Théry, 'Rapport introductif: la notion d'exécution', in *L'exécution: XXIIIème Colloque des Instituts d'études judiciaires, Lyon, vendredi 19 et samedi 20 novembre 1999* (Paris, L'Harmattan, 2001) 9, 13–9. See also his observations on Eugène Gaudemet's concept of performance: P Théry in H Beale, P Théry and G Dannemann, 'Emerging Themes', below ch 20, p 418.

[3] L Aynès, 'Rapport introductif' RDC 2005, 9.

unnecessary to go over the well-known moral, philosophical or economic arguments and it should be borne in mind that, in law, obligations are functional ties: they exist only in order to give satisfaction to the creditor and that satisfaction is, in principle, provided by performance of the obligation.

The chosen aim has been constant throughout the ages because its legitimacy cannot be denied. It is therefore understandable that the preference for performance is already incorporated in the Code civil and, even more clearly, in the whole of French private law.

All of which does not mean that the *Avant-projet* does not entail change or innovation. It is just that, perhaps here more than elsewhere, the *Avant-projet* is a work of continuity rather than of sudden change. And that is also true of the voluntary performance of contractual obligations (section I below) and of their enforced performance (section II below).

I. THE PREFERENCE FOR THE VOLUNTARY PERFORMANCE OF CONTRACTUAL OBLIGATIONS

Every contract is concluded by interest (for a cause). That interest marks the seriousness of the undertaking without which the contract would not exist. Once the contract is duly formed, two possibilities can be envisaged: either the interest in performance will still exist, which is the most frequent case, or it will disappear. The *Avant-projet* contemplates those two possibilities, but subjects them to the same rule. In other words, it favours the performance of the obligations whether the debtor retains his interest in the contract (section I(a) below) or whether he loses it (section I(b) below).

(a) Performance of the Contract in Which the Debtor has an Interest

A debtor who retains his interest in the contract must obviously perform it. What should be noted here is not that this rule is still included as an incontrovertible truth, but the way in which the draftsmen of the *Avant-projet* have expressed it. In this connection it is regrettable that the layout is faithful to the Code civil in that it is no better—ie the dispersal of the provisions concerning performance (i) and those on the classification of contractual obligations (ii).

(i) The Dispersal of Provisions on the Performance of Obligations

In the present Code civil the main provisions of general law on the performance of obligations are dispersed among Chapter III of Title III of Book

III devoted to 'the effects of obligations' and Chapter V of the same Title, relating to 'the extinction of obligations'.

The reform of the Code civil offered an excellent opportunity to bring them together so as to provide an overall consolidated view of performance. Indeed that appears to be what was envisaged because Chapter III of Sub-title I, as amended by the *Avant-projet*, includes a new Section 4 entitled 'The Performance of Obligations'. This initiative must be approved. Unfortunately, the wording is deceptive and the provisions remain dispersed. Or, rather, it has been compounded since the bipartite fragmentation in the Code civil has become tripartite in the *Avant-projet*.

The first fragmentation of provisions is explained by the fact that the concept of performance is perceived from two viewpoints between which the drafters of the *Avant-projet* have not differentiated: performance is at one and the same time an effect of contracts and a method of extinguishing obligations. This duality gives rise directly to two 'masses' already present in the Code civil. Performance is dealt with separately at first under the heading of 'Performance of Obligations' (draft articles 1152 to 1156-2),[4] then under the heading of 'Satisfaction' (articles 1219–1236), while satisfaction is defined as 'the performance of the subject-matter of the obligation' (article 1219). This complaint is more a matter of form than of substance because the provisions concerning satisfaction have, of course, the same aim in favour of the performance in kind of obligations—see, for example, article 1223(1) of the *Avant-projet*. The fact remains that a more consolidated layout would have been more readable and more consistent with the decision to create a Section devoted to the performance of obligations.

To those two 'masses' a third has now been added. While the Code civil includes in 'the effects of obligations' the rules relating to 'damages arising from the non-performance of the obligation' (articles 1146–1155), the *Avant-projet* excludes them completely, apart from a brief allusion in article 1158(1). There is a simple explanation for this. The draftsmen of the *Avant-projet* regarded damages as a form of reparation for the harm caused by non-performance of a contractual obligation (article 1340(2)) not as a method of performance by equivalent.[5] Consequently all the provisions relating to the judicial assessment of damages, and contractual arrange-

---

[4] In reality, Chapter III of the *Avant-projet* contains provisions relating to the performance of obligations outside Section 4, of which that is, however, the subject—see, for example, art 1134(3) which prescribes performance in good faith; and art 1149 which sets out the conditions in which the obligation of result and the obligation to take necessary steps are performed, a provision that ought to have formed part of the provisions on contractual liability.

[5] On this observation, see G Viney, 'Exposé des motifs: Sous-titre III. De la responsabilité civile (Articles 1340 à 1386)' in *Avant-projet de réforme du droit des obligations et de la prescription: Rapport remis au garde des Sceaux* (Paris, La documentation française, 2006) 159, 163 (see below pp 809, 815). On the difference between this observation and positive law, see, *inter alia*, Théry above n 2, 417 mentioning the case-law of the Commercial chamber of the Cour de cassation concerning a claim for damages against a company in difficulty.

ments relating to damages,[6] are found in the part on civil liability. In our opinion this choice merits respect and—this time—seems consistent.[7] It deserves respect in so far (and only in so far) as the special nature of contractual liability is preserved.[8] It is consistent because it is logical to deal together with concepts whose identity of nature is affirmed. The fact remains that, as one of the contributors to the *Avant-projet* has recognised, the structure adopted is not always readable.[9] Furthermore, it leaves outside the provisions relating to the law of contract one of the most widespread sanctions for the non-performance of contractual obligations.[10] Beyond these more or less justified technical reasons, the dispersal of the provisions on the performance of obligations shows that, faced with the monumental edifice of the Code civil, it is easier to add than to take away. The same applies to the classification of contractual obligations.

(ii) The Classification of Contractual Obligations

In the *Avant-projet* the rules for the performance of obligations follow two series of classifications, one already enshrined in the Code civil,[11] the other more modern.

The first classification, the origins of which go back to Roman law,[12] distinguishes between obligations to do, not to do, to give and to give for use. The distinction has not only been retained, but supplemented.

It has been retained although many French commentators deny the existence of the obligation to give, taking the view that the agreed transfer of title is a legal effect of the contract and not the subject-matter of an obligation; it takes place automatically.[13] Contrary to this opinion, the draftsmen of the *Avant-projet* consider that the obligation to give does exist. Its nature is as follows: passively, the debtor of an obligation to give undertakes to surrender his right of ownership; actively, the creditor

---

[6] On the last point see D Mazeaud, 'Les conventions portant sur la réparation' RDC 2007, 149.

[7] Cf M Faure-Abbad, 'La présentation de l'inexécution contractuelle dans l'avant-projet Catala' D 2007 Chron 165, 169–73.

[8] P Ancel, 'Présentation des solutions de l'avant-projet' RDC 2007, 19, 19–25; E Savaux, 'Brèves observations sur la responsabilité contractuelle dans l'avant-projet de réforme du droit de la responsabilité' RDC 2007, 45, 47–50.

[9] P Ancel, 'Quelques observations sur la structure des sections relatives à l'exécution et à l'inexécution des contrats' RDC 2006, 105, 110.

[10] See also G Rouhette, 'Regard sur l'*Avant-projet* de réforme du droit des obligations' RDC 2007, 1371, 1373–5.

[11] Arts 1126 and 1136–1145.

[12] See R Zimmermann, *The Law of Obligations* (Oxford University Press, 1996) 6. The renown of the classification owes a great deal to the glossators.

[13] See, for example, M Fabre-Magnan, *Les obligations 1: Contrat et engagement unilatéral* (Paris, PUF, 2008) no 85; F Terré, P Simler and Y Lequette, *Les obligations* (9th edn, Paris, Dalloz, 2005) no 267. *Contra* F Zenati and T Revet, *Les biens* (2nd edn, Paris, PUF, 1997), nos 131, 137; J Huet, 'Des différentes sortes d'obligations et, plus particulièrement, de l'obligation de donner, la mal nommée, la mal aimée' in *Etudes offertes à Jacques Ghestin* (Paris, LGDJ, 2001) 425.

benefits, on the conclusion of the contract, from a promise of ownership but becomes the proprietor only when the obligation to give has been performed.[14] Having been retained, the distinction is then amplified: first, on account of the enlargement of the scope of the obligation to give to include rights other than ownership; secondly, by adding to the traditional classification 'the obligation to give for use', the subject-matter of which is, according to article 1146 of the *Avant-projet*, 'a grant of permission to use a thing on condition of its return'.[15]

From our point of view, this classification is irrelevant. Whether the obligation is to do, not to do, to give or to give for use, the rule is that in principle it must be performed in kind, and regardless of whether performance is voluntary or, as we shall see, enforced. Consequently a question comes to mind: could not the classification be dispensed with? It is permissible to think so for two reasons: the first is that a comparative study shows that the distinction is in no way necessary for an understanding of the substance and the implementation of the performance of contractual obligations;[16] the second is that the *Avant-projet* adopts a more modern and, it seems, sufficient classification.

This second classification contrasts monetary obligations with obligations 'in kind', that is to say, those which do not concern a sum of money. This distinction has long been upheld by *le doyen* Carbonnier[17] and it is adopted by the *Avant-projet* in article 1147. This recognition is very welcome. It is true that all obligations, whether monetary or not, must in principle be performed in kind. However, the distinction is justified because the voluntary performance of monetary obligations follows specific rules inherent in money, and this justifies separate treatment by comparison with the rules common to all payments.[18] The draftsmen of the *Avant-projet* took account of this in articles 1225 to 1225-4 which deal with the nominal value of money and the different provisions for it, and in article 1226 concerning the currency of payment.[19] In sum, the distinction between monetary obligations and obligations in kind is clear, definite, useful and necessary. In our opinion, it ought not to have been added to the old classification in the Code civil, which it transcends, but ought to have replaced it.

---

[14] See the demonstration by T Revet, observations on Cass com 10 January 2006, RTD civ 2006, 343, 347. See also G Blanluet, 'Le moment du transfert de la propriété' in *1804–2004: Le Code civil, un passé, un présent, un avenir* (Paris, Dalloz, 2004) 409, 420.

[15] G Pignarre, 'L'obligation de donner à usage dans l'avant-projet Catala: *Analyse critique*' D 2007, Chron 384.

[16] Nor is the distinction made in the various European proposals for the harmonisation of contracts. This is not a trivial observation in view of the avowed ambition of promoting the influence of French civil law.

[17] J Carbonnier, *Les obligations* (22nd edn, Paris, PUF, 2000) no 10.

[18] See, for example, to that effect, P Malaurie, L Aynès and P Stoffel-Munck, *Les obligations* (3rd edn, Paris, Defrénois, 2007) nos 1075–1110.

[19] The special nature of the voluntary performance of monetary obligations is also shown by arts 7:101, 7:107, 7:108, 7:109 and 7:111 PECL.

Nothing is more normal than that preference should be given to the performance of an obligation in which the debtor still has an interest. However, the preference for performance goes further because the *Avant-projet* aims to 'save' contracts whose initial balance is modified to the point of losing all point for the debtor.

(b) The Performance of a Contract Which has Lost its Point for the Debtor

The *Avant-projet* sets up a system that has a clear purpose: it is better to have a contract performed, even if it is modified, than a contract whose imbalance is such that it risks being breached and then terminated. This system is a major innovation in relation to the Code civil, and it must be described (i) before it can be criticised (ii).

(i) Description of the System

The system set up by articles 1135-1 to 1135-3 of the *Avant-projet* is innovative but not revolutionary.

First of all, it is innovative on the practical level. Its novelty consists not so much in the fact that the parties are left free to stipulate a clause whereby they undertake to negotiate a modification of the contract where, as a result of supervening circumstances, the original balance of what the parties must do for each other is so disturbed that the contract loses all its point for one them. Article 1135-1 of the *Avant-projet* which provides for this clause is a descriptive provision that authorises nothing more than what is already permitted by the freedom to contract. Its novelty consists rather in the general way in which the court (the president of the tribunal de grande instance) is given power to order a new negotiation on application by the party for whom the contract has lost its point. The other practical novelty consists in establishing a priority in favour of the performance of the contract and to the detriment of the termination of the contract for the future, which is available only in the event of the failure of negotiations conducted in good faith—draft article 1135-3(2).

Secondly, the system is innovative on the theoretical level: first, in so far as it allows of no confusion between the binding force of the contract and its inviolability (binding force means that the parties are bound subject to the sanction of the law, nothing more;[20] it does not make the contract immutable); secondly, in so far as it takes into account the special nature of contracts which are performed over a period of time and which therefore need to be adjusted;[21] finally, in so far as it confers upon the court a power

---

[20] Y-M Laithier, *Etude comparative des sanctions de l'inexécution du contrat* (Paris, LGDJ, 2004) no 38.

[21] For the importance of the term in contracts see R Libchaber, 'Réflexions sur les effets du contrat' in *Mélanges offerts à Jean-Luc Aubert* (Paris, Dalloz, 2005) 211, 225–33.

that the Code civil did not give it. But on this last point, as on others, the novelty must be considered in context.

The proposed system is not revolutionary. First of all, because certain noteworthy judgments have been given against creditors for lack of good faith or of honesty where they sought performance of the contract as concluded, without agreeing to renegotiate it, while the interests of the other party were seriously compromised by the change in circumstances.[22] While it is true that in those decisions the court does not directly order the opening of negotiations—as provided for by article 1135-2 of the *Avant-projet*—the judgments at least provide the parties with an incentive. Secondly, and more importantly, the system is not revolutionary because the court is not given power to modify the contract—not even as an alternative if the negotiations fail.[23] In other words, these provisions are faithful to the liberal philosophy of the Code civil. The court does not restore the balance of the contract; it encourages the parties to do it themselves, which is quite different.

Some will regret that the plunge was not taken with judicial revision of contracts.[24] On that point we disagree, considering that, on the contrary, the proposed system is too generous as it stands.

(ii) Criticism of the System

This criticism does not relate to the actual principle of judicial intervention, although one may question the effectiveness of a negotiation imposed on the parties. The criticism is directed at the rules for such intervention and, in particular, the conditions for activating the system.[25]

For the court to be able to order a new negotiation, three conditions must be fulfilled. The first is the existence of a contractual imbalance subsequent to the conclusion of the contract. The second is that the imbalance originates from 'supervening circumstances'. The third is that the imbalance is so serious that 'the contract loses its point' for one of the parties. At first sight, these conditions seem strict. In reality, they lack precision and are incomplete.

First of all, the reference to the 'circumstances' causing the imbalance is imprecise. It ought to have been mentioned that those 'circumstances' are 'external'. To be even more precise, the *Avant-projet* ought to indicate that

---

[22] See, for example, F Terré et al, above n 13, no 467 and references cited there.

[23] Cf art 6:111(3)(b) PECL.

[24] See, to that effect, D Mazeaud, 'Observations conclusives' RDC 2006, 177, 193–4; D Tallon, 'Teneur et valeur du projet appréhendé dans une perspective comparative' RDC 2006, 131, 132 and 133.

[25] The woolliness surrounding the extent of the court's powers and what happens to the contract during the negotiations may also be noted. See, on the first point, D Fenouillet, 'Les effets du contrat entre les parties: ni révolution, ni conservation, mais un "entre-deux" perfectible' RDC 2006, 67, 75.

not only the occurrence, but also the progress of the events giving rise to the contractual imbalance must be beyond the control of the party pleading it.

Secondly, the imprecision affects the condition of the seriousness of the imbalance. Under article 1135-2 of the *Avant-projet*, in order for a party to apply to the court for a new negotiation the contract must have 'lost its point'. On reading this, we do not know whether the loss must be total or partial or whether, behind that formulation, what has to be established before the court is in reality the disappearance of the cause. However this may be, in view of the imperative of legal certainty,[26] one wonders whether it would not have been preferable to specify, as the criterion of seriousness, that performance of the obligation would be excessively onerous, taking account, where appropriate, of the value of the reciprocal obligation.[27] To put it another way, it would seem that the condition relating to value would be easier to assess—and therefore more predictable—than the condition concerning the 'point' of the contract.

However, the main reservation concerning the conditions laid down by the *Avant-projet* is the complete absence of any reference to the allocation of risks, which is one of the essential functions of a contract. In our opinion, it must be made clear that a contractual imbalance may under no circumstances be pleaded by the party who bears the risk of a supervening change in circumstances,[28] either because he gave an undertaking to that effect or because it is clear from the economic balance of the contract. This additional condition makes it possible to prevent opportunistic behaviour by the party who, following the materialisation of a risk that he must bear, seeks at best to pass part of the burden of the risk to the other party by means of negotiations that are successful or, at worst, to escape the entire risk once and for all if the negotiations he has applied for are opened and fail, since in that case he will have the right to terminate the contract for the future.

The foregoing criticisms could be met with the objection that, unlike other national laws, the system set up by the *Avant-projet* gives the court only the power to order a new negotiation and not the power to revise the contract. More exactly, the idea is as follows: as the effects of the system are modest, the ease with which it can be activated is acceptable.

This objection is not convincing for two reasons. First, because the effects of the system must not be played down. The court's decision gives rise to obligations to be fulfilled by the parties—to open negotiations and

---

[26] According to A Ghozi, 'Exposé des motifs: Effet des conventions, interprétation, qualification (art 1134 à 1143)' in *Avant-projet de réforme du droit des obligations et de la prescription: Rapport remis au garde des Sceaux* (Paris, La documentation française, 2006) 46, 48 (see below pp 543, 547), the condition that the contract has 'lost its point' is justified by the 'certainty of transactions'.

[27] This is the criterion adopted by art 6:111(2) PECL.

[28] See, also to that effect, on the basis of certain national laws, art 6:111(2)(c) PECL.

to conduct them in good faith—which, if not performed, give rise to civil liability. Secondly, because the system comes close to introducing in a general way 'financial force majeure'.[29] Article 1135-3(2) of the *Avant-projet* confers on each party the right to terminate the contract at no cost or loss if the negotiations fail in the absence of bad faith. It is true that this outcome is envisaged as an *ultimum remedium*, available only after the negotiations have been properly conducted. Nevertheless, the system virtually enables each of the parties to free himself very cheaply from his obligations. Consequently that is the reason why it is imperative that the conditions for activating the system be better defined. The same applies to observance of the binding force of the contract, which would be affected if the debtor could escape from his undertakings with complete impunity.

For the draftsmen of the *Avant-projet*, contractual obligations are to be performed in kind. This is obvious where the concluded contract still has some point for the parties. It is a priority objective where the contract loses its point for one of them because of changed circumstances. And as we shall find, it is also a priority objective where the contract is not performed.

II. THE PREFERENCE FOR THE ENFORCED PERFORMANCE IN KIND OF CONTRACTUAL OBLIGATIONS

Numerous provisions of the *Avant-projet* provide that, in the case of non-performance, the enforcement in kind of contractual obligations may be obtained. This applies to the obligation to give,[30] the obligation to do,[31] the obligation not to do[32] and the obligation to give for use.[33] To state the same rule, a more relevant and more useful layout would have consisted in making better use of the distinction made by the *Avant-projet* between monetary obligations and obligations 'in kind', by separating clearly the rules for the enforcement of each. However, works of legal scholar-ship—French[34] and foreign[35]—were illuminating.

However this may be, the draftsmen of the *Avant-projet* have elevated enforcement in kind to the level of a sanction of 'principle' which yields

---

[29] It is officially rejected in French law (see, eg, F Terré et al, above n 13, no 582), as in English law: see, eg, J Beatson, 'Increased Expense and Frustration' in FD Rose (ed), *Consensus ad idem: Essays in the Law of Contract in Honour of Guenter Treitel* (London, Sweet & Maxwell, 1996) 121.

[30] Art 1152(3).

[31] Arts 1154(1) and, by implication, 1151(4).

[32] Arts 1154-1 *in fine*, and 1154-2.

[33] Art 1155(3).

[34] See, for example, Malaurie et al, above n 18, nos 1128–36; Terré et al, above n 13, nos 1108–19.

[35] See, for example, T Weir, 'Non-Performance of a Contractual Obligation and its Con-sequences in English law' in L Vacca (ed), *Il contratto inadempiuto* (Turin, G Giappichelli, 1999) 71, 74–95. See also arts 9:101 and 9:102 PECL.

only to impossibility and the 'clearly personal character of the subject-matter of the obligation'. Whilst the choice that has been made is at odds with the letter of article 1142 Cc and the interpretation it is generally given by scholars, it conforms on the other hand to the prevailing case-law of the Cour de cassation, to the idealisation of enforcement in kind by most French commentators and is faithful to the tradition of continental European jurisdictions.[36] For all those reasons, the direction taken by the draftsmen will surprise no one. Therefore, to avoid what would in the end be a commentary on current French law,[37] we should like to concentrate on the principal silences in the *Avant-projet*. Some relate to the obstacles to enforced performance in kind (section II(a) below), the others to the associated contractual arrangements (section II(b) below).

(a) The Obstacles to Enforced Performance in Kind

Not all the silences in the *Avant-projet* have the same implications. Some are in fact imprecisions (i), while others are rejections (ii).

(i) Imprecise Obstacles

The *Avant-projet* contains two series of obstacles whose relative imprecision calls for a few remarks.

The first obstacle is impossibility. Fearing to state what is obvious, the drafters admit that they hesitated to mention it.[38] The obstacle was finally taken into account by the *Avant-projet*, but neither its nature nor its extent are made clear. In all probability, the legal nature of impossibility is dual. First there is the legal impossibility arising from the need to respect rights acquired in the subject-matter of the obligation by third parties in good faith. While it is true that the transfer of title to a purchaser creditor can be relied upon in relation to third parties, this rule does not succeed in protecting him effectively against the risk of alienation to a third party to whom the law grants its favours if he is in good faith.[39] This traditional—and opportune—limit is adopted by the *Avant-projet* in the context of unilateral promises of sale (article 1106(3)); pre-emption agreements (article 1106-1(3)); and, more generally, the obligation to give (draft article

---

[36] On all these points, see Laithier, above n 20, nos 17–48.

[37] Subject to the proposed provisions of articles 1106(2) and 1106-1(3) relating to the unilateral promise to contract and the pre-emption agreement, which are not in line with the case-law of the Cour de cassation, although the difference is less in the latter case: see, for example, Cass mixte 26 May 2006, Bull mixte no 4, D 2006, 1861 note P-Y Gautier, D 2006, 1864 note D Mainguy, Defr 2006, 1206 obs E Savaux, RDC 2006, 1080 obs D Mazeaud, RTD civ 2006, 550 obs J Mestre and B Fages; Cass civ (3) 14 February 2007, Bull civ III no 25, Defr 2007, 1048 obs Libchaber, RTD civ 2007, 366 obs P-Y Gautier.

[38] See the explanatory note under art 1154 of the *Avant-projet* (see below p 691).

[39] See, for example, Blanluet, above n 14, 422.

1153). Secondly, impossibility may be material. This it not indicated by the *Avant-projet*. However, one may argue on the basis of article 1154-1, which provides that 'a failure to observe an obligation not to do gives rise to damages by operation of law from the mere fact of the breach'. If, exceptionally, damages prevail, that is because non-performance is complete and enforced performance in kind is impossible. The same applies to, for example, the disclosure of information contrary to an undertaking of confidentiality, the non-performance of which entails irreversible consequences.

If material impossibility is found, it remains to determine its extent. Here again the *Avant-projet* is silent. Legal writers traditionally take the view that impossibility must be absolute. Strictly speaking, therefore, material impossibility should be found only in the case of non-performance with irreversible effects or where the subject-matter of the obligation is unique— unique in France? In the world? On the market? However, the case-law of the Cour de cassation is less intransigent than academic writing.[40] In those circumstances, is the lack of precision in the *Avant-projet* to be regretted? We do not think so. By leaving the concept of impossibility somewhat vague, the text allows the court case-by-case discretion and the power to adjust the rule to changing circumstances.

The second series of obstacles to enforced performance in kind includes the clearly personal character of the subject-matter of the obligations, ie respect for the debtor's liberty and for his dignity. This raises two questions, one concerning the presentation of the three obstacles, the other their substance. The first question is as follows: why have these factors been added together? Was it not sufficient to state as a limit either the personal character of the subject-matter of the obligation or respect for the debtor's liberty or for his dignity? The draftsmen of the *Avant-projet* explain why they wished to distinguish, on the one hand, the limit to indirect constraint procedures (monetary penalties) and, on the other hand, the limit to direct constraint procedures.[41] There is a further distinction. In the first case, it is the purpose of the order which is limited: in principle the court has power to order enforced performance in kind 'unless the subject-matter of the obligation has a clearly personal character' (draft article 1154(2)).[42] In the second case, what is limited is the execution of the order: it is possible to constrain the debtor to furnish the subject-matter of the obligation unless that compromises his liberty or dignity (draft article 1154(3)). We can illustrate the distinction: the first limit prohibits an order, on pain of a monetary penalty, requiring an artist to carry out the promised

---

[40] See Laithier, above n 20, no 46 and the references cited there.

[41] L Leveneur and H Lécuyer, 'Exposé des motifs: Exécution des obligations (art 1152 à 1156-2)' in *Avant-projet de réforme du droit des obligations et de la prescription: Rapport remis au garde des Sceaux* (Paris, La documentation française, 2006) 50, 52 (see below p 559).

[42] Impossibility is another limit to the court's power to order performance in kind.

work, but it does not prohibit an order requiring a building contractor to carry out the work he has promised; however, although the builder may be ordered by the court, the second limit prevents him from being obliged by force to furnish the subject-matter of the obligation because such direct constraint would encroach on his liberty.[43] No doubt the distinction is clear and instructive, but it does not seem to be useful.[44] The limits to enforced performance in kind are shared, but not lessened. For the distinction to have a point, no limit should have been placed on the court's power to order performance in kind, apart from impossibility. In other words, the court ought to have been able to order the debtor to perform his obligation in kind even where the subject-matter of the obligation is 'clearly personal'. And it is only at the later stage of execution of the judgment ordering performance in kind that this limit could, if need be, have found its place if it did not duplicate that relating to the debtor's liberty or dignity.

The second question relates to the respective substance of those obstacles. Let us pass over the first two quickly as they are very well known. The *Avant-projet* does not indicate what constitutes a 'clearly personal' obligation. Nowadays scholars give various definitions of the 'personal' obligation to do, but almost all of them boil down to the interpretation or creation of works of intellectual value.[45] This restrictive concept is *a priori* confirmed by the use of the adverb 'clearly'. With regard to respect for liberty, it is certainly necessary but nevertheless ambiguous because it can just as well be argued, on the one hand, that an order to perform an obligation in kind is in itself an encroachment on individual liberty, and one can just as well reply, on the other hand, that the obligation to perform which the debtor is ordered to carry out is, by definition, freely contracted. In short, reasoning in terms of liberty is not particularly illuminating. However, as in the previous case, it does not appear that the provision should modify the solutions currently accepted. In contrast, the obstacle arising from respect for the debtor's dignity is more worrying. The draftsmen of the *Avant-projet* do not breathe a word about it in spite of its novelty and the wording takes care not to be specific. It must be noted straight away that the compromise of an individual's dignity is not connected with the subject-matter of the obligation because, if that were the case, the contract would be contrary to public policy and therefore void. The compromise of dignity results from the enforced performance in kind of a valid contractual obligation. Having said that, concrete applications appear to be limited as yet. One could imagine, for example, that, on that basis, the enforced performance would be refused of a seller's obligation to deliver the property which serves as his home when he has no

---

[43] The example is given by Leveneur and Lécuyer, above n 41, 52 (see below p 559).

[44] For a more detailed account of the distinction and of criticism, see Laithier, above n 20, nos 32, 47–8.

[45] See, for example, Fabre-Magnan, above n 13, no 236.

other property of that kind and, furthermore, he is bankrupt. It is also possible to imagine that the eviction of a tenant unjustifiably occupying premises would be refused if he has no other accommodation. Thus what respect for individual liberty is not sufficient to prevent today,[46] could be prohibited tomorrow in the name of respect for dignity. This interpretation, whatever one may really think of it,[47] has the merit of giving substance to the distinction made by the *Avant-projet* between liberty and dignity.

These are the different elements which call for more precision. But not every silence is an omission. Sometimes it is the expression of a rejection.

(ii) The Rejected Obstacles

Mention should be made of two rejected factors which show that economic considerations have had little influence on the drafting of the rules of enforced performance in kind.

The most important missing factor is the disproportionate cost of enforced performance in kind. No provision of the *Avant-projet* provides for this sanction to be discarded on the ground that applying it would impose on the debtor in question an excessive financial burden having regard to, in particular, its actual point for the creditor . However, the contrary solution would not have been surprising in view of the place taken in the *Avant-projet* by the requirement of contractual balance.[48] It should be added that this limit to enforced performance in kind has long been advocated by certain writers who suggest that the judicial revision of disproportion should be based either on the court's power to assess the expediency of the sanction,[49] or more precisely, on the abuse of rights or the duty of good faith.[50] Finally, it should be added that the limit, widespread in comparative law,[51] has been adopted by article 9:102(2)(b) of the Principles of European Contract Law, which deprives the creditor of performance in kind where it 'would cause the debtor unreasonable effort or expense'.

However, it may be asked whether the court could not find, in the condition of 'possibility' laid down by article 1154(1) of the *Avant-projet*, the means of refusing to order performance in kind for reasons connected

---

[46] See Terré et al, above n 13, no 1118.

[47] Personally, I consider that dignity—which should be included among 'those indeterminate concepts which serve more as excuses than reasoned justifications', C Atias, *Philosophie du droit* (Paris, PUF, coll Themis, 1999) 207—has nothing to do with the rules of the performance of contractual obligations, any more than it has with the rest of contract law.

[48] See G Cornu, 'Introduction' in *Avant-projet de réforme du droit des obligations et de la prescription: Rapport remis au garde des Sceaux* (Paris, La documentation française, 2006) 19, 20 (see below pp 479, 481).

[49] See A Sériaux, *Droit des obligations* (2nd edn, Paris, PUF, 1998) no 63.

[50] See, for example, G Viney and P Jourdain, *Les effets de la responsabilité* (2nd edn, Paris, LGDJ, 2001) nos 20–1.

[51] This is particularly the case in English law and in German law: § 275(2) and (3) BGB.

with the cost of implementing it. This would mean enlarging the concept and adding to legal and material impossibility a third type: economic impossibility. This suggestion breaks with the dominant case-law of the Cour de cassation[52] and is probably not faithful to the intention of the draftsmen. But it revives a long French tradition, strikingly expressed by Pothier,[53] and which, provided it is properly framed,[54] would make it possible to avoid imposing a sometimes excessive sanction.

The other limit rejected by the *Avant-projet* concerns the effect of the duty to mitigate the damage. As everyone knows, the authors of the part dedicated to civil liability innovated by requiring the victim who

> had the possibility of taking reliable, reasonable and proportionate measures to reduce the extent of his loss or to avoid its getting worse.[55]

However, worded in that way, this duty has only a limited scope. Failure to comply entails a reduction in damages. On the other hand, the duty does not affect the availability of enforced performance in kind. In other words, it is not possible, it seems, to deprive the creditor of enforced performance in kind merely on the ground that he could have remedied the non-performance of which he is the victim by other 'reliable, reasonable and proportionate measures', and also less costly ones.

The choice made, which here again differs from the Principles of European Contract Law,[56] is possible but questionable. The profound justification of the duty to mitigate the loss consists in the will to manage resources efficiently. However, these economic considerations are not limited to assessing damages. They apply likewise to enforced performance in kind.[57] As the system is at present, a creditor who thinks he has failed in his duty to mitigate the loss will therefore be well advised not to claim damages, but rather to apply for performance in kind. In that way he will escape the consequences of his omission, whatever its pernicious effects.

---

[52] See, for example, Cass civ (3) 11 May 2005, Bull civ III, no 103, RTD civ 2005, 596 obs J Mestre and B Fages.

[53] R-J Pothier, *Traité du contrat de vente*, vol I (Paris/Orléans, Debure, Rouzeau-Montaut, 1781) no 68: 'if a person who intended to pull down his house sold me a certain beam or some other thing forming part of that house . . . nevertheless if the vendor changed his mind and, no longer wishing to pull down his house, refuses to deliver those things to me, I shall not be permitted to pull down his house in order to remove the things which he sold me which are attached to it, and in that case his obligation must give rise to damages: there is a public interest which is opposed to the demolition of a building; and furthermore *where the debtor must suffer from the performance of his obligation a harm much greater than the creditor may suffer from non-performance, it is fair that the creditor should in that case content himself with compensation for what he suffers from non-performance by an award of damages and that he should not be able to constrain the debtor in that case to perform the obligation exactly'* (emphasis added).

[54] For the possible criteria for assessing disproportion, see Laithier, above n 20, nos 316–8.

[55] Art 1373. On this subject, see P Jourdain, 'Présentation des dispositions de l'avant-projet sur les effets de la responsabilité' RDC 2007, 141, 146–7.

[56] Art 9:102(2)(d).

[57] For further observations, see Y-M Laithier, above n 20, no 303.

He is then free, once an order for performance in kind is obtained, to settle on the best terms.

Apart from these missing provisions concerning the obstacles to enforced performance in kind, there are other missing provisions relating to the power to arrange the rules governing it.

(b) Contractual Arrangements for Enforced Performance in Kind

Contractual arrangements for enforced performance in kind can have two opposite purposes: a clause may be stipulated in order to impose that sanction (i) or, on the contrary, to exclude it (ii).

(i) Clause Imposing Enforced Performance in Kind

The possibility for the parties to stipulate enforced performance in kind in the event of non-performance of a contractual obligation is not provided for by the *Avant-projet*. Perhaps this is an oversight, for it is true that this clause has hitherto received hardly any attention from French legal theorists.[58] Perhaps it is a deliberate choice, the authors considering that the primacy accorded to enforced performance in kind is sufficient. In fact, the usefulness of a clause for enforced performance in kind is obvious in a jurisdiction where the imposition of that sanction is a matter for the court's discretion,[59] but the point of such a clause is *a priori* doubtful where the creditor is widely recognised as having the right to obtain an order requiring a defaulting debtor to furnish in kind the subject-matter of the obligation due.

Nevertheless, in spite of the frequency and clarity with which the primacy of enforced performance in kind is asserted in the *Avant-projet*, a clause imposing that sanction would not necessarily be superfluous. The point of the clause is not in the exclusion of the limits laid down in the provisions. It would be absurd to remove the obstacle of impossibility. And to remove the obstacle of the 'clearly personal character' of the promised

---

[58] On the validity, usefulness and effectiveness of a clause for enforced performance in kind in French law, see Y-M Laithier, 'La prétendue primauté de l'exécution en nature' RDC 2005, 161, 165–71. In a recent case, the Cour de cassation seems to have accepted the validity of a clause for enforced performance in kind, see Cass civ (3) 27 March 2008, Bull Joly Sociétés 2008, 852 note R Libchaber, JCP 2008 II 10147 note G Pillet, RDC 2008, 734 obs D Mazeaud, RTD civ 2008, 475 obs B Fages: 'if the parties to a unilateral promise of sale are free to agree that non-performance by the promisor of his undertaking to sell may be converted in kind by the court's declaration of the sale, it must be found that the agreements entered into by the company Foncière Costa and the company Ogic did not stipulate that non-performance by the former of its "binding promise" and "binding undertaking" to sell would be converted by any means other than that provided for by art 1142 Cc'.

[59] See, for example, in US law, § 2-716(1) UCC: 'In a contract other than a consumer contract, specific performance may be decreed if the parties have agreed to that remedy.'

subject-matter of the obligation or the obstacle of personal liberty does not appear lawful. Article 1154(3) of the *Avant-projet* provides that:

> *In no case* may performance be obtained by recourse to any coercion which compromises a debtor's personal liberty or dignity. [emphasis added]

This is a form of words that, it would seem, renders the provision imperative. Consequently the point of the clause is not to remove the legal obstacles to enforced performance in kind, but to provide guidance for judicial interpretation. Thus the clause could define very strictly what the parties understand by material impossibility capable of precluding an order for enforced performance in kind, for example, by specifying how temporary impossibility is to be treated or by restricting impossibility to the loss of an article that is unique in the market, which is itself delimited. Precision would be all the more necessary in that, in the *Avant-projet*, impossibility is the only effective ground available to the court for not ordering a sanction it considers unfair.

As the clause has been shown to be moderately useful, should it be regretted that the *Avant-projet* does not deal with it? In our opinion, this omission is not a gap. First of all, freedom of contract gives the parties power to determine the terms of the contract in accordance with the rules of public policy and accepted moral standards. A clause for enforced performance in kind does not offend against those rules. On the contrary, it is conducive to the normally expected outcome of the conclusion of the contract. Secondly, being validly stipulated, the clause acquires binding force. It produces its effects and binds the court, which can neither set it aside nor misconstrue it. To sum up, the two fundamental principles of freedom of contract and binding force establish an adequate framework

With regard to a clause which aims to exclude enforced performance in kind, the conclusion is different.

(ii) Clause Excluding Enforced Performance in Kind

The *Avant-projet* does not rule on the validity of a clause whereby the creditor undertakes not to apply for enforced performance in kind. What should be inferred from this silence?

Beyond merely mentioning freedom of contract, several arguments may be adduced in support of the legality of a clause that excludes enforced performance in kind. To begin with, it must be observed that the binding force of the contract does not mean that the creditor will obtain enforced performance in kind in the event of non-performance. As has been said, binding force only means that the contractual bond between the debtor and the creditor is legally sanctioned. Article 1134(1) is the basis for the existence of a sanction, but it does not prescribe the type. Consequently two situations must be distinguished. In the first situation the creditor

waives any sanction, in which case no contract at all can exist. The debtor does not give an undertaking for anything. In the second situation the creditor waives only one or the other of the sanctions for non-performance of the contract, in which case it retains binding force. It must then be found that in the existing law the creditor's claim is dissociated from the right to enforced performance in kind, as proved not only by certain provisions applying to a debtor in difficulty, by also by judgments awarding damages to a creditor who, however, had sought judgment *in specie* against the party with whom he contracted. Finally, as a continuation of the last observation, the lawfulness of the clause excluding enforced performance in kind can be defended on condition that the creditor can instead obtain damages[60] of an amount representing the benefit promised and not furnished. If the damages are assessed by reference to the positive interest—the 'expectation interest' in common law terms—the sanction safeguards the creditor's economic interests and, more broadly, the economic exchange function of the contract.[61]

In spite of everything, and to confine ourselves strictly to the framework of the *Avant-projet*, it does not seem necessary to recognise the validity of a waiver in advance of enforced performance in kind. Two arguments can be put forward in support of this. First, article 1382-2 of the *Avant-projet* renders ineffective a clause whereby the debtor excludes reparation for the harm caused by a failure to perform one of his essential obligations. It is true that article 1382-2 relates to contractual liability. But, reasoning by analogy, it can be argued that a clause excluding enforced performance in kind should also be ineffective, at least where it relates to an essential obligation. If the coherence of the undertaking is actually the theoretical justification for the limit laid down by article 1382-2,[62] the limit must then apply in the same way to a debtor who excludes any reparation in the event of non-performance as to a debtor who excludes enforced performance in kind in the case of non-performance.[63] Secondly, as we know, the *Avant-projet* rejects the concept of performance by equivalent. Damages are conceived as the pecuniary compensation for harm and not as a mode of performance of the contractual obligation. If this theoretical choice is respected, it is hardly convincing to argue that a clause excluding enforced performance in kind is valid provided that the creditor obtains damages. This is no longer a satisfactory alternative because damages are not the monetary equivalent of performance of the contractual obligation. And this

---

[60] For this possibility, see arts 1154(4) and 1158.

[61] See Y-M Laithier, above n 20, nos 139, 257.

[62] See, to that effect, Mazeaud, above n 6, 155–7.

[63] Compare P Delebecque, 'L'exécution forcée' RDC 2006, 99, 101: 'the fact remains . . . that the sanction of enforced performance appears inherent in the obligation and to permit the debtor to free himself from it, even at the price of a compensation payment—but only one— *conceals a fundamental contradiction*' (emphasis added).

time the objection applies, whether the unperformed obligation is essential or not.

The fact remains that because of the uncertainty of the existing law and the controversy concerning the question, it would have been a good opportunity for the *Avant-projet* to include an express provision rendering the clause ineffective so as to consolidate the primacy accorded to enforced performance in kind.

By way of conclusion, it should be stressed that the direction chosen by the *Avant-projet* in favour of performance in kind arises, more or less consciously, from our concept of contract. For French jurists, the essential element of the contract does not consist in exchange or trust ('reliance'), but in consent. However, the expression of consent is generally confused with giving one's word, which is a precept very firmly anchored in our culture—in particular, our religious culture—and requires to be respected.

7

The Enforcement of Contractual Obligations: Comparative Observations on the Notion of Performance

LUCINDA MILLER*

I. INTRODUCTION

The topic of the 'enforcement of contractual obligations' invites a number of comparative observations, not least concerning the ambiguity of the expression itself. When a common law lawyer talks about the enforcement of a contractual obligation what she is referring to is whether there is an action available in the court for breach[1] of contract. In other words, it concerns the remedies[2] available to the creditor[3] on breach. However, bearing in mind that one normally is referring to a damages award,[4] an external observer might consider it a rather strange use of language whereby enforcement of the contractual obligation generally refers, not to

---

* Thanks to Michael Bridge for discussion on an earlier draft as well as enlightening discussion with participants at the Colloque on the *Avant-projet* in Oxford, March 2007.

[1] 'Breach' has a particular common law meaning that is not synonymous with 'non-performance', or *l'inexécution*. Non-performance will often amount to a breach, since the non-performance will often not have a legal excuse. However, where there is a legal excuse, such as frustration, there is no breach and different remedies apply: see GH Treitel, *Law of Contract* (11th edn, London, Sweet & Maxwell, 2003) 759.

[2] The term 'remedies' likewise belongs to the common law and traditionally has little meaning for the civilian. For the common lawyer it refers to the category of legal responses that are available to the 'victim' of a breach of contract, and will be used in this chapter to denote such a group of recourses.

[3] A further terminological precision is that, in contrast to France, it is only in the particular instance where a monetary sum is owed that the term creditor (and the corollary term debtor) is used in English legal language to denote the contractual relationship between the parties. However, this being understood, both terms will be used in this chapter, since they conveniently capture the obligational relationship for both jurisdictions.

[4] It will be seen that specific performance is an exceptional remedy in the common law.

the enforced performance of the primary obligation, but to the extinction of that obligation and monetary compensation in its place. One might consider it more appropriate to restrict use of the term to those instances where the obligation is enforced by the court through the remedy known as specific performance. Enforcement in this context encompasses not just the coercive element that is inherent in the language used, but also the fulfilment of the precise obligation under the contract, rather than any substitutionary award of damages. Nevertheless, as will be seen below, the common law understanding of the notion reflects the limited role occupied by performance within the legal system, and a particular understanding of 'obligation', which does not become subsumed within the idea that the contract has to be performed.

In France, the notion of 'enforcement' can be translated by the term *exécution*. The same term is also used to translate 'performance'; performance and enforcement thereby come together within the same conceptual category. This is significant since, from a French perspective, the 'enforcement of contractual obligations' is associated far more with the notion of performance than under the common law. As will be seen, this is a legal system that favours performance of the obligation over and above an award of damages. Thus, the way that each jurisdiction understands the notion of 'enforcement of contractual obligations' says much about the extent to which performance is pursued within each system.

The *Avant-projet de réforme du droit des obligations et de la prescription* provides an excellent opportunity to explore the concept of performance. The form and extent to which a legal system assures performance of the obligation agreed by the parties is a concept right at the very heart of contract law and reflects a number of central principles, not least the very notion of contract and contractual obligation, whilst also having implications for the role of the judge and the limits to party agreement. The following chapter is divided into two parts. The first part focuses on the extent to which performance of the contractual obligation is pursued in the *Avant-projet*, and the modalities under which this operates. The discussion is refracted through a common law lens and thereby adopts a comparative perspective. In so doing, one gains insight into the distinct theoretical backgrounds to each jurisdiction; these fundamental differences account for the role of performance in each. The chapter then moves on to discuss the proposed modifications to the penalty clauses rule, with analysis focusing on the extent to which such changes might impact on the performance of the contractual obligation. Again, it is through comparative eyes that the discussion is conducted. It is hoped that, through this form of analysis, processes of reflexivity and mutual understanding in this area of law will be engendered, an important by-product of any reform project being undertaken in Europe today, and particularly pertinent in the light of

current developments on a common contract law within the institutions of the European Community.[5]

II. *EXÉCUTION EN NATURE* AND THE *AVANT-PROJET*

(a) Proposed Article 1154; the Primacy of *exécution en nature*

The proposed article 1154 of the *Avant-projet* is a substantial reformulation of the current article 1142 Cc and, at first blush, its championing of *exécution en nature* (enforcement in kind) seems to reflect a dramatically distinct approach towards the remedies available for breach of contract. Article 1154(1) provides:

> If possible an obligation to do is to be performed in kind.[6]

Here, the primary role that performance is to play in relation to obligations *de faire* is clearly stated; unless impossible, the obligation is to be performed. Paragraph 2 further strengthens the position of *exécution en nature* since the court can supplement the order with an *astreinte* (a monetary penalty), or some other means of constraint. This is only prevented where the subject-matter (*prestation*) of the obligation is of a clearly (*éminemment*) personal character, although little guidance is given as to when the subject-matter would fall into this category. The portrait that a painter has been commissioned to paint is an obvious candidate,[7] but it is unclear as to the extent to which the adjectival use of 'clearly' might restrict other contenders.[8] One also might wonder whether such a restriction makes a substantive contribution to the earlier concept of impossibility. Impossibility seems flexible enough to encapsulate notions of moral impossibility, within which such prestations could be embraced. In paragraph 3, concerns as to the repressive potential of *exécution en nature* are revealed in the

---

[5] The debate was kicked off with the EC Commission's Communication: Commission (EC), 'European Contract Law' (Communication) COM (2001) 398 final, 11 July 2001. Ambiguities still surround the objectives and final form of European proposals. The most recent document to be published by the Commission is Commission (EC), 'Second Progress Report on the Common Frame of Reference' COM (2007) 447 final, 25 July 2007.

[6] 'L'obligation de faire s'exécute si possible en nature.'

[7] This is an illustration provided by L Leveneur and H Lécuyer, 'Exposé des motifs: Exécution des obligations (art 1152 à 1156-2)' in *Avant-projet de réforme du droit des obligations et de la prescription: Rapport remis au garde des Sceaux* (Paris, La documentation française, 2006) 50, 52 (see below p 559). It is also a category familiar to the common law, where restrictions to the remedy of specific performance also reflect a concern with forcing performance of personal obligations. In such instances, '[q]uestions of the adequacy of damages are irrelevant to th[e] issue': *Young v Robson Rhodes* [1999] 3 All ER 524, 534 (ChD).

[8] See Y-M Laithier, 'The Enforcement of Contractual Obligations: A French Perspective', ch 6 above, for a more detailed discussion of the *Avant-projet*'s limitations to *exécution en nature*.

restriction provided by that paragraph, prohibiting the remedy where it would compromise the personal liberty and dignity of the debtor.[9]

In this way, the limits to enforced performance are found within tight parameters, thus emphasising the importance attached to the performance of obligations in French law. This is further underlined by the final paragraph, in which one finally finds reference to an alternative to performance in kind. This paragraph provides that, in the absence of *exécution en nature*, an award of damages arises. For common law sensitivities it seems a belated appearance for the remedy of damages.

A comparison with its textual predecessor, current article 1142 Cc,[10] might suggest that the *Avant-projet* heralds a considerable volte-face in policy. However, the position of *exécution en nature* in France belies the actual words of the text. As is almost too well known to repeat, the codal principle has been subject to far-reaching juristic interpretation, stretching its meaning so far from its clear wording as to render it almost meaningless.[11] The result is the 'primauté de l'*exécution en nature*'[12] in French law, rather than the award of damages, which the provision itself seems to dictate.[13] One can go as far as to describe article 1142 as an exception to the general principle of specific performance[14] And not only does judicial and doctrinal interpretation of article 1142 rebut the actual words of the text; when read beside article 1 of the 1991 law on Civil Procedures of

---

[9] The reader is again directed to the contribution of Laithier (above n 8) who analyses in greater depth art 1154(2) and (3) of the *Avant-projet*.

[10] Art 1142 provides: 'Non-performance by the debtor of any obligation to do or not to do gives rise to damages' ('Toute obligation de faire ou de ne pas faire se résout en dommages et intérêts, en cas d'inexécution de la part du débiteur').

[11] It has been considered a mere 'safety valve': W Jeandidier, 'L'exécution forcée des obligations contractuelles de faire' RTD civ 1976, 700. Further references underline the hostile reception that has been given to this provision; G Baudry-Lacantinerie and L Barde, *Droit civil: Des Obligations*, vol I (3rd edn, Paris, Recueil J-B Sirey et Journal du Palais, 1906) no 433, comment on how the legislator would have done better not to have drafted art 1142 at all; A Tunc, note under CA Lyon 30 July 1946, D 1947, 377, draws attention to the rather tiresome nature of art 1142, even considering it contrary to the very notion of obligation. He considers that it should be limited to situations where *exécution en nature* is materially or morally impossible. See also Cass civ (3) 19 February 1970, Gaz Pal 1970.1.282: 'every *creditor* can demand performance of the obligation, where such performance is possible' ('tout créancier peut exiger l'exécution de l'obligation, lorsque cette exécution est possible'). And, more recently, Cass civ (1) 9 July 2003, appeal no 00-22202, unpublished.

[12] Y-M Laithier, 'La prétendue primauté de l'*exécution en nature*' RDC 2005, 161.

[13] Although the court has, at times, refused the award of *exécution en nature*, its decision resting on the text of art 1142; Cass civ (3) 24 June 1971, Bull civ III no 411. For further discussion, see below p 146.

[14] Eg V Lonis-Apokourastos, *La primauté contemporaine du droit à l'exécution en nature* (Presses Universitaires d'Aix-Marseille, 2003); F Terré, P Simler and Y Lequette, *Droit civil: les obligations* (9th edn, Paris, Dalloz, 2005) no 1017 state that 'the judge has gradually placed within parenthesis the terms of article 1142 so that the right to *exécution forcée* has become the guiding principle'. Also see comments by J Mestre and B Fages in RTD civ 2003, 709 who maintain that: 'nowadays, the path to *exécution forcée* is wide open to the courts, despite the restrictive terms of article 1142 Code Civil'.

Enforcement[15] it is nigh on impossible to assert that article 1142 states the French position towards *exécution en nature*.[16]

Thus, although reflecting a 'radical modification'[17] of the actual wording of the text, the substantive effect of proposed article 1154 is less innovative than the textual rewording suggests, and can instead be viewed as providing a more transparent articulation of the position of performance in the French legal landscape. For this it should be welcomed.

From a common law perspective, a number of observations can be made. First, the proposed article maintains the much-documented distinction between England and France in the area of contractual remedies for non-performance. As is well documented, the equitable remedy of specific performance in England is an exceptional remedy, with damages holding primary position. Despite some indication that the remedy was to receive more favourable treatment by the courts,[18] more recent case-law has affirmed the traditional resistance to its award.[19] Interestingly, its position seems threatened even within the category where traditionally specific performance has been routinely awarded. A Canadian common law case has raised doubts about the award in a contract for the sale of an interest in land[20] with the decision being seen favourably by some English commentators.[21] In light of the anachronistic separate treatment of land contracts,[22] it is possible that the Canadian approach will take root in England, thus limiting the award even further.

But the *Avant-projet* does not simply affirm the Anglo-French divergent positions. The textual reformulation is significant in the respect that it departs even further from the English position by granting the creditor more powers than previously available to enforce performance, should she

---

[15] Art 1 of Loi no 91-650 du 9 juillet 1991 portant réforme des procédures civiles d'exécution, JO 14 July 1991, provides that 'every creditor can, in accordance with the conditions set out by the law, compel the defaulting debtor to perform the obligations that are owed to him' ('tout créancier peut, dans les conditions prévues par la loi, contraindre son débiteur défaillant à exécuter ses obligations à son égard'). This 1991 law formally recognises the *astreinte* as a penalty for disobedience of a court order (Section VI arts 33–37).

[16] See Leveneur and Lécuyer, above n 7, 51 (see below p 557).

[17] *Ibid.*

[18] Eg *Beswick v Beswick* [1968] 1 AC 58 (HL).

[19] Eg *Co-operative Insurance Society v Argyll Stores (Holdings) Ltd* [1998] AC 1 (HL).

[20] *Semelhago v Paramadevan* [1996] 2 SCR 415 (Supreme Court of Canada). Here, the assumption that every piece of real estate was unique was explicitly rejected by the court. The court held that evidence would need to be provided in order to show that the piece of land could not be substituted by any other, and therefore that damages was inadequate. This decision goes against the almost entrenched rule that the purchaser of an interest in land is entitled to get the very parcel he bargained for. Investigation into whether damages are (in)adequate have been traditionally foreclosed; see R Sharpe, *Injunctions and Specific Performance* (Toronto, Canada Law Book Ltd, 1983) para 614.

[21] Eg D Harris, D Campbell and R Halson, *Remedies in Contract & Tort* (London, Butterworths, 2002) 176.

[22] Modern day housing can commonly comprise of identical lots, often purchased purely for their investment potential, making it difficult to sustain the argument that the uniqueness of land demands specific performance of the contract of sale.

so wish. Although the text refrains from the formulation of 'droit à . . .'[23] nevertheless its substantive effect seems indeed to furnish the creditor with a *right* to demand *exécution en nature*. The only limitations to this right come within the instances provided for by the proposed provision, as discussed above. The limitations appear far more restrictive than under the Code civil, where the court has been known on several occasions to refuse the award in those situations falling outside the categories in proposed article 1154. A detailed analysis by Laithier[24] demonstrates that there have been many instances where the Cour de cassation has refused the creditor's request for *exécution en nature*, and awarded damages in its place, thus challenging the 'myth' that article 1142 Cc has been treated as an exception, and *exécution en nature* a 'principle'.[25] Such situations are not confined to those instances concerning personal obligations, or to instances where the situation could be considered as outside the domain of *exécution en nature* and instead in that of *réparation en nature*.[26] Furthermore, it seems unlikely that notions such as *bonne foi* (good faith) or *abus de droit* (abuse of right) can now be used to curtail the creditor's choice. Under the Code civil such tools can, in theory,[27] act as a useful brake on the award in certain circumstances. It might well be equitable to consider the interests of the debtor, eg where the creditor pursues specific performance of the contract motivated by bad faith, or where the economic impact of the award might be economically disastrous to the debtor. However, the reformulation of article 1142 means a change in emphasis that will increase the possibility for *exécution en nature*, and decrease the possibility to circumvent the award. In other words, any notion that *exécution en nature* is a discretionary remedy seems to have been comprehensively abandoned. This change is crucial for the way that it alters the balance of powers between the judge and the parties—away from the court and in favour of

---

[23] The notes to proposed art 1154 state that the impersonal form was preferred to the 'droit à . . .' formula. Although the drafters are not explicit as to the rationale for such an objective formula, the decision not to grant the creditor a *subjective* right to performance has been welcomed. The formula avoids pitting the debtor's *subjective* fundamental rights to liberty and dignity against the creditor's subjective right to performance: M Faure-Abbad, 'La présentation de l'inexécution contractuelle dans l'avant-projet Catala' D 2007 Chron 165.

[24] Y-M Laithier, *Étude comparative des sanctions de l'inexécution du contrat* (Paris LGDJ, 2004) nos 28, 61.

[25] Although the more nuanced account by Laither might well need to be revised in the light of a recent, unambiguous decision by the Cour de cassation holding, in an *attendu de principe*, that the creditor can 'force' the debtor to perform where possible, thereby quashing the decision of the Court of Appeal of Paris which had adopted a more faithful interpretation of art 1142 and awarded damages; O Gout note under Cass civ (1) 16 January 2007, D 2007, 1119.

[26] For a discussion on the distinction between *l'exécution en nature* and *réparation en nature* see Laithier, above n 24, nos 49–64.

[27] Although little used in practice: G Viney and P Jourdain, *Traité de droit civil: Les conditions de la responsabilité* (2nd edn, Paris, LGDJ, 1998) nos 20–21 and cases cited in no 61. Contrast the use of the doctrine of abuse of rights in Québec: R Jukier, '*Banque Nationale du Canada v Houle* (SCC): Implications of an Expanded Doctrine of Abuse of Rights in Civilian Contract Law' (1992) 37 McGill LJ 221.

the creditor[28] and thereby signals the import of the modifications proposed.

With this in mind, one might conclude that English law takes a far more robust and pragmatic attitude. The wide discretionary nature of specific performance in England gives the court far greater flexibility to balance a number of different considerations. The House of Lords decision of *Co-operative Insurance v Argyll*[29] exemplifies the approach. Here the court considered relevant the debtor's behaviour, the commercial position (and therefore bargaining power) of each party, whether the award would be used as a bargaining chip, the economic impact of the award (either on the particular debtor, or on wider societal economic interests) and, more generally, the difficulties in supervising the award satisfactorily, as well as the adequacy of the award in comparison to damages. Such breadth of discretion seems driven from valid consideration by the *Avant-projet*.

From a comparative perspective it is also interesting to note that the concerns raised in *Co-operative Insurance* mirror those raised by another civilian jurisdiction, Québec, where the High Court was faced with facts almost identical to the House of Lords.[30] Article 1601 of the Civil Code of Québec in essence sets out specific performance as a right for the creditor but qualifies this to 'cases which admit of it'. This allows the court to assess each request on its merits, and provides powers of discretion reminiscent of those under English law. This illustration from Québec is another reminder of the unusual position of the *Avant-projet*, and marks it out from other civilian, as well as common law, jurisdictions.[31]

And the distinct approach taken by the *Avant-projet* is highlighted even further if one briefly turns to the Principles of European Contract Law (PECL). Article 9:102(1) PECL elevates specific performance into a right,[32] but then in paragraph 2 sets out the limitations to that right.[33] Of course, in a project such as the PECL, which houses under the one regulatory roof what is argued to be the best solutions from both the common and civil law approaches to contract law, one detects more than a glimmer of

---

[28] J Rochfeld, 'Remarques sur les propositions relatives à l'exécution et à l'inexécution du contrat: la subjectivation du droit de l'exécution' RDC 2006, 113.

[29] Above n 19.

[30] *Construction Belcourt Ltée v Golden Griddle Pancake House Limited* [1988] RJQ 716 (CS Que). The conclusion reached, however, in the Québec decision was the inverse to that in England; the court allowed the award of specific performance.

[31] Although the Québec legal system is of course influenced by its geographical proximity to the Canadian common law and, whilst resting on French law for its substantive rules, follows the style of legal reasoning more familiar to a common law jurisdiction. The discursive style of judgment does tend to encourage greater, or more explicit, consideration of the merits of specific performance in each case.

[32] The text provides: 'The aggrieved party is entitled to specific performance of an obligation other than one to pay money, including the remedying of a defective performance'.

[33] Art 9:102(1) and (2) PECL show how granting the creditor a *droit subjective* to *exécution en nature* can be compatible with limitations to that right which are concerned with the debtor's *droits subjectives*; see above p 146.

compromise between the two legal families. This is evident from the exceptions to the right to specific performance, which align themselves far more closely to the English position: exceptions that rest on, for example, a consideration of the effort or expense that the debtor would be subjected to—article 9:102(2)(b)—and whether it is reasonable for the creditor to obtain performance from another source—article 9:102(2)(d). These are clearly evocative of common law limitations to the award. Whilst recognising the common law bias of this author, it does nevertheless seem that these considerations allow a more pragmatic response to breach, allowing the court to make a balanced appraisal of both creditor and debtor interests. One might wonder as to the extent to which the more burdensome case load at the Cour de cassation, in comparison to the House of Lords, has had a part to play in the minimisation of discretion within the French system.[34]

Of course, one could argue that the common law court has the scales unevenly balanced with the interests of the debtor too often trumping those of the creditor.[35] The House of Lords decision of *Cooperative Insurance v Argyll*[36] again serves as example. But one might wonder whether in distancing itself from both the common law and the PECL, the *Avant-projet* has upset the balance too far in the opposite direction. If a principal objective of the *Avant-projet* is for a modernised French law of obligations to be once more influential across the world and to act as a possible lodestar for any future common European contract law,[37] whatever the final nature of the European project, then the unique stance will have to be heavily defended and withstand substantial resistance from the common law. Linked to such resistance will undoubtedly come the charge that the French position ignores the economically inefficient results that such an approach may generate.[38] It also raises questions as to how far the right to *exécution en nature* under the proposed reform is an accurate reflection of some of the purported guiding principles articulated within the reform itself–principles such as *justice contractuelle*, *esprit de solidarité* and a greater extension of *bonne foi*.[39]

---

[34] The average caseload each year in the Cour de cassation reaches a figure of more than 20,000; A Lacabarats, 'Chronique de la Cour de cassation' D 2007 Chron 889.

[35] One sometimes needs to remind oneself that, after all, the debtor is in breach of an obligation.

[36] Above n 19.

[37] Aspirations for the reform to convert the Code civil into 'an exportable model' and 'a passport allowing the French model to spread beyond our frontiers' have been articulated by D Mazeaud, 'Observations conclusives' RDC 2006, 177, 179. See also D Mazeaud, 'Les conventions portant sur la réparation' RDC 2007, 149, 151, maintaining that 'there is an absolute urgency to reform our Code in a manner that enables the French law of obligations to carry weight in the elaboration of the law of future generations'.

[38] The vigour with which *exécution en nature* has been pursued, despite the economic illogic to the award is demonstrated by Cass civ (3) 3 April 1996, Bull civ III no 91.

[39] P Catala, 'Présentation générale de l'avant-projet' in *Avant-projet de réforme du droit des*

(b) *Exécution en nature* and (Non)-Performance

It is to be welcomed that the *Avant-projet* has chosen to unite, under a considerably modified article 1184 Cc (proposed article 1158), the remedial choices of the creditor. This is contained in a tripartite arrangement (enforced performance, termination and damages) in place of the previously bipartite one that made no mention of damages. Proposed article 1158 is contained within Section 5, under the rubric of 'Non-Performance of Obligations and Termination of the Contract'. Although, from the viewpoint of a common lawyer, structural coherence and systematisation is not something that causes much anxiety, it nevertheless seems sensible to bring together the creditor's options (*moyens*) when faced with a non-performing debtor. One feels in comfortable remedies terrain. Whilst there may be differing opinions amongst common lawyers as to the *substantive* content of the law of remedies, the term is nevertheless universally understood as the bundle of legal (or self-help) actions[40] available to the creditor, who wishes to take measures in response to the debtor's non-performance of his contractual obligation.[41] The law of remedies is perceived in the common law system as a fairly coherent, systematic set of principles, suitable for self-standing scholarly attention, that are presented in a more or less uniform manner by the main textbook writers.[42] In this respect, therefore, article 1158 might be welcomed.[43] However, once united under article 1158, Section 5 then proceeds to deal only with the modalities for termination of the contract, and one finds, on the one hand, damages parachuted into the section on 'Civil Liability' and, on the other hand, *exécution en nature* nesting in Section 4, somewhat strangely under the heading of 'Performance of Obligations'.[44] The common lawyer is immediately struck by the choice of where to house this proposed principle of *exécution en nature* and it is to this that we now turn.

An initial comment arising from the inclusion of *exécution en nature* within Section 4 is that it is difficult for the common lawyer to conceive of specific performance in any meaningful context outside that of *breach*. Specific performance is a remedy, and hence necessarily supposes a breach of the contractual obligation. Thus, the exclusion of specific performance

---

obligations et de la prescription: Rapport remis au garde des Sceaux (Paris, La documentation française, 2006) 11, 12, 15 (see below pp 467, 475); G Cornu, 'Introduction' in *ibid*, 19, 20 (see below pp 481–3).

[40] In the ordinary, non-legal, sense of the word.

[41] See Harris et al, above n 21, 3.

[42] Most writers include remedies as the final chapter(s) in their works, at the end of a 'formation–performance–breach–remedies' continuum: eg Treitel, above n 1; MP Furmston, *Cheshire, Fifoot & Furmston's Law of Contract* (15th edn, Oxford University Press, 2007).

[43] As well as celebrated for putting an end to the peculiar foundations on which current parameters of contractual termination rest—the resolutory condition.

[44] Art 1158 does not even cross-reference to the relevant provisions on damages, or performance.

from the following Section that deals with *non-performance* is immediately striking. Indeed, on examination of the substance of the provisions within Section 4, any common law confusion seems justified since there seems little, if anything, contained within articles 1154 to 1154-2 of the *Avant-projet* that is not linked directly to the non-performance of the obligation.

The puzzled common lawyer is not alone. The drafting has been criticised within French circles where similar bewilderment as to the inconsistency of conceiving of *exécution en nature*, without situating it in the prior context of a non-performance by the debtor, has been recently articulated. The lament by Faure-Abbad shares a common law wavelength; 'the *Avant-projet* creates a Section on performance . . . only to deal exclusively with non-performance'.[45] And the decision creates a disjuncture between French law and the PECL, which incorporates the remedy of specific performance within Chapter 9, a chapter dedicated to non-performance.

But the structure of the *Avant-projet* seems indicative of the more central role that performance plays in French law, and offers an insight into a fundamental difference between civilian and common law systems. In the common law, although the notion of performance is at the heart of the contractual obligation,[46] it nevertheless becomes almost entirely subsumed within the notion of *non*-performance. This is not solely because remedies law played a large part in the development of the common law.[47] It is also largely due to the way that the common law develops through the accretion of case-law. In a system that does not formulate abstract, predetermined propositional statements of law, set out systematically in a code, but instead develops through the happenstance of litigation, questions concerning performance only become salient when parties are determining whether the action by the debtor is of the kind that constitutes breach—and thus whether a remedy is triggered. It thus only receives attention in the context of establishing the extent of non-performance. As a consequence, even when performance is recognised as an important 'interest',[48] either by the court or by academic commentary, it is almost entirely within the context of the appropriate remedial response that any discussion takes place.

In contrast, the new Section on 'Performance' in the *Avant-projet* reflects a more developed and sophisticated understanding of performance and signals its centrality within French law. Ensuring the performance of contractual obligations is a principle that forms a fundamental plank of the legal system, and does not just arouse theoretical interest in the context of

---

[45] M Faure-Abbad, above n 23, 168.

[46] As Friedmann reminds, '[t]he essence of contract is performance. Contracts are made in order to be performed. This is usually the one and only ground for their formation': D Friedmann, 'The Performance Interest in Contract Damages' (1995) 111 LQR 628, 629.

[47] The medieval writ system framed causes of action primarily in relation to the remedies that were being sought: D Ibbetson, *A Historical Introduction to the Law of Obligations* (Oxford University Press, 1999) ch 1.

[48] See discussion below p 152.

l'inexécution. In brief, the commitment to the principle stems from such things as philosophical and moral concerns with preserving the contractual obligation and *la parole donnée*;[49] alignment of *la force obligatoire*[50] with the principle that, as binding, the obligation must be enforced;[51] and the desire to minimise judicial intervention into the parties' agreement.[52]

Commitment to the principle also reflects the civilian understanding of obligation as a *lien* that unites both parties,[53] and this furthers the principle that preservation, rather than rupture, of the *lien*, or obligation, is an objective to pursue. The etymological root of the Latin word *obligatio*, which denotes a tying together (*ligare*) of bonds between the obligor and the obligee, is also significant to our understanding of performance in French law. It symbolises an essentially bilateral relationship, significant when viewed from either side of the contractual relationship. For the debtor, the obligation represents the duty to perform and, for the creditor, it denotes the right to receive performance. This 'double-sided' nature of obligation links the parties in the contractual relationship and, in practice, manifests itself in the ways that performance of the contract is, at all times, a goal to be furthered. For French law, where the obligor does not perform, the response of the law is not to encourage the rupture of the relationship but, instead, to provide a legal framework within which performance is encouraged. In conclusion, although *exécution en nature* arises in the context of non-performance, such performance that is ordered by the court can nevertheless be conceptually aligned with a party's spontaneous, or voluntary, performance in France.[54] Both are performed with the assistance

---

[49] G Rouhette, *Contribution à l'étude critique de la notion de contrat* (doctoral thesis, Paris, 1965) cited in Laithier, above n 24, nos 41, 63.

[50] The notion that contracts are binding, as encapsulated by art 1134(1) Cc, which provides that contracts 'which are lawfully concluded hold the place of the law itself for those who have made them' ('Les conventions légalement formées tiennent lieu de loi à ceux qui les ont faites').

[51] The notion of *force obligatoire* acts as explanatory tool for why *exécution en nature* is logically the primary remedy. Under this dominant reasoning, the fact that the contract is legally binding has relevance to the sanction that should be pronounced and, more specifically, that the appropriate remedy be *exécution en nature* since this ensures 'the utmost respect for the obligation': O Gout, above n 25, no 8. The two principles are said to be tied by 'un lien irréductible': D Mazeaud, 'Exécution forcée de l'obligation contractuelle de faire' RDC 2005, 323. Also, *exécution en nature* is 'l'effet le plus direct du principe de la force obligatoire': G Viney, 'Exécution de l'obligation, faculté de remplacement et *réparation en nature* en droit français' in M Fontaine and G Viney (eds), *Les sanctions de l'inexécution des obligations contractuelles, Etudes de droit comparé* (Bruylant LGDJ, 2001) 167, 182. A very recent decision of the Cour de cassation underlines this relationship between the two principles, the court basing its decision on the *double visa* of arts 1134 and 1142: see O Gout, above n 25. *Contra* Laithier who find the assimilation of contractual norm with sanction 'a most serious confusion'; see above n 12.

[52] Since the parties have agreed to perform, then to award another remedy would be contrary to *la volonté des parties*: Laithier, above n 12.

[53] 'The obligation is the legal bond that ties the creditor to the debtor' ('L'obligation est le lien de droit unissant le créancier au débiteur'): P Malaurie, L Aynès and P Stoffel-Munck, *Les Obligations* (2nd edn, Paris, Defrénois, 2005) no 1.

[54] One is reminded of how *exécution* captures a double meaning in English: performance *and* enforcement. See above p 142.

of the debtor and both preserve the contractual relationship between the parties. It is just the degree of coercion that differs. What is crucial to the French legal system is fulfilment of the contractual obligation—*la mise en force du contrat*.[55] With this in mind, the housing of article 1154 of the *Avant-projet* seems far less incongruous.

(c) Protection of the 'Performance Interest'

The incorporation of *exécution en nature* within Section 4, as opposed to subsequent Section 5 which deals with non-performance, also results in the separation of two remedies that the common lawyer tends to conceptualise only in conjunction with each other. A further comparative response might therefore be to bemoan the wasted opportunity for a 'coherent presentation' of remedies law that the *Avant-projet* offered to the drafters, and which has been encouraged amongst some French scholars.[56]

It is true that, in some respects, the category of remedies offers a useful prism through which to examine the recourses available to the creditor on breach. But one should be wary of ignoring the detrimental consequences that flow from a supposedly 'coherent' category of remedies.[57] One such consequence, and one that emphasises the relatively little weight given to the notion of performance in the common law, is that specific performance has little independence as a remedy. Instead, it holds a subsidiary position in relation to the award of damages, this being reflected in the rule that, outside certain contracts,[58] it is only awarded where damages are considered inadequate—which is rarely the case. The subsidiary position has both historical roots,[59] as well as a more modern-day buttressing—the latter encompassing the particular economic tendencies underlying English

---

[55] N Molfessis, 'Force obligatoire et exécution: un droit à l'*exécution en nature*?' RDC 2005, 37. Here, *exécution en nature* is not a sanction but *la mise en force du contrat* since the view is taken that you cannot punish someone for doing what they engaged to do.

[56] D Tallon, 'L'inexécution du contrat: pour une autre présentation' RTD civ 1994, 223. Tallon supports such a structure as a way for making French law more accessible to foreign jurists.

[57] Although Laithier considers that 'le systématisation cohérente et claire des "*remedies*" est un mythe': Laithier, above n 24, no 4.

[58] The paradigmatic, but somewhat anachronistic, example being the contract of the sale of an interest in land, see above p 145.

[59] Namely the division between common law and equitable jurisdictions. Despite the fusion of the courts in the 1873 and 1875 legislation, this historical legacy has heavily influenced the articulation of modern law principles. As a consequence, the bifurcation of jurisdictions, if no longer of an institutional nature, has nevertheless left an indelible mark on the common law mentality. In addition, the formulation of contractual principles took shape within the strictures of a particular type of contractual dispute. Since litigation remained the privilege of those with financial means, the courts primarily found themselves deciding issues pertinent to commercial parties. This commercial context of nineteenth-century embryonic contract law was instrumental in placing damages at the helm of the remedial structure.

law reasoning[60] which support the award of damages over that of specific performance. And, although contract cannot be reduced to solely economic significance, the common law notion of contract is less concerned with the obligational relationship between the parties to the contract than with the contract itself.[61] This more 'objectivised' contract is viewed as something of economic value—a bargain. On default by the debtor, there seems little justification to keep the parties 'yoked'[62] together, and damages, rather than specific performance, are seen as the remedy more befitting economic theory. But one might regret the way that assimilation of both remedies within the one theoretical framework has discouraged analysis of the particular nature and objective that each remedy seeks to promote; one might do well to question why the adequacy of one should be of any relevance to the availability of the other. In so doing, greater consideration might be given to the notion and role of performance in English law.

It seems that it is the conceptual category of 'remedies' that is largely responsible for creating a false unity out of different remedies that serve quite different aims. A unitary concept of remedies unites under the one term the very distinct 'interests' that each remedy seeks to protect. Within the remedies grouping is packed an assorted bunch of legal responses to non-performance. This somewhat sloppy categorisation is an obstacle to true analysis.[63] In this way, the separate treatment of damages and specific performance in the *Avant-projet* is valuable to the common lawyer since it encourages one to rethink the catch-all category of remedies and the different interests that each remedy seeks to protect.

In more recent years questions have indeed been raised within common law circles as to the appropriateness of assessing specific performance in relation to the (in)adequacy of damages. The underlying objective seems to be a desire to confront the fundamental question of how committed English law is to the notion that contracts entail a right to performance.[64] Whilst this scholarship has certainly raised the theoretical profile of performance in the common law, it will be seen that the conceptual framework in

---

[60] Which largely explains why the English assessment of 'adequacy' of damages, in relation to specific performance, more often than not rests simply on whether an accurate assessment of damages is possible, and thus on a pragmatic concern to avoid over, or under, compensation, rather than philosophical concerns about performing obligations. In this respect, the English rules on specific performance are often justified as being an economically efficient way of resolving the problem of the impossibility of calculating the expectation loss of the creditor. It seems that a feature of English law is the way that it lends itself to *ex post facto* generalisation and 'capture' by special interest groups such as economists.

[61] The conception of *obligation* is not 'double-sided' (as in France, see above p 151) but instead perceived solely from the viewpoint of the debtor. This emphasises the duty to perform and not the accompanying right of the creditor to receive performance.

[62] See dicta of Lord Hoffmann in *Co-operative Insurance*, above n 19, 16.

[63] P Birks, 'Rights, Wrongs, and Remedies' (2000) 20 OJLS 1 forcefully criticised the terminology of remedies and he showed how the notion of 'remedies' is prone to *destabilise* proper analysis.

[64] Eg C Webb, 'Performance and Compensation: An Analysis of Contract Damages and Contractual Obligation' (2006) 26 OJLS 41.

which this discussion takes place is nevertheless of a distinctly common law flavour; the problem is approached from the perspective of remedies, and, more specifically, that of the remedy of damages. As will be seen, this standpoint reflects the quite distinctive understanding of performance in English law, in comparison to that which has inspired the final form of the *Avant-projet*.

The discussion in England has largely centred on the extent to which English law protects what is known as the 'performance interest'.[65] Such 'performance interest' is said to arise at the time that the contract is formed and can be viewed as the creditor's *primary* right. Importantly, it is distinguished from her *secondary* right that arises, not at the time of conclusion of the contract, but at the moment of breach. This secondary right is not to have the contract performed, but rather, not to be left worse off as a result of the breach. In this way, the argument aims to illustrate how the two rights are conceptually quite distinct in nature and fulfil very different goals. As such, it would therefore seem meaningless to assess the appropriateness of specific performance in relation to whether damages are adequate or not. Each right instead demands a different form of protection. And it is cogently argued that specific remedies[66] best protect the interest in performance, whilst compensatory damages best protect the right not to be left worse off as a result of the breach.

If we follow this line of reasoning, one might add that specific remedies, unlike compensatory damages, do not *necessarily* depend on a breach of contract.[67] In practice, such claims will only be brought if the debtor has already breached the contract, or if it is anticipated that she will breach. But the creditor is asserting a right 'which in no way rests on the commission of any breach'.[68] It is a right that existed, not from the time of breach, but from the time that the contract was concluded. Thus, to return briefly to the *Avant-projet*, from the English perspective just outlined one could analyse Section 4 as recognition of the performance interest that has arisen at the time the contract was formed. The separate treatment of *exécution en nature*, outside of the context of *l'inexécution*, is logical if one remembers that one is asserting a right that does not depend on the debtor's non-performance. French law could thus be said to take the performance interest seriously.

Furthermore, if one agrees that primary and secondary rights are distinct, one must also accept that it is inappropriate to regard the secondary right as simply an alternative means of enforcing the primary interest,[69] or 'perfor-

---

65 The language of contractual 'interests', although familiar within Germany, only became common currency in the common law following publication of the influential article by L Fuller and W Perdue, 'The Reliance Interest in Contract Damages' (1936) 46 Yale LJ 52.
66 Namely, specific performance, injunctions and the action in debt.
67 Webb, above n 64, 50.
68 *Ibid*.
69 *Ibid*, 43.

mance interest'. In other words, compensatory damages should not be seen as protecting the interest in performance by means of a monetary equivalent for performance.[70] They are *not a substitute for performance*; they rather *compensate* for non-performance. Although the interest in having the contract performed has been considered the 'core of contract law',[71] as has been seen, traditional remedies law rules in England favour the award of compensatory damages, rather than the award of specific performance. Under this line of reasoning, therefore, one can argue that English law protects not the performance interest, but the interest in not being left worse off as a result of the breach.

For those who recognise that the performance interest is worthy of protection a problem arises (for both scholars and the courts) as to how best this is to be achieved. Rather than any noticeable advocates for an extension in the award of specific performance, common law attention has instead turned to ways in which a monetary award can better reflect the right that the claimant has to performance, as opposed to an award in compensation.[72] This creates difficulties in finding an appropriate way to measure this right to performance in monetary terms,[73] particularly if the distinction between primary and secondary right is to be upheld. The cost-of-cure assessment is generally deemed as the most appropriate way of reflecting performance in monetary terms. In other words, a sum of money for the cost of having the obligation fulfilled by a third party. However, this

[70] Likewise, some scholarship in France has fused contractual 'interests', straitjacketing performance and damages within the same theoretical structure. However, whereas within the English system the subsidiary position of specific performance forces conceptualisation of this remedy within a damages blueprint, in France it has been damages that have been analysed with a performance lens. In so doing, however, both systems have viewed damages as a substitute performance, or *exécution par équivalent*. For French *jurisprudence* see Cass soc 4 December 2002, RDC 2003, 53 obs P Stoffel-Munck, JCP 2002 I 186 obs G Viney, RTD civ 2002, 321 obs P-Y Gautier. The structural separation of damages from performance, and its conception as *réparation* in the *Avant-projet* makes a clear stand against this procrustean fit of damages within performance.

[71] Friedmann, above n 46, 629. See also B Coote, 'The Performance Interest, *Panatown*, and the Problem of Loss' (2001) 117 LQR 81, 82, who remarks that 'what distinguishes an effective contractual promise from any other is that it is intended to, and does in fact, confer on the promisee an enforceable legal right to have the promise performed'.

[72] In practice, the problem of protecting the performance interest usually arises in the context of third party contracts where a contracting party is trying to claim damages for a loss that has not been suffered by herself, but by a third party, eg *Linden Gardens Trust Ltd v Lenesta Sludge Disposals Ltd* [1994] 1 AC 85 (HL); *The Albazero* [1977] AC 774 (HL); *Alfred McAlpine Construction Ltd v Panatown Ltd* [2001] 1 AC 518 (HL). Since under English law a claim for anything more than nominal damages needs proof of loss, the issue is generally considered as to whether the claimant has suffered loss herself, or whether she can claim for the third party's loss. Thus the question as to whether the contractual party has a right to a monetary award by the very fact of non-performance, tends to get caught up in questions of loss, rather than any discussion on whether performance should be worthy of protection regardless of whether any loss has been suffered. It seems that if one is to accept the argument underlined above, then the notion of loss is redundant.

[73] Or, what has been described, rather awkwardly, as the 'performance interest damages award'; Webb, above n 64, 57.

raises two important points.[74] First, the rule that damages are designed to make the creditor no worse off after breach does not seem to mark a clear separation between primary and secondary rights, since surely the creditor is no worse off after breach if she can still expect the full economic equivalent of primary performance?[75] It seems that by suggesting that an appropriate measure of 'damages'[76] can be found to reflect the creditor's performance interest, the distinction between primary and secondary rights becomes susceptible to collapse.

Secondly, protecting the performance interest by way of a cost-of-cure sum of money begs a further question as to how performance by a third party can represent *the* performance agreed under the original contract. One author deals with this problem by finding implicit terms within the original contract; should a party not perform, then she is under an obligation under the contract to provide the claimant with the means to obtain this end product from a third party.[77] Not only does this seem to reconceptualise the notion of performance into the benefit of the end product, but it also seems an unnecessarily tortuous construction. A more convincing analysis of this remedy is the one traditionally taken; it is an action for termination of the principal contract and a claim for compensatory damages from the original contracting party. Under the 'duty'[78] of mitigation, the creditor would be obliged to find a new contractual party so as to minimise damages and, from the shadow of the first contract, a second, new, contract is formed with another contractual party.

Analysis of French law and of the *Avant-projet* raises similar difficulties with third party performance. The problem is demonstrated by examination of proposed article 1154-2, which also comes within Section 4 on Performance and indeed might be considered a particularly unusual candidate for this section. The provision brings together current articles 1143 and 1144 Cc—authorising the creditor to have the obligation performed by another

[74] Unfortunately, the confines of this chapter only allow a brief treatment of these points.

[75] It might be useful at this point to note that under the terminology introduced by Fuller and Perdue, above n 65, damages are viewed as protecting what is known as the 'expectation interest' which is traditionally seen as synonymous with the 'performance interest'. For a criticism of this inappropriate terminology see Friedmann, above n 46, 632. The debate seems to illustrate the problem as to how to distinguish between primary and secondary rights, when the former is being protected through a monetary award.

[76] Using the term 'damages' as a way to describe a monetary award that reflects the equivalent of performance, rather than compensation for non-performance, is not entirely satisfactory since it alludes to a compensatory element to the award.

[77] Webb, above n 64, 59.

[78] 'Duty' is misleading terminology since the creditor is not subject to any liability should he not so mitigate. Treitel, above n 1, 979; also M Bridge, 'Mitigation of Damages in Contract and the Meaning of Avoidable Loss' (1989) LQR 398, 399; and *Sotiros Shipping Inc and Aeco Maritime SA v Sameiet Solholt ('The Solholt')* [1983] 1 Lloyd's Rep 605, 608 (CA). It instead acts more as a 'disabling' device, preventing him from recovering those losses that he could have avoided, CJ Goetz and RE Scott, 'The Mitigation Principle: Toward a General Theory of Contractual Obligation' (1983) 69 Virginia Law Review 967.

person,[79] or to destroy anything done in contravention of a negative obligation. The cost of this is met by the debtor who may be ordered to pay the necessary sum in advance. It is clear that proposed article 1154-2 is deemed as 'one type' of a performance in kind.[80] In a similar fashion to the cost-of-cure award in England, this conceptualisation is problematic for the notion that the obligation under a contract between A and B is converted by the court into an obligation between A and C. This conflicts with the conception of *exécution en nature* as a *mise en force du contrat*. It is instead a *mise en force* of another contract with a different contractual party. As such, whilst it was argued above[81] that *exécution en nature* could be conceptually aligned with a voluntary performance by the debtor, it is difficult to extend the argument to the action encapsulated by article 1154-2. Hence, not only does it seem out of place in the new Section 4 concerning performance, but on closer examination the provision seems to be reformulating the essence of performance in much the same way that the cost-of-cure damages approach does in England—from fulfilment of the contractual obligation, to perception as the benefit of the *end product* of the contractual obligation.[82]

A further point relating to proposed article 1154-2 concerns the nature of the judicial discretion under this provision. If article 1154 of the *Avant-projet* establishes a 'right' to performance, as it seems to do, thus circumventing judicial powers of discretion to order damages (in favour of creditor choice), the proposed article 1154-2 in contrast is clearly facultative; the court *can* authorise the creditor to have the obligation performed by another party. However, it is unclear as to the nature of the considerations under which this power is to be exercised. It is possible that the inclusion of article 1154-2 within the provision on *performance* will encourage an approach which limits judicial discretion and favours the position of the creditor.

And once more French law stands apart from the PECL. In the section concerned with damages and interest, article 9:506 deals with what is termed a 'substitute transaction'. The very subtitle of the provision reflects

---

[79] Known as *remplacement par autrui*.

[80] Leveneur and Lécuyer, above n 7, 52. Its position within Section 4 itself affirms that art 1154-2 of the *Avant-projet* is to be embraced as a true instance of performance but the stance is further clarified in the notes to proposed art 1369, which distinguish arts 1143 and 1144 Cc from *réparation en nature* 'since articles 1143 and 1144 of the present Civil Code concern performance'.

[81] See above p 151–2.

[82] The provision also sits awkwardly alongside the principle of the sanctity of contract, since it allows the court to convert the debtor's obligation *de faire* into that of paying a sum of money, which, for many authors, is an obligation *de donner*; B Starck, H Roland and L Boyer, *Les Obligations: Contrat* (6th edn, Paris, Litec, 1997) nos 1625–6. The question as to whether the obligation to pay a debt of money constitutes one of *de faire* or *de donner* is discussed in Terré et al, above n 14, no 1009.

the common law position of the extinction of the original obligation and a new 'substitute' transaction being agreed.[83]

III. PENALTY CLAUSES AND PERFORMANCE

A discussion on the performance of contractual obligations also raises significant questions related to the penalty clause rules. For this reason the proposals of the *Avant-projet* in relation to this legal mechanism are particularly worthy of note.

Under English law, it is a well-known fact that the penalty clause is treated with hostility. Resistance towards the mechanism stems principally from allegiance to the compensatory principle of damages. As Lord Roskill states:

> Perhaps the main purpose of the law relating to penalty clauses is to prevent a plaintiff recovering a sum of money in respect of a breach of contract committed by a defendant which bears little or no relationship to the loss actually suffered by the plaintiff as a result of the breach by the defendant.[84]

It is considered that the creditor is sufficiently compensated by being indemnified for his actual loss, and thus clauses that are in the nature of a threat held over the other party *in terrorem*—as a security that the contract will be performed—have little place in the common law. They are thus disregarded.[85]

This does not mean that all clauses that set out in advance the sum which shall be payable by way of damages in event of breach are considered negatively. The liquidated damages clause, as distinguished from the penalty clause, is considered a *genuine pre-estimate of loss*—and deemed an extremely useful mechanism for allowing the parties to apportion loss between them. It 'is perfectly legitimate and indeed laudable'[86] to allow the parties to avoid costly, lengthy and hazardous litigation by effectively allocating risk in advance with a pre-estimate of the damages due in case of default. Such clauses are thus valid and the creditor is able to recover in the event of breach without having to prove actual damage.[87]

---

[83] As a point of interest, the EC Sales Directive—Council Directive (EC) 1999/44 on certain aspects of the sale of consumer goods and associated guarantees [1999] OJ L/171/12—does not envisage a third-party performance, at the seller's expense, should the seller deliver non-conforming goods. Instead there is implicit recognition that the buyer can terminate the contract by simple notification, and then go out on the market for substitute goods.

[84] *Export Credits Guarantee Department v Universal Oil Products* [1983] 1 WLR 399, 403 (HL).

[85] For the significance of this term see L Miller, 'Penalty Clauses in England and France: A Comparative Study' (2004) 53 ICLQ 79, 84.

[86] Treitel, above n 1, 212.

[87] *Wallis v Smith* (1882) 21 Ch D 243, 267 (CA) (Cotton LJ).

Of course, the distinction between liquidated damages and penalty clauses is not an easy one to draw and the amorphous boundary has led to a rich and complex body of case-law.[88] Nevertheless, the distinction remains: the common law dislike of the penalty clause, as mentioned, rests on the principle that a relationship between actual loss and compensation should be established. But the English position concerning penalty clauses is anomalous in its conflicting stance to a fundamental principle of English contract law that allows the parties to decide their contractual terms without interference from the court—freedom of contract. The tension between the penalty clause rules and this fundamental principle finds voice in the raft of inconsistencies that bedevil this area of law.[89] And, in practice, it is rare for the court to hold that the clause is invalid for its status as a penalty, particularly when the court is faced with a contract between commercial parties. A recent attempt to expand the instances in which the court could classify a clause as penal was given short shrift by the majority in the Court of Appeal.[90] So, despite judicial misgivings from time to time, the principle that the court will interfere with the contract where an agreed damages clause is classified as penal has stood the test of time, and the seemingly anachronistic rules remain firmly in place.

The roots of the principle can be found in the economic underpinning to contract law in England, which asserts its authority over any moral or philosophical considerations that might find positive outcomes in a principle that encourages fulfilment of the contractual obligation. In relation to the penalty clause, there are two interrelated strands to the economic arguments. The first, as already seen, is that compensation should do just that, compensate, and no more. The second strand captures the idea that it is not economically efficient to compel the party to perform. In brief, economists focus on the economic efficiency of legal rules, efficiency being treated as synonymous with wealth maximisation. Wealth maximisation, in Kaldor–Hicks terms,[91] has spawned the 'efficient breach' theory of contract.[92] The doctrine is at first beguiling. It states that the debtor should be able, and indeed encouraged, to breach his contract provided that the

---

[88] Rules to guide classification of agreed damages clauses were set out by the House of Lords in 1915 and still provide the key formula for distinguishing: *Dunlop Pneumatic Tyre Co Ltd v New Garage & Motor Co Ltd* [1915] AC 79, 87 (HL).

[89] See Miller, above n 85, 92–6.

[90] *Murray v Leisureplay plc* [2005] EWCA Civ 963, [2005] IRLR 946.

[91] 'Kaldor–Hicks' efficiency (named after the two eponymous economists) occurs only if the economic value of social resources is maximised. Efficiency is determined by whether one party is enabled to be better off by a change in policy to the extent that she is able, *in theory*, to adequately compensate the party, or parties, that would be made worse off. It can be analysed in relation to Pareto efficiency, which finds efficiency only where no one is worse off and at least one person is better off by the change in policy.

[92] It seems that the term was first used in an article by CJ Goetz and RE Scott, 'Liquidated Damages, Penalties and the Just Compensation Principle: Some Notes on an Enforcement Model and a Theory of Efficient Breach' (1977) 77 Columbia Law Review 554.

benefits he gains from breach exceed his loss, whilst still leaving the creditor in an economically stronger position than if he had performed the original obligation. The result is considered a positive outcome in terms of economic efficiency. Justification for breach is found at both the macro, as well as the micro level; the economic welfare of society as a whole, as well as that of the individual obligor, is increased. All this while leaving the economic integrity of the creditor intact. No one is left worse off by the breach and thus one arrives at what is termed a state of Pareto-optimal efficiency. It is clear that the English predilection for damages accords with such economic theory. If higher value can be obtained elsewhere, then it would be inefficient, and a waste of resources, to compel the obligor to perform. It also means that, since the penalty clause acts to compel performance (or deter breach), then its rejection should be upheld.

In appreciating that the penalty clause can act as additional weapon in the performance armoury, it would seem strange to denude it of its power if a system wants to encourage performance. In considering the position that the *Avant-projet* takes towards performance of contractual obligations, as outlined above, the modifications that are made in this area, indeed 'the most important innovations',[93] appear difficult to reconcile with the philosophy underpinning Section 4 discussed above.[94] For, as it will be seen, the reform has the potential to strip the clause of much of its coercive effect.

(a) The *clause pénale* within the Code civil

A brief exposition of the current position of the *clause pénale* seems necessary prior to any examination of the modifications proposed by the *Avant-projet*. The starting point in France is that the *clause pénale* is valid,[95] and, rather than hostility towards its coercive potential, it is deemed an admirable institution for the very fact that it encourages performance of contractual obligations. This being so, there are dangers inherent in such a comminatory contractual clause. This was given legislative recognition in 1975 when a law was enacted entrusting the judge with powers of intervention should the clause be deemed *manifestement excessive*.[96] The parameters of judicial intervention are contained within article 1152(2),

[93] G Viney, 'Exposé des motifs' in *Avant-projet de réforme du droit des obligations et de la prescription: Rapport remis au garde des Sceaux* (Paris, La documentation française, 2006) 161, 169 (see below pp 809, 831).

[94] See above p 154.

[95] Section VI of Chapter IV of Title III of the Third Book of the Code civil, entitled 'Des obligations avec clauses pénales', dedicates eight provisions to penalty clauses (arts 1226–1233).

[96] Loi no 75-597 du 9 juillet 1975 modifiant les art 1152 et 1231 du Code civil sur la *clause pénale*, JO 10 July 1975, 7076.

which allows the court, even on its own initiative, to reduce or increase the agreed penalty where it is manifestly excessive or derisory.[97]

Much ink has been spilt over the extent of judicial powers to modify the clause; the 1975 law triggered debate as to whether such powers of modification should be restricted to a 'true'[98] *clause pénale*, or instead, whether any clause that provides for payment of a sum in case of breach should fall within article 1152(2). By way of preface for the following observations on the *Avant-projet*, it should be noted that the 1975 legislation engendered much concern over the impact that such moderating powers would have on the *clause pénale*. The spectre of judicial modification was seen to weaken the repressive element of such mechanism, and in turn the clause's potential to encourage performance. This prompted one author to announce the 'death' of the clause.[99] Another immortalised its passing away in an article entitled 'Requiem pour une *clause pénale*'.[100]

In practice, the 1975 reform did not sound the death knell for the *clause pénale*. Judicial practice has not on the whole endorsed extension of moderating powers beyond those agreed damages clauses that are 'true' penalty clauses,[101] thus not only enforcing the coercive impact of the clause but also limiting any corrosion of *la force obligatoire* that was so feared by commentators of the time.[102] This means that where a clause is not classified as a penalty, then, in a fashion similar to English law, it is allowed to stand as a genuine pre-estimate of damages as agreed between the parties. Of course, the principal difference between jurisdictions remains: should the clause be considered a penalty, it is still treated as valid, but *may* be subject to judicial powers of modification.[103] And, importantly, when such powers are exercised it seems that the concept of *peine* in article

[97] 'Néanmoins, le juge peut, même d'office, modérer ou augmenter la peine qui avait été convenue, si elle est manifestement excessive ou dérisoire. Toute stipulation contraire sera reputée non écrite.'

[98] The influential thesis of D Mazeaud, *La notion de clause pénale* (Paris, LGDJ, 1992) 147, contends that a 'true' *clause pénale* is one that guarantees performance, rather than agreed compensation for non-performance. The essence of the clause is not *réparatrice*, but instead 'the *clause pénale* has as its objective, its function and its reason the performance of the principal and original obligation. It is concluded so as to guarantee such performance.'

[99] B Boubli, 'La mort de la *clause pénale* ou le déclin du principe de l'autonomie de la volonté' J not 1976, 1, 945.

[100] Y Letartre 'Requiem pour une *clause pénale*?' RJ com 1978, 101.

[101] Eg Cass civ (1) 9 January 1991, D 1991, 481 note G Paisant; Cass com 14 October 1997, Defr 1998, 328 obs D Mazeaud; Cass com (3) June 2003, appeal no 00-12580, unpublished. For a convincing argument that supports an extension of judicial moderating powers to any contractual clause that stipulates damages in case of non-performance see Cass soc 2 July 1984 and Cass civ (3) 5 December 1984, RTD civ 1985, 372 obs J Mestre.

[102] Eg G Paisant, 'Dix ans d'application de la réforme des articles 1152 et 1231 du Code civil relative à la *clause pénale* (loi du 9 juillet 1975)' RTD civ 1985, 647: 'in this way, a breach in the principle of the *force obligatoire* of agreements has been opened in 1975'; F Chabas, 'La réforme de la *clause pénale*' D 1976 Chron 229, considers that the law is: 'one of the first significant infringements of article 1134 Code civil'.

[103] The Cour de cassation controls judicial intervention and considers it exceptional; Mazeaud, above n 98, 53.

1152(2) encourages a reduction that does not reach actual loss suffered, for otherwise it would seem contrary to the very concept of *peine*. This approach has therefore maximised the coercive impact of the *clause pénale* in French law.

(b) *Avant-projet* Modifications

The reform makes some important changes to the mechanism of the *clause pénale* and one might even say that it banishes the clause into relative obscurity, in effect subsuming it into a unitary regime of agreed damages clauses.

First, in place of the current articles 1226–1233 Cc, which form a Section of the Code entirely devoted to regulation of the *clause pénale*,[104] we find a single article 1383. The following discussion demonstrates how this slimline regime, a diminution that has not gone unlamented,[105] leaves the *clause pénale* a shadow of its former hardy self. Furthermore, proposed article 1383 is incorporated into the Subtitle that deals with Civil Liability (Subtitle III of the third Title of Book III of the *Avant-projet*) and, more specifically, that Section which deals with agreements relating to reparation (Chapter 3 Section 3). The absence of any mention in the Section on Performance (discussed above[106]) augurs the extent to which the *Avant-projet* weakens the clause's potential to ensure performance.

The first two paragraphs of article 1383 of the *Avant-projet* at first seem to create a division between those clauses in paragraph 2 'whose purpose is to force the contractual debtor to perform'—the *clause pénale* (though interestingly not directly identified as such)[107] and those, in paragraph 1, 'where the parties have fixed in advance the reparation which will fall due'. But the division does not seem to have legal implications in respect of their treatment by the court. And this is where the reform makes substantial amendments, for it is now clear that *all* agreed damages clauses (in other words both 'pre-set reparation clauses' as well as penalty clauses) are to be subject to the discretionary judicial moderating powers,[108] thus, in one stroke of the drafters' pen, ending debate as to the reach of judicial modification powers. It should be emphasised that modification is possible

---

[104] See above n 95.

[105] D Mazeaud, above n 37, RDC 2007, 149 considers that the *clause pénale* has been relegated to the annals of history by the *Avant-projet*.

[106] See above p 152.

[107] Perhaps owing to the ambiguity that has hitherto surrounded the definition and nature of the *clause pénale*.

[108] The power to *increase* the amount of a clause, should it be derisory, has been omitted. The notes to art 1383 explain that this power is hardly ever used. Viney, above n 93, 169 (see below p 831) states that the rules provided by 1382-1 to 1382-4 seem adequate. For one example where the clause was increased by the court see Cass soc 5 June 1996, Bull civ V no 226, Defr 1997, 737 obs D Mazeaud.

regardless of whether the clause has a coercive intent, and thus regardless of whether the dangers inherent in such clauses justify judicial intervention to alter the parties' agreement. Any clause might find itself reduced if considered *manifestement excessive*. Thus, the *clause pénale* becomes just one variant of the ordinary contract term that sets compensation in advance.[109]

Thus the first point of enquiry concerning any clause, whatever its nature, is whether it is *manifestment excessive*, rather than whether it is a penalty clause or not.[110] If so, then it is at risk of moderation by the court. This regulator of judicial intervention—the manifestly excessive nature of the clause—seems to suggest far wider powers for the court than would be usual for an English judge. The theoretical backbone to English contract law is that the terms of an agreement should be upheld to the greatest extent possible, and thus should be subject to the minimal possible interference from the judiciary. A system of contract law committed to freedom of contract must reject controls over the content of the contract (including remedial provisions) as far as possible. The penalty clause rules are viewed as exceptions to this principle and thus should be interpreted in a restrictive fashion. In the recent Court of Appeal decision of *Murray v Leisureplay*[111] the leading speech by Lady Justice Arden illustrates an attempt to base the classification of an agreed damages clause on the factual difference between actual loss and amount stipulated; where discrepancy occurs, this would then need to be *justified*.[112] This approach was stifled by the majority since it threatened the overriding principle of *pacta sunt servanda* and would lead to an ill-desired increase in contracts subject to judicial scrutiny. Only where the clause is a clear attempt to deter breach, rather than compensate, should the penalty clause powers come into play. The extension in judicial discretion under the *Avant-projet* is therefore striking from the common law perspective, and seems to be far more concerned with the compensatory objectives of 'agreed damages clauses' rather than their ability to secure performance.

From the French perspective, however, the more expansive intervention might also be considered surprising. This is for two principal reasons. The first is related to the notion of *force obligatoire* as articulated within article 1134(1) Cc,[113] its numeration symbolically reproduced in the *Avant-projet*. In common with English law, the binding nature of contracts is a fundamental principle that forms the backdrop to contractual obligations. The

---

[109] Mazeaud, above n 37, RDC 2007, 161.

[110] In this way, the problems associated with classification of the clause remain a feature of English law only.

[111] Above n 90.

[112] 'The real question is whether the sums for which the parties have provided be paid on breach differ substantially from the sums that would be recoverable at common law and whether there is shown to be no justification for that', *Ibid*, [46].

[113] See above p 151.

Code civil currently provides a reminder of this in article 1152(1).[114] This paragraph provides:

> Where a contract provides that he who fails to perform it will pay a certain sum as damages, the other party may not be awarded a greater or lesser sum.[115]

The moderating powers of the judge, currently contained in the second paragraph of article 1152, are thereby seen as an *exception*[116] to the general rule of *intangibilité*, as underlined in the first paragraph of that same article. But the reform omits to make any such reference to this general principle of enforceability of the agreement between parties. Modification under the new rules is thus not presented as an exception to the binding nature of the parties' agreement.[117] The *Avant-projet* is surprising in this respect and although the impact of the proposals depend on the extent to which the court exercises its discretion, the judicial powers still need to be reconciled at a general level with article 1134 and the principle expounded therein, and, more specifically, with the persistent incantation of *la force obligatoire* as theoretical justification for *exécution en nature*.[118]

Secondly, the reform diminishes the coercive aspect of the clause. By extending the modification powers beyond those clauses that assure performance, *any* clause that might be *manifestly excessive* (in relation to loss) can be rewritten by the court. It can be argued that this decreases the incentive for the party to perform; the greater potential for judicial intervention, the less the defaulting party will be encouraged to perform. Furthermore, article 1383 omits what in practice seems an important element to the moderating judicial powers. Where the judge chooses to exercise his discretion, he can reduce the *peine*, and it seems that within the wording of this provision there are inherent limits to article 1152. The concept of *peine* encourages a reduction that does not fall to an amount equivalent to actual loss since this would seem contrary to the very conception of *peine*.[119] The new articulation of these rules adopts the

---

[114] Article 1152(1) is viewed as one example of *la force obligatoire du contrat* articulated by article 1134(1); J Thilmany, 'Fonctions et révisibilité des *clause pénales* en droit comparé' RIDC 1980, 17.

[115] 'Lorsque la convention porte que celui qui manquera de l'exécuter payera une certaine somme à titre de dommages-intérêts, il ne peut être alloué à l'autre une somme plus forte, ni moindre.'

[116] Art 1152(2) is seen as 'a violation in the principle of *la force obligatoire du contrat*', Cass com 3 June 2003, RDC 2004, 930 obs D Mazeaud.

[117] See also art 9:509(2) PECL which presents judicial modification as an exception to the rule of inviolability.

[118] See above p 151.

[119] '[T]o moderate does not mean to suppress': G Paisant, note under Cass civ (3) 9 January 1991, D 1991, 481. One scholar conducted interviews in 2005 with a group of French magistrates, all of whom stated that they would retain an extracompensatory element to a *clause pénale*, even after moderating it, since this accorded with the parties' intention to discourage breach: C Calleros, 'Damages and *Clauses Pénales* in Contract Actions: A Comparative Analysis of the American Common Law and the French Civil Code' (2006) 32 Brooklyn Journal of International Law 67.

language of sanction rather than *peine* and in so doing seems to permit a reduction to actual loss. Thus, an important coercive element to the clause is lost. In conclusion, in focusing on the disparity between actual loss and amount stipulated in an agreed damages clause, the *Avant-projet* has neglected the clause's potential to ensure performance of the contractual obligation. For the common lawyer, this seems to contradict the energy with which performance is pursued in Section 4.[120] It also seems to weaken the principal function of the contractual instrument itself—a tool to allocate risk between parties.

IV. CONCLUSION

The *Avant-projet* is an ambitious undertaking; it is the first comprehensive revision of the law of obligations and prescription since promulgation of the Code civil in 1804. The reform certainly brings 'vigour' and 'youth'[121] to this central area of private law and, as the examination of article 1154 of the *Avant-projet* has demonstrated, recasts core principles of contract law in a manner more faithful to the current legal framework. In light of current developments in European contract law,[122] such modern expression, indeed recodification, of the French law of obligations comes at a timely moment. The resulting reform[123] has the potential to act either as a bulwark against, or as a blueprint for, a future common European contract law.[124] Whatever the influence of the *Avant-projet* on the European stage, comparative reflection on the notion of performance provides a theoretical arsenal to counter those complacent about the challenges and legitimacy of European harmonisation. The opposing theoretical positions towards performance in England and France reflect jurisdictional settlements about fundamental values of contract law. Divergences relate to notions concerning the nature of obligation, the role of the court, limits to party autonomy, the legitimacy of economic theory, as well as historical circumstance and tradition. If a common contract law in Europe is to suppress diversity in the name of a more effective internal market, then one should take heed of the issues that this chapter examines. The notion of performance demonstrates just what is at stake in the Europeanisation of contract law.

---

[120] It also, from a common law perspective, seems to stand at odds with the *astreinte*, which buttresses the principle of performance in proposed article 1154(2). The *astreinte* acts as a 'form of judicially ordered penalty clause to enforce indirectly obligations to do or not to do': MP Michell, 'Imperium by the Back Door: The *Astreinte* and the Enforcement of Contractual Obligations in France' (1993) 51 University of Toronto Faculty Law Review 250, 259.

[121] Ph Rémy, 'Réviser le titre III du livre troisième du Code civil' RDC 2004, 1169.

[122] See above n 5.

[123] If given legislative approval.

[124] Whatever the final nature of such a project.

D

Termination for Non-performance and its Consequences

8

Termination of Contract:
A Missed Opportunity for Reform

MURIEL FABRE-MAGNAN

Termination of contract is a matter that is handled very badly by the Code civil. According to the principle stated in article 1134(2), contracts 'can be revoked only by the parties' mutual consent or on grounds which legislation authorises'.

The wording of this provision initially leads one to think—wrongly—that termination by the parties' mutual consent (*le mutuus dissensus*[1]) is the primary cause of revocation of contracts, whereas it is undoubtedly only very marginal, at any rate in the context of cases that are litigated. Termination of contract is, for the most part, termination desired by only one of the parties, and that party is not referred to by this article, which merely refers, in a subordinate and ill-defined way, to the possibility of termination on 'grounds which legislation authorises'.

Staying with the general law of contract,[2] it is necessary to refer to article 1184 Cc for the principal example of those grounds: termination of contract on the grounds of non-performance by one of the parties (*résolution pour inexécution* or 'termination for non-performance'). Article 1184(2) provides that

> the party who has not received the contractual performance has a choice between forcing the other party to perform the contract if that is possible, or seeking retroactive termination of the contract with damages.

If he opts for retroactive termination, this

> must be claimed by way of legal proceedings in court, and the defendant may be granted a period of time for performance depending on the circumstances.[3]

---

[1] See R Vatinet, 'Le mutuus dissensus' RTD civ 1987, 252.

[2] There are, in fact, numerous special laws which provide specific grounds for termination of contract, whether in matters relating to employment contracts, which is a good example of a special law for the termination of contract, or alternatively in connection with the law governing leases.

[3] Art 1184(3) Cc.

The inadequacy of the provisions of the Code civil is a result of the fact that the code is based on the model of a contract for instantaneous performance such as a contract of sale. Therefore, from the point of view of the Code civil, the problem of termination of contract only really relates to the situations where there is termination for non-performance.

The *Avant-projet de réforme du droit des obligations et de la prescription* preserves essentially the same structure and rests on the same fundamental model, such that this colloquium, which takes its format from the project, only raises the question of 'termination for non-performance', or the termination of the contract as a remedy for non-performance by one of the parties (section I below).

It is regrettable that the *Avant-projet*, like the present Code civil, is silent on one of the most current issues and most interesting developments in contract law, which would of itself have justified a reform of Title III of Book III: the question of termination of contracts of indefinite duration, not as a sanction for non-performance, but as an expression of the choice and of the right of each party to withdraw from this type of contract (section II below).

I. THE ONLY QUESTION CONSIDERED: TERMINATION OF CONTRACT AS A REMEDY FOR NON-PERFORMANCE BY ONE PARTY OF HIS OBLIGATIONS (TERMINATION FOR NON-PERFORMANCE)

In order to interpret and supplement the provisions of the Code civil, the French courts have created a whole system of rules governing termination of a contract for non-performance, setting out both the conditions for and the effects of this sanction.

(a) The Conditions for the Remedy

First, the courts have set out the necessary substantive conditions allowing one party to claim termination of the contract: there must be a sufficiently serious non-performance of the contract (a complete or partial failure of performance, defective performance, or even sometimes late performance), but it does not appear to be essential that such non-performance should be attributed to the fault of the non-performing party.[4]

---

[4] See in particular Cass civ (1) 4 February 1976, Bull civ I no 53. For example, termination would be possible even if the parties have agreed by common accord that they no longer want to perform the contract. See in particular Cass civ (1) 16 December 1986, Bull civ I no 301, RTD civ 1987, 750 obs J Mestre, which has been variously interpreted in the academic literature, and in which S paid K the amount of money necessary for the acquisition of a vehicle, provided that

Discussion has focused principally on the conditions under which use may be made of the possibility of termination. Where there is an express termination clause (*clause résolutoire expresse*), then in principle there is a right to termination once the debtor has been given formal notice to perform, and the creditor has exercised his right under the clause in good faith. By contrast, in the absence of an express termination clause, such a clause is implied,[5] but article 1184(3) Cc then provides that 'termination must be claimed by way of legal proceedings in court'; a notice to perform is thus not required, but instead it is necessary to have a judicial decision terminating the contract on grounds of non-performance, save where an exception from this requirement is expressly provided for by legislation.[6]

The courts have recently allowed certain exceptions to the need for a judicial decision terminating a contract. Thus the Cour de cassation has decided that where the conduct of one of the contracting parties is particularly seriously at fault, the other party may unilaterally terminate the contract without resorting to a court. Nevertheless, in cases where there is litigation, the courts must then examine whether the conduct of the one contracting party was sufficiently serious to justify the other in thus terminating it unilaterally. According to the Cour de cassation,[7]

> the serious nature of the conduct of one party to a contract may justify the other party in putting to an end that contract unilaterally at his own risk, and . . . the serious character of that conduct—any finding as to which by a professional regulatory authority does not bind the courts—does not necessarily exclude the need to give a period of notice.[8]

K would give S transport, but where, by mutual agreement, they decided to break off this arrangement; the Cour de cassation confirmed a judgment of the Cour d'appel in which K was ordered to make partial restitution of the money which she received, which could be interpreted as a partial retroactive termination of the contract.

[5] According to art 1184(1) Cc, 'a resolutory condition [*condition résolutoire*] is always implied in synallagmatic contracts, for the situation in which one of the two parties does not fulfil his obligations'.

[6] See art 1657 Cc which provides that 'in matters relating to sale of goods and personal effects, termination of the sale shall take place as of right and without the need for summons, in favour of the seller, after expiry of the period of time agreed for the goods to be collected'. It is often perishable goods that are at issue, and the time required to obtain a court decision would lead to irreversible damage. This provision is broadly related to the commercial practice known as *laissé pour compte* ('returned goods') which authorises the creditor in certain circumstances to go and find supplies elsewhere without waiting for the debtor to decide to perform his obligations.

[7] Cass civ (1) 13 October 1998, Bull civ I no 300, RTD civ 1999, 384 obs J Mestre, D 1999, 197 note C Jamin, D 1999 Somm 115 obs P Delebecque.

[8] The case concerned a doctor who was an anaesthetist and who had been granted the exclusive right in a certain clinic to perform the work falling within his area of specialisation for a period of thirty years. But the clinic put an end to their contractual relationship after fifteen years because of the fault and professional failings of the doctor. The Cour de cassation confirmed in the passage quoted in the text that the assessment made by the professional regulatory body (the French Medical Association) of the conduct of the doctor was not binding on the courts.

Termination without judicial intervention is therefore authorised in exceptional cases, as the Cour de cassation has since confirmed.[9] Nevertheless it is 'at the risk' of the person who initiates it, which means that the courts later assess the correctness of that termination, and must examine whether the conduct of the contracting party in question was sufficiently serious to justify retroactive termination of the contract.[10] They may therefore decide that the termination was justified,[11] or instead hold that responsibility should be shared;[12] and if they consider that termination was not justified, they may order the person responsible to pay damages.[13] The person who finds he has received notice of termination that he considers to be unjustified may bring an action before the judge dealing with interlocutory matters (*le juge des référés*) to ask him to order a continuation of the contractual relationship until the full court has given judgment on the merits.[14]

The *Avant-projet* confirms this case-law, and expressly provides very generally for the possibility of unilateral termination of contract for cases

---

[9] Cass civ (1) 20 February 2001, Bull civ I no 40, D 2001, 1568 obs C Jamin, D 2001 Somm 3239 obs D Mazeaud, RTD civ 2001, 363 obs J Mestre and B Fages, Defr 2001 article 37365 no 41 obs E Savaux: 'In the light of articles 1134 and 1184 of the Code civil; whereas the seriousness of the conduct of a party to a contract may justify the other party in putting that contract to an end unilaterally at his own risk, whether or not the contract is intended to be of indefinite duration'; Cass civ (1) 28 October 2003 Bull civ I no 211.

[10] See eg Cass civ (1) 28 October 2003, Bull civ I no 211; Cass civ (1) 20 February 2001, Bull civ I no 40, D 2001, 1568 note Ch Jamin.

[11] See eg Cass com 13 December 2005, appeal no 04-13374, unpublished; Cass civ (1) 13 October 1998, Bull civ I no 300.

[12] See eg Cass com 27 September 2005, appeal no 03-12472, unpublished.

[13] See Cass com 20 June 2006, appeal no 04-15785, unpublished. The case concerned contracts for the grant of trademark licences in relation to scarves, bandanas, stoles and hats for women. The licensor had renounced the contracts, on the basis of faults committed by the other contracting party, who then sued him for payment of licence fees and for damages. The licensor himself then counterclaimed the retroactive termination of the contracts on the grounds of the wrongful acts of the other parties, and compensation for the harm he had suffered. The Cour d'appel characterised the unilateral prospective termination of the contracts as wrongful, and ordered the licensor to pay various amounts by way of damages. The application for *cassation* of this decision was rejected.

[14] Cass civ (1) 29 May 2001, RTD civ 2001, 590 obs J Mestre and B Fages; see also B Fages, *Le comportement du contractant* (Presses universitaires Aix-Marseille, 1996) no 810: An anaesthetist found himself practising alone after the retirement of one of his colleagues. Since he had had a heart problem, he had a notice of leave of absence on health grounds sent to the clinic which then notified him of the renunciation of his contract with immediate effect. He therefore brought proceedings before the *juge des référés*, submitting that he had been the victim of a wrongful act which had involved a manifest infringement of the law. The Cour d'appel ordered the contractual relationship between the anaesthetist and the clinic to be maintained, under threat of a periodic penalty, and the latter were also prohibited from creating any obstacles to the exercise of the doctor's activity within the clinic. The Cour de cassation rejected the application for *cassation* of this judgment on the ground that 'there was thus a persistent disagreement concerning the performance of the contract, such that the decision taken in relation to [the claimant] at the time of his notice of leave of absence on health grounds, when the courts should first have been asked to rule on the disagreement between the parties, was unlawful'. In this way, the contracting party was clearly criticised for having taken a unilateral initiative without submitting the dispute to the courts.

of non-performance without judicial intervention. The relevant provision is the new article 1158 which, in its first paragraph, provides that:

> In all contracts, a person for whose benefit an undertaking has not been performed or has been performed only imperfectly, has the choice either to pursue performance of the undertaking, to instigate termination of the contract or to claim damages, and the latter may in some cases be recovered in addition to performance or termination of the contract.

Draft article 1158(2) adds that:

> Where a creditor opts for termination of the contract, he can either claim it from the court or by his own act put the defaulting debtor on notice to fulfil his undertaking within a reasonable time, failure to do so in the debtor leading to the creditor's right himself to terminate the contract.

Draft article 1158(3) then sets out the requisite procedure for this unilateral termination of the contract without judicial intervention:

> Where a debtor continues to fail to perform, the creditor can give him notice that the contract is terminated and on what grounds. In these circumstances, termination takes effect at the time of receipt of the notice by the other party to the contract.

When placed beside the present Code civil, the novel feature of the *Avant-projet* is therefore that it grants to a creditor who wants to terminate the contract a choice between judicial termination and unilateral termination. If a creditor opts for unilateral termination, he must first put the defaulting creditor on notice to fulfil his undertaking and allow him a reasonable time to do so before he possesses the right to terminate the contract by giving notice to that effect. It is to be noted that this right to termination is accompanied by an obligation to give reasons for termination: the draft provision states that the notice of termination must state 'on what grounds' it is based.

Unilateral termination is thus henceforth officially a possible 'remedy' for non-performance of a contract. This development is in harmony with European contract law, which is inspired by English law. The Principles of European Contract Law (PECL) drawn up in 1998 thus contain an article 9:301 entitled 'Right to Terminate the Contract', which provides that:

> A party may terminate the contract if the other party's non-performance is fundamental.

Article 9:303 adds that:

> A party's right to terminate the contract is to be exercised by notice to the other party.

The PECL even find room for anticipatory non-performance, a solution

that is offered by English law; while this is not provided for by the *Avant-projet*, it is possible that it would be accepted by the courts.[15]

The *Avant-projet* speaks of the 'right to terminate the contract'. The commentary under the draft article explains that the form of words 'the contract shall be deemed to be terminated' seemed less brutal and uncompromising than the form of words 'he declares that the contract is terminated'.[16] In fact, neither of these two forms of words is used and the text simply says that 'the creditor can give notice [to the debtor] that the contract is terminated'.

Choosing to terminate the contract unilaterally remains at the creditor's risk, and the debtor is free to contest that termination in court. Article 1158-1(1) of the *Avant-projet* thus provides that:

> The debtor may contest the creditor's decision before the court by claiming that any failure to perform which is alleged against him does not justify termination of the contract.

Article 1158-1(2) further provides that:

> Depending on the circumstances, the court may confirm the termination effected by the creditor or instead order performance of the contract, with the possibility of giving the debtor time to perform.

The court may in some cases order the contract to be performed under threat of periodic penalties for non-performance.

In contrast to a certain number of academic writings which suggest that the court ought also to intervene to supervise the fairness of contracts, the *Avant-projet* clearly opts instead for a less interventionist approach, and chooses to leave contracts in the hands of their parties. This choice then leads to a position where it is the person who is notified of the termination of his contract who has to bear the costs and the length of any proceedings, ie the party owing the obligation that has not been performed. This solution is not unfair if his failure to perform is confirmed, but it is not right that the cost and risk of initiating proceedings should dissuade him from objecting in a case where unilateral termination is not justified. Otherwise an unscrupulous creditor, having found a contract elsewhere that will be more advantageous to him, could find it to be a convenient way of releasing himself from his obligations by claiming non-performance on

---

[15] Art 9:304 PECL provides: 'Where prior to the time for performance by a party it is clear that there will be a fundamental non-performance by it the other party may terminate the contract'. See on this question, A Pinna, 'L'exception pour risque d'inexécution' RTD civ 2003, 31.

[16] Cf the explanatory note under art 1158 of the *Avant-projet* (see below p 695): unilateral termination of a contract could be rather a shock. It is useful to give it formal recognition, but with some care as to its form (thinking of the psychological side of the change). The form of words 'he declares that the contract is terminated' would be too downright. For the same result, one can make one-sided termination more tolerable by using a less 'unilateral' turn of phrase by saying 'the contract shall be deemed to be terminated.'

the part of the other contracting party, and could thereby recognise in practice a form of what is referred to in Anglo-American circles as 'efficient breach of contract'.[17]

(b) The Effects of the Remedy

As to the consequences of termination of a contract, the first question is whether termination is only prospective, ie whether it applies only to the future (without restitution in respect of past performance), or whether true *résolution* is involved, ie retroactive termination with restitution and counter-restitution.

The *Avant-projet* confirms the existing law on this point, but emphasises that, in practice, the principle is to prefer prospective termination. Thus article 1160-1(1) provides that if 'termination of the contract frees the parties from their obligations', and draft article 1160-1(2) and (3) add that:

> As regards contracts with performance successively or in instalments, termination takes effect for the future; the parties' undertakings cease from the time of service of proceedings for termination or from the time of notice of any unilateral termination.
>
> If the contract has been performed in part, anything so exchanged by the parties gives rise neither to restitution nor to any compensation as long as they conformed to the respective obligations of the parties.

What is both new and welcome is that Articles 1161 to 1164-7 then propose specific rules governing restitution following the destruction of a contract, in particular as a result of its termination by *résolution*.

A second question, which is more complex and not traditionally the subject of as much consideration, concerns the damages that are due in cases of non-performance.[18]

The measure of such damages should depend on whether the contract is terminated from the beginning (in which case in principle the damages should correspond only to the damage suffered by the creditor as a result of entering into the contract), or merely prospectively (in which case the creditor should in principle be put in the situation in which he would have been had the contract been performed properly).[19] French courts do not, however, appear always to respect these principles and, in particular, do

---

[17] On efficient breach of contract, see below p 176.

[18] See A Pinna, *La mesure du préjudice contractuel* (doctoral thesis, University of Paris II, 2006) who analyses in detail the different heads of damages owed by the defaulting debtor, distinguishing between the cases where retroactive termination of the contract does or does not take place.

[19] In the first case, an award is made of so-called *negative* damages, in the second of *positive* damages: for these concepts, see M Fabre-Magnan, *Les obligations 1: Contrat et engagement unilatéral* (Paris, PUF, 2008) nos 246, 252.

not treat the retroactive destruction of a contract as an obstacle to compensating the creditor of the obligation that has not been performed for the loss of his 'positive' or 'performance' interest.[20]

The creditor should not, however, be able to accumulate both termination of the contract and an award of damages to compensate him for what he would have obtained from the proper performance of that same contract (which is the solution accepted by English law). The termination of the contract will allow him to recoup his own performance (eg the price he has paid), and there would be unjust enrichment if he was able to profit from a contract without having given anything in return. Moreover, in the special situation where there is serious fault on the part of the debtor, the creditor might obtain damages to compensate the loss of opportunity of another contract under the law of delictual liability and in this way compensation for the profit which the latter would have brought. The amount of damages will therefore be the same.

Indeed it is desirable to assess the amount of damages for breach of contract as generously as possible; this is in order to ward off the covert, but nevertheless real, introduction into French law of the American idea of 'efficient breach of contract' which undermines the legal and anthropological value of a promise made.[21] This has been seen in action, for example, in the so-called 'recalculation' case,[22] in which the Cour de cassation refused to accept that PARE (*plan d'aide au retour à l'emploi*: a scheme for assistance in returning to employment) had any contractual value even though it had been signed by the job-seekers in question, and even though it appeared to contain undertakings on their part and on the part of ASSEDIC (the institution required to pay compensation).[23]

All these issues remain rather undeveloped in French law owing to the fact that, in general, quantification of damages is a matter within the 'sovereign power of assessment' of the lower courts. This means that few rules have emerged in the case-law to supplement the many gaps left by the Code civil; unfortunately, here the *Avant-projet* fails to make use of the opportunity to give any guidance beyond the present terms of article 1149 Cc. And this provision does not actually contain any concrete guidance of any real use, limiting itself to stating that:

> Damages due to the creditor are, in general, for the loss he has suffered and the gain of which he has been deprived.

---

[20] Cf Pinna, above n 18, 504, who cites in particular Cass com 14 December 1993, appeal no 91-21937, unpublished, which allows both retroactive termination of the contract and compensation for the profit that would have resulted from the performance of the contract.

[21] See Fabre-Magnan, above n 19, no 256.

[22] See A Supiot, 'La valeur de la parole donnée (à propos des chômeurs 'recalculés')' Droit Social 2004, 541.

[23] Cass soc 31 January 2007, Bull civ V no 15.

Certainly the *Avant-projet* uses a new form of words and introduces the idea of compensation in respect of loss of a party's positive interest, though without actually saying so. The new article 1370 states that in principle

> the aim of an award of damages is to put the victim as far as possible in the position in which he would have been if the harmful circumstances had not taken place. He must make neither gain nor loss from it.

However, the draft does not specify further either the amount of damages or the circumstances that would affect their assessment, notably the incidence of retroactive termination of contract. This new gap is no doubt due to a choice made by the group given responsibility for proposing the rules governing civil liability. Indeed, while the *Avant-projet* is to be congratulated for having stated clearly that non-performance of a contract is a source of liability and not a form of performance by equivalent means,[24] it is regrettable that it treats the two types of liability, delictual and contractual, in a single set of provisions[25] as this has the unfortunate result of depriving the part of the *Avant-projet* governing remedies for contractual non-performance of one of the principle sanctions that are available. Furthermore, and most importantly, the rules governing the two types of liability are actually entirely different, notably in relation to the quantification of damages. As a result, this is an issue that remains unjustifiably neglected.

However, the *Avant-projet* overlooks another issue that is even more important.

II. THE NEGLECTED ISSUE: TERMINATION OF CONTRACT AS A RIGHT FOR EACH PARTY TO EXTRICATE HIMSELF FROM A CONTRACT OF INDEFINITE DURATION (A RIGHT TO UNILATERAL PROSPECTIVE TERMINATION)

The general framework governing termination of contracts remains unchanged under the *Avant-projet*, and the existing article 1134 is repeated almost word for word in a new article with the same number. Contracts can still only be revoked (the new article simply adds 'modified or revoked' but that is not the point of our discussion) 'by the parties' mutual consent or on grounds [instead of reasons, but this probably does not change anything] which legislation authorises'.

---

[24] For further explanations as to this position, see M Fabre-Magnan, *Les obligations 2: Responsabilité civile et quasi-contrats* (Paris, PUF, 2007) no 9.
[25] As to the *Avant-projet de réforme du droit de la responsabilité civile*, see the special issue 1/2007 of the RDC, which publishes the proceedings of a colloquium organised by the Université Panthéon-Sorbonne (Paris I) on 12 May 2006.

The new article and the proposals of reform thus pass over in silence the most significant developments in contract law over the last fifteen years or so: the fact that contracts extend further and further over time, that litigation thus increasingly concerns contracts concluded for a long period, or more correctly for an unspecified period (notably, concession contracts, franchise contracts, distribution contracts, etc), and that these kinds of contracts have their own method of termination, independent of non-performance by one of the parties: unilateral prospective termination.

(a) Unilateral Prospective Termination of Contracts of Indefinite Duration

In fact, the courts have always accepted that parties to a contract of indefinite duration have the right to break off from it unilaterally. According to the classic form of words used by the Cour de cassation, it is a consequence of article 1134(2) Cc

> that, in contracts for continuing performance where the duration of the contract has not been specified, unilateral prospective termination is available to the parties in the absence of abuse sanctioned by paragraph 3 of the same text.[26]

This right is traditionally explained as resulting from the prohibition of contracts of indefinite duration, the parties thus always having to be able to withdraw from a contractual relationship at the end of a certain period of time. The rule and its justification, which are expressly laid down by article 1780 Cc in relation to employment contracts,[27] are therefore valid for all contracts. What is involved is the prospective termination (*résiliation*) of the contract, ie a termination of the contract applying only as to the future.

Under both the present Code civil and the *Avant-projet*, this right is therefore supposed to be included in the reasons or grounds for the termination of contract that are 'authorised by legislation', which is rather unforthcoming. In reality, the courts have not only established this right, but they have also refined the conditions under which it can be exercised and, more importantly, specified the circumstances in which one of the contracting parties is to be seen as abusing his right.

It is a pity that the *Avant-projet* did not make use of its opportunity to treat this point in greater depth, because it is one of the key issues in the development of modern contract law and one where the general law of contracts is most defective and incomplete. Moreover, the courts can be seen to be making increasing use of special legislation particular to certain types of contracts in order to provide models of reasonably well-balanced

---

[26] Cass com 31 May 1994, Bull civ IV no 194.

[27] According to art 1780(1): 'A person may undertake to provide his services only for a period of time or for a specified task.' Art 1780(2) Cc provides: 'Contracts of service made without determination of duration may always end at the choice of one of the contracting parties.'

regimes of termination.[28] Where it is possible, they even rely on the rules of competition law[29].

There is nothing very surprising about this new need. Legal scholars have identified a movement towards the contractualisation of society,[30] and as a result contract has made ever greater inroads even into areas of the law which have traditionally been highly resistant to the ideas of the will (*la volonté*) of the parties and to contract, as, for example in the case of family law or public law. So, for instance, civil pacts of solidarity (*le pacte civil de solidarité*), which fundamentally concern the status of persons[31] which is traditionally not alterable by an act of will, are expressly defined by article 515-1 Cc itself as 'contracts which are concluded between two persons'. Moreover, new forms of contract continue to arise that no longer constitute true contracts of exchange, but are rather something that one might call 'organisational contracts'.[32] In this way, emphasis is increasingly put on the relationship that is created by parties to a contract, and this is reflected by the emergence of ideas such as relational contracts (based on

[28] See for example the Loi no 96-588 du 1er juillet 1996 sur la loyauté et l'équilibre des relations commerciales, JO 3 July 1996, 9983, modified by the Loi no 2001-420 du 15 mai 2001 sur les nouvelles régulations économiques, JO 16 May 2001, 7776, which puts in place a general regime for the termination of established business relationships. According to article L 442-6, I of the Code de commerce, 'The following acts committed by any producer, trader, manufacturer or person listed in the trade register render the perpetrator liable and entail the obligation to redress the loss caused: . . . 5. Suddenly breaking off an established business relationship, even partially, without prior written notice commensurate with the duration of the business relationship and consistent with the minimum notice period determined by the multi-sector agreements in line with standard commercial practices. . . . The foregoing provisions do not affect the right to cancel without notice in the event of the other party failing to perform its obligations or in the event of *force majeure*'. The courts assimilate established business relationships to contracts of indefinite duration. For comment on this provision, see in particular L Idot, 'La deuxième partie de la loi NRE ou la réforme du droit français de la concurrence' JCP G 2001 I 343. See also P Vergucht, 'La rupture brutale d'une relation commerciale établie' RJ com 1997, 129.

[29] See in particular Cass com 24 October 2000, Bull civ IV no 163, RTD civ 2001, 141 obs J Mestre and B Fages; Cass com 6 June 2001, RTD civ 2001, 588 obs J Mestre and B Fages. See also M-E Tian-Pancrazi, *La protection judiciaire du lien contractuel* (Presses universitaires Aix-Marseille, 1996) 227.

[30] See primarily A Supiot, 'La contractualisation de la société' in Y Michaud (ed), *Qu'est-ce que l'humain?*, vol II (Paris, Odile Jacob, 2000) 157; similarly A Supiot, 'Un faux dilemme: la loi ou le contrat?' Droit Social 2003, 59, where he demonstrates that, if in practice there is a reduction in the prerogative of the legislator, this is not to the advantage of contract because freedom of contract has become the subject of a set programme and real agreements have been rendered secondary. See also M Mekki, *L'intérêt général et le contrat: Contribution à une étude de la hiérarchie des intérêts en droit privé* (Paris, LGDJ, 2004) no 1055. On the emergence of a contractual society, S Erbès-Seguin (ed), *Le contrat: Usages et abus d'une notion* (Paris, Desclée de Brouwer, 1999). See also, in relation to English law, H Collins, *The Law of Contract* (4th edn, London, LexisNexis Butterworths, 2003) especially ch 6, 'The Contractualization of Social Life'.

[31] It must furthermore henceforth be registered as a marginal note on the birth certificate. See the new art 515-3(1) resulting from the Loi no 2006-728 du 23 juin 2006 portant réforme des successions et des liberalités, JO 24 June 2006, 9513.

[32] P Didier, 'Le consentement avec l'échange: le contrat de société' Revue de jurisprudence commerciale November 1995 (special issue on *L'échange des consentements*) 75. See also P Didier, 'Brèves notes sur le contrat-organisation' in *L'avenir du droit: Mélanges en hommage à François Terré* (Paris, Dalloz/PUF/Juris-classeur, 1999) 635.

the idea suggested by Ian R Macneil[33]). Contract is becoming a means for the organisation of power or control,[34] and the duration of the relationships it creates is one of its essential elements.[35]

All these developments can be observed in abundance in the case-law and in special legislation, but there is no trace of it to be found in the draft law for the reform of the Code civil, which remains tied to the same old models as before. A new general law of contract, adapted to the modern development of contracts, would have been welcome to make up for this omission.

The main deficiency in the Code civil, which case-law and academic writings have tried to remedy, exists specifically in relation to termination of such contracts. Once contract becomes essential to certain persons and no longer constitutes merely an instrument for a one-off exchange, it becomes necessary to find ways by which it can be made both stable and durable. And if contract constitutes an instrument for the control of one party by the other, it becomes necessary to ensure that a proper balance in the relationship is re-established. These two objectives—ensuring stability and the re-establishment of balance—become of supreme importance when it comes to constructing the legal framework by which unilateral termination is permitted.

Both the courts and legal scholars have therefore tried to refine the present regime governing unilateral termination of contracts and have gradually forged the beginnings of a general law of unilateral prospective termination of contracts of indefinite duration.

While as a matter of general principle it remains the case that there is a right to break off from contracts of indefinite duration by a simple unilateral expression of intent, the Cour de cassation has accepted that this right to unilateral termination of contract can be abused (as in principle can all rights) and that such an abuse will be sanctioned.[36]

---

[33] See his first article: IR Macneil, 'The many futures of contracts' (1974) 47 Southern California Law Review 691; in France, see C Boismain, *Les contrats relationnels* (doctoral thesis, University of Nantes, 2004); A Cathiard, *L'abus dans les contrats conclus entre professionnels: L'apport de l'analyse économique du contrat* (Presses universitaires Aix-Marseille, 2006); H Muir Watt, 'Du contrat "relationnel"' in *La relativité du contrat: Actes du colloque, Nantes 1999* (Travaux de l'association Henri Capitant, Journées nationales, vol IV) (Paris, LGDJ, 2000) 169; H Bouthinon-Dumas, 'Les contrats relationnels et la théorie de l'imprévision' RID éco 2001, 339; Y-M Laithier, 'À propos de la réception du contrat relationnel en droit français' D 2006 Chron 1003.

[34] For an analysis of this theory A Supiot, 'La relativité du contrat en question' in *La relativité du contrat: Actes du colloque, Nantes 1999* (Travaux de l'association Henri Capitant, Journées nationales, vol IV) (Paris, LGDJ, 2000) 183. According to this author—and he develops this idea throughout his article—contracts are emerging whose 'primary objective is not to exchange specific goods, nor to seal an alliance between equals, but to regulate the exercise of a power'.

[35] See A Etienney, *La durée de la prestation: Essai sur le temps dans l'obligation* (doctoral thesis, University of Paris I, 2005).

[36] According to the general form of words used by the first Civil chamber of the Cour de cassation, 'it results from this provision [article 1134(2) Cc] that, in contracts whose performance takes place continuously, in which there is no provision as to duration, unilateral prospective

The criterion for determining whether there is such an abuse rests traditionally on the presence or absence of an intention to harm in the person exercising the right, but in the context of unilateral termination of contracts of indefinite duration the Cour de cassation has taken a broader view.[37] In particular, the courts have required a period of notice to be observed in order to allow the other party to the contract to make appropriate arrangements: if the contract has been in place for some time, a sudden termination will therefore generally constitute an abuse of the right to break off the relationship.[38] But the courts have gone further and have characterised conduct as abusive in the absence of a failure to provide notice of termination. Thus, termination of the contract may be abusive not only by reference to the procedure employed to effect that termination, but also substantively. In fact, adoption of this approach has begun to restrict the right to break off from the contract to certain situations. So, for example, in relation to distribution contracts it is possible to identify as abusive the case where a supplier has sought to break off the relationship after falsely leading its distributor to believe that the contract would be continued or renewed,[39] and in particular if it has required capital expenditure to be made by the latter shortly before this, without allowing time for depreciation of this expenditure by amortisation.[40]

termination is, *in the absence of any abuse sanctioned by para 3 of the same provision*, available to both parties' (emphasis added) (Cass civ (1) 5 February 1985, Bull civ I no 54). See also Cass com 31 May 1994, Bull civ IV no 194, JCP 1994 I 3803 obs G Virassamy.

[37] See Cass com 3 June 1997, Bull civ IV no 171: 'Abuse in the prospective termination of a contract does not consist solely of an intention to harm on the part of the party terminating.'

[38] See Cass com 5 December 1984, Bull civ IV no 332: 'by failing to investigate whether the grantor of a concession, who had the right to terminate the oral contract granting the concession, which was necessarily of indefinite duration in the absence of any express provision to the contrary, had observed a period of notice that was not too abrupt in terminating the contract, the Cour d'appel failed to provide a legal basis for its decision'; Cass com 8 April 1986, Bull civ IV no 58: 'While, in the absence of any agreement to the contrary, the company Tim had the right to put an end to the concession contract of indefinite duration, this was on condition that the exercise of that right should not be abusive; the Cour d'appel found that Tim had abruptly terminated its contract with the company Van Beurden Mode Agenturen by advising it a few days before the presentation of the summer collection in 1981 that that collection would not be entrusted to it; on this ground alone, and disregarding the grounds rightly criticised by the appeal in cassation, which are superfluous, the Cour d'appel has legally justified its decision.'

[39] See for example Cass com 5 April 1994, Bull civ IV no 149, JCP 1994 I 3803 obs C Jamin, D 1995, 355 note G Virassamy. See M Behar-Touchais and G Virassamy, *Les contrats de la distribution* (Paris, LGDJ, 1999) nos 349–56, and the academic literature and case-law cited there.

[40] See Cass com 5 April 1994, Bull civ IV no 149, where certainly the Supreme Court approved the Cour d'appel for 'having correctly stated that Vag France could terminate the contract without giving reasons', but where it also approved the first instance court for having nevertheless, on the facts, found that the termination was abusive to the extent that the grantee of the concession had agreed, on the grantor's request, significantly to increase its investment and advertising efforts; similarly Cass com 7 October 1997, Bull civ IV no 252, in a case where, if no abuse was found in the termination of the contract, this was because there was no adequate proof that the grantee of the concession was required to pay large amounts in investments, but that, on the contrary, he appeared to have acted spontaneously; see also Cass com 20 January 1998, Bull civ IV no 40, D 1998, 413 note C Jamin; Cass com 29 January 2002 and Cass com 9 April 2002, RTD civ 2002, 811 obs J Mestre and B Fages.

Another essential point, and one much debated in academic writings, is the question of the obligation to give reasons.[41] In the special regimes for unilateral prospective termination of contracts concluded for a long period, in particular in relation to employment contracts, a crucial consideration is the obligation, imposed on the person who seeks to end the contract unilaterally, to give reasons for his decision.[42] The obligation to give reasons is not a merely formal condition: the giving of reasons is as a general rule not done solely for informative purposes, but brings about a situation where only certain grounds for termination are authorised.[43] By thus restricting the right to break off from a contract, the obligation to give reasons can be a factor in giving stability to contractual relationships.

However, the case-law in this area remains unsettled.[44] Some judgments lead one to believe that there is a certain degree of supervision of the reasons for termination, or at least to conclude that the latter are not entirely a matter of discretion; so, for example, the Cour de cassation was able to criticise a Cour d'appel for accepting that termination was valid without making any finding to the effect that the grantee of the concession had been informed of the reasons for it.[45] Other decisions, by contrast, seem more reticent, and find

[41] See X Lagarde, 'La motivation des actes juridiques' in *La motivation: Actes du colloque, Limoges 1998* (Travaux de l'association Henri Capitant, Journées nationales, vol III) (Paris, LGDJ, 2000) 73; M Fabre-Magnan, 'L'obligation de motivation dans les contrats' in *Le contrat au début du XXI siècle: Etudes offertes à Jacques Ghestin* (Paris, LGDJ, 2001) 301. See also the discussion in RDC 2005, 533–614.

[42] Several special provisions impose an obligation to give reasons for termination. This is particularly the case in the context of labour law: dating from a law of 13 July 1973, there must be real and serious grounds for dismissal, which are for the court to assess, under threat of payment of compensation which may not be less than the last six months' salary (art L 122-14(4) Code du travail); it is also the same in the context of contracts of lease, termination of which by the lessor is subject to an obligation to give reasons. More generally, in the context of agencies of common interest (contracts by means of which the two parties intend to collaborate in the creation of a common client base), the person responsible for termination must show that he has a legitimate interest in so doing—see J Ghestin, C Jamin and M Billiau, *Traité de droit civil: Les effets du contrat—interprétation, qualification, durée, inexécution, effet relative, opposabilité* (3rd edn, Paris, LGDJ, 2001) nos 277–89; but in spite of several proposals in the academic literature—in particular G Virassamy, *Les contrats de dépendance: Essai sur les activités professionnelles exercées dans une dépendance économique* (Paris, LGDJ, 1986)—the Cour de cassation for the time being appears to refuse to extend this special regime to all contracts concluded for a long period. See for example, in the context of an exclusive concession, Cass com 7 October 1997, Bull civ IV no 252, D 1998, 413 note C Jamin; for a contract to operate as a medical practitioner, Cass civ (1) 25 June 1996, Bull civ I no 269). See Behar-Touchais and Virassamy, above n 39, no 358.

[43] The obligation to give reasons for termination is not in conflict with the right unilaterally to break off from a contract of indefinite duration. Certain rights may, in effect, be limited to particular situations, and thus subject to the giving of reasons, without the right itself being called into question. This is the case, to take one of many possible examples, in relation to the right to divorce, which cannot normally be exercised except in the cases and for the reasons that have been provided for by legislation.

[44] See D Mazeaud, 'Un petit plomb en moins dans l'aile du solidarisme contractuel . . .' D 2003, 93.

[45] Cass com 20 January 1998, Bull civ IV no 40, D 1998, 413 note C Jamin; in another

that the grantor of the concession may terminate the concession contract without giving reasons, provided that he observes the period of notice and does not abuse the right to terminate.[46]

In this way, a failure to give reasons is not seen in itself as an abuse of the right to break off from the contract.

The obligation to give reasons is nevertheless in harmony with wider developments in the law of contract. Indeed, as we have seen, it is not just that contract is increasingly becoming an arena for the exercise of power and control, but, in addition and in parallel, one can see that the nature of this power is changing. One author has thus been able to observe in all the traditional areas in which power is exercised (business, the family, the public sphere), a 'decline in unfettered power in favour of power tied to certain purposes', a decline that logically manifests itself in

> an increase in the controls put in place over those who possess power: controls which take effect in advance as in the development of obligations to give reasons; and controls which take effect after the event as with the growth of the role of the courts.[47]

Imposing an obligation on a party to give reasons for his decision to break off from the contract thus enables a court to assess the correctness of the exercise of what is evidently a power, and in particular to check whether termination is sufficiently justified to offset the significant harm which such a termination may cause the other contracting party. Moreover in the labour law context an evidential argument has been found to be a convincing justification for the imposition on the employer of an obligation to give reasons for termination: for, it is said, it is not fair for the party who receives notification of termination to bear the burden of proof as to any abuse of the right to break off the relationship given that it is person

judgment, while applauding the Cour d'appel for 'having stated correctly that [the grantor] could cancel the contract without giving reasons', the Cour de cassation accepts that termination may nevertheless be abusive if, as in the case before it, the grantor had failed in his duty of loyalty by failing to inform the grantee of the concession of his intentions (Cass com 5 April 1994, Bull civ IV no 149); See also, more recently, Cass com 2 July 2002, Bull civ IV no 113, D 2003, 93 obs D Mazeaud, RDC 2003, 154 obs M Behar-Touchais, although in the case itself such a duty to give reasons could be deduced from an express term of the contract.

[46] Cass com 7 October 1997, Bull civ IV no 252, the paragraph which is quoted having undoubtedly been taken from the judgment of the Cour d'appel. One may add to this picture the judgments relating to the very similar question of non-renewal of contracts concluded for a specific period. There too, the Cour de cassation has sometimes held that where 'no reasons were given for the refusal to renew the contract, even though it caused harm to [the commercial agent]', the Cour d'appel could properly make a finding as to 'its abusive character' (Cass com 27 October 1998, Bull civ IV no 256); but it usually finds that 'the grantor is not required to give reasons for its decision not to conclude a new contract of concession' (Cass com 4 January 1994, Bull civ IV no 13), or that the person responsible for terminating the contract 'did not have to give reasons for the non-renewal of the contract' (Cass com 25 April 2001, D 2001, 3237 obs D Mazeaud, RTD civ 2002, 99 obs J Mestre and B Fages).

[47] A Supiot, 'Les nouveaux visages de la subordination' Droit social 2000, 132.

attempting to terminate alone who has the relevant evidence at his disposal.[48]

Thus the elements of a new general law of contract can clearly be seen both in case-law and in academic writing, emerging from outdated paradigms and the obsolete view of a contract as being an instrument binding two abstract contracting parties and involving immediate performance.

(b) The Adaptation of the General Law of Contract to the Diversity of Contractual Instances

The difficulty was undoubtedly to avoid going from one abstract model to another, and instead to adapt the general law of contract to the diversity of possible contractual situations; it would to some extent have been a question of refining the existing general law. In particular, the new forms of protection, such as obligations to give reasons, should have been restricted to certain particular situations.

Neither the idea of a contract of dependence (*contrat de dépendence*)[49] nor that of a contract relating to a common interest (*contrat d'intérêt commun*)[50] have been adopted by the courts as the criterion to be used to give shape to a specific regime. But then neither of these two ideas give expression to the relevant criterion: the existence of factors justifying measures to ensure the stability of the contract.

An inflexible termination regime is necessary where contracts are essential to one's personal life. That is why, for example, in matters relating to the status of persons, stability is given to the institution of marriage by the enactment of strict termination criteria.[51] In patrimonial matters a contract must be provided with stability if one party obtains the greatest part of his means of existence from that contract, a consideration that could be the perfect criterion for establishing a special regime. What is usually at stake is his salary (in employment contracts), or, more generally the money he needs in order to live (eg under a subcontract), but it may

---

[48] See M Fabre-Magnan, 'Pour la reconnaissance d'une obligation de motiver la rupture des contrats de dépendance économique' RDC 2004, 573.

[49] See generally Virassamy, above n 42.

[50] The court refused to treat all concession contracts in the same way as agencies of common interest, so that the same protective régime will not always be imposed. See Cass com 7 October 1997, Bull civ IV no 252: 'whereas, first, a contract for an exclusive concession is not a agency of common interest'.

[51] Even if in that context too, aided by the trend towards liberalisation, certain countries, including European ones, are removing from their law the concept of the 'grounds' for a divorce, so that the marriage can be dissolved unilaterally, without even having to provide a reason. See most recently, Spanish Law 13/2005 of 1 July, concerning the amendment of the Civil code in matters relating to the right to contract a marriage (Ley 13/2005 de 1 de julio, por la que se modifica el Codigo Civil en materia de derecho a contraer matrimonio).

also be his accommodation (in a lease, for example, termination of which by the lessor is also subject to a legislative obligation to give reasons).

German law recognises a similar concept, which might be put to use in a new general law of contract, whether French or even European. In relation to self-employed persons, this law identifies a separate category of 'persons analogous to employees' (*arbeitnehmerähnliche Personen*), those being persons who are independent as a matter of law, but who are dependent economically.[52] Precise criteria have been developed by the courts and by legislation to delimit this category more precisely.

For example, this concept features expressly in the law on collective agreements (Tarifvertragsgesetz), § 12a(1) of which defines the concept of *arbeitnehmerähnliche Personen*[53] and which assimilates such a person to an employee where he is considered to be economically dependent and in need of social protection. This is principally the case where he works alone without the company of other employees and he receives from a single person on average more than half of his total income from his profession (a third is sufficient in the press, radio and television sectors).[54]

A similar way of thinking can also be found in other German legislative provisions, for example in the law governing employment tribunals, whose jurisdiction extends to persons comparable to employees such as 'quasi-salaried' commercial representatives; here the relevant legislation requires that such persons represent only one undertaking and do not earn on average more than €1,000 per month.[55]

---

[52] See A Supiot (ed), *Au-delà de l'emploi: Transformations du travail et devenir du droit du travail en Europe* (Paris, Flammarion, 1999) 32–3.

[53] According to this article: '(1) The provisions of this Law apply:
1. to persons, who are economically dependent and are in need of protection in social matters comparable to that of an employee (persons similar to employees), if they work for other persons on the basis of contracts for services or for a specific undertaking, provide the services owed in person and essentially without the assistance of employees and a) work predominantly for one person or; b) receive on average more than half their total earned income from one person; if it is not possible to calculate this in advance, then, unless otherwise agreed in a collective agreement, calculation shall be based on income during the previous six months, or where the work has been for a shorter time, that shorter time.
2. to the persons listed in no 1, for whom the persons similar to employees are working, as well as to the legal relations formed between them and the persons similar to employees through a contract for services or for a specific undertaking.'

[54] Cf § 12a(3) of the Tarifvertragsgesetz.

[55] § 5 Arbeitsgerichtsgesetz (Law on Labour Courts, ie employment tribunals) devoted to 'the concept of employee': '(3) Commercial representatives shall only be treated as employees within the meaning of this law if they belong to the group of persons for whom, under § 92a of the Commercial code, the lower limits of the contractual performance of the undertaking can be established, and if, during the last six months of the contractual relationship, or in the case of a shorter contract period, during that period, on average they have not received more than 1000 Euros per month as payment, including commission and expenses for any outlay incurred in the general running of the business on the basis of the contract. The Federal Ministry for Employment and Social Matters, and the Federal Ministry of Justice may in common accord with the Federal Ministry for the Economy and Technology adapt the earnings limits specified in sentence 1 to the current wages and prices index by means of regulations which do not require the approval of the Senate.'

The advantage of these types of criteria is that the situation is assessed by the court on a case-by-case basis, which is fairer. In fact, for a given type of contract, the weaker party is not always the one that one might anticipate. Dependence is certainly often associated with the type of contract under consideration, but not necessarily, and it may equally be the product of specific circumstances: for example, the fact that one of the parties was obliged to make significant capital expenditure; in such a case the other party should not be able to break off from that relationship lightly, without allowing the first party time for these expenditures to be amortised. Moreover, sometimes the party requiring protection is the creditor who finds himself faced with non-performance by the debtor, but sometimes it may be the debtor, as in the case where the creditor relies on an alleged failure to perform on the part of his contracting party in order to avoid having to meet his own obligations. It is therefore appropriate to leave to the court the task of assessing the specific situation on the facts.

To conclude, the *Avant-projet* has missed the opportunity of refining the general rules governing unilateral termination of contracts of indefinite duration by rendering them more appropriate to real situations, despite the fact that such a reform is desperately needed. Instead, the general theory of contract that it propose remains abstract and is at risk of withering away and thus causing an ever greater reliance on special sets of rules governing particular types of contract.

Yet, even the Conseil constitutionnel in its decision on civil pacts of solidarity stressed the legislator's obligation to fill the gap in the legal regime governing the termination of contracts of indefinite duration. It thus held, quite generally,

> that if the contract is the general law common to the parties, the freedom that flows from article 4 of the Declaration of the rights of man and of the citizen of 1789 justifies the existence of a situation where a private law contract of indefinite duration may be broken off unilaterally by one or the other of the contracting parties, but nevertheless there must be a guarantee that the other contracting party will receive notice and compensation for any harm which may result from the circumstances of the termination. In that respect, it is the duty of the legislator, because of the need to ensure the protection of one of the parties in certain types of contract, to specify the grounds on which such a prospective termination may take place, and the procedures through which it may be effected, particularly as regards notice.[56]

In this area of the law, then, everything remains to be done.

---

[56] Decision no 99-419 DC of 9 November 1999, JO 16 November 1999, 16962, concerning the Law on the Civil Pact of Solidarity.

9

'Termination' for Contractual Non-performance and its Consequences: French Law Reviewed in the Light of the Avant-projet de réforme

SIMON WHITTAKER

The remarkable feature of contract law is that it allows people (whether human or corporate) to change their legal relations, creating new rights and obligations for each other by agreement, however agreement is understood and whether these rights and obligations are specified by this agreement itself or arise from it by operation of law. As article 1134(1) Cc so strikingly expresses it, by their agreement the parties can create their own law, even though this law is both subordinate to the law of the land and is in principle restricted to themselves. Granting this private law-making power to contracting parties allows them to change legal facts, ie the world as perceived through the prism of the law, for the law re-creates the real world in its own images. This means that once the parties have made an agreement in the way which the law sees as contractual and lawful, in a certain sense nothing and no one can undo their act of creation: it forms part of the private legal history of the parties' relations. This does not mean, of course, that the law cannot *treat* the parties' legal relations in a way *as if* their contractual act of creation had not taken place, but to do so is a legal fiction which requires justification. Moreover, it is a fiction whose effect would be retroactive, and retroactivity in the unmaking of the parties' private law has in common with retroactivity in public law-making that it disappoints reasonable expectations and disrupts legitimate planning.

What actually happens after the creation of a contract depends, of course, principally on the parties themselves, though exterior circumstances

may also have a bearing. So, where they both perform their obligations perfectly, the latter are said to be discharged (ie they no longer 'bind' the parties) and other consequences may also flow—eg the ownership of property that is the subject-matter of the contract may be transferred. However, where one of the parties does not perform or does not perform perfectly, new questions arise as to the appropriate response of the law to this contractual failure in performance. The language used to denote this response is noticeably different in English and French law (putting aside mere differences in the language types themselves), the former referring to remedies for breach of contract (and exceptionally the frustration of the contract); the latter traditionally referring to the need to ensure performance (in the interest of the debtor as well as the interest of the creditor) or otherwise to sanction or excuse non-performance depending on the circumstances, this language overtly reflecting a sense of the moral dimension to obligations and their non-performance. Moreover, the way in which these two laws respond to contractual non-performance (be it 'imputable' or not) differs considerably, each response stemming from their different legal histories and from significantly different starting points of legal principle or of legal policy; and each of the various 'responses' (be they 'remedies' or 'sanctions') are inextricably linked to each other. As a result, any individual response to non-performance (whether 'specific enforcement', damages or 'termination for non-performance/breach') needs to be seen in the context of the much wider pattern.

The particular topic for my discussion—'termination' for contractual non-performance (which I shall use to refer to cases of imputable non-performance or breach, thereby excluding cases of 'excused non-performance' where French law recognises *force majeure* and English law the doctrine of frustration)—raises some particularly nice and difficult questions for both English law and French law, but in this chapter I shall focus my attention on the French law in the light of the proposed changes in the *Avant-projet de réforme du droit des obligations et de la prescription*. In this respect, both French and English law describe what happens to the legal relations between the parties as 'ending' or being 'terminated'. This reflects a wider way of speaking, it having become customary to describe contracts as though they are things: they have beginnings (their formation by the parties, which may be invalid and so lead to their being rescinded or annulled); middles (performance or non-performance), and ends (though here the language is much more varied in English: sometimes 'discharge', sometimes 'termination' and sometimes 'rescission'). Some authors—particularly in the French context—even draw implicit analogies with animate beings, so that contracts are 'born' and enjoy a life which—hopefully after a period of fulfilment—comes to an end. I have, however, increasingly come to think that at least as regards non-performance this way of describing what

happens to the relationship created by contracts is both inaccurate and unhelpful.

First, it is inaccurate, because contracts are not 'things', let alone animate things; they are the expression of a remarkable legal 'institution' which allows the creation of a special form of legal relationship. And while both French law and English law use language which suggests the ending of the relationship (either by the injured party/creditor[1] or by the court) on the ground of imputable non-performance (so, 'termination' or even 'rescission' in English law, *résolution* or *résiliation* in French law), this does not properly reflect the legal reality. For neither 'termination for breach' on the one hand or *résolution* or *résiliation* on the other bring the legal consequences of a contract to an end, whether this ending is described as being retroactive or merely prospective. For in both legal systems, the contract continues as a ground of a liability in damages which is considered (though not exclusively) contractual rather than extra-contractual;[2] and some aspects of the terms of the contract also survive, particularly where they are intended to govern liability, notably penalty and exemption clauses.[3]

Secondly, the language of 'termination' (and even more of *l'anéantissement du contrat* on *résolution*) is unhelpful, because it appears to lead logically to a set of consequences that arguably may not give proper effect to the substantive policy goals of the legal system in question. In this regard, French law has suffered severely from its historical legacies from Roman law and canon law, the first providing the basis of the implication of a 'resolutory condition' in article 1184(1), the second the judicial power of dispensing the parties from their obligations found in article 1184(2). It is the purpose of this chapter to suggest that the *Avant-projet de réforme* does not go far enough in addressing the problems created by this legacy and by the circumventions which French lawyers have used to deal with them. In all this, I do not intend to argue for the adoption of the common law position (nor the position of the Principles of European Contract Law) as such on the ground that either of them are in some general sense 'better'. Indeed, such a way of thinking would be more than usually wrong-headed given the different substantive orientations of English and French legal responses to contractual non-performance. However, I do suggest that the present approach of French lawyers merits reconsideration.

---

[1] In the following, I shall refer to the 'creditor' even though this is not the normal English legal term except as regards monetary obligations.

[2] For English law this is axiomatic given that liability is founded on the breach of contract. For French law see P Malaurie, L Aynès and P Stoffel-Munck, *Droit civil: Les obligations* (2nd edn, Paris, Défrénois, 2004) no 879; C Larroumet, *Droit civil: Les Obligations—Le Contrat* (5th edn, Economica, Paris, 2003) no 716. This is not the position taken by all French jurists, some of whom have denied the propriety of referring to *la responsabilité contractuelle*: see especially P Rémy, 'La responsabilité contractuelle: l'histoire d'un faux concept' RTD civ 1997, 323.

[3] See below p 198.

I. '*LA RÉVOLTE DU DROIT CONTRE LE CODE*'[4]

This is not the occasion to expose the position in the Code civil governing termination for non-performance except in outline. Its central feature, though, is important for my argument: the concept of *la condition résolutoire*. As has been explained in the French literature, the use of this concept and its treatment by articles 1183 and 1184 reflects a joint legal legacy.[5]

First, it reflects the reception into the debates of Romanist legal scholarship of the Roman practice of the use of express contract terms to govern the effect of failure to perform on the contract itself, these terms being known as *leges commissoriae*. However, by the time of the making of the Code civil, its draftsmen could see it as unnecessary to require the parties to make express provision. As a result, article 1183—which is contained in the section of the Code devoted to *conditions*—first defines a *condition résolutoire* as a condition whose fulfilment 'revokes the obligation, and puts things into the same state as if the obligation had not existed', it then being emphasised that in these circumstances 'it obliges the creditor to restore what he has received'. Then, article 1184(1) provides that such a condition is 'always to be understood in synallagmatic contracts to deal with the situation where one of the two parties fails to satisfy his undertaking'. So, the technique adopted by the Code civil is the insertion by law into synallagmatic contracts of a condition whose very nature requires that when it is satisfied (ie when the debtor's obligation is not performed) the effect on the contract is its retroactive dissolution (*résolution*), with restitution by the creditor and counter-restitution by the debtor. This effect is typically described by French jurists and courts as *l'anéantissement du contrat*, ie the complete destruction of the contract, and can be seen to stem from the adoption of the notion of *condition résolutoire* by the Code.

Secondly, the influence of the canon lawyers is seen in the requirement of the need for a creditor to go to court to ask for *résolution*.[6] This requirement—which does not follow the logic of the insertion of a *condition résolutoire* which would naturally take effect automatically without the intervention of either the creditor or the court[7]—appears to stem from the idea that once the law has recognised that the parties to a contract have created *obligations*, they should be kept to them unless they are dispensed from doing so by a body invested with public authority (here, the court) that can assess the relative morality of the behaviour of the parties.[8] A first

---

[4] Cf G Morin, *La révolte du droit contre le code: la révision nécessaire des concepts juridiques (Contrat, responsabilité, propriété)* (Paris, Sirey, 1945) who does not, however, refer to *résolution*.

[5] F Terré, P Simler and Y Lequette, *Droit civil: Les obligations* (9th edn, Paris, Dalloz, 2005) no 644; Malaurie et al, above n 2, no 875.

[6] 'La résolution doit être demandée en justice . . .': art 1184(3) Cc.

[7] Terré et al, above n 5, no 644.

[8] Malaurie et al, above n 2, no 875.

effect of the judicial nature of *résolution* is that it allows the *juges du fond*[9] to assess whether the debtor's non-performance is sufficiently serious to justify *résolution*, a decision that in the absence of total non-performance gives them a good deal of leeway as to the appropriateness of allowing *résolution* in limine.

However, article 1184(3) Cc goes further and allows French courts to refuse a creditor's request for *résolution* (even if the debtor's non-performance is sufficiently serious) and instead give the debtor further time to perform. Such a *délai de grâce* was justified at the time (and is still justified) on the ground of the possible need for 'humanity' in treatment of the contractual debtor (which is also reflected in article 1244 in the context of money obligations[10]), but even more it is seen as a way in which the law encourages the preservation of the contract and its performance. So, while article 1184(2) also recognises a right in the creditor to ask the court for performance of the contract as long as this is possible (instead of asking for *résolution* with damages where appropriate), article 1184(3) recognises in the debtor a certain lingering right to perform, even after a serious failure to do so.

Clearly, these features of article 1184 relate to the modern reinterpretation of the creditor's right to performance, a right which famously appears in articles 1143 and 1144 Cc as an exception to the seemingly general rule of damages found in article 1142; but it is nevertheless universally accepted by *la doctrine*, an acceptance that the *Avant-projet* recommends should be given legislative expression.[11] Here, article 1144 Cc is very significant and marks a particular contrast with the approach of the common law. For, if the creditor of an obligation wishes to gain 'performance' (ie, here, the receipt of the *prestation promise* by the debtor) but not *from* the debtor (notably, on the ground that he has lost confidence in his ability to perform in a satisfactory way), he can apply to the court for authority to have the obligation performed by a third party at the debtor's expense. To a common lawyer used to the law's encouragement of unilateral obtaining of a substitute performance through the doctrine of mitigation of damage, this is an odd provision: first, because obtaining a substitute performance is treated as an example of *exécution en nature* even though it is not performance *by the debtor*; but even more in the need for judicial permission before the substitute is obtained. However, article 1144 makes perfect

---

[9] Cass civ 5 May 1921, S 1921.1.298.

[10] S Whittaker, 'A Period of Grace for Contractual Performance?' in M Andenas, A De Leon Arce, M Grimaldi, B Markesinis, H-W Micklitz and N Pasquini (eds), *Liber Amicorum Guido Alpa: Private Law Beyond the National Systems* (London, British Institute of International and Comparative Law, 2007) 1083; C Jamin, 'Les conditions de la résolution du contrat: vers un modèle unique' in M Fontaine and G Viney (eds), *Les sanctions de l'inexécution des obligations contractuelles: Etudes de droit comparé* (Bruxelles, Bruyant and Paris, LGDJ, 2001) 451, 452, citing Tribun Favart in the course of the *travaux préparatoires* of the Code civil.

[11] Art 1154 of the *Avant-projet*.

sense in the French context and dovetails neatly with article 1184. For the effect of a creditor's obtaining a substitute performance at the expense of the debtor is to remove the debtor's *right to perform*, even if it gives effect to the creditor's *right to performance*. Similarly, a creditor who seeks to extricate himself from the contract by applying for *résolution judiciaire* may find that the court gives the debtor further time to perform and, if he does, the creditor must then perform his own reciprocal obligations. Articles 1144 and 1184 reflect the same policy of encouraging performance by the parties even though they do so from different starting-points. These provisions reflect a very particular vision of the significance of *la force obligatoire des contrats*.

However, while this policy of encouraging performance remains an important one, there has already been *une révolte du droit contre le Code* and from three directions.[12]

First, French courts have gradually recognised that the creditor may himself sometimes choose to terminate the contract on the ground of the debtor's non-performance despite the general requirement that *résolution* be judicial.[13] This was first recognised where *résolution* was considered urgent, where the parties' relationship was one of confidence (which had been lost), or where the creditor would otherwise suffer an irreparable loss.[14] However, in 1998 the Cour de cassation went very much further, declaring that

> the seriousness of the behaviour [*le comportement grave*] of a party to a contract can justify the other party in putting an end to it unilaterally at his own risk [*à ses risques et périls*].[15]

This 'unilateral breaking-off' (*rupture unilatérale*) from a contract by a creditor can affect contracts whose performance is instantaneous or over a period that is fixed or left undetermined.[16] The significance of a creditor acting *à ses risques et périls* is that if he purports to terminate a contract for non-performance, it remains open to the debtor to go to court and ask it to refuse to recognise the creditor's act of termination: if the court holds that the creditor acted within his rights, then it will uphold his earlier *rupture unilatérale*, but if not, his earlier action will itself constitute an imputable non-performance of his own contractual obligations. However, what is not yet clear is the exact significance of the central requirement that the debtor's non-performance is 'sufficiently serious'. Some authors argue that

---

[12] For the following, see Jamin, above n 10, 459–510.

[13] Terré et al, above n 5, nos 660–61. There are also legislative exceptions to the judicial nature of *résolution*, eg art 1657 Cc (refusal by buyer to accept goods).

[14] F Terré, P Simler and Y Lequette, *Droit civil: Les obligations* (8th edn, Paris, Dalloz, 2002) 639.

[15] Cass civ (1) 13 October 1998, Bull civ I no 300, D 1999, 197 note Jamin; Cass civ (1) 20 February 2001, D 2001, 568 note Jamin; similarly, Cass civ (1) 28 October 2003, Bull civ I no 211, RDC 2004, 273 note Aynès, 277 note Mazeaud; Terré et al, above n 5, nos 660–61.

[16] Cass civ (1) 20 February 2001, n 15 above; Terré et al, above n 5, no 660.

this requirement does not differ from the condition required by courts for their own termination of contracts for non-performance,[17] but others disagree, seeing the language used by the Cour de cassation as requiring some further wrongful element to the debtor's behaviour.[18] As to the effects of *rupture unilatérale* on the contract, the language used by the Cour de cassation is very neutral, as it avoids using either the term *résolution* or *résiliation,* and refers to the creditor's 'putting an end' to the contract.[19] *A priori*, the effect should depend on similar considerations as are taken into account by the courts in deciding the effects of their own termination of contracts.[20] Overall, many French jurists admit that under cover of merely qualifying article 1184 Cc, this new case-law allows creditors unilaterally to terminate the contract for serious non-performance in the face of the Code's provisions subject only to the possibility of later control by a court.[21]

Here, the *Avant-projet* recognises the latest case-law fully for its article 1158(2) and (3), providing that:

> Where a creditor opts for termination of the contract, he can either claim it from the court or by his own act put the defaulting debtor on notice to fulfil his undertaking within a reasonable time, failure to do so in the debtor leading to the creditor's right himself to terminate the contract.
>
> Where a debtor continues to fail to perform, the creditor can give him notice that the contract is terminated and on what grounds. In these circumstances, termination takes effect at the time of receipt of the notice by the other party to the contract.

Therefore, under the *Avant-projet* a creditor's unilateral power to terminate the contract is not overtly subjected to any substantive condition (such as urgency) beyond 'non-performance', but it is subjected to two procedural requirements aimed at protecting the debtor: (i) a prior notice by the creditor to perform within a reasonable period on pain of *résolution*, and (ii) if the debtor's failure persists, notice by the creditor of his act of *résolution* supported by his reason for doing so (this notice taking effect on its arrival at the debtor's address).[22] The first of these requirements gives the debtor a modest *délai de grâce* in common with the general requirement of *mise en demeure*; but the second requirement's demand of the giving of a stated reason for terminating would provide a practical route into challenging the creditor's unilateral act of *résolution* on the grounds of his bad faith. This means, of course, that there is a significant risk still for the

---

[17] Terré et al, above n 5, no 661; similarly, Jamin, note D 2001, 568.
[18] Aynès, above n 15.
[19] Cass civ (1) 20 February 2001, n 15 above.
[20] See above pp 190–91.
[21] Terré et al, above n 5, no 661.
[22] Both these conditions were suggested by D Mazeaud, note on Cass civ (1) 28 October 2003, RDC 2004, 273.

creditor: as article 1158-1 of the *Avant-projet* expressly provides, the debtor may contest the creditor's unilateral *résolution* on the ground that 'any failure to perform which is alleged against him does not justify termination of the contract' ('le manquement qui lui est imputé ne justifie pas la résolution du contrat'). It is unfortunate for this purpose that the *Avant-projet* does not explain further the situations where non-performance will or will not justify *résolution*, whether in the case of the creditor's purported unilateral act or the court's own decision. The only description of the 'non-performance' for these purposes is that it may be 'imperfect',[23] a description which makes clear that non-performance need not be total.[24] What we do not see is the outlining of the sorts of considerations that the courts actually take into account in their decision as to *résolution*, considerations which have been identified by *la doctrine*[25] but which were clearly thought to be inappropriate for codified legislation. Secondly, French courts accept that sometimes the effect of a creditor's request for the contract to be brought to an end takes effect only prospectively. Here, following the terminology used by the Code civil itself in the exceptional situations where this is recognised,[26] the creditor is said to effect the *résiliation* of the contract. The importance in French law of the prospective nature of *résiliation* is that there is no general dissolution of the contract with its concomitant obligations of restitution and counter-restitution by the parties. Instead, up until the time of non-performance the parties may keep the benefit of what each has done for the other under the contract (their *prestations*), though they are said to be released from their obligations for the future. Clearly, therefore, it is important to know how large is this exception to the retroactive dissolution of the contract under article 1183.

La doctrine seems to be in general agreement that *résiliation* (whether judicial or unilateral) can take place where performance of the contract is continuous or in instalments (*à exécution successive ou échéllonée*).[27] The justification for this exception usually advanced is that in these contracts restitution and counter-restitution is too difficult, a justification which is just as usually knocked down on the basis that while this may be true of specific restitution (*restitution en nature*) it is not true of restitution of an equivalent value (*restitution en valeur*).[28] Nevertheless, contracts of hire of goods, tenancies of land and employment all clearly fall within this

---

[23] Art 1158(1) of the *Avant-projet*.
[24] Cf Conseil national des barreaux, *Projet de rapport du groupe de travail chargé d'étudier l'avant-projet de réforme du droit des obligations et du droit de la prescription* (2006), 33, http://www.cnb.avocat.fr/PDF/2006-11-09_obligations.pdf, which criticises this description of non-performance as 'too vague'.
[25] Jamin, above n 10, 464–9.
[26] Arts 1636, 1638 and 1729 Cc.
[27] On this distinction, see J Ghestin, C Jamin and M Billau, *Traité de droit civil: Les effets du contrat* (2nd edn, Paris, LGDJ, 1994) nos 142–3.
[28] C Paulin, *La clause résolutoire* (Paris, LGDJ, 1996) 99.

exception as their performance takes place over a period of time. So, where a landlord seeks to end a tenancy for failure to pay rent (to the extent to which he is entitled to do so[29]), any termination of the contract takes effect only prospectively: the landlord does not have to return rent previously paid nor does the tenant have to pay any sum representing his enjoyment of the property. The contrast is with a contract whose performance is 'instantaneous', the example usually given being a contract of sale for cash or the commissioning of an agent for one task, where the classic effect of *résolution* applies.

The *Avant-projet* recognises this *jurisprudence* in article 1160-1, providing that:

> Termination of the contract frees the parties from their obligations.
>
> As regards contracts with performance successively or in instalments, termination takes effect for the future; the parties' undertakings cease from the time of service of proceedings for termination or from the time of notice of any unilateral termination.
>
> If the contract has been performed in part, anything so exchanged by the parties gives rise neither to restitution nor to any compensation as long as they conformed to the respective obligations of the parties.
>
> As regards contracts whose performance is instantaneous, termination of the contract is retroactive; each party must make restitution to the other in respect of what he has received, in accordance with the rules set out in section 6 of this chapter.

From the point of view of an English lawyer, the key element missing from the *Avant-projet*, though, are definitions of these categories of *contrats à exécution successive ou échelonnée* and *contrats à exécution instantanée*: even granted traditional French legislative style, this would have been helpful. Nevertheless, the effect of a recognised place for *résiliation* in the present law, which is still usually viewed as an 'exception', is very striking: for where *résiliation* is considered appropriate, the effect is to protect the reliance by either of the parties on the continuation of the contract, this reliance being disturbed prospectively only where the creditor gives the debtor notice to perform, the debtor continues to fail to perform, and the contract is subjected to *résiliation*. From an external viewpoint, the proper justification of the prospective effect of *résiliation* is the protection of reliance rather than any ostensible difficulty in restitution or counter-restitution.

At this stage, though, it may be useful to ask whether the impression which one still gains from the *Avant-projet* that *résolution* is the rule and *résiliation* the exception should be retained.[30] Surely the vast majority of

---

[29] There is a considerable protection for tenants against termination of their tenancies: Terré et al, above n 5, no 663.

[30] This way of thinking—which stems from the present form of the Code civil—can be seen as implicit from the use throughout articles 1157–1160 of the *Avant-projet* of the terminology of

types of contracts are *not* 'instantaneous' in the sense here intended. So, contracts whose performance extends over a period include not merely contracts of hire, contracts for services and of employment, but most contracts of agency, all contracts of insurance, contracts for the licensing of intellectual property, contracts for the loan of money at interest—and indeed, possibly *all* contracts made on credit,[31] as performance by the debtor of his monetary obligation is necessarily extended over a period. If this description of the relative significance of the two broad categories of contract is accurate, then the law should perhaps be stated in the form that *résiliation* is the rule, *résolution* the exception.

Thirdly, while not strictly speaking a 'revolt of the *law*' against the Code civil, contracting parties have avoided recourse to *résolution judiciaire* by inserting into their contracts express terms making provision for their *résolution* in certain circumstances.[32] The effect of such a *clause résolutoire* depends in part on its terms, but if widely and carefully drafted, in principle it can allow the creditor to 'dissolve' the contract unilaterally (ie without any need to give the debtor a further chance of performance through *mise en demeure* and without recourse to court) in the circumstances which it specifies (and so avoiding the *appréciation des juges du fond* as to the question of the seriousness of the debtor's failure to perform).[33] Where the term is valid,[34] the creditor's reliance on it can save time, expense and avoid the uncertainty of the scheme put in place by article 1184 Cc. However, these advantages come at a cost: for a *clause résolutoire* allows a creditor to avoid the various judicial and legal protections which article 1184 enshrines for debtors. Under the present law, the effect of the exercise by the creditor of his right under a *clause résolutoire* depends upon its terms and in particular it may provide for *résiliation* in *contrats à exécution successive*.[35] Where the effect of a credi-

---

résolution, and the way in which the *Avant-projet* brings in *résiliation*, as article 1160-1 states that '[d]ans les contrats à exécution successive ou échelonnée, la résolution vaut résiliation'. Cf the introduction to the provisions by J Rochfeld, 'Exposé des motifs: Inexécution des obligations' in *Avant-projet de réforme du droit des obligations et de la prescription: Rapport remis au garde des Sceaux* (Paris, La documentation française, 2006) 52, 55 (see below p 567) which states that 'it is proposed that legislation should establish the consequences of termination of the contract, by providing in principle for termination for the future, except for the case of contracts of instantaneous performance where termination is to be retroactive'.

[31] At times jurists refer to *contrat de vente au comptant* as typical of an instantaneous contract (which suggests the exclusion of sales on credit); at others, they say that *vente à terme* (where payment is deferred) can nevertheless be 'instantaneous' (eg B Starck, H Roland and L Boyer, *Obligations*, vol 2: *Contrat* (4th edn, Paris, Litec, 1993) no 116; Ghestin et al, above n 27, no 142).

[32] According to Jamin, above n 10, 483 the courts recognised the validity of *clauses résolutoires* from 1860.

[33] Malaurie et al, above n 2, no 888.

[34] A *clause résolutoire* may be invalid on the ground of special legislation (eg contracts of tenancy, above n 29) or subject to a test of fairness in the case of consumer contracts: art L 132-1 Code de la consommation.

[35] Paulin, above n 28, 103.

tor's invocation of such a *clause résolutoire* is the same as under article 1183 Cc, ie the retroactive dissolution of the parties' obligations together with restitution and counter-restitution, this does not prevent the creditor from obtaining damages for any further losses that the breach of contract has caused him. However, one of the striking effects of such a dissolution is that any title to property which has passed reverts to its transferor: indeed, this appears to be one of the great practical advantages of reliance on a *clause résolutoire* as its invocation can allow the creditor to avoid the debtor's insolvency.[36] Clearly, this proprietary restitutionary effect of *clauses resolutoires* has the potential to create considerable disruption to the certainty of title of third parties, and this is avoided in French law only by the presence of wide protections for the recipients of movable property in good faith under article 2279 Cc.[37] Nevertheless, it can be seen that the effect of valid reliance on a *clause résolutoire* is a drastic one and the analogy with penalty clauses which is often drawn in *la doctrine* an understandable one.[38] For this reason, legislation has sometimes rendered *clauses résolutoires* invalid or otherwise controlled their exercise, and the courts have taken a very strict approach to the interpretation of their ambit and subjected their use to a requirement of good faith.[39]

The *Avant-projet*'s provisions governing *clauses résolutoires* follow fairly closely the existing *jurisprudence* and put in place a number of protections for the debtor so as to make up for the absence of judicial involvement. So, article 1159 of the *Avant-projet* provides expressly for the effectiveness of *clauses résolutoires* and then that such a contract term must expressly identify the contractual undertakings whose non-performance may lead to termination of the contract and that *résolution* under such a term is subject to a condition of prior service of an unsuccessful notice to perform which itself clearly refers to the term. However, while article 1159 describes the effects of *clauses résolutoires* in terms of *résolution*, article 1160-1 provides that '[t]ermination of the contract frees the parties from their obligations' ('[d]ans les contrats à exécution successive ou échelonnée, la résolution vaut résiliation'), a provision which appears to govern *résolution* under a *clause résolutoire* as well as *résolution judiciaire*. This seems to intend therefore to replace the present position which allows the effect of a *clause résolutoire* to turn on its terms with a rule of law requiring termination under such a contract term to be retrospective.

---

[36] Jamin, above n 10, 488, referring to art 37 of the Loi no 85-98 du 25 janvier 1985 relative au redressement et à la liquidation judiciaires des entreprises, JO 26 January 1985, 1097, a provision now found in art L 622-13 of the Code de commerce.

[37] Terré et al, above n 5, nos 656, 662.

[38] *Ibid* no 662 in fine.

[39] *Ibid* nos 664.

II. *RÉSOLUTION* AND THE AVOIDANCE OF LOGIC

I have already drawn attention to the fact that one apparently logical consequence of use by the Code civil of the notion of *condition résolutoire* (that the dissolution occurs without the need to go to court) was itself directly averted by article 1184's express rule which states that *résolution* '*doit être demandée en justice*', requiring therefore both the creditor's application and a court's consent.[40] This way of thinking is confirmed by the *Avant-projet*'s abandonment of the 'debatable technique' of implied condition.[41] More generally, sometimes the modern law has avoided other aspects of the apparent logic of *résolution*, while at other times it has given it full effect.

(a) The Survival of Some Contract Terms after *résolution*

As already mentioned briefly above, French law recognises that the 'retro-active destruction' of a contract by *résolution* does not wipe out all its terms.[42] So, in particular, contract terms whose purpose is to regulate the consequences of non-performance (notably, exemption clauses and penalty clauses) survive; and, of course, the retroactive destruction of a contract under a *clause résolutoire expresse* does not wipe out *this* clause and with it the power of *résolution*. In all these cases, the survival of the terms can be justified on the basis of the parties' intentions—these clauses were intended to deal with the very situation to which *résolution* is *part of* the law's response to non-performance. Moreover, in the case of an exemption clause the survival of the contract term can (depending on its drafting) exclude recourse to extra-contractual liability under articles 1382–1384 Cc (where the law allows such an exclusion[43]) despite the 'destruction' of the contract: for if, as is generally acknowledged, the debtor's liability for con-tractual non-performance remains contractual even after *résolution*, then the rule of *non-cumul des responsabilités contractuelle et délictuelle* would exclude recourse to extra-contractual liability.[44]

However, there are other types of contract term that are also said to survive *résolution* that do not fall into exactly this category: arbitration clauses and choice of jurisdiction clauses.[45] While these clauses may relate to the circumstances that have given rise to *résolution*, their ambit may be

---

[40] See above p 190.

[41] Rochfeld, above n 30, 53, 54 (see below p 563).

[42] Terré et al, above n 5, no 653.

[43] In principle, such a clause will control both contractual and extra-contractual liability except for *dol* and *faute lourde*: Malaurie et al, above n 2, nos 986.

[44] This rule of *non-cumul* is recognised (with an exception for claims for personal injuries) by art 1341 of the *Avant-projet*.

[45] Terré et al, above n 5, no 654.

broader—and, indeed, relate to matters other than the contractual obligations in question. A likely reason for the recognition of their survival of *résolution* may be found in the fact that their nature reveals that the parties intended them to survive despite *résolution*: and the parties' intentions should be given effect on the basis of *la force obligatoire du contrat*. However, if this is indeed the principle, its impact could be wider. So, for example, the question has arisen of the effect of *résolution* on a clause of non-competition: should it survive? At present, the *jurisprudence* appears hostile,[46] but it could well be argued that this should depend upon the circumstances and in particular on the intentions of the parties. Similarly, the question has arisen of the effect of 'termination' for breach of contract terms imposing a duty of confidentiality, the Cour de cassation holding that a banker's duty of confidentiality survives *résiliation* of the contract.[47] Here too, the general position to be taken by French law (ie the position to be taken putting aside any considerations of public policy which may invalidate the term itself) should be that the question of the survival of the term after 'termination' should depend on the intentions of the parties as interpreted in the usual way: the logic of *résolution* should not defeat the intentions of the parties in the absence of a genuine contrary consideration of *ordre public*.[48]

How, though, can these surviving obligations be accounted for? In the view of Professor Fabre-Magnan in one of the few discussions to address this problem head-on,[49] 'one cannot deny that in these situations the contract has well and truly disappeared'.[50] So, in the case of an employee's continuing obligation of confidentiality after leaving the employment, the contract of employment no longer exists. Nevertheless, even after termination of the contract, certain of its obligations survive, this being clear from the contractual nature of the liability which is engendered if they are broken.[51] She concludes that

> In a way, those contractual obligations which form the contract's natural accessories survive its disappearance, and this shows that a contract creates a relationship between the parties whose significance is not necessarily exhausted by the fulfilment of its main obligations.[52]

There is a great deal here with which I agree, not least in the recognition of the relative effect of 'termination' and the distinction between the contract itself and the relationship that it engenders. What I am less clear about

---

[46] Eg Cass civ (1) 29 November 1989, Bull civ I no 245; Cass civ (1) 6 March 1996, Bull civ I no 118.
[47] Cass civ (1) 2 June 1993, Bull civ I no 197.
[48] Paulin, above n 28, 107.
[49] M Fabre-Magnan, *Les obligations* (Paris, PUF, 2004) no 191.
[50] '[O]n ne peut nier que, dans tous ces cas, le contrat a bel et bien disparu'.
[51] Fabre-Magnan, above n 49, no 191.
[52] *Ibid*.

is that it is helpful to express this in terms of the 'disappearance' of the contract and the survival of the relationship which it creates. Surely, if anything, the reality is better reflected by saying that, for example, the *relationship of employment* disappears, even though the contract itself—or certain elements of it at least—survives. According to this way of thinking, the contract triggers a relationship that may then take on a certain independent existence from it.

The *Avant-projet de réforme* does not seek to address these questions overtly, though interestingly in its elaborate provisions governing restitution after '*l'anéantissement*' ('the destruction') of contracts in the context of both annulment and *résolution*, it provides that the benefit of any security provided for performance of the contract's primary obligations is transferred to the obligation to make restitution:[53] here again, therefore, aspects of the contract continue to take effect even after its own 'destruction', in this situation without any evidence of party intention to this effect.

(b) Contractual Liability in Damages and its Measure

It has been noted above that French lawyers assume that liability for contractual non-performance remains contractual even if the contract is 'destroyed' by *résolution*.[54] Clearly, at some level, this is a logical contradiction, for if the contract is retroactively wiped out (with its accompanying restitutionary consequences), it can no longer provide a proper basis for a claim for damages.

For the most part, though, French jurists have not (to my knowledge) seen the issue of the classification of liability for non-performance after *résolution* as problematic (or, indeed, even interesting). However, Professor Fabre-Magnan draws attention to a related question in one of the few French discussions to consider the way in which an award of damages should reflect the special nature of contractual obligations. The relevant passage focuses on the distinction between two main interests in awards of contract damages: the 'positive interest' (or as a common lawyer would put it, the 'expectation' or 'performance' interest), which is satisfied where the aim of an award of damages is to put the creditor in the position as though the contract had been performed; and the 'negative interest' (to the common lawyer, 'reliance interest') which is satisfied where the aim of an award of damages is to put the creditor in the position as though the contract had not been made.[55] This distinction is not generally discussed by French lawyers,[56] owing principally to the generally perceived significance

---

[53] Art 1162-1(1) of the *Avant-projet*.
[54] See above p 189.
[55] Fabre-Magnan, above n 49, no 216.
[56] A further exception may be found in P Rémy-Corlay, 'Exécution et réparation: deux concepts' RDC 2004, 13, 27.

of *le principe de la réparation intégrale* (the principle of complete reparation of a claimant's harm) and the allocation to the *juges du fond* of a 'sovereign power of assessment' of a claimant's loss (and therefore his damages). However, in the course of this discussion, Professor Fabre-Magnan explains that a creditor faced with non-performance by a debtor has a choice between claiming performance (which could either be direct by asking the court to order *exécution forcée en nature* or indirect by authorising the creditor to have the debtor's obligation performed by a third party at the debtor's expense under article 1144) or claiming *résolution* of the contract with its concomitant restitutions.[57] She then argues that where the contract is subject to *résolution*, only damages based on the creditor's negative interest should be awarded, as he should be put in the position as though the contract had not been made,[58] thereby ensuring that the retroactive nature of *résolution* is reflected in the approach to damages: unlike the common law's position, after opting for *résolution* the creditor cannot recover damages to represent his 'positive' or 'performance' interest. This line of reasoning is certainly logical, and emphasises the very hard choice with which the creditor is faced: either get out of the contract entirely (losing whatever profit it may have brought) or keep the contract for the benefit of both parties.[59]

However, it seems to me that this line of argument takes the logic of retroactivity rather too far. For, as a matter of policy (and of French policy, to the extent to which it is distinct from the common law's), why should the debtor by failing to perform in a way which is sufficiently serious to attract *résolution* be able to force the creditor into choosing between claiming proper performance (whether the debtor or from a third party) or instead losing the benefit of whatever bargain he has made altogether? Putting it the other way around, by removing the liability of the debtor to pay the lost net profit[60] of the creditor and leaving him merely with a right to restitution, the law appears to reduce the *sanction* for the debtor's imputable non-performance. And, by so doing, it reduces the incentive on

---

[57] Fabre-Magnan, above n 49, no 216 (the parenthetic explanation is my own).

[58] *Ibid.*

[59] A similar position is taken by Larroumet who simply asserts that 'only the losses resulting from loss due to *résolution* must be the subject of compensation, for there must be a causal link between the *résolution* for which one of the parties is responsible and the loss established by the other': Larroumet, above n 2, no 716, citing as an example Cass civ (3) 20 December 1995, Bull civ III no 267 where the Cour de cassation quashed a court of appeal's decision allowing damages to the buyer of a house under a contract terminated for non-performance on the part of the seller based on the difference between the price paid and the cost of an equivalent house: the buyer was entitled only to compensation for the delay in being repaid the price of the house (and this was set at a legal rate of interest).

[60] The profit would be net because in principle the effect of *résolution* would be to attract restitution and counter-restitution and so (if perfectly achieved) many of the 'costs' for the creditor and for the debtor of performance would thereby already have been dealt with.

the debtor to perform (or to perform in conformity with the contract). In this way, the restriction on damages recoverable after *résolution* weakens *la force obligatoire des contrats*.

I shall give two possible examples, one involving *résolution* and the other *résiliation*.

First, let us take a contract for the sale of goods (an 'instantaneous contract' thereby attracting the possibility of *résolution*):[61] the goods are delivered, but are not in conformity with the contract (eg they are the wrong type or wrong colour) to an extent to which the law accepts that the buyer can 'terminate' the contract; the buyer is granted *résolution* by the court for serious non-performance and gets back the price, the seller receiving back the goods. But if the buyer bought the goods for €500 and they were then (or are now) worth €700, why should the seller's non-performance deprive the buyer of his bargain (ie €200)? Agreed, the buyer could (quite apart from commercial sales where there is *laissé pour compte*[62]) ask the court for an order for proper performance by the seller or for *remplacement* under article 1144 Cc. But if the non-performance is sufficiently serious, why not allow termination with restitution/counter-restitution *and* damages for the net lost bargain?

My second example is of a contract of loan of money (and let us assume not a consumer credit contract which would attract special protections in both English and French law). The contract is for loan of €100,000 with a modest (lawful) rate of interest payable and principal repayable monthly over a period of five years. After one year, the debtor fails to pay several times. There is an express *clause résolutoire* in the contract which stipulates for prospective termination (*résiliation*) by the creditor of the contract on the ground of such a continuing non-performance. Again, assuming the effect of such a clause would be indeed to allow *résiliation* by the creditor (so allowing him to keep the interest paid and any principal repaid until the relevant failures to pay), what other effects would flow from *résiliation*? Certainly, it would terminate the debtor's future duty to pay instalments of interest, and it would normally also mean that he would have to repay the principal in full (this is normally stipulated expressly by English contracts and, let us assume for present purposes, also in our hypothetical French contract). If this is the case, can the creditor recover damages reflecting the profit he would have made from the *whole* of the contract of loan, ie all the profit from the interest over the five years of repayment of the loan? Or would he have to be content merely with recovery of his principal and keeping the interest paid until termination? Here again, restricting a credit-

---

[61] See above pp 194–5.
[62] This enables a buyer to reject the goods and obtain substitutes elsewhere without recourse to court: Malaurie et al, above n 2, no 891.

or's award of damages to his 'negative interest' would deny him his bargain without any apparent justification.

However, if the force of this line of argument were followed by French law so as to allow a party who obtains *résolution* or *résiliation* to recover damages reflecting his net lost bargain, this would certainly be to allow legal policy to trump legal logic: for if the contract is 'destroyed', how can the purpose of damages be to put the creditor in the position as though the contract had been performed?

III. CONCLUDING OBSERVATIONS

There is no doubt that the present terms of the Code civil do not reflect the reality of the law governing termination for imputable non-performance as it is applied by French courts and carried into effect by the parties to French contracts. In this respect, the *Avant-projet de réforme* does set out clearly the possibility of a creditor's unilateral termination of the contract and that the effect of such a termination can be prospective rather than retrospective. However, the provisions of the *Avant-projet* are open to criticism on a number of counts. First, and in common with the present position, they do not give any guidance as to when non-performance is sufficiently serious to justify termination, whether this is judicial or extra-judicial.[63] Secondly, they state the law in a way which assumes that the general rule is that the effect of termination is retroactive, whereas it would appear that in fact it is prospective (though this point depends in part on one's understanding of concepts of 'instantaneous, continuous and instalment contracts', concepts that are left undefined by the *Avant-projet*).[64] Thirdly, where a contract is said to be terminated, whether prospectively or retrospectively, there remains no proper explanation of the survival of certain of its legal effects, notably where it deals with aspects of the effects of contractual non-performance. And, finally, the *Avant-projet* makes no attempt to deal with the question of the measure of damages properly obtainable by a creditor after termination of the contract for non-performance, though the position to be gleaned from *la doctrine* is that—logically—these are available only to put the creditor in the position as though the contract had not been made.[65] In my view, this last position gives preference to logic over legal policy; but until French lawyers generally, and, I would add, in their Code civil, make clear the distinction between the recovery of damages based on the creditor's positive/expectation/performance interest and his negative/reliance interest, the particular

---

[63] See above p 194.
[64] See above pp 195–6.
[65] See above pp 200–01.

case of damages after termination is likely to remain unclear. Unfortunately, while the provisions of the *Avant-projet* governing the assessment of damages do represent a considerable effort to set out the heads of recoverable loss,[66] they do not make use of such a fundamental distinction.

---

[66] Arts 1370–1377 of the *Avant-projet*.

E

The Effects of Contracts on Third Parties

10

Contracts and Third Parties in the Avant-projet de réforme

DENIS MAZEAUD

IN HIS WELL-KNOWN article, published in 1968 in the *Archives de philosophie du droit*,[1] Henri Battifol remarked that article 1165 Cc—which deals with the effects of contracts as regards third parties by providing that 'the binding force of contracts' affects 'only the parties to the contract'—expresses

> a blatant individualism [as a result of which] only relations between individuals are recognised . . .

However, he went on to note that

> one of the most striking evolutions of the subject in the 19th century was the continued development of the effects of contracts in relation to third parties.[2]

And he 'predicted' that this would continue:

> [A] contract cannot be regarded as a bond existing purely between individuals which concerns only the parties who have given their consent to it . . . more general interests [are] at stake . . . in the law of contracts . . . beyond even the simple fact, which has always been recognised, that the juridical acts of individuals have repercussions in their practical impact upon others who have relationships with them outside [the particular] act [in question] . . . it must also be said that contemporary developments have extended the truly legal consequences on third parties. These relationships [show] that contracts have to be placed within a [wider] web of social relationships.[3]

Almost forty years later, when one examines the provisions of *Avant-projet de réforme du droit des obligations et de la prescription* devoted to the effects of contracts in relation to third parties, one is struck both by the relevance and by the foresight of Batiffol's remarks. The individualist

---

[1] H Battifol, 'La crise du contrat' Archives de philosophie du droit 13 (1968), 13.
[2] *Ibid*, 18.
[3] *Ibid*, 27.

dimension, by virtue of which 'the contracting parties, masters of their own consent, may enter into obligations only reciprocally',[4] which was the driving force behind the law of contracts in the Code civil and which continues to permeate the current law, is certainly maintained. The notion that a contract deploys its effects of fact or of law in relation to third parties is, however, very clearly laid down; so much so that one may legitimately ask whether, in the *Avant-projet*, the classical principle of the relative effects of concluded contracts must now come to terms with what may be called the principle of the 'attractive' effects of contractual non-performance.

However, before turning to the substance of the *Avant-projet* on the effects of contracts as regards third parties, certain points should be highlighted.

First, it will be recognised that, from a quantitative viewpoint, the *Avant-projet* contains more than three times as many rules on this issue in comparison with the Code civil. Including not only those rules which are included in Section 7 of Chapter III of Sub-title I, entitled 'The Effects of Contracts as Regards Third Parties', but also the very radical article 1342 which has been inserted into Sub-title III, there are no fewer than twenty-three provisions devoted to relations beyond the contract, whereas even taking all its provisions into account the Code civil contained only seven. This increase is explained, essentially, by the concern of the drafters of the *Avant-projet*, whose objective was to modify the Code civil rather than the law of obligations, to ensure that the Code civil reflects French current law of contracts as faithfully as possible. Logically, this has led them to codify the rules forged by the Cour de cassation over several decades in relation to the impact of a contract beyond the parties, an impact that has never ceased to grow with the passage of time.

Secondly, from a structural point of view one can see a very clear improvement in the presentation of the issue of the effects of contracts in relation to third parties. This improvement proceeds, with the exception of article 1342 which has already been mentioned, through the regrouping into a single subdivision (Section 7 of Chapter III[5] of Sub-title I[6]) of all the rules covering the topic. This represents quite a striking contrast with the Code civil, in which the relevant rules are scattered over various Sections; not only, of course, in the Section entitled 'The Effects of Contracts as Regards Third Parties', but also in diverse Sections relating to consent and to proof. This improvement in presentation is accompanied, it should be noted, by the greater accessibility and intelligibility of these issues, as many of the solutions currently recorded in the *Bulletin des arrêts de la Cour de cassation* are also codified in the *Avant-projet*. Jurists, as well as those using

---

[4] *Ibid*, 18.
[5] 'The Effects of Contracts'.
[6] 'Contracts and Consensual Obligations in General'.

the justice system—for whom the law is made—can only rejoice in this structural renovation.

Moreover, it is to be noted from a comparative point of view that there is a profusion of rules relating to the effects of contracts as regards third parties in the *Avant-projet*. This contrasts with the relative reticence that projects for the harmonisation of European contract law have displayed in relation to this topic. In fact, with the exception of stipulations for the benefit of a third party and the doctrine of *simulation*, the UNIDROIT Principles (at the international level), the Principles of European Contract Law[7] and the Proposals for a European Code of Contract Law[8] do not contain any general rules governing the effects of contracts beyond the contracting parties.[9]

Finally, without prejudging the quality of the rules set out in the *Avant-projet*, it would appear to be permissible to note that the structure of these rules does not perfectly reflect the opposing principles which give life to the question at hand: the individualistic dimension of contracts on the one hand (which allows the channelling of the freedom of the contracting parties), and their economic and social dimensions on the other (which lead, under certain conditions, to the extension of the factual and obligational effects of contracts to third parties). The same point applies within these two guiding notions, which, it is to be admitted, have been presented in a somewhat academic form, but which have the merit of simplicity and intelligibility. The concepts of principle, application and exception are not respected in the *Avant-projet*, ceding their place to a structure that cannot be said to be a beacon of coherence. This defect has led me, by way of a conclusion to this chapter, to propose a new draft of the Section of the *Avant-projet* devoted to the effects of contracts as regards third parties.

Having made these preliminary remarks, it is now high time to outline, explain and assess the rules of the *Avant-projet* on the effects of contracts as regards third parties. In this regard, the statement of Pierre Catala (the guiding-force behind the draft) that the *Avant-projet* does 'not propose to

---

[7] On the PECL see (among other contributions) G Rouhette, I de Lamberterie, D Tallon and C Witz (eds), *Principes du droit européen du contrat* (Paris, Société de législation comparée, 2003); P Rémy-Corlay and D Fenouillet (eds), *Les concepts contractuels français a l'heure du droit européen des contrats* (Paris, Dalloz, 2003); C Jamin and D Mazeaud (eds), *L'harmonisation européene du droit des contrats* (Paris, Economica, 2001); C Prieto (ed), *Regards croisés sur les principes du droit européen du contrat et sur le droit français* (Presses universitaires Aix-Marseille, 2003).

[8] On these proposals see A Debet, 'Le Code européen des contrats, Avant projet' RDC 2003, 217; J-P Gridel, 'Sur l'hypothèse d'un Code européen des contrats: les propositions de l'académie des privatistes européens (Pavie)' Gaz Pal 2003, 240.

[9] For a comparison of the *Avant-projet* and the PECL see B Fauvarque-Cosson and D Mazeaud, 'L'avant projet de réforme du droit des obligations et de la prescription et les principes du droit européen du contrat: variations sur les champs magnétiques dans l'univers contractual' LPA 24 July 2006, no 146, 3. See also B Fauvarque-Cosson and D Mazeaud, 'L'avant-projet de réforme du droit des obligations et de la prescription' [2006] ULR 103.

break away from the original, but to adjust it'[10] cannot be taken literally, permeating this chapter to the exclusion of all else. Whilst the *Avant-projet* constitutes in quite a large measure a reproduction of the current law on this issue, which we will set out in section I belwo, it also involves in part the reform of the current law, which we will examine in section II.

I. REPRODUCING THE CURRENT LAW

The discussion of the essential elements of the *Avant-projet* relating to the effects of contracts as regards third parties which more or less reflect the current law (whether this is of legislative or judicial origin) is best organised around three guiding principles:

1. the relative effect of concluded contracts (section I(a));
2. the obligational effect of contracts in progress (section I(b));
3. the 'opposability' of contractual non-performance (section I(c)).

(a) The Relative Effect of Concluded Contracts

This principle is stated in two provisions of the *Avant-projet*. One may well ask oneself whether they are not in fact redundant.

First, article 1165, which is an almost entirely faithful reproduction of the provision of the Code civil; its numbering is unchanged and, while its wording is lightly amended, there is no change in meaning. As we all know, this provision, which sets out the principle of the relative effect of concluded contracts, denies the contracting parties the power to subject a third party to the binding ties of the contract without his consent.

This rule, which has been one of the pillars of France's contractual temple for many years, does not require many observations and we will therefore restrict ourselves to a few brief remarks. First, in relation to the basis of the rule, it is the fruit of the individualistic and consensualist vision of contract. At root, the principle of the relative effect of concluded contracts channels freedom of contract and, correlatively, preserves the independence of each individual, because

> [i]n private law, where individualistic considerations carry the day, a contract produces effects in principle only as regards the individuals who willed it to do so, as one set of individual wills cannot command other individual wills.[11]

---

[10] P Catala, 'Présentation générale de l'avant projet' in *Avant-projet de réforme du droit des obligations et de la prescription: Rapport remis au garde des Sceaux* (Paris, La documentation française, 2006) 11, 13 (see below pp 465, 471).

[11] F Terré, P Simmler and Y Lequette, *Droit civil: Les obligations* (Paris, Dalloz, 2005) no 482.

While

> the contracting parties are free to undertake obligations the one to the other . . .
> they cannot by contrast make a third party either debtor or creditor without his
> consent—this underlines the will of the law to sustain the independence and con-
> sequently the freedom of every individual.[12]

In short, 'the contracting parties are sovereign, but they are sovereign only
over themselves':[13] no one can therefore be contractually bound without
his knowledge or against his own free will.

Next, in relation to the effects of this principle, because the contracting
parties are authorised by article 1165 Cc to bind only themselves, the
creditor of a contractual obligation cannot demand performance from a
third party who has not participated in the conclusion of the contract that
has given rise to the obligation; and, reciprocally, a third party cannot
demand that a contractual debtor perform an obligation created by a
contract in the formation of which the third party has not participated.

Finally, in relation to the temporal scope of the rule, it is helpful to make
clear that the relative effect is that of a 'concluded' contract because, as has
been judiciously pointed out, article 1165 'is a provision aimed at a
particular moment: that of the formation of the contract'.[14] Once this stage
of the contractual process has passed, other rules intervene, complement or
replace the principle of relative effect in order to determine the effects of a
contract beyond its boundaries.

Now these explanations have been made, it is helpful to set out the rules
of the *Avant-projet* which constitute simple applications of the principle of
the relative effect of concluded contracts.

One such rule is to be found in article 1170 which relates to promises to
stand as surety (*promesse de porte-fort.*) This provision, which is currently
to be found in the Section on consent in article 1120 Cc, is still set out as
awkwardly in the *Avant-projet* as it was there, as a limitation on the
principle of relative effect. This is the result of a piece of defective drafting.
Article 1120, which has been placed immediately after the article excluding
promesse pour autrui, begins with the adverb 'Nevertheless'. This incorrectly
suggests that it constitutes an exception to this rule, an idea supported by
too many contemporary writings in the law of obligations, which also
present it in this way. Far from being an exception to this principle, the
provision governing *promesse de porte-fort* is a straightforward application
of the principle of relative effect since the third party whom the contracting
party (the 'surety') has undertaken will do something himself does not
become bound to do anything unless he manifests his will to this effect. In

---

[12] J-L Aubert, *Le contrat* (Paris, Dalloz, 2005) 98.

[13] J-L Aubert, Y Flour and E Savaux, *Droit civil: Les obligations, l'acte juridique* (Paris, Sirey,
2006) no 422.

[14] Aubert et al, above n 13, no 423.

reality, a *promesse de porte-fort* binds only the surety who undertakes that a third party will do something: the surety promises in the form of an *obligation de résultat* that the relevant performance will occur or, rather, the surety does not so much promise performance by the third party, but gives his own promise to ensure that the third party achieves the promised result. Thus, in line with the principle of the relative effect of concluded contracts, the third party retains complete freedom of action, despite the *promesse de porte-fort* given by another. Moreover, it is only if the third party agrees to undertake the accomplishment of the result promised by the surety that the third party will be contractually bound; and the contract will be taken to have been concluded at the time of the *promesse de porte-fort*. Consequently, and consistently with the principle of relative effect, the third party cannot be contractually bound by another in the absence of a manifestation of will on his part. The fact that the third party's possible future manifestation of will involves the formation of a contract as from the time of the *promesse de porte-fort* changes nothing: the third party cannot be contractually bound against his will.

It remains, then, to consider the exceptions—real or apparent—to the principle of relative effect, namely stipulations for the benefit of a third party which are governed by articles 1171 to 1171-4 of the *Avant-projet*, and 'direct actions for payment' (*l'action directe en paiement*) for which provision is made in article 1168.

First, with regard to the exception found in stipulations for the benefit of a third party, this was already envisaged by article 1121 Cc, which is also to be found in the Section on 'Consent'. This provision shows that the drafters of the Code civil 'understood that a contract can contain a stipulation for the benefit of a third party',[15] though they did not anticipate the extraordinary development of this concept, which was driven to a large extent by considerations relating to insurance law. It is this development which probably explains the giant leap brought about by the *Avant-projet*, which devotes five articles to stipulations for the benefit of a third party, while the Code civil dealt with it by article 1121 alone. This leap is no doubt explicable by the significant economic importance of the mechanism, on which many insurance contracts, in particular, rely.[16] No doubt this point also explains why the projects for the harmonisation of European contract law contain provisions dealing in detail with stipulations for the benefit of a third party.

Under the mechanism of stipulation for the benefit of a third party, a third party becomes the holder of a right (and so a creditor) as a result of a contract concluded between two other contracting parties. Here, therefore,

---

[15] Battifol, above n 1, 19.

[16] See M Grimaldi, 'Le contrat et le tiers' in *Libres propos sur les sources du droit: Mélanges en l'honneur de Philippe Jestaz* (Paris, Dalloz, 2006) 163, 168.

there is indeed a true exception to the principle of relative effect, because the third party

> whose will does not in any way participate in the putting in place of the operation, becomes creditor solely as a result of the agreement of wills which is formed apart from him.[17]

He acquires the contractual right solely as a result of the effect of the contract concluded by others and, from the conclusion of this contract onwards, the third party's acceptance constitutes neither a condition of validity nor a condition of effectiveness of the right created for his benefit. The sole effect of the third party's acceptance is to consolidate the right, by rendering the revocation of the stipulation impossible. This exception is much less surprising when one considers that it is for the benefit of third parties who become holders of a right as a result of the contract concluded by others. This remains true even though the Cour de cassation accepts that

> a stipulation for the benefit of a third party does not exclude the possibility that if he accepts its benefit its beneficiary may be bound by certain obligations[18]

because '[t]he beneficiary does not have a burden imposed upon him against his will, as he is at liberty to accept or refuse it'.[19] In other words, the rule set out in the case-law as an exception to the principle of the relative effect of concluded contracts in fact accords perfectly with this very principle.

The second exception to the principle of relative effect set out in the *Avant-projet* can be seen from article 1168(1), which provides that:

> Legislation grants to certain creditors the right to sue directly to obtain satisfaction from the debtor of their own debtor, up to an amount not exceeding the lesser of the sums owed by their own debtor or his debtor.

This doctrine was recognised by the Code civil, which dealt with it through a number of specific (though scattered) provisions. So, according to François,

> A direct action permits a creditor to pursue satisfaction of an obligation from a debtor of his own debtor by way of a personal right of his own, that is to say a right which is not transmitted through the assets of the 'intermediary' debtor.[20]

The boundaries of this action recognised by the current law are scarcely altered by the *Avant-projet*. Indeed, article 1168(1) has only a weak normative content, as it is essentially limited to a reminder that there is such a thing as special direct actions, that these are provided for by legislation and

---

[17] Aubert, above n 12, 101.

[18] Cass civ (1) 1 December 1987, D 1989 Somm com 233 obs J-L Aubert, RTD civ 1988, 532 obs J Mestre.

[19] A Bénabent, *Droit civil: Les obligations* (Paris, Monchrestien, 2005) no 251.

[20] J François, *Droit civil: Les obligations, régime général* (Paris, Economica, 2000) no 331.

one aspect of their traditional rules. Indeed, one may legitimately ask whether this provision is of any real significance and whether the *Avant-projet* could have dispensed with it, given that it does not really set out any legal rule.

It is said that these direct actions derogate from the principle of relative effect, in particular as regards what are called 'perfect' direct actions,[21] where the third party 'can demand performance in his favour of an obligation created by a contract in whose formation he has played no part'.[22] It is, however, far from clear that this in reality the case. In fact,

> it is not the will of the parties (to an insurance contract, a contract of hire or a sub-contract . . .) which creates the right for the benefit of the creditor who is the claimant under the direct action (*action directe*), but legislation alone.[23]

In other words, the third party becomes the holder of a right of his own not because the contracting parties have decided that he should have it without his knowledge, but because legislation has provided that he should have it. It is, however, true that that this type of action 'moves, for the benefit of the holder of the right, an effect of the contract as regards the creditor of one of the parties'[24] and therefore involves the contract having an obligational effect as regards a third party.

Following this examination of the first principle which governs the effects of contracts as regards third parties in the *Avant-projet*, we shall now move to the second: the obligational effect of contracts in progress.

(b) The Obligational Effect of Contracts in Progress

Strictly speaking, it is incorrect to say that there exists (either in the *Avant-projet* or in current French law) a 'principle' of the obligational effect of contracts in progress as regards third parties. On the contrary, there is rather a principle denying the obligational effect of contracts as regards third parties permeating current French law and which is maintained in the *Avant-projet* by article 1169, which provides that:

> In general, a person is not able to undertake engagements nor to make stipulations in his own name except for himself.

This neutralises *promesses pour autrui* and is a logical consequence of article 1165. For present purposes we shall content ourselves with noting that this provision which—save for the deletion of two commas—is an exact reproduction of article 1119 Cc (which was placed in the Section

---

[21] The situation in which the debt of the debtor of the holder of the *action directe* is burdened from the beginning in favour of the holder of the action.

[22] François, above n 20, no 334.

[23] Flour et al, above n 13, no 100.

[24] *Ibid*, no 460.

dealing with consent and in the chapter on the conditions for the validity of a contract) and that it expresses the idea, in the elegant words of Jean Carbonnier, that '[t]he parties must in general draw the contract around themselves'.[25] This notion has the consequence that, in principle, a successor in title on a particular basis (*ayant-cause à titre particulier*) does not—any more than any other third party—become the debtor of the obligations created by any contract concluded by his predecessor in relation to the property title that has passed to him.

It remains to be noted that, by way of exception to this principle, some provisions of the *Avant-projet* require third parties to perform contracts concluded by others not because the original contracting parties deliberately created obligations whose performance is imposed upon the third party (and which would therefore form an exception to the principle of the relative effect of concluded contracts), but because this extension of the ambit of a contract made by others stems from a legislative requirement or from the will of the third party in question. These rules, which we are not going to examine here, are therefore not so much exceptions to the principle of relative effect, but rather extensions of the obligational effect of contracts.

This extension of the obligational effect of contracts can, as we have noted, result from a legislative requirement to this effect. The *Avant-projet* (like the Code civil) provides several examples. A legal obligation on a third party to become involved in a contract in progress can be seen, on the one hand, in article 1165-3, which governs the transmission of contractual obligations on death. From a structural perspective, it is to be noted that in the Code civil transmissibility on death is governed by article 1122, which is placed in the Section on consent in the chapter dealing with the conditions of validity of contracts. Opportunely, the *Avant-projet* places this provision in the Section on the effects of contracts as regards third parties.

From a substantive point of view, under the current law, a contracting party's heir and his legatees succeed to his rights and obligations and his contractual debts, because they continue his legal personality. They become contracting parties instead of, and in place of, the deceased contracting party, because the contract which he concluded forms part of his assets and, as such, is transmitted to his universal successors in title (*ayant-cause à titre universel*). These heirs and legatees, who are third parties at the time of the conclusion of the contract, become contracting parties at the time of its performance. This rule does not in reality constitute a limit on the principle of relative effect because,

> the submission of the universal successor in title . . . to the obligations created by the contract is not in any way a result of the will of the original contracting parties. It is the effect . . . of legislation.[26]

---

[25] J Carbonnier, *Droit civil: Les obligations* (22nd edn, Paris, PUF, 2000) no 123.
[26] Aubert, above n 12, 115.

An examination of the provisions of the *Avant-projet* reveals certain differences when compared with the text of the Code civil. The exceptions mentioned by the Code civil ('in so far as the contrary is not expressed or does not result from the nature of the contract') are not expressly set out by the *Avant-projet*, but result implicitly from article 1165-3(1), which provides that the heirs succeed to the deceased's rights and obligations 'where they are not extinguished by the fact of his decease'.[27] Article 1165-3(2) adds that the heirs of a deceased person may take his place in the contracts to which he was party and whose performance is sought after his death as long as this substitution is established by legislation, provided for by contract or stipulated by the deceased in his testament. Contrary to current French law, the transmission of contracts in progress appears no longer to be automatic and requires either a legislative provision, a term making such provision in the contract transferred to the heirs, or a manifestation of unilateral will by the contracting party before his death.

Commentators have raised the issue of where the boundary lies between the rights and obligations transmitted 'automatically' to the heirs (the target of paragraph 1), and the substitution subject to conditions of the heirs for the deceased in contracts in progress (the target of paragraph 2 of the new provision) on the other.[28] In this regard, it is possible to argue that, on the one hand, automatic transmission applies in relation to contractual rights and obligations other than those created by a contract concluded *intuitu personae* and which are created and whose performance may be demanded before the death of the original contracting party, while, on the other hand, 'conditional' transmission applies only to those obligations the performance of which may be demanded after his death, notably because they were created by contracts involving successive or performance in instalments.[29]

However, the legal duty imposed on a third party to perform a contract in progress also results from article 1165-5(1) of the *Avant-projet*, which provides that a contract may be assigned without the consent of the other

---

[27] It should be noted that this provision makes express reference (in relation to the automatic transmission of obligations by reason of death) to the rules which govern family property law. The new article 786 Cc, which is the product of the reform of the law of succession, provides that an heir who accepts the inheritance 'may request to be discharged in whole or in part from his obligation to a successoral debt which he has legitimate reasons to be unaware of it at the time of acceptance, where the satisfaction of this debt would have the effect of gravely burdening his personal assets'.

[28] See for example L Aynès, 'Les effets du contrat à l'égard des tiers (art 1165 à 1172-3 de l'avant projet de réforme)' RDC 2006, 63, 64; D Artheil, 'L'effet des conventions à l'égard des tiers dans l'avant-projet de réforme du droit des obligations' LPA 15 November 2006, no 228, 11, 13.

[29] Thus, where an individual concludes a contract of sale and a contract of maintenance in relation to the property sold and he dies before paying the price under the contract of sale, his heir will be automatically bound to pay the price of the contract of sale and will be bound to perform the maintenance contract only if a term of the contract so provides or if the deceased so stipulates in his testament.

contracting party 'in situations provided for by legislation'. By virtue of the *cession forcée légale de contrat* (the compulsory transfer of a contract as a result of legislative provisions), a third party may become party to contract in the course of performance without the consent of the other contracting party and may demand that that party perform for his benefit the obligations created by a contract which he had not concluded with that other contracting party.

The new provision, by virtue of its generality and its lack of normative impact, is of little interest, indicating merely that instances of *cession forcée* exist. Once again, it would appear that the *Avant-projet* could have dispensed with this useless and long-winded provision.

That being said, we know that in current French law the following in particular are required: the transfer of a lease to the purchaser of a building by article 1743 Cc; the transfer of a contract of employment to the purchaser of a business by article L122-12 of the Labour Code; and the transfer of an insurance contract to the purchaser of the thing insured by article L121-10 of the Insurance Code.

These compulsory legislative transfers of contracts are traditionally seen as derogations from the principle of relative effect. These are not really, however, limitations of the principles of relative effect, but rather an extension of the obligational effect of contracts in progress. As Aubert remarks:

> [T]he submission of the transferee to the obligations created by the contract is not in any way a result of the will of the original contracting parties. It is a consequence . . . set by legislation.[30]

This legislative extension of the obligational effect of certain contracts in progress rests on considerations of technique and on considerations of legal policy. From the point of view of legal technique, a contract is transferred to a particular successor in title in spite of the absence of consent of the original contracting party from whom a person, who had not contracted with him, can demand the performance of the obligations created by a contract he had concluded with another person, because the contract that has been transferred cannot be disassociated from the property that has been transferred. The contract is 'viscerally' attached to the property in question and either is of interest only for the owner of the property that has been transferred or can be performed only by the owner of the property that has been transferred. In other words, the contract is transferred because it has been concluded *intuitu rei*. From the point of view of legal policy, these compulsory transfers by operation of law are justified by considerations inherent in *ordre public*, whether they relate to the protection of a person's home or of his or her employment.[31]

---

[30] Aubert, above n 12, 115.
[31] See eg Grimaldi, above n 16, 170–71.

The extension of the obligational effect of contracts in the *Avant-projet* derives, secondly, from the will of the new contracting party. This is the situation dealt with by assignment of the contract by agreement (*la cession conventionnelle du contrat*), governed by draft article 1165-4. This power given to third parties to join a contract in progress is not to be found in the Code civil, but it is not unknown to the law as it is applied which this provision reproduces faithfully. As the Cour de cassation has held,[32] an agreement for the assignment of a contract concluded between the assignor and assignee has no effect as against the other original contracting party (the *cédé*) in the absence of his consent to the assignment. In other words, a third party cannot as a result of the assignment of a contract become a contracting party and behave as such in relation to an original contracting party who has not given his consent: without the agreement of the contractual debtor, the assignee remains a third party in relation to him. It is to be regretted that the drafters of the *Avant-projet* did not provide more detail in relation to the requirement of the 'agreement' of the debtor—a defect also present in the current law. Does this mean a simple authorisation, pursuant to which the assignment results in the continuation of the original contract between the new contracting parties, or rather a consent which leads to the creation of a new contract? We still do not know, with a consequential cost in terms of legal certainty.

Just like the earlier examples of the obligational effect of contract, this does not constitute a limit on the principle of relative effect. Again, as Aubert observes:

> [T]he submission of the . . . assignee to the obligations created by the contract is not in any way a result of the will of the original contracting parties. It is the result . . . of a manifestation of will on the part of the contracting party which is distinct and authorised by legislation intervening, as the case may be, in conjunction with other wills, notably that of the assignee.[33]

It remains, now, to complete our examination of the traditional principles of the current law—restated by the *Avant-projet*—which determine the scope of the effects of contracts as regards third parties, to consider the third of these principles: the 'opposability' of contractual non-performance.

(c) The 'Opposability' of Contractual Non-performance

The principle of the opposability of contractual non-performance is absent from the Code civil, but has been constructed over the last few decades by

---

[32] Cass com 6 May 1997 Contrats Concur Consom 1977 comm no 146 obs L Leveneur, D 1997, 588 note M Billau and C Jamin, Defr 1997, 977 obs D Mazeaud, RTD civ 1997, 936 obs J Mestre.
[33] Aubert, above n 12, 115.

la doctrine on the basis of reported decisions of the Cour de cassation which have accepted it as reflecting the law. It may be expressed in two propositions, both of which have been codified by the *Avant-projet*.

The first of these two propositions is the rule of the opposability of contracts *against* third parties, which puts in other words the obligation imposed on third parties to respect contracts concluded by others as laid down by article 1165-2 of the *Avant-projet*. As a result of this provision, some of the effects of a contract as a social and economic fact can radiate beyond the circle of the contracting parties: a contract does not form an object of plunder for third parties, who must in their own legal and economic activities take account of and respect existing contracts which have been concluded by others. Moreover, if a third party contributes to the non-performance of a contract concluded by other people, then the creditor of the relevant obligation may—as the victim of the non-performance of this contract—bring an action in delict against the third party, who has made himself an accessory to the non-performance by the contractual debtor. In order to establish liability in the third party, the creditor must show that the third party knew of the existence of the contract which has been breached.

On further reflection, other provisions of the *Avant-projet* can perhaps be considered as applications of this first rule of the opposability of contracts against third parties, provided that one does not limit this rule to the situation where a third party is held liable as accessory to breach. These provisions are articles 1166 and the first article 1167-1(1), which govern *action oblique*.

An *action oblique* is an action by which a creditor claims in the name of his debtor from a third party—the debtor of the creditor's own debtor—satisfaction in respect of an obligation which the debtor had undertaken in favour of his creditor. This action is put forward awkwardly by the Code civil as an exception to the principle of the relative effect of concluded contracts: at present it is placed in the Code civil immediately after article 1165, which sets out the principle of relative effect, in article 1166 which begins with the word 'Nevertheless' ; this misleads one into thinking that it involves an exception to the principle of relative effect. This is doubly incorrect. On the one hand, because the *action oblique*

> permits the creditor to exercise in the place of the debtor not only contractual rights, but also extra-contractual rights. It is quite clear that in the latter case, one is not dealing with a derogation from the principle of the relative effect of contracts.[34]

On the other hand, and above all, because the creditor (who exercises the *action oblique*)

---

[34] François, above n 20, no 278.

does not act by virtue of his own right, [this action] only permits the creditor to exercise the rights and claims of the debtor in the place of the debtor and its effects are no different from those which would have been secured had the debtor brought the action himself . . . the *action oblique* is compatible with the principle of relative effect because its effects occur within the assets of the debtor and not in those of the creditor who acts in place of the debtor.[35]

We must therefore welcome heartily the disappearance of the adverb 'Nevertheless' in the text of the *Avant-projet* as this helpfully dissociates the *action oblique* from the principle of the relative effect of concluded contracts.

Some commentators, with whom we shall concur for present purposes, therefore propose that this action should be seen as an application of the principle of the opposability of a contract concluded by the creditor (claimant in the action) against the third party (defendant to the action):

The principle of opposability thus authorises a contracting party to insist upon his contractual right to require from the third party the performance of his obligation for the benefit of his creditor.[36]

In essence, one may consider that the contractual creditor sets up ('opposes') his contract against the debtor of his debtor, where this contract is threatened with non-performance by reason of the inertia of his own contractual partner. And article 1167-1, which sets out a rule designed to alleviate the relative inefficacy of the *action oblique*, would appear to support such an analysis. Under the current law, if an *action oblique* succeeds, the rights in question are added to the assets of the debtor of the claimant creditor and they are therefore 'the prey of all the creditors, of the claimant creditor, but also of the other creditors'.[37] Any product of an *action oblique* is not attributed directly to the claimant creditor, who does not have any preferential right in relation to the debt which is added to the assets of his debtor:

A payment which is effected by the debtor of his [ie the claimant creditor's] debtor does not enrich him personally; rather, it increases the assets of the debtor and therefore becomes the common security of all the creditors.[38]

By its new article 1167-1(1), the *Avant-projet* modifies the current law, as the creditor may require payment by deduction from the sums that have become part of the assets of the debtor in default as a result of his claim. This provision therefore accords priority to the claimant creditor over any other creditors and the *action oblique* will now therefore, like the *action paulienne*, have a relative effect.

---

[35] *Ibid.*
[36] Aubert, above n 12, 118.
[37] Carbonnier, above n 25, 118.
[38] A Sériaux, *Droit des obligations* (Paris, PUF, 1998) no 217.

The rule of the opposability of a contract against third parties has two exceptions which are not often discussed when the rule is considered.

The first is the *action paulienne* which is governed by article 1167 of the *Avant-projet* and by which a creditor may bring an action for a declaration that a contract concluded between his own debtor and a third party may not be relied upon against him on the basis of an act of fraud committed by his debtor which threatens his contract with non-performance. The current provisions relating to the *action paulienne* are fleshed out by the *Avant-projet* which in the case of non-gratuitous contracts imposes a requirement that the claimant creditor proves that the third party contracting with his debtor knew of the debtor's fraud: this codifies current case-law. But the current law is also modified in the interests of limiting disruption to any contract concluded by the debtor and the third party, as any action brought by the creditor must be brought within a period of three years from the time that he knows of the fraud committed by his debtor.

Secondly, the other exception to the rule as to opposability is set out in article 1165-1, which deals with the doctrine of *simulation*. From the point of view of its structural arrangement, it is to be noted that in the Code civil the provision which deals with this doctrine is to be found in the Section on the proof of obligations and satisfaction. From a formal point of view, one may remark that the provisions of the Code and of the *Avant-projet* are identical, bar one word.[39] As a matter of substance, according to the provisions of article 1165-1 of the *Avant-projet* (as also under article 1321 Cc), where contracting parties conclude a *contre-lettre*—that is to say a secret, but 'real' contract in which they express their true will, but hiding it by concluding another 'apparent' contract—a ostensible but false contract— third parties may elect to rely upon the apparent contract or upon the secret contract (the *contre-lettre)* depending upon how this best suits their own interest in the matter. As Professor Aynès has emphasised,[40] rather than saying, as the provision in the *Avant-projet* does, that such secret agreements 'have no effect against third parties', it is strictly more accurate to say that they cannot be set up against third parties.

The third principle in the *Avant-projet* which governs the effects of contracts as regards third parties[41] takes the form of a second proposition: the opposability of contractual non-performance by third parties. This rule, which is not known to the Code civil but was created by the Cour de cassation and taken up by article 1165-2 of the *Avant-projet*, grants third parties the ability to rely upon a contract concluded by others where its non-performance causes them harm, even though the rule does not recognise in them any 'right to demand performance'.

---

[39] Art 1321 Cc: 'elles n'ont *point* d'effet contre les tiers' (emphasis added); art 1165-1 of the *Avant-projet*: 'elles n'ont *pas* d'effet contre les tiers' (emphasis added).

[40] Aynès, above n 28, 64.

[41] Namely, the opposability of contractual non-performance.

Professor Aynès[42] wonders how a third party can rely upon a contract without demanding performance of it. Classically, one could reply that where a third party suffers harm caused by the non-performance of a contract and brings an action on the basis of extra-contractual liability, he relies upon the unperformed contract without actually demanding performance of it. As the nature of the claim shows, the claimant is acting as the victim suffering loss and not—as the principle of relative effect would forbid—as the creditor of an obligation created by a contract to which he is not a party. The right to damages which he obtains if his action succeeds cannot be assimilated to the contractual right to which only the other contracting party is entitled: it constitutes an extension and a projection of this contractual right, and in the event of non-performance its holder obtains a substitute for performance in the form of damages. To an extent, at least, the *Avant-projet* follows this classical approach, since article 1342(2) provides that where a third party suffers harm caused by the non-performance of a contract, if he elects to claim in delict he must prove that this contractual fault which caused the harm in question constitutes, in relation to him, 'one of the actions giving rise to liability'[43] required by the relevant cause of action, ie a delictual or quasi-delictual fault. This rule can be deduced from the principle of the relativity of contractual fault, for the application of this principle means that such a claim will fail where the harm in question has been caused by the non-performance of a contractual obligation which consists of 'a failure to accomplish the promised performance',[44] a failure by the debtor 'in relation to the obligational content of the contract',[45] which, in itself, 'is limited to the narrow circle of the contracting parties'[46] and which is 'assumed by the debtor for the benefit of the creditor alone and which has the contract as its sole foundation'.[47]

It should be noted, though, that this classical solution, reiterated by the *Avant-projet*, has been abandoned by the Assemblée plenière of the Cour de cassation which decided, on 6 October 2006, that,

> [a] third party to a contract may invoke a failure in contractual performance on the basis of delictual liability where this failure has caused him harm.[48]

---

[42] Aynès, above n 28, 64.

[43] Art 1342(2) of the *Avant-projet*.

[44] P Ancel, 'Les arrêts de 1998 sur l'action en responsabilité contractuelle dans les groupes de contrats, quinze ans après' in *Mélanges André Ponsard: La Cour de cassation, l'université et le droit* (Paris, Litec, 2003) 3, particularly no 35.

[45] J-P Tosi, 'Le manquement contractuel dérelativisé' in *Mélanges Michelle Gobert: Ruptures, mouvements et continuité du droit* (Paris, Economica, 2004) 479, no 7.

[46] Cass civ (1) 18 July 2000, RTD civ 2001, 146 obs P Jourdain.

[47] Cass com 8 October 2002, JCP 2003 I 152 obs G Viney.

[48] D 2006, 2825 note G Viney; JCP 2006 II 10181 obs M Billiau; and the numerous notes and commentaries published on this judgment in the Revue des contrats, see RDC 2007, 269, 279, 379, 531–631.

As laid down in this way (which could hardly be more broad in its terms), non-performance of a contractual obligation necessarily constitutes a failure upon which a third party may rely in order to bring an action in delict against the contractual debtor. In this way the Cour de cassation has proclaimed the identity of contractual and delictual fault and has accepted, at least to a certain extent, that a third party may demand performance in equivalent form of an unperformed contract in just the same way as the creditor.

To an extent, therefore, the Cour de cassation has sketched out the shape of a new rule relating to the effects of contracts as regards third parties: the 'attractive' effect of contractual non-performance, a rule that, as we shall see in the next section, permeates certain other provisions of the *Avant-projet* and would lead to real reform of current French law.

II. REFORM OF THE CURRENT LAW

Some of the rules set out in the *Avant-projet* bring about a noticeable reform of the current law, either because they forge a new rule relating to the effects of contracts as regards third parties—namely the attractive effect of contractual non-performance—or because they establish a rule which, while not unknown to the current law lacks detail and solidity—a rule we shall refer to, for present purposes, as the attractive effect of contractual groups.

(a) The Attractive Effect of Contractual Non-performance

A mini-revolution in contract law is brought about by article 1342(1) of the *Avant-projet*, which provides:

> Where non-performance of a contractual obligation is the direct cause of harm suffered by a third party, the latter can claim reparation from the contractual debtor on the basis of articles 1363 to 1366.[49] The third party is then subject to all the limits and conditions which apply to the creditor in obtaining reparation for his own harm.

If one may talk of a 'revolution' in relation to this provision, it is because under the current law the combination of the rules of relative effect and the opposability of contracts against third parties means that a contractual claim by a third party to a contract who is the victim of harm caused by non-performance of a contract remains exceptional. The nature of a third party's claim is, in principle, extra-contractual and, following the very

---

[49] These provisions govern contractual liability.

well-known decision in the *arrêt Besse*,[50] this is so even if there exists a link between him and the contract whose non-performance has caused him harm; such a link would exist where the third party is himself party to a contract which is dependent on the contract which has not been performed as they both work towards a single identical economic goal. Since this decision, the only third parties who may bring a claim in contract are those who are parties to a contract which is a member of a homogeneous[51] or heterogeneous[52] chain of contracts which transmit property rights, where this chain includes the contract that has not been performed. Moreover, this approach applies only in the domestic law: in the case of European or international chains of contracts, the Cour de cassation disavows any contractual claim on the part of the sub-purchaser.[53]

This approach is tied to the nature of the legal technique on which the contractual nature of the action is based, as the claimant's contractual action is transmitted as 'accessory' to the property title that is transferred to him as sub-purchaser or contractor; this transmission of the action allows a claim against the contracting partner of his own contracting partner on the same conditions and to the same extent that the latter enjoys. As a result of this 'accessory rights doctrine' (*la théorie de l'accessoire*), the third party, who is the claimant in the action, enjoys all the rights and claims that are available to the contracting party from the contract which that party has concluded with the defendant to the action.

This claim in contract, which is both exceptional and fragile in the current law, gains the status of a general principle under the *Avant-projet*. That this is the intended result can be seen from the commentary on article 1342(1) written by the drafters themselves, in which they state that 'the most balanced solution [to deal with the question of the nature of the claim brought by the third party victim] appeared to be to grant in principle'[54] a claim in contract. By means of article 1342, the *Avant-projet* therefore creates a new rule on the attractive effect of contractual non-performance because from now on a third party who is the victim of harm caused by the non-performance of a contract can always bring a claim in contract, this claim being subject to the general regime governing contractual liability, and the measure of recovery being determined by the content of the contract that has not been performed. The contract that has not been performed and which constitutes the basis of the third party victim's action

---

[50] Ass plén 12 July 1991, D 1991, 549 note J Ghestin, Defr 1991, 1301 obs J-L Aubert, JCP 1991 II 21743 obs G Viney, RTD civ 1991, 750 obs P Jourdain.

[51] Cass civ (1) 9 October 1979, RTD civ 1980, 354 obs G Durry.

[52] Ass plén 7 February 1986, D 1986, 293 note A Bénabent, JCP 1986 II 20616 obs P Malinvaud, RTD civ 1986, 364 obs J Huet, RTD civ 1986, 594 obs J Mestre, RTD civ 1986, 605 obs P Rémy.

[53] See Cass civ (1) 27 January 1993 Contrats Concur Consom May 1993, 1 note L Leveneur; Cass civ (1) 5 January 1999, D 1999, 3383 note C Witz, RTD civ 1999, 503 obs J Raynard.

[54] Note 1 to art 1342 of the *Avant-projet* (see below p 837).

therefore determines the regime of the action. Accordingly, in consequence of the attractive effect of contractual non-performance upon which the third party bases his claim, the defendant debtor may rely against the third party upon all the terms of the contract that deal with the consequences and sanctions of contractual non-performance.

The essential concern of the drafters of the *Avant-projet* in requiring a claimant third party to bring a claim in contract is the protection of the contractual expectations of the debtor against whom the third party brings his claim based on the non-performance of the contract. In essence, and as the drafters expressly indicated in their explanation of their thinking:

> [P]ractical considerations . . . require the compulsory application of the contractual regime wherever the basis of the action lies uniquely in a defendant's contractual failure to perform. This is in fact the only way in which third parties can be made subject to all the restrictions and limitations which the contract imposes on a creditor in order to obtain reparation in respect of his own harm.[55]

It is therefore clear that the drafters of the *Avant-projet* have considered the principle set out in article 1342(1) as being in the exclusive interest of the contractual debtor for whom the harm suffered by the third party is to be responsible.

Moreover, the contractual nature of the action brought by the third party avoids inappropriate distinctions in the legal treatment of different categories of third-party victim. On the one hand, third parties who bring such a claim would not be treated any better than a creditor who, *ex hypothesi*, can find that the rules governing his compensation are influenced and affected by the rules of the law of contract and by the terms set out in the contract that has not been performed. On the other hand, the claims of all third parties would conform to the same pattern because the contractual action would apply to all categories of harm suffered by a third party and in relation to all categories of third party claimant (a position that is not reached by the current law).

It may be asked, though, whether this really remarkable innovation brought about by the *Avant-projet* is at risk of being neutralised as a result of the application of other rules which it introduces. First, this is the case in relation to article 1172-1, which imposes a requirement that a third party who is a member of the contractual 'group' and who suffers harm will be bound by a term in the contract on which he is claiming only if it is reproduced in all the contracts forming part of the group and accepted by all the members of the group. *Ex hypothesi*, this condition will not be fulfilled in all cases: either a term found in the contract concluded by the debtor will not be found in the contract concluded by the third party victim or, while

---

[55] G Viney, 'Exposé des motifs: Sous-titre III. De la responsabilité civile (Articles 1340 à 1386)' in *Avant-projet de réforme du droit des obligations et de la prescription: Rapport remis au garde des Sceaux* (Paris, La documentation française, 2006) 159, 165 (see below pp 809, 819).

the term is to be found in both contracts, the third party may be able to establish that he did not accept it. Similarly, article 1172-2, which also concerns interdependent contracts, subjects the extension of contract terms which limit or exclude liability, arbitration clauses and jurisdiction clauses as against third parties only where they were 'aware of them . . . and made no reservation': in other words, it subjects the application of these types of contract terms to the condition that the third party tacitly consented to them. One may assume that these conditions will not be fulfilled when a defendant seeks to rely upon a clause limiting or excluding liability against a third-party victim. Finally, article 1382-3 sets out a general rule which applies where the defendant debtor and the third-party victim are not parties to the same group of interdependent contracts. It provides:

> In the contractual context, the party who is faced with a term excluding or limiting reparation must have been able to be aware of it at the time of concluding the contract.

This is a condition that, while not impossible to satisfy, is at least difficult to fulfil where a contractual claim is brought by a third party as the victim of harm caused by non-performance of a contract that is not part of a group with which his own contract is related. On the other hand, if in all these cases the restrictions governing the effectiveness of contract terms were not to be applied where an action is brought by a third party, the latter would be less well treated than a victim who was a contracting party, a result that would be unjust to say the least.

One may therefore legitimately ask whether this requirement of knowledge of a contract term is capable of ruining the effectiveness of article 1342 of the *Avant-projet*, whose rationale resides, as we know, in the protection of the contractual expectations of the debtor, defendant to any contractual action brought by a third-party victim. In fact, one may readily imagine that a third party who brings such an action will often not know of a term excluding liability or limiting the damages recoverable which has been included in the contract concluded by the defendant, who will therefore not be able to rely upon it. This means that the rule set out in article 1342 will therefore frequently be outflanked and the rule of the attractive effect of contractual non-performance deactivated, since the third party would be able to rely upon the non-performance of the contract while at the same time avoiding the application of the contractual regime, in particular any contract terms excluding or limiting liability. The third party would therefore be in a better position than the contractual creditor and the contractual expectations of the debtor will be fatally disappointed.

We will finish this short overview of the rules set out in the *Avant-projet* relating to the effects of contracts as regards third parties with a few words on a final group of provisions which establish the attractive effect of contractual groups.

(b) The Principle of the Attractive Effect of Contractual Groups

In a number of its provisions, the *Avant-projet* establishes the notion of 'interdependent contracts' by which is meant, in the words of article 1172:

> Contemporaneous or successive contracts whose performance is necessary for the putting into effect of a group operation of which they form part . . .

This was a notion which is completely absent from the Code civil, and which the courts have used only selectively and sparingly. While the *Avant-projet* does not endow this concept with a general sigificance, it gives it many more effects than is the case under our current law. In doing so, the *Avant-projet* carries out a 'macro-contractual' adaptation of the effects of contracts as regards third parties, founded on a realistic, dynamic and economic vision of contractual relations. In the vision of the *Avant-projet*, contracts are no longer to be viewed as one-offs and in isolation, but rather in the plural and in relation to each other. The *Avant-projet* adopts a more realistic perspective in relation to the economic relations that are often supported by contractual groups to an extent to which it may be argued that it establishes a principle of the attractive effect of groups of contracts.

As for the application of this principle, one may begin by noting the rule established by article 1172-2, which provides for the extension of certain contract terms—those excluding or limiting liability, arbitration clauses and jurisdiction clauses which are included in one of the contracts forming part of a contractual group—to all the parties to the other contracts in the group. The only condition for this extension is the tacit consent of the party against whom reliance is placed on such a clause.

Secondly, we should pause to consider direct actions for payment (*l'action directe en paiement*) created by article 1168(2). Having reminded us in article 1168(1) that such an action exists where legislation so provides, this paragraph adds an innovative rule by providing that a direct action for payment may be brought without any specific legislative provision where there is a contractual group and where the bringing of the action avoids the unjust impoverishment of the creditor. This is a remarkable innovation because under the present law the *action directe* does not—unlike the *action oblique* and the *action paulienne*—have the status of a general rule: it is not available to all the creditors of a contracting party. At present, in French law '[t]here are only specific and diverse direct actions'.[56] Thanks to the attractive effect of contractual groups, under the *Avant-projet* this position would be reversed where there are interdependent contracts. Moreover, we should note that the condition imposed by this provision, according to which the action must enable the unjust impoverishment of the creditor to be avoided, represents a return to

---

[56] Sériaux, above n 38, no 217.

the fundamental basis of direct actions and to a considerable extent merges with their raison d'être, which consists in permitting a third-party creditor to bring an action directly for the payment of his debt against the contracting partner of his own contracting partner: in sum, they require the performance for his benefit of a contract to which he is not a party in order to avoid the consequences of the insolvency of his own contracting partner. In order for his action to proceed, it therefore should be enough for him to show that it provides the sole means by which he can obtain payment of his debt.

A further application of the attractive effect of contractual groups is to be found in article 1165-5(2) which, exceptionally, permits the assignment by agreement of a contract which constitutes an integral part of an operation which forms an indivisible whole—such as the merger or division of companies and assets contributions—without the accord of the other contracting party being a condition for the validity of the assignment. So, in a case where a contract is assigned to a third party against the will of one of its contracting parties, the latter's protection is ensured by his right to 'withdraw' from the contract.

Finally, the clearest manifestation of this principle is to be found in article 1172-3, which provides that where one of the interdependent contracts forming part of a contractual group is affected by nullity, the parties to other contracts in the same group may treat them as lapsed. In relation to this provision, it would be simply astonishing if this result were limited to the situation where a contract is destroyed by nullity, given that under the current law, such a solution has already on several occasions been taken in other situations, notably cases of prospective termination (*résiliation*).[57]

Following on from these observations we propose, by way of conclusion, the following modifications[58] to the text of the *Avant-projet*:

Section 7: The effects of contracts as regards third parties

§1 – *The relative effect of concluded contracts*

Article 1165

Contracts bind only the contracting parties; they have no effect on third parties except in the situations and subject to the limitations explained below.

---

[57] For illustrations, see Cass com 15 February 2000, D 2000 Somm com 364 obs Ph Delebecque, Defr 2000, 118 obs D Mazeaud, RTD civ 2000, 325 obs J Mestre and B Fages; Cass civ (1) 4 April 2006, RDC 2006, 700 obs D Mazeaud.
[58] The modifications are indicated in italics in the body of the text.

Article 1166

A person may stand surety for a third party by promising that the latter will do something; if the third party refuses to do what the surety has promised that he will do or refuses to ratify the agreement, then the surety must pay compensation.

If the third party performs the act which has been promised or ratifies the surety's undertaking, the latter is released from any obligation, and the undertaking is retroactively validated as from the date on which it was originally made by him.

A third party who inherits from a person who has stood surety must fulfil the undertaking which the latter took on.

Article 1167

One of the parties to a contract (termed the 'promisee' ('stipulator')) may require an undertaking from the other (the 'promisor') to do something for the benefit of a third party beneficiary, on condition that where the latter is a future person he must be precisely identified or capable of being determined at the time of performance of the promise and that he has at this date the legal capacity to receive this benefit.

Article 1167-1

The promisee may freely revoke a stipulation which he has made for the benefit of a third party unless and until the latter accepts it.

Where the third party accepts the benefit of such a stipulation before its revocation, this renders the stipulation irrevocable once its maker or the promisor becomes aware of it.

Although enjoying from the time of acceptance a right to sue the promisor directly for performance of the undertaking, the beneficiary is deemed to have had this right as from the time of its creation by the contracting parties.

Article 1167-2

Revocation may be effected only by the promisee, or, after his death, by his heirs. The latter may do so only after a period of three months has elapsed from the date when they put the third party on notice to accept the benefit of the promise.

Revocation is effective as soon as the third party or the promisor become aware of it. Where it is made by testament, it takes effect from the moment of the testator's death. If it is not accompanied by a new designation of a beneficiary, revocation benefits the promisee or his heirs, as the case may be. A third party who was initially designated is deemed never to have benefited from the stipulation made for his advantage.

Article 1167-3

Acceptance can be made by the beneficiary or, after his death, by his heirs, sub-

ject to any contrary agreement. It may be express or implied. It can take place even after the death of the promisee or the promisor.

Article 1167-4

The promisee is himself entitled to demand performance from the promisor of the undertaking made for the benefit of a third party.

Article 1168

Legislation grants to certain creditors the right to sue directly to obtain satisfaction from the debtor of their own debtor, up to an amount not exceeding the lesser of the sums owed by their own debtor or his debtor.

§2 – *The obligational effect of contracts [in the course of performance]*

Article 1169

In general, a person is not able to undertake engagements nor to make stipulations in his own name except for himself.

Article 1170

Where the rights and obligations of a deceased person are not extinguished by the fact of his decease, they are transmitted to his heirs in accordance with the rules set out in the Title 'Succession' and the Title 'Gifts *inter vivos* and Testmants'.

Similarly, the heirs or legatees of a deceased person, or certain of them, are able to take the latter's place in the contracts to which he was party and whose performance is sought after his death, as long as this substitution is established by legislation, provided for by contract or stipulated by the deceased in his testament.

Article 1171

A contracting party cannot assign *inter vivos* his status as part to the contract without the express or implied consent of the other contracting party.

§3 – *The opposability of contractual non-performance*

Article 1172

Contracts may be invoked against third parties, who must respect them.

Article 1173

A creditor may exercise all the rights and actions of his debtor in the latter's name, with the exception of those which are exclusively personal to him.

A creditor does not justify his interest in bringing proceedings unless he establishes a failure in his debtor to perform which causes him loss.

Article 1173-1

A creditor who exercises the action oblique may be paid by deduction from the sums which, as a result of his claim, have become part of the assets of the debtor in default.

Article 1174

In addition, a creditor can challenge in his own name any juridical act made by his debtor in fraud of his rights, although in the case of a non-gratuitous act he can do so only if he establishes that the other party contracting with his debtor knew of this fraud.

A juridical act which has been declared fraudulent may not be invoked against creditors, so that the latter must not be prejudiced by any of its consequences. Where applicable, a third party who has acquired property under such an act is bound to make restitution in respect of what he has received through fraud.

A creditor may bring such an action only within a period of three years from the time when he became aware of the fraud.

Article 1174-1

Claims brought under the preceding article benefit [only] those creditors who initiated the proceedings and those who joined proceedings once they were already in motion.

Article 1175

A secret agreement hidden by the contracting parties behind another ostensible agreement can be effective only as between those parties; it has no effect on third parties.

Article 1176

Contracts may be invoked by third parties, who may take advantage of them, though they do not have a right to require their performance.

Article 1176-1

Where a third party who is the victim of harm caused by the non-performance of a contract, brings an claim in extra-contractual liability against the contractual debtor, the third party must prove the existence of one of the actions giving rise to liability envisaged by articles 1352 to 1362.

§4 – The attractive effect of contractual non-performance

Article 1177

Where non-performance of a contractual obligation is the direct cause of harm suffered by a third party, the latter can claim reparation from the contractual debtor on the basis of articles 1363 to 1366. The third party is then subject to all the limits and conditions which apply to the creditor in obtaining reparation for his own harm.

§5 – The attractive effect of contractual groups

Article 1178

Contemporaneous or successive contracts whose performance is necessary for the putting into effect of a group operation of which they form part are seen as inter-dependent to the extent specified below.

Article 1179

Contract terms which organise the relationship between the parties to one of the contracts within such a grouping do not apply to the other agreements except where they are reproduced in those agreements and accepted by the other contracting parties.

Article 1179-1

Nonetheless, the effect of certain types of contract term contained in one of the group contracts extends to the parties to the other contracts within the group, provided that those parties were aware of them at the time of their own contractual undertakings and that they made no reservation in this respect; and also to third parties who bring an action in contractual liability, as article 1342 paragraph 1 of the present Code permits them to do.

This is the case as regards contract terms which limit or exclude liability, arbitration clauses and choice of jurisdiction clauses.

Article 1180

A direct action may arise where it is the sole means of avoiding the unjust impoverishment of a creditor taking into account the link which unites the contracts in question.

Article 1181

The substitution of one party to a contract by another person can occur where the contract forms an integral part of an operation giving rise to an indivisible group of transactions, as in the case of the merger or division of companies and of assets contributions.

In the absence of contrary agreement, where such a transfer takes place without his consent, the other party to the contract may withdraw from the contract at the end of a period of reasonable notice.

Article 1182

Where one of the interdependent contracts is affected by nullity or terminated for non-performance (whether retrospectively or prospectively) the parties to other contracts in the same grouping can treat them as lapsed.

11

The Effects of Contracts on Third Parties: The Avant-projet de réforme in a Comparative Perspective

STEFAN VOGENAUER

THE *AVANT-PROJET de réforme du droit des obligations et de la prescription* contains a number of suggestions for a reform of the law pertaining to the effects of contracts on third parties. Professor Mazeaud has already given a comprehensive overview and an authoritative assessment of the proposed changes from the perspective of a French lawyer.[1] The purpose of this chapter is to subject some of these proposals to a comparative assessment. The *Avant-projet* and Professor Mazeaud's chapter touch on a wide variety of doctrines and legal institutions relating to the effects of contracts on third parties, and it is impossible to provide a comparative analysis of all of them within the confines of this contribution. Being forced to be selective, I will discuss the fundamental principle in this area of law, the 'relative effect' or 'relativity' of contract (section I) and some of the exceptions to this principle recognised by the *Avant-projet*, in particular the stipulation for the benefit of a third party (section II). By way of conclusion, I will briefly revisit the principle of 'relative effect' (section III).

I. REINFORCING RELATIVE EFFECT

The *Avant-projet* explicitly reaffirms the principle of relative effect of contracts, and it has been said to be one of the draft's achievements that the 'hallmark of the rule of relativity of contract remains'[2] and that '[t]he

---

[1] D Mazeaud, 'Contracts and Third Parties in the *Avant-projet de réforme*', see above ch 10. For a brief critique of the relevant provisions of the *Avant-projet* see L Aynès, 'Les effets du contrat à l'égard des tiers (art 1165 à 1172-3 de l'avant projet de réforme)' RDC 2006, 63, and also D Arteil, 'L'effet des conventions à l'égard des tiers dans l'avant-projet de réforme du droit des obligations' LPA 15 November 2006, no 228, 11.

[2] G Cornu, 'Introduction' in *Avant-projet de réforme du droit des obligations et de la prescription: Rapport remis au garde des Sceaux* (Paris, La documentation française, 2006) 19, 20 (see below p 483).

235

celebrated article 1165 maintains . . . its number and its substance, formulated differently'.[3] Article 1165 Cc, in its current version, is placed first in the Code's Section on 'The Effects of Contracts as regards Third Parties'. It states that:

> Agreements have effect only between the parties to them; they impose no burdens on third parties and confer benefits on them only in the case provided for in article 1121 [ie the stipulation for the benefit of a third party].

The slightly rephrased article 1165 of the *Avant-projet* provides that:

> Contracts bind only the contracting parties: they have no effect on third parties except in the situations and subject to the limitations explained below.

The principle of relative effect is not peculiar to French law. It is known to other legal systems belonging to the Romanistic family which copied the essence of article 1165 Cc. Thus article 1257(1) of the 1889 Spanish Código civil provides that 'contracts only produce effects as between the parties who conclude them',[4] and the Italian Codice civile of 1942, in its article 1372(2), contains a similar statement.[5] The 1900 German Civil Code provides in § 241(1) that by 'virtue of the relationship of obligation the creditor [ie *only* the creditor] is entitled to claim performance from the debtor [ie *only* the debtor]'. And it is well known that according to the English doctrine of privity of contract 'only a person who is a party to a contract can sue on it'[6] and a third person cannot be subjected to a duty by a contract to which he is not a party.[7] All these jurisdictions therefore agree that as a general rule contracts do not (to use the language of article 1165 Cc) 'confer benefits' on third parties, and that 'they impose no burdens' on such persons either. The second aspect of the principle of relativity is much less discussed than the first. In German law it is usually referred to as the prohibition of 'contracts to the detriment of third parties'.[8]

These apparent similarities should not disguise some differences as to the scope of the principle. It will be noted, for instance, that the German principle of *Relativität des Schuldverhältnisses* is wider than the French principle of relative effect. It concerns all 'relationships of obligations', and not only contractual ones. It can therefore be found in the 'General Part' of the Second Book of the BGB which applies to the entire law of obligations, ie those arising from contract, *negotiorum gestio*, delict and unjustified

---

[3] P Catala, 'La genèse et le dessein du projet' RDC 2006, 11, 16.

[4] 'Los contratos sólo producen efecto entre las partes que los otorgan . . .'

[5] 'Il contratto non produce effetto rispetto ai terzi che nei casi previsti dalla legge.'

[6] *Dunlop Pneumatic Tyre Co Ltd v Selfridge and Co Ltd* [1915] AC 847, 853 (HL) (Viscount Haldane LC).

[7] Law Commission, 'Privity of Contract: Contracts for the Benefit of Third Parties' (Law Com No 242, HMSO, 1996) 6.

[8] For references see P Gottwald in K Rebmann, FJ Säcker and R Rixecker (eds), *Münchener Kommentar zum BGB*, vol 2 (5th edn, München, CH Beck, 2007) § 328 para 188.

enrichment. The English doctrine of privity, on the other hand, only denies that a contract can confer rights or impose liabilities on third parties. It is thus narrower than the French principle which is generally held to be but a starting point for the discussion of further 'effects' on third persons.

There are also differences in the rationale underpinning the different versions of the principle of relative effect. The continental approach has two sources. The first one is the rule of Roman law, according to which no one can request a person to promise to another, *alteri stipulari nemo potest.*[9] The second one is the pronounced individualism of nineteenth-century lawyers. They wanted to safeguard the autonomy of the person and its freedom from unwanted intrusion. Persons who were not party to a contract should not only be free from incurring duties under it; they should not even be entitled to rights arising from it. Private autonomy reigned supreme, and the independence of a third person was valued even more highly than the benefits he might gain by acquiring a right from a contract concluded between others.[10] Similar thinking may have underpinned the English doctrine of privity of contract, which, although of older origin,[11] flourished only in the nineteenth century.[12] But English privity had (and still has) a theoretical basis as well. It is the rule that consideration has to move from the promisee: a third party, by definition, has never provided consideration.[13]

None of these reasons seem to be compelling for French legislation in the twenty-first century. Obviously, in the context of modern French law the Roman maxim *alteri stipulari* is as insignificant as the English doctrine of consideration. Neither is French contract law known for exaggerated individualism. Quite the contrary, it generally emphasises the social dimension of contract law much more heavily than other jurisdictions, and the drafters of the *Avant-projet* place themselves in this tradition.[14] French

---

[9] Ulpian Dig 45.1.38.17; Inst III.19.19.

[10] For a historical account see R Michaels in M Schmoeckel, J Rückert and R Zimmermann (eds), *Historisch-kritischer Kommentar zum BGB*, vol II (Tübingen, Mohr Siebeck, 2007) Preliminary remarks to § 241 paras 7, 21 and S Vogenauer in *ibid*, §§ 328–335 para 1. Independence of the individual and autonomy of will are still mentioned by French writers in this context today, eg M Grimaldi, 'Le contrat et le tiers' in *Libres propos sur les sources du droit: Mélanges en l'honneur de Philippe Jestaz* (Paris, Dalloz, 2006) 163, 167.

[11] D Ibbetson, *A Historical Introduction to the Law of Obligations* (Oxford University Press, 1999) 76–80, 140–41, 207–8; JH Baker, *An Introduction to English Legal History* (4th edn, London, Butterworths, 2002) 353–5.

[12] PS Atiyah, *The Rise and Fall of Freedom of Contract* (Oxford University Press, 1979) 413–4; VV Palmer, *Paths to Privity: The History of Third Party Beneficiary Contracts at English Law* (San Francisco, Austin and Winfield, 1992) 162–71.

[13] *Price v Easton* (1833) 4 B & Ad 433 (KB); *Tweedle v Atkinson* (1861) 1 B & S 393 (QB).

[14] P Catala, 'Présentation générale de l'avant-projet' in *Avant-projet de réforme du droit des obligations et de la prescription: Rapport remis au garde des Sceaux* (Paris, La documentation française, 2006) 11, 12 and 15 (see below pp 465, 467, 475), seeing it as the vocation of the Code civil to temper freedom of contract with 'a degree of contractual justice' and invoking the 'spirit of solidarity'; Cornu, above n 2, 20 (see below p 481) calls the 'desire for contractual fairness . . . one of the guiding ideas for the reform'.

lawyers, after all, attacked the principle of relative effect of contracts on the basis of the 'socialisation des contrats' as early as 1934.[15]

Nevertheless, the drafters of the *Avant-projet* chose, as we have seen, to reaffirm the principle by maintaining its prominence. This stands in marked contrast with other recent pieces of legislation and reform proposals in the area of contract law. Neither the new Dutch Civil Code with its 1992 book on contract law[16] nor the recent blueprints for a European or even a global contract law contain similar statements.[17] In fact, article 42 of the *Avant-projet* of the Academy of European Private Lawyers, co-ordinated by Professor Gandolfi, deliberately deviates from the formulation of articles 1165 Cc and 1372(2) Codice civile and states that a contract 'produces effects for the benefit of third parties as laid down in the provisions of the present chapter' which deals with the effects of contracts. By phrasing the provision in this way, the Academy intended to approach the issue of third party rights 'in an affirmative rather than in a negative way, so as to avoid according the character of exceptions to the rules referring to third parties'.[18]

In a similar vein, the part of the 2004 edition of the UNIDROIT Principles of International Commercial Contracts which relates to third party rights refrains from stating the principle of relative effect in its black letter rules. Despite the strong support of some members of the Working Group, the insertion of a draft article affirming the principle at the head of the Section was rejected by a narrow majority. The majority feared that laying too strong an emphasis on the principle of relativity might constitute an obstacle to the future development of the law.[19] As a result, the principle was relegated to the Official Comment to the Principles, where it is not even framed in normative language. The Comment instead states in an empirical fashion that:

> *Usually* contracts are intended by the parties to create rights and obligations between themselves. In such cases only the parties will acquire rights and duties under the contract.[20]

---

[15] R Savatier, 'Le prétendu principe de l'effet relatif des contrats' RTD civ 1934, 525, 540. Contra: A Weill, *La relativité des conventions en droit privé français* (Paris, Dalloz, 1939).

[16] But see s 2(1) of the 2002 Estonian Law of Obligations Act—which mirrors § 241(1) BGB—and s 8(2) of the Act ('A contract is binding on the parties').

[17] The Principles of European Contract Law (1995/2000) do not mention the principle of relative effect.

[18] G Gandolfi, 'Rapport du coordinateur sur les art. 42-88' in Academy of European Private Lawyers, *Code européen des contrats: Avant-projet, Livre premier* (Revised edn, Milan, Giuffrè, 2004) 123, 133.

[19] For references to the *travaux préparatoires* of the PICC see S Vogenauer in S Vogenauer and J Kleinheisterkamp (eds), *Commentary on the UNIDROIT Principles of International Commercial Contracts* (Oxford University Press, 2009) art 5.2.1 para 3.

[20] Official Comment to art 5.2.1, in the official edition of the PICC (Rome, UNIDROIT, 2004) 142 (emphasis added).

As a preliminary result it can be noted that the *Avant-projet*'s attachment to the principle of relative effect runs counter to an international trend. But it is too early to assess the merits of this decision on the part of the project's drafters. I will return to this issue in the final part of this contribution, after having discussed the exceptions from the principle of relativity that are recognised by the *Avant-projet*. For every lawyer knows that a principle is only worth as much as the exceptions to it permit.

II. REINFORCING EXCEPTIONS TO RELATIVE EFFECT

As is apparent from Professor Mazeaud's contribution, the *Avant-projet* qualifies the principle of relative effect by admitting a host of exceptions to it. The formulation of draft article 1165 itself is testimony to this. As opposed to the current article 1165 Cc, it does not only permit stipulations for the benefit of a third party, but it allows for all other exceptions and limitations set out in the Section on the 'Effects of Contracts as Regards Third Parties'. This part of my contribution deals with these exceptions from a comparative perspective. Only one of them, stipulations for the benefit of a third party, can be analysed in some detail (section II(a) below). A few comparative observations as to the other exceptions will be made in the concluding section of this part (section II(b) below).

(a) Stipulations for the Benefit of a Third Party

The *Avant-projet* dedicates almost the entire fourth part of the Section on the 'Effects of Contracts as Regards Third Parties' to stipulations for the benefit of a third party, the *stipulation pour autrui*. Article 1169 of the draft is a verbatim reproduction of article 1119 Cc. Draft articles 1171 to 1171-5 replace the current article 1121 Cc. So far, these provisions have not been met with great interest by French commentators.[21] This does not come as a surprise, given that the provisions of the *Avant-projet* on this topic merely intend to restate and order the case-law in the field.[22] The

---

[21] See the very brief remarks by Aynès, above n 1, 65; Arteil, above n 1, 16, 17; Mazeaud, above n 1, 212–13. The relevant provisions are not even mentioned by the reports of the Chambre de commerce et d'industrie de Paris, *Pour une réforme du droit des contrats et de la prescription conforme aux besoins de la vie des affaires* (2006), http://www.etudes.ccip.fr/archrap/pdf06/reforme-droit-des-contrats-kli0610.pdf, of the Conseil national des barreaux, *Projet de rapport du groupe de travail chargé d'étudier l'avant-projet de réforme du droit des obligations et du droit de la prescription* (2006), http://www.cnb.avocat.fr/PDF/2006-11-09_obligations.pdf, and of the Cour de cassation, *Rapport du groupe de travail de la Cour de cassation sur l'avant-projet de réforme du droit des obligations et de la prescription* (2007), http://www.courdecassation.fr/jurisprudence_publications_documentation_2/autres_publicatio ns_discours_2039/discours_2202/2007_2271/groupe_travail_10699.html.

[22] Catala, above n 14, 14 (see below p 471); Catala, above n 3, 17; JL Aubert and P Leclercq, 'Exposé des motifs: Effet des conventions à l'égard des tiers' in *Avant-projet de réforme du droit*

draft simply suggests a 'slight *retouching* which removes, by emphasising the essential, the minor problems which affect' the settled law.[23] Another reason for the relative lack of interest is probably that this part of the *Avant-projet* represents a great step forward, in terms of both clarity and accessibility, from the convoluted and almost incomprehensible article 1121 Cc. A comparative analysis, however, suggests that there is some scope for improvement.

(i) Tradition and Terminology: articles 1169 and 1171 of the Avant-projet

Article 1169 of the *Avant-projet* repeats the wording of the existing article 1119 Cc and provides that:

> In general, a person cannot undertake engagements or make stipulations in his own name except for himself.

The decision to retain this provision is based on two reasons. Article 1169 is intended to serve as a 'reminder', and it is meant to preserve the specific terminology of 'stipulation' in this area of the law.[24] Neither of these rationales is convincing.

In the first place, it is not entirely clear what exactly the provision shall remind the reader of. If draft article 1169 is merely supposed to restate a time-honoured formula without adding anything of substance it would be hollow. If it is meant to repeat the principle of relative effect[25] it would be superfluous and inaccurate. It would be superfluous because the current spatial distance between articles 1119 and 1165 Cc is already bridged by removing article 1119 Cc to the position now suggested. It would be inaccurate because, strictly speaking, the provision does not concern the *effect* of a contract on third parties, but deals with the prior question as to whether a contract in which one party stipulates a benefit for a third party is *valid* as such and thus with effect even between the parties themselves.[26] It is with good reason that article 1119 Cc has its place in the Code civil's Section on 'Consent'. If, finally, the provision is intended to resume a historical tradition it would be misleading. The formulation of article 1119 Cc can be traced back to the medieval jurists who grappled with the maxim *alteri stipulari nemo potest*:[27] in the few instances where Roman law accepted the validity of a promise for the benefit of a third party, the

---

des obligations et de la prescription: Rapport remis au garde des Sceaux (Paris, La documentation française, 2006) 62, 63 (see below p 591).

[23] Cornu, above n 2, 23 (see below p 489) (emphasis in the original).

[24] Explanatory note to art 1169 of the *Avant-projet*.

[25] This is suggested by Arteil, above n 1, 16.

[26] B Nicholas, *The French Law of Contract* (2nd edn, Oxford University Press, 1992) 180; Vogenauer, above n 10, §§ 328–335 para 43.

[27] For references to the glossators, Pothier and the *travaux préparatoires* of the Code civil see Vogenauer, above n 10, §§ 328–335 paras 27, 40, 43.

promise had to consist of a specific combination of the *verba promissoria* (the words indicating to whom the promise was made) and the *verba executoria* (the words indicating to whom the benefit was to be conferred). The first had to contain the name of the promisee; the second had to refer to the name of the third. A stipulation based on a request such as 'do you promise *Titius* to give *him* ten solidi' would accordingly be invalid, whilst a stipulation based on the request 'do you promise *me* to give *Titius* ten solidi' would be valid. But even a transaction based on the proper formula could only be valid in the instances where Roman law exceptionally permitted deviations from the principle *alteri stipulari nemo potest*. As a general rule, no one could enter into an engagement or stipulate in *one's own name* except for *oneself*—or, as the draftsmen of the Code civil translated in article 1119:

> On ne se peut, en général, s'engager, ni stipuler en *son propre nom*, que pour *soi-même* [emphasis added].

The provision only makes sense in the specific context of Roman law which knew both the *stipulatio* as a specific type of contract and the maxim *alteri stipulari nemo potest* as a rule of law. Modern contract law lacks this context and does not need a provision such as article 1119 Cc. In the words of François Terré, the 'alleged principle set out in article 1119 is not true anymore'.[28]

These historical considerations lead to the second, equally dubious, reason provided for retaining the provision. Preserving the language of *stipulation* evokes, of course, the oral contract of Roman law which could only be given validity by making it in the specific verbal form of question and answer. But clinging to the terminology of *stipulatio* is not only an unnecessarily retrograde step; it also suggests that the beneficiary's right flows from a unilateral promise made by the promisor. This impression is even strengthened by the explanation of the drafters who claim that the specific terminology of 'to stipulate' is particularly justified in this area of law, as opposed to 'the general meaning according to which it is a synonym for "to conclude" (to agree)'.[29] Article 1171 of the *Avant-projet* also emphasises the undertaking given by the promisor at the request of the promisee ('peut faire promettre à l'autre, le promettant').[30] Articles 1169 and 1171 thereby conceal the true origin of the beneficiary's right which, as is generally accepted in French law today, flows from the agreement of

---

[28] F Terré, P Simler and Y Lequette, *Droit civil: Les obligations* (9th edn, Paris, Dalloz, 2005) no 516.

[29] Explanatory note to art 1169 of the *Avant-projet*.

[30] The explanatory note to art 1171 of the *Avant-projet* confirms the emphasis on the 'special meaning' of the verb 'to stipulate'. It may be argued, however, that by referring to the 'contracting parties' the provision gives an indication as to the contractual origin of the beneficiary's right. For the full text of draft art 1171 see p 245 below.

the promisee and the promisor.[31] More recent accounts even abandon the language of 'stipulation pour autrui' altogether and rather speak of a 'contract conclu pour autrui'.[32]

Other modern codifications are more explicit as to the contractual origin of the third party's right. One of these is the German Civil Code. But even this retains traces of the uncertainty over the theoretical foundation of the right that prevailed throughout Europe up to the late nineteenth century. Initially, the draftsmen of the code intended to insert the provisions on third party rights into a part of the code that was supposed to deal with the effect of unilateral promises. Only later did they decide to ground the right in the contract of the original parties. They clarified this by phrasing § 328(1) BGB as follows:

> A *contract* may stipulate performance for the benefit of the third party, so that the third party acquires the right directly to demand performance [emphasis added].

The language of 'stipulate', however, betrays the difficulties the draftsmen had in overcoming the Roman law model. So does the heading of the respective title of the BGB which survived the reformulation of the actual provision. It does not refer to a 'contract' for the benefit to a third person, but to the 'promise of performance to a third party'.[33] Article 112(1) of the Swiss Obligationenrecht of 1911 shows the same tension: it lets the right vest in the beneficiary if 'a person who acts in his own name stipulates performance to a third for the benefit of the latter', and its German language version does so under the heading *Vertrag zugunsten eines Dritten* ('contract for the benefit of a third party')—whilst the French language version has the heading *Stipulations pour autrui*. Even the language of the Italian Codice civile of 1942 still sends out mixed signals.[34]

More recent legislators have found it much easier to emphasise the contractual origin of the beneficiary's right by using unequivocal language. Thus § 441(1) of the 1976 Civil Code of the German Democratic Republic—fortunately now a piece of legal history—simply provided that the 'partners [*sic!*] of a contract can agree that the right to performance directly vests in the third (beneficiary)'. According to article 6:253 of the new Dutch Civil Code, an 'agreement creates a right in the third to claim performance . . . if the agreement contains a requirement to this effect'. Article 5.2.1 of the 2004 UNIDROIT Principles of International Commercial Contracts is equally clear in providing that the parties 'may confer

---

[31] See only J Flour, JL Aubert and E Savaux, *Droit civil: Obligations*, vol I: *L'acte juridique* (10th edn, Paris, Dalloz, 2002) nos 467, 484; Terré et al, above n 28, nos 523, 526, 529.

[32] Grimaldi, above n 10, 168.

[33] 'Versprechen der Leistung an einen Dritten'. For the legislative history see Vogenauer, above n 10, §§ 328–335 para 68.

[34] Art 1411(1): '*Contratto* in favore di terzi. E valida *la stipulazione* a favore di un terzo . . .' (emphasis added).

by . . . agreement a right on a third party'.[35] The 1994 Civil Code of Québec even manages to combine the terminologies of contract and stipulation without denying the contractual origin when it says that a 'person may make a stipulation in a contract for the benefit of a third person'.[36]

Semantic considerations of this kind will not necessarily trouble the trained French lawyer who knows the intricacies of the doctrine of *stipulation pour autrui*. For foreign lawyers, however, the terminological conservatism of the *Avant-projet* does not only obscure the theoretical foundations of the doctrine. The archaic language also makes draft articles 1169 and 1171 unnecessarily difficult to understand.

(ii) The Validity of the stipulation pour autrui: *articles 1171 and 1125-2 of the* Avant-projet

Like article 1119 Cc, and displaying a similar loyalty to its Roman law origins, the first sentence of article 1121 Cc was intended to deal with the validity of a *stipulation pour autrui* as between the parties, and not with the question whether such an agreement can have an effect on third parties by creating a right in them.[37] According to the letter of article 1121 Cc, there is a 'numerus clausus' of transactions that can be validly made for the benefit of third parties. Such a *stipulation* is valid only 'where it is the condition of a stipulation which one makes for oneself or of a gift which one makes to another'.[38] As is well known, these requirements 'dissolved like sugar in water'[39] in the late nineteenth century.[40] The Cour de cassation held it to be sufficient that the promisee had a mere 'moral interest' in the performance of the promise to the beneficiary,[41] and such an interest was usually found without difficulty.

A similar development occurred in other continental jurisdictions at around the same time. Driven by a similar desire to keep pace with socio-economic progress, particularly with the emergence of life insurance for the benefit of dependents, the courts and legal writers in these legal systems overcame equally restrictive legislative requirements as to the validity of

[35] Art 6:110 PECL, however, is still headed 'Stipulation in Favour of a Third Party', although it grounds the beneficiary's right in the agreement of the parties.

[36] Art 1444(1): 'On peut, dans un contrat, stipuler en faveur d'un tiers.' See already art 1257(2) of the Spanish Código civil which applies if the 'contract contains a stipulation in favour of a third party'.

[37] Nicholas, above n 26, 182–4; Vogenauer, above n 10, §§ 328–335 para 43. See n 26 above.

[38] 'On peut pareillement stipuler au profit d'un tiers, lorsque telle est la condition d'une stipulation que l'on fait pour soi-même ou d'une donation que l'on fait à un autre.'

[39] Grimaldi, above n 10, 168.

[40] The story has frequently been told. For accounts in English see Nicholas, above n 26, 184–7; H Kötz, 'Rights of Third Parties: Third Party Beneficiaries and Assignment' in R David et al (eds), *International Encyclopedia of Comparative Law*, vol VII: *Contracts in General* (Tübingen, Mohr Siebeck, 1992) para 11.

[41] Cass civ 16 January 1888, DP 1888.1.77; Req 30 April 1888, DP 1888.1.291.

contracts in favour of third parties.[42] Twentieth-century legislation took account of this development. The only exception is the Italian Codice civile of 1942 which still requires that the promisee has an interest in the stipulation.[43] But this prerequisite was whittled away as early as 1956 when the Corte di cassazione declared a mere 'moral interest' to be sufficient.[44] Other modern civil codes and model laws recognise the general validity of contracts for the benefit of third parties, regardless of a particular interest on the part of the promisee or similar additional requirements.[45] The 1999 English Contracts (Rights of Third Parties) Act does not even touch on the issue. However, for English law the question of validity has never been of great importance since, as has been seen above, it was not subject to the pernicious influence of the Roman maxim *alteri stipulari nemo potest*. The doctrine of privity therefore only concerns the possibility of creating an enforceable right in the third party,[46] but it has never cast doubt on the validity of the agreement as between the parties.[47]

Thus, by abandoning the requirements of article 1121 Cc, article 1171 of the *Avant-projet* brings French law in line with an international trend. The explanatory note to draft article 1171 confirms that the very 'point of this leading provision is to make available the possibility of a stipulation for the benefit of a third party as a matter of principle'.[48] The drafters even wisely ensured that the old requirements cannot slip in through the back door, in the guise of *la cause*, a doctrine to which the *Avant-projet* clings with remarkable tenacity. Whilst the draft, in its article 1124, still provides that the 'validity of a contract presupposes that it has a real and lawful cause which justifies it', it immediately goes on to clarify in article 1125-2 that an

> undertaking entered into in exchange for a benefit agreed for a third party has this benefit as its cause, regardless of any moral or material interest that the party entering into the undertaking may find for himself.

At the same time as it abolishes the old requirements for the validity of the *stipulation d'autrui*, article 1171 of the *Avant-projet* codifies, for the first time in French law, two other prerequisites. They concern the person of the third party beneficiary. Both, however, have been long established in the case-law and in legal writings, and both conform to internationally accepted solutions. Draft article 1171 reads as follows:

---

[42] See Vogenauer, above n 10, §§ 328–335 paras 46–56 with references to Austria, France and the German territories.

[43] Art 1411(1): 'E valida la stipulazione a favore di un terzo, qualora lo stipulante vi abbia interesse.'

[44] Cass 24 October 1956, n 3869, Massimario di Giustizia Civile 1956, 1318.

[45] Art 112(2) OR; § 328(1) BGB; art 1444(1) Civil code of Québec; art 5.2.1 PICC; art 72(1) AEPL Code. See also, implicitly, art 1257(2) Spanish Código civil; art 6:253(1) NBW.

[46] See p 237 above.

[47] *Beswick v Beswick* [1968] AC 58, 71 (HL) (Lord Reid).

[48] Explanatory note to art 1171 of the *Avant-projet*.

One of the parties to a contract (termed the 'promisee', or 'stipulator') may require an undertaking from the other (the 'promisor') to do something for the benefit of a third party beneficiary, on condition that where the latter is a future person he must be precisely identified or capable of being determined at the time of performance of the promise and that he has at this date the legal capacity to receive this benefit.

The first condition concerns the question whether a stipulation can be made for the benefit of a future and/or indeterminate person. Article 1171 of the *Avant-projet* does not require the third party to be in existence or even conceived at the time of the conclusion of the contract—a view that prevailed under the *ancien droit*,[49] was mostly rejected during the nineteenth century,[50] regained the upper hand during the twentieth century[51] and is accepted in other legal systems as well.[52] The draft does, however, insist that the beneficiary 'must be precisely identified or capable of being determined at the time of the performance of the promise'. In doing so, it strikes the proper balance between commercial flexibility and legal certainty. On the one hand, the parties typically have an interest in making arrangements for the future, although it may not be entirely clear who exactly will benefit from their agreement at that stage or indeed whether any beneficiary will be in place at all—they thus will not always wish to name the beneficiary at the time of making the agreement. On the other hand, they usually do not intend to extend the circle of potential beneficiaries too widely. The promisor in particular will be interested in having some degree of predictability as to who might acquire a right against him. It is therefore appropriate to require that the beneficiary be at least 'capable of being determined at the time of the performance'.

In setting up this requirement, article 1171 of the *Avant-projet* is in step with other, relatively recent regimes providing for contracts in favour of third parties, such as the Civil Code of Québec which requires that the beneficiary 'need only be determinable' at the time when the stipulation is made,[53] or the UNIDROIT Principles with their requirement that the 'beneficiary must be identifiable with adequate certainty by the contract'.[54] The *Avant-projet* positively distinguishes itself from other pieces of legislation that do not address the question at all, eg the German and the Dutch

---

[49] E Lambert, *Du contrat en faveur de tiers: Son fonctionnement, ses applications actuelles* (Paris, Giard et Brière, 1893) 162–214.

[50] *Ibid*, 136–61.

[51] Terré et al, above n 28, no 535.

[52] Cf s 1(3) of the English Contracts (Rights of Third Parties) Act 1999, based on s 4 of the New Zealand Contracts (Privity) Act 1982; art 1445 Civil Code of Québec. For Germany see RG 9 March 1907, RGZ 65, 277, 280; BGH 20 June 1986, NJW-RR 1987, 114; BGH 3 May 1995, BGHZ 129, 297, 305. See also art 5.2.2 PICC and art 72(2) AEPL Code.

[53] Art 1445 Civil Code of Québec.

[54] Art 5.2.2 PICC.

civil codes.[55] It is also preferable to other instruments which, like the US Restatement 2nd Contracts, the Preliminary Draft of a European Contract Code by the Academy of European Private Lawyers, or the Principles of European Contract Law, merely state that the 'third person can be uniden-tified',[56] 'need not be identified at the time the agreement is concluded'[57] or that it 'is not essential . . . that he be identified' at that time,[58] without positively providing for the minimum threshold of determinability of the beneficiary. The *Avant-projet* fails, however, to provide any criteria as to when a third party 'is capable of being determined'. In this respect, the English Contracts (Rights of Third Parties) Act can serve as a model of certainty and clarity. It requires that the 'third party must be expressly identified in the contract by name, as a member of a class or as answering a particular description'.[59]

The second prerequisite codified by article 1171 of the *Avant-projet* is the beneficiary's capacity to receive the benefit. This presupposes only his general capacity to acquire and hold rights, but not the capacity to contract, as the third party only gains a right and incurs no duties under the stipulation in his favour.[60] This requirement is not discussed in the context of third party rights in other jurisdictions.[61] There, it seems that the general rules as to capacity to enjoy rights are considered to be sufficiently able to cover this issue.

(iii) The Possibility to Create a Right in the Third Party: article 1171-1(3) of the Avant-projet

In its third paragraph, article 1171-1 of the *Avant-projet* explicitly recog-nises that it is possible for a third party to acquire 'a right to sue the promisor' from the *stipulation* in his favour.[62] This does not necessarily follow from the proposition enounced in draft article 1171, ie that contracts for the benefit of a third party are, in general, valid.[63] It is perfectly possible for a legal system to hold that an agreement purporting

[55] German courts, however, soon developed the requirement that the beneficiary 'need not be identified, but has to be identifiable', see the references provided by R Jagmann in *Staudingers Kommentar zum Bürgerlichen Gesetzbuch* (2004 edn, Berlin, Sellier–de Gruyter) § 328 paras 14–6.

[56] Art 72(2) AEPL Code.

[57] Art 6:110(1)(3) PECL; but see the examples in the Official Comment D to art 6:110, p 319.

[58] § 308 Restatement 2nd Contracts. However, this does not refer to the validity of the contract, but to the conditions for the creation of a right in the beneficiary.

[59] S 1(3) of the Act; see also Law Commission, above n 7, para 8.1. The provision is modelled on s 4 of the New Zealand Contracts (Privity) Act 1982. Again, these rules do not concern the validity of the contract, but refer to the conditions of the enforceability of the third party's right.

[60] See, for the current position under the Code civil, Terré et al, above n 28, no 532.

[61] See, eg, Law Commission, above n 7, paras 8.1–8.17; § 308 Restatement 2nd Contracts; art 1445 Civil Code of Québec; for German law Gottwald, above n 8, § 328 para 24.

[62] For the full text of draft art 1171-1(3) see p 252 below.

[63] See p 244 above.

to benefit a third is valid as such and to acknowledge the reciprocal rights and duties of the parties arising from this agreement, whilst at the same time denying, at least in principle, that the third person acquires a right from the agreement. Indeed, this is, as we have seen before, precisely the traditional position under the English doctrine of privity.[64] French law, however, has never emphasised this distinction. The *ancien droit* took it for granted that in those exceptional cases where the *stipulation pour autrui* was valid the third party would normally acquire a right.[65] This view has lived on under the Code civil[66] whose laconic article 1121 Cc does not say anything about the rights, if any, created by the stipulation. The perspicuity of article 1171-1(3) of the *Avant-projet* in this respect presents a major step forward.

It also reconciles the letter of French law with what has been the state of legislative art throughout the continent since the second half of the nineteenth century.[67] The Swiss Obligationenrecht acknowledged as early as 1881 that the third party can 'claim performance',[68] and only a few years later article 1257(2) of the Spanish Código civil stated that if 'the contract contains a stipulation in favour of a third the latter can enforce performance'. § 328(1) BGB equally emphasises that the consequence of a contract in favour of a third party is that he 'acquires the right . . . to demand performance',[69] as do the twentieth-century codifications of Austria, Italy, Portugal and the Netherlands.[70] A similar solution was introduced in the common law jurisdictions, as they were gradually overcoming the doctrine of privity.[71] The English 1999 Contracts (Rights of Third Parties) Act, for instance, permits that a third party 'may in his own right enforce a term of the contract'.[72] It is no surprise therefore that the recent model laws aiming at a transnational contract law are equally explicit as to the possibility of creating a right in a third party.[73]

[64] See p 237 above.

[65] RJ Pothier, *Traité des obligations* (1761) in idem, *Traités de droit civil, et de jurisprudence françoise*, vol I (Paris/Orléans, Debure, 1781) no 73. For references to the earlier *ancien droit*, see Lambert, above n 49, 76–8, 83–96, 102.

[66] This is, for instance implicit in Req 30 April 1888, DP 1888.1.291 and Cass com 7 October 1997, D 1998 Somm 112 obs P Delebecque.

[67] For references to German territorial legislation up to the 1870s see Vogenauer, above n 10, §§ 328–335 para 64 note 319.

[68] Art 128(2) of the Swiss Obligationenrecht of 1881; see now art 112(2) OR.

[69] For the full text of § 328(1) BGB see p 242 above.

[70] § 881(2) ABGB (in the revised version of 1916); art 1411(2) Italian Codice civile of 1942; art 444(1) of the Portuguese Código civil of 1966; art 6:253(1) NBW.

[71] §§ 302(1), 304 Restatement 2nd Contracts; ss 4, 8 of the New Zealand Contracts (Privity) Act 1982. The old privity rule still lives on in Australia, cf *Trident General Insurance Co Ltd v McNiece Bros Pty Ltd* (1988) 165 CLR 107, 143, although it has been abolished by legislation in some Australian states, cf T Ciro and V Goldwasser, 'The Enforcement of Commercial Expectations in the Law of Privity and Compound Interest' in I Davies (ed), *Issues in International Commercial Law* (Hampshire, Ashgate, 2005) 123, 131.

[72] See s 1(1) of the Contracts (Rights of Third Parties) Act 1999.

[73] Art 6:110(1)(1) PECL; art 72(3)(1) AEPL Code; art 5.2.1 PICC.

(iv) The Requirements for the Creation of a Right in the Third Party: articles 1171 and 1171-1(3) of the Avant-projet

Having established that the parties can validly agree on a *stipulation pour autrui* and that they can confer a right on the third party, the *Avant-projet* sets out the requirements for the creation of such a right in articles 1171 and 1171-1(3). These prerequisites are an 'undertaking' of one of the contracting parties and an 'acceptance' of the beneficiary. Both merit further examination.

1. 'Undertaking' Leaving acceptance aside for a moment, it seems to follow from the two draft provisions in question that the third party's right arises from the 'undertaking' of the promisor, made to the promisee, to render performance for the benefit of the third.[74] As has been said before, the infelicitous terminology of 'stipulation' should not be taken to indicate that the *Avant-projet* does not require a contract for the benefit of the third. An agreement to confer a benefit on a third party is indeed what French writers usually presuppose for the creation of the right. Only few of them insist that the parties must have agreed to create a right in the third party.[75] Thus we witness, yet again, the tendency to equate the validity of the contract and the conferral of the right on the third party that can be traced back to the *ancien droit*: as a general rule, any valid agreement or *stipulation pour autrui* is taken to generate the right in the third party beneficiary.[76] As opposed to this, the Cour de cassation held as early as 1898 that

> one must not conclude [from article 1121 Cc] that every contract term that is capable of generating advantages for a third party generates a direct right of action of that party against the promisor, even if it has not been the intention of the contracting parties to confer such a right on the third party.[77]

Other legal systems also distinguish carefully between mere agreements to benefit a third person and agreements to create an enforceable right in the third party. The parties can agree to benefit a third person by conferring a right of action in him. But they can also agree to benefit this person without vesting such a right in him. In German law, only agreements belonging to the first group are categorised as 'genuine contracts in favour of a third party' (*echte Verträge zugunsten Dritter*) within the meaning of § 328(1) BGB. This provision explicitly envisages a contract to the effect that 'the third party acquires the right . . . to demand performance'.[78] In contrast to

---

[74] For the full text of draft arts 1171 and 1171-1(3) see p 245 above and p 252 below.
[75] See, eg, G Légier, 'Stipulation pour autrui' in *Jurisclasseur civil* (1995 edn) art 1121 et 1122, no 33.
[76] See p 247 above.
[77] Req 20 December 1898, DP 1899.1.320. See also Cass civ 20 December 1911, S 1914.1.297 note E Naquet and, implicitly, Cass civ 14 August 1878, DP 1879.1.57.
[78] See p 242 above.

this, agreements belonging to the second group are called 'spurious contracts in favour of a third party' (*unechte Verträge zugunsten Dritter*). The classical example would be the agreement that the seller delivers the goods directly to one of the buyer's customers. This is usually not meant to confer on the customer a right to sue the seller for performance. German law thus requires the agreement of the parties to confer a right, as opposed to a mere benefit, on the third party.

In preparing the 1999 Contracts (Rights of Third Parties) Act, the English Law Commission also discussed the various possible 'tests of enforceability' in detail.[79] It explicitly rejected the proposition that a third party should be able to enforce every contractual term which purports to confer a benefit on him. The Commission rather required that, as a minimum, the interpretation of the parties' agreement does not show that the parties did not intend the third party to have the right. The recommendation found its way into the somewhat convoluted subsections 1 and 2 of section 1 of the 1999 Act. These provide that:

> (1)   . . . a person who is not party to a contract (a "third party") may in his own right enforce a term of the contract if—
>   (a) the contract expressly provides that he may, or
>   (b) subject to subsection (2), the term purports to confer a benefit on him.
> (2)   Subsection (1)(b) does not apply if on a proper construction of the contract it appears that the parties did not intend the term to be enforceable by the third party.

The test of enforceability is thus, as is the case in German law and in other legal systems,[80] whether the parties have agreed to create a right in the third party. Whilst such an agreement has to be established positively by way of interpreting the contract in German law, section 1(2) of the English Act creates a presumption of enforceability: if a contractual term purports to confer a benefit on the third party, it will be presumed to create an enforceable right in him. The presumption can, however, be rebutted if the interpretation of the contract evinces that the parties did not intend this result.

The *Avant-projet* does not explicitly distinguish between mere agreements to confer a benefit on a third person and agreements to confer an actionable right on the third party. As has been seen, this is perfectly in line with the current *doctrine*, but it deprives French law of an analytical tool that other jurisdictions have found useful in establishing whether the third party has acquired an enforceable right. In addition, the lack of the distinction broadens the exception to the principle of relative effect to a greater extent than needed: since every agreement to confer a right on a third

---

[79] Law Commission, above n 7, paras 7.1–7.17, 7.52–7.53.
[80] See, eg, § 302 Restatement 2nd Contracts; art 112(2) OR; art 6:253(1) NBW; art 6:110(1) PECL; art 5.2.1 PICC.

party implies an agreement to confer a benefit on him, but the converse is not true, the *Avant-projet* seems to make a considerably greater number of transactions for the benefit of third persons enforceable than English or German law.

The *Avant-projet* does not mention whether the parties have to agree expressly to confer a benefit on the third party, or whether implied agreement is sufficient. This issue is controversial both in France and in other jurisdictions.[81] In France, Germany and the United States it is widely held that the parties can impliedly agree to benefit a third person.[82] English law also admits the possibility that the third party can enforce a term which is only implied in the agreement of the parties.[83] But the 1999 Act adopts a much stricter test than other jurisdictions. As has already been seen, it requires, as a minimum, a 'contractual term that purports to confer a benefit' on the third party,[84] and it imposes more burdensome requirements as to the identifiability of the third party.[85] As a result, many cases in which French courts imply a stipulation for the benefit of a third party would not create an enforceable right in the third under English law.[86]

The *Avant-projet* might have seized the opportunity to make it obvious that a *stipulation pour autrui tacite* or *implicite* is valid. After all, the draft explicitly refers to 'implied' consent, agreement, acceptance or renunciation at various points, even in the very Section on the effects of contracts on third parties.[87] Of course it might be argued that the possibility of an implicit stipulation for the benefit of another already follows from the application of the ordinary rules of interpretation of contracts. These accept the implication of terms, a general solution that is confirmed and perhaps strengthened by the decision of the *Avant-projet* to merge articles 1135 and 1160 Cc into a single provision, ie draft article 1135. This would not, however, exclude a reaffirmation of the general principle in the context of contracts for the benefit of third parties, as is done, for instance, in the UNIDROIT Principles. These make ample provision for the implication of terms.[88] Nevertheless, article 5.2.1 of the Principles explicitly provides that the parties 'may confer by express or implied agreement a right on a third party'.

2. The Function of the Beneficiary's 'Acceptance'   There remains the question whether creating a right in a third party requires his acceptance. This was

---

[81] Although, in line with what has just been said, the question in those other systems would rather be whether an implied agreement to confer a *right* is sufficient or not.

[82] Terré et al, above n 28, no 517; Flour et al, above n 31, no 472; Gottwald, above n 8, § 328 para 32; § 302(1)(b) Restatement 2nd Contracts.

[83] Law Commission, above n 7, para 7.6 note 6.

[84] S 1(1)(b) of the Act (see p 249 above).

[85] S 1(3) of the Act (see n 59 above).

[86] See p 267 below.

[87] Cf arts 1165-4, 1171-3, 1185, 1237, 1268, 2236 of the *Avant-projet*.

[88] Cf arts 4.8, 5.1.2 PICC.

frequently advocated by nineteenth-century jurists and courts in France.[89] However, the terms of article 1121 Cc, on a literal reading, do not impose such a prerequisite. The second sentence of the provision simply states that the right of the promisee to revoke the stipulation ceases to exist 'where the third party declares that he wishes to take advantage' of the stipulation.[90] And indeed, since the late nineteenth century, when the Cour de cassation abandoned its previous position and held that the beneficiary's right is created 'directly', 'personally' or 'immediately',[91] there has been broad consensus that acceptance is not constitutive for the right, but that the latter arises simply from the agreement of the parties.[92] This solution is shared by most other modern jurisdictions. Some provide so explicitly,[93] others implicitly: they contain provisions which would be difficult to reconcile with a requirement of acceptance.[94] Some make the point by stipulating 'that the third party acquires the right *directly* to demand performance',[95] others by simply not mentioning any requirement of acceptance at all.[96] The only exception is the Dutch Civil Code which, in its article 6:253(1), requires that 'the third accepts the agreement' of the parties. According to article 6:253(4), however, such acceptance is presumed if the right was granted irrevocably and gratuitously, and the third party was both aware of it and did not object immediately. Furthermore, the beneficiary's acceptance can be implied,[97] for instance from his claim for performance.[98]

The advantages of abandoning a requirement of acceptance are well known: the parties can confer a right upon the beneficiary without his knowledge, as is frequently done in the case of life insurance; it becomes possible to confer a right upon a minor, an unborn child or even a future person; the right is automatically transferred to the heirs of the beneficiary if the latter dies before having declared his acceptance; and, most importantly, the right against the promisor vests directly in the beneficiary and never enters the promisee's assets, not even just to pass through, so that the promisee's creditors or heirs cannot seize it in the event of his insolvency or

[89] For further references, also to the *travaux préparatoires*, see Vogenauer, above n 10, §§ 328–335 para 81.

[90] 'Celui qui a fait cette stipulation ne peut plus la révoquer, si le tiers a déclaré vouloir en profiter.'

[91] For references see Vogenauer, above n 10, §§ 328–335 para 86.

[92] Cass com 23 February 1993, RTD civ 1994, 99 obs J Mestre; Cass civ (1) 19 December 2000, D 2001, 3482 note I Ardeeff; Terré et al, above n 28, nos 523, 526; Flour et al, above n 31, no 483.

[93] Art 444(1) Portuguese Código civil; art 72(3)(1) AEPL Code.

[94] § 306 Restatement 2nd Contracts (see Comment a); art 6:110(2) PECL; art 5.2.2 PICC, cf Vogenauer, above n 19, art 5.2.1 para 28.

[95] § 328(1) BGB (emphasis added); in a similar vein § 881(2)(1) ABGB; art 1444(2) Civil Code of Québec.

[96] Art 1411(2)(1) Italian Codice civile; s 1 of the English Contracts (Rights of Third Parties) Act.

[97] HR 31 March 2006, NJ 2007, 20.

[98] HR 19 March 1976, NJ 1976, 407 (for the old Dutch Civil Code).

death.[99] The *Avant-projet* wants to retain these solutions. By emphasising the beneficiary's 'direct' right to sue the promisor in article 1171-1(3), it helpfully clarifies the established French position.

Rather confusingly, however, the *Avant-projet* does not discard the concept of acceptance in the context of the beneficiary's right entirely. Again, this is in line with the current position under French law. The declaration of the beneficiary 'that he wishes to take advantage' of the right, or, as is frequently said, his 'acceptance', deprives the promisee of his right to revoke the *stipulation* (see the second sentence of article 1121 Cc). As a consequence, the right is 'consolidated' because, as noted by Professor Aubert,

> his right is irrevocable, from which the conclusion has to be drawn, incidentally, that he can *from then on* act against the promisor . . . in order to ensure the protection of his right.[100]

Certainly, the acceptance can be made implicitly, for instance by bringing the action against the promisor, and it is said to apply retroactively, so that the right does not pass through the assets of the promisee.[101] Nevertheless, the passage just quoted creates the impression that only the 'acceptance' of the beneficiary makes the right enforceable. Article 1171-1(3) of the *Avant-projet*, co-drafted by Professor Aubert, reproduces this solution. It provides that the beneficiary is 'enjoying *from the time of acceptance* a right to sue the promisor directly for performance' (emphasis added), although it concedes at the same time that 'the beneficiary is deemed to have had this right as from the time of its creation':

> Although enjoying from the time of acceptance a right to sue the promisor directly for performance of the undertaking, the beneficiary is deemed to have had this right as from the time of its creation.[102]

But why is it not possible for the beneficiary simply to enjoy his right from the moment of its creation, ie from the conclusion of the contract between the parties? Why is it necessary first to postpone the enforceability of the right until acceptance, and then to ensure, by way of fiction, that it has retroactive effects? The argument advanced by Professor Aubert, namely that only an irrevocable right is enforceable, is a fallacy. This becomes immediately clear if the problem is looked at from a comparative perspective. Other legal systems do not find it difficult to assume that the

---

[99] Terré et al, above n 28, nos 526, 529; Flour et al, above n 31, nos 467, 482–3.

[100] Flour et al, above n 31, no 485: 'L'acceptation du tiers bénéficiaire fait disparaître cette faculté [de révoquer]: son droit devient irrévocable, d'où il faut conclure, d'ailleurs, qu'il peut *dès lors* agir, contre le stipulant, en exécution de ses obligations contractuelles, afin d'assurer la sauvegarde de son droit' (emphasis added).

[101] Flour et al, above n 31, no 485.

[102] 'Investi *dès lors* [ie dès l'acceptation] du droit d'agir directement contre le promettant pour l'exécution de l'engagement, le bénéficiaire est censé avoir eu ce droit dès sa constitution' (emphasis added).

beneficiary's right is vested and enforceable from the moment of the conclusion of the contract, at least unless the parties provide to the contrary. As long as the right is still revocable it may be 'inchoate' or 'incomplete', but it is nevertheless enforceable. The beneficiary *has* the right, and he is not only, as article 1171-1(3) of the *Avant-projet* suggests, 'deemed to have had' it retroactively.

The real concern of French law in this area rather seems to be the desire to ensure that no one acquires a right against his will. Requiring the acceptance by the third party provides a safeguard against this. By refusing to accept, the third party can prevent the imposition of an unwanted right on him.[103] That the requirement of acceptance has this function is manifest in the French cases where the right conferred upon a third person carries with it certain obligations. Here, the validity of the *stipulation pour autrui* depends on the acceptance by the third. Acceptance becomes constitutive for the creation of the right.[104]

Other legal systems have found a different and, it is submitted, more elegant way of complying with the ancient adage *beneficia non obtruduntur*. They forgo any requirement of acceptance, but recognise a right on the part of the third party to 'refuse', 'revoke' or 'renounce' the right conferred upon him.[105] § 333 BGB states that if 'the third party rejects, as against the promisor, the right acquired from the contract, the right is deemed not to have been acquired'. This is echoed by § 882(1) of the Austrian Civil Code as revised in 1916, by article 447 of the Portuguese Código civil, by article 6:110(2) of the Principles of European Contract Law and by article 5.2.6 of the UNIDROIT Principles.[106] § 306 of the US Restatement 2nd Contracts allows for a 'disclaimer' by the beneficiary which renders any duty of the promisor to him 'inoperative from the beginning'. Article 1411(3) of the Italian Codice civile provides for the 'refusal of the third person to avail himself' of the stipulation. It adds the presumption that in such cases performance has to be made for the benefit of the promisee, unless the parties have agreed otherwise.[107] This was, incidentally, also the view of the English Law Commission when it prepared

---

[103] See Terré et al, above n 28, no 519.

[104] Cass civ (1) 8 December 1987, D 1989 Somm com 233 obs JL Aubert; Terré et al, above n 28, no 523.

[105] The Cour de cassation employed the concept of renunciation as well, albeit, it seems, only in some older cases where an implicit *stipulation pour autrui* (see p 250 above) would have led to contractual liability, had the promisor not benefited from an explicit exemption clause. But once a contractual relationship was assumed, a potentially successful action in delict by the third would have been precluded under the doctrine of *non cumul*. The assumption of a 'tacit renunciation' prevented this result, see Cass com 19 June 1951, D 1951, 717 note G Ripert; Cass civ (2) 21 January 1959, D 1959, 101 note R Savatier; Cass civ (2) 23 January 1959, D 1959, 281 note R Rodière.

[106] However, neither art 447 Portuguese Código civil nor art 5.2.6 PICC provide for the consequences of renunciation, cf Vogenauer, above n 19, art 5.2.6 para 6.

[107] This solution was adopted in art 72(3)(1) and (2) AEPL Code. For a similar approach see art 1980 Civil Code of Louisiana.

the 1999 Act, although in the end it was thought that no legislative provision on the 'release given to the promisor by the third party' was necessary.[108]

This solution also relies on a fiction, but it is a fiction that only has to be invoked in exceptional cases, namely when the third party wants to renounce the right conferred on him. As opposed to this, the French solution is based on a double fiction which applies in the ordinary case where the third party intends to avail himself of the right. It is regrettable that the *Avant-projet* adheres to this tradition and does not explore the alternative approach.

(v) Revocation of the Stipulation: articles 1171-1 to 1171-3 of the Avant-projet

One of the most difficult questions with respect to contracts in favour of third parties relates to the power of revoking or modifying such agreements without the consent of the third party. The texts of article 1121 Cc and articles 1171-1 to 1171-3 of the *Avant-projet* do not deal with the problem in its entirety: they refer only to revocation of the stipulation and do not mention modification, as do other civil codes both in the French tradition and beyond.[109] Other regimes on third party rights are more explicit and allow that the stipulation be 'revoked or modified'.[110] The English Act of 1999 speaks of the possibility to 'rescind the contract, or vary it in such a way as to extinguish or alter [the beneficiary's] entitlement under that right, without his consent'.[111] Again, this is only a minor terminological issue, and no French lawyer doubts that revocation includes, *a fortiori*, modification. However, it is submitted that the *Avant-projet* misses an easy opportunity to be more explicit.

The issue of revocability (and I will follow the French approach and confine the following discussion mostly to revocation) arguably includes at least five different questions. First, is revocation possible at all? Secondly, what is the effect of revocation? Thirdly, who may revoke? Fourthly, how may revocation be effected? Fifthly, at what stage does the power to revoke cease to exist?

The first paragraph of article 1171-1 of the *Avant-projet* answers the first question in the affirmative. In doing so it is in line with article 1121 Cc and with all other major jurisdictions.[112] It provides that

---

[108] Law Commission, above n 7, paras 11.7–11.8.

[109] Cf art 1257(2) Spanish Código civil; arts 1446–8 Civil Code of Québec; art 112(3) OR; art 6:110(3) PECL.

[110] Art 1411(2)(1) Italian Codice civile; in a similar vein art 5.2.5 PICC. See also § 311 Restatement 2nd Contracts ('discharge or modification of a duty to an intended beneficiary'); § 328(2) BGB ('to take away or modify the right of the third party without his consent'); art 72(4) AEPL Code.

[111] S 2(1) of the English Contracts (Rights of Third Parties) Act 1999.

[112] See the references in the following footnotes.

The promisee may freely revoke a stipulation which he has made for the benefit for a third party unless and until the latter accepts it.

The answer to the second question is not provided by article 1121 Cc. French jurists generally assume that revocation destroys the beneficiary's right retroactively, and that, as a consequence, the right against the promisor arises *ab initio* in the promisee or his heirs, or, if a new beneficiary has been designated, in the latter.[113] The third and the fourth sentence of article 1171-2(2) of the *Avant-projet* are welcome clarifications of this position:

> If [revocation] is not accompanied by a new designation of a beneficiary, revocation benefits the promisee or his heirs, as the case may be. A third party who was initially designated is deemed never to have benefited from the stipulation made for his advantage.

Other jurisdictions have developed similar solutions,[114] although these are rarely spelt out in legislation.[115]

The third question, ie who may revoke, is more interesting from a comparative perspective, as it receives diverging answers in different jurisdictions. The first paragraph of article 1171-1 of the *Avant-projet*, quoted at the top of this page, follows article 1121 Cc in vesting the power of revocation in the promisee. The first half of the first sentence of the first paragraph of draft article 1171-2 reaffirms this proposition in a somewhat repetitive fashion.[116] The solution of the *Avant-projet* corresponds to the position of Swiss, Dutch, Italian and Spanish law and to the approach of the Principles of European Contract Law.[117] As opposed to this, the US Restatement, English law and the UNIDROIT Principles require the joint agreement of the contracting parties to revoke.[118] German law is unique in that it does not provide any default rule and leaves the entire issue of revocability to the discretion of the parties (§ 328(2) BGB). Accordingly, the person who holds the power to revoke can be determined only by interpretation of the original contract for the benefit of a third party which follows the ordinary rules of contractual construction. But it has been held that if the contract does not make any explicit or implicit provision to this

---

[113] Terré et al, above n 28, no 528.

[114] Gottwald, above n 8, § 330 para 18.

[115] But see art 1448(2) Civil Code of Québec ('Where a new beneficiary is not designated, revocation benefits the stipulator or his heirs') and art 1980 Civil Code of Louisiana ('In case of revocation . . . of the stipulation, the promisor shall render performance to the stipulator').

[116] For the full text of draft art 1171-2(1) see p 256 below.

[117] Art 112(3) OR; art 6:253(2) NBW; art 1411(2)(2) Italian Codice civile; for Spain, where the Código civil is silent on the question, see E Arroyo i Amayuelas 'Third Parties' in S van Erp and A Vaquer (eds), *Introduction to Spanish Patrimonial Law* (Granada, Editorial Comares, 2006) 123, 126; art 6:110(3) PECL.

[118] § 311(2) Restatement 2nd Contracts; s 2(1) of the English Contracts (Rights of Third Parties) Act 1999; art 5.2.5 PICC. Art 72(4) of the AEPL Code also requires the 'mutual consent' of the parties.

effect, the right can only be revoked by both parties acting together.[119] Only in the case of life insurance is there a presumption that, if the parties have not agreed otherwise, the power to revoke vests exclusively in the promisee.[120]

Looking at the typical interests of the parties, there is indeed a strong case to be made for a flexible solution to this question. As we have seen, revocation has the effect that the promisor has to render performance to the promisee or to a newly designated beneficiary, and not to the third person who was originally designated as beneficiary. In many cases this will not make any difference to the promisor, so it seems appropriate to give the promisee a unilateral power of revocation. In other cases, however, the promisor might have an interest in benefiting precisely the original benefi-ciary. Here it makes sense to require the promisor's consent for revocation of the right, and indeed this was stipulated by the Cour de cassation as early as 1877.[121] Other legal systems in the Romanistic tradition, such as Portugal, Louisiana and Québec, have codified this requirement.[122] The *Avant-projet* might have used the opportunity to insert a similar provision which would have reflected the existing state of the law more accurately.

However, the draft presents a great step forward by its partial break with the judge-made doctrine of the 'strictly personal character' of the right to revoke. According to this theory, the right can be exercised only by the promisee, and not by his creditors or heirs. With respect to life insurance contracts, this has long been abandoned for heirs who may revoke the policy if the beneficiary has not declared his acceptance of the policy within three months of having been formally invited to do so.[123] French writers have ever since advocated extending this rule to other contracts for the benefit of third parties,[124] and this is what the first paragraph of article 1171-2 of the *Avant projet* suggests:

> Revocation may be effected only by the promisee, or, after his death, by his heirs. The latter may do so only after a period of three months has elapsed from the date when they put the third party on notice to accept the benefit of the promise.

The rule strikes a fair balance between the interests of the heirs and those of the beneficiary. The latter needs to be protected against the heirs undoing a stipulation for his benefit, the existence of which he frequently had not even been aware of. The heirs, on the other hand, have an interest in knowing, after the lapse of a reasonable period, which assets belong to

---

[119] RG 24 May 1907, RGZ 66, 158, 162.
[120] § 159(1) Versicherungsvertragsgesetz.
[121] Req 30 July 1877, S 1878.1.55.
[122] Art 448(2) Portuguese Código civil; art 1979(2) Louisiana Civil Code ('If the promisor has an interest in performing, however, the stipulation may not be revoked without his consent'); art 1447(2) Civil Code of Québec. See also the second half of art 1411(3) Italian Codice civile.
[123] Art L 132-9(3) Code des assurances, introduced by the Loi du 13 juillet 1930 relative au contrat d'assurances, JO 18 July 1930, 8003.
[124] Flour et al, above n 31, no 485.

the estate and which do not. This solution may commend itself to other jurisdictions which still adhere to the doctrine of the 'strictly personal character' of the promisee's right to revoke, such as Québec.[125]

It might also be considered by other legal systems which do not adhere to the doctrine at all, such as German law. Contrary to a widely held view at the beginning of the twentieth century, there is now general consent amongst German lawyers that the power to revoke is not a 'strictly personal right' (*höchstpersönliches Recht*) of the promisee. It can therefore be exercised by his insolvency administrator or his heirs.[126] The promisee will frequently wish to avoid this result. In order to do so he has to agree with the promisor that the right should be irrevocable.[127] This, however, deprives him of the flexibility that he might wish to retain and which the power of revocation is generally meant to preserve. The French doctrine of the 'strictly personal character' avoids this result.

The fourth question in the context of revocation concerns how the right can be revoked, ie the requirements for a valid revocation. Article 1121 Cc is silent on this issue, but it is generally accepted that the promisee can revoke by express declaration, by way of a testamentary provision[128] or by conduct, eg by designating another beneficiary, assigning a life insurance contract or surrendering it to the insurer for cash.[129] In the case of life insurance, the promisee has a strong incentive to inform the insurer of his revocation, regardless of how it was made, because the latter will be released by a *bona fide* payment to the previously designated beneficiary.[130] As a general rule, however, it is not necessary that the promisor or the beneficiary have knowledge of the revocation in order for it to be effective.[131] This seems odd and may give rise to difficult issues of proof. The Civil Code of Québec avoids these problems. Its article 1448(1) provides that revocation of the stipulation has effect only 'as soon as it is made known to the promisor; if it is made by will, however, it has effect upon the opening of the succession'. A very similar solution has been elaborated by the German courts. They hold that revocation by one of the parties is effective only once it has reached the other party to the contract. Even a declaration to the beneficiary is not sufficient.[132] Communication to the promisor is normally not required if the promisee revokes by way of testamentary provision, a possibility explicitly provided for by § 332

---

[125] Cf art 1447(1) Civil Code of Québec: 'Only the stipulator may revoke a stipulation; neither his heirs nor his creditors may do so.'

[126] Jagmann, above n 55, § 328 para 74 and § 330 paras 31, 33.

[127] For details in the context of life insurance contracts see Jagmann, above n 55, § 330 paras 36–9; Gottwald, above n 8, § 330 paras 18–20.

[128] Req 20 July 1936, DH 1936.555; art L 132-8(6)(3) Code des assurances.

[129] Req 22 June 1891, S 1892.1.177 note JE Labbé.

[130] Art L 132-25 Code des assurances.

[131] Cass civ (1) 24 June 1969, D 1969, 544; Kötz, above n 40, para 44.

[132] RG 22 March 1932, RGZ 136, 49, 52; RG 17 February 1933, RGZ 140, 30, 32–4.

BGB.[133] For life insurance contracts, however, a different rule has been introduced by the General Life Insurance Conditions which are established by the insurance industry and approved by the Federal Regulatory Authority. According to these Conditions, testamentary revocation of the beneficiary's right is effective vis-à-vis the insurer only if made in writing and communicated to the insurer.[134] It is not sufficient that the will containing the testamentary revocation is presented to the insurer only after the death of the insured.[135]

Thus the *Avant-projet*, in the first two sentences of the second paragraph of its article 1171-2, does not only present marked progress over article 1121 Cc by tackling the issue of how revocation can be effected at all and by explicitly recognising the possibility of revocation made in a will. It also brings French law somewhat more in line with the solutions prevailing in other jurisdictions. This is done by requiring the promisor's knowledge of the revocation and by waiving this requirement for testamentary revocation. The latter takes effect from the moment of the death of the testator; the *Avant-projet* adds a new dimension, though, in making revocation effective even in those cases where only the beneficiary has knowledge of it. The two sentences in question run as follows:

> Revocation is effective as soon as the third party or the promisor become aware of it. Where it is made by testament, it takes effect from the moment of the testator's death.

The fifth question with respect to revocability is up to what moment in time the power to revoke exists. Currently, under the second sentence of article 1121 Cc, the promisee's right to revoke the stipulation ceases, once 'the third party has declared that he wishes to take advantage of it'. This declaration is commonly called 'acceptance', and this term is indeed used by article L 132-9(1) of the Code des assurances, according to which the stipulation of a life insurance for the benefit of a third party 'becomes irrevocable upon the beneficiary's express or implied acceptance'. Articles 1171-1 and 1171-3 of the *Avant-projet* propose introducing the language of 'acceptance' into the Civil code's regime of third party rights. This is perhaps unfortunate, given the potential for conceptual and terminological confusion inherent in the term.[136] In substance, however, the two provisions mainly reaffirm article 1121 Cc and codify the case-law of the Cour de cassation. The first two paragraphs of article 1171-1, strangely duplicating the same proposition, state that the beneficiary's acceptance renders the stipulation irrevocable. The second paragraph adds that either the

---

[133] This is also provided for by art 1412(1) Italian Codice civile, albeit only for the case that it is agreed that performance is to be made to the third person after the death of the promisee.

[134] § 13(3) Allgemeine Lebensversicherungsbedingungen; cf Jagmann, above n 55, § 328 para 72, § 330 para 12 and § 332 para 3.

[135] BGH 14 July 1993, NJW 1993, 3133, 3135.

[136] With respect to art 1171-1(3) of the *Avant-projet*, see p 252 above.

promisee or the promisor has to be aware of the acceptance for it to become effective. It provides:

> Where the third party accepts the benefit of such a stipulation before its revocation, this renders the stipulation irrevocable once its maker or the promisor becomes aware of it.

Article 1171-3[137] provides that acceptance can be made implicitly,[138] that it can still be declared after the death of the promisee,[139] the promisor or the beneficiary, and that in the latter case it may also be made by the heirs of the beneficiary, unless otherwise agreed.[140] In setting out the prerequisites and the effects of the beneficiary's acceptance so clearly, the *Avant-projet* presents itself once again as a major improvement over article 1121 Cc.

It also sets itself apart from other codifications which treat the issue in a much more cursory fashion. Whilst the Austrian Civil Code does not even touch on it, § 328(2) BGB is equally unhelpful by leaving the answer to the express or implied agreement of the parties—which will usually be impossible to ascertain.[141] Most civil codes simply echo article 1121 Cc and treat the beneficiary's acceptance as the cut-off point for revocability,[142] although in some jurisdictions this is held to be subject to the parties agreeing otherwise.[143] Occasionally it is added that acceptance can also be made by the heirs of the beneficiary, even after the death of the promisee or the promisor,[144] but this will usually need no exposition since it follows from the general rules on succession. The Italian Codice civile contains an original solution. As a general rule, acceptance by the beneficiary makes the stipulation irrevocable, as under article 1121 Cc.[145] However, in cases where performance can be demanded only after the promisee's death, most importantly in life insurance contracts, the promisee may revoke even after the beneficiary may have accepted the benefit. The stipulation will be

---

[137] 'Acceptance can be made by the beneficiary or, after his death, by his heirs, subject to any contrary agreement. It may be express or implied. It can take place even after the death of the promisee or the promisor.' Art 1171-3 of the *Avant-projet* also contains an unnecessary duplication in that it repeats the proposition that the beneficiary can accept the stipulation, already made in the first and the second paragraphs of art 1171-1.

[138] See already Req 25 April 1853, DP 1853.1.161; Req 2 April 1912, DP 1912.1.524.

[139] See already Cass civ 8 February 1888, DP 1888.1.193 (at 201); Req 22 June 1891, S 1892.1.177; art L 132-9(3) Code des assurances. For the insolvency of the promisee see Cass civ 27 March 1888, DP 1888.193 (at 199).

[140] See already Cass civ 8 February 1888, DP 1888.1.193 (at 201); Cass civ (1) 9 June 1998, RTD civ 1999, 836 obs Mestre; art L 132-9(3) Code des assurances.

[141] For a historical explanation see Vogenauer, above n 10, §§ 328–335 paras 99–100.

[142] Art 1257(2) Spanish Código civil; art 112(3) OR; art 448(1) Portuguese Código civil; arts 1978(2), 1979(1) Civil Code of Louisiana; art 6:253(2) NBW; art 1446 Civil Code of Québec; art 6:110(3)(b) PECL; art 72(4) AEPL Code.

[143] See H Kötz, *European Contract Law: Formation, Validity, and Content of Contracts; Contract and Third Parties* (Oxford University Press, 1997) 261 n 70 with references to Swiss and Dutch law.

[144] Art 1449 Civil Code of Québec.

[145] Art 1411(2) Italian Codice civile.

irrevocable only if the beneficiary accepts and the promisee has previously waived his power of revocation in writing.[146] In these instances it is therefore the promisee, and not the beneficiary, who has ultimate control over the moment when irrevocability sets in. Common law jurisdictions are generally more favourable to the beneficiary. Irrevocability is not only triggered if he expressly or impliedly accepts or 'assents' to the contract conferring a right upon him, but also if he 'materially changes his position in justifiable reliance on the promise' (§ 311(3) Restatement 2nd Contracts).[147] This idea was taken up by section 5 of the New Zealand Contracts (Privity) Act 1982. It was also introduced in the English Act of 1999 which accords great weight to the beneficiary's reliance and provides, in its section 2(1), that

> . . . where a third party has a right . . . to enforce a term of the contract, the parties to the contract may not, by agreement, rescind the contract, or vary it in such a way as to extinguish or alter his entitlement under that right, without his consent if—
> (a) the third party has communicated his assent to the term to the promisor,
> (b) the promisor is aware that the third party has relied on the term, or
> (c) the promisor can reasonably be expected to have foreseen that the third party would rely on the term and the third party has in fact relied on it.

Focusing on the beneficiary's justifiable reliance rather than on his acceptance seems to be a fairer solution, particularly if the promisor is aware of the reliance or should be aware of it. As a result, the reliance criterion has also found its way into the UNIDROIT Principles of International Commercial Contracts,[148] and it might be worth considering its implementation in the *Avant-projet*.

(vi) Rights of the Beneficiary

As mentioned above, a valid stipulation or contract for the benefit of a third party generates a direct and immediate right in the beneficiary which is directed against the promisor. Article 1121 Cc does not provide any information as to the content of the right. The *Avant-projet* is more explicit in this respect. Its article 1171 speaks of the undertaking of the promisor 'to do something for the benefit of a third party beneficiary', and article 1171-1(3) clarifies that the beneficiary acquires a 'right to sue the promisor directly for performance of the undertaking'. It seems to be implied that

---

[146] Art 1412(1) Italian Codice civile.

[147] See already § 143 of the Restatement 1st Contracts of 1932, but limited to creditor beneficiaries.

[148] See also art 5.2.5 PICC: 'The parties may modify or revoke the rights conferred by the contract on the beneficiary until the beneficiary has accepted them or reasonably acted in reliance on them.'

non-performance of the promisor's obligation will give rise to actions for the usual remedies for non-performance.

This is also the position in all other jurisdictions,[149] although few legislative provisions are as explicit as section 1(5) of the Contracts (Rights of Third Parties) Act 1999, according to which for

> . . . the purpose of exercising his right to enforce a term of the contract, there shall be available to the third party any remedy that would have been available to him in an action for breach of contract if he had been a party to the contract (and the rules relating to damages, injunctions, specific performance and other relief shall apply accordingly).

In one of the European contract law reform proposals it is stated, in a slightly less cumbersome fashion, that the 'third party can take any action against the promisor in the event of omitted, delayed or inexact performance, as if he himself had made the contract'.[150] Again, this is an issue that might as well be codified by the *Avant-projet* if a clear restatement of the law is desired.

Many regimes providing for contracts in favour of third parties recognise that the 'conferment of rights in the beneficiary includes the right to invoke a clause in the contract which excludes or limits the liability of the beneficiary'.[151] Only a few more recent legislative enactments make this explicit. One of them is section 1(6) of the English Act of 1999 which, as regards those cases to which the Act applies, supersedes a long line of case-law[152] and stipulates:

> Where a term of a contract excludes or limits liability in relation to any matter references in this Act to the third party enforcing the term shall be construed as references to his availing himself of the exclusion or limitation.

This does, however, require that the exclusion or limitation clause purports to protect the third party by naming him or identifying him in an appropriate manner.[153] The German courts go even further, although the BGB does not have any provision to this effect. They interpret an exclusion or limitation clause agreed between the parties as implicitly protecting third persons even if the clause does not mention any third party at all. However, this requires that the party for whose benefit the particular clause was inserted was under a duty to have regard to the welfare and interests of the third person and accordingly, as must have been apparent to the other

---

[149] See Comment a to § 307 Restatement 2nd Contracts; Official Comment to art 5.2.1 PICC; for German law Jagmann, above n 55, § 328 para 30.

[150] Art 73(1)(2) AEPL Code.

[151] Art 5.2.3 PICC.

[152] *Adler v Dickson* [1955] 1 QB 158 (CA); *Scruttons Ltd v Midland Silicones Ltd* [1962] AC 446 (HL); *New Zealand Shipping Co Ltd v AM Satterthwaite & Co Ltd* ('*The Eurymedon*') [1975] AC 154 (PC).

[153] Cf s 1(1)–(3) of the Act, see pp 246, 249 above.

party, had an interest in including the third within the scope of protection afforded by the clause.[154] A similar result is now explicitly provided for in the Dutch Civil Code.[155]

French discussions of the *stipulation pour autrui* do not normally mention the effect of exclusion and limitation clauses on third parties, and articles 1169 and 1171-4 of the *Avant-projet* do not touch on the issue. The problem is, however, of major relevance in cases where such a clause is not invoked by the third party, but by one of the contracting parties against the claim of a third person. This is the subject of a vigorous debate about the borderline between contractual and delictual actions, as will be seen from the discussion of article 1342 of the *Avant-projet* below.[156]

(vii) Defences of the Promisor

Although article 1121 Cc is silent on this issue, French law accepts that the promisor can raise against the beneficiary all the defences relating to the contract made in favour of the beneficiary which he would be able to assert against the promisee, such as nullity, non-performance by the promisee or compensation.[157] This view is also universally held in other jurisdictions,[158] and the *Avant-projet* would do well to codify it rather than omitting to deal with the issue.

(viii) Rights of the Promisee

Article 1121 Cc does not deal with the question whether any rights of the promisee flow from a *stipulation pour autrui*. French case-law and doctrine nevertheless recognise that the promisee is entitled to sue the promisor to render performance to the beneficiary.[159] This proposition is perfectly in line with the solution of other jurisdictions,[160] and it is codified in article 1171-4 of the *Avant-projet*:

> The promisee is himself entitled to demand performance from the promisor of the undertaking made for the benefit of a third party.

---

[154] BGH 7 December 1961, NJW 1962, 388.

[155] Arts 6:253(1), 6:257 NBW.

[156] See pp 266–7 below.

[157] Cass com 25 March 1960, Bull civ IV no 118; Terré et al, above n 28, no 526.

[158] § 334 BGB; § 882(2) ABGB; art 1413 Italian Codice civile; art 449 Portuguese Código civil; art 1982 Civil Code of Louisiana; § 309 Restatement 2nd Contracts; art 1450 Civil Code of Québec; s 3 Contracts (Rights of Third Parties) Act 1999; art 73(2) AEPL Code; art 5.2.4 PICC.

[159] Cass civ (1) 12 July 1956, D 1956, 749 note J Radouant; Cass civ (1) 14 December 1999, D 2000 Somm com 361 obs P Delebecque; Terré et al, above n 28, no 525.

[160] § 335 BGB; art 112(1) OR; art 1981(2) Civil Code of Louisiana; § 307 Restatement 2nd Contracts; art 6:256 NBW; s 4 Contracts (Rights of Third Parties) Act 1999 and *Beswick v Beswick* [1968] AC 58, 77 per Lord Reid (HL); for Spain see Arroyo i Amayuelas, above n 117, 127. See also art 6:110 PECL with Comment E ('It goes without saying . . .') and, for the PICC, Vogenauer, above n 19, art 5.2.1 para 36.

The draft does not, however, tackle the more controversial question of whether the promisee is also entitled to sue the promisor for damages or termination of the contract if the promisor is in breach. Whilst the promisee is everywhere entitled to sue for the damages he has suffered himself,[161] views differ as to the damages incurred by the beneficiary. The traditional position of the common law is that, subject to many exceptions, the promisee may recover only his own losses, not those of a third party,[162] but section 5 of the English Act of 1999 seems to assume that the promisee can also recover the beneficiary's loss. Civilian jurisdictions allow the promisee to sue for damages to be paid to the beneficiary.[163] The position is even more complex with respect to the promisee's right to rescind the contract which is widely thought to cease at the same time that his right of revocation is brought to an end.[164] Again, when taking a fresh look at the area, the *Avant-projet* might have taken the opportunity to clarify the issue.

(b) A Multitude of Further Exceptions

The *stipulation pour autrui* has long been recognised as an exception to the principle of relative effect. But the *Avant-projet* proposes codifying other exceptions as well, and it has a tendency to extend them. I will just highlight a few of the relevant doctrines in this part of the contribution: the *action directe* (section b(ii) below), the notion of contractual groups (section b(iii) below), and the idea that third parties have a contractual action for damages arising from non-performance by one of the contracting parties (section b(iv) below). It should, however, be mentioned beforehand that article 1165 of the *Avant-projet*[165] gives a slightly misleading picture. It suggests that all the provisions contained in the Section on the 'Effects of Contracts as regards Third Parties' are 'limitations' on the principle of relative effect. But many of the doctrines mentioned there are only apparent exceptions. This has already been elaborated by Professor Mazeaud, but it might be added that a comparative perspective confirms his view (section b(i) below).

(i) Apparent Exceptions

One of the doctrines which are only apparent exceptions to the principle of relative effect is *simulation*, provided for by article 1165-1 of the *Avant-projet*. German law treats the problem entirely as one of the validity of

---

[161] Jagmann, above n 55, § 335 para 6; Terré et al, above n 28, no 525.

[162] *Alfred McAlpine Construction Ltd v Panatown Ltd* [2001] AC 518 (HL).

[163] Jagmann, above n 55, § 335 para 5; Terré et al, above n 28, no 525. For a similar solution Comment b to § 307 Restatement 2nd Contracts.

[164] Kötz, above n 40, para 57.

[165] For the text of draft art 1165 see p 236 above.

agreement. Whilst the sham transaction is invalid, another 'hidden' or 'secret' bargain which the sham transaction served to disguise is valid (§ 117 BGB). Whether it has any effect on third parties is then determined according to the general rules.[166] English law deals with cases of *simulation* under very different headings. According to the context, they could raise questions of proof, the true content of the contract or of illegality. If third parties are concerned, issues of estoppel might arise.[167]

The question of *opposabilité* (article 1165-2 of the *Avant-projet*) is rather seen as one for the laws of property and delict or tort in other jurisdictions.[168] In German law, for instance, a contract has no proprietary consequences which could be 'opposed' to a third party. Reliance of the parties would be on a *right*, not on the contract. The 'relationship of obligation' concerns only the creditor and the debtor of a particular claim, it has 'relative' effect as between them (*inter partes*) and, in contrast to proprietary rights, no 'absolute' effect as against everyone. As a consequence, third persons do not have any duty to respect contractual relationships existing between others, and there is no delictual protection against interference with contractual claims, unless such interference is *contra bonos mores* (§ 826 BGB).[169] English law knows the corresponding tort of inducing breach of contract for cases where a 'third' person knowingly induces another to break a contract with the victim.[170]

Comparative lawyers have long observed that the so-called *actions indirectes*, ie the *action oblique* and the *action paulienne*, do not constitute exceptions to the principle of relative effect.[171] They concern the creditor's rights to bring the actions of his debtor and to revoke actions of his debtor which limit his assets with the intention to harm (see articles 1166 and 1167 Cc). The *Avant-projet* recognises that there is 'more than one subtle distinction between "third party creditors" and "third parties who are entirely foreign to the contract"'.[172] But its drafters do not act accordingly and retain the actions in the Section on the 'Effect of Contracts as regards Third Parties' (see draft articles 1166 to 1167-2). In other legal systems

---

[166] For the differences in approach see M Ferid, *Das französische Zivilrecht*, vol I: *Allgemeine Lehren; Recht der Schuldverhältnisse* (Frankfurt/Main, Alfred Metzner, 1971) 307–8.

[167] Nicholas, above n 26, 195.

[168] See, in a comparative perspective, R Wintgen, *Étude critique de la notion d'opposabilité: Les effets du contrat à l'égard des tiers en droit français et allemand* (Paris, LGDJ, 2004), and already R Krasser, *Der Schutz vertraglicher Rechte gegen Eingriffe Dritter: Untersuchungen zum Delikts- und Wettbewerbsrecht Deutschlands, Frankreichs und Belgiens* (Köln, Heymann, 1971) 299–300.

[169] From a comparative perspective Ferid, above n 166, 540, 548.

[170] *Lumley v Gye* (1853) 2 El & Bl 216, 118 ER 749 (QB); *OBG Ltd v Allan* [2007] UKHL 21, [2008] 1 AC 1.

[171] Ferid, above n 166, 541 n 16; Nicholas, above n 26, 193.

[172] Explanatory note above art 1166.

they are seen as special remedies of the laws of bankruptcy or insolvency which do not have a place in the general law of contract.[173]

The promise of the *porte-fort* found in article 1120 Cc is equally left in its current context by article 1170 of the *Avant-projet*. But the person who promises to another person that a third party will do something for the benefit of the second person does not bind the third party. The agreement containing the promise of the *porte-fort* is therefore no exception to the principle, although French law is not alone in dealing with it in this context.[174] Yet other legal systems simply treat it as a specific type of contract which is related to suretyship.[175]

(ii) Direct Actions: article 1168 of the Avant-projet

As opposed to the doctrines just mentioned, the *action directe* is a true exception to the principle of relative effect. It is a direct claim of a creditor against the debtor of his debtor.[176] The *Avant-projet* greatly extends the scope of the *action directe*. Rather than admitting it only in the limited number of cases where it is provided for by legislation, the draft turns it into a broad, subsidiary remedy that would apply in all those cases where an 'unjust impoverishment' of the creditor would otherwise occur (see article 1168(2) of the draft).

From a comparative perspective this is striking. Other legal systems recognise only a very limited number of direct actions, particularly in the case of claims by victims of road traffic accidents against the liability insurer of the motorist.[177] But as a general rule they admit contractual actions only against co-contractors, not against others who are further away in the 'contractual chain'. Such persons can be sued only in tort or delict. Whoever would go 'in search of an *action directe*' in, for instance, German law would end up disappointed.[178]

---

[173] See also the suggestion by Aynès, above n 1, 65 to deal with these problems in the context of the creditor's general securities; see also D Mazeaud, 'Observations conclusives' RDC 2006, 177, 185.

[174] Cf art 111 OR; § 880 a ABGB.

[175] For German law cf Ferid, above n 166, 544, 781.

[176] For a comprehensive account see S Whittaker, 'Privity of Contract and the Law of Tort: the French Experience' (1995) 15 OJLS 327, 343–54. From a German perspective, see HC Ficker, *Die Schadensersatzpflicht des Verkäufers und seiner Vormänner in der französischen Rechtsprechung* (Frankfurt/Main, Metzner, 1962).

[177] See, for English and German law, ss 151–3 of the Road Traffic Act 1988; § 3 Nr 1 Pflichtversicherungsgesetz of 5 April 1965. Both are incorporating art 6 of the Annex to the European Agreement of 20 April 1959 on mandatory liability insurance for motor vehicles.

[178] See the title and the conclusions of I Corbisier, 'À la recherche d'une "action directe" en droit allemand des obligations et des assurances' in M Fontaine and J Ghestin (eds), *Les effets du contrat à l'égard des tiers: Comparaisons franco-belges* (Paris, LGDJ, 1992) 325.

(iii) Contractual Groups: articles 1172 to 1172-3 of the Avant-projet

The *Avant-projet* also develops an 'innovative'[179] and 'new solution'[180] to the problem of 'complex' or 'interdependent' contracts. As is well known, in the late 1980s French courts allowed contractual claims for damages even in cases where the parties to the litigation did not have any direct contractual relationship, but where both of them had made contracts with other parties who, ultimately, formed part of a 'contractual group' or 'ensemble' or 'grouping'.[181] This line of cases was at least partially reversed by the Cour de cassation's decision in the *arrêt Besse* in 1991.[182] However, the *Avant-projet* proposes the introduction of the notion of 'interdependent contracts' into the Code civil for the first time. As a general rule, terms contained in one contract would not affect the other agreements in a contractual 'ensemble' (see article 1172-1 of the draft). But according to article 1172-2, the effect of limitation clauses, exclusion clauses, arbitration clauses and jurisdiction clauses contained in one of the contracts within the group would be supposed to extend to the parties to the other contracts within that group, provided that these parties were aware of these clauses at the time of their own contractual undertakings and did not object to them.

Again, this is a deviation from the principle of relative effect which is unheard of in other jurisdictions. They do not have a doctrine of 'group contracts'. Even if there is an economic and factual link between different contractual transactions, these are kept entirely separate in law. In such cases there are no exceptions to the general rule that contractual actions are brought between parties to a contract. Other parties have to sue in delict or tort.

(iv) Actions of Third Parties for Damages Arising from Non-performance of One of the Contracting Parties: article 1342 of the Avant-projet

The most striking acceptance of the conferral of contractual rights on third parties in the *Avant-projet* can be found in its article 1342. The provision is innovative enough to have generated huge interest amongst French lawyers.[183] The negligent or intentional non-performance of a contractual

---

[179] Aubert and Leclercq, above n 22, 64 (see below p 593).
[180] Catala, above n 14, 14 (see below p 473).
[181] Whittaker, above n 176, 354–7.
[182] Ass plén 12 July 1991, D 1991, 549 note J Ghestin.
[183] See Aynès, above n 1, 64; Arteil, above n 1, 11, n 8, and 17; P Ancel, 'Présentation des solutions de l'avant-projet' RDC 2007, 19, 27–30; J Huet, 'Observations sur la distinction entre les responsabilités contractuelle et délictuelle dans l'avant-projet de réforme du droit des obligations' RDC 2007, 31, 40; É Savaux, 'Brèves observations sur la responsabilité contractuelle dans l'avant-projet de réforme du droit de la responsabilité' RDC 2007, 45, 51–5; Mazeaud, above n 1, 223–6; Cour de cassation, above n 21, paras 60–62; P Sargos, 'The Work of the Cour de cassation on the *Avant-projet de réforme*', ch 18 below, 383, 395–6.

duty by one party can of course cause harm to a third person. It is accepted in all legal systems that the third party will then have an action in delict or tort if he can establish all the requirements of delictual or tortious liability. But in cases where fault cannot be established, where no protected right has been affected or where a delictual action would be less advantageous for other reasons the courts are frequently willing to extend the contractual liability of the party in breach. This is certainly the case in French law, for instance when the courts rely on a 'contractual ensemble' or find an 'implied stipulation for the benefit of another' who can accordingly sue for damages for breach of an *obligation de sécurité*.[184] These doctrines have always been controversial, but they have always been regarded as exceptions, and they had at least some inherent limitations. Article 1342(1) of the *Avant-projet* now suggests that contractual liability ought to be available to *all* third parties who suffer harm caused by non-performance of a contractual obligation, although they are subject to all the limits and conditions to the contractual claim which apply to the creditor. As an alternative route, the victim can, however, choose to pursue an action in delict if he can meet the requirements of delictual liability (article 1342(2) of the *Avant-projet*).

The solution of draft article 1342 does not only contradict the recent case-law of the Cour de cassation which, after some hesitation, has come down firmly in favour of only admitting a delictual action of third persons in such cases.[185] It is also surprising from a comparative perspective. In English law, no contractual liability would lie in these cases. Frequently, liability would lie in tort, but it would be difficult to establish it in cases of pure economic loss. In other legal systems, contractual liability might be established under the doctrine of 'contracts with protective effect for third parties' (*Verträge mit Schutzwirkung für Dritte* or *contratti con effetti protettivi a favore dei terzi*). There would be a right in the third party to sue a contractual party who was in breach of a contractual duty of care if the other party to the contract has an interest in the protection of the third party and it was foreseeable that the third party might be endangered by the breach. The Italian Corte di Cassazione, for instance, recognised such actions in favour of children who were injured by the negligence of doctors when the children's mothers were giving birth.[186] But these remedies are regarded as exceptional, and, especially in Germany, as controversial, at least in cases of pure economic loss. Most importantly, they would be

---

[184] See p 250 above.
[185] Ass plén 6 October 2006, D 2006, 2825 note G Viney. The decision has generated a flurry of comments, see, eg, the contributions in RDC 2007, 269, 279, 379, 531–631, especially the comparative remarks by C Popineau-Dehaullon, 'Regards comparatistes sur la responsabilité du contractant à l'égard d'un tiers, victime de l'inexécution du contrat' RDC 2007, 622.
[186] Cass 22 November 1993, no 11503, Nuova giurisprudenza civile commentata 1994 I 690; Cass 29 July 2004, no 14488, Danno e responsabilità 2005, 380. See, however, against invoking this doctrine in a similar case, Cass 22 January 1999, no 589, Danno e responsabilità 1999, 294.

available only if strict tests as to the proximity of the third party to the creditor of the contractual obligation and to the transaction itself are met.[187] In contrast to this, article 1342 of the *Avant-projet* turns the exception into a rule and envisages delictual liability as a mere alternative in cases where the rule does not reach satisfactory results.[188] It therefore deviates from the principle of relative effect to an unprecedented extent.

III. REINFORCING RELATIVE EFFECT?

The overview provided in the second part of this chapter shows that no other legal system recognises as many exceptions to the principle of 'relative effect' and construes them so widely. Professor Mazeaud, in his contribution, seems somewhat surprised that most of the rules contained in the Section of the *Avant-projet* dealing with 'The Effects of Contracts as Regards Third Parties' do not have a counterpart in other jurisdictions.[189] The reason for this is exactly that these jurisdictions do not consider it worthwhile to extend the effect of contracts on third persons to such an extent.

There is indeed not much left of the 'celebrated article 1165' Cc.[190] The ostensible reinforcement of the principle is hollow. For some time now, there have been suggestions to 'rethink' the principle of relativity.[191] The *Avant-projet* has not taken up this invitation. It has maintained the principle, and it has even reanimated the wholly outdated article 1119 Cc, whilst at the same time stretching the exceptions to a point where the only surviving aspect of the principle enounced in article 1165 Cc is precisely the one which the *Avant-projet* suggests to delete: 'Les conventions . . . ne nuisent point au tiers', ie agreements do not harm a third party. Maybe a new 'celebrated article 1165' should contain only the opening words of draft article 1165: 'Contracts bind only the contracting parties.' This is the remaining core of 'relative effect' as understood by the *Avant-projet*, and as accepted elsewhere in Europe.

---

[187] For a Franco-German comparison of this area see H Hengstenberg, *Ansprüche Dritter bei Schädigungen aus Vertragsverletzung im deutschen und französischen Recht* (München, Schubert, 1962).

[188] For a similar observation from a comparative perspective cf S Lorenz, 'La responsabilité contractuelle dans l'avant-projet: un point de vue allemand' RDC 2007, 57, 62.

[189] Mazeaud, above n 1, 209. In a similar vein P Didier, 'L'effet relatif' in P Rémy-Corlay and D Fenouillet (eds), *Les concepts contractuels français à l'heure des Principes du droit européen des contrats* (Paris, Dalloz, 2003) 187, 187–8, 197–200 and P Jestaz, 'Rapport de synthèse' in *ibid*, 263, 274.

[190] See n 3 above.

[191] Grimaldi, above n 10, 181.

F

The Definition of la faute

12

The Definition of la faute *in the* Avant-projet de réforme

JEAN-SÉBASTIEN BORGHETTI

FAULT IS ONE of those concepts that jurists find particularly difficult to define because they are not exclusively legal notions: legal or
juridical fault is just one type of fault among many others and co-
exists with moral fault, political fault, fault in a sporting context, etc. All
these particular types of fault are often seen as various instances of a single
overarching category. It is true that the basis for such an essentialist position which would postulate the existence of an absolute concept of fault
without any qualification or modification is debatable. Nevertheless, it is
clear that the word 'fault' forms a part of everyday language and that, as
such, it has a significance which is not primarily juridical.

Fault is certainly not the only term borrowed from everyday language
which is employed to designate a legal concept. The law of civil liability is
indeed very rich—though no more so than the other branches of the law—
in these ambiguous concepts which first have significance for the generality
of human beings before they identify a particular legal concept: harm,
causation or indeed defectiveness are further examples, along with fault. It
is inevitable as well as desirable that the law should borrow from everyday
language some, indeed the majority, of the terms that it uses. That
expresses the link between law and the reality for which it is called to
provide structure, reinforcement and direction—a link which should be
unbreakable.

These concepts, which are in a certain sense at the crossroads between
everyday language and legal language, nevertheless create particular difficulties in terms of their definition. Their legal meaning must be clearly
distinguished from their ordinary meaning. And at the same time, the first
of these meanings is subordinate to the second, so that there is a risk that
jurists may sometimes forget that the term they are using does not necessarily cover exactly the same fact situations as in everyday language. To
take just one example, borrowed from the law of civil liability, one may

wonder whether the problems that the concept of causation poses in French law might not be disentangled and clarified somewhat (although certainly not completely resolved!) if a clearer distinction were drawn between causation as a concept of everyday language and true legal causation.

In relation to fault, however, it should be recognised that jurists have long been careful to affirm the special character of the concept within their domain. Furthermore, that special character does not involve a single 'general' legal fault. That is to say, there is no such thing as 'legal fault' as a single concept. The concept of fault bears, so to speak, the full brunt of the division of the law into separate branches. Fault in administrative law is not to be confused with that in criminal law, and the latter is not to be confused with fault in civil law. In the context of this study, we shall restrict our discussion to civil fault, that is to say, fault as it is viewed in the law of civil liability.

Civil fault is certainly not to be confused with either fault in everyday language, or with other particular instances of fault, specific to certain areas or disciplines, such as moral fault or fault in the context of sport. However, this has not always been the case. It is plausible, in fact, that the drafters of the Code civil did not attribute any specific legal meaning to the word 'fault', as it features in article 1382.[1] At the time legal rules were not so clearly distinguished from social and moral norms as they are today. Over the following two centuries, however, the distinct character of civil fault has progressively been asserted, first in contrast to moral fault, and then in contrast to 'social' fault. This assertion of the 'autonomy' or independence of civil fault has been the means used to extend civil liability for fault, because it has made it possible to dissociate legal liability from moral, or even social, culpability. More recently, civil fault has asserted its independence from criminal fault, after nearly a century in which the two types of fault were treated as identical, even though that identity was debated and debatable.[2] To some extent, the history of civil fault since 1804 could thus be seen as one of its progressive assertion of independence, first in relation to non-legal types of fault, and then in relation to criminal fault.

Today, the distinct character of civil fault is no longer questioned. At a technical level, it is revealed in particular by the monitoring function of the Cour de cassation in relation to findings of fault.[3] This monitoring function dates back a long way, and it is precisely because of the work undertaken by the supreme court that the distinct character of civil fault in relation to

---

[1] Art 1382 Cc: 'Any human action whatsoever which causes harm to another obliges the one by whose fault it occurred, to make reparation for it.'

[2] See P Le Tourneau, *Droit de la responsabilité et des contrats* (6th edn, Paris, Dalloz, 2006) no 582.

[3] Supervision affirmed by Cass civ 15 April 1873, S 1873.1.174.

other types of fault has gradually been asserted. It is nevertheless remarkable that this assertion has taken place without there being any 'official' definition of civil fault or without any such definition becoming established.

Fault is not defined by the Code civil. This should not surprise us, since those drafting the French code, in contrast to those drafting the German one, for example, were not particularly keen on definitions. A definition of fault for the purposes of article 1382 would no doubt have appeared all the more superfluous to them because of the fact that they did not always establish a very clear distinction between legal concepts and those of everyday language, as has already been said, and that such a definition would no doubt have seemed to them to duplicate the work of the *Dictionnaire de l'Académie française.*

As the concept of civil fault became more refined and increasingly distinct from other types of fault, a definition could nevertheless have been established by the work of the courts. The Cour de cassation, in particular, could very well have been able to impose its definition of civil fault, by monitoring the process of characterisation of actions or omissions as fault by lower courts, but nothing of the kind occurred. This is no doubt a mark of the prudent approach adopted by the Supreme Court, which has preferred not to tie itself to a particular definition, which might have proved to be too narrow or poorly adapted to its task, whereas one of the great strengths of the concept of fault, in French law, is its extreme pliability and flexibility.

Moreover, to propose a single definition of civil fault is not as easy as it seems as there are in fact different types of civil fault. A distinction should be drawn, in particular, between intentional fault and unintentional fault, also characterised as recklessness or negligence. This distinction, which can be traced back to the classic distinction between (civil) delict and quasi-delict, is expressly identified in article 1383 Cc.[4] It is to be found in all the great legal systems. Thus in English law, the *tort of negligence* only concerns, as its name indicates, harm caused by negligent fault, whereas harm caused intentionally is compensated, if need be, via recourse to other specific torts. In German law, § 823(1) of the German Civil Code expressly distinguishes between harm caused intentionally (*vorsätzlich*) and harm caused negligently (*fahrlässig*).

It is true that in French law, as also in many foreign laws, and in particular in German law, the question whether harm has been caused by intentional or unintentional fault does not in principle lead to any difference in the regime applicable to reparation of that harm. However,

---

[4] Art 1383 Cc: 'Everyone is liable for the harm he causes not only by his intentional act, but also by his negligent conduct or by his imprudence.' Note also that Chapter II of Title IV of Book III of the Code civil, where the provisions devoted to what is today called extra-contractual civil liability are to be found, is entitled 'Concerning Delicts and Quasi-delicts'.

that does not mean that, conceptually, the two types of fault do not remain quite distinct. In consequence, the majority of legal systems refrain from suggesting a single definition of civil fault. Just to take one example, the German Civil Code proposes a definition of negligence,[5] but not a definition of civil fault in general.

This diversity within civil fault, while it might have contributed to dissuading the Cour de cassation from suggesting a definition, nevertheless did not discourage French academic writers from so doing. On the contrary, the definition of civil fault has given rise to some major works and has been the subject of famous controversies.[6] Today, however, the doctrinal debate has lost most of its vigour. Most authors sensibly share the same views and the search for a definition of fault, a compulsory section of any work dealing with civil liability for fault, principally aims to develop a form of words that makes it possible to take account, as precisely as possible, of the solutions worked out by the courts. Academic writers, in general, do not even attempt to question the conception of civil fault which emerges from the case-law.

It is in this context that the provisions of the *Avant-projet de réforme du droit des obligations et de la prescription* concerning civil liability are to be seen. These provisions have, in particular, the notable feature that they suggest a definition of civil fault. Article 1352 of the *Avant-projet* provides:

> A person must make reparation for the harm which he has caused through any type of fault.
>
> Fault consists of breach of a rule of conduct imposed by legislation or regulation or failure to conform to a general duty of care and diligence.
>
> Where a person's action falls within one of the situations governed by articles 122-4 to 122-7 of the Criminal Code no fault is committed.

The existence of a definition of civil fault in article 1352(2) is a perfect illustration of the pedagogical concern of the authors of the *Avant-projet*. It also illustrates their desire, not radically to transform the French law of obligations, but to rephrase it by integrating the fruits of case-law and, if need be, to amend it on the basis of the work undertaken by academic writers in the last two centuries in order to define and systematise the concepts used in the law of obligations. The definition of fault suggested by the *Avant-projet* fits perfectly within this approach to rewording the legislation, since it does indeed do no more than adopt the definition most often advanced by academic writers and considered to reflect the current status of the case-law. On reflection, however, this faithfulness to the existing law may be less complete than it seems. Above all, under cover of

---

[5] § 276(2): 'A person acts negligently if he fails to observe the relevant accepted standards of care.'

[6] See G Viney and P Jourdain, *Les conditions de la responsabilité* (3rd edn, Paris, LGDJ, 2006) nos 441 to 444-1.

ensuring continuity, the *Avant-projet* encourages and accentuates a development in the conception of fault, the basis for which might have deserved some discussion, particularly when compared with foreign laws.

The definition of fault suggested in article 1352(2) of the *Avant-projet* thus falls within the framework of an assumed faithfulness to the law as presently applied (section I below), while at the same time marking a definite evolution of that law (section II below).

I. ASSUMED FAITHFULNESS TO THE EXISTING LAW

The mere proposal to enact a legislative definition of civil fault marks a break with tradition. Nevertheless it is in essence a formal break. As to the substance, the *Avant-projet* is consistent with a continuation of the law as presently applied. First of all it endorses a purely objective conception of fault (section I(a) below). Then it maintains the definition of such an objective fault which the majority of academic writers deduce from a study of the case-law (section I(b) below).

(a) Endorsing the Objective Conception of Fault

In the middle of the twentieth century, a lively debate set the supporters of a subjective conception against those of an objective conception of fault.[7] For the first, fault is composed of two elements: a 'material' element and a mental element. The material element consists of the unlawfulness of the conduct contemplated, that is to say, its conflict with the law. As to the mental element, commonly designated as the condition of imputability, this consists of the mental ability of the agent to understand the scope of his acts and to assume responsibility for their consequences. The supporters of an objective concept of fault, by contrast, consider that the material element alone is sufficient to enable fault to be identified, without requiring any condition of imputability.

The subjective conception of fault reigned for a long time without any argument in French law, as it continues to do in many legal systems. The practical consequence of that was that infant children (*infantes*) and persons with mental problems could not commit any fault and therefore could not be made liable on the basis of articles 1382 and 1383 Cc. As a result, the victims of harm caused by such persons sometimes found themselves deprived of all compensation. This absence of compensation finally started to seem rather odd in the light of the ever-increasing tendency of French law to favour victims of harm. This led to the development of a purely objective conception of fault, championed by an influential sector,

---

[7] *Ibid*, nos 444 to 444-1.

and soon by a majority, of academic writers. This objective conception has progressively been adopted in the law as it is applied in practice, and has been endorsed both by legislation and the courts.[8] Today, the solution adopted is clear: the condition of imputability has disappeared from the conception of civil fault in French law. This situation, while it may still be the subject of certain criticisms,[9] henceforth has the weight of evidence on its side.[10]

It is not therefore surprising that this purely objective conception of civil fault should be confirmed by the *Avant-projet*. This emerges implicitly from draft article 1352, which does not make any reference to a condition of imputability. Most significantly, it emerges explicitly from article 1340-1 of the *Avant-projet*, which provides that

> A person who has caused harm to another while lacking understanding is none-theless obliged to make reparation for it.

The note which accompanies this article states that the working group chose to insert this provision after the general one stating the different instances of liability, rather than to amend the definition of fault given in article 1352. This makes it possible, according to the note, to avoid saying that a person lacking understanding can commit a fault. However, article 1340-1 does not appear to be designed as an independent ground of liability. Therefore, the liability of a person lacking understanding necessarily presupposes that his actions have been subsumed within one of the grounds of liability provided for in the *Avant-projet*, of which fault forms one part. And if a person lacking understanding can commit a fault, this confirms, in spite of the text of the note to article 1340-1, that the concept of fault, as defined by the *Avant-projet*, does not include any condition of imputability.

Such a conclusion is further confirmed by article 1351-1 of the *Avant-projet*, according to which the defence to liability arising when the fault of the victim has also contributed to the harm that has occurred does not apply to persons lacking understanding. This provision clearly favours the victim. Its objective is to counter the most highly criticised consequence of making fault an objective notion, which is the possibility of relying on the fault of a victim who lacks understanding as a defence against him.[11]

---

[8] *Ibid*, nos 585 to 593-3.

[9] See especially C Radé, 'Brefs propos sur une réforme en demi-teinte' RDC 2007, 77, 82.

[10] It is appropriate to point out that, according to certain authors, the condition of imputability should be distinguished from fault; see eg H and L Mazeaud and A Tunc, *Traité théorique et pratique de la responsabilité civile délictuelle et contractuelle*, vol 1 (5th edn, Paris, Montchrestien, 1957) no 390. They consider that it is an independent condition of liability for personal actions, distinct from fault. From this perspective, fault always had a strictly objective scope, and the legislature and case-law, starting from 1968, did no more than abolish the condition of imputability, without changing the definition of fault. See also Viney and Jourdain, above n 6, no 444-1.

[11] See especially Viney and Jourdain, above n 6, no 593-1.

On this point, the *Avant-projet* departs clearly and explicitly from the law as it is presently applied. But in so doing, it confirms that imputability is not an element of fault. In fact, if imputability were an aspect of fault, article 1351-1 could have contented itself with a reminder that a victim lacking understanding was not competent to commit a fault. By contrast, in deciding that a defence based on the victim's own fault cannot be asserted as against a victim lacking understanding, article 1351-1 implicitly confirms that the absence of understanding is no obstacle to a finding of fault.[12]

A final confirmation of the adoption of a purely objective conception of fault is to be found in article 1353 of the *Avant-projet* which provides:

> A legal person may commit a fault not only through its representative, but also by a failure in its organisation or operation.

This article confirms the existing law to the extent that it confirms that it is possible for a legal person to commit a civil fault, but it has the interesting feature that it transposes into civil law the idea of 'failure in its organisation or operation', borrowed from administrative law, which could make it easier to identify fault in a legal person. If a legal person is able to commit a fault, independently of any fault of its representative, it must mean that imputability is not an element in fault, for it is evident that there can be no question, in relation to a legal person, of a mental capacity to understand the scope of its acts.

Thus it is clearly apparent from articles 1340-1, 1351-1, 1352 and 1353 of the *Avant-projet* that the latter endorses the purely objective concept of fault which has already established itself in the law as presently applied. Moreover, it suggests a definition of the material element, the element to which civil fault may henceforth be reduced.

(b) Endorsing the Definition of Objective Fault Espoused by Academic Writers

Once it has been accepted that civil fault is a purely objective conception, independent of the state of mind of the actor, it is still necessary to establish how the material element, which henceforth will be the sole factor constituting fault, is to be defined. On this point, the text of the *Avant-projet* endorses the position adopted by the majority of academic writers (i). In so doing, it only very marginally challenges the solutions offered by the case-law (ii).

---

[12] Compare the interpretation offered by F Leduc, 'La responsabilité du fait personnel—la responsabilité du fait des choses' RDC 2007, 67, 69.

(i) Acceptance of the Definition of Fault Espoused by Academic Writers

It is well known that Planiol, more than a century ago, suggested that fault should be defined (with respect to its material element at least) as a breach of a pre-existing obligation.[13] Much ink has been spilt over this definition. The use of the term 'obligation', in particular, has been criticised, to the extent that the term, today at least, is used in reference to the contractual context. If, however, the term 'obligation' is replaced by that of duty, one arrives at a definition of fault as the breach of a pre-existing duty, which gets the vote of a good proportion of contemporary academic writers.[14]

It is true that certain authors criticise this definition of fault as the breach of a duty, or, if preferred, this definition of fault in terms of unlawfulness, since the infringement of a norm recognised by the law is generally classified as unlawful. These authors prefer in general to define fault as behaviour different from that of a reasonably diligent person—at one time charac-terised as the 'good father of a family' (*bon père de famille*).[15] Attention has, however, been drawn to the fact that the clash between these two definitions of fault is less a matter of substance than of the form of words used.[16] The authors who define fault as a 'departure from expected con-duct' necessarily refer to a norm, which finds its expression in the conduct of a good father of a family. Thus, in reality they are indeed defining fault as a breach of a rule. It therefore seems that almost all French academic writers agree, in substance if not in form, on a definition of fault as a breach of a norm recognised by the law.

Clearly this poses the question as to the identity of the norms recognised by the law, breach of which constitutes a civil fault. Academic writers are unanimous in considering that, first and foremost, the rules concerned are those norms of behaviour imposed by legislation or regulation. But irrespective of the respect required for duties imposed by legislation or regulation, a person may commit a fault if he does not demonstrate the care required in the circumstances in which he finds himself. This level of care is generally not demanded and set out in detail in any legal text, but many authors consider that there is a 'general norm of social conduct requiring individuals to behave with care and diligence in all circum-

---

[13] M Planiol, *Traité élémentaire de droit civil*, vol II: *Obligations, contrats, sûretés réelles* (3rd edn, Paris, LGDJ, 1949) no 947; M Planiol, 'Études sur la responsabilité civile' (1905) 34 Revue critique de législation et jurisprudence 277, 287.

[14] See the early contribution of A Rabut, *De la notion de faute en droit privé* (Paris, LGDJ, 1948) nos 13–4; R Savatier, *Traité de la responsabilité civile en droit français civil, administratif, professionnel, procédural*, vol 1: *Les sources de la responsabilité civile* (2nd edn, Paris, LGDJ, 1951) no 4.

[15] See in particular Mazeaud et al, above n 10, no 428; N Dejean de la Bâtie, *Responsabilité délictuelle* (C Aubry and CF Rau, *Droit civil français*, vol VI-2) (8th edn, Paris, Librairies tech-niques, 1989) no 22; P Brun, *Responsabilité civile extracontractuelle* (Paris, Litec, 2005) no 343.

[16] Viney and Jourdain, above n 6, no 443.

stances',[17] sometimes called a fundamental rule of behaviour or of civility.[18] The content of this norm is determined on a case-by-case basis by the courts, in the light of the factual circumstances of the case on which they are required to give judgment.

It is this conception of fault that is explicitly adopted by article 1352(2) of the *Avant-projet*, when it defines fault as

> breach of a rule of conduct imposed by legislation or regulation, or failure to conform to a general duty of care and diligence.

The *Avant-projet* openly follows the majority of academic writers and it does not seem, moreover, that the definition of fault it suggests has really been criticised, even by those who prefer to define fault in terms of a departure from expected behaviour. This is easily explicable, because this definition of fault is clearly along the lines pursued by the case-law, and very few would dissent from this.

(ii) Apparent Faithfulness to Case-law Solutions

Since the conception of fault espoused by the majority of academic writers is intended to correspond to the conception of this idea which has been adopted by the courts, the definition of fault given in article 1352(2) of the *Avant-projet* should logically agree with the solutions found in the case-law. And in fact, that seems to be the case.[19] Apparently, therefore, the *Avant-projet* does no more than confirm the current state of the law. In suggesting a definition of a notion which, until now, was getting on very well without one, it nevertheless takes the risk that it will fix immutably the identifying features of fault. It also inevitably opens up avenues for development.

1. Unchanging features   It emerges from the law reports that civil fault does indeed consist, in principle, of the breach of a rule of conduct imposed by legislation or a regulation, or failure to conform to a general duty of care and diligence— even if the courts, and in particular the Cour de cassation, do not always specify the nature of the duty that has been breached when they make a finding of fault. The majority of examples of fault currently recognised by the case-law are therefore capable of being subsumed within the definition proposed by the *Avant-projet*.

Nevertheless, the latter may in certain respects seem restrictive, since in addition to the breach of a rule of conduct imposed by legislation or

---

[17] *Ibid*, no 450.
[18] See in particular M Puech, *L'illicéité dans la responsabilité civile extracontractuelle* (Paris, LGDJ, 1973) no 25, who defines civil unlawfulness as the breach of a fundamental rule of behaviour implicit in arts 1382 and 1383 Cc.
[19] Leduc, above n 12, 68.

regulation, the only norm which it recognises, breach of which is liable to constitute fault, is the general duty of care and diligence.

Arguing *a contrario*, does this not mean that the breach of any other type of rule does not constitute fault within the meaning of article 1352 of the *Avant-projet*?[20]

If so, breach of a purely contractual rule would not constitute fault *per se*. On this point, article 1352 is in conformity with the solutions traditionally offered by French law, and differs from the most recent case-law, as it emerges from the judgment of the Assemblée plénière of the Cour de cassation of 6 October 2006.[21] However, it is known that article 1342 of the *Avant-projet* formally recognises one distinct example of liability being imposed independently of fault, when it allows a third party to seek reparation from a contracting party for the harm which non-performance by that party of a contractual obligation has directly caused him.[22]

Nor, according to article 1352 of the *Avant-projet*, would civil fault be constituted by a simple failure to comply with an ethical rule. There too, the *Avant-projet* does not really depart from the present solutions adopted by the case-law, even though the latter are not always entirely clear.[23] This being so, to the extent that many ethical rules are now enforced through administrative regulations (cf the Code of medical ethics, adopted by decree) and that those that are not can in certain cases be linked to the general duty of care and diligence, the terminology of article 1352 would not prevent a good number of breaches of ethical rules being characterised as civil faults, as is already the case today.

In defining the norms whose breach constitutes a civil fault, article 1352 of the *Avant-projet* is clearly intended to confirm for the most part the solutions currently provided by the courts. This assumed continuity is also marked by the absence of any reference to the distinction between faults of commission and faults of omission.[24] As is well known, this is an important distinction in many legal systems, and in particular in English law. In France, the question has been posed as to whether fault consisting in an omission should receive special treatment, but the response as a matter of principle which has been given to that question, by both academic writers and case-law, is negative.[25] Article 1352 of the *Avant-projet* implicitly

---

[20] See, in a similar vein, S Whittaker, 'La responsabilité pour fait personnel dans l'Avant-projet de réforme du droit de la responsabilité: donner voix aux silences du Code civil' RDC 2007, 89, 93.

[21] Ass plén 6 October 2006, Bull civ ass plén no 9, D 2006, 2825 note G Viney, JCP G 2006 II 10181 opinion Gariazzo and note M Billiau, Resp civ et assur 2006 Études 17 note L Bloch, RTD civ 2007, 123 obs P Jourdain.

[22] This provision departs from the solution adopted by the Assemblée plénière, since it provides for liability in relation to third parties which is contractual in nature in cases of contractual non-performance—subject to art 1342(2)—whereas the liability accepted by the judgment of 6 October 2006 is extra-contractual liability.

[23] Le Tourneau, above n 2, no 6760.

[24] Whittaker, above n 20, 98.

[25] Viney and Jourdain, above n 6, nos 452–6.

confirms this assimilation of faults of omission to faults of commission by not drawing any distinction between the two types of fault. From which one may observe that endorsement of the solutions already reached emerges both from what article 1352 says, and also from what it does not say.

Finally, it should be noted that article 1352(3) states that:

> Where a person's action falls within one of the situations governed by articles 122-4 to 122-7 of the Criminal code no fault is committed.

These provisions of the Criminal code define justifying events or defences: the existence of a legislative obligation or authorisation; the command of legitimate authority; a legitimate self-defence; and necessity. Now, although it is not mentioned in the present text of the Code civil, it is accepted today by both the courts and academic writers that certain defences recognised by criminal law also stand in the way of a finding of civil fault.[26] This is the solution formally accepted by article 1352(3).[27] Furthermore one may note that the text of the *Avant-projet* remains silent on such issues as the acceptance of risk and the consent of the victim, which are currently capable, in certain cases, of preventing liability being incurred by the person responsible for the harm. No doubt this is explicable not so much in terms of a desire to make a break with the solutions found in the law as it is presently applied, as by virtue of the fact that in the existing law these justifications have a very restricted field of application.[28]

The continuity between the definition of fault given by the *Avant-projet* and the solutions found in the law as presently applied is thus obvious and deliberate. Nevertheless, the simple fact of giving precise delimitation to the idea of fault, which the current case-law refrains from doing, is capable of giving rise to new developments in the case-law.

2. Possible changes   Article 1352 of the *Avant-projet* remains silent on a number of particular situations, in which a finding of fault is subject to specific rules under the law as presently applied.

First of all, the *Avant-projet* does not say anything about the abuse of rights. Now, it is known that where harm is caused during the exercise of a right, special criteria can be applied to the finding of fault.[29] Does the silence of the *Avant-projet* on this point mark a desire to abandon the idea of abuse of right, and the restriction of the concept of fault thereby entailed in certain circumstances? This is not clear. Undoubtedly one should rather see it as the exercise of a certain degree of prudence and the desire not to

---

[26] Brun, above n 15, nos 386–91.

[27] Taking account of the definition of fault given by art 1352(2), it must be conceded that the existence of a justification is an obstacle to a finding of fault, not because it would suppress the subjective culpability of the actor, which does not need to be taken into account, but because its effect is to make lawful the breach of a rule, which, otherwise, would be unlawful.

[28] Brun, above n 15, nos 392–4.

[29] *Ibid*, no 378.

take sides on an extremely delicate question. It does not mean that, taken literally, the text of the *Avant-projet* throws doubt on the possibility of assessing fault in a more restrictive way if the particular circumstances authorise the person responsible for the harm to depart from the care normally required in society.[30]

This process of questioning also applies to the more specific issue of abuses committed in the exercise of freedom of expression. The Cour de cassation, in a judgment of 27 September 2005,[31] decided that abuses of freedom of expression concerning individuals cannot be the subject of a legal action under article 1382 Cc and are exclusively the province of the special provisions of the Law of 29 July 1881 on the freedom of the press.[32] In so doing the Cour de cassation excluded freedom of expression concerning individuals from the scope of the rules on liability for ordinary fault. But the *Avant-projet* does not say anything about a possible limitation of the scope of article 1352, whether in relation to the very specific field of freedom of expression in relation to persons, or more generally in relation to cases where the exercise of a right or a fundamental freedom is at issue. It could therefore be interpreted as adopting a stance in favour of a generalised and uniform application of the rules on liability for fault, whatever the circumstances and activities at issue. From this point of view, the *Avant-projet* would mark a change, albeit subtle and implicit, from the current case-law, to the extent that it further reinforces the universality of the notion of fault and of its field of application.

Article 1352 of the *Avant-projet* also stays silent on the issue of fault in the context of sports. In the field of sporting activities, assessment of civil fault by the courts manifests a certain degree of specificity. Such fault does not arise automatically from the breach of a rule of sport, but presumes 'immoderation' in a sporting context, which is difficult to assimilate purely and simply to a failure to conform to the general duty of care or of diligence.[33] There too, then, a literal application of the text of the *Avant-projet* could cast doubt on the solutions currently achieved by the law.

Moreover, on the assumption that article 1352 of the *Avant-projet* comes into force, the question arises as to whether the simple fact of imposing a legislative definition of fault might influence judicial practice. Until now, the absence of any definition of fault has allowed the courts, and notably the Cour de cassation, to confirm the existence of fault in a given case without having to specify the elements on which they are relying in order to make this finding.

---

[30] From this point of view, the absence of any mention and of any special treatment of abuse of rights can be classed with the absence of any reference to the acceptance of risks and to the consent of the victim.

[31] Cass civ (1) 27 September 2005, Bull civ I no 348, D 2005, 768 note G Lécuyer, D 2006, 485 note T Hassler, RTD civ 2006, 126 obs P Jourdain.

[32] Loi du 29 juillet 1881 sur la liberté de la presse, JO 30 July 1881, 4201.

[33] Viney and Jourdain, above n 6, no 573-1.

This great freedom granted to the courts explains why the case-law sometimes recognises the existence of fault without giving reasons in cases where a failure to conform to the general standard of care and diligence, or even a departure from expected conduct, whatever it may be, appears at least doubtful. Thus the Cour de cassation has had occasion to confirm that the simple fact that one climber caused another climber to fall constitutes a fault within the meaning of article 1382 Cc.[34] Now, if a definition of fault were imposed by legislation, would the courts not be obliged to identify the elements constituting fault in accordance with the legislative definition, before recognising the existence of fault? In this case, they would be less free than before to accept the existence of fault on the grounds of expediency. In other words, the establishment of a legal definition of fault would be liable to limit the very large power the courts currently enjoy in determining whether or not there is fault. This would not, however, be an inevitable consequence of the establishment of a legal definition of fault, given the freedom which French courts tend to show in their handling of the texts: it is entirely possible that the legislative endorsement of a definition of fault would remain without any effect on judicial practice and in particular on the way in which the existence of fault is found.

In the end, there is no doubt that the definition of fault proposed by article 1352 of the *Avant-projet* is in line with the continuing development of the law as presently applied. In its essentials, the text of the *Avant-projet* confirms the present state of the law, and the modifications that it is liable to bring no doubt arise less from a deliberate desire to reform, than from the rigidity inherent in any legal definition, particularly where that definition relates to an idea which previously has been left to the free assessment of the courts. This continuity, however natural it may seem, is nevertheless open to criticism in certain respects to the extent to which it confirms and even gives support to the questionable way in which the French system of civil liability has developed.

II. CONFIRMATION OF A DEVELOPMENT

The definition of fault given by article 1352 of the *Avant-projet* is open to challenge to the extent that it reinforces a conception of fault that may be considered too general and abstract (section II(a) below). Furthermore, this provision confirms and supports a development which increasingly tends to make fault, no longer truly an event giving rise to liability, but rather a criterion for imputing responsibility to make reparation (section II(b) below).

---

[34] Cass civ (2) 18 May 2000, Bull civ II no 85, JCP G 2000 I 280 no 10 obs G Viney.

(a) Fault, an Increasingly Abstract and Disembodied Idea

As has already been seen, article 1352 of the *Avant-projet* gives formal recognition to an extremely general conception of civil fault: no distinction is made between intentional fault and unintentional fault, nor between faults of commission and faults of omission. Moreover, the idea of fault, as defined by this provision, is supposed to apply to all cases, without taking into account particular circumstances and in particular the exercise by the defendant of a right or of a fundamental freedom.

This extremely general conception of fault is further reinforced by the reference made to the general duty of care or diligence. It is symptomatic, in fact, that the *Avant-projet*, following the majority in academic writers, speaks of a single duty, which is applicable to all life's circumstances. Foreign laws also recognise the idea of a legal duty of care or of diligence, such as the *duties of care* in the *tort of negligence* in English law, or the *Verkehrssicherungspflichten* in German law. Usually, however, foreign laws provide for a number of duties and not a single duty, extending its remit across time and place. No doubt, these duties of care today cover all the significant activities undertaken by individuals and legal persons. Nevertheless, the system remains, in principle, a fragmented one: the law requires that a certain degree of care be taken, but not in all circumstances—only where an activity creates risks for others. In other words, not every failure to take care necessarily constitutes fault. Fault assumes that the circumstances justified the existence of a particular duty of care or concern.

In French law, by contrast, if academic writers and the case-law are to be believed, a citizen must demonstrate care in all circumstances. He must permanently be on guard, for any failure to take care is apt to make him liable. Even in the most innocuous circumstances, no relaxation is allowed, for any failure to take care is likely to cause harm that he will have to remedy. Little matter that the harmful consequences of such a lack of care were unforeseeable, or even out of the ordinary, in their nature or extent: the French law of civil liability, and the *Avant-projet* in its wake, prefer to apply the principle of 'equivalence of conditions' to determine questions of causation, and refuse to prioritise the interests protected or to distinguish between types of harm, so as to give priority to the compensation of some of them.[35] Nor is there any question that French law, at least officially, accepts the so-called 'principle of Aquilian relativity', according to which an infringement of a rule gives rise to an obligation to make reparation in respect of the harm which it causes only to the extent to which the harm is of the kind that the law in question was actually designed to avert.[36]

---

[35] Viney and Jourdain, above n 6, no 355.

[36] *Ibid*, no 441. Nevertheless, 'Aquilian relativity' appears to be a matter of common sense, at least where the rule infringed is a legislative rule or administrative regulation which is clearly intended to achieve a particular purpose.

This extremely wide conception of fault and of liability for fault, and the deliberate refusal to adopt a more nuanced approach, are so firmly anchored in French law that their adoption by the *Avant-projet* seems perfectly natural to a French lawyer. Nevertheless, one can question whether such a system, which deliberately ignores the complex and varied character of the real events to which the law of civil liability is applied, can properly be justified. There is, in fact, a considerable resort to fiction involved in affirming that a citizen must, in all circumstances, demonstrate care and diligence. From a physical and psychological point of view, this is clearly impossible. It would therefore be somewhat illusory to justify the excessively demanding character of French law in the name of the educative or preventative function of the law of civil liability. More generally, one may doubt whether every failure to take care, whatever the circumstances and the consequences, justifies imposing liability on the person responsible for that failure. Be that as it may, such a conception of fault deprives liability for fault of any moral basis, because it is not fair that all the harmful consequences of acts undertaken by individuals should be treated in the same way. There are moments when attention may legitimately be relaxed, because there is no foreseeable danger. There are others where a particular power enjoyed by a citizen or the exercise of a particular function (eg the provision of information), may justify and excuse a lower standard of care and a lower standard of attention to the interests of others. Nevertheless, in all these cases, article 1352 of the *Avant-projet* will allow a finding of civil fault to be made and as a result the imposition of liability.

By endorsing a purely abstract conception of fault, the *Avant-projet* in a way consummates the 'disembodiment' of the French law on civil liability. It is not a morally blameworthy failure of conduct on the part of the person concerned which justifies the imposition of liability, but rather digression from an abstract and disembodied standard of normality. One may legitimately regret this development. Foreign laws seem to us to be more realistic, adjusting the finding of fault to the circumstances and the types of interest at stake. It is true that, taking into account French legal traditions, it hardly seems realistic to consider the introduction into French law of a fragmented system of civil delicts, analogous to that known to English law[37]—nor indeed would it necessarily be desirable.[38] But, without going as far as that extreme solution, which would moreover have gone counter to the drafters' objective of being in harmony with the ongoing development of the law as presently applied, could not the *Avant-projet* have encouraged the timid advances made by the courts which sometimes seek to adapt the

---

[37] See, however, the perceptive plea made by P Rémy, 'Critique du système français de responsabilité civile' (1996) 31 Droit et cultures 31.

[38] G Viney, 'Pour ou contre un "principe général" de responsabilité civile pour faute' in *Le droit privé français à la fin du XXe siècle: Etudes offertes à Pierre Catala* (Paris, Litec, 2001) 555.

definition of fault and its application to particular circumstances (cf the solutions adopted in the contexts of abuse of rights and of freedom of expression)? Instead they have chosen to go in exactly the opposite direction.

Clearly the increasingly abstract and general character of the concept of fault is justified by reference to the need to provide compensation, or more precisely, to the ideology of compensation.[39] Certainly the purpose underpinning the development of the law of civil liability in this direction is praiseworthy. But does it not end up, nevertheless, perverting the logic of liability? Civil liability is not solely a mechanism for compensating harm. It is also—perhaps even primarily—a mechanism enabling a certain measure of justice to govern social interactions, by ensuring that reparation is made for unjustly caused harm. Current developments in French law increasingly tend to leave the idea of redressing injustice out of the equation.

Nevertheless it must be apparent that, pushed to its limits, a logic of reparation of this kind leads to a questioning of the traditional structure of civil liability. That is to say, if the only purpose of liability is to compensate the harm suffered, then making liability subject to the existence of an event giving rise to liability and causation may appear unnecessarily complicated. And in fact, that is what emerges implicitly from the *Avant-projet*, which seems ultimately to envisage fault less as an event giving rise to harm and thus to liability, but rather as a criterion justifying the imputation of an obligation to make reparation for the harm alleged by the claimant.

(b) Fault, Merely a Criterion for the Imputation of a Duty to Make Reparation?

Traditionally, the French law of civil liability has been centred on the person responsible for the harm. Conceptually speaking, the starting-point for liability is an event giving rise to liability—even if in practice, clearly, it is the occurrence of harm that in principle leads to the search for liability. The expression 'event *giving rise to*' is moreover a good indicator of this insistence on the source of the harm. The requirement of a causal link falls naturally within this logical framework, because an event, in order to be characterised as 'giving rise to' it, must have caused the harm at issue.

Formally speaking, the *Avant-projet* remains perfectly faithful to this classical conception of liability, and to the threefold scheme event/causal link/harm. Article 1352(1) of the *Avant-projet* is, however, worded in an unusual way, since on a literal reading it provides:

---

[39] Adopting the expression used by L Cadiet, 'Sur les faits et les méfaits de l'idéologie de la réparation' in *Le juge entre deux millénaires: Mélanges offerts à Pierre Drai* (Paris, Dalloz, 2000) 495.

Any type of fault imposes on its author the obligation to make reparation for the harm which he has caused.[40]

Surprisingly, the provision does not say that the person responsible for the fault must make reparation for the harm caused by his fault, but the harm which *he* has caused.

This rather unusual formulation is most likely not the result of any deliberate choice on the part of the drafters, and the latter are not intending to break with the traditional rule according to which fault imposes on the person responsible the obligation to make reparation for the harm caused by that fault, and only that harm. But even so, taken by itself, independently of the intention of those responsible for drafting, the wording of this provision opens up astonishing perspectives. Effectively, article 1352(1) of the *Avant-projet* disassociates fault and the fact of causing harm. Taken literally, it permits a citizen who has committed a fault to be ordered to make reparation for harm which he has caused, even if that harm is not a consequence of his fault. No doubt the French courts are not ready to accept such a solution, which let us repeat, undoubtedly was not the intention of those drafting the text. But it is possibility. The provision makes fault appear less as an event giving rise to harm, and therefore liability, than as an event justifying the imputation to the person responsible of an obligation to make reparation. Fault almost seems to be a pretext for a sanction. There is a movement from fault as a cause of harm to fault as a pretext for the imposition of the obligation to make reparation.

The causative role of fault thus becomes a secondary consideration. It is first and foremost envisaged as a source of reproach and sanction. This approach is to be found in other provisions of the *Avant-projet* which require a particular degree of fault in certain circumstances. Thus, according to article 1351, the fault of the victim only provides a partial defence to liability for the person responsible for personal injury if it is a serious fault. Along similar lines, according to article 1359-1, employees who have acted within the limits of their functions, for purposes that conform to their roles and without disobeying their employers' orders, cannot normally incur personal liability except in the case of intentional fault on their part. And article 1371, which allows the award of punitive damages, makes that subject to the existence of a manifestly deliberate fault. In each of these cases, the requirement of a particular degree of fault expresses the desire to impose a sanction. Fault thus leads to consequences less because of its causal role than because it provides grounds for blaming the person responsible, which justify the imposition of a sanction.

---

[40] This translation differs from the one made by John Cartwright and Simon Whittaker that is otherwise used throughout this chapter because it ingeniously suppresses the ambiguity prevailing in the original.

The problem with article 1352 is that it tends to generalise a way of thinking which views fault as grounds for imposing a sanction, while at the same time it perfects the objective approach to defining fault and definitively deprives it of any moral content. Now, the more one comes to understand that a particular degree of fault, characterised in a way which assumes proof of truly blameworthy behaviour may merit the imposition of a sanction, the more difficult it is to accept that all abstract failures to take care which fall within article 1352 should be grounds for imposition of a sanction. Nevertheless, this is what the text envisages. Moreover, the difficulties go beyond just the question of fault. The whole of the *Avant-projet* endorses a conception of liability that is completely centred on reparation. This finds expression in particular in its refusal to delineate clearly the concepts of harm and causal link. The overarching inspiration is obvious, conferring an absolute priority on reparation. In this respect, there seems to us to be a large gulf between French law and foreign laws, in particular English and German law: while the latter seek to retain civil liability within socially and economically acceptable limits, French law confers an absolute priority on the compensation of claimants who, entirely symptomatically, French jurists systematically characterise as victims.[41]

The definition of fault and the role attributed to it by the *Avant-projet*, seem to us to be exaggeratedly broad. Certainly the *Avant-projet* is entirely in keeping with the French law of civil liability, but one may regret that it has further accentuated the abstract and disembodied character of fault and that the opportunity was not taken to provide French law with mechanisms allowing civil liability to be placed within a more subtle framework, as is done by foreign law.

---

[41] Whittaker, above n 20, 99.

13

The Role of la faute *in the* Avant-projet de réforme

PAULA GILIKER

I. INTRODUCTION

T HE *AVANT-PROJET de réforme du droit des obligations et de la prescription* is of great interest to any lawyer working in the field of contract, tort or unjust enrichment. The French Civil Code of 1804 has long stood as a prime example of codification; one capable of organising and structuring the law of obligations, whilst able to adapt to the enormous socioeconomic and political changes of the last 200 years. In reality, of course, the law cannot be found solely in this one Code, but must be examined in the light of case-law, legislation and academic commentary. Nevertheless, the concept of a unified statement of principle as a first point of reference retains its appeal, and continues to intrigue a common law audience.[1]

The Code's qualities of brevity and adaptability are perhaps best seen in relation to the law of tort or delict.[2] In the course of the original five articles (articles 1382–1386 Cc), fault and strict liability principles are articulated in a manner that astonishes many common law commentators. In the words of one academic:

> The breadth of these provisions is truly staggering. They do not make use of a concept approaching our own duty of care in the tort of negligence. . . . Even more surprising, French law does not rule out from these delictual liabilities any particular type of harm.[3]

---

[1] One may note, with interest, the abandoned attempt of the English and Scottish Law Commissions in the 1960s to draft a code of contract law, see H McGregor, *Contract Code: drawn up on behalf of the English Law Commission* (Milan, Giuffre, 1993).

[2] Livre troisième, titre IV, Chapitre II: 'Des délits et des quasi-délits'.

[3] S Whittaker, 'Privity of Contract and the Law of Tort: The French experience' (1995) 15 OJLS 327, 331. See also T Weir, *A Casebook on Tort* (10th edn, Sweet and Maxwell, 2004) 3: 'Continental lawyers are more concise. The law of delict in the French Code civil consists of a

289

The very generality of *faute délictuelle*, as articulated in articles 1382 and 1383 Cc,[4] stands in contrast to the specificity of protected interests in § 823 of the German Civil Code[5] and the common law retention of a system of nominate torts, each with its own conditions of liability and level of duty. However, the survival of this brief section also raises concerns as to the extent to which the Code civil remains a true starting-point for lawyers in this area, in view of the necessary development and interpretation of these articles by the courts since 1804.

This chapter will examine the role of *faute* in the proposed *Avant-projet*. In so doing, I will concentrate on three main questions.[6] First, it will comment on the decision to treat contractual and delictual liability within the same section of the Code. This marks a significant restructuring of the original Code civil and raises the perennial question of the relationship between contract and tort in the law of obligations. Secondly, it will consider the relative importance of a general principle of *faute* in the law of delict. A large part of the liability section is devoted to liability arising without fault by the defendant. This reflects developments in the law of contract with the use of *obligations de garantie*[7] and, notably, the growth of liability for *fait de choses* (acts of things)[8] and *fait d'autrui* (acts of others)[9] in the law of delict. It remains a fundamental question whether a modern legal system should focus on fault and/or strict liability principles, and to what extent principles of corrective justice continue to dominate any

mere five short articles (and one very long one, thanks to Brussels). . . . These legislative provisions have naturally been elucidated or obscured by countless judicial glosses since their enactment . . . but despite the vast changes in social structure and physical environment which have taken place since their enactment . . . they have remained literally much as they were.' BS Markesinis, 'The Not So Dissimilar Tort and Delict' (1977) 93 LQR 78, 81 adds: 'the laconic provisions of some continental codes—the Code civil notable amongst them—are likely to appear to the common lawyer as manifesto-type declarations of rights to be treated with the appropriate degree of scepticism'.

⁴ Art 1382 Cc: 'Tout fait quelconque de l'homme, qui cause à autrui un dommage, oblige celui par la *faute* duquel il est arrivé à le réparer.' Art 1383 Cc: 'Chacun est responsable du dommage qu'il a causé non seulement par son fait, mais encore par sa négligence ou par son imprudence.'

⁵ § 823(1) BGB: 'Wer vorsätzlich oder fahrlässig das Leben, den Körper, die Gesundheit, die Freiheit, das Eigentum oder ein sonstiges Recht eines anderen widerrechtlich verletzt, ist dem anderen zum Ersatz des daraus entstehenden Schadens verpflichtet.'

⁶ There are clearly more than three questions which could be raised in this context, but to avoid any overlap with other chapters, I have sought to identify issues of interest to a mixed common/civil law audience and comparative tort lawyers. For an analysis of the definition of *faute* in the *Avant-projet*, see Jean-Sébastien Borghetti, 'The Definition of *la faute* in the *Avant-projet de réforme*', ch 12 above.

⁷ F Terré, P Simler and Y Lequette, *Droit civil. Les obligations* (9th edn, Paris, Dalloz, 2005) no 580.

⁸ Notably, *l'arrêt Teffaine* (Cass civ 18 June 1896, S 1897.1.17 note A Esmein, D 1897.1.433 concl Sarrut, note Saleilles) and *l'arrêt Jand'heur* (Ch réun 13 February 1930 DP 1930.1.57 note G Ripert, rapport Le Marc'hadour, S 1930.1.121 note P Esmein).

⁹ Notably, *l'arrêt Blieck* (Ass plén 29 March 1991, D 1991.324 note C Larroumet, D 1991 Chron 157 obs G Viney, JCP 1991 II 21673 concl H Dontenwille, note J Ghestin)—liability imposed on a day centre for mentally handicapped people when one of their members had started a fire in a forest.

modern law of tort/delict. Finally, the chapter will focus on one particular innovation of interest to common lawyers: article 1362 of the *Avant-projet* which imposes liability for dangerous activities. The proposed section is in clear contrast to modern developments in English tort law and is therefore worthy of particular attention in an Anglo-French study.

II. A RECATEGORISATION OF CONTRACTUAL AND DELICTUAL LIABILITY

The *Exposé des motifs* to the *Avant-projet*'s Sub-title on Civil Liability explains the connection between contractual and delictual liability: both seek to compensate, and non-performance of a contract may, in a broad sense, be described as a *fait illicite*.[10] Provided one accepts the commonality of the concept of *fait illicite*, or 'unlawful act', in contract and tort,[11] it is possible to identify common introductory provisions (articles 1340–1342), liability provisions (articles 1343–1351: 'Reparable loss', 'Causation', 'Defences'),[12] and principles of compensation (articles 1367–1383). Such a choice may seem surprising in a system that still adheres to the concept of *non-cumul*, the rule against the accumulation of actions (retained in article 1341 of the *Avant-projet*, save for personal injury claims). However, notably, Chapter II, Section 1 on 'Conditions of Liability' usefully draws together a core set of principles, avoiding repetition but emphasising the basic constituents of any civil liability claim. In setting out fundamental compensatory principles in a manner that clarifies existing law, whilst mixing recognition of jurisprudential developments with innovative new provisions,[13] litigants are offered a common reference point with considerably more detail and explanation than previously existed.

[10] G Viney, 'Exposé des motifs: Sous-titre III. De la responsabilité civile (Articles 1340 à 1386)' in *Avant-projet de réforme du droit des obligations et de la prescription: Rapport remis au garde des Sceaux* (Paris, La documentation française, 2006) 159, 163 (see pp 809, 815 below). See also G Viney and P Jourdain, *Les conditions de la responsabilité* (3rd edn, Paris, LGDJ, 2006) no 445.

[11] A point of contention—in the words of Huet, 'la matière est une des plus controversées qui soient': J Huet, RDC 2007, 31, who questions whether the link is rather artificial in reality.

[12] Such provisions again rest on the assumption that common definitions exist in contract and tort. Concern may be raised that the drafters do not, however, attempt a definition of the causal connection/*lien de causalité* (a task which is rejected as 'illusoire' by the *Avant-projet*). This would appear to mirror comments by certain English judges that it is simply a matter of common sense: see L Hoffmann, 'Causation' (2005) 121 LQR 592, 603: 'There is nothing special or mysterious about the law of causation. One decides, as a matter of law, what causal connection the law requires and one then decides, as a question of fact, whether the claimant has satisfied the requirements of the law. There is, in my opinion, nothing more to be said.' Yet as the ongoing debate between the *théorie de l'équivalence des conditions* and *théorie de la causalité adéquate* (see F Terré et al, above n 7, no 860) and English cases such as *Fairchild v Glenhaven Funeral Services Ltd* [2002] UKHL 22, [2003] 1 AC 32 and *Barker v Corus UK Ltd* [2006] UKHL 20, [2006] 2 AC 572 suggest, conceptual difficulties exist, and it is a pity not to recognise this more openly and seek greater clarity.

[13] Perhaps, most controversially, note the proposed introduction of punitive damages in art

The key question is whether the benefits of such a change outweigh the potential for confusion in drawing together two heads of liability in a manner which divorces contractual liability from alternative remedial responses, such as specific performance or termination of the contract. Separate sections of the *Avant-projet* still exist for delictual and contractual liability, together with a less distinct set of rules applying solely to personal injury claims. The result is very different from the succinct nature of the existing Code civil. It may be argued, however, that a modern legal system should attempt a more detailed clarification of its remedial structure. Whilst the provisions on the *effets de la responsabilité*/effects of liability may be detailed and complex in places, this reflects the law in practice. Further, if one is prepared to accept that the rules of 'harm' or 'loss' or causation are identical in contract and tort, any repetition would appear to be pointless. Article 1340 of the *Avant-projet* does, however, cause an external observer some thought. It is described as 'an announcement for later articles'[14] and describes both delictual and contractual liability as follows:

> (1) Any unlawful or abnormal action which has caused harm to another obliges the person to whom this is attributable to make reparation for it. [*responsabilité extracontractuelle*]
> (2) Similarly, any non-performance of a contractual obligation which has caused harm to its creditor obliges the debtor to answer for it' [*responsabilité contractuelle*].[15]

One must wonder how these general provisions interact with the more specific definitions of extra-contractual liability, set out in articles 1352–1362 of the *Avant-projet*, and contractual liability, set out in articles 1149 and 1163–1166 of the *Avant-projet*. Do they act as a starting-point? A point of reference in case of uncertainty? An interpretative tool?[16] Having seen how widely such general introductory provisions have been inter-

---

1371 of the *Avant-projet*, for which English law has long opposed recovery in contract law—see *Addis v Gramophone Co Ltd* [1909] AC 488 (HL) and Law Commission, *Aggravated, Exemplary and Restitutionary Damages* (Law Com No 247, HMSO, 1997)—and to which it has adopted a restrictive approach in tort: see *Rookes v Barnard* [1964] AC 1129 (HL). It remains, however, a topic of debate: see, most recently, R Cunnington, 'Should punitive damages be part of the judicial arsenal in contract cases?' (2006) 26 LS 369.

[14] 'Ce texte qui se présente comme une annonce de textes ultérieurs': Viney, above n 10, 171, n 1 (see p 834, n 1 below).

[15] Thanks must be given to the excellent English translation by John Cartwright and Simon Whittaker. The original is as follows:
(1) Tout fait illicite ou anormal ayant causé un dommage à autrui oblige celui à qui il est imputable à le réparer.
(2) De même, toute inexécution d'une obligation contractuelle ayant causé un dommage au créancier oblige le débiteur à en répondre.

[16] The Conseil national des barreaux, *Projet de rapport du groupe de travail chargé d'étudier l'Avant-projet de réforme du droit des obligations et du droit de la prescription* (2006), http://www.cnb.avocat.fr/PDF/2006-11-09_obligations.pdf, fears that it may become a 'source d'insécurité juridique persistante' and recommends its deletion.

preted in the past—consider, for example, the courts' treatment of article 1384(1) Cc discussed below—caution is perhaps needed in framing such introductory provisions. Certainly for a cautious common lawyer, steeped in a system requiring precision and exactitude in its legislative drafting, such statements provoke immediate concern as to their potential interaction with the more detailed provisions elsewhere in the Code.

III. GENERAL OR SPECIAL REGIMES OF LIABILITY: A RE-EXAMINATION OF *FAUTE* IN THE LAW OF DELICT

In setting out the law of *délit* and *quasi-délit* in five short articles in 1804, the Code civil provides what has been described as 'the prototype of a general clause system [which] remains the only undisputable one in the world today'.[17] This small section of the Code has been forced to respond to the enormous changes in French society from its pre-industrialised state in 1804, to industrialisation from around 1848 onwards and then to its modern position as a member of the Group of Eight (G8) major industrial nations.[18] Such developments say much about the ability of a legal system to adapt, and the interpretative skills of the judiciary in particular. One can understand, therefore, the scale of the task facing reformers re-examining the legacy of this section of the Code civil. Given the opportunity to redraft outdated provisions to reflect 200 years of legal, economic and social development, and recognising the clear theoretical shift from liberal ideas of fault to modern ideas of loss shifting and risk allocation, it is unsurprising that the new provisions are far more detailed than their predecessors. The inevitable question facing the reformer, however, is whether to use this opportunity to consolidate changes, originating either from the courts or the legislator, or to promote fresh provisions to reinvigorate and radicalise the Code. Arguably, modern developments, notably the increasing amount of European Community law directly affecting the law of obligations, render the brevity of 1804 impossible, but one fundamental choice must be whether to retain a general clause or to focus more on particular protected interests (as in German law) or specific causes of action (a characteristic of common law legal systems).

The extra-contractual liability provisions appear to reflect rather a mixed approach towards this latter question. The provisions are far more detailed than their predecessors and, although certain general clauses remain, they are supplemented by a more detailed breakdown of liability together with

[17] S Banakas, 'Liability for incorrect financial information: Theory and practice in a general clause system and in a protected interests system' (1999) 7 ERPL 261, 262. The detailed *Titre IV bis, De la responsabilité des produits défectueux* (arts 1386-1 to 1386-18 Cc) is not representative of the style of the Code.

[18] C Heywood, *The Development of the French Economy: 1750–1914* (Cambridge University Press, 1995).

provisions that deal with particular protected interests, most noticeably personal injury,[19] and by reference to specific forms of liability—nuisance ('Les troubles de voisinage' in article 1361 of the *Avant-projet*) and dangerous activities ('Les activités dangereuses' in article 1362 of the *Avant-projet*). There is an obvious contrast, also, between the provisions describing *faute* and strict liability, and the detailed provisions placed at the end of the 'Civil Liability' section which concern accident victims (based on the statute of 5 July 1985[20]) and the retention of the rather inelegant articles 1386-1 to 1386-18 Cc (product liability based on Directive 85/374[21]). These 'principal special regimes of liability or compensation', which reflect statutory intervention in relation to specific causes of injury, bear little relation to the principles stated in earlier sections and stand in their own right. It must be questioned, however, why only two such schemes are included—would it not be more logical to attempt a more comprehensive inclusion of such schemes, or leave them out of the Code? It is clear from the *Exposé des motifs* that the working group was very divided on this issue, and the end result bears all the hallmarks of a compromise.[22] Yet, more positively, it does result in the incorporation of two major protectionist forms of legislation within the Code civil. This will present future litigants with clearer and more accessible information of the compensatory structure. In view of the number of road accidents each year, this must be a positive development.[23] One wonders, however, whether product liability would, in the absence of the European Directive and subsequent litigation, be regarded as worthy of special attention in lieu of, for example, compensation for accidents at work or harm caused by criminal offences, which impact on a large section of the population. In reality, as soon as one inserts specific provisions relating to liability, one is forced to defend one's choices and the rationale on which such choices are made. At the very least, it would appear advisable for a clearer justification for the choices of these two particular forms of liability to be given.

A general statement of *faute* is nevertheless retained. The new version, given in article 1352 of the *Avant-projet*,[24] is far more detailed than its

---

[19] See arts 1341, 1351, 1373, 1379, 1382-1 of the *Avant-projet*.

[20] Loi no 85-677 du 5 juillet 1985 tendant à l'amélioration de la situation des victimes d'accidents de la circulation et à l'accélération des procédures d'indemnisation, JO 6 July 1985, 7584.

[21] Council Directive (EEC) 85/374 of 25 July 1985 on the approximation of the laws, regulations and administrative provisions of the Member States concerning liability for defective products [1985] OJ L/210/29.

[22] Viney, above n 10, 161 (see p 809 below).

[23] For example, the United Kingdom Department of Transport, *Road Deaths: EU Comparison 2001—Social Trends 34* (2001) indicated that the number of road deaths in France and the United Kingdom were 13.8 and 6.1 per 100,000 population, respectively. Art 1385 of the *Avant-projet* additionally extends the compensatory principles to treat drivers in the same manner as other victims and to include railway and tramway accidents.

[24] The original is as follows:
(1) Toute faute oblige son auteur à réparer le dommage qu'il a causé.

predecessor, article 1382 Cc;[25] the reformers having taken the opportunity to outline the standard of care needed (harm and causation are dealt with, of course, in the common sections). Article 1353 of the *Avant-projet* goes further to extend liability to a *défaut d'organisation or de fonctionnement*—utilising an administrative law concept to impose primary liability on companies, rather than identifying individual acts of misconduct.

In so doing, article 1353 of the *Avant-projet* marks a move from subjective individual responsibility to the more objective test of fault in the organisation or operation of the company. This is consistent with the fact that the majority of the new delict provisions focus not on *faute*, but strict liability (*responsabilité de plein droit*), and it is the express recognition and expansion of the current article 1384 which marks the most notable changes and innovations in this area of law. The drafters formally recognise that the centrality of the original concept of *faute* in the Code civil must in the twenty-first century give way to the notion of strict liability—strict liability for the actions of things, people, nuisances and even dangerous activities. This reflects, in part, case-law development over the last 200 years. In particular, the evolution of the concept of *fait des choses* (liability for the acts of things) from a general provision introducing liability for animals[26] and ruined buildings[27] to its modern broad interpretation demonstrates the significant interpretative powers of the courts in favour of strict liability principles.[28] It is of interest to note in the *Avant-projet* reference to a discussion as to the continued usefulness and appropriateness of maintaining liability under article 1384(1) Cc due to specific statutory provisions dealing with road accidents and the absence of equivalent provisions in other legal systems.[29] One suggestion was to replace it with a principle of strict liability for dangerous activities—it may be noted that the final version contains both provisions! In choosing to retain this form of liability, but to clarify its principles in articles 1354 and 1354-1 to 1354-4 of the *Avant-projet*, the reformers clearly indicate that *faute* must compete with the now codified principles of strict liability which favour victims' rights over those of defendants.

(2) Constitue une faute la violation d'une règle de conduite imposée par une loi ou un règlement ou le manquement au devoir général de prudence ou de diligence.

(3) Il n'y a pas de faute lorsque l'auteur se trouve dans l'une des situations prévues aux articles 122-4 à 122-7 du Code pénal.

See, for example, art 122-4 Code pénal:

(1) N'est pas pénalement responsable la personne qui accomplit un acte prescrit ou autorisé par des dispositions législatives ou réglementaires.

(2) N'est pas pénalement responsable la personne qui accomplit un acte commandé par l'autorité légitime, sauf si cet acte est mainfestement illegal.

[25] 'Tout fait quelconque de l'homme, qui cause à autrui un dommage, oblige celui par la *faute* duquel il est arrivé à le réparer.'

[26] Art 1385 Cc; art 1354-4 of the *Avant-projet*.

[27] Art 1386 Cc; omitted from the *Avant-projet* as outdated: see Viney, above n 10, 163, n 1.

[28] See Viney and Jourdain, above n 10, no 628 ; Terré et al, above n 7, nos 745–61.

[29] Viney, above n 10, 176, n 1 (see p 845, n 1 below).

This may be further seen in the provisions relating to *fait d'autrui* (liability for the acts of others), set out in articles 1355–1360.[30] This area of law, as contentious in the common law world as in civil law countries,[31] directly raises questions as to the extent to which one person should be held accountable for damages in the absence of fault. In comparison to common law systems, the current French position is very generous towards victims,[32] and the *Costedoat* decision protects employees to a perhaps surprising degree.[33] Inevitably, one finds little indication of such extensive liability in the wording of article 1384(5) Cc itself, both, one suspects, due to the fault-based focus of the 1804 Code and the fact that the scope of *fait d'autrui* is in practice a problem of industrialised nations where the potential for others to injure individuals becomes a significant social problem. The choice for the reformers was therefore clear: to re-emphasise individual responsibility, codify existing principles[34] or to set out a future framework for liability. The *Avant-projet* reflects the second and third options.

In so doing, a distinction is immediately drawn between:

(i) those having organisation, regulation or control over the way of life of minors or adults whose condition or situation requires some special supervision; and

(ii) those who organise and profit from the activity of other persons.

In so doing, the provisions bring together liability under article 1384(1) and (5) Cc, and give a theoretical framework for liability, which is to be welcomed. Articles 1355–1359 of the *Avant-projet* helpfully codify case-law developments in a clear and accessible way, and transform the Code from a virtually misleading source to one providing guidance to litigants and a useful starting-point for lawyers. Interestingly, *faute* does have a role—the actual culprit must be proved to have committed an act of a kind

---

[30] Note also the extension of fault liability to failures in the organisation or operation of a company in article 1353 of the *Avant-projet*, which additionally imposes liability on businesses for the acts of their employees.

[31] See *Lister v Hesley Hall Ltd* [2001] UKHL 22, [2002] 1 AC 215; *Bazley v Curry* [1999] 2 SCR 534 (Supreme Court of Canada); *Jacobi v Griffiths* [1999] 2 SCR 570 (Supreme Court of Canada); *New South Wales v Lepore* (2003) 212 CLR 511 (High Court of Australia).

[32] Most notably in relation to parental liability for their children: see Cass civ (2) 19 February 1997, Bull civ II no 56, JCP 1997 II 22848 concl R Kessous, note G Viney, D 1997, 265 note P Jourdain (*l'arrêt Bertrand*); Ass plén 13 December 2002, Bull civ Ass plén no 4, D 2003, 231.

[33] Ass plén 25 February 2000, JCP 2000 II 10295 rapp R Kessous and note M Billiau, JCP 2000 I 241 obs G Viney, D 2000, 673 note Ph Brun. In this decision, the court firmly rejected the previous rule that an employer could seek an indemnity from his employee. Although this has long been limited by legislation—see art 36(3) of the Loi du 13 juillet 1930 relative au contrat d'assurances, JO 18 July 1930, 8003 (now L 121-12(3) of the Code des assurances)—the decision confirmed that, provided the employee was acting in the course of his employment, the employer would take full responsibility for his actions. The employee would only be personally liable in the case of *faute personnelle*.

[34] Not necessarily noted for their clarity!

which would attract liability.[35] This marks a reversal of the case-law imposing liability without proof of fault on parents and reinstates fault as the trigger of liability, if not its whole justification. *Faute* might also be seen as relevant to article 1359-1 Cc which permits a claim against the employee himself in some circumstances. However, the terms of this provision clearly indicate that the aim is to ensure a solvent defendant for the victim, rather than any notion of accountability. The harshness which the *Costedoat* decision might cause to victims facing an insolvent or uninsured employer is thereby reversed.[36]

One might hesitate, however, at the potential scale of liability imposed under these two heads. We are informed that category (i) covers children and adults whose physical or medical condition or situation requires special supervision. This appears to narrow the scope of article 1384(1) Cc to focus on responsibility for the most vulnerable in society.[37] Some concern may be expressed, however, at the apparent vagueness of article 1358 of the *Avant-projet*, which imposes liability as follows:

> Other persons who take on the task of supervising another person in the course of business or by way of their profession are answerable for the action of the person directly behind the harm, unless they show that they did not commit any fault.

The explanatory note to this provision states that the text is aimed at child-minders, leisure centres or schools to whom a child is temporarily entrusted by its parents, but the phrase 'other persons' could extend beyond this.[38] It is common, for example, in England for law students to take on work experience prior to starting their studies at university, ie as minors. Would a solicitor or judge kind enough to allow the student to sit in his office to observe his work find himself potentially liable under article 1358 of the *Avant-projet*?[39] Is the rebuttable presumption of fault sufficient to deal with such problems? Much will depend how broadly the terms 'supervision' and 'in the course of the business or by way of their profession' are interpreted—a matter likely to be of particular concern to insurers and their clients.[40] Of course, this is a minor concern in view of the wide interpretative powers previously existing under article 1384(1) Cc.

[35] Art 1355.

[36] See M Fabre-Magnan, *Les Obligations* (Paris, Presses Universitaires de France, 2004) no 327, who suggests that the *Costedoat* decision in fact reduces the rights of victims by removing the possibility of targeting the employee should it be impossible to pursue the employer.

[37] Which currently extends, for example, to sporting organisations which organise, manage and control the activities of their members in competition: Cass civ (2) 22 May 1995, JCP 1995 II 22550 note J Mouly, JCP 1995 I 3893 obs G Viney, RTD civ 1995, 899 obs P Jourdain; Cass civ (2) 3 February 2000, JCP 2000 II 10316 note J Mouly.

[38] See Viney, above n 10, 177, n 5 (see p 849, n 1 below).

[39] Perhaps, more pertinently, would this cover schoolteachers, whose liability has, according to the drafters, been abolished?—see Viney, above n 10, 176 (see p 845 below).

[40] Le Tourneau, RDC 2007, 109, in contrast, expresses concern as to the rigidity of the provisions in this Section and questions whether they will permit judges sufficient freedom to develop the law to respond to novel situations as yet unforeseen.

The most noticeable extension of liability lies in article 1360 of the *Avant-projet*. This detailed article essentially extends strict liability to parties regulating or organising the professional or business activities of others, or who control the economic or financial activities of another business or professional person who is factually (if not legally) dependent on them. Although specific examples are given—doctors for the first option and parent companies and franchisors in the second—the wording is again very broad. The aim is to extend liability beyond the employer/employee context, recognising that, in modern conditions, economic dependency exists not solely within a contract of employment, but within a far greater range of models. As such, it marks a change from the traditionally broad interpretation of *commettant* (employer) and *préposé* (employee) used by the case-law, by which doctors might in any event be viewed as the *préposé* of the hospital.[41] Professor Viney comments that:

> This example of liability would be entirely new, but the members of the working group thought that it would be extremely useful to adjust the law of liability so as to reflect the radical changes which have occurred in the way in which economic relations are structured, as regards both production and distribution.[42]

To extend no-fault liability in this way must be considered very carefully, particularly when worded in such a broad manner. The insurance implications and economic burden on those operating through subsidiaries and franchisees clearly has to be considered, together with what is meant by 'control'[43] and 'factual dependency'. Without clear definitions of such terms, the scope of such a provision is difficult to determine, both for the parties who are potentially liable and their insurance providers, and gives rise to an unwelcome degree of uncertainty. One must question, practically, how much autonomy a parent company would have to grant a subsidiary to avoid such liability, and, theoretically, whether such liability can be said to be consistent with the very notion of separate legal identity on which such economic structures are based. This amounts to a significant extension of strict liability which, it is suggested, should be contemplated with great

---

[41] This is accepted in England, see *Cassidy v Ministry of Health* [1951] 2 QB 343 (QBD), and there is some support for this in France: see Cass crim 5 March 1992, Bull crim no 101, Resp civ et assur 1992 Comm 302, JCP 1993 II 22013 note F Chabas, RTD civ 1993, 137 obs P Jourdain. Note, however, that the decision to adopt a narrower definition of the employer/employee relationship in art 1359 of the *Avant-projet* than that currently used at law renders this problematic, and art 1360 of the *Avant-projet* a logical necessity.

[42] Viney, above n 10, 167 (see p 825 below).

[43] For criticism from the business community, see the reaction of the Chambre de commerce et d'industrie de Paris, *Pour une réforme du droit des contrats et de la prescription conforme aux besoins de la vie des affaires* (2006), http://www.etudes.ccip.fr/archrap/pdf06/reforme-droit-des-contrats-kli0610.pdf, 33, which expresses concern as to the impact such liability will have on insurance premiums for defendants. Note, also, the criticisms of B Fagès, RDC 2007, 115, who emphasises the particular difficulty of defining 'control' in a commercial context.

care, preferably following consultation and further consideration of the market impact of imposing liability on such parties.

IV. ARTICLE 1362: LIABILITY FOR *LES ACTIVITÉS DANGEREUSES*—A STEP TOO FAR?

Yet it is article 1362 of the *Avant-projet* that raises the most obvious concerns for a comparative tort lawyer, familiar with both civil and common law responses to this question. This article states the following:

> Without prejudice to any special regulation governing particular situations, a person who undertakes an abnormally dangerous activity is bound to make reparation for the harm which results from this activity even if it is lawful. An activity which creates a risk of serious harm capable of affecting a large number of people simultaneously is deemed to be abnormally dangerous. A person who undertakes an abnormally dangerous activity cannot escape liability except by establishing a fault in the victim in the circumstances set out in articles 1349 to 1351-1.[44]

It is described as 'a regime of liability suitable notably to deal with large-scale industrial catastrophes', such as the explosion at the AZF factory at Toulouse on 21 September 2001 in which 29 people died.[45] It bears some resemblance to the provisions in the US Restatement of the Law, Second, Torts, which reads:

> § 519. General Principle:
> (1) One who carries on an abnormally dangerous activity is subject to liability for harm to the person, land or chattels of another resulting from the activity, although he has exercised the utmost care to prevent the harm.
> (2) This strict liability is limited to the kind of harm, the possibility of which makes the activity abnormally dangerous.[46]

---

[44] 'Sans préjudice de dispositions spéciales, l'exploitant d'une activité anormalement dangereuse, même licite, est tenu de réparer le dommage consécutif à cette activité. Est réputée anormalement dangereuse l'activité qui crée un risque de dommages graves pouvant affecter un grand nombre de personnes simultanément. L'exploitant ne peut s'exonérer qu'en établissant l'existence d'une faute de la victime dans les conditions prévues aux articles 1349 à 1351-1.'

[45] See J Besset, Le Monde, 25 September 2001. In addition, more than 2,400 were injured, 8,000 suffered minor injuries, and 40,000 people were made homeless for several days.

[46] See also § 520. Abnormally Dangerous Activities: 'In determining whether an activity is abnormally dangerous, the following factors are to be considered: (a) existence of a high degree of risk of some harm to the person, land or chattels of others; (b) likelihood that the harm that results from it will be great; (c) inability to eliminate the risk by the exercise of reasonable care; (d) extent to which the activity is not a matter of common usage; (e) inappropriateness of the activity to the place where it is carried on; and (f) extent to which its value to the community is outweighed by its dangerous attributes.' Only the plaintiff's assumption of the risk is a defence to a strict liability action based on an abnormally dangerous activity; the fact that the plaintiff may have failed to use reasonable care for his own protection is irrelevant: § 523. Note also the proposed Draft Restatement of the Law, Third, Torts, § 20. Abnormally Dangerous Activities: '(a) An actor who carries on an abnormally dangerous activity is subject to strict liability for physical harm resulting from the activity. (b) An activity is abnormally dangerous if: (1) the activity creates a foreseeable and highly significant risk of physical harm even when reasonable care is exercised by all actors; and (2) the activity is not one of common usage.'

Whether an activity is ultra-hazardous is a question of law to be determined by the court.[47]

Both forms of liability are, however, in marked contrast to the English rule in *Rylands v Fletcher*,[48] which in fact inspired the US provision. The House of Lords chose, however, to confine this rule of strict liability by first limiting the tort to injury caused by an escape from land under the control of the defendant to the claimant's neighbouring land,[49] by requiring that the damage be foreseeable,[50] and finally by determining it to be an exceptional rule arising in extraordinary circumstances which was part of the common law tort of private nuisance.[51] In the words of Lord Goff:

> I incline to the opinion that, as a general rule, it is more appropriate for strict liability in respect of operations of high risk to be imposed by Parliament, than by the courts. If such liability is imposed by statute, the relevant activities can be identified, and those concerned can know where they stand. Furthermore, statute can where appropriate lay down precise criteria establishing the incidence and scope of such liability.
>
> It is of particular relevance that the present case is concerned with environmental pollution. The protection and preservation of the environment is now perceived as being of crucial importance to the future of mankind; and public bodies, both national and international, are taking significant steps towards the establishment of legislation which will promote the protection of the environment. . . . But it does not follow from these developments that a common law principle, such as the rule in *Rylands v Fletcher*, should be developed or rendered more strict to provide for liability in respect of such pollution. On the contrary, given that so much well-informed and carefully structured legislation is now being put in place for this purpose, there is less need for the courts to develop a common law principle to achieve the same end, and indeed it may well be undesirable that they should do so.[52]

---

[47] *Luthringer v Moore* (1948) 31 Cal.2d 489, 190 P.2d 1 (Supreme Court of California); *Beck v Bel Air Properties, Inc.* (1955) 134 Cal.App.2d 834 at 842, 286 P.2d 503 (Court of Appeal of California).

[48] (1865) 3 H & C 774 (Court of Exchequer); (1866) 1 LR 1 Ex 265 (Court of Exchequer Chamber); (1868) LR 3 HL 330 (HL). The case was finally resolved at House of Lords level, but the classic statement of principle was given by Blackburn J in the Court of Exchequer Chamber: 'We think that the true rule of law is that the person who for his own purposes brings on his lands and collects and keeps there anything likely to do mischief if it escapes, must keep it in at his peril, and, if he does not do so, is *prima facie* answerable for all the damage which is the natural consequence of its escape. He can excuse himself by shewing that the escape was owing to the plaintiff's default; or perhaps that the escape was the consequence of *vis major*, or the act of God; but as nothing of this sort exists here, it is unnecessary to inquire what excuse would be sufficient': (1866) LR 1 Ex 265, 279–80; affirmed in (1886) LR 3 HL 330.

[49] *Read v J Lyons & Co Ltd* [1947] AC 156 (HL) (inspector of munitions injured by an explosion of a shell whilst inspecting the defendants' munitions factory). In so doing, the House treated the rule as one regulating the mutual obligations of neighbours and not, as the first instance judge suggested, a strict liability rule for ultra-hazardous activities.

[50] *Cambridge Water Co v Eastern Counties Leather plc* [1994] 2 AC 264 (HL).

[51] *Transco plc v Stockport MBC* [2003] UKHL 61, [2004] 2 AC 1.

[52] Above n 50, 305. See also Law Commission, *Civil Liability for Dangerous Things and Activities* (Law Com No 32, HMSO, 1970), paras 14–6.

Whilst such a statement may be criticised as complacent, 'bland and some-what premature',[53] it does raise the question whether such problems may be better dealt with by specific legislative provisions rather than a general codal provision that will require elaboration by the courts. French law, like that of most industrialised countries, already possesses specific legislative provisions imposing strict liability, for example, on aircraft companies for harm caused to the land by their machines[54] and on nuclear energy under-takings for accidents on site.[55] Article 1362 of the *Avant-projet* does not prejudice these provisions and, indeed, the explanatory note to this provision states that '[t]he proposed scheme is very similar to that which inspires these special legal provisions'.[56] An obvious response is to question why, therefore, further special legal measures should not be implemented to cover other situations of public concern. A glance at the experience in the United States may also highlight some of the potential difficulties to which such a provision might give rise. As Nolan has recently noted,[57] US law has found it difficult to determine which activities are in fact classified as 'ultra-hazardous' and, in reality, the doctrine plays only a subsidiary role in modern tort law, in which a huge number of dangerous activities have been found to be outside the doctrine.[58] It is true that specific legislation runs the risk of gaps in the regulatory web which a general tort provision may overcome, but in view of the disagreement amongst economic theorists as to the merits of strict liability in this context,[59] one must wonder whether a general codal provision or specific legislation is the most appropriate mechanism for dealing with such disasters. If the risks of such disasters, as Stanton indicated in 1998,[60] are actually relatively small due to the high level of precautions undertaken, it is the provision of compensation for disaster victims that is the concern, rather than liability. Use of the prin-ciples of civil liability must therefore be considered carefully in the light of

---

[53] R Mullender and L Dolding, 'Environmental Law: Notions of strict liability' [1995] JBL 93, 97.

[54] Art L 141-2 of the Code de l'aviation civile: 'L'exploitant d'un aéronef est responsable de plein droit des dommages causés par les évolutions de l'aéronef ou les objets qui s'en détacheraient aux personnes et aux biens situés à la surface. Cette responsabilité ne peut être atténuée ou écartée que par la preuve de la faute de la victime.'

[55] See Convention de Paris du 29 juillet 1960 sur la responsabilité civile dans le domaine de l'énergie nucléaire.

[56] See Viney, above n 10, 179, n 2 (see p 851, n 4 below).

[57] D Nolan, 'The Distinctiveness of *Rylands v Fletcher*' (2005) 121 LQR 421, 448. For a more positive take on *Rylands* see J Murphy, 'The merits of *Rylands v Fletcher*' (2004) 24 OJLS 643.

[58] See GR Schwarz, '*Rylands v Fletcher,* Negligence and Strict Liability' in P Cane and J Stapleton (eds), *The Law of Obligations* (Oxford, Clarendon Press, 1998) 238. Stanton comments that the scope of its operation is in reality far more limited than that found under art 1384 Cc: KM Stanton, 'The legacy of *Rylands v Fletcher*' in NJ Mullany and AM Linden (eds), *Torts Tomorrow: A Tribute to John Fleming* (Sydney, LBC Information Services, 1998) 88, n 22.

[59] Should it be justified, for example, as resulting from the profit-making activities of the defendant thereby confining the principles to a certain category of claims, or due to the creation of non-reciprocal risks which could give rise to a huge extension of liability?

[60] Stanton, above n 58.

all other available options, and, it is suggested, such a general provision should only be adopted if found to possess advantages greater than specific legislative or codal provision,[61] which counterbalance the inevitable uncertainties which will result.[62]

V. CONCLUSION

In this chapter, I have focused on three controversial aspects of the *Avant-projet* concerning the future role of *faute* in the French law of obligations. I have sought to highlight areas where greater clarity is needed and, in particular, to identify potential areas of overlap which may lead to confusion and litigation, at a cost to litigants and society in general, whilst analysing critically some of the more radical extensions to the liability regime.

In so doing, it is important to recognise the value of the *Avant-projet* in providing a re-examination of the provisions governing *faute* of the Code civil in the light of over 200 years of legal development. The brevity of the existing delict section of the Code civil belies the complexity and dynamism of the current law, and the intricate legal frameworks that exist in practice. A restructuring of this section will never be easy, and the undertaking of such an endeavour is to be admired. The drafters have reviewed, updated and radicalised the role of *faute*, moving away from a notion of subjective individual fault to a system favouring strict liability in the interests of victims. In so doing, they reflect the significant changes that have occurred in the French, and, of course, European legal culture in the past two centuries. That said, it is suggested that having waited so long before implementing a full-scale reform of the Code civil, time spent in consultation, discussion and further reflection on the practical impact and theoretical coherence and consistency of the proposed reforms would not go unrewarded, and would be likely to promote wider acceptance of any resulting proposals.

---

[61] Note that liability for *fait des choses* continues to apply, having been retained under art 1354.

[62] See Stanton above n 58, 88–9: 'any introduction of a strict liability regime modelled on the lines of § 519 needs to weigh the advantages of a new strict liability remedy . . . against the efforts which would be involved in removing the uncertainties as to the boundaries within which the new doctrine would operate'.

G

Damages, Loss, and the Quantification of Damages

14

Damages, Loss and the Quantification of Damages in the Avant-projet de réforme

PAULINE RÉMY-CORLAY

THE PART OF the *Avant-projet de réforme de droit des obligations et de la prescription* that deals with civil liability[1] remains faithful to French tradition: it stays 'victimophile'. Nevertheless it cannot be said to reproduce the provisions of the present Code civil: it has ninety-two articles where the 1804 Code had only five. This should not be surprising, and a number of factors explain this marked increase. First of all the important role of case-law should be recognised, for the courts have worked hard to translate the few articles of the Code civil into a scheme adapted to the increasing complexity of the world in which we live, and whose contributions would be adopted into the Code (and in some cases reformulated) by the *Avant-projet*. Next, the Code did not contain all the legislation relating to civil liability, and the *Avant-projet* would bring within its scope the rules on traffic accidents from the Act of 5 July 1985[2] (in a modified form: drivers would be assimilated to other victims; rail and tramway accidents would also be included), alongside the rules relating to liability for defective products, which are already to be found in the Code civil but in an odd Book IV bis. The other special schemes (such as that for medical liability) remain outside the Code; this is regrettable in terms of the consistency of the law and of the ease of understanding these different schemes of liability

---

[1] Sub-title III of Title III of Book III, which might be called the '*Avant-projet* Viney'. This draft seems to be very different from the part relating to contract and quasi-contract, respectively Sub-titles I and II of what constitutes a new Title III of Book III on 'Obligations' (with the surprising disappearance of Book IV and a fortunate one of Book IV bis). It has the further benefit of its own *exposé des motifs*, distinct from the general *exposé*.

[2] Loi no 85-677 du 5 juillet 1985 tendant à l'amélioration de la situation des victimes d'accidents de la circulation et à l'accélération des procédures d'indemnisation, JO 6 July 1985, 7584.

or compensation;[3] but the inclusion of all the different schemes would undoubtedly have involved an enormous amount of work as a complete overhaul would have been necessary to ensure that the whole work was coherent and this was impossible to achieve within the time period allowed to the Working Group chaired by Professor Geneviève Viney.

The *Avant-projet* also includes in articles 1379-3 to 1379-8 the provisions of the Act of 5 July 1985 which, in relation to personal injury, sought to specify the different possible heads of damage, in order to identify those in relation to which third parties making direct payments to the victim (as in the case of social security and insurance) have a right of recourse against a person liable. The *Avant-projet* goes further, however, and notably introduces 'in advance' the right to such an indemnity of third parties making direct payment, item by item, which has just been adopted by article 25 of the recent Act on the Financing of Social Security.[4]

The number of articles relating to civil liability is further explicable by the fact that liability is interpreted broadly, including both delictual liability (referred to in the *Avant-projet* as 'extra-contractual' liability) and contractual liability. Certain special provisions therefore had to be inserted in order to explain how these two types of liability relate to each other, and to set out certain provisions specific to one or the other of them. Despite the *Avant-projet*'s claims that liability forms a single category, fortunately there has not been a complete unification of the regimes governing liability. The way in which the two types of liability are set out must appear particularly surprising to English lawyers—even those who are comparative lawyers. The apparent fusion of the two, which has existed in embryonic form in French law for more than a century, is vigorously advocated by a section of French legal scholars, in particular Professor Viney; it is therefore not surprising that it is to be found in the *Avant-projet*. Will this influence the development of French law? The answer to this remains uncertain when one compares the *Avant-projet* with European projects relating to delictual liability and in particular with the Principles of European Tort Law drawn up by the so-called 'Vienna Group'.[5] Our subject is limited to damages, loss

---

[3] See M Poumarède, 'Les régimes particuliers de la responsabilité civile, ces oubliés de l'avant-projet Catala' D 2006, 2420. Unfortunately it is not possible, given the constraints of space here, to deal with loss as an aspect of the various special regimes of liability or compensation, whether those integrated into the Code civil by the *Avant-projet*, or those which do not find a place there.

[4] Loi no 2006-1640 du 21 décembre 2006 de financement de la sécurité sociale pour 2007, JO 22 December 2006, 19315: this represents a very great advance in the compensation of victims of personal injury, rather in the spirit of the text produced by the Working Group chaired by Professor Viney. For comment see C Lienhard, 'Recours des tiers payeurs: une avancée législative signicative' D 2007, 452; P Jourdain, 'La réforme des recours des tiers payeurs: des victimes favorisées' D 2007, 454; as to this issue see P Jourdain, 'A propos de l'assiette des recours des tiers payeurs' in *Responsabilité civile et assurances: Etudes offertes à Hubert Groutel* (Paris, Litec, 2006) 189.

[5] European Group on Tort Law, *Principles of European Tort Law: Text and Commentary* (Wien, Springer, 2005).

and the quantification of damages; however, it will be seen that even from this perspective the confusion between the two sources of liability has significant consequences.

Thus there are two features that seem in particular to characterise the *Avant-projet*: as I have said, the first characteristic feature is that it gives preferential treatment to the 'victim' of harm. The use of the term 'victim' is itself not neutral.[6] The law is not focused on the person responsible for the damage, on the issue of liability, but rather on the victim, on his need for reparation. The Code civil did not refer to the 'victim', but, neutrally, to the person responsible for the harm: 'a person who causes harm to another'. Everything was focused on the conditions for his liability in a very general way: 'any human action whatsoever' (article 1382 Cc) or again 'his negligent conduct or his imprudence' (article 1383 Cc); liability for harm 'caused by the actions of persons for whom one is responsible, or by things which are in one's custody'. The other party was not named, being referred to simply as 'another'. By contrast, the *Avant-projet* is orientated towards the victim and the harm which he has suffered. It seems as though it is the conditions for obtaining reparation (for a right to reparation?) that are being studied, rather than the conditions for imposing liability. A person is a 'victim' simply because of the fact that he has suffered harm, whatever the cause may be; he may be a victim of bad luck or even of fate. Thus Chapter II of Sub-title III of the *Avant-projet* which establishes 'The Conditions for Liability' begins by defining 'reparable loss', the need for a causal connection and the defences available. Next follow the various 'grounds' of reparation. Several factors may play a role, depending on whether the liability is delictual (personal action, the actions of things, the actions of other people, nuisance, dangerous activities) or contractual (non-performance). This new presentation, which has the merit of delineating clearly the various sources of liability in spite of the 'super general clause' in article 1340 of the *Avant-projet*, evidences, so it seems to me, an emphasis on 'loss and harm'. No doubt this way of presenting things is simply the solution to a problem of form: first setting out what is common to the different types of liability, before following on with provisions specific to the different types of liability. Nevertheless, in contrast to the traditional way of presenting the conditions for liability (fault, harm, a causal relationship between the two), what is emphasised here is loss, immediately defined in the broadest possible manner in accordance with the French conception of 'full reparation'.

The emphasis on reparation also flows from the fact that, contrary to what is found in the Code civil, a chapter is devoted to a detailed examination of 'the effects of liability' (thirty-four articles!) and thus deals with

---

[6] See S Whittaker, 'La responsabilité pour fait personnel dans l'avant-projet de réforme du droit de la responsabilité: donner voix aux silences du Code civil' RDC 2007, 89, 98–9.

the quantification of damages. And this is certainly not a bad thing: French law as it stands suffers from the fact that no clear distinction is made between one type of reparable loss and another, and from the fact that, and perhaps as a result of this reason, the assessment of damages is made at large and is left to the 'sovereign assessment of the lower courts'. With good reason, the *Avant-projet* provides that 'the court must assess distinctly each of the heads of loss claimed of which it takes account' (article 1374). If this were to lead to a degree of supervision by the Cour de cassation, it would certainly be beneficial to the clarification and transparency of French law—requiring at least that the courts give an account of the factors taken into account in the quantification of damages. Nevertheless, it seems to me that the *Avant-projet* has not gone far enough in making a distinction between types of loss so as to give them an order of priority and to determine the way that they should be quantified. We are still a long way from McGregor on Damages![7]

One type of harm nevertheless demands special attention: personal injury. This is a natural consequence of victimophilia. The victim of personal injury is certainly the most to be pitied, and deserves preferential treatment, and so he alone (along with third-party victims of all types of harm) has the possibility of choosing between claiming in contract or in delict under article 1341(2) of the *Avant-projet*. Moreover, his veritable 'right to reparation' means that the fault of the victim of personal injury may not be taken into account unless it is of a certain degree: 'serious fault' is the expression used by article 1351 of the *Avant-projet*. Personal injury is the object of a very extended study of reparable losses, not for the purposes of excluding certain types of consequential loss, but rather to demonstrate that the reparation involved must cover all losses (articles 1379 to 1379-8 of the *Avant-projet*) without it being possible for an agreement to exclude or limit the reparation of personal injury (articles 1382-1 to 1382-4 of the *Avant-projet*). In the same spirit it is provided that a victim's duty to mitigate his own harm ceases to exist where the measures to be taken are of such a kind as to compromise his physical integrity (article 1373, in fine, of the *Avant-projet*). It is possible to see in this the first steps towards establishing

> a prioritisation of the interests protected by the system of liability, strengthening the protection of physical integrity. This was the basis of Starck's thesis, half a century ago, and it is to be found again today in Philippe le Tourneau's proposals for reform.[8]

I am not sure that this is the philosophy adopted by the *Avant-projet*: the proposed approach would be no more than a strengthening of the victim's

---

[7] H McGregor, *McGregor on Damages* (17th edn, London, Sweet & Maxwell, 2003).

[8] See Ph Remy, 'La responsabilité civile: étude de l'avant-projet Catala', forthcoming, which seeks to provide an 'optimistic' interpretation of the text.

right to reparation, without creating any real priorities (see article 1343 of the *Avant-projet*). Physical integrity must be protected more than other interests—in particular proprietary or financial interests (*intérêts patrimoniaux*)—but harm to this integrity makes all the losses consequent on physical damage, whatever they may be, fall within the same preferential system (see article 1379 of the *Avant-projet*).

The second distinguishing feature (if not the first), especially, it would seem, from the point of view of an English lawyer, is the fusion of delictual and contractual liability. This gives formal recognition to thesis of Brun, according to which liabilities in delict and in contract have the same function, even though they do not have the same basis.[9] On the one hand the same losses are reparable, whatever the source of liability may be: this maintains the existing rules, established by French case-law. On the other hand, according to the *Avant-projet*, reparation will have to take place in the same way whatever the type of liability: a court may in its discretion (article 1368) order reparation in kind (articles 1369 to 1369-1) or damages and they have the same objective: 'to put the victim . . . in the position in which he would have been if the harmful circumstances had not taken place', such that he should make 'neither gain nor loss from it' (article 1370). The *Avant-projet*, it seems to me, has not seized the chance it was given to make a distinction between the different types of harm, confining some to the sphere of contract and others to the sphere of delict. The question of 'pure economic' loss was not examined, and all losses remain reparable, whatever the source of the harm. Fusion also leads to a position where agreements concerning reparation are allowed in both spheres (articles 1382 to 1382-4).

One might therefore be surprised at article 1341 of the *Avant-projet*, which maintains the rule against concurrent claims where the harm suffered is not personal injury. What is the purpose of prohibiting concurrent claims if the rights of the victim are the same in both cases? This is only an apparent paradox: the process of fusion has not been complete. On the one hand, as we have seen, the different sources of liability have been maintained: delict and contract, and contractual 'non-performance' (article 1363) is distinct from the different 'grounds of delictual liability' (in articles 1352 to 1362). Above all, in terms of the overall system, even if all the types of losses can be compensated whether the action is brought in delict or contract, the distinctive character of liability in contract is partially taken into account. Only loss 'foreseeable at the time of contracting' will be subject to reparation (article 1366); contract terms limiting liability and other agreements bearing on reparation apply principally in the contractual context because 'in the extra-contractual context, a person cannot exclude

---

[9] A Brun, *Rapports et domaines des responsabilités contractuelle et délictuelle* (doctoral thesis, University of Lyon, 1931).

or limit the reparation in respect of harm which he has caused by his fault' (article 1382-4). It should be observed, though, that third-party victims—that is to say, those who are not parties to a contract—may claim reparation on a contractual basis and therefore have such clauses relied on against them (article 1342), at least if they were aware of them before entering into the contract (article 1382-3)! This quasi-fusion of liabilities (section II below) no doubt raises more questions and more grounds for objection than the 'victimophilia' from which this law suffers (section I below). The latter does not necessarily lead to the former.

I. A VICTIMOPHILE LAW ON REPARATION

The proposed French law looks more like a law on reparation than a law on liability—and this to the great advantage of victims. Where the victim suffers physical damage it even translates into a right to reparation.

(a) A Law on Reparation

The different 'grounds' of liability are completely forgotten when the question at hand is what harm is reparable. The *Avant-projet* opts, in accordance with French tradition, for a principle of 'full reparation', without any distinction being made between the different types of loss. Draft article 1343 reads:

> Any certain loss is reparable where it consists of the prejudicing of a legitimate interest, whether or not relating to assets and whether individual or collective.

A number of comments can be made about this.

First of all, the concept of 'full reparation' does not of itself necessarily imply the inclusion not only of 'harm' (defined in a footnote to article 1343 of the *Avant-projet* as 'the actual injuring of the victim's person or property'[10]) but also of 'all loss', understood as 'the prejudicing of a legitimate interest, whether or not relating to assets and whether individual or collective', without any distinction being made either as to the source of liability or as to the interests harmed. Although the principle of restitutio in integrum is one that is shared by other European laws (French, German and English law express it in very similar terms), it is applied, it seems, in very differing ways.

Subject to any provision or agreement to the contrary, each of the laws is concerned,[11] as article 1370 of the *Avant-projet* provides, to

---

[10] *Avant-projet de réforme du droit des obligations et de la prescription: Rapport remis au garde des Sceaux* (Paris, La documentation française, 2006) 173, n 2 (see p 839, n 2 below).
[11] See *McGregor on Damages*, above n 7, para 1-021, citing Lord Blackburn in *Livingstone v Rawyards Coal Co* (1880) 5 App Cas 25, 29 (HL): 'the sum of money which will put the party

put the victim as far as possible in the position in which he would have been if the harmful circumstances had not taken place. He must make neither gain nor loss from it.

But this does not necessarily include all the types of harm: in particular, neither 'moral harm' (dommage moral) nor future harm or the loss of a chance, nor indeed 'pure economic loss' seem necessarily to be included in the range of types of harm for which reparation may be claimed—which shows the truth of what Lord Hoffman observed in *Banque Bruxelles Lambert v Eagle Star Insurance Co*:

> Before one can consider the principle on which one should calculate the damages to which a plaintiff is entitled as compensation for loss, it is necessary to decide for what kind of loss he is entitled to compensation.[12]

And the introduction of reparation of a 'collective interest' raises a number of questions.

To summarise, it can be noted that since French law, on the one hand, makes no distinction between types of harm, instances of 'moral harm' have the potential to be compensated whatever the injury or damage that has been suffered. By contrast, English law reserves the payment of reparation for 'moral harm' to certain types of injury, excluding damage to property, and reserving it for certain types of tort (having caused personal injury, death, false imprisonment, defamation). Since the quantification of loss is in France left to the 'sovereign power of assessment' of the lower courts which do not have to provide an explanation of the various heads of loss, it is difficult to know the extent to which 'moral harm' is compensated where consequential on damage to property; but at any rate it is not excluded in principle.[13]

In the same way, the concept of 'pure economic loss' is not known to French law, and this type of harm can be compensated in the delictual context as well as in the contractual context, without it being considered to be more appropriate to the one rather than the other, or that there are types of delict which by their very nature involve economic loss (a loss that therefore falls within the range of reparable losses), and others whose

---

who has been injured, or who has suffered, in the same position as he would have been in if he had not sustained the wrong for which he is now getting his compensation or reparation'; § 249 BGB: 'A person who is under an obligation to make reparation must restore the situation that would have existed if the event giving rise to the obligation to make reparation had not occurred.'

[12] [1997] AC 191, 211 (HL).

[13] Reparation for 'moral harm' is permitted in the contractual context without it giving rise to any particular discussion—for example in the context of unemployment following breach of a contract of employment, G Viney and P Jourdain, *Les effets de la responsabilité* (2nd edn, Paris, LGDJ, 2001) no 93. For a discussion and an explanation of the development of English law on the question of whether there may be compensation for 'mental distress' in the contractual context, and in particular in the context of employment contracts, see *McGregor on Damages*, above n 7, paras 3-019 to 3-030.

function is not to compensate this type of loss. This sometimes causes problems in delimiting the spheres of contract and delict and also explains the maintenance of the rule against concurrent actions—and in particular makes it possible for third parties to intrude into a contract, as we shall see.[14] The English perspective seems to me to be more pragmatic in this respect: the cases, in relation to the tort of negligence, in which compensation of pure economic loss is permitted are justifiably restricted to situations where there is a 'virtual contract',[15] the persons who can claim such compensation therefore being determined in accordance with strict criteria.

Despite the 'Rules Special to the Reparation of Certain Types of Harm' (section 2 of Chapter III on the 'Effects of Liability' in the *Avant-projet*'s Sub-title III on 'Civil Liability'), it certainly seems that the general statement in article 1343 of the *Avant-projet* prevails over the special rules and that the court may take into account heads of harm other than those established by such special rules. This constitutes, therefore, a new 'general clause', which may lead, in the context of reparation, to abuses.

Article 1343 still requires that only loss that is certain may be compensated: in French law, this does not exclude either the reparation of future loss—provided that it is certain—or the loss of a chance. Articles 1345 and 1346 of the *Avant-projet* make provision for this effect, the latter article recalling that the quantification of the loss of a chance is not the same as 'the advantage which would have inured to the claimant's benefit if the chance had materialised'. Article 1375 of the *Avant-projet*, repeats what seems to have been accepted since a decision of 6 January 1993, according to which

> if the victim establishes that a head of loss has not yet been the subject of a claim on his part and the harm to him has increased, he can obtain supplementary reparation, whatever the stage of the proceedings reached, and if necessary by commencing a new action.[16]

This goes further than what is allowed in English or German law. The reparation of future loss, paid as a capital sum, is certainly accepted by English law,[17] but it does not seem that the law goes to the length of allowing a new action to be commenced, whether on the ground of an increase in harm, except in cases of continuing harm—but then it is because at the time the damages were assessed, the court did not take into account future

---

[14] See p 321 below.

[15] See *Hedley Byrne v Heller* [1964] AC 465 (HL). As to pure economic loss and whether or not it is accepted in the various different European countries, see M Bussani and VV Palmer (eds), *Pure Economic Loss in Europe* (Cambridge University Press, 2003).

[16] Cass civ (2) 6 January 1993, Bull civ II no 6. See also Cass civ (2) 5 January 1994, Bull civ II no 15; Viney and Jourdain, above n 13, no 79.

[17] See *McGregor on Damages*, above n 7, paras 9-024 to 9-029; furthermore it does not seem that future harm must always be certain, provided that it is probable.

harm—or, *a fortiori*, for a head of loss which was not the subject of the claim, without there being any increase in the initial harm.[18] In German law, periodic payments are principally reserved for certain types of harm: articles §§ 843(1) and 845 of the German Civil code permit it in personal injury cases for loss of income or increased expenses; § 844(2) allows them to dependents of the deceased victim; the periodic payment awarded is thus capable of being reviewed, as often as necessary, both to the advantage and to the disadvantage of the victim. By contrast, where damages are awarded as a capital sum, no revision is possible.[19]

If the position of French law is better explained by the *Avant-projet* than by the current law, by virtue of the obligation imposed on the court to quantify individually each of the heads of loss claimed (article 1374), the rule established is nevertheless open to challenge. It is at the very least curious that, in a system where the court is required to quantify damages taking all relevant considerations into account, as well as any reasonably foreseeable development in relation to the harm, and to assess that harm in order to make payment either in the form of a capital sum, or in the form of a periodic payment (article 1376), the bringing of a new action, in relation to the same set of facts, is allowed on the one hand because the harm has increased, without the claimant being required to show that that increase had not been taken into account in the original proceedings, and on the other hand, without any increase in harm, for a head of harm not taken into account in the original proceedings. This is difficult to justify, except as preferential treatment for the victim—which explains why only an increase in harm may be taken into account and not an improvement in the situation of the victim. Perhaps on this issue one might more usefully draw on the example offered by German law.

But this is no more than a restatement of the solutions already accepted by French law, whose scope is well known. Of greater concern, so it seems to me, is the introduction among heads of 'reparable harm' of the collective interest, without any further explanation either of this type of harm, or of the persons entitled to bring proceedings. Traditionally in French law it has been considered that only personal loss is reparable; certain associations and unions have been recognised as having the right to bring proceedings to assert a 'collective harm'. But class actions still do not exist in France— and seem to have been firmly rejected for the time being[20]—and it is hard

---

[18] *McGregor on Damages*, above n 7, paras 9-030 to 9-036; and see *Rowntree v Allen* (1936) 41 Com Cas 90 (KBD).

[19] BGH 8 January 1981, BGHZ 79, 187.

[20] The draft law 'for the benefit of consumers' of 8 November 2006 (as to which see D Fenouillet, 'Premières remarques sur le projet de loi en faveur des consommateurs' D 2006, 2987) which introduced a basis for a class action—solely for consumers who are natural persons, in the context of an action in contract solely intended to obtain reparation just for harm to their financial assets (material loss and loss of enjoyment of property, excluding actions compromising physical integrity)—has, so it seems, finally been buried. On 30 January 2007 the Government

to see why reparation of a possible collective interest should receive such a general endorsement. Does this mean that an action for any person suffering 'collective harm' is to be introduced by the *Avant-projet*, without their claim having to be limited to the harm which they themselves have personally suffered?

The very generality of draft article 1343, while in line with the traditional French approach, could be reconsidered: the way that the *Avant-projet* proceeds thereafter is undoubtedly more rational, in that it makes a clearer distinction between the different types of harm—losses resulting from personal injury, losses resulting from injury to property, etc. It enables prioritisation among the different types of loss to be made, some of them deserving fuller cover than others. This approach is also more suited to the new duty imposed on the court to quantify individually the heads of harm which it takes into account.

This last proposal, which is a departure from the existing law, is certainly one of the major advances of this part of the *Avant-projet*: France has often been mocked for the fact that it is impossible to understand the method of quantification of damages—a feature that certainly made this method 'unexportable'. It is true that in relation to personal injury, this approach to quantification was used only up to a point,[21] because of articles L 376-1 and L 454-1 of the Code de la sécurité sociale and article 31 of the Act of 5 July 1985.[22] These provisions restrict recourse actions for an indemnity brought by third parties who have made a direct payment to a victim suffering harm to his physical integrity, excluding those of a personal character 'relating to pain and suffering, whether physical or "moral" endured by the latter, to any aesthetic loss or to their loss of amenity' and 'those relating to the "moral harm" of their successors in title'. This gave rise to the need to separate out certain heads of harm. But the approach to doing so was not systematic. By contrast, a requirement that the courts quantify the various heads of harm separately would make their decisions more transparent, and would no doubt reduce their potentially arbitrary character—although that would not be removed completely, because quantification of 'moral harm', physical pain, future loss or the loss of a chance necessarily make assessment uncertain where no scale is established for the purpose. Would this enable the Cour de cassation to review the decisions of lower courts in this respect? First of all it is not clear that it wants to do so, but some review would be possible, if not of the quantification itself (by requiring, as in German law, grounds to be given for any differences from awards made by other courts in similar cases), then at least of the method of quantification: verification as to whether the heads of loss

withdrew it from the agenda for the day when it was due to be debated (6 February 2007); see F Rome, 'Action de groupe: tchao pantins!' D 2007, 425.

[21] Used, but not imposed.

[22] Loi no 85-677 du 5 juillet 1985, above n 2.

compensated were those permissible given the type of injury in question. It would also have to be accepted that certain heads of loss were reserved for certain types of injury, but this is not apparent from article 1343 of the *Avant-projet*.

(b) The Right to Compensation: Personal Injury

If, however, there is one area in which the type of injury is taken into account, it is the area of personal injury. The special rules applied in this area when compared with other types of harm are such that one can properly ask whether in fact the intention was to create a real right to compensation in this context, thus starting to establish a system of priorities for types of harm. In fact the terminology used by article 1379 of the *Avant-projet* tends to promote this way of thinking: 'In the case of personal injuries, the victim has the right to . . .' though the wording of draft article 1343 is more neutral: 'Any certain loss is reparable . . .'.[23]

First and foremost, an analysis of the provisions giving preferential treatment to the victim of personal injury suggests that there has been such a change in the nature of reparation.

Apart from the introduction of item-by-item indemnification for third parties making direct payment—which explains the fact that article 1379 of the *Avant-projet* enumerates the various types of reparable loss (an introduction, incidentally, which now represents the law as it is presently applied[24])—several aspects attract attention: first, unlike the situation with other types of injury, any fault on the part of the victim cannot be taken into consideration in order to provide a partial defence for the person responsible for some of the harm; next, the duty to mitigate the loss is limited where the measures to be taken are 'of a kind to have compromised his physical integrity'; finally, contract terms excluding or limiting the reparation of personal injured are prohibited.

The way in which the fault of the victim is taken into account by neighbouring legal systems seems to be rather different from the one proposed here: in English law, it appears that the account taken varies according to the type of tort, and not according to the type of injury: in the case of an intentional tort, there is no reduction in damages, by contrast to those cases in which the source of the harm is only negligence, or indeed where there is strict liability. Nor does § 254 of the German Civil Code draw any distinction according to the type of harm. The solution proposed by the *Avant-projet* thus seems to stand on its own: it aims to give further protection to the interests of the victim, since a serious fault will have to be

---

[23] Nevertheless, it may be noted that draft art 1380 on the reparation of losses resulting from damage to property uses this expression.
[24] Loi no 2006-1640 du 21 décembre 2006, above n 4.

shown on his part, and the courts will undoubtedly be less inclined to make a finding of this degree of fault if the victim is seriously injured.[25] Nevertheless, to the extent that the defendant can incur liability without fault, it could be considered unfair that the latter has to bear the burden of making reparation for all the physical harm suffered by a person who contributed to the occurrence of his own harm.[26] This is explicable only by reference to insurance law. The definition of a serious fault on the part of the victim remains to be established.

The duty to mitigate one's own harm has also been attenuated in the case of victims of personal injury. The duty to mitigate introduced by article 1373 of the *Avant-projet*, which differs from the present situation in French case-law is to be welcomed: it is similar to the position in both English law and § 254(2) of the German Civil Code, and furthermore responds to a concern to raise moral standards as a matter of both law and equity (not to allow a 'victim' to profit from a situation) as well as of economic logic. No doubt French law manifests itself as more cautious than English law; it is in this respect more like German law which requires that it must be shown that the victim is at fault in not seeking to mitigate his loss. This corresponds better to the general spirit of French law, which favours the compensation of victims. Moreover, the *Avant-projet* draws the natural conclusion to which this approach leads, to the effect that expenditure incurred in mitigation of the harm should be included in the award of damages (article 1344 of the *Avant-projet*). Nevertheless the proviso added at the end of draft article 1373, in fine (no duty to mitigate 'where the measures to be taken were of a kind to have compromised his physical integrity') was not perhaps justified given that the requirement of 'reliable, reasonable and proportionate measures' already provided a safeguard. It is understandable that the Avant-project does not adopt the English position which requires a claimant (victim) who has refused an operation contrary to medical advice to show that he has acted reasonably: this seems somewhat harsh to French eyes.[27] But the intermediate position found in German law, whereby the victim does not have a duty to accept an operation unless that measure is 'simple and safe, not connected with exceptional pain, and offers the certain prospect of cure or substantial improvement',

---

[25] Moreover it may be observed that in German law, where there is a general requirement to demonstrate fault on the part of a person who has suffered damage (§ 254 BGB), it seems that it is more difficult to make a finding of 'fault' on the part of the victim than of 'fault' on the part of the defendant to the action; see B Markesinis and H Unberath, *The German Law of Torts: A Comparative Treatise* (4th edn, Oxford, Hart, 2002) 110.

[26] This is nevertheless the solution currently adopted in relation to traffic accidents (art 3 of the Loi no 85-677 du 5 juillet 1985, above n 2): it is not possible to rely on the victim's own fault as a defence to an action, except for their inexcusable fault where it has been the sole cause of the accident—a provision which is thus more severe than the proposed art 1379. It is only the victim who is a driver, against whom his fault can be relied on as a general defence (art 4 of the Act). As to the *Avant-projet*, it would assimilate the victim who is a driver to other victims.

[27] *Selvanayagam v University of the West Indies* [1983] 1 WLR 585 (PC).

would perhaps have been enough.[28] The relevant German judgment adds that even a victim who is not obliged to undergo an operation still has the duty to undertake rehabilitation to make him capable of employment. This solution seems sensible and measured. The exclusion of the duty to mitigate in such circumstances, while it may once again express the special treatment shown to victims of personal injury, seems unduly radical.

The final feature demonstrating preferential treatment for victims of personal injury is the prohibition of contract terms limiting or excluding liability, such terms being accepted by the *Avant-projet* in the delictual context except where the defendant's liability is based on fault. Such a rule does not appear in English law where it seems that 'liquidated damages' have been reserved for matters relating to contract.[29] In a system providing a right of reparation for a victim of personal injury, it is natural that the latter may not renounce such reparation in advance, even in part. To provide that such a contract term is unlawful makes it possible to avoid abuse and pressure. On the other hand, it is not surprising to find that such clauses are permitted as regards delictual liability in respect of other types of harm in a system which, like ours, accepts that all the harm suffered, including pure economic loss, is reparable, whatever the legal basis relied on. It would therefore no doubt be possible to accept that the *Avant-projet* should go a bit further and recognise the legal validity of such terms, including those concerning fault liability, save for fault that is fraudulent, gross or inexcusable, at least in relation to the compensation of economic loss.

A rule should be noted which could, in comparison with the others, prove to be prejudicial to a victim of personal injury: in this context, article 1379-3 of the *Avant-projet* proposes use of index-linked periodic payments rather than payment of a capital sum for lost business or professional profits, the loss of physical maintenance and a loss incurred by requiring the help of a third party. This is in itself a good thing, since it allows the periodic payments to be revised 'if the harm becomes smaller or more extensive'.[30] But curiously, this solution is not then adopted for other types of harm, the introduction of a new action being permitted in such cases without provision for any reduction in the damages assessed (draft article 1375) and even if the compensation is awarded in the form of a periodic payment (article 1376 of the *Avant-projet*).

---

[28] BGH 13 May 1953, BGHZ 10, 18—the case is translated in W van Gerven et al, *Ius Commune Casebooks for the Common Law of Europe: Cases, Materials and Text on National, Supranational and International Tort Law* (Oxford, Hart Publishing, 2000) 795.

[29] See *McGregor on Damages*, above n 7, ch 13 and no 19-002: 'The clearest and undoubted distinctions between contract and tort lie in the exceptional cases where damages are not given strictly on the principle of awarding compensation. . . . [s]ince liquidated damages can only result from agreement, they apply to contract and cannot in the nature of things refer to tort.' Cf s 2(1) of the Unfair Contract Terms Act 1977 which invalidates the exclusion or limitation of 'business liability' in respect of personal injuries or death caused by negligence.

[30] Art 1379-3(2) of the *Avant-projet* (emphasis added).

II. A LAW OF REPARATION SEEKING THE FUSION OF CONTRACT AND DELICT

The other feature characterising the new system established by the *Avant-projet* is the fusion—at least in outward appearance—of delictual and contractual liability. This fusion is certainly not complete: contractual liability has a certain degree of independence or 'autonomy', and four provisions are devoted to it which establish the distinctive character of its regime. First, mere 'non-performance' of a contract is a ground for reparation, without there being any need for a separately identified element of fault. Article 1364 of the *Avant-projet* nevertheless restates the distinction between an obligation to take necessary precautions (obligation de moyens) and an obligation to achieve a particular result (obligation de résultat) which has been devised by academic writers and put into effect in the case-law. Next—thankfully—draft article 1366 retains the requirement of foreseeability of the reparable loss at the time of contracting.[31]

It is appropriate to examine how far these provisions suffice to enable contractual liability to retain its distinctive character (section II(a) below). Another problem arises from the fact that the text of the *Avant-projet* does not provide solely for reparation in damages, but also for 'reparation in kind'. It is therefore necessary to try to understand how such 'reparation in kind' may work concurrently with performance in kind, which is provided as the primary remedy for contractual non-performance, see especially articles 1154-1156 and 1158 of the *Avant-projet* (section II(b) below).

(a) The Distinctiveness of Contractual Liability?

Several factors are liable to undermine the distinctive character of contractual liability: on the one hand, there is the fact that draft article 1370 states a general rule for the assessment of damages without any recognition of a right to reparation in respect of the party's 'positive' or 'performance interest' for the contractual context; on the other, the fact that third parties are able to bring an action in contract; finally the absence of any distinction in the way in which force majeure is understood, depending on whether the context is contractual or delictual.

---

[31] However, it will be noted that there is a difference in language: the Code civil required the 'damages which were foreseen', or those which could have been foreseen at the time of the contract to be taken into account, and not the 'consequences of non-performance'. Nevertheless, the 'consequences of non-performance' may be harm caused just as much as damages payable—it even seems that harm caused is the initial consequence of non-performance. Foreseeable consequences may give rise to unforeseeable damages. But the courts had already undertaken this shift from foreseeing damages towards foreseeing harm.

Article 1370 of the *Avant-projet* is the general provision relating to the quantification of damages; and it governs equally both delictual and contractual liability. It states that

> Subject to special regulation or agreement to the contrary, the aim of an award of damages is to put the victim as far as possible in the position in which he would have been if the harmful circumstances had not taken place. He must make neither gain nor loss from it.

The proviso as to agreement to the contrary refers directly to the possibility that the parties may conclude agreements dealing with reparation including as regards delictual liability, unless it is fault based. However, although claims for personal injury may be brought in contract where the contract in question is directly concerned with the protection of the person, generally they are brought in delict and so the fact that clauses limiting liability are prohibited for personal injury as regards the latter does not deprive contract of its distinctive character.

It is apparent from article 1370 of the *Avant-projet* that the purpose attributed to contractual liability is the same as that given to delictual liability: to restore matters to the state they were in before the harm occurred—article 1366, which sets a limit to loss reparable (foreseeable loss), is not treated as a derogation from article 1370. However, I do not consider that this to be the primary purpose of contractual liability, which is instead principally concerned with enabling the creditor to obtain by means of reparation (it can be called reparation if so desired) the equivalent of what he would have obtained if the contract had been performed.[32] The creditor can thus ask to have taken into account not just the loss that he has suffered but also the profit that he has lost and in general all the benefits he has failed to gain. This is the position under both English and German law. The scope of damages in the contractual context is therefore, from this perspective, greater than in the delictual context: the creditor should receive the profit anticipated from the contract—even if, with respect to draft article 1366, this head of claim may seem more restricted owing to the limitation to foreseeable harm. It would be disconcerting, to say the least, if it were to be thought that under French law reparation can be made only in respect of a 'negative' or 'reliance loss', whereas everywhere else an award of damages in respect of the positive or performance interest is accepted.

It is true that there is no formal acknowledgement of this distinction in French law, but a reform of the law of obligations is precisely the time to provide a clear statement of the way in which damages should be calculated in the contractual context and to make a distinction between damages based on the negative/reliance interest and positive/performance interest. The form of words used by article 1370 of the *Avant-projet* could be

---

[32] See, for English law, *Robinson v Harman* (1848) 1 Exch 850, 855 (Ex); *McGregor on Damages*, above n 7, para 19-005.

retained if desired, provided that it is made clear that in the contractual context damages, although limited to foreseeable losses, should cover all the interests contemplated by the parties at the time of making the contract. Intrinsic interests, as Pothier said, without any specific statement to that effect by the parties; extrinsic interests if it appears from the circumstances of the case or the terms of the contract that the parties had them in mind, or should have had them in mind.

The fact that article 1340 of the *Avant-projet* proposes that the non-performance of a contractual obligation must have caused 'harm' to the creditor before the debtor is liable seems less likely to influence inter-pretation—provided at any rate that one does not understand the term 'harm' in the strict sense which is given to it by a footnote to article 1343 of the *Avant-projet* (harm to the person or the property of the victim),[33] but rather in a broader sense as any harm to the interests covered by the contract. As I have pointed out elsewhere,[34] before claiming a substitute for an interest, it is necessary for that interest to have been prejudiced. However, proof of loss does not appear to be a 'condition' for the imposition of contractual liability, but rather something that is necessary to establish the measure of damages. This would explain why there is no requirement to show a 'loss' before compelling performance of the contract in kind. And this makes it possible to reconcile, to some extent, article 1340(2) of the *Avant-projet*, which imposes liability for 'harm' caused to others, with draft article 1154(4), which provides that '[i]n the absence of performance in kind, an obligation to do gives rise to damages', and with article 1154-1 of the *Avant-projet*, under which

> A failure to observe an obligation not to do gives rise to damages by operation of law from the mere fact of the breach, without prejudice to the creditor's right to claim performance in kind for the future.

Before these damages can be assessed, it is necessary that an interest should have been harmed—which is generally the case where someone has failed to comply with their obligation not to do, at least if that is the principal obligation rather than a secondary one. The text of the *Avant-projet* allows such an interpretation.[35] Article 1340(2) is neutral when it says that, subject to the previously emphasised proviso as to the use of terminology,

> any non-performance of a contract which has caused harm to its creditor obliges the debtor to answer for it.

Nor does Chapter 2 governing 'The Conditions of Liability' refer to the need for loss in its provisions common to both types of liability, but solely

---

[33] See above, n 10.

[34] 'Exécution et réparation: deux concepts?' RDC 2005, 13.

[35] See M Faure-Abbad, 'La présentation de l'inexécution contractuelle dans l'avant-projet Catala' D 2007, 165.

defines the range of possible types of loss. Article 1363 of the *Avant-projet*, a provision that is specifically concerned with contractual liability, merely proposes that the creditor can claim reparation for his loss in cases of non-performance, without also making loss a condition of the making of a claim.[36] Loss may thus be understood primarily as an element necessary for the assessment of damages, and not as a condition of the imposition of liability in contract.

The other factor which risks making contractual liability lose its distinctive character[37] is the fact that no distinction is made between the delictual and the contractual contexts in defining force majeure and no consideration is given to the differing roles it plays there. *Force majeure* in matters relating to tort is principally a defence to liability; it demonstrates the absence of fault in cases where fault is required. In the contractual context, *force majeure* is principally a factor in the allocation of contractual risk: it makes it possible to release the party who is not required to bear the risk of *force majeure* preventing performance of his obligation. Furthermore, it is appropriate to make distinctions in relation to the very concept of force majeure: in the contractual context, it is the unforeseeability of the event at the time of making the contract that should be emphasised. By contrast, in the delictual context, it is the unavoidable character of the event that should be the main factor; the unforeseeable character of the event may be taken into account at the time the harm occurs (or more accurately at the time the fault is committed), but, it seems to me, only as a secondary consideration.

One may further doubt how far the distinctive character of contractual liability is maintained when one sees that such liability may henceforth be relied on by third parties who suffer harm as a result of non-performance of a contract. Article 1342 of the *Avant-projet* offers third parties an option between contractual and delictual liability. Having read the academic discussions which took place at the time of the drafting of the English Contracts (Rights of Third Parties) Act 1999, it is possible to imagine the reaction of English lawyers to such a measure! In reality, article 1342 is quite logical in the context of the recent history of French law: after the

---

[36] Something should no doubt also have been said about the giving of notice to perform (*mise en demeure*), established as a condition precedent to reparation only in cases of late performance and 'where it is necessary in order for non-performance to become manifest', the system for notification itself being contained in the part devoted to contractual obligations. Cf, as a matter of the law as presently applied, the gloss provided by Cass mixte 6 July 2007, appeal no 06-13823, to be published in Bull mixte, which states that the mere fact that there has been non-performance of the contract, and that it has caused loss gives a right to damages, even though the debtor may not have been given notice to perform.

[37] See Ass plén 14 April 2006, Bull civ nos 5 and 6, which put an end to the divergence between the Chambers of the court. According to these judgments, *force majeure* is defined in the contractual context, as being an event unforeseeable at the time of contracting, and unavoidable in relation to the performance of the contract. In the delictual context, the event considered must have these two characteristics at the time when the harmful event occurs.

invention of 'direct actions,' which are necessarily contractual, and of 'groups of contracts', it is known that the decision in the Besse case[38] put a brake on the availability of this action—the advantage of which was the fact that the terms of the contract could be used as a defence against third parties seeking to rely on non-performance of the contract. After this decision, third-party actions in delict thus resumed their significance, but with the law in the greatest possible disarray. The first and third Civil chambers of the Cour de cassation—the commercial Chamber taking an opposing view—rapidly accepted that any contractual fault causing harm to another person constituted delictual fault and so any term in the contract in question could not be used as a defence against such a third party claim. This is the final result of the unification of the two types of fault: considerable unpredictability for contracting parties. The solution nevertheless received the approval of the Assemblée plénière.[39] It is for this situation that draft article 1342 seeks to provide a remedy by offering a choice: an action in contract, but subject to the terms of the contract; or an action in delict, but with the need for proof of the circumstances giving rise to liability. All in all, I prefer the doctrine of 'groups of contracts': it had the advantage of enabling one to identify those having a right of action, other than by reference to the fact that they had suffered harm. That is all the more the case since, with article 1382-3 of the *Avant-projet* providing that

> [i]n the contractual context, the party who is faced with a term excluding or limiting reparation must have been able to be aware of it at the time of concluding the contract,

it will be easy for a third party to avoid these terms given that in general they will not have been aware of them. This would not be the case only if 'party' in this provision were to be understood in the strict sense of 'party to a contract' as then the terms could be used as a defence without it being necessary to show knowledge of them on the part of the third party.

(b) Reparation in Kind as Contrasted with Performance in Kind

The last point that I would like to emphasise[40] is the difficulty presented by the formal acceptance of 'reparation in kind' in the contractual context. This type of reparation, known in French law in the delictual context and worthy of being retained there, is difficult to distinguish from performance in kind in the contractual context. Indeed, I must admit that I have great difficulty in finding any way of distinguishing one from the other. Is the replacement of a defective product 'reparation' or 'enforced performance

---

[38] Ass plén 12 July 1991, Bull civ no 5.
[39] Ass plén 6 October 2006, Bull civ no 6.
[40] For further details see Rémy-Corlay, above n 34.

in kind'? And is 'reparation' as ordinarily understood the fact of getting the product repaired?

The system elaborated by articles 1368 and 1369 of the *Avant-projet* seems very different from that established by the provisions relating to contract. Thus, whereas article 1368 provides that

> [r]eparation of harm may at the court's discretion take the form of reparation in kind or of an award of damages and these two types of measures may be ordered concurrently so as to ensure full compensation of the victim's loss [emphasis added],

draft article 1158 provides that

> [i]n all contracts, a person for whose benefit an undertaking has not been per-formed or has been performed only imperfectly, has the choice either to pursue performance of the undertaking, to instigate termination of the contract or to claim damages, and the latter may in some cases be recovered in addition to per-formance or termination of the contract' [emphasis added].

This is also the effect of articles 1154 and 1154-1 of the *Avant-projet*. How can these contradictions be reconciled? If reparation in kind is too widely conceived, the principle of the primacy of performance in kind in contracting (according to which performance in kind cannot be refused by a court unless it is unreasonable having regard to the good faith of the contracting parties) is deprived of all its force even though this principle is affirmed elsewhere and is dear to French legal culture.[41] Even the drafting of the various articles encourages confusion. On the one hand it is stated that 'articles 1143 and 1144 of the present Civil code' are not relevant to a title concerning liability,[42] such that one should conclude that articles 1154 to 1154-2 of the *Avant-projet* do not give rise to issues of 'reparation', but rather of performance. On the other hand, a comparison between these provisions and draft articles 1369 and 1369-1 does not provide any grounds on which to base the proposed difference in treatment.

It would not have been unreasonable to link contractual liability to non-performance of the contract, rather than to delictual liability. Even though it may be accepted that in both contexts we are concerned with types of liability, one context does not come into play without non-performance of a contract—indeed, without the existence of a contract. Contractual liability therefore satisfies a particular need for the success of a system of contract, which cannot be ignored, and which the grouping together of the two types of liability can only blur. One of the consequences of this con-fusion has already been the acceptance by the Assemblée plénière that any contractual fault constitutes fault for the purposes of delict, without any delimitation of the third parties who can rely on non-performance; thus

---

[41] See, Faure-Abbad, above n 35.
[42] Explanatory note to art 1369 of the *Avant-projet*.

giving a death blow to the principle of the relativity of contract in the name of a dubious doctrine concerning the extent to which contract may be relied on as a defence to an action.[43] The *Avant-projet* has seen the dangers of this and it tries to provide a remedy, but I do not think that the grouping together of liabilities is the best way to highlight a distinction between the two which is so necessary for predictability in contract. One way of remedying this defect would be to go further in making a distinction between the different types of harm reparable, and to refuse to accept certain heads of reparation except in relation to certain types of liability: the distinction between contractual and delictual liability could thus be maintained in relation to the measure of damages. No doubt it would also be necessary, in order to ensure the predictable nature of reparation, to go more deeply into the methods of calculation, impose scales of awards, or at least—as in German law—require the lower courts to provide reasons for the awards of damages that they make by reference to other judicial decisions dealing with the same type of harm.

---

[43] See the thesis of R Wintgen, *Etude critique de la notion d'opposabilité: Les effets du contrat à l'égard des tiers en droit français et allemand* (Paris, LGDJ, 2004). See previously, in relation to such a 'death blow', R Savatier, 'Le prétendu principe de l'effet relatif des contrats' RTD civ 1934, 525.

15

Comparative Observations on the Introduction of Punitive Damages in French Law

SOLÈNE ROWAN*

I. INTRODUCTION

PUNISHMENT IS NOT, at least formally, an objective of the French law of damages. Instead, in both contract and tort, damages are awarded to compensate loss. The innocent party can expect to be returned, insofar as possible, to the position he would have been in had the breach of contract or the tort not been committed.[1] This is achieved exclusively by reference to his loss. The seriousness of the breach of contract or the tort and the extent of any profit accruing to the perpetrator are irrelevant.[2]

One of the principal innovations of the *Avant-projet de réforme du droit des obligations et de la prescription* relating the law of damages is the proposal that the existing regime should be supplemented by the introduction of punitive damages. Draft article 1371 provides as follows:

A person who commits a manifestly deliberate fault, and notably a fault with a view to gain, can be condemned in addition to compensatory damages to pay punitive damages, part of which the court may in its discretion allocate to the Public Treasury. A court's decision to order payment of damages of this kind must be supported with specific reasons and their amount distinguished from any

* I am indebted to Professor John Bell and Gregg Rowan for their comments on an earlier draft. The views expressed herein are mine alone. I would like to acknowledge the support received from the Arts and Humanities Research Council.

[1] Which, in a contractual context, equates to the contract having been performed in accordance with its terms. See art 1149 Cc.
[2] P Jourdain, 'Les dommages-intérêts alloués par le juge' in G Viney et M Fontaine (eds), *Les sanctions de l'inexécution des obligations contractuelles: Etudes de droit comparé* (Bruylant LGDJ, 2001) 263, 266–7. Cass civ (2) 8 May 1964, JCP 1965 II 14140 note P Esmein.

other damages awarded to the victim. Punitive damages may not be the object of insurance.[3]

The formal enactment of this provision would align French law more closely with English law. Whilst the principal purpose of damages in English civil law is also to compensate loss,[4] in certain narrowly drawn circumstances punitive damages may be awarded. The existence and scope of this remedy have long been controversial amongst English academic and practising lawyers alike. Punitive damages have been described by many as anomalous[5] and have famously been criticised as

> out of place, irregular . . . exceptional, unjust, unscientific, not to say absurd and ridiculous when classed among civil remedies . . . a monstrous heresy . . . an unhealthy excrescence, deforming the symmetry of the body of the law'![6]

In view of the exceptional nature of punitive damages and the controversy they arouse in England, one could be forgiven for wondering why the drafters of the *Avant-projet* have included article 1371. The ten lines of the *Exposé des motifs* to Sub-Title III give little away. In these circumstances, an insight may be gained from the analysis and assessment of the provision from a comparative perspective having regard to English law and its ongoing debate as to the role of punitive damages.

This chapter will commence with a discussion of the rationale underlying punitive damages, drawing in particular upon judicial observations in England. The model of punitive damages proposed in the *Avant-projet* will then be explored through the prism of English case-law. This will include analysis of the scope of draft article 1371, the requirement that French judges provide specific reasons for punitive awards and the method by which punitive damages should be quantified. Two further questions raised by article 1371, namely to whom punitive damages may be awarded and whether liability to pay such damages should be an insurable risk, will receive consideration. On both points article 1371 would take French law beyond the punitive damages regime operating in England. The reasons for these divergences will be examined. Finally, this chapter will explore whether the introduction of punitive damages in French law is desirable. It will be concluded that punitive damages do have a role to play in France and to this extent, article 1371 is welcome. The only cause for disappointment is that article 1371 fails to provide adequate guidance as to the operation of the remedy in several important respects.

---

[3] Translated into English by J Cartwright and S Whittaker.

[4] In tort, *Livingstone v Rawyards Coal Co* (1880) 5 App Cas 25, 39 (HL) (Lord Blackburn). In contract, *Robinson v Harman* (1848) 1 Exch 850, 855 (Court of Exchequer) (Baron Parke).

[5] *Rookes v Barnard* [1964] AC 1129, 1221 (HL) (Lord Devlin); *Broome v Cassell* [1972] AC 1027, 1086 (HL) (Lord Reid).

[6] *Fay v Parker* 53 NH 342 (1873) 382 (Supreme Court of New Hampshire) (Foster J).

II. THE RATIONALE UNDERLYING PUNITIVE DAMAGES

As a prelude to any meaningful debate on whether and when a jurisdiction should award punitive damages, a word must be said as to their underlying rationale. By definition, punitive damages are not compensatory. They are awarded independently of any loss suffered and go beyond the sum of money necessary to repair the harm caused to the victim.

Amongst English lawyers, it is widely accepted that punitive damages seek to punish and deter.[7] Punishment and deterrence reflect different preoccupations. The former sanctions the degree of culpability of the wrongdoer and the seriousness of his actions. It is based on retribution, looking back at his conduct. Deterrence, on the other hand, is concerned with influencing the future behaviour of the wrongdoer and others. An example is made of the wrongdoer's conduct. This is reflected by the title, 'exemplary damages', which is often used interchangeably with 'punitive damages'. Deterrence is a particularly important objective where there is evidence that the misconduct occurs on a regular basis and/or is widespread.

Aside from punishment and deterrence, two other frequently cited justifications for punitive damages merit mention. One is appeasement of the victim. A punitive award vindicates his rights and provides him with moral satisfaction.[8] Punitive damages also serve to mark a legal system's disapproval of a person's misconduct.[9] In *Kuddus v Chief Constable of Leicestershire Constabulary*,[10] Lord Nicholls stated that the underlying rationale of punitive damages 'lies in the sense of outrage which a defendant's conduct sometimes evokes, a sense not always assuaged fully by compensatory damages'.[11] He added that

> on occasion conscious wrongdoing by a defendant is so outrageous, his disregard of the plaintiff's rights so contumelious, that something more is needed to show that the law will not tolerate such behaviour.[12]

Punitive damages therefore vindicate the strength of the law.[13] The wrongdoer and others who might be tempted to engage in wrongful behaviour are taught that the law 'cannot be broken with impunity' and that 'tort does not pay'.[14]

Punishment, deterrence and vindicating the strength of the law are objectives more commonly associated with criminal law. In England, they lie at the margins of the civil law and even then are controversial. Approaching

---

[7] *Rookes v Barnard*, above n 5, 1221 (Lord Devlin).
[8] *A v Bottrill* [2003] UKPC 44, [2003] 1 AC 449 [29] (Lord Nicholls).
[9] GH Treitel, *The Law of Contract* (11th edn, London, Sweet & Maxwell, 2003) 935–6.
[10] [2001] UKHL 29, [2002] 2 AC 122.
[11] *Ibid*, [65].
[12] *Ibid*, [63].
[13] *Rookes v Barnard*, above n 5, 1226.
[14] *Ibid*, 1227.

draft article 1371 from this perspective, the most intriguing questions almost certainly relate to the circumstances in which punitive damages would be awarded under the *Avant-projet*.

III. THE CIRCUMSTANCES GIVING RISE TO PUNITIVE DAMAGES

Article 1371 of the *Avant-projet* provides that punitive damages may be awarded where a person commits 'a manifestly deliberate fault'. This concept is novel in French civil law and appears to add to the established scale of civil faults.[15] Its central feature is that the defaulting party must voluntarily commit the act or omission which constitutes the fault and intend, or at least be conscious of, the possible loss resulting from the same.[16] The term 'manifestly' appears to emphasise the need for certainty as to the defaulting party's motive. The circumstances in which punitive damages may be awarded are therefore limited. Negligence is insufficient, however gross. Only the deliberateness of the conduct of the defaulting party justifies objectives such as punishment and deterrence.

Article 1371 cites 'fault with a view to gain' as a preponderant instance of 'manifestly deliberate fault'. The *Exposé des motifs* to Sub-Title III of the *Avant-projet* elaborates upon a fault with a view to gain as being one 'whose beneficial consequences for its perpetrator would not be undone by the simple reparation of any harm which it has caused'.[17] This definition raises as many questions as it answers and, it is respectfully submitted, leaves unclear the circumstances in which punitive damages will be available. On one construction, liability would be established where the defaulting party intends to benefit from his fault. This would cast the net relatively widely. A narrower construction is that, as well as intending to benefit from his fault, the defaulting party must calculate that his act will yield a pecuniary advantage, even after any potential liability to compensate the victim is taken into account.

The key to understanding which of the two competing constructions of 'fault with a view to gain' was intended by the drafters of article 1371 lies in French academic literature on punitive damages. Commentators have long considered as 'shocking'[18] those breaches where the defaulting party

---

[15] *Faute simple, faute lourde, faute inexcusable, faute intentionnelle.*

[16] For a review of the debate relating to the scope of *faute intentionnelle*, see P Jourdain and G Viney, *Traité de droit civil, les conditions de la responsabilité* (3rd edn, Paris, LGDJ, 2006) nos 618–26.

[17] G Viney, 'Exposé des motifs: Sous-titre III. De la responsabilité civile (Articles 1340 à 1386)' in *Avant-projet de réforme du droit des obligations et de la prescription: Rapport remis au garde des Sceaux* (Paris, La Documentation française, 2006) 159, 168 (see below pp 809, 827).

[18] D Fasquelle, 'L'Existence de fautes lucratives en droit français' LPA 20 November 2002, no 232, 27, 28; P Jourdain, 'Rapport introductif' in 'Faut-il moraliser le droit français de la réparation du dommage? (à propos des dommages et intérêts punitifs et de l'obligation de

intends that, even taking into account any liability to compensate the losses which flow from his default, he will make a profit.[19] The element of calculation is regarded as being particularly objectionable. Awarding punitive damages in such circumstances removes the financial incentive which would exist if only compensatory damages were available. Although the point is not free from doubt and clarification would be welcome, it seems likely that the drafters intend to refer to such faults. This paper will proceed on this basis.

Another difficulty with the definition of 'fault with a view to gain' is that it is unclear whether it encompasses the situation where the defaulting party anticipates that his victim will not seek recompense as opposed to calculating that any compensatory liability will be more than offset by his profit.[20] Such passivity may be referable to the relative triviality of the loss or the cost and precariousness of legal proceedings. Where the defaulting party is in a dominant position, it may even be attributable to the victim's fear of reprisals. Alternatively, the defaulting party may hope that there will be no victim[21] or that there is no identifiable victim with *locus standi* to bring proceedings.[22] This kind of calculation is equally blameworthy and should be capable of attracting punitive awards.

Whilst the *Exposé des motifs* to Sub-Title III of the *Avant-projet* does not give examples of 'fault with a view to gain', the French literature on the subject suggests that such faults may be committed in a wide variety of domains. These encompass, amongst others, the law of privacy, unfair competition and environmental law.[23] A commonly cited example is that of the publication of images of a celebrity in a magazine or newspaper, intentionally invading his right to privacy in order to boost sales. The profit generated by the wrongful publication of the pictures may well exceed the compensable loss caused to the celebrity.[24] Similarly, in the field of *concurrence déloyale*, a company may commit a 'fault with a view to gain' by

minimiser son propre dommage)' LPA 20 November 2002, no 232, 3, 4; M Chagny, 'La notion de dommages et intérêts punitifs et ses répercussions sur le droit de la concurrence—Lectures plurielles de l'article 1371 de l'avant-projet de réforme du droit des obligations' JCP G 2006 I 149.

[19] Fasquelle, above n 18, 30, argues that 'la faute lucrative est généralement la conséquence d'un calcul de la part de l'auteur' and G Viney 'Projet de réforme du droit des obligations: les eléments clés en matière de droit de la responsabilité', Revue Lamy Droit Civil 2005 no 22 contends that punitive damages will be useful where 'le profit *attendu* de l'activité illicite est supérieur au montant de l'indemnisation des dommages réalisés' (emphasis added).

[20] Fasquelle, above n 18, 30.

[21] A typical example is that of airlines speculatively overbooking flights in anticipation of some passengers failing to travel.

[22] An obvious example is wrongful conduct which causes environmental harm: Fasquelle, above n 18, 30.

[23] *Ibid*, 28–9; Jourdain, above n 18, 4; S Carval, *La responsabilité civile dans sa fonction de peine privée* (Paris, LGDJ, 1995).

[24] See the German case of *Caroline of Monaco*, BGH 15 November 1994, BGHZ 128, 1, NJW 1995, 861, JZ 1995, 360.

deliberately denigrating a rival to strengthen its market position. The resulting benefit to the wrongdoing company may be exponentially greater than the compensable harm suffered by the rival. Another example is the wrongful causing of pollution, knowing that any eventual sanction is likely to be less onerous than the cost of disposing of the pollutant lawfully.[25]

The scope of article 1371 seems to encompass contract as well as tort. The article appears in Chapter III of Sub-Title III of the *Avant-projet*, 'The Effect of Liability', the provisions of which are mutually applicable to contract and tort. A possible instance of a 'fault with a view to gain' in a contractual context is that of an insurance company withholding a payment which is due to its insured so as to coerce him into a lower settlement, even though liability on the insurance policy is beyond question. The insurer's behaviour is particularly deserving of punishment because, in addition to the intentional breach of its contractual obligation to pay and the duty to act in good faith, it exploits the victim's vulnerability.[26] Another example may be that of a vendor who, in breach of a contract for the sale of goods, sells to a third party who has offered a higher price knowing that the compensation payable to the victim will be less than his eventual gain.

Punitive damages in a contractual context have the potential to bring French law into conflict with proponents of an economic analysis of the law.[27] A tenet of their 'efficient breach' theory is that breach should be encouraged where the benefit accruing from the same will exceed any potential compensatory liability. If, following the conclusion of an agreement, the promisor finds a better opportunity for the use of his resources, he should be allowed to escape from his obligation to perform subject to the full compensation of the promisee. Having pursued a more profitable activity elsewhere, he will be 'better off' whilst the promisee has lost nothing. To breach a contract equates to making a rational economic choice.

Turning to the circumstances in which punitive damages are awarded in English law, the starting point is the classic speech of Lord Devlin in *Rookes v Barnard*[28] in which the remedy was restricted to three situations: first, where there is 'oppressive or unconstitutional action by the servants of the government'. This category covers cases of abuse of executive power. For instance, courts have awarded punitive damages in cases of wrongful arrest,[29] false imprisonment and malicious prosecution;[30] second, where 'the defendant's conduct has been calculated by him to make a profit for

---

[25] Jourdain, above n 18, 4.

[26] See *Whiten v Pilot Insurance Co* [2002] 1 SCR 595 (Supreme Court of Canada).

[27] For a discussion of the law of remedies from an economic perspective in France, see Y-M Laithier, *Etude comparative des sanctions de l'inexécution du contrat* (Paris, LGDJ, 2004) and in England, see D Harris, D Campbell and R Halson, *Remedies in Contract and Tort* (2nd edn, London, Butterworths, 2002).

[28] Above n 5, 1226.

[29] Eg *Holden v Chief Constable of Lancashire* [1987] QB 380 (CA).

[30] Eg *Thompson v Commissioner of Police of the Metropolis* [1998] QB 498 (CA).

himself which may well exceed the compensation payable';[31] and third, where expressly authorised by statute.[32]

Lord Devlin's second category is in substance close to the 'fault with a view to gain' of article 1371 of the *Avant-projet*. It targets the wrongdoer who 'with a cynical disregard for a plaintiff's rights has calculated that the money to be made out of his wrongdoing will probably exceed the damages at risk'.[33] In practice, this has most commonly been makers of defamatory statements and landlords who wrongfully harass and/or evict their tenants.[34]

In the context of defamation, punitive damages have been awarded where publishers knowingly disseminate false allegations in the expectation that any liability to pay compensatory damages will be more than offset by their eventual profit. It is not sufficient that the wrongdoing publisher is engaged in an activity aimed at profit. He must be shown to have known that his statement was defamatory, or to have been reckless as to the same, and to have nonetheless published the libellous statement because the prospect of material advantage outweighed that of material loss.[35]

An example is *Broome v Cassell*.[36] The claimant was a distinguished retired naval officer. He brought claims in libel against the publisher and the author of a book which was presented as an authentic account of a wartime disaster. The defamatory statement was that the claimant bore a share of the responsibility for the disaster. The House of Lords upheld the jury's award of £15,000 by way of compensatory damages and £25,000 as punitive damages. On the facts, there was clear evidence that the defendants knew that they might be defaming the claimant but still went ahead with the publication of the book. There was sufficient calculation of profit by both defendants to justify a punitive award.

The second category of punitive damages enunciated by Lord Devlin is not limited to money making in the literal sense. It extends, for instance, to wrongfully depriving a person of an interest in property.[37] This includes landlords who wrongfully evict their tenants. For instance, in *Drane v Evangelou*,[38] the landlord sought to evict his tenant in order to re-let the

---

[31] Above n 5, 1226.

[32] *Ibid*, 1225. Lord Devlin cites s 13(2) of the Reserve and Auxiliary Forces (Protection of Civil Interests) Act 1951. In contrast, Lord Kilbrandon in *Broome v Cassell*, above n 5, 1133 doubted whether any existing statute contemplated the award of punitive damages in the proper sense.

[33] Above n 5, 1227.

[34] H McGregor, *McGregor on Damages* (17th edn, London, Sweet & Maxwell, 2003) paras 11-022 to 11-025.

[35] *Broome v Cassell*, above n 5, 1079 (Lord Hailsham): 'It is not necessary that the defendant calculates that the plaintiff's damages if he sues to judgment will be smaller than the defendant's profit. This is simply one example of the principle. The defendant may calculate that the plaintiff will not sue at all because he has not the money . . . or because he may be physically or otherwise intimidated.'

[36] Above n 5.

[37] *Rookes v Barnard*, above n 5, 1227 (Lord Devlin).

[38] [1978] 1 WLR 455 (CA).

demised residential property for more money. He entered the property during the temporary absence of the tenant who returned to find trespassers inside the property and his belongings outside in the yard. The Court of Appeal upheld a punitive damages award of £1,000 for trespass.

Lord Devlin's second category does not apply in a contractual setting. Punitive damages are not available for breach of contract, a rule that has prevailed since the decision in *Addis v Gramophone Company Limited*.[39] In this case, the House of Lords refused to award damages for the abrupt and oppressive way in which an employee's services were wrongfully dispensed with by his employer. The main objections to punitive damages being awarded for breach of contract are that such awards would affect commercial predictability and the concept of punishment is not easily applicable in the context of private agreements in which rights and duties are allocated by mutual consent.[40]

It is interesting to note that article 1371 of the *Avant-projet* and the English common law show equal keenness for limiting the circumstances in which punitive damages can be awarded. The prime function of the law of damages remains compensation and only in the rarest of circumstances will punishment be an additional aim. Both countries consider the same kind of conduct as being particularly reprehensible. No tolerance is shown towards a person who cynically disregards the victim's rights for profit. Such behaviour brings the law in disrepute and should be deterred.

Despite these obvious parallels, article 1371 is markedly wider in scope than Lord Devlin's second category. Its inclusion in the Code civil would see punitive awards available in France in both tort and contract. They would also be made regardless of the nature of the motives of the defaulting party. It should be remembered that 'fault with a view to gain' is but an instance of manifestly deliberate fault and is non-exclusive. This avoids a criticism which has been made by English commentators of Lord Devlin's second category, namely that it does not allow punitive damages to be awarded where the wrongdoer acts not for profit but maliciously.[41] A wrongdoer deserves punishment irrespective of whether he is compelled by malice or profit.

---

[39] [1909] AC 488 (HL).

[40] For a full discussion of the objections to punitive awards for breach of contract and their counter-arguments, see N McBride, 'A Case for Awarding Punitive Damages in Response to Deliberate Breaches of Contract' (1995) 24 Anglo-American Law Review 369; J Edelman, 'Exemplary Damages for Breach of Contract' (2001) 117 LQR 539 and R Cunnington, 'Should Punitive Damages be Part of the Judicial Arsenal in Contract Cases?' (2006) 26 LS 369.

[41] *Broome v Cassell*, above n 5, 1088, where Lord Reid thought that the distinction between greed and malice could be justified only by reference to authority. See also Lord Nicholls in *Kuddus*, above n 10, [67]. The Law Commission, *Aggravated, Exemplary and Restitutionary Damages* (Law Com No 247, HMSO, 1997) recommended that the 'category test' should be replaced by a more general principle whereby punitive damages would be awarded for any tort or equitable wrong which shows 'a deliberate and outrageous disregard' for the claimant's rights. In Australia, see *Uren v John Fairfax & Sons Pty* (1966) 117 CLR 118 (High Court of Australia).

IV. THE JUSTIFICATION FOR, AND ITEMISATION OF, PUNITIVE DAMAGES AWARDS

In addition to restricting the circumstances in which punitive damages can be awarded, the drafters of the *Avant-projet* have included two other safeguards. Article 1371 requires that a court's decision to order that punitive damages be payable must be supported by 'specific reasons' and 'their amount distinguished from any other damages awarded to the victim'. The combined effect of these provisions should be to prevent arbitrariness and excess. They will ensure that the defaulting party is given sufficient information to understand precisely why he has been punished and the monetary value of his punishment.

A wider implication of the adoption of article 1371 is likely to be the development of a body of case-law which should enable a better understanding of the circumstances in which punitive damages may be awarded and the amount of such damages. The insistence of article 1371 on full and transparent reasoning will allow the Cour de cassation to monitor the circumstances in which punitive awards are made. It will most likely intervene to ensure the uniform interpretation of 'manifestly deliberate fault' and 'fault with a view to gain'.[42] This will lead to greater consistency as to the kind of behaviour deserving punishment and may ultimately serve as a deterrent.

English courts, which are more familiar with specifically articulating the reasons underlying their orders than their French counterparts, are equally explicit when awarding punitive damages. Extra care is taken to explain the imposition of a penalty on a wrongdoer, not least because both the principle and amount of penal awards may well be the subject of appeal. Notwithstanding Lord Devlin's recommendation in *Rookes v Barnard*[43] that there should not necessarily be separate compensatory and punitive awards, the two types of damages can be, and generally are, itemised.[44]

It is perhaps regrettable that article 1371 stops short of requiring punitive orders to be justified in principle and does not specifically oblige courts to explain how they quantify punitive awards. Admittedly, any insistence that the quantum of punitive damages be expressly justified would pose a new challenge for the French judiciary. French *juges du fond* are unaccustomed to expressly setting out their methods of quantifying damages. The assessment process is entrusted entirely to the discretion of the court, both at first instance and in the courts of appeal. The Cour de cassation's appellate remit is limited to ensuring the proper application of the principle of 'full compensation'. The more a decision is reasoned, the more it is exposed to Cour de cassation intervention. It is disappointing that the

---

[42] Viney, above n 19.
[43] Above n 5, 1228.
[44] Law Commission, above n 41, para 1.116; *John v MGN Ltd* [1997] QB 586 (CA).

drafters of article 1371 did not take heed of criticism of this lack of transparency in the context of compensatory damages[45] by going further in relation to punitive damages. [46]

V. THE LEVEL OF PUNITIVE DAMAGES

The *Avant-projet* is silent as to the criteria to be taken into account by courts when faced with the task of quantifying punitive damages. This lack of specificity is unfortunate. Whilst subjectivity is inevitable in any evaluation of a person's conduct, courts would benefit from guidance. In the absence of any advice as to how punitive awards should be quantified, there is a risk of wide disparities. This omission has been criticised by a recently published practitioners' report on the *Avant-projet*, as has the apparent intention that article 1371 should provide no limit on the amount of punitive damages that may be awarded.[47]

If article 1371 is adopted, the principles applied by English courts when awarding punitive damages may, at least initially, be of assistance to French judges.[48] One such principle is that, whilst punitive awards should reflect the gravity of the wrongdoer's conduct, they should nonetheless be moderate. Any penalty must be the minimum necessary to achieve the dual purposes underlying the remedy, namely punishment and deterrence. In other words, courts should keep a sense of proportionality.[49]

An instance of the courts applying the principle of proportionality can be found in *John v MGN*.[50] A famous singer claimed punitive damages for defamation in respect of a newspaper article which erroneously stated that he followed a bizarre diet of chewing but not swallowing food. While the article was clearly defamatory, the Court of Appeal substituted the jury's punitive award of £275,000 with the sum of £50,000. Sir Thomas Bingham MR thought that the award made by the jury was 'manifestly excessive' and went 'well beyond the minimum sum needed' to punish the newspaper and deter it and others from similar behaviour.[51]

A second principle which has guided English courts contemplating an order that a wrongdoer pay punitive damages is that regard should be

---

[45] Jourdain, above n 2, 268–72; P Jourdain and G Viney, *Traité de droit civil: Les effets de la responsabilité* (2nd edn, Paris, LGDJ, 2001) nos 62–5.

[46] Carval, above n 24, no 317.

[47] Conseil national des barreaux, *Projet de rapport du groupe de travail chargé d'étudier l'avant-projet de réforme du droit des obligations et du droit de la prescription* (2006), http://www.cnb.avocat.fr/PDF/2006-11-09_obligations.pdf, 45–6.

[48] *Rookes v Barnard*, above n 5; McGregor, above n 34, paras 11-032 to 11-045.

[49] *Broome v Cassell*, above n 5, 1081, where Lord Hailsham said that juries should be 'fully aware of the danger of an excessive award'.

[50] Above n 44.

[51] *Ibid*, 625.

had to his means.[52] A small award might have no impact on a wealthy wrongdoer but could be difficult or impossible to bear for someone who is impecunious.

Thirdly, English courts give weight to the conduct of the parties up to the time of judgment. An apology or expression of regret from the wrongdoer, for instance, may be capable of reducing a punitive award.[53] Equally, the bad conduct of the victim can be relevant. He may, for example, have provoked the libel or have defamed the wrongdoer in reply.[54]

A fourth issue that would have to be addressed in France and on which guidance can be found in England is the relevance of the amount awarded as compensation. In English law, only if the compensatory award is inadequate to punish the wrongdoer for his outrageous conduct and deter others will a court order that punitive damages be paid.[55] Should a punitive award be made, any liability to pay compensation will be taken into account. This acknowledges that compensatory damages may have an incidental punitive effect. Punitive damages are in this way a remedy of last resort.

Fifthly, any criminal penalties should be taken into account. Punishing someone twice for the same conduct offends against basic principles of justice. A defendant who is ordered to pay a fine should not be punished a second time by being ordered to pay punitive damages for the same wrong.

Lastly, the extent of any profit made by the wrongdoer may be relevant.[56] This issue has received much attention in French literature on punitive damages.[57] It has been suggested that punitive damages can be an effective deterrent if their assessment is dependent on the profit made by the defaulting party.[58]

In England, the relevance of any profit resulting from the wrongful conduct is a matter of debate. *McGregor on Damages*, for instance, argues that the real purpose behind Lord Devlin's second category is not the punishment of the wrongdoer but the prevention of his unjust enrichment.[59] Punitive damages are described as a 'somewhat makeshift and arbitrary' method of preventing a wrongdoer's unjust enrichment, although 'it may be that the emergence of restitutionary damages will take away from Lord Devlin's second category and render it unnecessary'.[60] In the same vein, Lord Scott in *Kuddus v Chief Constable of Leicestershire Constabulary*

---

[52] *Ibid.*

[53] *Rookes v Barnard*, above n 5, 1226–7 where Lord Devlin held that 'everything which aggravates or mitigates the defendant's conduct is relevant'; *Design Progression Ltd v Thurloe Properties Ltd* [2004] EWHC 324 (Ch), [2005] 1 WLR 1 [147].

[54] *Broome v Cassell*, above n 5, 1071.

[55] *Rookes v Barnard*, above n 5, 1228.

[56] *John v MGN*, above n 44.

[57] Fasquelle, above n 18, 28; Conseil national des barreaux, above n 47, 45–6. Chagny, above n 18.

[58] Jourdain, above n 18, 4.

[59] McGregor, above n 34, para 11-046.

[60] *Ibid*, paras 11-028, 11-046.

opined that restitutionary damages could provide a substitute for Lord Devlin's second category.[61]

It is submitted that these views confuse the aims of punitive and restitutionary damages. Whilst punitive damages are capable of stripping a defaulting party of wrongfully obtained profit, this is ancillary to their intended purpose. As already noted, the objectives of punitive damages are punishment and deterrence. Any prevention of unjust enrichment is coincidental. It follows that, as in English law, punitive damages should be available in France even where the defaulting party's scheme proves to be unprofitable. His purpose, rather than whether such purpose is fulfilled, is all important.[62]

A further corollary of the absence of any association between the profit accruing to the defaulting party from his wrong and punitive damages is that any award need not be limited to the gains obtained. As Lord Diplock stated in *Broome v Cassell*:[63]

> [The second category] may be a blunt instrument to prevent unjust enrichment by unlawful acts. But to restrict the damages recoverable to the actual gain made by the defendant if it exceeded the loss caused to the plaintiff, would leave the defendant contemplating an unlawful act with the certainty that he had nothing to lose to balance against the chance that the plaintiff might never sue him, or if he did, might fail in the hazards of litigation. It is only if there is a prospect that the damages may exceed the defendant's gain that the social purpose of this category is achieved – to teach a wrongdoer that tort does not pay.

A final difficulty with linking punitive awards to the profit which derives from the act or omission of the defaulting party is that profit is seldom easy to measure. For instance, the profit generated by a defamatory statement published in a newspaper is rarely shown with precision. Overemphasis on profit could complicate or even undermine the assessment process. The extent of the ill-gotten gain of the defaulting party is therefore best considered as one criterion amongst others.

VI. TO WHOM MAY PUNITIVE DAMAGES BE AWARDED?

However French courts ultimately decide to quantify awards of punitive damages, they will face the equally important issue of whom the remedy should benefit. An intriguing feature of article 1371 of the *Avant-projet* is

---

[61] *Kuddus*, above n 10, [109]. But see *Borders (UK) Ltd v MPC* [2005] EWCA Civ 197, where punitive damages were awarded exclusively by reference to the profit made by the defendant. Nevertheless, the Court of Appeal recognised that the case should have been pleaded on a different basis. Their Lordships upheld the award for reasons of justice. This decision was criticised in R Cunnington, 'The Border between Compensation, Restitution and Punishment' (2006) 122 LQR 382.

[62] *Broome v Cassell*, above n 5, 1130; *Design Progression*, above n 53.

[63] Above n 5, 1130.

its proposal that there should be a judicial discretion to order that part of any punitive damages liability be paid to the public treasury. This achieves a compromise between two imperfect situations. On the one hand, diverting the full award to the state would divest the victim of any incentive to claim punitive damages. Few would claim such damages knowing that they could not thereby gain. On the other hand, any order that punitive damages be paid to the victim confers on him a substantial, largely unmerited, windfall benefit. In the context of unfair competition between rival businesses, there is obvious potential for negative consequences. If the victim of the unfair competition were to receive a punitive award, the effect would be to consolidate or even strengthen its financial position. There is an attendant risk of imbalance in the market place to the potential detriment of not only the wrongdoer but other unconnected commercial actors who have done nothing wrong.[64]

It is conceivable that the drafters of article 1371 also had in mind criticisms which have long been made of the *astreinte*, the full amount of which is awarded to the victim. It is a device used by courts to force parties to comply with their orders. The victim must be paid a specified sum of money for each period of time during which the default continues. Many commentators have argued that the *astreinte* has the perverse effect of unjustly enriching victims.[65]

Unfortunately, the *Avant-projet* provides no guidance as to when part of the punitive award should be directed to the state and in what proportion. It is possible that the drafters drew upon a theory propounded by Suzanne Carval some ten years before draft article 1371 saw the light of day. She contended that punitive damages do not necessarily unjustly enrich. Instead, such awards should be seen as remuneration. They are earned by bringing the conduct of the defaulting party before the courts.[66] The victim is thus 'paid' for the service he renders to society as a private prosecutor. Any award could be calculated so as to cover the victim's expenses and would include an element of reward to act as an incentive. Where, however, the award of punitive damages is large and goes beyond the remuneration deserved by the victim, Suzanne Carval recommended that the undeserved balance be diverted elsewhere.

While ingenious, Suzanne Carval's analysis is not without difficulties. Whether the state wishes to enlist citizens as private prosecutors is certainly debateable. There is clearly a risk that such a provision would both encourage and add to the arsenal of vexatious litigants. The concept of reasonable

---

[64] D Fasquelle, 'Exposé introductif—Concurrence déloyale: Amende civile ou dommages punitifs?' www.creda.ccip.fr.

[65] See Jourdain and Viney, above n 45, no 6-5; Y Chartier, *La réparation du préjudice dans la responsabilité civile* (Paris, Dalloz, 1983) no 767.

[66] Carval, above n 23, nos 318–23.

remuneration is also problematic, being subjective and difficult to determine.

More generally, the appropriateness of awarding anything at all to the state is itself questionable. Whilst conferring an undeserved windfall on the victim is intuitively undesirable, it is not obvious why the state is a more deserving beneficiary of any award. Ordering a payment into the public purse would be tantamount to imposing a fine.[67] The position might be different if the state's share of the award were diverted to a designated fund whose purpose were to counteract at a general level the negative consequences of the wrong. The application of this notion is particularly easy to imagine in respect of wrongs which cause environmental harm. In the prevailing political climate of increased environmental awareness and concern, such a scheme has obvious advantages. However, it goes beyond and is significantly more radical than the *Avant-projet* as currently drafted.

An additional difficulty with this aspect of article 1371 is that it is unclear whether the state itself or the victim will be responsible for enforcing the state's part of the award. The victim will clearly have no financial incentive to do so. Indeed, it may even be regarded as a burden which he would rather be without.

In England, there is no jurisdiction for part of an award of punitive damages made in the context of civil litigation to be allocated to the state. A scheme in which 33 per cent of the total award of punitive damages would be payable to the state was considered and rejected by the Law Commission. The cost of administration and enforcement was thought to be disproportionate to the amount of punitive damages in issue.[68] It was also believed that any such scheme would be vulnerable to abuse in *inter partes* settlement negotiations. The amount of compensatory or restitutionary damages could be inflated with a corresponding diminution in punitive damages, thereby preventing the state from receiving its due share of the punitive damages award.[69]

Insofar as article 1371 is concerned with avoiding the unjust enrichment of the victim, it should be welcomed. However, the lack of guidance to assist judges as to when and in what proportion the award should be diverted to the state is problematic. If nothing else, the English position has the advantage of being simple.

---

[67] D Fasquelle, 'La sanction de la concurrence déloyale et du parasitisme économique et le rapport Catala' D 2005 Chron 2666.
[68] Law Commission, above n 41, Part V para 1.158.
[69] *Ibid*, para 1.150.

VII. INSURANCE

Article 1371 of the *Avant-projet* would forbid insurance against the risk of being ordered to pay punitive damages. The reasoning underlying this prohibition is that if liability to pay punitive damages were an insurable risk, the impact of any award on the pocket of the defaulting party would be negated. This would correspondingly dilute the retributive and deterrent effects of the remedy. In the words of the *Exposé des motifs* to Sub-Title III of the *Avant-projet*, this rule is 'absolutely necessary to give to the award the punitive impact which constitutes its very raison d'être'.[70] It also achieves consistency with article L113-1(2) of the French insurance code which states that 'the insurer shall not be answerable for losses and damage caused by the insured's intentional fault or *dol*'.

In this respect, article 1371 diverges from English law, which allows awards of punitive damages to be insured against. In *Lancashire County Council v Municipal Mutual Insurance Ltd*,[71] Simon Brown LJ expressed the view that punitive damages were still 'likely to have punitive effect' despite insurance. A wrongdoer who makes an insurance claim in respect of liability to pay punitive damages would have to pay higher premiums subsequently and may even encounter difficulties obtaining renewal insurance.[72] The Law Commission, which recommended that punitive damages should be insurable, cited four main arguments. First, whilst there is a clear interest in punishing and deterring bad conduct as well as in offering appeasement to the victim, this is futile if the wrongdoer cannot pay. Tort victims are unlikely to claim punitive damages if the wrongdoer is impecunious. This would be obviated if a liability insurance policy were in place.[73] A second reason for allowing punitive damages to be an insurable risk is that the insurance industry, in controlling the availability and cost of such insurance, is in a position to exert significant pressure on present and future insured parties.[74] Third, the courts and legislature should not interfere lightly with commercial agreements.[75] Lastly, permitting insurance for punitive damages as well as compensatory damages would avert a risk of conflict between the insurer and the wrongdoing insured. Forbidding insurance would result in the wrongdoer seeking to maximise the size of any compensatory award if he could thereby achieve a commensurate diminution in any punitive award. An insurer would, of course, prefer the opposite outcome.[76]

It is submitted that at least some of the arguments advanced by the Law

---

[70] Viney, above n 17, 168 (see below p 827).
[71] [1997] QB 897 (CA).
[72] *Ibid*, 503–4.
[73] Law Commission, above n 41, Part V para 1.237.
[74] *Ibid*, para 1.238.
[75] *Ibid*, paras 1.242–1.246.
[76] *Ibid*, para 1.248.

Commission are weak and the *Avant-projet* is to be preferred. The first argument of the Law Commission misses the point. Only if a punitive award lands a direct blow on the wrongdoer's finances will his victim be appeased. Just as fines cannot be insured against, nor should punitive damages. If punitive damages are awarded by reference to the means of the wrongdoer, then unless he is insolvent, he will always be able to pay something, however moderate. The second argument, namely that the insurance industry is capable of exerting leverage over the wrongdoer, is equally unsatisfactory. It allows the insurer, rather than the court, to decide the punishment that should be visited on the wrongdoer.

It may ultimately be that the question of whether liability to pay punitive damages should be insurable is more theoretical than practical. As the Law Commission observed, it might be hard to find an insurance company willing to cover liability for punitive damages.

VIII. IS THE INTRODUCTION OF PUNITIVE DAMAGES IN FRENCH LAW DESIRABLE?

Having reviewed and commented on the manner in which the *Avant-projet* envisages introducing punitive awards, the merits and demerits of French law adopting such a remedy may now be considered. The *Exposé des motifs* to Sub-Title III of the *Avant-projet* describes the introduction of punitive damages as being 'cautious'. On one view, this betrays unease on the part of the drafters at the prospect of such a novel and potentially controversial provision being introduced into French law. Punitive damages have long been hotly debated amongst English practitioners and academic lawyers. In *Rookes v Barnard*, Lord Devlin thought that he could not get rid of punitive damages as he felt bound by precedent.[77] The speeches in *Broome v Cassell*[78] reveal considerable divergences of opinion on the desirability in principle of punitive damages as a civil law remedy. Current attitudes are no different. In *Kuddus v Chief Constable of Leicestershire Constabulary*,[79] the House of Lords expressed disappointment that the parties failed to invite them to consider whether punitive damages should ever be awarded.[80] Lord Nicholls and Lord Hutton thought that the remedy might have a valuable role in dealing with outrageous behaviour and the defence of civil liberties.[81] Lord Scott, however, regarded it as an anomaly that should be removed from English law.[82]

[77] Above n 5, 1226.
[78] Above n 5.
[79] Above n 10.
[80] *Ibid*, [31], [68], [72], [105].
[81] *Ibid*, [63], [75].
[82] *Ibid*, [121].

The formal recognition of punitive damages in France would certainly have far-reaching consequences, setting French law apart from other European civil law jurisdictions and international principles of tort law. Punishment is not a formal objective of the law of damages in neighbouring civil law jurisdictions such as Germany and Belgium.[83] Further, the concept of punitive damages has not been included in the Principles of European Tort Law.[84] Whilst these Principles recognise prevention as an additional aim of damages, and take into account the degree of the wrongdoer's fault in the assessment of damages for non-pecuniary loss where it significantly contributes to the grievance of the victim, punishment alone cannot be the basis for an award of damages.[85]

Reticence towards punitive awards can also be found in European Community private international law. The Regulation on the Law Applicable to Non-Contractual Obligations includes a provision to the effect that the application of a law designated by the Regulation leading to the award of an excessive amount of punitive damages may be regarded as being incompatible with the public policy of the forum.[86]

In contract law, article 1371 of the *Avant-projet* will isolate French law from the approaches of conventions regulating international trade as well as international principles of contract law. Punitive damages are unknown to the UNIDROIT Principles of International Commercial Contracts, the United Nations Convention on Contracts for the International Sale of Goods, and the Principles of European Contract Law prepared by the Commission on European Contract Law. [87]

Some observers have already made known their discontentment at the proposed introduction of punitive damages into French law. The report of the Commercial Chamber of Paris has unambiguously rejected the recognition of punitive damages.[88] One of its main criticisms is that retribution should be confined to criminal law, civil liability being exclusively concerned with compensation. The courts already have at their disposal efficient means of punishing a defaulting party, not least the power to order

---

[83] U Magnus (ed), *Unification of Tort Law: Damages* (The Hague, Kluwer Law International, 2001) 89–90 (Germany), 30 (Belgium); The European Group on Tort Law, *Principles of European Tort Law, Text and Commentary* (Vienna, Springer, 2005). Nevertheless, there is a tendency in these countries to take account of the conduct of the party in breach in assessing damages for non-pecuniary losses.

[84] The European Group on Tort Law, above n 83.

[85] Art 10:101 of the PETL, which recognises compensatory and preventative functions of damages; see Magnus, above n 83, 185–7; see also art 10:301 of the PETL.

[86] Regulation (EC) No 864/2007 of the European Parliament and of the Council of 11 July 2007 on the Law Applicable to Non-Contractual Obligations (Rome II), Recital 32. The discretion will depend on the circumstances of the case and the legal order of the Member State of the court seised.

[87] Art 7.4.2 PICC; art 74 CISG; art 9:502 PECL.

[88] Chambre de commerce et d'industrie de Paris, *Pour une réforme du droit des contrats et de la prescription conforme aux besoins de la vie des affaires* (2006), http://www.etudes.ccip.fr/archrap/pdf06/reforme-droit-des-contrats-kli0610.pdf, 119–22

compensation to cover all the detrimental consequences of a wrong. The report recommends that article 1371 be deleted.[89]

It is submitted that the admission of punitive damages into French law should not be so controversial. The idea of punishment in the civil sphere is already well known in France.[90] For instance, according to article 1150 Cc, if non-performance of a contractual obligation is deliberate or dishonest, the contract-breaker is liable to make reparation in respect of all the consequences flowing from the breach, even those that were not reasonably foreseeable at the time of the conclusion of the contract. Exclusion and limitation clauses may not be relied upon in such situations. Insurance is also forbidden for the deliberate non-performance of contractual obligations.

A further example of punishment in French civil liability is that pursuant to article 1152 Cc, penalty clauses are valid.[91] Although the courts have the power to reduce manifestly excessive agreed sums which are penal, any reduction is seldom to the extent that damages become purely compensatory. For the courts to make such a reduction would all but remove the coercive function of penalty clauses. Another example which reveals the latent presence of punishment in French civil law is the *astreinte*, whose purpose is to force defaulting parties to comply with court orders. In assessing the final sum to be paid, the persistence of the defaulting party in failing to comply and any bad faith are taken into account. Once again, insurance is forbidden.

La doctrine has also shown that there is a tendency on the part of *juges du fond*, consciously or otherwise, to vary the quantum of damages in accordance with the gravity of the defaulting party's conduct.[92] This practice is unspoken and is only made possible because the assessment of damages is a matter for the discretion of first instance and appeal courts. As long as the lower court decision is carefully drafted so as not to disclose any punitive intention, the Cour de cassation will not interfere with the damages awards of *juges du fond*. The scope of judicial discretion as to the quantum of damages is most apparent in respect of non-pecuniary loss (*dommage moral*) because there are no objective assessment criteria.[93]

If one accepts that retribution and compensation are not exclusive and hermetically sealed concepts in French civil law, punitive damages cease to be controversial. If, furthermore, punitive damages can serve the useful purpose of preventing behaviour that brings the law into disrepute where

---

[89] *Ibid*. See also S Piedelièvre, 'Les dommages et intérêts punitifs: une solution d'avenir' Resp civ et asssur 2001, 68, rejecting the introduction of punitive damages in French law long ago.

[90] Carval, above n 23, nos 18–198, who demonstrated more than ten years ago in her thesis on *peine privée* that punishment was informally present in many domains of French civil law and had a vital role to play in civil liability; Jourdain and Viney, above n 45, nos 4 to 6-5; Chartier, above n 65, nos 505–6; Jourdain, above n 2, 280–90.

[91] Jourdain, above n 2, 281–3; Carval, above n 23, no 12.

[92] Jourdain and Viney, above n 45, no 6; Chartier, above n 65, no 505.

[93] Chartier, above n 65, no 505; Jourdain, above n 2, no 7.

other remedies lack teeth, then they become desirable. The obvious example is faults with a view to gain. Suzanne Carval convincingly demonstrated more than ten years ago in her thesis on *peine privée* that a formalisation of the punitive function of civil liability would bring about a less arbitrary and more efficient system.[94] It is entirely possible that the introduction of article 1371 of the *Avant-projet* has been inspired by her ideas.

IX. CONCLUSION

The *Avant-projet* intends that punitive damages become a useful tool in French law, punishing and deterring reprehensible conduct such as faults with a view to gain. As the effects of such faults are not neutralised by compensatory damages, an additional remedy is needed to vindicate the strength of the law. It is regrettable, however, that draft article 1371 omits to provide detailed guidance as to how punitive damages will operate in practice. In particular, the failure to set out criteria to be taken into account in the quantification of punitive awards and the circumstances in which part of the award will be diverted to the state is unfortunate. This lack of direction may even be dangerous, having the potential to result in disparities between judicial decisions and arbitrariness. Punitive damages would then become all the more controversial, albeit for the wrong reasons.

Whether article 1371 will ever appear in the Code civil remains a matter for speculation. There is a real possibility that French legislators will be deterred by the controversy generated by the prospect of punitive awards. It may be that the sacrifice of article 1371 is necessary to ensure the smooth passage of other aspects of the *Avant-projet*. Alternatively, an intermediate compromise solution may be preferred. If the drafters are keen to target faults with a view to gain, the obvious candidate is restitutionary damages.[95]

Whilst any development which sees punitive damages replaced by restitutionary damages in a revised *Avant-projet* is outside the terms of reference of this paper, it is nonetheless legitimate to conclude with a cautionary note. Those tempted by a seemingly watered-down article 1371 should be under no illusions. Restitutionary damages must, by definition, be limited to gains accruing from wrongful conduct. They deprive the defaulting party of no more than his ill-gotten gains. A party tempted to commit a fault with a view to gain and faced with the prospect of

---

[94] See Carval, above n 2, who argued that compensatory damages were often inefficient to deter misconduct. The formal recognition and principled expansion of penal awards were recommended to tackle such problems.

[95] Restitutionary damages being damages reversing gains following the commission of a tort or breach of contract. For a general analysis of restitution for wrongs in England, see A Burrows, *Remedies for Torts and Breach of Contract* (3rd edn, Oxford University Press, 2005) ch 17.

restitutionary but not punitive damages may form the view that he has little to lose. This being the case, the deterrent effect at the core of article 1371 would be all but removed. Ultimately, the choice facing the drafters is one of policy.

H

Reforming the French Law of Prescription

16

Reforming the French Law of Prescription: A French Perspective

ROBERT WINTGEN*

THE MERITS OF French case-law, which has been able to fill the gaps in the 1804 Code civil and to adapt its provisions where changes appeared necessary, are frequently praised—and rightly so. However, this can hardly be said of the law of prescription. It appears to be generally accepted today that this branch of the law consists of rules that are anachronistic, confused, changeable and technically imperfect.[1]

The unsuitability of case-law for remedying the defects in the present system is easy to explain. First, the rules of law which contain figures are by nature more refractory than others that lend themselves to creative interpretation: thirty years is thirty years, and even the most ingenious interpreter will find it difficult to persuade anyone to the contrary. Secondly, in the area of prescription more than in other areas, the policy considerations pursued by the legislature that justify statutory rules are often not in line with the requirements of individual justice. In a case where the evidence appears irrefutable and the claimant had good reasons for not acting in time, the court will hesitate to apply strictly an absolute bar based on the risk of loss of evidence and the idea that the claimant was negligent in delaying bringing an action. Therefore a court confronted with special cases can hardly be expected to lay down a coherent set of general and impersonal rules governing prescription. However, experience shows that

---

* After completion of the manuscript, the law of prescription in the Code civil has been substantially revised by the Loi no 2008-561 du 17 juin 2008 portant réforme de la prescription en matière civile, JO 18 June 2008, 9856. References to the Code civil in this chapter are to the pre-reform state of the law.

[1] See A Bénabent, 'Le chaos du droit de la prescription extinctive' in *Mélanges dédiés à Louis Boyer* (Presses universitaires Toulouse, 1996) 123; P Courbe (ed), *Les désordres de la prescription* (Publications de l'Université de Rouen, 2000).

in France, as in other countries, such rules are preferable to a system where the question of prescription is abandoned to the discretion of the court.[2]

The extent of the defects in the present law explains why the *Avant-projet de réforme du droit de la prescription* drafted by Professor Philippe Malaurie differs clearly in spirit from the *Avant-projet de réforme du droit des obligations*. The latter is mainly confined, apart from a few selective alterations, to consolidating the law as it exists today, developed by contemporary case-law. So far as the law of prescription is concerned, what is proposed is a radical reform based largely on foreign and European models. However, the concern to preserve the French tradition is still present in this part of the reform. Consequently, certain traditional principles whose advantages do not appear to be beyond dispute have been retained.

Accordingly what is striking, on reading the *Avant-projet*, is that many things would change if it were adopted (section I). However, what is also striking is that certain things which could have changed would not change (section II).

I. WHAT WOULD CHANGE

The *Avant-projet* proposes a radical reform of prescription periods and major changes with regard to the causes of interruption and suspension.

(a) With Regard to Periods

The thirty-year prescription period which is now the general period is usually considered too long. It is true that, with regard to extinctive prescription, its scope has already shrunk away. The adoption of the ten-year prescription in commercial matters[3] and in the law of extra-contractual liability[4] has in effect made it possible in most cases to reduce the extinctive prescription period to reasonable limits.

Consequently the main defect in extinctive prescription periods is not their excessive duration, but that there are too many of them.[5] The multiplicity of periods makes the law of prescription very complex and gives rise to abundant argument concerning classification. No doubt this would be a

---

[2] Cf the French experience of the 'short period' of art 1648 Cc or the English experience, generally regarded as inconclusive, of the court's moderating power in this connection.

[3] Loi no 48-1282 de 18 août 1948 relative à la prescription des obligations entre commerçants à l'occasion de leur commerce, today article L 110-4 Code commercial. As the 10-year period also applies to mixed acts, it has in fact become the true general period.

[4] Loi no 85-677 de 5 juillet 1985 tendant à l'amélioration de la situation des victimes d'accidents de la circulation et à l'accélération des procédures d'indemnisation, JO 6 July 1985, 7584, today art 2271-1 Cc.

[5] Bénabent, above n 1, 124, lists eleven, 'save for omissions which it is impossible to avoid in this field'.

necessary evil if the differentiation of periods were the result of a coherent and rational policy pursued by legislature. That, however, is manifestly not the case. First, there are several radical differences between the periods applying to similar actions. The contrast between the 'short period' (now set at two years) in relation to hidden defects and the ten- or thirty-year prescription period for non-conformity with the contract in the law of sale is the example which is the best caricature of itself. Secondly, the duration of a prescription period is always somewhat arbitrary. Therefore it is hardly possible to justify rationally the need to distinguish between, for example, periods of three, four or five years.

The *Avant-projet* largely *unifies* the periods while permitting the parties to derogate from the statutory rules and agree on a period which would be more suited to their situation (article 2235).[6] It introduces a general extinctive period of three years (article 2274) which begins to run on the day when the creditor can act (article 2262), which means that he is aware of his right (article 2264). A ten-year period would be the acquisitive prescription period in relation to immovable property (article 2276) and, at the same time, the general extinctive period for certain specified actions (article 2275) and the back-stop extinctive prescription period applying to most actions. This back-stop period would begin to run on the date of the circumstances giving rise to the obligation and would not be subject to any interruption, suspension or agreements which extend its duration (article 2278(1)). Finally, a period of thirty years would be the back-stop period for actions for civil liability for the reparation of a loss arising from personal injury, from an act of barbarism or from damage to the environment (article 2278(2)).

The *Avant-projet* therefore abolishes the category of 'presumptive prescription' and that of 'non-suspendable periods'. Presumptive prescription, which only has the effect of establishing an ordinary presumption of satisfaction, is explained by the idea that failure to claim satisfaction over a certain period of time makes it probable that there was an earlier satisfaction which becomes more and more difficult to prove because of the loss of evidence. In reality, this idea is inherent in any prescription period. Without true conceptual autonomy of presumptive prescription periods, the particular rules governing them could appear to be unnecessary complications. As for non-suspendable periods, their legal nature and consequently their rules have always been the subject of debate.[7]

In relation to extinctive prescription, the *Avant-projet* combines a relatively short prescription period (three years)—with its starting point

---

[6] The right to derogate from the statutory rules is nevertheless kept within limits that are perhaps too narrow: not less than one year and not more than ten. The *Avant-projet* provides for a thirty-year prescription period for certain actions, so that the parties should also be able to extend the period to more than ten years.

[7] Cf Bénabent, above n 1.

delayed until the day when the creditor can act and which is suspended during periods when he would be unable to do so—and a longer period (ten or thirty years). In doing so, it does not merely harmonise the periods. It also generalises[8] the modern technique of *two-stage periods* which now seems to attract national legislatures more and more and which has been adopted by the UNIDROIT Principles and the Principles of European Contract Law (PECL).

The advantages of this system over the single-period system are obvious. First of all, it encourages the claimant to act rapidly where he can and prevents him from suspending for too long the sword of Damocles of an action over the defendant's head.[9] Secondly, it gives the defendant the certainty that, after a certain period and no longer, a new action cannot be brought. It is therefore better able to provide legal certainty than the single-stage system for two reasons: first, the single-stage system may appear excessively long where the creditor has all the information to act; secondly, it may sometimes lead to the indefinite postponement of the completion of prescription, either because the starting point has been deferred, or by the effect of grounds of suspension.[10]

Nevertheless the *Avant-projet* appears to have a number of technical shortcomings in the application of the two-stage system, particularly in relation to the *starting point of the periods*. Under article 2278 the starting point for the back-stop period is the date of the 'circumstances which gave rise to the obligation'. Unless this phrase is given a special meaning in relation to prescription, the rule appears unsuitable for certain types of contractual obligation. With regard to obligations coupled with a suspensive term, the starting point of the prescription period cannot be the date of the contract, which is the circumstance giving rise to the obligation, but only the date of expiry of the term. Otherwise the obligation would risk being prescribed even before the creditor could sue for performance. Likewise with regard to continuing obligations to do or not to do, it must

[8] This technique is not unknown in French law as it presently stands. It was adopted by the legislature in relation to liability for defective products and by case-law, which applies the short period for hidden defects and the general period together see Cass com 27 November 2001, Bull IV no 187.

[9] Regarding an action for nullity of a contract, the *Avant-projet* adopts another interesting technique permitting greater legal certainty: under art 1129-5, the party on whom confirmation or ratification rests may be given notice by the other party either to affirm or ratify, or to proceed with an action for nullity within a period of six months, on pain of losing the right.

[10] See eg Cass civ (1) 24 January 2006, Bull civ I no 28, D 2006, 626 note R Wintgen, D 2006 IR 395 obs I Gallmeister, D 2006 Pan 2643 obs S Amrani Mekki, JCP 2006 II 10036 note M Mekki, Gaz Pal 2006, 2566 note D Seysen-Guérin, Defr 2006, 583 obs E Savaux, AJ fam 2006, 116 obs Bicheron, RTD fam 2006, no 97 note J-R Binet, RJPF 2006-5/47 note J Casey, LPA 11 August 2006 no 160, 9 note Y Dagorne-Labbe, LPA 3 October 2006 no 197, 16 note P-A Bon, RDC 2006, 708 obs D Mazeaud, RTD civ 2006, 320 obs D Mazeaud and B Fages (action for nullity for fraud in renunciation of succession).

be observed that they are not extinguished ten years after the contract, but prescription begins to run only on the date of breach of the obligation.[11]

The prescription period of the general law does not run as long as the creditor[12] is unaware of the existence or extent of his claim. However, it would no doubt be expedient to treat the knowledge of his right that the creditor ought to have as actual knowledge,[13] particularly as the recent case-law seems to have taken that plunge already.[14]

A further question arises regarding the relevance of article 2275 of the *Avant-projet*, which replaces, for certain types of action, the thirty-year general period with a ten-year period. This exception is laid down, first, for actions claiming reparation of personal injury or any loss caused by an act of barbarism. However, while it is understandable that such actions, which protect essential values, have a longer back-stop period—thirty years instead of ten[15]—there appears to be no reason why the creditor should have ten years to bring an action when he has all the information to act. The exceptions laid down for actions on a builder's ten-year guarantee and actions for absolute nullity seem inconsistent with the general two-stage system. The introduction of ten-year prescription at a starting point that is often deferred and liable to suspension leads in actual fact to applying to those actions alone the back-stop period, also ten years, but at the objective starting point which is not liable to suspension. Finally, the ten-year prescription for obligations upheld by a judgment is justified according to the aims of prescription,[16] but there seems to be no rational justification for treating any other enforceable instrument as a judgment, contrary to the current case-law.[17]

---

[11] Cf art 14:203 PECL, which states that the period begins to run from the time when the debtor has to effect performance. It adds, with regard to continuing obligations, that the starting point is the date of breach of the obligation.

[12] Art 2264 of the *Avant-projet* refers to the 'debtor' instead of the creditor, but it is evident and also clearly follows from P Malaurie, 'Exposé des motifs' in *Avant-projet de réforme du droit des obligations et de la prescription: Rapport remis au garde des Sceaux* (Paris, La documentation française, 2006) 193, 200 (see below pp 881, 897), that only the creditor's ignorance can be such as to delay the starting point of prescription. Consequently this should be regarded as just a clerical error.

[13] The approach taken by the PICC, the PECL, English law, German law and, in French law, the present art 1386-17 Cc in relation to liability for defective products.

[14] In terms which are, however, somewhat inept. See Cass civ (3) 29 March 2006, Bull III no 88 which starts the prescription provided for by the present art 1304 Cc on the ground that the fraud 'could have been discovered', whereas the provision requires it to have been discovered. However, there is an enormous difference between 'discover' and 'could discover'. In that particular case, the fraud (arising from an untruthful advertising document) could nevertheless have been discovered on reading the contract and it is therefore possible to take the view that it 'ought' to have been discovered.

[15] Art 2278(2) of the *Avant-projet*.

[16] See R Libchaber, 'Le point sur l'interversion des prescriptions en cas de condamnation en justice' D 2006, 254.

[17] Cass mixte 26 May 2006, JCP G 2006 II 10129 note H Croze, D 2006, 1793 note R Wintgen.

The proposed changes in relation to the causes of interruption and suspension also call for qualified observations.

(b) The Causes of Interruption and Suspension

In the laws and academic codes that have adopted the two-stage system there are differences concerning the possibility of suspending or interrupting the long period. In German law all the causes of interruption and suspension apply to the long period. Consequently it is differentiated from the short period only by its objective starting point, which is the date when the right arose and not the date when the creditor knew or ought to have known of it. In essence, the same applies to the proposed English reform, save with regard to suspension in the case of disability, which applies only to the short period. Therefore the long period is not suspended on the ground of disability, but its point of arrival may be deferred in favour of a minor lacking legal capacity. The PECL allow as the only cause of suspension of the long period that arising from judicial proceedings, but they also provide for interruption by the effect of an acknowledgement of the right by the debtor and by attempted performance. The UNIDROIT Principles, on the other hand, disregard interruption by attempted performance, but allow suspension of the long period by judicial proceedings and interruption of the long period by acknowledgement (articles 10.4 and 10.5 PICC). Consequently the long period may be more or less rigid, depending on whether the emphasis is put on protection of the claimant's right or on legal certainty.

The solution proposed by article 2278 of the *Avant-projet* is, for its part, much more radical than those just mentioned. It states that:

> All actions become prescribed ten years after the circumstances which gave rise to the obligation, whatever its subject-matter, their starting-point or any interruption, suspensions or agreements which amend their duration.[18]

However, such a *general limitation period*, which would escape all causes of suspension and interruption, would have curious consequences. As it would not be suspended or interrupted by the institution of judicial proceedings, in could expire in the course of such proceedings. As it would not be interrupted by enforcement measures, it would have the effect of despoiling the most diligent creditors. And as it would not be interrupted where the debtor acknowledges the right, it would compel the creditor to bring an action before the court even if there were no dispute.

---

[18] The same provision states that 'crimes against humanity . . . are not subject to prescription' and that 'in the case of actions claiming civil liability for the reparation of a loss resulting from personal injury, from an act of barbarism or from damage to the environment, the period is thirty years'.

In contrast, the other innovations relating to the causes of suspension and interruption appear to be welcome. This applies, first, to the rule, based on the German reform and adopted by both the European Principles and the UNIDROIT Principles, that *judicial proceedings* entail the suspension and not, as in the existing law, the interruption of the period. Suspension during proceedings has, by comparison with interruption, the advantage of preventing the expiry of the period in the course of proceedings. However, the case-law now removes this risk by stating that interruption 'continues' during the proceedings and that the new period begins to run only at the end of the proceedings.[19] In other words, the existing law in reality combines interruption of the period by the institution of proceedings and suspension of the period for the duration of the proceedings.

However, suspension of the period seems sufficient. As a general rule, judicial proceedings end with a judgment on the substance of the case which has the authority of *res judicata* and it is that, not prescription, which presents an obstacle to a new action. In other cases, where the judgment does not relate to the substance of the case—eg lack of jurisdiction—it appears hardly appropriate to authorise the claimant to allow a new period, which is as long as the first, to elapse before finally bringing an action for a judgment on the substance. Having already brought an action that encountered a procedural obstacle of some kind, he should be in possession of all the information to enable him to bring the appropriate action quickly.

Two other provisions relating to the causes of suspension should also be mentioned. First, the *Avant-projet* provides that prescription is suspended as against any person who finds it *impossible to act* 'owing to an impediment caused by legislation, a contract or *force majeure*', but adds that 'where *force majeure* is temporary it is a ground of suspension of prescription only where it occurred within six months of expiry of its period' (article 2266 of the *Avant-projet*). Consequently the maxim *contra non valentem* is in this way codified and clarified as to its effects.

Secondly, the *Avant-projet* provides for suspension of the period by *negotiations* conducted in good faith (article 2264). This rule has also been enshrined in the PECL, but discarded by the UNIDROIT Principles, whose authors feared that it would give rise to uncertainty as to the concept of negotiations conducted in good faith. In view of this risk, it would perhaps be more appropriate to suspend prescription only if the negotiations take place within the months before expiry of the prescription period, as laid down in the cases where it is impossible to act.

Many things would therefore change if the *Avant-projet* were adopted. On the other hand, others would not.

---

[19] Eg Cass com 10 October 1995, Bull IV no 229.

II. WHAT WOULD NOT CHANGE

'The status quo is in the nature of the law. Nothing is more natural to boundaries than not to change', *le doyen* Carbonnier used to say. Even in the context of a substantial reform, therefore, it seems wise to 'save everything that it is not necessary to destroy'.[20] On two points, however, the *Avant-projet* could, and no doubt should, have gone further. The retention of certain provisions relating to the causes of suspension, and the retention of the unitary approach to extinctive and acquisitive prescription may be questioned.

(a) The Retention of Certain Provisions Relating to the Causes of Suspension

The *Avant-projet* retains all the traditional causes of suspension even though, as we have seen, their scope would be reduced because of the back-stop period, which cannot be suspended. It also retains the rule that prescription 'runs against a *vacant estate* even were it does not have the benefit of a curator' (article 2271 of the *Avant-projet* and article 2258 Cc). The rule has been criticised on the ground that it is inconsistent with the principle that prescription should not run where it is impossible to act.[21] However, a vacant estate is not necessarily the result of *force majeure* preventing the heirs from claiming it. Consequently the provision may be justified if it is interpreted as meaning that a vacant estate is not in itself a cause of suspension.

Like the present article 2252 Cc, article 2268 of the *Avant-projet* provides that prescription does not run against 'emancipated minors or adults subject to guardianship'. Although the rule is not unique in comparative law,[22] it has not persuaded the authors of the PECL or those of the UNIDROIT Principles and there are good reasons for doubting whether it is expedient to retain it.

First, persons with a disability have a legal representative who can act in their name; consequently it is not impossible for them to act. It is true that the representative may be negligent in the management of the affairs for which he is responsible, but that is a risk which persons with a disability customarily have to bear, subject only to an action for liability which is available against the representative. There seems to be no reason for distributing the risks relating to prescription in any other way.

[20] Cf P Catala, 'Présentation générale de l'avant-projet' in *Avant-projet de réforme du droit des obligations et de la prescription: Rapport remis au garde des Sceaux* (Paris, La documentation française, 2006) 11 (see below p 465).

[21] R Zimmermann, '"Extinctive" Prescription under the *Avant-projet*' [2008] ERPL 805.

[22] Suspension in favour of persons under a disability is known in English law and the Law Commission also proposes its retention: 'Limitation of Actions' (Law Com No 270, HMSO, 2001) paras 3.121, 3.133.

Secondly, the rule is not suitable for short prescription periods based on the idea of a presumption of satisfaction or the concern to protect the debtor against the accumulation of a periodic debt. That is why, in the existing law, these periods also run against persons under a disability 'save for their action against their guardians'.[23] As the *Avant-projet* abolishes all the present distinctions between the different short prescription periods for the sake of simplicity, it also abandons this exception. However, that amounts to replacing the old short prescription periods with the ten-year period[24] in all cases where the creditor is a person with a disability, but in those cases it appears excessively long.

Finally, although this cause of suspension is retained to the detriment of the security of commerce, persons with a disability would have much less protection under the provisions of the *Avant-projet* than in the existing law. Suspension would not apply to the long period of ten years. Further, the present article 475 Cc, which permits a minor to bring an action for liability against his guardian for five years from attaining majority, would have to be repealed if the *Avant-projet* were adopted.[25] It follows that the guardian of a minor could rob him with impunity until he reaches the age of eight years. An action for liability for earlier acts would in effect be barred on the day the minor reaches full age.

From the viewpoint of the protection of third-party interests and from that of a person with a disability, it would be more appropriate to suspend only the prescription period of an action for liability against the guardian until the end of legal incapacity.

The rule, also adopted by the *Avant-projet*, that prescription does not run *between spouses* is equally contentious. The reason traditionally put forward in support of this cause of suspension is the aim of maintaining peace in households. However, it is difficult to see how a cause of suspension of which the vast majority of married couples is unaware could strengthen conjugal peace. In any case, it seems doubtful whether peace would really be ensured if spouses were able to defer the settlement of their disputes. Neither divorce nor the winding-up of an estate will be made easier if spouses or their heirs are authorised to revive old disputes. The rule was understandable at a time when divorce was almost unknown and the wife was under the husband's authority;[26] today the rule seems an

---

[23] Art 2278 Cc.

[24] As we have seen, suspension would in effect apply only to the three-year period and not the long periods of ten or thirty years.

[25] If Malaurie, above n 12, 196 (see below p 889), is to be believed, the new provisions would apply to 'all prescriptions without exception—even for those belonging to family law, the law of succession, matrimonial property regimes or the law governing banking and finance'.

[26] Cf CBM Toullier and M Duranton, *Cours de droit français suivant le Code civil*, vol XI (3rd edn, Paris, Alex-Gobelet Libraire 1836) no 299, which justifies the provision with the idea that an action between spouses 'gives rise to dissension between them and perhaps fatal discord' but also with the married woman's 'state of dependence'.

anachronism.[27] Finally, assuming that a contemporary justification can be found for this cause of suspension, it seems hardly consistent not to extend the principle in favour of civil partners and persons cohabiting.

Therefore the *Avant-projet* appears imbued with a questionable conservatism in retaining these traditional causes of suspension. The same applies in relation to the retention of the unitary approach to acquisitive and extinctive prescription.

(b) The Retention of the Unitary Approach to Acquisitive and Extinctive Prescription

Both extinctive and acquisitive prescription have the effect of consolidating legal situations after a certain period of time has elapsed. Furthermore, the two principles are historically connected[28] and their regimes have a number of points in common. Consequently it is not unreasonable that they should be treated under a common title in the Code civil.

However, the unitary approach adopted by the 1804 Code is a source of confusion. In Chapter I it deals with 'General Provisions', some of which have meaning only for acquisitive prescription.[29] Chapter II, devoted to possession, contains, most importantly, provisions applying exclusively to acquisitive prescription,[30] whereas their wording suggests that they are general provisions.[31] The same applies to the provisions of Chapter III, relating to 'Cases which Prevent Prescription'. Chapter IV, which deals with causes interrupting or suspending prescription, mixes causes of suspension or interruption common to both types of prescription with those which are peculiar to one of them. The same confusion reigns in Chapter V, concerning 'The Periods of Time Required for Prescription'.

The *Avant-projet* retains this traditional structure and, with it, all the risks of confusion it entails. It does not succeed in ordering the rules relating to the two types of prescription in a rational way, eg by distin-

---

[27] Cf the Comments and Notes in O Lando, E Clive, A Prüm and R Zimmermann, *Principles of European Contract Law, Part III* (The Hague, Kluwer Law International, 2003) 190.

[28] On this point, see J Cartwright, 'Reforming the French Law of Prescription: An English Perspective', ch 17 below.

[29] Art 2226 Cc: 'There can be no prescription in relation to the domain of things which may not be owned or alienated.'

[30] Contra: F Zénati and S Fournier, RTD civ 1996, 339: the debtor would have possession of the claim, so that what is extinctive prescription from the viewpoint of the creditor is acquisitive prescription period from that of the debtor. Nevertheless, this concept appears debatable in relation to the idea of possession. The person claiming to be the creditor, not the debtor, is in possession of the claim. In addition, the latter may not know of the existence of his debt, a circumstance which appears to rule out the characteristic *animus* of possession. Furthermore, the theory does not take account of the existing law; eg, it is of no consequence whether the debtor's alleged 'possession' suffers from defects in relation to extinctive prescription.

[31] Eg art 2229 Cc: 'To be able to claim prescription, possession must be continuous, uninterrupted, uncontested, public, unequivocal and as proprietor.'

guishing between a general part on prescription in general and a special part for the two types of prescription. Failing a rational approach of that kind, the unitary approach, which has been rejected by all modern codifications, appears as a regrettable archaism of French law.

The only significant change in the structure of the title on prescription is the creation of a Section devoted to 'The Possession of Moveable Property' within Chapter V, which deals with the 'Periods of Time Required for Prescription'. This Section repeats articles 2279 and 2280 Cc, retaining their numbering and wording. However, it would have been useful to distinguish the evidential and the acquisitive functions of the rule that 'in the case of movable property, possession is equivalent to title' (draft article 2279(1)), particularly in order to make it clear that the acquisition of a movable property by possession presupposes the good faith of the possessor. It would also have been useful to indicate the prescription period applicable to the possessor of a movable property in bad faith. As there is no specific provision on this point, it will no doubt be necessary to apply the general period of three years. However, if that is the correct interpretation, draft article 2279(2), which lays down a three-year period in which to reclaim stolen or lost property, seems to become redundant.

These defects were no doubt inevitable, at least in part, because the aim of the authors of the *Avant-projet* was to 'reform' the Code 'without damaging either its structure or its form'.[32] However, one cannot help thinking that, in the area of prescription, it would have been desirable to go further.

---

[32] Catala, above n 20, 11 (see below p 465).

17

Reforming the French Law of Prescription: An English Perspective

JOHN CARTWRIGHT*

T
HE LAW OF prescription is not a topic on which comparative lawyers often focus. Such questions as why different legal systems might choose different prescription periods seem hardly to have a deep intellectual content. Whether two, three, five, ten or thirty years is the appropriate length of time for the period for prescription for a particular purpose seems to be a rather empty discussion.

Indeed, the English law on this subject is not a topic on which English lawyers (or, at least, our English law students) themselves focus sufficiently. There is a sense that it is a fringe topic which appears half-heartedly on our students' reading lists for each area of substantive law, often buried amongst the 'defences'. Our students have the idea that there is a rule that a right of action will in some sense be barred if the claimant delays too long; but that has the sound more of the law of procedure than of the real substance of the law of contract or tort: more for the practitioner than the student learning about substantive rights in private law. The reality, of course, is quite different. As with many issues of procedural law, there is a regrettable tendency to ignore their effect on substantive rights. And there are fundamental questions about the law of contract, tort and property which link directly into the law of prescription—or, rather, 'limitation of actions' as it exists within English law.

The approach taken in the current law in England—which is to be reformed if the Government ever gets round to implementing the Law Commission's recommendations made in 2001 (on which more will be said

---

* After completion of the manuscript the law of prescription in the Code civil has been substantially revised by the Loi no 2008-561 du 17 juin 2008 portant réforme de la prescription en matière civile, JO 18 June 2008, 9856. References to the Code civil in this chapter are to the pre-reform state of the law.

below)—is to focus on the *accrual of the cause of action*. Cases in which the fundamental issue was the running of the limitation period have forced the courts to focus on what constitutes the essential wrong giving rise to a claim: to determine the time of the accrual of the cause of action presupposes an understanding of the cause of action itself. For example, one needs to know what constitutes 'damage' for the purposes of an action in tort where as a result of defective design there is a physical change to a building (which therefore requires money to be spent on rectifying the defect) but where that change is not yet visible to the observer, and has not yet caused physical damage to any other item of property.[1] And the differences in the timing of accrual of causes of action in claims in contract and in certain torts (notably the tort of negligence) has been the breeding-ground for the development of the current approach in English law to the concurrence of actions in contract and tort. One of the most fundamental reasons for a claimant to wish to pursue an action in tort against a party with whom he has a contract (and where the act constituting the tort is also a breach of the contract) is because the tort action is still active when the contract action has become time-barred. This issue has forced the House of Lords to assess the proper relationship between contract and tort—to decide whether there is any objection in principle to allowing a claimant to use an action in tort to evade the policy reasons for barring the claim in contract; and their finding that there is no such objection in principle[2] increases the pressure for claimants to test the limits of tort in order to find remedies where their more obvious contract action can no longer succeed. These practical questions about whether a claimant will fail in an action to enforce his substantive rights just because of the passage of a particular period of time have direct consequences for the formulation of the claim to the rights in question, but also have consequences for the general development of the law in response to such issues being brought before the courts.

Questions of the application of the rules relating to time periods have also had the effect of focusing the French courts' minds on the dividing line between contract and tort. And so claimants who might be met with an objection that they had not brought their claim under a contract of sale within the requisite 'short time' will seek to bring their claim in tort.[3] Or in another case the claimant may seek to bring a claim in contract rather than tort because the longer limitation period of the general law is still available whereas the tort claim is now extinguished. In France the focus is sharper since the rule of *non cumul* means that there is in principle no concurrence of actions on the model now accepted in England—and so some funda-

---

[1] *Pirelli General Cable Works Ltd v Oscar Faber & Partners* [1983] 2 AC 1 (HL).
[2] *Henderson v Merrett Syndicates Ltd* [1995] 2 AC 145 (HL).
[3] Until 2005 an action under a contract of sale for rescission or reduction of price for certain defects in the goods had to be brought within a 'short period' (*bref délai*): art 1648 Cc. This was changed in 2005 to a period of two years from discovery of the defect.

mental questions of the proper characterisation of the contract/tort divide can arise out of a response to the differing prescription periods for the different actions.

From this one might take various starting-points for a consideration of the law of prescription—and, in particular, for a comparative view of the law. In the first place, one must look at the law of prescription within a legal system in the light of that system's substantive rights to which the pre-scription rules relate—or, put another way, a consideration of the approach to prescription might cast light on the substantive rights themselves. From that starting-point, one might therefore not necessarily expect a uniformity between legal systems in their rules of prescription, given that there are substantive differences to respect. On the other hand, the fact that all legal systems have a view that the passage of time must in some sense bar claims, and therefore all have some version of a law of prescription, points towards some convergence of the rules—at least in the sense that it is not obvious why one legal system would require a certain type of claim to be brought within a very short period (say, a year) and another legal system might allow an extremely long period (say, thirty years). Unless there is some other policy at play, under which the systems take fundamentally different views of the claimant/defendant balance (the system with the long prescrip-tion period seeking to give a greater scope of protection to its claimants in spite of their dilatory pursuit of potential claims), or has some other policy to encourage rather than discourage litigation, significant divergences seem undesirable.

In all of this one cannot avoid the hand of history: modern legal systems have devised their own particular approaches to prescription in the light of their own legal history. This might explain differences that are to be found in the current law. On the other hand, one cannot ignore the fact that there have been recent reviews of the law of prescription within various systems, and the natural thing these days is for reformers to take account of other legal systems. Comparative law, in some form or to some degree, has become a tool of the law reformer. We can see this within the *Avant-projet de réforme du droit des obligations et de la prescription* in relation most particularly to the proposals for the reform of the law of prescription. The Preamble to the section on prescription makes clear that aspects of the proposals for reform are inspired by the recent reforms of the German Civil Code and the proposals on prescription set out in the Principles of European Contract Law (PECL). For the English reader of the *Avant-projet*, however, it is also interesting to compare the Law Commission's proposals for the reform of English law in the field of limitation of actions. Indeed, the fact that there have been such proposals for reform in the several jurisdictions also raises some interesting general points of com-parison about the procedures for reform of the law.

I. SOME FUNDAMENTAL QUESTIONS (AND INSTINCTS?)
ABOUT THE LAW OF PRESCRIPTION

In any consideration of the law of prescription certain questions naturally arise. What is the scope of the law: is it concerned simply with the prevention of actions being brought after a certain time; or does the passage of time have the effect of changing the underlying right itself? Does it cover (and apply similarly to, or in different ways to) personal rights (and personal actions) and property rights (and property actions)? How absolute are the rules—for example, are the time periods fixed or can they be applied flexibly where the policies underlying them so require in the particular case, and in the light of the particular parties? Are they imposed as a matter of public policy, or can the parties themselves vary them by agreement? Can the running of time be interrupted—and, if so, what is the effect of such an interruption? What is the appropriate time period to set, and are there good reasons to set different periods for different purposes? And when does time start to run? We shall see some of the answers of the current (and proposed) law in France and in England to these questions later in this paper. Here we should first note some more general issues.

(a) Legal Instincts? Striking a Balance

That the passage of time has of itself an impact on civil law rights and remedies seems to be a matter of legal instinct. The Preamble to the section in the *Avant-projet* dealing with prescription states its importance in rather strong terms:

> More than any other doctrine, prescription marks man's relationship with time and with the law: it dominates all rules and all the law. Not only the law of obligations which forms its domain of choice, but also all other branches of the law, the whole of private law, public law, criminal law and the law of procedure.

Time changes things. On the practical level, it tends to reduce the availability and reliability of evidence. But on a more fundamental level, there is a balance to be struck between the parties whose rights are in issue: a claimant who has not pursued his rights might be held to have forfeited them, in the interests of the protection of the defendant who has been left undisturbed; yet is it right that without some formal change in the rights themselves, such as a formal release, the claimant should be held simply to have lost his rights by silence and inactivity? The instinct in favour of rules which allow the passage of time to have such an effect is strong: the need to temper legal rights and remedies in the light of the passage of time is obvious to most legal systems. But the details of such rules may differ depending on the rights in question—different rights might deserve different

protections against the passage of time, and in different circumstances. Just a brief glance at Roman law can give us some ideas about this.

(b) Roman Law: Instincts and Policies

The Roman lawyers saw the significance of the passage of time in relation, first, to title to property. As Gaius told us in the second century AD, it was already established by the time of the Twelve Tables in the fifth century BC that possession of property could mature into ownership after fixed time periods, through the doctrine of *usucapio*, although this had its limitations:[4]

> [O]nce *usucapio* is completed it becomes yours by full title. . . . Usucapion of movables is completed in one year, of lands and buildings in two: so the law of the Twelve Tables provides. We may also acquire by usucapion things which have been delivered to us by one who is not their owner . . . provided we have received them in good faith, believing the delivered to be their owner. This system appears to have been adopted in order to obviate the ownership of things being uncertain for too long, the periods of one or two years appointed for usucapion by the possessor being sufficient for the owner to seek out his property. But sometimes, though a man possess another's property in the best of faith, usucapion does not run in his favour, for example if he is in possession of a thing which has been stolen or taken by violence; for the law of the Twelve Tables forbids usucapion of a stolen thing, and the *L. Iulia et Plautia* that of a thing taken by violence . . .

So the passage of time ought as a matter of policy to give security of title to the possessor of property, who deserves to be preferred to the true owner as long as he took possession in good faith without notice of the defect in title. The time periods can differ between different types of property (two years for immovables, one year for movables), but the purpose of the time period is to strike a balance: to avoid uncertainty of ownership (in favour of the possessor) but to allow the true owner sufficient time to try to find his property and to assert his rights to it. Once it is complete, *usucapio* had the effect of vesting a new title in the possessor. But there were policies which tempered this—such as the rule that once an item of property has been stolen it cannot thereafter be usucapted by a possessor, even in good faith. The original owner's property rights should not be defeated in cases of theft—a rule which limited (in theory, at least) the usefulness of this doctrine for movables.[5] However, the *bona fide* possessor of land could

---

[4] *Inst Gai* 2.41–5. Translations are taken from F de Zulueta, *The Institutes of Gaius, Part I* (Oxford, Clarendon Press, 1946).

[5] *Inst Gai* 2.50: 'in the case of movables it does not readily happen that usucapion is open to their possessor in good faith, seeing that one who sells and delivers another's property commits theft'. In practice, this became a matter of the burden of proof: it would be for the original

more easily acquire title to it by the passage of time, since land could not in law be stolen—a rule which appears to have been aimed specifically at the rules of *usucapio*, to further a policy in favour of the *bona fide* possessor of land.[6] So, again, the operation of the rules relating to the passage of time varies between immovables and movables because of the different policies at play.

But as society changes, one can expect a development of the rules governing prescription. The time periods which were first fixed may no longer be appropriate. And one might even develop different views about the countervailing policies (such as whether the original owner should always be so categorically protected in the case of theft). By the sixth century AD the explanation of the rules of *usucapio* and its underlying policies had changed. After reciting the law which was set out by Gaius, Justinian's *Institutes* made clear that things have moved on:[7]

> Such was the decision of the ancients, who thought the times we have mentioned [one year for movables, two years for immovables] sufficient for owners to inquire after their property; but we have come to a much better decision from a wish to prevent owners being despoiled of their property too quickly, and to prevent the benefit of this mode of acquisition being confined to any particular locality. We have accordingly published a constitution providing that moveables shall be acquired by a use extending for three years, but immoveables by the 'possession of long time', that is, ten years for persons present, and twenty for persons absent; and that by these means, provided a just cause of possession precedes, the ownership of things may be acquired, not only in Italy, but in every country subject to our empire.

Moreover, the detail of the rules of prescription had been refined. For example, in the case of land, under the new doctrine of *longi temporis praescriptio*—'prescription of a long time'—successive periods of possession could be added together to make up the qualifying time period. And another doctrine, *longissimi temporis praescriptio*—'prescription of a very long time'—allowed the acquisition even of stolen property (and in

---

owner, asserting his rights after the passage of the year which would otherwise have deprived him of his ownership by *usucapio*, to show that the possessor had not acquired his property in good faith, or that it had been stolen: B Nicholas, *An Introduction to Roman Law* (Oxford, Clarendon Press, 1962) 123–4.

[6] *Inst Gai* 2.51: 'there is no obstacle to usucapion by a *bona fide* possessor, since the opinion once held that land can be stolen has been exploded'. The *squatter* would not be able to acquire title by *usucapio*, since he was not in good faith (he knew that he was taking possession of land to which he had no right). But the purchaser in good faith from the squatter was protected. This favours possessors of land in good faith who can therefore have a greater security that their belief in their title will be matched by legal reality and therefore encourages them to make proper use of the land, with only a time-limited risk of a 'true' owner being able to evict them.

[7] *Inst* 2.6 pr. The translation is taken from TC Sandars, *The Institutes of Justinian* (7th edn, Longmans Green, London, 1883).

circumstances where there were other defects negativing *usucapio*) after thirty or forty years.[8]

One can also notice that Roman law did not take a consistent view of the significance of the passage of time on property rights. *Usucapio* was a form of acquisitive prescription: a new title was created to replace the former owner's title which was extinguished. But when the newer form of 'possession for a long time' was introduced it was first seen as simply barring the civil law owner's rights to assert his title—a form of limitation of actions, rather than extinctive or acquisitive prescription. But in due course the view prevailed that the passage of the necessary time in all cases created a new title.[9]

Moreover, it did not seem self-evident to Roman lawyers that the right to bring a *personal* action should itself be time-limited, or that personal rights should themselves be extinguished by a passage of time. Some actions had a limitation period of a year, but it was only in the fifth century AD that a general limitation period of thirty years was introduced.[10] So the instinct of the Roman lawyers was to see that the possession of property deserved protection by reference to time; and that, within this, the acquisition of immovable property required a longer period than movable property; and that the consequence of time should be allow possession to mature into ownership. Personal claims eventually had limitation periods, too.

(c) English Law: Instincts and Policies

The instinctive starting-points of English lawyers are not very different. The first limitation periods were developed for land-related actions.[11] Fixed *dates* were used first.[12] The first fixed *periods* for land actions (sixty, fifty and thirty years for different land actions) were set by the Act of Limitation in 1540. Non-land actions were first given limitation periods in the Limitation Act 1623, and it was at this time that the main limitation period of six years was introduced but with many exceptions (different periods for some actions, and no period at all for others). It should be noted that in most cases the approach of English law was to use limitation periods to bar *actions*, even in the case of property claims, rather than to create new rights. English law did not develop the general notion of acquis-

---

[8] Nicholas, above n 5, 128–9; WW Buckland, *A Text-book of Roman Law* (3rd edn by P Stein, Cambridge University Press, 1963) 249–52.

[9] Nicholas, above n 5, 128.

[10] Nicholas, above n 5, 122; Buckland, above n 8, 689–90.

[11] For an account of the history of the law of limitation of actions in England, see Law Commission, 'Limitation of Actions', Consultation Paper No 151 (HMSO, 1998) paras 1.6–1.21.

[12] The day of Henry I's death in 1135 was the date used until a new date—Henry II's coronation in 1154—replaced it in 1235. Other particular dates were later substituted by statute.

itive prescription after the manner of the Roman *usucapio*, perhaps because
the approach to property rights was different from the civilian systems:
English law did not recognise ownership (*dominium*) of land, instead
basing title on relative possession (or 'seisin'). Losing a right of action based
on one's former possession was sufficient to leave the present possessor
with an enforceable right because his (factual) possession was sufficient to
give him an action against others, including anyone who sought to dis-
possess him.[13] That said, since 1833 the statutory provisions dealing with
limitation of land actions have provided that the effect of the passing of the
limitation period is not simply to bar the action but also to extinguish the
right. But it did not of itself create a new title to the land—although in
other contexts (easements and profits à prendre) English law has developed
acquisitive prescription.[14] In the more modern case, however, of registered
land, the effect of the passing of time is not to extinguish the former
owner's rights but to effect a transfer of them to the person who has
possessed the property adversely to the registered owner for the required
length of time, although under the most recent reform the mere passage of
time—however long—does not of itself either extinguish the registered
proprietor's title or confer any title on the possessor.[15] In England the
policy in favour of the registered proprietor of land (and, correspondingly,
against the squatter) is now at its all-time high. But it is also, in consequence, less open to challenge under the European Convention on Human
Rights.[16]

II. THE PRESSURES FOR REFORM IN MODERN FRENCH LAW AND ENGLISH LAW

(a) Problems in the Existing French Law

In the Preamble to the proposals of the *Avant-projet* on prescription,
Philippe Malaurie states the case for reform in unequivocal terms: 'In

---

[13] Nicholas, above n 5, 121.

[14] EH Burn and J Cartwright, *Cheshire and Burn's Modern Law of Real Property* (17th edn, Oxford University Press, 2006) 116, 616–28, 650–51.

[15] *Ibid*, 143–8. Not all estates in land are yet registered. Under the Land Registration Act 1925 the expiry of the limitation period (twelve years' adverse possession) resulted in the registered owner holding his title on trust for the new owner. Under the Land Registration Act 2002, however, the passing of time does not of itself change the rights to the land, but ten years' adverse possession gives a squatter the right to apply to be registered as the substitute owner but this can be resisted by the registered proprietor, and the squatter can only be registered if the proprietor is dilatory and allows him to remain in possession for a further two years. This significantly limits the possibility of a registered owner losing his title by adverse possession.

[16] The European Court of Human Rights first held that the regime relating to registered land before the reforms contained in the Land Registration Act 2002 was incompatible with art 1 of the First Protocol (deprivation of possessions): *JA Pye (Oxford) Ltd v UK* (App no 44302/02)

the view of everyone, the existing regime of prescription in civil matters possesses three essential defects of an equal seriousness': the excessive length of the prescription periods; the multiplicity of periods; and uncertainty and inconsistency as regards many of the rules governing the prescription regime. As a result,

> the law of prescription, which ought to contribute to the making of peace in human relations and support their dynamism, has become an abundant source of litigation.

Some of the details of the existing law and its problems have been high-lighted in Robert Wintgen's chapter.[17] The reader of the Preamble in the *Avant-projet* is left in no doubt that the most fundamental general objection to the present law is its complexity, and those of its features which tend to increase dispute and litigation. The first stated defect is the excessive length of the primary prescription period—thirty years. This of itself leaves claims open too long. But it is tempered by other shorter periods which in practice cut down the period; but then this is itself a defect in that it immediately increases the complexity of the law and so reduces its clarity and utility. Philippe Malaurie does not mince his words about the sheer complexity of the law:

> [T]his state of affairs has been called really chaotic and even a shambles, and it provides a basis for disregarding the law and a source of muddles and interminable arguments.

On one point that is sometimes criticised, however, no excuse is given—and no proposal is made for reform: the fact that prescription is both extinctive and acquisitive. In other words, the legal regime governing the law of prescription should continue to embrace both the extinction of actions, and the acquisition of rights to property. In consequence, the texts proposed by the *Avant-projet* retain the structure already contained in the Code—and rules governing both the nature and significance of *possession* of property are intermingled with rules governing the time after which actions (both generally, and actions to enforce specific kinds of rights) will be extinguished.

But an overriding purpose of the reform is to modernise the law on prescription; not simply to remove complexity and the potentiality for dispute, but to examine what a modern law of prescription should contain—and this involves departing from the models which have been inherited from history where they no longer represent the modern way of

---

(2006) 43 EHRR 3, but the Grand Chamber later reversed this by a majority of ten votes to seven: (2008) 46 EHRR 45.

[17] R Wintgen, 'The Reform of the French Law of Prescription: a French Perspective', see ch 16 above.

business (and so, for example, a thirty-year prescription period for the
extinction of actions is simply not appropriate in modern dealings), but
also bringing French law broadly into line with other modern legal systems.
As we have noted, the model is the German reform and the PECL.[18] But it
would equally well have been possible to look across to the proposals of
the English Law Commission, whose reasoning proceeds on many points
broadly in parallel with these other proposals for reform.

(b) Problems in the Existing English Law

The English Law Commission produced a Consultation Paper in 1998[19]
and a final Report recommending changes to the law on limitation of
actions in 2001.[20] The need for reform was stated by the Law Commission
in its Consultation Paper[21] in terms that are not far removed from those
that inspire the reform proposals of the *Avant-projet*: the English law on
limitation is 'incoherent' (it has developed in an ad hoc way over
centuries), 'needlessly complex' (a multiplicity of periods for different types
of action, and many complicated provisions relating to particular types of
case[22]), 'outdated' (time periods that are no longer appropriate in the
modern law), 'uncertain' (there are unsettled questions about the interpretation of some of the rules, and judicial discretion to override limitation
periods adds uncertainty), 'unfair' (the current law does not provide an
acceptable balance between certainty and justice) and 'wastes costs' (the
defects listed above result in unnecessary litigation). The Law Commission
reviewed the law—it took them 159 pages to set out the then current
law[23]—and formed the provisional view that[24]

> there should be a fundamental reform of the law of limitations in order to produce
> a modern code which is, so far as possible, simple, coherent, fair, up-to-date,
> clear and cost-effective.

This reform was proposed in its final form in the Report in 2001.

---

[18] Above p 361.
[19] Law Commission, above n 11.
[20] Law Commission, 'Limitation of Actions' (Law Com No 270, HMSO, 2001).
[21] Law Commission, above n 11, paras 11.1–11.14.
[22] The most common limitation period is six years from the accrual of the cause of action (tort,
breach of contract, sums recoverable by statute, distress of rent, action to enforce judgment), but
this is varied for personal injuries (three years from discoverability), negligence other than
personal injuries (later of six years from accrual and three years from discoverability but subject
to long-stop of fifteen years from breach of duty), defective products (three years from later of
accrual and discoverability but subject to a ten-year long-stop), claims for contribution (two
years from right to recover contribution), breach of contract where the contract was executed as
a deed (twelve years) and actions to recover land or by a mortgagor to redeem the mortgage
against the mortgagee in possession (twelve years).
[23] Law Commission, above n 11, Section A.
[24] *Ibid*, para 11.15.

It has already been noted that the English approach is to treat time as barring actions, rather than extinguishing rights (a law of limitation of actions, rather than of prescription); and that even in relation to land English law traditionally considered the passage of time as only extinguishing the former owner's title rather than creating a new title. One must raise a doubt about the proposal in the *Avant-projet* to continue the French approach to the unity of acquisitive and extinctive prescriptions. Roman law saw the rules relating to the acquisition of property through possession for a passage of time as quite separate from the rules (developed later and separately) for limitation of actions.[25] But the development of the English approach to this question is also illuminating. Although the history of limitation periods shows that land was covered first, English law was able to unify the rules relating to land and to other actions because in all cases— whether land, other property or personal actions—the English approach was to consider whether time should bar the claimant being able to pursue his action. And even though English law has gone further in relation to land, and developed the view that the action is extinguished (and therefore the title to land is extinguished) by the expiry of the limitation period, the essentially negative effect of the passage of time has given a unity to the rules relating to property and other actions in English law. The current statute on limitation periods, the Limitation Act 1980, therefore contains provisions relating to all kinds of actions, including actions relating to land. However, under the modern system of registered conveyancing, things have moved on. The effect of the expiry of the limitation period is no longer to extinguish title in relation to registered land. Since its effects are different, it is appropriate to remove the provisions from the general rules on limitation of actions, and to place them in the statutory context in which they belong—the Land Registration Act.[26] One should also notice that, although the English provisions in relation to actions relating to personal property are contained within the general provisions for limitation of actions, this is appropriate because English law protects such rights not by property actions (there is no *vindicatio*) but through the law of tort. An action to reclaim personal property (a chattel) is an action in the tort of conversion; and if the action is not brought within the prescribed limitation period (currently six years) it becomes too late to do so, and the title to the chattel is extinguished—thus (as in the case of the old land law rules) leaving the possessor unchallengeable in his possession.[27]

---

[25] Above p 365.

[26] Above, text to nn 15–16.

[27] Limitation Act 1980, s 3. In the case of stolen property, the thief can be sued in tort without any limitation period; but the claim against a third party is barred—and the claimant's title to the chattel is extinguished—six years after the first sale of the chattel to a purchaser in good faith: s 4.

III. THE PROPOSALS OF THE *AVANT-PROJET*—AND SOME
ENGLISH LAW COMPARISONS

There is not sufficient space here to discuss all aspects of the proposals in the *Avant-projet* in relation to the law of prescription. Some general issues about the reform proposals, and some particular proposals, will be mentioned—where appropriate drawing comparisons with English law, either the present law or the law as it would be if reformed in accordance with the Law Commission's proposals.

(a) Overview: A 'Limited Reform'?

The Preamble to the section of the *Avant-projet* on prescription states that this is not simply a 'limited reform'—but this is in relation to the complexity of the limitation periods.[28] One possibility would have been just to reduce the existing period of thirty years to ten and leave the rest of the law untouched. The *Avant-projet* is certainly more radical than that. However, it should be noted that the reform is limited in another respect: it reforms or replaces just those particular articles of the Code which present problems, and retains as much as possible of the structure and language of the existing provisions. Within Title XX, Chapters I (General Provisions), II (Possession), III (The Grounds on which Prescription is Impeded) are changed only incidentally. The other chapters, which relate to the substance of the proposed reforms, are amended, but always in as limited a way as possible. And there is deliberately no radical amendment to the positioning of the section on prescription within the Code, or the general coverage of the provisions (retaining the extinctive and acquisitive prescriptions within the single regime).[29] The only significant change of positioning is to remove to the section on civil liability the provision governing prescription of actions claiming civil liability,[30] which follows the practice in certain other cases of placing the rules relating to prescription of particular actions within the sections of the Code dealing with those actions.[31] However, this approach is not followed consistently.[32]

[28] P Malaurie, 'Exposé des motifs' in *Avant-projet de réforme du droit des obligations et de la prescription: Rapport remis au garde des Sceaux* (Paris, La documentation française, 2006) 193, 195 (see below pp 881, 885).

[29] *Ibid*, 194 (see below p 883-5).

[30] Art 1384 of the *Avant-projet*, moved from art 2270-1 Cc.

[31] Eg art 1304 Cc (actions claiming nullity for defect of consent); arts 1130 (actions for absolute and relative nullity), 1162-1 (obligation to make restitution following annulment or retroactive termination) of the *Avant-projet*.

[32] Art 2275 of the *Avant-projet* includes the ten-year prescription period for actions claiming civil liability for personal injury (whereas art 1384 has the general rule that actions claiming civil liability become prescribed after ten years commencing from the manifestation of the harm or its getting worse). And the prescription period for the decennial guarantee of building work is placed in art 2275 rather than with the primary provisions in arts 1792 to 1792-2 Cc.

(b) Limitation Periods

The three core issues for any regime of prescription or limitation of actions are the period of time that is necessary for the action to be barred (or, in the case of acquisitive prescription, for the right to be acquired); the time at which the period begins to run; and whether the period can be suspended or interrupted (ie the acts or facts which will either delay the running of the period or stop it—whether or not it then allows a period to start running again). First, we consider the time period; and then the starting-point and suspensions and interruptions.

The most obvious objection to the existing law on prescription in France is the excessive length of its principal (default) prescription period—thirty years. The *Avant-projet* proposes to reduce this to three years.[33] This is a radical reduction, which the Preamble recognises might be rather a surprise:[34] 'would not moving from thirty years to three years mean going from one extreme to another?'; and will not command universal approval: 'a reform of this breadth relies on the existence of great political courage for it will be met with an outcry of opposition'. But this is explained, justified and nuanced. The explanation is that in the modern world, in particular in the light of more rapid commercial transactions, three years is a sensible period for most actions; thirty years is outdated. It is justified by reference to the fact that the other legal systems and rules which are considered as comparable by the contributors to the *Avant-Projet* have also selected a three-year primary prescription period: the choice for the French Reform Proposals is explicitly 'inspired' by the similar provision in the reforms of the German Civil Code and the PECL. And there has to be a firm decision on a single default period (and three years is the best such period) in order to insist on simplification of the law. The choice of a three-year period is also nuanced because in fact there is no suggestion that there must be a single three-year period for all cases. Some situations are to be kept out of the new regime altogether.[35] And within the new regime there are in fact to be three periods: three years is the default period; but there are certain special situations for which three years is too short and ten years is to be the default period.[36] But even beyond this for all actions there are to be prescription periods of ten or thirty years from the circumstances which gave rise to the obligation—which act as long-stop prescription

[33] Art 2274.

[34] Malaurie, above n 28, 195, 196 (see below pp 887, 889).

[35] Art 2277 of the *Avant-projet* (this includes rules found in other Codes, and international treaties and rules of the European Union, but also 'periods equal to or lower then six months during which an action must be brought or a right exercised on pain of its extinction'—so existing short prescription periods are unaffected).

[36] Arts 2275 (civil liability for personal injury or loss caused by barbarism; actions claiming absolute nullity; enforcement of court decisions; the decennial guarantee of building works), 2276 (the *acquisitive* prescription period for immovable property: see further below pp 372–3).

periods where the default prescription period has not yet expired because there has been a delay in the starting-point or in the running of the period which would otherwise apply.[37]

Some complexity is therefore to be retained. But this is inevitable. The choice of a three-year primary default period is in keeping with the German reform. But it reflects the spirit of the times in that the English Law Commission also proposed a default three-year limitation period, and a long-stop period of ten years from the date on which the cause of action accrues or the date of the act or omission which gives rise to the claim.[38] But there are still further variations to these general rules in the case of certain particular types of claim. The details vary between the various reforms and reform proposals. But there is a general trend of convergence between them; and this is not surprising because the national reforms are responding to an inherited complexity in the multiple periods for pre-scription or limitation; and there are common points of reference amongst them. The French proposals refer to the German reforms and the PECL; but the German reforms were themselves built on the work of the PECL, and the English Law Commission in preparing its Consultation Paper considered the law of other jurisdictions—mostly other common law juris-dictions but including the proposals (as they then still were) for the reform of the German law.[39]

In the French and the English reform proposals there are some common underlying policies, not only in relation to the core period of three years, but also in seeing exceptions for certain types of interest—in particular, damages for personal injuries and interests in land. The *Avant-projet* proposes to retain the unified regime for both extinctive prescription (actions) and acquisitive prescription (property). But it is recognised that land must then be treated differently within the regime. Although the general rule for recovery of movables falls in line with the general rules for prescription, and is based on a three-year period,[40] such a period would be far too short for land. The principal proposal is therefore for an acquisitive prescription period of ten years, although a variant is offered: twenty years, but reduced to ten in favour of a possessor who acquired the property in good faith and under a transaction which on its face would transfer

---

[37] Art 2278 (ten years is the long-stop period except in case of civil liability for personal injury or loss caused by barbarism, where the period is thirty years. For crimes against humanity there is no prescription).

[38] The periods in the Law Commission's proposals (both the primary period and the long-stop period) were reached after a consideration of a range of possible lengths, see above n 11, paras 12.88–12.96, 12.109–12.113; but they acknowledged in discussing the primary period that 'the exact period to be chosen is obviously to some extent arbitrary': *ibid*, para 12.94.

[39] Law Commission, above n 11, Part X. The discussion of the German proposals for reform is at paras 10.168–10.173.

[40] Art 2279 of the *Avant-projet*.

ownership.[41] English law, too, allows claims for personal property to be subject to the same general limitation period as personal actions,[42] but regards land as deserving of special protection. The lengthier periods of adverse possession which were used in the old law were reduced over time, but still to give a longer period for actions to recover land (twelve years' adverse possession) than actions in respect of other claims (the core period is presently six years). The Law Commission proposed that the period for land actions be reduced to ten years.[43]

(c) The Starting-point for the Running of the Period

The length of the period, however, is only half the picture. It cannot be separated from the question of the time at which the period starts to run—and whether the period, once running, can be halted temporarily. Both the English and the French proposals for reform would change the law in this area, and would simplify it and improve it.

The starting-point for the current English law is that, in general, limitation periods begin to run when the cause of action accrues: that is, when a claim could first be made for its enforcement—which means, for example, when the damage occurs which completes the cause of action in a claim in negligence; but at the moment of breach in the case of a claim for breach of contract, since damage is not necessary for the cause of action to be complete. This has been seen as unfair to claimants in cases in which they could not reasonably have discovered their claim before the limitation period had already started—or had even already expired. Piecemeal reform was made to this rule over the years, in response to particular problems as they arose; and so in 1975 a reform was made to provide that in many cases of claims for damages for personal injuries, the limitation period should be not the usual six years from the cause of action accruing, but three years from the date on which the injured person had knowledge that his injury was significant, that the injury was attributable to the defendant's breach of duty, and of the defendant's identity—a shorter limitation period, but one which would only begin to run when it was discoverable by the claimant.[44] Similarly, in 1986 the period for claims for damages in the tort of negligence (other than for personal injury) was extended in cases where a period of three years from the discoverability of the elements necessary for his claim would lead to a period longer than the normal six-year period—but at the same time subject to a long-stop period of fifteen years

[41] Art 2276. The variant is in substance the Roman doctrine of the acquisition *bona fide* and *iusta causa* within *usucapio*.
[42] Above n 28.
[43] Since that Report there has now already been a change to the limitation rules for *registered* land: above n 15.
[44] Limitation Act 1975, s 1; now found in Limitation Act 1980, s 11.

from the act or omission giving rise to the claim.[45] These two reforms paved the way for the general approach of the Law Commission in its review of the law—and their Report in 2001 recommended a fundamental change to the general rule governing the starting-point of the time period. Time should no longer run as a general rule from the date on which the cause of action accrues, but instead should start only when the claimant could have discovered it: and this then allows the general period to be reduced from six years to three years. But there is also to be a long-stop limitation period of ten years from the date on which (generally) the action accrued—except for certain cases such as claims for personal injury where the long-stop period does not apply but the court is instead to be given a discretion to disapply the three-year primary limitation period.

The current French approach is different. The case-law has devised a rule that the starting point for the running of time for prescription is the day when the creditor can act,[46] an application of the maxim *contra non valentem agere non currit praescriptio* (prescription does not run against a person who is unable to act). However, what constitutes being 'able to act' depends on the nature of the action. In the case of a claim in delict there is a special rule[47] that the action becomes prescribed after ten years from the manifestation of the harm or its getting worse—and so the special ten-year period for extra-contractual civil liability has an inbuilt rule which delays the starting-point for the running of the period until the harm becomes manifest. However, in other cases, such as claims in contract, the time within which the creditor is able to act is the time within which his rights accrue,[48] which does not of itself depend on the state of knowledge of the claimant. So it would at first sight appear that time can run against the claimant even when he does not realise that he has a claim. However, in such cases French law moves this latter issue into the *suspensions* of the prescription period. Applying the principle that prescription does not run against a person who is unable to act, the period will be suspended when the creditor cannot act as a result of *force majeure*—which in this context has been interpreted by the case-law as including the case where the creditor is unaware of his right to act, as long as his ignorance has a legitimate cause.[49] In effect, then, the ignorance of the claimant, as long has he should not have discovered the truth, suspends the running of the prescription period. This seems to be a rather complicated way of achieving

[45] Limitation Act 1980, ss 14A, 14B, inserted by Latent Damage Act 1986.

[46] P Malaurie, L Aynès and P Stoffel-Munck, *Les Obligations* (2nd edn, Defrénois, Paris, 2005) no 1207.

[47] Art 2270-1 Cc, introduced by an amendment in 1985. The Cour de cassation had already held that the period in the case of an action in delict runs from the date when the victim could actually have been aware of the action giving rise to the harm: JurisClasseur Civil Code, arts 1382–1386, Fasc 222, *Régime de la réparation*, nos 166–7.

[48] JurisClasseur, above n 47, no 168.

[49] Malaurie et al, above n 46, no 1215. Ignorance of the law is not legitimate.

the result, but the use of suspension to delay from the outset the running of the prescription period in the case of the creditor's ignorance of his rights, rather than providing that the period has not yet started to run, is adopted by the PECL.[50]

The *Avant-projet* articulates some of these rules and reforms others. The basic rules that have been created by the case-law are to be written into the Code,[51] another example of the reform being used to bring the terms of the Code up to date. But time is not to run, or is suspended, for as long as the debtor is unaware of the existence or extent of the right against him.[52] And the rule of the current law under which an action for extra-contractual liability runs from the manifestation of the harm or its getting worse is to be extended to all cases of liability, to encompass claims in contract as well as in tort.[53]

(d) Suspensions and Interruptions

In addition to the case of suspension just mentioned—and which applies generally to any case where the claimant is unable to act owing to an impediment caused by legislation, a contract or *force majeure*[54]—the *Avant-projet* contains various provisions for suspension of the prescription period (which can then begin to run again when the cause of suspension ceases) or its interruption (which cancels the prescription and sets time running again).[55] The proposals are designed to simplify the existing (very complex) law in these areas. Some of the provisions which it maintains will be familiar to an English lawyer (and, indeed, lawyers in any jurisdiction), such as rules suspending the running of time against minors and those under a legal incapacity, although some points will not be familiar—such as the rule that time is suspended while the parties negotiate in good faith,[56] although for the French, as for the English, the issue of proceedings to

---

[50] Arts 14:203, 14:301.

[51] Arts 2262 ('The starting point for the running of time for prescription is the day when the creditor can act') and 2266 ('Time runs against a person who does not find it impossible to act owing to an impediment caused by legislation, a contract or *force majeure*').

[52] Art 2264.

[53] Art 1384, replacing art 2270-1 Cc (above n 47). This change is made deliberately to eliminate the distinction between contractual and extra-contractual liability: see the note which introduces art 1384 in the *Avant-projet*.

[54] This is a broader ground of suspension than accepted under English law or the Law Commission's proposals for reform, but (particularly in relation to *force majeure*) it fits well with the general French approach to permanent and temporary impossibility. A limitation contained in the *Avant-projet*—that temporary *force majeure* can suspend prescription only if it occurs within the last six months of the period—art 2266(2)—is novel, but is simply based on the German provisions: Malaurie, above n 28, 199 (see below p 897). It is also in art 14:303 PECL.

[55] Arts 2257–2271.

[56] Art 2264. Art 14:304 PECL contains a different rule, which delays the expiry of the period to one year after the last communication made in the parties' negotiations.

enforce the right is an event that interrupts (and does not merely suspend) prescription.[57]

(e) The Place of the Court and of the Parties

Two rules are proposed to regulate the relationship between the court and the parties. Prescription is a matter for the parties—its effect is relative to the parties and the court may not raise a plea of prescription on its own initiative.[58] And the parties are not only free to decide whether to take the point when it arises in litigation, but may also renounce the benefit of a completed prescription, and may agree to shorten or lengthen an extinctive prescription period. However, the freedom of contract here is limited: it may not be reduced below a year, nor extended to more than ten years.[59] This idea of giving a limited freedom to vary the period is found in the PECL[60] although there the limits are one year and thirty years (not ten years). The approach of the English Law Commission is, at first sight, more liberal, since their proposals would allow the parties a general freedom to contract out of the legislative limitation periods, although this is limited in certain particular cases—and any term which sought to vary a limitation period would have to satisfy the 'reasonableness' test of the Unfair Contract Terms Act 1977.[61]

IV. HARMONISATION OF THE LAW OF PRESCRIPTION?

One thing which emerges from a consideration of this topic is that there is a tendency in the modern European context to harmonise the law of prescription. This is an area where the work of the Commission on European Contract Law is having an impact: where there is a dissatisfaction within one of the European legal systems about an area on which the Commission has already reviewed the law of the several European legal systems on the topic and has proposed a text in the PECL,[62] there is a natural tendency to look at the PECL for inspiration. The *Avant-projet* does this explicitly— although it also (and even more so) draws inspiration from the recent German reform of the law on the subject. But the German reform in its

---

[57] Art 2260.
[58] Art 2238.
[59] Art 2235.
[60] Art 14:601.
[61] Law Commission, above n 20, paras 3.170–3.175. The current English law on this issue is unclear, but it seems likely that the courts would uphold a clause which reduces or extends the existing statutory periods.
[62] For the discussion in relation to prescription and limitation of actions, see the Comments and Notes in O Lando, E Clive, A Prüm and R Zimmermann, *Principles of European Contract Law, Part III* (The Hague, Kluwer Law International, 2003) ch 14.

final drafting was also inspired by the work contained in the PECL.[63] The English Law Commission, which did not yet have the benefit of the published PECL, also considered the current position in other systems in its own researches, not only common law systems but also French and German law and, in particular, the proposals for reform which were then being discussed in Germany.

There may be various reasons for this trend towards harmonisation in this area. There are some particular limitation periods in Directives affecting private law which therefore introduce common ideas into the separate systems. Most obviously, perhaps, the Directive on Defective Products[64] contained a mandatory limitation period of three years from the day on which the plaintiff became aware, or should reasonably have become aware, of the damage, the defect and the identity of the producer; and a long-stop period of ten years from the date on which the producer put into circulation the actual product that caused the damage.[65] The idea of using periods which run from a date of 'knowledge' or 'discoverability', coupled with a long-stop period to protect a defendant against open-ended claims which only come to light after a very long time, has been introduced in England in relation to claims in negligence for latent damage (other than personal injuries)[66] and has been picked up by the PECL[67] and now the *Avant-projet*.[68]

The details of the limitation rules will not, however, necessarily be identical. There is no single 'right' answer to whether the long-stop should be ten years or some other lengthy period.[69] Or whether the long-stop should apply in all jurisdictions to all causes of action or whether, for example, the policy in relation to particular claims (such as personal injuries) might be viewed within some jurisdictions as deserving of protection by a longer limitation period or even none.[70] Or the scope of the freedom of

---

[63] *Ibid*, 161, n 6.

[64] Council Directive (EEC) 85/374 of 25 July 1985 on the approximation of the laws, regulations and administrative provisions of the Member States concerning liability for defective products [1985] OJ L/210/29.

[65] *Ibid*, arts 10, 11.

[66] Latent Damage Act 1986; above, n 45. The Law Reform Committee, proposing the Act, mentioned the (then draft) long-stop provisions of the Directive on Defective Products, but noted that a long-stop had already been proposed or considered (but rejected) in relation to claims for personal injury by earlier reform committees in 1949 and 1974: Law Reform Committee 24th Report (Cmnd 9390, 1984) paras 4.10, n 13; 4.13. They also noted that an analogy is found in the Scottish twenty-year period of long negative prescription: Prescription and Limitation (Scotland) Act 1973, s 7.

[67] Art 14:307.

[68] Art 2278.

[69] Law Reform Committee 24th Report, above n 66, para 4.13, considered a range of periods, and thought that the ten-year long-stop in the draft Directive on Defective Products was probably too short; that twenty years would probably be too long, and so they settled on fifteen years. But in its recent deliberations the Law Commission rejected this and decided on the ten-year standard period: above n 38.

[70] The long-stop for claims for personal injury is thirty years under art 2278 of the *Avant-*

the parties to vary the statutory periods.[71] Or the effect of the parties' negotiations on the running of the period.[72] Or whether the court should have an overriding discretion to disapply the statutory periods.[73] And the policies in favour of claims for property, and the differentiation between personal property and land, may vary amongst jurisdictions, at least in part because of variations in *other* rules in the systems' regimes relating to property—how property rights are acquired and transferred. And there may well be differences in the consequences of completed time periods: for example, the distinction between the operation of time periods as defences to claims (limitation of actions) and their extinction of the substantive rights (extinctive prescription), based on the traditional answer to this question in the separate legal systems. But what appears clear from the present comparison is that there is a trend towards a similar approach to the passing of time, and even (broadly) to the periods of time which are appropriate in particular contexts, in jurisdictions which, having decided that their own rules—weighed down with the consequences of history—are unsatisfactory, engage in reform to meet modern needs.

V. POSTSCRIPT: THE PROPOSALS FOR THE REFORM OF THE LAW OF PRESCRIPTION AS AN ILLUSTRATION OF DIFFERENT APPROACHES TO LAW REFORM

The fact that there are such close parallels between the proposals for reform of the French law on prescription in the *Avant-projet* and the English Law Commission's proposals for reform of the law on limitation of actions offers an opportunity to take a slightly wider view of the comparisons between the methodology of law reform in the two jurisdictions.

The approach in England is for proposals to be brought forward by the Law Commission, a body established by statute (the Law Commissions Act 1965). The Commission's website gives details of their make-up and resources:[74]

> There are five Commissioners, all of whom work full-time at the Commission. The Chairman is a High Court judge, appointed to the Commission for up to three years. The other four Commissioners are experienced judges, barristers, solicitors or teachers of law. They are appointed by the Lord Chancellor and Secretary of State for Justice for up to five years, although their appointments may

---

projet, and art 14:307 PECL; under the English Law Commission proposals the normal ten-year long-stop would not apply to personal injury claims, and the court has a discretion to disapply the normal period of three years from discoverability.

[71] Above p 376.

[72] Above p 375.

[73] The Law Commission, after some debate, included a (structured) discretion in its proposals: Law Commission, above n 20, paras 3.156–3.169.

[74] See generally http://www.lawcom.gov.uk.

be extended. They are supported by the Chief Executive of the Commission and about 20 other members of the Government Legal Service, four or five Parliamentary Counsel (who draft the Bills to reform and consolidate the law), and about 15 research assistants (usually recently qualified law graduates), as well as a librarian and the Corporate Services Team.

The Commission may be invited by a Government department to undertake a review of a particular topic, or they may propose topics for consideration themselves—but a project must be approved before it is taken forward. Again, the Law Commission's own statement is:

> The Law Commissions Act 1965 requires the Commission to submit 'programmes for the examination of different branches of the law' to the Lord Chancellor for his approval before undertaking new work. Before making his decision, the Lord Chancellor invites the comments of the Ministerial Committee on the Law Commission.
>
> Before deciding which projects to take forward, the Law Commission takes views from judges, lawyers, Government Departments and the general public. For any programme of law reform the Commissioners must weigh up concerns about limited resources with competing claims for attention.

The project to reform the law on limitation of actions, 'with a view to its simplification and rationalisation', was proposed by the Law Commission to the Lord Chancellor in 1995.[75] The project was approved, and the Commission produced a Consultation Paper in 1998[76] and after public consultation the final Report was published in 2001.[77] The Government accepted the recommendations in principle in July 2002, but has not yet found time to finalise the legislation and bring it forward.

This procedure contrasts with the *Avant-projet*—but in a way that illustrates not only the difference in lawmaking but also the different significance that is given to the academic community in France. The *Avant-projet* was received by the Minister of Justice, but was not sponsored by the French Government in the way in which Law Commission projects are sponsored. It was put together by an eminent group of lawyers, mainly academics, but was a private initiative of the group, co-ordinated by Professor Pierre Catala. Its strength and significance derives from those who took part in the project and prepared it—in effect, this is a reform project driven by *la doctrine* (the academic community). The stages in the progress of the proposals for reform are clearly different, too: in the case of the *Avant-projet*, there was consultation amongst the group themselves in producing the proposals, and once published it is now being subjected to

---

[75] Law Commission, Sixth Programme of Law Reform (Law Com No 234, HSMO, 1995), 28.
[76] Law Commission, above n 11.
[77] Law Commission, above n 20. The Report lists at Appendix B the list of people and organisations who commented on the Consultation Paper, divided into members of the judiciary (10), academic lawyers (14), practitioners: barristers (23) and solicitors (20), government departments (13), doctors (26), individuals (14), insurers (10) and other organisations (48).

public discussion and consultation. Interest groups are now adding their own voice to the proposals for reform.[78] But they are responding to the final version of the working group—not being consulted during the formulation of the proposals. It should also be noticed that the scale of the Law Commission's work is larger: not simply in that it involves two separate stages (Consultation Paper and final Report), but also that each document is in itself far more detailed than the Preamble to the *Avant-projet* in its explanation of what is proposed, and why.[79]

There are clearly merits on both sides. On the English side, however, one might observe that the text of a final report is more final—it has already been subject to a process of consultation and therefore many of the likely objections can already have been anticipated and dealt with. It is also published with a draft Bill which, being drafted by one of the Parliamentary Draftsmen seconded to the Law Commission, is quite likely to form an acceptable basis for the introduction of legislation. In a sense, by working from within the system (albeit as an independent agency) the Law Commission ought to be well placed to effect its proposals. That said, however, there is a notable lack of speed in implementing Law Commission Reports—and the Report on limitation of actions illustrates this well: it was accepted by the Government in principle in 2002, but parliamentary time has not yet been found to bring forward legislation.[80] The English lawyer will watch with interest the speed of response to the proposals contained in the *Avant-projet de réforme*—and their implementation?[81]

---

[78] Eg reports have been published by the *Chambre de commerce et d'industrie de Paris*; and institutions representing the profession of *avocat* (*Conseil National des Barreaux, Ordre des avocats de Paris* and *Conférence des Bâtonniers*). See also the proceedings of a colloquium on the *Avant-projet* published in issue 1/2006 of the Revue des contrats.

[79] The Consultation Paper ran to 415 pages; the Report (excluding the draft Bill) to 220 pages.

[80] It was announced in Parliament on 9 January 2007 that the Department for Constitutional Affairs would 'consult in spring 2007 on the detailed content of a draft Bill to implement the Law Commission's recommendations.': Hansard HL vol 688 col WS8 (9 January 2007).

[81] For steps which have been taken to take forward the implementation of the *Avant-projet* after the preparation of this paper for the Oxford conference in March 2007, see S Vogenauer, 'The *Avant-projet de réforme*: an Overview', ch 1 above, pp 3, 17–20.

I

The Perspective of the Judiciary

18

The Work of the Cour de cassation on the Avant-projet de réforme

PIERRE SARGOS

THE PREMIER PRÉSIDENT of the Cour de cassation and the Procureur Général at the Cour de cassation decided to set up a working group, comprising judges of the five Civil chambers of the Cour de cassation (both the judges of the court, and the magistrates who act on behalf of the public interest in relation to cases before the court) and chaired by the author of this contribution. The task of the working group was to give an opinion on the *Avant-projet de réforme du droit des obligations et de la prescription* drafted by a group of French lawyers (academics, judges and practitioners) and known as the Projet Catala.

As regards methodology, at the end of a first plenary meeting the working group decided to divide into four sub-groups working on the broad thematic divisions of the *Avant-projet*. These sub-groups were to carry out specific studies on points falling within their theme, which would later be discussed at plenary meetings of the working group. Requests for views on the *Avant-projet* were then sent out to economic, trade union and professional organisations. The final report of the working group will be prepared in the course of June 2007.[1]

At the end of the first fortnight of March 2007, the date of the Oxford colloquium, it is of course not possible to give the final direction of that report, or even of the comments on particular points of the *Avant-projet*. One can only mention the concerns of the judges of the Cour de cassation with regard to their approach to this major reform, concerning no less major provisions of the Code civil—provisions that have been the object of only a few amendments since the entry into force of the Code civil in 1804

---

[1] The report was published after completion of the manuscript: Cour de cassation, *Rapport du groupe de travail de la Cour de cassation sur l'avant-projet de réforme du droit des obligations et de la prescription* (2007), http://www.courdecassation.fr/jurisprudence_publications_document-ation_2/autres_publications_discours_2039/discours_2202/2007_2271/groupe_travail_10699.html. This chapter reproduces the paper delivered at Oxford in March 2007.

and on which there has been very significant case-law involving, in particular, the Cour de cassation, especially in the area of contractual and delictual liability. In this regard, a question and a constitutional requirement may be drawn out.

The *question* is, of course, whether it is appropriate to carry out a reform of the law of obligations and the law of prescription in the short term in France at a time when a wider movement has been initiated in favour of the bringing together of European contract law—if not the civil law as a whole—with the aim of improving the working of the internal market. Thus in a recent resolution the European Parliament reaffirmed 'that a uniform internal market cannot be fully functional without further steps towards the harmonisation of civil law'.[2] It could therefore be tempting to wait and then transpose into French law what will have been decided by the European Union, following the example, for instance, of the transposition of the directive on liability for defective products[3] into French law.[4]

The advantage of waiting would undoubtedly be to avoid putting into place a transitional new law of obligations before the entry into force of European rules. Every new law necessarily requires a period of adaptation and gives rise to uncertainty as to its scope and interpretation by the courts; and this stage would happen again when the European contract law applies in the EU Member States, even if it is limited to a 'Common Frame of Reference' within the meaning that the Commission and the European Parliament give to that notion.

However, the temptation to 'follow passively' in that way would have serious disadvantages, in particular as regards the defence at a European level of the values with which the French conception of the law of obligations has for centuries been imbued. This conception is not a model in itself and must gain from other legal traditions—as indeed French law has often done—but it has a role to play in contributing to the building of a European contract law, in particular within the framework defined by the latest communications of the Commission.[5] One cannot contribute efficiently to building anew by merely referring to a model going back to

---

[2] Parliament (EC), 'Non-Legislative Resolution on European Contract Law and the Revision of the Acquis: the Way Forward', T6-0109/2006, 23 March 2006.

[3] Council Directive (EEC) 85/374 of 25 July 1985 on the approximation of the laws, regulations and administrative provisions of the Member States concerning liability for defective products [1985] OJ L/210/29.

[4] Loi no 98-389 du 19 mai 1998 relative à la responsabilité du fait des produits défectueux, JO 21 May, 7744 (establishing arts 1386-1 to 1386-18 Cc).

[5] Commission (EC), 'European Contract Law and the Revision of the Acquis: The Way Forward' (Communication) COM (2004) 651 final, 11 October 2004; Commission (EC), 'First Annual Progress Report on European Contract Law and the Acquis Review' COM (2005) 456 final, 23 September 2005. The acquis essentially concerns the protection of consumers about which the Resolution of the European Parliament, above n 2, stresses that 'with a view to raising public confidence in the internal market, it is necessary to deliver a high level of consumer protection'.

the society comprised of farmers and artisans at the beginning of the nineteenth century—a model which, whatever its merits, no longer corresponds to the evolutions and breaks with the past that have occurred since the Second World War in the fields of economics, international affairs (with, in particular, all the international instruments for the protection of human rights which are capable of interfering with some aspects of contract law, and, of course, the building of Europe), politics, the law (in particular, the increase in the number of codes, which causes a loss of 'readability' of the general principles of the law of contracts), and in social, health and environmental affairs. Influence means change, and in that respect one thinks of the influence acquired by German law since the reform of the law of obligations which came into force in January 2002, or by Dutch law whose reform of the Code civil is hailed as forming a model for the European Union.[6] On the other side of the Atlantic, the new Civil Code of Québec has also aroused much interest.

The initiative taken by French lawyers under the direction of Professor Catala in making proposals for the reform of the law of obligations must therefore be welcomed as showing a way out of the 'neolithic era' of national legal isolation and the way to a reasoned and reasonable study of necessary—if not absolutely essential—reforms of that law. One must in fact stress that this private initiative on the part of French lawyers is a continuation of other private initiatives which, this time at European level, have led to the preparation of proposals for European rules for the law of obligations with a recognised influence, even if some areas of contention inevitably exist. There are three European sources of unification of contract law. (i) The UNIDROIT Principles of International Commercial Contracts (PICC) were prepared, published in 1994 and revised in 2004, by the Institut International de Droit Privé, a non-governmental organisation, the seat of which is in Rome. (ii) The Principles of European Contract Law (2000) were prepared by a private commission established from 1980 around Professor Lando. (iii) The proposal for a European Contract Code of 2001 (sometimes called the 'Gandolfi Project') stems from a private initiative of the Académie des privatistes européens (the Academy of European Private Lawyers, also known as the 'Pavia group').

The 'Catala group' therefore falls within an established European methodology. This methodology is advocated by the Commission and approved by the European Parliament with the 'joint network on European contract law', which is due to submit the fruit of its discussions in the course of 2007. French academics are taking part in a number of groups responsible for drafting its provisions—in particular the Study Group on a European Civil Code ('Study Group'), the European Research Group on Existing EC Private Law ('Acquis Group'), and the Project Group on a

[6] Parliament (EC), above n 2.

Restatement of European Insurance Contract Law ('Insurance Group'), not forgetting the group set up by the Association Henri Capitant and the Société de législation comparée which aims to identify, and clarify, the fundamental principles that are to govern European contract law.

The *constitutional requirement* stems from a major concept of the French Conseil Constitutionnel which since 1999 has developed a theory of intelligibility and accessibility of the law,[7] further refined by a recent decision.[8] The Conseil Constitutionnel states

> that it falls upon the legislator fully to exercise the competence given to it by the Constitution, and, in particular, by article 34; the full exercise of this competence, as well as *the objective of intelligibility and accessibility of the law*, an objective with constitutional force which stems from articles 4, 5, 6 and 16 of the Declaration of the Rights of Man and of the Citizen of 1789, impose the obligation to adopt sufficiently precise and unambiguous provisions; indeed the legislator must protect persons subject to the law against any interpretation which would be contrary to the Constitution or against the risk of arbitrariness, without transferring to administrative or judicial authorities the task of setting up rules the making of which the Constitution entrusted to legislation alone.[9]

This objective of intelligibility and accessibility of the law, which is an important component of legal certainty, can undoubtedly be considered as applicable not only to new legislation, but also to old legislation which must be improved when, because of changes wrought by the passage of time, it has ceased to be reasonably intelligible and accessible. In French law, there is of course no control of constitutionality after a law has been promulgated, and it would be absurd to suggest that the Code civil is not in conformity with the Constitution, but when the law in force becomes opaque, this objective of intelligibility and accessibility may be a signal for, and a guide to, legislative reform. Yet—and this comment is a truism—the letter of the French law of obligations, set rigidly in two-hundred-year-old formulae, no longer reflects the state of the law in force in France for anyone who does not have a specialist's knowledge—and even then of case-law and academic works. This defect is all the more unacceptable given that the intelligibility and accessibility of the law must be appreciated not only as regards the French people, but as regards all the inhabitants of the European Union of which France is only a component. It is also possible that this defect explains, at least in part, the virulence of the 2004 and 2006 reports of the World Bank against the French legal tradition.[10]

---

[7] CC decision 99-421 DC of 16 December 1999, JO 22 December 1999, 19041.

[8] CC decision 2006-540 DC of 27 July 2006, JO 3 August 2006, 11541.

[9] Emphasis added. The first decisions referred to a principle of clarity which appeared to the Conseil to be redundant, if not tautological, and a source of confusion. The concept of intelligibility necessarily implies clarity of the law, so that the reference to the latter was abandoned in the most recent decision of 27 July 2006, above n 8.

[10] World Bank, *Doing Business in 2004: Understanding Regulations* (Washington DC, World Bank and Oxford University Press, 2004); World Bank, *Doing Business in 2006: Creating Jobs* (Washington DC, World Bank and International Finance Corporation, 2006).

In a US-style legal system, one would probably talk of the need for a 'restatement'. In a Romano-Germanic system of law, the only technique applicable is a redrafting of legislation that has become obsolete or incomplete; that is to say, insufficiently intelligible and accessible.

In the present state of its work—subject, of course, to the final decision which will be taken by all the members of the group together in a few weeks, and noting that it is not impossible that the final report may also make mention of diverging opinions in cases where unanimity has not been achieved on particular points—the working group considers that the *Avant-projet* is an opportune initiative.

On the substance and the form of this *Avant-projet*, the works of the group and the sub-groups are not sufficiently advanced to give definitive conclusions—in particular because they have not yet received replies to the requests for comments. However, it must be stressed that in its approach to the various aspects of the proposed reform, the working group intends to display a complete openness of mind, with no preconceived ideas or prejudice. Even as regards issues that have a long tradition in legislation or in the case-law, this group does not exclude in advance raising questions about any French legislative texts, so long as such questions contribute, on the one hand to intelligibility and accessibility of the law, and on the other hand to a better protection of the rights of persons in contractual relationships, whilst preserving a reasonable balance with the requirements of the economy, and finally, to bringing European laws closer. On this last point, one must stress the long-established and constant European tradition of the Cour de cassation which was the first among French courts with a mission to unify the interpretation of rules, and to lay down the principle of the primacy of Community law, even in relation to a national law adopted after the Treaty of Rome. It did so in the *Jacques Vabre* decision,[11] which the 1975 Annual Report of the Cour rightly stressed would be 'a milestone in the history of Community law'.[12] The decision held that the Treaty Establishing the European Community had an authority superior to that of national law, and set up its own legal order integrated into that of the Member States, with the result that it was directly applicable to the nationals of those states and binding on their courts, and that the provisions of that Treaty prevailed over national law even if the latter was adopted later.

It is subject to these preliminary observations that we shall proceed with what is only a partial survey of the main points on which the group and sub-groups were to conduct their examination, in relation to obligations (section I below) as well as civil liability (section II below), noting that the question of prescription, a factor in the extinction of rights of action that is

[11] Cass mixte 24 May 1975, Bull mixte no 4.
[12] *Rapport Annuel de la Cour de cassation 1975* (Paris, La documentation française, 1976) 93.

common to both contractual and delictual liability, will be examined within the second part.

I. THE REFORM OF THE LAW OF OBLIGATIONS

It may reasonably be thought that a number of choices made by the authors of the *Avant-projet* will be the object of a consensus within the group (apart from suggestions as to drafting in appropriate cases).

In the first place there are all the provisions which merely put into legislative shape interpretations of the courts, which have mostly been the subject of a wide consensus. Then there are the definitions given to a number of legal concepts and types of contracts or obligations. One thinks, for instance, of articles 1001-1 to 1103, 1105-1, 1106, 1106-1, 1144 to 1151 of the *Avant-projet*, with a special reference to the legislative recognition and the definition of notions of *obligations de moyens et de résultat* (obligation to take necessary steps and obligation of result) in article 1149 of the *Avant-projet*, which are also recognised by the UNIDROIT Principles.[13]

Such details follow European directions in relation to the necessity of having a clear, precise and comprehensive legal terminology[14] as well as the French constitutional requirement of intelligibility and accessibility of the law.

It is also likely that there will be a consensus regarding the explicit recognition of (i) the negotiation phase of contracts, (ii) offers and their specific regime, and (iii) duties to inform (although as regards the consequences of offers and duties to inform, differences of view may emerge), as well as of the primacy given, where possible, to performance in kind of obligations that must be undertaken (article 1154 of the *Avant-projet*). There again, the three European sources of unification of the law of contracts follow the same path.

Among the points that will give rise to more controversy within the group, one can logically identify in the first place the layout of the *Avant-projet*. At first glance, this point could be considered as being of only limited interest, but the quality of the layout is also part of the intelligibility and the accessibility of the law. It is well known that the layout of the Code civil is mediocre to the point that a member of the commission for reform of the Code civil, set up just after the end of the Second World War,

---

[13] Art 5.1.4 PICC.
[14] See Commission (EC), 'European Contract Law' (Communication) COM (2001) 398 final, 11 July 2001, paras 36–9; Commission (EC), 'A More Coherent European Contract Law: An Action Plan' (Communication) COM (2003) 68 final, 12 February 2003, paras 19–20.

exclaimed: 'there is no code the layout of which is worse drafted, and the titles of which more uncertain than the French code'.[15]

The layout of Title III of the Code civil is sub-divided into seven Chapters. The *Avant-projet* replaces it by two Subtitles, the first of which—and the most important, since Subtitle II deals with the limited area of quasi-contracts—is also sub-divided into seven Chapters which essentially follow the structure of the original layout, albeit with adaptations and in more detail, and with one innovation consisting of rationally bringing together in a new Chapter VI all the transactions relating to rights under obligations. At first glance, this last innovation appears fortunate in its principle—obviously the group will make its assessment as to its contents—but might there not be a question about moving to a final Chapter everything relating to proof? Would it not have been more suitable to proceed by bringing together the questions of form—at present in Section 5 of Chapter II—and of proof? More generally, should the structure of the layout itself not be revised, taking inspiration from the best of the three European sources of unification of the law of contracts—the UNIDROIT Principles, the Principles of European Contract Law and the Proposals for a European Contract Code?

Linked in a way to the layout, but giving rise to a much more fundamental problem, is the deliberate refusal of the authors of the *Avant-projet* to give, in a preliminary chapter, what could be called the guiding principles of contract law. These principles would take the place of the preliminary Chapter (articles 1101 to 1101-2 of the *Avant-projet*) dealing with the definitions of juridically significant facts and juridical acts. It is not that these definitions are unnecessary—indeed, the opposite is true. But to put them at the head of a large reform of the law of obligations shows an approach that could appear limiting, if not technocratic.

It is well known that the UNIDROIT Principles and the Principles of European Contract Law chose to underline the general principles, in particular contractual freedom—with necessary reasonable limits—and good faith. The Preliminary Draft of a European Contract Code is more reserved, but article 2 relating to 'contractual autonomy' is seen as a true guiding principle; its first paragraph is worded as follows:

> The parties can freely determine the contents of the contract, within the limits imposed by mandatory rules, morals and public policy, as established in the present Code, Community law or national laws of the Member States of the European Union, provided always that the parties thereby do not solely aim to harm others.[16]

And this same Draft Code gives great strength to good faith—in particular

---

[15] Commission de Réforme du Code civil, *Travaux de la Commission de réforme du Code Civil*, vol IV: *Année 1948–1949* (Paris, Sirey, 1950) 25.

[16] Art 2 AEPL Code.

articles 6 and 32. It may be added that the United Nations Convention of 1980 on the International Sale of Goods (the Vienna Convention) also adopts good faith.

Guiding principles may be detected in the Code civil with, in particular, the symbolic articles 1134 and 1135 Cc to which the Cour de cassation has given a dynamic interpretation that goes far beyond the simple effects of contracts. To take just one recent example, one can cite the developments of the 2005 Annual Report of the Cour de cassation[17] as underlining the importance of good faith at every stage of the life of a contract. This implies, in particular in contracts with performance successively or in instalments, an ethic of solidarity and of community of interests, which as long ago as the beginning of the twentieth century were defended by Demogue. These comments relate of course to a specific contract—the contract of employment—but may be transposed to many other 'successive performance' contracts. The notion of good faith must be connected to that of reason or reasonableness, brought to light by numerous international provisions and also referred to by the three European sources and in particular by the Principles of European Contract Law (eg article 2:104). The 2004 Annual Report of the Cour de cassation referred to the topicality and importance of this notion of reasonableness.[18]

Therefore the question arises, on which the group will take a position, of a preliminary Chapter, different from the one in the *Avant-projet*, setting out guiding principles. Such guiding principles, if they were adopted, could probably include the substance of articles 1134 and 1135 Cc and take their inspiration from the European sources of unification of the law of contracts, recent foreign codes—such as, for instance, the Civil Code of Québec, as regards good faith—and the case-law of the Cour de cassation. As to the contents of these guiding principles, one could probably think of: contractual freedom, subject to compliance with mandatory rules of national law not contrary to Community law and not pursuing a purpose breaching the European Convention on Human Rights;[19] the binding force of contracts, which are binding not only in respect of what they provide, but also for all the consequences which custom, equity or legislation give to the obligation according to its nature; the requirement of good faith understood in broad terms (loyalty, solidarity) applying at all stages of the life of a contract—negotiation, the provision of information, conclusion, performance, interpretation, amendment, renegotiation, breach and its consequences. Such a general wording would avoid the reference on numerous occasions to good faith or one of its components, loyalty—as the *Avant-projet* does—in respect

---

[17] *Rapport Annuel de la Cour de cassation 2005* (Paris, La documentation française, 2006) 221, 233–5.
[18] *Rapport Annuel de la Cour de cassation 2004* (Paris, La documentation française, 2005) 209.

of individual specific phases of the life of the contract, eg articles 1104, 1134 and 1176.

If this option of setting out the guiding principles of contracts—in particular as regards good faith combining loyalty and solidarity throughout the contract—were to be retained by the group, it would probably, as a logical consequence, give rise to an examination of the admission of unforeseeability, rejected by the *Avant-projet* which contents itself with setting out rules on renegotiation of the contract (articles 1135-1 to 1135-3), based on a concept that could appear imprecise, that of loss of any point for a party to proceed with a 'successive performance' contract.

The three European sources of unification of the law of contracts admit, with variations, unforeseeability allowing revision or termination of a contract. Article 6.2.2 of the UNIDROIT Principles thus develops the concept of 'hardship' and defines it as resulting from the occurrence of events fundamentally altering the equilibrium of the contract, unknown or not reasonably foreseeable at the time of the conclusion of the contract, beyond the control of the party suffering damage, and of which he has not assumed the risk. The Principles of European Contract Law also admit that changes in circumstances making the performance excessively onerous, occurring after the time of conclusion of the contract and not reasonably foreseeable by the party who has not undertaken the risk, may justify an ending or adaptation of the contract. The Proposals for a European Contract Code follow the same path with a notion of extraordinary or unforeseeable events. Does the duty of contractual good faith not give rise to a revision of the contract when upheavals change the initial contractual balance beyond all foreseeability and reasonable proportion—and one knows the importance of the demand for proportionality in modern law? The time of the well-known judgment *Canal de Craponne*, which three centuries ago saw the Cour de cassation recognise the inviolability of a price for the supply of water agreed, has passed; and we know in that respect the developments made in particular by the Commercial chamber.[20] The requirement of a contractual balance—which was the basis of the premonitory decision of the Cour d'appel d'Aix-en-Provence in 1873,[21] unfortunately quashed by the Cour de cassation in 1876[22]—was recognised by the European Court of Human Rights in *Hutten-Czapska v Poland*, which condemned a Polish law limiting rents to such an extent that owners could no longer maintain their building.[23] Would it not therefore be more coherent to admit in law that—since the principle of obligation to perform

---

[19] In this respect one thinks of the principle of non-discrimination in private law contracts: *Pla and Puncernau v Andorra* (App no 69498/01) ECHR, 13 July 2004.

[20] Cass com 3 November 1992, Bull civ IV no 338 (*Huard*).

[21] CA Aix-en-Provence 31 December 1873, see Cass civ 6 March 1876, Bull no 25.

[22] Cass civ 6 March 1876, Bull no 25.

[23] (App no 35014/97) ECHR, 19 June 2006; see also RTD civ 2006, 719.

contracts freely entered into must be maintained, even if this is more difficult—unforeseeability, clearly characterised, places an obligation on the parties to renegotiate or, failing that, allows the courts to adapt the contract or to end it?

On this last point, it can be noted that the role of the courts in contracts is conceived in a very minimalist way in the *Avant-projet*, in contrast to the three European sources of unification of the law of contracts and with the European Convention on Human Rights, which recognises the requirement of an effective access to the courts in case of a dispute: this means that the courts should have a wide jurisdiction, used of course with the guarantees of the right to be heard. The working group might wonder why the admission, for instance, of article 157(5) of the Gandolfi Proposal for a European Contract Code according to which

> After evaluating the circumstances and taking into consideration the interests and requests of the parties, the judge, with possible expert assistance, can alter or dissolve the contract as a whole or in its non-performed part and, if required, and it is the case, order return of goods or award damages for loss.

could not be acceptable in France? Also, does this mistrust of the courts not lead the authors of the *Avant-projet* to include superfluous provisions, such as for instance that of article 1158-1, allowing the debtor to dispute in court a decision of his creditor, whereas article 6(1) of the European Convention on Human Rights forms the basis of the right of every person to seise the courts of a dispute relating to his rights and obligations?

Another question of principle from the group could relate to the retention, indeed reinforcement, in the *Avant-projet* of that French peculiarity: the theory of cause (*la cause*) as a condition of validity of contracts—articles 1124 to 1126-1, which is more articles than in the present Code civil. Everything has been said since Planiol's famous anti-cause diatribe at the beginning of the twentieth century[24] on the false and unnecessary, or at the very least uncertain, ambiguous and obscure character of the concept of cause in contracts. (One thinks of the discussions about objective, subjective, determining, efficient, ultimate cause and of the uncertain boundaries with the subject-matter of the contract). Most European countries do not know of it; nor do the three sources of unification of the law of contracts. The Commission and the European Parliament, for their part, as has already been mentioned, have warned against terminology that is abstract and too vague, as this can lead to legal uncertainty.[25] The respect of the constitutional requirement of intelligibility of the law is also problematic.

---

[24] In 1891 in his annotated Code civil Fuzier-Herman had already underlined that the notion of cause 'constituted an unnecessary complication and a source of confusion'. See E Fuzier-Herman, *Code civil annoté*, vol II: *Article 711 à 1167* (Paris, Librairie de la société du recueil général des lois et de arrêts et du journal du Palais, 1891) 1027.

[25] See above n 14.

The notion of cause, as developed by the courts who tend to take into account the parties' interests in the contract, has a protective effect as regards the weak or injured party in French law, but is that effect not achieved by a wide acceptance of good faith, with its components of loyalty and solidarity, indeed even of proportionality, allowing a control of the contractual balance and its maintenance? A contract, or terms of a contract, can also be annulled by reference to the notion of subject-matter of the contract, which must not be unlawful—eg a contract attacking a human being's dignity. The group will have to query whether retaining cause is still of any use in an efficient contract law, and, more importantly a contract law anxious to come nearer to a European consensus.

The following points, on which the working group is likely to express an opinion, may also be mentioned:

- defects of consent, and in particular the notion of a situation of weakness (article 1114-3 of the *Avant-projet*), which meets the theory of the Court of Justice of the European Communities of the weaker party in a contract;[26]
- the general introduction of the notion of lapse of a contract (articles 1131 and 1172-3 of the *Avant-projet*), already accepted by the Cour de cassation in relation to collective agreements;[27]
- unilateral termination of a contract (article 1158 of the *Avant-projet*), which goes in the same direction as that of the three sources of unification of European contract law as well as, in certain aspects, the same direction as some case-law of the Cour de cassation; in particular in the case of termination of contracts of employment, which is the subject of considerable development;[28]
- the fixing of the price in contracts which provide for performance successively or in instalments (articles 1121-4 and 1121-5 of the *Avant-projet*);
- groups of contracts or interdependent contracts and their consequences (articles 1172 to 1172-3 of the *Avant-projet*);
- should the obligation to give, as regards the transfer of the thing, not be considered as an effect of the contract, rather than as the performance of an obligation, as is supported by a number of academic authors (articles 1152 to 1153-1 of the *Avant-projet*)?

---

[26] Joined cases 397/01 to 403/01 *Pfeiffer et al v Deutsches Rotes Kreuz, Kreisverband Waldshut eV* [2004] ECR I-8835.
[27] Cass soc 17 June 2003, Bull V no 198.
[28] *Rapport Annuel de la Cour de cassation 2003* (Paris, La documentation française, 2004) 323; *Rapport Annuel 2004*, above n 18, 252; *Rapport Annuel 2005*, above n 17, 263.

II. THE REFORM OF THE LAW OF CIVIL LIABILITY AND THE LAW OF PRESCRIPTION

Articles 1382 to 1386 Cc are often considered, in view of their lapidary character—apart from some additions to article 1384, in particular that resulting from the unfortunate law of 7 November 1922,[29] which the *Avant-projet* proposes to remove—as general principles around which a body of rules has been developed by the courts and legal authors. One must know these developments in order to gather, if not understand, the French law of extra-contractual liability. And the uninterrupted expansion of contractual liability since the founding judgment of the Cour de cassation[30] may also be seen as a development of the very brief general principles contained in articles 1134, 1135, 1146, and especially 1147, of that Code.

This shows that regarding this particularly sensitive area, the requirements of intelligibility and accessibility of the law, within the meaning of the Conseil Constitutionnel referred to above,[31] have to be looked at with caution.

The *Avant-projet*, drawing the conclusions of that situation—which suggests similarities between the French law on liability and a 'common law' system built on precedents, subject to the special legal regimes of liability such as that applying to traffic accidents or the European rules on liability for defective products—brings profound changes through sixty-four new articles (articles 1340–1386). The increase in the number of these articles, over 1000% in comparison with the original articles of the Code civil, is indeed significant, even if a number of them retain the theory of accepted solutions developed by the courts. However, for the reasons already given, that is to say, the fact that the work of the group is not yet complete, this contribution will be limited to identifying the main questions on which the group will, in all likelihood, be led to give its views.

The first question will be about the choice made to include everything relating to civil liability, whether contractual or extra-contractual, in a new Sub-title. The argument of some legal authors against the very concept of contractual liability (the sanction of contractual non-performance being then reduced to the sole function of enforced performance of the contract) is thus put aside in favour of a regime which, whilst defining both types of liability, strives to set up common rules, then specific rules for each type of liability, and deals with loss caused to third parties as well as with the specific case of harm to physical integrity of human beings. The group will, of course, give its views on those points, which are all the more important

---

[29] Loi du 7 novembre 1922 complétant l'article 1384 du code civil, JO 9 November 1922.
[30] Cass civ 21 November 1911, S 1912.1.73 and DP 1913.1.249 (*Compagnie Générale Transatlantique*).
[31] Above p 386.

because they are such as to bring major upheavals in a wide section of liability law, which means that its scope must be carefully measured.

If it is decided to retain the two types of liability, a difficulty arises from their combination in a number of cases. It is well known that the courts, in a formula inappropriately called the 'rule against accumulation', forbid the victim of a contractual loss to rely on the rules of extra-contractual liability, as for instance—and the temptation was strong before being condemned by the courts—the rules of liability for harm caused by the actions of things. The choice made by the *Avant-projet* is that of non-accumulation—unlike most of the laws of the countries of the European Union—with specific adjustments relating to the situation of third parties to the contract and personal injuries caused by a contractual non-performance.

As regards third-party victims of harm resulting directly from the non-performance of an obligation arising out of a contract, article 1342 of the *Avant-projet* gives them a choice between the contractual ground—in which case they will be subject to the limitations and conditions of the contract—or the extra-contractual ground, with the onus of proving one of the facts giving rise to liability provided by articles 1352–1362 the *Avant-projet*, ie fault, the action of things or animals, actions of other people, nuisance from neighbours, or dangerous activities.

One may query the suitability and potential difficulties of such an option. This choice first presumes that the victim has all the elements to assess the contract in order to make an enlightened choice; yet many contracts are not in writing or are governed by usage or customs the access and understanding of which are difficult for the non-initiated. It will also be necessary to resolve the conflicts of options in the case of two or more persons being liable for the harm, or of two or more victims, indeed of facts giving rise to liability which combine a contractual and non-contractual source. The apportionment of the amount of reparation between all the persons liable runs the risk of being delicate if not iniquitous—notwithstanding the provisions of article 1378 of the *Avant-projet* on the effect of two or more persons being liable—where one third-party victim has taken the option of the contractual ground and another of the extra-contractual ground.

Besides, is it not somewhat artificial, if not sophistic, to allow the qualification of a single fact as 'contractual fact' and 'delictual fact'? Would it not be preferable to look for a greater simplification to resolve the position of a third-party victim of the total or partial non-performance of a contract? Does any contract not give rise to the obligation not to cause harm to third parties, ie not to cause them to suffer a loss? Obviously, the mere performance of a lawful contract cannot in itself make the parties to a contract liable as regards third parties, given its relative effect, but are third parties not in some way automatically entitled, by virtue of this same relative effect, to rely on a wrong the non-performance of which causes them a loss?

The wording of the current article 1165 Cc that 'contracts . . . do not harm third parties' has traditionally been interpreted by the majority of legal authors as meaning simply that third parties are not bound by the contract. But does it not in fact have a stronger meaning than the mere relative effect of contracts, as the tribune Mouricault gave the legislative body to understand when he distinguished what binds and what causes harm, specifying that 'contracts do not bind those who were not party to them, *and* do not harm third parties'?[32] This comment would also raise a question about the wording of draft article 1165 which removes the reference to harm.

In this respect the judgment by the Assemblée plénière of the Cour de cassation, according to which 'a third party to a contract may invoke, on the delictual ground, a contractual breach if that breach caused him harm', is significant.[33] In that case there were the breaches of maintenance obligations arising out of a management lease agreement which made the action of the third party admissible. Does this wording not deserve to be recognised by the law—subject to the question of whether retaining the delictual ground for the third party's action is well founded?

The second of these adjustments relates to personal injuries caused by contractual non-performance. Third parties then always have a choice as to the ground for their action, as indicated above, but the second paragraph of article 1341 of the *Avant-projet* goes further since it opens up the same option to the other party to the contract who is the victim of such a personal injury. A kind of 'favour principle', following the example of that existing in favour of employees under employment law, is thus recognised.

Use of this option encounters the objections already developed. Furthermore, in the current state of the draft, the other party to the contract who opts for the delictual ground would not be bound by the requirements imposed on third parties taking the same option—in particular, the onus of proof as to the extra-contractual fact giving rise to liability.

One could ask oneself whether one should not go further in the autonomy of the regime applying to harm to the integrity of human beings, independently not only of the contractual or extra-contractual nature of the fact giving rise to liability, but also on whether the person responsible for the harm is a private or public person. The way private law and public law courts look at liability and reparation has come closer; however, a body of single rules which apply regardless of the court having jurisdiction—in the absence of a unification of litigation—would offer more guarantees, in particular as to the equality of treatment of victims. Moreover, the development, if not the explosion, of services to individuals capable of causing harm to them would be a unifying trend, but could create artificial distor-

---

[32] See PA Fenet (ed), *Recueil complet des travaux préparatoires du Code Civil*, vol XIII (Paris, Imprimerie de Ducessois etc, 1827) 422.
[33] Ass plén 6 October 2006, D 2006, 2825.

tions depending on whether or not the person supplying the service to the individual and that individual have a contractual relationship. Last, and not least, is there not an ethical need to set up a body of uniform rules, given the constitutional principle of respect of human dignity?

In matters of personal injury resulting from a medical act, the law on patient's rights[34] has already gone in the direction of unification since it makes no distinction either on the basis that there is a contractual relationship, or because of the nature of the person liable: all are liable when there is a fault, liability without fault being limited to specific cases (essentially harm attributed to medicines[35]). A general transposition could perhaps be possible on the basis of the principle of liability for fault —regardless of whether it is contractual or not or whether it lies with a private or public person—with clearly defined cases of liability without fault (essentially situations where there is currently a regime of strict liability or a 'safety obligation' of result).

Still on the topic of personal injuries, the setting-up of uniform rules of reparation by articles 1379–1381 and by article 1382-1 of the *Avant-projet* (prohibition of any exclusion or limitation of reparation) undoubtedly deserves approval as to its principle, subject to discussing its contents— what of the scale of disability referred to in draft article 1379-1?—and to extending them to administrative litigation.

The liability for the actions of things, as is well known, is not generally accepted by laws of the countries of the European Union and is of less use for victims because of certain special regimes—traffic accidents and defective products. Furthermore, if article 1362 of the *Avant-projet* on strict liability for harm resulting from a dangerous activity—which raises specific difficulties on which the group will give its views—were to be retained, the interest in maintaining an 'autonomous' liability for the actions of things would be reduced still further. Moreover, in the case of contractual liability, the very notion of liability for the action of a thing used for the performance of a contractual obligation does not make sense— and in fact nor does that of liability for the actions of other people—the party to the contract being responsible in principle for the service or the product, regardless, as far as the victim is concerned, of the part played by the thing or the person he uses or asks to intervene. One could therefore ask whether this French particularity of the liability for the actions of things should be retained, but one would have to identify the situations in which it still has a use—the absence of human action in the harm caused by the thing, and of special regimes.

Liability for actions of other people provided by draft articles 1355–1360 will no doubt also be given much attention by the working

---

[34] Loi no 2002-303 relative aux droits des malades et à la qualité du système de santé du 4 mars 2002, JO 5 March 2002, 4118.
[35] See art L 1142-1 Code de la santé publique.

group, in particular the provisions relating to obligations of employees and liability without an employment relationship.[36] Is it acceptable that an employee, who is only liable as regards his employer in case of gross fault— ie implying an intention to harm him—becomes his guarantor when he is insolvent or has no insurer and the unintentional fault committed by the employee was committed in the course of his employment and for purposes which conform to their roles?

Would the extension of the liability for actions of other people in the absence of an employment relationship not be based on imprecise criteria— supervision or organisation of an activity, economic advantage, dependence—such as to give rise to difficulties to subscribe to an effective insurance policy? The example (is it a good legislative technique to have recourse to such distinctive examples?) given by draft article 1360 of the doctor 'employed'—this term is arguable for the engagement of one in a liberal profession—by a healthcare establishment may not be pertinent in so far as the law on the rights of sick persons of 4 March 2002[37] requires insurance by healthcare establishments as well as by doctors, and where the courts carefully define the components of the respective liabilities of doctors and healthcare establishments. In the same way, the example given in the same article, of the liability of parent companies and those granting concessions for their subsidiaries and those granted the concession, may have perverse economic effects.

Article 1348 of the *Avant-projet*, which relates to the liability of identified members of a group for harm caused by one of them who is unascertained, will also deserve special attention. The wording as regards the notion of group is imprecise and potentially dangerous, indeed a source of iniquity— they will not necessarily be insured—for those who can be identified and who will have the heavy burden of proving that they could not be the perpetrators of the harm. Is the comparison made with hunting accidents, even independently from the existence of Les Fonds de garanties des assurances obligatoires de dommages (Guarantee Fund of Compulsory Damage Insurance), not questionable in so far as the group made up of huntsmen, who have to be insured, knowingly takes part in an intrinsically dangerous activity (could this not be a criterion of liability for members of a group)? But is it acceptable, for instance, that the identified member of a group of demonstrators formed more or less fortuitously runs the risk of being declared liable for the damage caused by some of them who remained unidentified? A recent judgment of the second Civil chamber of the Cour de cassation[38] has recently held that since a trade union has neither as its object nor mission the organisation or control of the activity of its members in the course of strikes or demonstrations in which the latter take part, the

---

[36] Arts 1359-1 and 1360 of the *Avant-projet*.
[37] Above n 34.
[38] Cass civ (2) 26 October 2006, D 2007, 204.

faults personally committed by them do not automatically make the trade union to which they belong liable.

The following points on which the working group will no doubt express its views can also be mentioned:

- Should one not, following the example of the reform of the law of obligations, give definitions of notions such as 'serious', 'gross' or 'inexcusable' fault, or also fault 'with a view to gain', referred to in a number of articles? It is true that the notion of fault and its various gradations is often a question of fact, or a combination of facts, resistant to any real definition, which explains why, with the exception of inexcusable fault, the Cour de cassation has not given a general definition. The definition of fault itself by draft article 1352:

  > a breach of a rule of conduct imposed by legislation or regulation or failure to conform to a general standard of care and diligence

  is indeed objective, but one may question whether it presents a real interest for the courts. On the other hand, fault with a view to gain allowing the award of punitive damages would perhaps deserve a definition that emphasises the idea of seeking an unlawful gain when committing the fault.
- Should one admit punitive damages, with the risks of excess which they carry (article 1371 of the the *Avant-projet*), although one can imagine that the awards would be allocated to Les Fonds de garantie des assurances de dommages?
- Is the possibility of reducing the amount of reparation when the victim could take measures—except where they would compromise his physical integrity—to reduce the extent of his loss or avoid its getting worse (articles 1373 and 1344 of the the *Avant-projet*)—although it is also provided by the Vienna Convention, advocated by the Principles of European Contract Law, and adopted by several jurisdictions—not such as to provoke delicate litigation and delays (calls for expert reports)? Should the statement as to the grounds referring to the victim's 'specified act of negligence' not be included in the main body of draft article 1373?
- Can the provisions relating to reparation and penalty clauses (articles 1382 and 1383 of the *Avant-projet*) be admissible outside the area of contract, even taking account of the general prohibition in the case of personal injury?
- Do articles 1369 and 1376 of the *Avant-projet* not give the courts an excessive, if not arbitrary, power, as regards the choice of reparation (in kind, in the form of damages, lump sum or periodic payments)? Is it not for the victim to select the kind of reparation he wishes, subject to the court having the power to decide otherwise but by a special, reasoned decision?

- Must the definition of *force majeure* (article 1349 of the *Avant-projet*) be different from the one given by two judgments of the Assemblée plénière of the Cour de cassation?[39]
- Should amendments be made to the '*loi* Badinter',[40] in particular as regards the driver's situation? As regards the basis of the recourse claims by third parties by way of subrogation, it should be noted that article 25 of the Law of 21 December 2006[41] has adopted the limitation of recourse claims for heads of loss individually, as proposed by article 1379-7 of the *Avant-projet*.

Finally, as regards prescription, the working group found itself confronted with a particular problem given that, in 2004, another working group within the Cour de cassation drafted a report on the harmonisations of prescription. These proposals will therefore have to be compared with those of the *Avant-projet*.

- Is it necessary, in particular, to reform at the same time extinctive prescription, acquisitive prescription and possession, the amalgamation of which in the Code civil is considered by some as artificial?
- Should the regimes of suspension and interruption of prescription be amended?
- Would it not be better to stick to a simpler reform consisting of reducing the period of thirty years? But in that case, which 'basic' period should be adopted as the extinctive prescription period—three years in the *Avant-projet*, or ten years in the 2004 proposal of the Cour de cassation?
- Are there not too many special prescription periods, or more generally, too many prescription rules, in the *Avant-projet* relating to the law of obligations and of liability (articles 1130, 1167, 1205 and 1384), which seems contrary to the concern for unification?
- Is the fixing of an absolute 'back-stop period' of ten years after the event giving rise to the obligation (article 2278 of the *Avant-projet*) constitutional? The decision of the Conseil Constitutionnel of 13 December 1985[42] comes to mind; this held that a provision which stated that the prescription period started running not from the day the harm was suffered but from the day the works were completed was in breach of the principle of equality as regards public duties. The loss may only appear well after the event which caused it. The question of conformity with the requirements of fair trial imposed by

---

[39] Ass plén 14 April 2006, D 2006, 1566, Defr 2006, 1212.
[40] Loi no 85-677 du 5 juillet 1985 tendant à l'amélioration de la situation des victimes d'accidents de la circulation et à l'accélération des procédures d'indemnisation, JO 6 July 1985, 7584.
[41] Loi no 2006-1640 de financement de la sécurité sociale pour 2007 du 21 décembre 2006, JO 22 December 2006.
[42] CC decision 85-198 DC of 13 December 1985, JO 14 December 1985, 14574.

the European Convention on Human Rights could also be raised. Following the same line of thought, one may question the reason why article 1384 excludes the date of stabilising of the injury as starting point for actions claiming civil liability whereas article L 1142-28 of the Code de la santé publique recognises it.

- Should so-called non-suspendable periods be retained?
- Could the contractual variation of prescription periods be acceptable? The recollection of them is so bad in the case of insurance contracts matters that the Law of 13 July 1930[43] had to prohibit them.

III. CONCLUSIONS

Without claiming that they are exhaustive, these are the main points for reflection by the working group on the *Avant-projet de réforme du droit des obligations et de la prescription*. These points may seem like a collection of unrelated comments, but this is unavoidable since, as already mentioned, the group has not yet taken a definitive position, and no one may speak for it in advance. The only certainty, at the time of the Oxford colloquium, is that the group feels strongly that reflecting on the reform of the law of obligations, liability and prescription (at least—for the latter—as to its length) is necessary for a better intelligibility and accessibility of French law and to achieve closeness within Europe.

---

[43] Loi du 13 juillet 1930 relative au contrat d'assurances, JO 18 July 1930, 8003.

J

Summaries of the Discussions and Emerging Themes

19

Summaries of the Discussions

SIMON WHITTAKER, STEFAN VOGENAUER AND
JOHN CARTWRIGHT*

I. DISCUSSIONS ON THE LAW OF CONTRACT: NEGOTIATION AND CAUSE (SIMON WHITTAKER)

THE CHAPTERS ON negotiation and renegotiation (Chapters 2 and 3 above) gave rise to a discussion on the contrast in approach between English and French law to the notion and significance of *la sécurité* and legal certainty in the respective systems, and the significance of acceptance or denial of a general principle of good faith in contracts.

First, the *Avant-projet* came in for criticism from Denis Mazeaud on the basis that it had failed to include a general provision requiring good faith and that this reflected a mistrust of judges: the statement by Alain Ghozi that '[h]ommage à la vertu du contrat, la solution est négociée' in his introduction to articles 1134–1143 contained a message of defiance to judges! A general principle of good faith could be used, inter alia, to deal with problems of the effects of changes of circumstances; the great advantage of leaving good faith undefined was that it did not limit and therefore reduce its field of application and usefulness. While this position found support around the table, other participants thought that it would be useful to have a series of definitions of good faith according to its distinct and various functions in the law. And the English participants saw a principal reason for English law's rejection of a principle of good faith as being the legal and transactional uncertainty to which it would give rise and that the resolution of these uncertainties would inevitably give too much power (and too internventionist a role) to courts: English law does recognise interference in contracts as made by their parties, but this interference is recognised only in specific circumstances.

In this respect, Philippe Théry noted that there had been a paradoxical

* We are particularly grateful to Ms Janice Feigher, *Avocat à la Cour* and Solicitor with Clifford Chance Paris, and Mr James Dingley, Solictor with Clifford Chance London, for providing us with notes of the discussions.

change in approach in French law. For during the same relatively recent period when French judges had gradually exercised more power in the supervision of the making and performance of contracts in general, their role in relation to agreements made in the family context had diminished dramatically. So, for example, agreements concluded by spouses in the course of divorce proceedings (which are compulsory where divorce takes place by mutual consent and under which they settle its personal and financial consequences) escape control by the Cour de cassation, a position approved by the majority of *la doctrine*: in Jean Carbonnier's words, consensual divorce should be '*tout-compris*' (an all-inclusive package). How different from the treatment of divorce under the Code civil of 1804 where the role of the courts was so central!

More generally, participants agreed that there was a contrast in approach (both as a matter of substance and of technique) between French and English lawyers and that this could be seen as reflecting a contrast in understanding as to the significance of *la sécurité* and legal certainty. For English lawyers, contractual certainty requires that parties to contracts know where they *will be* if they enter a contract; for at least some French lawyers, *la sécurité* has this sense but also one that the law will ensure that where they will be will be substantively fair.

The doctrine of *la cause* attracted both devoted adherents and convinced critics among the participants reflecting the contrast of positions adopted by Judith Rochfeld and Ruth Sefton-Green (Chapters 4 and 5 above). At a technical level, the *jurisprudence Chronopost* came in for criticism on the basis that it confused two conceptions of *la cause* in bilateral contracts: one which rests on the need for some counterpart (*une contrepartie*) to each party's obligation, and the other which rests on the motives of parties in entering the contract. For Judith Rochfeld, however, these two conceptions were necessarily linked as deciding what *is* the relevant 'counterpart' cannot be divorced from the intentions of the parties. Other participants thought that using *la cause* to review the fairness of contract terms was unhelpful at the level of legal technique as this role was obscured by the complex, more general doctrine of *la cause* of which it formed part.

However, Denis Mazeaud rallied to the defence of *la cause* in the hands of French judges as they used it to intervene in contracts (whether in the context of the control of terms or where there was said to be no *cause* on the ground of substantive inequality of bargain) only where there was a manifest abuse to be rectified. And speaking from a judicial perspective, Pierre Sargos noted that French judges *had* at present to make what they could of *la cause* given that it was there in the Code civil! However, from his own point of view, he agreed with Planiol that *la cause* was both barely comprehensible and redundant. Much better, in his view, to develop use of a principle of good faith in the interests of ensuring a proper balance between the contracting parties.

In concluding this discussion, Geneviève Viney noted that the Cour de cassation had used *la cause* as a means of ensuring a proper balance between contracting parties, thereby using it as a substitute for *la lésion*. She welcomed this development as a matter of substance, but considered that it put too much reliance on a single term (*la cause*) whose meaning within French law varied considerably. Rather than using this single concept, it would be better for French law to develop a number of legal mechanisms each adapted to its own purpose.

II. DISCUSSIONS ON THE LAW OF CONTRACT: ENFORCEMENT, TERMINATION AND EFFECTS ON THIRD PARTIES (STEFAN VOGENAUER)

The discussion of the papers dealing with the enforcement of contractual obligations (Chapters 6 and 7 above) was introduced by Mark Freedland who chaired the session and observed that Yves-Marie Laithier had sketched out a tough approach on enforcement. Lucinda Miller had then applied these notions and depicted a surprisingly tough approach to the equivalent of specific performance and a surprisingly gentle approach to the power of the judge to strike down penalty clauses. By way of explanation, Simon Whittaker highlighted the fundamental difference of approach between the French and English laws of contract. Whilst French law started from the right to perform or to choose the remedy, English law took the breach as a point of departure and explored the options available to remedy it. The rights-centred language of French law and of the *Avant-projet* thus reflected the idea of a right to performance as well as the corresponding duty to perform.

The speakers then focused on the historical and conceptual reasons for the English reticence to specific performance. But it was also clear that the discretion of the judges in this area is very wide. As Lucinda Miller explained, the parties cannot fetter it with a clause excluding (or, for that part, providing for) specific performance as a remedy. With respect to French law, Geneviève Viney cast doubt on Yves-Marie Laithier's argument that it follows from article 1382-2 of the *Avant-projet* that the parties cannot validly agree on an exclusion of specific performance in kind.

Finally, the strengths and weaknesses of the various approaches were discussed in the light of the economic analysis of law. The notorious case of *Co-operative Insurance Society Ltd v Argyll Stores (Holding) Ltd* [1998] AC 1 in which the House of Lords had not developed the economic argument was mentioned as an example for a scenario where specific performance would have been economically beneficial: the remedy could have saved both the shopping mall and the surrounding smaller shops which were dependent on it.

The papers on termination for non-performance and its consequences (Chapters 8 and 9 above) raised a number of terminological issues. To begin with, it was not at all clear whether the use of the concept of 'termination' was similar in the two jurisdictions concerned. One of the important questions was whether there is termination of the contract or termination of all the obligations between the parties. French law seemed to focus on the latter. It made an effort to protect long-term relationships between the parties by attempting to preserve the contract. As opposed to this, English law seemed to emphasise the contract as such, taking spot contracts as a paradigm that the parties should be allowed to terminate once they have given reasonable notice. This led to difficulties in relational contracts, such as contracts of employment or consumer credit agreements. Overall it would seem that English law is far too generous to creditors, the principle being that the creditor has a right to his performance. French law struck a balance by acknowledging both the creditor's right to performance and the debtor's right to perform.

One focal point of the discussion was whether the provisions of the *Avant-projet* were in line with the doctrine of efficient breach. Efficient breach might be encouraged by providing the possibility of extra-judicial termination which would make it possible to avoid costly litigation and thus set an incentive for efficient breach. But, as Ruth Sefton-Green pointed out, it is impossible to know in advance who would be the weak party and who would have to bear the cost of judicial termination. Furthermore, it was discussed whether the award of positive interest to the victim of a breach of contract would disencourage efficient breach. In this respect, Solène Rowan drew attention to the provisions of the *Avant-projet* which introduce punitive damages as a new remedy and which could be used to suppress efficient breaches.

The discussion of the papers on the effects of contracts on third parties (Chapters 10 and 11 above) focused on the wide expansion of contractual liability envisaged by the *Avant-projet*. This certainly went far beyond the solutions in other jurisdictions and, it was argued by some, distorted the borderline between contract and tort. Would it not have been easier simply to abandon the rule of *non-cumul*?

The approach of the reform proposals was particularly defended by Geneviève Viney. She suggested that there had been a long evolution towards a wide contractual liability, like in the cases of the *obligations de sécurité et d'information*. She admitted that preserving the rule of *non-cumul* had been contentious amongst the drafters, and she drew attention to the fact that, whilst the rule had been maintained as a matter of principle, the exceptions for corporal damages and in the cases covered by article 1342 of the *Avant-projet* were of such practical importance that there was not much left of the rule. Finally, she defended the controversial article 1342(1) of the *Avant-projet* as an application of common sense: it

should not be possible for the third party to enjoy the benefits of a contract, whilst at the same time being able to disregard the disadvantages
flowing from the position of a contractual party, such as short prescription
periods or exclusion clauses.

Even those participants who thought that the *Avant-projet* went much
too far in expanding contractual liability towards third parties conceded
that article 1342 simply followed the inherent logic of previous expansions
of contractual liability in French law. Given that these had been accepted it
seemed hard to resist the common-sense argument raised by Geneviève
Viney. Finally, Denis Mazeaud argued that the law concerning liability
should be less concerned with doctrinal classification than with the victim's
palpable need for redress. He suggested that in this regard the *Avant-projet*
properly reflected a certain French idea of private law.

III. DISCUSSIONS ON THE LAW OF DELICT AND OF PRESCRIPTION (JOHN CARTWRIGHT)

(a) Delict

Throughout the discussion of the sections of the *Avant-Projet* on delict it
was a very significant advantage to have as a participant in the colloquium
Geneviève Viney, who chaired the working group which drafted the Sub-
title on Civil Liability.

The discussion of the papers on the definition of *la faute* (Chapters 12
and 13 above) concentrated on two issues: the proposal in the *Avant-Projet*
to introduce into French law a definition of fault (*faute*); and a more
general comparative discussion of the role of tort law, and insurance in
relation to tort law.

There was some discussion as to whether article 1352(2) of the *Avant-
projet* was intended to be a complete definition, or merely illustrative. The
answer to this question affects significantly the translation of this text,
because the English rendering, perhaps more than the French original, has
to point in one direction or the other. The suggestion was that it is indeed a
constraining definition of fault—and Mme Viney said that it was designed
to make clear (in the face of ambiguous case-law) that there is no difference
between different sources of fault, whether the violation of a textual rule or
other duties. It is drafted in very general terms because a detailed list of the
different circumstances in which a party can be at fault would add a huge
number of (unnecessary) additional articles to the Code civil. The merits of
this were debated—and a counter-suggestion was made that if the article
was taken literally it might not cover every case, or at least would make it

difficult for the courts who would have to characterise explicitly the source of a defendant's duty of care and diligence.

There was a broad discussion of the relative roles of the law of tort and insurance—contrasting the wider scope of French liability with the more restricted law of tort in England, and noting the parallel in the use of insurance in the two jurisdictions: a more general use of third-party insurance in France to match a wider (and, much more often than in England, strict) liability. But although this demonstrated two different and irreconcilable philosophies, it was also argued that there has been a trend to expand strict liability in England, at least through cases which have widened the scope of vicarious liability. However, as one (English law) participant noted, if tort law has a normative effect on people's behaviour, we should be careful not to make people *too* careful: we want risk-taking, as long as it is reasonable.

The discussion of the papers on damage, loss and the quantification of damages (Chapters 14 and 15 above) focused largely on the merits (or otherwise) of the proposal to introduce punitive damages. Points made by several contributors were: whether the award of punitive damages (in *any* jurisdiction, including England where punitive damages are already accepted in relatively rare cases) would be contrary to the European Convention on Human Rights, although it was noted that the European Court of Human Rights had itself (in all but name) awarded punitive damages under articles 50 and 51 of the Convention; whether it was right to allow part of an award of punitive damages to be payable to the state, although it was noted that this had also been debated in 1991 in relation to the *astreinte* (monetary penalty for disobedience of court orders) but at that time Parliament had refused to accept a rule which would involve the state being enriched; and the most fundamental question—whether it was likely that the principle of punitive damages would be accepted in France. It was thought unlikely; but there was a suggestion that a form of restitutionary damages for *faute lucrative* (a tortious act designed to make a profit) might emerge, although this would be an imperfect solution in the eyes of those who wished to use the award of damages in the law of tort to provide both punishment the defendant's wrongdoing and an incentive to proper behaviour on the part of others.

A further topic of discussion arising from Pauline Rémy-Corlay's paper linked back to the earlier discussion of the definition of fault: the question of the use of broad and general definitions rather than more particularised statements in the Code. Here the issue was whether the *Avant-projet* should have been more detailed as regards the types of loss which can be compensated. One contributor suggested that this would have the inherent risk of limiting the scope of damages from its present, more flexible basis. Geneviève Viney indicated that the working group had consciously avoided

being too detailed: in any event, the *Avant-projet* had already increased the scale of legislative provision on delict from five to sixty-four articles!

(b) Prescription

The discussion about the proposed reforms of the law of prescription (Chapters 16 and 17 above) demonstrated some scepticism about the failure of the *Avant-projet* to separate out acquisitive and extinctive prescription. The importance of the subject was emphasised: as one participant said, it is a matter of the period during which one's rights endure, a fundamental question. And it was argued that it was most regrettable that there should be such differences amongst jurisdictions not only on prescription/limitation periods but also on such matters as the power of the courts in their operation of the rules, and whether the rules are matters of substance or of procedure, an issue which has a very significant bearing on the outcome of disputes in private international law.

As in some earlier topics, the discussion about prescription turned to the question of whether implementation of the proposals of the *Avant-projet* is likely. One (French) participant had some doubts: not about whether there would be a reform of the French law of prescription, but whether the particular proposals of the *Avant-projet* would be the preferred basis of the reform rather than the earlier and more modest reform proposal from a working group of the Cour de Cassation (referred to in President Pierre Sargos's paper).

This final discussion provoked the closing comment on the Colloquium by Stefan Vogenauer: whether or not the *Avant-projet* is to be enacted, in whole or in part, it constitutes a presentation of the French law of obligations and of prescription as it exists today and how it might be reformed—how some would like it to be reformed. That is of itself a very valuable resource.

20

Emerging Themes

HUGH BEALE, PHILIPPE THÉRY AND
GERHARD DANNEMANN

I. EMERGING THEMES IN THE LAW OF CONTRACT: NEGOTIATIONS AND CAUSE (HUGH BEALE)

A NUMBER OF THEMES have emerged from the four excellent papers we have heard. We also need to tease out what has not been said. We must read between the lines to expose unstated assumptions which may be very different.

Denis Mazeaud points out that contract law is not ideologically neutral.[1] There are undoubtedly conflicting ideologies within English contract law, and I am sure there are within French contract law. Insofar as it is possible to identify ideologies that predominate within a given system, it is very likely that the ideological differences between French contract law and English contract law are even greater.

The difficulty is to identify them. Just as when we compare legal terminology and concepts, it is hard to know whether we use different words to mean the same thing or the same words to mean different things. We also need to work out which are differences in substance and which are merely superficial, or result from differences in method rather than aim. For example, I find it hard to discuss law reform in terms of principles alone. I constantly ask both for statements of underlying policy and for concrete examples of how the rules under discussion would apply. In contrast, at least from the texts of the *Avant-projet* that I have seen, the French approach seems almost purely abstract, with few statements of policy or practical examples. This does not necessarily mean that the end result is different or even that English law reform is ultimately more 'pragmatic'. It may be no more than a different technique to arrive at the same end. But for me it creates difficulties in assessing the reform proposals.

I sense that behind rather similar words there are actually quite deep

---

[1] D Mazeaud, 'Contracts and Third Parties in the *Avant-projet de réforme*', above ch 10.

differences not only in meaning but of legal culture. The Lando Commission, when it produced the Principles of European Contract Law, managed to come up with a form of words that the members of the Commission could agree on despite their widely varying legal traditions. However, if they thought that the words would be interpreted similarly in each Member State, or even that they meant the same thing to each member of the Commission, I suspect they were fooling themselves.

Take an obvious example: good faith. Just as a standard, what does it require? Merely the absence of bad faith, as in the English phrase 'a purchaser in good faith'? Or does it require more—for example that a party must take into account the other party's legitimate interests as well as his own? That he must behave consistently and act with *cohérence*? Even that he must put the other party's interests ahead of his own? I suspect that academics from different jurisdictions have rather different ideas of what standard good faith requires.

In order to assess a proposed reform I feel particularly the need to ask: what is the reformer seeking to achieve? This is not just a question that arises with reform proposals: it can happen with case-law also. I will confess to having written off the doctrine of *cause*—except for *cause illicite*, which serves an evident purpose—as so much ritual incantation, as being as incomprehensible as the outer reaches of the English doctrine of consideration. From Professor Rochfeld's chapter[2] I now have a much better idea of the use that the French courts make of the doctrine. But from both the case examples she gives and some of the proposed articles of the Catala project I have the sense that the dominant philosophy underlying French contract law is rather different to that which underlies English contract law.

French law seems much more paternalist or concerned with perfectionism, preventing parties making bargains that in the long run are simply not worthwhile. English law is much more likely to take the attitude that parties who have made fools of themselves must bear the consequences, to refuse to intervene with a contract simply on the ground that it was a bad bargain. We tend to interfere only when there was something wrong with the procedure by which the contract was made, not merely on the ground that the resulting exchange was one-sided, even as wholly one-sided as it was in the French video-rental case. Of course there are exceptions, particularly in the hands of some judges—some of Lord Denning's remarks on unconscionability spring to mind—but the fundamental attitude or policy seems different to that in France.

If this is correct, we need to ask why. We must not, of course, resort to the old game of trading insults of the kind, 'English law is a law for tradesmen' versus 'French law is a law for peasants'. But nonetheless there may

---

[2] J Rochfeld, 'A Future for *la cause*? Observations of a French Jurist', above ch 4.

be a germ of truth there. For example, English contract law is conditioned, some would say distorted, by the very heavy diet of commercial cases that come before the higher courts—the only courts whose judgments are normally reported. The cases are often about high-risk contracts in rapidly fluctuating markets, and only too often the litigation is over whether a party who has made a bargain that has turned out to be unprofitable can escape from it and throw the market risk back onto the other party. The parties themselves often have no connection with England other than having chosen English law to govern their agreement—perhaps because of the alleged certainty of English law, perhaps because of the high reputation of English courts, who knows. Judgments that favour certainty over more communitarian notions of 'contractual justice' are hardly surprising.

In contrast, what types of cases do the French courts routinely handle? Would the same kind of rules be suitable for those cases? I suspect not, but without knowing the target it is hard to gauge whether the proposed reforms provide the most appropriate solution.

It may not just be a difference in the types of case the two systems aim to handle. It may also reflect a difference over what we want contract law to do. To a common lawyer, the contract provisions of the Code civil seem to tell legal subjects how they ought to behave. As has often been remarked before, a contract is envisaged as the law between the parties—and the law ought to be followed. The heavy emphasis on performance and on remedies aimed at preserving the contract seem to reflect these priorities. In contrast, English law seems less concerned to tell the parties what as good citizens or loyal businesspeople they ought to do. Rather it merely sets outer limits by proscribing what should not be done. Even then the law is frequently perfectly content to allow parties to 'play the rules'. That may not be commercially reasonable or what a person 'of tender moral conscience' would do, but often it is permitted by the courts. It has on occasion been constrained by particular doctrines but not, of course, by a general doctrine of good faith.

I have a final question about 'what it is that we are trying to do.' Are the reformers seeking solutions that will produce a good 'domestic law' for France? Or are they also seeking to produce a model that can be exported across Europe? The same question arises on both sides of the Channel. In England a frequent argument for law reform is that we should develop a good model, one which we hope will influence any future European legislation, rather than go our own way and risk having a 'European' solution foisted on us by Brussels. How pressing these concerns are in relation to general contract law it is hard to say. Certainly I do not expect to see a unified European Civil Code, or even Code of Contract Law, in my lifetime. But there may well be further directives, regulations, even optional instruments . . .

If export is the aim, then it becomes even more important to explain the purposes of the proposed reforms, and how they would work in practice.

II. EMERGING THEMES IN THE LAW OF CONTRACT: ENFORCEMENT, TERMINATION AND EFFECTS ON THIRD PARTIES (PHILIPPE THÉRY)

Previous chapters have stressed that the *Avant-projet* was a work of adjustment and not breaking away, and that it was, as Denis Mazeaud strongly insisted, the expression of a certain ideology and manifestation of certain sensitivities.[3] It can be added that, in spite of the unification of style on which Gerard Cornu worked, the *Avant-projet* is not so much a collective work as a collection of individual thoughts. These points have their importance.

Looking at the previous chapters, it has to be acknowledged that what is novel or not is not assessed similarly by everyone. Denis Mazeaud, when discussing provisions relating to contracts and third parties, made few references to the stipulation for the benefit of third parties. The audience will have understood that this text restates the settled law. Yet, this same stipulation for the benefit of third parties made up the essential part of Stefan Vogenauer's contribution.[4] It is perhaps a sign that the stipulation for the benefit of third parties has become more of an English than a French issue, in the same way, for instance, that trusts and similar techniques have become a French issue.

The first observation raised by the reports stems from role distribution. Let us begin with the distribution between the courts and the legislator: if one puts aside some radically new solutions—the possibility of third parties relying on contractual rules to claim reparation of the loss caused by the non-performance of a contract—one is in the presence of codification 'of constant case-law'. The provisions mirror the state of the law at the beginning of the twenty-first century, such as progressively established by the courts making up for the deficiencies of an ageing code. The 1804 Code civil, even if it did not break away with earlier law on every point, was a starting point. Is the *Avant-projet* anything else but a snapshot? Will the courts which developed most solutions look at this code as a new tool? Gerard Cornu defended the idea that the interpretation of new provisions should be less free because the will of the legislator is not so much a thing of the past.[5] Is this observation, which has not always restrained activist courts, pertinent for a work which is so nourished by case-law?

---

[3] Mazeaud, above n 1.

[4] S Vogenauer, 'The Effects of Contracts on Third Parties: the *Avant-projet de réforme* in a Comparative Perspective', above ch 11.

[5] G Cornu, *Droit civil: Introduction, personnes et biens* (9th edn, Paris, Montchrestien, 1999)

Muriel Fabre-Magnan made an observation when referring to 'relational' contracts which can be linked to that question.[6] She deplored the fact that the *Avant-projet* made no mention of them. Can it, however, be said that the philosophy of the proposals was in harmony with what she expected? It will be remembered that Jean Carbonnier, when examining the criticism often made of the Code civil that it had not given a special place to contracts of employment, answered succinctly: 'thank goodness'. Escaping from the rules of the Code, the contract was also escaping the risk of calcification to which they would have led.

This question of role distribution is not always easy either where courts and parties are concerned. There is a feeling that there is at the same time too much court and not enough court. The unilateral termination of contract is established in spite of the literal wording of article 1184 Cc but it is immediately specified that the question remains under the control of the court—as if the very particularity of legal life was not precisely there. Take an almost opposite situation where the court recognises to the debtor a kind of right of performance ('right of the debtor to perform').

The second observation relates to terminology. The *Avant-projet* adopts the traditional solution—in spite of the literal wording of article 1142 Cc— of the primacy of performance in kind. It must, however, be noted that the Commercial chamber—admittedly because of the requirements of insolvency proceedings—puts itself outside this trend. Applying article 1142 literally, it sees in any obligation in kind a potential monetary obligation that must, as any monetary debt, be declared in the proceedings.[7] But, subject to that exception which retains a certain mystery, the *Avant-projet* recognises a change of jurisdictional perspective: obligations must be performed in kind, except where they are too personal in character for the debtor to be forced to perform them.

However, does everyone understand the same thing when one talks of contractual performance? Nothing is less certain. Yves-Marie Laithier wondered whether dignity (article 1154) which may be an obstacle to performance in kind, would not prevent a tenant's expulsion.[8] One is at the very least on the fringe of the contract. Take the fact that English law,

---

no 406: 'The lawyers' task (at least the civil law lawyers') could today be to go back to the exegesis, at least for the coherent whole of the fundamental laws which amended the Code civil. Since 1964, extensive reforms have been carried out. The interpreter must get free from the fear of being the subject of reproaches which the scientific method made (with or without reason) to the exegetists of the 19th century: these criticisms are of no concern to us. . . . For this body of laws rethought and redrawn, our relationship with the law completely reversed. From 1964, a legislative move developed which contemporary lawyers must absorb. Interpretation youthfulness consists in going back to the exegesis of provisions in that vein . . .'

[6] M Fabre-Magnan, 'Termination of Contract: a Missed Opportunity for Reform', above ch 8.
[7] Cass com 20 July 1996, Bull civ IV no 192.
[8] Y-M Laithier, 'The Enforcement of Contractual Obligations: a French Perspective', above ch 6.

rather reserved on the question of specific performance, does not indulge in soul searching in this case. There is not only uncertainty as to what is contractual, but also as to what constitutes *performance* of the contract. Yves-Marie Laithier and Lucinda Miller are in agreement to define it as the creditor's satisfaction.[9] Muriel Fabre-Magnan probably sees something different there.[10] She strongly disputes the idea of efficient breach, which would be an unwelcome encouragement not to respect one's given word. As a result, the debtor is again in the main role: performance would be the completion by the debtor of what he promised.

It will be admitted that the argument is rather theoretical. However, according to the position taken, the limits of performance move, and with them the qualifications. Thus, the entering into an agreement with a third party in case of default on the part of the main debtor will at times fall within performance (the creditor is satisfied) and at others, will, at best, be only a remedy for a confirmed non-performance.

The third, and final observation is that it is not certain that the method of 'compartmentalised preparation', to use Denis Mazeaud's formula, is not without disadvantages. Yves-Marie Laithier deplored the fact that the provision did not develop such an important practical distinction between monetary obligations and obligations in kind. It is true that the Law of 9 July 1991[11] answers this concern to a large extent. However, it is perhaps not sufficient; a link between civil law and the law of performance would have been welcome, using as a starting point the idea of Eugène Gaudemet—which seems to me profoundly correct—that there is, between the different forms of performance (spontaneous, encouraged by means of a penalty clause or on pain of a monetary penalty, forced) a difference of form only, and not of substance.

On the other hand, one can be more critical of the provision which defines direct action. Not so much because it is merely descriptive, and therefore of doubtful value as a rule, but because it can only satisfy civil law lawyers by abstracting itself from the 'outside' world. The definition is so wide[12] that it includes enforcement measures for monetary debts. Far from being reserved to 'some creditors', this right is open to each of them (articles 2284 and 2285 Cc). The definition, instead of giving substance to the notion, leads to its dissolution.

---

[10] *Ibid*; L Miller, 'The Enforcement of Contractual Obligations: Comparative Observations on the Notion of Performance', above ch 7.

[10] Fabre-Magnan, above n 6.

[11] Loi no 91-650 du 9 juillet 1991 portant réforme des procédures civiles d'exécution, JO 14 July 1991.

[12] Art 1168 of the *Avant-projet*: 'The right to sue directly for payment of their debt against the debtor of their debtor, within the limit of both debts.'

III. EMERGING THEMES IN THE LAW OF DELICT
(GERHARD DANNEMANN)

Perhaps I should begin with a theme which, quite rightly, has *not* emerged as major topic from the four chapters on tort and the ensuing discussion. This is the issue of *non-cumul* of remedies in contract and tort, which distinguishes French from English law. In French law with its wide general clause and (theoretically) unlimited delictual liability for pure economic loss, such a doctrine can serve a useful function if contractual remedies are not always to be overlaid by delictual remedies. No such useful function can be served in English law, which shows a much smaller overlap between contractual and delictual liability, so that Lord Goff was right to reject a doctrine of *non-cumul* for English law in *Henderson v Merrett Syndicates Ltd*.[13]

A first theme that does emerge from the chapters and the discussion is the French notion of a law of damages which is common to contract and tort. The difference between French and English law is presently less noticeable than one could be lead to believe. On the one hand, English law has a respectable tradition of scholarly works on the law of damages as a subject in its own right.[14] On the other hand, in the present French Code civil, much of the law of damages is contractual law, and applied to delictual liability only by way of analogy. French courts have thus been free not to adopt for delictual claims some of the provisions on contractual losses, notably the limitation to foreseeable damage in article 1150 Cc. The picture looks quite different with the *Avant-projet*, which formulates one common law of damages for contract and tort. Where distinctions become necessary, they will have to be woven in, perhaps carefully, perhaps against the wording of the rules. I refer to the difficulty expressed in the chapter by Pauline Rémy-Corlay of distinguishing execution in kind of a contractual claim from reparation in kind under damages.[15] On the other hand, the experience of German law with its common law of damages for contract and tort in §§ 249–54 BGB is not too discouraging.

This leads to a second theme, which perhaps is even an overarching theme for the entire discussion. The present article 1382 Cc is the prototype of a very wide general clause, and it is essentially maintained in this generality by the *Avant-projet*. General clauses tend to have the disadvantage that they catch more than was bargained for by the legislator, whereas more specific rules (such as those used by English tort law and German law

---

[13] [1995] 2 AC 145 (HL).

[14] AI Ogus, *The Law of Damages* (London, Butterworths, 1973); H McGregor, *McGregor on Damages* (17th edn, London, Sweet & Maxwell, 2003). The first edition of 'McGregor' was John Mayne, *A Treatise on the Law of Damages* (London, H Sweet, 1856). See also J Sayer, *The Law of Damages* (London, W Strahan and M Woodfall, 1770).

[15] P Rémy-Corlay, 'Damages, Loss and the Quantification of Damages in the *Avant-projet de réforme*', above ch 14.

of delict) tend to have the disadvantage that they miss out on something important. If, for example, I cause an accident on the M25 motorway or on the Boulevard périphérique which leads to massive tailbacks, my fault can cause damage to thousands of motorists who arrive late for work or miss lucrative deals. French law with its wide delictual clause must therefore constantly keep an eye on limiting liability.

I have heard no one state in the chapters or in the discussion that the *Avant-projet* will do anything to reduce liability. On the contrary, I have heard many voices, many of them warning, which believe the opposite, namely that liability will be further extended.

We have learned from Jean-Sébastien Borghetti that the restatement in the *Avant-projet* has done nothing to limit the general clause as practised, and that on some occasions it may indeed have widened delictual liability.[16] Similar worries were expressed by Paula Giliker, generally about what she sees as the uncertainty created by some provisions, and more specifically about provisions on strict liability such as draft articles 1384(1) and 1360.[17] Pauline Rémy-Corlay had similar misgivings about the extension of what can be recovered as total reparation, and specifically about damages for violation of a collective interest, and towards third parties for breach of contract under article 1342.[18] In her cautious welcome of punitive damages, Solène Rowan has highlighted a number of problems related to the adoption of draft article 1371, including the *Avant-projet* being unspecific in general, and allowing punitive damages in contract law.[19]

In the past, French law has partially compensated for a generous general clause with more restrictive rules on causation and compensable loss, just as English and German law have overcome their tendency to be parsimonious by extending into compensation for pure economic loss which theoretically should not be available at all in those legal systems.

In its attempts to limit delictual recovery, French law has frequently resorted to notions of causation and recoverable loss as expressed in article 1151 Cc, a contractual provision which French courts have also applied to delictual liability. The provision presently reads:

> Even in the case where the non-performance of the agreement is due to the debtor's intentional breach, damages may include, with respect to the loss suffered by the creditor and the profit which he has been deprived of, only what is an immediate and direct consequence of the non-performance of the agreement.[20]

---

[16] J-S Borghetti, 'The Definition of *la faute* in the *Avant-projet de réforme*', above ch 12.

[17] P Giliker, 'The Role of *la faute* in the *Avant-projet de réforme*', above ch 13.

[18] Rémy-Corlay, above n 15.

[19] S Rowan, 'Comparative Observations on the Introduction of Punitive Damages in French Law', above ch 15.

[20] 'Dans le cas meme où l'inexécution de la convention résulte du dol du débiteur, les dommages et intérêts ne doivent comprendre à l' égard de la perte éprouvée par le créancier et du gain dont il a été privé, que ce qui est une suite immédiate et directe de l'inexécution de la convention.'

In my motorway example, I suspect that the damage suffered by the numerous motorists who, due to my fault, are stuck in a traffic jam would be considered *dommage indirecte* and thus ruled out. As Geneviève Viney has shown us, *dommage indirecte* has little to do with additional factors needed to produce damage, and is rather used methaphorically, as a shorthand for damage that cannot be recovered.[21] I understand it has been pensioned off in the *Avant-projet* on the ground of being not very helpful. I agree that the notion of *dommage indirecte* has little if any explanatory force. At the same time, I wonder why such an unhelpful notion should then become the controlling element in the new and controversial liability under article 1342 of the *Avant-projet*, the liability towards third parties for breach of contract.

One must also wonder which peg or shorthand will be available for French courts in the future for limiting liability. In one case,[22] a house built by the defendant had been erected taller than permitted by local by-laws. The claimant, the owner of a villa 50 metres away, required the top floor to be demolished on the ground that it obstructed his view. There was *faute* by the defendant, but the Cour de Cassation held the neighbour's loss to be *dommage indirecte* and explained that the statutory provisions aimed to protect only closer neighbours. The latter reason is, of course, an example for the scope of the rule theory which Jean-Sébastien Borghetti would like to see French courts embrace more openly.[23] That the court instead used *dommage indirecte* shows some existing problems in reasoning. Can there a more direct way of obstructing a view than by erecting a building which covers this view? But the case also shows the merits of having at least a shorthand for refusing recovery. Whereas 'the building was not *cause directe* for the loss of light' may be an acquired taste, to state that 'the building has not caused the loss of light' is plain ridiculous. So under the *Avant-projet*, French courts will at least have to find a new shorthand for rejecting recovery. And they will need such a shorthand even more urgently if delictual liability will indeed become even wider if the *Avant-projet* is adopted. One possible candidate is draft article 1343, the requirement of a *lésion d' un intérêt licite*, which once was used to fend off claims by mistresses, but which might find an entirely different field of application under the rules of the *Avant-projet*.

While this is mere speculation, we also know from English experience that dramatic changes in the setup of tortuous liability can go by almost unnoticed for some time. What might have appeared like a small twist in *Anns v Merton London Borough Council*[24] turned out to shift English law

---

[21] G Viney and P Jourdain, *Les conditions de la responsabilité* (3rd edn, Paris, LGDJ, 2006) no 359.
[22] Cass civ (3) 2 July 1974, D 1975, 61 note E Franck.
[23] Borghetti, above n 4.
[24] [1978] AC 728 (HL).

so far towards an almost French recovery for pure economic loss that the House of Lords pulled the emergency brake in *Murphy v Brentwood District Council*.[25] So some dangers lie ahead for French law if, under the *Avant-projet*, delictual liability is widened, and the most important shorthand for limiting recovery thrown overboard at the same time.

We do not know how French courts will react. I suppose they will do what Président Pierre Sargos has suggested in our discussion, namely react with pragmatism.[26] And that leads to a third emerging theme. Ultimately, our discussions are a showcase for the division of tasks between academics, legislators and judges. I have little doubt that the present draft would clarify much and make French law of delict more transparent. And although I sympathise with a number of concerns being raised about the *Avant-projet* being too unspecific, I would still think that it is much more specific on a number of issues than the present Code civil. What I doubt, though, is that the adoption of the *Avant-projet* would reduce the burden on courts to develop the law. Pragmatism may be a useful guide, but a lot of work would evidently have to be done during a phase of transition. Finally, I found it striking in the discussion that English and French law seem to agree on a role of judges who develop the law using common sense and pragmatism. Of course, English common sense and French common sense may not necessarily be the same.

---

[25] [1990] 1 AC 398 (HL).
[26] P Sargos, 'The Work of the Cour de Cassation on the *Avant-projet de réforme*', above ch 18.

Part III

Translating the
Avant-projet de réforme

21

Translating the Avant-projet de réforme

SIMON WHITTAKER AND JOHN CARTWRIGHT[1]

Anyone embarking on the translation of a legal text from the language used by one legal system to the language used by a second legal system must attempt to resolve (or at least come to terms with) a major tension between two competing aims. On the one hand, one must select those words and phrases in the language of composition which best give effect to the technical sense of the terminology used by the language translated in a way which is readily comprehensible to one's readers: here, the temptation is to use words commonly used by the legal system or legal systems with which the language of translation is closely associated (or perhaps even with which the translators are closely associated). On the other hand, one must not lose the technical subtleties, deform the analytical structure or more generally betray the legal thinking of the original text.

In the translation into English of the *Avant-projet de réforme*, set out in the Appendix to this volume, we have tried to resolve this tension bearing in mind both the nature of the text (or rather texts) involved and the characteristics of our likely readership. In this introductory essay, we will try to set out some of the difficulties we have encountered in the process and how we have tried to deal with them. We are conscious that some of our choices may not be the best ones and therefore would very much value suggestions as to other possibilities for the future.

---

[1] This chapter was drafted by Simon Whittaker, drawing on our discussions during the course of translating the *Avant-projet*. In preparing the translation we first discussed particular issues of language which we anticipated would arise in translating the text; then we divided the material by theme and each took responsibility for the first draft of roughly half of the French text. Finally, each of us reviewed the other's translation and we agreed the final text of the whole work. At each of these stages we encountered a range of issues, of which the most significant are described here.

I. GENERAL OBSERVATIONS

First, there are two kinds of text in the published edition of the *Avant-projet*: the preambles or introductory essays and notes (whether footnotes or interspersed with the text of the provisions) composed by the various contributors to the project on the one hand, and the draft legislative provisions suggested for reform of the Code civil themselves on the other.

The first kind of text includes the very general preambles by Pierre Catala introducing the project as a whole and by Gérard Cornu introducing the title on *Obligations*;[2] two rather more particular preambles introducing the proposals governing civil liability by Geneviève Viney and governing prescription by Philippe Malaurie;[3] and a series of introductory notes by the contributors to the project entrusted with the drafting (or rather the first drafting[4]) of particular sections of the *Avant-projet* governing obligations in general, contract and quasi-contracts.[5] These essays differ considerably in length, style and format (including the extent to which they use footnotes). So, in particular, the introductory essays by Catala, Cornu and Malaurie belong firmly to a grand legal rhetorical tradition, seeking by their style of language as much as by their invocation of earlier legislative reformers (notably, Portalis[6] and Carbonnier[7]) to emphasise the continuity of their undertaking, indeed, the traditional nature of their innovation. This kind of French style is, we found, really quite difficult to render in an English currently in use in the modern legal context and so instead we tried to capture the flavour of the French in our own translation. So, for example, at one point Cornu observes in referring to the importance of the binding force of contracts (expressed by article 1134 of the present Code civil) that:

> Au fond, l'ouverture à la modernité ne passe pas par le rejet des maximes qui font encore la force vive du contrat. L'article 1134 est toujours le même pilier. Il appartient aux citoyens.

We have rendered this as:[8]

---

[2] Below, pp 464–77 and 478–91 respectively.

[3] Below, pp 808–31 and 880–99 respectively.

[4] The parts of the *Avant-projet* governing contracts, obligations in general and quasi-contracts (which are attributed to and introduced by individual jurists or pairs of jurists) were all subject to editorial rewriting. As Catala explains (below, pp 469–71): '[the retouching] was undertaken by the original group of participants supplemented by volunteers depending upon the subject under debate; certain chapters required up to ten versions. . . . G. Cornu played a primordial role in the task of rewriting; any well-versed reader will recognise his style.'

[5] Below, pp 478–623.

[6] Below, pp 465, 467, 477 (in the General Presentation by Catala).

[7] Below, pp 465 (Catala), 618 (Cornu). Carbonnier is also invoked by other contributors in the particular preambles.

[8] Below, pp 480, 481. See another good example, in Catala's General Presentation, below,

Essentially, opening up to a modern perspective does not involve rejecting the maxims which are still the real strength of contract. Article 1134 is still the same mainstay. It is the citizen's birthright.

By contrast, while elegantly expressed, the introductory essay by Viney to the provisions governing civil liability prefers to explain in a rather more concrete way 'the significance of the choices which were made [by the working group which she chaired] on the most important issues'. A similar explanatory and perhaps somewhat less elevated style was adopted by most of the *Avant-projet*'s contributors in their introductory essays to their own sections. To reflect this stylistic difference, we have kept our own style more prosaic.

The second kind of text consists of the draft legislative provisions themselves. Clearly, the style of drafting of these is very different from most English legislative drafting, and so we have kept to this much more allusive style as far as possible, resorting to explanatory phrases rather than single words to translate French technical terms only where otherwise the translation would be incomprehensible.[9] We have not resorted to the expedients of using a rare English word or coining neologisms[10] to escape these difficulties, though we were sorely tempted to do so in the case of '*prestation*' (which exists in a somewhat rarefied manner in English, though not in English *law*) for reasons we shall later explain.[11] The main reason is our readership, which we see as including lawyers trained in the common law (including English lawyers), but also lawyers not so trained but who can read English (but not French) and are interested in law reform of the French Code civil. This wider readership emphasises the need already noted to avoid wherever possible the use of technical English law terms to translate technical French law terms, especially where the former have very particular English law or common law associations. Instead, we have tried to adopt a more neutral English (but not English law) terminology, where necessary this being explained in our own translators' footnotes (which

---

pp 466, 467: 'Le Code civil s'adresse de manière indifférenciée à tout citoyen, qu'il prend en charge de son premier à son dernier soupir, dans une égalité républicaine', translated as 'The Civil Code addresses all citizens alike, looking after them with Republican equality from their first breath to their last.'

[9] Eg our translation of *contre-lettres* in art 1165-1 of the *Avant-projet* as 'a secret agreement hidden by the contracting parties behind another ostensible agreement'. Another example of an explanatory translation may be found in the case of the term *interversion*, used, eg, in art 1162-2 which provides that '[l]e jugement d'annulation ou de résolution entraîne interversion de la prescription applicable à l'obligation de restitution'. This is rendered as '[a] court order which declares the annulment or the retroactive termination of a contract interrupts the original prescription period applicable to the obligation to make restitution and converts it into the prescription period provided by the general law'.

[10] Such as 'interversion' which has no technical meaning in English law—and very little meaning in English more generally, appearing in the *Oxford English Dictionary* as 'embezzlement' (which the French *interversion* does not mean) though stated by its *OED*'s editors as appearing *only* in a literary text of 1755.

[11] Below, p 440.

appear in square brackets). Of course, this involves a degree of compromise, both from the point of view of the full significance of the French term and from the point of view of the English used.

We shall give some examples of this later in the context of the effects of contractual obligations,[12] but here we would wish to mention one less prominent example of our avoidance of the apparently natural English 'equivalent'. So, for instance, we translate the French *bon père de famille* as 'good head of household'.[13] Here, we deliberately avoid using the very English phrase 'reasonable man': while the latter has the advantage of retaining the gender-bias (still surprisingly unremarked by most French lawyers), it loses the wider patriarchal flavour of the French (stemming of course from the French being itself a translation of the Latin *bonus paterfamilias*). Moreover, while the concept of 'reasonableness' is very familiar to French lawyers[14] (and has indeed sometimes been incorporated into French legislation as a result of its use by EC directives[15]), it is still seen by some as an alien import from the common law (with which it is rightly closely associated) and for this reason, if no other, is sometimes avoided by French legislation implementing an EC directive which uses it.[16] Given this sensitivity, we should not attempt to foist 'reasonableness' on the contributors to the *Avant-projet*! For similar reasons, we avoid translating *obligation de moyens* as 'obligation to take reasonable care', preferring instead 'obligation to take necessary steps'.[17]

For the remainder of this introductory essay, we wish to explain two further difficulties or types of difficulty which we have encountered: first,

---

[12] Below, pp 437–45.

[13] Art 1152-1 of the *Avant-projet*. See below, p 687.

[14] Eg G Viney and P Jourdain, *Les obligations, La responsabilité: conditions* (2nd edn, Paris, LGDJ, 1998; the volume forms part of J Ghestin (ed), *Traité de droit civil*) 354, who are content to refer to the standard of the *bon père de famille* in judging delictual fault for the purposes of arts 1382–1383 Cc as 'l'homme raisonnable, prudent et avisé, sûr de ses actes'.

[15] Eg art 1386-4 Cc (implementing Directive 1985/374/EEC concerning liability for defective products and defining 'defectiveness' of a product for this purposes of the special product liability in terms of 'la sécurité à laquelle on peut légitimement s'attendre . . . [compte tenu] . . . de l'usage qui peut en être *raisonnablement* attendu').

[16] Eg Directive 1999/44/EC of the European Parliament and of the Council of 25 May 1999 on certain aspects of the sale of consumer goods and associated guarantees uses 'reasonableness' and related words on four occasions, including the central definition of 'contractual non-conformity': arts 2(d) (definition of non-conformity partly in terms of 'reasonable expectation'), 2(3), 3(3) and 3(5) (the buyer's rights). However, the French implementing legislation substituted 'legitimate expectation' ('les qualités qu'un acheteur peut légitimement attendre') in this definition: art L 211-5 1 para 2 Code de la consommation (and see similarly art L 211-6 *ibid*) and expunged all reference to 'reasonableness' in setting out the consumer buyer's remedies. On French attitudes here see O Tournafond, 'Remarques critiques sur la directive européenne du 25 mai 1999 relative à certain aspects de la vente et des garanties des biens de consommation' D 2000 Chron 159 who considered that the 1999 Directive is 'essentially impregnated with woolly concepts foreign to our legal tradition', these concepts being (according to L Grynbaum, 'La fusion de la garantie des vices cachés et de l'obligation de délivrance opérée par la directive du 25 mai 1999' Contrats Concur Consom (May, 2000) 46) perceptibly 'Anglo-American'.

[17] Art 1149(2) of the *Avant-projet*.

the translation of French terms with multiple significances; and secondly, the translation of the various terms used to analyse and describe the effects of contractual obligations.

II. THE TRANSLATION OF FRENCH TERMS WITH MULTIPLE SIGNIFICANCE

There are, of course, a number of French terms which require translation in more than one way according to their context, and here we shall discuss only three.[18]

(a) 'de plein droit'

In general terms, the phrase *de plein droit* has the sense of some legal event that occurs automatically on the occurrence of an event or circumstance and so, 'by operation of law'. However, in the *Avant-projet de réforme*, it is used in two very different contexts.

First, *de plein droit* can be used to describe something that occurs by reason of the law itself and so without the need for judicial intervention or even, for example, one of the parties to a contract serving notice. This significance of *de plein droit* is very well caught by the negative reference to it in article 1184(2) of the present Code civil, which governs the mechanism of *résolution* (retroactive termination for contractual non-performance). Articles 1183 and 1184(2) first set out the mechanism of an implied 'resolutory condition' in all synallagmatic contracts for the situation of non-performance by one of the parties, but then articles 1184(2) and 1184(3) go on to avoid the logical effect of this device (ie automatic retroactive termination of the contract on satisfaction of the condition) by providing that, where one of the parties' undertakings has not been satisfied,

---

[18] *La cause* furnishes another example. In the context of contract we have translated *une cause* as 'a cause'—a 'non-translation' which draws attention by its very opaqueness to the peculiarity of the French concept; but in the context of the doctrine of *enrichissement sans cause* we have translated *sans cause* as 'unjustified' or 'without justification'. This translation certainly explains the thinking behind the latter doctrine in a way which makes it recognisable to a common lawyer (through familiarity with the idea of unjustified enrichment); but we cannot translate *la cause* in the contractual context as 'without justification' not least because art 1125 of the *Avant-projet* provides that 'L'engagement est sans justification, faute de cause réelle, lorsque, dès l'origine, la contrepartie convenue est illusoire ou dérisoire', given that we would be led to a translation which explains 'lack of justification' in terms of lack of justification. We recognise that our twofold translation of *la cause* and *sans cause* destroys the unity of approach between the doctrines of *la cause* in the contractual context and of *enrichissement sans cause* which Gérard Cornu celebrates (below, p 622 affirming that 'La présence de la cause dans le contrat répond à l'absence de cause dans le quasi-contrat'), but, with respect, we do not see this identification of the two doctrines as being prominent in *la doctrine* more generally.

le contrat n'est point résolu *de plein droit*. La partie envers laquelle l'engagement n'a point été exécuté a le choix ou de forcer l'autre à l'exécution de la convention lorsqu'elle est possible, ou d'en demander la résolution avec dommages et intérêts.

La résolution doit être demandée en justice, et il peut être accordé au défendeur un delai selon les circonstances.[19]

This provision could hardly be more emphatic. For, first, it states that in this situation 'the contract is not retroactively terminated *de plein droit*', but it then requires the creditor of the obligation which has not been performed to claim *résolution* (*alinéa* 2) and then adds emphatically that *résolution* must be sought from a court (*alinéa* 3). So, despite the logic of the implied 'resolutory condition', termination requires judicial intervention and does not occur by operation of law without more.

The *Avant-projet* does not deal with termination on contractual non-performance using the traditional device of 'implied resolutory condition', but instead allows the creditor of the obligation which has not been performed himself to terminate it, whether prospectively (*résiliation*) or retroactively (*résolution*).[20] However, the *Avant-projet* does use the phrase *de plein droit* at a number of points to refer to some legal effect or consequence of an action or an event which follows without the need of any further step (such as the giving of notice or judicial intervention) in the context of the incidence of restitution following annulment or retroactive termination,[21] liability in damages for non-performance of negative obligations,[22] the divisibility of joint and several obligations as between debtors,[23] and subrogation.[24] In all these contexts, we consider that this sense of *de*

---

[19] 'The contract is not retroactively terminated *de plein droit*. The party for whose benefit the undertaking has not been performed has a choice between forcing the other party to perform the contract [see below, p 436, on this translation] where it is possible or to claim retroactive termination of it with damages.

Retroactive termination must be claimed from a court, and there may be granted to the defendant a period of grace for performance according to the circumstances.'

[20] See arts 1158 to 1160-1 of the *Avant-projet* and see Whittaker, above, 193–4.

[21] Arts 1162 and 1163-5 of the *Avant-projet*, below, pp 696–7, 700–01. In the case of annulment of a contract, in principle both a claim for annulment and judicial intervention are still required (arts 1129, 1129-2, 1129-3, 1130 and 1130-1 of the *Avant-projet*) and so here the significance of the *obligation de restitution* arising *de plein droit* is that there is no need for further judicial order beyond annulment. In the case of *résolution*, the *Avant-projet* recognises both judicial and extra-judicial termination of the contract (art 1158 of the *Avant-projet*), though both need the service of notice by the creditor of the obligation in question. Here the significance of the *obligation de restitution* arising *de plein droit* is similarly that there is no need for *further* notice by the creditor of decision by the court.

[22] Art 1154-1 of the *Avant-projet*, below, pp 688–9. Here, its significance is that there is no need for the creditor to serve notice to perform on the debtor. Similarly, art 1381 of *the Avant-projet* provides that damages compensating loss resulting from delay in the payment of a sum of money are due 'only from the date of service of a notice to perform, except where legislation provides that they accrue *de plein droit*'.

[23] Art 1210 of the *Avant-projet*, below, pp 730, 731 and cf art 1224-1 (divisibility of obligation between heirs), below, pp 738, 739.

[24] Art 1259 of the *Avant-projet*, below, pp 760, 761.

plein droit is captured sufficiently by the English phrase 'by operation of law'.

Before moving on to a different significance of *de plein droit*, we should note that the drafters of the *Avant-projet* specifically *avoided* using this phrase in the context of set-off.[25] Article 1290 of the present Code civil states boldly that '[l]a compensation s'opère de plein droit par la seule force de la loi même à l'insu des débiteurs',[26] but its use of the phrase *de plein droit* has been criticised on the basis that set-off takes effect only after it is invoked by a debtor who has been sued.[27] For this reason, the drafters of the *Avant-projet* used the phrase *la compensation légale* (which is current in *la doctrine*) to distinguish set-off which arises by law from set-off which results from an order of the court or by contract, and we have followed this distinction by translating *la compensation légale* as 'set-off by law'.[28]

Secondly, the expresssion *la responsabilité de plein droit* is used in the context of civil (extra-contractual) liability. This expression first became current in the context of the liability of a *gardien* for the 'actions of things' in his keeping under article 1384(1) Cc and it brought with it a particular significance. Until the *affaire Jand'heur* in 1930,[29] it remained a matter of some dispute whether or not the *gardien* could escape liability by proving an absence of fault, this being suggested by the fact that it was sometimes said to be based on *une présomption de faute*.[30] However, this case established that the *gardien* possessed defences only of *force majeure* and *faute de la victime*, and the *Chambres réunies* of the Cour de cassation gave formal recognition to this by replacing the terminology *une présomption de faute* with *une presomption de responsabilité*.[31] However, as Viney and Jourdain have noted, from 1957 the Cour de cassation abandoned this terminology of 'presumption' (which suggested that this liability turned on an issue of proof) and adopted instead the expression *une responsabilité de plein droit* which 'removed any doubt on the question' whether liability remained grounded on fault.[32] Given this background, we think it right to translate this phrase as 'strict liability' (and describe a person bearing such a liability as being 'liable strictly'), as it is this characteristic of the liability that is uppermost in French minds when using the phrase,[33] whereas to an

---

[25] See the introductory note by J François and R Libchaber, below, pp 604, 605.

[26] 'Set-off takes effect by operation of law and by the mere force of the law even against the wishes of the debtors.'

[27] P Malaurie, L Aynès and P Stoffel-Munck, *Les obligations* (2nd edn, Paris, Defrénois, 2005) no 1191.

[28] Art 1241 of the *Avant-projet*.

[29] Ch réun 13 February 1930, S 1930.1.121 note Esmein, DP 1930.1.57 note Ripert.

[30] Ripert, *ibid*.

[31] Above n 29.

[32] Viney and Jourdain, above n 13, 607 referring to Cass civ 13 February 1957, Bull civ II no 89.

[33] See below, pp 472, 473 (P Catala); pp 820, 821 and 824, 825 (G Viney); arts 1354, 1355 and 1361 of the *Avant-projet*, below, pp 843, 845 and 848 respectively.

English reader the alternative translation of 'by operation of law' would not distinguish it sufficiently from any other liability, for *all* extra-contractual liabilities are imposed by the law's operation! Interestingly, it is to be noted that while the expression *une responsabilité objective* is also commonly used in *la doctrine* to denote a strict liability (in contrast to *une responsabilité subjective*, which requires proof of fault[34] and also suggests that any fault should be judged by the standard of the individual whose liability is in issue[35]), it is not used by the *Avant-projet* itself or by its contributors in their introductory notes.

(b) 'acte' and 'fait'

A rather more difficult series of questions arises in relation to the translation of *acte* and *fait*, terms that appear very regularly and at a number of different stages in the *Avant-projet* and its notes.

Let us start with the more straightforward uses. The term *acte juridique* occurs throughout the *Avant-projet* and refers to a voluntary act recognised by the law that is specifically undertaken to produce legal effects,[36] whether bilateral (such as a contract) or unilateral (such as a testament or *promesse unilatérale de vente*).[37] Although this broad categorisation of 'voluntary acts' is not common in the English context, its sense can be appreciated from the translation 'juridical act', the use of 'juridical' rather than 'legal' (or the more homely but clumsy 'act in law') drawing attention to the characteristic of the act as giving rise to legal consequences with the implication that these are intended.[38] However, where it is clear that the juridical act in question is necessarily contained in or evidenced by a document we have translated *acte* as 'instrument'; so *acte authentique* is translated as 'authenticated instrument' because here what is meant is not merely an act intended to produce legal effects, but an act contained in a document and authenticated which is so intended.[39] Similarly, *acte de cession* is rendered as 'instrument of assignment'.[40]

---

[34] See the discussion of the liabilities arising from non-performance of *obligations de moyens* and *obligations de résultat* in these terms in Viney and Jourdain, above n 31, 445–6.

[35] This is usually put in terms of an assessment '*in abstracto*' or '*in concreto*': ibid 350–54.

[36] Art 1101-1 of the *Avant-projet* and see similarly, J Flour, J-L Aubert and E Savaux, *Droit civil, Les obligations*, vol 1: *L'acte juridique* (12th edn, Paris, Sirey, 2006) no 55.

[37] Flour, Aubert and Savaux, above n 36, nos 489–503.

[38] Sometimes in the *Avant-projet* '*acte*' without the adjective is used in the same sense, and here we have kept to 'juridical act' where 'act' by itself would be unclear in the context. We have taken a similar approach to *l'acte législatif*, rendering this as 'legislative act'. Eg in Catala's General Presentation, 'L'acte législatif n'est pas un acte unilatéral mais collectif' is translated as 'A legislative act is not a unilateral act, but a collective one'. See below, pp 476, 477.

[39] See P Catala, Introduction to 'Validity–Form', below, pp 534, 535. Cf, however, below, n 60 explaining that French lawyers sometimes use *l'obligation* to describe the legal instrument in which an *acte juridique* is contained.

[40] H Synvet, Introduction to 'Transactions Relating to Rights Under Obligations' para 4, below, pp 608, 609.

Fait is more difficult. A first example of its use is as a complementary concept to *acte juridique*, ie *fait juridique* or *faits juridiques*. As article 1101-2 states:

> Les faits juridiques sont des agissements ou des événements auxquels la loi attache des effets de droit.

So, sometimes *faits juridiques* are things that a person does or fails to do (*agissements*, translated by us as 'conduct') or events to which the law attaches legal consequences. As the *Avant-projet* sets out (following in this respect French legal usage more generally), *faits juridiques* include not only *faits générateurs de responsabilité* but also *quasi-contrats*.[41] On turning to the range of *faits générateurs de responsabilité* we find that some of these require an action or omission on the part of the person to be held liable, as notably is the case with liability for *faute* under article 1352 of the *Avant-projet*, but this is also true of the liability of producers for harm caused by their defective products, who must have put the product into circulation;[42] but others do not, as is the case with the liability of a *gardien* for harm caused by the 'things within his keeping' and the liability of a person for harm caused by people under his control.[43] This very broad range of uses could have been dealt with in one of two ways: either we could simply translate *faits* throughout as 'facts' (or perhaps 'events'), or we could try to distinguish the significances of *faits* in the various situations where it is used, translating it as (as the case may be) 'facts', 'events' or 'actions'. Apart from simplicity, the advantage of the former is that it retains the formal unity of approach of the original; the disadvantage is that it renders *phrases* with a particular significance in French in a way which do not readily reveal this significance in the English. On balance, we found the second approach more convincing. So, *faits juridiques* is rendered as 'juridically significant facts' (the elaboration compared to the French being needed to explain the rather opaque 'juridical facts' and, indeed, to distinguish this category from 'juridical acts'); similarly, article 1284's statement that '[l]a preuve des actes et des faits d'où naissent les obligations peut être faite, selon les distinctions qui suivent, par écrit' appears in our translation as '[p]roof of acts and facts which give rise to obligations may be established, following the distinctions set out below, by writing'—the note to article 1284 linking this reference to *des actes et des faits* explicitly back to article 1101. However, *faits générateurs de responsabilité* [44] is translated as 'events giving rise to liability',[45] 'events'

---

[41] Art 1101-2 of the *Avant-projet*.
[42] Art 1386-11 1 Cc, incorporated by reference by Chapter IV, Section 2 of the part of the *Avant-projet* dedicated to civil liability.
[43] Arts 1354 to 1354-4 of the *Avant-projet*.
[44] Similarly, *fait générateur de l'obligation* as in art 2278 of the *Avant-projet*.
[45] Art 1342(2) of the *Avant-projet*.

being sufficiently broad to include within it all the various examples of civil liability set out in the *Avant-projet*.

By contrast, in the three classic phrases *le fait personnel, le fait des choses* and *le fait d'autrui*, we have translated *le fait* as 'action' or 'actions'. Clearly, this translation works best in the case of the first and the third of these. So, for example, the title to the section setting out a person's extra-contractual liability for fault is headed in French '*Le fait personnel*', which we translate as 'Liability for personal action';[46] similarly, '*Le fait d'autrui*' we translate as 'Liability for the actions of other people'.[47] In both these cases, translating *le fait* as 'fact' or 'event' would be meaningless ('liability for personal facts!'); and while 'liability for personal acts' is possible, it immediately would set up the risk of confusion with our principal trans-lation of *le fait juridique* as 'juridically significant fact' in contradistinction to *l'acte juridique* as 'juridical act'.[48] However, it is as regards liability for *le fait des choses* where our difficulty in translating '*le fait*' is at its most acute. So, notably, articles 1354 and 1354-1(1) provide that:

> On est responsable de plein droit des dommages causés par le fait des choses que l'on a sous sa garde.
>   Le fait de la chose est établi dès lors que celle-ci, en mouvement, est entrée en contact avec le siège du dommage.

Here, *le fait de la chose* cannot be translated as the 'fact of the thing' (nor even more by translating *le fait* as 'event' or 'circumstance') as these would be meaningless. We are faced, then, with using either 'action' (or a similar word such as 'deed'[49]), which would have the advantage of showing the connections with liability for personal actions and the actions of others, but the disadvantage of a degree of absurdity, given that 'things' do not act! On balance, we concluded that any absurdity involved was not inappropriate given that the idea of things 'acting' and being themselves 'causes' is present in this special (and almost uniquely French) basis of liability.[50] Finally, we translated *la responsabilité du fait des produits défectueux* as 'liability for defective products' and *un principe de responsabilité de plein droit du fait des activités dangereuses* as 'a principle of strict liability for dangerous activities': in both these phrases, a specific translation of '*fait*' is entirely redundant in English.

---

[46] Section 2, para 1, below, pp 840, 841. We add 'liability for' to 'personal action' rather than relying on the earlier heading (as does the French text, being *Dispositions propres à la responsabilité extra-contractuelle*).

[47] Title to Section 2, para 3, below, pp 842, 843.

[48] Above, p 432.

[49] We rejected 'act' for the same reason as is given at n 48.

[50] Other phrases using *fait* were sometimes translated in a way which circumvented the issue, so that, for example, in art 1354-2's statement that '[l]e gardien est celui qui a la maîtrise de la chose au moment du fait dommageable', *au moment du fait dommageable* was translated as 'at the time of its causing harm' (though elsewhere we have translated *le fait dommageable* as 'the harmful action': art 1360).

(c) 'contrat' and 'convention'

We found a particular difficulty in translating *la convention* in the *Avant-projet*, a difficulty that stems from its usage in the Code civil, for *la convention* is used in different ways in different places and, it must be said, in ways that are by no means entirely consistent.

First, we should note that it is often said that there is a distinction between *la convention* (defined as 'a meeting of minds between two or more persons intended to create legal effects') and *le contrat* (defined as such a meeting of minds but with the intention of creating *obligations*): this we shall refer to as the technical distinction. So, a 'release of a debt' (*une remise de dette*) is a *convention*, but not a *contrat*, as its purpose is to extinguish an obligation rather than to create it.[51] This distinction leads to a conclusion that *le contrat* forms a (very large) sub-category of *la convention*. However, while found in much of *la doctrine,* it is also accepted that

> the Code civil does not provide a general set of rules except for *le contrat*; but to a considerable degree this set of rules extends to all *conventions* for which *le contrat* provides the general background law [*le droit commun*].[52]

However, with respect, the strict categorisation between *conventions* and *contrats* in this sense does not appear to be reflected fully if one looks at the Code civil with a fresh eye; instead its provisions rather reflect the older (and ultimately Roman) distinction between *conventio* (an agreement, which may or may not be recognised by the law and given some legal force) and *contractus* (which is a particular type of legal relationship resting on *conventio*). So Zimmermann observes that in the famous pronouncements by Sextus Pedius and Ulpian[53] '[c]onventio . . . appears more or less to be a synonym for consensus'.[54] Zimmermann also notes that the French jurist of the second half of the seventeenth century, Jean Domat, took *les conventions* as the starting-point for his discussion of private law and defined them as

> les engagements qui se forment par le consentement mutuel de deux ou plusieurs personnes qui se font entr'eux une loi d'exécuter ce qu'ils promettent.[55]

Here, *les conventions* is used to describe those agreements which are given legal force and which involve 'undertakings' (*engagements*) (ie 'contracts' to an English lawyer): it is not given the technical meaning attributed to it

---

[51] M Fabre-Magnan, *Les obligations* (Paris, PUF, 2004) no 60.
[52] Flour, Aubert and Savaux, above n 36, no 80.
[53] Dig 2.14.1.3 and Dig 50.12.3 pr.
[54] R Zimmermann, *The Law of Obligations: Roman Foundations of the Civilian Tradition* (Oxford, Clarendon Press, 1996) 563.
[55] Liv I, Introduction.

by modern French jurists. The direct relationship of this statement in Domat to articles 1101 and 1134(1) Cc is obvious, although in article 1101 the drafters of the Code used *le contrat* instead of *la convention* and used *la convention* instead of the phrase *le consentement mutuel*.

What this means is that, in our view, an English translation should translate the significance of *la convention* in its various contexts in the *Avant-projet* (as in the Code civil) rather than hope to keep to a single translating word. So, in the definition of *contrat* in article 1102 of the *Avant-projet*, *la convention* should be translated into English as 'agreement'. However, at other times in the *Avant-projet* (as in the Code civil) *la convention* is used in a context which makes clear that it is not a mere agreement which is intended, but an agreement which is recognised as lawfully effective. This is most clear in articles 1134(1) and 1135 themselves. For, first, article 1134(1) makes little sense if it were held to state that 'agreements which are lawfully concluded take the place of legislation for those who have made them', but much more sense if it were to held to state that 'contracts which are lawfully concluded' have this effect, the reference to lawful conclusion being an echo of the fundamental provision at the very beginning of the Code civil, article 6, according to which 'on ne peut pas déroger par des conventions particulières aux lois qui intéressent l'ordre public et les bonnes mœurs'. Even more clear is article 1135, which defines the consequences of *les conventions* in terms of their obligational effect. This provision is incompatible with an understanding of *convention* as a mere agreement or a more technical understanding of *convention* as an agreement which does not *create* obligations! Conversely, the *Avant-projet* designates as *le contrat* an agreement which is 'extinctive' of rights and obligations—article 1121(2)—even though according to the technical distinction it would not be *un contrat* but only *une convention*. For this reason, we have translated *convention* here as 'contract', this being the closest equivalent in English. So, we translate *la convention* sometimes as 'agreement' and sometimes as 'contract' according to the context: see article 1102 (*convention* as 'agreement'), article 1108 (*convention* as 'contract' in context of conditions of validity) and article 1237 (*convention* as 'contract' in definition of *remise de dette*). For in English (and not merely in English law, putting aside its special meaning in public international law) 'contract' is the word used to describe an agreement given full legal force.[56]

---

[56] After concluding this work of translation (and writing this essay) we have had the benefit of seeing the work of A Tenebaum (gen ed), *Terminologie contractuelle commune* (Paris, Société de Législation Comparée, 2008) 19 which (inter alia) discusses most helpfully the usages of *contrat* and *convention* in the *acquis communautaire* and international instruments and compares these with their use of English.

III. TRANSLATING DIFFERENCE: THE ANALYTICAL STRUCTURE OF CONTRACTUAL *OBLIGATIONS* AND THEIR EFFECTS

We found the most difficult area for translation of the *Avant-projet* to be the terminology relating to contractual *obligations* and their effects, this terminology reflecting entirely the accepted usage of French lawyers more generally. We found this difficult because (in our view) this terminology expresses an analytical structure making up and surrounding the notion of *obligations*, their effects and the effects of their non-performance which is significantly different from the analytical approach adopted by English common law.

Let us start very simply and fundamentally with the provisions defining contracts and describing their effects. Article 1101 of the present Code civil starts the preliminary section of its part entitled 'Des contrats ou des obligations conventionnelles en général' by announcing that:

> Le contrat est une convention par laquelle une ou plusieurs personnes s'obligent, envers une ou plusieurs autres, à donner, à faire ou à ne pas faire quelque chose.

Article 1102 of the *Avant-projet* is even more general, replacing the reference to the three different types of obligation ('à donner, à faire ou à ne pas faire quelque chose') with the general phrase *à accomplir une prestation* (to whose translation we shall return).[57] Both formulations have in common that they define contracts in terms of an agreement (*une convention*) giving rise to obligations. Later in both the Code and the *Avant-projet,* article 1134(1) proclaims that 'contracts which are lawfully concluded take the place of legislation for those who have made them'; and article 1135 adds that:

> Les conventions[58] *obligent* non seulement à ce qui y est exprimé, mais encore à toutes les suites que l'équité, l'usage ou la loi donnent à *l'obligation* d'après sa nature.[59]

So, contracts create *obligations*, these being set by the parties or resulting from legislation, custom or equity, these provisions giving striking recognition to what is universally known as *la force obligatoire du contrat*. This last expression is usually translated into English as 'the binding force of contracts', but for the French lawyer (following here the civilian tradition more generally), use of the language of *obligation* possesses a series of consequences, both in terms of analysis and in terms of moral and, therefore, normative appeal.

[57] Below, p 440.
[58] See above, pp 435–6, for the translation of *convention* as 'contract'.
[59] 'Contracts create obligations not merely in relation to what they expressly provide, but also to all the consequences which equity, custom or legislation give to them according to their nature.'

First, at an analytical level, in the context of *le droit des obligations*, *une obligation* refers to the *whole* relationship linking the parties.[60] So, for example, Malaurie, Aynès and Stoffel-Munck define *une obligation* (and not merely a contractual obligation) as 'le lien de droit unissant le créancier au débiteur' and observe that

> [d]ans l'obligation, il existe . . . à la fois un aspect passif, la dette pesant sur le débiteur et un aspect actif, la créance dont le créancier est titulaire.[61]

We can notice also from this sentence that French lawyers describe the parties to a contractual *obligation*[62] as being *le créancier* (the person holding a right under the *obligation*) and *le débiteur* (the person bearing the duty under the *obligation*), the 'right under the *obligation*' itself being referred to as *la créance*, the duty as *la dette*. All these terms are found throughout the *Avant-projet de réforme* as they are in both the Code civil and in French law more widely.

Turning to the English law context, while 'obligation' can be found in a somewhat consciously civilian way (so, some works collecting together the law governing contract and torts, and sometimes also restitution/unjust enrichment, refer to themselves as concerning the 'law of obligations'[63]), generally in the contractual context 'obligation' is used by English lawyers as synonymous with duty (this being correlative to a contractual right) and is not used (as in French law) to designate the whole legal relationship between the parties to a contract or more generally. Moreover, while the language of rights and obligations is often used and readily comprehensible to English lawyers to describe aspects of the relationship of parties to a contract, their more natural and usual way of expressing the effects of contracts starts by setting out the contract's express and implied terms, this being supplemented (especially as regards certain types of contracts) by describing the contract's other legal incidents (eg the duty of good faith in contracts of partnership[64] or the rules as to discharge on variation in

---

[60] Flour, Aubert and Savaux, above n 36, nos 38 and 39 note that '*obligation*' is also found more generally in the sense of 'duty' (*le devoir*) and (particularly in commercial law) to refer to the legal document or instrument in which the 'juridical act' is contained. They then adopt for their own use in their work on *Les obligations* the meaning noted in the text.

[61] Malaurie, Aynès and Stoffel-Munck, above n 27, no 1. They distinguish *obligation* from a mere duty (*le devoir*) from whose breach an *obligation* arises: *ibid*.

[62] Interestingly, even though French works on *obligations* typically include treatment of what is termed variously *la responsabilité délictuelle* (now somewhat old-fashioned), *la responsabilité extra-contractuelle* (though this term is normally used where a contrast is to be drawn with *la responsabilité contractuelle*, which has itself become a controversial terminology or (most commonly) *la responsabilité civile*, the 'parties' to a claim on this ground are often not referred to as *le créancier* and *le débiteur*, but rather *la victime* and *l'auteur du dommage*.

[63] Eg AM Tettenborn, *Introduction to the Law of Obligations* (London, Butterworths, 1984); A Burrows (ed), *English Private Law* (2nd edn, Oxford University Press, 2007) possesses a part dedicated to the 'Law of Obligations'.

[64] *O'Neill v Phillips* [1999] 1 WLR 1092, 1098 (HL) (Lord Hoffmann).

contracts of suretyship[65]).[66] Furthermore, the normal English way of describing the parties to a contract is simply as the '(contracting) parties'. Where one needs to refer to one or other party to a contract, either the terminology attaching to the particular type of contract can be used (eg seller and buyer, or employer and employee) or (and typically in the context of a dispute) one can refer to the 'party in breach/default' and 'the injured/innocent party' or even (with an eye to future litigation) the 'defendant' and 'claimant', respectively. So, in looking at a particular aspect of a contract as between its parties and how it affects the parties given what has or has not occurred (and therefore what is in dispute), an English lawyer normally examines whether the parties have performed or are in breach or, as the case may be, whether any purported exercise of a contractual right under a contract (eg a right to vary the price in certain circumstances[67]) falls within its terms. As a result, it is no exaggeration to say that in English one can often describe a contract and its legal effects without using the language of obligation at all.

How, then, should we translate the French terminology of *obligation* in the *Avant-projet*? Here, we decided to opt for the simple expedient of translating *obligation* as 'obligation' despite its different normal usage in English, as it was important to retain the form and structure of the French analysis. For the same reason, we translated *le créancier* as 'creditor', *le débiteur* as 'debtor', and *la dette* as 'debt'[68] even though normally all these words are used in the English context only to describe someone with a right or duty relating to the payment of *money*, and often under a loan. Again, the convenience of adopting this pseudo-civilian terminology is obvious, both in terms of retaining the French structure and in giving the English translation the flavour of the more formal and conceptual French usage. And to the extent to which we use these English terms more broadly than they would be in the normal English context, their broader meaning is typically readily apparent from the context. Following on from this, we used a phrase rather than a word to describe *la créance*, being the 'right

---

[65] *Holme v Brunskill* (1877) 3 QBD 495 (CA).

[66] However, the English courts have made considerable use of implied terms in setting the incidents of particular types of contracts where a civil law system would instead rely on particular rules of the Civil Code or general principle (such as good faith): B Nicholas, 'Rules and Terms—Civil Law and Common Law' (1974) 48 Tul LRev 946.

[67] But notice that such a contractual right does not have any correlative duty in the other party, nor does it form part of an 'obligation' between the two. Indeed, in Hohfeldian terms (WN Hohfeld, *Fundamental Legal Conceptions as Applied in Judicial Reasoning*, ed WW Cook (New Haven, Yale University Press, 1946), such a right is a power.

[68] Eg frequently in the sections 'Joint and Several Obligations' (arts 1209, 1210, 1212); 'Indivisible Obligations' (arts 1216, 1217) and 'Satisfaction' (arts 1220, 1224). However, we translate *dette de valeur* as 'obligation of value', or more explicitly 'debt whose value is to be assessed' (art 1225) using here 'obligation' in the more narrow English sense so as to avoid the even more opaque 'debt of value'.

under a (contractual) obligation'.[69] So, for example, we translate article 1251 in the following way:

> La cession de créance est une convention par laquelle le créancier cédant transmet tout ou partie de sa créance à un tiers cessionnaire, par vente, donation ou autre titre particulier.

> Assignment is a contract by which the creditor (the assignor) transfers the whole or part of his rights under an obligation to a third party (the assignee) by sale, gift or by some other disposition.

However, French lawyers explore and expound *obligations* further and in a number of different directions. The *Avant-projet* therefore follows the Code civil in distinguishing between *obligations de faire* (obligations to do), *obligations de ne pas faire* (obligations not to do) and *obligations de donner* (obligations to give[70]), but adds a fourth category, *obligation de donner à usage* (obligation to give for use).[71] In the *Avant-projet* these are designations of different types of *obligations* according to their subject-matter (*l'objet*), this subject-matter being termed *la prestation*.[72] How, then, should we translate *prestation*? This elusive term is often translated in international instruments (such as the *Principles of European Contract Law*[73]) as 'the performance' but this is unsatisfactory as *la prestation* does not refer to the act (or omission) of performing (which is expressed in French as *l'exécution*) but rather the thing to be done or not done, to be given or given for use. While the word 'prestation' is used by Scottish lawyers in a similar sense to the one used by French law[74] and does appear in English dictionaries with the meaning of 'the performance of something promised',[75] it is not a word in current use in either English law or

---

[69] Eg arts 1244 and 1246 and generally in the chapter 'Transactions Relating to Rights Under Obligations' ('Des opérations sur créances') (arts 1251 to 1257-1).

[70] Arts 1144 and 1145 of the *Avant-projet*.

[71] Art 1146. The force of *obligation de donner* is actually more of an 'obligation to convey title' (B Nicholas, *The French Law of Contract* (2nd edn, Oxford, Clarendon Press, 1992) 154 noting that this usage stems from Roman law), but such a translation would immediately cause problems with the translation of *une obligation de donner à usage*, where *donner* has the sense of 'give' or 'transfer' but *not* of the conveyance of title.

[72] This appears especially from art 1121 which refers to the quadruple classification noted in the text and then states (in paragraph 2) that '[l]es prestations ainsi convenues caractérisent le contrat comme déclaratif, constitutif, translatif ou extinctif de droits et d'obligations'.

[73] Arts 7:104-7:109 PECL, where the terms *prestation, exécution* and *paiement* appearing in the French version of the *Principles* all appear at certain points in the English version as 'performance'.

[74] See, eg, *Kerr v Aitken* [2000] BPIR 278 (where a particular defence to liability to restore a bankrupt's property conveyed to his wife which uses the expression 'adequate consideration' was interpreted as referring to 'a reasonable prestation' for the property conveyed); *Armour v Thyssen Edelstahlwerke AG* [1991] 2 AC 339, 350–51 quoting *Cowan v Spence* (1824) 3 S 42 (new edn 28) ('rents and other prestations being duly paid'); *Herbert Clayton and Jack Waller Ltd v Oliver* [1930] AC 209, 221 (Lord Dunedin).

[75] *Oxford English Dictionary* 'prestation'.

everyday English more generally. In a translation,[76] therefore, we decided that in many contexts the most helpful translation of *la prestation* would be 'subject-matter of the obligation'. So, for example, article 1112-1(2) of the *Avant-projet* appears as:

> [L'erreur] est une cause de nullité qu'elle porte sur la prestation de l'une ou de l'autre partie.

> [Mistake] is a ground of nullity whether it bears on the subject-matter of the obligation of one party or of the other.

An example of the need to avoid translation of *la prestation* as 'performance' may be seen in articles of the *Avant-projet* where both *l'exécution* and *la prestation* are used,[77] such as article 1154(2):

> [L']exécution [d'une obligation de faire] peut être ordonnée sous astreinte ou un autre moyen de contrainte, sauf si la prestation attendue a un caractère éminemment personnel.

> [P]erformance [of an obligation to do] may be ordered by a court either on pain of a monetary penalty or of some other means of constraint, unless the subject-matter of the obligation has a clearly personal character.

and 1163:

> Les modalités de la restitution dépendent de la nature des prestations accomplies en exécution du contrat.

> The modalities of restitution depend on the nature of the subject-matter of the obligations effected in performance of the contract

However, while we have an explanatory approach, we have sometimes used slightly different wording. So, article 1135-1 of the *Avant-projet* reads:

> Dans les contrats à exécution successive ou échelonnée, les parties peuvent s'engager à négocier une modification de leur convention pour le cas où il adviendrait que, par l'effet des circonstances, l'équilibre initial des prestations réciproques fût perturbé au point que le contrat perde tout intérêt pour l'une d'entre elles.

> In contracts whose performance takes place successively or in instalments, the parties may undertake to negotiate a modification of their contract where as a result of supervening circumstances the original balance of what the parties must do for each other is so disturbed that the contract loses all its point for one of them.

---

[76] Cf S Whittaker, 'A Few Observations on the Plurality of Debtors and on their Release' in A Vaquer (ed), *La Tercera Parte de Los Principios de Derecho Contractual Europeo, The Principles of European Contract Law Part III* (Valencia, Tirant lo blanch, 2005) 23, 33–4 which argues in favour of using 'prestation' in the English version of the Principles of European Contract Law and similar documents.

[77] For perhaps the most extreme example, see art 1219, 'le paiement est l'exécution de la prestation due', discussed below, p 442.

Here, *des prestations réciproques* is translated as 'of what the parties must do for each other'. Similarly, in article 1122-1 of the *Avant-projet* we translate *prestations* as 'contents' of the obligations:

> Le défaut d'équivalence entre les prestations convenues dans un contrat commutatif n'est pas une cause de nullité, hormis le cas où la loi admet la rescision du contrat pour cause de lésion.

> A lack of equivalence in the agreed contents of the obligations in a commutative contract is not a ground of annulment except where the law allows rescission of the contract by reason of substantive inequality of bargain.

Putting aside other types of classification of *obligations* found in the *Avant-projet* (notably, as between *obligations de moyens* and *obligations de résultat*), the next stage to which we come in the French analysis is performance (*l'exécution*) or non-performance (*l'inexécution*) of *obligations*. This is, of course, a complex and rich area, both at a substantive level and in terms of difficulties of translation into English, and we shall confine ourselves to two points: the relationship between *l'exécution* and *le paiement* and the proper translation of *exécution en nature* and its related terms.

First, the section of the *Avant-projet* entitled *Du paiement* provided (for us) some of the most difficult provisions to be translated. So, first and foremost article 1219 provides that:

> Le paiement est l'exécution de la prestation due.[78]

The difficulty here is with *le paiement*, as 'payment' in English (and in English law) refers to the transfer of a sum of *money* in discharge or satisfaction of a debt (ie a duty to pay a certain some of money), whereas *le paiement* is not so restricted in this context (though it is in the context of *le paiement de l'indu*).[79] This, then, suggested translating *le paiement* as 'discharge', but while the *effect* of *le paiement* is indeed the discharge of an *obligation*, discharge is expressed in French normally by use of the verbs *acquitter* or *libérer*;[80] and *le paiement* describes rather the process which leads to this effect (though with one eye on this effect). For this reason, we chose 'satisfaction' as the closest English term to *le paiement* in this general sense, so that article 1219 is translated as

> Satisfaction is the performance of the subject-matter of the obligation.

---

[78] If one were to adopt the translating practice of the *Principles of European Contract Law*, noted above, p 440, this provision would appear as: 'Performance is the performance of the due performance'!

[79] S Whittaker, 'The Law of Obligations' in J Bell, S Boyron and S Whittaker (eds), *Principles of French Law* (2nd edn, Oxford University Press, 2008) 294, 427–8. For our translation of *le paiement* in the context of 'Undue payment' as 'payment', see arts 1330–1333 of the *Avant-projet*, below, pp 802–05.

[80] Eg arts 1221 and 1227-1 of the *Avant-projet* respectively in both of which we use 'discharge'.

This solution is, we concede, not entirely perfect, for while in this context it renders both the sense and generality of *le paiement*, in later provisions which are concerned with monetary obligations, we translate *le paiement* as 'payment'[81] as in these contexts 'satisfaction' is both awkward and unnecessarily general. To this extent, we lose the unity of *le paiement* in the contractual part of the *Avant-projet*.

Secondly, the *Avant-projet* declares boldly that '[l]'obligation de faire s'exécute si possible en nature'.[82] But how should one translate *exécution en nature* (which appears both in the text of the *Avant-projet* and in its notes) and *exécution forcée*, referred to emphatically by Leveneur and Lécuyer in the notes to the *Avant-projet*—although not in the provisions of the *Avant-projet* itself—as *exécution forcée directe*[83]? The temptation to an English lawyer is to see these expressions as the equivalent of English law's remedy of specific performance—and sometimes they do represent the closest equivalent there is—but this temptation has to be resisted for a number of reasons.

The most important reason is that while *exécution en nature* often does involve a court ordering a contractual debtor to perform his obligation, it does not always do so. The key example of this is provided by what is known as *la faculté de remplacement*, at present provided for by article 1144 of the Code civil and found in article 1154-2 of the *Avant-projet*. These provisions provide that a creditor of an obligation may apply to the court to be authorised to perform the obligation himself or to have the obligation performed by a third party at the expense of the debtor, hence 'replacing' the performance. This mechanism does not therefore involve performance of the obligation by the debtor (who simply pays money rather than doing what the obligation requires), but French lawyers do see it as *exécution en nature*. So, Leveneur and Lécuyer observe that:

> la faculté de remplacement des actuels articles 1143 et 1144 peut être maintenue quasiment en l'état: elle passait pour une atténuation de l'impossibilité de l'exécution forcée directe; elle est évidemment compatible, *a fortiori*, avec le nouveau principe posé du droit à l'exécution en nature, dont elle représente une modalité.[84]

So, *la faculté de remplacement* is a 'modality' (kind or type) of *exécution en nature,* even though not a true example of *exécution forcée directe*. Here, then, we see a contrast between *exécution en nature* which allows the creditor to obtain 'performance' (or perhaps rather, *la prestation*, the

---

[81] Eg art 1225-2.

[82] Art 1154(1) ('if possible an obligation to do is to be performed in kind').

[83] Below, p 558.

[84] Below, pp 558, 559; translated as: 'the right to obtain substitute performance at present provided for by articles 1143 and 1144 can be retained almost as it stands. It can pass muster as a means of making up for the lack of availability of direct enforced performance; a fortiori it is

subject-matter of the obligation) from a third party and *exécution forcée directe*, where the debtor is himself forced (under threat of monetary penalties) to perform. For this reason, we translate *exécution en nature* as 'performance in kind'.

However, in our view, neither should we translate *exécution forcée* (*directe*) as specific performance. First, specific performance in English law is a remedy with a specific scope, characteristics and force: it is restricted to duties to do or to convey title to property (negative duties being enforceable by injunction and duties to pay money by the action for the agreed sum); it is equitable and discretionary; and it is backed by the fearsome law of contempt of court. None of these features applies to *exécution forcée* and to mark this difference a neutral English expression is preferable: we chose 'enforced performance' or 'direct enforced performance' as the case may be.[85]

In concluding this discussion, we would like to note that the *Avant-projet* follows the traditional structure of French law in relation to the effects of an obligation. For, in principle, an obligation to do or not to do leads to 'performance in kind', seen not so much as a sanction for non-performance but rather as the logical putting into effect of the obligation itself. Secondly, however, the two other consequences of non-performance of an obligation are indeed seen as *sanctions*,[86] sanctions, ie for 'imputable non-performance' on the part of the debtor, and these are *résolution* (retroactive termination) or *résiliation* (prospective termination) of the contract and liability in damages. While both these 'sanctions' are subjected to considerable reform by the *Avant-projet* ('unilateral' termination of the contract for non-performance by the creditor being formally recognised and treated in principle as prospective[87] and contractual liability in damages being dealt with together with extra-contractual liability in damages[88]), what we do not see is the introduction into French law of either the language or the approach of 'remedy' for non-performance,[89] even though this is well known in France and has a certain following in *la doctrine*.[90] This is not, of course, a problem of translation. Rather, the retention of the language of sanction marks a consciously traditional French approach to contractual non-performance and an implicit rejection of the approach of the common law with which the language of remedy is rightly associated.

---

clearly also consistent with the new principle of a right to performance in kind, of which it forms one type'.

[85] These terms appear only in the notes to the *Avant-projet*, rather than the provisions themselves: below, pp 500, 501 and 558, 559.

[86] This language is particularly prominent in Sérinet's introductory note to the *Avant-projet*'s provisions on the restitutionary effects of *nullité* and *résolution*, below, pp 567–87.

[87] Arts 1158 to 1160-1 of the *Avant-projet* and see Fabre-Magnan, above, ch 8 and Whittaker, above, ch 9.

[88] Arts 1343 to 1351-1 of the *Avant-projet*.

[89] *Remède* is not used in the *Avant-projet* in this context and is used otherwise only twice: below, pp 502 and 590.

Appendix

Avant-projet de réforme du droit des obligations et de la prescription

Pierre Catala

Proposals for Reform of the Law of Obligations and the Law of Prescription

English translation by
John Cartwright and
Simon Whittaker

Avant-projet de réforme
du droit des obligations
et de la prescription
Pierre Catala

Proposals for Reform
of the Law of Obligations
and the Law of Prescription
Pierre Catala

English translation by
John Cartwright and
Simon Whittaker

Translators' Preface

We would first like to thank Professor Pierre Catala for inviting us on behalf of himself and of the other contributors to the *Avant-projet de réforme du droit des obligations et de la prescription* to translate its provisions into English. We have very much enjoyed this opportunity of bringing this expression of French private law *doctrine* to a wider audience.

We early took the view that it was important to include in the scope of our translation all the elements of the *Avant-projet* as presented to the French Minister of Justice in September 2005 (and later published by the Ministry[1]), including both the introductory preambles of the contributors and the notes which accompany the provisions themselves. These materials explain the general approaches and guiding principles of the contributors to the *Avant-projet* and the thinking behind many of the specific provisions.

We have endeavoured to translate the French legal terminology in a way which is both accurate and faithful to French legal thought and yet comprehensible to readers of English, whether or not they are familiar with the concepts of the civilian tradition. We have attempted to explain already some of the choices which we have made and how the most difficult of them stem from differences in some of the fundamental structural features of French law and the common law (to which many available English terms are so intimately related).[2] In this published edition of the translation, we have added some notes of our own to the text. These are of four types: some relate to the translation itself; some refer the reader to other parts of the *Avant-projet*; some expand the original references to French *doctrine* or case-law; and some seek to explain briefly those concepts or rules which are likely to be most unfamiliar to a person not trained in the civil law. All these translators' notes appear at the foot of the page in square brackets so as to be distinguished from the original footnotes.

Finally, we would like to thank Mlle Geneviève Helleringer of the Université de Paris I Panthéon-Sorbonne for her helpful comments on an earlier draft of our translation.

John Cartwright and Simon Whittaker

[1] P Catala (dir) Avant-projet de réforme du droit des obligations et de la prescription (Paris, La documentation Française, 2006).
[2] See above, pp 425ff.

Sommaire

Contents

452

458

Personnes ayant participé à la préparation de l'avant-projet

(par ordre alphabétique)

Pascal ANCEL – Professeur à l'Université de Saint-Étienne

Jean-Luc AUBERT – Conseiller honoraire à la Cour de cassation. Agrégé des Facultés de droit

Laurent AYNES – Professeur à l'Université de Paris 1

Alain BENABENT – Avocat au Conseil d'État et à la Cour de cassation. Agrégé des Facultés de droit

Philippe BRUN – Professeur à l'Université de Savoie

Rémy CABRILLAC – Professeur à l'Université de Montpellier 1

Pierre CATALA – Professeur émérite de l'Université de Paris 2

Gérard CORNU – Professeur émérite de l'Université de Paris 2

Philippe DELEBECQUE – Professeur à l'Université de Paris 1

Jean-Pierre DUMAS – Président de chambre honoraire à la Cour de cassation

Georges DURRY – Professeur émérite de l'Université Paris 2

Jérôme FRANCOIS – Professeur à l'Université de Paris 5

Alain GHOZI – Professeur à l'Université de Paris 2

Jacques GHESTIN – Professeur émérite de l'Université de Paris 1

Jean HAUSER – Professeur à l'Université de Bordeaux 4

Jérôme HUET – Professeur à l'Université de Paris 2

Patrice JOURDAIN – Professeur à l'Université de Paris 1

Pierre LECLERCQ – Conseiller honoraire à la Cour de cassation

Hervé LECUYER – Professeur à l'Université de Paris 2

Fabrice LEDUC – Professeur à l'Université de Tours

Yves LEQUETTE – Professeur à l'Université de Paris 2

Laurent LEVENEUR – Professeur à l'Université de Paris 2

Rémy LIBCHABER – Professeur à l'Université de Paris 1

Grégoire LOISEAU – Professeur à l'Université de Paris 1

Philippe MALAURIE – Professeur émérite de l'Université de Paris 2

Philippe MALINVAUD – Professeur émérite de l'Université de Paris 2

Didier MARTIN – Professeur à l'Université de Paris 11

Denis MAZEAUD – Professeur à l'Université de Paris 2

Judith ROCHFELD – Professeur à l'Université de Paris 11

Participants in the preparation of the Reform Proposals

(in alphabetical order)

Pascal ANCEL – Professor at the University of Saint-Etienne

Jean-Luc AUBERT – Honorary member of the Cour de cassation. Professor of law

Laurent AYNES – Professor at the University of Paris 1

Alain BENABENT – Counsel with right of audience before the Conseil d'État and the Cour de cassation. Professor of law

Philippe BRUN – Professor at the University of Savoie

Rémy CABRILLAC – Professor at the University of Montpellier 1

Pierre CATALA – Emeritus professor at the University of Paris 2

Gérard CORNU – Emeritus professor at the University of Paris 2

Philippe DELEBECQUE – Professor at the University of Paris 1

Jean-Pierre DUMAS – Honorary President of Chamber of the Cour de cassation

Georges DURRY – Emeritus professor at the University of Paris 2

Jérôme FRANCOIS – Professor at the University of Paris 5

Alain GHOZI – Professor at the University of Paris 2

Jacques GHESTIN – Emeritus professor at the University of Paris 1

Jean HAUSER – Professor at the University of Bordeaux 4

Jérôme HUET – Professor at the University of Paris 2

Patrice JOURDAIN – Professor at the University of Paris 1

Pierre LECLERCQ – Honorary member of the Cour de cassation

Hervé LECUYER – Professor at the University of Paris 2

Fabrice LEDUC – Professor at the University of Tours

Yves LEQUETTE – Professor at the University of Paris 2

Laurent LEVENEUR – Professor at the University of Paris 2

Rémy LIBCHABER – Professor at the University of Paris 1

Grégoire LOISEAU – Professor at the University of Paris 1

Philippe MALAURIE – Emeritus professor at the University of Paris 2

Philippe MALINVAUD – Emeritus professor at the University of Paris 2

Didier MARTIN – Professor at the University of Paris 11

Denis MAZEAUD – Professor at the University of Paris 2

Judith ROCHFELD – Professor at the University of Paris 11

Yves-Marie SERINET – Professeur à l'Université de Cergy Pontoise

Philippe SIMLER – Professeur à l'Université de Strasbourg 3

Philippe STOFFEL-MUNCK – Professeur à l'Université de Paris 1

Hervé SYNVET – Professeur à l'Université de Paris 2

Jean-Jacques TAISNE – Professeur à l'Université de Lille

Philippe THERY – Professeur à l'Université de Paris 2

Geneviève VINEY – Professeur à l'Université de Paris 1

Guillaume WICKER – Professeur à l'Université de Bordeaux 4

Yves-Marie SERINET – Professor at the University of Cergy Pontoise

Philippe SIMLER – Professor at the University of Strasbourg 3

Philippe STOFFEL-MUNCK – Professor at the University of Paris 1

Hervé SYNVET – Professor at the University of Paris 2

Jean-Jacques TAISNE – Professor at the University of Lille

Geneviève VINEY – Professor at the University of Paris 1

Guillaume WICKER – Professor at the University of Bordeaux 4

Présentation générale
de l'avant-projet

Pierre Catala

1) Le bicentenaire du Code civil a connu un immense retentissement dans la plupart des pays ayant la codification en partage, quelle que fût leur langue. Il donna lieu à d'innombrables manifestations, dont émergèrent, bien qu'elles fussent de taille et d'inspirations diverses, les noms de Portalis et de Carbonnier. Le fondateur et le rénovateur avaient en commun la culture historique, une connaissance approfondie des coutumes et des traditions qui forment « l'esprit des siècles », et le sentiment qu'« il est utile de conserver tout ce qu'il n'est pas nécessaire de détruire ». Ils n'étaient pas des faiseurs de systèmes, mais ne doutaient pas, cependant, que la loi soit, avant la jurisprudence, mère de l'ordre juridique. « La science du législateur consiste à trouver, dans chaque matière, les principes les plus favorables au bien commun ; la science du magistrat est de mettre ces principes en action, de les ramifier, de les étendre, par une application sage et raisonnée, aux hypothèses privées » (Discours préliminaire).

De ces deux noms accolés s'exhalait une double certitude : que le Code de 1804 constituait toujours un modèle idéal de législation civile ; qu'il était possible de le rénover sans dégrader sa structure ni sa forme. Jean Carbonnier l'avait démontré en transfigurant le livre premier avec le bonheur que l'on sait. Mais par-delà les propos agréables qui sonnèrent aux oreilles françaises, un autre message, le plus souvent tacite, nous était adressé ; il disait : qu'attendez-vous pour continuer la modernisation de votre code ?

2) À cette tâche, et dans la perspective du grand rendez-vous de 2004, **une poignée de civilistes** universitaires s'était attelée un an plus tôt. Le déclic provint d'un colloque organisé par la faculté de Sceaux qui mettait en parallèle le droit français avec les « principes européens du droit des contrats » issus des travaux de

General Presentation of the Reform Proposals

Pierre Catala

(1) The bicentenary of the Civil Code has created a considerable stir in most of the countries which share the principle of codification, whatever their language. It has given rise to innumerable gatherings—on different scales, and with different objects—but at which the names of Portalis[1] and Carbonnier[2] have stood out. The founder and the reformer had the same perspective of history, a deep understanding of the customs and traditions which make up the 'spirit of the centuries' and the sense that 'it is right to save everything that it is not necessary to destroy'. They did not themselves create systems of law, yet they had no doubt that legislation, rather than case-law, is the mother of legal order. 'The art of the legislator consists in finding, in each area, those principles which are most conducive to the common good; the art of the judge is to put these principles into action, to develop them and extend them, by wise and reasoned application, to individual cases' (Portalis, *Discours Préliminaire*).

Putting these two names side by side, we can be certain of two things: on the one hand, that the Code of 1804 always constituted an ideal model of civil legislation and, on the other, that it was possible to reform it without damaging either its structure or its form. This had been demonstrated by the evident success of Jean Carbonnier's transformation of its first book.[3] But beyond these remarks, which make pleasant hearing for French ears, there was another message for us, more often than not unspoken: what are you waiting for to continue the modernisation of your code?

(2) With the prospect of the great watershed of 2004, **a handful of civil law academics** started on this task a year earlier. This was triggered by a symposium organised by the Faculty at Sceaux, which set French law alongside the *Principles of*

---

[1] [Jean-Etienne-Marie Portalis (1745–1807) was one of the Commission of four charged by Napoleon with drafting the Civil Code. For a portrait and a brief biography, see P Malaurie, *Anthologie de la Pensée Juridique* (Paris, Editions Cujas, 1996) 143–5. The quotations in this paragraph are all taken from the the *Discours Préliminaire sur le Projet de Code Civil* (1799), reproduced in JEM Portalis, *Ecrits et Discours Juridiques et Politiques* (Presses Universitaires d'Aix-Marseille, 1988) 21 at 23, 34, 30 respectively. The *Discours Préliminaire* was signed by all four members of the Commission but was written by Portalis.]

[2] [Jean Carbonnier (1908–2003) was Professor and Dean (*Doyen*) at the University of Poitiers (1937-1955) and Professor at Paris (1955–1976). For a photograph and a brief biography written in 1996, see Malaurie, above, n 1, 281–6. His writing on the civil law and legal theory was very influential in France, and he was the draftsman of a number of reforms to the Civil Code within the field of family law since 1965.]

[3] [ie, the law of persons (including family law): above, n 2; see H Stalford, 'Family Law' in J Bell, S Boyron, S Whittaker, *Principles of French Law* (2nd edn, Oxford University Press, 2008) ch 8.]

M. Landö. Il paraissait en ressortir que si, sur certains points, notre droit était ou pouvait entrer en convergence avec la trame proposée pour l'Europe, sur d'autres points, cette dernière contrevenait davantage à notre tradition nationale. Dans la conjoncture du moment, ceci méritait à l'évidence d'être approfondi.

Le dessein de ceux qui s'assemblèrent pour y réfléchir n'était pas de s'opposer à qui ni à quoi que ce soit. Il était de passer au crible les Titres III et IV du livre troisième du Code civil pour en détecter les silences et pour distinguer, parmi les dispositions en vigueur, celles qui méritaient de demeurer en l'état, de celles qui appelaient une écriture nouvelle ou un pur et simple abandon. Ce faisant, nous suivions l'exemple de nos voisins allemands et néerlandais qui venaient de rénover leur code, tout comme nos cousins d'outre-atlantique québécois et latino-américains.

Au cœur du débat qui s'ouvrait, il y avait la place du Code civil dans l'ordre juridique privé. Est-il encore le droit commun par excellence, la constitution civile de la France ? S'il ne l'est plus, peut-on le rétablir comme tel, au centre d'un système de lois proliférant au gré des politiques nationale et communautaire et dont la complexité s'accroît tant qu'en bien des domaines sa connaissance devient l'apanage de quelques initiés ? Pour répondre à ces deux questions, il faut se faire **une certaine idée de la loi civile.**

3) « Les lois civiles, disait Portalis, disposent sur les rapports naturels ou conventionnels, forcés ou volontaires, de la rigueur ou de la simple convenance, qui lient tout individu à un autre ou à plusieurs ». Par ces simples mots, leur office se trouve dépeint dans sa généralité absolue. Alors que les lois du commerce laissent toute liberté aux seuls marchands pour les besoins de leur négoce, que la protection du consommateur lui est spécifiquement dédiée face au professionnel, la loi civile saisit ces mêmes personnes en dehors de leurs activités de marchand ou de consommateur. Le Code civil s'adresse de manière indifférenciée à tout citoyen, qu'il prend en charge de son premier à son dernier soupir, dans une égalité républicaine.

S'agissant des contrats, sa vocation est à la fois de tempérer par le souci d'une certaine justice contractuelle la liberté ouverte aux commerçants sans verser dans la mise sous tutelle du consommateur. Le droit civil est un droit d'équilibre, pareillement soucieux des intérêts en présence, sans *a priori* favorable à l'une ou l'autre partie. C'est à d'autres codes ou lois qu'incombe le soin de régler la balance contractuelle vers plus d'efficacité ou de sécurité, en fonction des situations juridiques en cause et de l'utilité sociale recherchée.

Accomplie dans cet esprit de juste milieu, la modernisation du Code civil le maintiendra comme pivot du droit privé, tronc robuste d'un arbre dont les branches procèdent et se ramifient sans se délier de leur souche. À cette fin, le Titre « Des obligations » doit être le siège de maximes générales qui édictent un droit commun actualisé, recouvrant et ménageant à la fois le particularisme des lois spéciales

European Contract Law produced by Professor Lando's working group.[1] What appeared to emerge was that, although on certain points our law fitted, or could develop to fit, the framework proposed for Europe, on other points, the latter contravened our national tradition rather more. In the present circumstances this seemed to merit further investigation.

Those who gathered to deliberate on this had no underlying purpose of opposing anyone, or anything. The intention was to examine Titles III and IV of the third book of the Civil Code closely, to determine where it was silent and to distinguish, among those provisions currently in force, those which merited being left as they were from those which needed to be rewritten, or quite simply abandoned. In this, we were following the example of our German and Dutch neighbours who had just reformed their codes, as had our transatlantic cousins in Quebec and Latin America.

At the heart of this opening debate was the place of the Civil Code within the private legal order. Does it still express the fundamental, general principles of law, the civil constitution of France? If not, could it be re-established as such, at the centre of a system of legislation which is proliferating at the whim of national and European Community politicians and growing in such complexity that the knowledge of particular areas becomes the prerogative of the few? To answer these two questions, we need to form **a clear idea of civil legislation.**

(3) 'Civil legislation', said Portalis, 'deals with relationships, whether natural or contractual, forced or voluntary, of a defined type or created to suit the occasion, linking each individual to another or others'.[2] These simple words serve to delineate its general purpose in the absolute. Whereas commercial law gives merchants every freedom in the pursuit of their deals, and consumer protection is specifically dedicated to the consumer as against the business or professional, the civil law deals with these same persons beyond their roles of merchant or consumer. The Civil Code addresses all citizens alike, looking after them with Republican equality from their first breath to their last.

When it comes to contracts, its vocation is to temper the freedom available to merchants with a concern for a degree of contractual justice, without becoming the over-protective guardian of consumers. The civil law is a law of equilibrium, concerned equally with all the interests before it without favouring *a priori* one party over the other. It is the concern of other codes or laws to regulate the contractual balance towards greater efficiency or certainty depending upon the legal contexts in question and their requisite social utility.

Undertaken in this spirit of the golden mean, the modernisation of the Civil Code will maintain this as the central tenet of private law, the robust trunk of a tree whose branches grow and spread out in turn without losing touch with their roots. To this end, the Title 'Obligations' should be the repository of maxims which will set out an updated statement of the general law to be applied, whilst at the same

---

[1] [O Lando and H Beale (eds), *Principles of European Contract Law, Parts I and II, Prepared by The Commission on European Contract Law* (The Hague, Kluwer Law International, 2000); O Lando, E Clive, A Prüm, R Zimmerman (eds), *Principles of European Contract Law, Part III, prepared by the Commission on European Contract Law* (The Hague, Kluwer Law International, 2003).]

[2] [*Discours Préliminaire*, above, p 465, n 1, 32.]

nouvelles. C'est ainsi que le code demeurera **le recours naturel du juge confronté au silence des statuts particuliers et des conventions, le fonds commun de notre raison juridique.**

4) Parrainé par l'Association Capitant, **le projet formé en 2003 est aujourd'hui achevé** avec l'aide du Ministère de la justice, trente mois après avoir été conçu. Pour aboutir dans ce délai, les quelques-uns du début n'auraient pu suffire ; il était indispensable de répartir le fardeau et d'assembler d'autres compétences. Notre première tâche fut de découper la matière et d'en confier les segments à des collègues particulièrement qualifiés, en posant un certain nombre de règles de temps et de forme. On estima rapidement nécessaire de former deux équipes distinctes, affectées l'une aux contrats et quasi-contrats et l'autre à la responsabilité civile. G. Viney se détacha du groupe initial et composa avec G. Durry une équipe de six universitaires au total qui prit en charge collectivement la responsabilité civile. Pour les contrats et les quasi-contrats, au contraire, un travail purement collectif paraissait irréalisable au regard de la masse des sujets à traiter. Le groupe initial assurerait donc la coordination d'un travail réparti, en s'adjoignant un nombre suffisant de coauteurs. Vingt-six universitaires et trois hauts magistrats à la retraite de la cour de cassation assumèrent la réfection du Titre III (obligations conventionnelles) subdivisé en dix-huit thèmes. Deux autres auteurs se consacrèrent respectivement aux quasi-contrats et à la prescription. Au total, **le programme mobilisa trente-sept personnes.**

Sa réalisation a connu globalement **quatre phases** qui se sont parfois chevauchées. Le premier temps (février-juillet 2003) fut dédié à la confection du programme : détermination des objectifs, découpage de la matière, ralliement des auteurs. Dans une seconde étape (septembre 2003 – avril 2004) ceux-ci accomplirent leur mission consistant à rédiger les articles du chapitre ou de la section qui leur était confié et un texte de présentation.

Chacune de ces contributions fut ensuite adressée à tous les intervenants, avec demande d'avis, de suggestions et de critiques : cette troisième phase constitua une sorte de « forum » d'une grande richesse grâce à la part qu'y prit la majorité des auteurs. On découvrit des lacunes et des doubles emplois, ainsi que certains articles du code actuel qui n'avaient pas été reclassés à la suite des modifications apportées au plan. On releva aussi quelques conflits d'opinion, plus rares qu'on n'aurait pu le craindre, dont la plupart connurent une solution consensuelle.

La troisième phase était prévue pour s'achever à l'automne 2004, mais elle se prolongea, en fait jusqu'à la fin. Il est vrai que la quatrième et dernière avait parallèlement commencé dès l'été 2004. Elle avait pour objet initial l'harmonisation d'une vingtaine de contributions forcément hétérogènes en la forme, à raison du style propre à chaque auteur. À quoi s'ajouta la charge de résoudre les difficultés apparues au cours de la phase trois et de retoucher de nombreux textes en raison des avis que le « forum » avait inspirés ; il y fut procédé avec le concours du groupe initial augmenté de quelques volontaires en fonction des sujets débattus ; certains

time subsuming specific new laws. In this way the Code will remain **the natural recourse of a judge faced with silence in the specific statutes or contracts, the common basis of our legal reasoning.**

(4) Sponsored by the *Association Capitant*,[1] **the project set up in 2003 has now been completed,** with the assistance of the Ministry of Justice, thirty months after its conception. Those who were there at the outset were too few for the project to succeed within this time; it was essential to spread the load and gather together those with other expertise. Our first task was to divide up the material and to entrust sections to colleagues who were particularly well qualified, whilst imposing a clear set of rules regarding time and form. We soon came to the view that it was necessary to form two distinct teams, one for contract and quasi-contracts and the other for civil liability. G. Viney moved from the initial group and, with G. Durry, formed a team of six academics in total who collectively took on civil liability. For contract and quasi-contracts, on the other hand, a purely collective approach seemed impossible, given the mass of topics to be handled. The initial group was to ensure therefore the oversight of a collaboration and was at the same time afforced by a sufficient number of co-contributors. Twenty-six academics and three senior judges who had retired from the Cour de cassation took on the rebuilding of Title III (Contractual Obligations), subdivided into eighteen topics. Two other contributors devoted themselves to quasi-contracts and prescription respectively. In total, **the project called thirty-seven people into action.**

There were **four phases,** in all, in carrying out the project. These sometimes overlapped. The first phase (February to July 2003) was dedicated to preparing the programme: determining the objectives, dividing up the material and gathering together the contributors. In a second phase (September 2003 to April 2004) they accomplished their task which consisted in drafting the articles of the chapter or section with which they had been entrusted and producing a text for presentation.

Each of these contributions was then presented to all the participants requesting their advice, suggestions and criticism: this third phase comprised a sort of 'forum' which was richly rewarding thanks to the part played by most contributors. Gaps and duplications were discovered as well as particular articles of the present Code which had not been reorganised following modifications to the plan. There were also some conflicts of opinion, rarer than one would have thought, most of which found a solution by agreement.

The third phase should have been completed by autumn 2004 but in fact continued through to the end of the project. It is fair to say that the fourth and final stage ran in parallel from summer 2004. Its initial objective was the harmonisation of around twenty contributions which were inevitably heterogeneous in form, given the personal style of each contributor. In addition there was the task of resolving those differences which became apparent during phase three and re-touching numerous texts in response to the advice given during the 'forum'; this was undertaken by the original group of participants supplemented by volunteers depending upon the subject under debate; certain chapters required up to ten versions... G. Cornu

---

[1] [*Association Henri Capitant des Amis de la Culture Juridique Française*; see *www.henricapitant.org.*]

chapitres connurent jusqu'à dix versions... Quant à l'œuvre de réécriture, G. Cornu y joua un rôle primordial ; tout lecteur averti reconnaîtra sa plume.

Pendant que le droit des contrats et des quasi-contrats prenait forme nouvelle, le groupe Viney-Durry achevait de reconstruire la responsabilité civile et Ph. Malaurie la prescription. C'est donc un avant-projet abouti qui, au seuil de l'été 2005, va être présenté aux pouvoirs publics et à la communauté juridique dans son ensemble, de la manière que voici. Un premier regard sur le projet en général sera suivi d'une introduction propre aux obligations conventionnelles par G. Cornu, puis d'un exposé des motifs où chaque auteur présentera la partie du projet qu'il a traitée ; tout ceci précédant le texte des nouveaux articles 1101 à 1339. La deuxième partie comportera une introduction de G. Viney sur la responsabilité civile, suivie des nouveaux articles 1340 à 1386. La troisième, relative à la prescription, contiendra une introduction de Ph. Malaurie en tête des articles 2234 à 2281.

5) Ces quelques pages ne sauraient empiéter sur les explications qui seront données au lecteur par les esprits les mieux avertis. Leur but n'est que de dégager quelques linéaments qui tissent **la logique** d'un projet considérable par son ampleur et la diversité de ses objets.

Un hommage, d'abord, doit être rendu aux sources, à commencer par la première d'entre elles, la loi. L'étude a montré que nombre de solutions du code Napoléon conservaient leur valeur après deux siècles d'application ; on les retrouvera soit sous la forme même dans laquelle nos ancêtres les avaient coulées, soit dans une rédaction mieux adaptée au goût du temps présent. Sous ce rapport, **l'avant-projet ne propose pas un code de rupture, mais d'ajustement.**

En ceci, il est redevable à la **doctrine** et à la **jurisprudence**. La première fut à l'origine de maintes trouvailles terminologiques habillant des innovations fondamentales : les obligations de moyens et de résultat pour n'en citer qu'une. L'avant-projet lui doit les nombreuses définitions qu'il a paru souhaitable de consacrer dans la loi, car la définition, si elle n'est pas *stricto sensu* normative, constitue un incomparable outil d'analyse et de qualification.

Pour grande cependant que soit la part due à la doctrine, celle de la jurisprudence l'emporte largement dans la substance de l'avant-projet. La stabilité des titres III et IV s'explique certes, en partie, par l'apparition de codes et de lois qui ont germé autour du Code civil, mais plus encore par l'œuvre de la Cour de cassation dans l'interprétation *praeter legem* du code lui-même. C'est elle qui a donné corps à la période précontractuelle, inventé la responsabilité du fait des choses, sculpté la stipulation pour autrui... On la retrouvera à chaque pas ou presque dans les pages qui suivent.

6) Mais l'empreinte du code Napoléon et l'emprunt fait aux sources interprétatives, pour importants qu'ils soient, sont loin de réduire l'avant-projet à l'étiage d'une codification à droit constant.

En certains points, et non des moindres, y figurent de **nouvelles règles contraires à**

played a primordial role in the task of rewriting; any well-versed reader will recognise his style.

While the law of contract and the law of quasi-contracts were taking on their new form, the Viney-Durry group completed their reconstruction of civil liability and P. Malaurie that of prescription. Thus it became possible to present successfully completed Reform Proposals to the public authorities and the legal community in early summer 2005 in its entirety, as you see. An initial overview of the project will be followed by a specific introduction to contractual obligations by G. Cornu. Then a preamble in which each contributor will present the part of the Proposals on which he or she worked. This will all be followed by the text of the new articles 1101 to 1339. The second part will comprise an introduction by G. Viney on civil liability, followed by the new articles 1340 to 1386. The third, relating to prescription, will contain an introduction by P. Malaurie, followed by articles 2234 to 2281.

(5) These few pages will not encroach on the explanations which will be offered to the reader by better informed minds. The intention is just to highlight some characteristics which weave together **the logic** of a project of such a considerable magnitude and diversity of subjects.

First of all we must pay respect to our sources, beginning with the first of these–legislation. Our study has shown that numerous solutions in the Napoleonic Code still retain their value after two centuries of application; they will be found either in just the same form as they were cast by our ancestors or re-drafted to suit present day taste better. In this connection, **the Reform Proposals do not propose to break away from the original, but to adjust it.**

In this the Proposals are indebted to **academic writing** and the **work of the courts.** The former was the source of much of the terminology for fundamental innovations; obligations 'to take necessary steps' and 'of result' to name but one.[1] The Reform Proposals also owe to academic writing the numerous definitions which it has seemed desirable to set out in the legislation, because definition, if not *stricto sensu* normative, constitutes an incomparable tool for analysis and characterisation.

But however great the debt to academic writing, the Reform Proposals owe far more to the work of the courts. Clearly the robustness of Titles III and IV is explained in part by the appearance of codes and legislation which have grown up around the Civil Code, but even more so by the work of the Cour de cassation in interpreting the Code beyond the words of the text themselves. This court has given substance to the pre-contractual period,[2] discovered the liability for the 'actions of things',[3] moulded stipulations for the benefit of third parties,[4] etc. It will be seen at almost every turn in the following pages.

(6) But the stamp of the Napoleonic Code and borrowings from interpretive sources, however considerable, are far from reducing the Reform Proposals to merely a low level of a codification of the law as it stands today.

On certain points—and not the least significant—there are **new rules which run**

[1] [Below, p 553, and article 1149.]
[2] [Below, p 499.]
[3] [Below, p 845.]
[4] [Below, p 591.]

la jurisprudence contemporaine. La promesse unilatérale oblige le promettant à conclure le contrat si l'acceptation du bénéficiaire intervient pendant le délai de l'option (art. 1106) ; la fonction de la cause s'épuise dans la formation du contrat, sans interférer avec son exécution (art. 1123 et 1124 combinés). L'engagement du délégué envers le délégataire rend indisponible la créance du délégant envers le délégué, qui ne peut être saisie ni cédée (art. 1284). Ailleurs, les textes proposés ne contrecarrent pas la jurisprudence, mais visent à la **clarifier** (restitutions), l'**encadrer** (consentement, cession de contrats), la **tempérer** par une règle de preuve (fixation du prix, art. 1121-4 et 1121-5), à **lui ouvrir des voies nouvelles** : action directe (art. 1168), contrats interdépendants (art. 1172 s.), cessions de créance future (art. 1252).

Il faut, enfin, prendre en compte les matières qui échappent au pouvoir du juge partout où **la loi seule peut créer le droit ou le transformer.** Elle seule peut substituer à l'article 1142 du Code civil une disposition de sens inverse (art. 1154 proposé), offrir au créancier insatisfait la faculté de résoudre unilatéralement le contrat (art. 1158), permettre au juge d'ordonner la renégociation d'une convention qui a perdu tout intérêt pour l'une des parties (art. 1135-2). Un texte légal est tout aussi nécessaire pour accorder une préférence aux créanciers qui exercent les actions oblique ou paulienne (art. 1167-1), de même que pour alléger les formes substantielles de la cession de créance (art. 1254-2).

Dans l'ordre de la responsabilité civile, c'est à la loi d'affirmer l'existence d'une responsabilité contractuelle, de créer un régime de responsabilité plus favorable aux victimes de dommages corporels (art. 1341, 1351, 1373, 1382-1), d'élargir la responsabilité de plein droit en matière d'activité anormalement dangereuse (art. 1362) et d'ouvrir la voie à des dommages et intérêts punitifs (art 1372). S'agissant de la **prescription**, il n'appartient qu'au législateur d'en fixer les délais, ou de redistribuer les rôles respectifs de l'interruption et de la suspension.

7) Cette palette qui, pour les besoins de l'exposé, décline les nuances allant de la continuité au changement, masque peut-être l'**unité du projet**. On la trouvera pourtant dans les multiples lignes de force qui ont guidé sa construction.

Un même **principe de cohérence** lie les conditions de validité du contrat à leurs sanctions (art. 1122 et 1124-1), et inspire, notamment, des règles de fond telles que l'article 1125, al. 2, d'interprétation (art. 1137) et de preuve (art. 1293). Par-delà ces manifestations ostensibles, une cohérence latente, que les introductions ci-après mettront en lumière, assemble les différentes pièces de l'avant-projet.

Le pouvoir de la volonté est proclamé. Son omnipotence est de principe en cas d'échange des consentements (art 1127 et 1136), y compris en matière de preuve

counter to current case-law. A unilateral promise to contract obliges the promisor to conclude the contract if the beneficiary accepts within the option period (article 1106); the function of the doctrine of 'cause' is fully explored in the formation of the contract without interfering with its performance (articles [1124] and [1125])[1] taken together). In a case of delegation the undertaking by the delegate in favour of the beneficiary of the delegation renders the right of the delegator unavailable against the delegate, so that it can no longer be subject to distraint nor assigned (article [1281]). Elsewhere, the proposed texts do not contradict case-law, but aim to **clarify** it (restitution), **provide a framework** for it (consent, assignment of contracts), **temper** it with a rule of proof (fixing of the price, articles 1121-4 and 1121-5), or **open up new solutions:** direct actions (article 1168), interdependent contracts (articles 1172 *et seq.*), and assignment of future rights under obligations (article 1252).

Lastly, we must take into account matters which are beyond the power of courts where **legislation alone can create or transform the law.** It alone can substitute in place of article 1142 of the Civil Code a contrary provision (the proposed article 1154), offer the unsatisfied creditor the right to terminate a contract unilaterally (article 1158), or permit the court to order the renegotiation of a contract which has lost all point for one of the parties (article 1135-2). Equally a legislative provision is necessary in order to give priority to creditors exercising *actions obliques* or *actions pauliennes*[2] (article 1167-1), and likewise to reduce the substantial formalities for the assignment of rights under obligations (article 1254-2).

Within the law of civil liability, it is for legislation to confirm the existence of contractual liability; to create a regime of liability which is more favourable to victims of personal injury (articles 1341, 1351, 1373, 1382-1); to broaden strict liability in the case of abnormally dangerous activities (article 1362) and to open the way to punitive damages (article 1372). On the question of **prescription** only the legislator can determine the time periods or redefine the respective roles of interruption and suspension.

(7) The fact that, for the purpose of presentation, this palette runs through every shade from continuity to change, perhaps masks the **unity of the Reform Proposals.** It is nonetheless to be seen in the many thematic strands which have come together to guide its construction.

The same **principle of consistency** links the conditions for the validity of a contract to their sanctions (articles 1122 and 1124-1) and inspires, in particular, basic rules such as article 1125 paragraph 2, and those of interpretation (article 1137) and of proof (article 1293). Beyond these obvious manifestations a latent consistency which the following introductions will bring to light, unites the different elements of the Reform Proposals.

The power of the human will is proclaimed. Its omnipotence is the overriding principle in the case of exchange of consent (articles 1127 and 1136), including in

---

[1] [In the course of translation we have discovered a small number of errors of cross-referencing in the published French text of the *Avant-projet*. We have sought to correct them, identifying any changes we have made by the use of brackets (as here).]

[2] [For an explanation of *actions obliques* and *actions pauliennes*, see below, p 589, nn 2, 3.]

(art. 1289), de responsabilité (art. 1382) et de prescription (art. 22 35). Parallèlement, les effets reconnus à la volonté unilatérale s'étoffent (art. 1101-1, 1121-4, 1121-5, 1158).

Mais s'il sacrifiait sans retenue à la liberté contractuelle, le Code civil perdrait la vertu d'équilibre qui est de son essence ; l'affirmation de cette liberté ne saurait aller sans des contrepoids générateurs de sécurité juridique. Ainsi un **devoir de loyauté**, implicite ou nommé, traverse de bout en bout la matière des obligations conventionnelles (art. 1104, 1110, 1120, 1134, 1176).

Allant plus loin, **un même esprit de solidarité** porte la loi civile à secourir la partie la plus faible par des dispositions générales qui ne se limitent pas au droit de la consommation. Telles sont les règles relatives à la forme, à la capacité et au pouvoir, que l'avant-projet développe sensiblement par rapport au Code civil. À côté d'elles, des mesures ponctuelles relevant du même esprit touchent aux conditions de validité du contrat (art. 1114-3, 1122-3, 1125 et suivants), à son interprétation (art. 1140-1), à son exécution (art. 1154, 1175), à sa cession (art. 1165-4) et à sa preuve (art. 1289 al. 3 et 1299). Semblablement, la responsabilité civile prend en considération le comportement de personnes dont l'état nécessite une surveillance particulière (art. 1356, 1357) et la prescription épargne celles qui sont empêchées d'agir (art. 2266).

8) Tel qu'il se présente, l'avant-projet s'efforce donc de faire une juste part à l'esprit des siècles et aux nécessités du temps présent, comme firent jadis les pères du code. Cette même combinaison s'imposant à ceux qui nous entourent, il n'est pas sans intérêt de regarder, au terme de notre démarche, dans quelle mesure son résultat recoupe les principes avancés par M. Landö. Le bilan apparaît mitigé.

Il est des convergences appréciables dans la formation du contrat, les vices du consentement et la représentation (bien que l'avant-projet soit plus complet sur ce dernier point). Également, dans les phases d'exécution, on trouve une faveur commune faite à l'exécution en nature du contrat, la trilogie des « moyens » disponibles face à la défaillance du débiteur (exécution, résolution, dommages-intérêts), ainsi que la faculté de résolution unilatérale. On se réjouira plus encore d'une identité de vue en matière de prescription.

Mais les « principes européens » omettent la cause comme justificatif de l'engagement, confèrent au juge le pouvoir de refaire le contrat (ce que les auteurs de l'avant-projet rejettent massivement), et admettent l'annulation du contrat par voie de notification au contractant. Ces mêmes principes admettent la preuve du contrat

the matter of proof (article 1289), liability (article 1382) and prescription (article 2235). In parallel, the effects recognised for unilateral acts of will have been strengthened (articles 1101-1, 1121-4, 1121-5, 1158).

But if it gave in completely to freedom of contract, the Civil Code would lose the virtue of balance which is its essence; the affirmation of this freedom could not proceed without a counterweight to generate legal certainty. Thus a **duty of loyalty**, implicit or expressed, runs from one end to the other through the subject-matter of contractual obligations (articles 1104, 1110, 1120, 1134, 1176).

Going further, **this same spirit of solidarity**[1] brings civil legislation to the rescue of the weakest party through general provisions which are not limited to consumer law. Such are the rules relating to form, capacity and power to act,[2] which the Reform Proposals develop markedly by comparison with the Civil Code. Alongside these, some particular measures, in the same spirit, concern the conditions of validity of contracts (articles 1114-3, 1122-3, 1125 *et seq.*), their interpretation (article 1140-1), their performance (articles 1154, 1175), their assignment (article 1165-4) and their proof (articles 1289 paragraph 3 and 1299). Likewise, civil liability covers the behaviour of those whose condition calls for special supervision (articles 1356, 1357) and the law of prescription spares those who are prevented from acting (article 2266).

(8) As presented, the Reform Proposals aim at an equitable balance between the spirit of the centuries and the needs of the present, as did the fathers of the Code in their day. As this same balance is necessary for every society today, it is not without interest to see, now we have completed our project, how far its outcome matches the principles advanced by Professor Lando. The answer appears to be mixed.

There is clear convergence on formation of contracts, defects of consent, and representation (although the Reform Proposals are more comprehensive on the last of these). Equally, during the stage of performance, we find a shared preference for enforcement of the contract in kind, the trilogy of 'measures' available in the face of a debtor's default (performance, termination, damages), and likewise the power of unilateral termination. The similarity of viewpoints on the subject of prescription will be even more pleasing.

However the *European Principles* do not include the doctrine of 'cause' as a justification for undertakings; they confer on courts the power to remake contracts (which the authors of the Reform Proposals overwhelmingly reject), and allow the annulment of a contract by notification to the other contracting party. These same Principles allow the proof of a contract by any form of evidence, and make joint

---

[1] [The idea of 'social solidarity' or simply 'solidarity' has long formed part of French legal thought; see eg L Duguit, *L'état, le droit objectif et la positive* (Paris, Fontemoing, 1901) 69-78. Recently, its role in relation to contract law in particular has become both more prominent and more controversial: see especially D Mazeaud, 'Loyauté, solidarité, fraternité: la nouvelle devise contractuelle?' in *L'avenir du droit, Mélanges Terré* (Paris, Dalloz, 1999) 603; C Jamin, 'Plaidoyer pour le solidarisme contractuel' in *Etudes offertes à J. Ghestin – Le contrat au début du XXIe siècle* (Paris, LGDJ, 2001) 441; J Cédras, 'Le solidarisme contractuel en doctrine et devant la Cour de cassation' in *Rapport annuel de la Cour de cassation* (2003) available at *www.courdecassation.fr*.]

[2] [Articles 1127 to 1128-2 (form); 1116 to 1120-1 (capacity and the power to act in the name of another).]

par tous moyens, et font de la solidarité le principe en matière civile. Ils disposent que la cession de créance ne requiert pas d'écrit ni aucune autre exigence de forme et qu'elle prend effet au moment de l'accord sans régler la question de son opposabilité aux tiers. Ces solutions, potentiellement dangereuses en matière civile et s'ajoutant à la judiciarisation des contrats, inspireront sans doute des réserves aux civilistes français.

9) L'acte législatif n'est pas un acte unilatéral mais collectif. Notre propos commun était de donner corps à une réforme générale du droit des obligations et de la prescription, dont l'urgente nécessité devrait s'imposer à l'esprit du législateur national. Notre espoir est que l'avant-projet serve l'entreprise qui donnera à la France un droit civil adapté à son époque et une voix dans le concert européen.

« Le plan que nous avons tracé de ces institutions remplira-t-il le but que nous nous sommes proposé ? Nous demandons quelque indulgence pour nos faibles travaux, en faveur du zèle qui les a soutenus et encouragés. Nous resterons au-dessous, sans doute, des espérances honorables que l'on avait conçues de notre mission : mais ce qui nous console, c'est que nos erreurs ne sont point irréparables ; une discussion solennelle, une discussion éclairée les réparera ». Par ces mêmes mots, Portalis concluait le discours préliminaire.

and several liability the principle in civil matters. They provide that the assignment of a right under an obligation requires neither writing nor any other formality and that it takes effect at the point of agreement without settling the question of its effect as against third parties. These solutions, potentially dangerous in civil matters and increasing judicial intervention in contracts, will, no doubt, inspire some reservations on the part of French civil lawyers.

(9) A legislative act is not a unilateral act, but a collective one. Our common intent was to give substance to a general reform of the law of obligations and prescription, the urgency of which should be impressed upon the mind of the national legislator. Our hope is that the Reform Proposals serve the purpose which will give France a civil law adapted to its time and a voice at the table of Europe.

'Will the plan which we have outlined for these institutions fulfil the objective which we set ourselves? We crave indulgence for our poor endeavours, in consideration of the zeal which has supported and encouraged us in our work. No doubt, we shall still fall short of the worthy hopes which were conceived for our task; but we are consoled by the fact that our errors are not beyond repair: formal discussion, enlightened discussion will repair them.' With these same words Portalis concluded his *Discours préliminaire*.[1]

---

[1] [*Discours Préliminaire*, above, p 465, n 1, 63.]

LIVRE TROISIÈME

TITRE III
DES OBLIGATIONS

Introduction

Gérard Cornu

Ce qui est dit, dans ce projet, du contrat et des obligations conventionnelles en général, n'est pas le fruit d'une reconstruction intégrale sur une table rase. Il s'agit d'une révision, d'une **révision d'ensemble**. Et c'est précisément parce qu'à cette échelle, aucun examen n'avait jamais été entrepris depuis 1804, qu'une telle épure a aujourd'hui des titres à entrer dans le paysage législatif.

La pérennité de la théorie générale du contrat dans le Code civil n'est pas une preuve de son obsolescence – il est heureux d'avoir ce monument législatif en héritage. Mais ce n'est pas non plus un brevet d'intangibilité. Le temps présent ouvre de nouvelles vues.

Selon l'idée qui a présidé dès 1965 à la réforme des régimes matrimoniaux et, dans le même esprit, à la refonte dans le Code du droit patrimonial et extrapatrimonial de la famille,[1] **le droit contractuel demande, à son tour, à être refondu dans le corps de droit auquel il appartient.** Au sein du Code civil, la recodification de cette partie se fait en relation avec les autres, afin que règne entre elles la concordance. Les dispositions générales consacrées aux restitutions après anéantissement du contrat ont été établies en contemplation de celles qui gouvernent l'indivision, les récompenses, le rapport et la réduction des libéralités (exemple entre beaucoup d'autres). Les mêmes notions, courant sous les mêmes mots, irriguent le tout. C'est un bienfait de la rénovation en lien.

Le contrat demeure la figure centrale. Une fois réglées sa formation et les conditions de sa validité, il introduit à la théorie des obligations conventionnelles en général : interprétation, exécution, inexécution, effets à l'égard des tiers, modalités, extinction, preuve. Cependant, sur le seuil de cette partie principale, une

---

[1] Tutelle des mineurs, droit des majeurs protégés, autorité parentale, filiation, divorce, successions en instance d'achèvement.

BOOK THREE

TITLE III
OBLIGATIONS

Introduction

Gérard Cornu

What is said, in these Reform Proposals, about contracts and about contractual obligations in general, is not the result of a completely new construction on a blank canvas. It is a revision, a **comprehensive revision**. And it is precisely because no examination has been undertaken of it on this scale since 1804, that this blue-print for action is entitled now to make its legislative debut.

The durability of the general doctrine of contract in the Civil Code does not prove its obsolescence – it is lucky to be the inheritor of this legislative monument. But nor is this a guarantee of inviolability. A new age opens up new perspectives.

In accordance with the idea which has governed since 1965 in the reform of matrimonial property regimes and, in the same spirit, in the recasting in the Code of family law (as regards both family assets and other rights),[1] **the law of contract, in its turn, requires to be recast within the legal framework to which it already belongs**. At the heart of the Civil Code, recodification of this part has to be done taking into account the other parts, so that harmony may reign between them. The general provisions concerning restitution after destruction of the contract have been constructed bearing in mind those which govern the joint ownership of property, transfers between spouses, hotchpot, and the setting aside of acts of generosity (amongst many other examples). The same notions, in the same terms, run throughout. This is a benefit which flows from the reform.

Contract remains the central figure. Once the formation and conditions of validity have been dealt with, the general doctrine of contractual obligations is introduced: interpretation, performance, non-performance, effects as regards third parties, the modalities of obligations, extinction, proof. However, before dealing with this main

---

[1] Guardianship of minors, the law of adults under legal protection, parental authority, descent, divorce, estates in the course of being wound up. [For the role of Carbonnier in the reform of family law, see above, p 465, n 2.]

présentation inaugurale offre le panorama des sources de toutes les obligations, et pas seulement des obligations conventionnelles, mais de toutes les obligations extracontractuelles (quasi-contrats et responsabilité civile). **Ce tableau met en perspective la division majeure des actes juridiques et des faits juridiques** sous les auspices de laquelle toutes leurs espèces s'ordonnent. Au sein des actes juridiques, la convention prend sa juste place aux côtés de l'acte juridique unilatéral et de l'acte collégial. Parmi les faits juridiques, formant antithèse, les quasi-contrats et la responsabilité civile font respectivement naître des obligations à partir d'avantages reçus sans droit ou de dommages causés sans droit. C'est le remploi amplifié et mis en exergue de la disposition-charnière de l'actuel article 1370.

Ces diverses espèces d'actes et de faits juridiques sont définies, comme le sont en suivant les diverses sortes de contrats. Mais le recours aux définitions légales est loin d'être systématique. C'est le privilège des figures juridiques de référence qui sont les clés du droit contractuel : espèces d'obligations, modalités, causes d'extinction, modes de preuve, opérations sur créance, etc. Les obligations forment une théorie à cause de l'ordre mis dans ces concepts pour la pratique.

Orientations de fond

Au fond, l'ouverture à la modernité ne passe pas par le rejet des maximes qui font encore la force vive du contrat. L'article 1134 est toujours le même pilier. Il appartient aux citoyens.

• Cependant, la liberté contractuelle et la force obligatoire du contrat doivent compter avec les **aspirations de la justice contractuelle**. La conscience contemporaine attend des progrès en ce sens. Telle est, primordialement, l'une des idées directrices de la révision. Le projet imprime à la justice dans le contrat tout l'élan compatible avec la sécurité juridique. Pour les majeurs pleinement capables, la rescision pour cause de lésion demeure encadrée, de même que l'erreur sur la valeur. Mais la violence n'a plus le seul visage de la contrainte physique ou morale, elle peut aussi résulter de la menace abusive d'une voie de droit ou de l'état d'extrême précarité dans lequel se trouve l'un des contractants, quand l'autre l'exploite pour en tirer un avantage manifestement excessif. Le dol est pris en considération non seulement s'il émane du cocontractant mais s'il est le fait du représentant de celui-ci ou même, en certaines circonstances, d'un tiers (art. 1113-2). Surtout, en renvoyant aux cas spécifiés dans lesquels une loi de protection autorise la révision judiciaire des clauses qui créent un déséquilibre excessif au détriment d'un contractant, le projet ouvre carrière à la théorie de l'imprévision en matière civile, pour le cas où l'équilibre initial des prestations serait gravement perturbé dans les contrats à exécution successive ou échelonnée. Quand les parties n'en conviennent pas à l'avance, une nouvelle négociation peut être ordonnée par le juge et déboucher sur une résiliation unilatérale (art. 1156 s.). Le même souci d'équilibre explique que, lorsqu'une convention a été établie sous l'influence dominante d'une partie, elle doit être interprétée en faveur de l'autre (art. 1140-1).

part, an opening presentation gives an overview of the sources of all obligations: not only contractual obligations, but all extra-contractual obligations (quasi-contracts and civil liability). **This picture puts in perspective the major division between juridical acts and juridically significant facts** under the aegis of which each species is organised. Within juridical acts contract takes its place alongside unilateral juridical acts and collegial juridical acts. Amongst juridically significant facts, by contrast, quasi-contracts and civil liability respectively give rise to obligations as a result of benefits received without right, or loss inflicted without right. This re-uses, in an extended and re-emphasised form, the key provision of the existing article 1370.

These various forms of juridical acts and juridically significant facts are defined, as are the different kinds of contracts in the sections which follow. But the use of legal definitions is far from systematic. Only legal terms of reference have this privilege, as they are the keys to the law of contract: types of obligation, modalities, grounds of extinction, kinds of evidence, transactions relating to rights under obligations, etc. Obligations form a coherent doctrine because of the system imposed on these concepts in practice.

Fundamental directions

Essentially, opening up to a modern perspective does not involve rejecting the maxims which are still the real strength of contract. Article 1134 is still the same mainstay. It is the citizen's birthright.

• However, freedom of contract and the binding force of contracts must take into account the **desire for contractual fairness**. These days we expect progress in this direction. This is, essentially, one of the guiding ideas of the reform. The Reform Proposals give as much impetus to contractual fairness as is compatible with legal certainty. For fully competent adults, rescission for gross undervalue remains restricted, as does mistake as to value. But duress has a new look: it is not limited to physical or moral pressure, but can also result from an improper threat to take legal proceedings, or to take advantage of the state of extreme weakness in which one of the parties finds himself, where the other exploits it to obtain a manifestly excessive advantage. Fraud is taken into account not only where it emanates from the other party, but also if it is done by his agent or even, in certain circumstances, by a third party (article 1113-2). Above all, in referring to particular cases in which a protective legislative rule authorises the judicial review of contract terms which create an excessive imbalance to the detriment of one party, the Reform Proposals open the way to a doctrine of unforeseeability[1] in private law, in cases where the initial balance of the content of the parties' obligations is gravely upset in contracts involving performance successively or in instalments. Where the parties do not first come to an agreement, new negotiations can be ordered by the court, and if no agreement is reached, unilateral termination for the future can follow (article [1135-1] *et seq.*). The same concern for balance explains why, where a contract has been formed under the dominant influence of one party, it must be interpreted in favour of the other (article 1140-1).

---

[1] [For 'unforeseeability' (*imprévision*) in public law by contrast with the proposal for private law, see below, p 547, n 2.]

• Toutes ces avancées de la justice contractuelle s'accompagnent – c'est une corrélation active – du **plus grand rayonnement donné à la bonne foi.** Établi pour gouverner l'exécution du contrat (art. 1134, al. 3), le principe de bonne foi étend sa loi sur sa formation même (négociation, pourparlers, 1104, al. 1, convention sur la durée de la prescription 1162). L'obligation de renseignement fait une entrée raisonnable dans le Code, et, au rang des modalités de l'obligation, l'accomplissement de la condition est sous l'égide de la loyauté (art. 1176). La faveur à la bonne foi circule dans tout le texte (V. encore art. 1120). Liberté dans la probité, la devise est de haute tradition.

• Phénomène plus nouveau, le dynamisme inventif des pratiques dans la ramification des actions économiques, demandait que soit relevé le défi de **la complexification des relations conventionnelles.** La relativité garde ses marques : les conventions ne lient que les parties contractantes (art. 1165). Mais elles-mêmes sont souvent liées dans une opération d'ensemble qui crée entre elles une interdépendance riche de conséquences (art. 1137). C'est au demeurant dans un tel cadre – si la cession de dette n'est pas isolément admise – que peut s'opérer un transfert de contrat (notamment par fusion ou scission de société) entraînant une substitution de contractant (art. 1165-2). Sous le même horizon, les opérations triangulaires sont toujours plus florissantes. La stipulation pour autrui et le porte-fort ont certes depuis longtemps droit de cité. Mais une réalité économique majeure anime la matière. Dans les patrimoines, la créance constitue une valeur, objet de propriété, source de garantie, matière de la circulation financière. Le projet tient pour essentiel de remembrer toutes les opérations sur créance dans le relief d'un chapitre nouveau (art. 1251 s.). Si la subrogation et la novation conservent leurs fortes assises, la délégation (à peine effleurée dans le code) se déploie dans toute sa polyvalence (art. 1275 s.) et, à l'heure électronique, la cession de créance accède à la simplicité qu'elle requiert. Évinçant *inter partes*, la remise de l'acte, l'établissement de l'écrit qui constate la cession opère à lui seul et par lui-même le transfert, et celui-ci est censé être accompli, sans notification, *erga omnes* (art. 1254). Dans le même esprit, les rigidités de l'individualisme absolu sont également refoulées sur d'autres points. Une ouverture est faite à l'action directe des créanciers (art. 1168). Mis au rang des actes juridiques, l'acte collégial doit être interprété à la lumière de l'intérêt commun (art. 1136). Quand enfin le projet propose d'écrire que les conventions légalement formées sont opposables aux tiers et que ceux-ci doivent les respecter, il est dans la même ligne, mais il se réfère en cela à d'autres acquis.

• All these advances in contractual fairness are accompanied – in direct correlation – by the **greater significance given to good faith**. First laid down to govern the performance of the contract (article 1134, paragraph 3), the principle of good faith extends its legislative sway also to cover the formation of the contract (negotiations, discussions, article 1104 paragraph 1; agreements on prescription periods applicable, article 1162). Obligations to inform make a sensible addition to the Code and, in the section dealing with the modalities of obligations, satisfaction of a condition is placed under the overriding requirement of loyalty (article 1176). This preference for good faith appears throughout the provisions (see also article 1120). 'Freedom and integrity' is our motto—a motto with a fine history.

• A more recent phenomenon, the creative dynamism of practices within the growing network of economic activity, required us to meet the challenge of **the increasing complexity of contractual relationships**. The hallmark of the rule of relativity of contract remains: contracts bind only their parties (article 1165). But contracts are often linked in a group operation which gives them an interdependence with significant consequences (article 1137). In fact, it is in this context—although there cannot generally be a transfer of just a debt—that there can be a transfer of a contract (in particular, in a corporate merger or division) entailing the substitution of a contracting party (article 1165-2). In the same field, three-party transactions flourish. Of course, stipulations for the benefit of third parties[1] and standing surety[2] have long had their rightful place. But an economic reality of major significance gives new life to this subject. Within a person's wealth,[3] a right under an obligation constitutes an asset, an object of ownership, which can be used as security, and is part of economic currency. The Reform Proposals regard it as essential to bring together all transactions relating to rights under obligations and highlight them in a new chapter (articles 1251 et seq.). Although subrogation and novation retain their well established bases, delegation (hardly touched upon in the Code) is used in its many forms (articles 1275 et seq.) and in this time of electronic transactions the assignment of rights under obligations is given the simplicity it needs. Abolishing, as between the parties, the requirement of delivery for its effectiveness, the drawing-up of a written document which records an assignment has the effect, in and of itself, of transferring the right, and the transfer is deemed effective, without notification, as regards third parties (article 1254). In the same spirit, the strict rules flowing from individualism are also suppressed on other points. There is now a place for creditors to have direct actions (article 1168). Given its place within juridical acts, collegial juridical acts must be interpreted in the light of the common interest (article 1136). And finally, when the Proposals recommend that it should be stated that contracts which are lawfully concluded may be invoked by and against third parties and that third parties must respect them,[4] they do so along the same lines but in this they refer to other settled legal elements.

---

[1] [See article 1171.]

[2] [See article 1170.]

[3] [The French concept of le patrimoine, here translated as 'wealth', does not have an exact counterpart in English law: it is the totality of rights which an individual possesses. See J Bell in Bell, Boyron and Whittaker, above, p 465, n 3, 271.]

[4] [This is a mixed reference to articles 1134 ('contracts which are lawfully concluded') and 1165-2 ('may be invoked...').]

• Sans contradiction, la reconnaissance de ces réalités va de pair avec la montée au jour – comme un pêcheur le dit de la remontée d'un filet – de données latentes confirmées déjà présentes dans la pensée juridique. La révision a puisé chez les interprètes (juges et auteurs), comme à des sources créatrices, le **consensus doctrinal** qui autorise une consécration légale (*communis opinio doctorum*). Elle n'a pas reversé dans la loi toutes les richesses jurisprudentielles et doctrinales, mais seulement filtré – laissant maintes données d'application à leur destin tracé – le noyau des accords. Ainsi le projet propose-t-il de consacrer – de déclarer – la liberté de la preuve des faits juridiques (art. 1287), le principe du consensualisme dans le choix des formes (art. 1127), celui du parallélisme des formes entre l'acte originaire et l'acte modificatif ou contraire (art. 1127-6), l'existence d'un ordre public de protection individuelle (art. 1129-1), l'ouverture à l'incapable agissant seul des actes courants autorisés par l'usage et des actes qui le concernent très personnellement (art. 117-1), l'affirmation au rang des dispositions générales que, pour faire une convention valable, il faut être sain d'esprit (art. 1109). Ainsi a-t-il donné corps dans le Code à la théorie de la qualification (ici à la qualification des actes juridiques, clé de l'analyse contractuelle (art. 1142 s.)), à la théorie générale de la représentation (art. 1119 s.), érigé le pouvoir d'agir au nom d'autrui, en condition spécifique de validité des actes accomplis par le représentant légal, judiciaire ou conventionnel (art. 1108, 1119 s.), caractérisé la capacité de jouissance face à la capacité d'exercice (art. 1116 et 1117), marqué les liens qui unissent les incapacités à l'assistance et à la représentation, fait la part des personnes morales, donné à l'illicéité le sens générique qui lui fait couvrir l'ordre public, les bonnes mœurs et les règles impératives (art. 1126, 1162-3), défini la dette de valeur (art. 1148), etc. Sur tous ces points d'accord, la coutume s'est en somme invitée dans la loi et le Code, puisant à ces sources autorisées, en sort revivifié.

Sur trois points controversés, on pourrait à la vérité douter de l'appui de l'opinion commune. Le projet demeure fidèle à la cause (art. 1124 s.), à l'obligation de donner et à son exécution par le seul échange des consentements (art. 1121, 1145, 1152 s.) ainsi qu'à la rétroactivité de la condition (art. 1182). Tout bien pesé, la conviction a prévalu que, dans l'interprétation régnante, la double fonction de la cause dans la justification de l'engagement est bien maîtrisée, comme le sont l'obligation de donner et son exécution assorties des nuances raisonnables qui en précisent l'application. En définitive, le maintien de ces notions crée beaucoup moins de problèmes que les expédients et les détours par lesquels il faudrait passer pour combler le vide creusé par leur suppression.

• Dans le prolongement de cette action « déclarative », le projet propose de **combler de nombreuses lacunes**, en introduisant dans le Code civil des règles qui, portées par des réflexions convergentes, sont elles aussi mûres pour une telle incor-

• Without doubt, the recognition of these real elements goes hand in hand with bringing to the light of day—as the fisherman says about bringing in his net—the unspoken elements shown to be already present in legal thinking. Our revision has drawn on interpretations given by both courts and writers, as well as on creative sources, the **shared understanding of legal scholarship** which justifies its recognition by legislation (*communis opinio doctorum*).[1] It has not transferred into legislative form all the riches of case-law and academic writing, but has only filtered the core of their shared understanding – leaving many elements to their own fate. And so the Proposals recommend that the following should be established—indeed, declared: that juridically significant facts may be proved in any way (article 1287); the principle of consensualism in the parties' choice of the form of the contract (article 1127); the correspondence of form between the original contract and that which modifies or revokes it (article 1127-6); the existence of a public policy of protection of individuals (article 1129-1); allowing a person lacking legal capacity, acting alone, to use juridical acts which are customarily available and juridical acts which concern him personally (article [1117-2]); and confirming amongst the general provisions that, to make a valid contract, one must be of sound mind (article 1109). And so it has given substance in the Code to the doctrine of classification (here, the classification of juridical acts, which is the key to the analysis of contracts (article 1142 *et seq.*)), and to the general doctrine of representation (article 1119 *et seq.*); it has established the power to act in the name of another as a special condition of validity of juridical acts entered into by a representative appointed by law, by the court or by agreement (articles 1108, 1119 *et seq.*); it has defined the legal capacity of enjoyment as contrasted with the capacity to exercise a right (articles 1116 and 1117); it has indicated the links between incapacity, and support and representation; it has made provision for legal persons; it has given a general meaning to unlawfulness which allows it to cover public policy, public morality and mandatory rules of law (articles 1126, 1162-3); it has defined an obligation of value (article 1148), etc. On all these points of agreement, custom has in fact been welcomed into legislation and the Code, drawing on these authorised sources, comes out revitalised.

On three controversial points, one might in reality doubt that there is any reliable common view. The Reform Proposals remain faithful to the doctrine of 'cause' (articles 1124 *et seq.*), to obligations to give and their performance by the simple exchange of consent (articles 1121, 1145, 1152 *et seq.*), and to the retroactive effect of conditions (article 1182). After the arguments had been weighed up, we became convinced that, according to the prevailing interpretation, the double function of 'cause' in justifying an undertaking is well established, as are obligations to give and their performance, together with sensible nuances which qualify their application. In fact, retaining these notions creates significantly fewer problems than the roundabout measures that would be necessary to fill the gap left by their removal.

• Continuing with this 'declarative' action, the Reform Proposals recommend that **several gaps should be filled,** by introducing into the Civil Code rules which rest on lines of thinking which come together to a similar point and make them ripe for

---

[1] [The *communis opinion doctorum*—the collected view of the learned (academic writers), known in France as *la doctrine*, is a significant source of law: J Bell and S Boyron in Bell, Boyron and Whittaker, above, p 465, n 3, 33-35. The *Avant-projet* would translate into the reformed legislative text many principles of existing law as it has been developed by *la doctrine*, as well as case-law developments.]

poration. Il reconnaît une vocation de principe à l'exécution en nature de l'obligation (art. 1154), ménage une place à la résolution unilatérale du contrat pour inexécution (art. 1158 s.), donne au droit de rétention, énoncé en son principe, une base légale dans le Code (art. 1156) et ses propositions, sur certains points, viennent en gerbe. Dessinant, pour la théorie générale, le profil de la négociation (art. 1045 s.), du contrat cadre (art. 1102-6), de l'accord de principe (art. 1104-1), de l'offre et de l'acceptation (art. 1105 s.), de la promesse unilatérale de contrat (art. 1106), du pacte de préférence (art. 1106-1), du contrat d'adhésion (art. 1102-5), du délai de réflexion et du délai de repentir (art. 1110-2), de la faculté de dédit (art. 1134-1), il donne corps à **l'ensemble des règles qui structurent la négociation contractuelle et la formation du contrat**, augment notable.

Éléments de méthode

Le comblement des lacunes dont le postulat est **l'enracinement dans le Code d'apports neufs**, conduit à la méthode de la révision. C'est en effet parce que celle-ci se déploie sur l'ensemble de la théorie générale que ses interventions, échelonnées de chapitre en chapitre, procèdent par mise au point, mise en valeur et en concordance, travaux de présentation, ouvrant la voie, dans la trame, à maintes innovations en harmonie.

• Ainsi le projet agence-t-il quelques **remodelages**. C'est en marquant la trilogie des sources de la compensation que s'ordonne le carré des quatre conditions essentielles de la compensation légale (art. 1241-1) au regard desquelles la compensation judiciaire et la compensation conventionnelle prennent leur juste place. La consignation de la chose due, au titre du paiement, a des chances d'aboutir à la libération du débiteur dès lors que les formalités auxquelles elle est associée (offre de paiement, mise en demeure) mettent à la charge du créancier des initiatives à défaut desquelles une issue raisonnable peut efficacement prospérer sous le contrôle du juge (art. 1233 s.). Jusqu'alors réduite à l'opposition de la condition suspensive et de la condition résolutoire, la théorie de la condition s'enrichit d'un troisième type, la condition extinctive qui, opérant pour l'avenir sans rétroactivité, répond à une utilité et pas seulement à la symétrie du terme extinctif (art. 1184-1). Au rang de ces mêmes obligations modales, figurent seules les obligations indivisibles, sur l'observation qu'entre créancier et débiteur, la dette est tenue de droit pour indivisible (règle pure et simple du paiement, art. 1224) et qu'elle se divise de plein droit entre leurs héritiers (règle successorale pure et simple). Enfin, la classification bipartite des obligations selon leur objet, d'une part, l'obligation de donner, d'autre part, les obligations de faire et de ne pas faire se prête à un approfondissement naturel qui fait émerger un troisième type d'obligation spécifiée par son objet, l'obligation de donner à usage. C'est en effet parce qu'il est de l'essence de l'usage de la chose d'autrui d'obliger à restitution celui qui en est constitué détenteur précaire qu'une **telle prestation est irréductible** à une aliénation (comme dans l'obligation de donner) et semblablement que le détenteur à usage ne reçoit d'autrui ni travail, ni ouvrage, ni entreprise (ni l'avantage d'une abstention, comme dans

incorporation. They invoke performance in kind of an obligation as a first principle (article 1154); make a place for unilateral termination of the contract for non-performance (articles 1158 *et seq.*), give rights of retention a legal basis in the Code, and state this as a matter of principle (article 1156); and they make a shower of other proposals on certain points. Laying out general doctrines of the shape of negotiations (articles [1104] *et seq.*), framework contracts (article 1102-6), agreements in principle (article 1104-1), offer and acceptance (articles 1105 *et seq.*), unilateral promises to contract (article 1106), pre-emption agreements (article 1106-1), standard-form contracts (article 1102-5), periods for reflection and periods for a change of mind (article 1110-2), rights of withdrawal (article 1134-1); and they give substance to **the totality of rules which give shape to contractual negotiations and the formation of contracts**, which is a notable addition to the Code.

Methodological issues

The filling of gaps, in which the purpose is **to embed in the Code new provisions,** leads on to the method of our revision. And it is because the method underpins the whole of the general theory that its application, from one chapter to another, proceeds by explanations of clarification and of the significance and of correspondence of the new texts, presentations which open the way, within this framework, to many harmonious innovations.

• Thus the Reform Proposals **remodel** a number of things. Setting out the trilogy of sources of set-off gives a context for the four essential conditions of set-off by law (article 1241-1) in relation to which set-off by order of the court, and set-off by contract take their proper place. Deposit with a public depositary of what is due under a contract by way of performance can result in the discharge of the debtor once the required formalities (tender of performance, giving notice to accept performance) put on the creditor the onus of taking steps in default of which a reasonable outcome can be given effect under the control of the court (articles 1233 *et seq.*). Hitherto limited to the contrast between suspensive conditions and resolutory conditions, the doctrine of conditions is enriched by a third type, the extinctive condition which, operating for the future without retroactive effect, is a notion employed for its usefulness, and not only to fit with the concept of an obligation being extinguished at the end of a period (article 1184-1). Amongst these same specially qualified obligations figure only indivisible obligations, noting that between creditor and debtor the debt is deemed to be indivisible (a straightforward rule of satisfaction: article 1224) and that by operation of law it is divisible between their heirs (a straightforward rule of succession). Finally, the bipartite classification of obligations by reference to their subject-matter—on the one hand, obligations to give, on the other hand obligations to do and not to do—lends itself to a natural further development which leads to the emergence of a third type of obligation defined by its subject-matter, obligations to give for use. And it is because it is of the essence of the use of a thing belonging to another to require the person who is its temporary holder to restore it, that an **obligation with a content of this kind cannot be reduced to** the alienation of property rights in the thing (as in the case of obligations to give), and similarly that the person who holds a thing for use does not receive from the other any labour, works or service (nor the benefit of any abstention from doing something, as in the case of obligations to do or not to do)

l'obligation de faire ou de ne pas faire) mais **spécifiquement une chose à restituer à son propriétaire après usage**, notion distinctive (art. 1102, 1121, 1146, 1155 s.).

• D'un autre côté, ont été opérés des **regroupements de règles** jusqu'alors dispersées, leur mise en facteur commun permettant de mettre en évidence leur généralité. Ainsi la forme des conventions devient le lieu de dispositions de synthèse (art. 1108, 1127 s.). Les restitutions après anéantissement du contrat (par nullité ou résolution) forment désormais un pôle de référence (art. 1161 s.). Le rapprochement de notions jusqu'alors non écrites tend au même résultat. Introduites ensemble dans le Code, l'inopposabilité, la caducité et la régularisation se caractérisent par comparaison, moyennant une définition (art. 1131 à 1133) de même que, relativement, l'obligation de moyens et l'obligation de résultat (art. 1149). Ces consécrations sont d'évidents progrès.

• Enfin, revues dans leur ensemble, les assises les mieux éprouvées du droit des obligations s'offrent d'elles-mêmes aux **retouches** légères qui effacent, par accent sur l'essentiel, les réserves mineures qui les affectent. Ainsi suffit-il d'effleurer d'un mot les définitions de la loi pour mettre au clair le fondement de toute présomption (art. 1314), la dispense spécifique qui découle des présomptions légales (art. 1317), le caractère toujours réfragable de celles qui sont abandonnées aux lumières des magistrats (art. 1318), l'effet tout à la fois apériteur et imparfait du commencement de preuve par écrit qui, rendant admissibles tous les modes de preuve, a besoin d'être corroboré par l'un d'eux (art. 1312), le climat consensuel de la remise de dette (art. 1237 s.), le mécanisme raffiné de la stipulation pour autrui (art. 1171 s.), le devoir de conscience sous l'obligation naturelle (art. 1151), au fond de l'intime conviction, la conscience du juge (art. 1287). On n'ira pas exagérer la portée de cette législation occasionnelle de performance (c'est la recodification qui fait l'occasion). Mais, chemin faisant, l'opportunité se présente de répondre à certaines attentes contemporaines, ainsi en mettant au large les volontés individuelles lorsqu'elles s'accordent, dans des limites du raisonnable, sur certaines adaptations (aménagement conventionnel des règles de preuve, art. 1289, ou des délais de prescription). Les mêmes aspirations invitent à donner ici et là du sens et de la souplesse grâce à des critères directifs : ainsi en marquant que le contrat s'interprète en raison et en équité (art. 1139), que le rattachement des contrats innomés aux contrats voisins se fait par analogie (art. 1103), que, dans le doute, la vraisemblance est un repli efficace et pertinent (art. 1287, 1293, 1314, 1317).

but **specifically a thing to be restored to its owner after use,** which is a distinct concept (articles 1102, 1121, 1146, 1155 *et seq.*).

• On the other hand, **rules** which have hitherto been dispersed have been **brought together,** and identifying their common links shows their true nature. And so the formal requirements for contracts provide the occasion for drawing things together in general provisions (articles 1108, 1127 *et seq.*). Restitution after destruction of a contract (by nullity or termination) now forms a point of reference (articles 1161 *et seq.*). Making connections between notions hitherto not written in the Code gives the same result. Introduced together into the Code, the general lack of effects of contracts in relation to third parties, lapse and regularisation of defects in a contract are distinguished, each being defined (articles 1131 to 1133), as are, respectively, obligations to take necessary steps and obligations of result (article 1149). Setting out these things is clearly a step forward.

• Finally, when subjected to a thorough review, even the most tried and tested settled rules of the law of obligations invite slight **retouching** which removes, by emphasising the essential, minor problems which affect them. And so it is sufficient to tidy up the legal definitions to make clear the basis of all presumptions (article 1314); what need not be proved in the case of legal presumptions (article 1317); the rebuttable nature of those which are left to the discretion of the courts (article 1318); the significant—but at the same time imperfect—effects of the 'beginning of proof by writing' which allows all other types of evidence to be admissible but needs to be corroborated by one other of them (article 1312); the consensual nature of the release of obligations (articles 1237 *et seq.*); the sophisticated mechanisms of stipulations for the benefit of third parties (articles 1171 *et seq.*); the moral duty in natural obligations (article 1151); and the duty in judges to act as they think right, following their inner conviction[1] (article 1287). We should not exaggerate the significance of what has been achieved by this drafting (it is the re-drafting of the Code that has given us the opportunity to do it). But, along the way, there was an opportunity to respond to certain current expectations; for example, by giving a significant place to the wills of the parties where they agree—within the limit of what is reasonable—on certain variations to the rules (contractual variation of the rules of proof: article 1289; or prescription periods). The same aspirations invited us here and there to give direction and flexibility by the use of guiding criteria: for example by making clear that a contract should be interpreted rationally and equitably (article 1139); that innominate contracts[2] should be linked with similar nominate contracts by analogy (article 1103); that, in cases of doubt, the more likely position is the appropriate and workable test (articles 1287, 1293, 1314, 1317).

---

[1] [The use of the 'inner conviction' is applied in the establishment of proof by the judge or jury in criminal matters: Code of Criminal Procedure, articles 304, 353, 427.]

[2] ['Nominate', or 'special', contracts are those types of contract (eg sale, hire, partnership) which have been classified in French law as embodying particular transactions, and whose incidents are set out in the Code or in other legislation. 'Innominate' contracts are those contracts which have not been so characterised, but which are governed by the general principles of contract law. The provisions of the Code which are the subject of the *Avant-projet* are provisions governing the general rules of contract law, rather than those governing special contracts. The theory of 'special' contracts is part of the inheritance from Roman law. See B Nicholas, *The French Law of Contract* (2nd edn, Oxford, Clarendon Press, 1992) 46-7.]

De façon comparable, la révision d'ensemble donnait l'occasion d'apporter des **clarifications** nécessaires, débouchant souvent sur de nouvelles solutions. Ainsi de définir le paiement (art. 1219), d'énoncer qu'il se prouve par tous les moyens (art. 1231), de mettre en facteur commun le caractère déterminant des vices du consentement (art. 1111-1), d'étendre à l'acte juridique unilatéral le principe de l'interprétation exégétique (art. 1136), de mesurer la valeur du silence dans la formation du contrat (art. 1105-6), de n'attacher qu'une nullité relative à l'absence de consentement (art. 1109-2), de donner en principe à la réception de l'acceptation ou la vertu de parfaire la formation du contrat (art. 1107).

Ces modifications ponctuelles sont inséparables des autres propositions. En effet, qu'elle soit regardée au fond ou dans sa méthode, la **révision d'ensemble** qui vient d'être exposée est liée par les **deux idées fondamentales qui l'animent**.

Les matières de la théorie générale ont été traitées en concordance. **Le principe de cohérence** est le premier trait de leur union. Quand le contexte y invite, il n'exclut pas certaines variations rédactionnelles. Mais les mêmes inspirations imprègnent tout le texte et, sous le texte, les notions de fond reviennent toujours avec le même sens. La théorie générale du contrat est, par nature, l'organisation d'une diversité, du simple au compliqué. On ne l'appauvrit pas ; on l'enrichit en assumant ce qui est nouveau, moyennant des simplifications, des amplifications et des redistributions, mais toujours dans un ordonnancement sans lequel les obligations conventionnelles en général n'existent pas. Les progrès du rail et de la route se font en réseau. Il en va de même pour le réseau contractuel. On modernise l'outil pour l'usager.

Relativement aux autres règles, dans le Code ou en dehors de lui, les dispositions de la théorie générale sont encore unies par leur même et singulière vocation. **Elles constituent le droit commun des contrats**. Elles laissent jouer, chacune en son domaine, les règles particulières aux espèces de convention qui y fleurissent. Mais elles ont en propre, d'une part, d'ériger en archétype les figures principales du droit des contrats qui sont au moins des repères, d'autre part d'ouvrir globalement à l'acte unilatéral et à l'acte collégial l'application en tant que de raison du droit des conventions (art. 1101-1), enfin de donner une solution résiduelle aux questions que le silence des lois laisse sans réponse, recours subsidiaire. Dès le seuil, l'article 1103 en pose le principe. Il a sa part dans le destin du Code civil dont on a célébré le bicentenaire.

In a similar way, comprehensive revision gave us the opportunity to provide necessary **points of clarification,** often opening up new solutions: for example, to define satisfaction (article 1219), to make clear that it can be proved by any form of evidence (article 1231); to identify as a common requirement of the defects in consent that they are decisive of the party's consent (article 1111-1); to extend to the unilateral juridical act an exegetical principle of interpretation (article 1136); to assess the significance of silence in the formation of a contract (article 1105-6); to provide that the absence of consent gives rise only to relative nullity (article 1109-2); to establish a principle that it is the receipt of acceptance that has the effect of completing the formation of a contract (article 1107).

These various modifications are inseparable from other proposals. Indeed, whether it is viewed in relation to its substance or its methodology, the **comprehensive revision** which we have just described is **based on two fundamental ideas.**

The subjects belonging to general contract doctrine have been considered together. The **principle of** consistency is the first link between them. Where the context so requires, this does not exclude certain differences in drafting. But the same ideas permeate the text and, beneath the text, the substantive notions always reoccur with the same significance. The general doctrine of contract is, of its very nature, the organisation of a diversity—from the simple to the complex. This is not to impoverish it; it is enriched by taking on what is new, together with simplification, amplification and re-alignment, but always in a structure without which contractual obligations in general could not exist. Rail and road make their progress through their networks. So it is too for the contractual network. The tool is modernised for the benefit of the user.

In relation to other rules, within the Code or outside it, the provisions of general doctrine are still united by their one purpose: **they form the general law for contracts.**[1] They allow the rules that are relevant to each particular kind of contract to have their own place. But they have their own place, on the one hand, to set up as model forms the principal elements of the law of contract which are at least landmarks; and on the other hand to open up the application of the law of contracts fully (as far as may be) to unilateral juridical acts and collegial juridical acts (article 1101-1), and to give a default solution to questions which are left unanswered by the silence of other legislative texts—by way of back-up. From the very beginning, article 1103 sets out the principle. It plays its part in the destiny of the Civil Code, whose bicentenary we have celebrated.

---

[1] [The notion of *le droit commun* ('the general law') is a very significant one in French private law in particular. Its significance is of the law applicable in the absence of special derogation or qualification. From this perspective, the Code civil forms the basis of *le droit commun* of French private law, this being qualified or supplemented by special legislation outside the Code. The 'general law for contracts' (*le droit commun des contrats* or *le droit commun contractuel*) designates the (private) law generally applicable to contracts, in the absence of special rules owing to the nature of the parties (contrast consumer law and commercial law) or the special nature of the type of contract in question (eg sale). See also above, p 489, n 2.]

Exposé des motifs
Source des obligations – Définitions (art. 1101 à 1103)

Gérard Cornu

I – De la source des obligations (art. 1101 à 1101-2)

Nouveau, le chapitre préliminaire par lequel s'ouvre le Titre III « Des obligations » est la conséquence de l'apparition, dans le Code, d'un titre regroupant le contrat, les quasi-contrats et la responsabilité civile. Il a précisément pour objet **la présentation inaugurale des trois sources principales d'obligation.**

Tableau d'ensemble, l'article 1101 reprend en l'élargissant la disposition charnière de l'article 1370 actuel. Ce texte d'origine introduit en effet, dans leur division majeure, « les faits personnels à celui qui se trouve obligé » (entendons les faits juridiques), à savoir, d'un côté les quasi-contrats, de l'autre les délits et quasi-délits, non sans avoir d'abord mis hors-série, accompagnés d'exemples, « les engagements qui résultent de l'autorité seule de la loi ».

L'article 1101 du projet n'omet pas de rappeler l'existence de tels engagements, mais son objet primordial, porté en tête du Titre « Des obligations » est d'ajouter aux faits juridiques les actes juridiques, au premier rang desquels le contrat, instauration d'ensemble.

Cette introduction aux sources principales d'obligations est **une mise en perspective**. Il est en effet essentiel de mettre au contact les unes des autres des **notions fondamentales qui sont coordonnées.** Plus précisément, de marquer la place du contrat dans la catégorie plus générale des actes juridiques et, semblablement, celle des quasi-contrats et autres faits générateurs d'obligation dans l'ensemble des faits juridiques.

Ainsi se manifeste le **parti législatif** qui déclare sa fidélité à la conception traditionnelle française. Le contrat est bien une espèce d'acte juridique, mais, dans la conception régnante, ici confirmée, **le contrat est et demeure la figure centrale.** C'est pourquoi le premier sous-titre du Titre Des obligations est centré sur le contrat, et c'est pour la même raison que, pour ordre, toutes les espèces d'actes et de faits sont d'abord situées dans l'ensemble cohérent qui les englobe.

La disposition de l'article 1101-1 s'attache en premier à définir les actes juridiques en général (al. 1) et à donner la définition particulière des trois éléments de la trilogie (al. 2, 3 et 4). La définition générale et celle de l'acte juridique conventionnel sont classiques, plus nouvelles celle de l'acte juridique unilatéral et de l'acte juridique collectif.

La considération de l'auteur de l'acte est une première donnée de leur différenciation : deux ou plusieurs personnes pour la convention ; pour l'acte

Preamble
The Source of Obligations – Definitions
(articles 1101 to 1103)

Gérard Cornu

I. The source of obligations (articles 1101 to 1101-2)

A new provision, the preliminary chapter with which Title III ('Obligations') opens, is the consequence of a new title in the Code bringing together contract, quasi-contracts and civil liability. To be precise, its object is **an initial presentation of the three principal sources of obligation.**

Giving an overview, article 1101 takes on and enlarges upon the key provision of article 1370 in the present Code. This provision on which we have drawn introduces, with a major division, 'the personal actions of the person who becomes subject to an obligation' (referring to juridically significant facts), that is, on the one hand quasi-contracts, and on the other hand delicts and quasi-delicts; having also separated out (with examples) 'the undertakings which arise merely from the authority of legislation'.

Article 1101 of the Reform Proposals does not fail to recall the existence of such obligations, but its principal object, placed as it is at the beginning of the Title 'Obligations' is to give a unity to juridically significant facts and juridical acts, and in particular to contracts.

This introduction to the principal sources of obligations seeks to **put them in perspective.** It is certainly essential to connect each of the **fundamental notions which are linked.** More particularly, to make clear the place of contract in the more general category of juridical acts and, in the same way, that of quasi-contracts and other events which give rise to obligations in the whole field of juridically significant facts.

Thus our **legislative choices are made** which declare their loyalty to the traditional French conception. Contracts are certainly a form of juridical act, but, in the prevailing view, here confirmed, **contracts are and remain the central figure.** That is why the first sub-title of the Title *Obligations* focuses on contracts, and it is for the same reason that, to give a proper order, all the forms of act and facts are first placed in the coherent whole in which they are incorporated.

The provisions of article 1101-1 set out first to define juridical acts in general (paragraph 1) and to give each of the trilogy its own definition (paragraphs 2, 3 and 4). The general definition, and that of contractual juridical acts, are classic; rather newer are the definitions of unilateral juridical acts and collective juridical acts.

The nature of the person who makes a juridical act is a primary concern in distinguishing between them: two or more persons for a contract; for a collective act, the members of the association (whether or not having separate legal personality).

collectif, les membres de la collectivité (dotée ou non de la personnalité juridique). En général accompli par une seule personne, l'acte juridique unilatéral peut aussi émaner de plusieurs personnes unies dans la poursuite d'un même intérêt (l'unité d'intérêt faisant reconnaître, malgré la pluralité d'auteurs, l'acte unilatéral).

Leur champ d'action les distingue surtout. L'ouverture est générale pour la convention (en harmonie avec la liberté des conventions). Au contraire, l'objet des décisions collectives s'inscrit dans la finalité particulière et la compétence spéciale de chaque type de collectivité (indivision, association, société, etc.). Quant à la **volonté unilatérale, elle n'a pas été érigée en source générale d'obligation.** Elle peut seulement prospérer sous l'égide de la loi ou (c'est une ouverture) de l'usage.

Fondamentalement, tous les actes juridiques se caractérisent, comme actes volontaires, par la direction que prend la volonté (car les faits juridiques peuvent aussi être volontaires). Dans l'acte juridique, la volonté est toujours tendue vers l'effet de droit consciemment perçu et recherché par son auteur (ce que traduisent les mots-clés « destinés », « en vue »).

Dans son alinéa final, l'article 1101-1 renvoie implicitement les actes juridiques unilatéraux et les actes collectifs aux dispositions spéciales qui les gouvernent respectivement, dans leur validité et leur effet. Mais, quand la raison le commande, **il leur rend subsidiairement applicable le régime général des conventions,** lequel apparaît ainsi, sous ce rapport, comme le **droit commun des actes juridiques.** Le contrat est bien, dans cet ensemble, la figure rayonnante.

L'article 1101-2 met en évidence que si, en eux-mêmes les faits juridiques sont dans une grande diversité, comme agissements (individuels ou collectifs) ou comme événements (faits divers particuliers, économiques, politiques, naturels, etc.) c'est toujours la loi qui leur attache l'effet de droit qu'elle détermine (lequel ne correspond évidemment pas s'il s'agit de faits volontaires, au propos délibéré de leur auteur).

L'article annonce enfin la division majeure entre les faits dommageables illicites, générateurs de responsabilité civile (sous-titre III) et les faits licites utiles, source d'obligation quasi-contractuelle (pour celui qui en profite sans y avoir droit (sous-titre II).

II – Définitions (art. 1102 s. à 1103)

La définition générale du contrat en tête du sous-titre « Du contrat et des obligations conventionnelles en général » est une idée des rédacteurs du Code de 1804. Ainsi que celle de la faire suivre de la définition particulière de plusieurs figures de contrat dont chacune est classée, de façon saisissante, par opposition à la figure antithétique, le contrat synallagmatique par opposition au contrat unilatéral, le contrat à titre onéreux par opposition au contrat à titre gratuit, le contrat commutatif par opposition au contrat aléatoire. Cette classification inaugurale répond à l'intention de mettre en place **les grandes familles de contrat au sein desquelles se rangeront les multiples contrats** dits spéciaux.

Dans leur justesse et leur clarté, certaines de ces définitions ne demandent qu'à être maintenues (contrat synallagmatique) ou effleurées d'une retouche (contrat unilatéral). L'opposition du contrat à titre onéreux et du contrat à titre gratuit

Generally created by a single person, unilateral juridical acts can also issue from more than one person, if they are united in furthering the same interest (the unity of interest showing that it is a unilateral act, in spite of the plurality of the people making it).

It is above all their sphere of activity which distinguishes them. For contracts it is general, in accordance with the principle of freedom of contract. By contrast, the object of collective decisions depends upon the particular purpose and special powers of each type of grouping (co-owners, associations, companies, etc.). **A person's unilateral will, however, has not been raised to the level of a general source of obligations.** It can work only within the principles established by legislation or (this is new) custom.

Fundamentally, given that they are acts of the will, all juridical acts are characterised by the direction taken by the will (because juridically significant facts can also be voluntary). In the case of juridical acts, the will is always directed towards the legal consequence which is deliberately realised and sought by the person who makes it (which is the meaning of the key words 'intended', 'with the aim').

In its final paragraph, article 1101-1 implicitly relates unilateral juridical acts and collective acts to special provisions which govern respectively their validity and their effects. But, whenever necessary, **as a secondary matter it makes the general contractual regime applicable**: this therefore appears, in this connection, as the **general law of juridical acts.** Within this group, contracts are certainly the shining feature.

Article 1101-2 makes clear that, if juridically significant facts are themselves very diverse, whether as behaviour (individual or collective) or events (various particular happenings—economic, political, natural, etc) it is always legislation which attaches to them the legal effect which it determines (which is not of course the case for voluntary actions, done intentionally).

The article finally announces the major division between harmful and unlawful actions, which give rise to civil liability (Sub-title III) and lawful, useful acts, which give rise to quasi-contractual obligations (on the person who benefits from them without any right to do so) (Sub-title II).

II. Definitions (articles 1102 to 1103)

The general definition of a contract at the very beginning of the Sub-title 'Contract and obligations created by agreement in general' is an idea of the draftsmen of the Code in 1804. So is the idea to follow it with particular definitions of several types of contract, each of which is categorised, in a striking fashion, by comparison with its contrasting type: synallagmatic contracts by contrast with unilateral contracts; onerous contracts by contrast with gratuitous contracts, commutative contracts by contrast with aleatory contracts. This initial categorisation follows the intention to put in place **the large families of contract, within which will be lined up manifold other contracts,** known as 'special' contracts.

In their exactness and their clarity, some of these definitions simply require to be retained (synallagmatic contracts) or retouched (unilateral contracts). The contrast between onerous contracts and gratuitous contracts derives from the emphasis

prend du sens par l'accent mis sur l'intention décisive (« entend ») relativement à une contrepartie (*animus donandi* pour le contrat à titre gratuit ; la poursuite d'une contrepartie pour le contrat à titre onéreux). Pour une modification voisine mais plus prononcée, la considération de l'équivalence initiale des prestations, dans la pensée des contractants, est le critère qui fait le départ entre le contrat commutatif et le contrat aléatoire.

Le catalogue actuel a seulement été complété par de nouvelles définitions énoncées, selon la même méthode, non point pour l'interprétation du texte mais en fonction de la nature propre de chaque figure, dans l'ensemble du système juridique. Ainsi est proposée l'opposition déjà connue mais non écrite du contrat consensuel et du contrat solennel. L'extrême importance pratique du contrat d'adhésion et du contrat cadre exigeait que leur définition soit élaborée, afin surtout que soient clarifiées, dans le contrat d'adhésion, la distinction entre le noyau imposé et l'éventuelle partie complémentaire négociée, et semblablement, dans le contrat cadre, la distinction de l'accord de base et des conventions d'application.

On retrouve dans l'article 1103 l'affirmation que **les règles énoncées au titre du contrat constituent le droit commun des contrats**. Le texte réserve, en l'illustrant d'exemples topiques, l'application à certains contrats des règles particulières qui les gouvernent, mais il marque sous cette réserve que la vocation des règles générales s'étend à toute espèce de contrat, nommé ou innommé. Quant à ces derniers, il ouvre un précieux **recours au raisonnement analogique** afin de combler avec discernement les lacunes des prévisions contractuelles.

On aura remarqué que, dans l'article 1102, ne figure plus la référence à la trilogie traditionnelle (donner, faire, ne pas faire). Mais on en retrouve les éléments à l'article 1121 qui précise l'objet du contrat. Ce transfert qui évite une redondance a surtout l'avantage de **compléter la trilogie**, car le contrat peut aussi avoir pour objet de concéder la détention d'une chose avec ou sans usage, **prestation spécifique qui ne se ramène ni à donner, ni à faire, ni à ne pas faire**.

Ainsi déployé, l'éventail des prestations a sa place naturelle dans l'objet du contrat, sans alourdir la définition générale préliminaire du contrat. Dans celle-ci, la référence est désormais faite à une **notion générique consacrée** qui enveloppe tous les cas. Toute obligation naissant d'un contrat a pour objet **l'accomplissement d'une prestation**.

Formation du contrat
(art. 1104 à 1107)

Philippe Delebecque,
Denis Mazeaud

Très précis sur les conditions de validité et les effets du contrat, les rédacteurs du Code civil de 1804 étaient, en revanche, restés silencieux sur ses conditions de

placed on the key element of intention ('expects') as to what is expected in return (*animus donandi* for gratuitous contracts; pursuit of something in return for onerous contracts). For a related, but more pronounced, amendment, the issue of the initial equivalence of the content of the obligations, as the parties see them, is the criterion which distinguishes between commutative contracts and aleatory contracts.

The present list has been filled out only by giving new definitions, following the same method, not for the interpretation of the text, but in accordance with the proper nature of each type of contract, within the whole of the legal system. And so the contrast—already well known, but not hitherto written in the Code—is offered between consensual contracts and formal contracts. The very great practical significance of standard-form contracts and framework contracts required their definition to be elaborated so that, in particular, in standard-form contracts the difference could be made clear between the imposed kernel of the contract and any supplementary part which may have been negotiated; and, similarly, in framework contracts the difference between the basic agreement and the implementation contracts.

In article 1103 we find the affirmation that **the rules set out in the title on Contract constitute the general law of contract.**[1] Giving particular examples by way of illustration, the text reserves the application of particular rules for certain contracts, but it notes within this reservation that the role of the general rules extends to all kinds of contract, nominate or innominate.[2] In relation to the latter, it sets out a valuable **appeal to reasoning by analogy** in order to fill in a discriminating manner the gaps in what the contract has provided.

It will have been noticed that, in article 1102, there is no longer any reference to the traditional trichotomy (obligations to give, to do and not to do). But their elements will be found in article 1121, which defines the subject-matter of a contract. Transferring them to that position avoids unnecessary repetition, and especially has the benefit that **the trichotomy can be supplemented,** because contracts can also have as their subject-matter the grant of permission to hold a thing, with or without a right to use it, **a specific content of obligation which cannot be reduced to giving, doing or not doing.**

Formation of Contracts (articles 1104 to 1107)

Philippe Delebecque,
Denis Mazeaud

Although they were very detailed about the conditions for the validity of contracts and their effects, the draftsmen of the Civil Code of 1804 said nothing about the

---

[1] [On the notion of 'the general law of contract' see above, p 491, n 1.]
[2] [On the distinction between nominate and innominate contracts, see above, p 489, n 2.]

formation, autrement dit sur la phase de rencontre des volontés. Le contraste est saisissant avec le luxe de détails dont font preuve le législateur français contemporain, notamment dans le domaine des contrats de consommation, et les projets d'harmonisation européenne du droit des contrats qui, eux, régissent avec une extrême minutie les différentes étapes qui conduisent de la simple intention de contracter à la conclusion de l'accord définitif.

Il a donc semblé légitime aux promoteurs de ce projet de combler cette lacune de notre Code et de prévoir des textes qui encadrent la formation du lien contractuel. Tel est l'objet des articles 1104 et suivants de cette section intitulée « De la formation du contrat ».

Quant à la structure de cette section, les rédacteurs se démarquant ainsi des textes élaborés au niveau européen et international qui visent à harmoniser ou à codifier le droit des contrats, ont délibérément opté pour des règles générales destinées à charpenter la rencontre des volontés et ont renoncé à réglementer avec moult précisions le processus de formation du contrat, étant entendu que dans ce domaine la liberté des futurs contractants doit pouvoir se déployer le plus largement possible et qu'une certaine marge d'appréciation doit être laissée au juge saisi de l'existence d'un contrat. Par ailleurs, il s'est agi d'envisager les différents procédés et étapes qui jalonnent le chemin qui conduit à la création du contrat. Ainsi, les textes proposés ont pour objet les différents actes unilatéraux ou bilatéraux qui sont le plus souvent utilisés et exploités dans la perspective de la conclusion d'un contrat.

Quant au fond, les règles élaborées puisent à plusieurs sources : la jurisprudence française rendue dans ce domaine, depuis deux siècles, d'abord ; certaines codifications européennes et internationales récentes (Allemagne, Pays-Bas, Québec), ensuite ; les projets d'harmonisation européenne et internationale du droit des contrats (Avant-projet de code européen des contrats-groupe Gandolfi ; Principes du droit européen du contrat-commission Landö ; Principes Unidroit), enfin. Par ailleurs, ces règles sont articulées autour d'un triptyque : liberté, loyauté, sécurité.

Liberté, en premier lieu, dans la période de négociation précontractuelle (articles1104 à 1104-2). Les négociateurs sont libres d'entrer en pourparlers, de mener leur négociation et d'y mettre fin comme et quand bon leur semble. En principe, leur responsabilité ne peut pas être recherchée à l'occasion de cette phase de négociation. En particulier, elle ne peut pas être engagée du seul fait que la négociation a été rompue et que cette rupture a provoqué un dommage pour un des négociateurs. Liberté, en deuxième lieu, au stade de l'offre et de l'acceptation. D'une part, l'offrant dispose d'un important pouvoir unilatéral de rétractation. D'autre part, le destinataire de l'offre ne peut pas, sauf circonstances

conditions for the formation of contracts—that is, about the phase where the parties' wills must meet. This is a striking contrast with the wealth of detail demonstrated by the French legislator of today, particularly in the field of consumer contracts, and the European harmonisation projects relating to the law of contracts, which regulate in minute detail the different stages leading from the simple intention to contract to the formation of the final agreement.

The promoters of these Reform Proposals therefore thought it right to fill this lacuna in our Code, and to include provisions covering the formation of contractual relationships. This is the object of articles 1104 *et seq.* in this section entitled 'Formation of contracts'.

As regards the structure of this section, its draftsmen have differed from the texts drawn up at the European and international level which aim to harmonise or to codify the law of contracts, and have deliberately opted for general rules which are destined to give shape to the meeting of wills, rejecting any very detailed regulation of the process of the formation of the contract. They have done so because in this area the freedom of contacting parties in the future must be maintained as widely as possible, and a certain margin of evaluation must be left to the court which has to decide on the existence of a contract. Moreover, one must keep in mind the different ways of proceeding and steps along the way leading to the creation of a contract. Therefore, the proposed provisions have as their subject-matter the different unilateral or bilateral juridical acts which are most commonly employed and made use of with the prospect of concluding a contract.

As to the substance, the rules as drafted draw on a number of sources: first, French case-law in this area over the last two centuries; then certain recent codes from countries in Europe and elsewhere (Germany, the Netherlands, Quebec); lastly, the European and international harmonisation projects relating to the law of contract (the draft European Contract Code of the Gandolfi group;[1] the *Principles of European Contract Law* of the Lando commission;[2] the *Unidroit Principles*[3]). And these rules are based on a trio of principles: freedom, loyalty and certainty.

First, **freedom** in the period of pre-contractual negotiations (articles 1104 to 1104-2). The negotiating parties are free to enter into discussions, to carry on their negotiations and to end them how and when they see fit. In principle, they will not incur liability in this negotiating phase. In particular, there will be no liability simply because the negotiations have been broken off and this breaking-off has caused harm to one of the negotiating parties. Freedom, in the second place, at the stage of offer and acceptance. On the one hand, the offeror has a significant unilateral power of revocation. On the other hand, the recipient of the offer cannot, save in exceptional circumstances, be bound contractually by proof of his

---

[1] [Academy of European Private Lawyers, *European Contract Code—Preliminary Draft* (Università Di Pavia, 2001). The English translation of the articles is reproduced in O Radley-Gardner, H Beale, R Zimmermann and R Schulze, *Fundamental Texts on European Private Law* (Oxford, Hart Publishing, 2003) 439-519. The Academy is headed by Professor Giuseppe Gandolfi.]

[2] [Above, p 467, n 1.]

[3] [UNIDROIT (International Institute for the Unification of Private Law), *Principles of International Commercial Contracts* (new edn, Rome, UNIDROIT, 2004); the text of the articles is available on *www.unidroit.org*.]

exceptionnelles, être contractuellement lié lorsqu'il fait preuve de passivité à réception de celle-ci. Liberté, en troisième lieu, quant aux instruments que les négociateurs peuvent exploiter dans la perspective de la conclusion de leur accord définitif : contrat de négociation, accord de principe, promesse unilatérale, pacte de préférence. Étant entendu que la « liste » n'est pas exhaustive et que le recours à d'autres instruments contractuels est possible.

Loyauté, en deuxième lieu. La liberté précontractuelle est, en effet, tempérée et canalisée par une exigence de loyauté destinée à imposer une certaine éthique lors de la période qui tend vers la conclusion d'un contrat, dans la mesure où la négociation contractuelle s'inscrit souvent dans la durée et se traduit souvent par d'importants investissements financiers. Aussi, la bonne foi guide les négociateurs lors de la négociation et singulièrement à l'occasion de sa rupture. De même, la liberté de conclure des petits contrats qui jalonnent et encadrent les pourparlers est canalisée par l'exigence de bonne foi.

Sécurité, en troisième lieu. Les règles proposées sont mues par l'impératif d'assurer la sécurité juridique lors de la période précontractuelle. Ainsi, d'abord, le pouvoir de révocation unilatérale de l'offrant est neutralisé lorsque son offre, adressée à personne déterminée, comportait son engagement de la maintenir pendant un délai précis. Dans ce cas de figure, la révocation de l'offre n'empêchera pas la formation du contrat si elle est acceptée dans le délai fixé, pas plus d'ailleurs que le décès de l'offrant ou son incapacité survenus pendant le délai d'acceptation. De même que la sécurité du destinataire de l'offre, concrètement le respect de sa croyance légitime dans le maintien de l'offre, est assurée par cette disposition, celle de l'offrant est promue par la règle qui prévoit que le contrat n'est conclu qu'à compter de la réception de l'acceptation. Ainsi, l'offrant n'est-il contractuellement lié que lorsqu'il a pu prendre effectivement connaissance de la volonté manifestée par son partenaire et ne peut pas être juridiquement engagé sans le savoir. Solution qui, par ailleurs, renforce automatiquement son pouvoir de révocation unilatérale. Ensuite, c'est la protection de la confiance légitime du bénéficiaire d'un pacte de préférence ou d'une promesse unilatérale de contrat que les règles nouvelles ont poursuivie comme objectif. En harmonie avec les textes relatifs à l'irrévocabilité unilatérale du contrat, à l'exécution forcée et dans le souci de ne pas priver d'intérêt les avant-contrats les plus utilisés dans la pratique contractuelle, la rétractation du promettant est sanctionnée de la façon la plus énergique qui soit. En effet, le refus du promettant de conclure le contrat promis ou la conclusion avec un tiers du contrat à propos duquel il avait consenti une priorité ou une exclusivité au bénéficiaire, ne font pas obstacle à la conclusion du contrat promis au profit du bénéficiaire.

failure to react on its receipt. Freedom, in the third place, as regards the instruments that the negotiating parties can use with a view to concluding their final agreement: a contract to negotiate; an agreement in principle; a unilateral promise to contract; and a pre-emption agreement. Of course this list is not exhaustive, and recourse can be made to other contractual mechanisms.

Secondly, **loyalty**. Pre-contractual freedom is indeed tempered and limited by a requirement of loyalty which is intended to impose a certain code of ethics in the period leading towards the conclusion of a contract, in so far as contractual negotiations are often marked by their length and often involve significant financial outlay. Also, the requirement of good faith provides guidance for negotiating parties during the negotiations, and especially at the moment of breaking them off. Similarly, the freedom to enter into minor contracts which mark out and provide a framework for the negotiations is constrained by the requirement of good faith.

Thirdly, **certainty**. The proposed rules are driven by the imperative to ensure legal certainty during the pre-contractual period. And so, first, an offeror's unilateral power of revocation is negatived when his offer, addressed to a particular person, carries his undertaking to maintain it during a specified period. In such a situation, the revocation of the offer will not prevent the formation of the contract if it is accepted within the specified period, nor will the offeror's death or incapacity during the period for acceptance. Just as certainty is assured by this provision for the recipient of the offer, and in particular respect for his legitimate belief that the offer will be maintained, so certainty for the offeror is promoted by the rule which provides that the contract is concluded only at the moment of receipt of the acceptance. Thus, the offeror is contractually bound only once he has actually been able to have notice of the will manifested by his partner, and cannot be bound in law without such knowledge. This solution, moreover, automatically reinforces his power to revoke his offer unilaterally. Secondly, the new rules aim to protect the legitimate expectations of the beneficiary of a pre-emption agreement or a unilateral promise to contract. In harmony with the provisions to the effect that one party may not unilaterally revoke a contract, and with the provisions governing enforced performance, and motivated by a concern not to undermine the preliminary contracts which are most commonly used in practice, the withdrawal by the offeror is sanctioned in the strongest possible manner. Indeed, the offeror's refusal to conclude the promised contract, or his concluding with a third party a contract of which he had given a preferential or exclusive right to the offeree, are not an obstacle to the conclusion of the promised contract with the offeree.

Validité du contrat – Consentement (art. 1108 à 1115-1)

Yves Lequette,
Grégoire Loiseau,
Yves-Marie Serinet

Selon un avis unanime, les dispositions relatives au consentement en vigueur dans le Code civil (articles 1109 à 1118) ne rendent compte de la matière que de façon imparfaite et incomplète.

Les textes, dont la rédaction originale demeure inchangée depuis 1804, envisagent les seules qualités de lucidité et de liberté que celui-ci doit revêtir afin que de la volonté de chaque contractant sorte un engagement valable.

De toute évidence, la perspective ainsi choisie s'avère doublement limitée au regard des questions que soulève cette condition essentielle de formation des conventions dans le droit contemporain.

D'une part, la présentation des codificateurs conduit à passer sous silence le processus d'expression et de rencontre des volontés, masquant ainsi la difficulté spécifique de l'absence totale de consentement.

D'autre part, elle n'ouvre à celui qui n'aurait pas contracté en pleine connaissance de cause et librement que les remèdes curatifs de l'annulation pour vice du consentement. Or, les développements récents du droit de la consommation ont montré, en marge du Code civil, que d'autres formes de protection permettaient, par une voie préventive, d'assurer d'une manière souvent plus efficace la même fonction de protection.

Au demeurant, sur le terrain le plus classique de la théorie des vices du consentement, il apparaît aujourd'hui que les textes initiaux ne traduisent le droit positif qu'en surface. Car les notions d'erreur, de dol et de violence ont connu des transformations profondes sous l'influence de débats doctrinaux nourris depuis la fin du XIXe siècle. Dans leur prolongement, une jurisprudence foisonnante et subtile, parfois jusqu'à l'excès, a considérablement ajouté au régime juridique de chacun des vices au point qu'il faille désormais y rechercher l'essentiel des règles applicables. Si, sur certains points, les choix prétoriens demeurent encore discutés, il n'en reste pas moins que, dans son ensemble, la construction jurisprudentielle a atteint un degré de maturité et de finesse suffisant pour servir de source

Validity of the Contract – Consent (articles 1108 to 1115-1)

Yves Lequette,
Grégoire Loiseau,
Yves-Marie Serinet

Everyone agrees that the provisions relating to consent currently in force in the Civil Code (articles 1109 to 1118) give only an imperfect and incomplete account of the matter.

The provisions, whose original wording has remained unchanged since 1804, address only the qualities of clarity and freedom that the consent must possess in order for the will of each contracting party to result in a valid undertaking.

Clearly this chosen perspective is limited in two respects with regard to the questions raised by this essential condition for the formation of contracts in the law today.

On the one hand, the presentation adopted by the draftsmen of the Code results in the process of the expression and meeting of the wills of the parties being passed over in silence, thereby masking the particular difficulty of total absence of consent.

On the other hand, it gives to the party who would not have contracted if he had had full knowledge, and had been free, only the remedy of annulment for defect of consent. Recent developments in consumer law, however, have shown, on the margins of the Civil Code, that other means of protection could take a preventive form and fulfil—often in a more effective manner—the same protective function.[1]

In fact, in the most classical areas of the doctrine of defects in consent, it is clear today that the original wording conveys the law as it really exists only on the surface. The concepts of mistake, fraud and duress have undergone very significant changes under the influence of lively academic debates since the end of the 19th century. Following on from these, an abundant and subtle case-law (sometimes too subtle) has added significantly to the legal rules governing each of the defects in consent to the point where that has become the place to find the core rules. Although, on certain points, the judicial developments are still debated, it is still the case that, overall, the edifice built by the judges has reached a sufficient degree of maturity and detail to serve as a source of inspiration for the drafting of new provi-

---

[1] [The Consumer Code, first adopted in 1993, gathered together a range of existing legislative provisions relating to consumers and consumer protection (but also, rather curiously, certain provisions which cover business-to-business transactions), and has since been further amended to include new similar provisions, often in order to implement European Directives. The current text may be seen (in French and with an English translation) in the section on 'Codes' on *www.legifrance.gouv.fr*. The first section (Book 1, Title 1) contains (eg) provisions governing information to be provided by one party to the other during the formation of a contract.]

d'inspiration à la rédaction de nouveaux textes. D'autant qu'en ce domaine, le droit positif français assure une meilleure protection et témoigne d'un plus grand perfectionnement technique que les diverses propositions de textes émises ailleurs sur le même sujet.

Pour ces différentes raisons, la rédaction d'une nouvelle section du Code civil qui aurait à traiter du consentement (articles 1109 à 1115-1) nécessiterait, dans l'esprit de ceux à qui elle a été confiée, d'une part, de combler les lacunes dans l'approche que les codificateurs de 1804 avaient eu de la matière en rédigeant de nouvelles dispositions relatives à l'existence et à l'intégrité du consentement et, d'autre part, de tirer toutes les conséquences des principales évolutions apportées par la jurisprudence à la construction du régime des différents vices du consentement en modifiant et complétant les textes actuellement en vigueur.

C'est ainsi que dans une Sous-section 1, il sera proposé d'adopter plusieurs textes généraux qui traitent de la question de l'existence du consentement. À ce titre, deux difficultés peuvent surgir, qui ne sont pas les plus fréquentes, mais font d'ordinaire l'objet d'un traitement peu satisfaisant par renvoi à des textes particuliers en dehors du cœur du droit des obligations ou par rattachement à des notions voisines quoique pourtant distinctes.

La première concerne l'absence de consentement de l'un des contractants. Elle correspond à la situation d'une personne juridiquement capable qui souffre d'une altération des facultés mentales et se trouve par là même hors d'état d'émettre un véritable consentement. Le contrat ne peut alors se former valablement à défaut d'une volonté réelle à l'origine de la déclaration de volonté. Afin de traiter cette situation, il est envisagé de généraliser à tous les actes juridiques une solution énoncée à l'article 901 du Code civil pour les libéralités et figurant déjà à l'article 489 du Code civil dans les dispositions relatives aux majeurs issues de la loi du 3 janvier 1968 rédigée par le doyen Carbonnier. Cette généralisation avait d'ailleurs déjà été envisagée par lui et permet de régler de façon uniforme la question de l'acte juridique conclu sous l'empire d'un trouble mental dans un nouvel article 1109.

La seconde difficulté est relative à l'absence de rencontre des consentements, lorsque les deux parties n'ont pas voulu la même chose. Il y a bien une apparence de contrat, mais celui-ci repose sur un malentendu, ce que l'on traite habituellement au titre de l'erreur-obstacle. Afin d'envisager cette situation qui, le plus souvent, reste étudiée avec la théorie de l'erreur, un article 1109-1 est prévu.

Enfin, une sanction uniforme est proposée à l'article 1109-2 du Code civil en cas d'absence de consentement. C'est la nullité relative qui se déduisait déjà de la conception moderne des nullités et résultait de la réforme du 3 janvier 1968. Outre qu'il met fin aux incertitudes et discussions sur une éventuelle résurgence de la

sions. This is all the more so, given that in this area the law as presently applied in France gives a greater degree of protection, and displays a higher degree of technical perfection than the various alternative proposals that have been published on this subject.

For these different reasons, the drafting of a new section of the Civil Code containing provisions on consent (articles 1109 to 1115-1) would need, in the view of those to whom the task has been entrusted, on the one hand, to fill in the gaps in the approach taken by the draftsmen of the 1804 Code to the topic, by drafting new provisions concerning the existence and integrity of consent; and, on the other hand, to draw all the conclusions from the main developments made by case-law to build up the rules governing the several defects of consent, by modifying and supplementing the provisions presently in force.

Therefore, in a first sub-section, it is proposed to adopt a number of general provisions dealing with the question of the existence of consent. In this, two difficulties can arise which are not the most common, but which are usually dealt with in a hardly satisfactory manner by cross-reference to individual provisions outside the core of the law of obligations, or by links to neighbouring concepts which, however, are distinct.

The first concerns the absence of consent of one of the parties. It corresponds to the situation where one person, with legal capacity, suffers a change in his mental faculties and so finds himself incapable of giving true consent. The contract can then not validly be formed because of the lack of a real will within the declaration of will. To deal with this situation, it is intended to generalise to all juridical acts a solution set out in article 901 of the Civil Code[1] for acts of generosity, and which already appears in article 489 of the Civil Code[2] within the provisions dealing with adults as a result of the Law of 3 January 1968,[3] drafted by *le doyen* Carbonnier.[4] This generalisation had also already been contemplated by him, and allows a uniform treatment of the question of juridical acts performed under the influence of a mental problem in a new article 1109.

The second difficulty relates to the absence of a meeting of consent, when the two parties have not intended the same thing. There is certainly the appearance of a contract, but this is based on a misunderstanding, which is usually discussed under the heading of mistake preventing a contract coming into existence. In order to provide for this situation which is most commonly studied within the doctrine of mistake, article 1109-1 is included.

Finally, a uniform sanction for the situation of absence of consent is proposed in article 1109-2 of the Civil Code. This is relative nullity which already follows the wider modern doctrine of nullities, and results from the reform of 3 January 1968. In addition to putting an end to the uncertainty and debate over a possible revival

---

[1] [Article 901 Cc: 'Pour faire une liberalité, il faut être sain d'esprit...' (In order to make an act of generosity, one must be of sound mind...).]

[2] [Article 489 Cc: 'Pour faire un acte valable, il faut être sain d'esprit...' (In order to make a valid transaction, one must be of sound mind...).]

[3] [Loi no 68-5 portant réforme du droit des incapables majeurs, JO 4 January 1968, 114.]

[4] [We do not translate *le doyen*. Without exact parallel in English, it is an honorific title which reflects not only the formal status as a present or former 'Dean' of a Faculty, but also a seniority in years and wisdom which of itself merits respect.]

notion d'inexistence du contrat, ce choix présente l'avantage d'homogénéiser ces sanctions avec celles qui sont classiquement retenues en matière de vices du consentement.

Ensuite, dans une Sous-section 2, les propositions visent à exposer, de façon plus détaillée, les règles destinées à assurer la qualité du consentement des contractants dans deux paragraphes inégalement novateurs.

Dans une première subdivision, sont insérées des dispositions nouvelles relatives aux mesures positives de protection du consentement. Leur fonction préventive justifie l'intitulé du paragraphe qui traite de l'intégrité du consentement. Sont ici successivement définis deux instruments que le droit de la consommation utilise de manière courante à cette fin bien que le premier ne s'y trouve pas strictement cantonné : l'obligation précontractuelle de renseignement d'une part (articles 1110 et 1110-1), les techniques tendant à différer la formation définitive du contrat que sont les délais de réflexion et de repentir d'autre part (article 1110-2). À chaque fois, il s'agit de favoriser la réflexion du contractant en lui permettant de prendre une décision éclairée et lui offrant le temps suffisant avant de s'engager définitivement et irrévocablement.

Il est apparu nécessaire de donner un cadre général à ces notions qui permette de dépasser, selon les cas, la diversité de leurs sources (jurisprudentielle ou légale) et l'éclatement de leurs régimes. En fixer le sens et les principaux caractères dans le droit commun des obligations du Code civil redonne à celui-ci ses pleines cohérence et dimension tout en créant un point d'ancrage vers les droits spéciaux plus techniques, notamment le droit de la consommation. Refaire du Code civil un Code pilote serait aussi une manière de répondre à la critique qui veut que la réglementation générale des contrats ait perdu sa vigueur et sa capacité créatrice au profit du droit de la consommation qui, plus nouvellement codifié, incarnerait le droit vivant...

Une seconde subdivision, de façon plus classique, redéfinit le régime des vices du consentement que le Code civil avait originellement prévu, en y intégrant les apports les plus substantiels du droit positif, en prenant parti sur certains points encore soumis à discussion et en s'efforçant de rassembler, par une mise en facteur commun, les éléments qui réunissent les mesures curatives de protection du consentement.

En tête puis en fin de paragraphe, figurent quatre dispositions générales. Reprenant la formule originaire du Code de 1804, louée pour sa valeur expressive particulièrement forte, un nouvel article 1111 regroupe la trilogie des vices du consentement en changeant simplement l'ordre de leur énumération afin de respecter celui qui sera suivi pour les présenter. À sa suite, l'article 1111-1 énonce la condition de détermination du consentement commune à tous ces vices dans un texte qui s'inspire d'un arrêt célèbre rendu à propos de l'erreur déterminante (Cass. civ., 28 janvier 1913, S. 1913, 1, 487). L'absence de distinction entre le vice

of the notion of the inexistence of the contract,[1] this choice provides the advantage of harmonising the sanctions with those which are classically retained for defects in consent.

Next, in a second sub-section, the proposals are intended to set out, in a more detailed manner, the rules designed to guarantee the quality of the contracting parties' consent in two paragraphs which are not equally novel in their provisions.

In a first sub-division there are new provisions relating to positive measures designed to protect the consent. Their preventive function justifies the title of the sub-division, which deals with the integrity of consent. Here are set out two mechanisms which are currently used by consumer law[2] to achieve this, even though the first is not confined to that: pre-contractual obligations to inform, on the one hand (articles 1110 and 1110-1); and, on the other hand, the techniques which tend to delay the final formation of the contract: periods allowing for reflection and for a change of mind (article 1110-2). At each stage it is necessary to promote the contracting party's ability to reflect, allowing him to take an informed decision and giving him enough time before he is finally and irrevocably bound.

It appeared necessary to give a general framework to these notions, going beyond their different origins (judicial or legislative) and their separate regimes. Fixing their meaning and their principal characteristics within the general law of obligations in the Civil Code gives the Code again a real coherence and standing whilst also creating an anchor-point for the more technical specialised areas of law, and in particular consumer law. Re-modelling the Civil Code as a legislative beacon would also be a way to respond to critics who say that the general rules of contract law have lost their force and their creative power in favour of consumer law which, having been codified more recently, embodies the living law.

A second, more classical, sub-division redraws the scheme of the defects in consent that were originally provided by the Civil Code, by integrating into it the most significant contributions made by the law as it is today, by taking a position on certain points which are still subject to debate, and by aiming to find the common threads between, and to bring together, the elements which link the remedial measures which further the protection of consent.

At the very beginning and then at the end of the sub-division are placed four general provisions. Taking up the original formulation of the Code of 1804, praised for its particularly strong expressive value, a new article 1111 gathers together the trio of the defects in consent, changing only their order so as to respect what follows in the detailed presentation. Following this, article 1111-1 sets out, for all the defects in consent, the requirement of decisiveness in relation to consent, in a provision which takes its inspiration from a famous decision on the subject of decisive mistake (Cass civ. 28 January, 1913, S. 1913, 1, 487). The absence of any

[1] [There has been a debate in French academic writing about whether a consequence of a mistake in the formation of a contract might be to render the contract inexistent rather than subject to the (judicial) sanction of nullity. See Carbonnier, *Droit civil*, vol 4 *Les Obligations* (22th edn, Paris, PUF, 2000) no 109.]

[2] [Eg the Consumer Code contains provisions for certain information to be provided to a consumer before the formation of a contract in Book 1, Title 1; and for periods for reflection in articles L121-26 and L121-33 (doorstep selling), and L312-5 and L312-14-1 (credit agreements for loans relating to real property).]

principal et incident est également soulignée cependant que les éléments de l'appréciation *in concreto* du caractère déterminant se trouvent énoncés, l'effet du vice sur le consentement devant se mesurer à l'égard de celui qui l'allègue. Par ailleurs, les articles 1115 et 1115-1 rappellent que l'erreur, le dol et la violence ouvrent classiquement l'action en nullité relative qui, tendant à la protection du contractant victime, ne court que du jour de la cessation du vice ou de sa découverte. La proximité des voies de droit qu'exprime l'expression traditionnelle de « *fongibilité* » des vices du consentement autorise les passerelles procédurales. Enfin, l'annulation du contrat s'obtient sans préjudice d'éventuels dommages et intérêts alloués cumulativement ou alternativement. Dol et violence ont en effet toujours présenté la structure dualiste d'un délit civil, pour celui qui l'exerce, et d'un vice du consentement, pour celui qui le subit. Mais on admet aujourd'hui encore que l'erreur provoquée par les agissements fautifs du cocontractant autorise une réparation sur le terrain délictuel. C'est ce que l'article 1115 alinéa 2, résume dans une formule générale dérivée de l'article 1382 (anc.) du Code civil.

À ces règles communes, s'ajoutent des dispositions spéciales propres à chaque vice du consentement.

C'est ainsi que l'erreur est d'abord réglementée, avec ses deux objets possibles que l'article 1110 (anc.) du Code civil envisageait dès 1804 : la substance de la chose et la personne du cocontractant (article 1112). À chaque fois, la qualité essentielle sur laquelle la méprise aura porté est celle en considération de laquelle les deux parties auront contracté (qualité convenue) ou qui, envisagée par l'une, aura été portée à la connaissance de l'autre (qualité entrée dans le champ contractuel ?). Conformément à une jurisprudence bien assise, développée en matière de vente d'œuvres d'art, il a été retenu que l'acceptation d'un aléa relativement à une qualité de la chose chassait l'erreur (article 1112-1. alinéa 2). Sont également reprises d'autres solutions, largement éprouvées, qui tiennent les erreurs de droit et de fait pour équivalentes et refusent, après analyse des comportements respectifs des parties, la prise en considération de l'erreur inexcusable (article 1112-3). Dans un esprit voisin, la simple erreur sur la valeur ou sur les motifs est tenue pour indifférente sous les conditions dégagées par la jurisprudence au terme d'une longue évolution prétorienne (article 1112-4).

Sur le terrain du dol, les propositions consacrent l'élargissement de la définition classique du vice qui s'évinçait de l'article 1116 (anc.) du Code civil à la réticence dolosive (article 1113-1), laquelle présente un intérêt pratique supérieur et permet de faire un lien avec l'obligation de renseignement précédemment organisée (article

distinction between principal and incidental defects of consent is also emphasised,[1] whereas it is made clear that the test of decisiveness is subjective, the effect of the defect being assessed in relation to the person who alleges it. Moreover, articles 1115 and 1115-1 are a reminder that mistake, fraud and duress give rise classically to an action for relative nullity for which time starts to run only from the day when the defect has ceased or has been discovered, given that it aims to protect the party who has been its victim. The closeness of the forms of legal action which are caught by the traditional description of the defects of consent as 'interchangeable'[2] allows them to be procedurally connected. Finally, annulment of a contract is without prejudice to any damages that might be awarded cumulatively with it, or in the alternative. Fraud and duress have of course always had a double aspect: a civil delict for the one who commits them, and a defect in consent for the one who suffers from them.[3] But today it is even admitted that a mistake induced by the other party's conduct which constitutes a fault justifies reparation in the delictual domain. This is summed up by article 1115, paragraph 2, in a general formula derived from (former) article 1382 of the Civil Code.

To these generally applicable rules are added specific provisions for each defect in consent.

And so the rules governing mistake are set out first, with the same two objects that the (former) article 1110 of the Civil Code has provided for since 1804: the substance of the thing and the person of the other party to the contract (article 1112). In each, the essential quality in respect of which the misunderstanding must have been made is that in consideration of which the parties have contracted (the agreed quality) or which was in the contemplation of one to the knowledge of the other (or should it be a quality which might be said to have entered the 'contractual sphere'?). In accordance with well-established case-law, developed within the field of the sale of works of art, the rule has been retained that if one party accepts the risk as to a quality of the thing, this excludes mistake (article 1112-1, paragraph 2). Other solutions, which are generally agreed upon, have also been retained: mistakes of law and of fact are treated as the same; and a mistake of one party which, in the light of the behaviour of both parties, was inexcusable is not taken into account (article 1112-3). In a similar spirit, a mere mistake of value or of motive has no effect, on the basis established by a long series of developments by the courts (article 1112-4).

In the area of fraud, the proposals give effect to the enlargement of the traditional definition of this defect in consent from the (former) article 1116 of the Civil Code to fraudulent non-disclosure (article 1113-1). This is of great practical significance, and allows a link to be made to the obligation to inform which has been set out

---

[1] [For the 'unworkable' distinction between *dol principal* ('principal fraud', giving rise to annulment of the contract) and *dol incident* ('incidental fraud', where the claimant would still have entered into some form of contact in spite of the proven fraud) see Nicholas, *The French Law of Contract*, above, p 489, n 2, 111.]

[2] [It is said that the defects in consent are 'interchangeable' ('*fongible*') because if a claimant brings his claim on the basis of one of the defects (eg fraud: article 1116 Cc) it is open to the court to decide the case on the basis of another (eg mistake: article 1110).]

[3] [This is a legacy of Roman law, where fraud (*dolus*) and duress (*metus*) gave rise to actions in delict, but also constituted defences to claims to enforce a contract: B Nicholas, *An Introduction to Roman Law* (Oxford, Clarendon Press, 1962) 176, 223.]

1110). Les rapports entre les deux notions sont encore clarifiés puisqu'il est énoncé que, lorsque l'intention de tromper fait défaut, le manquement à une telle obligation n'engage que la responsabilité de celui qui y était tenu. Sur le principe selon lequel le dol qui n'émanerait pas du cocontractant reste sans effet sur la validité du contrat, l'article 1113-2 apporte certains aménagements, parfois connus, afin de tenir compte de la possible intercession d'un tiers dans la conclusion de la convention. Au dol de l'une des parties, est assimilé celui de son représentant, gérant d'affaires, préposé ou porte-fort. En outre, l'article 1113-3 prévoit que l'erreur résultant d'un dol sera plus facilement sanctionnée qu'une erreur spontanée puisqu'on la tiendra toujours pour excusable et qu'elle ouvrira la nullité alors même qu'elle aurait porté sur la seule valeur ou sur de simples motifs. Toutefois, le texte réserve cette extension au seul cas d'une erreur « *provoquée* » par le dol ce qui, *stricto sensu*, ne sera pas généralisable à la réticence dolosive. Tacitement, la disposition conduit à entériner la jurisprudence *Baldus* (Cass. civ. 1re, 3 mai 2000, *Bull. civ.*, I, no 130), si, du moins, on veut bien en faire une lecture littérale.

Reste la violence. À son égard, les textes proposés reprennent, pour l'essentiel, les dispositions actuelles du Code civil (articles 1111 à 1114 anc.). Il est seulement procédé à quelques aménagements afin de tenir compte, notamment, des ajustements que la jurisprudence avait déjà dessinés à propos de l'emploi illégitime d'une voie de droit. L'innovation réelle provient de la consécration de l'idée d'exploitation abusive d'une situation de faiblesse provoquée par un état de nécessité ou de dépendance. L'opportunité de retenir en ce cas la violence, récemment débattue, se trouve reconnue sous la forme d'un nouvel article 1114-3 qui précise également les critères en fonction desquels ce cas particulier de violence sera apprécié.

Validité – Capacité et pouvoir (art. 1116 à 1120-2)

Jean Hauser,
Guillaume Wicker

La capacité des sujets de droit a été étrangement traitée, par les auteurs du Code civil, à propos de la conclusion des actes juridiques. C'était voir seulement le côté actif de la capacité alors que notre société, soucieuse parfois exagérément de principes, y verrait plutôt le côté passif du sujet. La capacité est d'abord une

earlier (article 1110). The relationship between these two notions is again made clear because it is provided that, where there is no intention to deceive, breach of the obligation gives rise only to a liability on the part of the one who was subject to the obligation. To the principle that fraud which does not originate in the other contracting party has no effect on the validity of the contract, article 1113-2 makes certain adjustments, some of them already well-known, in order to take into account the possible intervention by a third party in the formation of the contract. To fraud of one of the parties is assimilated that of his representative, as is that of a person who intervenes in his affairs without authority, his employee, or one standing surety for him. In addition, article 1113-3 provides that a mistake caused by fraud will be more easily sanctioned than a spontaneous mistake, because it is always excusable and it gives rise to the right to nullity even when it is a mistake simply of value or of mere motive. However, the wording reserves this extension for the sole case of a mistake 'provoked' by fraud which, strictly interpreted, will not extend to fraudulent non-disclosure. Implicitly, this provision leads to the ratification of the *Baldus* decision (Cass civ. (1), 3 May 2000, Bull. civ., I, n° 130[1]), at least if it is given a literal reading.

This leaves duress. In this area, the proposed provisions repeat, in essence, the present provisions of the Civil Code (former articles 1111 to 1114). There are just a few refinements to take account of, in particular, adjustments that the case-law has already made with regard to the illegitimate use of legal process. The real innovation is the acceptance of the idea of the wrongful exploitation of a situation of weakness caused by a state of necessity or dependence. Whether this should be treated as a case of duress has been the subject of recent debate, but the opportunity has been taken to recognise it, in the form of a new article 1114-3 which also defines the criteria by reference to which this particular form of duress will be assessed.

Validity – Capacity and Power to Act (articles 1116 to 1120-2)

Jean Hauser,
Guillaume Wicker

The capacity of legal actors as regards the making of juridical acts was dealt with strangely by the authors of the Civil Code. They considered only the positive aspect of capacity, whereas modern society, preoccupied—sometimes over-preoccupied—with principle, has considered more the negative side of the subject. Capacity is first and foremost a question of the law of persons. And so we can

---

[1] [In this case a purchaser of photographs by the celebrated photographer Baldus was not liable to the seller for fraud under article 1116 Cc where he knew that he was buying them at a derisory price: the reason given by the Cour de cassation was that there was no duty of disclosure on the buyer. See commentary by C Jamin at JCP 2001 II 10510.]

question de droit des personnes. Ainsi, peut-on se demander si le §1 du projet sur la capacité de jouissance ne trouverait pas plus sa place dans les articles phares du Code, désormais les articles 16 et s., plutôt que dans des articles consacrés au droit des obligations. La notion de « capacité naturelle » est maintenant familière à la doctrine dans ces matières et mériterait une place à part.

Pour autant, et faute d'une réforme globale du code, il n'était pas inutile d'affirmer le lien de la capacité de jouissance avec la personne elle-même et d'y mentionner les rares incapacités de jouissance qui peuvent frapper certaines personnes, essentiellement on le remarquera (art. 1116-2) pour des raisons limitées d'opposition d'intérêts. En même temps il n'était pas non plus inutile de mentionner la capacité de jouissance spéciale des personnes morales, sur laquelle le Code ne se prononçait pas, tout en précisant le contenu de cette capacité dans une formule dont la jurisprudence pourrait tirer profit. Le texte pourrait constituer l'amorce d'une théorie générale de la capacité des personnes morales qui trouverait bien sa place dans un code civil modernisé où ces personnes, apparues après le code de 1804, auraient enfin le statut qu'elles méritent. Enfin les effets de l'apparition d'une incapacité de jouissance de l'une des parties pendant un contrat justifiaient aussi une précision.

L'essentiel devait, à l'évidence, être consacré aux incapacités d'exercice. L'article 1117, qui affirme le principe et l'exception, aurait précisément pu être intégré ailleurs puisqu'il s'agit d'un principe général qui dépasse de beaucoup la conclusion des actes juridiques. Deux conséquences pratiques en découlent. C'était, tout d'abord, l'occasion de consacrer, au moins théoriquement, la possibilité d'organiser une future perte de l'incapacité d'exercice, prévue par le projet de réforme du droit des incapacités, en voie d'adoption, sous l'appellation de mandat de protection future.

C'était ensuite l'occasion de réaffirmer et généraliser ce que les textes et la jurisprudence ont progressivement dégagé : la capacité résiduelle de la personne protégée pour les actes conservatoires, les actes permis par la loi ou l'usage et les actes relatifs à la personne. Sur ce dernier point, particulièrement délicat, il a paru souhaitable de préciser la nécessaire distinction entre les conséquences personnelles de ces actes, soumises au principe d'autonomie, et les conséquences patrimoniales demeurées dans la sphère de la représentation. La jurisprudence aura inévitablement à préciser cette frontière.

Il a paru nécessaire de préciser l'effet de l'incapacité résultant de la minorité et le statut législatif en est sensiblement renforcé. Les conditions de la rescision pour lésion et ses effets sont assez nettement précisées ainsi que le droit d'agir en nullité des différentes parties à l'acte juridique. Le cantonnement de ce droit d'agir en nullité ou en rescision pourrait indirectement favoriser une certaine extension de la théorie des actes courants en ce que les tiers contractants se trouveraient mieux garantis contre d'éventuelles actions en restitution de la personne protégée.

L'ajout d'un important dispositif législatif à propos de la représentation traduit le souci de préciser une technique finalement assez peu étudiée, sous le prétexte que toute représentation ressemblerait à un mandat, ce qui est certainement faux pour la

wonder whether part 1 of the Reform Proposals on the capacity of enjoyment should not rather be placed in the leading articles of the Code (now article 16 *et seq.*) than in the articles dealing with the law of obligations. The notion of 'natural capacity' is now familiar to writers in that context, and would deserve to be treated separately.

However, since there is to be no overall revision of the Code, it was not unhelpful to confirm the link between the capacity for enjoyment and the person himself, and in this context to mention the exceptional cases of lack of capacity for enjoyment which can affect certain persons, essentially (as will be noticed: article 1116-2) for limited reasons where there are competing considerations. At the same time, it was not unhelpful either to mention the particular capacity for enjoyment of legal persons of which the Code made no particular mention but making clear the contents of this capacity in a formula on which the courts could draw. The text could form the beginnings of a general doctrine of capacity of legal persons, which would certainly have a place in a modernised civil code where these persons (who have come into existence after the 1804 Code) would at last have the status they deserve. Finally, the effect of a lack of capacity for enjoyment of one party arising during a contract would also justify clarification.

The most significant place, of course, should be given to lack of capacity in respect of the exercise of legal rights. Article 1117, which affirms both the principle and the exception, could certainly have been included elsewhere because it contains a general principle which goes far beyond the formation of juridical acts. Two practical consequences follow. First, this provided an opportunity to recognise formally, at least in theory, that a person may make arrangements for a future loss of capacity in respect of the exercise of legal rights, which was provided for in the proposal for the reform of the law of incapacity, currently in the process of being adopted, under the name of mandates for future protection.

Secondly, this provided an opportunity to reaffirm and generalise what legislation and case-law have gradually made clear: the protected person's residual capacity to enter into juridical acts for his own protection, juridical acts permitted by law or custom, and juridical acts relating to his own person. On this past point, which is particularly sensitive, it seemed desirable to make clear the necessary distinction between the personal consequences of such juridical acts, subject to the principle of autonomy, and their consequences for his estate, which remain within the scope of representation. Case-law will inevitably have to settle this borderline.

It seems necessary to make clear the effect of a lack of capacity which flows from minority, and its legal status is clearly strengthened. The conditions required for rescission for substantive inequality of bargain, and its consequences, are quite clearly set out, as are the right of different parties to a juridical act to sue for annulment. Setting parameters for this right to sue for annulment or rescission could indirectly lead to some widening of the doctrine of everyday transactions, in that third parties would find themselves with better protection against possible actions for restitution by the protected person.

The addition of a significant legislative provision in relation to representation flows from a concern to clarify a technique which, after all, is studied rather too little, on the basis that every representation resembles a mandate—which is certainly false in

représentation légale ou judiciaire et a provoqué d'importantes confusions, y compris en jurisprudence. Ainsi se trouve précisée la mission du représentant éventuel en fonction des catégories d'actes à réaliser à défaut de précisions suffisantes dans l'acte instituant la représentation. Les effets eux-mêmes de la représentation sur les pouvoirs du représenté sont détaillés en distinguant, ce qui n'était pas toujours clair, entre les effets de la représentation légale ou judiciaire et les effets de la représentation conventionnelle. Dans cette dernière est affirmé le principe qu'on ne peut accorder une représentation contre soi-même sauf à observer une loyauté minimum envers le représentant désigné.

La reprise, en les généralisant, des règles de l'opposition d'intérêts, bien connues des spécialistes du droit des incapacités, devrait donner naissance à une véritable théorie générale, jamais construite, alors que l'hypothèse concerne toutes les formes les plus diverses de représentations et pas seulement les cas de représentation d'un incapable.

Comme on l'a remarqué au départ la question de la capacité est une partie du droit des personnes plus qu'une partie du droit des obligations. La capacité à être partie à un rapport d'obligation n'est qu'un élément de la question plus vaste de la capacité de la personne à participer à la vie juridique en général et à la vie contractuelle en particulier. Le projet limité au seul droit des obligations laisse donc entière la question d'une refonte globale du Code civil dont la généralité de ce sujet demeure symbolique.

Validité – Objet
(art. 1121 à 1123)

Jérôme Huet,
Rémy Cabrillac

Dans son état actuel, l'objet du contrat figure dans une section 3 du chapitre II du livre III, intitulée « De l'objet et de la matière des contrats », qui comprend cinq articles (1126 à 1130). Les textes en question sont pour l'essentiel hérités de Pothier, Domat étant peu disert sur cette question de l'objet.

L'objet est peu évoqué dans les codifications récentes, officielles ou officieuses. Le *Code civil du Québec*, par exemple, ne lui consacre que deux articles (1412 et

the case of legal or judicial representation—and has given rise to serious confusion, even in the case-law. Therefore, we have made the task of any representative clear by reference to the categories of juridical acts to be entered into where the document creating the representation does not contain sufficient particularity. The effects, too, of representation on the powers of the person represented are laid out, distinguishing—and this was not always clear—between the effects of legal or judicial representation and the effects of contractual representation. In relation to this last form, the principle is affirmed that one cannot allow a person to act as one's representative against oneself, without fulfilling a minimum standard of loyalty in favour of the intended representative.

The repetition and generalisation of the rules governing conflict of interests, well known by specialists on the law of capacity, should give rise to a genuine general doctrine, never hitherto constructed, given that the examples concern all the diverse forms of representation, and not only the case of representation of a person who lacks capacity.

As mentioned at the outset, the question of capacity forms part of the law of persons, more than of the law of obligations. The capacity to be party to a relationship within the law of obligations is only one element of the much larger question of the capacity of a person to have a role in the legal sphere, and in the sphere of contracts in particular. The Reform Proposals, limited simply to the law of obligations, therefore leave untouched the question of a complete reform of the Civil Code, although the generality of this subject is symbolic.

Validity – Subject-Matter (articles 1121 to 1123)

Jérôme Huet,
Rémy Cabrillac

In the present arrangement, the subject-matter of contracts appears in section 3 of Chapter II of Book 3, under the heading 'The subject-matter and contents of contracts', which comprises five articles (1126 to 1130). These provisions are essentially inherited from Pothier, Domat not having been very forthcoming on the question of subject-matter.[1]

'Subject-matter' is not much used in recent codifications, whether official or unofficial. The *Civil Code of Quebec*, for example, gives it only two articles (1412

[1] [The writings of Jean Domat (1625-1696; *Les Lois civiles dans leur ordre naturel*, 1689) and Robert-Joseph Pothier (1699-1772; *Traité des obligations*, 1761) had a very significant influence on the drafting of the Civil Code of 1804. For a portrait and a brief biography of each, see Malaurie, above, p 465, n 1, 81-3, 103-4.]

1413). Les *Principes du droit européen des contrats* et le *Code de l'Académie des privatistes européens* n'évoquent que le contenu du contrat.

Une question préliminaire devait donc être tranchée, celle du maintien ou non de la notion d'objet. Ce maintien, ainsi que celui des exigences qui en découlent, a semblé nécessaire, en raison des conséquences importantes qui en découlent, ce dont témoigne une jurisprudence abondante ces dernières années, en particulier sur les questions d'existence ou de licéité de l'objet, ou encore de détermination du prix. De plus, la notion de contenu du contrat qui lui est parfois substituée ne paraît pas présenter une précision suffisante pour garantir la sécurité des relations contractuelles.

En conséquence, le projet propose de consacrer à l'objet du contrat une section 3 du chapitre II du sous-titre I du titre III, intitulée « De l'objet » et comprenant dix articles (1121 à 1122-3). Et, dans cette section, la terminologie traditionnelle a été conservée autant que faire se peut, tout en étant adaptée à la nouvelle distinction des obligations proposées par le projet : donner, donner à usage, faire ou ne pas faire (art. 1121).

Les textes existants nécessitaient, tout d'abord, un toilettage. Il convenait de modifier en l'intégrant à l'article 1121 l'actuel article 1127 qui implique l'obligation de donner à usage, reconnue désormais en tant que telle par le projet. Par ailleurs, l'actuel article 1130 al. 2, relatif à la prohibition des pactes sur succession future, a été supprimé, n'ayant plus sa place dans la théorie des obligations depuis que la prohibition figure à l'article 722.

L'actuel article 1128 concernant les « choses hors du commerce », dont la formule célèbre fait partie de notre patrimoine juridique, a été conservé. On a préféré la maintenir plutôt qu'établir une liste détaillée des choses hors commerce, ce qui aurait été hasardeux et inévitablement incomplet. Le sens du texte est à la fois suffisamment large et précis, comme en témoigne la jurisprudence. Il figure quasiment inchangé dans l'article 1121-1.

De même, la possibilité pour une chose future de constituer l'objet d'une obligation a été conservée (art. 1121-2 al. 3).

Un article annonçant les qualités nécessaires requises pour l'objet, en guise de transition, a été ajouté : l'objet doit être licite, possible, et exister au moment de la formation du contrat (art. 1121-2). De même, a été ajouté un article précisant les sanctions, en particulier pour distinguer entre l'illicéité de l'objet, frappée de nullité absolue, et l'absence de l'objet (art. 1122).

Au-delà de ces modifications, les principales innovations contenues dans le projet concernent les trois points suivants :

and 1413). The *Principles of European Contract Law* and the *Code of the Academy of Private Lawyers*[1] refer only to the content of contracts.

A preliminary question therefore needs to be addressed: whether or not the notion of subject-matter should be maintained. Maintaining it, and the other provisions which follow upon it, seemed to be necessary because of the significant consequences which flow from it, as witnessed by a wealth of case-law in recent years, in particular on the questions of the existence or lawfulness of subject-matter, or, again, the determination of the price. Moreover, the notion of the contents of contracts, which is sometimes substituted, did not seem to be sufficiently accurate to guarantee the certainty of contractual relationships.

In consequence, the Reform Proposals recommend that Section 3 of Chapter II of Sub-title I of Title II, headed 'Subject-matter', comprising ten articles (1121 to 1122-3), should be devoted to the subject-matter of contracts. And, in this section, the traditional terminology has been retained as far as possible, whilst being adapted to the new categories of obligations recommended by the Proposals: to give, to give for use, to do, or not to do (article 1121).

The present provisions first needed to be tidied up. It was appropriate, in combining it into article 1121, to modify the present article 1127 which refers by implication to the obligation to give for use—now recognised in its own right by the Reform Proposals. On the other hand, the present article 1130 paragraph 2, dealing with the prohibition of agreements for future rights of succession, has been deleted: it no longer belongs within the doctrine of obligations now that this prohibition appears in article 722.

The present article 1128 concerning 'things which may not be owned or alienated'—the famous expression which is part of our legal heritage[2]—has been preserved. We preferred to keep it, rather than to set out a detailed list of things which cannot be owned or alienated, which would have been hazardous and, inevitably, incomplete. The meaning of the legislative wording is sufficiently wide and, and the same time, sufficiently clear, as is shown by case-law. It appears almost unchanged in article 1121-1.

Similarly, the possibility for a future thing to be the subject-matter of an obligation has been preserved (article 1121-2, paragraph 3).

An article setting out the characteristics which must be fulfilled by the subject-matter has been added by way of transition: the subject-matter must be lawful, possible, and must exist at the moment of formation of the contract (article 1121-2). Similarly, an article has been added making clear its accompanying sanctions, distinguishing in particular between unlawfulness of subject-matter (which is sanctioned by absolute nullity) and absence of subject-matter (article 1122).

Beyond these amendments, the principal innovations contained in the Reform Proposals concern the three following points:

---

[1] [Above, p 499, nn 1, 2.]

[2] [This translates *choses hors du commerce*—things which are 'outside trade'. It and its opposite (things *dans le commerce*, things 'inside trade') are an inheritance from the Roman law distinction between things *in commercio* (possible objects of private ownership) and *extra commercium*: JAC Thomas, *Textbook of Roman Law* (Amsterdam, North-Holland, 1976) 159.]

1° Atteinte à un élément essentiel du contrat :

La jurisprudence qui a culminé avec l'arrêt Chronopost devait être incorporée dans le Code civil. Même si elle a été rendue sous le visa de l'article 1133 relatif à la cause, elle concerne davantage l'objet et figure désormais dans l'article 1121 alinéa 3.

2° Détermination de l'objet :

La question a suscité des controverses doctrinales et des initiatives jurisprudentielles sur lesquelles il est inutile de revenir.

Il a semblé judicieux de maintenir le principe de détermination dans les termes mêmes du Code, en ajoutant seulement, pour l'expliciter, que l'exigence a pour objet de ne pas laisser une des parties à la merci de la volonté de l'autre (art. 1121-3).

Mais il est apparu nécessaire de poser deux séries d'exception à ce principe. La première concerne le cas des contrats-cadre, notamment en matière de distribution. La disposition retenue offre aux contractants une certaine liberté, sous réserve d'un éventuel contrôle judiciaire *a posteriori*, solution inspirée des arrêts de l'Assemblée plénière de la Cour de cassation du 1er décembre 1995 (art. 1121-4). La seconde est propre aux contrats qui, comme le louage d'ouvrage ou le mandat, comportent une obligation de faire dont l'étendue ne peut pas être fixée dès la conclusion du contrat : la disposition retenue s'inscrit dans la ligne de la jurisprudence actuelle (art. 1121-5).

3° Défaut d'équivalence entre les prestations :

Le défaut d'équivalence entre les prestations des parties à un contrat commutatif n'est actuellement consacré dans le Code civil que dans une disposition relative à la lésion, figurant dans une section relative aux vices du consentement. Ce choix est critiqué par une majorité de la doctrine et il est apparu que le sujet avait davantage sa place dans la section relative à l'objet (art. 1122-1), ou une disposition spécifique est désormais dédiée aux clauses abusives.

Mais, pour éviter tout risque d'ambiguïté, le cas du défaut d'équivalence entre les prestations des parties à un contrat commutatif qui survient après l'exécution du contrat a été renvoyé aux dispositions relatives à l'effet des conventions figurant dans le chapitre III.

1. Undermining an essential element of a contract:

The case-law which culminated in the *Chronopost* decision[1] had to be incorporated into the Civil Code. Even though article 1133 was given as its formal legislative foundation (and this relates to 'cause'), it is more concerned with the subject-matter and now appears in article 1121 paragraph 3.

2. Ascertainment of the subject-matter:

This question has given rise to disagreement amongst academic writers, and to initiatives by the courts which it is not necessary to repeat here.

It seemed wise to maintain the principle of ascertainment in the same terms in the Code, just adding by way of explanation that the requirement is aimed at not leaving one of the parties at the mercy of the other party's choice (article 1121-3).

But it appeared to be necessary to set out two kinds of exception to this principle. The first concerns the situation of framework contracts, particularly those in the field of contracts of distribution. This provision gives the contracting parties a certain freedom, subject to possible judicial control afterwards, a solution inspired by the decisions of the *Assemblée plénière*[2] of the Cour de cassation on 1 December 1995[3] (article 1121-4). The second is peculiar to contracts, such as the hire of services or mandate, which include an obligation to do, the extent of which cannot be fixed at the time the contract is concluded: the provision given here is written along the lines of the current case-law (article 1121-5).

3. Lack of equivalence in the content of the parties' obligations:

The lack of equivalence in the content of the obligations of the parties to a commutative contract is at present provided for in the Civil Code only in one provision dealing with substantive inequality of bargain, which appears in a section on the defects in consent. The decision to place it there is criticised by a majority of writers, and it appeared that the subject belonged rather in the section relating to 'subject-matter' (article 1122-1), where a specific provision is now dedicated to unfair terms.

But, to avoid any risk of ambiguity, the case of the lack of equivalence in what the parties have to do under a commutative contract where this arises after the performance of the contract has been moved to the provisions concerning the effect of contracts which are placed in Chapter III.[4]

---

[1] [See below, p 525, n 2.]

[2] [The *Assemblée plénière* is a plenary court which contains representatives of each of the six chambers of the Cour de cassation (three civil chambers, one social, one commercial and one criminal). It sits to hear a case in which the decision of a lower court has already been quashed by one chamber of the Cour de cassation, but on a re-hearing another lower court has insisted on maintaining the same decision and a claim is brought to quash the second decision). On the *Assemblée plénière*, and the role of the Cour de cassation generally, see Nicholas, *The French Law of Contract*, above, p 489, n 2, 8-12.]

[3] [D 1996, 13 concl Joel note Aynès. In this decision, the *Assemblée plénière* held that parties to a long-term supply contract could validly set its future prices by references to the supplier's normal rate, provided that this power were not exercised abusively.]

[4] [Articles 1161 to 1164-7 (restitution following destruction of a contract).]

Validité – Cause
(art. 1124 à 1126-1)

Jacques Ghestin

Art. 1124.

Il s'agit d'affirmer que, conformément à notre tradition juridique, une cause réelle et licite reste une condition de validité du contrat. Ce choix implique toutefois d'éviter les deux écueils opposés d'une définition exagérément restrictive, qui lui enlèverait tout intérêt pratique, ou trop extensive, qui porterait atteinte à la sécurité juridique.

C'est la *cause de l'engagement* qui est prise en considération. Cette formulation relativement nouvelle évite, notamment, d'utiliser les dénominations, contestées par certains, et sans doute contestables, de cause de l'obligation, dite objective et abstraite, opposée à la cause du contrat, dite subjective et concrète. On a observé notamment que, dès l'instant qu'il suffisait, selon la jurisprudence la plus récente de la Cour de cassation, que l'une des parties ait poursuivi un but illicite ou immoral pour justifier l'annulation du contrat, alors même que l'autre l'avait ignoré, il semblait difficile de réserver à cette notion la qualification de cause du contrat par opposition à la cause de la seule obligation de l'une des parties. En outre, en tant que « manifestation de volonté (offre ou acceptation) par laquelle une personne s'oblige » (*Vocabulaire juridique*, ss. dir. G. Cornu), l'engagement semble plus apte à désigner l'acte qui donne naissance au contrat compris comme une opération juridique, voire économique, globale et non seulement, de façon analytique, à une ou plusieurs obligations juxtaposées.

L'article 1124 fait de la cause une *notion unitaire*. Elle est la justification de l'engagement, autrement dit la raison pour laquelle le droit positif lui reconnaît des effets juridiques (ce que certains auteurs appellent, en lui donnant ce sens, la « cause efficiente »). Conformément à la tradition du droit canonique l'obligation naît de la seule volonté de l'obligé à la condition de posséder une cause qui l'explique et la

Validity – Cause
(articles 1124 to 1126-1)

Jacques Ghestin

Article 1124

This confirms that, in accordance with our legal tradition, a real and lawful 'cause' remains a condition for the validity of a contract.[1] However, choosing this course makes it necessary to avoid two pitfalls at opposite extremes: a definition either so restrictive that it would lose all practical relevance, or so wide that it would endanger legal certainty.

It is the *'cause' of the undertaking* which is taken into account. This relatively recent formulation avoids, in particular, the use of the language—questioned by some, and no doubt it is open to question—of the 'cause' of the obligation (said to be objective and abstract), as opposed to the 'cause' of the contract (said to be subjective and concrete). In particular, we have seen that, as soon as the most recent decisions of the Cour de cassation held it to be sufficient that one of the parties had pursued an unlawful or immoral purpose in order to justify the annulment of the contract, even though the other did not know of it,[2] it seemed difficult to limit to this concept the characterisation of the 'cause' of the contract, rather than the 'cause' of just the obligation of one of the parties. Moreover, as a 'manifestation of will (offer or acceptance) by which a person undertakes an obligation' (*Vocabulaire Juridique*, edited by G. Cornu[3]), an undertaking seems more appropriate to identify the act which gives rise to a contract seen in the round as a juridical (or even economic) transaction, and not only, in a technical, analytical manner, one or more juxtaposed obligations.

Article 1124 gives a unitary notion to 'cause'. It is the justification for an undertaking, or in other words the reason why the law today recognises it as having legal consequences (some writers give it this meaning and call it the 'efficient cause'). In accordance with the traditions of Canon law, an obligation arises simply from the will of the person subject to it, as long as it has a 'cause' which explains and justifies

---

[1] [For a summary discussion of the present function of the doctrine of *la cause* in French contract law see S Whittaker, 'The Law of Obligations' in Bell, Boyron and Whittaker, above, p 465, n 3, 317 and 324. For opposing views as to the continuing role of *la cause* see Rochfeld, above, ch 4, and Sefton-Green, above, ch 5.]

[2] [Before 1998 the courts had required that the illegal motive of one party be known or even shared by the other before the contract was invalid on the basis of illegal 'cause'. But this was reversed by the Cour de cassation in Cass civ (1) 7 October 1998, JCP 1998 II 10202.]

[3] [Now 8th edn, Paris, PUF, 2007.]

justifie. Nous verrons qu'en définissant la cause comme la contrepartie convenue, pour apprécier sa réalité dans les contrats à titre onéreux, le projet prend également en considération, au moins implicitement, la « cause finale » de l'engagement, qui est l'intérêt poursuivi.

L'exigence d'une cause réelle et licite distingue ses *deux fonctions* : contrôle de l'existence et de la licéité de la cause dont les sanctions spécifiques sont précisées dans l'article suivant.

Art. 1124-1.

La nature relative ou absolue de la nullité correspond aux deux fonctions de la cause. En l'absence de cause de l'engagement c'est-à-dire, selon l'article 1125 du projet, lorsque « dès l'origine, la contrepartie convenue est illusoire ou dérisoire », il ne s'agit que de « la sauvegarde d'un intérêt privé » (article 1129-1, alinéa 2), ce qui réserve à la partie protégée la faculté de demander l'annulation ou de confirmer l'acte (article 1129-1, alinéa 3). Lorsque la cause de l'engagement est illicite, c'est-à-dire, selon l'article 1126, « lorsqu'il est contracté, par l'une au moins des parties, dans un but contraire à l'ordre public, aux bonnes mœurs, ou, plus généralement, à une règle impérative », « la sauvegarde de l'intérêt général » (article 1129-1, alinéa 1) impose que l'annulation puisse être « invoquée par toute personne justifiant d'un intérêt, ainsi que par le Ministère public » et qu'elle puisse « aussi être relevée d'office par le juge » (article 1129-2).

Art. 1124-2.

Ce texte reproduit en substance l'article 1132 du Code civil en précisant le sens qui lui est donné aujourd'hui par une jurisprudence et une doctrine unanime.

Art. 1125.

1) Le premier alinéa est essentiel. Il rappelle d'abord que *la cause est la justification de l'engagement et qu'elle doit être réelle.* Il précise ensuite que *l'appréciation de la réalité de la cause doit se faire au moment de la formation du contrat.* La cause, condition de validité, est ainsi expressément cantonnée à celle-ci, à l'exclusion de l'exécution du contrat, dont l'équilibre est préservé par d'autres voies. Enfin, et surtout, il détermine, conformément à la jurisprudence actuelle de la Cour de cassation, les conditions de l'absence de cause : *il faut et il suffit que la contrepartie convenue soit illusoire ou dérisoire.* C'est sur cette définition que repose l'équilibre entre la justice contractuelle et la sécurité juridique.

L'article 1102-2, alinéa 1 du projet dispose que « le contrat est à titre onéreux lorsque chacune de parties entend recevoir de l'autre un avantage en contrepartie de celui qu'elle procure ». Dans ce contrat l'engagement de chaque partie doit être ainsi justifié par « un avantage », c'est-à-dire la satisfaction d'un intérêt qui en est la cause finale. Pour préciser celle-ci, il faut, d'une part, rejeter une abstraction

it.[1] We shall see that, in defining 'cause' as what is agreed to be given in return in order to understand its real significance for onerous contracts, the Reform Proposals also take into account, at least implicitly, the 'final cause' of an undertaking, which is the benefit sought from it.

The requirement of a real and lawful 'cause' keeps separate its two functions: checking the existence and the lawfulness of the 'cause': the specific sanctions are set out in the following article.

Article 1124-1

The different forms of nullity, relative and absolute, correspond to the two functions of 'cause'. In the absence of a 'cause' of the undertaking—that is, under article 1125 of the Proposals, where 'from the beginning what is agreed to be given in return is illusory or derisory'—there is only a question of 'the safeguard of a private interest' (article 1129-1, paragraph 2), which limits to the protected party the right to ask for annulment or to confirm the transaction (article 1129-1, paragraph 3). Where the 'cause' of the undertaking is unlawful—that is, under article 1126, 'where it is entered into, at least by one of the parties, with a purpose contrary to public policy, public morality, or, more widely, a mandatory rule of law'—'the safeguard of the public interest' (article 1129-1, paragraph 1) provides that the annulment can be 'invoked by any person who can demonstrate an interest, as well as by the magistrate representing the public interest' and that it can 'also be raised by the court on its own initiative' (article 1129-2).

Article 1124-2

This provision reproduces in substance article 1132 of the Civil Code and makes clear the sense that is given to it today unanimously by case-law and academic writing.

Article 1125

1) The first paragraph is fundamental. It constitutes a reminder first that *'cause' is the justification for an undertaking and that it must be real.* It then makes clear that *the assessment of the reality of the cause must be made at the moment of formation of the contract.* As a condition of validity, 'cause' is therefore expressly restricted to this, and does not apply to performance of the contract, in which the balance between the parties is preserved by other means. Finally, and most importantly, it defines, in accordance with the present case-law of the Cour de cassation, the conditions for finding an absence of cause: *it is necessary and sufficient that what is agreed to be given in return is illusory or derisory.*[2] On this definition rests the balance between contractual fairness and legal certainty.

Article 1102-2, paragraph 1, of the Proposals provides that 'a contract is onerous where each of the parties expects to receive a benefit from the other in return for what he provides'. In this contract the undertaking of each party must therefore be justified by 'a benefit', that is, the fulfilment of an interest which is the 'final cause' of the contract. To make clear what this means, it is necessary (on the one hand) to

---

[1] [For an illuminating discussion of the treatment of *causa* by medieval lawyers (including canon lawyers) see J Gordley, *The Philosophical Origins of Modern Contract Doctrine* (Oxford University Press, 1991) 49-57.]

[2] [eg Cass civ (3) 18 July 2001, Bull civ III no 1001, Défrenois 2000, 1421 note Savaux (annulment for 'cheapness of price'; Cass civ (1) 10 May 2005, Bull civ I no 203.]

excessive, ne tenant aucun compte des mobiles, propres à chaque partie qui ont concrètement déterminé les volontés de chacune dans la recherche de son intérêt particulier, et, d'autre part, préserver le caractère de procédure bilatérale du contrat en refusant de faire dépendre sa validité de motifs personnels n'ayant pas été intégrés dans ce qui est fréquemment appelé le « champ contractuel » et qu'il est préférable de définir, de façon plus précise, comme la contrepartie convenue. En effet, pour que le caractère contractuel de la cause soit effectif, le motif déterminant de l'une des parties doit non seulement être connu, non seulement avoir été pris en compte par l'autre partie, mais il doit faire partie de la définition contractuelle de l'objet de la contrepartie. Il s'agit de l'objet de l'obligation ou de la prestation promise – ou exécutée lorsque l'exécution est concomitante de la formation – par l'autre partie.

La jurisprudence de la Cour de cassation montre que c'est par l'interprétation, très généralement subjective (recherche de la commune intention des parties) et exceptionnellement objective (détermination autoritaire du contenu du contrat), que la contrepartie convenue est d'abord précisée. À partir de là c'est de sa réalité, c'est-à-dire de ce qu'elle n'est ni illusoire, ni dérisoire, que dépend l'appréciation de l'existence ou de l'absence de la cause de l'engagement du demandeur en annulation.

La jurisprudence de la Cour de cassation montre également qu'elle détermine, toujours par voie d'interprétation, le périmètre à l'intérieur duquel doit être appréciée la réalité de la contrepartie convenue. Si la Cour de cassation n'admet pas la nécessité d'une contrepartie propre à chaque obligation née du contrat, voire à chaque clause de celui-ci, en revanche, elle prend souvent en considération un ensemble de contrats indivisibles. L'absence d'objet réel de la contre-prestation stipulée dans l'un d'eux, par exemple un prix purement symbolique, ne justifiera pas l'annulation pour absence de cause s'il est établi que le demandeur bénéficiait parallèlement d'une contrepartie convenue par le biais d'un autre contrat indivisible. Le contrôle de la réalité de la cause dépasse ainsi dans la pratique celui de l'existence de l'objet de la contre-prestation.

2) Le second alinéa vise à confirmer la jurisprudence « Chronopost » et des arrêts

reject an unduly abstract construction, not taking into account the motives of each party, which have in fact been decisive in each giving his consent in pursuit of his own individual interests; and (on the other hand) to preserve the present two-sided process of contracts in refusing to make their validity depend on personal motives which were not included in what is often called the 'contractual sphere' and which it is better to define, more accurately, as what is agreed to be given in return. Indeed, for 'cause' to be characterised as having contractual effect, the decisive motive of one of the parties must be not only known, not only taken into account, by the other party, but it must be included in the definition in the contract of the subject-matter of the exchange. It is the subject-matter of the obligation or its contents promised by the other party—or performed by him, where performance accompanies the formation of the contract.

The case-law of the Cour de cassation shows that it is by interpretation, most commonly subjective (looking for the parties' common intentions), and exceptionally objective (a compulsory determination of the contents of the contract), that what is agreed to be given in return is first identified. After that, its reality, that is, its not being illusory or derisory, determines whether the 'cause' of the undertaking of the party claiming annulment is held to exist or not.

The case-law of the Cour de cassation shows also that it defines, always by way of interpretation, the limits within which the reality of what is agreed to be given in return must be assessed. Although the Cour de cassation does not accept the need for an exchange for each and every obligation in the contract, nor for every term in it, it does still often take into account a group of contracts which are inseparable. The absence of real subject-matter of the exchange stipulated in one of them, for example a purely symbolic price, will not allow the annulment of that contract for absence of 'cause' if it is established that the claimant would at the same time benefit from an agreed exchange by means of another contract which is inseparably connected to it.[1] The review of the reality of 'cause' therefore in practice goes beyond the review of the existence of the subject-matter of the exchange.

2) The second paragraph is intended to confirm the *Chronopost* decision,[2] and the

---

[1] [eg Cass civ (1) 13 June 2006, D 2007, 277 note Ghestin. There, a musician and composer entered into three contracts for the commercial exploitation of his work: a publishing contract, a contract of assignment of his intellectual property rights and a contract of sale of sound-tracks which he made. The *Cour de cassation* quashed the lower court's decision annulling the last of these on the ground that its price of one franc was 'derisory' and that therefore his obligation to supply the sound-tracks lacked a *cause* on the basis that it ought to have considered whether this contract formed part of an 'indivisible wider economic group' which would provide a proper counterpart to his obligations.]

[2] [Cass com 22 October 1996, JCP 1997 II 22881, in which the Cour de cassation held that a limitation clause in a contract between a company and a courier firm (*Chronopost*) for the delivery of a letter should be struck out on the basis of article 1131 (absence of 'cause') because the clause contradicted the essential obligation undertaken by the courier firm in the contract (reliability and speed of delivery). The novelty of the case was that article 1131 was employed as a tool to strike out a single term rather than to invalidate the whole contract. It has been followed in later cases as a means of striking out particular unfair terms where there is no other legal basis for doing so (eg legislation protecting consumers and other non-professional parties against unfair terms).]

qui en ont fait ensuite application. Il met en œuvre, sans qu'il paraisse opportun de le dire expressément, une nécessité logique de cohérence. Son éventuel rattachement à un « principe » de cohérence sera le rôle de la doctrine.

Art. 1125-1.

Conformément à ce qui est admis par une jurisprudence constante et une doctrine unanime il faut assimiler à « la remise de la chose ou des fonds à celui qui s'oblige » celle qui est faite à un mandataire de ce dernier, ou même à un tiers dès lors que sa désignation résulte de la convention.

En droit romain l'emprunteur, qui n'avait pas reçu la somme d'argent qu'il s'était obligé à rembourser, ou n'en avait reçu qu'une partie, pouvait utiliser la *querella non numeræ pecuniæ*. L'obligation de restituer est liée à la remise de la chose qui était également une condition, héritée du droit romain, de formation des contrats réels. Cette catégorie de contrats est aujourd'hui, à tort ou à raison, contestée dans son principe même et la jurisprudence la plus récente de la Cour de cassation tend à en exclure les prêts consentis par des établissements financiers, qui étaient jusqu'à présent l'un des domaines de prédilection de la nullité pour absence de cause. L'article 1102-5 du projet ne définit que le contrat consensuel et le contrat solennel. Il est vrai que le contrat réel n'était pas davantage défini dans le Code civil et que sa consécration par la jurisprudence est déduite de la définition d'un certain nombre de contrats spéciaux tels que le prêt à usage (art. 1875), le prêt de consommation (art. 1892), le dépôt (art. 1919), et le gage (art. 2071).

Quant à la cause, en tout cas, c'est en fait celle de l'engagement de restitution qui est spécifique dans les contrats réels. Il est admis, en effet, par la jurisprudence et une doctrine largement majoritaire, que c'est la remise de la chose qui est la cause de l'obligation de restitution, au motif, souligné par un auteur (G. Rouhette, *Contribution à l'étude critique de la notion de contrat*, th. Paris, 1965, n° 147, p. 467), qu'il « est de simple bon sens qu'on ne saurait restituer une chose qui n'a pas été remise ». Un tel engagement serait donc dépourvu de justification.

Il est fréquent qu'un avant-contrat, une promesse de contrat, fixe les modalités essentielles du contrat réel à conclure par la remise des fonds ou de la chose, telles que, par exemple, la rémunération du dépositaire ou, dans le prêt d'argent, le taux d'intérêt et la date de restitution. L'article 1106 du projet traite de façon générale de « la promesse unilatérale de contrat... par laquelle une partie promet à une autre, qui en accepte le principe, de lui donner l'exclusivité pour la conclusion d'un contrat dont les éléments essentiels sont déterminés, mais pour la formation duquel fait seulement défaut le consentement du bénéficiaire » (alinéa 1). Contrairement à la jurisprudence actuelle de la Cour de cassation, mais conformément à une doctrine largement majoritaire, il consacre l'interdiction pour le promettant, « pendant le temps laissé au bénéficiaire pour exprimer son consentement »,

later decisions which have applied it. It puts in place, without needing to spell it out, a necessary, consistent logic. Its eventual connection with a 'principle' of consistency will be for academic writers to achieve.

Article 1125-1

In accordance with what is accepted by a consistent line of case-law, and the unanimous writings of scholars, 'delivery of the thing or the money to the party subject to the obligation' will also include delivery to the latter's agent, or even to a third party who is indicated in the contract.

In Roman law the borrower who had not received the sum of money which he had undertaken an obligation to repay, or who had received it only in part, could use the challenge 'that the money had not been paid over'.[1] An obligation to make restitution is linked to delivery of the thing, which was also a condition, inherited from Roman law, of the formation of 'real contracts'.[2] The underlying principle of this category of contracts is today, rightly or wrongly, disputed and the most recent case-law of the Cour de cassation tends to exclude from the category loans made by finance houses which until recently were one of the most common areas for nullity for lack of cause. Article 1102-5 of the Reform Proposals defines only consensual contracts and formal contracts. It is true that real contracts are not defined in the Civil Code either, and that that their formal recognition was deduced by the courts from the definition of a certain number of special contracts, such as loan for use (article 1875), loan for consumption (article 1892), deposit (article 1919) and pledge (article 2071).

As for 'cause', in any case, it is certainly the undertaking to return the thing which is particular to real contracts. It is indeed very generally accepted by case-law and scholars that it is the delivery of the thing which is the cause of the obligation to return it, since, as emphasised by one writer (G. Rouhette, *Contribution à l'étude critique de la notion de contrat*, doctoral thesis, Univerity of Paris, 1965, n° 147, p. 467), 'it is only good sense that one could not return something that has not first been delivered'. Such an undertaking would therefore have no justification.

Frequently a preliminary contract, a promise to enter into a contract, sets out the essential modalities of real contracts that are to be entered into by delivery of money or a thing—such as, for example, the remuneration of a depositee or, in the case of a loan of money, the rate of interest and the date for repayment. Article 1106 of the Reform Proposals deals in general terms with 'a unilateral promise to contract ... by which one party promises to another (and the latter accepts in principle) to give him the exclusive right to conclude a contract of which the essential elements are settled, but for the formation of which only the consent of the beneficiary is required' (paragraph 1). Contrary to the present case-law of the Cour de cassation, but in accordance with the broad majority of scholars, it makes clear that the promisor, 'during the period allowed to the beneficiary to express his agreement' may not by revocation prevent 'the contract which was promised from

---

[1] [Thomas, *Textbook of Roman Law*, above, p 517, n 2, 269.]

[2] [A 'real contract' (*contrat réel*) is a contract which is concluded only after delivery of a thing: the agreement of the parties is necessary, but it is not sufficient and no obligation to deliver the thing arises without delivery itself.]

528

d'empêcher par une rétractation « la formation du contrat promis » (alinéa 2) et l'inopposabilité « au bénéficiaire de la promesse » du « contrat conclu avec un tiers » (alinéa 3). Ce texte, malgré sa portée générale, peut ne pas sembler directement applicable à toutes les promesses de conclure un contrat réel, notamment un prêt, dont la formation se réalisera postérieurement par la remise des fonds ou de la chose. Ces promesses sont en effet souvent synallagmatiques et non pas unilatérales, elles n'ont pas pour objet l'exclusivité de conclure un contrat et, enfin, ce n'est pas « le consentement du bénéficiaire » qui « fait seulement défaut », mais la remise des fonds ou de la chose, ce qui est différent. Il paraît toutefois possible d'en déduire, par analogie, voire *a fortiori*, que la promesse de conclure un contrat réel impose, aux conditions qu'elle détermine, la remise des fonds ou de la chose qui formera celui-ci. Il suffit de préciser ici que cet avant-contrat n'est lui-même valable que si « l'engagement a une cause réelle et licite qui le justifie » (art. 1124).

Art. 1125-2.

Dans les contrats synallagmatiques commutatifs il est exceptionnel que la contrepartie soit convenue au profit d'un tiers. Il en est ainsi, cependant, lorsque celle-ci est définie dans un ensemble contractuel, par exemple pour justifier l'existence d'une contrepartie réelle à la vente d'un terrain moyennant un franc symbolique, parce que c'était sur celui-ci qu'était construite l'usine d'une société dont le vendeur était l'un des actionnaires et dont l'acheteur reprenait le passif. Les arrêts de la Cour de cassation, qui retiennent cette contrepartie comme étant la cause de l'engagement contesté, relèvent l'intérêt indirect du débiteur à celle-ci, sans en faire toutefois une condition de validité du contrat.

Comme le texte le précise, il est potentiellement applicable à l'ensemble des stipulations pour autrui. Dans la pratique, c'est principalement en matière de sûretés que la jurisprudence s'est prononcée sur cette question. La contrepartie convenue au profit d'un tiers dans le cautionnement, par exemple, peut être définie comme le crédit ou tout avantage consenti par le créancier au débiteur principal et subordonné à la fourniture de cette sûreté. Cet avantage convenu peut excéder, selon la commune volonté des parties, le versement immédiat des fonds par la banque sur le compte du tiers et comporter, par exemple, son engagement corrélatif de maintenir pendant une durée plus ou moins déterminée, mais déterminable, un certain concours financier. Le cautionnement manquerait de cause réelle lorsqu'il apparaîtrait, notamment par une clôture immédiate du compte, que, dès la formation du contrat, la banque n'avait pas pour objectif d'avoir une garantie au cas d'insolvabilité du débiteur principal mais seulement de substituer à ce dernier un débiteur solvable. La contrepartie convenue serait en effet illusoire (V. Ph. Simler, *Juris-Classeur Civil, Fasc. 20 : Contrats et obligations – Cause – Rôle pratique*, 15 juin 2002, n° 33, texte et jurisprudence citée).

L'article 1125-2 entend préciser que, conformément à la jurisprudence de la Cour de cassation, notamment à l'égard du cautionnement, l'avantage consenti au

being formed' (paragraph 2) and that a 'contract concluded with a third party' does not prejudice 'the beneficiary of the unilateral promise' (paragraph 3). This provision, in spite of its general wording, does not seem to be directly applicable to all promises to enter into a real contract, in particular a loan, whose formation will later occur on the handing over of money or a thing. Such promises are in effect often synallagmatic, and not unilateral; they do not have as their object an exclusive right to conclude a contract; and, finally, it is not the 'consent of the beneficiary' which is alone required, but the handing over of the money or the thing—which is a different matter. It is, however, possible to deduce by analogy—or even *a fortiori*—that a promise to enter into a real contract requires (on the conditions that it sets out) the handing over of the money or the thing which will conclude the contract. It is enough to make clear here that this preliminary contract is also valid only if 'the undertaking has a cause which is real and lawful which justifies it' (article 1124).

Article 1125-2

In synallagmatic commutative contracts it is exceptional for the parties to agree that what is to be given in return is for the benefit of a third party. This happens, however, where the exchange is defined in a contractual grouping, for example, to explain the existence of a genuine exchange on the sale of a plot of land for the symbolic price of one franc, because on this plot was constructed a factory belonging to a company of which the seller was one of the shareholders and whose liabilities the buyer was accepting. The decisions of the Cour de cassation, which accept this exchange as being the 'cause' of the disputed undertaking, find an indirect interest of the debtor in it without, however, making it a condition of validity of the contract.[1]

As the text makes clear, it is potentially applicable to all stipulations for the benefit of third parties. In practice, it is mainly in the field of surety contracts that case-law has pronounced on this question. What is agreed to be given in return, for the benefit of a third party, in contracts of guarantee, for example, can be defined as the giving of credit, or any benefit agreed by the creditor in favour of the principal debtor which was conditional on the provision of this guarantee. This agreed benefit may exceed, if the parties so agree, the sum immediately paid by the bank to the account of the third party, and may include, for example, his undertaking in return to maintain a certain level of financial support for a period which is more or less defined (as long as it is at least definable). The guarantee would be lacking a real 'cause' if it appeared—such as by an immediate closure of the account—that, from the formation of the contract, the bank did not intend to take security in case of insolvency of the principal debtor, but only to substitute the solvent debtor for the latter. The agreed exchange would in reality be illusory (See P. Simler, *Juris-Classeur Civil, Fasc. 20: Contrats et obligations - Cause - Rôle pratique*, 15 June 2002, n° 33, text and case-law there cited).

Article 1125-2 is intended to make clear that, in accordance with the case-law of the Cour de cassation, and in particular in relation to guarantees, the benefit agreed

---

[1] [Cass civ (3) 3 March 1993, Bull civ III no 28, Defrénois 1993, 325601 obs Y Dagorne-Labbé.]

530

débiteur principal constitue la cause nécessaire et suffisante de l'engagement de la caution, indépendamment de l'intérêt moral ou matériel poursuivi par celle-ci en raison de ses relations avec ce débiteur.

Art. 1125-3.

Contrairement à une formule fréquemment utilisée, y compris par la Cour de cassation, ce n'est pas seulement l'absence d'aléa qui permet de caractériser, dans ces conventions, une absence de cause. Les contrats synallagmatiques aléatoires, notamment les ventes d'un bien moyennant le paiement d'une rente viagère, ne sont annulés pour absence de cause que sur la constatation que, dès la formation du contrat, l'absence d'aléa rendait illusoire ou dérisoire, pour l'un des contractants, la contrepartie convenue. Il en est ainsi en particulier lorsque le montant de la rente est inférieur aux revenus du bien cédé ou lorsque l'espérance de vie du crédirentier, connue de l'autre partie, rendait dérisoire, dès l'origine, le montant des rentes à verser.

Art. 1125-4.

La question se posait de savoir si la cause dans les libéralités, et plus spécialement dans les testaments qui ne sont pas des contrats, devait être traitée dans cette section, soit directement, soit par renvoi aux dispositions spéciales aux libéralités. Le fait que les dispositions relatives à la licéité et la moralité de la cause soient communes aux deux catégories d'actes plaide en faveur d'une définition de l'existence de la cause dans les actes à titre gratuits, énoncée parallèlement à celle des actes à titre onéreux.

La formule proposée s'inspire de l'article 911 du projet du Doyen Jean Carbonnier, Pierre Catala, Jean de Saint Affrique et Georges Morin, sur les libéralités.

Selon l'article 1102-2, alinéa 2 du projet, « le contrat est à titre gratuit lorsque l'une des parties entend procurer à l'autre un avantage sans recevoir de contrepartie ». Il en résulte d'abord que c'est l'intention libérale abstraite qui permet de qualifier les actes à titre gratuit : donations et, *a fortiori*, libéralités testamentaires (alinéa premier). Il s'en déduit également que l'existence de la cause ne peut dépendre dans les libéralités de celle de la contrepartie convenue. L'alinéa second prend alors en considération, à titre de justification de l'engagement, l'intérêt – essentiellement moral dans les libéralités en l'absence de contrepartie matérielle – qui en est la cause finale. L'impératif de sécurité juridique destiné à protéger l'autre partie dans les contrats à titre onéreux n'a pas la même intensité à l'égard du bénéficiaire d'une libéralité, ce qui autorise à retenir ici, comme justification et cause de l'engagement, le motif ayant déterminé le disposant.

Examinant les donations et « les autres contrats où l'un seul fait ou donne et où l'autre ne fait et ne donne rien », Domat observait déjà que « l'engagement de celui qui donne a son fondement sur quelque motif raisonnable et juste, comme un service rendu, ou quelque autre mérite du donataire, ou le seul plaisir de faire du bien ». Ce motif, ajoutait Domat, « tient lieu de cause de la part de celui qui reçoit

for the principal debtor constitutes the necessary and sufficient 'cause' of the guarantor's undertaking, regardless of any moral or substantial interest that the guarantor party may find for himself because of his relationship with the debtor.

Article 1125-3

Contrary to an expression often used—even by the Cour de cassation—it is not only an absence of risk which can be characterised as an absence of 'cause' in such contracts. Synallagmatic aleatory contacts, such as sales of property providing for the payment of a life annuity, are annulled for absence of cause only where it is established that, from the moment of formation of the contract, the absence of risk made what is agreed to be given in return illusory or derisory for one of the contracting parties. This is so, in particular, where the level of annuity is lower than the income from the property transferred, or where the life expectancy of the annuitant, as the other party knew, rendered the sums to be paid from the beginning derisory.

Article 1125-4

The question arose as to whether 'cause' in acts of generosity, and especially in testaments, which are not contracts, should be dealt with in this section, either directly, or by reference to the special provisions on acts of generosity. The fact that the provisions relating to the lawfulness and morality of 'cause' are common to the two categories of transactions argues for a definition of the existence of 'cause' in gratuitous transactions, set out alongside that relating to onerous transactions.

The proposed wording is inspired by article 911 of the proposals by Professor Jean Carbonnier, Pierre Catala, Jean de Saint Affrique and Georges Morin,[1] to reform the law on acts of generosity.

According to article 1102-2, paragraph 2, of our Reform Proposals, 'a contract is gratuitous where one of the parties expects to provide a benefit to the other without receiving anything in return'. In consequence, first, it is the abstract gratuitous intention which allows gratuitous transactions to be so characterised: gifts and, a fortiori, testamentary acts of generosity (first paragraph). Secondly, it follows that in the case of acts of generosity the existence of 'cause' cannot depend on the existence of something agreed to be given in return. So the second paragraph takes into account, by way of justification for the undertaking, the interest—essentially moral, in acts of generosity, in the absence of anything substantial in return—which is its 'final cause'. The imperative of transactional certainty, designed to protect the other party in onerous contracts, does not have the same intensity with regard to the beneficiary of an act of generosity, which allows us to retain here, as justification and 'cause' of the undertaking, the disponor's decisive motive.

Examining gifts and 'other contracts where one party does or gives something, and where the other party does and gives nothing', Domat in his time observed that 'the undertaking of a person who gives has its basis in some rational and just motive, such as a service that has been performed, or some other deserving quality of the donee, or simply the pleasure of doing good'. This motive, added Domat, 'takes the

---

[1] [J Carbonnier, P Catala, J de Saint Affrique, G Morin, *Des libéralités: une offre de loi* (Paris, Defrénois, 2003).]

et ne donne rien » (Domat, *Les lois civiles dans leur ordre naturel*, 1re partie, titre I, section 1, p. 235).

Art. 1126.

Cet article vise à confirmer l'état actuel de la jurisprudence en la matière, qui semble satisfaisant. Il signifie, en particulier, que le but illicite poursuivi par l'une des parties suffit à imposer, pour « la sauvegarde de l'intérêt général » (article 1129-1, alinéa 1 du projet), la nullité absolue du contrat pour absence de cause licite, sans qu'il y ait à rechercher si l'autre partie avait poursuivi le même but ou si elle en avait connaissance.

En revanche, ce texte ne préjuge pas du contenu de l'ordre public ou des bonnes mœurs, notamment quant aux libéralités consenties afin de favoriser des relations adultères.

Art. 1126-1.

Les restitutions consécutives à l'annulation rétroactive du contrat sont régies par les dispositions générales des articles 1162, alinéa premier et 1162-3 du projet.

L'article 1126-1 vise à corriger l'injustice qui pourrait résulter du dommage causé à la partie innocente par l'annulation du contrat. Il fait application à ce cas particulier de l'article 1162 du projet selon lequel « lorsque l'annulation ou la résolution est imputable à l'une des parties celle-ci doit en outre » (outre les restitutions) « indemniser l'autre de tous dommages et intérêts ». Il précise toutefois *les conditions de cette indemnisation*. Selon son alinéa premier (« à l'insu de l'autre »), clairement précisé par son alinéa second, la simple connaissance du but illicite suffit à exclure, y compris pour la partie qui ne poursuivait pas elle-même un tel but, toute réclamation d'une indemnisation du préjudice causé par l'annulation du contrat.

Validité – Forme
(art. 1127 à 1128-2)

Pierre Catala

Dans son chapitre traitant des conditions essentielles pour la validité des conventions, le Code civil ne contenait aucune disposition relative à la forme. Celle-ci siégeait principalement au chapitre de la preuve et, sporadiquement, dans les textes

place of "cause" on the part of the one who receives and gives nothing' (Domat, *Les lois civiles dans leur ordre naturel*, 1st part, title 1, section 1, p. 235).

Article 1126

This article is intended to confirm the present state of case-law on the subject, which seems satisfactory. It indicates, in particular, that an unlawful purpose pursued by one of the parties is sufficient to give rise—for 'the safeguard of the public interest' (article 1129-1, paragraph 1 of the Reform Proposals)—to absolute nullity of the contract for absence of lawful cause, without the need to ask whether the other party pursued the same purpose or had knowledge of it.

On the other hand, this provision does not make any assumptions about the contents of the requirements of public policy or public morality, such as in relation to acts of generosity made to encourage adulterous relationships.

Article 1126-1

Restitution following the retroactive annulment of a contract is governed by the general provisions of articles 1162 (first paragraph) and 1162-3 of the Reform Proposals.[1]

Article 1126-1 is intended to correct the injustice which could result from harm caused to the innocent party by annulment of a contract. It applies to this particular situation article 1162 of the Proposals, under which 'Where annulment or termination is attributable to one of the parties, the latter must also' (in addition to the restitution) 'compensate the other for all his losses'. It sets out, however, *the conditions of this compensation*. According to the first paragraph ('without the knowledge of the other'), clarified by the second paragraph, the simple knowledge of the unlawful purpose is sufficient to exclude—even for the party who does not himself pursue that purpose—any claim for compensation for loss caused by the annulment of the contract.

Validity – Form
(articles 1127 to 1128-2)

Pierre Catala

In the chapter dealing with the essential conditions for the validity of contracts, the Civil Code contains no provision relating to form. Form was placed mainly in the chapter dealing with proof and, here and there, in the provisions which govern the

---

[1] [These provisions do indeed govern these issues, but there appears to be further treatment of them following art 1331 of the *Avant-projet*, which provides that restitution of money or property following annulment or retroactive termination (*résolution*) of the contract is to be seen as a form of recovery of an undue payment. On these questions more generally see Whittaker, above, ch 9.]

qui règlent l'opposabilité des conventions. Quant aux formes requises à fin de validité, on les trouvait spécifiées, acte par acte, et elles variaient de l'un à l'autre, en passant de l'écriture manuscrite à l'écrit simple sous seing privé et à la forme authentique. Personne ne doutait, cependant, qu'en droit français le consensualisme soit le principe et le formalisme l'exception. Fallait-il, dès lors, inscrire dans la partie de l'avant-projet consacrée à la formation des contrats une section dédiée à leur forme ? En prenant ce parti nous n'étions pas seuls puisque le code européen proposé par l'Académie de Pavie consacre son Titre IV aux formes du contrat (art. 34 à 38).

Il y avait en ce sens un argument déterminant : l'équivalence de l'écriture électronique avec les écritures traditionnelles, reconnue pas les lois 2000-230 du 13 mars 2000 et 2004-75 du 21 juin 2004.

L'histoire récente de l'écriture électronique est captivante par plusieurs de ses traits. À la demande d'une première directive européenne, le Code civil dut reconnaître la force probante de l'écriture et de la signature électroniques. Il en a admis le principe et posé les conditions dans les nouveaux articles 1316 à 1316-4, issus de la loi du 13 mars 2000. Il ne s'agissait alors que d'un formalisme *ad probationem*, qui ne reconnaissait pas la validité de la forme électronique pour les actes où l'écrit était exigé à peine de nullité. Mais la même loi, dans l'article 1317 nouveau, prévoyait que l'acte authentique « peut être dressé sur support électronique, s'il est établi et conservé dans des conditions fixées par décret en Conseil d'État ». Or, bien que les actes authentiques figurent au chapitre de la preuve dans le Code civil, il est clair que le formalisme de l'authenticité exige l'écriture à peine de nullité et pas seulement aux fins de preuve. L'article 1317 alinéa 2 préfigurait ainsi, pour l'écriture électronique, le passage du formalisme *ad probationem* au degré supérieur du formalisme *ad validitatem*.

C'est ce que fit la loi du 21 juin 2004 sur l'économie numérique qui intégra en droit français la directive européenne relative au commerce électronique. Deux nouveaux articles 1108-1 et 1108-2 apparurent dans le Code civil au chapitre des conditions essentielles pour la validité des conventions. Le formalisme désormais faisant ainsi son entrée au rang desdites conditions, méritait dès lors, comme cadre d'accueil, une section particulière de l'avant-projet où les deux articles précités prennent place sous les numéros 1127-2 et 1127-3.

Le premier de ces textes dispose que lorsqu'un écrit électronique est exigé pour la validité d'un acte juridique, il peut être établi et conservé sous forme électronique dans les conditions prévues aux articles 1316-1 et 1316-4 du Code civil (soit 1285-1 et 1286 de l'avant-projet). Il en résulte une identité de la forme solennelle et de la forme probante : une même forme peut convenir à plusieurs finalités. On le savait déjà par le rapprochement de textes : la forme authentique, requise à peine

effects of contracts in relation to third parties. Formalities required for validity were found set out, juridical act by juridical act, and varying from one to another: from handwritten documents, to signed documents and those in publicly authenticated form. No one doubted, however, that in French law consensualism is the principle, and formalism the exception. So was it necessary to write into the section of the Reform Proposals dealing with the formation of contracts a section dedicated to their form? In taking this course we were not alone, because the European code proposed by the Pavia Academy[1] devotes its Title IV to contractual formality (articles 34 to 38).

There was a decisive argument in favour: the equivalence of electronic writing to traditional writing, recognised by the Laws 2000-230 (13 March 2000) and 2004-75 (21 June 2004).

The recent history of electronic writing is fascinating in several respects. As required by a first European Directive,[2] the Civil Code had to recognise the probative force of electronic writing and electronic signatures. It accepted the principle, and laid down conditions in the new articles 1316 to 1316-4, stemming from the Law of 13 March 2000. At that stage it was only a question of formality by way of proof, and did not recognise the validity of electronic forms for juridical acts for which writing was required on pain of nullity. But the same Law, in the new article 1317, anticipated that an authenticated instrument 'may be drawn up in an electronic medium, if it is created and stored in the circumstances fixed by decree by the *Conseil d'État*'. Now, although authenticated instruments are placed in the chapter on proof in the Civil Code, it is clear that the formality requirements relating to authentication require writing on pain of nullity, and not only with a view to proof. Article 1317 paragraph 2 thus foreshadowed, for electronic writing, the passing from formality by way of proof to the higher requirement of formality by way of validity.

This was done by the Law of 21 June 2004 on the digital economy, which integrated into French law the European directive on electronic commerce.[3] Two new articles (1108-1 and 1108-2) appeared in the Civil Code in the chapter on the essential conditions for the validity of contracts. From that point formality made its entry into the list of those conditions, and from that (as a context to introduce it) deserved its own section in the Reform Proposals where the two articles mentioned above take their place as numbers 1127-2 and 1127-3.

The first of these texts provides that when electronic writing is required for the validity of a juridical act, it can be created and stored in electronic form in the circumstances provided for by articles 1316-1 and 1316-4 of the Civil Code (or 1285-1 and 1286 of the Reform Proposals). From this comes an equivalence of the form for validity and the form for proof: a single form may satisfy several ends. It was already clear from a comparison of texts: the publicly authenticated form, required on pain of nullity in the case of donations, is also required in land

---

[1] [Above, p 499, n 1.]

[2] [Directive 1999/93/EC of the European Parliament and of the Council of 13 December 1999 on a Community framework for electronic signatures.]

[3] [Directive 2000/31/EC of the European Parliament and of the Council of 8 June 2000 on certain legal aspects of information society services, in particular electronic commerce, in the Internal Market.]

de nullité dans les donations, l'est aux fins d'opposabilité dans les transactions immobilières. Eu égard à cette polyvalence, il importe donc que la loi précise le but de la forme qu'elle prescrit : tel est le sens de l'article 1297 du projet qui retouche l'article 1426 du Code civil.

La section proposée n'a pas pour seule raison d'être une structure d'accueil pour les nouvelles technologies de l'écriture. Son propos est plus général.

L'article 1127 proclame en termes exprès le principe du consensualisme. L'article 1127-4, en cohérence avec la section voisine des nullités, dispose que le régime de l'action en nullité pour défaut ou vice de forme dépend de la nature des intérêts que la forme entend protéger. Il fait ainsi application d'un principe général énoncé par l'article 1129-1, auquel obéissent parallèlement les articles 1122 (objet) et 1124-1 (cause).

L'article 1127-5 confirme qu'il existe, à côté des formes solennelles, des formes requises à des fins distinctes de preuve ou d'opposabilité, qui sont sans effet sur la validité des conventions.

L'article 1127-6 pose le principe du parallélisme des formes qui s'applique aux actes modifiant ou abrogeant une convention antérieure. Son emplacement, en fin de paragraphe, laisse à penser qu'il vaut pour toutes les manifestations du formalisme et pas seulement pour les formes exigées à peine de nullité.

Le paragraphe 2 de la section 5 se borne à accueillir sous le signe de la forme électronique les articles 1369-1 et suivants du Code civil, que la loi du 22 juin 2004 sur l'économie numérique a introduits dans un nouveau chapitre du code intitulé « Des contrats sous forme électronique ». Ce sont des textes d'inspiration consumériste qui entourent de formes protectrices les conditions de l'offre et de l'acceptation pour que le contrat soit valablement conclu.

Sanctions
(art. 1129 à 1133)

Philippe Simler

Les dispositions de cette rubrique sont principalement consacrées à la **nullité des actes juridiques** (§1) et se substituent à celles des articles 1304 à 1314 actuels du Code civil, ainsi qu'aux articles 1338 à 1340. S'y ajoutent, en se limitant à une définition, trois articles relatifs aux concepts de **caducité** (§2), d'**inopposabilité** (§3) et de **régularisation** (§4), qui étaient comme tels absents du code de 1804.

Ce dispositif a trouvé naturellement place à la fin du chapitre traitant des conditions de validité des conventions. Cette place est assurément plus pertinente que celle des actuels articles 1304 à 1314, à la suite des causes d'extinction des obligations, *a fortiori* que celle des articles 1338 à 1340, curieusement placés dans le chapitre traitant de la preuve des obligations.

transactions for the purposes of their being relied on as against third parties. Given this versatility, it is necessary that legislation set out the purpose of the formality that it requires; this is the meaning of article 1297 of the Reform Proposals which retouches article 1426 of the Civil Code.

The proposed section is not included only to provide a context for the introduction of the new technologies of writing. Its purpose is more general.

Article 1127 proclaims in express terms the principle of consensualism. Article 1127-4, consistently with the adjacent section on nullities, provides that the regime of the action for nullity for absence or defect of formality depends on the nature of the interests which the formality is intended to protect. It therefore applies a general principle set out in article 1129-1, which articles 1122 (subject-matter) and 1124-1 (cause) equally respect.

Article 1127-5 confirms that there are, alongside the forms required for validity, forms required for the separate purposes of proof or for reliance as against third parties, which do not affect the validity of contracts.

Article 1127-6 lays down the principle of parallel formalities, which applies to documents modifying or abrogating an existing contract. Its position, at the end of the section, shows that it applies all types of formality, and not only to formalities required on pain of nullity.

Paragraph 2 of section 5 is confined to incorporating, under the heading of electronic formalities, articles 1369-1 *et seq.* of the Civil Code, which the Law of [21] June 2004 on the digital economy introduced in a new title of the Code headed 'Contracts in electronic form'. These provisions, inspired by consumer protection concerns, deal with the formalities which protect the circumstances of the offer and acceptance to ensure that the contract is validly concluded.

Sanctions
(articles 1129 to 1133)

Philippe Simler

The provisions under this heading are mainly concerned with the **nullity of juridical acts** (§ 1) and replace those of articles 1304 to 1314 of the present Civil Code, as well as articles 1338 to 1340. In addition, but limited to giving a definition, there are three articles concerning the concepts of **lapse** (§ 2), **invalidity and third parties** (§ 3) and **regularisation** (§ 4), which were not as such included in the Code of 1804.

These provisions have found their natural place at the end of the chapter dealing with the conditions of validity of contracts. This position is certainly more appropriate than that of the present articles 1304 to 1314, which follow the grounds of extinction of obligations, and even more so that of articles 1338 to 1340, curiously placed in the chapter dealing with proof of obligations.

Par ailleurs, les actuels articles 1304 à 1314 sont pour l'essentiel (10 des 11 articles, et même, pour partie, le 11ᵉ) relatifs à l'hypothèse de l'incapacité. Celle-ci appelle des sanctions spécifiques, dont la place est à l'évidence dans la rubrique qui lui est propre (ce qui laisse entière la question du sort des textes actuels, qui resteraient de droit positif dans cette mesure, dans l'hypothèse de l'adoption du présent projet).

En définitive, les dispositions de la présente section ne sont que très peu redevables à l'existant. Elles consacrent cependant très largement, spécialement en ce qui concerne la théorie des nullités, les solutions du droit positif.

§1 – De la nullité

Les textes proposés constituent une consécration explicite de ce qu'il est convenu d'appeler la théorie moderne des nullités, par opposition à la théorie dite « organique » qui a eu largement cours au XIXᵉ siècle et qui a prévalu, dans certains cas (par exemple pour l'absence de cause), jusqu'à une époque récente. Cela résulte clairement du critère de distinction entre la nullité absolue et la nullité relative proposé à l'article 1129-1, à savoir : la sauvegarde, respectivement, de l'intérêt général ou d'un intérêt privé. Il est cependant précisé que si l'intérêt privé met en cause une valeur fondamentale, comme la protection du corps humain, la nullité est absolue.

Le régime des nullités ainsi définies est conforme aux solutions du droit positif. La nullité absolue peut être invoquée par toute personne justifiant d'un intérêt et peut être relevée d'office par le juge ; elle n'est pas susceptible de confirmation et se prescrit par l'actuel délai de droit commun. La nullité relative ne peut être invoquée que par celui que la loi protège et qui peut y renoncer en confirmant l'acte vicié, expressément ou tacitement, par exemple en l'exécutant en pleine connaissance de cause ; elle se prescrit, sauf dispositions particulières, par un délai plus bref, actuellement de cinq ans, mais qui pourrait être ramené à trois ans.

Dans tous les cas, la nullité est prononcée par le juge. Mais il est précisé, ce qui apparaît à première vue très novateur, que les parties peuvent la constater d'un commun accord. En réalité tel était déjà le cas, mais ce qui va sans dire vaut parfois d'être expressément formulé. Si les parties à une convention valable peuvent, ce dont personne ne doute, y renoncer par un *mutuus dissensus*, combien plus sûrement doivent-elle pouvoir constater l'inefficacité d'une convention viciée. La reconnaissance explicite de cette faculté est de nature à les inciter à éviter d'inutiles contentieux. A été écartée, au contraire, la possibilité d'une annulation unilatérale qui serait simplement notifiée à l'autre partie, celle-ci ayant alors la faculté de la contester. Une telle solution est proposée pour la résolution (art. 1158). Dès lors que la nullité n'a pas pu faire l'objet du constat mutuel ci-dessus évoqué, le contentieux est inévitable et il paraît alors plus juste d'en imposer l'initiative à celui qui demande la nullité qu'à celui qui la conteste.

Moreover, the present articles 1304 to 1314 essentially relate to a case of lack of capacity (10 of the 11 articles and even, in part, the 11th). This gives rise to specific sanctions, which obviously belong in their own section (which leaves untouched the question of the fate of the present texts, which would remain to this extent from the law as it is presently applied, if the present Reform Proposals are adopted).

In fact, the provisions of this section owe very little to the existing provisions. But very largely, and in particular in relation to the doctrine of nullities, they formally establish the solutions of the law as it is presently applied.

§ 1 Nullity

The proposed provisions form an explicit establishment of what is generally called the modern doctrine of nullities, as contrasted with the so-called 'organic' doctrine which was generally accepted in the 19th century and which prevailed until recently in certain cases (for example, for absence of 'cause').[1] This follows clearly from the distinguishing criterion between absolute nullity and relative nullity, proposed in article 1129-1; that is, the safeguard of (respectively) the public interest or a private interest. It is, however, made clear that if the private interest raises an issue of a fundamental value, such as the protection of the human body, nullity is absolute.

The regime of nullities, so defined, is in accordance with the solutions of the law as it is presently applied. Absolute nullity may be invoked by any person who can demonstrate an interest, and may be raised by the court on its own initiative. It is not susceptible to affirmation, and becomes prescribed after the general time period set under the present law.[2] Relative nullity may be invoked only by a person protected by the relevant legislation and who can renounce it by affirming the vitiated juridical act, expressly or impliedly, for example by performing it with full knowledge of the defect. Except as otherwise specifically provided, it becomes prescribed after a shorter period—presently five years, but this would be reduced to three years.

In all cases, nullity is decreed by the court. But it is provided that—and this seems at first sight to be novel—the parties may establish it by common consent. In reality this is already the case, but what goes without saying is sometimes worth being expressly stated. If the parties to a valid contract may renounce it by an agreement to dissolve the agreement—which no one doubts—how much more certain is it that they can establish that a vitiated contract shall have no effect. The explicit recognition of this power is meant to encourage parties to avoid unnecessary litigation. On the other hand, we have ruled out the possibility of a unilateral annulment which would be simply notified to the other party, with the latter then having the right to challenge it. Such a solution is proposed for termination for non-performance (article 1158).[3] If nullity has not been able to be settled by the parties' mutual agreement, mentioned above, litigation is unavoidable and it then seems fairer to require the party who seeks nullity to take the first steps, rather than the party who challenges it.

---

[1] [For a discussion of the doctrine of nullities, see Nicholas, *The French Law of Contract*, above, p 489, n 2, 77-80.]

[2] [For the proposals for the reform of the law on prescription, see below, pp 880-915.]

[3] [See below, p 565.]

Le projet tend par ailleurs à combler la lacune du dispositif législatif relative à la question de l'étendue de la nullité. On sait que la jurisprudence était parvenue à des solutions satisfaisantes par une interprétation convergente, mais peu respectueuse de leur lettre, des articles 900 et 1172 du Code civil. Exprimant l'idée de *favor contractus*, l'article 1130-2 du projet pose en principe la nullité partielle de l'acte dont une clause ou une partie seulement est viciée, sauf preuve du caractère déterminant de cette clause ou partie. Ce critère subjectif, requérant une recherche d'intentions, est cependant lui-même écarté dans les cas où la loi répute non écrite une clause ou encore si la finalité protectrice de la règle violée exige le maintien de l'acte.

Le caractère rétroactif reconnu à la nullité, qui induit le principe de restitution des prestations déjà exécutée, est conforme aux solutions en vigueur, tout en renvoyant à une rubrique traitant de manière plus précise des restitutions.

§2 – De la caducité

La caducité existe et comporte de nombreuses facettes : caducité des libéralités, dans diverses circonstances, caducité d'un acte dépendant d'un autre qui est lui-même annulé ou résolu, caducité du mariage, même, en cas de changement de sexe d'un époux... Elle ne peut être assimilée à aucun autre concept, tel que la nullité ou la résolution. Elle mérite donc une place dans le Code civil.

Sa définition est cependant difficile. S'il est aisé de la différencier de la nullité ou de la résolution, il l'est moins de la définir positivement. Ses causes sont très diverses. Ses effets, au surplus, sont variables, puisqu'elle est tantôt rétroactive, tantôt non. Elle apparaît en quelque sorte comme une forme résiduelle d'inefficacité pour toute autre cause que l'absence d'une condition de validité ou l'inexécution. Aussi est-il proposé de n'inscrire dans le Code civil qu'une définition, en des termes suffisamment larges pour permettre d'embrasser des hypothèses diverses.

The Reform Proposals aim, moreover, to fill a gap in the legislative provisions relating to the question of the scope of nullity. We know that the courts have arrived at satisfactory solutions by a convergent interpretation of articles 900 and 1172 of the Civil Code—although it hardly respects their letter.[1] Expressing the idea of favouring the validity of the contract, article 1130-2 of the Proposals sets out the principle of partial nullity of the juridical act of which only one term or one part is defective, unless there is proof of the decisive character of this term or part. This subjective requirement, which calls for an investigation of intentions, is however itself removed in a situation where a legislative provision strikes out a clause, or again if the protective purpose of the rule which has been violated requires the continuation of the juridical act.

The retroactive character which is recognised for nullity, and which gives rise to the principle of restitution of what has already been done in performance, is in accordance with the solutions already in force, whilst referring to a section dealing with restitution in a more precise manner.

§ 2 Lapse

Lapse exists in many forms: lapse of acts of generosity, in various circumstances; lapse of a juridical act which depends on another which is itself annulled or retroactively terminated; even lapse of a marriage in case of change of sex of one spouse, etc. It cannot be assimilated to any other concept, such as nullity or termination. It therefore deserves a place in the Civil Code.

Its definition is, however, difficult. Although it is easy to distinguish it from nullity or termination, it is less so to define it in positive terms. Its grounds are very diverse. Its effects, moreover, vary, since it is sometimes retroactive, sometimes not. It appears in some sense to be a residual form of ineffectiveness for grounds other than absence of a condition of validity, or non-performance. And it is proposed to write into the Civil Code only a definition, in terms sufficiently wide to allow it to include the different cases.

---

[1] [Article 900 provides that 'In any disposition *inter vivos* or by testament, impossible conditions (which are those contrary to legislation or public morality) are struck out' (literally, 'deemed not written'); article 1172 provides that 'Any condition of an impossible thing, or one which is contrary to good morals or prohibited by legislation, is a nullity and renders a nullity the contract on which it depends.' The courts' 'convergent interpretation' of these provisions (the first of which suggests that only the unlawful condition itself is a nullity, whereas the second suggests that nullity affects the whole contract) rests the effect of the unlawfulness of a condition on the question whether the particular unlawful condition was one on which the parties intended their contract should depend: eg Cass civ (3) 24 June 1971, Bull civ III no 405.]

§3 – De l'inopposabilité

La définition de l'inopposabilité qui est proposée est celle communément admise : elle distingue clairement les parties et les tiers, seuls protégés par ce concept.

Force est de reconnaître cependant qu'elle n'est pas en harmonie avec son emploi, souvent contestable, au reste, dans diverses situations. La formulation d'une définition précise pourra contribuer à d'utiles clarifications.

§4 – De la régularisation

Ce concept appelle des observations semblables. La régularisation est mentionnée par divers textes législatifs. La définition qui est proposée est de nature à en permettre l'application dans d'autres hypothèses, non expressément prévues.

Effet des conventions, Interprétation, Qualification
(art. 1134 à 1143)

Alain Ghozi

Le chapitre III énonce les règles applicables aux effets des obligations. Il les organise en sept sections dans un ordre logique. Sont ainsi exposés successivement le contenu de l'accord, la manière de l'interpréter, la qualification qui en résulte, les diverses obligations qu'il engendre, les règles propres à leur exécution ou à leur inexécution et la résolution qui peut s'ensuivre. Il s'enrichit de nombreuses dispositions nouvelles à même de régler des problèmes révélés par la pratique : certaines se trouvaient il est vrai implicitement contenues dans les dispositions de principe en la matière tandis que d'autres, par adjonction, sont originales. Ainsi, notamment, du régime de la faculté de se dédire, du traitement des difficultés d'exécution du fait du changement des circonstances économiques, de l'encadrement du comportement

§ 3 Invalidity and third parties

The definition of the general lack of effect of contracts ('inopposability'[1]) with regard to third parties is that which is generally accepted: it distinguishes clearly between the contracting parties and third parties, the latter of whom are alone protected by this concept.

We have to recognise, however, that it is not in conformity with its usage, often disputed, moreover, in different situations. The formulation of a precise definition could make a useful contribution by way of clarification.

§ 4 Regularisation

This concept calls for similar observations. Regularisation is mentioned in various legislative provisions. The definition which is proposed is meant to permit its application in other situations, which have not been expressly provided for.

The Effects of Contracts; Contractual Interpretation and Contractual Classification (articles 1134 to 1143)

Alain Ghozi

Chapter III sets out the rules governing the effects of obligations. It organises them in a logical order in seven sections. So the following are set out in turn: the contents of agreements; the way in which they should be interpreted; the classification of contracts as so interpreted; the different types of obligations which they create; the rules applicable to performance and non-performance of these obligations; and retroactive termination of the contract on non-performance. This chapter benefits from a number of new provisions so as to be able to regulate problems which have become apparent in practice: while it is true that some of these may be found implicitly within provisions of principle governing the area, others are added to them and are completely new. This is the case in particular as regards the regime governing rights of withdrawal; the treatment of difficulties of performance as a result of a change in economic circumstances; the framework for unilateral lawful

---

[1] [The concept of (*in*)*opposabilité* is well understood by French lawyers, although not easily translated by a single term in English. It is commonly used in discussing the general 'relative effect' of a contract in relation to third parties (cf art 1165 of both the Civil Code and the *Avant-projet*) and covers the question of whether and when a contract may be relied on *against* a third party, as well as when it can be relied on *by* a third party. See Nicholas, *The French Law of Contract*, above, p 489, n 2, 170-1.]

unilatéral licite, de la consécration des ensembles contractuels dans leurs diverses formes et de l'introduction de l'obligation de donner à usage. Ainsi encore de l'aménagement de la faculté de résiliation unilatérale en cas d'inexécution du contrat, de la clarification du régime des clauses résolutoires, des restitutions après anéantissement du contrat. Et pour ce qui est de l'effet des conventions à l'égard des tiers, la promesse de porte-fort et la stipulation pour autrui sont elles aussi ordonnées ; les principes de la cession de contrat sont enfin affirmés. Chacun de ces points mérite quelques approfondissements. Ainsi, pour commencer, de la force obligatoire et de l'interprétation.

Les articles 1134 et 1135 ont constitué les axes autour desquels des pans entiers de la relation contractuelle se sont ordonnés : effet obligatoire de l'engagement, contenu de cet engagement et pouvoir des volontés sur lui. Avec, dans le prolongement nécessaire, en section 2, les règles d'interprétation de ces engagements.

Sans changer cette architecture, qu'une pratique séculaire a consacrée dans ses principes, il est apparu opportun de l'enrichir dans ses deux composantes : le contenu de l'engagement, c'est l'apport de la section 1, et, en section 2, l'articulation de l'interprétation avec la qualification.

Sur le premier point, deux innovations se sont imposées : le pouvoir des volontés d'organiser leur désengagement et celui de traiter les suites des difficultés d'exécution si graves qu'elles font perdre à la relation contractuelle son intérêt.

Régime de la faculté de se dédire

L'article 1134-1 appréhende explicitement la possibilité de se dédire : si cette faculté est le plus souvent unilatérale, il n'est pas rare qu'elle soit bilatérale, chacune des parties s'étant réservé la possibilité de se délier au regard de son intérêt pour le contrat. Prolongeant l'article 1134, cette disposition signifie qu'il ne saurait y avoir de dédit qui n'ait été autorisé, dans son existence et ses conditions de mise en œuvre, par la convention des parties, l'usage ou la loi selon les circonstances. Par voie réflexe, elle invite les parties à prévoir le dédit, consécration de leur pouvoir sur l'engagement qui les oblige, sans exclure qu'il puisse résulter de l'usage, comme c'est d'ailleurs le cas dans certaines pratiques du commerce par exemple. Le lien intellectuel avec les dispositions relatives à l'étendue de l'engagement est ainsi maintenu. Il est même renforcé par une remise en ordre de textes jusque-là mal agencés dans le code : ainsi l'article 1135, qui fonde l'incorporation dans l'accord des compléments qui lui sont apportés par la loi, l'usage et l'équité, se trouve

behaviour; the formal recognition of the various forms of contractual groupings; and the introduction of obligations to give for use. This is also true of the treatment given to the unilateral right to terminate the contract prospectively on the ground of contractual non-performance; of the clarification of the regime governing termination clauses; and of restitution consequential on the destruction of the contract. And the effects of contracts as regards third parties, of promises to stand as surety[1] and of stipulations for the benefit of third parties are also properly arranged and finally the principles governing the assignment of contracts are declared. Each of these points deserves some further elucidation. So, to start with, the binding force of contracts and contractual interpretation.

Articles 1134 and 1135 have furnished the axes around which great areas of the relationship created by contracts have been ordered: the binding force of contractual undertakings, the content of these undertakings and the power of the parties' wills over them, together with a necessary further treatment in section 2 of the rules governing the interpretation of undertakings.

Without changing this overall framework, whose principles have been approved by time-honoured practice, it appeared appropriate to elaborate it both as regards the content of undertakings (which is dealt with in section 1) and the creation of a link between contractual interpretation and contractual classification (which is dealt with in section 2).

As regards the former, two innovations are introduced: the power of the parties' wills to provide for their release and to provide for the consequences of problems of performance which are so serious that the contractual relationship has lost its point.

The regime governing the right of withdrawal

Article 1134-1 explicitly acknowledges the possibility of withdrawal by the parties. While such a right of withdrawal is mostly unilateral, it is not unusual for it to be bilateral, each of the parties reserving the possibility of withdrawing from the contract if it suits his interest. Developing the position set out in article 1134, article 1134-1 means that withdrawal is not possible unless both its existence and the circumstances in which it may take place are authorised by the contract itself, by custom or by legislation as the case may be. By way of corollary, article 1134-1 invites the parties to make express provision for withdrawal, which gives formal recognition to their power over their binding undertakings, but it does not rule out the possibility that such a right may arise by custom, as is the case for example in certain commercial contexts. A theoretical link is in this way maintained with those legal provisions which concern the extent of a party's undertaking; indeed, it is reinforced by putting the provisions which are at present rather awkwardly arranged in the Code into a proper order. So article 1135, which forms the basis for incorporation into the agreement of a contract's incidents attaching to it by law,

---

[1] [Here 'surety' is used in the loose English sense to cover any situation by which a person undertakes a responsibility in respect of another person's action or performance. It is not used in the technical English sense of 'guarantee' by which a person undertakes a *secondary* liability in respect of a principal debtor's *primary* liability.]

prolongé logiquement par l'ancien article 1160 qui en devient l'alinéa second : on doit en effet suppléer dans le contrat les clauses qui y sont d'usage, quoiqu'elles n'y soient pas exprimées.

Conséquences de la survenance d'un déséquilibre grave en cours d'exécution

Le pouvoir des parties est sollicité dans un autre domaine : la prévention contractuelle des difficultés d'exécution à venir, ou, à défaut, l'organisation d'une renégociation sous l'impulsion du Juge : c'est l'apport des articles 1135-1 et suivant introduits dans notre législation civile.

À ceux qui ne se lassent pas de regretter l'absence du traitement de l'imprévision en droit civil français, il faut rappeler que le contrat, acte de prévision par essence, se doit de prévoir les difficultés, et qu'il n'est de solution meilleure que celle qui aura été négociée par les parties concernées elles-mêmes. Aussi n'est-il pas fait allusion délibérément à l'imprévision. Le succès jamais démenti du contrat de transaction comme mode alternatif de résolution des litiges et de nos jours les appels au développement de la médiation comme autre mode négocié de solution en témoignent suffisamment. La pratique le sait bien d'ailleurs qui stipule des clauses de renégociation en cas de survenance de difficultés graves. Aussi, placée au centre du dispositif, la négociation des parties est une fois encore sollicitée mais il est cependant apparu nécessaire de l'encadrer lorsqu'elle intervient dans ces situations pour envisager et le silence des parties et l'échec de leur négociation. Tel est l'apport de ces dispositions.

Les parties sont encouragées à stipuler des clauses de renégociation de leur contrat pour le cas où il adviendrait que par l'effet des circonstances l'équilibre initial de leurs prestations fût perturbé au point que le contrat perde tout intérêt pour l'une d'entre elles (art 1135-1). Gage de la sécurité des transactions, la modification est liée à la perte de l'intérêt au contrat, à la fois mesure et preuve de la gravité du déséquilibre. Hommage à la vertu du contrat, la solution est négociée. À défaut de pareille clause, hypothèse qu'on ne saurait négliger, la partie qui perd son intérêt au contrat peut demander au juge, le président du tribunal de grande instance, qu'il ordonne la négociation salvatrice (1135-2). Et l'échec, exempt de mauvaise foi,

custom or equity is taken to its logical conclusion by adding the former article 1160 as its second paragraph to the effect that, even if they are not expressly included, terms which are customary may supplement the contract.

The consequences of a supervening serious imbalance arising in the course of performance of the contract

The parties' power is invoked in another area: the prevention by express contractual provision of future difficulties in performance, or, in its absence, the organisation of a procedure for renegotiation of the contract at the direction of the court. This is introduced into our civil legislation by articles 1135-1 *et seq.*[1]

Those who do not tire of regretting the absence of rules governing the effect of supervening unforeseeable events in French civil law[2] should remember that a contract is a juridical act which is by its nature an act of foresight and must therefore itself foresee and provide for such difficulties, and that there is no better solution than one which will have been negotiated by the parties in question themselves. Therefore, there is deliberately no provision made for unforeseeable events. The success of settlement as an alternative means of resolving disputes which has always been recognised and in our own day calls for the development of mediation as another negotiated means of resolution of disputes bears sufficient witness to this. Furthermore, practitioners know this well, and include renegotiation clauses to deal with the situation of supervening serious difficulties. Also, negotiation by the parties is once again to be encouraged by placing it at the centre of the law itself, though it was thought necessary to structure the circumstances in which negotiations should take place in these situations so as to deal both with cases where the parties themselves have been silent on the matter and where the parties' negotiations have broken down. This is the purpose of the provisions as proposed.

Parties to contracts are encouraged to include renegotiation clauses in their contracts to govern cases where a change of circumstances has the effect of disturbing the original balance of what is required of them under the contract to the extent that the contract loses all its point for one of them (article 1135-1). In order to guarantee the certainty of transactions, modification is tied to the loss of point to the contract, and this test acts both as a measure of the seriousness of the imbalance and as its proof. The solution to the problem of supervening circumstances is therefore found in negotiation, thereby solving a contractual difficulty through contract itself. In the absence of an express renegotiation clause (a possibility which ought not to be ignored), a party for whom a contract loses its point may apply to the court (specifically, to the President of the *tribunal de grande instance*[3]), which

---

[1] [On these provisions see Fauvarque-Cosson, above, ch 2 and Cartwright, above, ch 3.]

[2] [There is a doctrine of *imprévision* (unforeseeable events) in French *administrative* law, under which a private party, in a contract with a public party or for the provision of a public service, may be awarded an indemnity against the additional costs incurred in continuing to perform the service in the public interest, in the face of an unforeseeable supervening event which gravely undermines the economy of the contract: see Nicholas, *The French Law of Contract*, above, p 489, n 2, 208-10.]

[3] [*Tribunaux de grande instance* are courts of first instance in civil matters, situated throughout France.]

ouvrirait à chaque partie la faculté de demander la résiliation sans frais ni dommages (1135-3) : l'intérêt au contrat disparu, celui-ci peut disparaître. Implicitement, celui qui tiendra au contrat, saura faire les concessions nécessaires pour allouer à son cocontractant le minimum d'avantages pour l'encourager à poursuivre leur relation contractuelle.

Par ce dispositif original, il est fait écho aux dispositions de l'article 900-2, en tenant compte du caractère onéreux de la situation concernée ; l'unité d'inspiration des solutions applicables aux conséquences des changements de circonstances est ainsi établie, gage de l'harmonie du dispositif.

Interprétation ; actes unilatéraux ; ensembles de contrats interdépendants

Ainsi vivifiées, les dispositions générales, en tant qu'elles définissent le contenu de l'engagement, se prolongent logiquement par celles qui ont trait à leur interprétation, et, on l'a dit, par les rapports qu'elles entretiennent avec la qualification : c'est l'apport de la section 2 :

Instrument à la disposition du juge pour dégager la portée de l'engagement, les dispositions relatives à l'interprétation ont été actualisées en tenant compte de l'apport considérable de la jurisprudence, ici encore utilisée comme le laboratoire de l'épreuve nécessaire de la règle à la satisfaction des besoins de notre temps. Aussi fidèle à la méthode du Code, a-t-on exposé de manière à la fois analytique et successive les méthodes d'interprétation de l'obligation et de l'acte, de l'acte unilatéral (1136 al 2) puis de l'acte collectif qui recouvre toutes les décisions et délibérations d'un groupe (1136 al 3), autre nouveauté, ensuite de l'acte et du contrat, et enfin, autre nouveauté encore, du contrat puis de l'ensemble contractuel (1137 al 2). De la sorte les différentes innovations de la pratique, en matière d'acte collectif et de montage contractuel notamment, sont désormais formellement évoquées par notre droit, et consacrées à présent. Ces règles sont heureusement complétées par celles relatives aux effets de ces contrats interdépendants (art 1172 et s) de sorte que notre code comporte désormais un cadre complet pour ces innovations de la pratique, leur conférant de la sorte une prévisibilité et une clarté qui leur faisait défaut jusque-là.

Ces dispositions innovent encore en fournissant des outils de contrôle de l'équilibre contractuel. Parce que le contrat ne saurait constituer un instrument d'asservissement, il doit être interprété en raison d'abord, et aussi en équité. Il y a donc lieu de rechercher d'abord la raison d'être de l'engagement car elle donne la

may order a negotiation aimed at saving the contract (article 1135-2). If this fails, and putting aside cases of bad faith, either party would have the right to claim the prospective termination of the contract without payment of expenses or damages (1135-3): once the point of the contract has disappeared, so too should the contract itself. Implicit in this is that a person who wishes to see the contract maintained will have to make those concessions which are necessary to allow the other party a minimum of benefit to encourage him to carry on with their contractual relationship.

This innovative provision echoes those found in article 900-2 of the Civil Code[1] by its taking into account the burdensome nature of the situation in question. It therefore establishes the same way of thinking underlying the solutions governing the consequences of changes in circumstances, and this ensures consistency in the law as a whole.

Contractual interpretation; unilateral juridical acts; interdependent contractual groupings

Once reinvigorated in this way, the general provisions which define the content of the parties' contractual undertakings find their logical development in other provisions which deal with their interpretation, and, as has been said, in the relationship which they bear with the contract's classification. This is the concern of section 2.

Contractual interpretation is the means available to judges to draw out the significance of a party's undertaking and the legal provisions governing interpretation have been brought up to date by drawing on the considerable contribution made by the courts, here used as the necessary testing ground for rules to see if they satisfy contemporary needs. These provisions are also faithful to the Code's general method, for the Reform Proposals set out analytically and in turn the methods of interpretation of obligations and of juridical acts; unilateral acts (article 1136 paragraph 2), and collective acts—a new category which includes all decisions and resolutions of a group (article 1136 paragraph 3); then juridical acts and contracts; and then finally (and again an innovation) contracts and contractual groupings (article 1137, paragraph 2). In this way, the various innovations arising from practice, as regards collective acts and the structure of contractual arrangements in particular, would in future be formally alluded to and given effect by our law. These rules are nicely supplemented by those governing the effects of interdependent contracts (article 1172 et seq.) with the result that our Code would contain a complete framework for these innovations arising from contractual practice, and this would confer on them a predictability and a clarity which they have hitherto lacked.

These provisions are also innovative in that they create the tools by which the balance of the contract can be reviewed. Since contracts must not serve as an instrument of slavery, they must be interpreted first rationally and then equitably. As a result, a court should look for the rationale of a party's undertaking, for this gives

---

[1] [Article 900-2 allows the beneficiary of a gift or legacy to apply to the court to modify any conditions or burdens which attach to it where their performance has become significantly difficult or significant prejudicial as a result of a change of circumstances.]

mesure de ce que les parties ont voulu, de leur intérêt, volonté qui ne saurait déboucher sur l'inéquitable (1139).

Contrôle de l'unilatéralisme licite

Dans le même mouvement, l'acte établi sous l'influence dominante d'un seul, hypothèse fréquente dans les contrats de consommation, d'adhésion, mais aussi dans les relations de la distribution notamment, doit s'interpréter en faveur de l'autre (1140-1). Cette solution complète harmonieusement le dispositif original d'encadrement de la fixation unilatérale du prix, autre innovation proposée par l'avant-projet : il oblige son auteur à s'en justifier en cas de contestation, (1121-4 et 1121-5). Par ce renversement de la charge de la preuve, les rapports sont rééquilibrés ; le titulaire du pouvoir d'agir seul est contraint à la modération puisqu'il sait devoir se justifier sur simple contestation.

Qualification

Corrélativement il y avait lieu de pallier le silence du Code en matière de qualification (1142 et s) dès lors que l'innovation contractuelle multiplie les figures originales, puisant dans le modèle du contrat nommé pour concevoir des accords innommés, voire *sui generis*. Les principes en sont énoncés, qui doivent guider le juge et limiter l'incertitude de son intervention. En particulier a-t-on consacré le mécanisme de la conversion par réduction (1143 nouveau). Aussi s'est-on attaché à articuler ces dispositions avec celles du nouveau Code de procédure civile. De la coordination de ces règles nouvelles, il ressort un véritable corpus à même d'encadrer l'imagination contractuelle pour lui donner la sécurité qui assure son développement.

Diverses espèces d'obligations (art. 1144 à 1151)

Didier R. Martin

La classification des obligations – ou leur spécification – est un exercice délicat. Car

a clear indication of what the parties intended, the real point of their contract; but their intention should not be allowed to spill over into the unfair (article 1139).

The control of lawful dominance of one party over the other

In the same spirit, a juridical act which is made under the dominant influence of one of its parties, which is often the case in consumer contracts and standard-form contracts, but also especially in distribution contracts, must be interpreted in favour of the other party (article 1140-1). This rule complements consistently a new and innovative provision which sets a legal framework for the unilateral determination of the price by one of the parties to a contract by requiring that party to justify his decision if it is challenged (articles 1121-4 and 1121-5). This reversal of the burden of proof rebalances the parties' relationship, as a party who possesses the power to act unilaterally is forced to behave moderately as he knows that he has to justify himself merely on being challenged.

Contractual classification

As a corollary, it is appropriate to remedy the silence of the Code on the subject of the classification of contracts (article 1142 *et seq.*). These provisions are necessary now that innovations in contract-making give rise to lots of fresh patterns, relying on the idea of nominate contracts[1] so as to construct new unnamed and even sui generis agreements. The Reform Proposals set out the principles which the courts must use as their guide for the classification of these arrangements and these principles will reduce the uncertainty surrounding the courts' involvement. In particular, it makes formal provision for the technique of judicial reclassification of a contract if the parties' own classification cannot be given effect (this being termed 'conversion by reduction',[2] and given effect by a new article 1143). Also, care has been taken to relate these provisions to those found in the New Code of Civil Procedure.[3] As these new rules are carefully coordinated, the resulting body of law is able to set certain boundaries for the parties' contractual imagination and so give it the certainty needed to ensure its development.

The Various Types of Obligations (articles 1144 to 1151)

Didier R. Martin

The classification of obligations, or their distribution into species, is a difficult

---

[1] [On the distinction between nominate and innominate contracts see above, p 489, n 2.]
[2] [The translation here is rather more extended in order to convey the meaning of the original text.]
[3] [See below, p 681, for this relationship.]

il tend à exprimer, en peu de mots et de figures, les types généraux sous lesquels se rangent, ou auxquels se raccordent, en dépit de leur extrême diversité, les obligations légales ou volontaires. Est-ce la difficulté de l'entreprise qui a détourné les concepteurs du Code civil de s'y risquer ? L'expérience de l'enseignement et de la pratique du droit démontre cependant l'intérêt majeur d'un tel travail qui éclaire la théorie des obligations en l'enrichissant des concepts fondateurs de son objet même.

Traditionnellement, les obligations sont réparties en trois espèces élémentaires. Celle qui prescrit une action, un fait positif : c'est l'obligation de faire. Celle qui prescrit, à l'inverse, une abstention : c'est l'obligation de ne pas faire, avers et antithèse de la précédente. Celle, enfin, qu'on dénomme obligation « de donner », dont un courant doctrinal nie la spécificité, mais qui est, en réalité, irréductible à toute autre pour exprimer le devoir qu'on assume de transférer un droit réel ou personnel. L'affinement de la pensée donne aujourd'hui à comprendre qu'entre les deux archétypes (faire/ne pas faire et donner) s'insinue une variété mal diagnostiquée jusque-là et qu'il convient de qualifier (ne serait-ce qu'à raison de ses nombreuses et importantes applications pratiques) : l'obligation de donner à usage dont la marque, exclusive, est d'emporter devoir, pour ses bénéficiaires, de restitution de la chose ou de son équivalent au terme de l'usage convenu.

Ces types universels sont, du reste, eux-mêmes susceptibles de caractéristiques particulières ou communes qu'une classification des obligations doit, au second degré – en seconde détente – refléter. À cet égard, deux binômes majeurs s'imposent par leur vertu – et leur force – structurantes. L'un tient à l'objet de la prestation : il oppose l'obligation monétaire à celle qui ne porte pas sur une somme d'argent et qu'on dénomme, par une limpide abstraction, « en nature » : c'est que l'argent, étalon et contrepartie universels de tout, ne se prête pas au traitement juridique commun des autres objets de prestation. L'autre s'ordonne sur la finalité de l'obligation : il met en vis-à-vis l'obligation de résultat – de produire la satisfaction promise – et l'obligation de moyens, qui est de faire au mieux par les soins d'une diligence appropriée. Pur produit du génie juridique national, cette distinction, qui tolère des nuances intermédiaires, transcende les espèces d'obligations dont elle règle la portée.

Restait, en dernière ligne, à spécifier trois variétés atypiques d'obligations. L'obligation de valeur, d'abord, qui se règle, en argent, sur la valeur d'un bien à son échéance ou, en nature, sur ce qui convient aux besoins d'une personne ou aux soins d'une chose. L'obligation de sécurité, ensuite, qui reflète, dans une société de précaution, l'aspiration à une active sauvegarde contractuelle de l'intégrité de la

exercise. For its aim is to give expression in a few words and notions to general categories within which are ranged, or to which are related, despite their extraordinary diversity, all legal or voluntary obligations. Was it the difficulty of this undertaking which led those who conceived the Civil Code to avoid risking it? Nevertheless, the experience of teaching and of legal practice bears witness to the major interest of such a work which would illuminate the doctrine of obligations and at the same time enrich the fundamental concepts of its very subject-matter.

Traditionally, obligations are divided into three elementary kinds. An obligation which requires an action, a positive act, is an 'obligation to do.' Inversely, an obligation which requires an abstention, is an 'obligation not to do', this being the obverse and antithesis of the first. Finally, there is an obligation termed 'to give' and while its distinctiveness is denied by a line of thinking in legal scholarship, this obligation cannot be reduced to any other in order to give expression to what one agrees to do in transferring a real or personal right. A process of refinement of the thinking behind these traditional categories has led today to an understanding that between the two archetypes (obligations to do/not to do and obligations to give) there lies a further variety of obligations, one which had previously lain undetected, but which it is now agreed should be classified, if for no other reason than for its numerous and important practical applications. This third category is 'obligations to give for use' and its distinguishing and entirely special feature is that it brings with it a duty in those who benefit from its performance to restore the thing or its equivalent at the end of the period of the use which was agreed.

These universal categories are, moreover, themselves liable to possess particular or common characteristics which the classification of obligations at a second stage—at second blush—must reflect. In this respect, two major terms with two elements have become current owing to their structural qualities and force. The first relates to the nature of the subject-matter of a debtor's obligation and contrasts monetary obligations with those which do not concern a sum of money and which are called—rather laconically and abstractly—obligations 'in kind'. Here, it is the nature of money—which acts as a universal measure and equivalent of everything—which does not lend itself to a legal treatment which is shared with other kinds of subject-matter of obligations. The other centres on the purpose of obligations and contrasts 'obligations of result'—to produce the benefit which was promised—and 'obligations to take necessary steps', which are to do as well as one can with the use of appropriate care. The pure product of our nation's legal genius,[1] this distinction, which allows intermediate nuances between its two poles, transcends the different kinds of obligations whose full significance it governs.

This leaves at a secondary level the specification of three untypical varieties of obligations. First, 'obligations of value' which are concerned, if in money, with the value of property on its maturity; or, if in kind, with what is necessary for a person's maintenance or looking after a thing. Secondly, 'safety obligations' which, in the context of a careful society, reflect an aim of an active contractual safeguarding of the integrity of a party's person and property. Finally, 'natural

---

[1] [The distinction between 'obligations of result' (*obligations de résultat*) and 'obligations to take necessary steps' (*obligations de moyens*) was first drawn explicitly by R Demogue, *Traité des obligations en général* (Paris, Librairie Arthur Rousseau, 1923) vol V, 536 ff.]

personne et de ses biens. L'obligation naturelle, enfin : devoir de conscience, elle borde la frontière du juridique et ne doit sa positivité éventuelle qu'au bon vouloir du débiteur ; elle n'est qu'une prescription virtuelle, un pointillé où s'épuise le concept même d'obligation.

Exécution des obligations (art. 1152 à 1156-2)

Laurent Leveneur,
Hervé Lécuyer

Le Chapitre III du Titre III sera plus logiquement organisé en comprenant une section intitulée « De l'exécution des obligations » (question qui est actuellement traitée dans deux sections consacrées à l'obligation de donner, puis à l'obligation de faire ou de ne pas faire). Cette section viendra après celle relative aux diverses espèces d'obligations, et avant les dispositions portant sur l'inexécution des obligations et la résolution du contrat.

Exécution de l'obligation de donner (Articles 1152 à 1153-1)

Il n'est pas proposé de modifier le grand principe de transfert de propriété par le seul échange des consentements, qui ne soulève pas de difficultés pratiques et que l'on retrouve d'ailleurs aux articles 938 et 1583. Tout au plus la rédaction donnée aux articles 1152-1 et 1152-2 utilise-t-elle, pour plus de clarté, les mots délivrer et délivrance, au lieu de livrer et livraison (comme dans les actuels articles 1136 et 1138), ces derniers termes pouvant être ambigus : la livraison de l'actuel article 1138 est en effet en réalité la délivrance, c'est-à-dire le fait de mettre la chose à la disposition du cocontractant. Les rédacteurs du Code civil avaient utilisé les mots *délivrance* (art. 1603 et s.) et *livraison* comme des synonymes. Il est proposé de ne parler que de délivrance.

obligations', which concern those duties which one's conscience imposes, and which exist at the edge of the law's frontiers and which take up their potential for reality only with the goodwill of the debtor. Such an obligation is no more than a virtual requirement, a dotted-line where the very concept of obligation wears thin.

The Performance of Obligations (articles 1152 to 1156-2)

Laurent Leveneur,
Hervé Lécuyer

The third chapter of Title III will be more logically organised by including a section entitled, 'The performance of obligations' (an area of the law which is at present dealt with in two sections dedicated to obligations to give, and then to obligations to do and not to do). This section will come after the one concerning the various types of obligations, and before the provisions governing the non-performance of obligations and retroactive termination of the contract.

The performance of obligations to give (articles 1152 to 1153-1)

It is not proposed that the fundamental principle of transfer of title by the mere exchange of consent should be modified, as this does not give rise to difficulties in practice and as it is also found in articles 938 and 1583 of the Civil Code.[1] At the very most articles 1152-1 and 1152-2 have been drafted in the interests of greater clarity using the words *délivrer* and *délivraison* instead of *livrer* and *livraison*[2] (as are used in the current articles 1136 and 1138), as the latter are possibly ambiguous: *livraison* for the purposes of the current article 1138 is actually in reality *délivraison*, that is to say, the act of putting the thing at the disposition of the other party to the contract. The draftsmen of the Civil Code used the words *délivraison* (article 1603 *et seq.*[3]) and *livraison* as synonyms, but it is proposed that only *délivraison* should be used.

---

[1] [Article 938 provides that 'A gift which is duly accepted is complete on the mere agreement of the parties; and the ownership of objects given is transferred to the donee without the need for any other handing over.' Article 1583 makes a parallel provision for the transfer of ownership in contracts of sale.]

[2] [It is difficult to catch in English the significance of this reformulation. Both *délivrer* and *livrer* have the sense of the English word 'deliver': the reason for the change in French terminology is given by the draftsmen.]

[3] [These provisions concern the obligations of a seller in a contract of sale.]

Ce principe de transfert immédiat soulève d'autant moins de difficultés qu'il est toujours loisible aux parties de le différer, par une clause. Ces clauses sont répandues en matière immobilière surtout. Il connaît par ailleurs quelques exceptions légales (ex., art. 1585 sur la vente de choses de genre à mesurer). La rédaction du nouvel article 1152 réserve ces hypothèses.

L'obligation de conserver la chose jusqu'à la délivrance en y apportant tous les soins d'un bon père de famille du fameux article 1137 actuel est reprise à l'article 1152-1. La mise en demeure et ses conséquences sur la charge des risques (article 1139 d'aujourd'hui) le sont à l'article 1152-2 et 1152-3. Les articles 1140 et 1141 se retrouvent sous les numéros 1153-1 et 1153.

Exécution de l'obligation de faire ou de ne pas faire (article 1154 à 1154-2)

Une modification radicale est proposée pour la rédaction du célèbre article 1142. Il s'agit de tenir compte du fait que les exceptions et tempéraments apportés à la règle formulée par l'actuel article 1142 sont devenus si importants que le principe peut désormais être présenté d'une façon inversée, plus conforme à la réalité. Spécialement depuis que des textes (Lois du 5 juillet 1972, puis du 9 juillet 1991) ont consacré l'astreinte, il est bien difficile de continuer à proclamer que « Toute obligation de faire ou de ne pas faire se résout en dommages et intérêts, en cas d'inexécution de la part du débiteur ».

Sans doute l'astreinte n'est-elle qu'un procédé indirect de contrainte, ce qui permet en général à la doctrine d'essayer de la concilier avec le principe de l'article 1142, qui n'interdirait que la contrainte directe sur la personne du débiteur. Mais il n'empêche que l'astreinte assortit toujours une condamnation du débiteur à exécuter en nature l'obligation, et comme le domaine de l'astreinte est très vaste, il n'est plus possible de laisser entendre dans le Code civil que l'inexécution n'ouvrirait droit qu'à des dommages et intérêts au créancier...

En outre, on peut remarquer que la contrainte directe est elle-même assez souvent

The principle of immediate transfer of title to which reference has already been made raises even fewer difficulties given that it is always permissible for the parties to postpone transfer by an express term. Terms of this sort are very widespread, above all in the context of land transactions. In addition, there are some legislative exceptions to the principle, for example, in the case of sale of generic property sold by weight, number or measure as provided by article 1585 of the present Code. These qualifications are retained by the new article 1152 as drafted.

The obligation to look after the thing until delivery using all the care of a good head of household[1] which is currently found in the famous article 1137 is set out in article 1152-1. Notice to the contractual debtor to perform and its effects on the incidence of risk (at present contained in article 1139) are to be found in articles 1152-2 and 1152-3. Articles 1140 and 1141 are renumbered as articles 1153-1 and 1153.

The performance of obligations to do or not to do (articles 1154 to 1154-2)

A radical modification is proposed in redrafting the well-known article 1142. The point of the change is to take account of the fact that the exceptions and qualifications made to the rule set out in article 1142 as currently drafted have become so considerable that the reality is better reflected by stating the principle in the opposite way from the present position. It would be indeed very difficult to continue to proclaim that 'a debtor's non-performance of an obligation to do or not to do gives rise to liability in damages,' especially since legislative provisions (the Laws of 5 July 1972 and then of 9 July 1991) have formally recognised monetary penalties for disobedience of court orders.[2]

Doubtless such monetary penalties provide merely an indirect means of constraint on contractual debtors to perform, and this generally allows scholars to try to reconcile them with the principle found in article 1142, which only forbids the direct and personal constraint of debtors. But this does not prevent every court order of a debtor to perform his obligation specifically from being backed by a monetary penalty for disobedience, and since the scope of application of monetary penalties is very wide indeed, it is no longer possible to let it be understood from the Civil Code that contractual non-performance gives a creditor only a right to damages.

Furthermore, it may be observed that direct constraint is itself quite often possible,

---

[1] [The 'good head of household' (*bon père de famille*) is an inheritance from Roman law (*bonus paterfamilias*), and is the notional standard employed in French law to designate the conduct of a person who exercises a proper degree of care and diligence in his conduct or dealings in so far as they affect other persons or their property. It approximates to the English standard of the 'reasonable man': Nicholas, *The French Law of Contract*, above, p 489, n 2, 51, and is employed in a number of provisions of the Civil Code in relation to the obligation to look after property belonging to another; eg articles 450 (adminstration of a minor's property by his guardian), 601 (use of property by usufructary), 1137 (transferor of property pending its delivery), 1728 (use of property by borrower). See also above, p 428.]

[2] [These monetary penalties are termed *astreintes* and are payable on breach of a court order to the person in whose favour it was made: see further S Whittaker, 'Civil Procedure' in Bell, Boyron and Whittaker, above, p 465, n 3, ch 4(1) at 117-18.]

possible : expulsion du locataire qui doit restituer les lieux en fin de bail, saisie-appréhension d'un meuble que le débiteur doit livrer ou restituer...

La nouvelle rédaction proposée pour l'article 1142, qui devient l'article 1154, pose donc le principe de l'exécution en nature lorsqu'elle est possible (ceci est une allusion directe à l'actuel article 1184, qui envisage, en alternative à la résolution, l'exécution forcée de la convention « lorsqu'elle est possible »), et laisse implicitement aux lois sur la procédure (actuellement, essentiellement la loi du 9 juillet 1991 et le décret du 31 juillet 1992) le soin de régler les procédés de contrainte directe (ex. expulsion ; saisie-appréhension) ou surtout indirecte (astreinte) permettant d'obtenir cette exécution en cas d'inexécution de la part du débiteur.

Le plus délicat est d'exprimer les limites du droit à l'exécution forcée par contrainte directe, d'une part, et au moyen de l'astreinte, d'autre part, limites qui reposent sur la même idée, mais semble-t-il avec une intensité différente : on ne peut contraindre par la force un entrepreneur à effectuer les travaux promis (atteinte excessive à la liberté individuelle), alors qu'on peut le lui enjoindre sous astreinte ; mais l'astreinte cesse d'être possible si la prestation présente un caractère éminemment personnel (l'exemple classique est celui de l'œuvre qu'un artiste s'est engagé à réaliser).

En revanche la faculté de remplacement des actuels articles 1143 et 1144 peut être maintenue quasiment en l'état : elle passait pour une atténuation de l'impossibilité de l'exécution forcée directe ; elle est évidemment compatible, *a fortiori*, avec le nouveau principe posé du droit à l'exécution en nature, dont elle représente une modalité. Le nouvel article 1154-2 proposé reprend en substance les dispositions des articles 1143 et 1144 actuels.

Quant à l'article 1145 (dommages et intérêts en cas de violation de l'obligation de ne pas faire, sans mise en demeure), il n'est pas proposé de le modifier. Mais son contenu est intégré à l'article 1154-1.

Inexécution des obligations (art. 1157 à 1160-1)

Judith Rochfeld

Les propositions émises au sein de cette section sont assises sur l'état de la matière,

as in the case of the eviction of a tenant who has to give up possession of the property at the end of the lease, and the mechanism of distraint of movable property which a debtor is under an obligation to deliver or restore.

The new version proposed for article 1142 (which becomes article 1154) therefore sets out the principle of performance in kind where it is possible (this being a direct allusion to article 1184 as currently drafted, which provides for enforced performance of an agreement 'where it is possible' as an alternative to its retroactive termination for non-performance). Implicitly, this leaves to the legislation on civil procedure (at present, essentially the Law of 9 July 1991 and the Decree of 31 July 1992) the task of regulating the procedural mechanisms of direct constraint (for example, eviction or seizure of movable property) and above all indirect constraint (monetary penalties) by which performance may be obtained on a debtor's failure to perform.

Most awkward is how to give expression to the limitations on the creditor's right to enforced performance by direct constraint on the one hand, and by means of the imposition of monetary penalties for non-performance on the other, as while these limitations rest on the same idea, they appear to do so to a different degree: one cannot constrain by force a building contractor to perform the works which he has promised as this would be an excessive restriction on personal liberty, but one can order him to so on pain of monetary penalty; but monetary penalties themselves cease to be possible if the subject-matter of the debtor's obligation possesses a clearly personal character (the classic example being of an artist undertaking a commission[1]).

On the other hand, the right to obtain substitute performance at present provided for by articles 1143 and 1144 can be retained almost as it stands. It can pass muster as a means of making up for the lack of availability of direct enforced performance; a fortiori it is clearly also consistent with the new principle of a right to performance in kind, of which it forms one type. The proposed new article 1154-2 in substance picks up the provisions at present found in articles 1143 and 1144.

Finally, it is not proposed that article 1145 (which provides for damages for failure to perform an obligation not to do something without any prior notice to perform) should be modified, but its content is integrated into article 1154-1.

The Non-Performance of Obligations (articles 1157 to 1160-1)

Judith Rochfeld

The proposals advanced within this section find their foundations in the present

---

[1] [The allusion is to a famous real example, the *affaire* *Whistler*: Cass civ 14 March 1900, S 1900.1.489 note anon.]

tel qu'issu des textes initiaux et des apports de la jurisprudence (1). Elles tentent de pallier les lacunes existantes et de répondre aux nécessités d'évolution qui ont pu se faire jour depuis 1804 (2). Elles tracent, à ces fins, plusieurs directions (3).

§1 – L'état de la matière

La matière de l'inexécution des obligations et de la résolution du contrat (régie par l'article 1184 du Code civil) est assise sur plusieurs fondements traditionnels :

– la résolution est justifiée par le mécanisme de la condition résolutoire,

– la résolution s'inscrit comme implicite dans tous contrats synallagmatiques,

– la résolution est conçue comme judiciaire.

La philosophie juridique qui l'entoure s'impose comme spécifique, en tant qu'émanation de la pensée des rédacteurs du Code civil, et s'articule autour de deux idées :

– le principe fondamental de la force obligatoire du contrat et le moralisme contractuel : le contrat doit s'appliquer quelles que soient les circonstances et difficultés rencontrées. En conséquence, seuls les cas d'inexécution très grave, voire de faillite totale d'exécution, justifient qu'on l'anéantisse. Il est alors nécessaire de recourir au juge afin qu'il contrôle ce seuil de gravité,

– la protection du débiteur de l'obligation inexécutée et l'humanisme contractuel : le débiteur ne doit pas subir une sanction, trop vite assénée et sans contrôle, de la part de son partenaire contractuel.

§2 – Les lacunes de la matière et les nécessités de changement

a) Les lacunes relatives aux prévisions initiales du Code

– la résolution est la seule mesure prévue pour l'ensemble des contrats ;

– les autres mesures ne sont invoquées que dans des textes spéciaux épars, alors même qu'elles ont été généralisées en principes applicables à tous contrats

state of law in the area resulting in the original articles of the Civil Code and from the work of the courts (section 1). They attempt to remedy existing gaps and to respond to the needs for development which have come to light since 1804 (section 2). To this end the proposals follow a number of directions (section 3).

§1 The present state of the law

The law concerning non-performance of obligations and retroactive termination[1] of a contract (governed by article 1184 of the Civil Code) rests on several traditional foundations:

– termination is justified by recourse to the technique of a 'resolutory condition';

– termination is implicitly written into all synallagmatic contracts;

– termination is conceived of as requiring judicial intervention.

The legal theory which surrounds it demands our attention as it is rather special, reflecting clearly the thinking of the draftsmen of the Civil Code and turning on two central ideas:

– the fundamental principle of the binding force of contracts and contractual morality: a contract must still be applied whatever the circumstances or difficulties encountered. As a result, the destruction of a contract is justified only in the case of very serious non-performance, or indeed, a complete failure to perform. It is therefore necessary for recourse to be had to the court so that it may make sure that the threshold of seriousness needed for termination is satisfied;

– protection of a debtor in breach and contractual humanity; a debtor must not suffer a sanction which is inflicted by the other party to the contract too quickly and without any external control.

§2 Gaps in the present law and the need for change

(a) Gaps in the original provisions of the Code

– retroactive termination for non-performance is the only measure provided for all types of contracts;

– other measures are referred to only by a few particular legal provisions, even if these have been generalised into principles applicable to all synallagmatic contracts

---

[1] [*Résolution* of the contract is here translated explicitly as 'retroactive termination', although it will be called simply 'termination' where it is clear in context that the remedy being discussed has a retroactive character. *Résiliation* of the contract is in French law not retroactive, and is generally translated in this work as 'prospective termination' (although again it is sometimes simply 'termination' where the context makes it clear). On these see Whittaker, above, ch 9. The English lawyer naturally assumes that 'termination' has only a prospective character, whereas French law (as most civil law systems) starts from the position that an event of non-performance which is sufficiently serious to justify termination of the contract should have retroactive effect, each party making restitution in order to arrive at the *status quo ante*. See GH Treitel, *Remedies for Breach of Contract* (Oxford, Clarendon Press, 1988) ch IX.]

synallagmatiques par la jurisprudence et la pratique (exception d'inexécution ; théorie des risques) ;

– aucune disposition ne régit la résolution conventionnelle alors que celle-ci s'est également généralisée en pratique.

b) Les lacunes relatives aux conditions d'application

– l'article 1184 asseoit la résolution sur un mécanisme discutable, la condition résolutoire ;

– cette assise donne sa place au texte, au sein des règles relatives aux obligations conditionnelles (Chapitre IV « Des diverses espèces d'obligations », Section première « Des obligations conditionnelles », §3 « De la condition résolutoire »). Cette place est en conséquence également discutable et se prête à une réévaluation ;

– l'article 1184 ne précise pas les conditions d'application de la résolution : il ne dit rien du seuil d'inexécution propre à entraîner la résolution, se contentant de viser le « cas où l'une des parties ne satisfera point à son engagement ». Le constat peut être étendu à l'exception d'inexécution dont il faudrait plus précisément cerner le seuil d'intervention.

c) Les lacunes relatives aux effets

– l'article 1184 ne précise rien quant à l'étendue des effets de la mesure : rétroactifs ou non ; touchant ou non l'ensemble du contrat ;

– la résolution est traditionnellement conçue comme rétroactive, conformément à son fondement revendiqué de « condition résolutoire » ;

– la doctrine et la jurisprudence en ont néanmoins créé une variante : la « résiliation » ou plus exactement, résolution pour l'avenir, qui écarte la rétroactivité et ne produit effet que pour l'avenir. Néanmoins, le critère de distinction entre la résolution totale et rétroactive et la résolution partielle dans le temps n'est pas très explicite. Lorsqu'un critère est posé, il réside dans le caractère successif de l'exécution du contrat, critère discutable en ce qu'il repose sur la considération de la difficulté spécifique d'organiser des restitutions pour un contrat qui a duré ;

– rien n'est dit des suites de l'application de ces diverses mesures, notamment de l'organisation des restitutions et du fondement de ces dernières.

by the case-law and legal practice (as in the case of the defence of non-performance,[1] and the consequences of *force majeure* on the contract as a whole[2]);

– no legal provision governs termination of a contract under an express contract term even though this is also very widespread in practice.

(b) Gaps in the conditions required for termination for non-performance

– article 1184 sets the foundation of termination on the debatable technique of 'resolutory condition';

– this foundation determines its position in the Code, within the rules governing conditional obligations (Chapter IV 'Different types of obligations', section 1 'Conditional obligations', sub-section 3 'resolutory conditions'). As a result, this position is equally debatable and invites reassessment;

– article 1184 does not set out the detailed conditions for termination of the contract: it says nothing about the threshold of seriousness of non-performance appropriate to attract termination, limiting itself to the 'situation where one of the parties has not satisfied his undertaking'. This same point could also be made as regards the defence of non-performance where there is also a need to set out clearly the threshold for intervention.

(c) Gaps concerning the effects of termination

– article 1184 sets out no details as to the extent of the consequences of this measure, whether or not it is retroactive and whether it affects all or only part of the contract;

– termination is traditionally understood as being retroactive, following its stated basis in a 'resolutory condition';

– both legal scholarship and the courts have nevertheless created a variant on this position by recognising prospective termination[3] which is not retroactive, taking effect only for the future. Nevertheless, the criterion on which the distinction between complete and retroactive termination of the contract and termination which is partial because prospective is drawn is not very clear. Where a criterion is suggested, it is found in the successive character of performance of the contract, a criterion which is debatable as it rests on reflections about the particular difficulty found in dealing with restitution in contracts continuing over a period;

– nothing is said about the consequences of these various measures, notably, the basis of and rules governing restitution.

---

[1] [This defence—the *exception d'inexécution,* formerly often known as the *exceptio non adimpleti contractus*—allows a party to a bilateral contract faced with the non-performance by the other party to suspend performance of his own obligations in certain circumstances. Recognised in the pre-revolutionary law, it is not found in the Civil Code as a general proposition but may be glimpsed there from particular examples, eg articles 1612, 1613 Cc (sale). See further, Nicholas, *The French Law of Contract,* above, p 489, n 2, 213-6.]

[2] [This phrase translates *'la théorie des risques'* which is the name given to the set of rules governing a synallagmatic contract where one party's obligation becomes impossible owing to *force majeure.*]

[3] [*Résiliation*: see above, p 561, n 1.]

d) Les influences du droit européen

– les principes de droit européen des contrats prévoient uniquement la résolution unilatérale actionnée par le créancier, sur le modèle de nombreux pays voisins (chap. 9, art. 9 : 301), ce qui place le droit français en décalage.

§3 – Les directions proposées

a) Les directions quant à la place du texte

– la référence à la condition résolutoire disparaissant, il est possible de placer la section régissant l'inexécution à la suite de celle consacrée à l'exécution du contrat (Section 4 : de l'exécution des obligations, articles 1152 à 1156-2 ; section 5 : de l'inexécution des obligations et de la résolution du contrat, articles 1157 à 1160-1).

b) Les directions pour pallier les lacunes initiales des dispositions du code civil

– il est proposé d'établir textuellement l'existence de l'exception d'inexécution et de ses conditions d'application, notamment de son seuil d'intervention (inexécution totale ; article 1157) ;

– il est proposé d'intégrer la « théorie des risques » dans la résolution, en tant que celle-ci constituerait la mesure répondant à l'inexécution du contrat, quelle qu'en soit la cause (article 1158) ;

– il est proposé d'établir textuellement la possibilité de prévoir une clause de résolution et de régir les conditions d'application de cette dernière, ainsi que ses effets (article 1159).

c) Les directions quant au choix entre résolution judiciaire et unilatérale

– il est proposé d'opter pour le maintien du choix, pour le créancier, entre exécution forcée, dommages et intérêts et résolution (article 1158) ;

– il est proposé d'ouvrir, au créancier qui choisirait la résolution, une option entre résolution judiciaire et résolution unilatérale. Dans le cas où il opterait pour cette dernière, celle-ci interviendrait après mise en demeure du débiteur de s'exécuter et écoulement d'un délai raisonnable à cet effet. En cas de carence de ce dernier, la résolution serait constatée par une notification du créancier, exposant les motivations de la rupture (article 1158) ;

– il est proposé d'ouvrir au débiteur la possibilité de critiquer judiciairement *a posteriori* la décision du créancier, par contestation de l'existence des manquements qui lui sont imputés (article 1158-1).

(d) Influences of European law

– the *Principles of European Contract Law* make provision exclusively for unilateral termination of the contract by the creditor on the ground of non-performance following the model of a number of our neighbouring countries (Chapter 9, paragraph 9:301) and this shows French law to be out of step with others.

§3 The directions proposed

(a) The direction proposed for the position in the legislation of the provisions governing termination

– once the reference to 'resolutory condition' disappears, it becomes possible to place the section governing non-performance after the one dedicated to performance of the contract (Section 4 – The performance of obligations, articles 1152 to 1156-2; Section 5 – The non-performance of obligations and termination of contracts, articles 1157 to 1160-1).

(b) The directions proposed to remedy the gaps in the original provisions of the Civil Code

– it is proposed that legislation should establish the defence of non-performance and its conditions of application, notably as to the threshold of non-performance it requires (total non-performance; article 1157[1]);

– it is proposed that the wider consequences of *force majeure* should be integrated into the law governing termination of the contract for non-performance, in as much as the latter will constitute the measure in response to non-performance of the contract, whatever was the cause of this non-performance (article 1158);

– it is proposed that legislation should establish the possibility of parties to a contract agreeing to a termination clause, setting the conditions for its application and its effects (article 1159).

(c) The directions proposed as to the choice between termination of the contract by the court and by unilateral act of the creditor

– it is proposed to opt for the maintenance of a choice for a creditor between enforced performance, damages and termination of the contract (article 1158);

– it is proposed to grant to a creditor who chooses termination an option between termination by the court and termination by his own unilateral act. In the situation where he opts for the latter, termination takes effect after giving the debtor notice to perform and after the expiry of a reasonable period of delay for this purpose. Where performance is not forthcoming, termination may be effected by notification by the creditor setting out his reasons for the break-up (article 1158);

– it is proposed to grant to a debtor the possibility of contesting in retrospect before a court the creditor's decision to terminate, on the basis of denying the existence of the failures to perform which are alleged against him (article 1158-1).

---

[1] [In fact, there is no reference to 'total non-performance' in article 1157.]

d) Les directions quant au régime des effets de la résolution

– il est proposé d'établir textuellement le moment de prise d'effet de la résolution : à celui de l'assignation en résolution, lorsque celle-ci est judiciaire ; à celui de la réception de la notification, lorsque celle-ci est unilatérale (articles 1158 et 1160-1) ;

– il est proposé d'établir textuellement les effets de la résolution en prévoyant un principe de résolution pour l'avenir, sauf l'hypothèse de rétroactivité relative aux contrats à exécution instantanée (article 1160-1 et règles relatives aux restitutions, section 6) ;

– il est proposé de poser un critère de modulation de ces effets tenant au caractère divisible de l'exécution du contrat (article 1160).

Restitutions après anéantissement du contrat (art. 1161 à 1164-7)

Yves-Marie Serinet

Les règles relatives aux restitutions après anéantissement rétroactif du contrat en suite de son annulation ou de sa résolution ne font actuellement l'objet d'aucune disposition propre dans le Code civil, si l'on excepte, sans doute, l'article 1312 relatif aux restitutions qui suivent la rescision de la convention pour le vice d'incapacité. Encore faudrait-il ajouter immédiatement que la rédaction de ce dernier texte est postérieure à 1804 puisqu'elle résulte d'une loi du 18 février 1938.

(d) The directions proposed as to the regime governing the effects of termination

– it is proposed that legislation should establish the point in time when termination of the contract takes effect, putting it at the time of bringing an action for termination[1] where the latter is judicial, and putting it at the time of receipt of the creditor's notification where it is unilateral (articles 1158 and 1160-1);

– it is proposed that legislation should establish the consequences of termination of the contract, by providing in principle for termination for the future, except for the case of contracts of instantaneous performance where termination is to be retroactive (article 1160-1 and see Section 6 for the rules governing restitution);

– it is proposed to set a basis for the tailoring of the effects of termination according to the divisible character of performance of the contract (article 1160).

Restitution Following the Destruction of a Contract (articles 1161 to 1164-7)

Yves-Marie Serinet

The rules concerning restitution[2] after the retroactive destruction[3] of a contract resulting from its annulment or its termination are not at present the subject of any provision of their own in the Civil Code, excepting, of course, article 1312 of the Code as it stands concerning restitution following rescission of a contract for the defect of incapacity. And one must add at once that the formulation of this latter provision postdates 1804 as it is derived from the Law of 18 February 1938.

---

[1] [Technically, this time is *assignation*, ie the service of the formal document which sets out the purpose and legal grounds of the claim: New Code of Civil Procedure, article 55.]

[2] [The French term *restitution* has a fairly non-technical significance of a giving back (of money or property) and is used by extension to refer to recovery in kind of something which ought to have been returned but has not been. It is not, however, used (as it is often used by English or US lawyers) to refer to a *distinct* body of law ('the law of restitution') seen as the complementary third element within the law of obligations to contract and tort; but (as will appear from Serinet's discussion) it can refer to grounds of recovery which an English lawyer would see as 'restitutionary' (such as recovery of undue payments). For further discussion of this, see S Whittaker, 'The Law of Obligations' in Bell, Boyron and Whittaker, above, p 489, n 2, 417-23.]

[3] ['Destruction' might appear unusual to an English reader, but it translates *anéantissement*, a term which in French law encompasses the retroactive cancellation of a contract on different grounds, which have their own separate terms (annulment—*nullité* for defects in formation such as fraud or mistake; and retroactive termination—*résolution* for certain events of non-performance).]

La question des restitutions n'a pourtant pas été ignorée des codificateurs puisque, dans la réglementation de plusieurs autres institutions, on trouve des règles spéciales qui organisent la mise en œuvre de ce mécanisme. Tel est le cas, tout particulièrement, des dispositions du Code civil relatives à la répétition de l'indu auxquelles il est coutumier de renvoyer en la matière (articles 1376 et s. C. civ.), des règles qui déterminent les effets de la garantie contre l'éviction (articles 1630 et s.) dont on dit qu'elles fixent un régime dérogatoire de restitution, des textes applicables aux actions édiliciennes (articles 1644 et s. puisque ces actions sont, par nature, considérées comme ayant pour vocation d'organiser une restitution, ou encore du régime applicable au réméré (articles 1659 et s.) ou à la rescision de la vente pour cause de lésion (articles 1674 et s.), à cet égard encore significatif.

Dans la rédaction des projets de textes ici présentés, ces dispositions éparses du Code civil, pour la plupart inchangées depuis 1804, peuvent servir de source d'inspiration et de rédaction dans l'élaboration de nouveaux textes. Il ne semble pas, cependant, qu'elles soient directement transposables à la matière des restitutions après annulation ou résolution. Car leur esprit est soit trop particulariste s'agissant des règles relatives à certaines formes spéciales d'anéantissement dans la vente, soit trop différent, s'agissant des règles qui régissent les restitutions dans la répétition de l'indu.

Il a été démontré par d'importants travaux doctrinaux récents (c. *Guelfucci-Thibierge, Nullité, restitutions et responsabilités, thèse Paris l, préface de J. Ghestin, L.G. D.J., 1992 ; M. Malaurie, Les restitutions en droit civil, thèse Paris II, préface de G. Cornu, Paris, Cujas, 1991*) que la matière des restitutions *lato sensu* subit l'attraction de plusieurs branches du droit extérieures au droit des obligations (le droit des biens) ou, à l'intérieur du droit des obligations, de disciplines autres que le droit des contrats (droit de la responsabilité civile, quasi-contrats avec les théories de la répétition de l'indu et de l'enrichissement sans cause). Or, les finalités du droit des biens lorsqu'il traite de la théorie des fruits, des impenses ou de l'accession,

Even so, the issue of restitution was not unknown to the codifiers since special rules are found in the Code which organise the way in which it should operate in the rules surrounding several other legal doctrines. This is the case, in particular, as to the provisions of the Civil Code concerning recovery of undue payments to which it is customary to refer in this respect (articles 1376 *et seq.* of the Civil Code); of the rules which determine the effects of the guarantee against eviction (article 1630 *et seq.* of the Civil Code[1]) which are said to set out a regime which qualifies the normal position governing restitution; of those provisions which apply to a buyer's actions in respect of latent defects[2] (article 1644 *et seq.* of the Civil Code) since these actions are considered as naturally aimed at providing for restitution; or even of the set of rules governing a seller's option to repurchase (article 1659 *et seq.* of the Civil Code) or even more significant for this purpose, rescission of a contract of sale for gross undervalue (article 1674 *et seq.* of the Civil Code).

In drafting the proposed legislative provisions which are set out here, these sparse provisions in the Civil Code, which for the most part remain unchanged since 1804, can serve as a source of inspiration and of wording of the new provisions. However, it does not seem that they can be directly transposed to the context of restitution on annulment or termination of a contract.[3] For their way of thinking is either too specialised, as in the case of rules governing certain special kinds of termination of contracts of sale, or too different as in the case of the rules governing restitution in respect of undue payments.

Important recent work by scholars (cf. C. Guelfucci-Thibierge, *Nullité, restitutions et responsabilités*, doctoral thesis, University of Paris I, preface by J. Ghestin, (L.G.D.J., Paris 1992); M. Malaurie, *Les restitutions en droit civil*, doctoral thesis, University of Paris II, preface by G. Cornu, (Cujas, Paris 1991)) has shown that the area of restitution understood in a broad sense attracts the attention of several branches of law outside the law of obligations (*viz.* the law of property) or, within the law of obligations, of regulation other than by the law of contracts (*viz.* the law of civil liability, quasi-contract with its theories of recovery of undue payments and unjustified enrichment[4]). Now, the aims of the law of property in governing the theoretical basis of rights to fruits,[5] expenses incurred in maintaining another's

---

[1] [This 'guarantee' protects a buyer of property from defects in the title.]

[2] [These are sometimes (as in Serinet's text) termed the *actions édiliciennes*, this name evoking their historical origin in the edict of the ancient Roman magistrates, the curile aediles: see Thomas, *Textbook of Roman Law*, above, p 517, n 2, 287.]

[3] [As we have already noted (above, p 533, n 2) there appears to be a disharmony with the approach outlined here and the approach provided by article 1331 of the *Avant-projet* which provides simply that 'Restitution may take place where the debt which justified payment has subsequently been *annulled or retroactively terminated*, or loses its justification in any other way' (emphasis added).]

[4] ['Unjustified enrichment' (*enrichissement sans cause*) in French law does not form the legal foundation or general rationale for recovery on legal grounds (as for many scholars it does in English law as regards restitutionary recovery), but rather itself provides a distinct though potentially broad legal ground of recovery: on this see Bell, Boyron and Whittaker, above, p 465, n 3, 398-403.]

[5] [See articles 547 ff Cc.]

comme les finalités de la responsabilité civile quand elle définit les conditions de la réparation du préjudice, qu'il soit contractuel ou délictuel, ne sont pas celles des restitutions après annulation ou résolution rétroactives. Ce qui a d'ailleurs fait dire qu'il existerait une *summa divisio* entre les restitutions normales, celles qui interviennent dans l'usufruit, le prêt, voire le réméré ou la condition résolutoire, et les restitutions anormales, celles qui jouent pour la revendication, la nullité et la résolution, la répétition de l'indu ou le retour de l'absent. À ce premier clivage, vient s'en ajouter un autre. Il conduit à distinguer les restitutions intervenant dans le domaine contractuel, qui subissent à certains égards l'influence du contrat annulé ou résolu et imposent une réciprocité dans le retour à l'état antérieur lorsque l'exécution intermédiaire a été bilatérale, de celles qui interviennent hors le domaine contractuel qui présentent le plus souvent un caractère unilatéral.

Pour toutes ces raisons, il semble aujourd'hui opportun, sinon indispensable, de définir un régime cohérent propre aux seules restitutions consécutives à l'annulation ou la résolution, c'est-à-dire à l'anéantissement rétroactif du contrat.

Aussi cherchera-t-on ici à présenter des règles générales qui, synthétisant les propositions doctrinales les plus avancées ainsi que les solutions les mieux admises en jurisprudence ou susceptibles d'être recueillies dans les dispositions éparses du Code civil, répondent à la finalité commune objective d'un retour au *statu quo ante* qui soit le plus fidèle possible.

La nature broussailleuse de la matière devrait gagner en clarté à être ainsi retaillée selon les lignes classiques du jardin à la française.

Dans la perspective ainsi dessinée, il est proposé d'introduire la section 6 traitant de la matière (articles 1161 à 1164-7) par un article 1161 qui déterminerait, dès le seuil, le domaine d'application des règles nouvellement édictées. Une telle disposition liminaire permettrait en effet de définir la mesure dans laquelle les multiples hypothèses de restitution que le Code civil a déjà réglementées se trouvent soumises à ce corps de règles générales.

À la suite de quoi, le régime des restitutions après anéantissement du contrat se subdiviserait en trois paragraphes fixant respectivement les principes qui gouvernent la catégorie des restitutions après anéantissement du contrat, les

property[1] or property acquired through accession,[2] in common with the aims of civil liability, whether contractual or delictual, in defining the conditions of reparation for loss, are not the same as those of the rules governing restitution following annulment or retroactive termination of a contract. Moreover, it must be said that a *summa divisio* would be between normal restitution, which takes place in the context of usufruct, loan, and even where there is an option to repurchase or in the context of an 'express resolutory condition', and abnormal restitution, which occurs in the context of claims for one's own property,[3] nullity or termination of a contract, recovery of undue payments and recovery of property by a person presumed absent who reappears.[4] To this first division, another then follows on, as it leads to a distinction between restitution which takes place in a contractual context, which is affected in certain respects by the influence of the contract which has been annulled or terminated and which requires reciprocity in returning the parties to the *status quo ante* if both sides to the contract have meanwhile performed, and restitution which takes place outside the contractual context which is usually one-sided.

For all these reasons, it now seems appropriate, if not absolutely necessary, to set out a coherent legal regime solely to govern restitution following the annulment or termination, that is, on the retroactive destruction of a contract.

Furthermore, we shall seek in these proposals to put forward general rules which, by creating a synthesis of the most advanced proposals put forward by legal scholars together with the solutions most frequently reached by the case-law which are compatible with the sparse provisions of the Civil Code, answer the common and objective aim of returning the parties to the *status quo ante* as faithfully as possible.

In this way, the untidy undergrowth of the present law should be pruned and cleared, retrained according to the classical lines of a French garden.

Following this way of thinking, it is proposed that Section 6 which is to govern this area (articles 1161 to 1164-7) should be introduced by article 1161 which would at the outset determine the domain of application of the newly promulgated rules. This introductory provision could make clear the extent to which this new set of rules would govern the numerous cases of restitution which are already regulated by the Civil Code.

Following on from this, the legal regime applying to restitution following the destruction of a contract would be divided into three parts fixing respectively the principles which govern the category of restitution on destruction of a contract,

---

[1] [This phrase translates the French '*impenses*' by including an explanation drawn from arts 815–13 Cc.]

[2] [See art 546 Cc.]

[3] [This phrase translates *revendication*; and see arts 2279 and 2280 Cc.]

[4] [This situation is dealt with by articles 118 to 119 Cc.]

modalités de ces restitutions et les règlements complémentaires que l'on désigne parfois sous l'expression évocatrice de « *compte de restitution* ».

C'est ainsi que, dans un **premier paragraphe**, il est proposé d'adopter plusieurs textes énonçant les principes communs à ce type de restitution.

Dans une première disposition, l'article 1162, le mécanisme général des restitutions après anéantissement se trouve défini.

Quant à son domaine d'application, il semble rationnel que l'existence, la signification, et l'étendue d'un éventuel effet rétroactif soient fixées dans les sections traitant respectivement de la nullité et de la résolution. Ainsi, la fiction de la rétroactivité jouera-t-elle systématiquement pour l'annulation et de façon plus réduite pour la résolution puisqu'elle y est limitée aux contrats à exécution instantanée. Cette solution, pragmatique et conforme à la différence de nature des deux sanctions, paraît opportune. Ainsi s'explique que le texte évoque sans restriction les suites de l'annulation, toujours rétroactive, mais limite son application à la résolution aux seules hypothèses dans lesquelles elle produit cet effet.

Du point de vue de sa portée, la disposition pose le principe d'une restitution « *intégrale* », couramment admis, en vertu duquel chacun ne doit recevoir ni plus ni moins que ce qu'il avait fourni. La restitution doit être « *réciproque* » lorsque le contrat est synallagmatique. Il ne faudrait pourtant pas prendre au pied de la lettre l'image si suggestive du *contrat synallagmatique renversé* proposée par le doyen Carbonnier, car la restitution dépend surtout de ce qui a été exécuté, le cas échéant par chacun, durant la période intermédiaire. Ainsi, le calcul des restitutions n'est pas global mais analytique et suppose que l'on détermine, pour chaque obligation exécutée, la somme des avantages directs ou indirects reçus qui feront l'objet de la restitution. La réciprocité ne joue que dans la fusion de ces articles en compte et dans les éventuelles garanties que cela implique. En tout état de cause, la restitution s'impose également dans les contrats qui ne sont pas bilatéraux, ce qu'exprime la locution « *s'il y a lieu* ». Enfin, il est précisé que la restitution est emportée « *de plein droit* » par l'annulation ou la résolution rétroactive. Il s'agit d'insister sur le caractère automatique des restitutions et d'indiquer qu'il n'y a pas lieu de distinguer deux types d'actions et deux prétentions qui en seraient l'objet, l'anéantissement et la restitution, ce qui a une incidence sur le régime procédural applicable.

De façon tout aussi générale, le texte réserve en son deuxième alinéa la possibilité d'obtenir des dommages et intérêts aux conditions ordinaires de la responsabilité civile. Il tend ainsi à montrer que la restitution ne relève pas, précisément, de la même logique et n'obéit pas aux mêmes conditions puisqu'elle demeure un mécanisme strictement objectif.

the different forms which restitution may take and supplementary rules which are often designated by the evocative expression 'restitutionary accounting'.[1]

So, it is intended that the **first part** should contain several provisions which would announce the principles which are common to this type of restitution.

First, in article 1162 the general mechanism for restitution on destruction of a contract is defined.

As to its area of application, it seems logical that the existence, the significance and the extent of any retroactive effect should be fixed in the sections dealing with nullity and termination respectively. In this way, the fiction of retroactivity will come into play systematically on annulment, but only in a reduced way on termination as it is limited there to contracts of instantaneous performance. This solution appears appropriate as it is both practical and accurately reflects the different natures of the two sanctions. And this explains the fact that the provision sets out the consequences of annulment without any restrictions as it is always retroactive, but restricts its application to termination to those situations in which it has this effect.

From the point of view of its significance, article 1162 declares a principle of 'full restitution,' a principle which is already accepted and by which each person must receive neither more nor less than he earlier provided. Restitution must be 'reciprocal' where the contract is synallagmatic. However, the attractive metaphor of a 'reversed synallagmatic contract' suggested by *le doyen* Carbonnier[2] should not be taken too literally, as restitution depends above all on what one or both parties have performed during the intervening period. In this way, the quantum of restitutionary recovery is to be assessed analytically rather than at large and its theoretical basis is a calculation of the sum of all direct or indirect advantages received in respect of each obligation which has been performed, and this sum will form the basis of recovery. Reciprocal restitution arises only in the putting together of these various partial elements and subject to the guarantees which these imply. Be this as it may, restitution is imposed equally as regards contracts which are not bilateral, which explains the phrase 'where applicable' found in the first part of article 1162. Finally, it is made clear that restitution takes effect 'by operation of law' on annulment or retroactive termination of a contract. This emphasises the automatic character of restitution and indicates that there is no room for a distinction between two types of actions or claims of which it might be the object, one for destruction of the contract on the one hand and for restitution on the other: this has an effect on which rules of civil procedure are relevant.

In a really very general way, the wording of the second paragraph of article 1162 reserves to a claimant the possibility of obtaining damages subject to the ordinary conditions of civil liability. In this way it tends to show that restitution does not follow precisely the same logic and does not obey the same conditions as it remains a mechanism strictly detached from fault.

---

[1] [This phrase (which is not intended to evoke any technical common law mechanism such as the 'account of profits' found in *A-G v Blake* [2000] UKHL 45; [2001] 1 AC 268) translates '*compte de restitution*.']

[2] [See Carbonnier, *Droit civil*, vol 4 *Les Obligations*, above, p 507, n 1, no 107. For the honorific reference '*le doyen*', see above, p 505, n 4.]

Deux règles techniques, mais d'une importance pratique considérable, viennent ensuite consacrer des solutions dégagées par la jurisprudence (article 1162-1).

D'une part, il est prévu que l'obligation de restitution bénéficie du report des garanties qui auront été stipulées pour le paiement de l'obligation primitive. C'est la consécration d'une solution dégagée, en dehors de tout texte, à propos du cautionnement consenti pour garantir les remboursements des échéances d'un prêt. Puisque l'on admet depuis longtemps que la sûreté couvre la restitution des sommes prêtées lorsque le contrat est annulé.

D'autre part, la question de la prescription de l'obligation de restitution se trouve tranchée dans le sens d'un arrêt récent de la Cour de cassation qui a refusé d'appliquer, en ce cas, les règles de la répétition de l'indu *(Cass. civ. 1re, 24 septembre 2002 : Bull. civ. I, n° 218, p. 168)*. Il semble en effet naturel que les restitutions après anéantissement puisent à cet égard leur même régime dans les règles de la nullité ou de la résolution puisqu'elles en découlent de plein droit.

Puis, sont regroupées en un texte des propositions qui fixent, à plusieurs égards, le rôle du juge dans l'octroi des restitutions après anéantissement du contrat (article 1162-2).

Il semble tout d'abord légitime de donner au juge la possibilité de statuer d'office sur les restitutions puisque celles-ci sont virtuellement comprises dans la demande d'annulation ou de résolution comme étant l'un des effets de cette sanction *(V. en ce sens, Cass. civ. S, 29 janvier 2003 : pourvoi 01-03185, J.C.P. 2003, II, 10116)*. Au demeurant, on peut se demander si, dans les conclusions écrites, demander la nullité ne signifie pas au premier chef, dans l'esprit du plaideur, demander restitution. Quoiqu'il en soit, le texte ne va pas jusqu'à imposer au juge une obligation à cet égard qui aurait pu pourtant paraître logique. Il appartiendra donc aux parties de formaliser leurs demandes sur ce point, sauf au juge à décider de suppléer leur carence. Cela leur laisse également la possibilité de revenir devant lui ultérieurement pour le cas où la question n'aurait pas été tranchée. Ainsi s'explique, la disposition, naturelle au demeurant, du troisième alinéa qui rappelle l'interversion de la prescription découlant du jugement au profit de la prescription de droit commun. À défaut, le risque, très théorique, existerait que la demande de restitution se trouve rapidement prescrite alors que l'anéantissement aurait été prononcé.

After this come two rules which are technical but of a considerable practical importance and which are drawn from solutions adopted by the case-law (article 1162-1).

First, it is provided that an obligation of restitution benefits by extension from any security stipulated for performance of the original obligation. This marks the formal acceptance of the solution worked out in the absence of any legislative provision as regards contracts of guarantee concluded to cover the reimbursement of repayments of a loan. It has long been accepted that the security covers restitution of the sums borrowed if the contract is annulled.

Secondly, the issue of prescription of an obligation to make restitution is dealt with following the lead of a recent judgment of the Cour de cassation which refused to apply in the circumstances the rules applicable to recovery of undue payments (Cass civ. (1) 24 September 2002, Bull. civ. I, no. 218, p. 168).[1] It appears natural in fact in this respect that restitution following the destruction of a contract should draw on the same regime for its rules as regards nullity and retroactive termination as these both ensue by operation of law.

Following on from this come a group of proposals put together in one legal provision, which sets out the role of the court in a number of respects in awarding restitution after the destruction of a contract (article 1162-2).

From the first it seems legitimate to give to courts the possibility of deciding issues of restitution on their own initiative[2] since these issues are to all intents and purposes included within any claim for annulment or for termination of a contract as they form one of the consequences of these sanctions (see, in this sense, Cass civ. Sect. 29 January 2003, *pourvoi* 01-03185, JCP 2003.II.10116). All the same, it could be asked whether, in a written submission, a claim for nullity has the primary significance in the mind of the claimant of a claim for restitution. Be that as it may, the provision proposed (article 1162-2) does not go as far as to impose on courts an obligation here, even though this could appear to be logical. It is therefore for the parties to set out formally their claims in this respect, though a court may decide to make up for their failure to do so by ordering restitution on its own initiative. This also leaves the parties the possibility of returning to the court later if the question of restitution was not previously determined. This also explains the provision, which is a natural one, in the third paragraph which provides that a judgment of annulment or termination interrupts any existing prescription period and converts it into the thirty-year prescription period of the general law.[3] In the absence of such a provision, a risk—if only a theoretical one—would exist that a claim for restitution would run out of time very quickly after the pronouncement of the contract's destruction.

---

[1] [Recovery of undue payments is governed by articles 1386 to 1371 Cc.]

[2] [This translates '*d'office*': the traditional English expression is 'of its own motion' but this was replaced in modern English civil practice in 1998.]

[3] [This sentence paraphrases the French which uses the notion of '*l'interversion de la prescription*', a technical notion which refers both to the interruption of the normally applicable prescription period and its replacement by the thirty year prescription period found in article 2262 Cc. On this notion, see J Flour, J-L Aubert, Y Flour and E Savaux, *Les obligations*, vol 3 *Le rapport d'obligation* (2nd edn, Paris, Armand Colin, 2001) no 495 (though used in a different context).]

Quant au deuxième alinéa, il pose le principe d'un compte judiciaire de restitution dont les articles se compensent à la condition, bien sûr, que cette compensation soit techniquement possible puisqu'on ne saurait additionner ou soustraire que des choses de même nature.

Traditionnellement, le mécanisme de la restitution intégrale connaît deux limites qui se justifient par des considérations subjectives de moralité et d'équité. Elles méritent d'être maintenues comme des soupapes qui viennent tempérer la rigueur du principe.

À cet égard, la disposition de l'article 1162-3 exprime la transposition souhaitée de l'adage *Nemo auditur...* Il s'ensuit un élargissement de la portée du refus de restitution qui concernera toute contravention consciente à l'ordre public et aux bonnes mœurs là où, d'ordinaire, les seuls comportements immoraux se voyaient sanctionnés par la jurisprudence.

Quant à la mesure de sauvegarde instaurée en faveur de l'incapable (article 1312), elle subsiste mais à une place différente que lui réserve la nouvelle section du Code civil relative à la capacité des parties contractantes et au pouvoir d'agir au nom d'autrui (article 1117-5). Le texte ancien est repris sous réserve d'une très légère simplification dans la rédaction puisque le terme général d'« *incapable* » y remplace désormais ceux de « *mineur et majeur en tutelle* ». Si le maintien de cette protection se justifie en équité, sa spécificité explique qu'elle soit traitée avec les autres règles relatives à l'incapacité.

Dans un **deuxième paragraphe**, sont abordées les différentes **modalités de la restitution**.

Une première disposition (article 1163) énonce le principe qui commande la détermination des deux formes possibles de la restitution.

L'exécution d'une prestation contractuelle ouvre droit à une restitution en nature, soit à l'identique soit par équivalent. Lorsqu'elle est impossible, s'y substitue une restitution en valeur. Il y a donc deux modes de restitution. En sorte que l'impossibilité de restituer en nature ne doit plus jamais, mais la jurisprudence était en ce sens depuis longtemps, être considérée comme un obstacle à la restitution. Par ailleurs, il importait de relever que la restitution en nature peut elle-même avoir lieu sous deux formes qui dépendent de la nature de la chose à restituer. S'agissant des corps certains, elle se fait à l'identique. Pour les choses de genre, la maxime *Genera non pereunt* exprime l'idée qu'elle peut se faire par un équivalent de même nature (Ex. une tonne de sable pour une autre tonne de sable précédemment livrée).

Il apparaît ainsi que la forme de la restitution dépend prioritairement de la nature des prestations accomplies en exécution du contrat, ce que les articles suivants permettent d'illustrer. Subsidiairement, elle peut encore être affectée par les évènements qui sont intervenus durant la période intermédiaire qui a séparé l'accomplissement de la prestation à répéter de l'annulation ou de la résolution.

The second paragraph poses the principle of a judicial process of restitutionary accounting where restitution and counter-restitution are set-off against each other subject to the condition, of course, that this set-off is technically possible since one can only add or subtract things of the same nature.

Traditionally, giving practical effect to the principle of full restitution has two limitations, justified by subjective considerations of morality and of fairness. They deserve to be preserved as safety-valves which can temper the strictness of the principle.

In this respect, the terms of article 1162-3 give effect to the long-desired putting into law of the maxim *nemo auditur suam propriam turpitudinem allegans* ('A person who relies on his own wrong-doing shall not be given audience'). This reflects an enlargement of the ambit of denial of restitution which will apply to any knowing failure to conform to public policy or public morality in circumstances where usually at present only immoral behaviour is sanctioned by the courts.

The protection put in place for a person suffering from incapacity (article 1312 of the present Civil Code), remains, but elsewhere, being allocated a place in the new section of the Civil Code concerning the capacity of the contracting parties and the power to act in the name of another (article 1117-5). The long-standing wording of article 1312 is repeated except for a very slight simplification in the drafting as the general expression 'a person lacking capacity' in future will replace 'minor and adult subject to guardianship'. While maintaining this protection is justified as a matter of fairness, its particular characteristics explain why it should be treated with other rules governing incapacity.

The **second part** tackles the different **modalities of restitutionary recovery**.

The first provision (article 1163) declares the principle on the basis of which a court is to decide between the two possible forms of restitution.

The actual performance of the subject-matter of a contractual obligation gives rise to a right to restitution in kind, either to recover exactly the same thing or an equivalent substitute. Where restitution in kind is impossible, it is replaced with an obligation to make restitution of its value. There are therefore two kinds of restitution. In this way, the impossibility of making restitution in kind should never in future be considered as an obstacle to restitution, even though the case-law has actually taken this position for a long time. In other respects, it must be noted that restitution in kind can itself take place in one of two forms depending on the nature of the thing which is the object of restitution. As regards ascertained physical property, it takes effect by way of restitution of the very same property. As regards generic property, the maxim *genera non pereunt* ('generic property cannot perish') expresses the idea that restitution in kind can take effect by an equivalent of the same nature (for example, a ton of sand for another ton of sand previously delivered).

Thus it appears that the form of restitution depends primarily on the nature of subject-matter of the contractual obligations which have been performed, as the articles following article 1163 illustrate. Secondarily, it can also be affected by events which take place during the period between performance of the obligation in question and the annulment or retroactive termination of the contract.

Avec plus de détails, les articles 1163-1 à 1163-6 déclinent la proposition générale précédemment formulée.

Ainsi, lorsque l'obligation a été de faire ou de ne pas faire (article 1163-1), la restitution se réalise logiquement en valeur puisque telle est, alors, la seule forme possible de restitution. L'évaluation doit se faire sans tenir compte des stipulations du contrat. Toutefois, pour éviter qu'une même prestation ne bénéficie d'une double rémunération, il y a lieu de tenir compte des encaissements extérieurs déjà réalisés par celui qui l'a accomplie (Ex. dans les affaires de pompistes de marque, lorsque le pompiste a agi en qualité de mandataire et a déjà perçu des dividendes à la revente sur les produits) ou des avantages indirects qu'il en a retiré (Ex. dans un contrat d'apprentissage, la formation dispensée en plus du prix).

Quand l'obligation a été de donner une chose de genre, la restitution se fait par équivalent. Ce régime de restitution s'applique naturellement à l'obligation monétaire (article 1163-2). Le texte souligne que la monnaie est le bien fongible par essence et que le principe du nominalisme monétaire (article 1895 C. civ.), maintenu par la jurisprudence, s'applique. Mais l'article 1163-4 s'y réfère explicitement pour les autres choses de genre en l'assortissant néanmoins d'une option. Rien, pourtant, ne paraît interdire ici la restitution en nature sous forme d'équivalent. Mais sachant qu'elle peut s'avérer totalement inutile pour celui auquel on restitue, il semble naturel d'offrir à ce dernier un choix. Il est à noter que l'article 587 civ. prévoit un choix identique, en matière de quasi-usufruit, mais au bénéfice de celui qui rend la chose, à savoir l'usufruitier. La logique de la nullité et de la résolution conduit à renverser la règle sachant que, du fait de leur caractère fongible, il sera toujours possible pour le restituant de se procurer des choses équivalentes afin de satisfaire à son obligation.

Si l'obligation a été de donner un corps certain (article 1163-3), la restitution se fait en nature lorsque la chose existe encore entre les mains de celui qui l'a reçue. L'impossibilité d'une telle restitution « *naturelle* » n'interdit cependant pas toute forme de restitution. Celle-ci interviendra en valeur si la chose n'est plus individualisable du fait de sa destruction, sa transformation ou son incorporation. Dans le premier cas, une restitution complète doit être opérée que la destruction de la chose ait été fortuite ou résulte d'un acte volontaire de celui qui l'a reçue, ce qui correspond à la jurisprudence qui ne fait plus cette distinction et traite les deux situations à l'identique. Une telle solution est d'ailleurs conforme à l'idée que celui qui a détenu la chose pendant la période intermédiaire était le mieux placé pour l'assurer. Enfin, une dernière disposition envisage la situation où l'atteinte subie par le corps certain n'aura été que partielle. Une option est alors ouverte pour tenir compte de ce qu'une restitution partielle pourrait avoir perdu tout intérêt pour

Articles 1163-1 to 1163-6 draw out in more detail the significance of the general proposition which has already been stated in article 1163.

So, where the obligation in question was to do or not to do (article 1163-1), logically restitution is effected by transfer of its value as this is the only form of restitution which is possible. Its assessment must be made without taking account of the terms of the contract. Nevertheless, in order to avoid double recovery in respect of the same contractual performance, account may be taken of third-party benefits already received by the person who has performed (for example, in the case of tied petrol stations, where a petrol retailer acts as agent and has already received a commission on resale of the products) and of indirect advantages which have been drawn from it (for example, in a contract of apprenticeship, where training is received over and above the contractual agreed sum).

Where the obligation in question was to give generic property, restitution is effected by transferring equivalent property. This regime of restitution applies to monetary obligations by their nature (article 1163-2). The wording of this provision emphasises that money is fungible by its very essence and that the principle of the nominal value of money (found in article 1895 of the present Civil Code and maintained by the case-law), applies. But article 1163-4 refers to it explicitly as regards other generic property, though it nevertheless adds an option. ... However, there is no reason why in this type of case restitution in kind should take place by way of transfer of equivalent property, but given that this can turn out to be totally useless for the person who is claiming restitution, it seems natural to offer the latter a choice. It is to be noted that article 587 of the present Code provides an identical choice in the context of quasi-usufruct, but for the benefit of the person who restores the thing after use, that is to say, the usufructuary.[1] The logic of nullity and of retroactive termination of a contract leads to a reversal of the rule since a person who has benefited from performances of a fungible obligation will always be able to obtain an equivalent thing so as to fulfil his own restitutionary obligation.

Where the obligation in question was to give ascertained property (article 1163-3), restitution takes effect in kind if the thing still exists in the hands of its recipient. However, the impossibility of such a restitution *in natura* does not prevent all forms of restitution: there can be restitution of its value if the thing is no longer identifiable as a result of its destruction, its transformation or its incorporation into other property. In the first situation, restitution in full must be ordered whether the destruction of the thing was accidental or results from a voluntary act of the person who received it, this reflecting the case-law which no longer distinguishes between them two situations, treating them identically. Moreover, this solution fits with the idea that a person who holds a thing between performance of the primary contractual obligation and accrual of an obligation to make restitution is better placed to insure it. Finally, the last provision of article 1163-3 deals with the situation where any damage to ascertained property received is only partial. Here, an option is available to take account of the fact that partial restitution could be

---

[1] [Article 587 Cc concerns the situation where a usufruct includes property which cannot be used without being consumed (such as money, grain or liquor): the usufructuary may consume it, but on condition that he restores to the owner *either* things of the same quantity and quality *or* their value as at the time of making restitution.]

celui à qui l'on restitue. Dans ce cas, comme cela est prévu par de nombreux textes de droit spécial, il lui est permis de préférer la restitution intégrale en valeur.

À la suite de cet inventaire, l'article 1163-5 préconise l'adoption de deux dispositions complémentaires qui visent à simplifier le processus de retour au *statu quo ante* en évitant de recourir à la restitution en valeur. Tel est le cas lorsqu'il y a eu perte fortuite de la chose si elle était assurée ou perte imputable à un tiers. Tel est le cas, encore, lorsque la chose à restituer a été revendue. À chaque fois, la restitution en valeur paraît techniquement s'imposer. Mais il semble à la fois plus efficace et aussi juste de faire primer le jeu de la subrogation réelle à l'image de ce que prévoit l'article 1380 civ. pour la répétition de l'indu. Aussi la restitution se reportera-t-elle de plein droit, suivant les circonstances, sur l'indemnité ou le prix, voire sur la créance d'indemnité ou de prix.

Enfin, l'article 1163-6 définit la méthode d'évaluation des restitutions en valeur. En énonçant que le juge doit estimer la valeur de la chose au jour où il se prononce, suivant son état au jour du paiement de l'obligation, il fait application de la théorie de la dette de valeur. La solution est cohérente avec la manière dont seront indemnisées les plus et moins-values. Elle est également conforme avec le procédé d'évaluation de l'avantage qui a résulté de l'exécution d'une obligation de faire ou de ne pas faire (article 1163-1).

Le troisième paragraphe, détermine les règlements complémentaires qui, le cas échéant, s'ajoutent aux restitutions principales et composent le compte de restitution. Dans cette catégorie les sorts respectivement réservés aux accessoires, aux frais ainsi qu'aux plus-values et moins-values doivent être réglés.

S'agissant des accessoires, il est prévu que celui qui restitue soit comptable non seulement du principal de chaque obligation payée mais encore de ses accessoires du jour du paiement (article 1164). Contrairement au régime institué par les textes issus du droit des biens (article 549 civ. sur les fruits) ou traitant de la répétition de l'indu (article 1378 civ.), le caractère objectif des restitutions après anéantissement postule de tenir compte de tous les accessoires sans avoir égard à la bonne ou mauvaise foi des parties (c. *Guelfucci-Thibierge, Nullité, restitutions et responsabilités, th. préc., n° 802*). Celle-ci ne joue que pour une éventuelle indemnisation

pointless for the person to whom restitution is destined. In this situation, therefore, a claimant may opt to receive full restitution of its value instead, in keeping with a number of special legislative provisions to the same effect.

Following this series of provisions, article 1163-5 recommends the adoption of two complementary provisions which are aimed at simplifying the process of return of the parties to the *status quo ante* while at the same time avoiding recourse to restitution of value. A case in point would be where the thing which was lost through accident was insured or where its loss was attributable to a third party's action. A further case would be where the thing subject to restitution has been resold. In both situations, restitution of its value appears to be technically necessary, but it seems both more effective and fairer to see this as a case for the application of the doctrine of real subrogation,[1] reflecting the provision contained in article 1380 of the present Code as regards recovery of undue payments.[2] Furthermore, any compensation or price received (or to be received) in respect of a thing subject to an obligation of restitution will also be subject to restitution by operation of law.

Finally, article 1163-6 defines the method of assessment of awards of restitution of value. By stating that the court must assess the value of the thing as at the date of its decision according to its condition as at the date of satisfaction of the obligation by the claimant, it forms an application of the general doctrine of obligations of value. This approach is consistent with the way in which depreciation or appreciation of the thing is to be compensated and also conforms to the method of evaluation of the benefit which results from performance of an obligation to do or not to do (article 1163-1).

The third part sets out the rules for supplementary payments which in an appropriate case are to be added to the principal restitutionary recovery and which together make up a process of restitutionary accounting. It is here that the rules governing expenses incurred in relation to the thing to be restored, its accessories and its appreciation or depreciation in value are set out.

In the case of accessories, it is provided that a person who must make restitution is accountable not merely in respect of the principal subject-matter of any obligation performed for his benefit but also in respect of its accessories as at the date of satisfaction (article 1164). In contrast to the regime set up by the Code for the law of property (article 549 C. civ. concerning fruits) or dealing with recovery of undue payments (article 1378 C. civ.), the strict nature of restitution after destruction of a contract requires that account should be taken of all accessories of the thing in question, regardless of the good or bad faith of the parties (Cf. Guelfucci-Thibierge, *Nullité, restitutions et responsabilités, supra*, no. 802), which is relevant only to the

---

[1] [In French law, subrogation is 'real' where property acquired as a substitute for other property which is governed by a particular system of rights remains governed by that system of rights (or does so to a degree). It is recognised by the law only in certain cases: P Malaurie and L Aynès, *Les biens* (2nd edn, Paris, Defrénois, 2005) no 141.]

[2] [This article provides that where a person in good faith sells property which he has received unduly, he is liable to make restitution only of the price which he received for the property.]

complémentaire. Aussi convient-il de faire partir le calcul du jour de l'exécution du contrat (le « paiement » de chaque obligation) afin de déterminer l'avantage supplémentaire qui en est résulté. La règle *Lauxius vixit...* n'a pas à s'appliquer puisque de toute façon les dettes de revenus (fruits ou intérêts accumulés) se compenseront à hauteur de la plus forte des deux sommes dans les contrats synallagmatiques.

Naturellement, les accessoires varient selon la nature des prestations accomplies en exécution du contrat. Lorsqu'une somme d'argent doit être restituée (article 1164-1), ils comprendront les intérêts au taux légal, ce qui est une solution classique, mais encore les taxes acquittées sur le prix. On doit logiquement les comprendre comme celles-là seules qui auront été effectivement payées entre les mains de celui qui restitue le prix. Pour l'essentiel, la TVA se trouve ici visée lorsqu'elle a été en complément du prix. Il faudra ensuite, pour celui qui la restitue, la récupérer auprès du Trésor. Lorsque la restitution porte sur une chose autre qu'une somme d'argent (article 1164-2), les accessoires comprennent les fruits ou la jouissance procurée par cette chose. Il s'agit de revenir sur une solution adoptée récemment par la Cour de cassation *(Cass. ch. mixte, 9 juillet 2004 : D. 2004, p. 2175, note Ch. Tuaillon, J.C.P. 2004, I, 173)* après bien des hésitations *(Cass. civ. re, 11 mars 2003, Bull. civ., I, n° 74 et Cass. civ. 3e, 12 mars 2003, Bull. civ., III, n° 63, D. 2003, p. 2522)*. Contrairement à ce qui a été décidé afin, on peut le penser, de simplifier le calcul des restitutions complémentaires, il semble plus logique et équilibré de rembourser la jouissance du bien, quelle que soit la nature du contrat. Celle-ci s'analyse en effet comme un équivalent économique aux fruits qu'il aurait pu produire *(R. Wintgen, L'indemnité de jouissance en cas d'anéantissement rétroactif d'un contrat translatif, Defrénois 2004, article 3794-2, p. 692 et s.)*. D'ailleurs, lorsque la chose n'est pas frugifère, la Cour de cassation acceptait autrefois la compensation forfaitaire entre les intérêts et cette jouissance. En effet les intérêts correspondent à la fois à une rémunération pour la jouissance et la fructification de l'argent. Au surplus, la solution actuelle n'est pas en accord avec le principe de rétroactivité et l'idée qu'il convient d'anéantir tous les effets, directs ou indirects, de l'exécution du contrat.

possibility of supplementary compensation.[1] Also it is right to set the point of the calculation of their value as at the date of performance of the contract (the 'satisfaction' of each obligation) in order to determine any additional benefit which is derived from it. The maxim *lautius vixit non est lucupletior* ('a person who lives luxuriously does not become richer') is not to be applied in this context as in any event any debt relating to income from the thing (whether its fruits or any accumulated interest) will in synallagmatic contracts be set off at the level of the higher of the two sums.[2]

Of course, accessories vary according to the nature of the subject-matter of the contractual obligation which has been performed. Where a sum of money must be restored (article 1164-1), they consist of interest at the rate set by law (which is the standard solution) but also of any taxes paid in respect of the price. Logically one must include these only where they have been actually paid by the person who returns the price. In essence, the main concern here is VAT which has been paid on the price. Furthermore, it will be necessary for the person who has to make restitution in respect of such a payment to claim it back from the tax authorities. Where restitution concerns a thing other than a sum of money (article 1164-2), its accessories consist of its fruits or the enjoyment to which it has given rise. Here, it is proposed that the solution recently adopted by the Cour de cassation (Ch. mixte 9 July 2004, D 2004.2175 note C. Tuaillon, JCP 2004.I.173) after considerable earlier hesitation (Cass civ. (1) 11 March 2003, Bull. civ. I no. 74 and Cass civ. (3) 12 March 2003, Bull. civ. III no. 63, D 2004.2522) should not be followed. In contrast to what was most recently held, it could be thought that in the interest of simplifying the calculation of any supplementary restitution a more logical and balanced approach would require recovery in respect of enjoyment of the thing transferred whatever the nature of the contract. In practice this would consist of a financial equivalent of the fruits which it could have produced (R. Wintgen, *L'indemnité de jouissance en cas d'anéantissement rétroactif d'un contrat translatif*, Défrenois 2004, article 3794-2, p. 692 *et seq.*). Moreover, where the thing in question does not produce fruits, the Cour de cassation formerly used to impose a set-off at a fixed rate between interest payable on money sums to be returned and such an enjoyment. Indeed, interest corresponds both to remuneration for enjoyment of and the fruit to be garnered from money. Furthermore, the solution which is at present adopted by the Cour de cassation does not accord with the principle of the retroactive effects of annulment and termination and the idea that they destroy all the direct or indirect effects of performance of a contract.

[1] [This is the case because a person in bad faith will be at fault for the purposes of civil liability under the general law of delictual liability at present contained in articles 1382 to 1383 Cc.]

[2] [The maxim refers somewhat obliquely to the problem of following the logical nature of fruits so as to oblige a person who uses property to return not merely the property itself, but also its fruits when the period of his possession ceases: this logic would encourage a person to use up any fruits so as to avoid the risk of returning them, to the detriment of the management of the property. This logic is therefore avoided by French law, which recognises an 'amnesty' as regards the restoration of fruits for the benefit of a possessor in good faith. A possessor is 'in good faith' for these purposes where he possesses the property as its owner by virtue of a conveyance of property of whose defects he is unaware. See articles 549-550 Cc and Malaurie and Aynès, *Les biens*, above, p 581, n 1, no 516.]

S'agissant des frais, les textes reprennent une distinction doctrinale *(V. M. Malaurie, th. préc., p. 205)* proposée entre les frais occasionnés par le contrat (Ex. frais d'étude, frais d'acte, droits d'enregistrement, de publicité foncière, droits de mutation ou de consignation...) et les frais afférents à la chose dont on peut dire qu'ils sont engagés *intuitu rei* (Ex. frais d'assurance de la chose, charges relatives au bien...). Leur traitement est nettement différencié puisque le régime des premiers demeure clairement soumis aux règles de la responsabilité délictuelle (article 1163-3) tandis que celui des seconds, objectif, demeure dans le giron des restitutions (article 1163-4).

Reste la question des plus et moins-values. Il est proposé d'adopter des dispositions qui synthétisent les principes admis en la matière, quoique la jurisprudence ne soit pas toujours très claire ni fixée *(V. C. Guelfucci – Thibierge, Nullité, restitutions et responsabilités, th. préc., n° 808 et s. « M. Malaurie, th. préc., p. 215 et s.).*

Une règle commune d'évaluation au jour de la restitution est adoptée dans les deux cas (article 1164-6) qui est cohérente avec le mode de calcul précédemment énoncé pour la restitution intégrale en valeur. En ce qui concerne les plus-values, elles reviennent toutes à celui qui doit recevoir la restitution, l'équilibre patrimonial étant rétabli au moyen d'une indemnité qui va rémunérer l'augmentation de valeur ayant résulté du fait du restituant (article 1164-4). Du côté des moins-values, les choses sont rendues assez complexes par la nécessité de conjuguer deux idées différentes : d'une part, la nécessité d'une harmonie dans les régimes applicables à la perte totale fortuite et à la détérioration ou perte partielle ayant la même origine, puisqu'entre l'une et l'autre la différence n'est que de degré ; d'autre part, le souci d'une corrélation entre les différents types de plus et moins-values, lorsque du moins il est possible d'établir entre eux une relation de réciprocité. Or, les augmentations ou diminutions de valeur de la chose ont une origine variable (matérielle, juridique, économique ou monétaire), provenant parfois de celui qui restitue mais lui demeurant dans d'autres cas extérieures *(V. M. Malaurie, th. préc., p. 219 et s., et p. 237 et s.).* Compte tenu de ces éléments, il est proposé d'introduire un article 1164-5 qui dispose que celui qui doit restituer la chose répond des dégradations et détériorations qui en ont diminué la valeur ou entraîné sa perte, sans distinction d'origine. De la sorte, les hypothèses de détérioration fortuites suivront le sort de la perte totale de la chose qui impose, en ce cas, une restitution en valeur (article 1163-3). De même, l'usure normale du bien résultant de son utilisation sera indemnisée alors qu'aucune faute ne serait imputable au restituant. Les deux solutions sont en tout point conformes aux positions prises par la jurisprudence sur la question *(Cass. com., 21 juillet 1975, D. 1976, p. 582, note E. Agostini et P.*

As regards expenses, the provisions which are proposed pick up a suggested distinction found in scholarly writing (see Malaurie, *supra*, p. 205) between expenses incurred in relation to the contract itself (for example, the cost of any preliminary investigations, the cost of drawing up any legal document, of the necessary registration of rights, of publicity in relation to immovable property, of notarial impositions[1] or of the formal deposit of payment with a third party[2] etc.) and expenses incurred specifically in relation to the thing itself (for example, the cost of insuring the thing and any charges arising from it). Their treatment is very clearly differentiated as the regime governing the first category is clearly found in the rules of delictual liability (article 1163-3) whereas the second category where fault is irrelevant is brought under the aegis of the law governing restitution (article 1163-4).

There remains only the question of the increase or decrease in value of the thing. Here, it is proposed that provisions should be adopted which would synthesise the accepted principles in the area, even though the case-law is not always either clear or settled (see Guelfucci-Thibierge, *Nullité, restitutions et responsabilité, supra*, no. 808 *et seq.*; Malaurie, *supra*, p. 215 *et seq.*).

The same rule for assessment as at the date of making restitution is adopted for both situations (article 1164-6), a rule which is consistent with the method of calculation for cases of full restitution of value as previously noted. Any increase in value of the thing inures to the benefit of the person to whom it must be returned, though the relative position of the parties can be adjusted by means of an award of compensation where the increase in value results from an act of the person returning the thing (article 1164-4). In the case of decreases in value of the thing, the position is made quite complex by the need to marry two different ideas: on the one hand, the need for harmony of regimes applicable to cases of total accidental loss and to cases of accidental deterioration or partial loss, since the difference between the two is merely one of degree; on the other hand, the desire for a correlation between different types of increases or decreases in value, at least where it is possible to establish a reciprocal relationship between the two. Increases or decreases in value of the thing have a variety of causes (whether physical, legal, economic or monetary), often stemming from an act of the person who must return the thing, but in other cases arising from external circumstances (see M. Malaurie, *supra*, p. 219 *et seq.* and p. 237 *et seq.*). Taking these factors into account, a new article 1164-5 provides that a person who must make restitution of a thing is responsible for its being damaged or its deterioration where these have reduced its value or caused its loss, whatever their cause. In this way, cases of accidental deterioration would be treated in the same way as cases of total loss of the thing, where restitution of value is required (article 1163-3). Even so, normal wear and tear of the thing resulting from use are to be compensated even where no fault is attributable to the person who must return the thing. Both these solutions conform in every way to the positions taken by the case-law on the question (Com. 21 July

---

[1] [This translates '*droits de mutation*' which refer to all the taxes and impositions collected by a notary on behalf of the State and local authorities on the change of ownership of property.]

[2] [This is apparently the significance of the reference to '*consignation*', being an allusion to *offres réelles avec consignation* as provided for by articles 1257 to 1258 Cc.]

Diener, Cass. civ. 1ʳᵉ, 2 juin 1987, Bull. civ. nᵒ 183, Defrénois, 1988, art. 34202, nᵒ 13, p. 373, obs. J.-L. Aubert). À l'inverse, l'obsolescence de la chose faisant suite à l'écoulement du temps ne donnera pas lieu à restitution puisqu'il ne s'agit pas, à proprement parler, d'une dégradation ou détérioration de la chose, lesquelles ne s'entendent que d'une atteinte matérielle à son intégrité. La corrélation entre plus et moins-value est assurée puisque, dans les deux cas, celles qui ont une origine économique ou monétaire ne sont pas restituables. La seule différence concerne la prise en charge par le restituant des pertes partielles et dégradations fortuites qui ne trouvent pas leur contraire du côté des plus-values. Elle permet d'harmoniser les règles valant pour la perte totale et les moins-values fortuites.

Effet des conventions à l'égard des tiers
(art. 1165 à 1172-3)

Jean-Luc Aubert,
Pierre Leclercq

Dans un esprit de clarification et de modernisation, cette section rassemble en cinq paragraphes les différents éléments qui constituent la substance traditionnelle de la question de l'*effet obligatoire du contrat*, traditionnellement gouvernée par le principe dit de l'*effet relatif*.

Leur objet est donc de mieux définir la situation des tiers par rapport à la convention conclue par deux ou plusieurs personnes et de tenir compte des besoins révélés par la pratique contractuelle moderne. À cette fin, il est d'abord proposé de regrouper les différents aspects de la question, que le Code civil abordait de façon quelque peu dispersée. Ensuite, sur le fondement du travail réalisé par la jurisprudence et la doctrine, le projet invite à des dispositions plus nombreuses et plus explicites sur cette matière qui se trouve au cœur de la vie du contrat. Enfin, diverses innovations sont proposées pour combler diverses lacunes ou insuffisances du Code.

Le **premier paragraphe** énonce, sous l'intitulé « Dispositions générales » les deux principes qui commandent la matière, mettant en lumière la différence de portée de la convention au regard des parties contractantes, d'une part, et des tiers, d'autre part.

L'article 1165 affirme que « les conventions ne lient que les parties

1975, D 1976.582 note E. Agostini and P. Diener; Cass civ. (1) 2 June 1987, Bull. civ. no. 183, *Défrenois* 1988, art. 34202, no. 13, p. 373, obs. J.-L. Aubert). On the other hand, obsolescence of the thing subject to restitution which results from lapse of time does not give rise to any distinct restitutionary recovery, as properly speaking this does not involve either damage to or deterioration of the thing itself, as these both are understood to apply only to an alteration of its physical state. A proper correlation between increases and decreases in value is assured as in both cases those which have a economic or monetary origin are not the subject of restitution. The sole difference relates to the bearing of the cost by the person liable to make restitution of any partial loss of the thing or its accidental damage which find no counterpart as regards increases in value. This allows the rules governing total loss and accidental decreases in value to be harmonised.

The Effects of Contracts as regards Third Parties
(articles 1165 to 1172-3)

Jean-Luc Aubert,
Pierre Leclercq

Inspired by a concern to clarify and to modernise, this section brings together in five parts the different elements which constitute the traditional subject-matter relating to the question of the *obligational effects of contracts*, traditionally governed by the principle of their *'relative effect '*.[1]

The aim of these provisions is therefore to define better the position of third parties in relation to a contract concluded by two or more other persons and to take account of the clear needs of modern contractual practice. To do so, we first recommend that the different aspects of the position of contractual third parties should be rearranged, the Civil Code at present treating them in a rather scattered way. Secondly, the work of both the courts and legal writers leads us to recommend more numerous and more explicit provisions to govern an area which lies at the very heart of contracts. Finally, we put forward various changes to fill various gaps or inadequate treatments in the present Code.

Under the heading 'General provisions,' the **first part** sets out the two principles which govern this area, making very clear the difference in significance of a contract as regards the contracting parties on the one hand and as regards third parties on the other.

Article 1165 affirms that 'contracts bind only the contracting parties', thereby

---

[1] [For discussion of these provisions see Mazeaud, above, ch 10 and Vogenauer, above, ch 11.]

contractantes... », ce qui cantonne, sous réserve d'exceptions et de nuances qui seront précisées dans la suite des dispositions, l'effet obligatoire du contrat à ceux-là seuls qui le concluent.

L'article 1165-1 ajoute que « les conventions sont opposables aux tiers... », consacrant le principe d'*opposabilité* des contrats *erga omnes* qu'avaient dégagé peu à peu doctrine et jurisprudence. Le texte souligne le double sens de cette opposabilité qui joue tant à l'encontre des tiers qu'à leur profit, sous la réserve essentielle, à ce dernier égard, qu'ils ne peuvent exiger l'exécution du contrat, ce qui permet de distinguer de façon radicale l'effet obligatoire de l'opposabilité.

Le **deuxième paragraphe** précise, de façon innovante, les déplacements possibles de l'effet obligatoire du contrat de l'une des parties contractantes à un tiers, consacrant ainsi l'éventualité d'une *substitution de parties* au contrat.

C'est l'effet, classique, des transmissions à cause de mort (art 1165-2).

C'est aussi la conséquence, entre vifs, d'une *cession de la qualité de partie au contrat* dont il est proposé de consacrer expressément la possibilité, tout en la subordonnant à l'accord du cocontractant (art. 1165-3).

Cette exigence comporte cependant des *exceptions* : d'une part, elle n'a lieu de s'appliquer qu'autant que la loi ne dispose pas autrement ; d'autre part, elle est écartée dans le cas des contrats faisant partie d'une opération constitutive d'un ensemble indivisible (fusions de sociétés, apports partiels d'actifs...). Du moins le cocontractant qui n'a pas donné son accord au transfert du contrat reste-t-il alors en droit, sauf convention contraire, de se retirer du contrat transmis.

Le **troisième paragraphe** règle les différentes actions dont la loi ouvre le bénéfice aux tiers-créanciers d'un contractant. On y retrouve l'*action oblique* et l'*action paulienne*, mais aussi l'*action directe* dont il est ainsi proposé de consacrer expressément la notion et d'en marquer, du même coup, les limites.

restricting the obligational effect of contracts to only those who have made them, subject to the exceptions and qualifications which are set out in detail in the subsequent provisions.

Article [1165-2] adds that 'contracts may be invoked by and against third parties', thereby formally adopting the principle of the 'opposability' of contracts as against the whole world, a principle which has been worked out bit by bit by legal writers and the courts. The wording of this provision underlines the double significance of this notion of 'opposability' which applies as much against third parties as for their benefit, with the essential qualification as to the latter that they cannot require performance of the contract, thereby allowing the fundamental distinction between the obligational effect of contracts and their opposability.

The **second part** sets out in an innovative way the possibility of transfer of the obligational effects of a contract from one of the contracting parties to a third party, and so gives formal recognition to the possibility of *substitution of parties* to a contract.

The classic example of this may be found in the effect of transmissibility of contracts on death (article [1165-3]).

Assignment *inter vivos* of the status of being a party to a contract is a further example of this and it is proposed that this possibility should be expressly recognised, though it may take place only where the other party to the contract consents (article [1165-4]).

However, there are *exceptions* to this requirement, which is not to apply where legislation provides to the contrary nor where the contract in question forms part of an operation which sets up an indivisible collection of transactions (as in the case of mergers of companies,[1] or assets contributions, etc.). At all events, a party to a contract who has not agreed to the transfer of the contract by the other party retains the right to withdraw from the contract on transfer, subject to contrary agreement.

The **third part** regulates the different actions which legislation grants to third parties to a contract who are creditors of one of its parties. Here we find once again *actions obliques*[2] and *actions pauliennes*,[3] but also 'direct actions', a notion which it is therefore proposed should be expressly recognised and at the same time delineated.[4]

---

[1] [We have translated *sociétés* as 'companies' but it can include partnerships and other non-incorporated associations: see A Bell, 'Commercial Law' in Bell, Boyon and Whittaker, above, p 465, n 3, ch 11 at 463 ff.]

[2] [An *action oblique* is an action brought by a creditor of a party to a contract by which the former exercises the latter's contractual or other rights with a view to satisfying his own claim.]

[3] [These actions allow a creditor of a party to a contract to challenge any transaction made by the latter in fraud of the creditor's rights. The name derives from the Latin *actio Pauliana* which is post-classical Roman: WW Buckland, *A Textbook of Roman Law* (3rd edn, Cambridge University Press, 1963) 596.]

[4] [See below, p 591. For discussion in English of *actions directes* in French law, see S Whittaker 'Privity of Contract and the Law of Tort: The French Experience' (1995) 15 Oxford Journal of Legal Studies 327.]

Pour ce qui a trait aux deux premières, les textes proposés reprennent les différentes solutions élaborées par la jurisprudence sous deux importantes réserves. D'une part, dans le but de porter remède à la relative inefficacité de l'*action oblique*, l'article 1167-1, al. 1er permet aux créanciers qui ont agi de se faire payer par prélèvement sur les sommes qui, au résultat de leur recours, entrent dans le patrimoine du débiteur négligent. D'autre part, pour limiter la perturbation de la stabilité du contrat qu'elle engendre, l'*action paulienne* est enfermée dans un délai de deux ans à compter de la connaissance que les créanciers ont eu de la fraude commise par le débiteur.

Quant à l'*action directe*, la notion en est formellement affirmée en même temps que le principe de son assise purement légale (art. 1168, al. 1er). Toutefois, il est proposé d'admettre une telle action, en dehors des prévisions expresses de la loi et en considération du lien qui unit les contrats, « lorsqu'elle permet seule d'éviter l'appauvrissement injuste du créancier » (art. 1168, al. 2).

Le **quatrième paragraphe** traite du *porte*-fort et de la *stipulation pour autrui*.

Il s'agit ici, pour l'essentiel, de mettre en forme et en ordre les acquis de la jurisprudence qui, sur la base des articles 1120 et 1121, a fixé le régime de ces deux mécanismes.

Pour la *promesse de porte-fort* (art. 1170), c'est l'ensemble des effets de ce mécanisme qui est mis en lumière, avec les risques que court le porte-fort (al. 1er, qui reprend, en la précisant, la disposition de l'article 1120 du Code civil), et la perspective de sa libération totale s'il obtient ce qu'il a promis (al. 2). Le texte invite à consacrer l'obligation pour le tiers qui hérite du porte-fort d'exécuter l'engagement souscrit par son auteur (al. 3).

Quant à la *stipulation pour autrui*, c'est l'ensemble de la construction élaborée par la jurisprudence qui se trouve consacré. En particulier, l'article 1171-1 met en lumière le cœur de ce mécanisme : libre révocabilité de la stipulation tant qu'elle n'a pas été acceptée par le tiers (al. 1er) ; irrévocabilité de la stipulation dès que l'acceptation du tiers intervient avant la révocation (al. 2) ; droit direct du tiers contre le promettant pour l'exécution de l'engagement souscrit par celui-ci (al. 3). Parti a été pris, aussi, de mieux organiser certaines situations dont le règlement demeurait insatisfaisant. Ainsi l'article 1171-2 énonce-t-il, après avoir posé que la révocation peut émaner des héritiers du stipulant après son décès, que ceux-ci ne peuvent exercer ce droit de révocation que trois mois après avoir vainement mis en demeure le bénéficiaire d'accepter. Ainsi encore, l'article 1171-3 précise-t-il *in fine*, que l'acceptation peut émaner des héritiers du bénéficiaire après le décès de celui-ci (sauf stipulation contraire) et qu'elle « peut intervenir même après le décès du stipulant ou du promettant ».

As to the content of the two first of these, the articles which are proposed take up the different solutions worked out in the case-law with two important qualifications. On the one hand, article 1167-1 paragraph 1 is intended to remedy the relative ineffectiveness of *actions obliques* and therefore allows creditors who have brought proceedings of this kind to be paid out of the sums which have become part of the assets of the debtor in default as a result of their claim. On the other hand, in order to limit their disruptive effect on contractual certainty, *actions pauliennes* are be brought within two years of the date of knowledge by the creditors of the fraud committed by the debtor.

Finally, the concept of a 'direct action' is formally recognised, but it is expressly provided that direct actions arise only where legislation so provides (article 1168 paragraph 1). Nevertheless, it is proposed that such an action should be allowed even in the absence of any express legislative provision where there is a link uniting the contracts in question and 'where it is the sole means of avoiding the unjust impoverishment of a creditor' (article 1168 paragraph 2).

The **fourth part** deals with promises to stand as surety for another[1] and stipulations for the benefit of third parties.

Essentially, here it is a matter of putting into proper shape and order the accepted regimes which the case-law has established for these two doctrines on the basis of articles 1120 and 1121.

For promises to stand surety for another (article 1170), this involves clarifying all the effects of this doctrine, setting out the risks which the surety runs (paragraph 1 which picks up and adds detail to the proposition found at present in article 1120 of the Civil Code), and the prospect of his complete release if what he has promised occurs (paragraph 2). The provision proposes that formal recognition should be made of the obligation for a surety's heir to perform the undertaking which the surety took on (paragraph 3).

As to stipulations for the benefit of third parties, this involves the formal recognition of all the elaborate structure worked out by the case-law. In particular, article 1171-1 casts light on the core elements of the doctrine: the freedom to revoke the promise until it has been accepted by the third party (paragraph 1); the irrevocability of the promise as soon as it has been accepted before revocation (paragraph 2); and the direct right of the third party to obtain performance from the promisor of the undertaking which he has made (paragraph 3). Views have also been taken of a number of issues so as to organise the regulation of certain situations which is at present unsatisfactory. So, having stated that the heirs of a promisee may revoke the promise after the latter's death, article 1171-2 provides that such heirs can exercise this right of revocation only at the end of three months following their putting the third party on notice to accept the benefit of the promise to no effect. So too, the final part of article 1171-3 makes clear that (subject to contrary agreement) acceptance may be made by the heirs of the third party beneficiary of the contract after the latter's death and that it 'can take place even after the death of the promisee or the promisor.'

---

[1] [This phrase translates *porte-fort*, on which see above, p 545, n 1.]

Enfin, le **cinquième paragraphe** innove en consacrant la prise en compte de l'éventuelle interdépendance de plusieurs contrats réalisant un ensemble (art. 1172 à 1172-3).

Cette interdépendance est caractérisée par l'appartenance des contrats considérés à une même opération d'ensemble et par la nécessité de leur exécution pour la réalisation de celle-ci (art. 1172).

Il est proposé d'attacher à cette interdépendance un effet élargi de certaines des clauses figurant dans l'un ou l'autre des contrats interdépendants, en dépit de l'absence d'acceptation expresse de celles-ci par les autres contractants. Du moins faut-il que ces derniers en aient eu connaissance lors de leur engagement et qu'ils n'aient pas formulé de réserves. La présomption d'acceptation ainsi posée ne peut cependant s'appliquer qu'à certaines clauses limitativement énumérées : clauses relatives à la responsabilité, clauses compromissoires et clauses d'attribution de compétence (art. 1172-1).

Le projet ajoute deux précisions importantes :

D'abord, qu'en dehors des cas ainsi prévus l'extension de l'effet d'une clause stipulée dans l'un des contrats aux autres contrats de l'ensemble suppose que ladite clause ait été reproduite dans ceux-ci et acceptée (art. 1172-2).

Ensuite, que la nullité de l'un des contrats interdépendants autorise les parties aux autres contrats de l'ensemble à se prévaloir de la caducité de ceux-ci (art. 1172-3).

Obligations conditionnelles, à terme, alternatives et facultatives (art. 1173 à 1196)

Jean-Jacques Taisne

§1 – Des obligations conditionnelles

Le contentieux que suscite trop souvent le recours à la condition met en évidence les imperfections de la codification actuelle. L'abondance de certaines définitions, les éléments contradictoires qui s'y glissent parfois, nuisent à la clarté de notions essentielles et, si la prolixité caractérise certains développements, les textes font défaut sur d'autres points, sollicitant ainsi l'imagination de la jurisprudence. Pour ces raisons, deux préoccupations fondamentales doivent orienter le travail de refonte des textes. En premier lieu, le souci de la simplification ; en second lieu, le souci d'assurer aux parties une parfaite prévisibilité des conséquences du recours à la condition.

A priori ces deux objectifs appellent des méthodes différentes : le premier postulerait

Finally, the **fifth part** is innovative in that it gives formal recognition to the potential significance of the interdependence of two or more contracts making up a contractual grouping (articles 1172 to 1172-3).

This interdependence rests on membership of the contracts in question of a group devoted to the same overall operation and on a requirement that their performance contributes to its achievement (articles 1172).

It is proposed that the existence of such an interdependence would give certain contract terms contained in one or other of the interdependent contracts a wide effect, even if they are not expressly accepted by the other contracting parties, as long as the latter were aware of them at the time of their own undertaking and as long as they had not expressed any reservation in this respect. However, the presumption of acceptance which is established in this way applies only to certain contract terms which are set out in an exhaustive list: terms governing liability, arbitration clauses and choice of jurisdiction clauses (article [1172-2]).

The Reform Proposals add two important clarifications:

First, outside the situations specifically provided for in this way, the extension of the effect of a contract term contained in one of the contracts to other contracts in the grouping assumes that such a term was reproduced in the latter contracts and accepted by their parties (article [1172-1]).

Secondly, the nullity of one of the interdependent contracts authorises the parties to the other contracts in the group to treat them as lapsed (article 1172-3).

Conditional, Time-Delayed, Alternative and Discretionary Obligations (articles 1173 to 1196)

Jean-Jacques Taisne

§1 Conditional obligations

Disputes which arise all too often relating to conditions highlight the imperfections of the present codification. The multiplicity of certain definitions, and contradictory elements which sometimes creep in, do damage to the clarity of fundamental notions. Although certain developments are characterised by their wordiness, the legislative provisions are short on other points, leaving them to the imagination of the courts. For these reasons, two fundamental concerns have to guide the work of redrafting the legislative provisions. First, a concern to simplify them; and secondly, a concern to allow the parties to have a clear picture of the consequences of the use of a condition.

At first sight these two aims call for different methods: the first would require a

un élagage sérieux, le second à l'inverse une réglementation complète et minutieuse. Il est cependant possible d'atteindre un équilibre. Sur de nombreux points, la référence à la commune intention des parties permet de trancher toute difficulté et de conférer au régime de l'obligation conditionnelle la souplesse désirable. Mais il convient également, et à raison même du rôle reconnu à la volonté des parties, d'aider ces dernières à prendre une pleine conscience des points qui pourraient entre elles faire difficulté.

Le présent projet propose en premier lieu de supprimer des textes superflus : ainsi, conformément à l'opinion déjà défendue en 1946/1947 par la Commission de réforme du code civil :

– les textes relatifs à la classification des conditions casuelles, potestatives ou mixtes (art. 1169 à 1171), seul demeurant le texte prohibant la condition potestative de la part du débiteur, rédigé en harmonie avec l'article 944 par hypothèse non touché ;

– les textes relatifs au mode d'accomplissement des conditions positives ou négatives (art. 1176-1177) qui expriment des vérités d'évidence découlant de l'actuel article 1175 lui-même déduit de l'article 1156.

Il écarte de même du champ de la condition l'article 1184 qui depuis longtemps lui était devenu totalement étranger.

À l'inverse, le projet propose d'introduire dans la théorie générale de l'obligation conditionnelle les dispositions qui lui manquent. La Commission de réforme du code civil avait envisagé à cet égard des textes relatifs, après accomplissement de l'événement, au sort des actes d'administration ou des perceptions de fruits. Il convient de s'en inspirer. Tout autant il est utile d'y ajouter, à l'invitation de la jurisprudence, des textes consacrés à la renonciation à la condition.

En dernier lieu le projet suggère de compléter les textes actuels, soit pour préciser le régime d'une sanction (nullité de l'obligation sous condition potestative de la part du débiteur), soit pour généraliser à toutes les conditions l'obligation de loyauté qui

serious pruning, the second the opposite—a complete and detailed set of provisions. However, it is possible to achieve a balance. On numerous points, reference to the common intention of the parties allows us to resolve any difficulty and to give the regime of conditional obligations a desirable flexibility. But it is also necessary, for the very reason of the role which is attributed to the will of the parties, to assist the latter to obtain a full understanding of the points which could give rise to difficulty between them.

The present Proposals recommend first that superfluous provisions should be deleted—that is, in accordance with the idea already championed in 1946/1947 by the Commission for the Reform of the Civil Code:[1]

– the provisions concerning the classification of conditions which depend on chance, or are potestative, or mixed (articles 1169 to 1171)[2]; all that remains is the provision prohibiting a condition which is potestative on the part of the debtor, drafted in harmony with article 944[3] which is not, of course, altered;

– the provisions concerning the methods of satisfaction of positive or negative conditions (articles 1176-1177) which set out matters which are self-evident as a result of the present article 1175 (itself deduced from article 1156).

It also removes from the field of conditions article 1184, which has long been entirely alien to it.[4]

On the other hand, the Reform Proposals recommend the introduction into the general doctrine of conditional obligations of provisions which are presently missing. The Commission for the Reform of the Civil Code had contemplated in this respect provisions which, after the event has occurred, concern the fate of administrative measures or the taking of fruits. It is helpful to take inspiration from these. Moreover, it is useful to add, following the lead taken by the courts, provisions relating to the renunciation of a condition.

Finally, the Reform Proposals suggest making additions to the existing provisions, either to identify the remedial regime (nullity of an obligation which is dependent on a potestative condition on the part of the debtor); or to extend to all conditions

---

[1] [In 1945 the French Government appointed a Commission to prepare a revision of the Civil Code: decree no 45-1194 of 7 June 1945. The Commission produced a number of reports: *Travaux de la commission de réforme du Code civil* (Paris, Sirey, 1945-1957), but its proposals were not implemented.]

[2] [A ' (purely) potestative condition' is one which depends for its fulfilment on the will of one of the parties and renders the obligation a nullity: articles 1170, 1174 Cc. By contrast, a 'casual condition' (one which depends on chance as defined by article 1169 Cc), a 'mixed condition' (defined by article 1171 Cc as one which is dependent on the will of one of the parties and the will of a third party) and a 'simply potestative condition' (defined by legal scholars as one which depends for its fulfilment partly on the will of one of the parties and partly on an external event) do not invalidate the contract: on these see Nicholas, *The French Law of Contract*, above, p 489, n 2, 159 – 69.]

[3] [Article 944 provides that conditional *inter vivos* gifts are a nullity where the satisfaction of the condition depends solely on the will of the donor.]

[4] [Article 1184 Cc provides for *résolution* for contractual non-performance and rests on the implication of a 'resolutory condition' in all synallagmatic or bilateral contracts. The *Avant-projet* deals with *résolution* by its articles 1157 – 1160-1 which do not preserve reference to such an implied condition.]

n'est littéralement posée jusqu'ici que pour la condition suspensive, soit enfin pour faire apparaître, distincte de la condition résolutoire, une condition simplement extinctive, ce qui clarifie implicitement l'attribution controversée des risques dans les transferts sous condition résolutoire.

Sur un point particulier le projet tourne le dos au modèle laissé par la Commission de réforme du Code civil. L'abandon par elle du principe de rétroactivité de la condition suspensive accomplie, décidé à la suite d'un revirement, n'a pas emporté la conviction ; la rétroactivité se justifie à la fois sur un plan rationnel et sur un plan pratique et l'écarter oblige nécessairement à prévoir que durant l'incertitude le débiteur devra se comporter conformément à la bonne foi et sans rien faire qui porte atteinte aux intérêts de l'autre partie, formules que l'on peut trouver vagues et compliquées. Il est à noter que le code du Québec conserve la rétroactivité (art. 1506) et que toutes les législations ou propositions « européennes » contemporaines qui s'en écartent, la rétablissent tout de même sur volonté expresse des parties. Le présent projet procède en ordre inverse ; fidèle au droit actuel, il retient la rétroactivité, sauf à nuancer ses *effets* ou permettre aux parties de l'écarter si elles le jugent préférable.

§2 – Des obligations à terme

L'actuelle codification suscite peu de difficultés, mais paraît squelettique au regard des codifications plus récentes : Québec et surtout Liban. Il est donc proposé de faire apparaître expressément les notions de termes certain et incertain et de termes suspensif et extinctif.

§3 – Des obligations à plusieurs objets

Ici encore le code suscite peu de difficultés. Il est essentiellement proposé de le rédiger de façon plus actuelle et de faire apparaître l'obligation facultative.

Obligations solidaires et indivisibles (art. 1197 à 1217)

Pierre Catala

La matière des obligations plurales est celle à laquelle l'avant-projet apporte le moins d'atteinte : la plupart des articles du Code civil y sont conservés à la lettre ou

the obligation of loyalty which has hitherto been expressly set out only for suspensive conditions; or, finally, to create a new form of condition, distinct from resolutory conditions—conditions which are merely extinctive. This implicitly settles the disputed question of risk allocation in the case of a transfer made under a resolutory condition.

On one particular point the Reform Proposals reject the model bequeathed by the Commission for the Reform of the Civil Code. The Commission's giving up of the principle of retroactivity of satisfied suspensive conditions,[1] which was settled on following a change of opinion, has not been convincing; retroactivity is justified on both theoretical and practical grounds, and removing it inevitably requires a provision that during the period of uncertainty the debtor must behave in accordance with good faith and without doing anything which harms the interest of the other party—tests which may be uncertain and difficult to apply. It should be noted that the Quebec Code retains retroactivity (article 1506) and that all the present 'European' legislation or proposals for reform which remove it, still allow it to be restored if the parties expressly so provide. Our Reform Proposals take the opposite path; faithful to the present law, they retain retroactivity, but qualify its *effects*, or allow the parties to reject it altogether, if they think it preferable.

§2 Time-delayed obligations

The present Code gives rise to few difficulties, but seems rather skeletal by comparison with more recent codes: Quebec and, in particular, Libya. It is therefore proposed to make express provision for the notions of fixed and uncertain delay-points , and suspensive and extinctive delay-points.

§3 Obligations with more than one subject-matter

Here again the Code gives rise to few difficulties. In essence, it is proposed to draft it in a more contemporary style, and to make provision for discretionary obligations.

Joint and Several Obligations, and Indivisible Obligations
(articles 1197 to 1217)

Pierre Catala

The subject of plural obligations is the one which the Reform Proposals challenge the least: most of the articles of the Civil Code are preserved to the letter, or are

---

[1] [The retroactive effect of suspensive conditions once satisfied is provided by art 1179 Cc.]

s'y retrouvent en substance à travers des regroupements et des retouches rédactionnelles.

Dans le cas des obligations solidaires, rien n'est changé à la solidarité active. Quant à la solidarité passive, une seule proposition nouvelle apparaît à l'article 1211, sur laquelle l'interprétation pourra se fonder pour affiner l'analyse de la modalité.

Une autre innovation attendue tient à la disparition de l'obligation *in solidum* en matière de responsabilité civile. Son siège n'étant pas au titre des obligations conventionnelles, c'est l'article 1378 au sous-titre de la responsabilité civile qui consacre sa disparition.

Le seul débat important relatif aux obligations solidaires a porté sur les conditions de la solidarité. Une opinion fortement argumentée soutenait que la solidarité devait devenir le principe en matière civile, sauf convention contraire, entre les codébiteurs tenus d'une obligation commune (et de même activement entre créanciers).

On eût aligné de la sorte la loi civile sur la règle commerciale. Cette opinion n'a pas convaincu la majorité du groupe de travail, auquel il a semblé que les risques et les profits de ce renversement radical étaient mal mesurés et difficilement mesurables. Il paraissait en pleine dysharmonie avec l'esprit de protection du consommateur, que le Code civil n'est pas tenu d'épouser mais dont il doit tenir compte. On pouvait craindre de désagréables surprises pour les codébiteurs civils dont l'un serait admis au bénéfice des lois relatives au surendettement.

Cette réforme, au surplus, aurait créé une distorsion quant à la solidarité entre les codébiteurs et les cautions dans la perspective où celles-ci sont placées par l'article 2294 du projet de réforme des sûretés. En bref, l'opinion majoritaire a estimé que le maintien de la présomption actuelle poserait moins de problèmes que son inversion.

included again in substance with only some rearrangement and drafting amendments.

In the case of joint and several obligations, no changes are made to active solidarity (joint and several *creditors*). In relation to passive solidarity (joint and several *debtors*), just one new proposal appears in article 1211, which will form a basis for interpretation to refine the analysis of this modality.

Another long-awaited reform is the abolition of obligations *in solidum* in the case of civil liability. Their place is not in the section dealing with contractual obligations, and so it is article 1378, in the sub-section on civil liability, which deals with its abolition.[1]

The only significant debate regarding joint and several obligations has been about the conditions for their incidence. One forcefully-put argument was that, unless the parties contracted out of it, joint and several obligations should become the principle in the civil law between co-debtors liable for a common obligation (and similarly for joint and several creditors).

This would have had the result that the civil law legislation would be aligned with the rule in commercial law.[2] This argument did not convince the majority of the working group; they thought that the risks and the rewards of this radical reversal were not well calculated, and were difficult to calculate. It appeared to be quite out of harmony with the spirit of consumer protection which the Civil Code is not required to espouse but of which it should take account. One could imagine some unpleasant surprises for co-debtors under the civil law where one of them became subject to the laws protecting against excessive debts.[3]

Such a reform, moreover, would have created an imbalance as regards joint and several liability between co-debtors and sureties, given the position in which the latter are placed by article 2294 of the proposals to reform the law on sureties.[4] In short, the majority opinion was that to maintain the present presumption would give rise to fewer problems than its reversal.

---

[1] [For the distinction between obligations *in solidum* and *solidarité*, see p 861, n 1 on article 1378, below.]

[2] [The Cour de cassation has declared that 'joint and several liability [*la solidarité*] applies by operation of law to obligations of a commercial nature': Cass com 16 January 1990, JCP 1991 II 21748. For the place of commercial law (*droit commercial*) in French law, by contrast with the civil law (*droit civil*) see A Bell in Bell, Boyron and Whittaker, above, p 465, n 3, 453-61.]

[3] [The argument here concerns a situation where one debtor is released under the law governing excessive debts of individuals (*lois relatives au surendettement des particuliers*, found in article L 331-1 ff Code de la consommation), whereas other co-debtors (not released under this law) would remain jointly and severally liable.]

[4] [Proposals to add a new fourth book to the Code civil, in order to reform the law of sureties, were published in 2005 by a working group chaired by Professor Michel Grimaldi. These proposals included as draft article 2294 a provision that, in the absence of agreement to the contrary, a surety should be severally liable or jointly and severally liable (*solidaire*), depending on whether it arises under the civil law or commercial law. In 2006 a more modest reform of the Code civil was effected than had been proposed by the working group, and the provision on joint and several liability was not included: Ordinance no 2006-346 of 23 March 2006, made under the authority of the Law no 2005-842 of 26 July 2005, article 24.]

S'agissant des obligations indivisibles, il est apparu que le régime de l'obligation indivisible n'appelait aucun changement. En revanche l'obligation divisible n'est pas une modalité de l'obligation mais fait partie de sa nature lorsque l'indivisibilité n'est pas imposée par la force des choses, de la loi ou de la convention. On a donc supprimé le paragraphe du Code civil relatif à l'obligation divisible, la règle de l'actuel article 1220 étant reportée à l'article 1224-1 dans le chapitre du paiement.

Extinction des obligations (art. 1228 à 1250)

Jérôme François,
Rémy Libchaber

Le chapitre V du titre III du livre III du Code civil, consacré à l'extinction des obligations, se révèle globalement adapté aux besoins actuels. En règle générale, il aura suffi d'un toilettage davantage que d'une refonte.

La subrogation et la novation ont été écartées de ce chapitre, la première en raison de son effet purement translatif, la seconde en raison de son rapprochement prépondérant avec la notion d'opération sur créance. L'une et l'autre sont réglementées au chapitre suivant.

L'article 1218, qui est le texte d'annonce du chapitre V, écarte par ailleurs des institutions qui ne sont pas assimilables aux autres causes d'extinction de l'obligation. Il s'agit de la nullité, de la résolution, de la perte de la chose, de l'effet de la condition résolutoire, qui figurent actuellement à l'article 1234 du Code civil. Les autres causes d'extinction conservent leur validité, sous réserve d'aménagements de fond ou de forme.

SECTION 1 : DU PAIEMENT

Les dispositions relatives au paiement ont exigé une attention soutenue. L'éviction du paiement avec subrogation a nécessité une refonte du plan d'ensemble. Celui-ci comprend désormais quatre paragraphes. Après les dispositions générales (§1), trois autres paragraphes sont consacrés à l'imputation (§2), à la preuve (§3) et à la consignation avec offre de paiement et mise en demeure (§4).

Après avoir envisagé la notion de paiement, les dispositions générales (§1) évoquent les questions relatives aux personnes, à l'objet du paiement et à son régime.

Pour ce qui concerne la notion, le projet se contente de poser à l'article 1219 une définition générique et reprend ensuite à l'article 1220 l'actuel article 1235 relatif à la répétition de l'indu.

As regards indivisible obligations, it appeared that the regime for indivisible obligations did not call for any change. On the other hand, a divisible obligation is not a modality of obligation but is part of its very nature when indivisibility is not imposed by virtue of the subject-matter, legislation or contract. We have therefore deleted the paragraph of the Civil Code relating to divisible obligations; the rule which is at present contained in article 1220 is transferred to article 1224-1 in the chapter on satisfaction.

Extinction of Obligations (articles [1218] to 1250)

Jérôme François,
Rémy Libchaber

Chapter V of Title III of Book III of the Civil Code, which is devoted to the extinction of obligations, appears on the whole suitable for present requirements. As a general rule, it will be sufficient to tidy it up, rather than re-draft it.

Subrogation and novation have been removed from this chapter—the former because its effect is simply to effect a transfer, the latter because its close parallel with the idea of transactions relating to rights under obligations. These are both regulated by the provisions of the following chapter.

Article 1218, which is the headline provision of Chapter V, also excludes other legal institutions which cannot be likened to the other grounds of extinction of obligations—nullity, retroactive termination, loss of the thing, the effect of resolutory conditions—which appear at present in article 1234 of the Civil Code. The other grounds of extinction remain valid, although with some amendment relating to their substance or their form.

SECTION 1: SATISFACTION[1]

The provisions concerning satisfaction called for some attention throughout. The removal of satisfaction with subrogation necessitated a re-drafting of the whole structure, which now comprises four sections. After the general provisions (§ 1), three other sections are given over to allocation (§ 2), proof (§ 3), and deposit with a public depositary together with offer of satisfaction, and notice to perform (§ 4).

After discussing the notion of satisfaction, the general provisions (§ 1) raise questions concerning persons, the subject-matter of satisfaction and its regime.

As regards the notion, the Reform Proposals are limited to giving at article 1219 a generic definition, and then repeating at article 1220 the present article 1235 concerning the restitution of satisfaction that was rendered without being due.

---

[1] [For discussion of this translation of '*le paiement*' see above, p 442.]

Les innovations ne sont pas plus importantes pour ce qui concerne les personnes, excepté l'article 1222. Son premier alinéa synthétise la jurisprudence actuelle en insistant sur la bonne foi du débiteur. Le second réserve le paiement électronique, pour lequel il est requis du créancier qu'il garantisse la sécurité du mode de paiement proposé.

Quant à l'objet du paiement, le projet conserve dans ses articles 1223, 1224 et 1224-1 les dispositions des actuels articles 1243, 1244 et 1220 C. civ., à ceci près que la dation en paiement, dépourvue à ce jour de support textuel, est désormais définie à l'article 1223, al. 2.

Surtout, des règles spécifiques aux obligations monétaires ont été ajoutées. Ainsi, l'article 1225 consacre le principe du nominalisme monétaire. Celui-ci concerne en effet toutes les obligations libellées en monnaie alors qu'il n'est à ce jour prévu que dans des dispositions particulières (voir notamment l'article 1895 relatif au prêt). Mais le principe du nominalisme ne fait obstacle ni à l'indexation (dont le principe est rappelé à l'article 1225-1), ni à la dette de valeur (art. 1225-2), ni, bien évidemment, à la production d'intérêts et à leur éventuelle capitalisation (art. 1225-3 et 1225-4). En outre, un article nouveau (1226) a été créé concernant la monnaie de paiement, qui reprend les apports jurisprudentiels en la matière.

Enfin, s'agissant du régime du paiement (le lieu, la date, les délais de grâce, la qualité de la chose et les frais du paiement), les dispositions du Code civil actuel ont été largement reprises.

Le paragraphe 2 est consacré à l'imputation des paiements, laquelle a été rationalisée sans modification substantielle. Il est désormais distingué entre l'imputation d'un paiement partiel sur une dette unique (art. 1228) et l'imputation d'un paiement, total ou partiel, sur une pluralité de dettes (art. 1228-1 à 1230).

Le paragraphe 3 relatif à la preuve du paiement est nouveau dans la forme comme dans le fond. L'article 1231 consacre le principe de la preuve par tous moyens, qui s'impose comme la solution la plus raisonnable en pratique, surtout à l'égard des obligations monétaires. De plus, à cette règle de preuve, ont été réunies les présomptions de libération (art. 1232 et 1232-1) traitées dans le Code civil actuel au titre de la remise de dette, elle-même réformée par le projet (cf. ci-dessous).

SECTION 2 : DE LA REMISE DE DETTE

Les présomptions de libération du débiteur ayant été traitées avec la preuve (cf. ci-dessus), la perspective d'ensemble de la section a été revue. Après un article (1237) définissant la remise de dette et mettant en lumière son caractère conventionnel, ses effets sont réglementés. Il s'agit d'un simple toilettage des dispositions actuelles du Code civil, avec incorporation à l'article 1239-1, al. 2, de la règle jurisprudentielle relative à la remise de dette consentie au cofidéjusseur solidaire.

The innovations in relation to persons are no more significant either—except for article 1222. Its first paragraph synthesises the present case-law in requiring the good faith of the debtor. The second makes a special provision for satisfaction by electronic means, in requiring the creditor to guarantee the security of the proposed method of satisfaction.

As regards the subject-matter of satisfaction, the Reform Proposals retain in articles 1223, 1224 and 1224-1 the provisions of articles 1243, 1244 and 1220 of the present Civil Code, apart from the fact that delivery by way of satisfaction—which has hitherto had no textual authority—is now defined in article 1223, paragraph 2.

Moreover, specific rules relating to monetary obligations have been added. Article 1225 formally recognises the principle of payment of the numerical sum specified in the contract. This concerns all obligations worded in currency, whereas hitherto it has been dealt with only in particular provisions (see especially article 1895 in relation to the contract of loan). But the principle of payment of the numerical sum does not prevent the use of indexation (there is a reminder of the principle at article 1225-1); nor of a debt whose value is to be assessed (article 1225-2); nor, of course, of the charging of interest and its capitalisation (article 1225-3 and 1225-4). In addition, a new article (1226) has been drafted concerning the currency of payment, which takes up the contributions of the courts to this topic.

Finally, as regards the regime for satisfaction (place, time, grace periods, the quality of the thing and the costs of satisfaction), the provisions of the present Civil Code have largely been repeated.

Section 2 is dedicated to the allocation of payments, which has been rationalised without significant amendment. There is now a distinction between the allocation of the partial payment of a single debt (art. 1228) and the allocation of payment (in full or in part) in respect of more than one debt (articles 1228-1 to 1230).

Section 3, dealing with proof of satisfaction is new both in form and in substance. Article 1231 formally recognises the principle of proof by all forms of evidence, which is used because it is the most sensible rule in practice, especially with regard to monetary obligations. Moreover, alongside this rule of proof have been set the presumptions of release (articles 1232 and 1232-1) which are dealt with in the present Civil Code under the heading of release of an obligation—which is also reformed by our Proposals (see below).

SECTION 2: RELEASE OF AN OBLIGATION

The presumptions of the release of the debtor have been dealt with alongside proof (cf. above), and so the overall arrangement of the section has been reviewed. After an article (1237) defining the release of a debt and highlighting its contractual character, rules are set out for its effects. This is just a tidying-up of the present provisions of the Civil Code, incorporating in article 1239-1, paragraph 2, the rule devised by the courts relating to the release which is granted to a joint and several co-surety.

SECTION 3 : DE LA COMPENSATION

Cette section a été entièrement repensée, avec une subdivision interne entre la compensation en général (§1) et celle des dettes connexes (§2).

Concernant la compensation en général (§I), les diverses modalités développées par la jurisprudence sur la base des dispositions insuffisantes du Code civil ont été introduites avec leur régime juridique propre. Sont désormais distinguées les compensations légale, judiciaire et conventionnelle.

Dans le cas de la compensation légale, les règles du Code civil ont été reprises dans leur ensemble. Toutefois, la déclaration figurant actuellement à l'art. 1290 C. civ., aux termes de laquelle la compensation s'opère de plein droit, a été écartée comme résultant d'une erreur de rédaction dénoncée depuis longtemps. De ce fait, l'art. 1243 du projet adopte une nouvelle rédaction adaptée aux besoins du commerce juridique.

Quant à la compensation judiciaire, qui n'a qu'une assise indirecte dans le Nouveau Code de procédure civile (art. 70, al. 2, et 564), elle fait son entrée dans le Code civil. A ce titre, les art. 1246 et 1246-1 du projet en définissent la notion et le régime, sur la base des règles jurisprudentielles actuelles.

Enfin, la possibilité de compenser conventionnellement, en dehors des conditions légales, est prévue par l'art. 1247.

À cette typologie distinguant entre ces trois compensations, est ajoutée une modalité particulière et autonome de compensation, celle des dettes connexes (§II). Dans ce cas, la compensation, de quelque nature qu'elle soit (légale, judiciaire ou conventionnelle), peut produire ses effets en dehors des conditions posées au paragraphe I. Ce régime d'exception, très important en pratique, est désormais précisé aux articles 1248 et 1248-1, lesquels codifient les apports de la jurisprudence moderne.

SECTION 4 : DE LA CONFUSION

Les articles 1249 et 1249-1 reprennent les dispositions des actuels articles 1300 et 1301, à un mot près. S'agissant des effets de la confusion, l'article 1249 prend le parti d'affirmer le caractère définitif de l'extinction opérée par la confusion, alors que la jurisprudence arbitre parfois en faveur d'une simple paralysie. La rédaction proposée renoue avec l'intention du codificateur de 1804, qui avait rangé la confusion parmi les causes d'extinction de l'obligation.

SECTION 3: SET-OFF

This section has been completely re-thought, with an internal sub-division between set-off in general (§1), and set-off of connected debts (§2).

In relation to set-off in general (§1), the various forms developed by the courts on the basis of the inadequate provisions of the Code Civil have been introduced within their own legal regime. Distinctions are now made between set-off by law, by order of the court, and by contract.

In the case of set-off by law, the rules of the Civil Code have been taken up in their entirety. However, the declaration which appears in article 1290 of the present Civil Code, to the effect that set-off operates by operation of law, has been removed, on the basis that it results from a drafting error which has long been criticised. Therefore, article 1243 of the Reform Proposals adopts a new form of wording, suited to the needs of the legal industry.

Set-off by order of the court, which has only an indirect basis in the New Code of Civil Procedure (articles 70, paragraph 2, and 564), makes its appearance in the Civil Code. In this respect, articles 1246 and 1246-1 of the Reform Proposals define its notion and its regime, on the basis of the rules which are today established in the case-law.

Finally, the possibility of set-off by contract, outside the circumstances prescribed by legislation, is provided for at article 1247.

To this classification, which distinguishes between these three forms of set-off, is added a particular and separate form of set-off: set-off of connected debts (§2). In this case, set-off, of whatever nature (by operation of law, by order of the court, or by contract) may have effects beyond the circumstances set out in section I. This exceptional regime, very important in practice, is now set out in articles 1248 and 1248-1, which codify the modern judicial developments.

SECTION 4: MERGER

Articles 1249 and [1250] take up the provisions of articles 1300 and 1301 of the present Code, almost to the word. Dealing with the effects of merger, article 1249 takes the position of affirming the absolute character of the extinction effected by merger, whereas the courts sometimes deliver judgments in favour of its simple paralysis. The proposed form takes up again the intention of the draftsman of the 1804 code, who placed merger amongst the grounds of extinction of an obligation.

De la consignation avec offre de paiement
(art. 1233 à 1236)

Philippe Théry

Même s'il est rare qu'un créancier refuse le paiement qui lui est dû, le code doit permettre un paiement forcé à l'initiative du débiteur qui entend se libérer. Cette procédure est organisée autour des idées suivantes :

● Puisque la procédure peut mener à la libération du débiteur, il faut assurer le sérieux de l'offre de paiement en imposant au débiteur de consigner la chose due, de sorte que le créancier puisse la retirer sans formalité particulière.

● La libération du débiteur est acquise si le créancier, ayant eu connaissance de l'offre, ne l'a pas contestée. S'il n'est pas certain que l'offre est connue du créancier, la libération du débiteur passer par un contrôle du juge.

● Les textes distinguent selon la nature de la chose consignée. Lorsqu'il s'agit d'autres biens qu'une somme d'argent, ils pourront, en l'absence de retrait dans un délai raisonnable, être vendus à l'initiative du débiteur et leur prix consigné au profit du créancier.

● Enfin, il a paru équitable d'écarter la règle selon laquelle la reconnaissance de la dette interrompt la prescription. Il en résulte notamment que le débiteur pourra se faire restituer la chose consignée si le créancier a laissé s'écouler le délai de prescription.

Opérations sur créances
(art. 1251 à 1282)

Hervé Synvet

Le chapitre VI du projet de réforme est profondément neuf.

En la forme il regroupe, pour la première fois, des opérations jusqu'à présent dispersées : la cession de créance est traitée dans le Code civil actuel comme une variété de vente (art. 1689 et s.) ; la subrogation personnelle est rattachée au paiement (art. 1249 et s.) ; la novation est envisagée comme un mode d'extinction

Deposit With a Public Depositary Together With an Offer of Satisfaction
(articles 1233 to 1236)

Philippe Théry

Although a creditor will rarely refuse to accept satisfaction which is owed to him, the Code must permit enforced satisfaction on the initiative of the debtor who intends to discharge himself. This procedure is constructed around the following ideas:

• Since the procedure may lead to the discharge of the debtor, it is important to ensure that the tender of satisfaction is serious, by requiring the debtor to deposit what is due, so that the creditor may take it without any particular formality.

• Discharge of the debtor is effected if the creditor, having known about the offer, does not challenge it. If it is not certain whether the offer was known about by the creditor, the discharge of the debtor must go before the court for assessment.

• The provisions draw a distinction according to the nature of the thing that is deposited. Property, other than a sum of money, if it is not taken within a reasonable period, may be sold on the initiative of the debtor and the price paid deposited to the account of the creditor.

• Finally, it seemed fair to abandon the rule under which acknowledgment of a debt interrupts the running of time for the purpose of prescription. The main consequence is that the debtor may require restitution of what he has deposited if the creditor has allowed the full prescription period to elapse.

Transactions Relating to Rights Under Obligations
(articles 1251 to 1282)

Hervé Synvet

Chapter VI of the Reform Proposals is fundamentally new.

In its arrangement, it brings together for the first time transactions which have hitherto been scattered: assignment is treated in the present Civil Code as a kind of sale (articles 1689 *et seq.*); personal subrogation is joined with satisfaction (articles 1249 *et seq.*); novation is seen as a method by which obligations are extinguished

des obligations (art. 1271 et s.) ; la délégation est simplement évoquée, au détour des dispositions consacrées à la novation (art. 1275 et 1276). Or, considérées sous l'angle économique, ces opérations entretiennent des liens de parenté étroits : la créance y est considérée comme un élément d'actif, appelé à circuler ou à constituer la base de la création de nouveaux rapports d'obligation. Dans un Code civil rénové, il y a donc lieu d'organiser, de façon plus homogène, le commerce juridique des créances.

Au fond, le régime des quatre opérations évoquées est aujourd'hui marqué par l'obsolescence, ou pèche par insuffisance de précision. La circulation des créances constitue une partie non négligeable de l'économie moderne. Elle relève de l'activité quotidienne des professionnels de l'argent et du crédit. Ceux-ci ont un besoin impératif d'efficacité, de sécurité et de rapidité. Force est de reconnaître que les textes du Code civil présentent aujourd'hui, sous ce rapport, de préoccupantes insuffisances. En réponse, des régimes particuliers ont été mis en place, dans des lois spéciales puis dans d'autres codes. Si l'on souhaite que le Code civil ne devienne pas le conservatoire d'un répertoire ancien, mais constitue la base légale du commerce juridique en matière de créances, il faut proposer une rénovation profonde des solutions. C'est ce qui a été fait dans le présent projet.

S'agissant de la cession de créance, elle est conçue, non plus comme une variété de vente, mais, de façon plus abstraite et générale, comme « *une convention par laquelle le créancier, cédant, transmet tout ou partie de sa créance à un tiers cessionnaire* » (art. 1251). Tout acte à titre particulier est propre à cette fin. Cette définition, large, permet d'accueillir, sans difficulté, la cession à titre de garantie (art. 1257-1). Innovation majeure, qui permettrait au droit français de combler le retard qu'il a malheureusement pris par rapport à plusieurs de ses homologues européens.

Un deuxième élément de modernisation est la consécration de la possibilité de céder des créances futures (« *à naître* », dit l'article 1252 : peu importe, par exemple, que le contrat dont procédera la créance ne soit pas encore conclu, ni même en projet, au moment de la cession). Et l'efficacité de l'opération est encouragée par l'indication qu'il suffit que l'acte de cession comporte les éléments permettant, **le moment venu**, l'identification de la créance cédée (art. 1252). Ce sont ainsi les « flux de créances » dont la transmission pourra désormais être organisée, avec une bonne sécurité juridique, sous l'empire du Code civil.

La troisième nouveauté est l'abandon du trop célèbre article 1690. L'exigence d'une notification par acte extrajudiciaire (ou son substitut qu'est l'acceptation du débiteur dans un acte authentique) constituait une formalité lourde et, souvent, décourageante. Le système proposé est profondément différent. Il repose sur une règle de forme (« *à peine de nullité, la cession de créance doit être constatée par écrit* » : art. 1253) et une distinction. Aussi bien dans les rapports entre les parties qu'à l'égard des tiers, la transmission de la créance est acquise dès la conclusion de

(articles 1271 *et seq.*); delegation is simply mentioned in the course of the provisions dealing with novation (articles 1275 and 1276). Viewed from an economic perspective, however, these transactions are very closely related: in each, the right under an obligation is seen as an asset, given circulation or constituting the basis for the creation of new obligations. In a renewed Civil Code it is therefore appropriate to organise, in a more consistent way, the dealings recognised by the law in relation to rights under obligations.

In essence, the regime of the four transactions which have been mentioned is today marked by obsolescence, or is weak because of a lack of clarity. Dealing in rights under obligations constitutes a not insignificant part of the modern economy. It forms the daily activity of financiers and credit houses. These have a pressing need for effectiveness, security and speed. We have to recognise that the provisions of the Civil Code today are worryingly inadequate in this regard. As a response to this, particular regimes have been put in place, in special legislation and in other codes. If we want to avoid the Civil Code becoming the repository of outdated lists of rules, rather than forming the legal basis of the dealings recognised by the law in relation to rights under obligations, we have to propose a fundamental renewal of the solutions. This is what has been done in these Proposals.

Assignment is seen no longer as a kind of sale but, in a more abstract and general form, as 'a contract by which the creditor (the assignor) transfers the whole or part of his rights under an obligation to a third party (the assignee)' (article 1251). Any transaction by an individual may be used to achieve this. This definition, wide as it is, allows the inclusion, without any difficulty, of an assignment by way of guarantee (article 1257-1). This is a significant reform, which would allow French law to reverse its backwardness which has unfortunately developed in comparison with several of its European counterparts.

A second element of modernisation is the formal acceptance of the possibility of assigning future rights (those 'yet to come into existence', says article 1252; it therefore does not matter, for example, that the contract which will give rise to the right has not yet been concluded, and is not even in draft, at the moment of the assignment). And the effectiveness of the transaction is encouraged by saying that it is sufficient that the instrument of assignment contains the details enabling the assigned right to be identified **when the time comes** (article 1252). And so the transfer of 'debt flow' may now be effected with clear legal certainty under the Civil Code.

The third novelty is the abandonment of the infamous article 1690.[1] The requirement of notification by an extrajudicial instrument (or its substitute, the acceptance by the debtor in a publicly authenticated instrument) constituted a burdensome—and often discouraging—formality. The proposed scheme is fundamentally different. It rests on a rule of formality ('On pain of nullity, an assignment must be effected in writing': article 1253) and a distinction. As between the parties, as much as in relation to third parties, the transfer of a right under an obligation is

---

[1] [Article 1690 provides that the assignee acquires rights enforceable against third parties only by notice of the assignment given to the debtor, or by an acceptance of the assignment made by the debtor in an authenticated instrument.]

l'acte (art. 1254). Les formalités à fin d'opposabilité disparaissent. Une règle de preuve, relative à la date de l'acte (art. 1254, al. 2) permet de conjurer le risque d'antidate. En revanche, s'agissant de l'opposabilité de l'opération au débiteur cédé, une notification écrite (mais sans intervention nécessaire d'un officier public) est exigée : il faut que le débiteur sache, sans ambiguïté, entre les mains de qui il doit payer.

Si l'on ajoute à cela que l'article 1257 règle de façon précise la question, souvent contentieuse, de l'opposabilité des exceptions, il est permis de penser que le nouveau régime de la cession de créance répond aux besoins de ses utilisateurs et fera revenir dans le giron du droit commun des opérations qui l'avaient quitté.

Dans ses dispositions relatives à la subrogation personnelle, le projet de réforme constitue largement une œuvre de consolidation. Consolidation quant à la fonction de la subrogation : celle-ci est devenue un mécanisme de transmission des créances, concurrent de la cession, ce qui justifie le transfert de la matière de la section consacrée au paiement vers ce nouveau chapitre embrassant l'ensemble des opérations sur créances. La définition maintient toutefois le lien avec la tradition, en soulignant que la subrogation se produit au profit de celui qui paye (art. 1258). Consolidation également quant au régime : les cas de subrogation légale sont conservés à l'identique, même si l'ordre est modifié pour tenir compte de leur importance pratique respective (art. 1259) ; l'exigence de concomitance entre la subrogation et le paiement est assouplie, selon les chemins déjà tracés par la jurisprudence (art. 1260, al. 3) ; l'effet translatif est accusé, à la fois dans son étendue (créance et accessoires) et quant à l'opposabilité aux tiers (dispensée de formalité, y compris lorsqu'est en cause l'opposabilité du transfert des sûretés qui accompagnent la créance).

Le neuf concerne la subrogation « *ex parte debitoris* ». Tout d'abord, l'article 1261, al. 1er, du projet renverse la jurisprudence classique selon laquelle la subrogation ne se produit que si le paiement est fait par le subrogé lui-même, et non si le débiteur emprunte pour payer sa dette à un créancier disposé à délivrer une quittance précisant l'origine des deniers. Ensuite, le second alinéa du même article tranche la question, discutée, des conditions auxquelles le débiteur peut imposer la subrogation au profit d'un nouveau prêteur, appelé à « refinancer » l'opération (à un taux naturellement plus favorable). Le respect de la force obligatoire des conventions a fourni le critère : encore faut-il, pour que le débiteur puisse subroger seul, que la dette soit échue ou que le terme soit en sa faveur.

La novation reçoit une définition qui, jusqu'à présent, lui faisait défaut. C'est « *une convention qui a pour objet de substituer à une obligation qu'elle éteint, une obligation différente qu'elle crée* » (art 1265). Est ainsi mis en lumière l'effet substitutif de l'opération, qui s'oppose à l'effet translatif de la cession de créance et de la subrogation personnelle. Est également soulignée la nécessité d'une différence

effected at the moment that the instrument is executed (article 1254). The formalities with a view to enforceability against different persons are removed. One rule of proof, relating to the date of the instrument (article 1254, paragraph 2) allows the risk of antedating to be avoided. On the other hand, relying on the transaction against the debtor requires written notification (but without any requirement for a public official to become involved): the debtor must know, without any ambiguity, towards whom he must satisfy his obligation.

If one adds to this that article 1257 deals in precise terms with the often disputed question of the raising of defences, we may think that the new regime for assignment responds to the needs of users, and brings back into the fold of the general principles of the law some transactions which had abandoned it.

In the provisions dealing with personal subrogation, the Reform Proposals constitute, on the whole, a work of consolidation. Consolidation in relation to the function of subrogation: it has become a mechanism for the transfer of rights under obligations, alongside assignment, which justifies the transposition of the subject-matter from the section dealing with satisfaction to this new chapter which embraces all transactions in the benefit relating to rights under obligations. The definition maintains, however, the link with tradition, by underlining that subrogation operates to the benefit of a person who satisfies a liability (article 1258). Consolidation, too, in relation to the regime: the various kinds of subrogation by operation of law are retained without any change, although their order is modified to take account of their respective practical importance (article 1259); the requirement of co-existence of subrogation and satisfaction is relaxed, along the lines already drawn by the courts (article 1260, paragraph 3); the effect by way of transfer is emphasised, both in its extent (the right under an obligation and its ancillary rights) and with regard to it being relied upon as against third parties (removal of the requirement of formality, including in the situation where the issue is the enforceability of the transfer of securities which are attached to the right under the obligation).

What is new is subrogation on the initiative of the debtor. First, article 1261, paragraph 1, of the Reform Proposals reverses the classical approach taken by the courts under which subrogation is effected only if the satisfaction is rendered by the substitute creditor himself, and not if the debtor borrows in order to satisfy his debt to a creditor who is willing to issue a receipt specifying the source of the funds. Secondly, the second paragraph of the same article settles the much debated question about the conditions under which the debtor may require subrogation in favour of a new lender, called upon to 'refinance' the transaction (at an interest rate which is, of course, more favourable). Respect for the binding force of contracts has provided the principle: for the debtor to be able to effect the subrogation on his own, it is still necessary for the debt to have fallen due or the period for payment to have been set for his benefit.

Novation is given a definition which hitherto it has lacked. It is '*a contract which has as its subject-matter the substitution of one obligation (which it extinguishes) with a different obligation (which it creates)*' (article 1265). This therefore emphasises the substitution effected by such a transaction, by contrast with the transfer effected by assignment and personal subrogation. It also underlines the

entre les deux obligations successives, même si, en cas de novation par changement d'objet, l'article 1266, 3°, indique qu'« *il y a novation quelle que soit la différence instituée entre l'ancienne et la nouvelle obligation* » (on espère que cette précision coupera court à une jurisprudence aléatoire sur les circonstances exclusives de novation).

La nouveauté du régime mis en place ne touche pas la classification proposée entre les différentes manières dont s'opère la novation (on retrouve la trilogie novation par changement de débiteur, novation par changement de créancier, novation par changement d'objet), ni l'exigence d'une volonté de nover dépourvue d'équivoque. Elle tient à la liberté reconnue aux parties d'organiser, par avance, la novation, pour en faire un instrument efficace de gestion des créances, susceptible de constituer une alternative utile à la cession. Deux dispositions sont à cet égard essentielles. L'article 1270, al. 1er, tout d'abord, selon lequel « *la novation par la substitution d'un nouveau créancier peut avoir lieu si le débiteur a, par avance, accepté que le nouveau créancier soit désigné par le premier* ». L'article 1271, ensuite, par l'exception qu'il introduit à l'effet extinctif de la novation quant aux sûretés : « *à moins que ces dernières n'aient été ou ne soient expressément réservées du consentement de tous les intéressés* ». Par la souplesse ainsi introduite, le droit français permettrait aux professionnels d'utiliser, à l'instar de leurs homologues sur des places concurrentes, la novation comme cadre juridique d'opérations de refinancement.

La délégation aurait sans doute pu continuer à s'épanouir dans la discrétion, à l'abri des rigidités qu'induit inévitablement l'intervention législative. Après tout, l'essentiel est ici la liberté contractuelle, qui est notamment appelée à s'exercer sur la détermination de l'objet de l'obligation du délégué. Il a néanmoins été jugé utile de fixer dans le Code civil les contours de l'institution, à la fois pour éviter les incertitudes liées à certaines discussions doctrinales et pour combattre des initiatives jurisprudentielles peu propices à l'essor de la délégation. Dans cet esprit, l'article 1276 précise que « *la délégation est valable alors même que le délégant n'est pas débiteur du délégataire ou que le délégué n'est pas débiteur du délégant* » : on ne pourra nier, désormais, que le délégué ait la faculté de s'engager « à découvert ». La question de l'inopposabilité des exceptions est réglée prudemment, avec à la fois l'introduction de la notion d'« *engagement expressément stipulé indépendant* » et la réserve de la convention contraire aux solutions proposées. L'essentiel est le résultat : les parties pourront, par des clauses adéquates, priver le délégué de la possibilité de se prévaloir d'exceptions tenant à des rapports de droit étrangers à celui qui l'unit au délégataire, ce qui correspond à l'une des utilités de la délégation. L'article 1281, al. 1er, aux termes duquel « *l'engagement du délégué envers le délégataire rend indisponible la créance du délégant envers le délégué, qui ne peut être ni cédée ni saisie* » tire les conséquences de la rigueur particulière que peut revêtir l'obligation du délégué. Celui-ci ne doit pas être exposé à payer deux fois : d'abord à un cessionnaire ou à un créancier saisissant venant aux droits du délégant ; ensuite au délégataire, auquel il ne pourrait opposer d'exception tirée de ses rapports avec le délégant. Est ainsi proposé un système cohérent, de nature à faire de la délégation un mécanisme sûr.

need for a difference between the two successive obligations—although, in the case of novation by change of subject-matter, article 1266, paragraph 3, says that '*there is a novation, regardless of any particular difference between the old and the new obligations*' (it is to be hoped that this clarification will put a stop to doubts in the case-law about there being limits to what can constitute novation).

The novelty of the regime which is put in place does not concern the proposed classification of the different ways in which novation is effected (we see the familiar trichotomy: novation by change of debtor, novation by change of creditor, novation by change of subject-matter); nor the requirement of the unequivocal will to novate. It relates to the freedom given to the parties to arrange the novation in advance, in order to make it an effective instrument to manage rights under obligations, capable of being a useful alternative to assignment. Two provisions are key in this respect. Article 1270, paragraph 1, in the first place, under which '*novation by substitution of a new creditor may take place if the debtor has agreed in advance that the new creditor will be appointed by the old*'. Article 1271, secondly, in the exception which it introduces to the extinctive effect of novation as regards securities: '*as long as these have not been, and are not, expressly preserved by the agreement of all those interested*'. As a result of the flexibility which is thus introduced, French law would allow businesses and professionals, like their counterparts with whom they are in competition, to use novation as a legal framework for refinancing transactions.

Delegation could no doubt have continued to blossom away from the rigidity which is inevitably induced by legislative intervention. After all, the essential thing here is contractual freedom, which is particularly expected to be called into play in relation to the determination of the subject-matter of the delegate's obligation. However, it was thought useful to lay down in the Civil Code the outlines of delegation, in order both to avoid the uncertainty flowing from certain academic debates, and to combat initiatives taken by the courts which are hardly going to assist in the development of delegation. In this spirit, article 1276 sets out that '*delegation is valid even if the delegator is not a debtor of the beneficiary, and if the delegate is not a debtor of the delegator*': in the future, one will not be able to deny that the delegate has the power to undertake the obligation 'without cover'. The question of what defences may not be raised is regulated carefully, with at the same time the introduction of the notion of an '*undertaking which is expressly stipulated as independent*', and the exception of contracting out of the proposed solutions. The result is key: the parties will be able, by suitable contract terms, to deprive the delegate of the possibility of taking advantage of defences linked to legal relations which are outside those which link him to the beneficiary, which is one of the advantages of delegation. Article 1281, paragraph 1, the terms of which provide '*The delegate's undertaking in favour of the beneficiary renders the right under the delegator's obligations in favour of the beneficiary unavailable; it may not be assigned nor subject to distraint*' draws the conclusions from the peculiar strictness which may apply to the obligation of the delegate. He must not be exposed to the requirement to render satisfaction twice—first to an assignee or to a judgment creditor enforcing the rights of the delegator, and then to the beneficiary, against whom he would not have the right to raise defences arising from his relationship with the delegator. And so a coherent system is proposed, which will make delegation a secure mechanism.

Preuve des obligations
(art. 1283 à 1326-2)

Philippe Stoffel-Munck

Le projet de réforme n'apporte pas de bouleversement au chapitre des preuves, Les principes et distinctions guidant la matière depuis 1804 ont démontré leur valeur et sont ancrés dans la pratique sans soulever de difficultés majeures.

Nulle nécessité de toucher au fond n'existant, la prudence a commandé de s'abstenir de toute audace gratuite pour une question d'usage aussi quotidien. Ainsi, il a semblé préférable de renoncer à avancer une définition générale de la preuve ou à prendre position sur la question encore controversée de l'exigence de loyauté dans sa recherche. Cette prudence était d'autant mieux possible que la loi du 13 mars 2000 avait déjà fait œuvre de réforme, adaptant le Code aux nouvelles technologies et `portant plusieurs précisions importantes, spécialement quant à la notion d'écrit et de signature.

Sur le fond, le projet de réforme se borne donc à transposer l'acquis jurisprudentiel pour compléter le corps actuel des principes légaux ou à apporter quelques précisions mineures inédites, comme la soustraction de l'écrit électronique à la règle du double original (art. 1296).

Sur la forme, en revanche, une clarification est souvent apparue utile, tant à propos du plan du chapitre que sur le détail de ses dispositions.

Quant au fond, tout d'abord, le projet conserve donc les principes traditionnels :

• le mécanisme d'attribution du fardeau de la preuve reste le même (art. 1283) ;

• la distinction de la preuve des faits et des actes juridiques est maintenue (art. 1284) ;

• la définition de l'écrit et de la signature nécessaires à la preuve littérale est reprise de la loi du 13 mars 2000 (art. 1285 à 1286) ;

• le principe de la liberté de preuve des faits s'inscrit dans la loi (art. 1287), et l'exigence d'une preuve littérale des actes juridiques est conservée (art. 1306) ;

• la licéité des conventions sur la preuve est affirmée, conformément à la jurisprudence et sous certaines limites (art. 1289) ;

• la règle prétorienne indiquant que « nul ne peut se constituer de titre à lui-même » passe dans la loi (art. 1299).

Proof of Obligations
(articles 1283 to 1326-2)

Philippe Stoffel-Munck

The Reform Proposals make no major upheavals in the chapter on proof. The principles and distinctions which have guided this subject since 1804 have demonstrated their value and are grounded in practice without giving rise to any significant difficulties.

There being no need to touch the substance, wisdom counsels us to abstain from gratuitously bold gestures in a matter of such everyday common practice. And so it seemed preferable to decline to set out a general definition of proof or to take a position on the question—still controversial—of the requirement of loyalty in its establishment. This wise course was all the more possible because the Law of 13 March 2000[1] had already introduced reform, adapting the Code to new technologies and containing several significant clarifications, especially as regards the notions of writing and signature.

In substance the Reform Proposals are therefore limited to bringing in the existing case-law to supplement the present body of legislative principles, or to introducing certain new minor details, such as the disapplication of the rule of double originals in the case of electronic writing (article 1296).

In relation to form, on the other hand, clarification has often seemed beneficial, with regard to both the structure of the chapter and the detail of its provisions.

As to substance, first, the Proposals retain the following traditional principles:

• the mechanism for attributing the burden of proof remains the same (article 1283);

• the distinction between proof of facts and of juridical acts is maintained (article 1284);

• the definition of writing and of a signature, necessary for written proof, is taken up from the Law of 13 March 2000 (articles 1285 to 1286);

• the principle of liberty in the forms of evidence is written into the legislative texts (article 1287), and the requirement of written evidence of juridical acts is preserved (article 1306);

• the lawfulness of contracts about proof is affirmed, in accordance with the case-law and within certain limits (article 1289)

• the judge-made law to the effect that 'no-one may establish evidence in his own favour' is given legislative force (article 1299)

[1] [Law no 2000-230, introducing provisions into the Code civil (esp articles 1316 to 1316-4 and 1317) in order to implement Directive 1999/93/EC of the European Parliament and of the Council of 13 December 1999 on a Community framework for electronic signatures; see also the discussion above, p 535.]

Sur la forme, ensuite, le projet remodèle le plan du chapitre consacré aux preuves de façon à mieux faire apparaître les grandes divisions intellectuelles de la matière. Il se compose de quatre sections.

La section première est consacrée aux « dispositions générales » (art. 1283 à 1290). Véritable « titre préliminaire », il concentre les principes gouvernant l'ensemble de la preuve des obligations. Les autres sections règlent chaque mode de preuve à titre particulier.

La section deuxième définit les conditions de forme de la preuve par écrit, également dénommée preuve littérale, et fixe sa valeur (art. 1291 à 1305). Elle distingue classiquement le titre authentique de l'acte sous seing privé et règle le sort des copies et actes recognitifs. Cette section ne contient pas d'innovation particulière par rapport au droit positif, hormis la soustraction de l'écrit électronique à la règle du double original (art. 1296). Elle fixe en revanche plusieurs solutions jurisprudentielles. Est ainsi expressément indiqué que l'exigence d'une mention de la part de celui qui s'engage constitue une simple condition de preuve de l'acte (art. 1297).

La section troisième fixe le champ de l'exigence d'une preuve par écrit. Pour l'essentiel elle reprend les articles 1341 à 1348 du Code civil actuel, ajoutant simplement, conformément à la jurisprudence, que le commencement de preuve par écrit doit être complété (art. 1312).

La section quatrième détaille les règles propres aux présomptions, à l'aveu puis au serment. Elle ne contient pas d'innovation majeure au regard du droit positif, intégrant simplement au texte plusieurs solutions prétoriennes. Ainsi, se trouve reprise la jurisprudence admettant que les présomptions du fait de l'homme puissent résulter d'indices graves et précis *ou* concordants (art. 1318), cet article ajoutant que de telles présomptions sont toujours susceptibles de preuve contraire. Le mécanisme de la présomption légale est également précisé (art. 1317).

Sur la forme, également, le projet de réforme tente de clarifier certaines règles sans en toucher le sens. L'exemple le plus net en est la reformulation de la règle ancestrale portée à l'actuel article 1341 du Code civil. Là où celui-ci dispose qu'« il doit être passé acte devant notaires ou sous signatures privées de toutes choses excédant une somme ou une valeur fixée par décret », le nouveau texte dispose plus simplement qu'« il doit être constitué une preuve par écrit des actes juridiques excédant une somme ou une valeur fixée par décret » (art. 1306) ; la notion de preuve par écrit étant précisément définie dans la section précédant celle qu'ouvre le nouvel article.

S'agissant des preuves, l'espoir des rédacteurs du projet est ainsi d'avoir clarifié le vocabulaire, les concepts et la formulation des règles, d'en avoir ordonné plus logiquement l'exposé et actualisé le fond par intégration de l'apport prétorien. Une meilleure compréhension du droit positif devrait en résulter, sans modification notable de son contenu tant les besoins de la pratique paraissent satisfaits en l'état actuel de la matière.

In relation to form, then, the Proposals re-model the structure of the chapter dedicated to proof in such a way as to show more clearly the major theoretical divisions of the subject. It is composed of four sections.

The first section is dedicated to 'general provisions' (articles 1283-1290). A genuinely 'introductory section', it focuses on the principles governing the whole area of proof of obligations. The other sections make provisions for each method of proof one by one.

The second section defines the requirements of form of proof by writing, equally referred to as written proof, and establishes its significance (articles 1291 to 1305). It draws the classical distinction between a publicly authenticated instrument and a signed document, and makes provision for the consequences of copies and formal acknowledgments. This section does not contain any particular innovation by comparison with the existing law, apart from removing electronic writing from the ambit of the rule of double originals (article 1296). On the other hand, it adopts several judicial solutions. And so it is expressly provided that the requirement of a statement by the party undertaking an obligation constitutes just one condition for proof of the document (article 1297).

The third section establishes the domain for the requirement of proof by writing. In its essentials, it carries over articles 1341 to 1348 of the present Civil Code, simply adding (in accordance with case-law) that the beginning of proof by writing must be supplemented (article 1312).

The fourth section sets out in detail the rules peculiar to presumptions, admission, and then oaths. It does not contain any significant innovation with respect to the current law, simply integrating into the provisions several judge-made solutions. And so one finds the case-law taken up which accepts that presumptions of fact relating to human action may result from evidence which is weighty and definite *or* corroborative (article 1318), this article adding that such presumptions may always be rebutted. The mechanism of legal presumptions is also made clear (article 1317).

In relation to form, too, the Reform Proposals seek to clarify certain rules without changing their meaning. The clearest example of this is the reformulation of the ancient rule which appears in article 1341 of the present Civil Code. Where this provides that 'A juridical act must be entered into before a notary, or under the parties' signatures, for any things which exceed a sum of money or a value fixed by decree', the new text provides more simply that 'Proof in writing is required for juridical acts which exceed a sum of money or a value fixed by decree' (article 1306); the notion of proof in writing being defined precisely in the section preceding that which opens with the new article.

With regard to proof, the hope of the draftsmen of the Reform Proposals is therefore to have clarified the vocabulary, the concepts and the formulation of the rules, to have ordered the presentation in a more logical manner, and to have brought the substance up to date by integrating the courts' contributions. This should give a better understanding of the current law, without any significant change in its content, given that the needs of practitioners seem to be well satisfied with the existing state of the subject.

Quasi-contrats (art. 1327 à 1339)

Gérard Cornu

Les quasi-contrats demeurent dans le projet, comme ils le sont dans le Code civil, une source d'obligation. Sans doute, ce point est-il, en législation, sujet à controverse. Mais, dans le parti législatif d'où le projet tire sa raison d'être et sa mesure, leur maintien allait de soi. Il aurait fallu adhérer à une ambition maximaliste qui n'est pas la sienne pour bouleverser la théorie des sources d'obligation au point d'en éliminer le quasi-contrat, entre le contrat et le délit. Aujourd'hui tout le monde sait que loin d'être obsolète, cette classification s'accorde avec la division majeure des actes juridiques et des faits juridiques que le tableau des sources présente en tête du projet (art. 1101 s.) : d'un côté, les actes juridiques conventionnels, unilatéraux ou collectifs, de l'autre les faits juridiques dommageables ou profitables.

Justement, c'est la notion même de quasi-contrat telle qu'elle ressort de l'analyse lumineuse de Jean Carbonnier qui légitime – qui exige – son maintien. Ce n'est pas un fourre-tout. C'est un concept. De même que la juridiction gracieuse n'est plus tout ce qui n'est pas la juridiction contentieuse, mais, en parallèle, une fonction juridictionnelle définie, de même les quasi-contrats ne sont pas un amalgame de faits résiduels informes. Face au dommage causé sans droit, un avantage reçu sans droit : en ce point commun se rejoignent tous les quasi-contrats. D'où la définition générale donnée en premier (art. 1327). Au sein de cette catégorie générique, viennent naturellement s'ordonner les deux applications particulières spécifiques de la tradition, gestion d'affaires et paiement de l'indu, ainsi que, venant de la coutume, le principe général que nul ne doit s'enrichir sans cause au détriment d'autrui. L'ensemble est cohérent.

Quasi-Contracts (articles 1327 to 1339)

Gérard Cornu

Quasi-contracts remain a source of obligations in the Proposals, as they do in the existing Civil Code.[1] This position is of course controversial in terms of legislative scope, but it flows naturally from the approach to law-making which forms the Proposals' intellectual foundations and which sets their boundaries. It would have been necessary to adopt a maximalist ambition which the Proposals do not espouse to overturn the doctrine of the sources of obligations to the point of getting rid of quasi-contracts, coming as they do between contract and delict. Today, everyone is aware that, far from being obsolete, this classification fits well with the major distinction between juridical acts and juridically significant facts which are listed as sources of obligations at the very beginning of the Proposals (article 1101 *et seq.*): so, on the one hand, there are juridical consensual acts, either unilateral or collective; on the other, there are juridically significant facts, either ones which cause harm or ones which confer benefits.

Deservedly, it is the concept of quasi-contract itself as so lucidly analysed by Jean Carbonnier,[2] which justifies, indeed, demands its inclusion.[3] It is not a mere rag-bag collection, but possesses a conceptual integrity. In the same way that the civil courts' jurisdiction to hear non-contentious applications no longer consists merely of all matters which are not for its contentious jurisdiction, but possesses its own distinct, parallel function,[4] so too quasi-contracts are not an amalgam of shapeless, left-over situations. Whereas civil liability is concerned with harm caused without right, quasi-contracts are concerned with advantages received without right; this is the point which unites all quasi-contracts and from which the general definition given first in the Proposals stems (article 1327). From this central element of this broad category flow naturally the two particular and specific applications which are traditionally recognised—management of another's affairs and undue payments—as does the customary general principle that no-one must enrich themselves at the expense of another without justification. The whole is entirely coherent.

---

[1] [See arts 1371 – 1381 Cc.]

[2] [See Carbonnier, *Droit civil*, vol 4 *Les obligations*, above, p 507, n 1, nos 297 ff.]

[3] [For a discussion in English of the category of '*quasi-contrats*' in French law and whether or to what extent it constitutes a law of restitution or unjustified enrichment in a common law sense, see S Whittaker, 'The Law of Obligations' in Bell, Boyron and Whittaker, above, p 465, n 3, 417 – 23.]

[4] [Here, the author's analogy draws a distinction between the civil courts' *juridiction en matière gracieuse* (for non-contentious matters) and *juridiction contentieuse* (for contentious matters). Article 25 of the New Code of Civil Procedure provides that a court gives judgment *en matière gracieuse* when in the absence of a dispute it is seized of an application which is required by law in order to allow the court to exercise its control over the matter in question. Examples of this may be found in the case of adoption or divorce at the joint request of both spouses: S Whittaker in Bell, Boyron and Whittaker, above, p 465, n 3, 93.]

L'autre raison de ne pas bouleverser la matière est la valeur même des apports de la tradition et de l'interprétation. Le régime de la gestion d'affaires et celui du paiement de l'indu sont faits de solutions logiques et de bon sens. Les dispositions qui les énoncent sont, en grande partie, simples, claires et fermes. Beaucoup d'articles conservent leur teneur originaire. Quant à la théorie générale de l'enrichissement sans cause, diminutif moins ambitieux et plus raisonnable de la théorie ouverte de l'enrichissement injuste, et techniquement encadrée par la subsidiarité (art. 1338), elle sort directement de l'enseignement doctrinal et de la jurisprudence. C'est la consécration d'un acquis, non d'une avancée imprudente.

Pourtant, la révision marque la matière de son empreinte. Sur de nombreux points elle a puisé dans l'interprétation régnante des solutions d'accord qui sont de véritables progrès. Que la gestion d'affaires puisse consister en des actes matériels et pas seulement en des actes juridiques (art. 1328), qu'elle puisse être entreprise non seulement dans l'intérêt exclusif d'autrui mais dans l'intérêt commun d'autrui et du gérant (art. 1329) sont d'heureuses extensions portées par un consensus. Un autre consensus opportun est d'assimiler au paiement par erreur, le paiement sous la contrainte (art. 1332) ou l'abandon d'une sûreté à la suppression du titre (*ibid.*). D'autres retouches, dans le détail, mettent en relief des points décisifs. Notion clé, l'utilité de la gestion devait être exposée au premier rang des conditions de l'obligation du maître de l'affaire (art. 1328-3). La référence au corps certain devait remplacer celle – non pertinente – au bien meuble corporel dans l'article 1334 et l'hypothèse de la mauvaise foi avait à être envisagée et réglée à l'article 1334-1.

Cependant le projet contient de véritables innovations:[1] l'idée de tenir compte, dans l'indemnisation du gérant des pertes qu'il aurait subies, à l'exclusion de toute rémunération (art. 1328-1) et surtout le renvoi bien inspiré à l'enrichissement sans cause des actions du gérant qui ne répondent pas exactement aux conditions de la gestion d'affaires (art. 1329-1). Ce rachat subsidiaire montre bien le lien qui unit, dans l'ensemble des quasi-contrats, l'illustration spécifique de la gestion d'affaires et la théorie générale dotée d'une vocation résiduelle. Enfin, hors série, les règles de

---

[1] Elles ont été retenues sur les suggestions de M. A. Benabent.

The other reason against radical reform is the valuable contribution which tradition and interpretation can bring to the subject. The sets of rules relating to management of another's affairs and undue payments are made up of a number of solutions to problems which are both logical and sensible. The provisions which introduce them are to a large extent simple, clear and confident. Many of the articles retain their original import. And the general doctrine of *unjustified* enrichment—which is the more modest, more reasonable and much narrower version of the very open-ended doctrine of *unjust* enrichment—is kept in check technically by the requirement of subsidiarity (article 1338), all this coming from lessons drawn from scholarly writing and the case-law. The Proposals here mark the formal recognition of established principle, rather than an unwise leap forward.

Nevertheless, our revision of the legislation does make a certain impact on the area. On a number of points it relies on the prevailing interpretation of solutions on which everyone agrees to make real progress. It is certainly a happy extension of the ambit of management of another's affairs and one attracting a wide consensus, that it can consist of physical action and not merely juridical acts (article 1328) and that it can be undertaken not merely in the exclusive interest of another person but also in the common interest of another person and of the person intervening (article 1329). Other opportune and agreed changes may be found in the assimilation of payment under duress to payment by mistake (article 1332) and of release of security to cancellation of a creditor's instrument of title (*ibid.*). Other retouching of details puts in relief some crucial points. The key notion of the utility of the management undertaken had to be set out as the first and foremost of the conditions of the obligation of the person benefiting from it (article 1328-3). Use of the term 'ascertained property' had to replace the inappropriate reference to corporeal movable property found in article 1334 of the existing Code and the position where bad faith is present had to be raised and regulated by article 1334-1.

However, the Proposals do contain some real innovations:[1] the idea of calculating the compensation due to a person managing another's affairs taking into account the losses which he thereby suffers but not including any amount for his remuneration (article [1328-3][2]) and above all the truly inspired recourse to recovery on the ground of unjustified enrichment where the actions of a person managing another's affairs do not exactly fulfil the conditions for the application of the doctrine of management of another's affairs (article 1329-1). This supplementary relief shows clearly the relationship (found as regards all the quasi-contracts) between the specific example of management of another's affairs and the general doctrine of unjustified enrichment which is endowed with a subsidiary role.[3] Finally, special

---

[1] These were retained at the suggestion of M A. Bénabent.

[2] [The original here cites art 1328-3, but art 1328-2 appears to be the appropriate provision.]

[3] [Recovery under the doctrine of unjustified enrichment (*enrichissement sans cause*) is subsidiary in the sense that in general a person may not rely on it where he possesses an effective action on some other legal ground against the 'enriched' person: see further S Whittaker, 'The Law of Obligations' in Bell, Boyron and Whittaker, above, p 465, n 3, 437-38]

restitution sont étendues au cas où le paiement de ce qui était dû perd ensuite sa cause par l'effet d'une annulation ou d'une résolution. Ce cas sort de l'épure. Le paiement n'était pas indu, mais il devient sans cause. Il entre ainsi dans la logique de l'absence de cause, ce qui justifie l'extension analogique.

L'observation en revient fondamentalement à l'unité de la matière. La figure traditionnelle de la gestion d'affaires apparaît bien dans la fidélité à ses origines et le droit fil de l'étymologie comme un quasi-mandat. Mais c'est la théorie de la cause qui, en dernière analyse, unit la trilogie. Le paiement est indu à la condition qu'il ne procède ni d'une intention libérale, ni d'une obligation naturelle, ni d'une autre cause (art. 1330 al. 2). Semblablement, l'enrichissement est sans cause lorsque (et parce que) la perte de l'appauvri ne procède ni de son intention libérale envers l'enrichi, ni de l'accomplissement d'une obligation dont il serait tenu envers lui en vertu de la loi, du jugement, du contrat ou de la poursuite d'un intérêt personnel (art. 1337). De son côté, la gestion du gérant d'affaires est sans titre. Ce fondement radical commun pourrait conduire à penser que, si l'on doutait de la légitimité de la cause en matière contractuelle, celle-ci pourrait trouver un appui dans les quasi-contrats, ce qui découvrirait un point de cohérence au cœur de la théorie générale des obligations. La présence de la cause dans le contrat répond à l'absence de cause dans le quasi-contrat.

provision is made so as to extend the rules governing restitution[1] so as to apply to the case of payment which was due at the time it was made but which becomes unjustified by reason of annulment or retroactive termination of a contract. Strictly speaking, this situation falls outside the doctrine: the payment was not undue, but it becomes unjustified. It therefore rests on reasoning from an absence of justification[2] and this is a good reason for making an analogous extension to the rules of restitution.[3]

This observation leads us back to the fundamental unity of this area. The traditional features of management of another's affairs seem very faithful to its origins, the law still revealing its etymological origins in quasi-mandate. But in the final analysis it is the doctrine of legal justification ('*la cause*') which unites the trio of management of another's affairs, undue payment and unjustified enrichment. A payment is undue if it does not flow either from an intention to confer a gratuitous benefit, from performance of a natural obligation, or from any other justification (article 1330 paragraph 2). Similarly, an enrichment is unjustified only where (and because) loss to the person at whose expense the enrichment is made does not stem from his intention to confer a gratuitous benefit on the person enriched, nor the fulfilment of an obligation which he owes him in law, as a result of a court order, under a contract or from the pursuit of his own personal interest (article 1337). In its turn, the management of another's affairs is unsupported by any authority to do so. This common fundamental basis could lead it to be thought that, although the legitimacy of the notion of 'justification' ('*la cause*') is doubtful in the contractual context, it could find some support in the law of quasi-contracts, and that this would reveal an element of consistency at the heart of the general theory of the law of obligations. The requirement of a justification for a contract corresponds to the absence of justification in quasi-contract.

---

[1] [See articles 1161 ff of the *Avant-projet*.]

[2] [However, *absence* of *cause* (a condition for the validity of a contract) for the purposes of annulment and *enrichissement sans cause* have not traditionally been viewed as linked in this way.]

[3] [Cf the provision made in articles 1161 – 1164-6 of the *Avant-projet* providing special rules for restitution following annulment or termination of a contract, above, p. 569, n 3, where this apparent double regulation is noted.]

Chapitre préliminaire
De la source des obligations
(Articles 1101 à 1101-2)

Art. 1101*

Les obligations naissent d'actes ou de faits juridiques.

Certaines obligations naissent également de l'autorité seule de la loi, comme les obligations de voisinage et les charges publiques** dont il est traité dans les matières qui les concernent.

> Notes : * C'est le remploi et l'élargissement de l'article 1370 c. civ. actuel.
>
> ** Ainsi la tutelle (V. art. 427 c. civ.)

Art. 1101-1

Les actes juridiques sont des actes de volonté destinés à produire des effets de droit.

L'acte juridique conventionnel ou convention est l'accord conclu entre deux ou plusieurs personnes en vue de produire de tels effets.

L'acte juridique unilatéral est un acte accompli par une seule ou plusieurs personnes unies dans la considération d'un même intérêt en vue de produire des effets de droit dans les cas admis par la loi ou par l'usage.

L'acte juridique collectif est la décision prise collégialement par les membres d'une collectivité.

L'acte unilatéral et l'acte collectif obéissent, en tant que de raison, pour leur validité et leurs effets, aux règles qui gouvernent les conventions.

Art. 1101-2

Les faits juridiques sont des agissements ou des événements auxquels la loi attache des effets de droit.

Le fait qui procure à autrui un avantage auquel il n'a pas droit constitue un quasi-contrat. Les obligations qui en découlent sont régies par le Sous-titre Des quasi-contrats.

Le fait qui cause sans droit un dommage à autrui oblige son auteur à le réparer. Cette obligation est régie par le Sous-titre De la responsabilité civile.

Preliminary Chapter
The Source of Obligations
(Articles 1101 to 1101-2)

Art. 1101*

Obligations arise either from juridical acts or from juridically significant facts. [1]

Certain obligations also arise simply by legislation, such as duties between neighbours, and public duties,** which are set out in their proper sections.

> *Notes: *This re-uses and expands article 1370 of the present Civil Code.*

> ** *For example guardianship (see art. 427 C.civ)*

Art. 1101-1

Juridical acts are exercises of will which are intended to produce legal effects.

A contractual juridical act—or contract[2]—is an agreement formed between two or more persons with the aim of producing such effects.

A unilateral juridical act is an act done by one person, or a number of persons acting together, with the aim of producing legal effects in circumstances accepted by legislation or by custom.

A collective juridical act is a decision taken collectively by the members of an association.

Unilateral acts and collective acts are governed, as far as may be, as regards their validity and their effects, by the same rules as apply to contracts.

Art. 1101-2

Juridically significant facts consist of conduct or events to which legislation attaches legal consequences.

An action which confers on another a benefit to which he has no right constitutes a quasi-contract. The obligations which flow from it are governed by the Sub-title *Quasi-contracts.*[3]

An action which, without legal right, causes harm to another gives rise to an obligation to make reparation in the person who does it. This obligation is governed by the Sub-title *Civil liability.*[4]

---

[1] [For the translation of *faits juridiques* as 'juridically significant facts' see above, p 433.]
[2] [We generally translate by the English term 'contract' both *contrat* and *convention*. See further above, pp 435-6.]
[3] [Below, p 799.]
[4] [Below, p 809.]

Notes complémentaires sur le chapitre préliminaire :

1) Il fait sonner le mot source, ce qui n'est pas inutile.

2) Il met en perspective la division majeure des actes juridiques et des faits juridiques.

3) De même que l'article relatif aux actes juridiques en distingue les trois espèces, de même l'article consacré aux faits juridiques distingue les faits dommageables et les quasi-contrats, et dans chaque ordre, la terminologie moderne est mise en correspondance avec les notions traditionnelles.

4) L'une et l'autre concernées, la responsabilité délictuelle et la responsabilité civile contractuelle, sont, dès ce moment, rapprochées sous couvert de la responsabilité, ce qui annonce un parti essentiel du projet.

5) Inspirée d'une suggestion de Carbonnier et d'une opposition scientifiquement exacte « dommage causé » sans droit, « avantage procuré » sans droit, la définition du quasi-contrat est ici dessinée dans ses éléments essentiels. La définition plus élaborée a sa place dans l'article 1327 du projet.

6) Les quasi-contrats ont leur place naturelle après les contrats (Sous-titre II), ce qui permet de mettre une certaine distance entre les contrats et l'ensemble regroupé des faits dommageables et manquements contractuels source de responsabilité civile.

Supplementary notes on the preliminary chapter:

1) The word source should be emphasised; it is not insignificant.

2) It gives a perspective on the principal division between juridical acts and juridically significant facts.

3) Just as the article dealing with juridical acts distinguishes between three types, so the article dedicated to juridically significant facts distinguishes between actions causing harm, and quasi-contracts and, in each category, the modern terminology is linked to the traditional notions.

4) Both delictual liability and contractual liability are, at this point, brought together under the umbrella of 'liability', as a key element of the Reform Proposals makes clear. ¹

5) Inspired by a suggestion of Carbonnier,² and by a doctrinally correct contrast between 'harm caused' without right, and 'benefit conferred' without right, the essential elements of the definition of quasi-contracts are here outlined. The more detailed definition is found in article 1327 of the Proposals.

6) Quasi-contracts have their proper place after contracts (Sub-title II), which allows a certain distance between contracts and the whole group of sources of civil liability: harmful actions, and contractual failures to perform.

---

¹ [See below, p 815 on the controversy of reference to 'contractual liability'.]
² [Cf Carbonnier, *Droit civil*, vol 4, *Les obligations*, above, p 507, n 1, no 297.]

Sous-titre I

Du contrat et des obligations conventionnelles en général (Articles 1102 à 1326-2)

Chapitre I
Dispositions générales

Section 1
Définitions
(Articles 1102 à 1103)

Art. 1102

Le contrat est une convention par laquelle une ou plusieurs personnes s'obligent envers une ou plusieurs autres à accomplir une prestation.

Art. 1102-1

Le contrat est synallagmatique ou bilatéral lorsque les contractants s'obligent réciproquement les uns envers les autres.

Il est unilatéral lorsqu'une ou plusieurs personnes s'obligent envers une ou plusieurs autres sans qu'il y ait d'engagement réciproque de celles-ci.

Art. 1102-2

Le contrat est à titre onéreux lorsque chacune des parties entend recevoir de l'autre un avantage en contrepartie de celui qu'elle procure.

Sub-Title I

Contracts and Obligations Created by Agreement in General
(Articles 1102 to 1326-2)

Chapter I
General Provisions

Section 1
Definitions
(Articles 1102 to 1103)

Art. 1102

A contract is an agreement[1] by which one or more persons undertake the accomplishment of its subject-matter[2] in favour of one or more others.

Art. 1102-1

A contract is synallagmatic or bilateral where the parties undertake reciprocal obligations in favour of each other.

It is unilateral where one or more persons undertake obligations in favour of one or more others without there being any reciprocal undertaking on the part of the latter.

Art. 1102-2

A contract is onerous where each of the parties expects to receive a benefit from the other in return for what he provides.

[1] [Here the text draws a formal distinction between a *contrat* ('contract') and a *convention* (here translated as 'agreement'): see above, p 625, n 2.]

[2] [For the translation of *prestation* (here, the 'subject-matter' of the agreement), see above, p 440.]

Le contrat est à titre gratuit lorsque l'une des parties entend procurer à l'autre un avantage sans recevoir de contrepartie.

Art. 1102-3

Le contrat est commutatif lorsque chacune des parties s'engage à procurer à l'autre un avantage qui est regardé comme l'équivalent de celui qu'elle reçoit.

Il est aléatoire lorsque les parties, sans rechercher l'équivalence de la contrepartie convenue, acceptent une chance de gain ou de perte pour chacune ou certaines d'entre elles, d'après un événement incertain.

Obs. : Il est tenu compte de l'article 1964 c. civ.

Art. 1102-4

Le contrat est consensuel lorsqu'il se forme par la seule manifestation des consentements quel qu'en soit le mode d'expression.

Le contrat est solennel lorsque sa formation est subordonnée, à peine de nullité, à des formalités déterminées par la loi.

Art. 1102-5

Le contrat d'adhésion est celui dont les conditions, soustraites à la discussion, sont acceptées par l'une des parties telles que l'autre les avait unilatéralement déterminées à l'avance.

Un tel contrat peut, cependant, leur adjoindre des conditions particulières sujettes à négociation.

Art. 1102-6

Le contrat cadre est un accord de base par lequel les parties conviennent de négocier, nouer ou entretenir des relations contractuelles dont elles déterminent les caractéristiques essentielles.

Des conventions d'application en précisent les modalités d'exécution, notamment la date et le volume des prestations, ainsi que, le cas échéant, le prix de celles-ci.

Art. 1103

Les contrats, soit qu'ils aient une dénomination propre, soit qu'ils n'en aient pas, sont soumis à des règles générales qui sont l'objet du présent titre.

Des règles particulières à certains contrats sont établies, soit sous les titres du présent code relatifs à chacun d'eux, soit par d'autres codes et lois, notamment dans les matières touchant au corps humain, aux droits intellectuels, aux opérations commerciales, aux relations de travail et à la protection du consommateur.

A contract is gratuitous where one of the parties expects to provide a benefit to the other without receiving anything in return.

Art. 1102-3

A contract is commutative where each of the parties undertakes to provide a benefit to the other which is regarded as the equivalent of that which he receives.

It is aleatory where the parties, without seeking equivalence in what they agree to exchange, accept a chance of gain or of loss for each or some of them, depending upon an uncertain event.

Comment: Here account is taken of article 1964 of the present Civil Code.

Art. 1102-4

A contract is consensual where it is formed by the mere outward signs of the parties' consents in whatever form they may be expressed.

A contract is formal where its formation is subject to formalities prescribed by law on pain of nullity.

Art. 1102-5

A standard-form contract[1] is one whose terms are not discussed but are accepted by one of the parties in the form that the other party unilaterally determined in advance.

Such a contract can, however, be supplemented by particular terms which have been negotiated.

Art. 1102-6

A framework contract is a basic agreement by which the parties agree to negotiate, to form or to maintain a contractual relationship whose essential characteristics they will determine.

Implementation contracts determine the modalities of performance under a framework contract, in particular the date and quantity of what is required by the obligations and, if necessary, its price.

Art. 1103

Contracts are subject to the general rules contained in this title, whether or not they have their own denomination.

Rules particular to certain contracts are laid down, either in the titles of this Code dealing with each of them, or by other codes and laws, and particularly in areas dealing with the human body, intellectual property rights, commercial transactions, labour relations and consumer protection.

---

[1] ['Standard-form contract' translates *contrat d'adhésion*, more literally 'a contract to which one adheres' and whose conclusion therefore involves no or little choice. The notion of *contrat d'adhésion* was identified early by French jurists, being attributed to R Saleilles, *La déclaration de volonté* (Paris, F Pichon, 1901) 229 ff. See further J Flour, J-L Aubert and E Savaux, *Droit civil, Les obligations* 1. *L'acte juridique* (12th edn, Paris, Sirey, 2006) 128ff.]

Les contrats innommés sont soumis par analogie aux règles applicables à des contrats comparables, dans la mesure où leur spécificité n'y met pas obstacle.

Section 2
De la formation du contrat
(Articles 1104 à 1107)

§1 – De la négociation

Art. 1104

L'initiative, le déroulement et la rupture des pourparlers sont libres, mais ils doivent satisfaire aux exigences de la bonne foi.

L'échec d'une négociation ne peut être source de responsabilité que s'il est imputable à la mauvaise foi ou à la faute de l'une des parties.

Art. 1104-1

Les parties peuvent, par un accord de principe, s'engager à négocier ultérieurement un contrat dont les éléments sont à déterminer, et à concourir de bonne foi à leur détermination.

Art. 1104-2

Le régime des accords destinés à aménager le déroulement ou la rupture des pourparlers, est soumis aux dispositions du présent sous-titre.

§2 – De l'offre et de l'acceptation

Art. 1105

La formation du contrat requiert la rencontre de plusieurs volontés fermes et précises de s'engager.

Art. 1105-1

L'offre est un acte unilatéral déterminant les éléments essentiels du contrat que son auteur propose à personne déterminée ou indéterminée, et par lequel il exprime sa volonté d'être lié en cas d'acceptation.

Art. 1105-2

L'offre peut être librement révoquée tant qu'elle n'est pas parvenue à la connaissance de son destinataire ou si elle n'a pas été valablement acceptée dans un délai raisonnable.

Innominate contracts[1] are subject by analogy to the rules applicable to comparable contracts, as long as there is no obstacle to it in their own special features.

Section 2
Formation of Contracts
(Articles 1104 to 1107)

§ 1 Negotiations[2]

Art. 1104

The parties are free to begin, continue and break off negotiations, but these must satisfy the requirements of good faith.

A break-down in negotiations can give rise to liability only if it is attributable to the bad faith or fault of one of the parties.

Art. 1104-1

The parties may, by an agreement in principle, undertake to negotiate at a later date a contract whose elements are still to be settled, and to work in good faith towards settling them.

Art. 1104-2

The rules governing agreements which are intended to provide for the conduct or breaking-off of negotiations are subject to the provisions of this sub-title.

§ 2 Offer and acceptance

Art. 1105

The formation of a contract requires the meeting of the definite and certain will to be bound on the part of more than one person.

Art. 1105-1

An offer is a unilateral act defining the essential elements of the contract which the person making it proposes to a particular person or to persons generally, and by which he expresses his will to be bound if it is accepted.

Art. 1105-2

An offer may be revoked freely as long as it has not come to the knowledge of the person to whom it was addressed, or if it has not been validly accepted within a reasonable period.

---

[1] [On the distinction between nominate and innominate contracts, see above, p 489, n 2.]
[2] [For discussion of these provisions, see Fauvarque-Cosson, above, ch 2 and Cartwright, above, ch 3.]

Art. 1105-3

L'offre devient caduque à défaut d'acceptation dans le délai fixé par son auteur, ainsi qu'en cas d'incapacité ou de décès de celui-ci survenu avant toute acceptation. Elle tombe également lorsque son destinataire la refuse.

Art. 1105-4

Cependant, lorsque l'offre adressée à une personne déterminée comporte l'engagement de la maintenir pendant un délai précis, ni sa révocation prématurée ni l'incapacité de l'offrant ni son décès ne peut empêcher la formation du contrat.

Art. 1105-5

L'acceptation est un acte unilatéral par lequel son auteur exprime la volonté d'être lié dans les termes de l'offre.

Une acceptation non conforme à l'offre est dépourvue d'effet, sauf à constituer une offre nouvelle.

Art. 1105-6

En l'absence de dispositions légales, d'aménagements conventionnels, d'usages professionnels ou de circonstances particulières, le silence ne vaut pas acceptation.

§3 – De la promesse unilatérale de contrat et du pacte de préférence

Art. 1106

La promesse unilatérale de contrat est la convention par laquelle une partie promet à une autre, qui en accepte le principe, de lui donner l'exclusivité pour la conclusion d'un contrat dont les éléments essentiels sont déterminés, mais pour la formation duquel fait seulement défaut le consentement du bénéficiaire.

La rétractation du promettant pendant le temps laissé au bénéficiaire pour exprimer son consentement ne peut empêcher la formation du contrat promis.

Le contrat conclu avec un tiers est inopposable au bénéficiaire de la promesse, sous réserve des effets attachés aux règles assurant la protection des tiers de bonne foi.

Art. 1106-1

Le pacte de préférence pour un contrat futur est la convention par laquelle celui qui reste libre de le conclure, s'engage, pour le cas où il s'y déciderait, à offrir par priorité au bénéficiaire du pacte de traiter avec lui.

Le promettant est tenu de porter à la connaissance du bénéficiaire toute offre relative au contrat soumis à préférence.

Art. 1105-3

An offer lapses if it is not accepted within the period fixed by the person who makes it or in the case of his incapacity or death before its acceptance. It is also extinguished if the offeree rejects it.

Art. 1105-4

However, where an offer addressed to a particular person includes an undertaking to maintain it for a fixed period, neither its premature revocation nor the incapacity or death of the offeror can prevent the formation of the contract.

Art. 1105-5

Acceptance is a unilateral act by which a person expresses his will to be bound on the terms of the offer.

An acceptance which does not conform to the offer has no effect, apart from constituting a new offer.

Art. 1105-6

In the absence of legislative provision, agreement between the parties, business or professional usage or other particular circumstances, silence does not count as acceptance.

§ 3 Unilateral promises to contract and pre-emption agreements

Art. 1106

A unilateral promise to contract[1] is a contract by which one party promises another (and the latter accepts in principle) to give him the exclusive right to conclude a contract of which the essential elements are settled, but for the formation of which only the consent of the beneficiary is required.

Revocation by the promisor during the period allowed to the beneficiary to express his agreement cannot prevent the contract which was promised from being formed.

A contract concluded with a third party does not prejudice the beneficiary of the unilateral promise, apart from the effect of any rules designed to protect third parties in good faith.

Art. 1106-1

A pre-emption agreement is a contract by which a party remains free to decide whether to enter into a contract, but undertakes that, if he does so decide, he will first offer to the beneficiary of the agreement the right to deal with him.

The promisor is bound to bring to the notice of the beneficiary any offer relating to the contract which is the subject of the pre-emption right.

---

[1] [The 'unilateral promise to contract' bears the hallmarks of an 'option contract' in English law. It is in common use in the context of conveyancing in France, as the first (binding contractual) stage in the sale of land. Under Law no 63-1241 of 19 December 1963 a unilateral promise to sell immovable property (*promesse unilatérale de vente*) is void if not entered into before a notary or, if entered into as a private document, registered within ten days of its acceptance by the beneficiary. This requirement is designed to ensure that the transaction comes to the notice of the tax authorities. See Nicholas, *The French Law of Contract*, above, p 489, n 2, 60, 65-6.]

Le contrat conclu avec un tiers est inopposable au bénéficiaire de la préférence, sous réserve des effets attachés aux règles assurant la protection des tiers de bonne foi.

§4 – De la date et du lieu de formation

Art. 1107

Faute de stipulation contraire, le contrat devient parfait par la réception de l'acceptation ; il est réputé conclu au lieu où l'acceptation est reçue.

Chapitre II
Des conditions essentielles pour la validité des conventions

Art. 1108

Quatre conditions sont essentielles pour la validité d'une convention :

– le consentement des parties contractantes ;

– leur capacité de contracter ;

– un objet qui forme la matière de l'engagement ;

– une cause justifiant l'engagement.

S'y ajoute, pour l'acte accompli par le représentant d'une partie, le pouvoir d'agir au nom de celle-ci.

La forme des conventions est exposée aux articles 1127 et suivants.

> *Note : Le terme « pouvoir » est polysémique, mais c'est au sein de la représentation qu'il apparaît dans son sens spécifique le plus pur (Carbonnier et Gaillard) au rang des conditions de validité de l'acte accompli par le représentant. Il mérite donc bien d'être annoncé à ce titre dans l'article 1108. C'est une condition occasionnelle (au cas de représentation) mais, dans cette hypothèse, elle est essentielle.*
>
> *La notion de pouvoir apparaît aussi sur la tête de la personne capable qui agit elle-même. Mais c'est une autre notion, et, comme condition, elle est distribuée, dans chaque institution, par les règles qui la gouvernent. Exemple : les « pouvoirs » des époux en vertu des régimes matrimoniaux, les « pouvoirs » du propriétaire, de l'usufruitier, du détenteur précaire, etc. Au titre des conventions en général, ce n'est pas une condition générale de validité. On en fait abstraction.*

A contract concluded with a third party does not prejudice the beneficiary of the pre-emption agreement, apart from the effect of any rules designed to protect third parties in good faith.

§ 4 The date and place of formation

Art. 1107

In the absence of agreement to the contrary, a contract is completed by receipt of the acceptance. It is deemed formed at the place where the acceptance is received.

Chapter II
The Essential Conditions for the Validity of Contracts

Art. 1108

Four conditions are essential for the validity of a contract:

– the consent of the contracting parties;

– their capacity to contract;

– a subject-matter of the undertaking;

– a cause which justifies the undertaking.

In addition, for a juridical act effected by the representative of one party, there must be the power to act in the party's name.

The form of contracts is set out in articles 1127 *et seq.*

> *Note: the term 'power' has many meanings, but it is within the law of representation that it appears in its most pure, particular meaning (Carbonnier[1] and Gaillard[2]) amongst the conditions of validity for acts done by representatives. It therefore deserves to be set out in this title in article 1108. It is a condition which applies only sometimes (in the case of representation) but, in that situation, it is essential.*

> *The notion of power also appears in the case of a person with legal capacity who acts on his own account. But that is a different notion and, as a condition of validity, it is arranged in each area of law by the rules which govern it. For example, the 'powers' of spouses by virtue of the matrimonial property regimes; the 'powers' of an owner, usufructuary, holder by permission, etc. It is not a general condition of validity in relation to contracts in general. We shall leave it aside.*

---

[1] [J Carbonnier, *Droit civil: Introduction* (27th edn, Paris, PUF, 2002) no 162.]
[2] [E Gaillard, *Le pouvoir en droit privé* (Paris, Economica, 1985).]

Section 1
Du consentement
(Articles 1109 à 1115-1)

Sous-section 1 : De l'existence du consentement

Art. 1109

Pour faire une convention valable, il faut être sain d'esprit.

C'est à celui qui agit en nullité de prouver l'existence d'un trouble mental au moment de l'acte.

Art. 1109-1

Il n'y a point de consentement lorsque les volontés ne se sont pas rencontrées sur les éléments essentiels du contrat.

Art. 1109-2

L'absence de consentement entache la convention de nullité relative.

Sous-section 2 : De la qualité du consentement

§1 – De l'intégrité du consentement

Art. 1110

Celui des contractants qui connaît ou aurait dû connaître une information dont il sait l'importance déterminante pour l'autre a l'obligation de le renseigner.

Cette obligation de renseignement n'existe cependant qu'en faveur de celui qui a été dans l'impossibilité de se renseigner par lui-même ou qui a légitimement pu faire confiance à son cocontractant, en raison, notamment, de la nature du contrat, ou de la qualité des parties.

Il incombe à celui qui se prétend créancier d'une obligation de renseignement de prouver que l'autre partie connaissait ou aurait dû connaître l'information en cause, à charge pour le détenteur de celle-ci de se libérer en prouvant qu'il avait satisfait à son obligation.

Seront considérées comme pertinentes les informations qui présentent un lien direct et nécessaire avec l'objet ou la cause du contrat.

Art. 1110-1

Le manquement à une obligation de renseignement, sans intention de tromper, engage la responsabilité de celui qui en était tenu.

Section 1
Consent
(Articles 1109 to 1115-1)

Sub-section 1: Existence of consent

Art. 1109

In order to make a valid contract, one must be of sound mind.

A party who brings an action for nullity must prove the existence of a mental problem at the time of the juridical act.

Art. 1109-1

There is no consent where the parties' wills have not met on the essential elements of the contract.

Art. 1109-2

An absence of consent taints the contract with relative nullity.[1]

Sub-section 2: Quality of consent

§ 1 Integrity of consent

Art. 1110

If one of the parties knows or ought to have known information which he knows is of decisive importance for the other, he has an obligation to inform him of it.

However, this obligation to inform exists only in favour of a person who was not in a position to inform himself, or who could legitimately have relied on the other contracting party, by reason (in particular) of the nature of the contract or the relative positions of the parties.

A party who claims the benefit of an obligation to inform has the burden of proving that the other party knew or ought to have known the information in question, but it is then for that other party to show that he has fulfilled his obligation in order to escape liability.

Information is relevant if it has a direct and necessary link with the subject-matter or the cause of the contract.

Art. 1110-1

In the absence of an intention to deceive, a failure to fulfil an obligation to inform gives rise to liability in the party subject to it.

---

[1] [For an explanation of the difference between 'relative nullity' and 'absolute nullity' see P Simler, above, p 539 and below, articles 1129-1 ff.]

640

Art. 1110-2

Dans certaines conventions déterminées par la loi, le consentement ne devient définitif et irrévocable qu'à l'expiration d'un délai de réflexion ou de repentir.

Le délai de réflexion est celui jusqu'à l'expiration duquel le destinataire de l'offre ne peut consentir efficacement au contrat.

Le délai de repentir est celui jusqu'à l'expiration duquel il est permis au destinataire de l'offre de rétracter discrétionnairement son consentement au contrat.

§2 – Des vices du consentement

Art. 1111

Il n'y a pas de consentement valable, si le consentement n'a été donné que par erreur, ou s'il a été surpris par dol ou extorqué par violence.

(art. 1109 actuel)

Art. 1111-1

L'erreur, le dol et la violence vicient le consentement lorsqu'ils sont de telle nature que, sans eux, l'une des parties ou son représentant n'aurait pas contracté ou aurait contracté à des conditions différentes.

Leur caractère déterminant s'apprécie eu égard aux personnes et aux circonstances.

Art. 1112

L'erreur n'est une cause de nullité de la convention que lorsqu'elle tombe sur la substance de la chose qui en est l'objet ou sur la personne du contractant.

Art. 1112-1

L'erreur sur la substance de la chose s'entend de celle qui porte sur les qualités essentielles en considération desquelles les deux parties ont contracté, ou, semblablement, l'une d'elles, à la connaissance de l'autre.

Elle est une cause de nullité qu'elle porte sur la prestation de l'une ou de l'autre partie.

L'acceptation d'un aléa sur une qualité de la chose exclut l'erreur relative à cette qualité.

Art. 1112-2

L'erreur sur la personne s'entend de celle qui porte sur des qualités essentielles du cocontractant.

Elle n'est une cause de nullité que dans les contrats conclus en considération de la personne.

Art. 1112-3

L'erreur sur la substance ou sur la personne est une cause de nullité, qu'elle soit de fait ou de droit, à moins qu'elle ne soit inexcusable.

Art. 1110-2

In certain contracts as fixed by legislation, consent is final and irrevocable only at the end of a period of reflection or a period allowed for a change of mind.

A *period for reflection* is one until the expiry of which the offeree cannot give his effective consent to the contract.

A *period allowed for a change of mind* is one until the expiry of which the offeree may freely revoke his consent to the contract.

§ 2 Defects in consent

Art. 1111

There is no valid consent if the consent has been given only by mistake, or if it has been ensnared by fraud, or extracted by duress.

(art. 1109 of the present Code)

Art. 1111-1

Mistake, fraud and duress vitiate consent where they are of such a nature that, without them, one of the parties or his representative would not have contracted, or would have contracted on different terms.

Their decisive character is assessed in the light of the person and of the circumstances.

Art. 1112

Mistake is a ground of nullity of the contract only where it is about the substance of the thing which is its subject-matter or about the person of the other contracting party.

Art. 1112-1

Mistake about the substance of the thing means that which bears its essential qualities which the two parties had in mind on contracting or, alternatively, which one of the parties had in mind to the knowledge of the other.

It is a ground of nullity whether it bears on the subject-matter of the obligation of one party or of the other.

Acceptance of a risk about a quality of the thing rules out mistake in relation to this quality.

Art. 1112-2

A mistake about the person means one which bears on the essential qualities of the other contracting party.

It is a ground of nullity only as regards contracts entered into on account of personal considerations.

Art. 1112-3

Mistake about the substance or the person is a ground of nullity, whether it is a mistake of fact or of law, as long as it is not inexcusable.

Art. 1112-4

Lorsque, sans se tromper sur les qualités essentielles de la chose, un contractant fait seulement de celle-ci une appréciation économique inexacte, cette erreur sur la valeur n'est pas, en soi, une cause de nullité.

Art. 1112-5

L'erreur sur un simple motif, étranger aux qualités essentielles de la chose ou de la personne, n'est une cause de nullité que si les parties en ont fait expressément un élément déterminant de leur consentement.

Art. 1113

Le dol est le fait pour un contractant de surprendre le consentement de l'autre par des manœuvres ou des mensonges.

Obs. : Reprise du verbe de l'article 1111 (1109 c. civ.)

Art. 1113-1

Constitue également un dol la dissimulation intentionnelle par un contractant d'un fait qui, s'il avait été connu de son cocontractant, l'aurait dissuadé de contracter, au moins aux conditions convenues.

Art. 1113-2

Le dol est semblablement constitué s'il émane du représentant, gérant d'affaires, préposé ou porte-fort du cocontractant, ou même d'un tiers sous l'instigation ou avec la complicité du cocontractant.

Art. 1113-3

L'erreur provoquée par le dol est toujours excusable. Elle est une cause de nullité alors même qu'elle porterait sur la valeur de la chose qui en est l'objet ou sur un simple motif du contrat.

Art. 1114

Il y a violence lorsqu'une partie s'engage sous la pression d'une contrainte qui lui inspire la crainte d'exposer sa personne, sa fortune ou celles de ses proches à un mal considérable.

Art. 1114-1

La menace d'une voie de droit ne constitue une violence qu'en cas d'abus. L'abus existe lorsque la voie de droit est détournée de son but ou brandie pour obtenir un avantage manifestement excessif.

Art. 1114-2

La violence vicie le consentement de la partie qui s'oblige, qu'elle ait été exercée par l'autre ou par un tiers, et non seulement lorsqu'elle a été exercée sur la partie contractante mais encore lorsqu'elle l'a été sur son conjoint ou sur l'un de ses proches.

La seule crainte révérencielle envers le père, la mère ou autre ascendant, sans qu'il y ait eu de violence exercée, ne suffit point pour annuler le contrat.

Obs. : C'est le remploi de trois articles actuels : 1111, 1113, 1114.

Art. 1112-4

In the absence of a mistake about the essential qualities of the thing, where a party makes only an inaccurate valuation of it, this mistake of value is not, of itself, a ground of nullity.

Art. 1112-5

Mistake about mere motive, extraneous to the essential qualities of the thing or of the person, is a ground of nullity only if the parties have expressly made it a decisive element of their consent.

Art. 1113

Fraud is an act of a party in ensnaring the other's consent by scheming or lies.

Comment: Repetition of the verb in article 1111 (1109 of the present Code).

Art. 1113-1

It is also fraud where one party intentionally conceals a fact which, if it had been known by the other party, would have deterred him from contracting, at least on the terms which they agreed.

Art. 1113-2

Fraud is equally established where it originates from the other party's representative, a person who manages his affairs, his employee, or one standing surety for him, or even from a third party acting at the instigation of, or with the complicity of, the other party.

Art. 1113-3

A mistake induced by fraud is always excusable. It is a ground of nullity even where it bears on the value of the thing which is the subject-matter of the contract, or on a person's mere motive.

Art. 1114

There is duress where one party contracts under the influence of pressure which makes him fear that his person or his wealth, or those of his near relatives, might be exposed to significant harm.

Art. 1114-1

A threat of legal action constitutes duress only when it is abused. It is abused where the legal process is deflected from its proper aims or is exercised in order to obtain a manifestly excessive advantage.

Art. 1114-2

Duress vitiates the consent of the contracting party, regardless of whether it has been applied by the other party or by a third party, and not only where it has been committed against the contracting party but also where it has been applied against his spouse or one of his near relatives.

Dutiful respect for one's father, mother or other older relative is not of itself sufficient for annulment of the contract without any duress being committed.

Comment: This re-uses three current articles: 1111, 1113, 1114.

Art. 1114-3

Il y a également violence lorsqu'une partie s'engage sous l'empire d'un état de nécessité ou de dépendance, si l'autre partie exploite cette situation de faiblesse en retirant de la convention un avantage manifestement excessif.

La situation de faiblesse s'apprécie d'après l'ensemble des circonstances en tenant compte, notamment, de la vulnérabilité de la partie qui la subit, de l'existence de relations antérieures entre les parties ou de leur inégalité économique.

Art. 1115

La convention contractée par erreur, dol ou violence donne ouverture à une action en nullité relative.

Indépendamment de l'annulation du contrat, la violence, le dol ou l'erreur qui cause à l'une des parties un dommage, oblige celui par la faute duquel il est arrivé à le réparer.

Les actions fondées sur un vice du consentement procèdent d'une seule et même cause qui les rend fongibles.

Art. 1115-1

Le délai de l'action en nullité ne court dans les cas de violence que du jour où elle a cessé ; dans le cas d'erreur ou de dol, du jour où ils ont été découverts.

Section 2
De la capacité des parties contractantes et du pouvoir d'agir au nom d'autrui
(Articles 1116 à 1120-2)

§1 – De la capacité de jouissance

Note : Il y a lieu de mettre l'accent sur la capacité des parties contractantes en marquant la division entre la capacité de jouissance et la capacité d'exercice (§2) et, comme l'accessoire joint au principal, le pouvoir d'agir au nom d'autrui (§3).

Art. 1116

Pour être valable un engagement requiert, en la personne du contractant, la capacité de jouissance, aptitude à être titulaire d'un droit.

Art. 1114-3

There is also duress where one party contracts under the influence of a state of necessity or of dependence, if the other party exploits this situation of weakness by obtaining from the contract a manifestly excessive advantage.

A situation of weakness is assessed by reference to all the circumstances, taking particular account of the vulnerability of the party who submits, the pre-existing relations between the parties, and their economic inequality.

Art. 1115

A contract entered into by mistake, fraud or duress gives rise to an action for relative nullity.[1]

Independently of any annulment of the contract, duress, fraud or a mistake which causes harm to one of the parties gives rise to an obligation on the party by whose fault it was caused to make reparation for it.

Actions based on a defect in consent arise from the same, unique cause of action and this makes them interchangeable.[2]

Art. 1115-1

In the case of duress, the period for bringing an action for nullity runs only from the day when it ceased; in the case of mistake or fraud, it runs only from the day when they were discovered.

Section 2
The Capacity of the Contracting Parties and the Power to Act in the Name of Another
(Articles 1116 to 1120-2)

§ 1 Capacity for enjoyment of legal rights

Note: There is good reason to emphasise the capacity of the contracting parties by indicating the distinction between the capacity to enjoy legal rights and the capacity to exercise one's rights (§ 2) and, following on from the latter, the power to act in the name of another (§ 3).

Art. 1116

To be valid an undertaking requires, in the person of the contracting party, the capacity for enjoyment, the ability to hold legal rights.

---

[1] [For an explanation of the difference between 'relative nullity' and 'absolute nullity' see P Simler, above, p 539 and below, articles 1129-1 ff.]

[2] [For the notion of 'interchangeability'—*fongibilité*—see above, p 509, n 2.]

Note : Plus léger, le parti d'inclure une définition au fil de la phrase s'inspire du précédent exemplaire de la définition de la tutelle (art. 427). L'essentiel est de donner une idée de la capacité de jouissance comme participation à l'activité juridique.

Art. 1116-1

Toute personne physique possède, en tant que sujet de droit, une capacité de jouissance générale.

Celle-ci n'est restreinte que par les incapacités et interdictions particulières établies par la loi relativement à certains actes.

Art. 1116-2

Ainsi il est interdit, sauf autorisation de justice, à quiconque exerce une fonction ou occupe un emploi dans un établissement hébergeant des personnes dépendantes ou dispensant des soins psychiatriques de se rendre acquéreur d'un bien ou cessionnaire d'un droit appartenant à une personne admise dans l'établissement, non plus que de prendre à bail le logement occupé par cette personne avant son admission dans l'établissement.

Pour l'application du présent article, sont réputées personnes interposées, le conjoint, les ascendants et les descendants des personnes auxquelles s'appliquent les interdictions ci-dessus édictées.

(art. 1125-1 actuel)

Art. 1116-3

Les personnes morales sont dotées d'une capacité de jouissance spéciale.

Celle-ci recouvre les actes utiles à la réalisation de leur objet, tel qu'il est défini par les statuts, dans le respect des règles applicables à la personne morale considérée, ainsi que les actes qui sont les accessoires des précédents.

Note : Par opposition à « possède » (pour les personnes physiques, art. 1116-1 ci-dessus), il peut être intéressant de faire sonner le terme « dotées » pour les personnes morales.

Art. 1116-4

La capacité de jouissance des personnes futures est réglée aux titres Des successions et Des libéralités du présent code.

Art. 1116-5

L'incapacité de jouissance ou l'interdiction atteignant l'une des parties à un contrat en cours d'exécution rend ce contrat caduc, à moins qu'il ne puisse être mené à bonne fin par les autres parties.

§2 – De la capacité d'exercice

Art. 1117

Toute personne physique qui n'est pas déclarée incapable par la loi, peut contracter par elle-même sans assistance ni représentation.

Note: To give a lighter touch, the decision to include a running definition is inspired by the existing example of the definition of guardianship (art. 427 C. civ.). Its purpose is to give an idea of the capacity for enjoyment as a participant in activities for which the law provides.

Art. 1116-1

As a legal actor, every natural person possesses a general capacity for enjoyment.

This is limited only by special incapacities and prohibitions established by law in relation to certain types of juridical acts.

Art. 1116-2

Thus, anyone who holds an office or employment in an establishment in which dependent persons reside, or which provides psychiatric treatment, is prohibited, without judicial authorisation, from procuring the acquisition of property or the assignment of a right belonging to a person admitted to the establishment, and from taking a lease of the residence occupied by such a person before his admission to the establishment.

For the purposes of this article the spouse and relatives (both ascendant and descendant) of the persons to whom the above prohibition applies are also deemed to be included.

(art. 1125-1 of the present Code)

1116-3

Legal persons are endowed with a special capacity for enjoyment of legal rights.

This covers juridical acts which are effective to accomplish their objects as defined by their constituent instruments, in accordance with the rules applicable to the legal person in question, as well as transactions which are ancillary to those referred to above.

Note: By contrast with 'possess' (for natural persons: art. 1116-1 above), it may be interesting to emphasise the term 'endowed with' for legal persons.

Art. 1116-4

The capacity of future persons for enjoyment is governed by the titles *Succession* and *Acts of Generosity* in this Code.

Art. 1116-5

A lack of capacity for enjoyment, or a declaration of legal incapacity, affecting one of the parties to a contract in the course of performance causes the contract to lapse, unless it can be fully completed by its other parties.

§ 2 Capacity for exercise of legal rights

Art. 1117

Every natural person who is not declared by law to lack capacity may contract, by himself, without support or a representative.

Une personne physique peut passer tout acte propre à organiser la protection et la gestion de ses intérêts pour le cas où elle deviendrait incapable d'exercer ses droits, dans le respect des principes énoncés au Livre premier du présent code.

Note : Il paraît nécessaire d'énoncer, pour les personnes physiques, ce qu'est la capacité d'exercice. C'est le principe.

Art. 1117-1

Sont incapables de contracter, dans la mesure définie par la loi :

• les mineurs non émancipés ;

• les majeurs protégés au sens de l'article 490 du présent code.

(art. 1124 actuel)

Art. 1117-2

La personne protégée par une incapacité d'exercice peut néanmoins, agissant seule, accomplir les actes nécessaires à la conservation de ses droits, les actes spécifiés par la loi ainsi que les actes courants autorisés par l'usage.

Note : C'est l'exception à l'exception (d'où l'ordre des articles).

Elle peut aussi, si elle jouit d'un discernement suffisant, passer les conventions relatives à sa personne et à celle de ses enfants, dans le respect des dispositions figurant au Livre premier du présent code ou dans des lois particulières.

Toutefois, les conséquences patrimoniales de ces conventions relèvent du régime de protection applicable à la partie protégée.

Une personne physique peut passer tout acte propre à organiser la protection et la gestion de ses intérêts pour le cas où elle deviendrait incapable d'exercer ses droits, dans le respect des principes énoncés au Livre premier du présent code.

Art. 1117-3

Le mineur ne peut se soustraire aux engagements qu'il a pris dans l'exercice de sa profession, ni aux obligations qui résultent de son délit ou quasi-délit.

La simple déclaration de majorité, faite par le mineur, ne fait pas obstacle à la restitution.

(cf. art. 1306 à 1310 actuels)

A natural person may enter into any juridical act appropriate to the arrangement of the protection and management of his interests in the situation where he becomes incapable of exercising his legal rights, in accordance with the principles set out in the first Book of this Code.

Note: For natural persons it seems necessary to state the capacity to exercise legal rights. This is the position in principle.

Art. 1117-1

The following lack capacity to contract, to the extent defined by law:

* minors who have not been emancipated; [1]
* adults who are protected within the meaning of article 490 of this Code.[2]

(art. 1124 of the present Code)

Art. 1117-2

A person who is protected by a lack of capacity to exercise his rights may nevertheless, acting independently, enter into juridical acts which are necessary to preserve his legal rights, acts which are specified by law, and day to day transactions which it is customary to do.

Note: This is an exception to the exception—hence the order of the articles.

If he has sufficient understanding, he may also enter into contracts relating to his person and the person of his children, in accordance with the provisions set out in the first Book of this Code or in particular legislative provisions.

However, the consequences of such contracts on the estate of a protected person are governed by the applicable rules of the relevant protective regime

A natural person may enter into any juridical act necessary to protect or manage his interests for the situation where he may become incapable of exercising his rights, in accordance with the principles set out in the first Book of this Code.

Art. 1117-3

A minor may not escape from undertakings which he has entered into in the exercise of his business or profession, nor obligations which flow from his delictual conduct, whether deliberate or not.

The fact that the minor has declared that he is an adult does not constitute an obstacle to restitution.

Cf. arts 1306 to 1310 of the present Code.

---

[1] [A minor may be 'emancipated' before attaining the age of majority (18 years); marriage emancipates him by operation of law; and he can be emancipated by the court (*le juge des tutelles*) on the proposal of one or both of his parents (or, in the case of an orphan, the proposal of the family council). He then has legal capacity for most purposes, but must obtain permission in certain circumstances, such as in order to marry: articles 476-482, 487 Cc.]

[2] [Article 490 provides a protective regime for those whose mental faculties are impaired by illness, infirmity, or weakness due to their age; and those whose physical capabilities are impaired in such a way as to prevent them expressing their will.]

Art. 1117-4

Le mineur n'est plus recevable à contester l'engagement qu'il avait souscrit pendant sa minorité, lorsqu'il l'a ratifié une fois majeur, que cet engagement fût nul ou seulement sujet à restitution.

Art. 1117-5

Les restitutions dues à un incapable sont réduites à proportion du profit qu'il a retiré de l'acte annulé.

(art. 1312 c. civ. modifié)

Art. 1118

La simple lésion, lorsqu'elle ne résulte pas d'un événement casuel et imprévu, donne lieu à rescision contre toutes sortes de conventions, en faveur du mineur non émancipé et du majeur protégé dans les cas prévus aux articles 491-2 et 510-3 du présent code.

Le rachat de la lésion peut toujours être proposé par la partie qui a bénéficié de la convention.

Obs. : Comparer art. 1305 actuel.

Art. 1118-1

Les personnes capables de s'engager ne peuvent opposer l'incapacité de ceux avec qui elles ont contracté, lorsque cette incapacité est destinée à assurer leur protection.

(art. 1125 c. civ. modifié)

Ces mêmes personnes peuvent faire obstacle à une action en nullité relative ou en rescision engagée contre elles, en montrant que l'acte était utile à la personne protégée et exempt de lésion ou qu'il a tourné à son profit.

Elles peuvent aussi opposer à l'action en nullité ou en rescision la ratification de l'acte par le cocontractant devenu ou redevenu capable.

Art. 1118-2

Lorsque l'incapacité d'exercice est générale, la loi assure la représentation ou l'assistance de la personne protégée.

Art. 1117-4

Where after attaining his majority a minor ratifies an undertaking entered into during his minority, he may no longer contest its validity, whether it was a nullity, or merely gave rise to restitution.

Art. 1117-5

Restitution which is due to a person lacking capacity is reduced to the extent of any benefit which he has obtained from the juridical act which is annulled.

(art. 1312 C. civ., amended)

Art. 1118

A substantive inequality of bargain, where it does not result from a fortuitous and unforeseen event, of itself gives rise to rescission in various different types of contract, in favour of a minor who has not been emancipated,[1] and an adult protected in the situations provided for by articles 491-2[2] and 510-3[3] of this Code.

Repurchase to undo the inequality can always be proposed by the party who has benefited from the contract.

Comment: Compare art. 1305 of the present Code.

Art. 1118-1

Persons with capacity to contract may not raise the lack of capacity of those with whom they have contracted where their lack of capacity is designed to protect them.

(art. 1125 C. civ., amended)

Such persons may defend an action taken against them for relative nullity[4] or rescission by showing that the juridical act benefited the protected person, and did not embody a substantive inequality or that he has made a profit from it.

They may also set up against the action for nullity or rescission the fact that the contracting party ratified the transaction after gaining or regaining his capacity.

Art. 1118-2

Where a lack of capacity to exercise rights is general, legislation ensures that the protected person has a representative or supporter.

---

[1] [See above, p 649, n 1 for an explanation of 'emancipation'.]

[2] [Article 491-2 provides that an adult placed under judicial protection (*la sauvegarde de justice*—the lightest form of intervention to protect an adult) may rescind transactions on account of a substantive inequality of bargain.]

[3] [Article 510-3 provides that, in the case of an adult who is under *curatelle*—a form of protection of which restricts the power to enter into significant transactions—a transaction properly entered into by the protected party without the supervision of his *curator* is liable to be rescinded by him on account of a substantive inequality of bargain.]

[4] [See above, p 639, n 1.]

Art. 1118-3

Les personnes capables de contracter peuvent conférer à un tiers pouvoir de les représenter.

Art. 1118-4

Les personnes morales contractent par l'intermédiaire de leurs représentants.

§3 – Du pouvoir d'agir au nom d'autrui

Art. 1119

Les conventions conclues par ceux qui ont reçu de la loi, du juge ou d'une convention mission de représenter une partie contractante obéissent à une condition complémentaire.

Note : C'est le rappel de l'article 1108 dans la version proposée.

Le représentant légal, judiciaire ou conventionnel n'est fondé à agir que dans la sphère des actes qui entrent dans la capacité de jouissance du représenté et dans la limite des pouvoirs qui lui ont été conférés.

Art. 1119-1

Le représenté est seul engagé par les actes accomplis par le représentant dans la limite de ses pouvoirs.

Mais le représentant répond des fautes qu'il a pu commettre dans l'exercice de ces pouvoirs, notamment s'il en résulte une cause de nullité de l'acte accompli au nom du représenté.

Art. 1119-2

Lorsque la mission du représentant est conçue en termes généraux, elle n'embrasse que les actes d'administration.

Lorsqu'elle est conçue en termes exprès, le représentant ne peut accomplir que les actes pour lesquels il est habilité et ceux qui en sont l'accessoire.

Art. 1119-3

L'acte accompli par un représentant hors de ses pouvoirs est nul. Le représenté peut toutefois le confirmer, s'il en a la capacité.

Les mêmes règles s'appliquent à l'acte par lequel le représentant se rend coupable d'un détournement de pouvoir au détriment du représenté, à moins que le tiers n'ait contracté de bonne foi.

Art. 1120

L'établissement d'une représentation légale ou judiciaire dessaisit pendant sa durée le représenté des pouvoirs transférés au représentant.

La représentation conventionnelle laisse au représenté l'exercice de ses droits, sous réserve de son devoir de loyauté envers son représentant.

Note : L'adjonction de cette réserve est prudente.

Art. 1118-3

Persons with capacity to contract may confer on a third party a power to represent them.

Art. 1118-4

Legal persons enter into contracts through their representatives.

§ 3 The power to act in the name of another

Art. 1119

Where a person is given the task of representing one of the contracting parties by law, by court order, or by contract, the resulting contract must comply with the following further condition.

Note: This links back to the proposed form of art. 1108.

A legal, judicially-appointed or contractual representative is not entitled to enter into transactions except within the scope of those juridical acts which are within the capacity for enjoyment of the person whom he represents, and within the powers which have been conferred upon him.

Art. 1119-1

A person who is represented is bound only by transactions entered into by his representative within the limits of his powers.

But the representative is liable for any fault which he was able to commit in the exercise of these powers, in particular if it causes a ground of nullity of the juridical act entered into in the name of the representative.

Art. 1119-2

Where the task of the representative is defined in general terms, it is limited to necessary managerial acts.

Where it is defined expressly, the representative may only enter into those transactions for which he is authorised, and those which are incidental to them.

Art. 1119-3

A juridical act entered into by a representative outside his powers is a nullity. However, a person who is represented may ratify it, if he has the capacity to do so.

The same rules apply to a juridical act by which the representative makes himself liable for a misuse of his power to the detriment of the person he represents, unless a third party entered into the contract in good faith.

Art. 1120

As long as it lasts, legal or judicial representation takes away from the person represented the powers which have been transferred to the representative.

Contractual representation leaves the person represented the power to exercise his rights, subject to his duty of loyalty towards his representative.

Note: The addition of this reservation is sensible.

Art. 1120-1

Il est interdit au représentant d'agir au nom et pour le compte des deux parties au contrat, ou de contracter lui-même avec le représenté, à moins que la loi ne l'autorise ou ne permette au juge de l'autoriser.

L'interdiction pourrait être autrement levée, par l'accord exprès du représenté ou, dans le cas d'un groupement, par une décision licite de ses membres.

Art. 1120-2

Le représentant ne peut entreprendre ou poursuivre la mission à laquelle il est appelé s'il est atteint d'une incapacité ou frappé d'une interdiction.

Il ne peut la poursuivre en cas de révocation conventionnelle ou judiciaire de sa mission.

Section 3
De l'objet
(Articles 1121 a 1122-3)

Art. 1121

Le contrat a pour objet une chose dont une partie s'engage à céder la propriété ou à concéder l'usage, ou qu'elle s'oblige à faire ou à ne pas faire. La détention de la chose peut être également transférée sans qu'en soit concédé l'usage, notamment à titre de dépôt ou de garantie.

> *Note : Cet alinéa est dans le prolongement de l'article 1127 actuel : « Le simple usage ou la simple possession d'une chose peut être, comme la chose même, l'objet du contrat », mais il est plus exact. Car si l'usage peut ainsi être l'objet du contrat (sa concession), la possession, res facti et non res juris ne peut l'être. Le texte désigne en réalité la détention (et le terme est d'autant plus riche qu'il implique l'obligation de restitution). Dans la version proposée, la détention est un point commun aux contrats qui la concèdent avec l'usage (bail, prêt à usage ; cf. plus loin, art. 1146, 1155 s., les obligations de donner à usage) et aux contrats qui confèrent la détention sans droit d'usage (gage, dépôt).*

Les prestations ainsi convenues caractérisent le contrat comme déclaratif, constitutif, translatif ou extinctif de droits et d'obligations.

Est réputée non écrite, toute clause inconciliable avec ces éléments essentiels.

Art. 1120-1

It is forbidden for a representative to act in the name and on behalf of both parties to a contract, or himself to contract with the person whom he represents, unless legislation so permits, or allows a court so to permit.

This prohibition can be waived, by express agreement of the person represented or, in the case of a group, by a lawful decision of its members.

Art. 1120-2

A representative may not undertake or continue to exercise the task which has been entrusted to him if he suffers from a lack of capacity or is legally prohibited from doing so.

He may not continue if his task is cancelled by contract or by the court.

Section 3
The Subject-Matter of Contracts
(Articles 1121 to 1122-3)

Art. 1121

A contract has as its subject-matter a thing the property in which one party undertakes to transfer, or to grant the right to use it; or something which the party undertakes to do or not to do. The right to hold the thing can also be transferred without there being a grant of the right to use it, for example by way of deposit or guarantee.

> *Note: This paragraph is an extended version of the present article 1127: 'The mere use or possession of a thing can, like the thing itself, be the subject-matter of a contract'. But it is more accurate. For if a right to use something can in this way be the subject-matter of a contract (the permission), possession in fact, and not merely in law, can be too. The text actually refers to the right to hold a thing ('detention', and that word carries such a greater meaning, because it implies an obligation to restore the thing). In the proposed version, a right to hold the thing is a common factor in contracts which grant it together with the right to use (leases, loans for use; see, later, arts. 1146, 1155 et seq.: obligations to give for use) and contracts which grant a right to hold without a right to use (pledge, deposit).*

The contents of the obligations so agreed characterise contracts as declaring, creating, transferring or extinguishing legal rights and obligations.

Any clause which is inconsistent with these essential elements is struck out.[1]

---

[1] [This translates a (technical) French notion that the clause is 'deemed not to have been written': cf S Gaudemet, *La clause réputée non écrite* (Paris, Economica, 2006). The same phrase appears in articles 1125, 1226-4, 1379-8 and 1383.]

Observation générale : Il est utile de conserver les notions et les termes traditionnels (chose, donner, faire, ne pas faire, matière de l'engagement, commerce) mais en les mettant en correspondance avec l'usage actuel (prestations, éléments essentiels, ces termes et expressions revenant d'ailleurs dans maints autres textes). Tout le réseau est cohérent.

Art. 1121-1

Il n'y a que les choses qui sont dans le commerce qui puissent être l'objet d'une convention.

Art. 1121-2

La chose qui forme la matière de l'engagement doit être licite.

Elle doit être possible et exister au moment de la formation du contrat.

Néanmoins, les choses futures peuvent être l'objet d'une obligation.

Art. 1121-3

L'obligation doit avoir pour objet une chose déterminée ou déterminable, à la condition que, dans ce dernier cas, l'étendue de l'engagement ne soit pas laissée à la seule volonté de l'une des parties.

Art. 1121-4

Dans les contrats à exécution successive ou échelonnée, il peut toutefois être convenu que le prix des prestations offertes par le créancier sera déterminé par celui-ci lors de chaque fourniture, fût-ce par référence à ses propres tarifs, à charge pour lui, en cas de contestation, d'en justifier le montant à première demande du débiteur faite par écrit avec avis de réception.

Art. 1121-5

Si l'étendue d'une obligation de faire n'est pas déterminée au moment du contrat, ni déterminable ultérieurement selon des critères extérieurs à la volonté des parties, le prix peut, après l'exécution, en être fixé par le créancier à charge, pour celui-ci, en cas de contestation, d'en justifier le montant à première demande du débiteur faite par écrit avec avis de réception.

General observation: It is worth keeping the traditional notions and terms (thing, give, do, not to do, subject-matter of the undertaking, commerce [capable of being owned or alienated[1]]), but linking them with terms in current use (contents of the obligations, essential elements: these terms and expressions reappear, moreover, in many other provisions). The whole network is coherent.

Art. 1121-1

Only things which are capable of being owned or alienated[2] can be the subject-matter of a contract.

Art. 1121-2

A thing which forms the subject-matter of the undertaking must be lawful.

It must be possible and must be in existence at the moment when the contract is formed.

However, future things can be the subject-matter of an obligation.

Art. 1121-3

An obligation must have as its subject-matter a thing which is ascertained or ascertainable, as long as, in the latter case, the extent of the undertaking is not left to the decision of one of the parties alone.

Art. 1121-4

In contracts which provide for performance successively or in instalments,[3] it may nevertheless be agreed that the prices to be paid by the person entitled to the benefit of performance[4] are to be fixed by him at the time of each supply, such as by reference to his own tariffs; and in case of dispute he has the burden of justifying the amount on the first request, made in writing by recorded delivery, of the person providing such a benefit.

Art. 1121-5

If the extent of an obligation to do is not ascertained at the time of the contract, nor ascertainable at a later stage in accordance with criteria which do not depend upon the will of the parties, its price may be fixed by the person entitled to the benefit of performance once the obligation has been performed; and in case of dispute he has the burden of justifying the amount on the first request, made in writing by recorded delivery, of the person providing such a benefit.

---

[1] [For the traditional French concepts of *choses hors du commerce*—things which are 'outside trade'—and the opposite (things *dans le commerce*, things 'inside trade'), which we translate as 'things which are capable of being owned or alienated', see above, p 517, n 2.]

[2] [Ibid.]

[3] [On these terms, see Whittaker, above, p 195.]

[4] [The person 'entitled to the benefit of performance' is referred to as the 'creditor' (*créancier*) in French law, but this terminology is misleading to the English reader who thinks of a 'creditor' in a narrower sense (the beneficiary of a money obligation). However, we have more generally used the French terminology for ease of reading. See further above, p 439.]

Art. 1121-6

Dans les cas prévus aux deux articles qui précèdent, le débiteur qui n'a pas obtenu de justification dans un délai raisonnable pourra se libérer en consignant le prix habituellement pratiqué.

Art. 1122

L'illicéité de l'objet entache la convention de nullité absolue.

L'absence d'objet est sanctionnée par une nullité relative.

Art. 1122-1

Le défaut d'équivalence entre les prestations convenues dans un contrat commutatif n'est pas une cause de nullité, hormis le cas où la loi admet la rescision du contrat pour cause de lésion.

Art. 1122-2

Cependant, la clause qui crée dans le contrat un déséquilibre significatif au détriment de l'une des parties peut être révisée ou supprimée à la demande de celle-ci, dans les cas où la loi la protège par une disposition particulière, notamment en sa qualité de consommateur ou encore lorsqu'elle n'a pas été négociée.

Obs. : Le dernier membre de la phrase est inspiré par les principes Landö.

Art. 1123

Le défaut d'équivalence entre les prestations convenues dans un contrat commutatif, qui survient au cours de l'exécution du contrat, relève des dispositions figurant au chapitre III du présent Titre, relatif à l'effet des conventions.

Section 4
De la cause
(Articles 1124 à 1126-1)

Art. 1124

La convention est valable quand l'engagement a une cause réelle et licite qui le justifie.

Art. 1121-6

In the situations set out in the preceding two articles, a person who is entitled to receive, but who has not received, a justification within a reasonable period may free himself from liability by depositing the customary price with a public depositary.

Art. 1122

Unlawfulness of the subject-matter taints the contract with absolute nullity.

Absence of any subject-matter is sanctioned by relative nullity.[1]

Art. 1122-1

A lack of equivalence in the agreed contents of the obligations in a commutative contract is not a ground of annulment except where legislation allows rescission of the contract by reason of substantive inequality of bargain.[2]

Art. 1122-2

However, a contract term which creates a significant imbalance in the contract to the detriment of one of the parties may be revised or struck out at the request of that party, in situations where legislation protects him by means of a particular provision—notably because he is a consumer, or where the clause has not been negotiated.

Comment: The last part of the sentence is inspired by the Lando principles.[3]

Art. 1123

A lack of equivalence in the contents of the obligations agreed in a commutative contract arising during its performance falls to be governed by the provisions contained in Chapter III of this Title, dealing with the effects of contracts.

Section 4
Cause
(Articles 1124 to 1126-1)

Art. 1124

A contract is valid where the undertaking has a cause which is real and lawful which justifies it.

---

[1] [For the distinction between absolute nullity and relative nullity see above, P Simler, p 539 and arts 1129-1 ff.]

[2] [Cf article 1118.]

[3] [Cf O Lando and H Beale, *Principles of European Contract Law*, Parts I and II (The Hague, Kluwer Law International, 2000) article 4:110(1). This is itself based on EC Council Directive 93/13/EEC OF 5 April 1993 on Unfair Terms in Consumer Contracts.]

Art. 1124-1

L'absence de cause est sanctionnée par une nullité relative de la convention. L'illicéité de la cause entache celle-ci de nullité absolue.

Art. 1124-2

La convention n'est pas moins valable quoique la cause n'en soit pas exprimée.

Il incombe à celui qui conteste la cause implicite d'en prouver l'absence ou l'illicéité.

Art. 1125

L'engagement est sans justification, faute de cause réelle, lorsque, dès l'origine, la contrepartie convenue est illusoire ou dérisoire.

Note : Le terme « convenue » comprend la référence au contenu du contrat (son économie).

Est réputée non écrite toute clause inconciliable avec la réalité de la cause.

Art. 1125-1

L'engagement de restituer une chose ou une somme d'argent a pour cause la remise de la chose ou des fonds à celui qui s'oblige.

Lorsque la valeur fournie est d'un montant inférieur à celui de l'engagement, ce dernier doit être réduit à la mesure de sa cause, à moins que cette différence ne soit justifiée dans la convention.

Art. 1125-2

L'engagement pris en contrepartie d'un avantage convenu au profit d'un tiers a pour cause cet avantage, indépendamment de l'intérêt moral ou matériel que celui qui s'oblige peut y trouver pour lui-même.

Art. 1125-3

Les contrats aléatoires sont dépourvus de cause réelle lorsque, dès l'origine, l'absence d'aléa rend illusoire ou dérisoire pour l'un des contractants la contrepartie convenue.

Art. 1125-4

Il n'y a pas de donation ni de testament à défaut d'intention libérale.

Les libéralités sont dépourvues de cause réelle en l'absence du motif sans lequel leur auteur n'aurait pas disposé.

Art. 1126

L'engagement est sans justification, faute de cause licite, lorsqu'il est contracté, par l'une au moins des parties, dans un but contraire à l'ordre public, aux bonnes mœurs, ou, plus généralement, à une règle impérative.

(cf. art. 1162-3 actuel)

Art. 1124-1

Absence of cause is sanctioned by relative nullity of the contract. Unlawfulness of cause taints the contract with absolute nullity.[1]

Art. 1124-2

A contract is no less valid for the cause not being expressed.

A person who disputes the cause which has not been expressed has the burden of proving its absence or unlawfulness.

Art. 1125

Where from the beginning what is agreed to be given in return is illusory or derisory, the undertaking is not justified for lack of real cause.

Note: The term 'agreed' refers to the content of the contract (the bargain).

Any term of the contract which is incompatible with the real character of its cause is struck out.

Art. 1125-1

An undertaking to return a thing or to repay a sum of money has as its cause the delivery of the thing or the money to the party subject to the obligation.

Where the value handed over is lower than that required by the undertaking, the scope of the obligation must be reduced to match the cause, as long as the difference is not justified from the contract.

Art. 1125-2

An undertaking entered into in exchange for a benefit agreed for a third party has this benefit as its cause, regardless of any moral or material interest that the party entering into the undertaking may find for himself.

Art. 1125-3

Aleatory contracts have no real cause where, from the beginning, the absence of any risk makes the agreed exchange illusory or derisory for one of the parties.

Art. 1125-4

There can be no gift or testament in the absence of an intention to confer a gratuitous benefit.

The conferral of gratuitous benefits does not have any real cause in the absence of a motive without which the party conferring the benefit would not have done so.

Art. 1126

An undertaking is not justified for lack of lawful cause where it is entered into, at least by one of the parties, with a purpose contrary to public policy, public morality, or, more widely, a mandatory rule of law.

(cf. art. 1162-3 of the present Code)

---

[1] [For the distinction between absolute nullity and relative nullity see P Simler, above, p 539 and below, articles 1129-1 ff.]

Art. 1126-1

La partie qui contracte dans un but illicite* a l'insu de l'autre doit l'indemniser de tout préjudice causé par l'annulation du contrat.

Toute réclamation est exclue quand les deux parties avaient connaissance de l'illicéité.

Note* : Illicéité comprend immoralité dans la disposition qui précède.

Section 5
De la forme
(Articles 1127 a 1128-2)

§1 – Dispositions générales

Art. 1127

En principe, les conventions sont parfaites par le seul consentement des parties, sous quelque forme qu'il soit exprimé.

Art. 1127-1

Par exception, les actes solennels sont assujettis à l'observation de formalités déterminées par la loi, et dont l'inobservation est sanctionnée par l'annulation de l'acte, à moins que celui-ci ne puisse être régularisé.

Art. 1127-2

Lorsqu'un écrit est exigé pour la validité d'un acte juridique, il peut être établi et conservé sous forme électronique dans les conditions prévues au chapitre sept du présent Titre.

Dans le cas où une mention manuscrite est requise de la part de celui qui s'oblige, il peut l'apposer sous forme électronique si les conditions de cette apposition sont de nature à garantir qu'elle ne peut être effectuée que par lui.

Art. 1127-3

Il est fait exception aux dispositions de l'article précédent pour les actes sous seing privé relatifs au droit de la famille et des successions et pour les actes sous seing privé relatifs à des sûretés personnelles ou réelles, de nature civile ou commerciale, sauf s'ils sont passés par une personne pour les besoins de sa profession.

Art. 1126-1

A party who enters into a contract with a purpose which is unlawful* without the knowledge of the other must compensate all the loss caused by the annulment of the contract.

There can be no claim where both parties knew of the unlawfulness.

Note*: Unlawfulness includes immorality in the provision just mentioned.

Section 5
Form
(Articles 1127 to 1128-2)

§ 1 General provisions

Art. 1127

As a general rule, contracts are completely formed by the mere consent of the parties regardless of the form in which this may be expressed.

Art. 1127-1

Exceptionally, solemn juridical acts are required to comply with those formalities which are prescribed by law, and failure to comply results in the act being annulled unless the defect can be cured.[1]

Art. 1127-2

Where writing is required for the validity of a juridical act, it may be created and stored in electronic form on the basis set out in chapter seven of this Title.

In circumstances where a person undertaking an obligation is required to add something in his own hand, he may do so in electronic form if the circumstances of this are such as to guarantee that it could have been done only by him.

Art. 1127-3

The provisions of the preceding article do not apply to signed juridical acts relating to family law and the law of succession, nor to signed juridical acts relating to personal or real guarantees, whether made under civil law or commercial law,[2] unless they are entered into by a person for the purposes of his business or profession.[3]

---

[1] [Cf article 1102-4.]

[2] [For the place of commercial law (*droit commercial*) in French law, by contrast with the civil law (*droit civil*) see Bell, Boyron and Whittaker, above, p 465, n 3, 431-41.]

[3] [The French concept of *profession* extends more broadly than the English 'profession' to cover economic activity in general, and is therefore translated throughout as 'business or profession'.]

Art. 1127-4

Le régime de l'action en nullité pour défaut ou vice de forme, lorsqu'il n'est pas déterminé par la loi, dépend de la nature des intérêts que la forme vise à protéger.

Art. 1127-5

Les formes requises aux fins de preuve ou d'opposabilité sont sans effet sur la validité des conventions.

Art. 1127-6

Les conventions qui ont pour objet de modifier une convention antérieure ou d'y mettre fin sont soumises aux mêmes règles de forme que celle-ci, à moins qu'il n'en soit autrement disposé ou convenu.

§2 – De la forme des contrats électroniques

Art. 1128

Quiconque propose, à titre professionnel, par voie électronique, la fourniture de biens ou la prestation de services, met à disposition les conditions contractuelles applicables d'une manière qui permette leur conservation et leur reproduction. Sans préjudice des conditions de validité mentionnées dans l'offre, son auteur reste engagé par elle tant qu'elle est accessible par voie électronique de son fait.

L'offre énonce en outre :

1° Les différentes étapes à suivre pour conclure le contrat par voie électronique ;

2° Les moyens techniques permettant à l'utilisateur, avant la conclusion du contrat, d'identifier les erreurs commises dans la saisie des données et de les corriger ;

3° Les langues proposées pour la conclusion du contrat ;

4° En cas d'archivage du contrat, les modalités de cet archivage par l'auteur de l'offre et les conditions d'accès au contrat archivé ;

5° Les moyens de consulter par voie électronique les règles professionnelles et commerciales auxquelles l'auteur de l'offre entend, le cas échéant, se soumettre.

(art. 1369-1 actuel)

Art. 1128-1

Pour que le contrat soit valablement conclu, le destinataire de l'offre doit avoir eu la possibilité de vérifier le détail de sa commande et son prix total, et de corriger d'éventuelles erreurs, avant de confirmer celle-ci pour exprimer son acceptation.

L'auteur de l'offre doit accuser réception sans délai injustifié et par voie électronique de la commande qui lui a été ainsi adressée.

La commande, la confirmation de l'acceptation de l'offre et l'accusé de réception sont considérés comme reçus lorsque les parties auxquelles ils sont adressés peuvent y avoir accès.

(art. 1369-2 actuel)

Art. 1127-4

Where they are not determined by law, the rules applicable to the action for nullity for absence of, or defect in, formality depend on the nature of the interests which the requirement of form is intended to protect.

Art. 1127-5

Formalities required for the purpose of evidence of a juridical act or its effect on third parties do not prejudice the validity of the contract in question.

Art. 1127-6

Contracts whose purpose is to modify or terminate an earlier contract must comply with the same rules of formality as the earlier contract, unless there is a legal provision or agreement to the contrary.

§ 2 The form of electronic contracts[1]

Art. 1128

A person who, in a business or professional capacity, makes a proposal in electronic form for the supply of goods or services, must provide the applicable contractual terms in a form which will permit their retention and reproduction. Without prejudice to the conditions of validity mentioned in the offer, the offeror remains bound by it as long as the offer is available to him in electronic form.

An offer must set out in addition:

1. The different steps that must be completed to conclude the contract in electronic form;

2. The technical mechanisms by which the user, before the conclusion of the contract, may identify errors in the data entry, and correct them;

3. The languages proposed for the conclusion of the contract;

4. Where the contract is to be archived, the circumstances in which the offer is to store it and the conditions for access to the stored contract;

5. If the offeror intends to be bound by any business, professional or commercial rules, the means by which these may be consulted in electronic form.

(art. 1369-1 of the present Code)

Art. 1128-1

In order that a contract may be validly concluded, the offeree must have had the possibility of verifying the detail of his order and the total price, and to correct any errors, before confirming this to give his acceptance.

The offeror must without unnecessary delay acknowledge receipt of such an order which has been addressed to him in electronic form.

The order, the confirmation of acceptance of the offer, and the acknowledgement of receipt are deemed to have been received when the parties to whom they are addressed can obtain access to them.

(art. 1369-2 of the present Code)

---

[1] [As Catala explains above, p 535, these provisions stem from EC legislation.]

Art. 1128-2

Il est fait exception aux obligations visées aux 1° à 5° de l'article 1128 et aux deux premiers alinéas de l'article 1128-1 pour les contrats de fourniture de biens ou de prestation de services qui sont conclus exclusivement par échange de courriers électroniques.

Il peut, en outre, être dérogé aux dispositions de l'article 1128-1 et des 1° à 5° de l'article 1128 dans les conventions conclues entre professionnels.

(art. 1369-3 c. civ. modifié)

Section 6
Des sanctions
(Articles 1129 a 1133)

§1 – De la nullité

Art. 1129

La convention qui ne remplit pas les conditions requises pour sa validité est nulle.

Art. 1129-1

La nullité est dite absolue ou d'ordre public lorsque la règle violée est ordonnée à la sauvegarde de l'intérêt général.

Elle est dite relative ou de protection lorsque la règle violée est ordonnée à la sauvegarde d'un intérêt privé. Toutefois, lorsque l'intérêt privé procède d'une valeur fondamentale, comme la protection du corps humain, la nullité revêt un caractère absolu.

> *Note : Les termes « absolu » et « relatif » ont tellement de sens différents qu'il peut être utile de les éclairer par un équivalent d'usage et de les introduire par le mot « dite ».*

Art. 1129-2

La nullité absolue peut être invoquée par toute personne justifiant d'un intérêt, ainsi que par le Ministère public ; elle peut aussi être relevée d'office par le juge.

La nullité absolue ne peut être couverte par la confirmation de l'acte ; celui-ci doit être refait.

> *Note : A l'article 1129-2 : harmonisation avec le Code de procédure civile : les parties « soulèvent », le juge « relève ».*

Art. 1128-2

There is an exception to the obligations referred to in paragraphs 1 to 5 of article 1128 and to the first two paragraphs of article 1128-1 for contracts for the supply of goods or services which are concluded exclusively by exchange of electronic communications.

In addition, the provisions of article 1128-1 and paragraphs 1 to 5 of article 1128 may be excluded in contracts concluded between business or professionals.

(art. 1369-3 C. civ, amended)

Section 6
Sanctions
(Articles 1129 to 1133)

§ 1 Nullity

Art. 1129

A contract which does not satisfy the conditions required for its validity is a nullity.

Art. 1129-1

Nullity is said to be absolute or a matter of public policy where the rule that has been violated is prescribed for the safeguard of the public interest.

It is said to be relative or protective where the rule that has been violated is prescribed for the safeguard of a private interest. However, where the private interest originates in a fundamental value, such as the protection of the human body, the nullity takes on the character of being absolute.

> *Note: The terms 'absolute' and 'relative' are of such different meanings that it is better to make them clear by an example of how they are used, and by introducing them by the words 'said to be'.*

Art. 1129-2

Absolute nullity may be invoked by any person who can demonstrate an interest, as well as by the magistrate representing the public interest;[1] it may also be raised by the court on its own initiative.

Absolute nullity cannot be remedied by affirmation of the juridical act, which must be entered into afresh.

> *Note: In article 1129-2: harmonisation with the Code of Civil Procedure: the parties 'rely on', the court 'raises'.*

[1] [In France a magistrate representing the public interest (the *ministère public*) may intervene in litigation between private individuals, as well as himself initiating proceedings on private law matters where the public interest so requires. See S Boyron 'Judicial Personnel' in Bell, Boyron and Whittaker, above, p 465, n 3, ch 3, 60-61.]

Art. 1129-3

La nullité relative ne peut être invoquée que par celui que la loi entend protéger. Le titulaire de l'action peut y renoncer et confirmer la convention.

Art. 1129-4

L'acte de confirmation ou ratification d'une obligation contre laquelle la loi admet l'action en nullité n'est valable que lorsqu'on y trouve la substance de cette obligation, la mention du motif de l'action en nullité, et l'intention de réparer le vice sur lequel cette action est fondée.

À défaut d'acte de confirmation ou ratification, il suffit que l'obligation soit exécutée volontairement après l'époque à laquelle l'obligation pouvait être valablement confirmée ou ratifiée.

La confirmation, ratification, ou exécution volontaire dans les formes et à l'époque déterminées par la loi, emporte la renonciation aux moyens et exceptions que l'on pouvait opposer contre cet acte, sans préjudice néanmoins du droit des tiers.

(art. 1138 c. civ. modifié)

Si l'action en nullité appartient à plusieurs titulaires, la renonciation de l'un n'empêche pas les autres d'agir.

Art. 1129-5

Celui dont dépend la confirmation ou la ratification peut être mis en demeure par l'autre partie soit de confirmer ou ratifier, soit d'agir en nullité dans un délai de six mois, à peine de forclusion.

Art. 1129-6

Le donateur ne peut réparer par aucun acte confirmatif les vices d'une donation entre vifs, nulle en la forme ; il faut qu'elle soit refaite en la forme légale.

(art. 1139 actuel)

La confirmation ou ratification, ou exécution volontaire d'une donation par les héritiers ou ayants cause du donateur, après son décès, emporte leur renonciation à opposer soit les vices de forme, soit toute autre exception.

(art. 1140 actuel)

Art. 1130

L'action en nullité absolue se prescrit par dix ans et l'action en nullité relative par trois ans, à moins que la loi n'en ait disposé autrement.

Art. 1129-3

Relative nullity can be invoked only by a person for whose protection the legislation is designed. The party who has the right to the action for nullity may renounce it and affirm the contract.

Art. 1129-4

An act of affirmation or ratification of an obligation for which legislation allows an action for nullity is valid only where it identifies the substance of the obligation, the ground of action for nullity, and the intention to rectify the defect on which the action is based.

In the absence of an act of affirmation or ratification, it is sufficient that the obligation is performed voluntarily after the time when the obligation may be validly affirmed or ratified.

Affirmation, ratification or voluntary performance in the forms and at the time fixed by legislation imply waiver of the grounds of claim and defences that a person might otherwise raise to the juridical act, without, however, prejudice to the rights of third parties.

(art. [1338] C. civ., amended)

If a number of persons have the right to the action for nullity, waiver by one does not bar the action of the others.

Art. 1129-5

The party on whom affirmation or ratification rests may be given notice by the other party either to affirm or ratify, or to proceed with an action for nullity within a period of six months, on pain of losing the right.

Art. 1129-6

A donor cannot by a confirmatory instrument remedy the defects in an *inter vivos* donation which is a nullity by virtue of defects in formality.[1] The donation must be made again in the form required by law.

(art. [1339] of the present Code)

Affirmation or ratification, or voluntary performance of a donation by the heirs or successors in title of the donor after his death implies their waiver of any right to object to it based either on a defect of form or on any other basis.

(art. [1340] of the present Code)

Art. 1130

An action for absolute nullity becomes prescribed after a period of ten years, and the action for relative nullity after a period of three years, unless legislation otherwise provides.

---

[1] [In French law a *donation* is a contractual transaction. Article 931 Cc requires (on pain of nullity) *inter vivos* donations to be entered into before a notary, although there are well-established exceptions, most notably where a gift which has been carried out by physical delivery of a movable is recognised as valid. The formality is required in order to ensure that the gift is publicly recorded for the purpose of gift tax and rules relating to the inheritance of family property.]

L'exception de nullité ne se prescrit pas si elle se rapporte à une convention qui n'a reçu aucune exécution.

Art. 1130-1

La nullité est prononcée par le juge, à moins que les parties à l'acte ne la constatent d'un commun accord.

Art. 1130-2

Lorsque la cause de nullité n'affecte qu'une clause de la convention, elle n'emporte nullité de l'acte tout entier que si cette clause a constitué un élément déterminant de l'engagement des parties ou de l'une d'elles.

La convention est maintenue si la finalité de la règle violée exige son maintien ou si la loi répute non écrite une clause qui, dès lors, ne lie pas le débiteur.

Les mêmes règles s'appliquent au cas ou la nullité n'affecte qu'une partie de l'acte.

Art. 1130-3

La convention nulle est censée n'avoir jamais existé.

Les prestations exécutées donnent lieu à restitution en nature ou en valeur, selon les distinctions énoncées aux articles 1161 à 1164-7.

§2 – De la caducité

Art. 1131

La convention valablement formée devient caduque par la disparition de l'un de ses éléments constitutifs ou la défaillance d'un élément extrinsèque auquel était subordonnée son efficacité.

La caducité produit effet, suivant les cas, rétroactivement ou pour l'avenir seulement.

Obs. : S'applique à l'acte unilatéral (V. art. 1101 in fine).

§3 – De l'inopposabilité

Art. 1132

La convention qui ne remplit pas toutes les conditions de sa pleine efficacité à l'égard des tiers leur est inopposable.

Art. 1132-1

L'inopposabilité est relative. N'annulant pas la convention elle-même, elle en neutralise les effets à l'égard des personnes qui sont en droit de ne pas en souffrir, à charge pour elles d'établir la circonstance qui justifie cette inefficacité, comme par exemple la commission d'une fraude ou le défaut de publication d'un acte.

A defence based on nullity does not become prescribed if it relates to a contract which has not yet been in any way performed.

Art. 1130-1

Nullity is declared by the court, unless the parties to the juridical act establish it by common consent.

Art. 1130-2

Where the ground of nullity affects only one term of the contract, it does not give rise to nullity of the whole juridical act unless this term formed a decisive element of the parties' undertaking, or of one of them.[1]

The contract continues in force if the purpose of the rule which has been violated requires its continuation, or if legislation strikes out a clause which will not thereafter bind the debtor.

The same rules apply to a case where nullity affects only one part of the juridical act.

Art. 1130-3

A contract which has been annulled is deemed never to have existed.

Performance which has been rendered gives rise to restitution, either in kind or according to its value, in the different situations set out in articles 1161 to 1164-7.

§ 2 Lapse

Art. 1131

A contract which has been validly formed lapses on the disappearance of one of its constituent elements, or on the failure of an external element to which its effectiveness was made subject.

The effect of such a lapse is either retroactive or only for the future, depending on the circumstances.

Comment: This applies to unilateral acts: see the end of art. 1101.

§ 3 Invalidity and third parties

Art. 1132

A contract which does not fulfil all the conditions for its full effect with regard to third parties cannot be set up against them.

Art. 1132-1

This lack of wider effect is relative. It does not annul the contract itself, but merely neutralises its effects as against persons who have a right not to be prejudiced by it—and such persons have the burden of establishing the circumstances which justify this lack of effect, such as for example the commission of a fraud or the failure to publicise the juridical act.

---

[1] [Cf the note as to the position of the Cour de cassation in this type of situation, above, p 541, n 1.]

§4 – De la régularisation

Art. 1133

Lorsque la loi l'autorise, la régularisation restitue son plein effet à un acte par la suppression de l'imperfection qui l'affecte ou par l'accomplissement de la formalité requise.

Chapitre III
De l'effet des conventions

Section 1
Dispositions générales
(Articles 1134 et 1135)

Art. 1134

Les conventions légalement formées tiennent lieu de loi à ceux qui les ont faites.

Elles ne peuvent être modifiées ou révoquées que de leur consentement mutuel, ou pour des raisons que la loi autorise.

Elles doivent être exécutées de bonne foi.

Art. 1134-1

Les parties peuvent, aux conditions de leur convention, de l'usage ou de la loi*, se réserver la faculté de se dédire ou l'accorder à l'une d'elles**.

Notes :

* La faculté de dédit est ici supposée résulter d'une clause mais son exercice est assujetti à des conditions que déterminent, selon les cas, la loi, l'usage ou la convention.

** La faculté de dédit est, en général, unilatérale. Rien n'exclut cependant qu'elle soit à l'occasion établie réciproquement.

Art. 1135

Les conventions obligent non seulement à ce qui est exprimé, mais encore à toutes les suites que l'équité, l'usage ou la loi donnent à l'obligation d'après sa nature.

(art. 1135 actuel)

On doit, notamment, suppléer dans le contrat les clauses qui y sont d'usage, quoiqu'elles n'y soient pas exprimées.

§ 4 Regularisation

Art. 1133

Where legislation so authorises, regularisation restores its full effect to a juridical act by the removal of the defect which affects it, or by the completion of any formality required.

Chapter III
The Effects of Contracts

Section 1
General Provisions
(Articles 1134 and 1135)

Art. 1134

Contracts which are lawfully concluded take the place of legislation for those who have made them.

They can be modified or revoked only by the parties' mutual consent or on grounds which legislation authorises.

They must be performed in good faith.

Art. 1134-1

The parties may reserve to themselves or to one of themselves** a right of withdrawal from the contract, this right being exercised under the conditions set by the contract itself, by custom or by legislation.*

Notes:

* A right of withdrawal is here assumed to result from an express contract term, but its exercise is subjected to conditions which are set by legislation, custom or the contract depending on the circumstances.

** A right of withdrawal is, in general, one-sided, but nothing prevents one from being established reciprocally on occasion.

Art. 1135

Contracts create obligations not merely in relation to what they expressly provide, but also to all the consequences which equity, custom or legislation give to them according to their nature.

(art. 1135 of the present Code)

Notably, contracts should be supplemented by customary terms, even if they are not expressed.

Obs. : C'est l'article 1160 actuel, qui paraît mieux venu dans le sillage de l'article 1135.

Art. 1135-1

Dans les contrats à exécution successive ou échelonnée, les parties peuvent s'engager à négocier une modification de leur convention pour le cas où il adviendrait que, par l'effet des circonstances, l'équilibre initial des prestations réciproques fût perturbé au point que le contrat perde tout intérêt pour l'une d'entre elles.

Art. 1135-2

À défaut d'une telle clause, la partie qui perd son intérêt dans le contrat peut demander au président du tribunal de grande instance d'ordonner une nouvelle négociation.

Art. 1135-3

Le cas échéant, il en irait de ces négociations comme il est dit au chapitre I du présent Titre.

Leur échec, exempt de mauvaise foi, ouvrirait à chaque partie la faculté de résilier le contrat sans frais ni dommage.

Obs. : Ces textes éludent l'imprévision et se bornent à une référence aux circonstances (cf. art. 900-2 c. civ.). Ils sont fondés sur la perte de l'intérêt au contrat : étant dans le titre onéreux cette formule paraît plus adaptée à la situation que celle de l'article 900-2. Ils sont en cohérence avec les dispositions préliminaires du chapitre I relatives à la négociation.

Section 2
De l'interprétation et de la qualification
(Articles 1136 à 1143)

§1 – De l'interprétation

Art. 1136

On doit dans les conventions rechercher quelle a été la commune intention des parties contractantes, plutôt que de s'arrêter au sens littéral des termes.

Comment: This is the present text of article 1160, which appears better following on from article 1135.

Art. 1135-1[1]

In contracts whose performance takes place successively or in instalments, the parties may undertake to negotiate a modification of their contract where as a result of supervening circumstances the original balance of what the parties must do for each other is so disturbed that the contract loses all its point for one of them.

Art. 1135-2

In the absence of such an express term, a party for whom a contract loses its point may apply to the President of the *tribunal de grande instance* to order a new negotiation.

Art. 1135-3

Where applicable, these negotiations should be governed by the rules provided by Chapter I of the present Title.

In the absence of bad faith, the failure of the negotiations gives rise to a right in either party to terminate the contract for the future at no cost or loss.

Comment: These legislative provisions avoid recourse to the idea of unforeseeability and are limited to referring to a change of circumstances (cf. article 900-2 of the Civil Code). They are based on the loss of any point to the contract and as they are included within the category of non-gratuitous contracts, their formulation appears more apt than does article 900-2.[2] They are consistent with the introductory provisions of Chapter I governing negotiations.

Section 2
Interpretation and Classification (Articles 1136 to 1143)

§ 1 Interpretation

Art. 1136

In interpreting contracts one should look for the common intention of the contracting parties at the time rather than staying at the literal meaning of the words.

---

[1] [For discussion of this and the following provisions see Fauvarque-Cosson, above, ch 2, Cartwright, above, ch 3, and Laithier, above, ch 6.]

[2] [This article makes provision for judicial amendment of conditions of gifts or legacies which have become extremely difficult or seriously harmful as a result of a change of circumstances.]

Note : Il est essentiel de maintenir en alinéa de tête, la disposition actuelle de l'article 1156, pilier et règle mémorable qui a la force coutumière d'un adage. Elle proclame le principe de l'interprétation, le principe exégétique que l'esprit l'emporte sur la lettre.

Ce choix fondamental est d'autant plus précieux, que sans méconnaître les différences spécifiques, la lecture de la loi contractuelle a toujours été considérée – et aujourd'hui encore – comme le modèle de celle de la loi étatique (au moins en première lecture).

On doit semblablement dans l'acte unilatéral, faire prévaloir l'intention réelle de son auteur.

Note : Sous-entendu sur le sens littéral, mais cela est compris dans le semblablement.

Dans l'interprétation d'une décision collégiale, on doit faire prévaloir le sens le plus conforme à l'intérêt commun des membres de la collectivité.

Art. 1137

Toutes les clauses des contrats s'interprètent les unes par rapport aux autres, en donnant à chacune le sens qui respecte la cohérence de l'acte tout entier.

Dans l'ensemble contractuel qu'ils forment, les contrats interdépendants s'interprètent en fonction de l'opération à laquelle ils sont ordonnés.

Art. 1138

Les clauses claires et précises ne sont pas sujettes à interprétation, à peine de dénaturation de l'acte.

Art. 1138-1

Quels que généraux que soient les termes dans lesquels une convention est conçue, elle ne comprend que les choses sur lesquelles il paraît que les parties se sont proposées de contracter.

(art. 1163 actuel)

Art. 1138-2

Lorsque dans un contrat on a exposé un cas pour l'explication de l'obligation, on n'est pas censé avoir voulu par là restreindre l'étendue que l'engagement reçoit de droit aux cas non exprimés.

(art. 1164 actuel)

Note : Il est essentiel de maintenir le parallèle historique entre ces deux dispositions complémentaires, relatives à deux maladresses de rédaction : énoncé trop général ou énoncé trop particulier...

Art. 1139

Le contrat s'interprète en raison et en équité.

Art. 1139-1

Lorsqu'une clause est susceptible de deux sens, on doit plutôt l'entendre dans celui

> *Note: It is essential to maintain as the leading paragraph the provision contained in article 1156 of the present Code, an important pillar of the law and a memorable rule which has the customary force of an adage. It proclaims the principle for the interpretation of contracts, an exegetical principle which places the spirit of the contract over its letter.*
>
> *This fundamental choice is especially valuable given that (apart from particular differences) the proper approach to reading contracts, which provide the law for their parties, has always been and is still considered as the model of how at least to approach the reading of legislation, which constitutes the law for the State.*

Similarly, in the case of a unilateral juridical act, effect must be given to the genuine intention of the person who makes it.

> *Note: This is implied underneath the literal meaning of the words, but this is implicit from use of the word 'similarly'.*

In the case of interpretation of a collegial decision, effect must be given to the meaning which most conforms to the common interest of the members of the group.

Art. 1137

All contract terms are to be interpreted by reference to each other, giving to each the meaning which makes sense of the contract as a whole.

Within the contractual groupings which they form, interdependent contracts are to be interpreted in relation to the overall operation to which they contribute.

Art. 1138

Contract terms which are clear and unambiguous are not to be the object of interpretation so as to avoid distorting the nature of the juridical act.

Art. 1138-1

However general the terms in which an contract is cast, it covers only those matters which the parties appear to have had in mind on contracting.

> *(art. 1163 of the present Code)*

Art. 1138-2

Where a contract explains an obligation by setting one example of its application, the parties are not deemed on this ground to have intended to restrict the ambit of their undertaking to this case alone where it would extend to other examples which are not expressed.

> *(art. 1164 of the present Code)*
>
> *Note: It is essential to maintain the historic parallel between these two complementary provisions, which concern two instances of clumsy drafting, one where a statement is too general, one where it is too particular.*

Art. 1139

Contracts are to be interpreted rationally and equitably.

Art. 1139-1

Where a term of a contract may bear two meanings, it should be understood in the

avec lequel elle peut avoir quelque effet, que dans le sens avec lequel elle n'en pourrait produire aucun.

(art. 1157 actuel)

Art. 1139-2

Les termes susceptibles de deux sens doivent être pris dans le sens qui convient le plus à la matière du contrat.

(art. 1158 actuel)

Art. 1139-3

Ce qui est ambigu s'interprète par ce qui est d'usage dans le lieu où le contrat est passé et par la pratique des parties.

(art. 1159 c. civ. modifié)

Art. 1140

Dans le doute, le contrat s'interprète contre celui qui a stipulé et en faveur de celui qui a contracté l'obligation.

(art. 1162 actuel)

Art. 1140-1

Toutefois, lorsque la loi contractuelle a été établie sous l'influence dominante d'une partie, on doit l'interpréter en faveur de l'autre.

Art. 1141

L'interprétation du contrat se fonde sur l'analyse de l'ensemble de ses éléments. La méconnaissance de ses éléments essentiels constitue une dénaturation.

> *Note : C'est un classique : jurisprudence constante, mais sous un énoncé plus législatif. On ne peut reprendre dans la loi le développement jurisprudentiel qui place l'interprétation du contrat sous l'appréciation souveraine des juges du fond, et la dénaturation, erreur de droit, sous la censure de la Cour de cassation. Un tel développement se place en effet sous le rapport de la répartition du pouvoir juridictionnel entre les juges du fait et le juge du droit. La disposition proposée dit la même chose, mais en donnant l'explication fondamentale de la répartition, en somme, pourquoi l'interprétation est appréciation de fait et pourquoi la dénaturation erreur de droit. Ce qui relève du fond, du droit civil pur.*

way which gives it some effect rather than in the way according to which it would produce no effect.

(art. 1157 of the present Code)

Art. 1139-2

Contract terms which may bear two meanings must be understood in the sense which best accords with the subject-matter of the contract.

(art. 1158 of the present Code)

Art. 1139-3

An ambiguous term is to be interpreted by reference to what is customary in the place where the contract was made and to any previous dealings of the parties.

(art. 1159 C. civ., amended)

Art. 1140

In case of doubt, a contract is to be interpreted against a person who has stipulated an obligation and in favour of a person who has undertaken it.

(art. 1162 of the present Code)

Art. 1140-1

Nevertheless, where the contractual bond has been created as a result of the dominating influence of one of the parties, the contract should be interpreted in favour of the other party.

Art. 1141

A contract is to be interpreted on the basis of all its elements taken together. Any misconstruction of its essential elements constitutes a distortion of its nature.[1]

> *Note: This reflects the classic position, drawing on settled case-law but put in the form of a legislative declaration. On the other hand, no legislative expression can be given to the case-law which places the interpretation of contracts in the sovereign power of assessment of the lower courts ('juges du fond'[2]), and sees a distortion by them of the nature of the contract as a mistake of law and therefore proper for the censure of the Cour de cassation. This sort of development forms part of the division of judicial competences between the lower courts, which decide issues of fact, and the highest court, which decides issues of law. The proposed provision says the same thing, but by way of giving a fundamental explanation of this division of function, that is, in sum, why interpretation is a matter for factual assessment and why the distortion of the nature of the contract by a lower court counts as a mistake of law; or, put another way, what involves the merits of a case and what involves questions of pure civil law.*

---

[1] [We have translated '*dénaturation*' as 'distortion of its nature'. The main significance of this designation is that *dénaturation* constitutes a ground of overturning (*cassation*) of a decision of a lower court by the Cour de cassation, as explained in the original note.]

[2] [The expression *juges du fond* is used by French lawyers to refer to the civil courts of first instance and appeal (who are judges of both fact and law), in contrast to the Cour de cassation at the apex of the civil pyramid whose role is to police the decision-making of these lower courts, quashing their decisions on various grounds, notably of law, as the text explains.]

L'intérêt de cette disposition est de faire consoner la règle qu'elle énonce avec la définition de l'objet du contrat (même référence aux éléments essentiels du contrat, à la nature, réseau central cohérent. Cf. art. 1124).

§2 – De la qualification

Note : La qualification peut intervenir à trois niveaux. Lorsque les parties donnent elles-mêmes une dénomination à leur accord, il y a lieu de prendre en considération, comme donnée de base, cette qualification conventionnelle. Dans le cas particulier que réserve l'article 12 alinéa 3 du Code de procédure civile, elle s'impose même au juge : il en est ainsi lorsque, « en vertu d'un accord exprès et pour les droits dont elles ont la libre disposition », elles lient le juge par la dénomination qu'elles ont choisie. En ce dernier cas, la qualification originale est seule à considérer.

En dehors de ce cas, il entre dans l'office du juge (c'est un devoir) soit de qualifier le contrat litigieux lorsque les parties n'ont rien prévu, soit dans le cas contraire, de restituer à la convention litigieuse sa véritable qualification, « sans s'arrêter à la dénomination que les parties en auraient proposée » si elle est inexacte (art. 12 préc. al. 2).

La qualification ou la requalification émane alors des juges du fond. Sous le contrôle de la Cour de cassation, cette qualification juridictionnelle peut être censurée pour erreur de droit.

Si l'on fait abstraction des règles de droit processuel, le point de droit substantiel qui a sa place dans le Code civil est de préciser sur quels critères de fond repose le contrôle juridictionnel de la qualification (et donc également celle-ci) : il se fonde sur les éléments essentiels du contrat, plus précisément sur les éléments essentiels que, dans la réalité, les parties ont donné pour base à leur accord.

Art. 1142

Lorsque les parties ont donné à leur accord une dénomination, il y a lieu de la suivre.

Lorsqu'elle est inexacte, le juge redresse cette qualification hors le cas où elle s'impose à lui. Pour requalifier, il se fonde sur les éléments que les parties, dans la réalité, ont donné pour base à leur accord.

The particular interest of article 1141 is that the rule which it sets out is in harmony with the definition of the 'subject-matter' of contract (where there is the same reference to the essential elements of contracts, to their very nature: a coherent network. Cf. article [1121]).

§ 2 Classification

Note: Classification can take place at three levels. Where the parties themselves give a particular denomination to their agreement, then it is right to take this agreed classification as the proper starting-point. In the special case dealt with by article 12 paragraph 3 of the New Code of Civil Procedure, such an agreed classification actually binds the court: this is the case where 'by virtue of an express agreement and as regards rights over which they have an unrestricted power of disposition', the parties can bind the court by the denomination which they have chosen. Here, therefore, the parties' own initial classification is the only one of which account should be taken.[1]

Outside this situation, it is the role—indeed, the duty—of a court to classify any contract which is the subject-matter of litigation either where the parties have failed to do so or, where on the contrary they have done so, to restore to the contract in dispute its true legal classification, 'without stopping at the denomination which the parties had proposed for it' if it is inaccurate (article 12 paragraph 2 of the New Code of Civil Procedure).

Classification or reclassification of a contract is a matter for the lower courts, but this judicial classification takes place under the control of the Cour de cassation, which may censure it for mistake of law.

Putting aside rules arising from the law of civil procedure, the important legal point which is properly included within the Civil Code is to set out clearly the substantive grounds of the Cour de cassation's review of classification by the lower courts, and, therefore, also of classification itself. This is based on a contract's essential elements, more precisely, on those essential elements which were genuinely put forward as the foundation of their agreement by the parties.

Art. 1142

In general, a denomination given to an agreement by its parties shall be followed.

However, a court shall rectify this classification where it is inaccurate, except in the situation where it is binding on it. Where a court reclassifies a contract, it shall do so on the basis of those elements which the parties have genuinely given as the foundation of their agreement.

---

[1] [This very special example is found in the context of civil procedure. Where the parties to litigation have expressly agreed to restrict their dispute to any point of law or ground of claim, then this classification binds the court (subject to the qualifications noted in the text). This rule therefore forms an exception to the general (and quite complex) sharing of responsibility between the parties and the court as to the legal basis or bases on which a court can or should decide a dispute: see S Whittaker in Bell, Boyron and Whittaker, above, p 465, n 3, 87-89.]

Note : cf. N.C.P.C. art. 12, al. 3 : « Toutefois, il (le juge) ne peut changer la dénomination ou le fondement juridique lorsque les parties, en vertu d'un accord exprès et pour les droits dont elles ont la libre disposition, l'ont lié par les qualifications et points de droit auxquels elles entendent limiter le débat ».

Art. 1142-1

S'il advient que le contrat soit modifié dans l'un de ses éléments essentiels, il y a lieu de lui donner la qualification nouvelle qui en découle.

Art. 1143

L'acte nul faute de répondre aux conditions de la validité correspondant à la qualification choisie par les parties subsiste, réduit, s'il répond aux conditions de validité d'un autre acte dont le résultat est conforme à leur volonté.

Note : C'est une application de la maxime potius ut valeat, ici par voie de requalification.

Section 3
De diverses espèces d'obligations
(Articles 1144 à 1151)

Art. 1144

L'obligation de faire a pour objet une action, comme la réalisation d'un ouvrage ou une prestation de services, ainsi dans l'entreprise ou le louage de services ; celle de ne pas faire une abstention, ainsi de la non-concurrence, du non-rétablissement, de la non-divulgation ou de la non-construction.

Art. 1145

L'obligation de donner a pour objet l'aliénation de la propriété ou d'un autre droit, comme dans la vente, la donation, la cession de créance ou la constitution d'usufruit.

Art. 1146

L'obligation de donner à usage a pour objet la concession de l'usage d'une chose à charge de restitution, comme dans le bail ou le prêt à usage ; elle n'a pas lieu dans les conventions qui concèdent la détention sans droit d'usage, comme le gage et le dépôt.

Note: cf. article 12 paragraph 3 of the New Code of Civil Procedure: 'Nevertheless, a court cannot change the denomination or the legal basis of a claim where the parties have restricted its decision-making by their choice of a particular legal classification or particular legal issues to which they intend to limit their dispute by virtue of an express agreement and as regards rights over which they have an unrestricted power of disposition.'

Art. 1142-1

If one of the essential elements of a contract is later varied a court shall give the contract any new classification which this entails.

Art. 1143

Where a juridical act would otherwise be a nullity for failing to satisfy the conditions of validity governing the legal classification which the parties have chosen to give it, nevertheless it may continue to exist in a reduced form as long as it complies with the conditions of validity of another juridical act whose result conforms to the intentions of the parties.

Note: This is an application of the maxim res magis valeat quam pereat, *here given effect by a process of reclassification.*

Section 3
Different Types of Obligations
(Articles 1144 to 1151)[1]

Art. 1144

The subject-matter of an obligation to do is an action, such as the effecting of works or the supply of services, as in the building context or contracts for services; the subject-matter of an obligation not to do is an abstention, as in the case of duties not to compete, not to re-establish one's business, not to breach a confidence or not to build on a parcel of land.

Art. 1145

The subject-matter of an obligation to give is the alienation of ownership or of some other right, as in the case of sale, gift, assignment or the creation of a usufruct.

Art. 1146

The subject-matter of an obligation to give for use is a grant of permission to use a thing on condition of its return, as in the case of hire or loan for use; it does not arise in the case of contracts which grant permission to hold a thing without any right to use it, as in the case of pledge or deposit.

---

[1] [For discussion of various provisions of the *Avant-projet* on classification of obligations, performance and non-performance see Laithier, above, ch 6.]

Note : L'obligation de donner à usage ne se réduit ni à l'obligation de donner ni à l'obligation de faire. Elle correspond à un concept autonome ; elle constitue une catégorie distincte qui se caractérise : par la nature spécifique et limitée du droit conféré, un droit d'usage, et par l'obligation de restitution. Autrement dit, et en deux mots, elle fait un détenteur précaire ; non pas un propriétaire, non pas le débiteur d'une somme d'argent, mais un usager tenu à restitution. La summa divisio « donner », « faire », devrait faire place à la trilogie « donner », « donner à usage » et « faire » (ou ne pas faire).

Linguistiquement l'expression « donner à usage » qui est assez concise pour avoir sa place dans le premier alinéa de l'article 1101-1 entre « donner » et « faire », est heureuse car elle évoque « donner à bail » et « prêt à usage ». Or, justement, le bail et le prêt à usage sont les deux applications topiques de l'archétype « donner à usage ».

Art. 1147

L'obligation est monétaire quand elle porte sur une somme d'argent. Toute autre obligation est dite en nature.

Les obligations monétaires, en toutes devises, sont fongibles, sauf disposition ou convention contraire.

Art. 1148

L'obligation de valeur est de fournir au créancier, en argent ou en nature, un avantage économique variable selon les circonstances, qui lui garantit, dans le temps, une satisfaction appropriée, moyennant l'actualisation de son montant au jour de son exécution.

L'obligation de valeur est monétaire quand son objet est de fournir une somme d'argent déterminable à la date de l'exigibilité ; elle est en nature quand son objet est de pourvoir aux besoins d'une personne ou aux soins d'une chose, sauf, dans ces deux cas, à être convertie, par convention ou décision judiciaire, en une obligation monétaire révisable.

Art. 1149

L'obligation est dite de résultat lorsque le débiteur est tenu, sauf cas de force majeure, de procurer au créancier la satisfaction promise, de telle sorte que, ce cas excepté, sa responsabilité est engagée du seul fait qu'il n'a pas réussi à atteindre le but fixé.

L'obligation est dite de moyens lorsque le débiteur est seulement tenu d'apporter les soins et diligences normalement nécessaires pour atteindre un certain but, de telle sorte que sa responsabilité est subordonnée à la preuve qu'il a manqué de prudence ou de diligence.

Note : Très souvent les parties ne précisent pas expressément à quoi elles s'engagent (résultat ou moyen). Sans doute vaut-il mieux éviter le verbe « s'engager ». Une expression neutre paraît préférable ; par exemple « être

Note: Obligations to give for use are not capable of being reduced either to obligations to give or to obligations to do. They constitute an independent concept and create a distinct category which is characterised by the specific and limited nature of the right which is conferred (a right to use) and by the obligation to return the thing. In other words and in a nutshell, it makes a person a permitted holder of a thing: not its owner, nor either a debtor of a sum of money, but a user bound to restore it. The grand dichotomy between obligations 'to give' and 'to do' must therefore give place to a trichotomy, distinguishing between obligations 'to give', 'to give for use' and 'to do' (or 'not to do').

Linguistically, the expression 'to give for use', which is concise enough to fit into the first paragraph of article 1101-1 between 'to give' and 'to do', is a nice one as it evokes both 'to give by way of hire' and 'to loan for use'. This is just right, as hire and loan for use are the two contexts in which this overarching category of 'giving for use' is best exemplified.

Art. 1147

An obligation is monetary where it concerns a sum of money. All other obligations are termed obligations in kind.

Monetary obligations in any currency are fungible, except where the law or a contract otherwise provide.

Art. 1148

An obligation of value requires the supply to its creditor, either in money or in kind, of an economic advantage variable according to the circumstances which in time secures for him an appropriate satisfaction by giving him an amount calculated as at the date of its performance.

An obligation of value is monetary where its subject-matter is to supply a sum of money ascertainable at the time when payment is due; an obligation of value is in kind where its subject-matter is to provide for the needs of a person or care of a thing, unless in these cases it is converted into a revisable monetary obligation either by agreement or by a judicial decision.

Art. 1149

An obligation is termed an 'obligation of result' where the debtor is bound to procure for the creditor a promised satisfaction except for cases of *force majeure*,[1] so that, with this exception, his liability arises from the mere fact that he has not succeeded in accomplishing this set purpose.

An obligation is termed an 'obligation to take necessary steps' where the debtor is bound merely to take the care and precautions normally necessary to accomplish a certain purpose, so that his liability arises only on proof of a failure to take care or precaution.

Note: Very frequently parties to a contract do not specify expressly the kind of engagement which they are taking on (whether to accomplish a result or to take care). It is certainly better to avoid use of the verb 'to undertake'. It

---

[1] [For a definition of *force majeure*, see art 1349 of the *Avant-projet*, below, p 841.]

tenu » qui vaut dans le silence des parties. Dans une vue pragmatique la différence spécifique tient au régime de la preuve. Sans doute est-il préférable de le marquer, en s'aventurant à concilier le critère de fond et le critère de preuve.

Art. 1150

L'obligation de sécurité, inhérente à certains engagements contractuels, impose de veiller à l'intégrité de la personne du créancier et de ses biens.

Art. 1151

L'obligation naturelle recouvre un devoir de conscience envers autrui. Elle peut donner lieu à une exécution volontaire, sans répétition, ou à une promesse exécutoire de s'en acquitter.

Note : Le devoir de conscience n'a pas besoin d'être qualifié légitime : il se suffit effectivement à lui-même.

Section 4
De l'exécution des obligations
(Articles 1152 à 1156-2)

§1 – De l'obligation de donner

Art. 1152

L'obligation de donner s'exécute en principe par le seul échange des consentements.

Toutefois son exécution peut être différée par la volonté des parties, une disposition de la loi ou la nature des choses.

Elle s'exécute en nature quel que soit son objet, corporel ou incorporel.

Son exécution rend le créancier titulaire du droit transmis et met à ses risques et périls la chose objet de ce droit, encore que la tradition n'en ait pas été faite.

(cf. art. 1138 al. 2 et 1302 al. 1 c. civ.)

Art. 1152-1

L'obligation de donner emporte celle de délivrer la chose et de la conserver jusqu'à la délivrance, en y apportant tous les soins d'un bon père de famille.

(cf. art. 1136 c. civ.)

La perte de la chose libère le débiteur de ses obligations, à charge pour lui de prouver

would seem that a more neutral expression is preferable, for example, 'to be bound by,' which works equally well where the parties are silent as to the content of their obligation. From a practical point of view, the particular difference lies in the rules governing proof. It is certainly preferable to draw attention to this, by attempting to put together the basis of the distinction between the two types of obligation both in terms of substance and in terms of proof.

Art. 1150

A safety obligation, which is inherent in certain contractual undertakings, requires its debtor to look after the integrity of the creditor's person or property.

Art. 1151

A natural obligation involves a moral duty towards another person. It may be performed voluntarily and, where it is, the debtor may not claim restitution of what he has given or in respect of what he has done; it may also be the object of an executory promise of discharge.

Note: There is no need to qualify the moral duty as legitimate: it is actually enough by itself.

Section 4
The Performance of Obligations
(Articles 1152 to 1156-2)

§ 1 Obligations to give

Art. 1152

In principle an obligation to give is performed by the mere exchange of consent.

Nevertheless, its performance may be deferred by agreement of the parties, by a legislative provision or by the nature of the things to which it relates.

Obligations of this type are performed in kind, whatever their subject-matter, whether corporeal or incorporeal.

Their performance gives the creditor an entitlement to the right conveyed and puts the thing which is the object of this right at his risk, even if it has not yet been physically handed over.

(cf. art. 1138 para. 2 and 1302 para. 1 C. civ.)

Art. 1152-1

An obligation to give comprises an obligation to deliver the thing and to look after it until delivery, taking all the care of a good head of household.

(cf. art. 1136 C. civ.)

Loss of the thing discharges a debtor of his obligations, as long as he shows that this

qu'elle a eu lieu sans sa faute. Il est cependant tenu, s'il y a quelques droits ou actions en indemnité par rapport à cette chose, de les céder à son créancier.

(cf. art. 1303 c. civ.)

Art. 1152-2

Lorsque le débiteur est mis en demeure de délivrer la chose, celle-ci reste ou passe à ses risques.

(cf. art. 1138 al. 2 c. civ.)

En cas de perte de la chose, le débiteur en demeure doit la restitution du prix, à moins que la chose n'eût également péri chez le créancier si elle lui avait été délivrée.

(cf. art. 1302 al. 2 c. civ.)

Art. 1152-3

Le débiteur est mis en demeure soit par une sommation ou un acte équivalent dont il ressort une interpellation suffisante, soit, si la convention le prévoit, par la seule échéance du terme.

(cf. art. 1139 al. 2 c. civ.)

Art. 1153

Si la chose que l'on s'est obligé de donner à deux personnes successivement, est purement mobilière, celle des deux qui a été mise en possession réelle est préférée et en demeure propriétaire, encore que son titre soit postérieur en date, pourvu que la possession soit de bonne foi.

Art. 1153-1

Les effets de l'obligation de donner un immeuble sont réglés au titre De la Vente et au titre Des Privilèges et Hypothèques.

§2 – Des obligations de faire ou de ne pas faire

Art. 1154

L'obligation de faire s'exécute si possible en nature.

Son exécution peut être ordonnée sous astreinte ou un autre moyen de contrainte, sauf si la prestation attendue a un caractère éminemment personnel.

En aucun cas, elle ne peut être obtenue par une coercition attentatoire à la liberté ou à la dignité du débiteur.

À défaut d'exécution en nature, l'obligation de faire se résout en dommages-intérêts.

occurred without his fault. However, he must cede to the creditor any rights or actions for compensation in respect of the thing.

(cf. art. 1303 C. civ.)

Art. 1152-2

Where a debtor is put on notice to deliver the thing, risk remains with or passes to him.

(cf. art. 1138 para. 2 C. civ.)

If the thing is lost, a debtor who has been put on notice to deliver must return the price, unless the thing would have perished in the keeping of the creditor if it had been delivered in any event.

(cf. art. 1302 para. 2 C. civ.)

Art. 1152-3

A debtor is put on notice to perform by formal demand, by an equivalent act which gives sufficient warning, or, where this is provided for by the contract, by mere expiry of the time for performance.

(cf. art. 1139 para. 2 C. civ.)

Art. 1153

If a person undertakes obligations one after another to give the same purely movable property to two persons, as between the latter it is the person who has effective possession who is to be preferred and he becomes its owner even if his title is later in date, provided that his possession was in good faith.

Art. 1153-1

The effects of obligations to give immovable property are governed by rules provided in the Title 'Sales',[1] and in the Title 'Charges and Mortgages'.[2]

§ 2 Obligations to do and not to do

Art. 1154[3]

If possible an obligation to do is to be performed in kind.

Its performance may be ordered by a court either on pain of a monetary penalty or of some other means of constraint, unless the subject-matter of the obligation has a clearly personal character.

In no case may performance be obtained by recourse to any coercion which compromises a debtor's personal liberty or dignity.

In the absence of performance in kind, an obligation to do gives rise instead to damages.

---

[1] [Arts 1582–1701 Cc.]

[2] [Arts 2130–2133 Cc. However, that Title was repealed and replaced by provisions in a new Book 4 of the Code civil ('Sureties'), by *ordonnance* no 2006-346 of 23 March 2006.]

[3] [For discussion of this and the following provisions see Miller, above, ch 7.]

690

Note : Le renversement du principe est bienvenu. Sans doute vaut-il mieux l'énoncer objectivement plutôt que par le biais d'un « droit à ».

Faudrait-il ajouter « lorsque cela est possible » ? Il y a le pour et le contre (précaution ou évidence). Si le pour l'emportait, on pourrait envisager d'énoncer : « L'obligation de faire ou de ne pas faire s'exécute si possible en nature ».

Le renversement est d'autant plus admissible qu'il n'éradique pas ce qu'il y a d'irréductible dans l'exclusion de la coercition sur la personne. D'où la proposition du troisième alinéa qui serre de très près la maxime « Nemo praecise cogi ad factum ».

Le terme « prestation » évoque bien l'action personnelle du débiteur qui le met hors d'atteinte de l'astreinte ou de l'injonction.

Art. 1154-1

L'inobservation d'une obligation de ne pas faire se résout de plein droit en dommages-intérêts du seul fait de la contravention, sauf le droit pour le créancier d'en exiger à l'avenir l'exécution en nature.

Art. 1154-2

Le créancier peut être autorisé à faire exécuter lui-même l'obligation ou à détruire ce qui a été fait par contravention à celle-ci. Le tout aux dépens du débiteur, qui peut être condamné, le cas échéant, à avancer les sommes nécessaires à cette exécution.

§3 – De l'obligation de donner à usage

Art. 1155

L'obligation de concéder l'usage d'une chose impose de la délivrer et de la maintenir en état de servir pendant un certain temps à l'issue duquel le détenteur est tenu de la restituer ; le tout sauf stipulation ou disposition contraire.

Ces obligations peuvent porter sur un bien corporel ou incorporel.

Elles s'exécutent en nature.

Art. 1155-1

En cas de conflit entre plusieurs personnes prétendant à l'usage de la chose, celui dont le titre est premier en date doit être préféré.

Art. 1155-2

Lorsque les parties n'ont pas prévu de délai pour la restitution de la chose, elle doit

Note: This reversal of the statement of principle is welcome.[1] It is certainly better to declare it in an impersonal form rather than by means of the formula that the creditor 'has the right to...'

Should it have been added that performance in kind is available 'where it is possible'? There are pros and cons (should one be cautious or is it too obvious?). If the arguments in favour were found convincing, one could envisage a provision such as 'An obligation to do or not to do is to be performed in kind if possible.'

The reversal of the statement of principle is even more welcome in that it does not get rid of the irreducible minimum which is found in the ruling out of personal coercion. In this way the proposition found in the third paragraph follows very closely the maxim 'Nemo praecise cogi ad factum' ('No-one can be compelled to perform in kind an obligation to do').

The phrase 'subject-matter of the obligation' refers equally to the personal action of a debtor which puts him beyond range of the imposition of a monetary penalty and of a direct order to perform.

Art. 1154-1

A failure to observe an obligation not to do gives rise to damages by operation of law from the mere fact of the breach, without prejudice to the creditor's right to claim performance in kind for the future.

Art. 1154-2

A creditor may be authorised to arrange for performance of a obligation himself or to destroy anything done in contravention of a negative obligation. The cost of these arrangements is to be borne entirely by the debtor who may in an appropriate case be ordered to pay any necessary sum of money in advance.

§ 3 Obligations to give for use

Art. 1155

An obligation to grant permission to use a thing requires its delivery and its maintenance in a fit state for its use during a certain period of time at the end of which its holder is bound to return it. These rules are subject to agreement or legislative provision to the contrary.

These obligations may relate either to corporeal or incorporeal property.

They are to be performed in kind.

Art. 1155-1

Where there is a conflict between several persons claiming use of a thing, the person whose title is first in time is to be preferred.

Art. 1155-2

Where the parties have not made provision as to the period at the end of which the

---

[1] [The 'reversal' is a reference to the present apparent statement of the general principle found in art 1142 Cc with the exceptions found in arts 1143 and 1144.]

être restituée dans un délai raisonnable et, sauf urgence, après un préavis donné au débiteur.

Art. 1156

Le détenteur est cependant fondé à retenir la chose jusqu'au complet paiement des sommes qui lui sont dues au titre d'une créance jointe à la chose.

Section 5
De l'inexécution des obligations et de la résolution du contrat
(Articles 1157 à 1160-1)

Art. 1157

Dans un contrat synallagmatique, chaque partie peut refuser d'exécuter son obligation tant que l'autre n'exécute pas la sienne.

Lorsque l'inexécution résulte d'une force majeure ou d'une autre cause légitime, le contrat peut être pareillement suspendu si l'inexécution n'est pas irrémédiable.

À l'exception d'inexécution, l'autre partie peut répliquer en prouvant en justice que la suspension du contrat n'est pas justifiée.

> *Obs. :*
>
> *1) La référence aux contrats synallagmatiques, domaine de l'exception paraît nécessaire (surtout par opposition à l'article 1158).*
>
> *2) La mise en valeur de l'inexécution fortuite ou légitime (service national, maternité, grève, cas plus particuliers) peut être utile (et c'est l'occasion de faire état du caractère non irrémédiable de l'inexécution, postulat de la suspension).*
>
> *3) La mise en facteur commun de la preuve contraire en justice, sous une forme générique, paraît opportune.*

Art. 1158

Dans tout contrat, la partie envers laquelle l'engagement n'a pas été exécuté, ou l'a été imparfaitement, a le choix ou de poursuivre l'exécution de l'engagement ou de provoquer la résolution du contrat ou de réclamer des dommages intérêts, lesquels peuvent, le cas échéant, s'ajouter à l'exécution ou à la résolution.

thing is to be returned, it must be returned after a reasonable period and, except in urgent cases, after giving notice to the debtor.

Art. 1156

However, a holder of a thing given to him for use is entitled to keep it until any sums due to him arising from a debt attached to it have been fully paid.

Section 5
Non-Performance of Obligations and Termination of Contracts
(Articles 1157 to 1160-1)

Art. 1157

In synallagmatic contracts, either party may refuse to perform his obligation to the extent to which the other does not perform his own obligation.

Where non-performance results from *force majeure*[1] or some other legitimate ground, the contract may be similarly suspended if the non-performance is not incapable of being remedied.

In reply to a defence of non-performance,[2] the other party may establish before a court that suspension of the contract was not justified.

Comments:

(1) The reference to synallagmatic contracts appears necessary as this is the context in which the defence of non-performance may arise (and especially by way of contrast to article 1158).

(2) Giving prominence to unavoidable or legitimate non-performance (national service, pregnancy, strikes, and more particular situations) is useful (and this is the occasion to note the non-irremediable nature of non-performance on which suspension of the contract depends).

(3) Making proof to the contrary before a court a common factor in a general way seems appropriate.

Art. 1158[3]

In all contracts, a person for whose benefit an undertaking has not been performed or has been performed only imperfectly, has the choice either to pursue performance of the undertaking, to instigate termination of the contract or to claim damages, and the latter may in some cases be recovered in addition to performance or termination of the contract.

[1] [For a definition of *force majeure*, see art 1349 of the *Avant-projet*, below, p 841.]
[2] [On this defence, see above, p 563.]
[3] [For discussion of this provision and its successors, see Fabre-Magnan, above, ch 8; Whittaker, above, ch 9 and Miller, above, ch 7.]

Quand il opte pour la résolution, le créancier peut soit la demander au juge, soit, de lui-même, mettre en demeure le débiteur défaillant de satisfaire à son engagement dans un délai raisonnable, à défaut de quoi il sera en droit de résoudre le contrat.

Lorsque l'inexécution persiste, le créancier notifie au débiteur la résolution du contrat et les raisons qui la motivent. Celle-ci prend effet lors de la réception de la notification par l'autre partie.

> *Obs. :*
>
> *1) Dans un premier alinéa charnière, il est utile d'ouvrir l'éventail de toutes les possibilités.*
>
> *2) La résolution est elle-même à double voie. Pourquoi fermer la résolution judiciaire en ouvrant la résolution unilatérale ? C'est l'occasion de marquer que le créancier prend ce parti à ses risques et périls.*
>
> *3) La résolution unilatérale a de quoi choquer. Elle est utile à consacrer mais avec des ménagements de forme (en pensant au côté psychologique de l'innovation). La formule « il déclare que le contrat sera résolu » serait trop catégorique. Pour un même résultat, on peut arrondir l'initiative par un tour moins « unilatéraliste » en énonçant « il tiendra le contrat pour résolu ».*

Art. 1158-1

Il est loisible au débiteur de contester en justice la décision du créancier en alléguant que le manquement qui lui est imputé ne justifie pas la résolution du contrat.

Le juge peut, selon les circonstances, valider la résolution ou ordonner l'exécution du contrat, en octroyant éventuellement un délai au débiteur.

Art. 1159

Les clauses résolutoires doivent expressément désigner les engagements dont l'inexécution entraînera la résolution du contrat.

La résolution est subordonnée à une mise en demeure infructueuse, s'il n'a pas été convenu qu'elle résulterait du seul fait de l'inexécution. La mise en demeure n'est efficace que si elle rappelle en termes apparents la clause résolutoire.

En toute hypothèse, la résolution ne prend effet que par la notification qui en est faite au débiteur et à la date de sa réception.

Art. 1160

La résolution peut avoir lieu pour une partie seulement du contrat, lorsque son exécution est divisible.

Art. 1160-1

La résolution du contrat libère les parties de leurs obligations.

Dans les contrats à exécution successive ou échelonnée, la résolution vaut résiliation ; l'engagement des parties prend fin pour l'avenir, à compter de l'assignation en résolution ou de la notification de la résolution unilatérale.

Where a creditor opts for termination of the contract, he can either claim it from the court or by his own act put the defaulting debtor on notice to fulfil his undertaking within a reasonable time, failure to do so in the debtor leading to the creditor's right himself to terminate the contract.

Where a debtor continues to fail to perform, the creditor can give him notice that the contract is terminated and on what grounds. In these circumstances, termination takes effect at the time of receipt of the notice by the other party to the contract.

> *Comments:*
>
> *(1) In the crucial first paragraph, it is useful to set out the full range of possibilities.*
>
> *(2) Termination therefore possesses two tracks. Why close off judicial termination on opening the way for unilateral termination? It is to be noted, however, that a creditor who chooses the latter does so at his own risk.*
>
> *(3) Unilateral termination of a contract could be rather a shock. It is useful to give it formal recognition, but with some care as to its form (thinking of the psychological side of the change). The form of words 'he declares that the contract is terminated' would be too downright. For the same result, one can make one-sided termination more tolerable by using a less 'unilateralist' turn of phrase by saying 'the contract shall be deemed to be terminated.'*

Art. 1158-1

The debtor may contest the creditor's decision before the court by claiming that any failure to perform which is alleged against him does not justify termination of the contract.

Depending on the circumstances, the court may confirm the termination effected by the creditor or instead order performance of the contract, with the possibility of giving the debtor time to perform.

Art. 1159

Termination clauses must expressly identify the contractual undertakings whose non-performance will lead to termination of the contract.

Termination of the contract may take place only after the service of a notice to perform, which has not been complied with, unless it was agreed that termination may arise from the mere act of non-performance. A notice to perform counts for this purpose only if it reminds the debtor of the termination clause in clear terms.

In all cases, termination takes effect only on actual notification to the debtor and on the date of its receipt.

Art. 1160

Where its performance is divisible, a contract may be terminated merely in part.

Art. 1160-1

Termination of the contract frees the parties from their obligations.

As regards contracts with performance successively or in instalments, termination takes effect for the future; the parties' undertakings cease from the time of service of proceedings for termination or from the time of notice of any unilateral termination.

Si le contrat a été partiellement exécuté, les prestations échangées ne donnent pas lieu à restitution ni indemnité lorsque leur exécution a été conforme aux obligations respectives des parties.

Dans les contrats à exécution instantanée, elle est rétroactive ; chaque partie restitue à l'autre ce qu'elle en a reçu, suivant les règles posées à la section 6 ci-après du présent chapitre.

Section 6
Des restitutions après anéantissement du contrat
(Articles 1161 à 1164-7)

Art. 1161

Les restitutions après anéantissement, par annulation ou résolution du contrat, sont gouvernées par les règles qui suivent.

Ces règles sont applicables, sauf disposition ou convention particulière, aux autres cas de restitution, notamment la caducité lorsqu'elle produit un effet rétroactif.

> *Note : La multiplicité des hypothèses de restitution rend nécessaire que soit dès le seuil déterminé le domaine d'application des règles édictées pour les restitutions après anéantissement du contrat.*

§1 – Principes

Art. 1162

L'annulation et la résolution rétroactive du contrat emportent, de plein droit, la restitution intégrale et s'il y a lieu réciproque des avantages reçus en exécution du contrat.

Lorsque l'annulation ou la résolution est imputable à l'une des parties, celle-ci doit en outre indemniser l'autre de tous les dommages et intérêts.

If the contract has been performed in part, anything so exchanged by the parties gives rise neither to restitution nor to any compensation as long as they conformed to the respective obligations of the parties.

As regards contracts whose performance is instantaneous, termination of the contract is retroactive; each party must make restitution to the other in respect of what he has received, in accordance with the rules set out in section 6 of this chapter (below).

Section 6
Restitution Following Destruction of a Contract
(Articles 1161 to 1164-7)

Art. 1161[1]

Restitution following the destruction of a contract, whether by way of annulment or retroactive termination, is governed by the following rules.

Except where legislation or a special agreement so provides, these rules apply to other cases of restitution, notably lapse[2] where it has a retroactive effect.

> *Note: the multiplicity of situations in which restitution may arise makes it necessary to determine at the outset the domain of application of the rules set out for restitution following the destruction of a contract.*

§ 1 Principles

Art. 1162

The annulment or the retroactive termination of a contract involves the full and, where applicable, reciprocal restitution by operation of law of any benefit received in performance of the contract.

Where annulment or termination is attributable to one of the parties, the latter must also compensate the other for all his losses.[3]

---

[1] [See the extensive explanatory introduction to these provisions by A Serinet, above, pp 567 ff.]

[2] [In French law, 'lapse' (*caducité*) can affect gifts (eg article 1088 Cc which concerns gifts made in contemplation of a marriage which does not take place) or legacies (see art 1042 Cc governing the case of a legacy in respect of property which is totally destroyed during the lifetime of the testator).]

[3] [The final words of the French text here refer to the compensation of '*tous les dommages et intérêts*' but this confuses what is compensated (harm or loss (*le dommage* or *le préjudice*): see arts 1370 ff of the *Avant-projet*) with the means of compensation (damages). For this reason, we have translated *dommages et intérêts* here as 'losses' rather than 'damages'. The legal basis for such an award of compensation would be delictual liability for fault, at present contained in arts 1382-3 Cc, this being implicit in the French term *imputable* (translated as 'attributable') which assumes the existence of fault.]

Art. 1162-1

L'obligation de restitution bénéficie des garanties stipulées pour le paiement de l'obligation primitive.

Elle se prescrit par le même délai que la nullité ou la résolution qui l'emporte.

Art. 1162-2

Le juge, saisi d'une action en nullité ou en résolution, peut statuer d'office sur les restitutions quand même il n'en aurait pas été requis.

Il prononce la compensation judiciaire des dettes fongibles de restitution.

Le jugement d'annulation ou de résolution entraîne interversion de la prescription applicable à l'obligation de restitution.

Art. 1162-3

Celui qui a sciemment contrevenu à l'ordre public, aux bonnes mœurs ou, plus généralement à une règle impérative, peut se voir refuser toute restitution.

§2 – Modalités de la restitution

Art. 1163

Les modalités de la restitution dépendent de la nature des prestations accomplies en exécution du contrat.

Art. 1163-1

Après l'exécution d'une obligation de faire ou de ne pas faire, la restitution a lieu en valeur.

Le montant de la restitution est calculé en tenant compte des avantages directs et indirects que les parties ont pu retirer de l'exécution du contrat, suivant leur estimation au jour de la restitution.

Art. 1162-1

An obligation to make restitution brings with it the benefit of any guarantees stipulated in respect of satisfaction of the original obligation.

An obligation to make restitution is subject to prescription on expiry of the same period as the nullity or retroactive termination to which it relates.

Art. 1162-2

A court seized of an action for annulment or for termination of a contract may on its own initiative decide on issues of restitution even where it has not been required to do so by the parties' claims.

In its decision, a court may set off[1] any fungible restitutionary debts.

A court order which declares the annulment or the retroactive termination of a contract interrupts the original prescription period applicable to the obligation to make restitution and converts it into the prescription period provided by the general law.[2]

Art. 1162-3

Restitution may be refused to a person who has knowingly violated public policy, public morality or, more generally, any mandatory rule.

§ 2 The modalities of restitution

Art. 1163

The modalities of restitution depend on the nature of the subject-matter of the obligations effected in performance of the contract.

Art. 1163-1

After performance of an obligation to do or not to do, restitution takes place of its value.

The amount of restitution is calculated taking into account the direct and indirect benefits which the parties were able to derive from performance of the contract, assessed as at the date of restitution.

---

[1] [The term used here is *'compensation judiciaire'* which draws a contrast with *compensation légale* (by which set-off occurs in certain circumstances automatically as provided by arts 1289 ff Cc) or *compensation conventionelle* (where set-off is provided for by the terms of an agreement). *Compensation judiciaire* can arise where a court holds that, even though one of the debts is not liquidated, set-off should take effect in the interests of protection of the other party by reason of the relationship between the two obligations: see A Bénabent, *Droit civil, Les obligations* (10th edn, Paris, Montchrestien, 2005) 572 ff. In the context of art 1162-2(2), an explicit reference to the judicial nature of set-off is redundant in English.]

[2] [The words 'interrupts the original prescription period applicable to the obligation to make restitution and converts it into the prescription period provided by the general law' explain—if long-windedly—the French term *'interversion'*: see above, p 575, n 3.]

Art. 1163-2

La restitution d'une somme d'argent se fait par équivalent. Elle n'est alors que la somme numérique énoncée au contrat.

Art. 1163-3

La restitution d'un corps certain se fait en nature lorsque la chose existe encore entre les mains de celui qui l'a reçue.

Elle se fait en valeur lorsque la chose n'est plus individualisable en raison de sa destruction volontaire ou fortuite, sa transformation ou son incorporation.

Lorsque la chose n'a été qu'en partie détruite, transformée ou incorporée, celui à qui la restitution est due peut préférer, ou la restitution intégrale en valeur, ou une restitution partielle et son complément en valeur.

Art. 1163-4

La restitution d'une chose de genre autre qu'une somme d'argent se fait par équivalent à moins que celui auquel elle est due ne préfère en recevoir la valeur.

Art. 1163-5

Lorsque la chose à restituer est périe fortuitement ou par le fait d'un tiers, la restitution se reporte de plein droit sur l'indemnité d'assurance ou de responsabilité ou sur la créance d'indemnité par subrogation.

Lorsque la chose à restituer a été vendue, la restitution se reporte de plein droit sur le prix ou la créance du prix de la vente par subrogation.

Art. 1163-6

Dans tous les cas où la restitution n'a pas lieu en nature ou par subrogation, le juge estime la valeur de la chose au jour où il se prononce, suivant son état au jour du paiement de l'obligation.

§3 – Règlements complémentaires

Art. 1164

La restitution porte sur le principal de la prestation accomplie et ses accessoires du jour du paiement.

Art. 1164-1

Les accessoires de la somme d'argent à restituer comprennent les intérêts au taux légal et les taxes acquittés entre les mains de celui qui a reçu le prix en complément de celui-ci.

Art. 1163-2

Restitution of a sum of money is effected by way of an equivalent. It consists of simply the numerical sum specified in the contract.

Art. 1163-3

Where ascertained physical property remains in the hands of the person who has received it, restitution must be made in kind.

Restitution is to be made of its value where the thing is no longer identifiable by reason of its voluntary or accidental destruction, its transformation or its incorporation into other property.

Where only part of the thing has been destroyed, transformed or incorporated into other property, the person to whom restitution is due may elect either full restitution of its value or partial restitution in kind with the value of the balance.

Art. 1163-4

Restitution of generic property other than a sum of money is to be made by rendering equivalent property unless the person to whom it is due prefers to receive its value.

Art. 1163-5

Where the thing which is subject to restitution has perished accidentally or by the act of a third party, restitution relates by operation of law to any compensation resulting from insurance or civil liability, or to any right to indemnity arising by way of subrogation.

Where a thing which is subject to restitution has been sold, restitution relates by operation of law to the price received or to the right to recover the price by way of subrogation.

Art. 1163-6

In all situations where restitution is not made in kind or by way of subrogation, the court shall assess the value of the thing as at the date of its decision on the basis of its condition as at the date of satisfaction of the obligation.

§ 3 Supplementary regulations

Art. 1164

Restitution relates to the principal subject-matter of the obligation which is accomplished and its accessories as at the date of satisfaction.

Art. 1164-1

The accessories of a sum of money which is subject to restitution consist of interest at the legal rate and any taxes on the price paid to the person who received the price.

Art. 1164-2

Lorsque la restitution porte sur une chose autre qu'une somme d'argent, les accessoires comprennent les fruits et la jouissance qu'elle a procurés.

La restitution des fruits naturels, industriels ou civils, s'ils ne se retrouvent pas en nature, a lieu selon une valeur estimée à la date du remboursement, suivant l'état de la chose au jour du paiement de l'obligation. Lorsque les revenus procèdent pour partie de l'amélioration de la chose par celui qui la rend, la restitution se fait en proportion de ceux qu'elle aurait produits dans son état initial.

La restitution de la jouissance est estimée par le juge au jour où il se prononce.

Art. 1164-3

Les frais occasionnés par le contrat peuvent être mis à la charge de celle des parties à qui l'annulation ou la résolution serait imputable.

Art. 1164-4

Les frais afférents à la chose peuvent donner lieu à restitution.

Celui auquel la chose est restituée doit tenir compte à celui qui la rend de toutes les dépenses nécessaires à la conservation de la chose.

Il doit aussi lui tenir compte des dépenses qui ont amélioré l'état de la chose dans la mesure où il en résulte une augmentation de sa valeur.

Art. 1164-5

Inversement, celui qui doit restituer la chose répond des dégradations et détériorations qui en ont diminué la valeur ou entraîné sa perte.

Art. 1164-6

Les plus-values et les moins-values advenues à la chose restituée sont estimées au jour de la restitution.

Art. 1164-2

Where restitution concerns a thing other than a sum of money, its accessories consist of its fruits[1] and the enjoyment to which it has given rise.

Restitution of natural, industrial or civil fruits[2] which do not still exist in kind is made according to their value assessed as at the date of reimbursement, and on the basis of the condition of the thing as at the date of satisfaction of the obligation. Where any income generated results in part from improvement of the thing by the person making restitution, then it is to be made in proportion to the income which would have been produced by the thing in its original condition.

Restitution in respect of enjoyment is to be assessed by the court as at the date of its decision.

Art. 1164-3

Expenses occasioned by the contract can be put to the account of the party who is responsible for the annulment or retroactive termination.

Art. 1164-4

Expenses relating to the thing itself can be the object of restitution.

The person to whom restitution is made must give credit to the person making restitution for all necessary expenses incurred in the maintenance of the thing.

He must also give credit in respect of any expenses incurred in improving the condition of the thing to the extent to which this has led to an increase in its value.

Art. 1164-5

By way of corollary, a person who makes restitution of a thing is responsible for any degradations or deteriorations which have reduced its value or caused its loss.

Art. 1164-6

Increases and decreases in value which affect the thing subject to restitution are assessed as at the date of its restitution.

---

[1] [The main significance of 'fruits' in French law (following Roman law) is that where a usufruct is created they are the perquisite of the 'usufructuary' rather than the owner of the property.]

[2] [This tripartite categorisation of 'fruits' is well known to the civil law legal systems and is set out by arts 582–586 Cc. 'Natural fruits' of property include those produced spontaneously by land and the products and offspring of animals; 'industrial fruits' (or perhaps better, the 'fruits of labour') are those which are obtained as a result of cultivation, such as sown corn; 'civil fruits' include rents on houses and interest on loans. The distinction between natural and civil fruits is Romanist, there being a reference to the offspring of animals (but not slaves) constituting 'fruits' by natural law in Justinian: *Institutes* II.1.37. See Thomas, *Textbook of Roman Law*, above, p 517, n 2, 203.]

Section 7
De l'effet des conventions à l'égard des tiers
(Articles 1165 à 1172-3)

§1 – Dispositions générales

Art. 1165

Les conventions ne lient que les parties contractantes ; elles n'ont d'effet à l'égard des tiers que dans les cas et limites ci-après expliqués.

> *Note : Cette annonce globale paraît préférable à l'opposition réductrice de « prodesse » et « nocere ».*

Art. 1165-1

Les contre-lettres ne peuvent avoir leur effet qu'entre les parties contractantes ; elles n'ont pas d'effet contre les tiers.

Art. 1165-2

Les conventions sont opposables aux tiers ; ceux-ci doivent les respecter et peuvent s'en prévaloir, sans être en droit d'en exiger l'exécution.

§2 – De la substitution de contractant et du transfert du contrat

Art. 1165-3

Les droits et obligations d'une personne défunte, lorsqu'ils ne s'éteignent pas par le fait de son décès, adviennent à ses héritiers selon les règles posées aux Titres Des successions et Des donations entre vifs et des testaments.

Semblablement, les héritiers ou légataires du défunt, ou certains d'entre eux, pourront prendre sa place dans les contrats auxquels il était partie et dont l'exécution se poursuit après son décès, si cette substitution est édictée par la loi, prévue par une convention ou stipulée par le défunt dans son testament.

Art. 1165-4

Un contractant ne peut sans l'accord exprès ou tacite de son cocontractant, céder entre vifs à un tiers sa qualité de partie au contrat.

Section 7
The Effects of Contracts as regards Third Parties
(Articles 1165 to 1172-3)

§ 1 General provisions[1]

Art. 1165

Contracts bind only the contracting parties: they have no effect on third parties except in the situations and subject to the limitations explained below.

Note: This global statement appears preferable to an analytical contrast between 'benefiting' and 'harming' third parties.

Art. 1165-1

A secret agreement hidden by the contracting parties behind another ostensible agreement[2] can be effective only as between those parties; it has no effect on third parties.

Art. 1165-2

Contracts may be invoked by and against third parties; the latter must respect them and can take advantage of them, though they do not have a right to require their performance.

§ 2 The substitution of contracting parties and the transfer of contracts

Art. 1165-3

Where the rights and obligations of a deceased person are not extinguished by the fact of his decease, they are transmitted to his heirs in accordance with the rules set out in the Title 'Succession' and the Title 'Gifts *inter vivos* and Testaments'.

Similarly, the heirs or legatees of a deceased person, or certain of them, are able to take the latter's place in the contracts to which he was party and whose performance is sought after his death, as long as this substitution is established by legislation, provided for by contract or stipulated by the deceased in his testament.

Art. 1165-4

A contracting party cannot assign *inter vivos* his status as party to the contract without the express or implied consent of the other contracting party.

---

[1] [For discussion of these provisions see Mazeaud, above, ch 10 and Vogenauer, above, ch 11.]

[2] [The words 'A secret ... ostensible agreement' translate (and explain) the French term *'contre-lettres'* which has no *terminological* equivalent in English practice, though 'counter letter' is found in French Canadian practice.]

Art. 1165-5

Il est fait exception à ce principe dans les cas prévus par la loi.

Hormis ces cas, la substitution de contractant s'opère lorsque le contrat fait partie intégrante d'une opération formant un ensemble indivisible, telles que les fusions ou scissions de sociétés, les apports partiels d'actifs.

Sauf convention contraire, il appartient au cocontractant, lorsque le transfert a eu lieu sans son accord, de se retirer du contrat au terme d'un préavis raisonnable.

§3 – Des actions ouvertes aux créanciers

Note : Les créanciers sont, bien sûr, des tiers mais il y a plus qu'une nuance entre les « tiers créanciers » et les « tiers étrangers ».

Art. 1166

Les créanciers peuvent, au nom de leur débiteur, exercer tous les droits et actions de celui-ci, à l'exception de ceux qui sont exclusivement attachés à la personne.

Note : Cette formulation fait mieux valoir la différence entre l'action oblique et l'action paulienne.

Ils ne justifient de leur intérêt à agir qu'à charge de prouver que la carence de leur débiteur leur cause préjudice.

Art. 1167

Les créanciers peuvent aussi, en leur nom personnel, attaquer les actes faits par leur débiteur en fraude de leurs droits, à charge d'établir, s'il s'agit d'un acte à titre onéreux, que le tiers cocontractant a eu connaissance de la fraude.

L'acte déclaré frauduleux est inopposable aux créanciers, de telle sorte que ceux-ci ne doivent souffrir d'aucun de ses effets. Le cas échéant, le tiers acquéreur est tenu de restituer ce qu'il avait reçu en fraude.

L'action ne peut être exercée que dans les trois ans qui suivent la connaissance que les créanciers ont de la fraude.

Art. 1167-1

Les créanciers qui exercent l'action ouverte à l'article 1166 sont payés par prélèvement sur les sommes qui, par l'effet de leur recours, rentrent dans le patrimoine du débiteur négligeant.

Art. 1165-5

Exceptions are made to this principle in situations provided for by legislation.

Outside these situations, the substitution of one party to a contract by another person can occur where the contract forms an integral part of an operation giving rise to an indivisible group of transactions, as in the case of the merger or division of companies and of assets contributions.

In the absence of contrary agreement, where such a transfer takes place without his consent, the other party to the contract may withdraw from the contract at the end of a period of reasonable notice.

§ 3 Actions available to creditors[1]

Note: Creditors are, of course, third parties but there is more than one subtle distinction between 'third party creditors' and 'third parties who are entirely foreign to the contract'.

Art. 1166

A creditor may exercise all the rights and actions of his debtor in the latter's name, with the exception of those which are exclusively personal to him.

Note: This formulation brings out better the difference between the action oblique *and the* action paulienne.[2]

A creditor does not justify his interest in bringing proceedings unless he establishes a failure in his debtor to perform which causes him loss.[3]

Art. 1167

In addition, a creditor can challenge in his own name any juridical act made by his debtor in fraud of his rights, although in the case of a non-gratuitous act he can do so only if he establishes that the other party contracting with his debtor knew of this fraud.

A juridical act which has been declared fraudulent may not be invoked against creditors, so that the latter must not be prejudiced by any of its consequences. Where applicable, a third party who has acquired property under such an act is bound to make restitution in respect of what he has received through fraud.

A creditor may bring such an action only within a period of three years from the time when he became aware of the fraud.

Art. 1167-1

A creditor who exercises the action provided by article 1166 may be paid by deduction from the sums which, as a result of his claim, have become part of the assets of the debtor in default.

---

[1] ['Creditors' is to be understood in a broad sense as the person to whom a contractual duty is owed, rather than only restricted to obligation to pay money; see above, p 439.]

[2] [For an explanation of *actions obliques* and *actions pauliennes*, see above, p 589, nn 2, 3.]

[3] [The reference to the 'interest in bringing proceedings' alludes to the requirement in art 31 of the New Code of Civil Procedure which makes a general requirement of a 'legitimate interest in the success or failure of an allegation' for all actions (with exceptions).]

L'action ouverte à l'article 1167 profite aux seuls créanciers qui l'ont intentée et à ceux qui se sont joints à l'instance.

Art. 1167-2

Quant à leurs droits énoncés au titre Des successions et au titre Du contrat de mariage et des régimes matrimoniaux, les créanciers doivent se conformer aux règles qui y sont prescrites.

Art. 1168

Certains créanciers sont investis par la loi du droit d'agir directement en paiement de leur créance contre un débiteur de leur débiteur, dans la limite des deux créances.

L'action directe est également ouverte lorsqu'elle permet seule d'éviter l'appauvrissement injuste du créancier, compte tenu du lien qui unit les contrats.

§4 – Du porte-fort et de la stipulation pour autrui

Art. 1169

On ne peut, en général, s'engager ni stipuler en son propre nom que pour soi-même.

> *Note : L'avantage de conserver cet article de tête, en rappel, est, d'une part, de conserver ici le terme « stipuler » dans son sens spécifique (faire promettre) qui a, ici, toute sa valeur, même s'il est aujourd'hui minoritaire relativement au sens générique dans lequel il est synonyme de conclure, (convenir).*

Art. 1170

Néanmoins, on peut se porter fort pour un tiers, en promettant le fait de celui-ci ; sauf l'indemnité contre celui qui s'est porté fort si le tiers refuse d'accomplir le fait promis ou de ratifier l'engagement.

Si le tiers accomplit le fait promis ou ratifie l'engagement, le porte-fort est libéré de toute obligation, et l'engagement est rétroactivement validé à la date à laquelle il a été souscrit.

> *Note : Il est préférable de maintenir dans le premier alinéa la teneur actuelle de l'art. 1120 parce qu'il met en premier, et en vedette, le risque de l'opération de porte-fort et son effet propre (celui qu'il produit en lui-même et à lui seul) : la charge de l'indemnité. C'est une annonce comminatoire. La ratification est un autre acte juridique qui vient ensuite (quand il vient) et sort alors son effet propre.*

Le tiers qui hérite du porte-fort doit remplir l'engagement de son auteur.

Claims brought under article 1167 benefit only those creditors who initiated the proceedings and those who joined proceedings once they were already in motion.

Art. 1167-2

In the case of the rights set out in the Title 'Succession' and the Title 'Contracts of marriage and matrimonial property regimes', creditors must obey the rules which are detailed in those titles.

Art. 1168

Legislation grants to certain creditors the right to sue directly to obtain satisfaction from the debtor of their own debtor, up to an amount not exceeding the lesser of the sums owed by their own debtor or his debtor.

A direct action may also arise where it is the sole means of avoiding the unjust impoverishment of a creditor taking into account the link which unites the contracts in question.

§ 4 Standing surety[1] and stipulations for the benefit of third parties

Art. 1169

In general, a person is not able to undertake engagements nor to make stipulations in his own name except for himself.

> Note: The advantage of preserving this article at the beginning as a reminder, is, on the one hand, to preserve the expression 'to stipulate' in its specific sense (requiring a person to promise something) which has here all its force, even though today this usage is much less frequent compared to its general meaning according to which it is a synonym for 'to conclude' (to agree).

Art. 1170

Nevertheless, a person may stand surety for a third party by promising that the latter will do something; if the third party refuses to do what the surety has promised that he will do or refuses to ratify the agreement, then the surety must pay compensation.

If the third party performs the act which has been promised or ratifies the surety's undertaking, the latter is released from any obligation, and the undertaking is retroactively validated as from the date on which it was originally made by him.

> Note: It is preferable to maintain in the first paragraph the present tenor of article 1120 of the Civil Code since it puts forward first and very prominently the risk which standing surety entails and its own particular consequence (which it has in and by itself): viz. the burden of paying compensation. It therefore acts as a warning declaration. Where it takes place, ratification is a distinct juridical act which occurs after a person has stood surety and which possesses its own consequences.

A third party who inherits from a person who has stood surety must fulfil the undertaking which the latter took on.

---

[1] [On use of the phrase 'standing surety' see above, p 545, n 1.]

Art. 1171

L'un des contractants, nommé stipulant, peut faire promettre à l'autre, le promettant, d'accomplir une prestation au profit d'un tiers bénéficiaire, à condition que celui-ci, serait-il une personne future, soit précisément désigné, ou puisse être déterminé lors de l'exécution de la promesse et qu'il ait, à cette date, la capacité de recevoir.

> *Note : L'intérêt de cette disposition de tête est d'ouvrir, dans le principe, l'éventualité d'une stipulation pour autrui. C'est également de nommer les protagonistes de cette opération triangulaire, notamment le stipulant, en écho au verbe stipuler maintenu dans l'art. 1169, ce qui permet, au passage, de le définir dans ce sens de précision.*

Art. 1171-1

Tant que le tiers n'a pas accepté le bénéfice de la stipulation faite en sa faveur, celle-ci peut être librement révoquée par le stipulant.

Quand elle intervient avant la révocation, l'acceptation rend la stipulation irrévocable dès que son auteur ou le promettant en a eu connaissance.

Investi dès lors du droit d'agir directement contre le promettant pour l'exécution de l'engagement, le bénéficiaire est censé avoir eu ce droit dès sa constitution.

> *Note : Dépouillée de tous les détails, cette disposition est réduite à l'essentiel. Il semble en effet capital d'articuler tous les ressorts du mécanisme juridique de la stipulation pour autrui tels que les a ciselés la jurisprudence prétorienne de la fin du XIXe siècle. C'est le noyau – le joyau – des arrêts de 1888 : la libre révocation de la stipulation pour autrui jusqu'à l'acceptation. L'irrévocabilité de la stipulation résultant de l'acceptation en temps utile, et la rétroactivité de l'acceptation, tout cela autour d'un axe : le droit direct.*

Art. 1171-2

La révocation ne peut émaner que du stipulant, ou, après son décès, de ses héritiers. Ceux-ci ne peuvent y procéder qu'à l'expiration d'un délai de trois mois à compter du jour où ils ont mis le bénéficiaire en demeure de l'accepter.

La révocation produit effet dès lors que le tiers bénéficiaire ou le promettant en a eu connaissance. Lorsqu'elle est faite par testament, elle prend effet au moment du décès. Si elle n'est pas assortie d'une nouvelle désignation bénéficiaire, la révocation profite, selon le cas, au stipulant ou à ses héritiers. Le tiers initialement désigné est censé n'avoir jamais bénéficié de la stipulation faite à son profit.

Art. 1171

One of the parties to a contract (termed the 'promisee' ('stipulator')) may require an undertaking from the other (the 'promisor') to do something[1] for the benefit of a third party beneficiary, on condition that where the latter is a future person he must be precisely identified or capable of being determined at the time of performance of the promise and that he has at this date the legal capacity to receive this benefit.

> *Note: The point of this leading provision is to make available the possibility of a stipulation for the benefit of a third party as a matter of principle. Equally, it is to set the terminology used to describe the protagonists of this triangular transaction, notably, the promisee ('stipulator'), and in this way echoes the verb 'to stipulate' which is retained by article 1169, which allows it to be given this special definition.*

Art. 1171-1

The promisee may freely revoke a stipulation which he has made for the benefit of a third party unless and until the latter accepts it.

Where the third party accepts the benefit of such a stipulation before its revocation, this renders the stipulation irrevocable once its maker or the promisor becomes aware of it.

Although enjoying from the time of acceptance a right to sue the promisor directly for performance of the undertaking, the beneficiary is deemed to have had this right as from the time of its creation by the contracting parties.

> *Note: This provision is stripped of unnecessary detail and reduced to its essentials. It appears to be of capital importance to set out clearly all the crucial elements of the legal doctrine of stipulations for the benefit of third parties as they were carved out by the reforming case-law at the end of the nineteenth century. The splendid nub of this case-law is to be found in the judgments of the Cour de cassation in 1888, which established that a stipulation for the benefit of a third party is revocable until it is accepted.[2] Both the irrevocability of a stipulation on acceptance within an appropriate time, and the retroactive effect of acceptance, revolve around the central axis of the beneficiary's direct right.*

Art. 1171-2

Revocation may be effected only by the promisee, or, after his death, by his heirs. The latter may do so only after a period of three months has elapsed from the date when they put the third party on notice to accept the benefit of the promise.

Revocation is effective as soon as the third party or the promisor become aware of it. Where it is made by testament, it takes effect from the moment of the testator's death. If it is not accompanied by a new designation of a beneficiary, revocation benefits the promisee or his heirs, as the case may be. A third party who was initially designated is deemed never to have benefited from the stipulation made for his advantage.

---

[1] [Here we translate *prestation* as 'something': on this word, see above, p 440.]
[2] [Cass civ 16 January 1888, DP 1888.1.77; Cass civ 8 February 1888, DP 1888.1.193.]

Art. 1171-3

L'acceptation peut émaner du bénéficiaire, ou, après son décès, de ses héritiers, sauf stipulation contraire. Elle peut être expresse ou tacite. Elle peut intervenir même après le décès du stipulant ou du promettant.

Art. 1171-4

Le stipulant est lui-même fondé à exiger du promettant l'exécution de son engagement envers le bénéficiaire.

§5 – De l'effet des contrats interdépendants

Art. 1172

Les contrats concomitants ou successifs dont l'exécution est nécessaire à la réalisation d'une opération d'ensemble à laquelle ils appartiennent sont regardés comme interdépendants dans la mesure ci-après déterminée.

Art. 1172-1

Les clauses organisant les relations des parties à l'un des contrats de l'ensemble ne s'appliquent dans les autres conventions que si elles y ont été reproduites et acceptées par les autres contractants.

Art. 1172-2

Toutefois, certaines clauses figurant dans l'un des contrats de l'ensemble étendent leur effet aux contractants des autres conventions, pourvu que ceux-ci en aient eu connaissance lors de leur engagement et n'aient pas formé de réserves.

Il en est ainsi des clauses limitatives ou exclusives de responsabilité, des clauses compromissoires et des clauses d'attribution de compétence.

Art. 1172-3

Lorsque l'un des contrats interdépendants est atteint de nullité, les parties aux autres contrats du même ensemble peuvent se prévaloir de leur caducité.

Art. 1171-3

Acceptance can be made by the beneficiary or, after his death, by his heirs, subject to any contrary agreement. It may be express or implied. It can take place even after the death of the promisee or the promisor.

Art. 1171-4

The promisee is himself entitled to demand performance from the promisor of the undertaking made for the benefit of a third party.

§ 5 The effects of interdependent contracts

Art. 1172

Contemporaneous or successive contracts whose performance is necessary for the putting into effect of a group operation of which they form part are seen as interdependent to the extent specified below.

Art. 1172-1

Contract terms which organise the relationship between the parties to one of the contracts within such a grouping do not apply to the other contracts except where they are reproduced in those contracts and accepted by the other contracting parties.

Art. 1172-2

Nonetheless, the effect of certain types of contract term contained in one of the group contracts extends to the parties to the other contracts within the group, provided that those parties were aware of them at the time of their own contractual undertakings and that they made no reservation in this respect.

This is the case as regards contract terms which limit or exclude liability, arbitration clauses and choice of jurisdiction clauses.

Art. 1172-3

Where one of the interdependent contracts is affected by nullity, the parties to other contracts in the same grouping can treat them as lapsed.

Chapitre IV
Des modalités de l'obligation

Section 1
Des obligations conditionnelles
(Articles 1173 à 1184-1)

§1 – De la condition en général

Art. 1173

L'obligation est conditionnelle lorsqu'on la fait dépendre d'un événement futur et incertain.

L'événement auquel est suspendue la naissance de l'obligation est une condition suspensive ; celui dont dépend sa disparition est, selon le cas, une condition résolutoire ou extinctive.

Note : L'opposition de la condition suspensive et de la condition résolutoire (rétroactive) s'enrichit (V. Carbonnier) si l'on y ajoute une troisième espèce, la condition extinctive (non rétroactive).

Art. 1174

Toute condition d'une chose impossible ou illicite est nulle et rend nulle la convention qui en dépend.

Note : Illicite : terme générique préférable à l'énumération actuelle de l'article 1172 c. civ.

Toutefois la convention peut être maintenue et la condition réputée non écrite lorsqu'en réalité celle-ci n'a pas été pour les parties un motif déterminant de contracter.

Note : L'exception ouvre, a posteriori, une appréciation judiciaire (ce qui correspond à la pratique).

De même, la condition de ne pas faire une chose impossible ne rend pas nulle l'obligation contractée sous cette condition.

Note : Regroupement dans le même article du principe (alinéa 1) et des deux exceptions qu'il souffre (al. 2 et 3).

Art. 1175

Est nulle toute obligation contractée sous une condition dont la réalisation dépend de la seule volonté du débiteur ; mais cette nullité ne peut être poursuivie lorsque l'obligation a été exécutée en connaissance de cause.

Chapter IV
Modalities of Obligations

Section 1
Conditional Obligations
(Articles 1173 to 1184-1)

§ 1 Conditions in general

Art. 1173

An obligation is conditional where it is made to depend on a future, uncertain event.

An event until which the creation of the obligation is suspended is a *suspensive condition*; an event on which the obligation is terminated is either a *resolutory condition* or an *extinctive condition*.

> Note: The contrast between suspensive conditions and resolutory (retroactive) conditions is enriched (see Carbonnier[1]) if one adds a third kind, extinctive conditions (which are not retroactive).

Art. 1174

Any condition which rests on a thing that is impossible or unlawful is a nullity and nullifies the contract which depends upon it.

> Note: 'unlawful': a general term, preferable to the present detailed list of article 1172 of the Code.

However, the contract can be maintained and the condition struck out where in reality the condition was not a decisive reason for the parties' having entered into the contract.

> Note: The exception gives rise, a posteriori, to a judicial evaluation (which corresponds to existing practice).

Likewise, a condition which rests on not doing something which is impossible does not nullify the obligation undertaken subject to the condition.

> Note: This puts together in the same article the principle (paragraph 1) and its two exceptions (paragraphs 2 and 3).

Art. 1175

Any obligation undertaken subject to a condition whose satisfaction depends upon the will of the debtor alone is a nullity. But nullity on this ground cannot be claimed where the obligation has been performed in full awareness of the position.

---

[1] [Carbonnier, *Droit civil*, vol 4 *Les Obligations*, above, p 507, n 1, no 137.]

Note : Contraction en un seul article de ce qui regarde la condition ci-devant nommée potestative.

Art. 1176

Les parties ont un devoir de loyauté dans l'accomplissement de la condition.

Note : Dans l'art. 1177-1 proposé, le verbe coopérer convient mal à la condition casuelle (qui existe même si elle n'est plus nommée). Le devoir de loyauté paraît concerner aussi bien la défaillance que l'accomplissement de la condition : d'où le terme générique « événement » qui les réunit.

Art. 1177

La condition est réputée accomplie si celui qui avait intérêt à sa défaillance en a empêché l'accomplissement.

Elle est réputée défaillie si son accomplissement a été provoqué par la partie qui y avait intérêt.

Note : Source éventuelle de litige, les mots « au détriment de l'autre partie » ne paraissent pas utiles.

Art. 1178

La partie dans l'intérêt exclusif de laquelle la condition a été stipulée est libre d'y renoncer unilatéralement, tant que la condition n'est pas accomplie. Jusqu'à ce moment les parties peuvent également, d'un commun accord, renoncer à la condition stipulée dans l'intérêt de chacune.

Toute renonciation rend l'obligation pure et simple.

Note : Réunion en un seul article de tout ce qui concerne la renonciation, ce qui permet la mise en facteur commun de la proposition finale (dernier alinéa).

Dans cet article, un renversement paraît plus logique. Ce qui mérite d'être mis en relief c'est la renonciation unilatérale particulière à un cas. La renonciation conventionnelle qui est générale est une évidence.

Art. 1179

Le créancier peut, avant que la condition soit accomplie, exercer tous les actes conservatoires de son droit et agir contre les actes du débiteur accomplis en fraude de ses droits.

Note : Cette disposition vient mieux, semble-t-il, après l'art. 1178 et avant celle-ci qui règle la transmission et la cession de l'obligation.

Art. 1180

Les obligations conditionnelles sont transmissibles à cause de mort sauf si la volonté des parties ou la nature de l'obligation y fait obstacle ; sous cette même restriction, les créances conditionnelles sont cessibles entre vifs.

Note: A shorter form, in a single article, about what has hitherto been known as a potestative condition.[1]

Art. 1176

The parties have an obligation of loyalty with regard to the satisfaction of the condition.

Note: In the proposed article [1176] the verb 'co-operate' is not well suited to a condition whose satisfaction depends on chance (this still exists, although no longer specifically identified by name). The obligation of loyalty seems to fit equally well the failure of a condition and its satisfaction: hence the general term 'event' applies to both.

Art. 1177

A condition is deemed to have been satisfied if the party who is interested in its failure has obstructed its satisfaction.

It is deemed to have failed if its satisfaction has been caused by the party who had an interest in this occurring.

Note: To avoid possible dispute, the words 'to the detriment of the other party' are better not included.

Art. 1178

The party for whose exclusive benefit a condition has been stipulated is free to renounce it unilaterally, as long as the condition has not been satisfied. Until that moment the parties may also, by agreement, renounce a condition stipulated for the benefit of each.

Any renunciation renders the obligation unconditional.

Note: This puts together in a single article everything concerning renunciation, which allows the final proposition to be a given as a common factor (last paragraph).

In this article a reversion of order seems more logical. Unilateral renunciation, which is available only in a particular situation, deserves to be given prominence. Renunciation by agreement between the parties, which is generally available, is obvious.

Art. 1179

Before the condition is satisfied, the creditor may take all measures necessary to preserve his rights, and take action against any juridical acts effected by the debtor in fraud of his rights.

Note: This provision seems to go better after article 1178, and before that which governs succession to, and assignment of, obligations.

Art. 1180

Conditional obligations are transmissible on death, unless the parties have otherwise provided, or the nature of the obligation prevents it. With this same restriction, the benefit of conditional obligations is assignable *inter vivos*.

[1] [See above, p 595, n 2, on 'potestative conditions' and its related concepts.]

Note : La formule de l'art. 1179 proposé n'est pas heureuse et elle est incomplète. Conditionnelles, les obligations n'en sont pas moins activement et passivement des éléments du patrimoine. Mais si la transmissibilité concerne les dettes aussi bien que les créances, la cessibilité est propre aux créances. L'exception est commune aux deux cas.

§2 – De la condition suspensive

Art. 1181

L'obligation contractée sous une condition suspensive est celle qui dépend ou d'un événement futur et incertain, ou d'un événement actuellement arrivé, mais encore inconnu des parties.

(art. 1181, al. 1 actuel)

L'obligation ne peut être exécutée avant l'événement ou la connaissance qu'en ont eu les parties.

(cf. art. 1181, al 2 et 3 c. civ.)

Art. 1182

En cas de défaillance de la condition l'obligation est caduque ; elle est réputée n'avoir jamais existé.

En cas d'accomplissement de la condition l'obligation est réputée avoir existé depuis le jour où l'engagement a été contracté.

Toutefois la rétroactivité ne remet en cause ni les actes d'administration ni les actes de jouissance accomplis dans la période intermédiaire.

Note : Le parallèle de la défaillance et de l'accomplissement dans le même article semble assez éclairant, et l'atténuation de la rétroactivité est en facteur commun (ce n'est peut-être pas très utile mais ce n'est pas gênant).

Art. 1182-1

Lorsque l'obligation a été contractée sous une condition suspensive, la chose qui fait la matière de la convention demeure aux risques du débiteur qui ne s'est obligé de la livrer que dans le cas de l'accomplissement de la condition.

(art. 1182, al. 1 actuel)

Si la chose est entièrement périe, l'obligation est éteinte.

Si la chose s'est détériorée, le créancier a le choix ou de résoudre le contrat, ou d'exiger la chose dans l'état où elle se trouve, sans diminution du prix.

Le tout sous réserve des dommages et intérêts qui pourraient être dus au créancier selon les règles de la responsabilité civile lorsque la perte ou la détérioration de la chose sont imputables à la faute du débiteur.

Note: The wording of article 1179 is not felicitous and is incomplete. Although conditional, such obligations are no less active and passive elements of a person's estate.[1] But although transmissibility relates to both the duties and rights arising under obligations, assignment is limited to rights. The exception is common to both.

§ 2 Suspensive conditions

Art. 1181

An obligation contracted under a suspensive condition is one which depends on either a future, uncertain event, or an event which has already happened but is not yet known to the parties.

(art. 1181 para. 1 of the present Code)

The obligation cannot be performed before the event or the parties' knowledge of it.

(cf. art. 1181 paras 2 and 3, C. civ.)

Art. 1182

If the condition fails, the obligation lapses; it is deemed never to have existed.

If the condition is satisfied, the obligation is deemed to have been in existence from the date when the contract was entered into.

However, this retroactivity does not cast any doubt on the validity, either of administrative acts or of acts by which the parties exercised their rights, in the intervening period.

Note: The parallel between the failure and satisfaction of the condition in the same article seems quite illuminating, and they have in common the limiting of the effect of retroactivity (this is perhaps not very helpful, but it is not too awkward).

Art. 1182-1

Where an obligation has been contracted under a suspensive condition, the thing which is the subject-matter of the contract remains at the risk of the debtor, who has the obligation to deliver it only when the condition is satisfied.

(art. 1182 para.1 of the present Code)

If the thing perishes in its entirety, the obligation is extinguished.

If the thing deteriorates, the creditor has a choice between retroactively terminating the contract, and requiring the thing as it is, without reduction of price.

This is all without prejudice to any award of damages which may be due to the creditor under the rules of civil liability where the loss or deterioration of the thing are attributable to the fault of the debtor.

---

[1] ['Estate' here translates *le patrimoine*: on this term, see above, p 483, n 3. The reference here to 'active' and 'passive' elements is to the estate's assets (property and the benefit of obligations) and liabilities (debts and the burden of obligations in general).]

§3 – De la condition résolutoire

Art. 1183

La condition résolutoire ne suspend pas l'exécution de l'obligation tant que l'événement prévu n'est pas arrivé ; elle en opère la révocation lorsque cet événement arrive.

> *Note : Ne vaut-il mieux pas commencer par ce qui distingue la condition résolutoire de la condition suspensive ? Le reste du §3 est ainsi consacré à la résolution.*

Art. 1184

Dans ce dernier cas la résolution s'opère rétroactivement ; elle remet les choses au même état que si l'obligation n'avait pas existé et oblige le créancier à restituer ce qu'il a reçu, selon les règles posées par les articles 1161 à 1164-7.

> *Note : Il n'est pas nécessaire, semble-t-il, de réserver une stipulation contraire. Car la condition extinctive qui suit n'est qu'une condition résolutoire non rétroactive à la disposition des parties.*

Toutefois, le créancier est dispensé de restituer les fruits qu'il a perçus avant l'événement et les actes d'administration qu'il a accomplis pendant la même période sont maintenus.

§4 – De la condition extinctive

> *Note : C'est un parallèle avec le terme extinctif.*

Art. 1184-1

La condition extinctive est celle qui fait dépendre l'extinction de l'obligation d'un événement futur et incertain. La condition extinctive n'opère que pour l'avenir.

Section 2
Des obligations à terme
(Articles 1185 à 1188)

§1 – Du terme en général

Art. 1185

Le terme est un événement futur et certain qui affecte une obligation née soit en retardant son exécution soit en y mettant fin.

Il peut être exprès ou tacite, ainsi quand il résulte implicitement de la teneur de l'engagement.

Le terme peut être une date déterminée ou son échéance être inconnue bien qu'il soit sûr qu'elle adviendra.

§ 3 Resolutory conditions

Art. 1183

A resolutory condition does not suspend the performance of the obligation until the anticipated event occurs; it effects its revocation when this event occurs.

Note: Would it not be better to begin with what distinguishes a resolutory condition from a suspensive condition? The remainder of Section 3 is dedicated to retroactive termination.

Art. 1184

In this latter situation termination has retroactive effect; it restores things to the same state as if the obligation had never existed, and requires the creditor to make restitution of what he has received, under the rules set out in articles 1161 to 1164-7.

Note: It does not seem to be necessary to qualify this by reference to contrary contractual provision: an extinctive condition, as explained below, is simply a resolutory condition that is not retroactive according to the parties' own provisions.

However, the creditor is not required to make restitution in respect of the fruits which he took before the event, and administrative acts which he has undertaken in the same period are maintained.

§ 4 Extinctive conditions

Note: This has a parallel in extinctive time delays.

Art. 1184-1

An extinctive condition is one which subjects the extinction of the obligation to a future, uncertain event. An extinctive condition has effect only for the future.

Section 2
Time-Delayed Obligations
(Articles 1185 to 1188)

§ 1 Delay-points in general

Art. 1185

A 'delay-point' is a future, certain event which affects an obligation which has already come into being, either by delaying its performance, or by putting an end to it.

It may be express or tacit, such as where it results implicitly from the content of the undertaking.

The delay-point may be a fixed date, or its occurrence may be unknown as long as it is certain that it will happen.

Art. 1186

Lorsque les parties indiquent seulement un délai constitué par un nombre de jours, de mois ou d'années, le calcul est opéré à compter du jour du contrat sauf dispositions légales ou conventionnelles différentes. Toutefois le jour à partir duquel on commence à compter n'entre pas dans le délai.

Art. 1186-1

Si les parties sont convenues de différer la détermination du terme, ou de laisser à l'une d'elles le soin d'y procéder, et que le terme ne soit pas déterminé à l'expiration d'un délai raisonnable, le juge pourra le fixer suivant les circonstances.

§2 – Du terme suspensif

Art. 1187

Ce qui n'est dû qu'à terme ne peut être exigé avant l'échéance du terme ; mais ce qui a été payé d'avance ne peut être répété.

Le créancier à terme peut exercer tous les actes conservatoires de son droit et agir contre les actes du débiteur accomplis en fraude de ses droits.

(cf. art. 1180 c. civ. et 1179 ci-dessus)

Art. 1187-1

Le terme suspensif est présumé convenu dans l'intérêt du débiteur, à moins qu'il ne résulte de la convention ou des circonstances qu'il a été établi en faveur du créancier ou dans l'intérêt commun des deux parties.

Celui dans l'intérêt exclusif duquel le terme a été stipulé, peut y renoncer unilatéralement.

Art. 1187-2

Le débiteur ne peut pas réclamer le bénéfice du terme lorsqu'il ne fournit pas les sûretés promises au créancier ou qu'il diminue par son fait celles qu'il lui a données.

Il est également déchu du bénéfice s'il devient insolvable ou s'il est déclaré en liquidation judiciaire.

§3 – Du terme extinctif

Art. 1188

Le terme extinctif met fin à l'engagement pour l'avenir. Jusqu'à l'échéance du terme, l'obligation produit le même effet que si elle était pure et simple.

Art. 1186

Where the parties indicate only a period of time by reference to a number of days, months, or years, the period is calculated from the date of the contract, in the absence of contrary provision fixed by legislation or by the agreement of the parties. However, the day from which the calculation begins is not itself included in the period.

Art. 1186-1

If the parties agreed to postpone fixing the delay-point, or to leave it to one of them, and if the delay-point has not been fixed after a reasonable period, the court may fix it according to the circumstances.

§ 2 Suspensive delay-points

Art. 1187

Whatever is due only on arrival of the delay-point may not be demanded before the expiry of the period which it sets; but whatever has been paid in advance may not be claimed back.

The creditor whose rights will arise on arrival of the delay-point may take all measures necessary to preserve his rights, and take action against any juridical acts effected by the debtor in fraud of his rights.

(cf. arts 1180 C.civ and 1179 above)

Art. 1187-1

A suspensive delay-point is presumed to have been agreed for the benefit of the debtor, as long as the contract or the surrounding circumstances do not show that it was fixed in favour of the creditor or for the common benefit of both parties.

The party for whose exclusive benefit the delay-point has been stipulated may renounce it unilaterally.

Art. 1187-2

A debtor may not claim the benefit of the delay-point if he does not provide the securities he promised to the creditor or by his own action reduces the value of those which he has provided.

He is also deprived of the benefit if he becomes insolvent or is declared to be in liquidation by the court.

§ 3 Extinctive delay-points

Art. 1188

An extinctive delay-point puts an end to an undertaking for the future. Until the arrival of the delay-point, the obligation has the same effect as if it were unconditional.

Section 3
Des obligations alternatives et facultatives
(Articles 1189 à 1196)

§1 – Des obligations alternatives

Art. 1189

L'obligation est alternative lorsqu'elle porte, au choix, sur l'une des deux prestations qu'elle renferme, de telle sorte que l'accomplissement de l'une suffit à libérer le débiteur.

Si l'une des prestations est impossible ou illicite dès le moment de l'engagement, l'obligation se concentre sur l'autre.

Art. 1190

Le choix appartient au débiteur s'il n'en est pas autrement convenu.

Lorsqu'une partie n'exerce pas, dans le délai fixé ou dans un délai raisonnable, le choix qui lui appartient, celui-ci revient, après mise en demeure, à l'autre partie.

Le choix est définitif.

(cf. art. 1190 c. civ.)

Art. 1191

Le débiteur ne peut ni choisir ni être contraint d'exécuter partie d'une prestation et partie de l'autre.

Obs. : Extension du 1191 c. civ.

Art. 1192

Le débiteur qui a le choix doit, si l'une des prestations devient impossible, même par sa faute, exécuter l'autre.

Si, dans le même cas, les deux prestations deviennent impossibles à exécuter et que ce soit, pour l'une d'elles, par la faute du débiteur, celui-ci doit au créancier la valeur de la prestation qui est restée la dernière.

Obs. : Version nouvelle du 1193 c. civ.

Art. 1193

Le créancier qui a le choix de la prestation doit, si l'une devient impossible à exécuter, accepter l'autre, à moins que cette impossibilité ne résulte de la faute du débiteur auquel cas le créancier peut exiger à son choix la prestation qui reste ou la valeur de la prestation devenue impossible.

Si dans le même cas les deux prestations deviennent impossibles à exécuter et que le débiteur soit en faute à l'égard de l'une d'elles ou des deux, le créancier peut exiger la valeur de l'une ou l'autre prestation.

Obs. : Version nouvelle du 1194 c. civ.

Section 3
Alternative and Discretionary Obligations
(Articles 1189 to 1196)

§ 1 Alternative obligations

Art. 1189

An obligation is alternative where it gives a choice between one of two possible subject-matters which it embodies, in such a way that the satisfaction of one of them is sufficient to discharge the debtor.

If one of the subject-matters of the obligation is impossible or unlawful from the moment of the contract, the obligation applies to the other.

Art. 1190

The debtor has the choice, if it has not been otherwise agreed.

Where a party does not make the choice as he is entitled to do within the period which has been fixed or within a reasonable period, the choice passes to the other party after he has given notice to make his choice.

A choice, once made, is final.

(cf. art. 1190 C. civ.)

Art. 1191

The debtor may neither choose, nor be required, to perform part of one of the alternative subject-matters of the obligation and part of the other.

Comment: Extension of art. 1191 C. civ.

Art. 1192

If one of the alternative subject-matters becomes impossible, whether or not through his own fault, the debtor must perform the other.

If, in the same situation, performance of both subject-matters becomes impossible, and this is, as to one of them, through the fault of the debtor, he owes to the creditor the value of the performance which remained longest in being.

Comment: New version of art. 1193 C. civ.

Art. 1193

A creditor who has the choice between alternative subject-matters of an obligation must, if one becomes impossible to perform, accept the other, as long as the impossibility is not the fault of the debtor; in that case the creditor has the choice between requiring performance of the subject-matter which remains, or the value of the subject-matter which has become impossible.

If in the same situation performance of both subject-matters becomes impossible and if the debtor is at fault with regard to one or both of them, the creditor may require the value of one or other subject-matter.

Comment: New version of art. 1194 C. civ.

Art. 1194

Lorsque toutes les prestations deviennent impossibles à exécuter sans la faute du débiteur, l'obligation est éteinte.

Obs. : Extension du 1195 c. civ.

Art. 1195

Les mêmes principes s'appliquent au cas où il y a plus de deux prestations comprises dans l'obligation alternative.

(art. 1196 c. civ. modifié)

§2 – **Des obligations facultatives**

Art. 1196

L'obligation est facultative lorsqu'ayant pour objet une certaine prestation, le débiteur a néanmoins la faculté, pour se libérer, d'en fournir une autre.

L'obligation facultative est éteinte si l'exécution de la prestation principale devient impossible sans la faute du débiteur.

Section 4
Des obligations solidaires
(Articles 1197 à 1212)

§1 – **De la solidarité entre les créanciers**

Art. 1197

L'obligation est solidaire entre plusieurs créanciers, lorsque chacun est en droit de demander le paiement du total de la créance, et que le paiement fait à l'un d'eux libère le débiteur, encore que le bénéfice de l'obligation soit partageable et divisible entre les divers créanciers.

(art. 1197 c. civ modifié)

Art. 1197-1

La solidarité ne se présume pas ; il faut qu'elle soit expressément établie.

Art. 1198

Il est au choix du débiteur de payer à l'un ou l'autre des créanciers solidaires, tant qu'il n'a pas été poursuivi par l'un d'eux.

Art. 1194

Where without the fault of the debtor performance of all the subject-matters becomes impossible the obligation is extinguished.

Comment: Extension of art. 1195 C. civ.

Art. 1195

The same principles apply to the situation where there are more than two subject-matters comprised within the alternative obligation.

Comment: Art. 1196 C. civ., amended.

§ 2 Discretionary obligations

Art. 1196

An obligation is discretionary where, although it has a particular subject-matter as its object, the debtor nevertheless has the right to discharge himself by providing another.

A discretionary obligation is extinguished if, without the fault of the debtor, the performance of the principal subject-matter of the obligation becomes impossible.

Section 4
Joint and Several Obligations
(Articles 1197 to 1212)

§ 1 Joint and several creditors[1]

Art. 1197

An obligation is joint and several amongst a number of creditors where each has the right to require contractual satisfaction in full, and satisfaction in favour of one of them discharges the debtor, even if the benefit of the obligation is divisible and may be shared between several creditors.

(art. 1197 C. civ., amended)

Art. 1197-1

The joint and several nature of an obligation is not presumed: it must be expressly provided for.

Art. 1198

The debtor has a choice between performing in favour of one or another of the creditors who have the joint and several benefit of the obligation, as long has he has not been sued by one of them.

---

[1] [As often in the translation, we use 'creditor' in the wider (French) sense of the person entitled to the benefit of performance, not restricted to the beneficiary of a money obligation: see above, p 439.]

Néanmoins, la remise qui n'est faite que par l'un des créanciers solidaires ne libère le débiteur que pour la part de ce créancier.

Semblablement, la confusion ou la compensation qui s'opère entre le débiteur et l'un des créanciers n'éteint l'obligation que pour la part de ce créancier.

(art. 1198 c. civ. modifié)

Art. 1199

Tout acte qui interrompt ou suspend la prescription à l'égard de l'un des créanciers solidaires, profite aux autres créanciers.

(art. 1199 c. civ. modifié)

§2 – De la solidarité de la part des débiteurs

Art. 1200

Il y a solidarité de la part des débiteurs, lorsqu'ils sont obligés à une même chose, de manière que chacun puisse être contraint pour la totalité, et que le paiement fait par un seul libère les autres envers le créancier.

(art. 1200 actuel)

Art. 1201

L'obligation peut être solidaire quoique l'un des débiteurs soit obligé différemment de l'autre au paiement de la même chose ; par exemple, si l'un n'est obligé que conditionnellement, tandis que l'engagement de l'autre est pur et simple, ou si l'un a pris un terme qui n'est point accordé à l'autre.

(art. 1201 actuel)

Art. 1202

La solidarité ne se présume pas ; elle ne peut résulter que de la loi, d'une convention ou des usages du commerce.

(cf. art. 1378 ci-dessous, Sous-titre III De la responsabilité civile.)

Art. 1203

Le créancier d'une obligation solidaire peut s'adresser à celui des débiteurs qu'il veut choisir, sans que celui-ci puisse lui opposer le bénéfice de division.

(art. 1203 c. civ. modifié)

Les poursuites faites contre l'un des débiteurs n'empêchent pas le créancier d'en exercer de pareilles contre les autres.

Obs. : Le nouvel article 1203 amalgamerait les dispositions des articles 1203 et 1204 c. civ.

Art. 1204

Si la chose a péri par la faute de l'un ou de plusieurs des débiteurs, les autres

However, any release of the debt which is given by only one of two or more joint and several creditors discharges the debtor only with regard to that creditor.

Similarly, merger or set-off between the debtor and one of the creditors extinguishes the obligation only with regard to that creditor.

(art. 1198 C. civ., amended)

Art. 1199

Any act which interrupts or suspends prescription with regard to one of two or more joint and several creditors operates for the benefit of the other creditors.

(art. 1199 C. civ., amended)

§ 2 Joint and several debtors[1]

Art. 1200

There is joint and several liability amongst debtors where they are under obligations to do the same thing such that the totality of it may be enforced against each of them, and satisfaction by only one discharges the others with regard to the creditor.

(art. 1200 of the present Code)

Art. 1201

An obligation may be joint and several even though one of the debtors may have a different obligation from the other as regards the accomplishment of the same thing; for example, if one has only a conditional obligation, whilst the obligation of the other is unconditional; or if one has a delay-point on his obligation which is not given to the other.

(art. 1201 of the present Code)

Art. 1202

Joint and several liability is not presumed; it may result from legislation, contract or commercial custom.

(cf. art. 1378 below: Sub-title III, Civil liability)

Art. 1203

The creditor of a joint and several obligation may require performance by any of the debtors he may choose—and the latter may not raise against him any claim to limit his share of liability.

(art. 1203 C. civ., amended)

An action brought against one of the debtors does not prevent the creditor from bringing a similar action against the others.

Comment: The new article 1203 brings together the provisions of articles 1203 and 1204 of the present Code.

Art. 1204

If the thing is lost through the fault of one or more of the debtors, the others

---

[1] [See below, p 861, n 1 on the distinction between *solidarité* or *obligation solidaire* (translated here as joint and several liability) and *obligations in solidum*.]

demeurent obligés pour la valeur de la chose ; mais ils ne sont point tenus des dommages et intérêts, sauf s'ils étaient en demeure au temps de la perte.

(art. 1205 c. civ. modifié)

Art. 1205

Les poursuites faites contre l'un des débiteurs solidaires interrompent ou suspendent la prescription à l'égard de tous.

Les mêmes effets s'attachent à la mise en demeure.

(art. 1206 c. civ. modifié)

Art. 1206

La demande d'intérêts formée contre l'un des débiteurs solidaires fait courir les intérêts à l'égard de tous.

(art. 1207 actuel)

Art. 1207

Le codébiteur solidaire poursuivi par le créancier peut opposer toutes les exceptions qui résultent de la nature de l'obligation, et toutes celles qui lui sont personnelles, ainsi que celles qui sont communes à tous les codébiteurs.

Il ne peut opposer les exceptions qui sont purement personnelles aux autres codébiteurs ou à l'un d'eux.

(art. 1208 actuel)

Art. 1208

Lorsque l'un des débiteurs succède au créancier, ou lorsque le créancier succède à l'un des débiteurs, la confusion n'éteint l'obligation que pour la part du débiteur confondu.

(art. 1209 c. civ. modifié)

Art. 1209

Le créancier qui consent à la division de la dette de l'un des codébiteurs, conserve son action solidaire contre les autres, mais sous la déduction de la part du débiteur qu'il a déchargé de la solidarité.

(art. 1210 actuel)

Art. 1210

L'obligation solidaire se divise de plein droit entre les débiteurs, qui n'en sont tenus entre eux que chacun pour sa part.

Le débiteur qui a payé la dette commune ne peut répéter contre chacun des autres que sa part.

(art. 1213 et 1214 c. civ. amalgamés et retouchés)

Art. 1211

Les codébiteurs sont mutuellement garants de leur solvabilité.

La part de l'insolvable se répartit par contribution entre les autres, y compris celui

remain under an obligation with regard to its value; but they are not liable in damages unless they had been put on notice to perform at the time of the loss.

(art. 1205 C. civ., amended)

Art. 1205

An action brought against a single joint and several debtor interrupts or suspends the running of prescription with regard to all.

The same effects follow from service of a notice to perform.

(art. 1206 C. civ., amended)

Art. 1206

A claim for interest made against a single joint and several debtor causes interest to run against all.

(art. 1207 of the present Code)

Art. 1207

A joint and several debtor sued by the creditor may raise all the defences which arise by virtue of the nature of the obligation, and all those which are available to him personally, as well as those which are common to all the debtors.

He may not raise defences which are purely personal to the other debtors, or to any one of them.

(art. 1208 of the present Code)

Art. 1208

Where one of the debtors becomes successor in title to the rights of the creditor, or where the creditor becomes subject to the duties of one of the debtors, merger extinguishes the obligation only on the part of the debtor whose rights and obligations have become merged.

(art. 1209 C. civ., amended)

Art. 1209

A creditor who consents to the division of the share of the debt of one of the debtors retains his action against the others jointly and severally, but after deduction of the share of the debtor whose joint and several liability he has discharged.

(art. 1210 of the present Code)

Art. 1210

A joint and several obligation is divisible by operation of law as between the debtors, each of whom is liable only for his own share.

A debtor who has satisfied a joint debt may claim from the others only their own respective shares.

(arts 1213 and 1214 para. 2 C. civ. merged and amended)

Art. 1211

The debtors stand as mutual guarantors as regards their solvency.

The share of an insolvent party is divided amongst the others, including one who

qui a fait le paiement ou qui a été précédemment déchargé de la solidarité par le créancier.

> *(art. 1214 al. 2 et 1215 c. civ. modifiés)*

Art. 1212

Si l'affaire pour laquelle la dette a été contractée solidairement ne concerne que l'un des codébiteurs, celui-ci est seul tenu de la dette vis-à-vis des autres, de telle sorte qu'il n'a aucun recours contre eux s'il l'a payée et que ceux-ci, s'ils l'ont payée, peuvent la recouvrer contre lui.

> *(art. 1216 c. civ. modifié)*

Section 5
Des obligations indivisibles
(Articles 1213 à 1217)

> *Dans un chapitre consacré aux modalités de l'obligation, seules les obligations indivisibles et non les obligations divisibles sont des obligations modales, soit entre codébiteurs, soit surtout (c'est la performance spécifique) à l'égard des héritiers (d'où d'ailleurs le regroupement des effets en un article).*

> *La divisibilité de l'obligation après décès n'est pas une modalité de l'obligation. Le principe est la division de plein droit entre les héritiers, des dettes et des créances du défunt.*

> *Quant à la règle énoncée (sous forme d'ailleurs assez surprenante) à l'alinéa 1 de l'article 1220 du code civil, c'est à fois le droit commun et le sens commun. Le débiteur ne peut contraindre le créancier à recevoir un paiement partiel. La règle concerne le paiement (cf. infra art. 1224-1).*

Art. 1213

L'obligation est indivisible lorsqu'elle a pour objet une prestation dont l'exécution n'est pas susceptible de division, soit matérielle, soit intellectuelle.

> *(art. 1217 c. civ. modifié)*

Art. 1214

L'obligation est indivisible, quoique la chose ou le fait qui en est l'objet soit divisible par sa nature, si le rapport sous lequel elle est considérée dans l'obligation ne la rend pas susceptible d'exécution partielle.

> *(art. 1218 actuel)*

has satisfied the debt or who has already been discharged from the joint and several liability by the creditor.

(arts. 1214 para. 2 and 1215 C. civ., amended)

Art. 1212

If the matter for which the debt has been entered into jointly and severally concerns only one of the debtors, he alone is liable for the debt as regards the others, with the result that he has no recourse against them if he has satisfied it himself; and the others, if they have satisfied it, may recover against him.

(art. 1216 C. civ., amended)

Section 5
Indivisible Obligations
(Articles 1213 to 1217)

In a chapter such as this dedicated to the modalities of obligations, only indivisible obligations (and not divisible obligations) constitute modes of obligation. This is the case whether as between co-debtors or as regards heirs, where it has a particular function (this leads to their effects being grouped in a single article).

The divisibility of obligations after death is not a mode of obligation. The rule is division of the deceased's duties and rights under an obligation by operation of law between heirs.

The rule set out (in a rather surprising form, it should be noted) in paragraph 1 of article 1220 of the Civil Code[1] forms both the general law and reflects common sense. The debtor may not require the creditor to accept partial satisfaction. The rule concerns satisfaction (cf. below, art. 1224-1).

Art. 1213

An obligation is indivisible where it has as its object a subject-matter whose performance is not capable of division, either physically or conceptually.

(art. 1217 C. civ., amended)

Art. 1214

An obligation is indivisible, even if the thing or the act which forms its subject-matter is of its nature divisible, if the basis on which it is set out in the obligation renders it incapable of partial performance.

(art. 1218 of the present Code)

---

[1] [This provides that an obligation which is capable of division must be discharged as between the creditor and debtor as if it were indivisible. It is moved to the second paragraph of the new article 1224, below.]

Art. 1215

Chacun des débiteurs d'une obligation indivisible en est tenu pour le tout.

Il en est de même pour chacun des héritiers de celui qui est tenu d'une telle obligation.

(art. 1222 et 1223 c. civ. modifiés)

Art. 1216

L'hériter du débiteur, assigné pour la totalité de l'obligation, peut demander un délai pour mettre en cause ses cohéritiers, à moins que la dette ne soit de nature à ne pouvoir être acquittée que par lui, qui peut alors être condamné seul, sauf son recours en indemnité contre ses cohéritiers.

(art. 1225 c. civ. actuel)

Art. 1217

Chaque héritier du créancier peut exiger en totalité l'exécution de l'obligation indivisible.

Il ne peut seul faire la remise de la totalité de la dette ; il ne peut recevoir seul le prix au lieu de la chose. Si l'un des héritiers a seul remis la dette ou reçu le prix de la chose, son cohéritier ne peut demander la chose indivisible qu'en tenant compte de la portion du cohéritier qui a fait la remise ou qui a reçu le prix.

(art. 1224 c. civ. actuel)

Chapitre V
De l'extinction des obligations

Art. 1218

Les obligations s'éteignent :

– par le paiement,

– par la remise de dette,

– par la compensation,

– par la confusion,

– par la novation et la prescription qui sont l'objet de dispositions particulières.

Art. 1215

Each debtor of an indivisible obligation is bound to the whole.

It is the same for each heir of a person who is bound by such an obligation.

(art. 1222 and 1223 C. civ., amended.)

Art. 1216

An heir of the debtor, if sued with respect to the totality of the obligation, may ask for time to join the other successors to the proceedings, as long as the debt is of such a nature that it cannot be discharged by him alone—in which case judgment may be given against him alone, subject to recourse by way of indemnity against his other co-heirs.

(art. 1225 of the present Code)

Art. 1217

Each heir of the creditor may require total performance of an indivisible obligation.

He may not alone grant a release relating to the totality of the debt; he may not alone receive the value of a thing in place of the thing itself. If one of the heirs has alone released the debt or received the value of the thing, his co-heir may not require the indivisible thing without giving credit for the share of the heir who has granted the release or who has received the value.

(art. 1224 of the present Code)

Chapter V
Extinction of Obligations

Art. 1218

An obligation is extinguished:

– by satisfaction,

– by release of the debt,

– by set-off,

– by merger,

– by novation and prescription, which are covered by their own separate provisions.

Section 1
Du paiement
(Articles 1219 à 1236)

§1 – Dispositions générales

Art. 1219

Le paiement est l'exécution de la prestation due.

Art. 1220

Tout paiement suppose une dette ; ce qui a été payé sans être dû, est sujet à répétition.

La répétition n'est pas admise à l'égard des obligations naturelles qui ont été volontairement acquittées.

(art. 1235 actuel)

Art. 1221

Une obligation peut être acquittée par toute personne qui y est intéressée, telle qu'un coobligé ou une caution, et par ceux qui agissent au nom du débiteur.

L'obligation peut même être acquittée par un tiers qui n'y a pas un intérêt personnel, sauf le droit pour le créancier de refuser le paiement, s'il y a un intérêt légitime. Hors ce cas, le tiers peut demander son remboursement sur le fondement de la subrogation conventionnelle ou en vertu d'un recours personnel.

(art. 1236 c. civ. modifié)

Art. 1221-1

Pour payer valablement, il faut être capable ou régulièrement représenté.

Néanmoins le paiement d'une somme d'argent ne peut être répété contre le créancier qui l'a consommée de bonne foi.

(art. 1239 c. civ. modifié)

Art. 1221-2

Le paiement doit être fait au créancier ou à son représentant.

Le paiement non conforme à l'obligation est néanmoins valable si le créancier le ratifie ou s'il en a profité.

Art. 1222

Le paiement fait de bonne foi entre les mains d'un créancier apparent est valable.

En cas de paiement électronique, le créancier garantit au débiteur la sécurité du mode de paiement proposé.

Section 1
Satisfaction[1]
(Articles 1219 to 1236)

§ 1 General provisions

Art. 1219

Satisfaction is the performance of the subject-matter of the obligation.

Art. 1220

Satisfaction presupposes a debt: where satisfaction has been given without being due, it is subject to a claim for restitution.

A claim for restitution is not allowed as regards natural obligations which have been discharged voluntarily.

(art. 1235 of the present Code)

Art. 1221

An obligation may be discharged by any person who has an interest in doing so, such as a co-debtor or a surety, and by those who act in the name of the debtor.

An obligation may even be discharged by a third party who has no personal interest in doing so, subject to the creditor's right to refuse the tender of performance if he has a legitimate interest in so doing. Outside this situation the third party may require reimbursement on the basis of contractual subrogation or by virtue of a personal recourse.

(art. 1236 C. civ., amended)

Art. 1221-1

Valid satisfaction may be given only by a person who has capacity, or is properly represented.

However, satisfaction by means of payment of a sum of money may not be claimed back from a creditor who has used it in good faith.

(art. 1239 C. civ., amended)

Art. 1221-2

Satisfaction must be made to the creditor or his representative.

Satisfaction which does not conform to the obligation is still valid if the creditor ratifies it or has benefited from it.

Art. 1222

Satisfaction made in good faith to the apparent creditor is valid.

In the case of satisfaction by electronic means, the creditor guarantees to the debtor the security of the proposed method of satisfaction.

---

[1] [On the translation of *paiement* (here, 'satisfaction'), see above, p 442.]

Art. 1223

Le créancier ne peut être contraint de recevoir une autre chose que celle qui lui est due, quoique la valeur de la chose offerte soit égale ou même plus grande.

Néanmoins, les parties peuvent s'accorder pour que le paiement se fasse par la dation d'une prestation différente.

Art. 1224

Le débiteur ne peut forcer le créancier à recevoir en partie le paiement d'une dette.

(art. 1244 actuel)

Même si elle est susceptible de division, la dette doit toujours être exécutée entre le créancier et le débiteur comme si elle était indivisible.

Note : C'est le remploi de l'actuel article 1220 c. civ. (1ʳᵉ phrase) qui renforce l'idée.

Art. 1224-1

Sauf si elle est indivisible, la dette se divise de plein droit entre les héritiers du créancier et du débiteur. Ceux-ci ne peuvent demander la dette ou ne sont tenus de la payer que pour les parts dont ils sont saisis ou dont ils sont tenus comme représentant le créancier ou le débiteur.

Note : La première phrase est l'énoncé du principe de divisibilité. La seconde, tirée de l'art. 1220 c. civ. actuel, en est le développement.

Art. 1225

Le débiteur d'une obligation monétaire n'est tenu que de la somme numérique énoncée au contrat, à moins qu'il ne s'agisse d'une dette de valeur.

Art. 1225-1

Le montant de la somme due peut également varier en vertu d'une clause d'indexation.

Celle-ci obéit aux dispositions du code monétaire et financier.

Art. 1225-2

Le montant de l'obligation de somme d'argent peut même être fixé autrement qu'en unités monétaires ayant cours, dès lors que la liquidation s'en fait au jour du paiement, le tout conformément aux règles spécialement prévues par la loi.

Art. 1225-3

Si l'obligation est productive d'intérêts, légaux ou conventionnels, ceux-ci peuvent eux-mêmes produire des intérêts, ou par une demande judiciaire, ou par une convention spéciale, pourvu que, soit dans la demande, soit dans la convention, il s'agisse d'intérêts dus au moins pour une année entière.

(art. 1154 c. civ. modifié)

Art. 1225-4

Néanmoins, les revenus échus tels que fermages, loyers, arrérages de rentes perpétuelles ou viagères, produisent intérêts du jour de la demande ou de la convention.

Art. 1223

The creditor cannot be required to accept a thing different from that which is owed to him, whether the value of the thing offered is equal to it or even higher.

However, the parties may agree that satisfaction will be made by the delivery of a different performance.

Art. 1224

The debtor cannot require the creditor to accept partial satisfaction of a debt.

(art. 1244 of the present Code)

Even if it is capable of division, a debt must always be discharged as between the creditor and the debtor as if it were indivisible.

Note: This makes use of the present article 1220 C. civ. (1st phrase) which reinforces the idea.

Art. 1224-1

Unless it is indivisible, a debt is divided by operation of law between the heirs of the creditor and the debtor. They may claim performance of the debt or are bound to pay it only as regards the share which belongs to them, or in relation to which they are bound, as representing either the creditor or the debtor.

Note: The first phrase sets out the principle of divisibility. The second, drawn from the present art. 1220 C. civ., develops it.

Art. 1225

A debtor of a monetary obligation is liable only for the sum of money set out in the contract, unless it is a debt whose value is to be assessed.

Art. 1225-1

The amount of the sum due may also vary in accordance with an indexation clause.

Such a clause must satisfy the requirements of the Monetary and Financial Code.

Art. 1225-2

The amount of an obligation to pay a sum of money may even be fixed other than in present units of currency, as long as the sum to be paid is calculated at the date of payment; and this must all satisfy the special rules provided by legislation.

Art. 1225-3

If the obligation attracts the payment of interest, whether under legislation or under a contract, the interest may be compounded if either an application is made to court or the parties make particular provision by agreement, provided that the application or the agreement relate to interest that has been outstanding for at least a complete year.

(art. 1154 C. civ., amended)

Art. 1225-4

However, overdue payments of income such as farm rents, other rents, and arrears of perpetual or life annuities bear interest from the date of the claim or the agreement.

La même règle s'applique aux restitutions de fruits et aux intérêts payés par un tiers au créancier en acquit du débiteur.

(art. 1155 actuel)

Art. 1226

Le paiement en France d'une obligation de somme d'argent se fait dans la monnaie qui y a cours. Toutefois, si l'obligation procède d'un contrat international ou d'un jugement, il est possible de prévoir que l'exécution se fera en France en unités monétaires étrangères.

Art. 1226-1

Le paiement doit être exécuté dans le lieu désigné par la convention. Si le lieu n'y est pas désigné, le paiement, lorsqu'il s'agit d'un corps certain et déterminé, doit être fait dans le lieu où était, au temps de l'obligation, la chose qui en fait l'objet.

Les aliments alloués en justice doivent être versés, sauf décision contraire du juge, au domicile ou à la résidence de celui qui doit les recevoir.

Hors ces cas, le paiement doit être fait au domicile ou à la résidence du débiteur.

(art. 1247 actuel)

Art. 1226-2

Le paiement doit être fait sitôt que la dette devient exigible.

Toutefois, compte tenu de la situation du débiteur et en considération des besoins du créancier, le juge peut, dans la limite de deux années, reporter ou échelonner le paiement des sommes dues.

Par décision spéciale et motivée, le juge peut prescrire que les sommes correspondant aux échéances reportées porteront intérêt à un taux réduit qui ne peut être inférieur au taux légal ou que les paiements s'imputeront d'abord sur le capital.

En outre, il peut subordonner ces mesures à l'accomplissement, par le débiteur, d'actes propres à faciliter ou à garantir le paiement de la dette.

Les dispositions du présent article ne s'appliquent pas aux dettes d'aliments.

Art. 1226-3

La décision du juge, prise en application de l'article 1226-1 suspend les procédures d'exécution qui auraient été engagées par le créancier. Les majorations d'intérêts ou les pénalités encourues à raison du retard cessent d'être dues pendant le délai fixé par le juge.

Art. 1226-4

Toute stipulation contraire aux dispositions des articles 1226-1 et 1226-2 est réputée non écrite.

The same rule applies to claims for restitution in respect of fruits[1] or interest paid by a third party to the creditor in discharge of the debtor.

(art. 1155 of the present Code)

Art. 1226

Payment in France of a sum of money due must be made in the money current there at the time. However, if an obligation arises under an international contract, or under a judgment, it is possible to provide that payment will be made in France in foreign currency.

Art. 1226-1

Satisfaction must be rendered in the place fixed by the contract. If the place was not so fixed, satisfaction which relates to specific and ascertained property must be rendered in the place where the thing which was its subject-matter was at the time when the obligation was undertaken.

Unless the court orders otherwise, maintenance payable under a court order must be paid at the place of domicile or residence of the person entitled to receive it.

Outside these situations, satisfaction must be rendered at the place of domicile or residence of the debtor.

(art. 1247 of the present Code)

Art. 1226-2

Satisfaction must be rendered as soon as the obligation becomes enforceable.

However, depending on the situation of the debtor and the needs of the creditor, a court may defer payment, or allow it to be made in instalments, for a period no greater than two years.

By a special, reasoned decision, a court may order that sums corresponding to deferred instalments will bear interest at a reduced rate (not lower than the legal rate of interest) or that any payments made will first be allocated to repayment of capital.

In addition, the court may make its decision on these matters subject to the debtor entering into whatever juridical acts may be necessary to facilitate or secure payment of the debt.

The provisions of this article do not apply to debts in relation to maintenance payments.

Art. 1226-3

A court order made under article 1226-1 suspends any enforcement procedures which have been initiated by the creditor. The interest payable or penalties incurred by reason of the delay cease to be payable during the period fixed by the court.

Art. 1226-4

Any contractual provision contrary to the provisions of articles 1226-1 and 1226-2 is struck out.

---

[1] [On fruits, see above, p 703, n 2.]

Art. 1227

Le débiteur d'un corps certain et déterminé est libéré par la remise de la chose en l'état où elle se trouve lors de la livraison, pourvu que les détériorations qui y sont survenues ne viennent point de son fait ou de sa faute, ni de celle des personnes dont il est responsable, ou qu'avant ces détériorations il ne fût pas en demeure.

(art. 1245 actuel)

Art. 1227-1

Si la dette est une chose qui n'est déterminée que par son espèce, le débiteur ne sera pas tenu, pour être libéré, de la donner de la meilleure espèce ; mais il ne pourra l'offrir de la plus mauvaise.

(art. 1246 actuel)

Art. 1227-2

Les frais du paiement sont à la charge du débiteur.

(art. 1248 actuel)

§2 – De l'imputation des paiements

Art. 1228

Le débiteur d'une dette qui porte intérêt ou produit des arrérages, ne peut point, sans le consentement du créancier, imputer le paiement qu'il fait sur le capital par préférence aux arrérages ou intérêts : le paiement fait sur le capital et intérêts, mais qui n'est point intégral, s'impute d'abord sur les intérêts.

(art. 1254 actuel)

Art. 1228-1

Le débiteur de plusieurs dettes a le droit de déclarer, lorsqu'il paye, quelle dette il entend acquitter.

(art. 1253 actuel)

Art. 1228-2

À défaut d'imputation par le débiteur, les parties peuvent imputer conventionnellement le paiement sur une dette. Si l'imputation est portée sur une quittance délivrée par le créancier, sa réception par le débiteur ne peut faire présumer son acceptation.

Art. 1229

Faute d'imputation dans les conditions précédentes, le paiement doit être imputé selon les dispositions suivantes :

1° dans le cas où le débiteur est tenu de dettes échues et non échues, l'imputation se fait en priorité sur les premières ;

2° si plusieurs dettes sont échues, l'imputation se fait en priorité sur la dette que le débiteur avait le plus d'intérêt à acquitter ;

Art. 1227

A person who has a duty to provide specific and ascertained property is discharged by the delivery of the thing in its present state at the time of delivery, provided that any deterioration in it is not a consequence of his action or his fault, nor of those persons for whom he is responsible, and as long has he was not already on notice to perform before the deterioration.

(art. 1245 of the present Code)

Art. 1227-1

If a debt relates to a thing which is determined only by its kind, the debtor shall not be bound to provide the best thing of that kind in order to be discharged; but he may not offer the worst.

(art. 1246 of the present Code)

Art. 1227-2

The costs of satisfaction are borne by the debtor.

(art. 1248 of the present Code)

§ 2 Allocation of payments

Art. 1228

The debtor of a debt which carries interest or is in arrears may not, without the consent of the creditor, allocate a payment he makes to the capital in preference to the arrears or interest. Payment is attributed to both capital and interest but if payment is incomplete it is first allocated to interest.

(art. 1254 of the present Code)

Art. 1228-1

A debtor who owes more than one debt has the right at the time of payment to declare which debt he intends to discharge.

(art. 1253 of the present Code)

Art. 1228-2

Failing allocation by the debtor, the parties may by agreement make provision for the allocation of payments in respect of a debt. If the allocation is made on a receipt delivered by the creditor, its reception by the debtor does not raise a presumption that he accepts it.

Art. 1229

Failing allocation in the ways set out above, a payment must be allocated according to the following provisions:

1. Where the debtor is liable in respect of both overdue and not overdue debts, payment is allocated first to the former.

2. If more than one debt is overdue, payment is allocated first to the debt which the debtor has the greatest interest in discharging.

3° si ces dettes échues sont d'égale nature, l'imputation se fait sur la plus ancienne ; si elles sont contemporaines, elle se fait proportionnellement ;

4° si l'imputation se fait seulement sur des dettes non échues, les règles 2° et 3° doivent être suivies.

Art. 1230

En cas de pluralité de dettes, l'imputation sur l'une quelconque d'entre elles suit la règle de l'article 1228, si nécessaire.

§3 – De la preuve du paiement

Art. 1231

Le paiement se prouve par tous moyens.

Art. 1232

La remise volontaire par le créancier au débiteur du titre original sous signature privée, ou de la copie exécutoire, fait présumer la remise de la dette ou le paiement, sauf preuve contraire.

La remise à l'un des débiteurs solidaires du titre original sous signature privée ou de la copie exécutoire a le même effet au profit de ses codébiteurs.

Art. 1232-1

La remise de la chose donnée en nantissement ne suffit pas à faire présumer la remise de la dette.

Note : Ces dispositions correspondent aux actuels articles 1282, 1283, 1284 et 1286, figurant dans la section consacrée à la remise de dette. Or ces dispositions nous paraissent davantage relever de la libération du débiteur, qu'elles font présumer. D'où le rattachement au paiement, et à sa preuve.

§4 – De la consignation avec offre de paiement et mise en demeure

Note : Le titre (long) marque la liaison de la consignation, de l'offre de paiement et de la mise en demeure.

Art. 1233

Lorsqu'à l'échéance le créancier refuse de recevoir son paiement, le débiteur peut consigner la chose due entre les mains d'une personne habilitée à la recevoir.

La consignation vaut paiement (1), si les conditions de celui-ci sont réunies. (2) La libération s'opère comme il est indiqué ci-après.

Notes :

(1) La règle de droit civil qui gouverne l'ensemble vient en tête.

3. If the debts are of a similar kind, payment is allocated to the oldest; if they are of the same age, the allocation is pro rata.

4. If the allocation is made only to debts which are not outstanding, rules 2 and 3 must be followed.

Art. 1230

In the case of multiple debts, allocation to any of them follows the rule in article 1228, if necessary.

§ 3 Proof of satisfaction

Art. 1231

Satisfaction may be proved by all forms of evidence.

Art. 1232

A voluntary delivery by the creditor to the debtor of the original signed instrument, or of the court order, raises a presumption that the debt has been released or satisfied, subject to proof to the contrary.

Delivery to one of two or more joint and several debtors of the original signed instrument, or of the court order, has the same effect in favour of the co-debtors.

Art. 1232-1

The re-delivery of a thing that was given as security is not sufficient to raise a presumption that the debt has been released.

> *Note: These provisions correspond to the present articles 1282, 1283, 1284 and 1286, which appear in the section dealing with release of a debt. However, they seem to relate more to release of the debtor, where they create a presumption. Therefore, they are put together with satisfaction and its proof.*

§ 4 Deposit with a public depositary together with an offer of satisfaction, and notice to perform

> *Note: The (long) title emphasises the link between deposit with a public depositary, offer of satisfaction, and notice to perform.*

Art. 1233

Where the creditor refuses to accept performance on the due date, the debtor may place what is due in the custody of a person authorised to receive it.

Such a deposit constitutes satisfaction (1) if it fulfils the latter's conditions. (2) The debtor is discharged as set out below.

> *Notes:*
>
> *(1) The general rule of the civil law is placed first.*

(2) Ce renvoi global évite de reprendre les conditions 1° à 5° de l'art. 1258 c. civ. actuel.

Art. 1234

Le débiteur doit notifier la consignation au créancier en lui faisant une offre de paiement conforme aux modalités convenues.

Art. 1234-1

Lorsque la chose consignée est une somme d'argent le débiteur est libéré, capital et intérêts, si, à l'expiration d'un délai de deux mois à compter de la notification à la personne du créancier, celui-ci n'a pas contesté l'offre de paiement.

Art. 1234-2

Si la notification n'a pas été faite à la personne du créancier, le débiteur peut, sur requête, demander au juge de l'exécution de déclarer libératoire son offre de paiement, sous réserve du droit, pour le créancier, d'en demander la rétractation.

Art. 1235

Lorsque la chose consignée est un bien autre qu'une somme d'argent, l'offre de paiement met en demeure le créancier d'avoir, dans le délai de deux mois à compter de la notification, soit à retirer la chose consignée, soit à contester l'offre.

Note : La distinction des modalités de la notification n'est pas reprise, mais la conséquence est moins grave (il y a une suite).

Art. 1235-1

Faute, pour le créancier, d'avoir pris dans le délai l'une ou l'autre initiative, le débiteur peut, sur autorisation du juge de l'exécution, le créancier entendu ou appelé, faire vendre aux enchères publiques la chose consignée, et le prix de celle-ci est déposé pour le compte du créancier, déduction faite des frais de la vente.

Jusqu'à ce moment, la chose consignée est aux risques du créancier.

Art. 1236

La notification de l'offre n'interrompt pas la prescription.

(2) This general reference avoids the need to set out conditions 1 to 5 of article 1258 of the present Code.[1]

Art. 1234

The debtor must notify the creditor that he has made the deposit as an offer of satisfaction in accordance with any agreed conditions.

Art. 1234-1

Where the thing which is deposited is a sum of money, the debtor is discharged, as to both capital and interest, if, at the end of a period of two months from the notification to the creditor personally, the creditor has not challenged the offer of satisfaction.

Art. 1234-2

If the notification was not made to the creditor personally, the debtor may bring proceedings to ask the court entrusted with enforcement to declare that the effect of his offer of satisfaction was to discharge him, subject to the right of the creditor to demand its withdrawal.

Art. 1235

Where the thing which is deposited is property other than a sum of money, the offer of satisfaction gives formal notice to the creditor, within a period of two months from the notice, either to receive the thing that has been deposited, or to challenge the offer.

(Note: Distinctions in the conditions for notification are not repeated, but this has no serious consequences)

Art. 1235-1

If the creditor has not within that period taken one or other course of action, the debtor may obtain permission from the court entrusted with enforcement, at a hearing at which the creditor was heard or of which he was given notice, to arrange for the sale by public auction of the thing which was deposited, and the price paid for the thing is deposited to the account of the creditor, after deduction of the costs of the sale.

Until that moment, the deposited thing is at the creditor's risk.

Art. 1236

Notification of the offer does not stop time running for the purpose of prescription.

---

[1] [Art 1258 sets out seven conditions for an offer of satisfaction to be valid: (1) that it be made to the creditor with capacity to receive it (or someone authorised to receive it for him); (2) that it be made by a person with capacity to give satisfaction; (3) that it be for the totality of the sum due by way of performance, interest, etc; (4) that any date for satisfaction stipulated in favour of the creditor have passed; (5) that the condition under which the debt was contracted have occurred; (6) that the offer be made at the place agreed for satisfaction and (in the absence of contrary agreement about the place of payment) either to the creditor personally, or to his domicile, or to the domicile chosen for performance of the contract; (7) that the offer be made by an authorised public officer.]

Après l'expiration du délai de prescription, le débiteur peut demander la restitution de la chose déposée.

Après cette date, la demande de rétractation de la décision déclarant le débiteur libéré cesse d'être recevable.

> *Note : L'offre de paiement constitue formellement une reconnaissance de la dette. Toutefois, le débiteur est contraint de recourir à la procédure de paiement forcé parce que le créancier n'a pas voulu recevoir le paiement. Dans ces conditions, il ne paraît pas choquant de dire que la prescription en cours n'est pas interrompue.*

Section 2
De la remise de la dette
(Articles 1237 à 1239-1)

Art. 1237

La remise de dette est la convention par laquelle le créancier libère le débiteur de son obligation avec l'accord, exprès ou tacite, de celui-ci.

Art. 1238

La remise de dette convenue avec l'un des codébiteurs solidaires libère tous les autres, à moins que le créancier n'ait expressément réservé ses droits contre ces derniers.

Dans ce dernier cas, il ne peut plus agir en paiement de la dette que déduction faite de la part de celui auquel il a fait la remise.

Art. 1239

La remise de dette accordée au débiteur principal libère les cautions ; celle accordée à la caution ne libère pas le débiteur principal.

Art. 1239-1

La décharge accordée à l'une des cautions ne libère pas les autres.

Si les cautions sont solidaires, les autres ne restent tenues que déduction faite de la part du cofidéjusseur libéré.

Ce que le créancier a reçu d'une caution pour la décharge de son cautionnement doit être imputé sur la dette et tourner à la décharge du débiteur principal et des autres cautions.

On expiry of the prescription period, the debtor may require restitution of the thing that he had deposited.

After that date, no application may be made to set aside the order which discharged the debtor.

> Note: The offer of satisfaction constitutes a formal acknowledgment of the debt. However, the debtor is obliged to follow the procedure for forced satisfaction since the creditor is not willing to accept performance. In such a case, it does not seem to be surprising to say that a prescription period, already underway, is not interrupted.

Section 2
Release of Debts
(Articles 1237 to 1239-1)

Art. 1237

Release of a debt is a contract by which the creditor discharges the debtor from his obligation with the latter's express or implied agreement.

Art. 1238

The release of one of two or more joint and several debtors discharges all the others, unless the creditor has expressly reserved his rights against them.

In the latter situation, he may sue for satisfaction only after deduction of the share of the party whom he has released.

Art. 1239

Release of a debt granted to a principal debtor discharges any sureties; but a release granted to a surety does not discharge the principal debtor.

Art. 1239-1

Discharge of one of several sureties does not discharge the others.

If the sureties are joint and several, the others remain liable only to the extent which remains after deduction of the share of the co-surety who has been discharged.

Anything received from a surety in return for the discharge of his suretyship obligation must be set against the debt and pro tanto discharges the principal debtor and the other sureties.

Section 3
De la compensation
(Articles 1240 à 1247)

Art. 1240

Lorsque deux personnes se trouvent débitrices l'une envers l'autre, les deux dettes s'éteignent par compensation jusqu'à concurrence de la plus faible, selon les règles ci-après.

§1 – De la compensation en général

Art. 1241

La compensation peut être légale, judiciaire ou conventionnelle.

Art. 1241-1

La compensation légale n'a lieu qu'entre deux dettes réciproques et fongibles, également liquides et exigibles.

> *Note : Les quatre conditions de base sont groupées. Le terme fongible est ici approprié ; « fongibles ou du même genre », la précision chemin faisant a son intérêt et « genre » va mieux « qu'espèce ».*

Sont fongibles les dettes qui ont pour objet une somme d'argent ou une certaine quantité de choses du même genre.

Les dettes ayant pour objet des choses de genre et dont le prix est réglé par un marché organisé peuvent se compenser avec des sommes liquides et exigibles.

> *(art. 1291 c. civ. modifié)*

Art. 1241-2

Le terme de grâce ne fait pas obstacle à la compensation.

Art. 1242

Toutes les dettes sont compensables quelles que soient les causes de l'une et de l'autre à l'exception de celles qui ont pour cause des aliments ou une autre créance insaisissable.

> *Note : « compensable » marque mieux qu'il s'agit bien ici de la nature de la dette.*

Art. 1243

Le moyen de la compensation légale doit être invoqué par le débiteur poursuivi. En ce cas, les dettes se trouvent éteintes à concurrence de leurs quotités respectives, à l'instant où elles ont coexisté avec les qualités requises.

Art. 1243-1

La caution peut opposer la compensation de ce que le créancier doit au débiteur principal ; mais le débiteur principal ne peut opposer la compensation de ce que le créancier doit à la caution.

Section 3
Set-Off
(Articles 1240 to 1247)

Art. 1240

Where two persons owe each other debts, the two debts are extinguished by set-off, up to the limit of the lower of the two, in accordance with the rules set out below.

§1 Set-off in general

Art. 1241

Set-off can be effected by law, by order of the court, or by contract.

Art. 1241-1

Set-off is effected by law only in the case of two mutual fungible debts which are both liquidated and enforceable.

> *Note: The four essential conditions are put together. The term fungible is here appropriate; 'fungible or of the same generic kind', the definition in passing is important, and 'generic kind' is better than 'form'.*

Debts are fungible where their subject-matter is a sum of money or a certain quantity of things of the same generic kind.

Debts whose subject-matter is generic and whose price is fixed in a regulated market may be set off against sums which are liquidated and enforceable.

(art. 1291 C. civ., amended)

Art. 1241-2

A period of grace for payment does not prevent set-off.

Art. 1242

All debts may be set off against each other, whatever their legal grounds, save only for maintenance debts and other non-distrainable debts.

> *Note: 'may be set off' emphasises that this depends on the nature of the debt.*

Art. 1243

A claim for set-off by law must be raised by the debtor in the action brought against him. In such a situation, the debts are extinguished as far as their respective values correspond, at the moment when they are both in existence together with the necessary attributes.

Art. 1243-1

A surety may take advantage of set-off as regards the debts owed by the creditor to the principal debtor; but the principal debtor may not take advantage of set-off as regards the debts owed by the creditor to the surety.

Le débiteur solidaire ne peut pas opposer la compensation de ce que le créancier doit à son codébiteur.

(art. 1294 actuel)

Art. 1244

Lors de la cession de l'une des créances compensables à un tiers, le débiteur cédé peut opposer la compensation au cessionnaire à moins qu'il n'y ait expressément renoncé par un acte écrit.

Obs. : Concordance avec l'article 1257.

Art. 1244-1

La compensation ne peut pas s'opérer entre deux créances si l'une devient indisponible du fait qu'elle est saisie avant que la créance réciproque ne soit liquide et exigible.

Art. 1245

Lorsqu'il y a plusieurs dettes compensables dues par la même personne, on suit, pour la compensation, les règles établies pour l'imputation par l'article 1228-1.

(art. 1297 actuel)

Art. 1245-1

Celui qui a payé une dette compensable, ne peut plus, en exerçant la créance dont il n'a point opposé la compensation, se prévaloir, au préjudice des tiers, des privilèges ou hypothèques qui y étaient attachés, à moins qu'il n'ait eu une juste cause d'ignorer la créance qui devait compenser sa dette.

(art. 1299 actuel)

Art. 1246

La compensation peut être opposée en justice par la partie dont la créance n'est pas encore liquide et exigible, à la condition, dans ce dernier cas, que le juge puisse prononcer la déchéance du terme. La compensation produit ses effets à la date de l'introduction de la demande reconventionnelle.

Art. 1246-1

La compensation judiciaire suit pour le surplus les règles de la compensation légale.

Art. 1247

Les parties peuvent convenir d'éteindre leurs dettes réciproques. Cette compensation n'opère qu'à la date de leur accord.

§2 – De la compensation des dettes connexes

Art. 1248

Lorsque deux dettes sont connexes, le juge ne peut écarter la demande en compensation au motif que l'une d'entre elles ne réunit pas les conditions de liquidité et d'exigibilité.

A joint and several debtor may not take advantage of set-off between his creditor and one of his co-debtors.

(art. 1294 of the present Code)

Art. 1244

If a right under an obligation, which is capable of being set off, is assigned to a third party, the debtor of the obligation which has been assigned may take advantage of the set-off against the assignee unless he has expressly renounced in writing the right to do so.

Comment: In harmony with article 1257.

Art. 1244-1

There can be no set-off between two rights arising under obligations if one becomes unavailable by reason of having been enforced before the reciprocal right becomes liquidated and enforceable.

Art. 1245

In the case of more than one debt owed by the same person and liable to set-off, the same rules are used for set-off as for the allocation of payments under article 1228-1.

(art. 1297 of the present Code)

Art. 1245-1

In enforcing the right to the obligations in respect of which he did not take advantage of set-off, a person who has paid a debt which was liable to set-off may not take advantage of charges or mortgages attached to it to the prejudice of third parties, unless he had good reason for being unaware of the right to the obligation which could have been set off against his debt.

(art. 1299 of the present Code)

Art. 1246

Set-off may be taken advantage of in court proceedings by a party who has a right under an obligation which is not yet liquidated and enforceable on condition (in the latter case) that the court is able to declare that the delay set for its enforcement has expired. Set-off takes effect at the date when the counter-claim is made.

Art. 1246-1

Set-off by order of the court follows in other respects the rules set down for set-off by law.

Art. 1247

The parties may agree to extinguish their mutual debts. Such set-off takes effect only on the date of their agreement.

§ 2 Set-off of connected debts

Art. 1248

In the case of two connected debts, the court may refuse a request for set-off only if one of them does not satisfy the requirements of being liquidated and enforceable.

Art. 1248-1

La transmission ou la saisie de l'une des créances connexes ne fait pas non plus obstacle à la compensation.

Section 4
De la confusion
(Articles 1249 et 1250)

Art. 1249

Lorsque les qualités de créancier et de débiteur se réunissent dans la même personne, il se fait une confusion de droit qui éteint définitivement l'obligation.

(art. 1300 actuel)

Art. 1250

La confusion qui s'opère dans la personne du débiteur principal profite à ses cautions.

Celle qui s'opère dans la personne de la caution n'entraîne pas l'extinction de l'obligation principale.

Celle qui s'opère dans la personne d'un codébiteur solidaire ne profite aux autres que pour la part dont il était débiteur.

Chapitre VI
Des opérations sur créances

Section 1
De la cession de créance
(Articles 1251 à 1257-1)

Art. 1251

La cession de créance est une convention par laquelle le créancier cédant transmet tout ou partie de sa créance à un tiers cessionnaire, par vente, donation ou autre titre particulier.

Art. 1252

Peuvent être cédées des créances nées ou à naître. En cas de cession d'une créance future, l'acte doit comporter les éléments permettant, le moment venu, l'identification de la créance cédée.

Art. 1248-1

Transmission or attachment of one of two or more connected rights under obligations does not prevent set-off.

Section 4
Merger
(Articles 1249 and 1250)

Art. 1249

Where the same person becomes both creditor and debtor of the same obligation, there is a merger by operation of law which extinguishes the obligation absolutely.

(art. 1300 of the present Code)

Art. 1250

A merger which takes place in relation to the principal debtor benefits his sureties.

A merger which takes place in relation to a surety does not cause the principal obligation to be extinguished.

A merger which takes place in relation to one of two or more joint and several debtors enures to the benefit of the others only in relation to his share of the debt.

Chapter VI
Transactions Relating to Rights Under Obligations

Section 1
Assignment of Rights Under Obligations
(Articles 1251 to 1257-1)

Art. 1251

Assignment is a contract by which the creditor (the assignor) transfers the whole or part of his rights under an obligation to a third party (the assignee) by sale, gift or by some other disposition.

Art. 1252

Both existing rights and rights yet to come into existence may be assigned. In the case of assignment of a future right, the instrument must include details enabling the assigned right to be identified when the time comes.

Art. 1253

À peine de nullité, la cession de créance doit être constatée par écrit, sans préjudice des cas où la forme authentique est exigée.

Art. 1254

Entre les parties, sauf convention contraire, l'établissement de l'acte suffit, par lui-même, à opérer la transmission de la créance.

Dès ce moment, le transfert de la créance est réputé accompli à l'égard des tiers et leur est opposable sans formalité. En cas de contestation, de la part de ceux-ci, sur la date de la cession, la preuve de son exactitude incombe au cessionnaire qui peut la rapporter par tous les moyens.

(cf. art. 1689 c. civ.)

Note : La règle est la même « inter partes et erga omnes » ; la mise en facteur commun souligne l'alignement, innovation marquante du texte.

Art. 1254-1

Toutefois, le transfert d'une créance future n'a lieu qu'au jour de sa naissance, tant entre les parties qu'à l'égard des tiers.

Art. 1254-2

La cession de créance ne devient opposable au débiteur que par la notification qui lui en est faite, sur papier ou sous forme électronique, par le cédant ou par le cessionnaire.

Art. 1254-3

Le conflit entre cessionnaires successifs d'une même créance se résout en faveur du premier en date. La preuve de la date se rapporte par tout moyen.

Art. 1255

Sauf clause contraire, la cession d'une créance comprend les accessoires de celle-ci, tels que caution, privilège et hypothèque, dont le cessionnaire peut se prévaloir sans autre formalité.

(art. 1692 c. civ. modifié)

Art. 1256

Celui qui cède une créance doit en garantir l'existence au temps du transfert, quoiqu'il soit fait sans garantie.

(art. 1693 actuel)

Il ne répond de la solvabilité du débiteur que lorsqu'il s'y est engagé, et jusqu'à concurrence seulement du prix qu'il a pu retirer de la cession de sa créance.

(art. 1694 actuel)

Lorsqu'il a promis la garantie de la solvabilité du débiteur, cette promesse ne

Art. 1253

On pain of nullity, an assignment must be effected in writing, without prejudice to the situations where the execution of a publicly authenticated document is required.

Art. 1254

Unless they otherwise agree, as between the parties the execution of the instrument is sufficient of itself to effect the transfer of the right.

From that moment, the transfer of the right is deemed to take place as regards third parties, and can be relied on against them without further formality. In the event of a challenge by the latter as to the date of the assignment, the burden of proof of its accuracy lies on the assignee, who may establish it by any form of evidence.

(cf. art. 1689 C. civ.[1])

Note: The rule is the same, between the parties and against third parties. Drawing these together underlines the similarity, a notable innovation of the provision.

Art. 1254-1

However, the transfer of a future benefit takes effect only on the day when it comes into existence, as between the parties as well as as against third parties.

Art. 1254-2

An assignment may be relied on against the debtor only once it has been notified to him by the assignor or the assignee in written or electronic form.

Art. 1254-3

Priority between successive assignees of the same right under an obligation is accorded to the earliest in time. Proof of the time may be established by any form of evidence.

Art. 1255

In the absence of contrary provision, assignment of the right under an obligation includes its accessory rights, such as to a guarantee, charge or mortgage; the assignee may take advantage of these without any further formality.

(art. 1692 C. civ., amended)

Art. 1256

The assignor of a right under an obligation must guarantee its existence at the time of the transfer, even if it is made without guarantee.

(art. 1693 of the present Code)

He is not answerable for the solvency of the debtor unless he has undertaken to be so, and then only up to the value of the sum he was able to obtain for the assignment.

(art. 1694 of the present Code)

Where he has promised to guarantee the solvency of the debtor, the promise

---

[1] [Article 1689 Cc (placed in the Title on the contract of sale) provides that in the transfer of a right under an obligation, or of a right or an action against a third party, the transfer takes place as between the assignor and the assignee by handing over the instrument of title.]

s'entend que de la solvabilité actuelle ; elle peut toutefois s'étendre au temps à venir, mais à la condition que le cédant l'ait expressément spécifié.

(art. 1695 c. civ. modifié)

Art. 1257

Lorsqu'il accepte la cession par un acte écrit, le débiteur cédé peut expressément renoncer à opposer au cessionnaire tout ou partie des exceptions qu'il aurait pu opposer au cédant.

À défaut d'une telle acceptation le débiteur peut opposer au cessionnaire toutes les exceptions inhérentes à la dette, y compris l'intransmissibilité de l'obligation, ainsi que les clauses de règlement des différends.

Il peut se prévaloir à l'encontre du cessionnaire de la compensation des dettes connexes dans ses rapports avec le cédant.

Il peut également opposer au cessionnaire l'extinction de la créance pour toute cause antérieure à la date à laquelle la cession de celle-ci lui a été rendue opposable.

Art. 1257-1

Une créance peut être cédée en propriété sans stipulation de prix à titre de garantie. Elle fait retour au cédant lorsque le cessionnaire a été rempli de ses droits ou que l'obligation garantie est éteinte pour une autre cause.

Section 2
De la subrogation personnelle
(Articles 1258 à 1264-2)

Art. 1258

La subrogation dans les droits du créancier au profit de la tierce personne qui le paie s'opère, en vertu de la loi ou de la convention, par substitution du créancier subrogé au créancier primitif.

(art. 1249 c. civ. modifié)

Note : La définition proposée à l'article 1258 du projet paraît trop doctrinale et trop abstraite. On conçoit qu'elle veuille montrer, comme on l'admet aujourd'hui, que la subrogation recèle une cession de créance. Mais elle ne met pas assez en relief que la subrogation demeure, à la base, une modalité du paiement (face traditionnelle déjà éclipsée par le déplacement du texte qui a été éloigné du paiement). Surtout, il n'apparaît pas aussitôt, concrètement, que, légale ou conventionnelle, la subrogation est toujours un mécanisme qui se produit au profit de celui qui paye. Ce paiement initial déclencheur d'un avantage en faveur du solvens qui fait l'avance des fonds est un point commun central. C'est la clé du mécanisme subrogatoire. Il est bon qu'elle apparaisse

extends only to his current solvency; it may be extended as to the future, but only if the assignor has expressly so specified.

(art. 1695 C. civ., amended)

Art. 1257

Where he agrees to an assignment by a written instrument, the debtor may expressly waive the right to raise against the assignee all or some of the defences that he could have raised against the assignor.

In the absence of such agreement the debtor may raise against the assignee all the defences inherent in the debt, including its non-assignability, as well as any dispute resolution clauses.

He may take advantage, as against the assignee, of the set-off of connected debts which arose in his dealings with the assignor.

As against the assignee he may also rely on the extinction of the debt on any ground which arose before the date on which the assignment became capable of affecting him.

Art. 1257-1

A right under an obligation may be assigned by way of guarantee, without charging any price. The assigned right reverts to the assignor where the assignee has had his own rights satisfied or the guaranteed obligation is extinguished on some other ground.

Section 2
Personal Subrogation
(Articles 1258 to 1264-2)

Art. 1258

Subrogation to the rights of a creditor in favour of a third party who satisfies a liability takes effect, either by virtue of legislation or of a contract, by placing the substitute creditor in the position of the original creditor.

(art. 1249 C. civ., amended)

Note: The definition proposed in article 1258 of the Reform Proposals may seem too academic and too abstract. It is clear that it is seeking to show that—as is accepted today—subrogation conceals an assignment. But it does not really highlight the fact that, at its root, subrogation remains a particular way of satisfying the obligation (the traditional viewpoint which has been masked by having separated this provision from those on satisfaction). Moreover, it is not self-evident that, whether operating by law or by agreement, subrogation is always a mechanism which works to the benefit of the party who satisfies the obligation. The initial satisfaction of the obligation, triggering a benefit in favour of the party who advances the payment by way of satisfaction, is a central element in all cases. It is the key to the mechanism

dès le début dans la définition de tête. Elle est d'ailleurs bien à sa place dans l'actuel article 1243 c. civ.. C'est tout le climat de la subrogation. Ce canevas court dans toutes les applications : le « profit » à qui fournit les fonds. Au demeurant, la transmission de la créance (qui est un effet commun) est bien mise en valeur dans l'article 1262 du projet (il y aurait donc une redite à maintenir l'article 1258 du projet). En revanche, il n'est sans doute pas inutile, dans l'article de tête, de montrer que la subrogation personnelle, terme de haute densité juridique, consomme la substitution d'un créancier à un autre dans le rapport contractuel (terme courant immédiatement intelligible).

NB : Une préférence pour parler du « créancier subrogé », plutôt que du « subrogé » par opposition au « créancier primitif ».

Art. 1259

La subrogation a lieu de plein droit :

1) au profit de celui qui, étant tenu avec d'autres ou pour d'autres au paiement de la dette, avait intérêt de l'acquitter ;

2) au profit de l'héritier bénéficiaire qui a payé de ses deniers les dettes de la succession ;

3) au profit de celui qui, étant lui-même créancier, paye un autre créancier qui lui est préférable ;

4) au profit de l'acquéreur d'un immeuble, qui emploie le prix de son acquisition au paiement des créanciers auxquels cet immeuble était hypothéqué.

La subrogation a également lieu dans les cas prévus par des lois spéciales.

(art. 1251 c. civ. modifié)

Note : Propositions pour une présentation plus logique :

a) la subrogation légale avant la subrogation conventionnelle ;

b) le droit commun (art. 1259 c. civ.) avant les lois spéciales ;

c) dans l'énumération de l'article 1259, le 3° actuel est promu au premier rang ; c'est le cas ordinaire le plus pur et, en pratique, le plus important.

Art. 1260

La subrogation conventionnelle s'opère à l'initiative du créancier lorsque celui-ci, recevant son paiement d'une tierce personne, la subroge dans ses droits contre le débiteur.

Cette subrogation doit être expresse.

Elle doit être consentie en même temps que le paiement, à moins que, dans un acte antérieur, le subrogeant n'ait manifesté la volonté que son cocontractant lui soit subrogé lors du paiement. La concomitance de la subrogation et du paiement peut être prouvée par tous moyens.

of subrogation. It is right that it should appear at the forefront of the headline definition. And it is in its rightful place in the present article 1243 of the Civil Code. It is the natural habitat of subrogation. This basic framework runs through all of its applications: the 'benefit' for the one who advances the funds. Incidentally, the transfer of the right under the obligation (which is a common consequence) is given real significance in article 1262 of the Reform Proposals (it would be a needless repetition to keep article 1258 of the Proposals). On the other hand, it is no doubt no bad thing, in the very first article, to show that personal subrogation, a term of deep legal significance, completes the substitution of one creditor for another in the contractual relationship (a common term, immediately understood).

N.B. We prefer to speak of the 'subrogated creditor' rather than 'the subrogated person', by way of contrast with the 'original creditor'.

Art. 1259

Subrogation takes place by operation of law:

(1) in favour of a person who, being bound with others or on behalf of others to satisfy a debt, had an interest in discharging it;

(2) in favour of an heir who has paid from his own funds the debts owed by the estate;

(3) in favour of a person who, being himself a creditor, pays another creditor whose right is prior to his own;

(4) in favour of the purchaser of a building who applies the purchase price to the satisfaction of creditors in whose favour the building was mortgaged.

Subrogation takes place also in certain situations set out in particular legislative enactments.

(art. 1251 C. civ., amended)

Note: Recommendations which give a more logical presentation:

a) subrogation by law before subrogation by contract;

b) the general law applicable (art. 1259 C. civ.) before special legislative rules;

c) in the list in article 1259, the third item in the present Code is promoted to the top of the list: this is the normal, most straightforward case and in practice the most important.

Art. 1260

Subrogation by contract takes effect on the initiative of the creditor where, on receiving satisfaction from a third party, the creditor substitutes the third party for himself as against the debtor.

This type of subrogation must be express.

It must be agreed upon at the same time as the satisfaction, unless, in an earlier juridical act, the party who subrogates has indicated his intention that the other contracting party should be subrogated to him at the time of satisfaction. The co-existence of the subrogation and the satisfaction may be proved by any form of evidence.

*Note : La rédaction ici proposée demeure très proche de l'article 1250 1°
c. civ. actuel. Elle marque l'initiative du créancier désintéressé par le tiers
solvens.*

Art. 1261

Sous les mêmes conditions, la subrogation conventionnelle a lieu à l'initiative du
débiteur lorsque celui-ci, empruntant une somme à l'effet de payer sa dette, subroge
le prêteur dans les droits du créancier avec le concours de celui-ci. En ce cas, la
quittance donnée par le créancier doit indiquer l'origine des fonds.

La subrogation peut même être consentie par le débiteur sans le concours du
créancier, mais à la condition que la dette soit échue ou que le terme soit en faveur
du débiteur. À peine de nullité de la subrogation, l'emprunt et la quittance sont
constatés par un acte ayant date certaine ; il doit être déclaré dans l'acte d'emprunt
que la somme a été empruntée pour faire le paiement, et dans la quittance que le
paiement a été fait des deniers fournis à cet effet par le nouveau créancier.

*Note : « même » a sa valeur, dès lors que l'alinéa qui précède se rapporte bien
à la subrogation à l'initiative du débiteur.*

Art. 1262

La subrogation transmet à son bénéficiaire, dans la limite de ce qu'il a payé, la
créance et ses accessoires, y compris les sûretés qui la garantissent. Le créancier
subrogé dispose de tous les droits et actions liés à la créance qui appartenaient au
créancier primitif, à l'exception des droits exclusivement attachés à la personne de
celui-ci.

Art. 1263

Toutefois, la subrogation ne peut nuire au créancier lorsqu'il n'a été payé qu'en
partie ; en ce cas, il peut exercer ses droits, pour ce qui lui reste dû, par préférence à
celui dont il n'a reçu qu'un paiement partiel, sauf convention contraire.

(art. 1252 c. civ. modifié)

Art. 1264

Lorsque la subrogation est consentie par le créancier, la transmission de la créance
ne devient opposable au débiteur qu'au moment où celui-ci en est informé.

Art. 1264-1

Le débiteur peut opposer au créancier subrogé toutes les exceptions inhérentes à la
dette, y compris l'intransmissibilité de l'obligation, ainsi que les clauses de
règlement des différends, et se prévaloir à son encontre de la compensation des
dettes connexes dans ses rapports avec le créancier primitif.

Il peut également lui opposer l'extinction de la dette pour toute cause antérieure à
la subrogation ou, en cas de subrogation consentie par le créancier, à la date à
laquelle il a été informé de celle-ci.

Note: The form of words proposed here remains very close to article 1250(1) of the present Civil Code. It emphasises the initiative of the creditor whose interest is paid off by a third party.

Art. 1261

On the same conditions, subrogation by contract takes place on the initiative of the debtor where the latter, borrowing a sum of money in order to satisfy his debt, subrogates the lender to the creditor's rights with the latter's consent. In this case, the receipt given by the creditor must indicate the source of the funds.

Subrogation may even be agreed by the debtor without the consent of the creditor, but only where the debt has fallen due or the period for payment was set for the debtor's benefit. On pain of nullity of the subrogation, the loan and the receipt must be established by an instrument with a set date; it must be declared in the instrument of loan that the sum has been borrowed in order to have the debt satisfied, and in the receipt that the satisfaction has been effected from funds provided for this purpose by the new creditor.

Note: 'even' is significant, since the preceding paragraph is also concerned with subrogation on the initiative of the debtor.

Art. 1262

Subrogation transfers to its beneficiary, up to the limit of the satisfaction which he has rendered, the right under the obligation and its ancillary rights, including the benefit of securities guaranteeing it. A subrogated creditor enjoys all the legal rights and rights of action linked to the rights under the obligation which formerly belonged to the initial creditor, apart from rights which belonged to him only personally.

Art. 1263

However, subrogation cannot prejudice the creditor where he has received satisfaction only in part; in this situation, he may exercise his rights, as regards what still remains outstanding to him, in priority to the person from whom he has received only partial satisfaction, unless the parties agree otherwise.

(art. 1252 C. civ., amended)

Art. 1264

Where subrogation is agreed by the creditor, the transfer of the right under the obligation becomes enforceable against the debtor only from the moment when the debtor is informed of it.

Art. 1264-1

As against a subrogated creditor, the debtor may raise all the defences inherent in the debt itself, including the prohibition on assignment of the obligation and dispute resolution clauses, and may rely on the right to set off related debts which arise in his dealings with the original creditor.

He may also rely on the extinction of the debt on any ground which arose before subrogation or, in the case of subrogation with the consent of the creditor, before the date on which he was informed of it.

Art. 1264-2

La subrogation est opposable aux tiers dès le paiement qui la produit. Cette opposabilité s'étend, sans autre formalité, au transfert des sûretés qui garantissent la créance.

Lorsque la subrogation est consentie par le créancier, ou par le débiteur avec le concours du créancier, il n'est pas requis que l'acte ait date certaine. En cas de contestation, la preuve de la date incombe au créancier subrogé, qui peut la rapporter par tous moyens.

Section 3
De la novation
(Articles 1265 à 1274)

Art. 1265

La novation est une convention qui a pour objet de substituer à une obligation qu'elle éteint, une obligation différente qu'elle crée.

> *Note : La novation est toujours une <u>convention</u>, même si ce n'est pas toujours entre le créancier et le débiteur de l'obligation primitive. Entre celle-ci et l'obligation nouvelle, il y a toujours une <u>différence</u>. Il semble préférable que ces deux termes soient présents dans la définition inaugurale, de même que les verbes « éteindre » et « créer ».*

Art. 1266

La novation s'opère de trois manières :

1) lorsqu'un nouveau débiteur est substitué à l'ancien qui est déchargé par le créancier ;

2) lorsque, par l'effet d'un nouvel engagement, un nouveau créancier est substitué à l'ancien, envers lequel le débiteur se trouve déchargé ;

3) lorsque le débiteur contracte envers son créancier une nouvelle dette qui est substituée à l'ancienne, laquelle est éteinte ; en ce cas, il y a novation quelle que soit la différence instituée entre l'ancienne et la nouvelle obligation.

> *Note : c'est la teneur même de l'actuel article 1271 c. civ., « le roc ».*

Art. 1267

La novation n'a lieu que si l'obligation ancienne et l'obligation nouvelle sont l'une et l'autre valables, à moins qu'elle n'ait pour objet déclaré de substituer un engagement valable à un engagement entaché d'un vice.

Art. 1268

La novation ne se présume pas ; il faut que la volonté de l'opérer résulte clairement de l'acte.

> *(art. 1273 actuel)*

Art. 1264-2

Subrogation may be relied on as against third parties from the time of the satis-faction which gave rise to it. This effect extends, without the requirement of any further formality, to the transfer of any security guaranteeing the obligation.

Where subrogation is effected with the agreement of the creditor or by the debtor with the consent of the creditor, there is no requirement that the instrument have a set date. In case of dispute, the burden of proof of the date lies on the subrogated creditor, who may establish it by any form of evidence.

Section 3
Novation
(Articles 1265 to 1274)

Art. 1265

Novation is a contract which has as its subject-matter the substitution of one obligation (which it extinguishes) with a different obligation (which it creates).

> *Note: Novation is always a <u>contract</u>, although it is not always between the creditor and the debtor of the original obligation. Between that obligation and the new one there is always some <u>difference</u>. It seems better to have these two terms in the opening definition, as well as the verbs 'extinguish' and 'create'.*

Art. 1266

Novation takes place in three ways:

(1) where a new debtor is substituted for the old, who is discharged by the creditor;

(2) where, in consequence of a new undertaking, a new creditor is substituted for the old, as against whom the debtor is released;

(3) where the debtor contracts with his creditor for a new debt which takes the place of the old, which is extinguished. In this situation, there is a novation, regardless of any particular difference between the old and the new obligations.

> *Note: This is essentially the same as article 1271 of the present Code, 'the rock'.*

Art. 1267

Novation is effected only if the old and the new obligations are both valid, unless it has expressly as its subject-matter the substitution of a valid undertaking for an undertaking which was tainted by a defect.

Art. 1268

Novation cannot be implied. The intention to effect it must be shown clearly in the instrument.

> *(art. 1273 of the present Code)*

Art. 1269

La novation par la substitution d'un nouveau débiteur peut s'opérer sans le concours du premier débiteur.

(art. 1274 actuel)

Note : On remarque que le premier débiteur n'est pas partie à la novation, mais que celle-ci est toujours une convention.

Art. 1270

La novation par la substitution d'un nouveau créancier peut avoir lieu si le débiteur a, par avance, accepté que le nouveau créancier soit désigné par le premier.

En cas de contestation sur la date de la novation, la preuve en incombe au nouveau créancier, qui peut la rapporter par tous moyens.

Art. 1271

L'extinction de l'obligation ancienne s'étend à tous ses accessoires, y compris les sûretés qui la garantissent, à moins que ces dernières n'aient été ou ne soient expressément réservées du consentement de tous les intéressés.

Note : Nouvelle, cette disposition générale est bienvenue. Le principe qu'elle énonce justifie que les dispositions qui suivent apparaissent comme des applications.

Art. 1272

La novation faite entre le créancier et l'un des codébiteurs solidaires libère les autres.

(art. 1281 al. 1 actuel)

Art. 1273

En ce cas, les sûretés réelles garantissant l'ancienne créance ne peuvent être réservées que sur les biens de celui qui contracte la nouvelle dette, sauf convention contraire avec tel codébiteur.

(art. 1280 actuel)

Art. 1274

La novation faite entre le créancier et la caution ne libère pas le débiteur principal. Elle ne libère pas davantage les autres cautions, sauf convention contraire.

Note : Cette disposition reproduit exactement la « dernière jurisprudence ».

Art. 1269

Novation by substitution of a new debtor may take place without the consent of the first debtor.

(art. 1274 of the present Code)

Note: One may notice that the first debtor is not a party to the novation, but that the novation is still a contract.

Art. 1270

Novation by substitution of a new creditor may take place if the debtor has agreed in advance that the new creditor will be appointed by the old.

In case of dispute about the date of the novation, the burden of proof lies on the new creditor, who may establish it by any form of evidence.

Art. 1271

Extinction of the old obligation extends to all its ancillary rights and obligations, including the securities which guarantee it, as long as these have not been, and are not, expressly preserved by the agreement of all those interested.

Note: This is new. As a general provision, it is welcome. The principle which it sets out shows that the provisions which follow constitute its application.

Art. 1272

A novation entered into between the creditor and one of two or more joint and several debtors discharges the others.

(art. 1281 para. 1 of the present Code)

Art. 1273

In this situation, any real security which guarantees the old obligation may be preserved only over the property of the party who undertakes the new obligation, unless such a co-debtor otherwise agrees.

(art. 1280 of the present Code)

Art. 1274

A novation entered into between the creditor and a surety does not discharge the principal debtor. Nor does it discharge the other sureties, unless the contract otherwise provides.

Note: This provision reproduces exactly the 'latest case-law'.

Section 4
De la délégation
(Articles 1275 à 1282)

Art. 1275

Il y a délégation lorsque, sur ordre d'une personne, le délégant, une autre personne, le délégué, s'engage envers une troisième personne, le délégataire*, qui l'accepte comme débiteur.

> *Note : *Ressort essentiel de la délégation, l'engagement du délégué envers le délégataire et l'acceptation, par ce dernier, de la délégation, doivent figurer dans la définition de tête.*

Art. 1276

La délégation est valable alors même que le délégant n'est pas débiteur du délégataire ou que le délégué n'est pas débiteur du délégant.

Art. 1277

La délégation a pour objet, selon ce que les parties déterminent, l'une des opérations suivantes.

Art. 1278

Lorsque le délégant est débiteur du délégataire et que celui-ci le décharge expressément, la délégation opère un changement de débiteur.

Cette délégation confère au délégataire un droit direct et indépendant contre le délégué, qui ne peut lui opposer les exceptions dont le délégant aurait pu se prévaloir.

Art. 1279

Lorsque le délégant est débiteur du délégataire et que celui-ci ne le décharge pas expressément, cette délégation simple donne au délégataire un second débiteur en qualité de débiteur principal.

Quand la délégation est faite pour donner au délégataire un second débiteur, le paiement par le délégué libère le délégant.

Art. 1279-1

Si l'obligation du délégué résulte d'un engagement expressément stipulé indépendant, celui-ci ne pourra pas opposer au délégataire les exceptions dont aurait pu se prévaloir le délégant ou qu'il aurait pu lui-même opposer au délégant, à moins qu'il n'en soit autrement convenu.

Si le délégué, à la demande du délégant, a promis de payer ce que celui-ci doit au délégataire, il pourra opposer à ce dernier les exceptions du délégant, à moins qu'il n'en soit autrement convenu.

Section 4
Delegation
(Articles 1275 to 1282)

Art. 1275

Delegation occurs where, on the order of one person (the delegator) another person (the delegate) undertakes in favour of a third party (the beneficiary of the delegation*), who accepts him as debtor.

> Note: *An essential element of delegation, the undertaking of the delegate in favour of the beneficiary, and the acceptance by the latter of the delegation, must appear in the initial definition.

Art. 1276

Delegation is valid even if the delegator is not a debtor of the beneficiary, and if the delegate is not a debtor of the delegator.

Art. 1277

In accordance with the determination of the parties, delegation has as its subject-matter one of the following transactions.

Art. 1278

Where the delegator is debtor of the beneficiary and the latter releases him expressly, delegation effects a change of debtor.

Such a delegation confers upon the beneficiary a direct, independent right against the delegate, who may not raise against him any defences of which the delegator could have availed himself.

Art. 1279

Where the delegator is debtor of the beneficiary and the latter does not release him expressly, this simple delegation provides the beneficiary with another debtor with the status of principal debtor.

Where the delegation is made in order to provide the beneficiary with another debtor, performance by the delegate discharges the delegator.

Art. 1279-1

If the obligation of the delegate is a result of an undertaking which is expressly stipulated as independent, he may not raise against the beneficiary the defences of which the delegator could have availed himself, or which he could have raised himself against the delegator, in the absence of agreement to the contrary.

If the delegate, at the delegator's request, has promised to satisfy the debt owed by the latter to the beneficiary, he may raise against the beneficiary the delegator's defences, in the absence of agreement to the contrary.

Art. 1279-2

Lorsque le délégant est débiteur du délégataire, il demeure tenu, alors même que celui-ci l'aurait déchargé, soit qu'il ait garanti l'insolvabilité du délégué, soit que le délégué se trouve soumis à une procédure d'apurement de ses dettes lors de la demande en paiement.

Art. 1280

Lorsque le délégué est débiteur du délégant, il appartient aux parties de décider s'il s'engage à payer au délégataire ce qu'il doit au délégant ou s'il souscrit envers lui un engagement expressément stipulé indépendant.

L'opposabilité des exceptions se règle alors comme il est dit à l'article précédent.

Art. 1281

L'engagement du délégué envers le délégataire rend indisponible la créance du délégant envers le délégué qui ne peut être ni cédée ni saisie.

Si une contestation s'élève sur la date de la délégation, la preuve incombe au délégué qui la rapporte par tous moyens.

Le paiement fait par le délégué au délégataire le libère à l'égard du délégant.

Le tout sauf convention différente des parties.

Art. 1282

La simple indication faite, par le débiteur, d'une personne qui doit payer à sa place n'emporte point novation ni délégation.

Il en est de même de la simple indication faite, par le créancier, d'une personne qui doit recevoir pour lui.

(art. 1277 c. civ. modifié)

Chapitre VII
De la preuve des obligations

Note : La théorie générale des preuves gouverne l'ensemble du droit privé. Elle aurait sa place naturelle dans le Titre préliminaire du Code civil, solution actuellement hors de portée. Le Titre des Obligations mérite d'en accueillir une bonne partie, d'abord en raison de la généralité inhérente à la matière (sous laquelle se profile le droit commun de l'acte juridique et du fait juridique) et aussi pour ne pas bouleverser le travail des praticiens, préoccupation essentielle. Au demeurant, beaucoup de règles particulières de preuve sont énoncées dans le code avec la matière qu'elles concernent (filiation, régime matrimoniaux, possession, etc.). Le mieux, en l'état, serait l'ennemi du bien. Un esprit pragmatique domine toute la matière.

Art. 1279-2

Where the delegator is debtor of the beneficiary, he remains bound—even where the latter would have released him—if he has guaranteed the solvency of the delegate, or the delegate is subject to a procedure for cancellation of his debts at the time of the demand for satisfaction.

Art. 1280

Where the delegate is debtor of the delegator, it is for the parties to decide whether he should undertake to satisfy the beneficiary as to what he owes the delegator, or whether he should undertake in his favour an undertaking which is expressly stipulated as independent.

The ability to raise defences is governed by the rules set out in the preceding article.

Art. 1281

The delegate's undertaking in favour of the beneficiary renders the right under the delegator's obligations in favour of the beneficiary unavailable; it may not be assigned nor subject to distraint.

If there is a dispute about the date of the delegation, the burden of proof lies on the delegate, who may use any form of evidence to establish it.

Satisfaction rendered by the delegate in favour of the beneficiary discharges him in relation to the delegator.

All these provisions are subject to different agreement of the parties.

Art. 1282

A simple indication by the debtor of a person who should perform in his place does not constitute either novation or delegation.

The same is true of a simple indication by the creditor of a person who should receive the performance on his behalf.

(art. 1277 C. civ., amended)

Chapter VII
Proof of Obligations

Note: the general doctrine of proof applies to the whole of private law. Its natural place would be in the Preliminary Title of the Civil Code, a solution which is not now possible. The Title on Obligations can incorporate a large part—first because of the inherent generality of the subject-matter (within which is outlined the general law of juridical acts and juridically significant facts), and also to avoid upsetting the work of practitioners, an essential concern. It should be noted that many specific rules of proof are set out in the Code alongside the subject-matter with which they are concerned (descent, matrimonial property regimes, possession, etc). As things are, the best would be the enemy of the good. A spirit of pragmatism runs throughout.

Section 1
General Provisions
(Articles 1283 to 1290)

Art. 1283

A person who claims the performance of an obligation has the burden of proving it.

In return, a person who claims to have been discharged must establish the satisfaction or the circumstances which have given rise to the extinction of his obligation.

> *Note: Art. 1315 of the present Code. It is wise not to make any change to this text. The harmony between the Civil Code and the New Code of Civil Procedure (article 9[1]) does not do any harm.*

Art. 1284

Proof of juridical acts and facts[2] which give rise to obligations may be established, following the distinctions set out below, by writing, by witnesses, by presumptions, by admission or by oath.

> *Note: This introductory provision sets out the range of methods of proof, and introduces the idea that the rules for proof are not identical for juridical acts and for juridically significant facts; and that they may also differ from one form to another.*
>
> *The reference to acts and facts which give rise to obligations is an allusion to the very first article of the Title on Obligations (article 1101).*
>
> *The reference to proof by writing introduces the following article, in which (with a simple inversion) the equivalent formula 'written proof' appears (an opportunity to be taken to include a synonym).*

Art. 1285

Proof by writing, or written proof, results from a series of letters, characters, numbers or any other signs or symbols with an intelligible meaning, whatever be their medium or their means of transmission.

> *Note: The definition of proof by writing comes immediately after the list of the different forms of proof. This definition is necessary because of the inclusion of writing in an electronic form—and this requires clarification. The definition of the other forms appears in the provisions which concern them, and from which they cannot be separated.*
>
> *The doubling-up proposed by the contributors to the Reform Proposals is interesting, but the advantage of repeating with only a slight qualification (by inversion of the words used) the terms of the existing article 1316 is, on the one hand, as we have already seen, to confirm the identity of proof by writing and written proof; and on the other hand to make a link with the preceding article.*

---

[1] [Article 9 of the New Code of Civil Procedure provides that it lies on each party to prove the facts necessary for the success of his claim.]

[2] [For the translation of *faits* as 'facts' see above, p 433.]

Art. 1285-1

L'écrit sous forme électronique est admis en preuve au même titre [et possède la même force probante] que l'écrit sur support papier, sous réserve que puisse être dûment identifiée la personne dont il émane et qu'il soit établi et conservé dans des conditions de nature à en garantir l'intégrité.

(art. 1316-1 actuel)

Art. 1286

La signature nécessaire à la perfection d'un acte juridique identifie celui qui l'appose. Elle manifeste le consentement des parties aux obligations qui découlent de cet acte. Quand elle est apposée par un officier public, elle confère l'authenticité à cet acte.

Lorsqu'elle est électronique, elle consiste en l'usage d'un procédé fiable d'identification garantissant son lien avec l'acte auquel elle s'attache. La fiabilité de ce procédé est présumée, jusqu'à preuve contraire, lorsque la signature électronique est créée, l'identité du signataire assurée et l'intégrité de l'acte garantie, dans des conditions fixées par décret en Conseil d'État.

(art. 1316-4 actuel)

Note : Le bloc de ces quatre articles a ici sa place : 1) pour ne pas le séparer de la définition de base qu'il complète d'ailleurs ; 2) si l'on admet que les règles concernant l'écrit sous forme électronique ne concernent pas exclusivement la preuve des actes juridiques, mais ont une portée générale et donc, à l'occasion, pour la preuve des faits juridiques.

Art. 1287

La preuve des faits est libre ; elle peut être rapportée par tous les moyens.

Hors les cas où la loi la détermine, la valeur des preuves est appréciée en conscience par le juge.

Dans le doute, le juge s'en tient à la plus forte vraisemblance.

Note : Le principe de la liberté de la preuve concerne traditionnellement les faits juridiques. L'ériger en principe commun aux actes et aux faits juridiques n'est pas compatible avec l'existence (et le maintien nécessaire) des restrictions particulières à la preuve des actes juridiques.

Il ne paraît pas nécessaire de définir la preuve, notion élémentaire qui tombe sous le sens (commun), quand au contraire tout énoncé théorique tombe dans la controverse (vérité du fait ou de l'allégation ? tant d'autres débats possibles).

Une proposition relative à la loyauté de la preuve soulève aussi beaucoup de problèmes (réflexion à approfondir).

En revanche la référence à l'intime conviction (ici nommée « conscience » en appel de discussion), tout en réservant les exceptions légales, pourrait être opportune, de même qu'une disposition sur le doute et la plus forte vraisemblance. La règle du melius jus survole la preuve en tous ses domaines (comp. la preuve de la propriété).

Art. 1285-1

Writing in electronic form is admissible as evidence on the same basis (and has the same probative force) as writing on paper, provided that it is possible properly to identify the person from whom it originates and that it is created and stored in such circumstances as will guarantee its integrity.

(art. 1316-1 of the present Code)

Art. 1286

The signature which is required in order to complete a juridical act must identify the person who places it on the document. It demonstrates the consent of the parties to the obligations which arise from the act. Where it is placed on the act by a public official, it confers authenticity on it.

Where it is in electronic form, it should use a reliable process of identification, guaranteeing its link with the juridical act to which it is attached. The reliability of the process is presumed, in the absence of proof to the contrary, where the electronic signature is created, the identity of the signatory is ensured, and the integrity of the juridical act is guaranteed, in the circumstances fixed by decree in the *Conseil d'État*.

(art. 1316-4 of the present Code)

Note: This group of four articles belongs here: (1) in order not to separate it from the core definition which it supplements; (2) if it is accepted that the rules concerning writing in electronic form do not apply solely to the proof of juridical acts, but have a general significance including, therefore, sometimes proof of facts giving rise to liability.

Art. 1287

Proof of facts is at large and it may be established by any means.

Outside situations where legislation otherwise so determines, the weight of evidence is assessed by courts as they think right.

In case of doubt, the court takes the one more likely to be true.

Note: The principle of the freedom of proof concerns traditionally juridically significant facts. Making it a principle common to juridical acts and juridically significant facts would not be compatible with the existence (and the necessary maintenance) of special restrictions on the proof of juridical acts.

It does not seem necessary to define 'proof', an elementary notion which is perfectly obvious when, on the contrary, every theoretical term is mired in controversy (truth of a fact or of an allegation? and so many other debates are possible).

A proposal concerning 'loyalty' in establishing proof also gives rise to many difficulties (something to be thought through further).

On the other hand, the reference to the inner conviction (here described in terms of 'thinking right' to prompt discussion), whilst putting aside legislative exceptions, could be useful—just as a provision on doubt and the balance of likelihood. The rule of the 'best legal right' runs through the law of proof in all its spheres (cf. proof of ownership).

Art. 1288

La preuve des actes juridiques est assujettie à des règles particulières touchant à la forme de la preuve par écrit, à l'exigence d'une preuve littérale et à l'admissibilité de la preuve testimoniale.

> *Note : établissant, dans leur principe, les restrictions qui affectent la preuve des actes juridiques (par opposition à celle des faits juridiques), cette disposition en précise les objets et, par là, annonce les titres des sections 2 et 3.*

Art. 1288-1

Les présomptions, l'aveu et le serment obéissent à des règles générales.

> *Note : Il s'agit de règles de preuve communes aux actes et aux faits juridiques. L'intérêt est d'annoncer la section 4 :*

Art. 1289

Les conventions relatives à la preuve sont licites.

Néanmoins, elles ne peuvent ni écarter ni affaiblir les présomptions établies par la loi et ne peuvent davantage modifier la foi que la loi attache à l'aveu ou au serment.

Elles ne peuvent davantage établir au profit de l'une des parties une présomption irréfragable attachée à ses propres écritures.

> *Note : En ouvrant le champ aux conventions relatives à la preuve, il paraît nécessaire d'en marquer les limites. C'est ce que propose le nouvel article 1316-3.*

> *On aura remarqué que la disposition relative aux tailles (art. 1333) ne figure pas dans cette version du projet. Elle n'est plus en usage.*

> *Comme le suggèrent les auteurs du projet, les dispositions relatives à la confirmation méritent sans doute d'être déplacées (art. 1338, 1339, 1340 actuels). D'où, en tout, un gain de trois loges d'articles.*

Art. 1290

L'administration judiciaire de la preuve et les contestations qui s'y rapportent sont régies par le Code de procédure civile.

Art. 1288

Proof of juridical acts is subject to special rules concerning the form of proof by writing, the requirement of written proof, and the admissibility of oral evidence.

> *Note: Laying down, as to their principles, the restrictions affecting the proof of juridical acts (as opposed to juridically significant facts), this provision identifies them and thereby introduces the subjects of Sections 2 and 3.*

Art. 1288-1

Presumptions, admissions and oaths are governed by general rules.

> *Note: This refers to the rules of proof common to juridical acts and juridically significant facts. The aim is to introduce Section 4.*

Art. 1289

Contracts relating to proof are lawful.

However, they must neither remove nor weaken the presumptions set by legislation, nor must they modify the entitlement to rely on admission or oath, as provided by legislation.

Nor may they establish, in favour of one of the parties, an irrebuttable presumption resting on his own writing.

> *Note: Since we open up the possibility of contracts relating to proof, it seems necessary to set the limits. This is what the new article [1289] proposes.*
>
> *It will be noticed that the provision relating to tallies (article 1333 of the present Code[1]) does not appear in this version of the Proposals. It is no longer in use.*
>
> *As the contributors to the Reform Proposals suggest, the provisions regarding affirmation should no doubt be moved (articles 1338, 1339, 1340 of the present Code).[2] That would free up the space of three articles in all.*

Art. 1290

The application by the courts of the rules of proof, and disputes relating to them, are governed by the New Code of Civil Procedure.

---

[1] [This is a reference to the use of a 'tally' (*taille*)—a stick of wood, marked with notches to record the quantity of goods supplied, which was cut lengthways through the notches, each of the parties retaining one part as proof of the supply. Art 1333 Cc provides that they constitute evidence as between parties who are accustomed to using tallies.]

[2] [Moved to arts 1129-4 to 1129-6 of the *Avant-projet*.]

Section 2
Des formes de la preuve par écrit des actes juridiques
(Articles 1291 à 1305)

Note : Le titre actuel « De la preuve littérale » est trop général : certaines dispositions relatives à la preuve littérale figurent dans la section 3. Il est trop vague : les exigences de la loi ici énoncées concernent précisément et exclusivement les formes de la preuve par écrit (et non l'exigence d'une preuve littérale. V. la section 3).

La section pourrait également avoir pour titre : « Des formes de la preuve littérale des actes juridiques » (à voir).

Art. 1291

La preuve par écrit d'un acte juridique peut être préconstituée en la forme authentique ou sous seing privé.

Art. 1292

L'acte, soit authentique, soit sous seing privé, fait foi entre les parties, même de ce qui n'y est exprimé qu'en termes énonciatifs, pourvu que l'énonciation ait un rapport direct à la disposition. Les énonciations étrangères à la disposition ne peuvent servir que d'un commencement de preuve.

(art. 1320 actuel)

Art. 1293

Lorsque la loi n'a pas fixé d'autres principes, et à défaut de convention valable entre les parties, le juge règle les conflits de preuve littérale en déterminant par tous moyens le titre le plus vraisemblable, quel qu'en soit le support.

(art. 1316-2 actuel)

§1 – Du titre authentique

Note : Question de terminologie. On peut dire indifféremment « titre » ou « acte » authentique. Mais « titre » est un terme de prestige qui convient bien à l'authenticité. L'usage traditionnel ne s'y trompe pas. On peut donc le conserver. L'ennui est que le « titre original » dont il est question à propos des copies peut être un acte sous seing privé (rien n'est parfait). La pratique n'est pas déroutée par ces équivalents qui lui sont familiers.

Section 2
The Forms of Proof by Writing of Juridical Acts
(Articles 1291 to 1305)

Note: The present title, 'Written proof', is too general; certain provisions relating to written proof appear in Section 3. It is too vague: the legislative requirements set out here concern exactly, and only, the forms of proof by writing (and not the requirement of written proof. See Section 3).

The section could equally well be entitled 'The forms of written proof of juridical acts' (see below).

Art. 1291

Proof by writing of a juridical act may be established by its being created in a publicly authenticated[1] form or by signature.

Art. 1292

The act, whether publicly authenticated or just signed, constitutes proof as between the parties, even as regards what is set out in it in only declaratory terms, provided that the declaration has a direct relation with the transaction. Declarations which are not related to the transaction can have effect only as a beginning of proof.[2]

(art. 1320 of the present Code)

Art. 1293

Where legislation has not laid down other principles, and in the absence of a valid contract between the parties, the court settles conflicts between written evidence by deciding (using any form of evidence) which is the more convincing instrument, whatever its medium.

(art. 1316-2 of the present Code)

§ 1 Authenticated instruments

Note: There is a question of terminology. One can speak indifferently of an authenticated 'instrument' or 'document'. But 'instrument' is a prestigious term which suits public authentication well. The traditional use of the term is not misleading. So we can retain it. The problem is that the 'original instrument' which is referred to in relation to copies can be just a signed document (nothing is perfect). Practitioners are not misled by these similarities, with which they are familiar.

[1] [For the notion of a document being 'authenticated' by a public official, such as a notary (*notaire*), see above, art 1286 and below, art 1294.]

[2] [The notion of a 'beginning of proof [in writing]' (*commencement de preuve [par écrit]*), used in a context where there is a requirement of written proof, is of a written document which is not of itself sufficient in law to constitute the required proof, but which can be used as supplemented by a form of proof outside the writing. See below, art 1312, and (for examples of the beginning of proof by writing, arts 1302 and 1303).]

Art. 1294

L'acte authentique est celui qui a été reçu par des officiers publics ayant le droit d'instrumenter dans le lieu où l'acte a été rédigé, et avec les solennités requises.

Il peut être dressé sur support électronique s'il est établi et conservé dans des conditions fixées par décret en Conseil d'État.

(art. 1317 actuel)

Art. 1294-1

L'acte qui n'est pas authentique par l'incompétence ou l'incapacité de l'officier, ou par un défaut de forme, vaut comme écriture privée, s'il a été signé des parties.

(art. 1318 actuel)

Art. 1294-2

L'acte authentique fait pleine foi de la convention qu'il renferme entre les parties contractantes et leurs héritiers ou ayants cause.

Néanmoins, en cas de plaintes en faux principal, l'exécution de l'acte argué de faux sera suspendue par la mise en accusation ; et, en cas d'inscription de faux faite incidemment, les tribunaux pourront, selon les circonstances, suspendre provisoirement l'exécution de l'acte.

(art. 1319 actuel)

§2 – De l'acte sous seing privé

Art. 1295

L'acte sous seing privé, reconnu par celui auquel on l'oppose, ou légalement tenu pour reconnu, a, entre ceux qui l'ont souscrit et entre leurs héritiers et ayants cause, la même foi que l'acte authentique.

(art. 1322 actuel)

Art. 1295-1

Celui auquel on oppose un acte sous seing privé est obligé d'avouer ou de désavouer formellement son écriture ou sa signature.

Ses héritiers ou ayants cause peuvent se contenter de déclarer qu'ils ne connaissent point l'écriture ou la signature de leur auteur.

(art. 1323 actuel)

Art. 1295-2

Dans le cas où la partie désavoue son écriture ou sa signature, et dans le cas où ses héritiers ou ayants cause déclarent ne les point connaître, la vérification en est ordonnée en justice.

(art. 1324 actuel)

Art. 1294

An authenticated instrument is one which has been received by public officials who have the right to draw up instruments in the place where the instrument was drafted, and with the required formalities.

It may be drawn up in an electronic medium if it is created and stored in the circumstances fixed by decree in the *Conseil d'État*.

(art. 1317 of the present Code)

Art. 1294-1

An instrument which is not authenticated by reason of the lack of authority or incapacity of the official, or a defect in its form, takes effect as a private written document, if it has been signed by the parties.

(art. 1318 of the present Code)

Art. 1294-2

An authenticated instrument constitutes conclusive proof of the contract which it contains, as between the contracting parties and their heirs or successors.

However, in case of a criminal complaint of forgery, the performance of the instrument alleged to be forged is suspended when the indictment is laid; and, where an allegation of forgery is made in other proceedings, the court may, in an appropriate case, make a provisional order suspending the performance of the instrument.

(art. 1319 of the present Code)

§ 2 Signed documents

Art. 1295

A signed document, acknowledged by the person against whom it is relied upon or deemed by the law to have been so acknowledged, has, as between those who have signed it and their heirs and successors, the same probative force as a publicly authenticated instrument.

(art. 1322 of the present Code)

Art. 1295-1

A person against whom a signed document is relied upon is required formally either to admit or to deny his writing or his signature.

His heirs or successors may simply declare that they do not recognise the writing or the signature of the person making them.

(art. 1323 of the present Code)

Art. 1295-2

In a situation where a party denies his writing or his signature, and where his heirs or successors deny that they recognise them, an assessment of its authenticity is ordered by the court.

(art. 1324 of the present Code)

Art. 1296

Les actes sous seing privé qui contiennent des conventions synallagmatiques ne sont valables que s'ils ont été faits en autant d'originaux qu'il y a de parties ayant un intérêt distinct.

Il suffit d'un original pour toutes les personnes ayant le même intérêt.

Chaque original doit contenir la mention du nombre des originaux qui en ont été faits. Néanmoins, le défaut de mention que les originaux ont été faits doubles, triples, etc., ne peut être opposé par celui qui a exécuté de sa part la convention portée dans l'acte.

Ces dispositions ne s'appliquent pas aux actes accomplis sous forme électronique.

(art. 1325 c. civ. modifié)

Art. 1297

La preuve d'un acte juridique par lequel une seule partie s'engage envers une autre à lui payer une somme d'argent ou à lui livrer un bien fongible doit résulter d'un titre qui comporte la signature de celui qui souscrit cet engagement ainsi que la mention, écrite par lui-même, de la somme ou de la quantité en toutes lettres et en chiffres. En cas de différence, l'acte sous seing privé vaut pour la somme écrite en toutes lettres.

(art. 1326 actuel)

Art. 1298

Les actes sous seing privé n'ont de date contre les tiers que du jour où ils ont été enregistrés, du jour de la mort de celui ou de l'un de ceux qui les ont souscrits, ou du jour où leur substance est constatée dans les actes dressés par des officiers publics, tels que procès-verbaux de scellés ou d'inventaire.

(art. 1328 actuel)

Art. 1299

Les écrits émanant de celui qui se prétend créancier ne font pas preuve de l'obligation qu'ils énoncent, sauf les dérogations résultant de la loi, de l'usage ou de la convention.

En ces deux derniers cas, ces écrits n'ont que valeur de présomptions et indices.

Art. 1300

Les écrits font preuve contre leur auteur ; mais celui qui veut en tirer avantage ne peut les diviser.

Art. 1300-1

Les registres et papiers domestiques ne font pas un titre pour celui qui les a écrits. Ils font foi contre lui : 1° dans tous les cas où ils énoncent expressément un paiement reçu ; 2° lorsqu'ils contiennent la mention expresse que la note a été faite pour suppléer le défaut du titre en faveur de celui au profit duquel ils énoncent une obligation.

(art. 1331 c. civ. modifié)

Art. 1296

A signed document which embodies a synallagmatic contract is valid only if it has been made in as many originals as there are parties with a distinct interest.

One original is sufficient for all persons who have the same interest.

Each original must include a reference to the number of originals which have been made. However, the failure to refer to the fact that there are two, three (etc.) originals may not be relied upon by a party who has performed his part of the contract which is contained in the document.

These provisions do not apply to transactions entered into in electronic form.

(art. 1325 C. civ., amended)

Art. 1297

Proof of a juridical act by which one party alone undertakes towards another to pay him a sum of money or to deliver to him fungible property, must be given by an instrument which bears the signature of the one who undertook the obligation, as well as a statement, written in his own hand, of the sum or the quantity in both words and numbers. In case of a discrepancy between the two, the signed document is evidence of the sum written in words.

(art. 1326 of the present Code)

Art. 1298

Signed documents take effect against third parties only from the date when they have been registered, from the date of the death of the person who signed them (or of any one of multiple signatories), or from the date when their substance is established by instruments drawn up by public officials, such as records of sealing or of inventory.

(art. 1328 of the present Code)

Art. 1299

Written documents originating from a person who claims to be a creditor do not constitute proof of the obligation to which they refer, except in cases provided by legislation, custom or contract.

In the latter two cases, the written documents have the force only of presumption and inference.

Art. 1300

A written document can be used as evidence against the person who wrote it; but one who wishes so to use it must take the whole document, not in part.

Art. 1300-1

Private legers and papers do not constitute evidence in favour of the person who wrote them. They are evidence against him: first, in any case where they expressly refer to the receipt of a payment; secondly, where they contain express mention that the note has been made in order to remedy the defect of evidence in favour of the person for whose benefit they refer to an obligation.

(art. 1331 C. civ., amended)

Art. 1300-2

L'écriture mise par le créancier à la suite, en marge ou au dos d'un titre qui est toujours resté en sa possession, fait foi, quoique non signée ni datée par lui, lorsqu'elle tend à établir la libération du débiteur.

Il en est de même de l'écriture mise par le créancier au dos, ou en marge, ou à la suite du double d'un titre ou d'une quittance, pourvu que ce double soit entre les mains du débiteur.

(art. 1332 actuel)

§3 – Des copies de titres et actes recognitifs

Art. 1301

Les copies, lorsque le titre original subsiste, ne font foi que de ce qui est contenu au titre, dont la représentation peut toujours être exigée.

(art. 1334 actuel)

Art. 1302

Lorsque le titre original n'existe plus, les copies font foi d'après les distinctions suivantes :

1° Les copies exécutoires ou premières expéditions font la même foi que l'original : il en est de même des copies qui ont été tirées par l'autorité du magistrat, parties présentes ou dûment appelées, ou de celles qui ont été tirées en présence des parties et de leur consentement réciproque.

2° Les copies qui, sans l'autorité du magistrat, ou sans le consentement des parties, et depuis la délivrance des copies exécutoires ou premières expéditions, auront été tirées sur la minute de l'acte par le notaire qui l'a reçu, ou par l'un de ses successeurs, ou par officiers publics qui, en cette qualité, sont dépositaires des minutes, peuvent, en cas de perte de l'original, faire foi quand elles sont anciennes.

Elles sont considérées comme anciennes quand elles ont plus de trente ans.

Si elles ont moins de trente ans, elles ne peuvent servir que de commencement de preuve par écrit.

3° Lorsque les copies tirées sur la minute d'un acte ne l'auront pas été par le notaire qui l'a reçu, ou par l'un de ses successeurs, ou par officiers publics qui, en cette qualité, sont dépositaires des minutes, elles ne pourront servir, quelle que soit leur ancienneté, que de commencement de preuve par écrit.

4° Les copies de copies pourront, suivant les circonstances, être considérées comme simples renseignements.

(art. 1335 actuel)

Art. 1303

La transcription d'un acte sur les registres publics ne pourra servir que de commencement de preuve par écrit ; et il faudra même pour cela :

1° Qu'il soit constant que toutes les minutes du notaire, de l'année dans laquelle

Art. 1300-2

Writing placed by the creditor at the end, in the margin, or on the back of an instrument which has always been in his possession is evidence, even though he has not signed or dated it, where it tends to show the discharge of the debtor.

The same is the case for writing placed by the creditor on the back, in the margin, or at the end of the duplicate of an instrument or a receipt, provided that the duplicate is in the debtor's possession.

(art. 1332 of the present Code)

§ 3 Copies of instruments and formal acknowledgments

Art. 1301

Where the original instrument is in existence, copies constitute evidence only of the contents of the instrument, of which production can always be required.

(art. 1334 of the present Code)

Art. 1302

Where the original instrument is no longer in existence, copies constitute evidence in accordance with the following distinctions:

1. Copies certified for enforcement or top office copies have the same probative force as the original. So have copies which have been made with the authority of a judicial officer, with the parties present or having been properly summoned, or those which have been made in the presence of the parties and with their mutual consent.

2. Copies which, without the authority of a judicial officer, or without the consent of the parties, and after the delivery of the copies certified for enforcement or top office copies, have been made as an official record of the document by the notary who has received it, or by one of his successors, or by public officials who, in that capacity, are authorised to hold official records, may, in case of loss of the original, be used as evidence where they are ancient.

They are considered as ancient where they are more than thirty years old.

If they are less than thirty years old, they can only serve as a beginning of proof by writing.

3. Where copies which have been made as an official record of a document were not made by the notary who received it, or by one of his successors, or by public officials who, in that capacity, are authorised to hold public records, they can serve—whatever their age—as only a beginning of proof by writing.

4. Copies of copies may, in an appropriate case, be considered simply as information.

(art. 1335 of the present Code)

Art. 1303

The transcription of a document into a public register can serve only as a beginning of proof by writing; and for this it is also necessary:

1. That it be clear that all the notary's records for the year in which the document

l'acte paraît avoir été fait, soient perdues, ou que l'on prouve que la perte de la minute de cet acte a été faite par un accident particulier ;

2° Qu'il existe un répertoire en règle du notaire, qui constate que l'acte a été fait à la même date. Lorsqu'au moyen du concours de ces deux circonstances la preuve par témoins sera admise, il sera nécessaire que ceux qui ont été témoins de l'acte, s'ils existent encore, soient entendus.

(art. 1336 actuel)

Art. 1304

En cas de perte du titre original, la copie fidèle et durable d'un acte sous seing privé peut suffire à en prouver l'existence.

Art. 1305

Les actes récognitifs ne dispensent pas de la représentation de l'acte primordial, à moins que sa teneur n'y soit spécialement relatée.

Ce qu'ils contiennent de plus que l'acte primordial, ou ce qui s'y trouve de différent n'a aucun effet.

Néanmoins, s'il y avait plusieurs reconnaissances conformes, soutenues de la possession, et dont l'une eut trente ans de date, le créancier pourrait être dispensé de représenter l'acte primordial.

(art. 1337 actuel remployé)

Section 3
De l'exigence d'une preuve par écrit et de la preuve testimoniale des actes juridiques (Articles 1306 à 1313)

Note : Le titre actuel n'est pas satisfaisant. Le titre proposé serre le contenu des dispositions de la section qui pose d'abord l'exigence d'une preuve littérale et règle ensuite la preuve testimoniale.

Art. 1306

Il doit être constitué une preuve par écrit des actes juridiques excédant une somme ou une valeur fixée par décret.

Aucune preuve par témoins n'est reçue des parties à l'acte contre et outre son contenu, ni sur ce qui serait allégué avoir été dit avant, lors ou depuis l'acte, encore qu'il s'agisse d'une somme ou valeur moindre.

Le tout sans préjudice de ce qui est prescrit dans les lois relatives au commerce.

Art. 1307

La règle ci-dessus s'applique au cas où l'action contient, outre la demande du capital

appears to have been made have been lost, or that it is proved that the loss of the record of this document has been caused by a specific accident;

2. That there be a register, in proper order, on the part of the notary, which establishes that the document was made at the particular date. If, by reason of these two conditions being satisfied, proof by witnesses is admissible, it is necessary that those who were witnesses of the instrument, if they are still living, be heard.

(art. 1336 of the present Code)

Art. 1304

In case of loss of the original instrument, a faithful and durable copy of a signed instrument may suffice to prove its existence.

Art. 1305

A formal acknowledgment does not dispense with the requirement to produce the original document, unless its content is set out in detail in the acknowledgment.

Anything contained in the acknowledgment which goes beyond the original document, or which is different from it, has no effect.

However, if there are a number of identical acknowledgments, supported by possession, of which one dates back thirty years, the creditor may be excused from producing the original document.

(art. 1337 of the present Code, re-used)

Section 3
The Requirement of Proof in Writing and Witness Evidence of Juridical Acts
(Articles 1306 to 1313)

Note: The title in the present Code is not satisfactory. The proposed title fits the contents of the provisions of this section, which sets out first the requirement of written proof and then governs witness evidence.

Art. 1306

Proof in writing is required for juridical acts which exceed a sum of money or a value fixed by decree.

No witness evidence is admissible from the parties to the document against or beyond its contents, nor of what may be alleged to have been said before, at the time of, or since the juridical act, even in the case of a lesser sum or a lower value.

This is all without prejudice to the legislative provisions relating to commercial transactions.

Art. 1307

The above rule applies to the situation where the action contains, in addition to the

une demande d'intérêts qui, réunis au capital, excèdent le chiffre prévu à l'article précédent.

(art. 1342 actuel)

Art. 1308

Celui qui a formé une demande excédant le chiffre prévu à l'article 1306 ne peut plus être admis à la preuve testimoniale, même en restreignant sa demande primitive.

(art. 1343 actuel)

Art. 1309

La preuve testimoniale sur la demande d'une somme même inférieure à celle qui est prévue à l'article 1306 ne peut être admise lorsque cette somme est déclarée être le restant ou faire partie d'une créance plus forte qui n'est point prouvée par écrit.

(art. 1344 actuel)

Art. 1310

Si, dans la même instance, une partie fait plusieurs demandes dont il n'y ait point de titre par écrit, et que, jointes ensemble, elles excèdent la somme prévue à l'article 1306, la preuve par témoins n'en peut être admise, encore que la partie allègue que ces créances procèdent de différentes causes, et qu'elles se soient formées en différents temps, sauf si ces droits proviennent par succession, donation ou autrement, de personnes différentes.

(art. 1345 actuel)

Art. 1311

Toutes les demandes, à quelque titre que ce soit, qui ne seront pas entièrement justifiées par écrit, seront formées par un même exploit, après lequel les autres demandes dont il n'y aura point de preuves par écrit ne seront pas reçues.

(art. 1346 actuel)

Art. 1312

Les règles ci-dessus reçoivent exception lorsqu'il existe un commencement de preuve par écrit.

On appelle ainsi, s'il rend vraisemblable le fait allégué, tout écrit émané de celui contre lequel la demande est formée, ou de celui qu'il représente.

Peuvent être considérées par le juge comme équivalant à un commencement de preuve par écrit les déclarations faites par une partie lors de sa comparution personnelle, son refus de répondre, ou son absence à la comparution.

(art. 1347 c. civ. modifié)

Tous autres modes de preuve devenant admissibles, le commencement de preuve par écrit doit être corroboré par au moins l'un d'entre eux pour que la preuve de l'acte soit complète.

claim for capital, a claim for interest which, when added to the capital, exceeds the sum provided for in the preceding article.

(art. 1342 of the present Code)

Art. 1308

A person who has formulated a claim exceeding the sum provided for in article 1306 is no longer allowed to adduce witness evidence, even if he reduces his original claim.

(art. 1343 of the present Code)

Art. 1309

Witness evidence in support of a claim for a sum even below that provided for in article 1306 is not admissible where such sum is declared to be the balance or to form part of a larger debt which is not proved by writing.

(art. 1344 of the present Code)

Art. 1310

If, in the same proceedings, a party makes a number of claims, none of them supported by a written instrument, and which, taken together, exceed the sum provided for in article 1306, witness evidence may not be given in support of them even where the party claims that his rights arise from different grounds and that they arose at different times, unless the rights arise from different persons by succession, donation, or otherwise.

(art. 1345 of the present Code)

Art. 1311

All claims, whatever their basis, which are not entirely justified by writing must be contained in the same writ; after this, other claims of which there is no evidence in writing are inadmissible.

(art. 1346 of the present Code)

Art. 1312

There is an exception to the above rules where there is a 'beginning of proof by writing'.

It is so called where there is writing, which suggests that the alleged fact is likely to be true and which originates from the party against whom the claim is made, or from his representative.

The court may accept as equivalent to a beginning of proof by writing, declarations made by one party in giving evidence, his refusal to reply, or his failure to appear to give evidence.

(art. 1347 C. civ., amended)

All other forms of evidence become admissible, but the beginning of proof by writing must be corroborated by at least one of them to complete the proof of the instrument.

Section 1
Dispositions générales
(Articles 1283 à 1290)

Art. 1283

Celui qui réclame l'exécution d'une obligation doit la prouver.

Réciproquement, celui qui se prétend libéré doit justifier le paiement ou le fait qui a produit l'extinction de son obligation.

> *Note : art. 1315 actuel. Il est prudent de ne pas toucher à ce texte. L'harmonie entre le Code civil et le Code de procédure civile (art. 9) ne nuit pas.*

Art. 1284

La preuve des actes et des faits d'où naissent les obligations peut être faite, selon les distinctions qui suivent, par écrit, par témoins, par présomption, par aveu et par serment.

> *Note : Ce texte d'annonce ouvre l'éventail des modes de preuve et introduit l'idée que les règles de preuve ne sont pas les mêmes pour les actes et les faits juridiques, et qu'elle peuvent d'ailleurs différer d'un mode à l'autre.*

> *La référence aux actes et faits d'où naissent les obligations fait écho à l'article de tête du Titre des Obligations (art. 1101).*

> *La référence à la preuve par écrit introduit l'article qui suit, dans lequel, moyennant une simple inversion, peut apparaître la formule équivalente « preuve littérale » (occasion à conserver de poser la synonymie).*

Art. 1285

La preuve par écrit ou preuve littérale résulte d'une suite de lettres, de caractères, de chiffres ou de tous autres signes ou symboles dotés d'une signification intelligible, quels que soient leur support et leurs modalités de transmission.

> *Note : La définition de la preuve par écrit vient aussitôt après l'énumération des modes de preuve. Cette définition est nécessaire à cause de la consécration de l'écrit sous forme électronique, lequel exige des précisions. La définition des autres modes apparaît dans les dispositions qui les concernent et en sont inséparables.*

> *Le dédoublement proposé par les auteurs du projet est intéressant, mais l'avantage de reprendre à une nuance près (l'inversion) la teneur de l'actuel article 1316 est, d'une part, on l'a vu, d'affirmer la synonymie entre preuve par écrit et preuve littérale, d'autre part, de faire le lien avec l'article qui précède.*

Note : Le commencement de preuve par écrit ne fait pas à lui seul la preuve de l'acte allégué. Il doit être complété par un élément de preuve extérieur à l'écrit qui le constitue.

Art. 1313

Les règles ci-dessus reçoivent encore exception lorsque l'une des parties, soit n'a pas eu la possibilité matérielle ou morale de se procurer une preuve littérale de l'acte juridique, soit a perdu le titre qui lui servait de preuve littérale, par suite d'un cas fortuit ou d'une force majeure.

Elles reçoivent aussi exception lorsqu'une partie ou le dépositaire n'a pas conservé le titre original et présente une copie qui en est la reproduction fidèle et durable. Est réputée durable toute reproduction indélébile de l'original qui entraîne une modification irréversible du support.

(art. 1348 c. civ. modifié)

Section 4
Règles particulières aux présomptions, à l'aveu et au serment
(Articles 1314 à 1326-2)

§1 – Des présomptions

Art. 1314

Les présomptions sont des conséquences que la loi ou le magistrat tire d'un fait connu à un fait inconnu, en tenant celui-ci pour certain sur le fondement du fait qui le rend vraisemblable.

(art. 1349 c. civ. modifié)

Art. 1315

La présomption légale est celle qui est attachée, par une loi spéciale, à certains actes ou à certains faits ; tels sont :

1° les actes que la loi déclare nuls, comme présumés faits en fraude de ses dispositions, d'après leur seule qualité ;

2° les cas dans lesquels la loi déclare la propriété ou la libération résulter de certaines circonstances déterminées ;

3° l'autorité que la loi attribue à la chose jugée ;

4° la force que la loi attache à l'aveu de la partie ou à son serment.

(art. 1350 actuel)

Art. 1316

L'autorité de la chose jugée n'a lieu qu'à l'égard de ce qui a fait l'objet du jugement.

Note: The beginning of proof by writing cannot of itself constitute proof of the alleged transaction. It must be supplemented by a form of proof outside the writing which constitutes it.

Art. 1313

There is a further exception to the above rules where one of the parties either could not physically or morally secure written proof of the juridical act, or has lost the instrument which constituted his written proof following an act of God or *force majeure.*

There is also an exception where one party or the depositee has not retained the original instrument and presents a copy which is a faithful and durable reproduction of it. Any indelible reproduction of the original which involves an irreversible change of medium is deemed to be durable.

(art. 1348 C. civ., amended)

Section 4
Rules Specific to Presumptions, Admissions and Oaths
(Articles 1314 to 1326-2)

§ 1 Presumptions

Art. 1314

Presumptions are the consequences that legislation or the court draws from a known fact about an unknown fact, holding the latter to be certain on the basis of the fact which renders it likely to be true.

(art. 1349 C. civ., amended)

Art. 1315

A legal presumption is one which is attached by a particular legislative provision to certain acts or certain circumstances, such as:

1. juridical acts which legislation declares to be a nullity, as presumed to have been made in fraud of its provisions from their nature alone;

2. situations in which legislation declares ownership or discharge as a consequence of certain defined circumstances;

3. the authority which legislation attributes to a judgment;

4. the force which legislation attributes to an admission made by a party, or his oath.

(art. 1350 of the present Code)

Art. 1316

The authority of a judgment applies only with respect to the subject-matter of the

Il faut que la chose demandée soit la même ; que la demande soit fondée sur la même cause ; que la demande soit entre les mêmes parties, et formée par elles et contre elles en la même qualité.

(art. 1351 actuel)

Art. 1317

La présomption légale dispense celui au profit duquel elle est établie de la preuve du fait qu'elle prend en considération, quand le fait qui rend celui-ci vraisemblable est certain.

Nulle preuve n'est admise contre la présomption de la loi, lorsque, sur le fondement de cette présomption, elle annule certains actes ou dénie l'action en justice, à moins qu'elle n'ait réservé la preuve contraire et sauf ce qui sera dit sur le serment et l'aveu judiciaires.

(art. 1352 c. civ. modifié)

Art. 1318

Les présomptions qui ne sont pas établies par la loi sont abandonnées aux lumières et à la prudence du magistrat, qui ne doit admettre que des présomptions graves et précises ou concordantes, et dans les cas seulement où la loi admet des preuves testimoniales, à moins que l'acte ne soit attaqué pour cause de fraude ou de dol.

De telles présomptions admettent toujours la preuve contraire.

(art. 1353 c. civ. modifié)

§2 – De l'aveu

Art. 1319

L'aveu qui est opposé à une partie est ou extrajudiciaire ou judiciaire.

(art. 1354 actuel)

Art. 1320

L'allégation d'un aveu extrajudiciaire purement verbal est inutile toutes les fois qu'il s'agit d'une demande dont la preuve testimoniale ne serait pas admissible.

(art. 1355 actuel)

La valeur probante d'un tel aveu est appréciée souverainement par le juge.

Art. 1321

L'aveu judiciaire est la déclaration que fait en justice la partie ou son fondé de pouvoir spécial.

Il fait pleine foi contre celui qui l'a fait ;

Il ne peut être divisé contre lui ;

Il ne peut être révoqué, à moins qu'on ne prouve qu'il a été la suite d'une erreur de fait. Il ne pourrait être révoqué sous prétexte d'une erreur de droit.

(art. 1356 actuel)

judgment. The subject-matter of the claim must be the same; the claim must have the same ground; the claim must be between the same parties, and brought by and against them in the same capacity.

(art. 1351 of the present Code)

Art. 1317

A legislative presumption exempts the party in whose favour it has been established from proof of the fact to which it applies, where the fact which renders it likely to be true is certain.

No evidence is admissible against a legislative presumption where, on the basis of this presumption, it nullifies certain juridical acts or prevents a legal action from being brought, unless the legislation allows proof to the contrary and with the exception of what will be said on oaths and judicial admissions.

(art. 1352 C. civ., amended)

Art. 1318

Presumptions which are not established by legislation are left to the wisdom and good sense of the court, which must allow only presumptions which are weighty and definite or corroborative, and only in the situations where legislation allows witness evidence, unless the juridical act is challenged on the grounds of fraud or deceit.

Such presumptions may always be rebutted by proof to the contrary.

(art. 1353 C. civ., amended)

§ 2 Admissions

Art. 1319

An admission which is relied on against a party may be extrajudicial or judicial.

(art. 1354 of the present Code)

Art. 1320

An allegation of a purely oral extrajudicial admission serves no purpose in any case where the claim is such that witness evidence would not be admissible.

(art. 1355 of the present Code)

The probative force of such an admission is determined by the court in its unfettered discretion.

Art. 1321

A judicial admission is a declaration made in court by a party or his special representative.

It constitutes conclusive evidence against the party who made it.

It may not be divided against him.

It may not be revoked, unless it is proved to have been made in consequence of a mistake of fact. It may not be revoked on account of a mistake of law.

(art. 1356 of the present Code)

§3 – Du serment

Art. 1322

Le serment judiciaire est de deux espèces :

1° Celui qui est déféré d'office par le juge à l'une ou à l'autre des parties ;

2° Celui qu'une partie défère à l'autre pour en faire dépendre le jugement de la cause : il est appelé *décisoire*.

(art. 1357 actuel)

Art. 1323

Le serment peut être déféré d'office par le juge à l'une des parties, soit pour en faire dépendre la décision de la cause, soit seulement pour déterminer le montant de la condamnation.

La valeur probante d'un tel serment est appréciée souverainement par le juge.

(art. 1366 actuel)

Art. 1324

Le juge ne peut déférer d'office le serment, soit sur la demande, soit sur l'exception qui y est opposée, que sous les deux conditions suivantes ; il faut :

1° Que la demande ou l'exception ne soit pas pleinement justifiée ;

2° Qu'elle ne soit pas totalement dénuée de preuves.

Hors ces deux cas, le juge doit ou adjuger ou rejeter purement et simplement la demande.

(art. 1367 actuel)

Art. 1324-1

Le serment déféré d'office par le juge à l'une des parties ne peut être par elle référé à l'autre.

(art. 1368 actuel)

Art. 1324-2

Le serment sur la valeur de la chose demandée ne peut être déféré par le juge au demandeur que lorsqu'il est d'ailleurs impossible de constater autrement cette valeur.

Le juge doit même, en ce cas, déterminer la somme jusqu'à concurrence de laquelle le demandeur en sera cru sur son serment.

(art. 1369 actuel)

Art. 1325

Le serment décisoire peut être déféré sur quelque espèce de contestation que ce soit.

(art. 1358 actuel)

Art. 1325-1

Il ne peut être déféré que sur un fait personnel à la partie à laquelle on le défère.

§ 3 Oaths

Art. 1322

Judicial oaths are of two kinds:

1. One which is required by the court on its own initiative of one or other party;

2. One which one party requires of the other on which to make the outcome of the case depend: this is known as *decisive*.

(*art. 1357 of the present Code*)

Art. 1323

An oath may be required of one of the parties by the court on its own initiative, either to make the outcome of the case depend upon it, or simply to settle the value of the award.

The probative force of such an oath is determined by the court in its unfettered discretion.

(*art. 1366 of the present Code*)

Art. 1324

The court may require an oath on its own initiative in relation either to the claim or to a defence which is raised against it, only on the two following conditions:

1. The claim or the defence must not be conclusively established; and

2. It must not be completely lacking in evidence.

Apart from these two situations, the court must either accept or reject the claim outright.

(*art. 1367 of the present Code*)

Art. 1324-1

An oath required of one of the parties by the court on its own initiative cannot be required by that party of the other.

(*art. 1368 of the present Code*)

Art. 1324-2

An oath on the value of the claim may be required by the court of the claimant only where it is impossible by other means to establish the value.

In such a case the court must also establish the sum up to which the claimant will be believed in his oath.

(*art. 1369 of the present Code*)

Art. 1325

A decisive oath may be required on any matter in dispute.

(*art. 1358 of the present Code*)

Art. 1325-1

It may be required only as to a fact which is personal to the party of which it is required.

(art. 1359 actuel)

Art. 1325-2

Il peut être déféré en tout état de cause, et encore qu'il n'existe aucun commencement de preuve de la demande ou de l'exception sur laquelle il est provoqué.

(art. 1360 actuel)

Art. 1325-3

Celui auquel le serment est déféré, qui le refuse ou ne consent pas le référer à son adversaire, ou l'adversaire à qui il a été référé et qui le refuse, doit succomber dans sa demande ou dans son exception.

(art. 1361 actuel)

Art. 1325-4

Le serment ne peut être référé quand le fait qui en est l'objet n'est point celui des deux parties, mais est purement personnel à celui auquel le serment avait été déféré.

(art. 1362 actuel)

Art. 1326

Lorsque le serment déféré ou référé a été fait, l'adversaire n'est point recevable à en prouver la fausseté.

(art. 1363 actuel)

Art. 1326-1

La partie qui a déféré ou référé le serment ne peut plus se rétracter lorsque l'adversaire a déclaré qu'il est prêt à faire ce serment.

(art. 1364 actuel)

Art. 1326-2

Le serment ne forme preuve qu'au profit de celui qui l'a déféré ou contre lui, et au profit de ses héritiers et ayants cause ou contre eux.

Néanmoins, le serment déféré par l'un des créanciers solidaires au débiteur ne libère celui-ci que pour la part de ce créancier ;

Le serment déféré au débiteur principal libère également les cautions ;

Celui déféré à l'un des débiteurs solidaires profite aux codébiteurs ;

Et celui déféré à la caution profite au débiteur principal.

Dans ces deux derniers cas, le serment du codébiteur solidaire ou de la caution ne profite aux autres codébiteurs ou au débiteur principal que lorsqu'il a été déféré sur la dette, et non sur le fait de la solidarité ou du cautionnement.

(art. 1365 actuel)

(art. 1359 of the present Code)

Art. 1325-2

It may be required at any stage of the proceedings, and even when there is no beginning of proof of the claim or of the defence in respect of which it is brought.

(art. 1360 of the present Code)

Art. 1325-3

A person of whom an oath is required, who refuses it or does not consent to refer it in turn over to his opponent, or the opponent to whom it is referred and who refuses it, must lose his claim or his defence.

(art. 1361 of the present Code)

Art. 1325-4

An oath may not be referred over to the other party where the fact to which it relates is not one common to the parties, but is purely personal to the one of whom the oath was initially required.

(art. 1362 of the present Code)

Art. 1326

Where the required (or referred) oath has been taken, the opponent cannot be heard to establish that it is false.

(art. 1363 of the present Code)

Art. 1326-1

The party who has required or referred an oath may no longer withdraw it where his opponent has declared that he is ready to take the oath.

(art. 1364 of the present Code)

Art. 1326-2

An oath constitutes evidence only in favour of the party who has required it, or against him, and in favour of his heirs and successors or against them.

However, an oath required by one of two or more joint and several creditors of the debtor discharges the debtor only in relation to that creditor;

an oath required of the principal debtor also discharges his sureties;

one required of one of two or more joint and several debtors benefits his co-debtors;

and one required of a surety benefits the principal debtor.

In the last two situations, an oath by a joint and several co-debtor or by a surety benefits the other co-debtors or the principal debtor only where it has been required in relation to the debt, and not in relation to the joint and several nature of the liability, or the fact of the suretyship.

(art. 1365 of the present Code)

Sous-titre II

Des quasi-contrats
(Articles 1327 à 1339)

Art. 1327

Les quasi-contrats sont des faits purement volontaires, comme la gestion sans titre de l'affaire d'autrui, le paiement de l'indu ou l'enrichissement sans cause dont il résulte, un engagement de celui qui en profite sans y avoir droit, et parfois un engagement de leur auteur envers autrui.

Notes :

1) L'article 1370 reprend le canevas actuel de l'article 1371. La référence à l'auteur des faits rend superflue la précision « de l'homme ». L'engagement de celui qui profite de ces faits envers leur auteur vient en premier, car il est commun à tous les quasi-contrats (et inhérent à la notion) tandis que l'engagement de l'auteur des faits est occasionnel (et en pratique propre à la gestion d'affaires). La gestion sans titre signifie sans mandat ni titre légal ou judiciaire d'intervention dans les affaires d'autrui.

2) L'article 1370 ainsi énoncé développe la définition esquissée dans l'article 1101-2 alinéa 2 au titre de la source des obligations.

3) Les deux espèces particulières de quasi-contrats et la théorie générale de l'enrichissement sans cause ont pour point commun un avantage reçu par une personne qui n'y a pas droit (critère de regroupement suggéré par Carbonnier).

4) L'insistance « gestion sans titre de l'affaire d'autrui » est marquée pour mettre en valeur un point commun à tous les quasi-contrats : <u>sans</u> titre, <u>indu</u>, <u>sans</u> cause.

Il n'est bien entendu question que de la gestion d'affaires dans la section qui lui est consacrée (mais on aurait pu concevoir d'intituler le chapitre : « De la gestion sans titre de l'affaire d'autrui ». Pourquoi pas ?

Sub-Title II

Quasi-Contracts
(Articles 1327 to 1339)

Art. 1327

Quasi-contracts are purely voluntary actions, such as the management of the affairs of another person without authority, payment of a debt which is not due or unjustified enrichment, which result in a duty in a person who benefits from them without having a right to do so, and sometimes in a duty in the person intervening to the person so benefited.

Notes:

(1) Article 1370 reuses the existing basic structure of article 1371. The reference to a person whose actions confer a benefit renders the qualification of 'action' as 'human' superfluous. The duty of a person who benefits from these actions towards the person intervening comes first, for it is shared by all quasi-contracts (and is inherent in the notion itself) while the duty of the person who intervenes only sometimes arises (and in practice belongs to the law of management of another person's affairs). 'Management of the affairs of another person without authority' means without any mandate, nor any legislative or judicial status which confers a right to intervene in another person's affairs.

(2) So stated, article 1370 develops the definition sketched out in article 1101-2 paragraph 2 in the Title on the Source of Obligations.[1]

(3) The common element of the two individual examples of quasi-contracts and the general doctrine of unjustified enrichment is a benefit received by a person who has no right to it (a criterion grouping them together suggested by Carbonnier[2]).

(4) The provision's insistence that the management of another's affairs be 'without authority' is made in order to highlight a common element for all quasi-contracts, being <u>without</u> legal title, <u>undue</u>, or <u>without</u> a justification.

This is not to be understood with certainty as regards the section which is dedicated to the management of another person's affairs (but it could be thought that the chapter should be entitled 'Management without authority in the affairs of another person'. Why not?

---

[1] [See above, p 625.]
[2] [Carbonnier, *Droit civil*, vol 4, *Les obligations*, above, p 507, n 1, no 307.]

Chapitre I
De la gestion d'affaires

Art. 1328

Celui qui, spontanément, se charge à titre bénévole de l'affaire d'autrui, à l'insu ou sans opposition du maître de cette affaire, se soumet, dans l'accomplissement des actes juridiques ou matériels de sa gestion, à toutes les obligations d'un mandat exprès qu'il en aurait reçu.

> *Note : Le caractère gratuit du mandat résulte suffisamment du fait que la rémunération du gérant ne figure pas au nombre des obligations du maître de l'affaire. L'utilité de la gestion est une condition de ces obligations qui est marquée à leur propos, ce qui suffit. L'adjonction des actes matériels est désormais classique.*

Art. 1328-1

Il doit continuer la gestion de l'affaire et de ses dépendances jusqu'à ce que le maître de l'affaire ou son héritier soit en état d'y pourvoir lui-même ou qu'il puisse s'en décharger sans risque de perte.

> *Note : C'est le remploi de deux dispositions : c. civ. art. 1372 et 1373*

Art. 1328-2

Les circonstances qui l'ont conduit à se charger de l'affaire peuvent autoriser le juge à modérer les dommages-intérêts qui résulteraient d'une gestion défectueuse.

> *Note : C'est à quelques mots près la disposition de l'art. 1374, al. 2 actuel. Cette souplesse mérite d'être conservée car elle oriente le juge vers les circonstances variables qui ont présidé à l'intervention (sa nécessité, l'esprit de son auteur, etc.).*

Art. 1328-3

Celui dont l'affaire a été utilement gérée doit remplir les engagements que le gérant a contractés en son nom, l'indemniser de tous les engagements personnels qu'il a pris, lui rembourser toutes les dépenses utiles ou nécessaires qu'il a faites et, à l'exclusion de toute rémunération, lui tenir compte des pertes qu'il a subies.

> *Note : « utilement » : c'est le mot clé qui est à sa place en tête des obligations du maître qui sont subordonnées à l'utilité de la gestion ; la référence aux pertes subies est bien venue.*

Art. 1329

Les règles de la gestion d'affaires s'appliquent semblablement lorsque la gestion est

Chapter I
Management of Another Person's Affairs

Art. 1328

Where a person takes on of his own accord another person's affairs without the latter's knowledge or opposition and without hope of reward, he is bound in accomplishing any juridical acts or physical action which this entails to all the obligations which he would have owed if he had enjoyed an express mandate to act.

> Note: The gratuitous nature of mandate is made out sufficiently from the fact that remuneration of the person managing another's affairs does not feature as one of the obligations of the person whose affairs are managed. The utility of the management is a condition of these obligations and this is made sufficiently clear in this context. The inclusion of physical actions is by this provision henceforth made standard.

Art. 1328-1

Such a person must continue to manage the other's affairs (and any related matters) until the latter or his heir is in a position to see to them himself or until he can rid himself of them without the risk of loss.

> Note: This reuses two provisions: art. 1372 and 1373 C. civ.

Art. 1328-2

The circumstances which led to a person taking on another person's affairs may justify a court in reducing the damages which would otherwise result from his deficient management.

> Note: This wording is very close to what is provided by article 1374 paragraph 2 of the present Code. This flexibility is worth keeping as it directs the court towards the various circumstances which can surround any intervention (its necessity, the thinking of the person intervening etc.).

Art. 1328-3

A person whose affairs have been managed usefully must fulfil any undertakings which the person intervening contracted in his name, compensate him for any personal undertakings which he took on, reimburse him for all useful or necessary expenses which he incurred, and account for any losses which he has suffered, though without any allowance being made for his remuneration.

> Note: 'usefully': this is the key word and is placed at the very beginning of the obligations of the person whose affairs have been managed, thereby subjecting them to a condition that his management was useful; the reference to 'losses suffered' is welcome.[1]

Art. 1329

The rules governing management of another's affairs apply in a similar way where

[1] [Article 1375 Cc makes no reference to reimbursement of a person who intervenes for losses suffered, though this has been accepted by the courts.]

entreprise non dans l'intérêt exclusif d'autrui mais dans l'intérêt commun d'autrui et du gérant.

Dans ce dernier cas, la charge des engagements, des dépenses et des pertes se répartit à proportion des intérêts de chacun.

Art. 1329-1

Si l'action du gérant ne répond pas aux conditions de la gestion d'affaires mais tourne néanmoins au profit du maître de cette affaire, celui-ci doit indemniser le gérant selon les règles de l'enrichissement sans cause.

> *Note : C'est la reprise, à quelques nuances de formulation près, d'une suggestion intéressante.*

Chapitre II
Du paiement de l'indu

Art. 1330

Celui qui reçoit, par erreur ou sciemment, ce qui ne lui est pas dû, s'oblige à le restituer à celui de qui il l'a indûment reçu.

> *Note : C'est l'article 1376 actuel, texte de base très clair qui correspond typiquement au quasi-contrat.*

Si toutefois il prouve que le paiement procède d'une intention libérale, d'une obligation naturelle ou d'une autre cause, il n'y a pas lieu à restitution.

> *Note : C'est une adjonction d'évidence, mais plutôt opportune (effet de cohérence avec diverses autres dispositions).*

Art. 1331

Il y a lieu à restitution lorsque la dette qui avait justifié le paiement est par la suite annulée ou résolue, ou perd d'une autre façon sa cause.

> *Note : Point d'interrogation : cette disposition sort du domaine du quasi-contrat. C'est une <u>extension</u> à des cas qui appartiennent à la théorie des nullités (des sanctions). Cette extension est d'ailleurs aujourd'hui contestée (Civ. 1re 24 septembre 2002, D. 2003 369).*

this is undertaken in the common interest of himself and another person, rather than in the exclusive interest of such another person.

Where the former is the case, the burden of any undertakings, expenses or losses is shared in proportion to each person's interest.

Art. 1329-1

If the action of a person intervening does not fall within the requirements of the doctrine of management of another's affairs but does nevertheless result in an advantage to the person whose affairs are managed, the latter must compensate the person intervening according to the rules governing the doctrine of unjustified enrichment.

Note: This takes up an interesting suggestion, though its formulation has been refined.

Chapter II
Undue Payment

Art. 1330

Where a person receives something which is not due to him, either knowingly or by mistake, he has an obligation to restore it to the person from whom he received it unduly.

Note: This is the present wording of article 1376, a very clear, basic provision which fits squarely within quasi-contract.

Nevertheless, no obligation to make restitution arises where the recipient establishes that the payment resulted from an intention to confer a gratuitous benefit, from performance of a natural obligation, or from any other justification.

Note: This is an obvious addition, but even so appropriate, given that it creates consistency with various other provisions.

Art. 1331

Restitution may take place where the debt which justified payment has subsequently been annulled or retroactively terminated, or loses its justification in any other way.

Note: Quaere: does this provision go beyond the area of quasi-contract? It marks an extension of cases which belong to the doctrine of the nullity of contracts (notably as regards its sanctions). This extension is moreover at the moment a matter of dispute (Cass civ. (1) 24 September 2002, D 2003.369).[1]

---

[1] [As has earlier been noted (above, p 569, n 3), this provision appears to regulate very generally by reference to the recovery of undue payments restitution after annulment or retroactive termination of a contract, which is regulated specially by articles 1161 – 1164-6 of the *Avant-projet*.]

Art. 1332

Lorsqu'une personne, par erreur ou sous la contrainte* a acquitté la dette d'autrui, elle peut se faire rembourser soit par le véritable débiteur**, soit par le créancier, sauf si celui-ci, par suite du paiement, a supprimé son titre ou abandonné une sûreté***.

Notes :

* Adjonction aujourd'hui généralement admise.

** L'attribution de cette option est intéressante.

*** La référence à l'abandon d'une sûreté est également intéressante.

Art. 1333

S'il y a eu mauvaise foi de la part de celui qui a reçu, il est tenu de restituer tant le capital que les intérêts ou les fruits, du jour du paiement.

(art. 1378 actuel)

Art. 1334

Si la chose indûment reçue est un corps certain, celui qui l'a reçu doit le restituer en nature, s'il existe, ou sa valeur au jour de la restitution, s'il est péri ou détérioré par sa faute ; il est même garant de sa perte par cas fortuit, s'il l'a reçu de mauvaise foi.

Note : C'est l'art. 1379 actuel mais avec référence à un corps certain (dans la teneur actuelle, le bien meuble corporel pourrait être une chose de genre, ce qui est non pertinent dans cette disposition).

Art. 1334-1

Si celui qui a reçu de bonne foi a vendu la chose, il ne doit restituer que le prix de la vente ; dans le cas contraire, il en doit la valeur au jour de la restitution.

Note : C'est l'art. 1380 actuel moyennant l'adjonction de l'hypothèse contraire de la mauvaise foi.

Art. 1335

Celui auquel la chose est restituée doit tenir compte, même au possesseur de mauvaise foi, de toutes les dépenses nécessaires et utiles qui ont été faites pour la conservation de la chose.

Note : C'est la disposition actuelle de l'art. 1381.

Art. 1332

Where a person by mistake or under duress* has discharged another person's debt, the former can elect to be reimbursed either by the true debtor** or by the creditor, except where as a result of payment the latter has cancelled his instrument of title or released any security.***

Notes:

   * *This addition is now generally accepted.*

   ** *The grant of this option is interesting.*

   *** *The reference to the release of any security is also interesting.*

Art. 1333

If a person who receives what is not due is in bad faith, he is bound to make restitution of the capital together with any interest or fruits accruing from the date of payment.

   (art. 1378 of the present Code)

Art. 1334

If the thing which is unduly received consists of ascertained property, where it still exists its recipient must make restitution in kind, but where it has perished or deteriorated by his fault, then he must restore its value as at the date of making restitution; where its recipient received it in bad faith he must in addition guarantee the payor against loss even in the case of unavoidable accident.

   Note: This is the present text of article 1379 but with a reference to ascertained property (its present form refers to 'movable corporeal property' which could consist of generic property and is not appropriate in this context).

Art. 1334-1

If a person sells a thing which he received in good faith, he must make restitution only of the price which he received for it; but where he was not in good faith, he must make restitution of its value as at the date of doing so.

   Note: This is the present wording of article 1380 with the addition of the contrary hypothesis of bad faith.

Art. 1335

A person to whom restitution is made must account to its former possessor for all necessary and useful expenses incurred in looking after the thing, even where he possessed it in bad faith.

   Note: This provision is at present found in article 1381.

Chapitre III
De l'enrichissement sans cause

Art. 1336

Quiconque s'enrichit sans cause au détriment d'autrui doit à celui qui s'en trouve appauvri une indemnité égale à la moindre des deux sommes auxquelles s'élèvent l'enrichissement et l'appauvrissement.

Note : Cette formule traditionnelle, en jurisprudence, paraît préférable à « dans la mesure de l'enrichissement corrélatif ».

Art. 1337

L'enrichissement est sans cause lorsque la perte subie par l'appauvri ne procède ni de son intention libérale en faveur de l'enrichi, ni de l'accomplissement des obligations dont il est tenu envers lui, en vertu de la loi, du jugement ou du contrat, ni de la poursuite d'un intérêt purement personnel.

Note : Cette formulation qui développe le titre du chapitre, est plus simple et plus claire que la démarche inverse (« l'avantage n'est pas injustifié ») et permet de regrouper tous les cas d'absence de cause.

Art. 1338

L'appauvri n'a pas d'action quand les autres recours dont il disposait se heurtent à des obstacles de droit comme la prescription*, ou lorsque son appauvrissement résulte d'une faute grave de sa part**.

Notes :

* La subsidiarité de l'action de in rem verso est indiquée dans sa conséquence principale.

** La réserve de la faute grave est proche de la jurisprudence.

Art. 1339

L'enrichissement et l'appauvrissement s'apprécient au jour de la demande. Toutefois, en cas de mauvaise foi de l'enrichi, l'enrichissement s'appréciera au temps où il en a bénéficié.

Note : Cet article final est utile

Chapter III
Unjustified Enrichment

Art. 1336

Any person who is enriched without justification at the expense of another person must indemnify the person who is thereby made the poorer to an amount equal to the lesser sum as between the enrichment and the impoverishment.

> Note: This traditional formulation found in the case-law seems to be preferable to 'to the extent of the correlative enrichment'.

Art. 1337

An enrichment is unjustified where the loss suffered by the person at whose expense it is conferred does not stem from his intention to confer a gratuitous benefit on the person so enriched, nor from the fulfilment of any obligation which he owes him under legislation, as a result of a court order, or under a contract, nor from the pursuit of his own purely personal interest.

> Note: This formulation, which expounds the title of the chapter itself, is simpler and clearer than the inverse way of putting the matter ('a benefit is not unjustified') and allows the cases of absence of justification to be grouped together.

Art. 1338

A person at whose expense a benefit is conferred has no action where another means of recourse available to him encounters a legal obstacle such as prescription*, or where his detriment results from his own serious fault.**

> Notes:
>
> * The subsidiarity of the action de in rem verso ['action in respect of benefits conferred']¹ is here indicated by its principal effect.
>
> ** Making an exception for serious fault is close to the position adopted by the case-law.

Art. 1339

The enrichment and the impoverishment are to be assessed as at the date of the claim. Nevertheless, where the person enriched was in bad faith, his enrichment shall be assessed at the time when he derived the benefit from it.

> Note: This final article is useful.

---

¹ [This Latin phrase is still much used to describe claims based on the ground of unjust or unjustified enrichment in the French context. Its origins are indeed Roman, but its development into a general action to redress enrichment is later (see R Zimmermann, *The Law of Obligations, Roman Foundations of the Civilian Tradition* (Oxford, Clarendon Press, 1990) 878-84).]

Sous-titre III

De la responsabilité civile
(Articles 1340 à 1386)

Exposé des motifs

Geneviève Viney

L'objet du présent rapport consiste à rendre compte de l'essentiel des débats qui se sont déroulés au sein du groupe de travail chargé de la rédaction du Titre IV « De la responsabilité ». Il tend à expliciter le sens des choix qui ont été faits sur les points les plus importants. Il est complété par les notes et observations qui accompagnent le texte lui-même.

I. – L'une des difficultés auxquelles a été affronté le groupe consistait à déterminer **le niveau de généralité auquel il convenait de se placer pour sélectionner les dispositions à insérer dans le code civil.**

1°) En particulier, il a fallu prendre parti sur le point de savoir s'il convenait d'inclure, à côté des dispositions générales qui relèvent de ce qu'il est convenu d'appeler « le droit commun », certains **régimes spéciaux** de responsabilité.

Les avis étaient très partagés à ce sujet. Certains ont émis l'opinion que ces régimes n'auraient pas leur place dans le code civil et que le parti, pris en 1998, d'y insérer le texte transposé de la directive du 25 juillet 1985 sur la responsabilité du fait des produits défectueux serait regrettable, tandis que d'autres ont fait valoir qu'il est souhaitable que le code civil reflète les tendances marquantes du droit contemporain et que les dispositions les plus couramment appliquées par les tribunaux y figurent.

Finalement, il a été décidé de laisser hors du code civil la plupart des régimes spéciaux de responsabilité ou d'indemnisation qui sont réglementés par des lois

Sub-Title III

Civil Liability
(Articles 1340 to 1386)

Preamble

Geneviève Viney

The purpose of this preamble is to give an account of the essential features of the discussions which took place within the working group charged with the drafting of Title IV of the Civil Code, 'Civil Liability'. Our intention is to explain the significance of the choices which were made on the most important issues. It is supplemented by notes and comments which accompany the text itself.

I. One of the difficulties facing the group consisted of deciding **the level of generality considered appropriate to be adopted in selecting provisions to be inserted into the Civil Code.**

(1) In particular, a view had to be taken on the issue whether it was appropriate to include certain **special regimes** of liability side by side with the general provisions which arise from what it is conveniently termed 'the general law'.[1]

Opinion was very divided on this question. Certain members of the group expressed the view that these special regimes should have no place in the Civil Code and that the decision, taken in 1998, to insert the legislative provisions implementing the European Directive of 25 July 1985 on liability for defective products[2] into this Code was regrettable; others instead emphasised that it is desirable that the Civil Code should reflect the characteristic tendencies of the modern law and that the legal provisions most frequently applied by courts should find a place there.

In the end, it was decided to leave outside the Civil Code most of the special regimes of liability or of compensation which are at present regulated by special

---

[1] ['The general law' translates *le droit commun* (cf above, p 491, n 1) here belonging to the law of liability in general as explained in the text.]

[2] [Council Directive 1985/374/EEC of 25 July 1985 on the approximation of laws, regulations and administrative provisions of the Member States concerning liability for defective products.]

particulières[1] mais de ne pas proposer d'en extraire les articles 1386-1 à 1386-18[2] que le groupe a laissés intacts puisque le législateur français ne peut désormais modifier ces textes sans l'assentiment des autorités européennes. En revanche, la majorité s'est prononcée en faveur de l'inclusion des dispositions réglementant le droit à indemnisation des victimes d'accidents de la circulation terrestre, en apportant d'ailleurs à celles-ci des modifications de forme et de fond importantes par rapport à la loi du 5 juillet 1985.

2°) C'est, en second lieu, à propos de la réglementation de **l'indemnisation du dommage corporel** qu'il est apparu difficile de concilier l'impératif d'une rédaction claire et concise avec la volonté d'apporter les précisions techniques nécessaires pour définir les droits et les obligations des parties. Notamment, la liste des préjudices indemnisables (article 1379) et surtout celle des prestations ouvrant droit au recours des tiers payeurs (article 1379-5 et 1379-6) peuvent paraître d'une facture peu élégante. La première semble pourtant indispensable. Quant à la seconde, elle reproduit l'actuel article 29 de la loi du 25 juillet 1985 et l'article L. 131-2 du code des assurances auxquels on aurait pu songer à renvoyer purement et simplement, mais, pour des raisons de commodité, la majorité des membres du groupe a jugé préférable de l'intégrer dans le code qui, de ce fait, contient l'ensemble des règles applicables à cette question de l'indemnisation du dommage corporel, si importante en pratique.

II. – Le choix d'une **construction** adaptée à la matière a soulevé d'emblée la question de **la place à assigner respectivement aux questions relatives à la responsabilité contractuelle et à la responsabilité extra-contractuelle.** Fallait-il maintenir la réglementation de la responsabilité contractuelle à la place que lui avaient assignée les rédacteurs du code civil ? Était-il, au contraire, préférable de regrouper l'ensemble sous un titre unique intitulé « De la responsabilité » ? Les membres du groupe, divisés sur ce point, ont laissé ce problème en suspens tant que les solutions n'ont pas été arrêtées sur le fond. C'est seulement après avoir rédigé l'ensemble et constaté que les règles communes aux deux branches de la responsabilité l'emportent très largement, qu'ils ont adopté, à la majorité, le second

---

[1] Notamment celles qui réglementent la responsabilité des compagnies aériennes pour les dommages causés au sol par les appareils, celle des exploitants de téléphériques pour les dommages subis par les tiers, celle de l'exploitant d'un réacteur nucléaire, etc. Il en va de même pour les textes régissant l'indemnisation des accidents du travail, des dommages résultant d'infractions ou d'attentats terroristes, de transfusions contaminées par le virus HIV, de l'amiante, etc.

[2] Cette proposition n'a pas recueilli l'unanimité.

legislation,[1] but not to recommend removing from it the existing articles 1386-1 to 1386-18[2] which the working group left untouched since the French legislator cannot in future amend these without the approval of the European institutions. On the other hand, the majority of the group declared itself in favour of the inclusion in the Code of provisions regulating the right to compensation of victims of motor-vehicle accidents, at the same time making important changes to these both at a formal and substantive level compared to the Law of 5 July 1985.[3]

(2) Secondly, it was in relation to the regulation of **compensation for personal injuries** where it appeared difficult to reconcile the requirement of a clear and concise form of words with the desire to introduce the technical elaborations which were considered necessary to define the parties' rights and obligations. Notably, the list of losses attracting compensation (article 1379) and above all the list of the benefits supplied by a third party to a victim which may give rise to a right of recourse in that third party (articles 1379-5 and 1379-6)[4] can appear as a rather inelegant construction. However, the first of these seems to be indispensable. The second reproduces the current provisions of article 29 of the Law of 25 July 1985 and article L. 131-2 of the Insurance Code and while it may be thought that one could simply cross-refer to these provisions directly, the majority of the members of the group decided that it was it preferable for reasons of convenience to include them within the Code so that it would contain all the rules applicable to the issues of compensation of personal injuries, these being so important in practice.

II. Choosing a **structure** suitable for this material raised at once the question of **the respective places to be assigned to issues relating to contractual and to extra-contractual liability.** Was it necessary to keep the rules governing contractual liability in the place assigned to it by the draftsmen of the Civil Code? Or was it instead preferable to re-categorise all this material under a single heading entitled 'Liability'? The members of the working group, who were divided on this point, put this problem aside until they had settled the substantive legal issues. It was only after having drafted the whole area and having found that to a considerable extent the rules common to the two branches of liability prevailed over all of it that the

---

[1] Notably, laws which govern the liability of airline companies for harm caused by their machines in the course of flight; the liability of operators of cable-cars for harm caused to third parties; the liability of operators of nuclear reactors, etc. It follows from this that other legislative provisions are also excluded, such as those governing compensation for accidents at work, harm caused by criminal offences or terrorist attacks, from transfusions of blood contaminated with the HIV virus, from asbestos, etc. [It is to be noted that here a distinction is being drawn between those legislative schemes which impose *responsabilité* (ie civil liability in damages) and those schemes which introduce rights of compensation which in principle do not involve the imposition of liability except in a fund set up for this purpose (*indemnisation*).]

[2] This recommendation was not unanimous. [These provisions of the Code implement the Product Liability Directive, above, p 809, n 4.]

[3] [Law no 85-677 of 5 July 1985 *tendant à l'amélioration de la situation des victimes d'accidents de la circulation et à l'accélération des procédures d'indemnisation* which at present governs the rights of motor-vehicle accident victims to compensation.]

[4] [This sentence translates by explanation the French '*prestations ouvrant droit au recours des tiers payeurs.*' A *tiers payeur* is any person (not being the victim/claimant nor the defendant) who pays over a sum or sums of money or provides services ['*prestations,*' here in the sense of 'things supplied'] to the victim/claimant. They include payments made by private insurers or by semi-public Social Security Funds (*Caisses de sécurité sociale*).]

parti.[1] Un chapitre intitulé « Dispositions préliminaires » a été placé en exergue afin de régler les relations entre les deux branches de la responsabilité.

Suivent deux chapitres consacrés respectivement aux conditions (chapitre deux) et aux effets (chapitre trois) de la responsabilité, suivi du dernier chapitre intitulé « Des principaux régimes spéciaux de responsabilité ou d'indemnisation ».

À propos des conditions de la responsabilité (chapitre deux), l'accord s'est fait assez facilement pour reconnaître que le préjudice réparable, le lien de causalité et les causes d'exonération se définissent de la même façon en matière contractuelle et extracontractuelle, ce qui a conduit à les regrouper dans une section 1 intitulée « Dispositions communes aux responsabilités contractuelle et extracontractuelle ». En revanche, le fait générateur de la responsabilité a fait l'objet de dispositions distinctes pour la responsabilité extracontractuelle, d'une part, la section 2 traitant successivement du « fait personnel », du « fait des choses », du « fait d'autrui », des « troubles de voisinage » et des « activités dangereuses », et pour la responsabilité contractuelle, d'autre part, la section 3 ne faisant pas cette distinction.

Le chapitre III, consacré aux effets de la responsabilité, comporte une section 1 intitulée « Principes » qui traite de « la réparation en nature » (§1), des règles générales concernant l'évaluation et les modalités de l'indemnisation sous forme de « dommages-intérêts » (§2) et de l'incidence de la pluralité de responsables (§3). Quant à la section 2, elle apporte des précisions concernant les règles applicables à la réparation de certaines catégories de dommages, à savoir « l'atteinte à l'intégrité physique » (§1), « l'atteinte aux biens » (§2), et le retard dans le paiement d'une somme d'argent (§3). La section 3 définit le statut des conventions portant sur la réparation, soit qu'elles l'excluent ou la limitent (§1), soit qu'elles en fixent forfaitairement le montant (§2). Une dernière section, très brève, est consacrée à la prescription de l'action en responsabilité.

Le chapitre IV consacré aux régimes spéciaux est divisé en deux sections, l'une consacrée à l'indemnisation des victimes d'accidents de la circulation et l'autre, à la responsabilité du fait des produits défectueux.

III. – **Sur le fond,** les membres du groupe n'ont pas cherché à innover systématiquement. Au contraire, ils ont consacré la plupart des solutions qu'a dégagées la jurisprudence pour compléter les dispositions très elliptiques qui figuraient dans le code civil. Toutefois, ils n'ont pas voulu non plus se limiter à proposer une « codification à droit constant », estimant qu'ils devaient prendre parti sur les questions délicates à propos desquelles la jurisprudence est divisée ou contestée par la doctrine. Ils n'ont pas hésité non plus à écarter les dispositions qui leur sont apparues périmées[2] ou même seulement inopportunes,[3] ni à en introduire

---

[1] Certains demeurent cependant réticents car ils estiment que cette présentation ne fait pas ressortir assez nettement le particularisme de la responsabilité contractuelle.

[2] Comme la responsabilité de l'artisan du fait de ses apprentis prévue actuellement par l'article 1384 alinéa 6 ou la responsabilité du propriétaire d'un bâtiment pour les dommages causés par le défaut d'entretien ou le vice de construction résultant de l'article 1386.

[3] Comme celle qu'a introduite la loi du 7 novembre 1922 à l'alinéa 2 de l'article 1384.

majority of the group's members adopted the latter course of action.[1] A chapter entitled 'Introductory provisions' was then placed at the very beginning so as to govern the relationship between the two branches of liability.

Following this introductory chapter come two chapters dedicated respectively to the conditions (chapter two) and effects (chapter three) of liability, then a final chapter entitled 'The principal special regimes of liability or compensation'.

As regards the conditions of liability (chapter two), it was quite easily agreed that reparable losses, causation and defences are defined in the same way in the contractual and extra-contractual contexts and this leads to their being grouped together in section 1, entitled 'Provisions common to contractual and extra-contractual liability'. By contrast, the various events which attract the imposition of liability were the object of distinct treatment so that as regards extra-contractual liability on the one hand, section 2 treats in turn 'liability for personal action', 'liability for the actions of things', 'liability for the actions of other people', 'liability for nuisance' and 'liability for dangerous activities', while, as regards contractual liability on the other hand, section 3 makes no similar division.

Chapter III is dedicated to the effects of liability: its first section entitled 'Principles' deals with (§1) 'reparation in kind'; (§2) general rules concerning the assessment and methods of compensation by way of 'damages'; and (§3) the circumstances in which two or more persons are liable. Its second section makes detailed provision as to the rules applicable to the reparation of certain categories of harm, that is, (§1) 'personal injury'; (§2) 'damage to property'; and (§3) delay in payment of sums of money. Its third section defines the legal position of agreements relating to reparation, whether they (§1) purport to exclude or limit it or (§2) set in advance a fixed sum of money. A final, very brief section is dedicated to the prescription period governing liability actions.

Chapter IV is dedicated to the special legislative regimes and is divided into two sections, one dealing with the compensation of victims of traffic accidents and the other liability for defective products.

III. **As regards matters of substance,** the members of the group did not seek to innovate in a systematic way. Instead, they have given formal expression to most of the solutions which have been worked out in the case-law to complete the highly elliptical provisions which appear in the present Civil Code. Nevertheless, the members of the group did not wish to limit themselves to recommending a mere 'codification of established law', as they considered that they ought to take a view on those finely balanced questions on which the courts are divided or academic writers do not agree. Nor did they hesitate to expunge legal provisions which appeared outdated[2] to them or even merely inappropriate,[3] nor to introduce new

---

[1] However, certain members remained hesitant as they considered that this way of arranging the law does not bring out clearly enough the special features of contractual liability.

[2] As in the case of liability of an artisan for the actions of his apprentices at present provided for by article 1384(6) or liability of an owner of a building for harm caused by a failure in its maintenance or defect in its construction stemming from article 1386.

[3] As in the case of the legal provision inserted as article 1384(2) by the Law of 7 November 1922 [which concerns the liability of occupiers of premises or holders of movable property in respect of damage caused to third parties by fire arising on the premises or from the movable property].

de nouvelles lorsqu'elles leur ont semblé de nature à accorder le droit positif aux exigences de la vie contemporaine.[1]

Nous nous bornerons à signaler dans ce rapport les positions qui paraissent les plus marquantes.

1°) La position du groupe concernant le concept de responsabilité contractuelle

On sait qu'un courant doctrinal récent nie le rattachement des dommages-intérêts contractuels au concept de responsabilité.[2] Les auteurs qui défendent ce point de vue estiment que ces dommages-intérêts constituent une simple modalité de l'exécution des obligations contractuelles, ce qui les amène à écarter l'exigence d'un dommage pour justifier leur octroi et à proposer de soumettre au régime extracontractuel toutes les condamnations à réparer les suites dommageables de l'inexécution.

Cette vision des choses, qui est contredite par une jurisprudence très majoritaire, n'a pas emporté l'adhésion de la majorité de la doctrine. Elle n'a pas été retenue par les membres du groupe. Ceux-ci estiment en effet qu'il est nécessaire de maintenir, au profit du créancier insatisfait, à côté du droit d'exiger l'exécution ou de demander la résolution du contrat, la possibilité d'obtenir réparation des dommages que lui a causés l'inexécution. Cette troisième voie leur paraît tout à fait autonome par rapport aux deux autres, aussi bien quant aux conditions imposées au demandeur pour s'y engager que quant aux résultats qu'il peut en attendre. Étant la seule qui garantisse le créancier contre les conséquences préjudiciables de la défaillance contractuelle, elle est indispensable à sa protection. Par ailleurs, son objectif indemnitaire et le fait qu'elle résulte d'une inexécution – c'est-à-dire d'un fait illicite, au sens large – permet de la rattacher au concept de responsabilité, sans pour autant condamner les particularités de son régime qui s'expliquent par le souci de préserver les prévisions des parties et d'éviter la dénaturation du contrat.

2°) Toutefois, cette option en faveur de l'admission d'une véritable responsabilité contractuelle pose un redoutable problème en droit positif, celui des **relations entre les deux régimes de responsabilité, contractuelle et extracontractuelle.**

---

[1] Par exemple celles qui figurent aux articles 1358, 1360, 1362, 1371, 1373, et 1379-7... du texte proposé.

[2] Pour un exposé particulièrement complet de cette doctrine, voir Philippe REMY, « La responsabilité contractuelle » : histoire d'un faux concept, Rev. trim. dr. civ. 1997 p. 323.

Cette position a été développée d'abord par Philippe le Tourneau. Elle a été reprise ensuite par Denis Tallon.

provisions where they appeared suitable to adapt the positive law to the demands of modern life.[1]

In this preamble we shall confine ourselves to drawing attention to the most striking positions which we have adopted.

(1) The position of the group on the concept of contractual liability

It is well known that a recent line of thinking in legal scholarship denies the idea that contractual damages should be linked to the concept of liability.[2] [3] Those writers who defend this point of view consider that these damages constitute merely a kind of performance of contractual obligations, and this leads them to deny that there should be a requirement of harm for their award and to propose that all court orders which do concern reparation for the harmful consequences of contractual non-performance should be governed by the extra-contractual regime.

This way of looking at things, which is contradicted by a large majority of the case-law, has not attracted the adherence of the majority of legal scholars and it was not adopted by the members of the working group. Indeed, they considered that an unsatisfied creditor of a contractual obligation must keep the advantage of obtaining reparation for the harm which non-performance has caused him as well as his right to demand performance or to claim retroactive termination of the contract. The first of these three routes appeared to them entirely independent of the other two, both as regards the conditions required of a claimant for its use and the results which it may entail. It is the only route which guarantees a creditor against the harmful consequences of a contractual failure to perform and it forms an indispensable part of his protection. Moreover, its purpose in compensating a claimant and the fact that it results from non-performance—that is to say, an act which is, in a broad sense, unlawful—allow it to be attached to the concept of liability without denying that the regime which governs it possesses special features which are to be explained by the desire to protect the expectations of the parties and to avoid distorting the nature of the contract.

(2) Nevertheless, the group's decision to accept the genuine nature of contractual liability leads to a daunting problem facing the law, the problem of the **relationship between the two regimes of liability, contractual and extra-contractual.**

---

[1] For example, those provisions which figure in arts 1358, 1360, 1362, 1371, 1373 and 1379-7 of the *Avant-projet*.

[2] For a particularly complete review of this doctrinal position, see Philippe Rémy, '"La responsabilité contractuelle": histoire d'un faux concept', RTC civ 1997, 323. This position was first developed by Philippe le Tourneau. [For whose views, see P Le Tourneau and L Cadiet, *Droit de la responsabilité et des contrats* (Paris, Dalloz, 2001) 196 ff.] It was then taken up by Denis Tallon ['L'inexécution du contrat: pour une autre présentation' RTD civ 1994, 223].

[3] [While we have used 'liability' to translate '*responsabilité*', the French term has a more moral resonance than the rather more neutral English term. However, such a difference between a morally-loaded term for extra-contractual (or sometimes, delictual) liability and a morally neutral term for contract is not the basis for the minority doctrinal position explained in the text of the Preamble].

Traditionnellement, le droit français prohibe ce qu'on appelle le « cumul » des régimes de responsabilité, c'est-à-dire en réalité la possibilité, pour la victime d'un dommage contractuel, de choisir de préférence l'application du régime délictuel. Pour justifier cette interdiction, on invoque généralement le fait que les règles relevant de cette branche de la responsabilité risqueraient de déjouer les prévisions des contractants et de tenir en échec les clauses du contrat.

Les membres du groupe étaient divisés sur l'opportunité de consacrer dans le code cette « règle du non-cumul » qui est ignorée par la plupart des droits étrangers. Toutefois, il a été décidé, à la majorité, de l'inscrire à l'article 1341, en lui apportant cependant une exception très importante au profit des victimes de dommages corporels. Il a paru en effet souhaitable de permettre à celles-ci d'opter en faveur du régime qui leur est le plus favorable, à condition toutefois qu'elles soient en mesure d'apporter la preuve des conditions exigées pour justifier le type de responsabilité qu'elles invoquent.

L'article 1342 prévoit, quant à lui, l'hypothèse dans laquelle l'inexécution d'une obligation contractuelle est à l'origine d'un dommage subi par un tiers. Actuellement, la jurisprudence tend à reconnaître très largement dans ce cas la responsabilité du débiteur, mais, quant à la nature de cette responsabilité, elle reste particulièrement hésitante. La plupart des arrêts la qualifient de « délictuelle » ou « extracontractuelle », n'hésitant pas à affirmer que le seul manquement au contrat suffit à établir une faute délictuelle ou un fait de la chose dès lors qu'il a causé un dommage à un tiers. Toutefois, lorsque la propriété d'une chose a été transmise par une chaîne de contrats, l'acquéreur est alors doté d'une « action directe nécessairement contractuelle » contre tous les maillons antérieurs de la chaîne de distribution. En outre, dans quelques espèces, la Cour de cassation a jugé que l'obligation contractuelle de sécurité profite, non seulement au créancier, mais également aux tiers, sans préciser pour autant si l'action du tiers victime est soumise alors au régime contractuel ou au régime extracontractuel. Ces solutions trahissent donc l'incertitude des juges qui n'a d'égale d'ailleurs que celle de la doctrine, les auteurs se montrant très embarrassés pour proposer des solutions cohérentes.

Traditionally, French law prohibits what is called the 'accumulation'[1] of regimes of liability, that is to say in reality, the possibility for a victim of a contractual harm to choose the application of the delictual regime instead. In order to justify this ban, reliance is generally placed on the fact that to allow the rules governing this branch of liability to apply as between parties to a contract would risk frustrating their expectations and rendering the terms of their contract of no effect.

The members of the working group were divided on the appropriateness of giving formal recognition in the Code to this 'rule against accumulation' which is not found in the majority of foreign laws. Nevertheless, it was decided by a majority to write it into the Code in a new article 1341, though also providing a very important exception for the benefit of victims of personal injuries as it appeared desirable to allow the latter to opt for whichever regime is more favourable to them as long as they are in a position to establish the circumstances required to justify the type of liability on which they rely.

In its turn, article 1342 provides for the situation where non-performance of a contractual obligation causes harm to a third party. At present, the courts tend to recognise liability in a contractual debtor very widely here, but they remain particularly unsure as to nature of the liability. The majority of decisions classify liability here as 'delictual' or 'extra-contractual', and do not hesitate to declare that a mere failure in performance of a contract is enough to establish delictual fault or an 'action of a thing' as long as it has caused harm to a third party.[2] Nevertheless, where ownership of a thing has been transmitted down a chain of contracts, its acquirer becomes endowed with a 'direct and necessarily contractual action' against all the earlier members of the chain of distribution.[3] Furthermore, in some cases, the Cour de cassation has held that a contractual safety obligation benefits not merely its contractual creditor, but also any third party, without making clear in doing so whether the third party victim's claim is subjected to the contractual or to the extra-contractual regime.[4] These solutions reveal therefore the uncertainty of the courts on this question, an uncertainty which is moreover felt equally by legal scholars, legal writers showing themselves rather at a loss to put forward a consistent approach for the resolution of these problems.

---

[1] [Here we translate 'cumul' as 'accumulation'. Strictly speaking, 'cumul' refers to the mixing of the rules drawn from the two regimes of liability, some from contract and some from delict and therefore the rule of 'non-cumul' forbids any such mixing. 'Concours' is the proper term to refer to the possibility for a person of claiming in the same proceedings in delict as well as alternatively in contract; and the notion of having an 'option' refers to a choice between claiming on one or the other basis. However, 'non-cumul' is used in French legal writing to refer to the denial in principle of all three of these possibilities, which have in common allowing a party to a contract to rely on the delictual provisions of the Civil Code against his contracting partner. For a discussion of the terminology see R Rodière, 'Etudes sur la dualité des régimes de responsabilité, Deuxième partie—La combinaison des responsabilités' JCP 1950 I 868. Although we translate 'cumul' as 'accumulation' here, at other times we prefer the more familiar terminology of 'concurrence'.]

[2] [See eg Cass civ (1) 15 December 1998, Bull civ no 368; Cass civ (1) 18 July 2000, Bull civ I no 221; Cass civ (1) 13 February 2001, Bull civ I no 35.]

[3] [The leading case is Cass civ (1) 9 October 1979, affaire Lamborghini, D 1980 IR 222 obs Larroumet; GP 1980 1 249 note Planqueel.]

[4] [A leading example may be found in Cass civ (1) 17 January 1995, D 1995, 350 note P Jourdain.]

C'est pourquoi il a paru indispensable de lever ces incertitudes.

Pour le faire, les membres du groupe sont partis de deux constatations.

Tout d'abord, la tendance à admettre largement la responsabilité du débiteur vis-à-vis des tiers auxquels il a directement causé un dommage par sa défaillance contractuelle correspond à une aspiration qui semble juste et qui d'ailleurs est étayée, sur le plan théorique, par l'admission du principe « d'opposabilité du contrat ». C'est pourquoi il a été décidé de consacrer cette responsabilité par une disposition explicite (à l'article 1342 alinéa 1er).

En revanche, il est clair que la soumission de cette responsabilité au régime extracontractuel risque à la fois de déjouer les prévisions des parties en écartant l'application des clauses du contrat qui ne sont pas compatibles avec ce régime (notamment celles qui écartent ou allègent les obligations ou les responsabilités ou qui désignent la juridiction compétente ou la loi applicable) et de conférer ainsi aux tiers qui invoquent le contrat pour fonder cette responsabilité, une position plus avantageuse que celle dont peut se prévaloir le créancier lui-même. Or cela semble particulièrement anormal.

C'est donc l'application du régime extracontractuel qui fait difficulté. Or cette application, que l'on justifie généralement en invoquant le fameux principe de l'« effet relatif du contrat », n'est en réalité nullement imposée par l'article 1165 du code civil. Des très nombreux et importants travaux consacrés à ce principe, il ressort en effet que sa portée se limite à deux conséquences essentielles. Au moment de la conclusion du contrat, il interdit aux parties de lier les tiers et, au moment de l'exécution, il leur réserve le droit d'exiger celle-ci. En revanche, il ne commande nullement le choix du régime de responsabilité à appliquer en cas d'inexécution.

Pour définir celui-ci, ce sont par conséquent les considérations pratiques qui doivent l'emporter. Or celles-ci commandent **d'imposer l'application du régime contractuel dès lors que le fondement de l'action réside uniquement dans un manquement au contrat.** C'est en effet la seule façon de soumettre les tiers à toutes les limites et conditions que le contrat impose au créancier pour obtenir réparation de son propre dommage.

En revanche, si le tiers peut établir à la charge du débiteur, outre la défaillance contractuelle, un fait générateur de responsabilité extracontractuelle, il n'y a alors aucune raison de le priver de l'action destinée à faire reconnaître cette responsabilité.[3]

Ce sont les solutions que propose de consacrer l'article 1342 alinéas 1 et 2 du projet présenté.

---

[3] Certes, cela laisse au tiers un avantage par rapport au créancier, mais cet avantage semble normal puisque le tiers n'a pas consenti aux éventuelles limitations du droit à réparation que le créancier a acceptées. Or il a subi un dommage contre lequel il n'avait aucun moyen de se prémunir.

This is why it appeared so absolutely necessary that these uncertainties should be removed.

In order to do so, the members of the group proceeded from two starting-points.

First, the tendency in many cases to hold a debtor liable to third parties to whom he has directly caused harm by his contractual failure to perform reflects an aim which seems fair and which is, moreover, supported at a theoretical level by the law's acceptance of the principle of the 'opposability of contracts.'[1] This is the reason why formal recognition was given to this liability by an express provision (found in article 1342 paragraph 1).

On the other hand, it is clear that subjecting liability in this situation to the extra-contractual liability regime risks frustrating the expectations of the parties by not applying any contract terms which are seen as incompatible with this regime (notably, those which exclude or limit a party's obligations or liability or which choose the competent jurisdiction or applicable law) while at the same time giving third parties who rely on the contract to ground their claim a more advantageous position than the creditor himself. This seems particularly anomalous.

The difficulty therefore stems from applying the extra-contractual regime to a third party's claim. Now, this application is usually justified by invoking the famous principle of 'the relative effect of contracts', but actually it is not required by article 1165 of the Civil Code at all.[2] Drawing on the numerous important studies which have been dedicated to this principle, it becomes clear that the significance of article 1165 is limited to two essential consequences: at the stage of the formation of the contract, it forbids contracting parties from binding third parties and, at the stage of performance, it reserves to the parties the right to demand performance. What it does not do is to make any requirement as to the proper regime of liability to be applied in the case of non-performance.

This being the case, practical considerations must be brought to bear in order to decide which regime should apply and these require **the compulsory application of the contractual regime wherever the basis of the action lies uniquely in the defendant's contractual failure to perform.** This is in fact the only way in which third parties can be made subject to all the restrictions and limitations which the contract imposes on a creditor in order to obtain reparation in respect of his own harm.

On the other hand, if a third party can prove that a contractual debtor has done something beyond his mere contractual failure to perform and this attracts extra-contractual liability there is no longer any reason to deprive him of an action whose purpose is to establish this liability.[3]

These are the solutions which article 1342 paragraphs 1 and 2 of the Proposals recommend should be formally adopted.

---

[1] [On this principle, see above, p 543, n 1, 589.]

[2] [Cf Mazeaud, above, p 221.]

[3] Certainly, this leaves the third party at an advantage as compared with the creditor, but this advantage seems normal since the third party has not consented to any limitations on his right to compensation which the creditor may have accepted. Moreover, he has suffered a harm against which he had no means of protecting himself.

3°) Une autre caractéristique importante des textes présentés réside dans **la faveur** qu'ils manifestent **à l'égard des victimes de dommages corporels ou d'atteintes à la personne.**

Cette tendance apparaît à l'article 1341 qui, dans son alinéa 2, autorise ces victimes à choisir le régime qui leur est le plus favorable, sans se heurter à la règle du non-cumul des responsabilités contractuelle et extracontractuelle.

On la retrouve également à l'article 1351 qui prévoit que, si elles ont commis des fautes en relation avec leur propre dommage, ces fautes ne seront retenues contre elles pour amputer leur droit à réparation que si elles sont « graves ».

Elle inspire encore l'article 1373 qui refuse au juge le pouvoir de réduire l'indemnisation en raison d'un refus de soins, même lorsque ceux-ci auraient été de nature à limiter les conséquences du dommage et l'article 1382-1 qui interdit de stipuler par convention toute restriction de l'indemnisation du dommage corporel.

Enfin l'aménagement de l'indemnisation de ce type de dommage par les articles 1379 à 1379-8 apparaît dans l'ensemble favorable aux victimes.

4°) Un autre domaine dans lequel un certain nombre d'innovations ont été proposées est celui de **la responsabilité extracontractuelle du fait d'autrui.**

On sait que depuis l'arrêt BLIECK rendu par la Cour de cassation en assemblée plénière le 29 mars 1991, la jurisprudence a profondément modifié les applications de ce type de responsabilité, sans toutefois être parvenue jusqu'à présent à stabiliser la matière.

Pour tenter de le faire, les membres du groupe ont estimé qu'il convenait d'abord d'indiquer les deux fondements possibles de la responsabilité du fait d'autrui qui sont, d'une part, le fait de régler le mode de vie des personnes soumises à une surveillance particulière en raison de leur état, et, d'autre part, le fait d'encadrer et d'organiser l'activité d'autrui dans l'intérêt personnel de celui qui exerce ce contrôle (article 1355).

Dans tous les cas, il est apparu nécessaire d'exiger la preuve d'un fait de nature à engager la responsabilité de l'auteur direct du dommage (article 1355 alinéa 2). Cette condition n'est pas conforme à la jurisprudence actuelle relative à la responsabilité des père et mère qui est désormais admise dès lors qu'est établi un simple « fait causal » du mineur.

a) Les personnes dont il est nécessaire de régler le mode de vie sont, d'une part, les mineurs et, d'autre part, les majeurs dont l'état nécessite une surveillance particulière en raison d'un handicap ou de précédents judiciaires.

(3) Another important characteristic of the provisions put forward lies in **the preferential treatment** which they clearly show **towards victims of personal injuries.**

This tendency can be seen in article 1341 whose second paragraph empowers a victim of personal injuries to choose the regime of liability which is most favourable to him without falling foul of the rule against the 'accumulation' of contractual and extra-contractual liability.

It is also to be found in article 1351 which provides that any fault committed by a victim of personal injuries which has contributed to his own harm will not count against him so as to cut down his right to reparation unless it is 'serious'.

This tendency also lies behind article 1373's denial of any power in the courts to reduce a claimant's compensation on the ground of his refusal to accept treatment, even where the latter is of a nature to limit the effects of his harm, and of article 1382-1 which forbids any contractual restriction on compensation for personal injury.

Finally, the arrangements for compensation for this type of harm put in place by articles 1379 to 1379-8 seem as a whole favourable to victims.

(4) Another area in which a certain number of innovations is proposed is the area of **extra-contractual liability for another person's action.**

As is well-known, since the *Assemblée plénière* of the Cour de cassation handed down its judgment in the *Blieck* case on 29 March 1991,[1] the courts have profoundly changed the range of application of this kind of liability, though so far without achieving much stability in the area.[2]

In order to try to do so, members of the group considered that it was appropriate first to indicate the two possible bases of liability for another person's action being, on the one hand, the factual regulation of the way of life of people subjected to special supervision owing to their condition, and, on the other, the factual structuring and organising of the activity of another person in the interest of the person who exercises this control (article 1355).

For all situations, it appeared necessary to require proof of action on the part of the third party of a kind which would attract liability in a person who had directly caused harm (article 1355 paragraph 2). This condition does not reflect existing case-law governing the liability of fathers and mothers for their minor children which is at present imposed as soon as a simple 'causal act' is established on the part of the latter.

(a) Persons whose way of life must be regulated are, first, minors and, secondly, adults whose condition requires some special supervision by reason of their disability or as a result of a judicial decision to this effect.

---

[1] [Ass plén 29 March 1991, *Blieck*, D 1991, 324 note Larroumet, JCP 1991 II 21673 concl Dottenwille.]
[2] [For a brief discussion of these cases in English see S Whittaker, 'The Law of Obligations' in Bell, Boyron and Whittaker, above, p 465, n 3, 397 – 399.]

Parmi les personnes chargées d'une responsabilité de plein droit pour le fait d'enfants mineurs, les père et mère ont été placés en première ligne. Il a semblé nécessaire de lier cette responsabilité à l'exercice de l'autorité parentale, mais c'est là la seule condition qui a été maintenue, la cohabitation de l'enfant avec ses parents ayant été, en revanche, écartée en raison des difficultés que suscite sa définition et des anomalies auxquelles avait conduit l'application de cette exigence lorsqu'elle était interprétée de manière rigoureuse.[1]

En cas de décès des parents, le tuteur assumerait la même responsabilité. Cette désignation, de préférence au conseil de famille, s'inspire de considérations pratiques. Le tuteur est facilement identifiable par la victime et il peut prendre l'assurance destinée à garantir ce risque.

Enfin il est prévu que la responsabilité incombe également à « la personne physique ou morale chargée, par décision judiciaire ou administrative, ou par convention de régler le mode de vie du mineur ». Cette disposition désigne, outre les associations d'action éducative, établissements ou organismes de rééducation chargés par le juge de l'assistance éducative ou par le juge des enfants ou un tribunal pour enfants de prendre en charge le mineur en danger ou délinquant, les instituts médico-éducatifs ou établissements scolaires auxquels les parents ont confié l'enfant en pension par contrat.

Le texte précise que ces différents cas de responsabilité ne s'excluraient pas l'un l'autre, mais pourraient se cumuler (article 1356 *in fine*).

Une responsabilité analogue pèserait sur « les personnes physiques ou morales chargées, par décision judiciaire ou administrative ou par convention, de régler le mode de vie » des majeurs « dont l'état nécessite une surveillance particulière ». Il s'agit, non seulement des majeurs en tutelle, mais aussi des jeunes adultes ayant fait l'objet d'une mesure de placement à la suite d'une infraction ou des malades mentaux hospitalisés selon les modalités prévues par le titre 1er du Livre II de la 3e partie du code de la santé publique (articles 3211-1 et suivants).

Ces responsabilités seraient encourues de plein droit et ne pourraient être écartées que par la preuve d'une cause étrangère présentant les caractères de la force majeure.

---

[1] En effet, elle favorisait alors celui des père et mère qui avait quitté l'enfant au détriment de celui qui s'en occupait effectivement.

Fathers and mothers were placed at the head of the list of those persons on whom strict liability for the acts of minor children is imposed. It seemed necessary to tie this liability to the exercise of parental authority, but this is the only condition which is retained from the Civil Code, for by contrast cohabitation of the minor with the parents was jettisoned on the ground of the difficult issues raised by its definition and the problems to which the application of this requirement has led where it has been interpreted strictly.[1]

Where his parents have died, a child's guardian takes over the same liability. This ascription of liability, in preference to the family council, is inspired by practical considerations, the guardian being easily identifiable by a victim and being able to take out insurance to cover the risk of liability.

Finally, it is provided that liability is also borne by 'the physical or legal person charged by judicial or administrative decision, or by agreement, with regulating the minor's way of life.' This provision refers to educational institutions for children with special needs and to teaching establishments to whom parents have entrusted their child as a boarder under a contract, as well as to associations for educative action, establishments or organisations for re-education charged by a Judicial Officer for Educative Action,[2] a Children's Judicial Officer or a Children's Court to take charge of a minor who was in danger or who had committed a criminal offence.

The wording of the provision makes clear that these different cases of liability are not mutually exclusive, but may apply concurrently (article 1356 *in fine*).

An analogous liability is borne by 'a physical or legal person charged by judicial or administrative decision, or by agreement, with regulating the way of life' of adults 'whose condition requires some special supervision.' This deals not merely with adults who are subject to guardianship,[3] but also with young adults who have been made the subject of a placement order following commission of a criminal offence and with mental patients who have been hospitalised in the circumstances provided for by Title 1 of Book II of the third part of the Code of Public Health (articles 3211-1 *et seq.*).

These liabilities would be strict and could be avoided only by proof of an external event which possesses the attributes of *force majeure*.[4]

---

[1] Indeed, it then favoured the parent who had abandoned the child to the detriment of the one who actually looked after him.

[2] [This translates *juge de l'assistance éducative:* the translation 'judicial officer' is preferred to 'judge' as the person acts non-judicially even though forming a member of the *magistrature* and therefore a *juge* in French terms: similarly for *juge des enfants*.]

[3] [In French law, 'guardianship' (*tutelle*) involves a person looking after the person and/or the affairs either of a child or an adult where the circumstances so require: see arts 390 (minors); 490, 492 (adults) Cc.]

[4] [See below, p 841.]

En outre, il a semblé utile de prévoir que toute autre personne – c'est-à-dire celle qui n'encourt pas la responsabilité prévue aux articles 1356 et 1357, mais qui assume, à titre professionnel, une mission de surveillance d'autrui – répond du fait de l'auteur direct à moins qu'elle prouve n'avoir pas commis de faute.

b) Parmi les applications de **la responsabilité fondée sur l'encadrement et l'organisation de l'activité d'autrui par une personne qui profite de cette activité**, il est un cas tout à fait classique, celui du commettant dont la responsabilité serait admise aux mêmes conditions qu'aujourd'hui.

En revanche, le projet prévoit de modifier la situation personnelle du préposé. Sa responsabilité ne serait pas écartée purement et simplement, comme l'a admis l'assemblée plénière de la Cour de cassation par son arrêt COSTEDOAT du 25 février 2000. Elle deviendrait subsidiaire par rapport à celle du commettant, ce qui apparaît plus protecteur de l'intérêt des victimes, tout en assurant une protection suffisante au préposé.

En outre, parce que les relations commettant-préposé ont été redéfinies de manière relativement stricte, un autre cas de responsabilité pour autrui a été prévu à la charge des professionnels qui encadrent ou contrôlent l'activité d'autres professionnels en situation de dépendance économique, que ceux-ci soient des membres de professions libérales comme, par exemple, le médecin qui travaille au profit d'une clinique, ou des commerçants, comme la filiale qui dépend d'une société mère, le concessionnaire ou le franchisé qui exerce son activité en partie au profit du concédant ou du franchiseur. La responsabilité du professionnel dominant serait alors engagée lorsque le fait dommageable commis par celui qui est en situation de dépendance serait en relation directe avec l'exercice du contrôle.

Ce cas de responsabilité serait tout à fait nouveau, mais les membres du groupe ont pensé qu'il serait extrêmement utile pour ajuster le droit de la responsabilité aux transformations qui ont affecté les structures économiques, aussi bien dans le secteur de la production que dans celui de la distribution. Il permettrait en effet de faire peser une part des responsabilités encourues à la suite des dommages causés à l'occasion des activités économiques sur les véritables décideurs, ce qui serait à la fois plus juste vis-à-vis des professionnels en situation de dépendance et plus protecteur des victimes.

Furthermore, it seemed useful to provide that any other person—that is to say any person who does not incur liability under articles 1356 and 1357, but who takes on the task of supervising another person in the course of business or by way of his profession—is liable for the action of the person who directly caused the harm unless he proves that he committed no fault.

b) The really classic case of employers[1] falls within the new category of **liability based on the structuring or organisation of another person's activity by a person who benefits from this activity** and their liability would remain imposed on the same basis as at present.

On the other hand, the Reform Proposals envisage a change to the personal position of employees, as their liability would not simply be ruled out as was held by the *Assemblée plénière* of the Cour de cassation in its judgment in *Costedoat* on 25 February 2000;[2] instead it would become subsidiary to liability in their employers, this seeming to be more protective of the interests of victims while at the same time ensuring a sufficient protection for employees.

Moreover, since the Reform Proposals redefine the relationship of employer/ employee in quite a strict way, they provide a further case of liability for another person's action to cover the situation where a professional person or business regulates or controls the activity of another professional or business who is economically dependent on them, whether the latter are members of a liberal profession (such as, for example, a doctor who works for a private hospital) or traders (such as a subsidiary company which is dependent on its parent company or a person acting under a concession or franchise who exercises his activity partly for the benefit of the person granting the concession or the franchisor). Liability in the dominant professional or business would then be imposed where a harmful act is committed by the person who is dependent on him and is directly related to the exercise of his control.

This example of liability would be entirely new, but the members of the working group thought that it would be extremely useful to adjust the law of liability so as to reflect the radical changes which have occurred in the way in which economic relations are structured, as regards both production and distribution. It would allow the imposition of some part of the liabilities incurred as a result of harm caused in the course of economic activities on the real decision-makers, which would be fairer to dependant professionals or businesses and at the same time more protective of victims.

---

[1] [The translation of *commettant* by 'employer' and *préposé* by 'employee' is not perfect. The central idea is one of a 'relationship of subordination' between the two parties, and while this does mean that it necessarily includes a relationship of employment (in the technical sense of a contract of employment (*contrat de travail*)) and would not normally include relationships created by a contract for services (where the provider of the service acts independently) it may include other relationships: see S Whittaker, 'The Law of Obligations' in Bell, Boyron and Whittaker, above, p 465, n 3, 395. The *Avant-projet* recommends a stricter definition of the relationship *commettant/préposé* in article 1359 in terms of 'a power to give orders or instructions in relation to the fulfilment of the duties of the employee'.]

[2] [Ass plén 25 February 2000, *arrêt Costedoat*, D 2000, 673 note Brun.]

5°) Parmi les innovations proposées, il convient de signaler encore l'introduction d'un nouveau cas de **responsabilité de plein droit**, celle **qui incomberait à l'exploitant d'une activité anormalement dangereuse** pour les dommages consécutifs à cette activité (article 1362).

Cette disposition a été particulièrement discutée au sein du groupe. Ses partisans ont fait valoir qu'elle rapprocherait le droit français de la plupart des droits des pays voisins et qu'elle serait en harmonie avec la jurisprudence administrative qui est en ce sens. Pourtant, certains membres du groupe ont objecté que d'autres dispositions, en particulier celles qui concernent la responsabilité du fait des choses, la rendraient à peu près inutile. À quoi il a été rétorqué que ce texte concernerait essentiellement les catastrophes industrielles alors que la responsabilité du fait des choses est mieux adaptée aux dommages entre particuliers.

Finalement, il a été décidé de maintenir cette règle pour le cas de dommages de masse résultant d'activités présentant des risques graves.

6°) En ce qui concerne les **fonctions assignées à la responsabilité,** les textes proposés accordent la première place à la réparation, conformément au droit actuel.

Toutefois, une disposition (l'article 1372) ouvre prudemment la voie à l'octroi de **dommages-intérêts punitifs.** Elle soumet le prononcé de cette sanction à la preuve d'une « faute délibérée, notamment d'une faute lucrative », c'est-à-dire d'une faute dont les conséquences profitables pour son auteur ne seraient pas neutralisées par une simple réparation des dommages causés. Elle exige également une motivation spéciale et impose au juge de distinguer les dommages-intérêts punitifs des dommages-intérêts compensatoires. Enfin elle interdit leur prise en charge par l'assurance, ce qui est indispensable pour donner à cette condamnation la portée punitive qui constitue sa raison d'être.

Quant à la **prévention**, elle n'est pas présentée comme l'une des fonctions spécifiques de la responsabilité. Cependant, une place discrète lui a été réservée, sous le couvert de la réparation en nature. En effet, l'article 1369-1 dispose que « Lorsque le dommage est susceptible de s'aggraver, de se renouveler ou de se perpétuer, le juge peut ordonner, à la demande de la victime, toute mesure propre à éviter ces conséquences, y compris au besoin la cessation de l'activité dommageable ».

La même idée inspire également l'article 1344 aux termes duquel « les dépenses exposées pour prévenir la réalisation imminente d'un dommage ou pour écarter son aggravation ainsi que pour en réduire les conséquences constituent un préjudice réparable dès lors qu'elles ont été raisonnablement engagées ».

(5) Among the innovations being proposed, particularly worthy of note is a new example of **strict liability**[1] where liability **would be imposed on a person undertaking an abnormally dangerous activity** for harm consequential on this activity (article 1362).

This provision was the subject of considerable discussion within the group. Its advocates emphasised that its inclusion would bring French law closer to the majority of neighbouring countries and would be consonant with the case-law of the administrative courts which is to the same effect.[2] However, certain members of the group objected that other provisions, in particular those which concern liability for the actions of things, would make it almost useless. To this argument it was countered that the new provision would overwhelmingly be concerned with industrial disasters whereas liability for the actions of things is more apt to deal with harm taking place between individuals.

In the end it was decided to retain this rule for the situation of catastrophic harm caused by activities bearing special risks.

(6) As regards the **purposes attributed to the imposition of liability,** the draft provisions recommend that first place be given to reparation, following the position of the present law.

Nevertheless, by article 1372 cautious provision is made to open the way for the award of **punitive damages.**[3] This provision subjects the pronouncement of this sanction to proof of a 'deliberate fault, and notably a fault with a view to gain', that is to say, a fault whose beneficial consequences for its perpetrator would not be undone by the simple reparation of any harm which it has caused. It also requires a court to give a special reason or reasons[4] for such an award and to distinguish between those damages which are punitive and those which are compensatory. Finally, it forbids their being covered by insurance, a rule which is absolutely necessary to give to the award the punitive impact which constitutes its very raison d'être.

Prevention, for its part, is not put forward as one of the specific purposes of liability. However, an unobtrusive place has been reserved for it under the cover of reparation in kind. So article 1369-1 provides that 'Where harm is liable to become worse, to reoccur or to linger, a court may, at the request of the victim, order any measure appropriate to avoid these consequences, including if need be an order for the discontinuation of the harmful activity in question.'

The same idea also inspires article 1344 according to which 'expenses incurred in order to prevent the imminent occurrence of harm, to avoid its getting worse, or to reduce its consequences, constitute a reparable loss as long as they were reasonably undertaken.'

[1] [We translate *'une responsabilité de plein droit'* as 'strict liability', though it literally refers to a liability imposed 'by operation of law': see above pp 431-2.]

[2] [See, notably, CE 1 Aug 1919, *arrêt Regnault-Desroziers*, D 1920 II 1 note Appleton and, for discussion in English, D Fairgrieve, *State Liability in Tort: a Comparative Study* (Oxford University Press, 2003) 138-42.]

[3] [For discussion of this proposal see Rowan, above, ch 15.]

[4] [Here, the terminology used by the *Avant-projet* is technical: *une motivation spéciale* requires a court to give a special reason, a failure to provide which would lead to *cassation*: New Code of Civil Procedure, art 455.]

828

7°) Parmi les textes proposés pour guider les juges dans l'évaluation des dommages-intérêts, la plupart entérinent les positions de la jurisprudence actuelle.

On signalera cependant une disposition qui n'est d'ailleurs pas sans rapport avec l'article 1344 qui vient d'être cité. Il s'agit de l'article 1373 qui **autorise le juge à réduire l'indemnisation lorsque la victime, par une négligence caractérisée, a laissé un dommage s'aggraver sans réagir ou n'a rien fait pour le réduire.**

La reconnaissance de cette possibilité de modération répond au souci de responsabiliser les victimes. Elle est admise aujourd'hui par la plupart des droits des pays voisins de la France ainsi que par la Convention de Vienne sur la vente internationale de marchandises[1] et les Principes du droit européen du contrat préconisent son adoption.[2]

On soulignera que, dans le texte proposé, il ne s'agit que d'une possibilité laissée à l'appréciation du juge et que l'exercice de cette faculté est subordonnée à la constatation que la réduction du dommage pouvait être obtenue par des « mesures raisonnables et proportionnées ». En outre, il est précisé, on l'a déjà souligné, qu'aucune réduction ne peut être admise lorsque ces mesures seraient de nature à porter atteinte à l'intégrité physique de la victime. Autrement dit, le refus de soins ne peut jamais motiver une diminution de l'indemnisation des préjudices résultant d'un dommage corporel.

8°) Les dispositions concernant « **les conventions portant sur la réparation** » proposent plusieurs changements par rapport au droit actuel.

Elles consacrent d'abord la **validité des clauses excluant ou limitant la réparation, même si elles affectent une responsabilité de nature extracontractuelle** (article 1382), sauf lorsque cette responsabilité est fondée sur une faute (article 1382-4, alinéa 2).

Cette validation en matière extracontractuelle concerne principalement les conventions portant sur les responsabilités entre voisins ou entre personnes qui entreprennent une activité en commun sans être liées par un contrat de société ou d'association.

Une première limite à la validité des clauses restrictives de responsabilité ou de réparation affecte l'indemnisation du dommage corporel qui ne pourrait être amputée conventionnellement (article 1382-1). Or cette solution, qui est réclamée depuis longtemps par une doctrine quasi-unanime, n'a jamais jusqu'à présent été affirmée clairement par la jurisprudence.

Une autre disposition propose de considérer comme nulles les clauses restrictives de responsabilité stipulées par un professionnel au détriment d'un consommateur lorsqu'elles ne sont compensées par aucune « contrepartie réelle, sérieuse et clairement stipulée ». Elle est tout à fait dans la ligne des solutions qui se dégagent des recommandations de la Commission des clauses abusives.

[1] Art. 77 CVIM.
[2] Article 9-505.

(7) Among the legal provisions which are proposed to guide courts in their assessment of damages, the majority confirm the present positions taken by the courts.

However, one provision deserves to be mentioned, not least because it is not unrelated to article 1344, which has just been quoted. This is article 1373, which **authorises a court to reduce a victim's compensation where the latter has by a specified act of negligence allowed his own harm to get worse without reacting or doing anything to reduce it.**

The recognition of this possibility of reducing a victim's compensation responds to a desire to make victims responsible for themselves. This is accepted today by the majority of the laws of countries neighbouring to France as well as by the Vienna Convention on the International Sale of Goods,[1] and the *Principles of European Contract Law* recommend its adoption.[2]

It should also be noted that the provision which is proposed creates merely a possibility for a court and that the exercise of its discretion is conditional on its finding that a reduction of the harm could have been achieved by 'reasonable and proportionate measures'. Furthermore, as has already been underlined, it is made clear that no reduction could be allowed where the measures would be of a nature to compromise the victim's physical integrity. In other words, a refusal of health care could never be a ground for a diminution in compensation for losses resulting from personal injury.

(8) The provisions which deal with '**agreements relating to reparation**' put forward several changes from the existing law.

First, they formally recognise the **validity of contract terms which exclude or limit reparation, even if these concern extra-contractual liability** (article 1382), except where this liability is based on fault (article 1382-4 paragraph 2).

In the extra-contractual context, this recognition principally concerns agreements relating to liabilities between neighbours or between persons who undertake a common activity without being bound by a contract of partnership or association.

A first limitation on the validity of contract terms which restrict liability or reparation concerns compensation for personal injuries which would be incapable of being cut down by agreement (article 1382-1). This solution, which has been advocated for a long time by an almost unanimous body of scholarly opinion, has never been clearly confirmed by the courts.

Another provision recommends that contract terms which are included in a contract by a professional or business to the detriment of a consumer are to be deemed a nullity where they are not balanced by some 'something real, significant and clearly stipulated in return'. This is quite in line with the solutions which are to be drawn from the recommendations of the Commission on Unfair Contract Terms.[3]

---

[1] Article 77 CISG.
[2] Article 9-505.
[3] [This Commission (the *Commission des clauses abusives*) has a research and advisory function under legislation now contained in the Consumer Law Code. However, while the courts may take its recommendations into account in their decisions under the legislation governing unfair terms in consumer contracts, they are not bound by them.]

Le texte consacre également certaines solutions d'ores et déjà admises par la jurisprudence, notamment l'inefficacité des clauses limitatives ou exonératoires de responsabilité en présence d'un dol ou d'une faute lourde et la nullité de celles qui ont pour effet de libérer le débiteur contractuel de toute responsabilité pour les conséquences du manquement à l'une de ses obligations essentielles. Il subordonne enfin l'opposabilité de la clause, en matière contractuelle, à la possibilité pour la victime d'en prendre connaissance avant la formation du contrat et, en matière extracontractuelle, à une « acceptation non équivoque ».

Mais les innovations les plus importantes concernent les clauses qui sont aujourd'hui désignées couramment par l'expression de « clauses pénales » et qu'il est proposé d'appeler « **Conventions de réparation forfaitaire et clauses pénales** ». Le groupe estime en effet qu'il n'est pas nécessaire de maintenir les articles 1226 à 1230, 1232 et 1233, qui ne sont plus guère appliqués. Il souhaite au contraire conserver le pouvoir de révision judiciaire introduit en 1975 mais pense que celui-ci n'est nécessaire que dans le sens de la modération des clauses « manifestement excessives ». En revanche, pour les clauses « dérisoires », la réglementation prévue aux articles 1382-1 à 1382-4 paraît suffisante.

La possibilité de réduire judiciairement la réparation prévue au contrat lorsqu'il y a eu exécution partielle, que permet l'actuel article 1231, mérite également d'être maintenue.

9°) En proposant d'introduire dans le code civil les dispositions définissant **le droit à indemnisation des victimes d'accidents de la circulation**, les membres du groupe ont souhaité apporter à celles-ci certaines modifications.

La plus importante concerne **le sort du conducteur victime d'une atteinte à sa personne**. Le moment paraît en effet venu d'assimiler le conducteur aux autres victimes, en ne retenant contre lui, pour le priver d'indemnisation, que sa « faute inexcusable », à condition qu'elle ait été la « cause exclusive de l'accident ».

Certes, en 1985, cette assimilation a pu être considérée comme prématurée, les conséquences de la réduction des causes d'exonération n'ayant pas encore été mesurées, mais une nouvelle étape paraît s'imposer aujourd'hui. En effet les

The provision which is proposed also formally recognises certain solutions which are already accepted by the courts, notably the ineffectiveness of contract terms which exclude or limit liability in the case of fraud or other dishonesty,[1] gross fault, and the nullity of terms which try to free a contractual debtor from any liability for the results of failure to perform one of his essential obligations. Finally, it subjects the ability of a person to rely effectively on a clause to a condition that the victim could have known of it before the conclusion of the contract (where the clause is sought to have contractual effect) and to a condition of 'unequivocal acceptance' outside such a contractual context.

However, the most important innovations relate to clauses which are at present termed 'penalty clauses'[2] and which it is proposed should be called '**Agreements for a pre-set reparation**[3] **and penalty clauses**'. The working group considers in fact that it is not necessary to retain articles 1226 to 1230, 1232 and 1233 of the present Civil Code, which are hardly ever applied. By contrast, it does wish to preserve the judicial power of review of penalty clauses introduced by legislation in 1975,[4] but thinks that it is necessary only in the direction of the reduction of clauses which stipulate sums which are 'manifestly excessive'. As to clauses stipulating for the payment of 'derisory' sums, the rules provided by articles 1382-1 to 1382-4 appear to be adequate.

The possibility of a court's reducing the reparation provided for by the contract where a debtor's failure to perform is only partial (and which is at present allowed by article 1231 of the Civil Code) equally deserves to be retained.

9) At the same time as recommending the insertion into the Civil Code of the legal provisions which define **the rights to compensation of victims of traffic accidents,** the members of the group wished to modify them in certain respects.

The most important respect concerns **the fate of a driver who is a victim of personal injuries.** The time seems to have come to treat drivers in the same way as other victims, so that their compensation is denied them only where they have committed an 'inexcusable fault' which was the 'exclusive cause of the accident'.

Certainly, in 1985,[5] such an assimilation of drivers and other victims could have been thought premature given that the effects of reducing the defences for those liable for traffic accidents had not yet been assessed, but a further step forward

---

[1] ['Fraud or other dishonesty' translates *dol*, whose core significance is one of 'deceit' or 'dishonesty' but extends as far as bad faith and, therefore, the deliberate breaking of a contract.]

[2] [The category of *clauses pénales* overlaps with but is not identical to the common law's 'penalty clauses' whose definition has evolved by way of contrast with 'liquidated damages clauses' which are valid at common law, whereas penalty clauses are not.]

[3] [This expression translates '*réparation forfaitaire*'.]

[4] [Article 1152(2) Cc, introduced by article 1 of the Law no 75-597 of 9 July 1975, which provides that 'Nevertheless, a court may, even of its own initiative, reduce or increase the penalty which has been agreed, if the latter is manifestly excessive or derisory. Any agreement to the contrary is deemed not to have been written'.]

[5] [This is the date of the legislation introducing a special legislative regime for the victims of traffic accidents: above, p 811.]

conducteurs sont exposés aux risques de la circulation exactement comme les piétons, les cyclistes et les passagers. Une prise en charge de leur indemnisation par l'assurance obligatoire, dont la raison d'être est précisément la garantie de ces risques, semble donc logique et nécessaire. D'ailleurs, la jurisprudence est déjà parvenue, dans un certain nombre de cas, à ce résultat.

De même, l'exclusion des accidents de chemin de fer et de tramway, admise en 1985, ne paraît plus guère justifiable. On constate d'ailleurs que la jurisprudence refuse désormais presque systématiquement d'admettre l'exonération de la SNCF en cas d'accident corporel, les causes étrangères invoquées pour écarter la responsabilité qu'elle encourt sur le fondement d'un manquement à son obligation de sécurité de résultat n'étant pratiquement jamais considérées comme présentant les caractères de la force majeure, même s'il s'agit de fautes de la victime, a fortiori de cas fortuits ou de faits d'un tiers. L'application du même régime de responsabilité à toutes les victimes d'accidents de la circulation dans lesquels sont impliqués des véhicules terrestres à moteur paraît donc s'imposer pour des raisons de simplicité et d'équité.

Enfin l'interprétation très étroite que la Cour de cassation adopte aujourd'hui de la faute inexcusable de la victime rend inutile le maintien de la disposition concernant spécialement les enfants et les personnes âgées ou handicapées. Pour toutes les victimes, il paraît suffisant d'exiger la preuve de leur faute inexcusable afin de refuser ou de limiter leur indemnisation.

Les explications contenues dans ce rapport ne portent que sur les questions qui apparaissent les plus importantes. Elles doivent être complétées par celles qui accompagnent le texte lui-même.

appears necessary today. In fact drivers are exposed to traffic risks in exactly the same way as pedestrians, cyclists and passengers. The taking on of their compensation by way of compulsory insurance whose very reason is precisely the guaranteeing of these risks seems therefore both logical and necessary. Moreover, the courts have in a number of cases already reached this very result.

Similarly, the exclusion from the special regime of railway and tramcar accidents which was conceded in 1985 scarcely appears justifiable any longer. Moreover, it is to be noted that the courts have for a while almost systematically refused to accept any defences by SNCF[1] to claims for personal injuries, any exterior causes which it invokes to escape liability which it incurs on the basis of a failure in its safety obligation of result being practically never found to count as *force majeure*, even if they concern the victim's own fault and even more as regards acts of God or acts of third parties. The application of the same regime of liability to all the victims of accidents which involve an earth-bound motorised means of transport is therefore appropriate as a matter both of simplicity and of fairness.

Finally, the very strict interpretation which the Cour de cassation today adopts of the notion of the inexcusable fault of a victim of a traffic accident[2] means that there is no longer any need to maintain the special provisions for children and for old or handicapped persons.[3] For all victims, it appears to be enough to require proof of their inexcusable fault before their compensation is refused or limited.

The explanations contained in this preamble concern only the most clearly important questions. They will be supplemented by those which accompany the text of the provisions itself.

---

[1] [*Société Nationale des Chemins de Fers Français*, ie the French State railway company, whose legal position is stretched across public and private law.]

[2] [This is relevant under the present law to contributory fault by persons other than drivers (and specially treated persons as explained in the following note) under article 3(1) of the Law of 5 July 1985. The Cour de cassation has defined 'inexcusable fault' for this purpose as 'a voluntary fault of an exceptional seriousness which exposes without any reason the person who commits it to a danger of which he ought to have been aware': Ass plén 10 November 1995, Bull civ AP no 6.]

[3] [Under article 3(2) and 3(3) of the Law of 5 July 1985 the contributory fault of road accident victims who are less than sixteen or more than seventy years old or who suffer from a registered disability of 80% or more is a ground of reduction of their damages only where they 'voluntarily sought the injury suffered', notably, by suicide or its attempt.]

Chapitre I
Dispositions préliminaires

Ce chapitre est particulièrement important car il prend parti sur des questions fondamentales et très controversées :

Il exige un fait illicite ou anormal pour fonder la responsabilité, mais précise que ce fait n'exige pas le discernement.

Il consacre la notion de responsabilité contractuelle ainsi que la règle du non-cumul des responsabilités contractuelle et extracontractuelle qu'il écarte cependant en cas de dommage corporel.

Il permet à un tiers au contrat de demander réparation du dommage causé par l'inexécution d'une obligation contractuelle mais soumet alors le tiers aux règles de la responsabilité contractuelle à moins qu'il ne soit en mesure de démontrer l'existence d'un fait susceptible d'engager la responsabilité extracontractuelle du défendeur. Dans cette dernière hypothèse, le tiers dispose d'un choix entre les deux régimes.

Art. 1340[2]

Tout fait illicite ou anormal ayant causé un dommage à autrui oblige celui à qui il est imputable à le réparer.

De même,[3] toute inexécution d'une obligation contractuelle ayant causé un dommage au créancier oblige le débiteur à en répondre.

Art. 1340-1[4]

Celui qui a causé un dommage à autrui alors qu'il était privé de discernement n'en est pas moins obligé à réparation.

Art. 1341

En cas d'inexécution d'une obligation contractuelle, ni le débiteur ni le créancier ne peuvent se soustraire à l'application des dispositions spécifiques à la responsabilité contractuelle pour opter en faveur de la responsabilité extracontractuelle.

---

[2] Ce texte, qui se présente comme une annonce des textes ultérieurs, utilise la notion de « fait illicite ou anormal » pour introduire les dispositions relatives à la responsabilité extracontractuelle.

[3] Cette formule vise à marquer l'identité des deux responsabilités en dépit de l'utilisation de deux mots différents (répondre, réparer) pour des raisons de style.

[4] Le groupe a choisi d'intégrer cette disposition après le texte général d'annonce des différents cas de responsabilité plutôt que de modifier la définition de la faute donnée à l'article 1352. Cette solution permet d'éviter de dire que la personne privée de discernement peut commettre une faute. Par ailleurs, elle donne à la responsabilité de l'aliéné (et éventuellement de l'infans) une portée générale valant pour tous les faits générateurs de responsabilité extracontractuelle et même pour la responsabilité contractuelle.

On remarquera que l'article 1351-1 écarte l'exonération pour faute de la victime lorsque celle-ci est privée de discernement. Les membres du groupe estiment en effet que l'exonération pour faute de la victime est une peine privée qui ne doit, par conséquent, s'appliquer qu'aux personnes conscientes des conséquences de leurs actes.

Chapter I
Introductory Provisions

This chapter is particularly important as it takes a position on the fundamental and most controversial questions.[1]

It requires an unlawful or abnormal action to ground liability, but makes clear that this action does not require any understanding in its perpetrator.

The chapter formally recognises the notion of contractual liability as well as the rule against the accumulation of contractual and extra-contractual liability which it rules out except for the case of personal injuries.

It allows a third party to a contract to claim reparation for the harm caused to him by the non-performance of a contractual obligation but in that case subjects the third party's claim to the rules of contractual liability as long as he is able to show the existence of circumstances of a kind which would attract extra-contractual liability in the defendant. Where this is the case, the third party has a choice between the two regimes of liability.

Art. 1340[2]

Any unlawful or abnormal action which has caused harm to another obliges the person to whom this is attributable to make reparation for it.

Similarly,[3] any non-performance of a contractual obligation which has caused harm to its creditor obliges the debtor to answer for it.

Art. 1340-1[4]

A person who has caused harm to another while lacking understanding is nonetheless obliged to make reparation for it.

Art. 1341

In the case of non-performance of a contractual obligation, neither the debtor nor the creditor may escape the application of legal provisions specifically governing contractual liability by opting in favour of extra-contractual liability.[5]

---

[1] [For discussion of some of the issues arising, see Borghetti, above, ch 12 and Giliker, above, ch 13.]

[2] This article, which is put forward as an announcement for later articles, uses the notion of 'unlawful or abnormal action' to introduce the provisions governing extra-contractual liability.

[3] This expression seeks to make clear the identity of the two liabilities despite the use of different words (to be answerable for, to make reparation for) chosen for reasons of style.

[4] The working group chose to insert this provision after the general text announcing the different instances of liability rather than to amend the definition of fault given by article 1352. This solution allows one to avoid saying that a person lacking understanding can commit a fault. Moreover, it bears a general significance for the liability of persons suffering from a mental disorder (and possibly of infants) which is valid for all the actions which give rise to extra-contractual liability and even for contractual liability. It is to be noticed that article 1351-1 rules out any exclusion of liability on the ground of fault in the victim where the latter lacks understanding. The members of the group consider that in effect such exclusion of liability on the ground of the victim's fault acts as a private penalty which must therefore be applied only to those persons who are conscious of the consequences of their actions.

[5] [This provision gives legislative recognition to the 'rule against accumulation' (*règle de non-cumul*), explained at p 817 above.]

Toutefois, lorsque cette inexécution provoque un dommage corporel, le cocontractant peut, pour obtenir réparation de ce dommage, opter en faveur des règles qui lui sont plus favorables.

Art. 1342[1]

Lorsque l'inexécution d'une obligation contractuelle est la cause directe d'un dommage subi par un tiers, celui-ci peut en demander réparation au débiteur sur le fondement des articles 1363 à 1366. Il est alors soumis à toutes les limites et conditions qui s'imposent au créancier pour obtenir réparation de son propre dommage.

Il peut également obtenir réparation sur le fondement de la responsabilité extracontractuelle, mais à charge pour lui de rapporter la preuve de l'un des faits générateurs visés aux articles 1352 à 1362.

Chapitre II
Des conditions de la responsabilité

Section 1
Dispositions communes
aux responsabilités contractuelle
et extra-contractuelle

§1 – Le préjudice réparable

La définition du préjudice réparable reste assez générale, mais l'allusion à la lésion d'un intérêt collectif paraît utile, notamment pour permettre la réparation du préjudice écologique.

[1] Ce texte est le résultat de longues réflexions...
Suite à la communication des travaux du groupe 10 sur les effets du contrat à l'égard des tiers, la solution la plus équilibrée a semblé être d'ouvrir par principe aux tiers une action en réparation leur permettant de se prévaloir de l'inexécution du contrat lorsqu'elle leur a causé un préjudice (ce qui est actuellement admis par la Cour de cassation sous l'angle de l'assimilation des fautes), mais en soumettant alors le tiers à toutes les contraintes nées du contrat (clauses limitatives ou exclusives de responsabilité, clauses de compétence, limite de la prévisibilité du dommage...). Cette solution répondrait à l'argument le plus souvent invoqué contre l'assimilation des fautes (qui, actuellement, permet au tiers à la fois de se fonder sur le contrat, et d'en éluder tous les inconvénients). Elle conduirait également à faire disparaître toutes les controverses et distinctions liées aux chaînes et aux groupes de contrats, ainsi que d'absorber la situation des victimes par ricochet. Cependant, le groupe maintient la possibilité pour le tiers qui souhaite échapper aux contraintes d'un contrat auquel il n'a pas été partie de se fonder sur la responsabilité extracontractuelle, mais il doit alors prouver toutes les conditions nécessaires à la mise en jeu de cette responsabilité.

Nonetheless, where such a non-performance causes personal injury, the other party to the contract can, in order to obtain reparation for this harm, opt in favour of the rules which are more favourable to him.

Art. 1342[1]

Where non-performance of a contractual obligation is the direct cause of harm suffered by a third party, the latter can claim reparation from the contractual debtor on the basis of articles 1363 to 1366. The third party is then subject to all the limits and conditions which apply to the creditor in obtaining reparation for his own harm.

He may equally obtain reparation on the basis of extra-contractual liability, but on condition that he establishes one of the events giving rise to liability envisaged by articles 1352 to 1362.

Chapter II
The Conditions of Liability

Section 1
Provisions Common to Contractual and Extra-Contractual Liability

§ 1 Reparable loss

The definition of reparable loss remains quite general, but the allusion to the prejudicing of a collective interest seems useful, notably in order to serve as a basis for the reparation of environmental damage.

[1] This text is the result of lengthy consideration....
After receiving notice of the work of Group 10 of the wider working group on the effects of contracts as regards third parties, the most balanced solution appeared to be to grant in principle an action for reparation to third parties allowing them to rely on non-performance of the contract where it has caused them a loss (this being at present accepted by the *Cour de cassation* by means of the assimilation of contractual and delictual fault), but by subjecting the third party to all the restrictions which arise from the contract (limitation or exclusion clauses, jurisdiction clauses, the extent of the forseeability of harm, etc.). This solution would address the argument which is most often put against the assimilation of contractual and delictual fault (which at the moment allows a third party to base a claim on the contract but at the same time avoid its disadvantages). It would also lead to the extinguishing of all the controversies and the distinctions tied to chains of contracts and contractual groups, as well as mopping up the cases dealing with indirect victims. Nevertheless, the working group preserves the possibility for a third party who wishes to escape the restrictions of a contract to which he has not been a party to rely on extra-contractual liability, but he must then establish all the conditions which this liability requires for its imposition. [On 'chains of contracts' and 'contractual groups' see Mazeaud, above, p 227; S Whittaker, 'Privity of Contract and the Law of Tort: The French Experience' (1995) 15 Oxford Journal of Legal Studies 327. 'Indirect victims' translates '*les victimes par ricochet*'. So, for example, a person who is killed in a road accident is *la victime*—or sometimes *la victime directe* as in article 1385-4 of the *Avant-projet*—whereas his relatives or others who suffer grief, loss of dependency or some other financial loss owing to his death are *les victimes par ricochet*].

Il semble également souhaitable de consacrer des dispositions spéciales aux dépenses effectuées pour minimiser les conséquences du fait dommageable et à la perte d'une chance.

Art. 1343[1]

Est réparable tout préjudice[2] certain consistant dans la lésion d'un intérêt licite, patrimonial ou extrapatrimonial, individuel ou collectif.[4]

Art. 1344

Les dépenses exposées pour prévenir la réalisation imminente d'un dommage ou pour éviter son aggravation, ainsi que pour en réduire les conséquences, constituent un préjudice réparable, dès lors qu'elles ont été raisonnablement engagées.

Art. 1345

Le préjudice futur est réparable lorsqu'il est la prolongation certaine et directe d'un état de chose actuel.[6]

Lorsque la certitude du préjudice dépend d'un événement futur et incertain, le juge peut condamner immédiatement le responsable en subordonnant l'exécution de sa décision à la réalisation de cet événement.[7]

---

[1] Une discussion s'est engagée sur l'opportunité de donner dans le Code une définition du dommage (ou du préjudice) réparable, qui fait actuellement défaut. En dépit de la difficulté de cette définition, le groupe décide de ne pas laisser passer l'occasion.

Le groupe décide, après discussion, de consacrer deux textes à deux points discutés: les dépenses effectuées pour prévenir la réalisation d'un dommage, et la perte d'une chance. En revanche, il n'apparaît pas utile de consacrer un article spécial aux pertes d'exploitation.

[2] Dans toute la mesure du possible, le groupe a essayé de donner des sens distincts aux termes « dommage » et «préjudice », le dommage désignant l'atteinte à la personne ou aux biens de la victime et le préjudice, la lésion des intérêts patrimoniaux ou extrapatrimoniaux qui en résulte.

[4] Le terme « collectif » a été introduit afin de permettre aux tribunaux d'admettre notamment l'indemnisation du préjudice écologique. Cependant le groupe n'a pas pris parti sur le point de savoir qui peut agir en réparation (individus lésés, associations regroupant ceux-ci...). Il a estimé que cette question relève plutôt de la procédure.

[6] Cette formule est empruntée à certains arrêts de la Cour de cassation.

[7] Cette solution, admise par la jurisprudence au profit des victimes séropositives menacées par le SIDA, paraît généralisable.

It also seems desirable to dedicate some special provisions to expenses which are incurred to mitigate the consequences of a harmful act and to loss of a chance.

Art. 1343[1]

Any certain loss[2] is reparable where it consists of the prejudicing of a legitimate interest, whether or not relating to assets[3] and whether individual or collective.[4]

Art. 1344

Expenses incurred in order to prevent the imminent occurrence of harm, to avoid its getting worse, or to reduce its consequences, constitute a reparable loss as long as they were reasonably undertaken.[5]

Art. 1345

Future loss is reparable where it consists of the certain and direct continuation of a present state of affairs.[6]

Where the certainty of a loss depends on a future and uncertain event, the court may give immediate judgment against the person responsible, though subjecting the execution of its decision to the occurrence of the event.[7]

---

[1] A discussion took place as to the appropriateness of providing in the Code a definition of reparable harm ['*dommage*'] (or of reparable loss ['*préjudice*']), which at the moment it lacks. Despite the difficulty of doing so, the working group decided not to miss this opportunity.

The group decided after discussion to dedicate two provisions to two debated points: expenses incurred to prevent harm occurring and loss of a chance. On the other hand, it did not seem useful to dedicate a special article to loss of profits.

[2] As far as possible, the working group tried to give distinct meanings to the terms 'harm' ['*dommage*'] and 'loss' ['*préjudice*']: harm designates the actual injuring of the victim's person or property, whereas 'loss' designates the prejudice to the victim's interests which is thereby caused, whether or not relating to his assets.

[3] [Literally, 'whether patrimonial or extrapatrimonial'. 'A patrimonial damage is one which damages the victim's estate ('*le patrimoine*'), his property or his wealth': M Fabre-Magnan, *Les obligations* (Paris, PUF, 2004) no 254. As its name suggests, extra-patrimonial interests consist of all those which do not relate to a person's property or wealth, their damaging being personal and termed *dommage moral* ('moral damage'). *Dommage moral* is a fairly broad category with no common law equivalent, but it includes grief, upset or mental distress, loss of amenity, loss to reputation, loss of privacy, and ecological damage: P Malaurie, L Aynès and P Stoffel-Munck, *Les obligations* (2nd edn, Paris, Defrénois, 2005) no 248.]

[4] The term 'collective' was introduced in order to permit the courts to accept the compensation of environmental damage. Nonetheless, the group did not take a view on the question as to who can claim reparation for this sort of loss (whether individual persons harmed, associations of groups of such persons, etc.). It considered that this question was one of procedure. [The reason, therefore, for the lack of its resolution here stems, therefore, from the contrast between the Civil Code (which deals with substantive law) and the Code of Civil Procedure.]

[5] [On the present denial of a 'duty of mitigation' by French law see S Le Pautremat, 'Mitigation of Damage: A French Perspective' (2006) 55 ICLQ 205; S Whittaker, 'Contributory Fault and Mitigation, Rights and Reasonableness: Comparisons between English and French law' in L Tichý (ed) *Causation in Law* (Prague, 2007) 147.

[6] This form of words is borrowed from certain judgments of the *Cour de cassation* [eg Req 1 Jun 1932, DP 1932.1.102 rapp E Pilon, S 1933.3.49 note H Mazeaud].

[7] This solution which has been accepted by the courts for the benefit of HIV victims who are threatened by AIDS, seems capable of generalisation.

Art. 1346

La perte d'une chance constitue un préjudice réparable distinct de l'avantage qu'aurait procuré cette chance si elle s'était réalisée.

§2 – Le lien de causalité

Il paraît illusoire de chercher à définir le lien de causalité par une formule générale. En revanche, l'affirmation de la responsabilité solidaire des membres d'un groupe d'où émane le dommage, lorsque l'auteur n'est pas identifié, semble utile, cette solidarité étant susceptible de s'appliquer dans des circonstances diverses.

Art. 1347

La responsabilité suppose établi un lien de causalité entre le fait imputé au défendeur et le dommage.

Art. 1348

Lorsqu'un dommage est causé par un membre indéterminé d'un groupe, tous les membres identifiés en répondent solidairement sauf pour chacun d'eux à démontrer qu'il ne peut en être l'auteur.[1]

§3 – Les causes d'exonération

Le texte consacre la notion de cause étrangère en se contentant d'énumérer les faits d'où elle provient. En revanche, il définit la force majeure en reprenant l'une des formulations mises au point par la Cour de cassation.

Les modifications par rapport aux solutions actuelles concernent la faute de la victime dont l'effet exonératoire est exclu lorsque l'auteur est privé de discernement et atténué lorsqu'elle subit un dommage corporel. En revanche, il est précisé que la faute intentionnelle de la victime la prive de toute réparation.

Art. 1349

La responsabilité n'est pas engagée lorsque le dommage est dû à une cause étrangère présentant les caractères de la force majeure.

La cause étrangère peut provenir d'un cas fortuit, du fait de la victime ou du fait d'un tiers dont le défendeur n'a pas à répondre.

La force majeure consiste en un événement irrésistible que l'agent ne pouvait prévoir ou dont on ne pouvait éviter les effets par des mesures appropriées.

Art. 1350

La victime est privée de toute réparation lorsqu'elle a recherché volontairement le dommage.

[1] Ce texte, qui évoque la jurisprudence bien connue sur les accidents de chasse, pourrait apporter une solution dans bien d'autres situations, en particulier en cas de dommages causés par un produit distribué par quelques entreprises, toutes identifiées, lorsqu'on ne peut établir laquelle d'entre elles a vendu le produit même qui est à l'origine des préjudices subis par les victimes.

Art. 1346

Loss of a chance constitutes a reparable loss distinct from the advantage which would have inured to the claimant's benefit if the chance had materialised.

§ 2 Causation

It seems pointless to try to define the requirement of a causal connection by a general formula. On the other hand, the declaration of the joint and several liability of members of a group from whose activities a harm emerges (where the actual person who caused the harm is not identified) seems useful, this joint and several liability being capable of applying in a variety of situations.

Art. 1347

Liability rests on a causal connection between an action attributable to the defendant and the harm.

Art. 1348

Where harm is caused by an unascertained member of a group, all its identified members are answerable for it jointly and severally, except that any one of them may escape liability by showing that his own actions were not implicated.[1]

§ 3 Defences

The text of the following provisions formally recognises the notion of an external cause but at the same time is content to do so by setting out the circumstances in which it arises. On the other hand, it defines force majeure *by taking up one of the formulations refined by the Cour de cassation.*

The modifications proposed when put beside the present solutions concern fault in the victim, whose exempting effect is excluded where the victim lacks understanding and reduced where he suffers personal injuries. On the other hand, it makes clear that any intentional fault of the victim deprives him of any claim to reparation.

Art. 1349

Liability is not imposed where the harm is due to an external cause which qualifies as *force majeure*.

An external cause may arise from an act of God, from an action of the victim, or from an action of a third party for whom the defendant is not responsible.

Force majeure consists of an unpreventable event which the defendant could not foresee or whose consequences he could not avoid by appropriate measures.

Art. 1350

A victim cannot recover any reparation where he deliberately sought the harm.

---

[1] This text, which invokes the very well-known case-law on hunting accidents, should also provide a solution in many other situations, in particular in the case of harm caused by a product distributed by several identified businesses, but where it cannot be established which of them sold the product which was the source of the losses caused to the victims.

Art. 1351

L'exonération partielle ne peut résulter que d'une faute de la victime ayant concouru à la production du dommage.[1] En cas d'atteinte à l'intégrité physique, seule une faute grave peut entraîner l'exonération partielle.[2]

Art. 1351-1

Les exonérations prévues aux deux articles précédents ne sont pas applicables aux personnes privées de discernement.

Section 2
Dispositions propres à la responsabilité extra-contractuelle

§1 – Le fait personnel

Une définition de portée générale de la faute est proposée ainsi qu'une précision concernant la faute de la personne morale qui peut tenir à son organisation ou à son fonctionnement.

Art. 1352

Toute faute oblige son auteur à réparer le dommage qu'il a causé.

Constitue une faute la violation d'une règle de conduite imposée par une loi ou un règlement ou le manquement au devoir général de prudence ou de diligence.

Il n'y a pas de faute lorsque l'auteur se trouve dans l'une des situations prévues aux articles 122-4 à 122-7 du Code pénal.[3]

Art. 1353

La faute de la personne morale s'entend non seulement de celle qui est commise par un représentant, mais aussi de celle qui résulte d'un défaut d'organisation ou de fonctionnement.[4]

---

[1] Des discussions ont eu lieu pour déterminer s'il convient d'écrire « de son propre dommage », ce qui aurait pour effet de condamner l'opposabilité de la faute de la victime initiale aux victimes par ricochet (solution admise par la Cour de cassation qui s'est prononcée sur ce point en assemblée plénière en 1981). La rédaction choisie présente l'avantage de laisser ouverte la possibilité d'une évolution.

[2] Cette solution n'est pas admise actuellement en droit positif. C'est une manifestation de faveur à l'égard des victimes de dommages corporels.

[3] Définissant les faits justificatifs.

[4] La notion de « défaut d'organisation ou de fonctionnement », couramment admise par les juridictions administratives, paraît utilement transposable en droit privé.

Art. 1351

A partial defence to liability can apply only where the victim's fault contributed to the production of the harm.[1] In the case of personal injury, only a serious fault can lead to a partial defence.[2]

Art. 1351-1

The defences provided for in the two preceding articles may not be relied on against persons lacking understanding.

Section 2
Provisions Special to Extra-Contractual Liability

§ 1 Liability for personal action

Here, the group recommends a general definition of fault, coupled with a clarification that fault in a legal person may relate either to its organisation or to its operation.

Art. 1352

A person must make reparation for the harm which he has caused through any type of fault.

Fault consists of breach of a rule of conduct imposed by legislation or regulation or failure to conform to a general duty of care and diligence.

Where a person's action falls within one of the situations governed by articles 122-4 to 122-7 of the Criminal Code no fault is committed.[3]

Art. 1353

A legal person may commit a fault not only through its representative, but also by a failure in its organisation or operation.[4]

---

[1] Discussion took place to decide if it is appropriate to write 'for his harm', which would have had the effect of refusing to allow the initial victim's fault to prejudice indirect victims (the solution accepted by the Cour de cassation which so held on this point in *Assemblée plénière* in 1981). The form of words chosen offers the advantage of leaving open the possibility of development.

[2] This solution is not at present accepted in the law as it stands. It is a manifestation of the special treatment of victims of personal injuries.

[3] These provisions define justifying circumstances [for the purposes of criminal responsibility. They provide for defences of self-defence and of necessity.].

[4] The notion of a 'failure in organisation or operation', which is at present used by the administrative courts, seems usefully to be transplanted into private law. [On the administrative law see Y Gaudemet, *Traité de droit administratif*, vol 1, *Droit administratif général* (16th edn, Paris, LGDJ, 2001) 806-807 and (in English) Fairgrieve, *State Liability in Tort: a Comparative Study*, above, p 827, n 2, 103–105.]

§2 – Le fait des choses[1]

Ce paragraphe vise à consacrer les solutions jurisprudentielles admises actuellement.

Art. 1354

On est responsable de plein droit[3] des dommages causés par le fait des choses que l'on a sous sa garde.

Art. 1354-1

Le fait de la chose est établi dès lors que celle-ci, en mouvement, est entrée en contact avec le siège du dommage.

Dans les autres cas, il appartient à la victime de prouver le fait de la chose, en établissant soit le vice de celle-ci, soit l'anormalité de sa position ou de son état.

Art. 1354-2

Le gardien est celui qui a la maîtrise de la chose au moment du fait dommageable.

Le propriétaire est présumé gardien.

Art. 1354-3

Ni le vice de la chose, ni le trouble physique du gardien ne constituent une cause d'exonération.

Art. 1354-4

Les articles 1354 à 1354-3 sont applicables aux dommages causés par les animaux.

§3 – Le fait d'autrui

La liste de cas de responsabilité pour autrui est assez profondément modifiée par rapport au droit actuel. Les régimes spéciaux de responsabilité de l'artisan pour le fait de ses apprentis et de l'instituteur par le fait de ses élèves sont supprimés.

Les cas retenus se rattachent à deux modèles différents. Certains sont fondés sur le contrôle du mode de vie des mineurs et des majeurs dont l'état ou la situation nécessite une surveillance particulière. D'autres visent les personnes qui contrôlent l'activité d'autrui et profitent de celle-ci. Au second modèle

---

[1] Une discussion a eu lieu au sein du groupe au sujet de l'utilité et de l'opportunité du maintien du régime de la responsabilité du fait des choses tel qu'il a été construit par la jurisprudence sur le fondement de l'article 1384 al. 1er du code civil.

Cette construction a perdu une partie de son intérêt depuis la promulgation de la loi du 5 juillet 1985 sur l'indemnisation des victimes d'accidents de la circulation.

En outre, aucun autre pays ne connaît un régime semblable et il apparaît, par comparaison avec les droits étrangers, d'une grande sévérité. Certains se demandent donc s'il ne serait pas souhaitable de le remplacer par un principe de responsabilité de plein droit du fait des activités dangereuses, comme celui qu'admet la jurisprudence administrative. Cette solution rapprocherait le droit français de la plupart des autres droits européens.

[3] Cette précision est apportée pour indiquer clairement qu'il n'y a pas d'exonération possible pour absence de faute.

§ 2 Liability for the actions of things[1]

This paragraph seeks to give formal recognition to existing case-law solutions.[2]

Art. 1354

A person is liable strictly[3] for harm caused by the action of things within his keeping.

Art. 1354-1

An action of a thing is established wherever, while moving, it comes into contact with the person or property which is harmed.[4]

In other situations, it is for the victim to prove the action of the thing, by showing either its defect, or the abnormality of its position or of its condition.

Art. 1354-2

The keeper of a thing is the person who has control of it at the time of its causing harm.

The owner of a thing is presumed to be its keeper.

Art. 1354-3

It is no defence to a keeper of a thing to show its own defect nor any physical problem in himself.

Art. 1354-4

Articles 1354 to 1354-3 apply to harm caused by animals.

§ 3 Liability for the actions of other people

The list of situations in which liability is imposed for the actions of other people is profoundly changed from the position under the present law. The special regimes of liability of artisans for the actions of their apprentices and of teachers for the actions of their pupils are abolished.

The situations where liability is preserved follow two different models. Some are founded on the control over the way of life of minors or over adults whose condition or situation require some special supervision. Other situations concern persons who organise and profit from the activity of another person.

---

[1] Discussion took place within the group as to the usefulness and the appropriateness of maintaining the special regime of liability for the actions of things as it has been built up by case-law on the basis of art 1384(1) of the Civil Code.

This construction lost part of its significance after the enactment of the Law of 5 July 1985 on the compensation of traffic accident victims [see above, p 811, n 3].

Furthermore, no other country recognises a similar special regime and by comparison with foreign laws it appears very harsh. Some members of the group wondered whether it would be desirable to replace it with a principle of strict liability for dangerous activities, like the one accepted by French administrative courts. Such a solution would draw French law closer to most of the other European national laws.

[2] [For an introduction in English to this case-law, see S Whittaker, 'The Law of Obligations' in Bell, Boyron and Whittaker, above, p 465, n 3, 382–393.]

[3] This clarification is made in order to indicate that no defence is available on proving an absence of fault.

[4] ['person or property which is harmed' translates '*siège du dommage*', literally, the 'seat' or 'locus of the damage'.]

sont rattachées non seulement la responsabilité du commettant pour le fait de son préposé, mais aussi celle des personnes physiques ou morales qui encadrent l'activité des professionnels non préposés et sont intéressées à cette activité.

Ces responsabilités sont strictes. Elles ne sont pas subordonnées à la preuve de la faute du responsable, mais à celle d'un fait qui aurait été susceptible d'engager la responsabilité personnelle de l'auteur direct s'il n'avait pas agi sous le contrôle d'autrui.

La responsabilité personnelle du préposé ne peut être engagée qu'à la condition que la victime ne puisse obtenir réparation ni du commettant ni de son assureur. En revanche celle des professionnels non préposés dont répond autrui demeure soumise au droit commun.

Art. 1355[2]

On est responsable de plein droit des dommages causés par ceux dont on règle le mode de vie ou dont on organise, encadre ou contrôle l'activité dans son propre intérêt.[3]

Cette responsabilité a lieu dans les cas et aux conditions prévues aux articles 1356 à 1360. Elle suppose la preuve d'un fait de nature à engager la responsabilité de l'auteur direct du dommage.

Art. 1356

Sont responsables des dommages causés par un enfant mineur :

– ses père et mère en tant qu'ils exercent l'autorité parentale,

– le tuteur en cas de décès de ceux-ci,

– la personne physique ou morale chargée par décision judiciaire ou administrative ou par convention, de régler le mode de vie du mineur. Cette responsabilité peut se cumuler avec celle des parents ou du tuteur.[4]

Art. 1357

Est responsable des dommages causés par un majeur dont l'état ou la situation[5] nécessite une surveillance particulière la personne physique ou morale chargée, par décision judiciaire ou administrative ou par convention, de régler son mode de vie.

---

[2] Cet article est un texte d'annonce des différents cas de responsabilité du fait d'autrui.

[3] Une hésitation s'est manifestée au sujet du choix entre «profit », « avantage » et « intérêt ». Ce dernier terme a été préféré parce que plus neutre que les autres et susceptible d'englober le cas de l'aide bénévole.

[4] ? ? ? ? ? ? Cette possibilité de cumul est actuellement écartée par la Cour de cassation. Elle a fait l'objet de discussions au sein du groupe de travail.

[5] L'état désigne une déficience physique ou mentale, tandis que la situation vise, par exemple, le cas de l'incarcération ou du contrôle exercé par une autorité judiciaire ou une personne déléguée par celle-ci.

This second model underpins not only employers' liability for the actions of their employees,[1] but also the liability of physical or legal persons who organise and have an interest in the activity of professionals or businesses (not being their employees).

These liabilities are strict. They do not rest on proof of fault in the person to be held liable, but on proof of an action which would have attracted a personal liability in the person directly behind the harm if he had not acted under another person's control.

Employees are not to be liable personally unless the victim is unable to obtain reparation either from his employer or the latter's insurer. On the other hand, the liability of professionals or businesses who are not employed, for whom another person is answerable, remains governed by the general law.

Art. 1355[2]

A person is liable strictly for harm caused by persons whose way of life he governs or whose activity he organises, regulates or controls in his own interest.[3]

This liability may arise in the situations and subject to the conditions provided for by articles 1356 to 1360. It rests on proof of an action of a kind which would attract liability in a person who caused the harm directly.

Art. 1356

The following are liable for harm caused by their minor children:

– fathers and mothers to the extent to which they exercise parental authority;

– guardians in the case of the death of both parents;

– the physical or legal person charged by judicial or administrative decision, or by agreement, with regulating the minor's way of life. This liability may arise concurrently with liability in a minor's parents or guardian.[4]

Art. 1357

A physical or legal person is liable for harm caused by an adult whose condition or situation[5] require some special supervision where they are charged by judicial or administrative decision, or by agreement, with regulating the adult's way of life.

---

[1] [See above, p 825, n 1 on 'employer' and 'employee'.]

[2] This article is an introductory provision of the different situations of liability for the actions of others.

[3] Some doubt was expressed as to whether to choose 'profit', 'advantage' or 'interest'. This last term was preferred as being more neutral than the others and more capable of including the case where a person helps another without reward.

[4] *Sed quaere*. This possibility of concurrence is presently rejected by the *Cour de cassation*. [See eg Cass crim 15 June 2000, Bull crim no 232.] It was the subject of discussion within the working group.

[5] 'Condition' relates to a person's physical or mental deficiencies, whilst 'situation' envisages the case, for example, of a person being imprisoned or controlled by judicial authority or its delegate.

Art. 1358

Les autres personnes qui assument, à titre professionnel, une mission de surveillance d'autrui, répondent du fait de l'auteur direct du dommage, à moins qu'elles ne démontrent qu'elles n'ont pas commis de faute.[1]

Art. 1359

Le commettant est responsable des dommages causés par son préposé. Est commettant celui qui a le pouvoir de donner des ordres ou des instructions en relation avec l'accomplissement des fonctions du préposé .[2]

Le commettant n'est pas responsable s'il prouve que le préposé a agi hors des fonctions auxquelles il était employé, sans autorisation et à des fins étrangères à ses attributions.[3] Il ne l'est pas davantage s'il établit que la victime ne pouvait légitimement croire que le préposé agissait pour le compte du commettant.[4]

Art. 1359-1

Le préposé qui, sans commettre une faute intentionnelle, a agi dans le cadre de ses fonctions, à des fins conformes à ses attributions et sans enfreindre les ordres de son commettant ne peut voir sa responsabilité personnelle engagée par la victime qu'à condition pour celle-ci de prouver qu'elle n'a pu obtenir du commettant ni de son assureur réparation de son dommage.[5]

Art. 1360[6]

En l'absence de lien de préposition, celui qui encadre ou organise l'activité professionnelle d'une autre personne et en tire un avantage économique est responsable des dommages causés par celle-ci dans l'exercice de cette activité. Il en est ainsi notamment des établissements de soins pour les dommages causés par les médecins qu'ils emploient. Il appartient au demandeur d'établir que le fait dommageable résulte de l'activité considérée.

[1] Ce texte vise, par exemple, l'assistance maternelle, le centre de loisirs ou l'école à laquelle un enfant a été confié temporairement par ses parents.

[2] Cette définition est plus étroite que celle qui est admise aujourd'hui par la jurisprudence. Cela s'explique par l'existence d'autres cas de « contrôle de l'activité d'autrui » (voir article 1360).

[3] Cette formule est celle qu'a utilisée l'assemblée plénière dans son arrêt du 19 mai 1988.

[4] Ce texte reprend une jurisprudence bien établie. Il procède de l'idée que si la victime est de mauvaise foi, le commettant doit être exonéré même s'il n'y a pas cumul des trois conditions qui, dans la première phrase, sont constitutives de l'abus de fonctions exonérant le commettant.

[5] Cette disposition propose de modifier la solution adoptée par l'Assemblée plénière de la Cour de cassation dans son arrêt Costedoat du 25 février 2000. Au lieu d'écarter la responsabilité personnelle du préposé, elle la rend subsidiaire par rapport à celle du commettant..

[6] Les hypothèses visées par les deux alinéas de cet article ne sont pas exactement les mêmes:

L'alinéa 1er désigne les « salariés libres » c'est-à-dire ceux qui ne reçoivent pas « d'ordres ni d'instructions » (par exemple le médecin salarié).

L'alinéa 2 vise essentiellement les rapports franchiseurs-franchisés, sociétés mères-filiales (d'où la précision « bien qu'agissant pour son propre compte »).

Art. 1358

Other persons who take on the task of supervising another person in the course of business or by way of their profession are answerable for the action of the person directly behind the harm, unless they show that they did not commit any fault.[1]

Art. 1359

Employers are liable for harm caused by their employees. Employers are persons who have the power to give orders or instructions in relation to the performance of the work or duties of their employees.[2]

Employers are not liable on this basis if they prove that their employees acted outside the sphere of their duties for which they were engaged, without authority and for purposes outside their own roles.[3] Nor are they liable if they prove that the victim could not legitimately believe that the employee was acting on behalf of the employer.[4]

Art. 1359-1

Employees who, without committing an intentional fault, have acted within the limits of their functions, for purposes which conform to their roles and without disobeying their employers' orders, cannot incur personal liability towards their victims unless the latter on their side establish their inability to obtain reparation for their harm from the employer or his insurer.[5]

Art. 1360[6]

Apart from cases involving a relationship of employment, a person is liable for harm caused by another person whose professional or business activity he regulates or organises and from which he derives an economic advantage where this occurs in the course of this activity. This includes notably the liability of healthcare establishments for harm caused by the doctors to whom they have recourse. The claimant must show that the harmful action results from the activity in question.

[1] This text concerns, for example, child-minders, leisure centres or schools to whom a child is temporarily entrusted by its parents.

[2] This definition is narrower than the one which is at present accepted by the courts. This is explained by the existence in the Reform Proposals of other cases of 'control over the activity of another person' (see article 1360). [On the broader understanding of '*préposé*' under the present law, see above, p 825, n 1.]

[3] This formula is the one used by the *Assemblée plénière* of the *Cour de cassation* in its judgment of 19 May 1988 [Bull Crim 1988 no 218.].

[4] This text reflects a well-established line of case-law. It starts from the idea that if the victim is in bad faith, the employer must be excused from liability even if the standard three conditions for this (which are set out in the first part of the article and define an employee's abuse of functions) are not satisfied.

[5] This provision recommends that the solution adopted by the *Assemblée plénière* of the *Cour de cassation* in the *Costedoat* case of 25 February, 2000 [Bull 2000 AP No 2 p 3], be amended. Instead of ruling out personal liability of employees, it renders it subsidiary to the liability of employers.

[6] The situations envisaged by these two paragraphs are not exactly the same:

The first paragraph refers to 'independent workers', that is, those who do not receive 'either orders or instructions' (for example, a salaried doctor).

The second paragraph is concerned essentially with the relationships of franchisors and franchisees and parent companies and their subsidiaries (hence the clarification 'even though acting on his own account').

De même, est responsable celui qui contrôle l'activité économique ou patrimoniale d'un professionnel en situation de dépendance, bien qu'agissant pour son propre compte, lorsque la victime établit que le fait dommageable est en relation avec l'exercice du contrôle. Il en est ainsi notamment des sociétés mères pour les dommages causés par leurs filiales ou des concédants pour les dommages causés par leurs concessionnaires.

§4 – Les troubles de voisinage

Le régime construit par la jurisprudence est maintenu. En revanche, son domaine est modifié car il est apparu que la responsabilité de l'entrepreneur pour les dommages causés aux voisins du maître de l'ouvrage relève d'une autre logique.

Art. 1361

Le propriétaire, le détenteur ou l'exploitant d'un fonds, qui provoque un trouble excédant les inconvénients normaux du voisinage, est de plein droit responsable des conséquences de ce trouble.

§5 – Les activités dangereuses[3]

Cette disposition est innovante. Elle est destinée à doter le droit français d'un régime de responsabilité adapté notamment aux catastrophes industrielles de grande ampleur.

Art. 1362

Sans préjudice de dispositions spéciales[4], l'exploitant d'une activité anormalement dangereuse, même licite, est tenu de réparer le dommage consécutif à cette activité.

Est réputée anormalement dangereuse l'activité qui crée un risque de dommages graves pouvant affecter un grand nombre de personnes simultanément.[5]

---

[3] On a vu (supra p 844 note 1) qu'une discussion a eu lieu au sein du groupe au sujet de l'opportunité de maintenir la responsabilité du fait des choses ou d'adopter un modèle du type « responsabilité du fait des activités dangereuses » connu par beaucoup de droits étrangers. Pour certains, le fait d'avoir opté en faveur du maintien de la responsabilité du fait des choses ne laisserait d'utilité à l'admission d'une responsabilité de plein droit du fait des activités dangereuses que si ce régime est caractérisé par une limitation plus stricte des causes d'exonération (que prévoit l'alinéa 2). Pour d'autres, les dispositions des articles 1354 à 1354-4, d'une part, et 1362, d'autre part, ne s'appliqueraient pas aux mêmes situations : voir, à ce sujet, le rapport introductif, III, 5°.

[4] Il s'agit des textes instituant une responsabilité de plein droit à la charge de certains exploitants, notamment les compagnies aériennes pour les dommages causés au sol par les appareils, les exploitants de téléphériques pour les dommages causés aux tiers, les exploitants de réacteurs nucléaires pour les accidents survenus sur le site, etc. Le système proposé est très proche de celui qui inspire ces textes particuliers. A terme, on peut donc prévoir que certains d'entre eux pourraient disparaître, absorbés par la disposition générale.

[5] L'hypothèse visée est celle des dommages de masse, par exemple ceux qui résultent d'un accident industriel comme celui qui a détruit l'usine AZF à Toulouse.

Similarly, a person who controls the economic or financial[1] activity of a business or professional person who is factually dependent on that person even though acting on his own account, is liable for harm caused by this dependent where the victim shows that the harmful action relates to the first person's exercise of control. This is the case in particular as regards parent companies in relation to harm caused by their subsidiaries or as regards those granting a concession in relation to harm caused by a person to whom the concession is granted.

§ 4 Liability for nuisance[2]

Here, the regime of liability built up by the courts is maintained. On the other hand, its ambit is modified for it appeared that the liability of a building contractor for harm caused to the neighbours of the person commissioning the building work rests on another rationale.

Art. 1361

A person who owns, holds or exploits land and who causes a nuisance exceeding the normal inconveniences to be expected of neighbours, is liable strictly for the consequences of this nuisance.

§ 5 Liability for dangerous activities[3]

This provision is innovative. It is intended to provide for French law a regime of liability suitable notably to deal with large-scale industrial catastrophes.

Art. 1362

Without prejudice to any special regulation governing particular situations,[4] a person who undertakes an abnormally dangerous activity is bound to make reparation for the harm which results from this activity even if it is lawful.

An activity which creates a risk of serious harm capable of affecting a large number of people simultaneously is deemed to be abnormally dangerous.[5]

---

[1] ['Patrimonial'; see above, p 483, n 3.]

[2] [For discussion of the private law governing liability for nuisance (*troubles de voisinage*) see P Malaurie and L Aynès, *Droit civil, Les biens*, above, p 581, n 1, nos 1069-1075.]

[3] It was seen (above, p 845, n 1) that a discussion took place within the group as to the appropriateness of maintaining the category of liability for the actions of things or whether instead to adopt a model of the type known by many foreign laws which rests on 'liability for harm caused by dangerous activities'. In the view of some members, having once decided to retain liability for the actions of things there was no point in creating a strict liability for dangerous activities unless the latter regime were to be distinguished by a stricter set of defences (as set out by paragraph 2). In the view of others, the provisions contained in articles 1354 to 1354-4 on the one hand, and in article 1362 on the other, would not apply to the same situations: see further on this subject, the introductory report at section III(5).

[4] This qualification concerns legal provisions imposing strict liabilities on certain operators, notably, air companies for harm caused to land by their machines, telecommunications companies for harm caused to third parties, nuclear energy undertakings for accidents on site, etc. The proposed scheme is very similar to that which inspires these special legal provisions. In the end, one might therefore expect that some of the latter might be absorbed by the general provision and disappear.

[5] The situation envisaged here is of catastrophic harm, for example, the harm which results from an industrial accident such as the one which destroyed the AZF factory at Toulouse [on 21 September 2001].

L'exploitant ne peut s'exonérer qu'en établissant l'existence d'une faute de la victime dans les conditions prévues aux articles 1349 à 1351-1.

Section 3
Dispositions propres à la responsabilité contractuelle[1]

Le fait générateur de la responsabilité contractuelle est l'inexécution qui s'apprécie en fonction de la portée de l'engagement. Un renvoi à l'article 1149 qui définit les obligations de moyens et de résultat est donc apparu nécessaire. Toutefois une autre rédaction de ce texte est proposée afin d'éviter toute redondance[2]

Le rôle de la mise en demeure est, par ailleurs, précisé.

Après discussion, le refus de la réparation du dommage contractuel imprévisible a été consacré.

Art. 1363

Le créancier d'une obligation issue d'un contrat valablement formé peut, en cas d'inexécution,[3] demander au débiteur réparation de son préjudice sur le fondement des dispositions de la présente section.

Art. 1364

Dans le cas où le débiteur s'oblige à procurer un résultat au sens de l'article 1149, l'inexécution est établie du seul fait que le résultat n'est pas atteint, à moins que le débiteur ne justifie d'une cause étrangère au sens de l'article 1349.

Dans tous les autres cas, il ne doit réparation que s'il n'a pas effectué toutes les diligences nécessaires.

---

[1] Sur la place faite à la spécificité de la responsabilité contractuelle, voir le rapport introductif, II et III, 1°.

[2] Cette rédaction est la suivante

« L'obligation est de résultat lorsque le débiteur s'engage à atteindre le but défini par le contrat. L'obligation est de moyens lorsque le débiteur s'engage seulement à fournir les soins et diligences normalement nécessaires à la réalisation de ce but. Cette obligation est plus ou moins étendue relativement à certains contrats dont les effets à cet égard sont expliqués sous les titres qui les concernent » (Cette dernière phrase est reprise de l'article 1137 actuel du code civil).

[3] L'inexécution est ici entendue dans un sens général qui englobe l'exécution défectueuse ou tardive.

A person who undertakes an abnormally dangerous activity cannot escape liability except by establishing a fault in the victim in the circumstances set out in articles 1349 to 1351-1.

Section 3
Provisions Special to Contractual Liability[1]

The event which forms the basis of contractual liability is non-performance of the contract and this is itself assessed as a function of the content of the contractual undertakings. For this reason, reference should be made to article 1149 which defines 'obligations to take necessary steps' and 'obligations of result'. All the same, another version of this text is proposed in order to avoid any redundance.[2]

This section also makes clear the role of giving notice to perform.

After discussion, it was decided to include a formal denial of reparation for unforeseeable contractual harm.

Art. 1363

A creditor of an obligation arising from a validly concluded contract can claim from the debtor reparation for his loss in the case of its non-performance[3] on the basis of the provisions contained in the present section.

Art. 1364

Where a debtor undertakes to procure a result within the meaning of article 1149, non-performance is established from the mere fact that the result is not achieved, unless the debtor justifies this failure by reference to an external cause within the meaning of article 1349.

In all other situations, a debtor must make reparation only if he has failed to use all necessary care.

---

[1] On the place assigned to the special characteristics of contractual liability, see the Preamble, II and III(1).

[2] This version is as follows:
'An obligation is termed an "obligation of result" where the debtor undertakes the accomplishment of an aim defined by the contract. An obligation is termed an "obligation to take necessary steps" where the debtor undertakes merely to use the effort and care which are normally necessary for the accomplishment of this aim. This type of obligation is more or less onerous in the case of certain types of contracts whose effects in this respect are explained in the Titles which deal with them' (this last phrase is taken from article 1137 of the present Civil Code).

[3] Non-performance for this purpose is to be understood in a broad sense so as to include both defective and late performance.

Art. 1365

La réparation du préjudice résultant du retard suppose la mise en demeure préalable du débiteur. La mise en demeure n'est requise pour la réparation de tout autre préjudice que lorsqu'elle est nécessaire pour caractériser l'inexécution.[1]

Art. 1366

Sauf dol ou faute lourde de sa part, le débiteur n'est tenu de réparer que les conséquences de l'inexécution raisonnablement prévisibles lors de la formation du contrat.

Chapitre III
Des effets de la responsabilité
Section 1
Principes

Art. 1367

La créance de réparation naît du jour de la réalisation du dommage ou, en cas de dommage futur, du jour où sa certitude est acquise.

Cette disposition est destinée à clarifier le droit positif qui, sur ce point, est ambigu.

Art. 1368

La réparation peut, au choix du juge, prendre la forme d'une réparation en nature ou d'une condamnation à des dommages-intérêts, ces deux types de mesures pouvant se cumuler afin d'assurer la réparation intégrale du préjudice.

La notion de « réparation en nature » est consacrée, y compris en matière contractuelle.

§1 – La réparation en nature

Ce paragraphe ne réglemente que les mesures de réparation en nature stricto sensu. Celles qui sont prévues par les actuels articles 1143 et 1144 concernent l'exécution et ne relèvent donc pas du titre « De la responsabilité ».

---

[1] La réglementation de la mise en demeure est renvoyée au groupe qui travaille sur l'exécution du contrat.

Art. 1365

Reparation for loss resulting from delay in performance presupposes a prior notice to perform made to the debtor. As regards reparation for any other loss, a notice to perform is required only where it is necessary in order establish that the debtor has indeed failed to perform.[1]

Art. 1366

Apart from cases of his deliberate or dishonest non-performance or gross fault, a debtor is liable to make reparation only for the consequences of non-performance which were reasonably foreseeable at the time of the conclusion of the contract.

Chapter III
The Effects of Liability
Section 1
Principles

Art. 1367

A right of reparation accrues as at the date when harm takes place or, in the case of future harm, the date when its occurrence has become certain.

> *This provision is intended to clarify the existing law which is ambiguous on this point.*

Art. 1368

Reparation of harm may at the court's discretion take the form of reparation in kind or of an award of damages and these two types of measures may be ordered concurrently so as to ensure full compensation of the victim's loss.

> *The notion of 'reparation in kind' is in this way formally recognised, including for the contractual context.*

§ 1 Reparation in kind

> *This paragraph governs only measures of reparation in kind in the strict sense. Those which are envisaged by articles 1143 and 1144 of the present Civil Code concern performance and are not therefore relevant to a title concerning 'liability'.*

---

[1] The rules governing 'notice to perform' ['*mise en demeure*'] were referred to the group working on the performance of contracts. [On the role of notice to perform in establishing the existence of a failure to perform by the debtor, see R Libchaber, 'Demeure et mise en demeure en droit français' in M Fontaine and G Viney (eds) *Les sanctions de l'inexécution des obligations contractuelles, Etudes de droit comparé* (Bruxelles, Bruyant, and Paris, LGDJ, 2001) 113, 129 ff.]

Art. 1369

Lorsque le juge ordonne une mesure de réparation en nature, celle-ci doit être spécifiquement apte à supprimer, réduire ou compenser le dommage.

Art. 1369-1

Lorsque le dommage est susceptible de s'aggraver, de se renouveler ou de se perpétuer, le juge peut ordonner, à la demande de la victime, toute mesure propre à éviter ces conséquences, y compris au besoin la cessation de l'activité dommageable.

Le juge peut également autoriser la victime à prendre elle-même ces mesures aux frais du responsable. Celui-ci peut être condamné à faire l'avance des sommes nécessaires.

§2 – Les dommages-intérêts

Les principales innovations prévues concernent les dommages-intérêts punitifs qui sont autorisés à certaines conditions (article 1371), la possibilité de réduire l'indemnisation lorsque la victime n'a pas fait preuve d'une diligence suffisante pour réduire le dommage ou en éviter l'aggravation (article 1373) ainsi que l'obligation pour le juge d'évaluer distinctement chacun des chefs de préjudice allégués (article 1374) et la possibilité qui lui est reconnue, dans des circonstances particulières, d'affecter les dommages-intérêts à une mesure de réparation spécifique. (article 1377)

Art. 1370

Sous réserve de dispositions ou de conventions contraires, l'allocation de dommages-intérêts doit avoir pour objet de replacer la victime autant qu'il est possible dans la situation où elle se serait trouvée si le fait dommageable n'avait pas eu lieu. Il ne doit en résulter pour elle ni perte ni profit.[2]

Art. 1371

L'auteur d'une faute manifestement délibérée, et notamment d'une faute lucrative, peut être condamné, outre les dommages-intérêts compensatoires, à des dommages-intérêts punitifs dont le juge a la faculté de faire bénéficier pour une part le Trésor public. La décision du juge d'octroyer de tels dommages-intérêts doit être spécialement motivée et leur montant distingué de celui des autres dommages-intérêts accordés à la victime. Les dommages-intérêts punitifs ne sont pas assurables.

---

[2] La réserve des dispositions ou conventions contraires permet de rendre ce texte compatible avec ceux sur la clause d'indemnisation forfaitaire (article 1383) ainsi qu'avec les dispositions légales ou réglementaires limitant la réparation de certains dommages. Par ailleurs, elle devrait assurer la compatibilité avec l'article suivant concernant les dommages-intérêts punitifs.

Art. 1369

Where a court orders a measure of reparation in kind, the latter must be specifically suitable to extinguish, reduce or make up for the harm.

Art. 1369-1

Where harm is liable to become worse, to reoccur or to linger, a court may, at the request of the victim, order any measure appropriate to avoid these consequences, including if need be an order for the discontinuation of the harmful activity in question.

Equally, a court may authorise the victim himself to take such measures at the expense of the person liable. The latter may be ordered to pay in advance an amount needed for this purpose.

§ 2 Damages[1]

The principal innovations envisaged here concern punitive damages which are authorised on certain conditions (article 1371); the possibility of reducing the victim's compensation where he has not shown that he took sufficient care in mitigating his own harm or preventing it from getting worse (article 1373); the imposition of a duty in courts to evaluate distinctly each of the heads of loss which are claimed (article 1374); and the recognition that a court may in special circumstances allocate damages to a specific measure of reparation (article 1377).

Art. 1370

Subject to special regulation or agreement to the contrary, the aim of an award of damages is to put the victim as far as possible in the position in which he would have been if the harmful circumstances had not taken place. He must make neither gain nor loss from it.[2]

Art. 1371

A person who commits a manifestly deliberate fault, and notably a fault with a view to gain, can be condemned in addition to compensatory damages to pay punitive damages, part of which the court may in its discretion allocate to the Public Treasury. A court's decision to order payment of damages of this kind must be supported with specific reasons and their amount distinguished from any other damages awarded to the victim. Punitive damages may not be the object of insurance.

---

[1] [See the discussion by Remy-Corlay, above, ch 14 and (on punitive damages in particular) Rowan, above, ch 15.]

[2] The qualification as regards regulation or agreement to the contrary allows this text to be rendered compatible with those governing clauses for a pre-set reparation (article 1383) as well as with legal or regulatory provisions limiting reparation in respect of certain types of harm. In addition, it ought to ensure consistency with the following article concerning punitive damages.

Art. 1372

Le juge évalue le préjudice au jour où il rend sa décision, en tenant compte de toutes les circonstances qui ont pu l'affecter dans sa consistance comme dans sa valeur, ainsi que de son évolution raisonnablement prévisible.

Art. 1373

Lorsque la victime avait la possibilité, par des moyens sûrs, raisonnables et proportionnés, de réduire l'étendue de son préjudice ou d'en éviter l'aggravation, il sera tenu compte de son abstention par une réduction de son indemnisation, sauf lorsque les mesures seraient de nature à porter atteinte à son intégrité physique.

Art. 1374

Le juge doit évaluer distinctement chacun des chefs de préjudice allégués qu'il prend en compte. En cas de rejet d'une demande relative à un chef de préjudice, le juge doit motiver spécialement sa décision.

Art. 1375

Si la victime établit qu'un chef de préjudice n'a pas fait encore l'objet d'une demande de sa part ou que son dommage s'est aggravé, elle peut obtenir en tout état de cause une réparation complémentaire, le cas échéant par l'introduction d'une action nouvelle.

Art. 1376

L'indemnité peut être allouée au choix du juge sous forme d'un capital ou d'une rente, sous réserve des dispositions de l'article 1379-3.

Art. 1377

Sauf circonstances particulières justifiant l'affectation par le juge des dommages-intérêts à une mesure de réparation spécifique,[2] la victime est libre de disposer comme elle l'entend des sommes qui lui sont allouées.

§3 – Incidence de la pluralité de responsables

Les solutions retenues sont très proches de celles qu'admet aujourd'hui la jurisprudence.

---

[2] Le texte ne définit pas ces « circonstances particulières ». L'un des cas où l'affectation des dommages-intérêts est le plus souvent préconisée est celui des atteintes à l'environnement.

Art. 1372

The court must assess the victim's loss as at the date of its judgment, taking into account all the circumstances which could affect its constituent elements, their value and its reasonably foreseeable future development.

Art. 1373

Where the victim had the possibility of taking reliable, reasonable and proportionate measures to reduce the extent of his loss or to avoid its getting worse, the court shall take account of his failure to do so by reducing his compensation, except where the measures to be taken were of a kind to have compromised his physical integrity.[1]

Art. 1374

The court must assess distinctly each of the heads of loss claimed of which it takes account. Where a claim concerning a particular head of loss is rejected, the court must give specific reasons for its decision.

Art. 1375

If the victim establishes that a head of loss had not already been the object of a claim by him or that his harm has become worse, he may obtain in any case a supplementary reparation, where appropriate by means of bringing a new action.

Art. 1376

A court may in its discretion award compensation either in a lump sum or by way of periodic payments, subject to the provisions contained in article 1379-3.

Art. 1377

Except where particular circumstances justify the allocation by the court of damages to a specific means of reparation,[2] the victim is free to dispose of the sums awarded to him as he thinks fit.

§ 3 The circumstances in which two or more persons are liable

The solutions adopted are very close to those at present accepted by the courts.

---

[1] [On this new 'duty to mitigate' see above, p 839, n 5.]

[2] The text does not define these 'particular circumstances'. One of the cases where the allocation of damages is most often advocated is the case of environmental damage.

860

Art. 1378

Tous les responsables d'un même dommage sont tenus solidairement[1] à réparation.

Si tous les co-auteurs ont vu leur responsabilité retenue pour faute prouvée, leur contribution se fait en proportion de la gravité de leurs fautes respectives.

Si aucun des co-auteurs n'est dans ce cas, ils contribuent tous par parts égales.

Sinon, la contribution est, en fonction de la gravité des fautes respectives, à la charge des seuls co-auteurs dont la faute est prouvée, qu'elle l'ait été par la victime, ou qu'elle le soit seulement à l'occasion d'un recours.[2]

Art. 1378-1[3]

Est irrecevable le recours en contribution contre un proche de la victime lorsqu'il n'est pas assuré et que le recours aurait pour effet de priver directement ou indirectement celle-ci, en raison de la communauté de vie qu'elle entretient avec le défendeur au recours, de la réparation à laquelle elle a droit.

Est également irrecevable le recours d'un débiteur d'indemnisation exercé contre la succession de la victime directe ou contre l'assureur de celle-ci.

---

[1] Il a paru inutile de maintenir la distinction entre obligation in solidum et solidarité.
[2] Sur ce dernier point, la solution proposée est différente de celle que consacre la jurisprudence actuelle.
[3] Ce texte étend des solutions qui ont été admises par la jurisprudence en matière d'accidents de la circulation.

Art. 1378

All persons liable for the same harm are held jointly and severally[1] liable to make reparation for it.

If all those who have caused the same harm were held liable on the basis of proven fault, their contribution is to be assessed in proportion to the seriousness of their respective faults.

If none of those liable are within this category, their contributions must be made in equal parts.

Where neither of these situations is the case, then the contribution of each person liable is to be assessed as a function of the seriousness of their respective faults where proved whether by the victim or merely at the stage of any claim for contribution.[2]

Art. 1378-1[3]

A claim for contribution is not admissible against a victim's relative where the latter is not insured and where the claim would have the effect directly or indirectly of depriving the victim of his rightful compensation because of their shared life together.

A claim for contribution by a person held liable to compensate is equally inadmissible against the victim's estate or his insurer.

---

[1] It seemed useless to maintain the distinction between *obligations in solidum* and *solidarité*. [In the present French law, recovery by a claimant in full against one of a number of persons civilly liable for the same harm is termed the *droit de poursuite du créancier* ('creditor's right of pursuit') and is found where the potential defendants owe *obligations solidaires* (this being termed *solidarité*) or where they owe *obligations in solidum* (sometimes termed *solidarité imparfaite*). This duplication of analysis stems from the Code civil's narrow provision for *obligations solidaires*, which exist only where they are expressly stipulated or by special legislative authority (article 1202 Cc), though there are some important legislative impositions of *solidarité*, for example, as regards those found jointly guilty of more serious criminal offences as to their civil liability to their victims: articles 375-2 and 480-1 of the New Code of Criminal Procedure. Apart from attracting the *droit de poursuite*, *solidarité* has certain other consequences which are termed 'secondary;' for example, a claim made against any one of the persons liable interrupts the running of the prescription period for all (article 1206 Cc) and interest accrues against all the persons liable from the time when *one* person's obligation falls due (article 1207 Cc). We have translated '*solidairement*' as 'jointly and severally liable' (and its related expressions of *solidarité* and *obligations solidaires* similarly) as this is the closest common law expression, as they have in common that all those liable for the same harm are liable in full as against the claimant, subject to any claim for contribution or an indemnity *inter se*, even though in both English and French law both the terminology and the incidents of these categories differ. For further discussion see S Whittaker, *Liability for Products, English law, French Law, and European Harmonisation* (Oxford University Press, 2005) 546-51.]

[2] On this last point, the solution proposed is different from the one adopted by existing case-law. [The *Cour de cassation* has held that where a 'co-author' of the same harm has been held liable *without* fault (for example, as *gardien* of a thing under article 1384(1) Cc), he can recover *in full* against any person liable on the basis of fault for the same harm to the primary claimant (Cass civ (3) 5 December 1984, JCP 1986 II 20543 note Dejean de la Bâtie) and conversely, a co-author held liable on the basis of fault as a matter of law cannot recover *any* contribution against a person also liable to the primary claimant without fault (Cass civ (2) 19 November 1970, JCP 1971 II 16748).]

[3] This provision extends solutions accepted by the courts in the context of traffic accidents.

Section 2
Règles particulières à la réparation de certaines catégories de dommages

§1 – Règles particulières à la réparation des préjudices résultant d'une atteinte à l'intégrité physique

> *Les dispositions qui suivent ont pour objet de donner un véritable cadre juridique à l'indemnisation du dommage corporel qui est aujourd'hui à peu près abandonnée au pouvoir souverain des juges du fond. Elles visent à restaurer dans ce domaine à la fois la sécurité juridique, l'égalité entre les justiciables et l'efficacité de la réparation.*

Art. 1379

En cas d'atteinte à son intégrité physique, la victime a droit à la réparation de ses préjudices économiques et professionnels correspondant notamment aux dépenses exposées et aux frais futurs, aux pertes de revenus et aux gains manqués, ainsi qu'à

la réparation de ses préjudices non économiques et personnels tels que le préjudice fonctionnel,[2] les souffrances endurées, le préjudice esthétique, le préjudice spécifique d'agrément, le préjudice sexuel et le préjudice d'établissement.

Les victimes par ricochet ont droit à la réparation de leurs préjudices économiques consistant en des frais divers et pertes de revenus ainsi que de leurs préjudices personnels d'affection et d'accompagnement.

Le juge doit distinguer dans sa décision chacun des préjudices économiques ou personnels qu'il indemnise.[4]

Art. 1379-1

L'ampleur du préjudice fonctionnel est déterminée selon le barème d'invalidité établi par décret.

Art. 1379-2

Le dommage corporel doit être apprécié sans qu'il soit tenu compte d'éventuelles prédispositions de la victime dès lors que celles-ci n'avaient pas déjà eu de conséquences préjudiciables au moment où s'est produit le fait dommageable.[5]

---

[2] On pourrait désigner ce préjudice par d'autres expressions telles que « préjudice physiologique » ou « déficit fonctionnel ».

[4] Cette énumération des chefs de préjudice est utile, non seulement pour obliger les juges du fond à motiver suffisamment leurs décisions sur la réparation, mais aussi pour permettre l'imputation du recours des tiers payeurs poste par poste, ainsi que le prévoit l'article 1379-7.

[5] Cette question de l'influence des prédispositions de la victime a donné lieu à une jurisprudence très complexe. La formule proposée exprime la position qui paraît adoptée aujourd'hui par la plupart des arrêts.

Section 2
Rules Special to the Reparation of Certain Types of Harm

§ 1 Rules special to the reparation of losses resulting from personal injuries

The purpose of the following provisions is to give a proper legal framework to the assessment of compensation for personal injuries which is now almost entirely abandoned to the unfettered discretion of the lower courts.[1] Their intention is to restore to this area legal certainty, an equal treatment to all litigants and the effectiveness of reparation.

Art. 1379

In the case of personal injuries, the victim has the right to reparation for his financial, business or professional losses and in particular to those losses which relate to expenses incurred and future outlay, to loss of income and to lost profits, as well as to reparation for his non-financial and personal losses such as physical impairment,[2] pain and suffering, disfigurement, any specific lost pursuit or pleasure, sexual impairment and any costs of investigation of the injury.

Indirect victims[3] have the right to reparation of their financial losses which consist of various expenses and lost income as well as their personal losses of love and affection, and companionship.

In giving judgment, a court must set out distinctly each of the financial or personal losses for which it awards compensation.[4]

Art. 1379-1

The extent of physical impairment is to be determined according to a scale of disability established by decree.

Art. 1379-2

Personal injuries must be assessed without taking into account any possible predispositions of the victim as long as these had not already caused any prejudicial consequences at the time when the harmful action took place.[5]

---

[1] [On the role of the *juges du fond* see above, p 679, n 2.]

[2] This loss could be described by other expressions such as 'physiological loss' of 'functional impairment'.

[3] [On 'indirect victims' see above, p 837, n 1.]

[4] This enumeration of the heads of loss is useful, not only so as to oblige lower courts to give sufficient reasons for their decisions on reparation, but also so as to allow the attribution to each individual head of loss of recourse claims by third parties who have indemnified the victim as is provided for by article 1379-7.

[5] The question of the impact of a victim's predisposition has given rise to a very complex case-law. The formula which is recommended expresses the position apparently adopted by the majority of current decisions.

Art. 1379-3

L'indemnité due au titre du gain professionnel manqué, de la perte de soutien matériel ou de l'assistance d'une tierce personne se fait, sauf décision contraire spécialement motivée, sous forme de rente indexée. Le juge a la liberté du choix de l'indice.[1]

Le juge peut d'ores et déjà prévoir que la rente sera révisée en cas de diminution ou d'aggravation du dommage, à condition de préciser explicitement la périodicité et les conditions de la révision.

Art. 1379-4

Les tiers payeurs qui ont versé à la victime d'un préjudice résultant d'une atteinte à son intégrité physique les prestations énumérées limitativement ci-après disposent d'un recours subrogatoire contre la personne tenue à réparation ou son assureur par imputation sur les droits de la victime.

Art. 1379-5[3]

Ouvrent droit à recours les prestations suivantes, lorsqu'elles ont un lien direct avec le fait dommageable :

1. Les prestations versées par les organismes, établissements et services gérant un régime obligatoire de sécurité sociale et par ceux qui sont mentionnés aux articles 1106-9, 1234-8 et 1234-20 du code rural ;

2. Les prestations énumérées au §II de l'article Ier de l'ordonnance no 59-76 du 7 janvier 1959 relative aux actions en réparation civile de l'État et de certaines autres personnes publiques ;

3. Les sommes versées en remboursement des frais de traitement médical et de rééducation ;

4. Les salaires et les accessoires du salaire maintenus par l'employeur pendant la période d'inactivité consécutive à l'événement qui a occasionné le dommage ;

5. Les indemnités journalières de maladie et les prestations d'invalidité versées par les groupements mutualistes régis par le code de la mutualité, les institutions de prévoyance régies par le code de la sécurité sociale ou le code rural et les sociétés d'assurance régies par le code des assurances.

Art. 1379-6

Lorsqu'il est prévu au contrat, le recours subrogatoire de l'assureur qui a versé à la victime une avance sur indemnité du fait de l'accident peut être exercé contre la personne tenue à réparation dans la limite du solde disponible après paiement des

---

[1] Cette disposition devrait entraîner l'abrogation de l'article 1er de la loi du 27 décembre 1974 relative à la revalorisation des rentes indemnitaires en matière d'accidents de la circulation.

[3] Les articles 1379-5 et 1379-6 reproduisent les articles 29, 33, alinéa 3 de la loi du 5 juillet 1985 et l'article L 131-2 du code des assurances. Ils pourraient être remplacés par un simple renvoi à ces textes (voir, à ce sujet, le rapport introductif, I, 2°), mais le groupe a préféré reproduire ceux-ci pour des raisons de commodité pratique et afin de consacrer la solution donnée par l'assemblée plénière de la Cour de cassation le 1er décembre 2003 au sujet des prestations indemnitaires versées par les assureurs de personnes.

Art. 1379-3

Compensation due under the headings of business or professional lost profits, of loss of physical maintenance or loss incurred by requiring the help of a third party is to be awarded in the form of index-linked periodic payments, unless the court decides otherwise for special reasons. The court possesses a discretion as to which index is to be used for this purpose.[1]

The court may provide in its judgment that any periodic payment shall be revised if the harm becomes smaller or more extensive, on condition that it expressly sets out the period within which and the conditions on which such a revision is to take place.

Art. 1379-4

Third parties[2] who have paid the victim the benefits set out in the following list in respect of a loss caused by his personal injury enjoy a subrogated claim against the person held liable or his insurer by way of attributing to them the victim's own rights.

Art. 1379-5[3]

The following benefits give rise to a right of recourse where they have a direct link to the harmful action attracting liability:

1. Benefits supplied by organisations, bodies or services operating a compulsory regime of social security and by those which are mentioned in articles 1106-9, 1234-8 and 1234-20 of the Rural Code;

2. Benefits listed at §II in article 1 of the Ordinance no. 59-76 of 7 January 1959 on actions for civil reparation brought by the State and certain other public bodies;

3. Sums paid by way of the reimbursement of the cost of medical treatment and rehabilitation;

4. Salaries and their incidental costs which an employer continues to pay during a period of inactivity following an event which caused the harm;

5. Daily sickness payments and invalidity benefits paid by friendly societies governed by the Code of Friendly Societies, provident institutions governed by the Code of Social Security or the Rural Code and insurance companies governed by the Insurance Code.

Art. 1379-6

Where it is so provided in the contract, a subrogatory recourse of an insurer which has made the victim an advance payment on his compensation arising from the occurrence of the accident can be brought against the person held liable to make reparation up to the extent of the funds available after payment of the third parties

[1] This provision ought to lead to the abrogation of article 1 of the Law of 27 December 1974 concerning the revaluation of compensatory periodic payments in the area of road accidents.

[2] [This translates 'tiers payeurs', on which see above, p 811, n 4.]

[3] Articles 1379-5 and 1379-6 reproduce articles 29 and 33(3) of the Law of 5 July 1985 and article 131-2 of the Insurance Code. They could be replaced with a simple cross-reference to these provisions (see on this subject the Preamble I(2)) but the working group preferred to reproduce them here for reasons of practical convenience and so as to give formal recognition to the solution provided by the *Assemblée plénière* of the *Cour de cassation* on 1[9] December 2003, Bull civ AP no 7 on the subject of compensatory benefits paid by personal insurers.

tiers visés à l'article 1379-4. Il doit être exercé, s'il y a lieu, dans les délais impartis par la loi aux tiers payeurs pour produire leurs créances.

Dans les contrats d'assurance garantissant l'indemnisation des préjudices résultant d'une atteinte à la personne, l'assureur peut être subrogé dans les droits du contractant ou des ayants droit contre le tiers responsable, pour le remboursement des prestations indemnitaires prévues au contrat. Les prestations sont réputées avoir un caractère indemnitaire, lorsque, même calculées en fonction d'éléments prédéterminés, elles se mesurent au préjudice subi et en dépendent dans leurs modalités de calcul et d'attribution.

Art. 1379-7[1]

Les recours subrogatoires des tiers payeurs s'exercent poste par poste dans la limite de la part d'indemnité mise à la charge du responsable réparant les chefs de préjudices qu'ils ont contribué à indemniser par leurs prestations. Ces recours s'exercent dans les mêmes conditions si le juge n'a réparé que la perte d'une chance.

Art. 1379-8

Hormis les prestations mentionnées à l'article 1379-5, aucun versement effectué au profit de la victime en vertu d'une obligation légale, conventionnelle ou statutaire, n'ouvre droit à une action contre la personne tenue à réparation ou son assureur.[2]

Toute disposition contraire aux prescriptions des articles 1379 à 1379-8 est réputée non écrite à moins qu'elle ne soit plus favorable à la victime.

§2 – Règles particulières à la réparation des préjudices résultant d'une atteinte aux biens

Ces règles reproduisent des solutions admises par la jurisprudence et généralement approuvées par la doctrine.

Art. 1380

En cas de destruction ou de détérioration d'un bien, la victime a droit, sans déduction au titre de la vétusté, à une indemnité lui permettant le remplacement ou la remise en état du bien. Il n'est pas tenu compte de la plus-value éventuellement inhérente à la réparation.

Si toutefois le coût de la réparation est plus élevé que celui du remplacement, la victime ne peut exiger que ce dernier.

---

[1] L'adoption de cette disposition entraînerait l'abrogation de l'article 31 de la loi du 5 juillet 1985 et la modification des articles 736-1 alinéa 3 et 454-1 alinéa 3 du code de la sécurité sociale.

[2] Cette disposition reprend l'article 33, alinéas 1 et 2 de la loi du 5 juillet 1985.

designated by article 1379-4. Where applicable, it must be brought within the periods allowed by legislation for third parties to claim their rights.

In contracts of insurance which guarantee compensation for losses resulting from personal injury, the insurer can be subrogated to the rights of the policy-holder or his successors in title against a third party liable for his harm so as to obtain the reimbursement of compensatory benefits provided for by the contract. These benefits are deemed to have a compensatory nature where they are measured by reference to and depend for their manner of calculation and attribution on the loss suffered by the victim even if they are calculated as a matter of predetermined elements.

Art. 1379-7[1]

Recourse claims by third parties by way of subrogation are to be brought for each head of loss individually up to the limit of the share of the compensation attributed to the person liable and which make reparation for the heads of losses which they have partially compensated by providing their benefits. These recourse claims are to be brought subject to the same conditions if a court has made reparation only for the loss of a chance.

Art. 1379-8

Apart from the benefits mentioned in article 1379-5, no supply of a benefit to the victim gives rise to a right of action against the person liable or against his insurer, whether these are made by virtue of a legislative, contractual or institutional obligation.[2]

Any contractual provision contrary to the requirements of articles 1379 to 1379-8 is struck out unless it is in favour of the victim.

§ 2 Rules special to the reparation of losses resulting from damage to property

These rules reproduce the solutions adopted by the case-law and which are generally approved by legal writers.

Art. 1380

Where property is destroyed or physically damaged, the victim has the right to compensation which would allow him to replace it or to put it back as it was before this occurred without any deduction on the ground of its age. No account is to be taken of any increase in value which may arise as a result of repair.

Nevertheless, the victim may choose only the cost of replacement where this is exceeded by the cost of repair.

---

[1] The adoption of this provision would lead to the abrogation of article 31 of the Law of 5 July 1985 and the amendment of articles 736-1(3) and 454-1(3) of the Social Security Code.
[2] This provision reflects article 33(1),(2) of the Law of 5 July 1985.

Art. 1380-1

Lorsque le bien ne peut être ni réparé, ni remplacé, la victime a droit à la valeur de celui-ci dans son état antérieur au dommage, estimée au jour de la décision. Le responsable peut exiger que le bien lui soit remis dans son état actuel. Il en est de même lorsque celui-ci, destiné à la vente, n'est plus en état d'être vendu.

Art. 1380-2

Si, nonobstant les réparations, le bien a perdu une partie de sa valeur, la victime a droit à une indemnité de dépréciation.

Elle a droit, en outre, à l'indemnisation des dommages consécutifs à la privation de jouissance et, le cas échéant, des pertes d'exploitation.

§3 – Règles particulières à la réparation des préjudices résultant du retard dans le paiement d'une somme d'argent

Ces règles sont celles qu'énonce l'actuel article 1153. En revanche, celles qui figurent à l'article 1153-1 n'ont pas leur place dans le Code civil, mais dans le Code de procédure civile.

Art. 1381[2]

L'indemnisation du préjudice résultant du retard dans le paiement d'une somme d'argent consiste en une condamnation aux intérêts au taux légal.

Ces dommages-intérêts sont dus sans que le créancier soit tenu de justifier d'aucune perte. Ils ne sont dus que du jour de la mise en demeure,[3] excepté dans le cas où la loi les fait courir de plein droit.

Le créancier auquel son débiteur en retard a causé un préjudice supplémentaire, peut obtenir des dommages-intérêts distincts des intérêts moratoires de la créance.

Section 3
Les conventions portant sur la réparation

§1 – Conventions excluant ou limitant la réparation

Il est proposé d'autoriser les clauses restrictives de responsabilité en matière extracontractuelle dès lors que la responsabilité n'est pas fondée sur la faute. En revanche, les différentes limitations que la jurisprudence a introduites ou que la doctrine a proposées pour limiter la validité ou l'efficacité de ces clauses en matière contractuelle sont consacrées.

---

[2] Ce texte reprend presque intégralement l'article 1153 actuel. Simplement, dans le dernier alinéa « indépendant du retard » a été remplacé par « supplémentaire » et la réserve, assez mystérieuse, des « règles particulières au commerce et au cautionnement » a été supprimée.

[3] La définition de la mise en demeure (sommation de payer...) n'est pas reprise. Elle devra être élaborée par le groupe chargé de l'exécution.

Art. 1380-1

Where the property cannot either be repaired or replaced, the victim has the right to its value in the state in which it was before it was damaged as calculated at the date of the court's decision. The person liable can demand that the property be handed over to him in its present state. This is also the case where property which was intended for sale is no longer in a fit state to be sold.

Art. 1380-2

If the property has lost part of its value despite its repair, the victim has the right to compensation for this depreciation.

He also has the right to compensation for harm consequential on his being deprived of the enjoyment of his property and, in an appropriate case, for consequential loss of profits.

§ 3 Rules special to the reparation of losses resulting from delay in payment of sums of money

These rules are those which are set out by article 1153 of the present Code. On the other hand, those which at present feature in article 1153-1 do not belong to the Civil Code but to the New Code of Civil Procedure.[1]

Art. 1381[2]

Compensation for loss resulting from delay in the payment of a sum of money consists of an award of interest at the rate set by legislation.

These damages are due without the creditor needing to justify any loss. They are due only from the date of service of a notice to perform[3] except where legislation provides that they accrue by operation of law.

Where a creditor facing delay in performance by his debtor suffers a further loss he may recover damages distinct from his award of interest for delay in payment.

Section 3
Agreements Relating to Reparation

§ 1 Agreements excluding or limiting reparation

It is proposed that contract terms which limit extra-contractual liability should be authorised where liability is not based on fault. On the other hand, the various restrictions which the case-law has introduced or which are recommended by legal writers to restrict the validity or effectiveness of these terms in a contractual context are formally recognised.

---

[1] [Article 1153-1 Cc provides, inter alia, that 'in every area, condemnation to payment of an indemnity includes interest at the legal rate in the absence of any claim or special order by a court and makes other provision governing the process of awards of interest.]

[2] This provision reproduces almost entirely the present article 1153. It is merely that in the last paragraph 'independent of any delay' is replaced with 'further' and the rather mysterious exception provided for 'special rules governing trade and guarantees' has been expunged.

[3] The definition of notices to perform (formal demands for payment etc) is not set out. It will be worked out by the group charged with 'performance'.

Des dispositions spéciales ont été prévues afin d'imposer l'acceptation de la clause par la personne qui doit en subir les conséquences.

Art. 1382

Les conventions ayant pour objet d'exclure ou de limiter la réparation sont en principe valables, aussi bien en matière contractuelle qu'extracontractuelle.[1]

Art. 1382-1

Nul ne peut exclure ou limiter la réparation d'un dommage corporel dont il est responsable.[2]

Art. 1382-2

Un contractant ne peut exclure ou limiter la réparation du dommage causé à son cocontractant par une faute dolosive ou lourde ou par le manquement à l'une de ses obligations essentielles.[4]

En l'absence de contrepartie réelle, sérieuse et clairement stipulée, un professionnel ne peut exclure ou limiter son obligation de réparer le dommage contractuel causé à un non-professionnel ou consommateur.[5]

Art. 1382-3

En matière contractuelle, la partie à laquelle est opposée une clause excluant ou limitant la réparation doit avoir pu en prendre connaissance avant la formation du contrat.

Art. 1382-4

En matière extracontractuelle, on ne peut exclure ou limiter la réparation du dommage qu'on a causé par sa faute.[6]

Dans les autres cas, la convention n'a d'effet que si celui qui l'invoque prouve que la victime l'avait acceptée de manière non équivoque.

[1] La reconnaissance de la validité des conventions restreignant une responsabilité de nature délictuelle est une innovation importante par rapport au droit actuel. Elle concerne principalement les relations entre voisins ou entre personnes qui exercent une activité en commun sans avoir conclu un contrat de société ou d'association. Cette validité est admise par de nombreux droits étrangers.

[2] Cette solution n'a pas jusqu'à présent été affirmée explicitement par la jurisprudence, bien qu'elle soit prônée presque unanimement par la doctrine.

[4] Ces solutions sont aujourd'hui consacrées par la jurisprudence.

[5] Cette solution peut paraître nouvelle. En réalité, elle est tout à fait dans la ligne des positions adoptées par la Commission des clauses abusives.

[6] Cette disposition limite sérieusement la portée du principe posé par l'article 1382.

Special provision is made so as to require the acceptance of a contract term by the person who is to be subjected to its effects.

Art. 1382

In principle agreements whose purpose is to exclude or to limit reparation are valid both as regards contractual and extra-contractual liability.[1]

Art. 1382-1

No person may exclude or limit the reparation in respect of personal injury for which he is responsible.[2]

Art. 1382-2

A party to a contract cannot exclude or limit the reparation for harm caused to his co-contractor by his deliberate, dishonest[3] or gross fault or by a failure to perform one of his essential obligations.[4]

A person acting in the course of business or a profession cannot exclude or limit his obligation to make reparation for a contractual harm caused to a consumer or to a person not in business or a profession in the absence of something real, significant and clearly stipulated in return.[5]

Art. 1382-3

In the contractual context, the party who is faced with a term excluding or limiting reparation must have been able to be aware of it at the time of concluding the contract.

Art. 1382-4

In the extra-contractual context, a person cannot exclude or limit the reparation in respect of harm which he has caused by his fault.[6]

In other situations, an agreement is effective only if the person relying on it proves that the victim accepted it in an unequivocal way.

[1] The recognition of the validity of agreements which restrict liability of a delictual nature marks an important innovation in relation to the existing law. It principally concerns the relations between neighbours or other persons who take part in a common activity without having made a contract of partnership or of association. This validity is accepted by many foreign laws.

[2] This solution has not so far been explicitly adopted by the courts, even though it is almost unanimously advocated by legal writers.

[3] [We have translated *dol* as 'deliberate, dishonest' as the word covers both in the French context: see above, p 831, n 1.]

[4] These solutions are formally accepted by the courts today.

[5] This solution may look new. Actually, it is well within the line of positions taken by the Commission on Unfair Contract Terms [on which see above, p 829, n 3.].

[6] This provision limits significantly the impact of the principle posed by article 1382 of the Reform Proposals.

§2 – Conventions de réparation forfaitaire et clauses pénales

Il a paru inutile de maintenir la distinction entre clause pénale et clause d'indemnisation forfaitaire ainsi que les dispositions des actuels articles 1226 à 1230, 1232 et 1233 qui ne sont presque jamais appliquées et dont la signification est controversée. En revanche, les deux systèmes de révision judiciaire réglementés actuellement par les articles 1152 et 1231 sont maintenus, à l'exception de la faculté de révision à la hausse d'une pénalité manifestement dérisoire qui ne semble guère utilisée.

Art. 1383

Lorsque les parties ont fixé à l'avance la réparation due, le juge peut, même d'office, modérer la sanction convenue si elle est manifestement excessive.

Le juge dispose du même pouvoir à l'égard des clauses dont l'objet est de contraindre le débiteur contractuel à l'exécution.

Lorsque l'engagement a été exécuté en partie, la sanction convenue peut, même d'office, être diminuée par le juge à proportion de l'intérêt que l'exécution partielle a procuré au créancier, sans préjudice de l'application de l'alinéa précédent.

Toute stipulation contraire est réputée non écrite.

Section 4
La prescription de l'action en responsabilité

La disposition qui figure aujourd'hui à l'article 2270-1 est reprise à l'exception du mot « extracontractuelle ». Il est donc proposé de soumettre à la même prescription l'action en responsabilité contractuelle et l'action en responsabilité extracontractuelle.

Art. 1384

Les actions en responsabilité civile se prescrivent par dix ans à compter de la manifestation du dommage ou de son aggravation, sans égard, en cas de dommage corporel, à la date de la consolidation.[3]

---

[3] Cette précision n'est pas conforme à la jurisprudence de la Cour de cassation qui a introduit, contrairement au texte, cette référence à la date de consolidation.

§ 2 Agreements for pre-set reparation and penalty clauses

It seemed pointless to maintain the distinction between penalty clauses and contract terms setting a compensation in advance[1] since the provisions contained in articles 1226 to 1230, 1232 and 1233 of the existing Code are hardly ever applied and their meaning is controversial. On the other hand, the two sets of rules providing for judicial revision of sums set by contract terms at present found in articles 1152 and 1231 are retained, with the exception of the possibility of increasing the amount of a penalty which is manifestly derisory which seems hardly ever to be used.

Art. 1383[2]

Where the parties have fixed in advance the reparation which will fall due, the court may, even on its own initiative, reduce the agreed sanction if it is manifestly excessive.

The court enjoys the same power as regards contract terms whose purpose is to force the contractual debtor to perform.

Without prejudice to the preceding paragraph, where an undertaking has been performed in part, the agreed sanction for its non-performance may be reduced by the court, even on its own initiative, in proportion to the benefit which the partial performance has produced for the creditor.

Any stipulation to the contrary is struck out.

Section 4
Prescription of Actions Claiming Liability

The legal provision which appears today as article 2270-1 of the Code is repeated except for the word 'extra-contractual'. It is therefore recommended that actions claiming liability should be subject to the same prescription period whether they are contractual or extra-contractual.

Art. 1384

Actions claiming civil liability become prescribed after ten years commencing from the manifestation of the harm or its getting worse, though in the case of personal injuries without having regard to whether their effects have stabilised.[3]

---

[1] [This translates '*clause d'indemnisation forfaitaire*'. We have avoided using the language of 'liquidated damages clauses' as being too loaded with common law significance].

[2] [For discussion of this provision see Miller, above, ch 7, p 162.]

[3] This detail does not conform to the case-law of the Cour de cassation which has introduced this reference to the date of stabilising of the injury contrary to the wording of the provision itself. [An example of this case-law may be found in Cass civ (2) 4 May 2000, Bull civ II no 75.]

Chapitre IV
Les principaux régimes spéciaux
de responsabilité ou d'indemnisation

Section 1
L'indemnisation des victimes d'accidents
de la circulation

Les dispositions qui suivent sont proches des articles 1 à 6 de la loi du 5 juillet 1985. Elles s'en séparent cependant sur trois points :

Le conducteur est assimilé aux autres victimes ;

Les accidents de chemin de fer et de tramway sont assimilés aux autres accidents dans lesquels un véhicule terrestre à moteur est impliqué ;

La disposition concernant spécialement les enfants, les personnes âgées et les personnes handicapées est supprimée, toutes les victimes ne pouvant se voir opposer que leur faute inexcusable si elle a été la cause exclusive de l'accident.

Art. 1385

Les victimes d'un accident de la circulation dans lequel est impliqué un véhicule terrestre à moteur ainsi que ses remorques ou semi-remorques sont indemnisées des dommages imputables à cet accident par le conducteur ou le gardien du véhicule impliqué, même lorsqu'elles sont transportées en vertu d'un contrat.

Ne constitue pas un accident de la circulation celui qui résulte de l'utilisation d'un véhicule immobile et dans une fonction étrangère au déplacement.

En cas d'accident complexe, chaque véhicule intervenu à quelque titre que ce soit dans la survenance de l'accident y est impliqué.

Même lorsqu'un seul véhicule est impliqué dans un accident, toute victime peut demander réparation à l'un des débiteurs de l'indemnisation, y compris le gardien au conducteur ou le conducteur au gardien.[5]

---

[5] Ces trois derniers alinéas explicitent des solutions que la jurisprudence a dégagées depuis 1985.

Chapter IV
The Principal Special Regimes of Liability or Compensation

Section 1
Compensation for the Victims of Traffic Accidents[1]

These provisions follow very closely articles 1 to 6 of the Law of 5 July 1985. They differ from them, however, on three points:

Drivers are treated in the same way as other victims;[2]

Railway and tramway accidents are treated in the same way as other accidents in which a motor-vehicle is involved;

The provision which deals specially with children, old people and handicapped people is expunged, so that all victims cannot be faced with a defence of their own contributory fault unless this was inexcusable and was the exclusive cause of the accident.[3]

Art. 1385

The victims of a traffic accident in which an earth-bound motor-vehicle is involved (including trailers and articulated lorries) are to be compensated for harm attributable to the accident by the driver or keeper[4] of the vehicle involved, even where they were being carried under a contract.

For this purpose, a traffic accident does not include an accident which results from use of a stationary vehicle which is unrelated to its function of transportation.

In the case of a complex accident, every vehicle which was part of the accident's occurrence in whatever way is implicated in it.

Even where only one vehicle is involved in an accident, any category of victim may claim reparation from one of those liable to compensate, including the keeper against the driver or the driver against the keeper.[5]

---

[1] [For a brief introduction to this law see S Whittaker, 'The Law of Obligations' in Bell, Boyron and Whittaker, above, p 465, n 1, 400 – 403 and further R Redmond-Cooper, 'The Relevance of Fault in Determining Liability for Road Accidents: the French Experience' (1989) 38 ICLQ 502.

[2] [At present, by art 4 of the Law of 5 July 1985, *any* fault on the part of a driver of a motor-vehicle (or those who claim through them) can reduce or extinguish the liability of another driver or *gardien*.]

[3] [Cf above, p 833, n 3 explaining how this contrasts with the present position.]

[4] ['Keeper' translates '*gardien*', this being a reference to the law governing liability of 'keepers' for the actions of the 'things': see above, p 431.]

[5] These three last paragraphs make explicit solutions which the case-law has worked out since 1985.

Art. 1385-1

Les victimes ne peuvent se voir opposer le cas fortuit ou le fait d'un tiers même lorsqu'ils présentent les caractères de la force majeure.

Art. 1385-2

Les victimes sont indemnisées des préjudices résultant des atteintes à leur personne, sans que puisse leur être opposée leur propre faute à l'exception de leur faute inexcusable si elle a été la cause exclusive de l'accident.

Toutefois, dans le cas visé à l'alinéa précédent, les victimes ne sont pas indemnisées par l'auteur de l'accident des préjudices résultant des atteintes à leur personne lorsqu'elles ont volontairement recherché le dommage qu'elles ont subi.

Art. 1385-3

La faute commise par la victime a pour effet de limiter ou d'exclure l'indemnisation des préjudices résultant d'une atteinte à ses biens ; l'exclusion de l'indemnisation doit être spécialement motivée par référence à la gravité de la faute.

Les fournitures et appareils délivrés sur prescription médicale donnent lieu à indemnisation selon les règles applicables à la réparation des atteintes à la personne.

Lorsque le conducteur d'un véhicule terrestre à moteur n'en est pas le propriétaire, la faute de ce conducteur peut être opposée au propriétaire pour l'indemnisation des dommages causés à son véhicule. Le propriétaire dispose d'un recours contre le conducteur.

Art. 1385-4

Les préjudices des victimes par ricochet sont réparés en tenant compte des limitations ou exclusions opposables à la victime directe.

La faute de la victime par ricochet lui est opposable dans les conditions visées aux articles 1385-2 et 1385-3.[2]

Art. 1385-5

Les débiteurs d'indemnisation sont tenus solidairement envers la victime.

Lorsque des tiers sont responsables d'un accident de la circulation sur le fondement du droit commun, ils sont également tenus solidairement.

Le conducteur ou le gardien d'un véhicule terrestre à moteur impliqué dans un accident de la circulation dispose d'un recours subrogatoire contre d'autres conducteurs ou gardiens de véhicules impliqués ou contre des tiers responsables de l'accident en vertu du droit commun. De même, le responsable d'un accident de la circulation sur le fondement du droit commun peut exercer un recours subrogatoire contre les conducteurs ou gardiens de véhicules impliqués dans l'accident.

---

[2] Ce texte consacre et étend la jurisprudence qui admet l'opposabilité de la faute de la victime par ricochet conductrice.

Art. 1385-1

Act of God or act of a third party may not be raised as a defence against victims of a traffic accident even where these circumstances possess the characteristics of *force majeure*.

Art. 1385-2

Victims of a traffic accident are to be compensated for losses resulting from their personal injury without being faced with a defence of their own contributory fault unless the latter was both inexcusable and the exclusive cause of the accident.

Nevertheless, in the situation envisaged by the preceding paragraph, victims are not to be compensated by the author of the accident for losses resulting from their personal injury where they deliberately sought the harm which they suffered.

Art. 1385-3

Fault committed by the victim has the effect of limiting or excluding his compensation in respect of losses resulting from damage to property; an exclusion of compensation must be specifically justified by reference to the seriousness of his fault.

Apparatus or other things supplied under a medical prescription to the victim give rise to compensation according to the rules applicable to personal injuries.

Where the driver of an earth-bound motor vehicle is not its owner, this driver's fault can be relied on as a defence against the owner as regards the compensation of damage caused to his vehicle. The owner possesses a recourse claim against the driver.

Art. 1385-4

Losses suffered by indirect victims are the subject of reparation taking into account any restrictions or exclusions faced by the direct victim.[1]

Fault in the indirect victim may be relied on against him subject to the conditions provided for in articles 1385-2 and 1385-3.[2]

Art. 1385-5

Those owing compensation are liable jointly and severally to the victim.

Where third parties are liable for a traffic accident on the basis of the general law, they are also liable jointly and severally.

A driver or keeper of an earth-bound motor vehicle involved in a traffic accident possesses a recourse claim by way of subrogation against other drivers or keepers of vehicles involved or against third parties liable for the accident under the general law. Equally, a person liable for a traffic accident on the basis of the general law can bring a recourse claim by way of subrogation against the drivers or keepers of vehicles involved in the accident.

---

[1] [See above, p 837, n 1 for a brief explanation of this terminology of 'direct' and 'indirect' victim.]

[2] This legal provision formally recognises and extends case-law which accepts that fault in a driver who suffers loss as an indirect victim of an accident may be relied on against him.

La contribution à la dette d'indemnisation se règle selon les dispositions des articles 1378 et 1378-1.

Section 2
La responsabilité du fait des produits défectueux

Articles 1386-1 à 1386-18 actuels du code civil devenant 1386 à 1386-17, les termes « du présent titre », qui figurent dans plusieurs de ces articles, devant être remplacés par « de la présente section ».

Contribution to the compensation payable for these purposes is governed by the provisions found in articles 1378 and 1378-1.

Section 2
Liability for Defective Products

The existing articles 1386-1 to 1386-18 of the Civil Code become 1386 to 1386-17, the terms 'of the present title' which figure in several of these articles having to be replaced with 'of the present section'.

LIVRE TROISIÈME

TITRE XX
DE LA PRESCRIPTION ET DE LA POSSESSION
(Articles 2234 à 2281)

Exposé des motifs

Philippe Malaurie

Plus que toute autre institution, la prescription mesure les rapports de l'homme avec le temps et avec le droit : elle domine toutes les règles et tous les droits. Pas seulement le droit des obligations qui constitue son domaine d'élection, mais aussi toutes les autres branches du droit, l'ensemble du droit privé, du droit public, du droit pénal et de la procédure. Les dispositions du Code civil relatives à la prescription s'appliquent à tous les autres codes et à toutes les lois, sauf exceptions précisées dans le présent avant-projet. La prescription est pour tous les praticiens, tous les usagers du droit et tous les acteurs de l'activité humaine d'une importance considérable.

1 – Les défauts du droit français de la prescription civile.

Le régime actuel de la prescription en matière civile présente, de l'avis unanime, trois défauts essentiels, d'une égale gravité.[2]

---

[2] A. BENABENT, *Le chaos du droit de la prescription extinctive*, Et. L. Boyer, Presses universitaires Toulouse, 1996, p. 123 et s. ; B. FAUVARQUE-COSSON, *Variations sur le processus d'harmonisation du droit à travers l'exemple de la prescription extinctive*, R.D.C., 2004 801 et s. ; V. LASSERRE-KIESOW, *La prescription, les lois et la faux du temps*, JCP éd. N, 2004 1225 ; *Les désordres de la prescription*, ouv. Collectif sous la direction de P. Courbe, P.U., Rouen, 2000.

BOOK THREE

TITLE XX
PRESCRIPTION AND POSSESSION
(Articles 2234 to 2281)

Preamble

Philippe Malaurie

More than any other doctrine, prescription marks man's relationship with time and with the law: it dominates all rules and all the law. Not only the law of obligations which forms its domain of choice, but also all other branches of the law, the whole of private law, public law, criminal law and the law of procedure. The provisions of the Civil Code relating to prescription are applicable to all other Codes and all other laws, except for the exceptions made clear in these Reform Proposals. Prescription is of considerable importance for all practitioners, for all users of the law and for all the actors in human activity.[1]

1. Defects of the French law of civil prescription

In the view of everyone, the existing regime of prescription in civil matters possesses three essential defects of an equal seriousness.[2]

---

[1] [For discussion of the provisions of the *Avant-projet* governing prescription see Wintgen, above, ch 16 and Cartwright, above ch 17.]

[2] A. BENABENT, *Le chaos du droit de la prescription extinctive*, Et. L. Boyer, Presses universitaires Toulouse, 1996, p. 123 *et seq.*; B. FAUVARQUE-COSSON, *Variations sur le processus d'harmonisation du droit à travers l'exemple de la prescription extinctive*, R.D.C., 2004 801 *et seq.*; V. LASSERRE-KIESOW, *La prescription, les lois et la faux du temps*, JCP éd. N, 2004 1225; *Les désordres de la prescription*, ouv. Collectif sous la direction de P. Courbe, P.U., Rouen, 2000.

En premier lieu, ses longueurs excessives qui ont pour conséquence une stagnation de l'activité humaine : longueur égale langueur. Plus personne ne peut comprendre que la prescription de droit commun soit encore aujourd'hui d'une durée de trente ans (C. civ., art. 2262). Beaucoup d'autres délais sont aussi trop longs. L'accélération de l'histoire, idéologie contemporaine souvent exacte, appelle une abréviation des délais.

Le second défaut, aussi généralement relevé, est la multiplicité des délais, allant de trois mois (diffamations et injures par voie de presse) à trente ans et même à l'imprescriptibilité, en passant par toutes sortes de délais intermédiaires (six mois, un, deux, trois, quatre, cinq, dix, vingt ans) : un vrai chaos a-t-on dit, et même un capharnaüm, source d'ignorance du droit, de désordres et d'interminables discussions.

Le troisième défaut, moins souvent dénoncé, réside dans les imprécisions et mêmes les incohérences de son régime : point de départ, interruption, suspension, rôles respectifs de la loi, de la jurisprudence et du contrat, office du juge, liberté contractuelle, incertitudes qui apparaissent même dans les concepts. À côté de la prescription proprement dite, existent en effet des nébuleuses de prescriptions qui en sont plus ou moins proches : délais préfix, délais de forclusion, délais de garantie, sans parler des délais de procédure. Ces incertitudes constituent une cause de procès fréquents.

La prescription, qui devrait être un élément de pacification des rapports humains et de leur dynamisme, est ainsi devenue en raison de sa longueur excessive, de sa multiplicité et de ses incertitudes une cause de stagnation de l'activité et une source abondante de litiges.

Dans ses défauts contemporains, il n'est pas fait mention d'un particularisme du droit français de la prescription, à la fois acquisitive et extinctive, car on peut considérer que ce trait important de la notion française de la prescription présente plus d'avantages que d'inconvénients. En raison de son histoire et de sa structure, le droit français en a une conception unitaire qui apparaît dans sa définition et dans son régime.

2 – Questions préalables : la méthode.

Toute réforme appelle des questions préliminaires de méthode. Il ne sera pas fait état ici des discussions théoriques sur la prescription, si célèbres soient-elles, lorsque n'y sont pas attachées de conséquences pratiques ; par exemple, pour la prescription extinctive, savoir si elle éteint le droit ou seulement l'action en justice, question qui intéresse seulement les conflits de lois dans l'espace ; ou bien le langage : faut-il parler de prescription extinctive, ou libératoire, ou négative, ou bien d'usucapion ou de prescription acquisitive ? Dans l'actuel avant-projet, la langue et la terminologie du Code ont été maintenues telles quelles car elles donnent satisfaction. Ou

First, the excessive length of its periods which lead to a stagnation in human activity: length is to be equated with languor. No-one can understand any longer why the prescription period of the general law should today still last for thirty years (article 2262 of the Civil Code). Many of the other periods are also too long. The frequently accurate notion found in contemporary ideology that history is accelerating calls for the shortening of these periods.

The second defect, which is also generally noted, is the multiplicity of periods, which extend from three months (as regards defamation and published libel) to thirty years and even to a point where prescription vanishes, and passing all sorts of intermediate periods (six months and one, two, three, four, five, ten, and twenty years): this state of affairs has been called really chaotic and even a shambles, and it provides a basis for disregarding the law and a source of muddles and interminable arguments.[1]

The third and less frequently denounced defect lies in the lack of detail and even inconsistencies found in its surrounding regime: as to the prescription periods' starting-point, their interruption, suspension, the relative roles of legislation, case-law and contractual provision, the proper role of courts, contractual freedom, and even uncertainties revealed in the concepts which are used. As well as prescription properly so-called, there also exists a hazy cloud of prescriptions which are more or less related to it: non-suspendable periods, foreclosure periods, guarantee periods, quite apart from periods governing the stages of legal proceedings. These uncertainties constitute a cause of frequent litigation.

In this way, because of its excessively long periods, their multiplicity and their uncertainty the law of prescription, which ought to contribute to the making of peace in human relations and support their dynamism, has become an abundant source of litigation.

Among the defects which it now possesses, we do not include a special feature of the French law of prescription, that is, that prescription is both acquisitive and extinctive, as it may be thought that this important feature of the French notion of prescription offers more advantages than disadvantages. As a result of its history and its structure, French law has a unified conception of prescription as is clear both from its definition and from its surrounding regime.

2. Preliminary issues: method

Every reform raises preliminary issues of method. This is not the place for an exposition of the theoretical discussions which have taken place on the subject of prescription, however famous they may be, unless they have some practical effect. For example, in the case of extinctive prescription, does it extinguish the right or merely the legal action, a question which concerns only the conflict of laws? Or in the case of the language used, should one refer to extinctive prescription, or rather to liberating or negative prescription, or to usucapion or acquisitive prescription? In the present Proposals, the language and terminology of the Civil Code have been retained as they are, since they are generally seen as satisfactory. To take another

---

[1] [For an account of the circumstances in which the various long, medium and short prescriptions apply, see Malaurie, Aynès and Stoffel-Munck, *Les obligations*, above, p 839, n 3, nos 1201-1206.]

bien encore la place de la prescription dans le Code : faut-il la déplacer ; par exemple, la mettre après le Titre III du Livre III (*Du contrat et des obligations conventionnelles en général*) en créant un Titre III bis avec des articles 1364-1 et suivants ? Ce déplacement a été jugé lourd, inutile et contraire à l'unité des prescriptions – acquisitives et extinctives – qu'il convient de conserver. A donc été maintenue la place actuelle de la prescription, située à la fin du Code, dans le Titre XX du Livre III, dont l'intitulé est également conservé (actuels articles 2219 à 2281). Précisément dans les dispositions préliminaires du Chapitre V du Titre III du Livre III du Code, énumérant les causes d'extinction des obligations, est annoncé le renvoi de la prescription à un titre particulier du Livre III (actuel art. 1234 ; disposition reprise par l'avant-projet, art. 1218 nouveau).

3 – Questions préalables : la politique législative.

Plus difficiles sont les questions de politique législative.

D'abord ont été délibérément écartés de l'avant-projet de réforme tous les délais de prescription énoncés par les traités internationaux et le droit européen, qui, en raison de leur supériorité sur le droit interne, ne peuvent être modifiés par la loi française, ce qui n'est pas sans inconvénient ; non en raison de leur longueur, jamais excessive, mais de leur diversité (un, deux ou trois ans) qui ne répond pas à une politique rationnelle et simplificatrice, mais au coup par coup, presque sur mesure, avec tous les inconvénients résultant de la multiplicité des délais.

Il a été aussi jugé utile d'écarter de l'avant-projet le droit pénal, la procédure civile, les voies d'exécution, le droit de la presse, le droit cambiaire, ceux des procédures collectives, de la famille, des successions et des régimes matrimoniaux, qui ont chacun une prescription dont le particularisme est marqué, sauf qu'aucun délai ne devrait dépasser la durée maximale de dix ou trente ans selon les cas, à l'exception des cas d'imprescriptibilité qui devraient être maintenus.

Ont aussi été écartés tous les délais égaux ou inférieurs à six mois pendant lesquels un droit doit être exercé ou une action introduite, à peine de déchéance ; par exemple, dans le régime de la copropriété immobilière, la contestation par un copropriétaire d'une décision de l'assemblée générale, qui doit à peine de déchéance être introduite dans un délai de deux mois (art. 42, al. 2, L. 10 juillet 1968). Ce n'est pas à proprement parler une prescription.

4 – Durée de la prescription.

Le premier problème législatif que soulève la prescription est la détermination de sa durée, étant acquis qu'il convient d'abréger au moins celle de droit commun et de diminuer, autant qu'il est possible, le nombre des prescriptions.

5 – Une réforme limitée ?

Il a paru indispensable de ne pas se cantonner à diminuer la durée de la prescription de droit commun qu'aujourd'hui tout le monde trouve excessive. Cette position minimale présenterait pourtant des avantages : d'abord, de faciliter la réforme, comme toute solution simple. En outre, un consensus général accepterait aisément

example, what is the proper place for the law of prescription within the framework of the Civil Code? Should it be moved, for example, putting it after Title III of Book III (Contracts and Obligations Created by Agreement in General) by creating a Title IIIB with articles numbered 1364-1 *et seq.*? This rearrangement was considered to be awkward, useless and contrary to the unified nature of acquisitive and extinctive prescription which it is thought should be maintained. So too, therefore, the present place of prescription ought to be maintained, being situated at the end of the Code in Title XX of Book III whose heading is also preserved (articles 2219 to 2281 of the present Code). In actual fact, cross-reference to the special title of Book III governing prescription (article 1234, a provision retained by the working group as article 1218) is made in the introductory provisions of Chapter V of Title III of Book III of the Code.

3. Preliminary issues: the policy pursued by the legislation

More difficult are issues of the policy to be pursued by the legislation.

First, all periods of prescription set out in international treaties or European law were deliberately excluded from the Reform Proposals since they are superior to internal law and cannot be modified by French legislation, even though this is not without its disadvantages, not because of their length (which is never excessive) but because of their diversity (one, two or three years), a diversity which reflects a piecemeal approach rather than a rational and simplifying policy, each being made one by one almost specially for each purpose with all the disadvantages which stem from a multiplicity of periods.

It was also considered useful to exclude from the Reform Proposals criminal law, civil procedure, means of enforcing judgments, press law, law governing banking and finance, the law governing collective procedures, family law, the law of succession and matrimonial property regimes, each one of which possesses rules of prescription whose special features are marked, except that no period ought to exceed a maximum of ten or thirty years as the case may be, with the exception of those situations where prescription is ruled out which ought to be retained.

We have also excluded all the periods which are less than or equal to six months during which a right must be exercised or an action brought on pain of expiry; for example, as regards the regime governing co-ownership of immovable property, challenges to decisions of general assemblies of co-owners, which must be brought on pain of expiry within a period of two months (Law of 10 July 1968, article 41, paragraph 2). These are not prescription periods properly so-called.

4. The duration of prescription

The first problem which prescription raises for the legislator is the setting of its duration, it being agreed that it is appropriate to curtail at least the period set by the general law and to reduce the number of periods as much as possible.

5. A limited reform?

It appeared indispensable to us that we should not restrict ourselves to reducing the prescription period set by the general law which today everyone considers excessively long, even if this minimal position would indeed present some advantages: first—and in common with every simple solution—it would make reform easy. Furthermore, a general consensus would easily accept the amendment of article

la modification de l'actuel article 2262 du Code civil en réduisant le délai à dix ans ; malgré l'avantage de la simplicité et du consensus, cette solution ne serait cependant qu'une réformette ; la réforme du droit de la prescription appelle une vision d'ensemble beaucoup plus drastique.

6 – Trois ans.

L'actuelle proposition posant une prescription de droit commun d'une durée de trois ans s'est fortement inspirée des règles nouvelles réformant le *Bürgerliches Gesetzbuch* (B.G.B.) (L. 26 novembre 2001, entrée en vigueur le 1er janvier 2002[1] et des propositions énoncées par les *Principes du droit européen des contrats*[2] prévoyant un délai unique de trois ans pour la prescription extinctive, qui la dissocierait donc de la prescription acquisitive, où un délai de trois ans serait évidemment inconcevable et pour laquelle il faudrait prévoir un délai de dix ans. Sans doute, ce système est-il surprenant au premier abord : passer de trente ans à trois ans, ne serait-ce pas aller d'un extrême à l'autre ?

Mais il présente de nombreux avantages, notamment les suivants : d'abord, il traduirait le nouvel esprit du droit civil des pays faisant partie de l'Union européenne et du droit communautaire contemporain (et dont la réforme du Code civil s'inspire chaque fois qu'il est utile) : non seulement une tendance à une certaine unification, mais surtout, de plus en plus attaché à la rapidité des opérations contractuelles et l'on comprend que les milieux d'affaires allemands (non, semble-t-il, tous les universitaires) y soient attachés. En outre, il présente les mérites de la simplification, qui en rendrait la connaissance facile, ce qui est particulièrement précieux dans une société devenue aussi complexe que la nôtre.

En apparence, le B.G.B., les *Principes européens*, et *Unidroit* ne connaissent qu'un seul délai. Cette simplification comporte une part d'illusions ; le droit allemand lui-même lui apporte de nombreuses exceptions (famille, successions, réparation du préjudice corporel dans la responsabilité délictuelle), sans compter celles provenant des droits international et européen. Sont également, en partie, un leurre, la brièveté et l'exclusion du contentieux, en raison notamment du régime particulier que le droit allemand prévoit pour le point de départ de la prescription.

7 – Pourquoi trois prescriptions ?

On a été amené à proposer une pluralité de délais, malgré les inconvénients qui en résultent, pluralisme réduit à trois : le droit commun (trois ans), un autre délai (dix ans) pour les prescriptions particulières, et un délai-butoir de dix ou de trente ans, à compter du fait générateur de l'obligation, pour la totalité des prescriptions, sans

---

[1] J. BAUERREIS, *Le nouveau droit de la prescription* (dans le BGB), RIDC, 2002, p. 1023 et s. ; V. LASSERRE-KIESOW, *loc. cit.*)
[2] Version française traduite par G. Rouhette, *Société de législation comparée*, 2002 ; cf. aussi : *Principes d'Unidroit*, cités par B. Fauvarque-Cosson, op. cit. p. 811.

2262 of the present Civil Code so as to reduce the period of prescription to ten years. However, despite these advantages of simplicity and general acceptability, this solution would be no more than a mini-reform. Reform of the law of prescription calls for a much more drastic and all-encompassing vision.

6. Three years

The present proposals which put forward a general prescription period of three years are very much inspired by the new rules which modified the German Civil Code (the B.G.B.) (Law of 26 November 2001 which came into force on 1 January 2002[1]) and the proposals set out by the *Principles of European Contract Law*[2] which envisage a single period of three years for extinctive prescription. Such a period would, however, require a certain separation of this law from the law governing acquisitive prescription where a period of three years would clearly be inconceivable and for which it would be necessary to provide a period of ten years. Without doubt, at first such a scheme would come as rather a surprise: would not moving from thirty years to three years mean going from one extreme to another?

But such a move would have a number of advantages, notably the following. First, it would give expression to the new way of private law thinking in countries which form part of the European Union and of modern EC law (from which reform of the Civil Code is inspired whenever it is appropriate). This way of thinking does not merely involve a tendency towards a degree of unification but above all an increasing awareness of the rapidity of contractual transactions, and so it is understandable that German business circles (if not, it would seem, all university jurists) are in favour of it. Furthermore, such a change has the merit of simplification, which would make it more easily accessible which is a particularly valuable characteristic in a society which has become as complex as our own.

At first sight, the German Civil Code, the *Principles of European Contract Law*[3] and the *Unidroit Principles*[4] recognise only a single prescription period. This simplification is partly illusory; German law itself has made very many exceptions to this position (in the context of family law, the law of succession, compensation for personal injuries in delictual liability) quite apart from those which stem from international or European law. The brief periods allowed for litigation before it is excluded are also partly a mirage notably because of German law's special set of rules governing the starting-point of prescription periods.

7. Why three prescription periods?

Despite the resulting disadvantages, we have become persuaded to recommend a variety of periods of prescription, but a variety reduced to three: a general rule of three years, a different period of ten years for special situations, and a back-stop period of ten or thirty years running from the events which give rise to the

---

[1] J. BAUERREIS, Le nouveau droit de la prescription (dans le BGB), RIDC, 2002, p. 1023 *et seq.*; V. LASSERRE-KIESOW, *loc. cit.* [See further (in English) R Zimmermann, *The New German Law of Obligations, Historical and Comparative Perpsectives* (Oxford University Press, 2005) ch 4.]

[2] The French version translated by G. Rouhette, *Société de législation comparée*, 2002; cf. also the *Unidroit Principles*, cited by B. Fauvarque-Cosson, *op. cit.*, p. 811.

[3] [See above, p 467, n 1].

[4] [See above, p 499, n 3.]

exception, même celles qui relèvent du droit de la famille, des successions, des régimes matrimoniaux ou du droit cambiaire.

De toute façon, une réforme de cette ampleur supposera un grand courage politique car elle soulèvera un tollé d'oppositions. Pourquoi, par exemple, diront les assurances et la Sécurité sociale, passer d'un délai de deux ans, qui donnait satisfaction à tout le monde, à trois ans ? À l'inverse, les salariés protesteront lorsque la prescription des dettes périodiques, telles que le salaire, passera de cinq à trois ans. Réponse : il faut absolument simplifier notre droit ; pour échapper à sa fragmentation, il faut trancher dans le vif.

8 – Liberté contractuelle.

L'ensemble de ces règles devrait être assoupli par un élargissement de la liberté contractuelle, comme le font actuellement le droit allemand, les principes du droit européen des contrats et l'avant-projet français de réforme du droit des obligations. Notre droit fait actuellement une distinction entre les clauses relatives à la prescription. Celles dont l'objet est d'allonger le délai sont en principe nulles parce que, au moins lorsque la prescription est longue, elles seraient l'équivalent d'une renonciation prohibée par la loi (art. 2220). Au contraire, les clauses restrictives sont valables si elles ne privent pas en fait le créancier du droit d'agir en justice.

Le principe nouveau devrait être, sans distinctions, la liberté à l'égard de la prescription, sauf butoirs dans l'abréviation et l'allongement des délais.

9 – Liberté contractuelle et ordre public.

Les deux butoirs limitant la possibilité d'abréger ou d'allonger par l'effet du contrat la durée de la prescription extinctive auraient pour conséquence de retirer ses effets pervers à la récente jurisprudence de la Cour de cassation prévoyant que l'énumération légale des causes d'interruption de la prescription n'est pas d'ordre public et que les parties peuvent y déroger.[1]

10 – Interruption du délai de prescription.

La première cause d'interruption de la prescription prévue par le droit actuel (art. 2244 à 2247, c. civ.) est la citation en justice. Depuis la fin du XIXe siècle, la jurisprudence a interprété de manière très extensive cette notion de citation en justice ; l'élargissement prétorien de la principale cause d'interruption est à la fois le résultat et la cause d'un abondant contentieux. Sont ainsi multipliées et rallongées les causes d'interruption de la prescription, ce qui est contraire à un des objectifs du présent avant-projet, tendant à en réduire la durée, à en simplifier le régime et à faire disparaître autant que possible les incertitudes du droit.

---

[1] Cass. civ. 1, 25 juin 2002, *Bull. civ.* I n° 214 ; D. 2003 195, note crit. Ph. Stoffel-Munck.

obligation governing all prescription without exception—even for those belonging to family law, the law of succession, matrimonial property regimes or the law governing banking and finance.

Anyway, a reform of this breadth relies on the existence of great political courage for it will be met with an outcry of opposition. For example, insurance companies and social security institutions will ask why one should move from a prescription period of two years to three years given that the former meets with universal satisfaction. Conversely, employees will protest if the prescription of periodic debts (such as salaries) changes from five to three years. Our response is that it is absolutely necessary for the law to be simplified: to escape its fragmentation we must take drastic action.

8. Freedom of contract

The entire body of these rules ought to be made more flexible by extending the impact of freedom of contract, as at present is the case with German law, the *Principles of European Contract Law* and also the French Reform Proposals for the law of obligations. At present our law draws a distinction in relation to contract terms governing prescription: those whose purpose is to extend a prescription period are in principle a nullity because, at least where the period is a long one, they would be equivalent to its renunciation, a renunciation which is forbidden by legislation (article 2220 of the Civil Code); by contrast, restrictive contract terms are valid as long as in fact they do not deprive a creditor of his right to act.

The new principle ought to be one of party freedom in relation to prescription without any distinctions, apart from checks on the shortening or lengthening of the periods which it sets.

9. Freedom of contract and public policy

The two checks which limit the possibility of shortening or lengthening the duration of extinctive prescription periods by contract would have as their consequence the removal of the perverse effects of the recent case-law of the Cour de cassation according to which the legislative enumeration of grounds of interruption of prescription is not considered a matter of public policy and therefore may be derogated from by the parties.[1]

10. The interruption of prescription[2]

The first ground of interruption of prescription recognised by existing law (articles 2244 to 2247 of the Civil Code) is bringing an action. Since the end of the nineteenth century, the courts have interpreted the notion of bringing an action in a very extensive way: this judicial enlargement of the principal ground of interruption of prescription is at the same time the result of and the cause of a good deal of litigation. In this way the grounds of interruption of prescription are multiplied and extended and this is contrary to one of the aims of the present Proposals which intend to reduce its duration, to simplify its regime and as much as possible to do away with the law's uncertainties.

---

[1] Cass civ (1) 25 Jun. 2002, Bull. civ. I, no. 214; D 2003.195 note P. Stoffel-Munck.

[2] [That is, where the running of the prescription period is halted on the occurrence of some act or event which is recognised by the law as sufficient to interrupt the prescription; when the period begins to run again, it starts afresh without taking into account the time which had already passed.]

Comme la récente réforme du droit allemand des obligations, il conviendrait de transformer la plupart des causes actuelles d'interruption de prescription en causes de suspension, et de n'admettre que deux causes d'interruption, peu susceptibles d'équivoque, la reconnaissance par le débiteur du bien fondé de la prétention du créancier et la mise en œuvre des voies d'exécution par le créancier. Il suffirait de reprendre le texte actuel de l'article 2248, en ajoutant que la reconnaissance du débiteur peut être tacite, par exemple : « *La prescription est interrompue par la reconnaissance même tacite que le débiteur ou le possesseur fait du droit de celui contre lequel il prescrivait* ». La citation en justice cesserait donc d'être une cause d'interruption de la prescription, qui deviendrait suspendue pendant la durée de la procédure.

11 – Disparition de l'interversion de la prescription extinctive.

Le premier effet produit actuellement par l'interruption de la prescription et qui doit être maintenu, est l'effacement de tous les effets antérieurs de la prescription ; une nouvelle prescription recommence à courir, de la même durée que l'ancienne. Le droit actuel prévoit aussi que certaines interruptions (non toutes) produisent une interversion de certaines prescriptions (non de toutes) : lorsqu'il s'agit d'une courte et, surtout, d'une très courte prescription fondée sur une présomption de paiement ou même lorsqu'il s'agit d'une dette périodique, l'interruption de la prescription vaut interversion si le débiteur a reconnu l'existence de son obligation par un acte écrit et chiffré et s'est engagé à la payer : à la courte prescription qui a été interrompue est substituée une nouvelle prescription, celle du droit commun. Pour fonder cette règle, les tribunaux invoquent généralement les dispositions de l'article 2274, qui pourtant ne disent rien de tel.

Cette institution prétorienne, pour traditionnelle qu'elle soit, est compliquée, paraît inopportune et devrait être abandonnée. Elle est un nid à procès, car l'incertitude continue à régner sur ses conditions : quelles sont les prescriptions susceptibles d'interversion ? Quel acte d'interruption vaut interversion ? Faut-il toujours pour qu'il y ait interversion une reconnaissance écrite et chiffrée du débiteur ? En outre, l'intérêt de cette institution apparaît surtout à l'égard des très courtes prescriptions dont la disparition rendrait l'interversion inutile. Enfin, l'interversion a pour conséquence d'allonger le délai nécessaire pour prescrire, ce qui est contraire à l'un des principaux objectifs de cette proposition de réforme.

In common with the recent reform of the German law of obligations, it is appropriate to convert the majority of what are now grounds of interruption of prescription into grounds of its suspension,[1] and to recognise only two grounds of interruption which do not attract ambiguity: acknowledgement by a debtor of the validity of his creditor's allegation and action by the creditor to enforce his rights. It would be enough to reproduce the present wording of article 2248, adding that an acknowledgment by a debtor can be implied, for example: 'Prescription is interrupted by an acknowledgment, even if implied, by a debtor or a person in possession, of the right of the person against whom time is running.' Therefore bringing an action would cease to be a ground of interruption of prescription, which would instead become suspended while any proceedings lasted.

11. The disappearance of the conversion of one extinctive prescription period into another[2]

The first effect which the interruption of prescription at present produces, and which ought to be retained, is the wiping away of all the previous consequences of prescription, so that a new period of prescription of the same duration as before starts to run. Existing law also provides that some (but not all) interruptions result in the conversion of some (but not all) prescription periods into a different prescription period. Where a short—and, above all, very short—prescription period based on a presumption of satisfaction is involved, or even where a periodic debt is involved, an interruption of prescription is deemed to lead to its conversion in this sense as long as the debtor has acknowledged the existence of his obligation by a written instrument recording the amount of the debt and has undertaken to satisfy it. In these circumstances, a new prescription period—the period of the general law—is substituted for the short prescription which has been interrupted. To give a legal basis for this rule, the courts generally invoke the provisions set out in article 2274 which actually say nothing of the kind.[3]

However traditional it may be, this judicial doctrinal construction is complicated, appears inconvenient and ought to be abandoned. It is a breeding-ground for litigation, for uncertainty continues to reign as to where it applies: which prescriptions are liable to conversion? What type of act of interruption is to count as attracting conversion? For such a conversion, is it always necessary for there to be a written acknowledgement which records the amount of the debt made by the debtor? Furthermore, the significance of this doctrine appears above all in relation to very short prescriptions whose disappearance would render conversion useless. Finally, conversion has the effect of lengthening the periods necessary for prescription, which is contrary to one of the principal aims of these Reform Proposals.

[1] [That is, the running of the prescription period is halted, but when it begins to run again it resumes at the point within the period at which it had reached when it was suspended.]

[2] ['Conversion of one ... period into another' translates *interversion*, a notion which is not known in the English law of limitation of actions: see above, p 575, n 3.]

[3] [The principle of *interversion* has been deduced from article 2274 Cc, para 2, which provides that the prescription period ceases to run where there is a written acknowledgment of the debt which establishes its value. This can be seen as analogous to a novation of the debt, under which the debtor's new undertaking constitutes a new ground of claim by the creditor and therefore sets a new period of prescription running: Malaurie, Aynès and Stoffel-Munck, *Les obligations*, above, p 839, n 3, no 1211. The term '*interversion*' does not appear in the Code civil.]

La récente réforme allemande des dispositions du B.G.B. intéressant le droit des obligations et les *Principes du droit européen des contrats* l'ont aujourd'hui purement et simplement abandonnée.

Cette exclusion de l'interversion de la prescription extinctive ne devrait pas s'appliquer à l'hypothèse toute différente de l'interversion applicable à l'usucapion (art. 2253 de l'avant-projet, 2238 actuel, C. civ.). Ainsi, le détenteur précaire qui, en principe, ne peut usucaper (art. 2251 de l'avant-projet, 2236 actuel) peut le faire s'il intervertit son titre, en affirmant qu'il n'est pas un détenteur précaire et que, désormais, il possède pour son compte. Les régimes de la prescription extinctive et de l'usucapion ne sont pas identiques.

12 – Suspension.

La suspension de la prescription n'efface pas le délai déjà couru ; elle en arrête temporairement le cours. Une fois la suspension achevée, la prescription reprend son cours, en tenant compte du délai déjà couru.

La suspension a, dans notre histoire, beaucoup évolué ; en outre, dans plusieurs de ses aspects, son régime actuel comporte de nombreuses incertitudes. La réforme devrait faire disparaître ces incertitudes, autant qu'il est possible, et tenir pour acquises certaines de ses évolutions.

Notre Ancien droit liait étroitement la suspension à l'équité, telle que le juge pouvait l'apprécier : une prescription était, au cas par cas, suspendue chaque fois que le juge estimait que tel ou tel événement rendait impossible l'exercice du droit ; conformément à leur conception du droit, attachée à la majesté et à l'exclusivité de la loi, les rédacteurs du Code civil ont entendu faire disparaître le caractère prétorien de la suspension, qui était, en effet, gros des risques d'incertitude et d'arbitraire ; ils ont donc décidé qu'il ne pouvait y avoir de suspension que lorsque la loi l'avait prévu : art. 2251 : « *La prescription court contre toutes personnes à moins qu'elles ne soient dans quelque exception établie par une loi* ».

La cause de suspension la plus importante tient à la tutelle pour incapacité (minorité ou tutelle des majeurs) et n'est exclue que pour les très courtes prescriptions, qui ne sont pas suspendues, sauf le recours de l'incapable contre son tuteur (art. 2278, C. civ.).

Dans le droit actuel, le principe de légalité domine donc en apparence la suspension de la prescription qui n'existe que dans les conditions prévues par la loi. La jurisprudence a pourtant, de deux manières différentes, porté atteinte à ce légalisme. D'une part, il est des cas où la prescription devrait être suspendue si l'on avait appliqué strictement la loi, mais ne l'est pas parce qu'il s'agit d'un délai préfix. D'autre part et à l'inverse, il est des cas où la prescription est suspendue par les

And today the recent German reform of the provisions of the German Civil Code concerning the law of obligations and the *Principles of European Contract Law* have simply abandoned it.

This rejection of the conversion of an extinctive prescription period ought not to be carried over to the completely different situation of conversion which applies in the case of usucapion (article 2253 of the Reform Proposals; article 2238 of the present Civil Code). So, a holder of property with the permission of its owner is in principle unable to acquire it by usucapion[1] (article 2251 of the Reform Proposals; article 2236 of the present Civil Code), but he can do so if he converts his own title, by declaring that he is no longer a permitted holder and for the future will possess it on his own account. The regimes governing extinctive prescription and usucapion are not identical.

12. Suspension

The suspension of prescription does not wipe out the period which has already run; it stops time running temporarily. Once the suspension has ended, the prescription period resumes its course, taking into account the period which has already run.

Our law governing suspension has developed a lot over time, and its present regime possesses many uncertainties. Reform ought to get rid of these uncertainties as far as possible and recognise as established some of these developments.

French law before the Revolution tied suspension strictly to equity which it was in the power of the courts to assess, so that a period of prescription was suspended on a case-by-case basis whenever the court thought that one or another event made the exercise of a right impossible. In keeping with their concept of law and their attachment to the majesty and the exclusivity of legislation, the draftsmen of the Civil Code sought to get rid of the judicial character of suspension which was in reality replete with the risk of uncertainty and arbitrariness and so they decided that there could be no suspension unless legislation had so provided. As article 2251 states: 'Prescription runs against all people unless they fall within an exception established by legislation.'

The most important ground of suspension relates to guardianship for incapacity (whether during minority or where an adult so requires) and this applies to all prescription periods except those which are very short which are not suspended (though without prejudice to any subsequent recourse by the incapable person against his guardian) (article 2278).

Under the present law, the principle of legality—that law should rest on legislation—therefore apparently dominates suspensions of prescription which exist only in the circumstances set by legislation. However, the courts have undermined this position in two different ways. On the one hand, there are cases where a prescription period ought to have been suspended if the legislative rule had been strictly applied, but where it was not on the basis that the case concerned non-suspendable periods. On the other hand (and conversely), there are cases where

---

[1] ['*Usucapion*' is the traditional name for the acquisition of property by possession for the prescription period. It is not the name given by the Code, but the general approach to acquisitive prescription is based on the Roman law of *usucapio*. For the Roman law, see Thomas, *Textbook of Roman Law*, above, p 517, n 2, 157-65, and Cartwright, above, pp 363-5.]

juges, alors qu'aucune disposition légale ne l'avait prévu, par application de la règle *contra non valentem...*

13 – *Suppression des délais préfix.*

La jurisprudence, souvent en l'absence de tout texte, a admis l'existence de « délais préfix » qui ne peuvent être suspendus, même pour cause d'incapacité ; par exemple, le délai de deux ans pendant lequel la rescision d'une vente d'immeuble pour cause de lésion peut être introduite, comme le prévoit expressément l'art. 1676, alinéa 2, du Code civil. De même, bien qu'aucun texte ne l'ait prévu, la jurisprudence décide qu'est un délai préfix le délai de trois ans pendant lequel un meuble perdu ou volé peut être revendiqué (art. 2272, al. 2 c. civ.).[2] Souvent aussi, mais non toujours, la jurisprudence décide que le juge peut soulever d'office l'expiration d'un délai préfix.

Aucun critère précis ne permet de déterminer quels délais sont ou ne sont pas préfix. Sur ce point également, le droit actuel de la prescription extinctive souffre d'incertitudes, causes de contentieux et de discussions parfois interminables. La réforme devrait faire disparaître la notion de délai préfix, sauf que la loi peut expressément décider, comme elle le fait dans l'article 1676 du Code civil, que, contrairement au droit commun, tel ou tel délai court contre les incapables.

14 – *Contra non valentem.*

Une jurisprudence abondante, ancienne et presque constante restitue au juge en matière de prescription extinctive le pouvoir créateur et modificateur des prescriptions que l'Ancien droit lui avait conféré et que le Code civil avait probablement voulu lui retirer.

Elle a ressuscité la maxime d'équité *Contra non valentem agere non currit prescriptio* : la prescription ne court pas contre celui qui a été empêché d'agir. Ainsi, la jurisprudence retarde-t-elle le point de départ de la prescription, lorsque le créancier ne peut agir pour cause de force majeure et même lorsque le créancier ignorait l'existence de son droit si cette ignorance avait une cause légitime : comme dans l'Ancien droit, il s'agit d'une mesure d'équité, très circonstanciée. La Cour de cassation énonce cette règle prétorienne, dans un attendu de principe assez souvent répété presque de la même manière : « *la prescription ne court pas contre celui qui est dans l'impossibilité d'agir par suite d'un empêchement quelconque résultant soit de la loi, soit de la convention ou de la force majeure* ».[3]

La jurisprudence applique cette règle d'équité de façon circonstanciée. Un de ses critères est de s'attacher au moment où apparaît l'impossibilité d'agir. Les juges n'appliquent la règle que si cette impossibilité d'agir n'est apparue que dans les

---

[2] Cass. crim., 30 oct. 1969, J.C.P. G 1970, II, 16333, note G. Goubeaux.
[3] V. par exemple: Cass. civ. 1re, 22 déc. 1959, J.C.P. 1960, II, 11494, note signée P. E.

a prescription period was suspended by the court even though this was not provided for by any legislative provision, by application of the rule *contra non valentem* ('prescription does not run against a person who is unable to act').[1]

13. *The suppression of non-suspendable periods*

The courts have accepted, often in the absence of any legislative authority, the existence of 'non-suspendable periods' which cannot be suspended even on the ground of incapacity, for example, the two-year period during which an action for rescission of a contract of sale of immovable property on the ground of gross undervalue may be brought as expressly provided for by article 1676 paragraph 2 of the Civil Code. Similarly, even though no legislative provision so provides, the case-law holds that the period of three years during which movable property which is lost or stolen may be reclaimed (article 2272 paragraph 2 of the Civil Code) is also a non-suspendable period.[2] Furthermore, often—though not always—the case-law holds that a court may raise the issue of the expiry of a non-suspendable period on its own initiative.

There is no precise criterion on the basis of which one can determine which periods are or are not non-suspendable. On this point too, the existing law of extinctive prescription suffers from uncertainty, which is a cause of litigation and often interminable arguments. Reform ought to get rid of the notion of a non-suspendable prescription period, without prejudice to the possibility of legislation deciding otherwise expressly—as indeed it does in the case of article 1676 of the Civil Code which provides in derogation from the general legal position that this or that prescription period runs against incapable persons.

14. *Contra non valentem*

In the area of extinctive prescription a very old, very abundant and almost unwavering case-law has restored to the courts the creative and corrective power with which pre-Revolutionary law had endowed them and which the Civil Code had probably intended to remove from them.

Case-law has resuscitated the equitable maxim *contra non valentem agere non currit praescriptio*: prescription does not run against a person who is unable to act. Therefore, the courts are able to hold back the starting-point of prescription where the creditor was unable to act owing to force majeure and even where the creditor was unaware of the existence of his right if this ignorance had a legitimate ground: as in the pre-Revolutionary law, the courts intervene as equity demands and in the light of the particular circumstances. The Cour de cassation announces this judge-made rule in a formal legal ground of principle which it quite often repeats in almost the same way: 'prescription does not run against a person who finds it impossible to act as a result of any impediment whether this results from legislation, from an agreement or from force majeure.'[3]

The courts apply this equitable rule in a very contextual way. One of the criteria used by the courts relates to the moment when the impossibility to act appears. The courts apply the rule only if this impossibility to act appeared only at the very end

---

[1] [For the operation of this rule, see below, sub 14.]
[2] Cass crim. 30 Oct. 1969, JCP 1970.II.16333 note G. Goubeaux.
[3] E.g. Cass civ. (1) 22 Dec. 1959, JCP 1960.II.11494 note P.E.

derniers temps du délai ; au contraire, ils en refusent l'application si le créancier a joui d'un délai suffisant après la disparition de cet obstacle.[1]

La récente réforme allemande du droit des obligations dans le B.G.B. a entendu légaliser la règle en la précisant par des chiffres : la force majeure empêchant le créancier d'agir n'est une cause de suspension de la prescription que si elle est intervenue dans les six mois précédant l'expiration du délai de prescription (§206 ; cf. aussi les *Principes du droit européen des contrats*, art. 14 303, 2). Le présent avant-projet s'est inspiré de cette règle.

15 – Office du juge.

« *Les juges ne peuvent pas suppléer d'office le moyen résultant de la prescription* ». La règle énoncée par l'art. 2223 s'applique même lorsque la prescription est d'ordre public. Elle traduit un consensus général et doit être maintenue. Il n'y a de discussion en doctrine que pour les délais préfix ; la notion et l'institution de délai préfix disparaissant, la discussion devient sans objet.

16 – Point de départ de la prescription.

Le principe est que le point de départ du délai de prescription est, non le jour où la créance est née, mais celui où le créancier peut agir. Par exemple, à l'égard des créances successives (ex. les loyers), la prescription court à compter de chaque échéance ; de même pour une dette à terme, le jour où le terme est échu.

À l'égard des dettes non exigibles, la loi prévoit que le point de départ de la prescription est retardé : pour une dette à terme, au jour où le terme est échu ; pour une dette sous condition suspensive, au jour où la condition est réalisée (art. 2257 c. civ.) ; à l'égard d'une action en nullité pour vice du consentement, du jour où le vice a cessé ou de celui où la victime en a eu connaissance (art. 1304, al. 2 c. civ.) ; mais des butoirs s'imposent ; même si la victime du vice du consentement ignorait que son consentement avait été donné par erreur, extorqué par violence ou surpris par dol, l'action est prescrite après un délai butoir : dix ans après la conclusion du contrat. Pour les actions en responsabilité civile extracontractuelle, la prescription de trois ans (dans l'actuel avant-projet) court du jour où la victime pouvait agir, c'est-à-dire eu connaissance du dommage, de son étendue ou de son aggravation (art. 2270-1 c. civ.) ; mais même si la victime n'a pas eu connaissance du dommage, de son étendue et de son aggravation, l'action est prescrite par un délai butoir de dix ans à compter de la commission du fait dommageable, délai qui est porté à trente ans s'il s'agit d'un préjudice corporel ou résultant d'un acte de barbarie ou d'un dommage causé à l'environnement.

---

[1] V. Par exemple: Cass. com, 11 janv. 1994, *Bull. civ.* IV, n° 22 ; *RTD civ.* 1995, 114, obs. J. Mestre : « *la règle selon laquelle la prescription ne court pas contre celui qui est dans l'impossibilité d'agir par la suite d'un empêchement quelconque résultant soit de la loi, soit de la convention ou de la force majeure, ne s'applique pas lorsque le titulaire de l'action disposait encore au moment où cet empêchement a pris fin, du temps nécessaire pour agir avant l'expiration du délai de prescription.* ».

of the prescription period and so they refuse to apply it if the creditor enjoyed a sufficient period to sue after the disappearance of the obstacle.[1]

The recent German reform of the law of obligations in the German Civil Code intended to give a legislative basis for the rule by providing detailed figures: so, force majeure which prevents the creditor from acting is not a ground of suspension of prescription unless it took place in the six months preceding the expiry of the prescription period (B.G.B. paragraph 206 and cf. the Principles of European Contract Law, article 14.303(2)). The present Reform Proposals are inspired by this rule.

15. The role of the court

'A court cannot raise a plea of prescription on its own initiative.' This rule set out by article 2223 applies even where prescription is a matter of public policy. It meets with general agreement and ought to be retained. It is debated by legal writers only as regards non-suspendable periods of prescription and so if the notion and doctrine of non-suspendable periods of prescription were to disappear, this debate would lose its point.

16. The starting-point of the prescription period

The principle is that the starting-point of a prescription period is the day when the creditor can act rather than the day when his right arises. For example, as regards successive rights (such as in the case of rent), prescription runs from the day when each payment falls due; similarly, for a debt whose payment is deferred, it is the day when the period of credit expires.

As regards debts which are not enforceable, legislation provides that the starting-point of prescription is held back: for a debt whose payment is deferred, to the day when the period of credit expires; for a debt subject to a suspensive condition, to the day when the condition is satisfied (article 2257 of the Civil Code); as regards an action for annulment on the ground of defect in consent, to the day when the defect ceased or to the day when the victim became aware of it (article 1304 paragraph 2 of the Civil Code). But some back-stops are necessary here; so even if a victim of a defect in consent was unaware that his consent was given by mistake, or obtained by fraud, or extracted by duress, his action becomes prescribed after a back-stop period of ten years from the formation of the contract. For actions claiming extra-contractual liability, the prescription period of three years (in the present Proposals) runs from the day when the victim was able to act, that is, when he became aware of the harm, its extent or its worsening (article 2270-1 of the Civil Code). But even if the victim was unaware of the damage, its extent and its worsening, his action becomes prescribed after a back-stop period of ten years from the commission of the action which caused the harm, a period which is extended to thirty years if it involves personal injury or results from an act of barbarism or harm to the environment.

---

[1] E.g. Cass com. 11 Jan. 1994, Bull. civ. IV no. 22, RTDCiv. 1995.114 comments J. Mestre: 'the rule according to which prescription does not run against a person who finds it impossible to act as a result of any impediment whether this results from legislation, from an agreement or from force majeure does not apply where at the time when this impediment has ended the person with the right of action still has the time necessary to act before the expiry of the prescription period'.

La plupart des dispositions actuelles du Code civil relatives au point de départ de la prescription devraient donc être maintenues, sauf à ajouter une règle prévoyant une date butoir lorsque le créancier a ignoré l'existence du vice du consentement ou la victime l'existence, l'étendue ou l'aggravation du dommage.

17 – Effet de la prescription.

La prescription libératoire a essentiellement un effet extinctif ; cependant, le payement d'une dette prescrite ne peut jamais être répété, ce que les tribunaux expliquent parfois par la survie d'une obligation naturelle (art. 1239 c. civ.). L'explication est contestable, car il importe peu que le *solvens* ait commis une erreur en ignorant la prescription qui le libérait. Aussi conviendrait-il d'ajouter un alinéa 3 à l'article 1235 du Code civil, énonçant que « *le payement d'une dette prescrite ne peut être répété* ».

18 – Droit transitoire.

La jurisprudence a adopté des règles simples pour le droit transitoire, dont l'actuel avant-projet s'est inspiré.

19 – Numérotation.

La simplification du droit de la prescription aurait pour conséquence la disparition de nombreux articles du Code civil. Il a été jugé utile de maintenir le numéro de l'article 2279, enraciné dans la culture et la mémoire nationales, comme les articles 544 et 1134.

Chapitre I
Dispositions générales
(Articles 2234 à 2242)

Art. 2234

La prescription est un moyen d'acquérir ou de se libérer par un certain laps de temps, et sous les conditions déterminées par la loi.

Art. 2235

On peut renoncer à une prescription acquise.

La durée de la prescription extinctive peut être abrégée ou allongée par accord des parties ou de leurs représentants légaux ; mais elle ne peut être réduite à moins d'un an ni étendue à plus de dix ans.

The majority of the present provisions of the Civil Code governing the starting-point for the running of prescription periods ought therefore to be retained, except that a rule should be added providing a back-stop date for the situation where a creditor was unaware of the existence of a defect in consent or a victim was unaware of the existence, extent or worsening of the harm.

17. The effect of prescription

Liberating prescription has an essentially extinctive effect. However, payment of a debt which has become prescribed can never be claimed back, a rule which the courts often explain as the result of a natural obligation (article 1239 of the Civil Code). This explanation is debatable as it does not matter whether or not the person paying was mistaken in being unaware of the expiry of the prescription which had in fact released him. Thus it is appropriate to add a third paragraph to article 1235 of the Civil Code stating that 'payment of a debt once prescribed cannot be recovered.'

18. Transitional provisions

The case-law has adopted simple rules by way of transitional provisions from which the present Proposals take their inspiration.

19. Numbering

The simplification of the law of prescription would have the effect of getting rid of many articles of the Civil Code. It was thought useful to retain the number of article 2279—which is deeply rooted in national culture and memory in the same way as articles 544 and 1134.[1]

Chapter I
General Provisions
(Articles 2234 to 2242)

Art. 2234

Prescription is a means of acquiring something or of being freed after a certain lapse of time and subject to conditions set by legislation.

Art. 2235

A person may renounce the benefit of a completed prescription.

The duration of an extinctive prescription period can be shortened or prolonged by the agreement of the parties or of their legal representatives, but it may not be reduced below a year nor extended to more than ten years.

---

[1] [Article 1134 Cc is also within the scope of the amendments proposed by the *Avant-projet*, but its numbering is similarly retained.]

Art. 2236

La renonciation à la prescription est expresse ou tacite ; la renonciation tacite résulte d'un fait qui suppose l'abandon du droit acquis.

Art. 2237

Celui qui ne peut aliéner ne peut renoncer à la prescription acquise.

Art. 2238

Les juges ne peuvent pas suppléer d'office le moyen résultant de la prescription, lors même qu'elle intéresse l'ordre public.

Art. 2239

La prescription peut être opposée en tout état de cause, même devant la cour d'appel, à moins que la partie qui n'aurait pas opposé le moyen de la prescription ne doive, en raison des circonstances, être présumée y avoir tacitement renoncé.

Art. 2240

Les créanciers, ou toute autre personne ayant intérêt à ce que la prescription soit acquise, peuvent l'opposer, ou l'invoquer encore que le débiteur ou le propriétaire y renonce.

Art. 2241

Les choses qui ne sont pas dans le commerce échappent à toute prescription.

Art. 2242

L'État, les collectivités locales et les établissements publics sont soumis aux mêmes prescriptions que les particuliers, et peuvent également les opposer ou les invoquer.

Chapitre II
De la possession

Art. 2243

La possession est la détention ou la jouissance d'une chose ou d'un droit que nous tenons ou que nous exerçons par nous-mêmes, ou par un autre qui la tient ou qui l'exerce en notre nom.

Art. 2244

Pour pouvoir prescrire, il faut une possession continue et non interrompue, paisible, publique, non équivoque, et à titre de propriétaire.

Art. 2236

Renunciation of a prescription period may be express or implied; an implied renunciation results from an action which assumes the abandonment of the right to be acquired by prescription.

Art. 2237

A person cannot renounce a prescription period if he does not have the legal right to dispose of property.

Art. 2238

A court may not raise a plea of prescription on its own initiative even where it is a matter of public policy.

Art. 2239

A plea of prescription may be put in defence at any stage in the proceedings, even before the Court of Appeal, unless the party who failed to do so earlier ought to be presumed in the circumstances to have impliedly renounced his right to do so.

Art. 2240

Creditors or any other person having an interest in the completion of a period of prescription may put it in defence or invoke it even where the debtor or the owner have renounced the right to do.

Art. 2241

Things which may not be owned or alienated may not be subject to any form of prescription.

Art. 2242

The State, local authorities and public bodies are subject to the same prescriptions as individuals and equally may put them in defence or invoke their benefit.

Chapter II
Possession

Art. 2243

Possession is the detention or enjoyment of a thing or a right which we hold or which we exercise ourselves or through another person who holds or exercises it in our name.

Art. 2444

In order for prescription to take place, possession must be continuous and uninterrupted, peaceful, public, unequivocal and as an owner.

Art. 2245

On est toujours présumé posséder pour soi, et à titre de propriétaire, s'il n'est prouvé qu'on a commencé à posséder pour un autre.

Art. 2246

Quand on a commencé à posséder pour autrui, on est toujours présumé posséder au même titre, s'il n'y a preuve du contraire.

Art. 2247

Les actes de pure faculté et ceux de simple tolérance ne peuvent fonder ni possession ni prescription.

Art. 2248

Les actes de violence ne peuvent fonder non plus une possession capable d'opérer la prescription.

La possession utile ne commence que lorsque la violence a cessé.

Art. 2249

Le possesseur actuel qui prouve avoir possédé anciennement, est présumé avoir possédé dans le temps intermédiaire, sauf la preuve contraire.

Art. 2250

Pour compléter la prescription, on peut joindre à sa possession celle de son auteur, de quelque manière qu'on lui ait succédé, soit à titre universel ou particulier, soit à titre gratuit ou onéreux.

Chapitre III
Des causes qui empêchent la prescription

Art. 2251

Ceux qui possèdent pour autrui ne prescrivent jamais par quelque laps de temps que ce soit.

Art. 2245

A person is always presumed to possess something for himself and as its owner unless it is proved that he started to possess it on behalf of another person.

Art. 2246

Where a person starts to possess something on behalf of another he is always presumed to possess it on the same basis, unless there is proof to the contrary.

Art. 2247

Acts which are merely permitted or which are simply tolerated cannot support either possession or prescription.

Art. 2248

Nor can acts of force[1] provide a basis for possession capable of attracting prescription.

Effective possession may arise only when any force has ceased.

Art. 2249

A present possessor who shows that he was formerly in possession is presumed to have been in possession during the intervening period, subject to proof to the contrary.

Art. 2250

In order to complete the period set for prescription, a person may add to his own period of possession any time of possession by his predecessor in title by whatever way in which he succeeded him, whether universally or individually,[2] and whether gratuitously or for value.

Chapter III
The Grounds on which Prescription is Impeded

Art. 2251

A person who possesses property on behalf of another person can never benefit from prescription however much time elapses.

---

[1] [The French is *actes de violence*, but here '*violence*' is used in a non-technical sense of 'force' rather than the narrower meaning of 'duress' as a defect of consent in the formation of a contract: above, article 1114.]

[2] ['Universal succession' refers to the situation where a person acquires ownership of property as part of a larger body of property, notably in the case of inheritance of an estate by an heir; 'individual succession' occurs where a person acquires ownership of property by way of a single transaction or transaction, as in the case of sale.]

Ainsi, le locataire, le dépositaire, l'usufruitier et tous autres qui détiennent précairement la chose du propriétaire, ne peuvent la prescrire.

Art. 2252

Les héritiers de ceux qui tenaient la chose à quelqu'un des titres désignés par l'article précédent ne peuvent non plus prescrire.

Art. 2253

Néanmoins, les personnes énoncées dans les articles 2251 et 2252 peuvent prescrire, si le titre de leur possession se trouve interverti, soit par une cause venant d'un tiers, soit par la contradiction qu'elles ont opposée au droit du propriétaire.

Art. 2254

Ceux à qui les locataires, dépositaires et autres détenteurs précaires ont transmis la chose par un titre translatif de propriété peuvent la prescrire.

Art. 2255

On ne peut prescrire contre son titre, en ce sens que l'on ne peut se changer à soi-même la cause et le principe de sa possession.

Art. 2256

On peut prescrire contre son titre, en ce sens que l'on prescrit la libération de l'obligation que l'on a contractée.

Chapitre IV
Des causes qui interrompent ou qui suspendent le cours de la prescription

Section 1
Des causes qui interrompent la prescription

Art. 2257

La prescription peut être interrompue ou naturellement ou civilement.

So, tenants, depositees, usufructuaries and all other persons who hold property as a result of its owner's permission cannot acquire it by prescription.

Art. 2252

The heirs of those who have held property on one of the legal bases indicated by the preceding article cannot acquire it by prescription either.

Art. 2253

Nevertheless, the persons referred to by articles 2251 and 2252 can acquire property by prescription if the basis of their possession changes either for a reason originating from a third party or as a result of the opposition which they have mounted to the rights of the owner.

Art. 2254

Persons to whom tenants, depositees and other persons who have held a thing with its owner's permission have conveyed it may acquire it by prescription.

Art. 2255

A person may not rely on prescription inconsistently with his own title, in the sense that he cannot himself change the legal ground or the principle of his own possession.

Art. 2256

A person may rely on prescription inconsistently with his own title in the sense that he can be freed by prescription from an obligation which he has contracted.

Chapter IV
The Grounds on which the Running of Prescription is Interrupted or Suspended

Section 1
The Grounds on which Prescription is Interrupted

Art. 2257

Prescription can be interrupted either naturally or civilly.[1]

---

[1] [This distinction is Roman in its origin. The *Avant-projet* goes on to define its significance in the modern French context, but it is worth noting that the 'civil interruptions' were so-called as they arose from the Roman civil law (for example through a legal claim against the possessor) and 'natural' as in the simple case of loss of possession: Thomas, *Textbook of Roman Law*, above, p 517, n 2, 160.]

Art. 2258

Il y a interruption naturelle, lorsque le possesseur est privé pendant plus d'un an de la jouissance de la chose, soit par l'ancien propriétaire, soit même par un tiers.

Art. 2259

Il y a interruption civile lorsque le débiteur ou le possesseur reconnaît, même tacitement, le droit de celui contre lequel il prescrivait.

Art. 2260

La prescription est également interrompue par un acte d'exécution tel qu'un commandement ou une saisie.

Art. 2261

L'interruption efface la prescription ; elle en fait courir une nouvelle de même durée que l'ancienne.

Obs. : L'article 2253, relatif à une autre hypothèse d'interversion est maintenu.

Section 2
Du cours de la prescription et des causes qui le suspendent

Art. 2262

La prescription a pour point de départ le jour où le créancier peut agir.

Art. 2263

Elle ne court pas :

À l'égard d'une créance qui dépend d'une condition, jusqu'à ce que la condition arrive ou défaille ;

À l'égard d'une action en garantie, jusqu'à ce que l'éviction ait lieu ;

À l'égard d'une créance à jour fixe, jusqu'à ce que ce jour soit arrivé.

Art. 2264

Elle ne court pas ou est suspendue, tant que les parties négocient de bonne foi.

Il en est de même tant que le débiteur ignore l'existence ou l'étendue de la créance.

Art. 2265

La suspension de la prescription en arrête temporairement le cours sans effacer le délai déjà couru.

Art. 2258

A natural interruption occurs where a possessor of a thing is deprived of its enjoyment for more than a year either by its former owner or even by a third party.

Art. 2259

A civil interruption occurs where a debtor or a possessor of a thing acknowledges the right of the person against whom time is running, even where this acknowledgement is implied.

Art. 2260

Prescription is also interrupted by an act of enforcement such as the service of a summons or seizure of the thing.

Art. 2261

Interruption wipes out time already run for prescription and it causes a new period to run of the same duration as the previous one.

> *Comment: article 2253, which is concerned with another different situation where a prescription period is converted, is retained.*

Section 2
The Running of Time for Prescription and the Grounds on which it is Suspended

Art. 2262

The starting-point for the running of time for prescription is the day when the creditor can act.

Art. 2263

Time does not run:

in the case of a right under an obligation which is subject to a condition, until that condition is fulfilled or fails;

in the case of an action on the guarantee of title, until dispossession has taken place;

in the case of a right under an obligation which is set for a fixed day, until that day arrives.

Art. 2264

Time does not run or is suspended while the parties negotiate in good faith.

The same rule applies for as long as the debtor is unaware of the existence or extent of the right against him.

Art. 2265

The suspension of prescription halts the running of time temporarily without wiping out time already run.

Art. 2266

La prescription court contre toute personne qui n'est pas dans l'impossibilité d'agir par suite d'un empêchement résultant de la loi, de la convention ou de la force majeure.

La force majeure, lorsqu'elle est temporaire, n'est une cause de suspension que si elle est intervenue dans les six mois précédant l'expiration du délai de prescription.

Art. 2267

La prescription est suspendue pendant le procès jusqu'à son achèvement.

Art. 2268

Elle ne court pas contre les mineurs non émancipés et les majeurs en tutelle.

Art. 2269

Elle ne court pas entre époux.

Art. 2270

Elle est également suspendue contre l'héritier bénéficiaire à l'égard des créances que l'héritier a contre la succession.

Art. 2271

Mais elle court contre une succession vacante, quoique non pourvue de curateur.

Elle court encore pendant les délais pour exercer l'option successorale.

Art. 2266

Time runs against any person who does not find it impossible to act owing to an impediment caused by legislation, a contract or *force majeure*.

Where *force majeure* is temporary it is a ground of suspension of prescription only where it occurred within six months of expiry of its period.

Art. 2267

Prescription is suspended during the course of proceedings until their conclusion.

Art. 2268

Time does not run against unemancipated minors[1] or adults subject to guardianship.[2]

Art. 2269

Time does not run as between husband and wife.

Art. 2270

Equally, the running of time is suspended against an heir with benefit of inventory[3] as regards rights which the heir possesses against the estate.

Art. 2271

But time runs against a vacant estate even where it does not have the benefit of a curator.[4]

It also runs during the time set for an heir to decide whether or not to accept an estate.[5]

---

[1] [For the emancipation of minors, see above, p 649, n 1.]

[2] [For the guardianship of adults, see above, p 823, n 3.]

[3] [On death, the heir may declare that he or she accepts the benefit of his or her inheritance subject to the 'benefit of inventory' (termed *'l'acceptation de la succession à concurrence de l'actif net'*), the 'inventory' being an estimate of the assets and debts of the deceased. This limits the heir's own personal liability: see articles 787 ff Cc as inserted by the Law no 2006-728 of 23 June 2006, article 1, which reformed the law of succession.]

[4] [A vacant estate is one where there is no heir who has accepted the succession: article 809 Cc (as inserted by the Law cited above, n 3. The 'benefit of a curator' refers to the possibility in these circumstances of appointment of another person (the *curateur*) to manage the estate: article 809-1 ff Cc as inserted by the Law cited above, n 3.]

[5] [An heir may accept or reject the succession, the Code civil providing that he or she cannot be forced to make an election before the expiry of 4 months from the 'opening' of the succession, ie the date of decease: articles 720 and 768 ff Cc esp 771 as inserted by the Law cited above, n 3.]

Chapitre V
Du temps requis pour prescrire
Section 1
Dispositions générales

Art. 2272

La prescription se compte par jours, et non par heures.

Art. 2273

Elle est acquise lorsque le dernier jour du terme est accompli.

Art. 2274

Toutes les actions sont prescrites par trois ans, sans que celui qui allègue cette prescription soit obligé d'en rapporter un titre ou qu'on puisse lui opposer l'exception déduite de la mauvaise foi.

Section 2
Des prescriptions particulières

Art. 2275

Toutefois, se prescrivent par dix ans :

1. les actions en responsabilité civile, tendant à la réparation d'un préjudice corporel ou de tout préjudice causé par des actes de barbarie ;

2. les actions en nullité absolue ;

les actions relatives à un droit constaté par un jugement ou un autre titre exécutoire.

3. les actions en responsabilité ou en garantie du constructeur d'un ouvrage engagées en vertu des articles 1792 à 1792-2.

Chapter V
The Periods of Time
Required for Prescription

Section 1
General Provisions

Art. 2272

Prescription is to be counted in days and not in hours.

Art. 2273

It is completed when the last day of the period has ended.

Art. 2274

All actions become prescribed after three years. A person who claims the benefit of such a prescription does not have to adduce any legal basis for it nor can he be faced with a defence alleging his bad faith.

Section 2
Special Prescription Periods

Art. 2275

Nevertheless, the following become prescribed after ten years:

1. actions claiming civil liability whose aim is the reparation of personal injury or any loss caused by an act of barbarism;

2. actions claiming absolute nullity;

actions relating to a right upheld by a court's decision or by some other authority whose decision brings a right of enforcement;[1]

3. actions claiming liability or the benefit of a guarantee against a builder of a work employed under articles 1792 to 1792-2.[2]

---

[1] [Before, for example, a creditor can enforce a right against the property of his debtor, he must have the benefit of a *'titre exécutoire'* that is, the right of enforcement. The main source of such a right is found in the decisions of courts, and these must expressly grant it by a form of words known as *la formule exécutoire*: New Code of Civil Procedure, article 502. However, French law has long recognised that formal decisions by *notaires* also grant such a right of enforcement: *Loi* du 25 Ventôse An XI, article 19 and see J Vincent and J Prévault, *Voies d'exécution et procédures de distribution* (19th edn, Paris, Dalloz, 1995) nos 39-44.]

[2] [These are references to existing provisions of the Code civil.]

Art. 2276

La propriété immobilière est acquise par une possession de dix ans.

Variante : La propriété immobilière est acquise par une possession de vingt ans. Toutefois, ce délai est réduit à dix ans lorsque le possesseur a acquis l'immeuble de bonne foi et par juste titre.

Art. 2277

Les règles énoncées par ce titre s'appliquent sans préjudice des dispositions du Nouveau Code de procédure civile, du Code pénal, du Code de procédure pénale, du Livre I, des Titres I et V du Livre III du présent Code, des Livres V et VI du Code de commerce, de la loi du 29 juillet 1881 sur la liberté de la presse, des traités internationaux ratifiés par la France et des règles de l'Union européenne.

Elles ne s'appliquent pas non plus aux délais égaux ou inférieurs à six mois pendant lesquels une action doit être introduite ou un droit exercé, à peine de déchéance.

Section 3
Du délai maximum des prescriptions extinctives

Art. 2278

Néanmoins, sauf à l'égard des crimes contre l'humanité, qui sont imprescriptibles, toutes les actions sont prescrites dix ans après le fait générateur de l'obligation, quels qu'en soient l'objet, le point de départ, les interruptions, les suspensions et les conventions qui en modifient la durée.

À l'égard des actions en responsabilité civile ayant pour objet la réparation d'un préjudice corporel ou résultant d'un acte de barbarie ou d'une atteinte à l'environnement, ce délai est de trente ans.

Section 4
De la possession mobilière

Art. 2279

En fait de meubles, la possession vaut titre.

Néanmoins celui qui a perdu ou auquel il a été volé une chose peut la revendiquer pendant trois ans à compter du jour de la perte ou du vol, contre celui dans les mains duquel il la trouve ; sauf à celui-ci son recours contre celui duquel il la tient.

Art. 2276

Immovable property is acquired after its possession for ten years.

Variation: Immovable property is acquired after its possession for twenty years. Nevertheless, this period is reduced to ten years where the possessor acquired the property in good faith and under a transaction which on its face would transfer ownership.

Art. 2277

The application of the rules set out in this Title is without prejudice to the provisions of the New Code of Civil Procedure, the Criminal Code, the Code of Criminal Procedure, to Book I, Titles I and V of Book III the present Code, to Books V and VI of the Commercial Code, to the Law of 29 July 1881 on the freedom of the press, to international treaties ratified by France and to rules of the European Union.

They do not apply either to periods equal to or lower than six months during which an action must be brought or a right exercised on pain of its extinction.

Section 3
The Maximum Period for Extinctive Prescription

Art. 2278.

Nevertheless, and without prejudice to the position governing crimes against humanity which are not subject to prescription, all actions become prescribed ten years after the event which gives rise to the obligation, whatever its subject-matter, their starting-point or any interruptions, suspensions or agreements which amend their duration.

In the case of actions claiming civil liability for the reparation of a loss resulting from personal injury, from an act of barbarism or from damage to the environment, the period is thirty years.

Section 4
The Possession of Movable Property

Art. 2279

In the case of movable property, possession is equivalent to title.

Nevertheless, a person who has lost or from whom has been stolen a thing may reclaim it for a period of three years starting from the day of its loss or theft, from the person in whose hands he finds it, without prejudice to any recourse by the latter against the person from whom he holds it.

Art. 2280

Si le possesseur actuel de la chose volée ou perdue l'a achetée dans une foire ou dans un marché, ou dans une vente publique, ou d'un marchand vendant des choses pareilles, le propriétaire originaire ne peut se la faire rendre qu'en remboursant au possesseur le prix qu'elle lui a coûté.

Le bailleur qui revendique, en vertu de l'article 2102, les meubles déplacés sans son consentement et qui ont été achetés dans les mêmes conditions, doit également rembourser à l'acheteur le prix qu'ils lui ont coûté.

Section 5
Droit transitoire

Art. 2281

La loi qui allonge la durée de la prescription est sans effet sur une prescription acquise ; elle s'applique lorsque l'action n'était pas prescrite à la date d'entrée en vigueur de la loi.

Lorsque la loi réduit la durée de la prescription, la prescription commence à courir du jour de l'entrée en vigueur de la loi, sans que la durée totale puisse excéder la durée prévue par la loi antérieure.

Art. 2280

If the present possessor of a stolen or lost thing bought it at a fair, at a market, at a public auction, or from a trader selling similar things, the original owner can have it returned only if he reimburses its possessor with the price which it cost him.

A landlord who under article 2102[1] reclaims movable property removed from the premises without his consent and which has been bought in the same circumstances must also reimburse the buyer for the price which it cost him.

Section 5
Transitional Provisions

Art. 2281

Any legislative provision which lengthens the duration of a prescription period has no effect on a prescription which is already completed; it applies to actions which have not become prescribed at the time of entry into force of the legislation in question.

Where legislation reduces the duration of a prescription period, time starts to run from the day of entry into force of the legislation as long as this does not lead to the total duration of the prescription exceeding that set by the previous law.

---

[1] [This is a reference to a provision which existed in the Code civil when the *Avant-projet* was published. It has now been replaced by the new article 2332 within Book 4 of the Code civil ('Sureties'), by *ordonnance* no 2006-346 of 23 March 2006.]

Index

References such as '178–9' indicate (not necessarily continuous) discussion of a topic across a range of pages. Wherever possible in the case of topics with many references, these have either been divided into sub-topics or only the most significant discussions of the topic are listed. Because the entire volume is about 'obligations', 'contract' and the *'Avant-projet'*, the use of these terms (and certain others occurring throughout the work, notably commencing 'contractual …') as an entry point has been minimised. Information will be found under the corresponding detailed topics.

./P